BRD
North American **Brewers Resource Directory**

Institute for Brewing Studies

BRD

North American **Brewers Resource Directory**

Compiled by Institute for Brewing Studies
David Coy, Managing Editor

1996–1997
Thirteenth Edition

Completely Updated

Published by Brewers Publications, Boulder, Colorado

North American Brewers Resource Directory 1996–1997
Compiled by the Institute for Brewing Studies
Copyright 1996 by the Association of Brewers, Inc.

Managing Editor: David Coy
Copy Editors: Kim Adams and Theresa Duggan

ISBN 0-937381-48-9
Printed in the United States of America

Published by Brewers Publications,
a division of the Association of Brewers:
PO Box 1679, Boulder, CO 80306-1679, U.S.A.
(303) 447-0816 • FAX (303) 447-2825
info@aob.org • http://www.aob.org/aob

Direct all inquiries/orders to the above address.

All rights reserved. Except for use in a review, no portion of this book may be reproduced in any form without the expressed written permission of the publisher.

Neither the Institute for Brewing Studies nor Brewers Publications assumes any responsibility for the use or misuse of information in this book.

Cover design by Stephanie Johnson
Cover photo courtesy of Abita Brewing Company

Table of Contents

Preface vii
Introduction 1
1 **Calendar of Events** 2
2 **United States Craft-Brewing: 1995 Industry in Review** 8
3 **Canadian Craft-Brewing: 1995 Industry in Review** 42
4 **Brewing Industry Statistics** 49
   United States Craft-Brewing Index 50
   United States Openings, Closings, Operating 51
   Canadian Craft-Brewing Index 52
   Canadian Openings, Closings, Operating 53
   United States and Canadian Craft-Brewing Industry Percentage Annual Growth 54
   United States Craft-Brewing Industry Annual Dollar Volume 54
   Top 50 United States Craft-Brewing Companies in 1995 55
   United States Regional Breweries: Estimated Total Taxable Shipments 56
   United States Microbreweries: Estimated Total Taxable Shipments 57
   United States Brewpubs: Estimated Total Taxable Shipments 62
   United States Contract Brewing Companies: Estimated Sales 73
   Canadian Regional Breweries: Estimated Total Taxable Shipments 76
   Canadian Microbreweries: Estimated Total Taxable Shipments 76
   Canadian Brewpubs: Estimated Total Taxable Shipments 77
   United States Large Brewers' Shipments 79
   United States Large Brewers' Market Share 80
   United States Imports: Sales 81
   Leading Imported Beer Brands 82
   Charts from the Beer Institute's *Brewers Almanac* 83
   Charts from R. S. Weinberg & Associates 110
   Brewing Operations Ratios 113
5 **United States Breweries** 114
   Index by State and Type of Brewery 114
   Alphabetical Listing by State 129
6 **Canadian Breweries** 187
   Index by Province and Type of Brewery 187
   Alphabetical Listing by Province 190
7 **North American Contract Brewing Companies** 199
   Index by State/Province 199
   Alphabetical Listing by State/Province 202

Table of Contents

8 Mexican Breweries **210**
    Index by State 210
    Alphabetical Listing by State 212

9 Caribbean Breweries **213**
    Index by Country 213
    Alphabetical Listing by Country 215

10 Brewing Equipment Manufacturers and Suppliers **217**
11 Packaging Equipment Manufacturers and Suppliers **240**
12 Restaurant and Pub Equipment Suppliers **248**
13 Brewing Consultants **254**
14 Marketing, Point-of-Sale, and Merchandise Suppliers and Consultants **260**
15 Malt Suppliers **267**
16 Hop Suppliers **274**
17 Yeast Suppliers and Laboratories **278**
18 Miscellaneous Ingredient and Material Suppliers **280**
19 Control Agencies, Laws, and Regulations **285**
    Bureau of Alcohol, Tobacco, and Firearms 286
    United States 289
    Canada 315
    Alcohol Content Limits by State 321
    BATF Compliance Matters 322

20 State Excise Taxes **334**
21 Brewing Associations **337**
22 Brewing Schools and Courses **343**
23 Brewing Books and Journals **346**
24 Brewing Libraries **365**
25 Beer Style Guidelines **367**
Equipment Index **384**
Index **406**
Advertising Index **429**

Preface

Welcome to the thirteenth annual edition of the *North American Brewers Resource Directory*, compiled by the Institute for Brewing Studies. We completed the first directory in 1984 when the Institute was less than one year old and North American microbreweries and brewpubs numbered fewer than twenty.

Today, with the publication of the 1996–1997 edition, there are more than eight hundred small breweries in North America. Moreover, three of the original microbreweries listed in the 1984 edition have since grown well beyond the 15,000-barrel microbrewery definition, establishing a new generation of middle-tier producers known as regional specialty brewers.

Now that "microbrew" is a household word, many breweries that produce these beers have far exceeded the "micro" definition. "Microbrew," in its current usage, refers more often to a market segment than it does to a brewery size. For this reason, the Institute for Brewing Studies now uses the term "craft-brewing industry" to refer to the entire group of companies established to brew and sell full-flavored, specialty beers. This category includes pubbreweries, microbreweries, regional specialty brewers, and contract brewing companies. Although almost every large and traditional regional brewery has introduced its own craft-brew look-alike beer during the last two years, the Institute for Brewing Studies reserves the terms "craft brewer" or "craft brewery" for those companies whose flagship brands are specialty beers.

Up through the 1970s and early 1980s the trend of brewing industry consolidation seemed unstoppable, with larger breweries buying out smaller producers at an alarming pace. As the number of United States breweries declined from 750 after Prohibition to less than forty by 1980, industry analysts predicted just a handful of breweries would remain in existence by the year 2000.

Fortunately, thanks to the fearless, dedicated pioneers of North America's modern craft-brewing renaissance, the tide has turned. If the craft-brewing industry's growth continues through the next ten years at the same pace as the past ten years, there will be more than six thousand microbreweries and brewpubs on the continent by 2005, an average of more than one hundred per state and province!

While this may seem absurd, it is certainly not implausible. California currently supports more than one hundred craft breweries. With the combination of expected market expansion for full-flavored beers and population growth throughout the state, California could easily be home to several hundred small breweries by the end of the decade.

This current *Brewers Resource Directory* gives you access to specialized statistical data, state tax information, brewpub law information, every North American brewery, and every supply company you will need to help you succeed in today's rapidly growing craft-brewing industry. In addition, inside you will find a calendar of brewing-industry events, national and international brewing schools, state and federal regulatory agencies, and books and journals related to brewing beer professionally. All these listings are in a data-base format so that the most current information is included.

However, the increasing number of breweries also means that the number of beer brands is on the rise. There's more than 7,500 brands on the market as this edition of the *Brewers Resource Directory* goes to press — a 93 percent increase over what was in last year's edition. In order to keep the book contained in one volume and still be able to include all the growing listings, the "Beer Brand Index" has been put on disk and is being sold separately. Formatted for either the Macintosh or PC, the disk allows easy access to the most up-to-date beer brand information available. To order the "Beer Brand Index" disk, use the order form in the back of this book.

The Institute for Brewing Studies would like to thank the Beer Institute, R. S. Weinberg and Associates,

Preface

and *Beer Marketer's Insights* for generously allowing us to reprint several of their charts in chapter 4.

The *Brewers Resource Directory* and its vast resources are the fruits of the tremendous efforts of a dedicated team of staff members of the Institute for Brewing Studies, Brewers Publications, and the Association of Brewers' Production Department.

I would like to thank David Coy, managing editor; Elizabeth Gold, Brewers Publications publisher; Tyra Segars, Association of Brewers graphics/production director; Shawn Steele, information systems administrator; Theresa Duggan and Kim Adams, copy editors; Chris Lowenstein, advertising assistant; and Keith Villa Ph.D., brewing scientist for Coors Brewing Co. All of these people were invaluable in their assistance with the logistical and practical aspects of compiling this information.

I would also like to thank Charlie Papazian, Association of Brewers president and Institute for Brewing Studies founder, for contributing his "Beer Style Guidelines." Thanks also to Jim Neighbors, IBS administrator; Kate Hanley, IBS administrative assistant; Casey Koehler, former circulation director; and Anna DeLigio, circulation coordinator.

Finally, the quality of the updated information in the *Brewers Resource Directory* is a testament to the generous assistance of every brewery and company composing the brewing industry's allied trades. By filling out and returning our Brewery Surveys and Supplier Directory Listing forms you helped make the *1996–1997 North American Brewers Resource Directory* the most useful source of information available on North American brewing. Thank you very much and cheers!

— David Edgar
Director, Institute for Brewing Studies

Introduction

The craft-brewing industry has enjoyed steady, strong growth, especially during the last eight years. While some may argue that a few cities or states may be near a saturation point in terms of the number of craft-brewed brands available in their marketplaces, the case could also be made that American beer drinkers' tastes continue to change and broaden. Growth, even in a microbrewery-dense market like Portland, Oregon, or Boston, Massachusetts, may still be decades from leveling off.

Many states, counties, and cities across the continent are more than ready for new handcrafted, quality beers. The opportunities are ripe.

That notwithstanding, do not underestimate the real amount of effort involved in building a profitable brewing company.

Look at the history of the industry; look at the most successful microbreweries. The people behind these young companies managed to get their breweries where they are today because of unyielding dedication and a tremendous capacity for hard work. If you talk to them, many will tell of working fifty- to sixty-hour weeks for several years with no days off.

As a craft brewer, your number-one priority should be quality control. Gone are the days when just being a microbrew was enough to guarantee steady sales for a new brewery. Craft-brew consumers have become much more knowledgable about beer and subsequently much less forgiving of "idiosyncracies" — while at the same time, being blessed with a larger number of brands from which to choose.

We cannot emphasize enough the importance of brewing a quality product that customers can rely on to be consistent. In addition, the chances for success in this business improve if you can offer consumers beer styles that are different than what is already available in your target market.

Another reality of the development of this market is that word-of-mouth advertising is no longer a sufficient means for maintaining consistent sales growth. In some parts of the country the shelves are getting craft beer crowded. How you market your beer has become more and more important — as the need increases for you to distinguish your brands from your competitors!

Nonetheless, the time is right, and the market is ready for new small breweries. If you start with a solid, well-researched business plan, good financial backing, and an experienced head brewer, you're on the right track. Moreover, if you're patient and persistent, willing and able to sacrifice a lot of time and sweat, then your chances of succeeding are good.

In terms of number of facilities, brewpubs represent the largest and fastest-growing segment of the craft-brewing industry, and they will continue to do so. Microbreweries face the predicament of a limited number of tap handles and available shelf space in the marketplace. Brewpubs, on the other hand, compete first with other restaurants and bars. It's important to understand, however, that another brewpub opening in a city that you are planning one for is more beneficial than detrimental to your planned project. It will increase local awareness and appreciation of full-flavored beer (unless it sells poor quality beer).

Gathering quality information and making decisions based on research minimizes risks and maximizes profits. A brewer makes thousands of decisions and will do much better making informed decisions. To this end, the Institute for Brewing Studies has compiled the *1996–1997 North American Brewers Resource Directory*. It can help with the research in locating a specific piece of equipment, finding a brewing school, and many other aspects of your project.

Whether you are a brewer, CEO, marketing director, plant manager, secretary, administrator, contract brewer, investor, beer wholesaler, or someone trying to get involved in the craft-brewing industry, the *Brewers Resource Directory* belongs on your desk.

It's a combination Yellow Pages and almanac of the craft-brewing industry, and much more.

1 Calendar of Events

June 12–15: World Beer Cup^{SM}, Vail, CO. Contact: Association of Brewers (303) 447-0816, info@aob.org

June 12–16: Le Mondial de la Biere, Vieux-Port de Montreal, Quebec, Canada. Contact: Pierre Lalumière (514) 722-9640, marois@login.net

June 13–16: Georgia Beer Wholesalers Association, annual convention, Marriott Bay Point, Panama City Beach, FL.

June 15: 3rd Annual Wichita Festival of Beers — Leukemia Society's Cure 2000 campaign, Kansas Coliseum, Wichita, KS. Contact: Beverly Moore, (316) 838-7707, ext. 1222.

June 15–16: Herbfarm Northwest Microbrewery Festival, Fall City, WA. Contact: Cindy Satler (206) 784-2222.

June 17–28: Brewing Microbiology and Microscopy, Siebel Institute of Technology, Chicago, IL.

June 19–21: Heartland Brewfest III, Adel, IA. Contact: Old Depot Brewery (515) 993-5064.

June 21–23: Midwestern Technical Conference, sponsored by Districts St. Paul–Minneapolis and Milwaukee. Contact: Jerry Hilton (414) 781-6100.

June 22: Second Annual Great New Jersey Craft Beer Festival, Action Park, Vernon, NJ. Contact: (800) 351-ALES.

June 22: Second Annual Summerfest 1996, Roseville, CA. Contact: Mark Hernandez (916) 261-1117.

June 29–30: Colorado Brewers' Festival, Fort Collins, CO. Contact: (970) 484-6500.

June 29: KQED International Beer and Food Festival, San Francisco, CA. Contact: Julie Becker (415) 553-2157, julie_becker@qm.kqed.org

July 1–3: Sensory Evaluation of Beer, Chicago, IL. Contact: Siebel Institute of Technology (312) 279-0966.

July 6: Savannah Suds II, River Street, Hyatt Regency, Savannah, GA. Contact: Mark Weisner (800) 689-3440.

July 8–12: Microbrewery and Pub Brewery Operations, Chicago, IL. Contact: Siebel Institute of Technology (312) 279-0966.

July 19–20: Great Eastern Micro Festival, Stoudt's Brewery, Adamstown, PA. Contact: (717) 484-4387.

July 19–20: International Beer Festival, Burlington, VT. Contact: Vermont Brewers' Association (802) 388-0727.

July 20: California Small Brewers Festival, Mountain View, CA. Contact: (800) 965-BEER.

July 20: Hayward/Russell City Blues & Brew Festival, Hayward/Alameda, CA. Contact: Mike Nash (510) 537-4341, marketng@ncacomputers.com

July 20: Sierra Brewfest, Nevada City, CA. Contact: (916) 265-6124.

July 20–26: Grain to Glass (seven-day course), Woodland, CA. Contact: American Brewers Guild (916) 753-0497 or (800) 636-1331.

July 27: Fifth Annual Rocky Mountain Beer Festival, Snowmass Village, CO. Contact: (970) 923-2000.

Calendar of Events

July 29–August 1: "Boots-On" Practicum (four-day course), Woodland, CA. Contact: American Brewers Guild (916) 753-0497 or (800) 636-1331.

July 31–August 4: Oregon Brewers Festival, Portland, OR. Contact: (503) 628-1227.

August 3: Fat Tire Festival, North Lake Tahoe, CA.

August 5–16: Fifty-sixth Short Course in Brewing Technology, Siebel Institute of Technology, Chicago, IL. Contact: (312) 279-0966.

August 6: MBAA District Rocky Mountain, New Belgium Brewing Co., Fort Collins, CO.

August 6–10: Great British Beer Festival: CAMRA's Annual Real Ale Fest, London, England. Contact: (011-44) 1727 867201.

August 10: HopFest, Pleasanton, CA. Contact: Linda Chew (510) 843-7625.

August 13: District St. Paul–Minneapolis MBAA golf outing, Dahlgren CC, Chaska, MN.

August 17–19: International Beer Festival, San Jose, CA. Contact: Kevin Lytle (408) 236-2258.

August 19–23: Microbrewery and Pub Brewery Operations, Chicago, IL. Contact: Siebel Institute of Technology (312) 279-0966.

August 26–28: Beer and Brewing: An Executive Overview, Chicago, IL. Contact: Siebel Institute of Technology (312) 279-0966.

August 30–31: Sprecher Fest, Glendale, WI. Contact: (414) 964-2739.

August 31–September 1: Second Annual Mount Snow Brewer's Fest, Mount Snow, VT. Contact: (800) 245-SNOW, (802) 464-3333.

September 2–6: Tenth Annual Northwest Ale Festival, Seattle, WA. Contact: Larry Bush (206) 634-1433.

September 3–6: Association Latinoamericana de Fabricantes de Cerveza, Alaface, Guatemala City, Guatemala.

September 3–October 4: Intensive Brewing Science and Engineering, Woodland, CA. Contact: American Brewers Guild (916) 753-0497 or (800) 636-1331.

September 3–November 8: Seventy-first Diploma Course in Brewing Technology. Contact: Siebel Institute of Technology (312) 279-0966.

September 3–November 15: Craftbrewers Apprenticeship Program, Woodland, CA. Contact: American Brewers Guild (916) 753-0497 or (800) 636-1331.

September 6–8: San Diego Street Scene: Food, Drink, and Music Festival, San Diego, CA. Contact: (619) 557-8490.

September 7: New York Beerfest 4 Under the Brooklyn Bridge. Contact: (718) 855-7882, ext. 21.

September 14–15: How to Open a Brewpub or Microbrewery, Woodland, CA. Contact: American Brewers Guild (916) 753-0497 or (800) 636-1331.

September 14–15: Second Annual River City Real Beer Festival, Richmond, VA. Contact: Bud Hensgen, Mid-Atlantic Association of Craft Brewers (703) 527-1441, budh@2erols.com

September 18: District St. Paul–Minneapolis MBAA at G. Heileman Brewing Co., La Crosse, WI.

September 19: District Milwaukee MBAA TBA.

September 19–21: National Beer Wholesalers Association Fifty-ninth annual convention, Marriott Hotel, San Francisco, CA. Contact: (703) 683-4300.

September 19–26: Drinktec-Interbrau '97, Munich Trade Fair Center, Munich, Germany. Contact: Kallman Associates (201) 652-70706.

September 20–21: Stoudt's Great Eastern Micro Festival, Adamstown, PA. Contact: (717) 484-4387.

September 20–22: Oldenberg's Beer Camp, Oldenberg Brewery, Fort Mitchell, KY. Contact: Emma Obertate (800) 426-3841.

September 21: MBAA District Rocky Mountain Fall Technical Seminar, Anheuser Busch, Fort Collins, CO.

September 21: Colorado Springs Microbrewers Exposition, Colorado National Bank parking lot. Contact: Downtown Colorado Springs Inc. (719) 632-0553.

September 21: Sixth Annual Steamboat Fall Foliage Festival & BrewFest, Steamboat Springs, CO. Contact: (970) 879-0880.

Calendar of Events

September 26–28: Fifteenth Annual Great American Beer Festival, Denver, CO. Contact: (303) 447-0816.

September 30–October 1: Brewing Microbiology and Microscopy, Siebel Institute of Technology, Chicago, IL.

September 30–June 4, 1997: Masterbrewers Program (Correspondence), Woodland, CA. Contact: American Brewers Guild (916) 753-0497 or (800) 636-1331.

October 5–6: Rock, Rhythm & Brews. Contact: (503) 867-3660.

October 6–9: Master Brewers Association of the Americas 109th Annual Convention, Queen Elizabeth Hotel, Montreal, Quebec, Canada. Contact: MBAA (414) 774-8558.

October 10: Thirteenth Annual Calistoga Beer & Sausage Fest and Chili Chaser, Calistoga, CA. Contact: Shirley Lauborough (707) 942-6333, ca94515@aol.com

October 11–13: Newport Microbrew Festival, Newport, OR. Contact: Esther Pinto (503) 265-8578.

October 14: Suncoast Brewers' Luncheon club meeting at George Pappas Restaurant, Largo, FL. Contact: Jack Meister (813) 785-6118.

October 15–27: MBAA Brewing and Malting Course, Madison, WI. Contact: MBAA office (414) 774-8558.

October 18–20: Great Northwest Microbrewery Invitational, Seattle, WA. Contact: Dennis Masel (206) 232-2982.

October 19: Pacific Coast Festival, Santa Barbara, CA.

October 19–25: Grain to Glass (seven-day course), Woodland, CA. Contact: American Brewers Guild (916) 753-0497 or (800) 636-1331.

October 20: MBAA District Ontario Technical Meeting, Labatt Breweries of Canada, London, Ontario.

October 20–22: MBAA District Southeastern Fall Meeting, the Stroh Brewery, Tampa, FL. Contact: Stroh Brewery (813) 972-8524.

October 20–31: MBAA Brewing and Malting Technology Course, Madison, WI.

October 25: Third Annual Charleston International Beer Festival, Charleston, SC. Contact: Mark Weisner (800) 689-3440.

October 28: MBAA District Rocky Mountain, Coors Brewing Co., Golden, CO.

October 28–31: "Boots-On" Practicum (four-day course), Woodland, CA. Contact: American Brewers Guild (916) 753-0497 or (800) 636-1331.

October 31: MBAA District Milwaukee, TBA.

November 3–5: Second International Beer Marketer's Symposium^{SM}, Vancouver, British Columbia, Canada. Contact: Sheri Winter, Association of Brewers (303) 447-0816, info@aob.org

November 8: MBAA District Pittsburgh, regular business meeting, Jones Brewing Co., Wauwatosa, WI. Contact: (414) 774-8558.

November 8–12: Brewers' Association of America, Fifty-fifth Annual Convention, New Orleans, LA. Contact (908) 280-9153.

November 9: Third Annual Rhode Island International Beer Expo, Providence Convention Center, Providence, RI. Contact: Maury Ryan, Festivals of America, Ltd. (401) 272-0980, RICider@aol.com

November 15: MBAA District St. Paul–Minneapolis, Stroh Brewery Co., St. Paul, MN.

November 18–20: Beer and Brewing: An Executive Overview, Chicago, IL. Contact: Siebel Institute of Technology (312) 279-0966.

November 18–20: InterBev, North America's premier tradeshow, Houston, TX. Contact: (202) 463-6794.

November 21: MBAA District Milwaukee, Annual Old Timers Night, Miller Brewing Co., Milwaukee, WI.

November 25–27: Sensory Evaluation of Beer, Chicago, IL. Contact: Siebel Institute of Technology (312) 279-0966.

December 2–13: Fifty-seventh Short Course in Brewing Technology, Siebel Institute of Technology, Chicago, IL. Contact: (312) 279-0966.

December 7–8: How to Open a Brewpub or Microbrewery, Washington, DC. Contact: American Brewers Guild (916) 753-0497 or (800) 636-1331.

Calendar of Events

December 7–8: Sales, Marketing and Distribution, Washingtion, DC. Contact: American Brewers Guild (916) 753-0497 or (800) 636-1331.

December 16–20: Practical Brewery Engineering Siebel Institute, Chicago, IL.

1997

January 6–17: Fifty-eighth Short Course in Brewing Technology. Contact: Siebel Institute of Technology (312) 279-0966.

January 6–June 4: Masterbrewers Program (Residential), Woodland, CA. Contact: American Brewers Guild (916) 753-0497 or (800) 636-1331.

January 20–22: Sensory Evaluation of Beer, Chicago, IL. Contact: Siebel Institute of Technology (312) 279-0966.

January 20–24: Advanced Microbiology, Chicago, IL. Contact: Siebel Institute of Technology (312) 279-0966.

January 20–24: Microbrewery and Pub Brewery Operations, Chicago, IL. Contact: Siebel Institute of Technology (312) 279-0966.

January 27–April 4: Seventy-second Diploma Course in Brewing Technology. Contact: Siebel Institute of Technology (312) 279-0966.

February 10–12: Beer and Brewing: An Executive Overview, Chicago, IL. Contact: Siebel Institute of Technology (312) 279-0966.

February 17–March 20: Intensive Brewing Science and Engineering, Woodland, CA. Contact: American Brewers Guild (916) 753-0497 or (800) 636-1331.

February 17–May 9: Craftbrewers Apprenticeship Program, Woodland, CA. Contact: American Brewers Guild (916) 753-0497 or (800) 636-1331.

February 24–March 7: Brewing Microbiology and Microscopy, Chicago, IL. Contact: Siebel Institute of Technology (312) 279-0966.

March 17–28: Beer Packaging Course, Chicago, IL. Contact: Siebel Institute of Technology (312) 279-0966.

March 22–23: How to Open a Brewpub or Microbrewery, Seattle, WA. Contact: American Brewers Guild (916) 753-0497 or (800) 636-1331.

March 22–23: Quality Assurance for the Micro or Pub Brewery, Seattle, WA. Contact: American Brewers Guild (916) 753-0497 or (800) 636-1331.

March 22–23: Sales, Marketing and Distribution, Seattle, WA. Contact: American Brewers Guild (916) 753-0497 or (800) 636-1331.

March 22–26: Institute for Brewing Studies' National Craft-Brewers Conference and Trade Show, Seattle, WA. Contact: Nancy Johnson, Institute for Brewing Studies, (303) 447-0816, ext. 131, info@aob.org

April 7–18: Brewing Microbiology and Microscopy, Chicago, IL. Contact: Siebel Institute of Technology (312) 279-0966.

April 12–18: Grain to Glass (seven-day course), Woodland, CA. Contact: American Brewers Guild (916) 753-0497 or (800) 636-1331.

April 14–16: Beer and Brewing: An Executive Overview, Chicago, IL. Contact: Siebel Institute of Technology (312) 279-0966.

April 21–24: "Boots-On" Practicum (four-day course), Woodland, CA. Contact: American Brewers Guild (916) 753-0497 or (800) 636-1331.

April 21–May 2: Fifty-ninth Short Course in Brewing Technology. Contact: Siebel Institute of Technology (312) 279-0966.

May 5–9: Basics of Brewery Engineering, Chicago, IL. Contact: Siebel Institute of Technology (312) 279-0966.

May 12–16: Essential Quality Control for Brewers, Chicago, IL. Contact: Siebel Institute of Technology (312) 279-0966.

May 12–16: Microbreery and Pub Brewery Operations, Chicago, IL. Contact: Siebel Institute of Technology (312) 279-0966.

May 12–30: British Ale Technology, Chicago, IL. Contact: Siebel Institute of Technology (312) 279-0966.

May 19–23: Essential Quality Control for Brewers, Chicago, IL. Contact: Siebel Institute of Technology (312) 279-0966.

May 19–23: Microbreery and Pub Brewery Operations, Chicago, IL. Contact: Siebel Institute of Technology (312) 279-0966.

Calendar of Events

May 24–29: Twenty-sixth Annual International Congress of the European Brewery Convention (EBC) Maastricht, Netherlands. Contact EBC, PO Box 510, 2380 BB, Zoeterwoude, Netherlands 31 71 45 60 47.

May 28–30: Sensory Evaluation of Beer, Chicago, IL. Contact: Siebel Institute of Technology (312) 279-0966.

June 2–13: Brewing Microbiology and Microscopy, Chicago, IL. Contact: Siebel Institute of Technology (312) 279-0966.

June 16-27: Sixtieth Short Course in Brewing Technology. Contact: Siebel Institute of Technology (312) 279-0966.

June 21–25: American Society of Brewing Chemists Annual Meeting Hyatt Hotel, Palm Springs, CA.

June 30–July 2: Sensory Evaluation of Beer, Chicago, IL. Contact: Siebel Institute of Technology (312) 279-0966.

June 30–July 18: British Ale Technology, Chicago, IL. Contact: Siebel Institute of Technology (312) 279-0966.

July 7–11: Basics of Brewery Engineering, Chicago, IL. Contact: Siebel Institute of Technology (312) 279-0966.

July 14–18: Essential Quality Control for Brewers, Chicago, IL. Contact: Siebel Institute of Technology (312) 279-0966.

July 14–18: Microbreery and Pub Brewery Operations, Chicago, IL. Contact: Siebel Institute of Technology (312) 279-0966.

July 21–25: Essential Quality Control for Brewers, Chicago, IL. Contact: Siebel Institute of Technology (312) 279-0966.

July 21–25: Microbreery and Pub Brewery Operations, Chicago, IL. Contact: Siebel Institute of Technology (312) 279-0966.

July 28–August 8: Brewing Microbiology and Microscopy, Chicago, IL. Contact: Siebel Institute of Technology (312) 279-0966.

August 11–22: Sixty-first Short Course in Brewing Technology. Contact: Siebel Institute of Technology (312) 279-0966.

August 25–27: Beer and Brewing: An Executive Overview, Chicago, IL. Contact: Siebel Institute of Technology (312) 279-0966.

August 25–September 12: British Ale Technology, Chicago, IL. Contact: Siebel Institute of Technology (312) 279-0966.

September 1–19: German Beer Technology, Chicago, IL. Contact: Siebel Institute of Technology (312) 279-0966.

September 2–October 4: Intensive Brewing Science and Engineering, Woodland, CA. Contact: American Brewers Guild (916) 753-0497 or (800) 636-1331.

September 2–November 7: Seventy-third Diploma Course in Brewing Technology. Contact: Siebel Institute of Technology (312) 279-0966.

September 2–November 14: Craftbrewers Apprenticeship Program, Woodland, CA. Contact: American Brewers Guild (916) 753-0497 or (800) 636-1331.

September 17–18: World Beer Symposium Hotel Bayerischen Hof Munich, Germany. Contact: Rudiger Ruoss (011-41) 81/23 78 05.

September 19–26: Drinktec Interbrau Munich Trade Fair Centre Munich, Germany.

September 21–24: National Beer Wholesalers Association Sixtieth Annual Convention, Bally's Hotel, Las Vegas, NV. Contact: (703) 683-4300.

September 29–October 10: Brewing Microbiology and Microscopy, Chicago, IL. Contact: Siebel Institute of Technology (312) 279-0966.

October 11–15: MBAA Annual Convention, Hyatt Regency, Baltimore, MD.

October 20–31: Beer Packaging Course, Chicago, IL. Contact: Siebel Institute of Technology (312) 279-0966.

November 10–14: Advanced Microbiology, Chicago, IL. Contact: Siebel Institute of Technology (312) 279-0966.

November 17–19: Beer and Brewing: An Executive Overview, Chicago, IL. Contact: Siebel Institute of Technology (312) 279-0966.

Calendar of Events

November 24–26: Sensory Evaluation of Beer, Chicago, IL. Contact: Siebel Institute of Technology (312) 279-0966.

December 1–12: Sixty-second Short Course in Brewing Technology. Contact: Siebel Institute of Technology (312) 279-0966.

December 15–19: Essential Quality Control for Brewers, Chicago, IL. Contact: Siebel Institute of Technology (312) 279-0966.

December 15–19: Microbreery and Pub Brewery Operations, Chicago, IL. Contact: Siebel Institute of Technology (312) 279-0966.

1998

September 24–26: National Beer Wholesalers Association Sixty-first Annual Convention, Hyatt Regency, Chicago, IL. Contact: (703) 683-4300.

2 United States Craft-Brewing: 1995 Industry in Review

A Million Barrels More for Craft Brewers
Over 50 Percent Growth the Second Year in a Row!

There's no more questioning the significance of the domestic craft-brewing renaissance. America's tastes are changing in the direction of all-malt beers. Just as consumers have experienced with specialty coffees and fine wines, once you have become accustomed to drinking the full-flavored varieties — and discover what a pleasure a beer with flavor can be — there's no going back to regular old adjunct-brewed beer. There's simply no comparison.

In almost every state, local brewing and local beers are slowly but surely becoming the rule instead of the exception. Just under two hundred brewpubs and ninety microbreweries opened in the United States last year, the majority of them in states not previously well known for craft brewing. The list of states with ten or more brewpubs and microbreweries opening in 1995 contains the usual suspects like California, Colorado, Florida, Oregon, and Washington, as well as the not-so-usual ones, such as Michigan, New York, Pennsylvania, South Carolina, and Texas.

While the craft-brewing industry took fifteen years to first reach the milestone of 1,000,000-barrel sales in a year (1992), in its current momentum it added on 1,000,000 barrels in *new* sales last year alone. In 1995 the U.S. craft-brewing industry's sales grew 50 percent for the second straight year. The total combined sales of brewpubs, microbreweries, regional specialty breweries, and contract brewing companies reached 3,780,000 barrels, with total share of the U.S. beer market increasing from 1.3 percent to 2 percent.

No, Not IPA, IPO!

A new acronym for many brewers and beer lovers alike was heard flowing from their lips during 1995 as five major craft-brewing companies released Initial Public Offerings. Rock Bottom Restaurants was first to get the ball rolling with its $34 million offering in February. Redhook Ale Brewery generated tremendous interest in this industry when the stock from its $33 million IPO in August jumped in value immediately upon release.

In November the going-public procession continued as Boston Beer issued a $76 million offering, and as Pete's Brewing issued a $51 million offering. Hart Brewing followed in December with its $44 million IPO. The first quarter of 1996 saw two more offerings, this time from Nor'Wester Brewery in January (formerly known as Willamette Valley Brewing Co.) and Maryland's Frederick Brewing Co. in March.

Pretty soon you'll be able to invest in craft-brewing mutual funds ...

Micros and Regionals Losing Independence

Big deals were struck during 1995 as Miller Brewing Co. purchased a majority share of the Austin, Texas, regional-level Celis Brewery in March and followed suit in New England by buying 50 percent of the rapidly growing Shipyard Brewery in November. Two other pioneering Pacific Northwest brewers gave up the reins during the fall: the Ponzi family sold its BridgePort Brewing Co. to Texas's Gambrinus Co., the importer best known for helping make Corona a household word and more recently purchasing the traditional regional Spoetzl Brewery (Shiner Beer).

"We call them the suit of the month club," BridgePort's Nancy Ponzi said last summer, referring to the parade of companies courting them with offers to purchase the company or to assist it in a public offering. Several months later, she and husband Dick Ponzi finalized the deal with Gambrinus.

Also, Bert and Sherry Grant sold their pioneering Yakima Brewing and Malting Co. to UST Inc., a Fortune 500 conglomerate that includes U.S. Tobacco and Stimson Lane Vineyards, a holding company representing Washington State's Chateau St. Michelle Winery. Brewmaster Bert Grant will retain his position and Sherry Grant will also stay as the brewery's public relations director.

Late in the year, California's Gordon Biersch brewery-restaurant chain sold a controlling interest in the company for $20 million to Fertitta Enterprises, which has an interest in several Las Vegas casinos.

Another Portland, Oregon, brewer, Widmer Brewing Co., sold a minority share of the company for $10 million to Desai Capital Management, a New York investment firm that has provided financing for other fast-growing companies such as Snapple Beverages. Widmer plans to use the capital to build a new 250-barrel brewery complete with its first-ever bottling line and initial capacity for producing 140,000 barrels.

Add to this list Stroh Brewery Co. owning — or having the option to own — part of Pete's Brewing Co. This was revealed in documents filed for Pete's public offering process, according to *Beer Marketer's Insights*. Stroh has warrants for 1.140 million shares, which, if exercised, would amount to 10.1 percent of the company, making it Pete's largest shareholder. The warrants were provided in exchange for cost-reductions as part of Pete's new contract arrangement with Stroh.

Coors is the only one of the big three brewers that has not yet bought into a micro- or craft-brewery. It appears inevitable that the company will, though, in light of President Leo Keilly's statement to the audience at the Brewers Association of America convention last November. "We're looking for partners," he told the gathering of regional brewers. Coors did announce a different sort of partnership, as it agreed to handle distribution in the West for F. X. Matt's Saranac family of craft-style beers.

There is one historical footnote to add to this. Miller's parent company, Philip Morris, first purchased 51 percent of the brewery in 1969. It then bought the other 49 percent one year later.

The Rise of the Chain Gang

The idea of franchising brewpubs has long attracted speculation. Yet almost every brewpub prides itself on its uniqueness and individuality — the *polar opposite* of franchise-style homogeneity and mass appeal. Today, however, with fresh, full-flavored beer approaching a level that could be considered mass appeal — and brewpubs' proven success of the "fresh beer and good food" concept — franchises may be just around the corner.

Can the success of one brewpub concept be replicated in another city in a different region? The emergence of successful brewpub chains appears to indicate the answer to be "Yes!" In fact, more than 15 percent of the new brewpubs opened in 1995 were started by companies already owning at least one other brewpub.

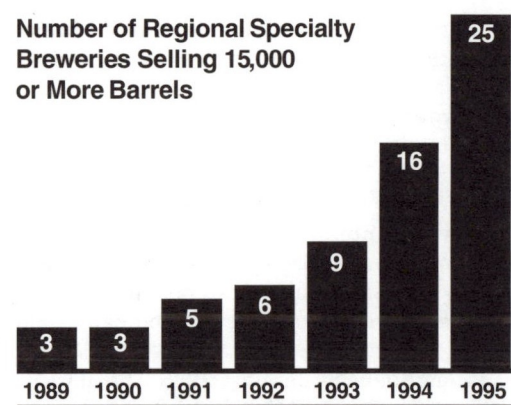

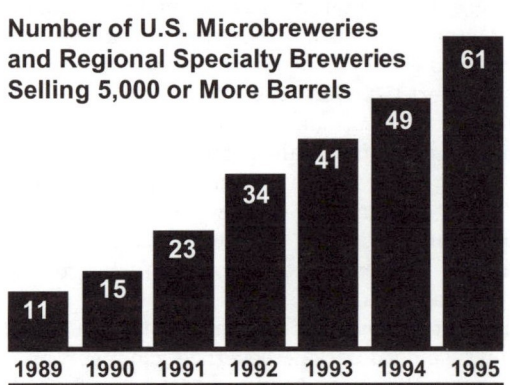

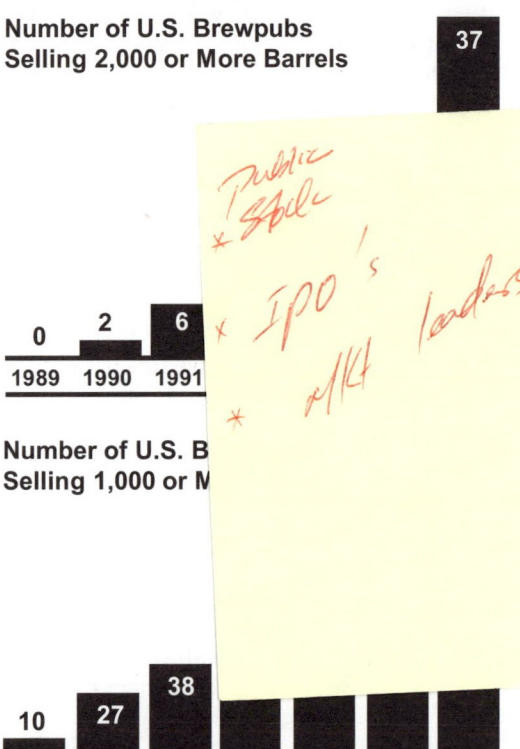

Rock Bottom Restaurants Inc. opened five brewpubs in five states, extending eastward as far as Chicago and Cleveland. Hops Grill and Bar added four more Florida brewpubs to bring its total to fourteen. McMenamin's Breweries ventured out of Oregon for the first time, building three brewpubs in the Seattle area and one in Vancouver, Washington.

The newest interstate chain to appear is the Tacoma, Washington-based Ram International/Big Horn Brewing Co. group. After opening its first in Salem, Oregon, in September, the company followed with one Big Horn Brewing Co. each in Texas, Colorado, and Idaho by January 1996. The more established Wynkoop Brewing Co. in Denver plans six new brewpubs in six different states stretching from Green Bay, Wisconsin, to Savannah, Georgia. Each one will be under a different name and be a joint venture with local partners (see "Mountain West" section).

Also brewing up new ventures is the eighteen-restaurant California Cafe company. Its first brewpub, Alcatraz Brewing Co., opened in Indianapolis, Indiana, last year. It plans three more under the Alcatraz moniker during 1996, to open in Chicago, Lower Downtown Denver, and the greater Washington, D.C., metropolitan area.

"We went into Indianapolis thinking it'll be a secondary market," said Alcatraz's beverage manager Michael Merriman. "We figured we would have a long, hard education process, and that was absolutely not the case." He added that they discovered a long learning curve for new site selection due to the tangled web of individual states' restrictions that can be difficult to ferret out.

Large-Brewery Craft Beers Show Mixed Results

It appears that the imitation microbrew beers from large breweries may not be a serious threat to independent craft brewers after all — or not yet, at least. In late 1995 Miller announced to its distributors that it will be discontinuing its Reserve line of brands such as Amber Ale and Velvet Stout. Scott Barnum, the head of Miller's American Specialty and Craft Beer division, said the company will instead place more emphasis on its craft-brewer partnerships.

One of the large brewer's focus groups learned that large brewery brands attempting to imitate brands from small breweries face a credibility gap among consumers. In addition, other research showed that when these large-brewery "high-price niche beers" succeed in initially attracting entry-level consumers, many retailers then encourage their customers to "trade-up" to the real micro and regional beers.

Coors's three new seasonal beers in 1994 — Eisbock, Weizen, and Oktoberfest — did not return for a second chance in 1995. The Colorado brewer instead tried several other approaches. First, it added the first Killian's brand extension with Killian's Brown Ale. Next, it opened its own draft-only microbrewery, SandLot Brewery at Coors Field baseball stadium in Denver, hiring veteran microbrewers away from Hubcap Brewery and H. C. Berger Brewing Co. (With its partner, Rounders Restaurant, next door, SandLot functions more as a brewpub than micro.) Then during the fall, Coors unveiled its Blue Moon line of specialty beers, including Honey Blonde Ale, Nut Brown Ale and Belgian White Ale, contract-brewed at F. X. Matt — the brewer for many other well-known contract-brewed craft beers.

Coors also added another red beer last year, Red Light, offering red-heads a lighter alternative.

Anheuser-Busch raised the eyebrows of many microbrewers with its release of Crossroads, an unfiltered German-style wheat beer. While its use of a German yeast strain and resulting slight banana aroma gave the beer a true German-wheat character, the brand's packaging failed to even mention the word "German" or to explain why the beer was so cloudy. The brand was discontinued months after its introduction.

A-B bounced back in the fall with the announcement of a new line of craft-style beers called "American Originals." Starting with recipes from the company's archives, the company reissued beers it hadn't made since prior to Prohibition, including Faust all-malt lager, Münchener amber lager, and Black and Tan, a porter. This time the packaging, incorporating the brands' original graphics, also explained the beers' styles. These were followed by Michelob Amber Bock and Christmas Beer, a dark lager and the company's first seasonal beer in many decades.

A-B also introduced its first regional brand, Zeigenbock, an amber bock beer brewed and distributed only in Texas. It may likely duplicate this approach with its breweries in other regions of the country. Both A-B and Coors appear to be following a "throw a lot of things at the wall and see what sticks" strategy.

S&P Corp. (Pabst/Pearl/Falstaff/Olympia) threw its hat into the ring, introducing Red Bone Red Lager. Stroh Brewery Co. continues to extend its Augsburger line, adding Augsburger Alt in 1995.

Genesee may provide the best example of a large brewery that has used specialty-type beers to boost its bottom line. According to a report by analyst Gabelli and Co., the combination of its J. W. Dundee's Honey Brown Lager and Michael Shea's brands sold approximately 150,000 barrels in 1995, close to 10 percent of the brewery's production.

Meanwhile, the "red rain" of new brands with the word "red" in their name appears to be subsiding. Having flooded various sectors of the market, from

JOIN THE INSTITUTE
The Power of Membership

Three excellent reasons why you should belong to the Institute for Brewing Studies:

1. Information
We research and publish information on all topics affecting brewers: alerts on legislative and tax issues, technical brewing data, new products and statistics, and operating information.

2. Fellowship
Our membership is more than 3,000 strong. These are 3,000 members in a community with common interests.

3. Membership Benefits
Benefits include a year's subscription to **The New Brewer**, substantial discounts for the National Craft-Brewers Conference and Trade Show, representation to associations and the media, Brewmaster for Hire, On-line Brewers Forum, Small Brewers Insurance, *Alcohol Issues Alert* quarterly updates (Brewery Member only), facts and figures on the industry, grass roots initiatives on issues and more.

Complete the membership application below and begin receiving all the benefits of membership in the Institute for Brewing Studies.

Membership to the Institute for Brewing Studies

Join the Institute and start receiving your benefits immediately. Just mark the appropriate membership category below and complete your address information. Thank you for your participation.

Corporate Membership

☐ Operating Brewer (includes all microbreweries, pubbreweries, regional breweries, large breweries and contract brewing companies). Estimate taxable production for current year and check appropriate category. Please remit in U.S. funds.

　　_____ 1 to 15,000 bbl./yr.　　$195
　　_____ 15,001 to 1 million bbl./yr. $325
　　_____ 1 million plus bbl./yr.　$1,400

☐ Allied Trade to the Brewing Industry (includes suppliers, associations, schools, consultants, etc.): $275

☐ Brew-on-Premise: $195

Individual Membership
(Includes breweries in planning.)

☐ $135

Subscription Only to *The New Brewer*

United States:
☐ $55 one-year　　☐ $99 two-year

Canada and International:
☐ $65 one-year　　☐ $119 two-year

Method of Payment:

☐ Check enclosed (must be in U.S. funds)

Charge to:
☐ Visa　　　　　　☐ MasterCard

Acct. No. _____

Exp. Date _____

• Make checks payable to: Institute for Brewing Studies. Prices effective through 12/31/97. Contact: (303) 447-0816, orders@aob.org or FAX (303) 447-2825 for credit card orders.

Important: Please indicate your industry affiliation.

☐ Operational brewery
☐ Brewery in planning
☐ Contract brewing company
☐ Distributor or importer

☐ Equipment manufacturer
☐ Industry consultant
☐ Ingredients supplier

☐ Association, government agency, school or library
☐ Publication editor or writer
☐ Other: _____

Please complete the following:

Name _____

Title _____

Company _____

Address _____ City _____

State/Province _____ Zip/Postal Code _____ Country _____

Telephone _____

Return this form to: Institute for Brewing Studies, PO Box 1510, Boulder, CO 80306-1510, U.S.A.; or FAX (303) 447-2825.

popular priced to super-premium, the plethora of tinted beers may have been of greater benefit to companies selling caramel color (or "Gravymaster," as one microbrewer puts it) than to their parent breweries.

Here Comes Wine and Spirits

Heard enough about pseudo microbrews from large breweries? Well, it no longer ends there. Spirits companies and wineries are also gearing up for their piece of the action. Brown Forman introduced its Jack Daniels 1866 Classic Amber Lager in late 1994. The brand was one of the fastest-growing craft-style beers, racking up 20,000-barrel sales during its first calendar year on the market. The company brewed 10 percent of product at its own Tennessee microbrewery and contracts the rest at Hudepohl-Schoenling Brewing Co.

Seagram's began test brewing Coyote Amber Lager, produced at one of the Stroh facilities. The New Orleans–based Sazerac spirits company released Pelican brand beers produced at Abita Brewing Co. California's Benzinger Winery is building its own brewery. Add the aforementioned sale of Yakima Brewing/Grant's Ales to the group that owns Chateau St. Michelle.

Wine and spirits and the craft-brewing industry are far from strangers to each other, as more and more microbrews have been using wine and spirits wholesalers to get their products to market. The continuing consolidation amongst beer wholesalers is likely encouraging this trend. Wine and spirits wholesalers tend to be larger than most beer wholesalers, averaging just three per state, and are used to carrying a large number of specialty niche brands — although this does not necessarily guarantee better performance than you will get from a traditional beer wholesaler. According to Douglas Metz, president of the Wine and Spirits Wholesalers Association, the top three distributors of 1994 for Pete's Brewing Co. were all wine and spirits wholesalers.

Cask-Conditioning Coming of Age?

Gradually, more and more American breweries are warming up to the concept, so to speak, of cask-conditioned ale. Cask-conditioned ale is defined as ale that is unpasteurized and unfiltered, conditioned and served without any artificial carbonation, and poured at cellar temperature (55 to 60 degrees F). It has been the cause célebre of Britain's CAMRA (Campaign for Real Ale), a consumer organization that helped to inspire the North American craft-brewing boom.

"True" cask beers or "real ales" require a trained cellarmaster who is responsible for the continuing maturation of the beer at the pub, after it has left the brewery. While some of the so-called cask-conditioned beers sold by today's craft brewers may not be considered "true" cask beers by CAMRA's standards, many are nonetheless approaching this goal by selling hand-pump-drawn, keg-conditioned ales. Here is a *partial list* of companies selling cask-conditioned ales in one form or another:

Brewpubs: Commonwealth Brewing Co., Goose Island Brewing Co., Sherlock's Home, Gritty McDuff's Brewpub, Oliver Breweries/Wharf Rat Camden Yards, Walnut Brewery, Rock Bottom Breweries, Wynkoop Brewing Co., John Harvard's Brewhouse, and Back Bay Brewing Co.

Microbreweries/Regional Breweries: BridgePort Brewing Co., Pike Brewing Co. (formerly Pike Place Brewing), Oregon Brewing Co./Rogue Ales, Emerald Isle Brew Works, Yards Brewing Co., Lind Brewing Co., St. Arnold Brewing Co., Atlantic Coast Brewing Co., Oxford Brewing Co., Shipyard Brewery and Wild Goose Brewery

Also, Boston Beer Co. has been "test-conditioning" and test-marketing Cask Ale, a "cask" version of its Boston Ale brand, in selected accounts in New England. President Jim Koch said Boston Beer is developing a product that will not require a cellarmaster after it is delivered to accounts by utilizing sterile filling technology at Hudepohl-Schoenling Brewing Co.

Along with Rhode Island's Emerald Isle Brew Works, the new Philadelphia microbrewery, Yards Brewing Co., in Philadelphia, Pennsylvania, is one of two breweries in the United States producing exclusively cask- or keg-conditioned ales. "It changes a little from bar to bar," said owner Tom Kehoe. Because their Yards Extra Special Bitter is "higher-maintenance" than other brands, Kehoe and co-owner Jon Bovit have to hand-pick the accounts that sell the ale.

Pacific Northwest

Redhook Ale Brewery had a great year with 155,000 barrels sold, reflecting a 66 percent increase. Its share of the craft-brewing market increased from 3.7 to 4.1 percent. Redhook began work on its new brewery in Portsmouth, New Hampshire, last summer, slated to be on line by the third quarter of 1996. This is the first time a successful craft brewer from one region of the country has set up a brewery in another region. Redhook added a new year-round brand, Redhook Rye ale, an unfiltered ale brewed with rye malt. It is the first rye beer from a regional-level craft brewery in the United States. Continuing its wild streak, the brewery unveiled Double Black Stout, an imperial stout brewed with Starbucks coffee (added after primary fermentation). While not the first-ever coffee beer (McMenamin's and Colorado's Mountain Sun brewpubs preceded it), it is the first coffee beer bottled for interstate distribution.

Hart Brewing Co. also enjoyed another tremendous year, posting a 70 percent increase for a total of 123,100 barrels sold. Hart's marketshare of the craft-brewing total increased from 2.9 to 3.3 percent as it passed Anchor Brewing Co. to become the fifth largest craft-brewing company in the nation. Hart opened its third brewing facility, a combination microbrewery and brewpub, in downtown Seattle in February 1995. The company added one new seasonal beer, Kölsch, brewed in the German Kölsch style.

Full Sail Brewing Co. upped the ante for brewery size amongst its regional specialty brethren as it fired up a new 200-barrel brewhouse, part of a 250,000-barrel capacity facility in Hood River, Oregon, that came on line in April 1995. Full Sail sold 71,500 barrels for a 36 percent increase over 1994. The company introduced a regular packaging of seasonal beers beginning with India Pale Ale in the summer followed by Red Ale in the fall.

Widmer Brothers Brewing Co. enjoyed a 40 percent increase with a total of 69,000 barrels sold, led by its Widmer Hefeweizen, the largest-selling draft craft-brew in Oregon. Still selling draft only during 1995, Widmer Brothers will bring this era to a close as it begins distributing bottled product during 1996. The company spent half the year test-brewing batches at G. Heileman's Milwaukee brewery, but was unsatisfied with the results (the brewery was later sold to Miller's Jacob Leinenkugel Brewing Co.). Undaunted by the experience, Widmer opened a number of new markets throughout the Rockies, Midwest and East Coast.

Widmer finally opened its Gasthaus brewpub it had been planning, attached to its Russell Street facility, and announced plans for a new, larger brewery to built across the street this year. Between also raising capital and adding the folksier "Brothers" to its corporate name, the brewery found time to introduce three new beers, Spezial Amber ale and the seasonals Widberry, in summer, and Winternacht black ale, in winter.

Portland Brewing Co.'s sales jumped to 62,000 barrels, a 68 increase for the year. Portland added Wheat Berry Ale, brewed with Oregon marionberries, during the summer and later reintroduced its old Portland Porter brand under the new moniker Haystack Black.

Oregon Ale and Beer Co., the contract-brewing subsidiary of Boston Beer Co., sold 35,000 barrels in its first full year on the market. Oregon Ale and Beer recently attracted the wrath of the Oregon Brewers Guild, which issued a press release attacking the company for its use and trademark of the term "Oregon's Original Ale" and marketing its brands as "microbrewed" when all of the bottled product is produced by Portland's giant Blitz-Weinhard brewery.

Nor'Wester Brewery & Public House (formerly Willamette Valley Brewing Co.) continued its rapid rise with 33,000-barrel sales, posting a 96 percent increase. Nor'Wester's public-stock philosophy of "turning beer enthusiasts into brewery owners" has built the company a strong and loyal following of shareholders. President Jim Bernau tells the story.

Jim Bernau, Nor'Wester Brewery

We've had a lot of good luck. There's a lot of myths about our industry that the consumers are continually revealing to not be true. "It's gotta slow down," people say. But it's not happening. The base keeps growing and that leads to significant volume increases.

Oregon leads the nation in total per-capita craft beer consumption at 10 percent of the market. And it's continuing. Our distributor is predicting a growth rate of 52 percent, which is significant given the volumes.

I think the main reasons for Nor'Wester's success are that we have very effective distribution and we produce products that craft-beer consumers want to buy. Our Raspberry Weizen, which we introduced in 1995, is now the fifth-ranked bottled craft beer sold in this market. Our hefeweizen is ranked first. Now, Raspberry Weizen for a dyed-in-the-wool craft brewer is not in their top ten list. But the customer is really interested. It's the state's leading fruit beer.

The third reason is our Northwest message. We celebrate the great outdoors on our labels, and the company also contributes to environmental causes such as the Adopt-a-River program.

Capacity is now our biggest constraint. There's only a 41,000-barrel capacity in Portland. But I own capacity in the other breweries I founded this year through a holding company called Microbreweries Across America. By the end of 1996 we should have a combined total of a 156,000-barrel capacity. The new breweries include Aviator Ales, Woodinville, Washington; Bayhawk Ales,

Irvine, California; and Mile High Brewing Co./ Timberline Ales in Denver, Colorado. We'll brew Nor'Wester beers at all of those facilities. I am the common link on the board of all of these companies as their original founder.

There's one more we're working on in Saratoga Springs, New York, where we'll be brewing in June. That will have a 100-barrel system, our largest brewery, along with a 220-bottles-per-minute Krones line.

We recently issued our IPO — a $7 million offering. Nor'Wester's existing stockholders made out pretty well. The initial stock sold for $1.20 per share. Then we did a reverse split, making the effective price $1.99, and then the stock was valued by the market at $7 per share. This affected just the original investors in Nor'Wester. The other breweries are separate and each one is a beer-enthusiast-owned company.

It was very gratifying to show our investors this level of return in that short amount of time. I had started by selling stock in the Regulation A offering by myself. People thought it was funny, but it really worked. We now have eight thousand beer enthusiasts in the market who own this company.

That's the concept I started with at the winery years ago. It's a very powerful concept of combining your investor with your market. Many people told me it's the only investment where they can drink themselves to profitability. They do enjoy their ownership.

Hefeweizen accounts for 46 percent of volume, Raspberry Weizen accounts for 29 percent, followed by Best Bitter at 10 percent, Blacksmith Porter at 8 percent, and Dunkel Weizen at 7 percent. The hefeweizen is a really approachable, almost transitional micro, as is the Raspberry. I think we're getting a lot of people trying our product who usually drink industrial beers, particularly among women. I think women are offended by the advertising of industrial brewers. And women are a powerful force — they do most of the shopping. Women are exercising a lot more economic independence than they used to. Also they're conscientious to value and are more interested in the quality than in the effect of the product.

We're introducing two new brands this year, Honey Weizen and Oregon Amber. We currently sell 58 percent of our beer in Oregon, 21 percent in Washington, and 11 percent in California. In Oregon and Washington we use the A-B distribution network. In Colorado we use Coors. In the Northeast we're building our network through Miller distributors. I'm referring to the independent family-owned businesses that distribute these products.

We try and select the best wholesalers for the market — those that have a lot of penetration for the market and high standards of treating the product properly. In California we chose a liquor distributor because it was the only company willing to commit to delivering the beer cold.

We spend at least 12 percent on sales support. How we spend it is important — primarily on point-of-sale materials in accounts. We don't buy radio or TV time and we do very little newspaper advertising.

We do programmed pricing throughout the year to generate consumer interest. We offer some targeted distributor incentives but not often. Our largest distributor, Maletis, refuses to accept incentives. He said, "If we can't do our job within our margin then something's wrong. If you want to spend money, spend it on the product or on talking to customers."

I believe that we're going to see an entire country of beer consumers choosing to buy locally brewed, high-quality lagers and ales, and the megatrend is now clearly established. And I believe there is enough market for all of us large and small to focus on meeting the market's needs. There are lots of areas with unmet needs, both in terms of geography and product style.

Oregon's Deschutes Brewery enjoyed another great year as sales hit 31,600 barrels, marking a 60 percent increase. Oregon Brewing Co./Rogue Ales had a tremendous 1995 as well with 26,000 barrels in sales, posting a 74 percent increase. Two new Rogue brands were introduced, Hazelnut Brown Nectar, based on a homebrewer's recipe created for an American Homebrewers Association® national conference, and Cran'n'Cherry, a fall release brewed with cherries and cranberries. Rogue's output bumps it up to the regional specialty category, as does that of Alaskan Brewing and Bottling Co. Alaskan sold just under 22,000 barrels for a 56 percent increase for the year. President Geoff Larson shares the story of this Great Northern pioneer.

Geoff Larson, Alaskan Brewing Co.

I think the industry itself has grown, and its momentum is pulling us along. In Alaska we have to maintain the highest quality beer possible. Our compatriots are doing the same but we have an added cost burden here. All our raw materials have to be shipped one thousand miles north. Then we make the beer and ship it one thousand miles south and compete with our brethren in the Northwest who don't have those freight costs.

The industry is higher-priced quality, and in Alaska it's even higher, so we always try to be 15 percent better. We've been trying to hold to that since the beginning.

We grew 68 percent in 1995. We anticipate the same growth for the next three to four years and we're gearing up for it. Our Alaskan Amber is 65 percent of all our sales. After that our Pale Ale and our new year-round release, Frontier Amber Ale, are running neck and neck. We sell 50 percent draft.

Many Northwest brewers are broadening their base by going into a lot of markets. I don't see us doing the same. We want our customers treated to a good solid brand with a lot of support. We try to provide them with the freshest product as we are generating increased volume. I think that's why we're the fourth-largest-selling draft craft-brewed beer in Washington State — and we're in only eight of the twenty-eight counties. We sell fifty-fifty in Alaska and Washington. We want to cover all of Washingon State, but only after we're sure we can supply it. Ultimately, we'll add Oregon, Montana, and Idaho, but that's still far off.

Our distributors range from specialty houses that concentrate on high-end wines and micros to A-B distributors. We support them. They see discounting as a tool to get sampling. We try to get our products out at the best value possible, while competing with inherent costs of location. We do post-offs, but less frequently than others. We try more to keep a low price point on a day-in-day-out basis.

We don't do incentives. We're probably one of the most simple of all the craft brewers in that respect. There are a few of us who don't do the standard beer game ploys. The success of the industry has brought it full circle. Craft brewers use a lot of the same techniques that this industry originally was spawned in reaction against. Maybe it's a coming of age, the changing of the marketplace, with the sheer volume — or it could be more a change of the consumer, which is now more mainstream. It's not just beer aficionados who drink these beers now. It's mom and dad, too.

Last year we installed a 150-barrel brewhouse, which has been up and running since July. We're looking at ultimately 100,000-barrel capacity. We had it designed for additional brewhouse vessels, so it's expandable.

We funded it through debt. Our bank has been with us pretty much from the beginning. It took them a while at first. Manufacturing is unique in this state since Alaska is more of a raw materials producer. Secondly, since a significant part of our sales was outside Alaska, their concern was "how can you compete against people in the lower forty-eight?" Our bank has been a partner in more ways than one, especially in making us aware of financial tools available to us in the state of Alaska.

Everyone has their partners of one type or another that, over time, they have built to a confidence level in terms of the degree of financial success of the company.

We've been brewing twenty-four hours a day, seven days a week for the past three years. The minute the week finished we'd clean the brewhouse, get it emptied, and drop another batch. Our record for number of batches in a week for the plant was forty-two! The first time we watched our new brewhouse and saw the meter running, collecting the same amount of wort in just fifteen minutes instead of the eight hours it used to take to create, we were in heaven. It's nice now, finally, to be off that gerbil-wheel track. The new brewery was supplied by JVNW. I think it was the largest they've ever done. My first was from them eleven years ago.

We still have a twenty-four-hour coverage because we still need to be monitoring tanks and yeasts counts and the like, although brewing is only between Monday and Friday. We're very happy with the new equipment. The expansion came through fairly on schedule — only one week off of what was planned. That's a testament to the crew and to Dayton's (Dayton Canaday, head brewer) gray hairs.

Now that our old 11-barrel system is waiting in the wings, we get to play with some new beers. I have no idea what our brewers want to do — but they're going to have some fun, and that'll be fun for us, as well as for the consumer. Last year we were in our growth throes. Now we're able to do more of what we want in terms of brewing new styles. The brewery has thirty full-time employees.

We want everybody in Alaska to be proud of what we do here, while being mindful that when someone puts down their $6.99 for a six-pack they're voting with hard-earned cash, and we're responsible for giving them a fair value.

We are living in interesting times. I don't see any clouds looming on the one- or two-year horizon, but the mists are out there.

For a great bottle of wine, some people are willing to pay as much as $900 a bottle. For quality beers, it's just an extra buck. A fresher pint can be much more easily purchased and for only a dollar more. With the craft beer market at just 2 percent and imports at 5 to 6 percent, I'm not afraid of large brewers coming into it. With all of their marketing and advertising telling consumers about better beer, they're broadening the market for everybody. For a very small investment a consumer can have a taste experience that, with a very good wine, could cost hundreds of dollars, but with beer we're only talking about a few quarters' price difference.

And finally, BridgePort Brewing Co. increased by 6 percent with 19,000 barrels in sales in 1995.

Microbreweries

Sales at Grant's Yakima Brewing and Malting Co. were flat for the year at 11,500 barrels. The new marketing director, Shawn Burns, explained that the Yakima brewery was shut down from mid-November through the end of the year. This enabled it to implement Chateau St. Michelle's new plan for reeling in Grant's distribution network from thirty-nine states back to just nine. Burns reported that by March 1996 Grant's sales in those nine states had already returned to the same level as prior to the pull-back. The states where Grant's Ales are still distributed include Washington, Oregon, Alaska, California, Hawaii, Arizona, Nevada, Montana, and Idaho. It will reappear in two of its former East Coast markets during 1996, Georgia and Connecticut, the home state of its parent company UST Inc.

Hale's Ales opened its third brewery, a combination microbrewery and brewpub, in the Fremont district of Seattle. Still draft-only, Hale's was down 2 percent for the year with 9,500 barrels in sales. The McMenamin's Edgefield Brewery increased 2 percent, with 5,200 barrels sold for the year. Seattle contract-brewing company Jet City Brewing Co. sold 4,600 barrels, a 4 percent increase. Seattle's Maritime Pacific Brewing Co. continued a steady pace of growth with 4,500 barrels, for 19 percent above 1994 sales.

Sales by neighboring Pike Brewing Co. (formerly Pike Place Brewing Co.) held steady at the 2,000-barrel mark, while it's contract-brewed volume dipped 32 percent, down to 2,000 barrels. This trend will likely boomerang back the other direction now that Pike has restructured its contract arrangement. The company discontinued its dual-contracting with both Vermont's Catamount Brewing Co. and Indiana's Indianapolis Brewing Co., consolidating production at Minnesota Brewing Co., the facility known for brewing Pete's Wicked brands during the last several years.

Fish Brewing Co., Olympia, Washington, sold 2,000 barrels for 67 percent growth for its second full year in business. Alaska's Bird Creek Brewery also hit 2,000 barrels, doubling its 1994 output. Star Brewing Co., Portland, Oregon, increased 52 percent for its second calendar year, achieving 1,800 barrels in sales. Star added a new twist to the fruit beer basket with its Pineapple Ale released last summer.

Brewpubs

Rock Bottom Brewery's Portland outlet became the region's largest selling brewpub with 2,300-barrel sales. Seattle's Big Time Brewing Co. was up 19 percent for the year with 1,600 barrels sold. Steelhead Brewing Co., Eugene, Oregon, was down 14 percent with 1,500 barrels. Newcomer Birkebeiner Brewing, Spokane, Washington, did well with 1,400 barrels in sales. Wild River Brewing, Cave Junction, Oregon, increased 33 percent, selling 1,000 barrels.

The McMenamin's chain of brewpubs added four more brewpubs, making fourteen total (plus Edgefield) by year's end. All four new operations were in Washington State, with one in Vancouver and three in or near Seattle. McMenamin's combined sales of all its breweries exceeds 15,000 barrels. Besides the breweries the company owns twenty taverns that also serve as outlets for its trademark "live, unfiltered ales." President Mike McMenamin and brewery manager Keith Mackie shed light on this empire of casual-atmosphere pubbreweries.

Mike McMenamin, McMenamin's Breweries

This week we'll open our fifteenth brewpub in Tigard. It's the first building we've ever built from the ground up. We also plan a brewpub for the Fremont area of Seattle, scheduled for mid-May. Then we have two larger projects. One is the Crystal Ballroom in Portland. It will feature a pub and an Edgefield-sized brewery on the first two floors and a concert hall in the ballroom on the third level. The other is the Kennedy School in Northeast Portland. The concept will be similar to Edgefield, albeit smaller. It's another good old historic building-complex we can have a lot of fun with. We'll have a theater there, plus lodging, a brewery, pub, and community center.

It's the people in the company that make McMenamin's what it is. For whatever reason, the people that tend to drift toward our company are extremely creative and interesting folks. With the size of the company there's now room for advancement. And we try to pay fairly, and have profit sharing and health plans. We're trying to make the restaurant business a legitimate occupation for people — which obviously we feel it is — instead of a job that you do when you're in between other things in your life. We now have employees buying houses, getting married, and having kids. It's more of a viable company.

Hammerhead pale ale, Terminator stout, and Ruby raspberry ale are our three best selling beers. Hammerhead has made a steady rise over the years. Our IPA is also a real strong seller. Overall we produced over 150 different brands of beer last year. The specialty beers make it fun and exciting for the brewers.

We don't have plans to go into other states yet. We'd like to do something in California. From a management perspective it makes sense to expand gradually. I don't think we can open up more than six or seven in a year and still manage to keep it fun for our employees.

At Edgefield we're working on a distillery this year, where we'll have a little bar where people can taste the products. We'll make brandy, which will take five years, as well as some quick stuff, like a grappa. Plus we'll experiment, like by distilling zinfandel and blending it back with the zinfandel wine from the same vintage. We're still moving through the licensing. We also hope to be able make some whiskey, but that will require a legislative change first.

We don't advertise much, have much point of sale, or sell our beers to outside accounts. It's getting intense with the competition here in the Northwest. And for breweries to keep growing, you have to keep coming up with more advertising and sales, etc. That's not as fun for us as it is in keeping the beer at our pubs and selling it ourselves. At least that's what we know.

Our menu consists of low-key, everyday, survival food with a lot of fun thrown in, and now pastas and salads. Food is 65 percent of our business, but we still like to keep it simple. That way, the people who work in the pubs can learn to do everything — cooking or waiting — and have the flexibility to be able to work in different areas.

Specialty beers have been our whole philosophy ever since we opened. We have ten taps for our own beers at all our pubs. Five are consistent and the other five are constantly rotated. It challenges the people that come in to always try something new and it challenges the brewers. Changing beers keeps an edge to brewing and keeps everybody learning.

For us, the cost of a new brewpub — if you include the land and building — is $1 million. If not, including leasehold/property improvements, fixtures, and equipment, it's in the $400,000 to $500,000 range. We still use Grundy tanks. To brew three times a week on a Grundy system is a full-time job for one person. I like the size because then you can have one person do everything, from ordering raw materials to milling to mashing, cleaning, kegging with time leftover to do the paperwork. When a person is trained on one of these systems, he's really schooled in what brewing is all about. And with the small batches — ten to twelve kegs per batch — it allows you to do specials all the time. It's only good for a week or two before the supply runs out.

We've expanded through company cash flow and bank debt. We have great banking relationships. Once the bank gets comfortable with what you're doing, they're a great friend. Now there's more of a track record for our brewpubs. Cash flow made Edgefield possible. We couldn't get bank money early because that was a scary project — from everybody's perspective.

Overall McMenamin's employs between seven hundred and eight hundred people. The downside is I can't know everybody on a first-name basis anymore, but the upside is there are a lot of opportunities for people. Our philosophy is we just do what we feel is right and it keeps us moving forward.

I think on the small brewpub side of things, it's unlimited. Ten years ago I was thinking it'll hit the wall fast and that'll be it. It's already gone full circle now. It's a blast. We're making our own beer, wine, and distilled products. It's quite an amazing thing. No one really thought that way before.

Keith Mackie, McMenamin's Breweries

We spend around $75,000 for a complete 6-barrel system installed, piecing together Grundy tanks wherever I find them. Recently we bought an entire container load of thirty-eight Grundys from England, which worked out to a cost of $1,000 apiece. We modify them ourselves to our own specs which costs another $800 to $1,000 per tank. We use Journeyman Metal Services, a new company out of Eugene, Oregon, for our boilers, mash tuns, vorlauf tanks, CIP piping, and any other sanitary stainless equipment.

John Richen and I are the two brewery general managers. There are two other managers underneath us, and then the ranks of individual brewers at all of the brewpubs. We have two jack-of-all-trades utility brewers who can brew at any of our breweries, plus a few keg washers at Edgefield, and several delivery drivers.

Usually after they've been with us for a while our brewers are experienced in brewing at four to five of our breweries. We try to get the job done, whatever that takes. Even the managers still brew about once a week.

On a monthly basis we get the brewers together by region, and have meetings in which we conduct tastings. We'll taste everybody's seasonal beer, like a bock in springtime, or if there's a new recipe everybody's brewing. Our customers, management, and staff at the different brewpubs are our best resource when it comes to detecting problems. Usually it's a pouring problem, if the beer pours too foamy or too flat, or if a customer returns it. We can easily track down the source. That's the nice thing about having all our beer served in our own places.

We use an English ale yeast strain that's repitched for eight to ten generations. We check everybody's culture for bacteria and wild yeast on a weekly basis.

We did a few different things last year. One was a chamomile tea beer that was nice. We experimented with using oat hulls, which are flavorless but act like little spacers in your mash — very helpful in a wheat beer. One new beer we won't do again is garlic ale. A brewer slipped that one by us without getting the appropriate approval. I said "You put *what* in the beer?" We ended up dumping five of the eleven kegs because no one was willing to drink it, except for the true garlic lovers.

Our brewers have been working a lot lately developing variations on hefeweizens, porters, and IPAs. We don't want to copy anybody. Rather, our intention is to give it a different twist.

Newcomer in the brewpub-chain realm is Tacoma, Washington-based RAM International/Big Horn Brewing Co., who opened three brewpubs in three different states in 1995. Brewery Manager David

Hollow explains the company's approach and its future plans.

David Hollow, RAM International/Big Horn Brewing Co.

We have twenty-one restaurants in six states. In the Northwest, because consumers are not very supportive of chain restaurants, they're all under different names, such as C. I. Shenanigan's, Murphy's, RAM Border Cafe, and Lakewood Bar and Grill. In Texas they're all known as Humperdinck's.

Our first brewpub opened September 15th, 1995, in Salem, Oregon. It was a remodel of a restaurant we had for twenty years known as Border Cafe. Since then we added brewpubs in Denver, Colorado (in the Denver Tech Center); Arlington, Texas (across from the Six Flags amusement park); and Boise, Idaho. In each case we retain the name of the existing restaurant and add Big Horn Brewing of Texas, of Colorado, or of Idaho, etc.

This year we'll open in Spokane, Washington, because we finally got the law changed in this state. Since we already owned retail establishments in Washington, the existing law would have required us to give up our liquor licenses, shut down for days, and reopen all of them as brewpubs — all just to open a single brewpub. We managed to appease most of the groups initially opposed to it; however, the lobbyists from Redhook and Hart breweries wouldn't accept the new law until it included a 2,400-barrel brewpub production cap. We'll have to live with that.

We're remodeling two more of our existing units this year, a C. B. & Potts restaurant in Fort Collins, Colorado, and one in Puyallup, Washington. We'll add new brewpubs in Dallas, Texas, Tucson, Arizona, and in 1997, Tacoma, Washington.

We have an overall sports theme package, including pool tables and a game room. We had originally estimated sales averaging 7 barrels per seat per year but we've gone well beyond that. We expect three of the four locations to go over 2,000 barrels this year. Business at our Denver site is already averaging 40 barrels per week. And with winter numbers currently exceeding projections, we're adding more capacity to the brewpubs in Colorado, Texas, and Idaho — two to three conditioning/serving tanks to each. Since these weren't originally planned for, they'll have to bring each tank into the walk-in cooler in three pieces, and finish the welding in there.

We use New World Brewing Systems out of Florida. They've been helpful with any problems that have come up, whether they were originally their fault or ours. Our cost, since it was a volume buy, was $180,000 per 15-barrel system, including four fermenters and five serving tanks.

In designing the beers, we did four and a half months of weekly blind taste tests with control groups. We were looking for broad appeal, yet distinctive beers. The owners spent three years researching the concept. They saw what everyone was doing wrong, especially with the lack of consistent quality and beers not being very distinctive. For example, we use more than one

---

PACIFIC NORTHWEST: 1995 OPENINGS AND CLOSINGS
STATES: Alaska, Washington, and Oregon

Companies listed as opened include all those that began selling their own beers during the 1995 calendar year.

† Denotes microbrewery with on-site restaurant or pub.

‡ Also operates as brew-on-premise.

MICROBREWERIES (9)
Alaska
Midnight Sun Brewing Co., Anchorage
Washington
Aviator Ales Brewery, Woodinville
Buchanan Brewing Corp., Oroville
Captains City Brewing Co., Coupeville
Ellensburg Brewing Co., Ellensburg
Hale's Ales Brewery and Pub (No. 3), Seattle †
Hart Brewing Co., Seattle †
Orchard Street Brewing Co., Bellingham
Tapps Brewing Co., Sumner
Youngs Brewery, Centralia (opened 1994)

BREWPUBS (23)
Alaska
Cusacks Brewpub and Roaster, Anchorage
Regal Eagle/North Slope Brewing Co., Eagle River
Oregon
Bend Brewing Co., Bend
Bank Brewing Co., Coos Bay
Big Horse Brewpub, Hood River
Big Horn Brewing Co. of Oregon/RAM International, Salem
Cascade Lakes Brewing Co., Redmond
Cascade Microbrewery and Public Firehouse, Salem
Fields Restaurant and Brewpub, Eugene
Mount Angel Brewing Co., Mount Angel
Siletz Brewing Co., Siletz
Spencers Brewhouse and Restaurant, Springfield

Washington
Boundary Bay Brewing Co., Bellingham
C. J.'s Brewpub Inc., Vancouver
Engine House No. 9/The Power Station, Tacoma
Issaquah Brewhouse/Eagle River Brewing Co., Issaquah
La Conner Brewing Co., La Conner
Mount Baker Brewing Co., Bellingham
McMenamin's — Mill Creek, Mill Creek
McMenamin's on the Columbia, Vancouver
McMenamin's — Roy Street, Seattle
McMenamin's — Six Arms, Seattle
Power House Restaurant and Brewery, Puyallup

CLOSINGS (YEAR OF OPENING IN PARENTHESES)
1 Brewpub
Willamette Brewing Co., Salem, OR (1991)

yeast. If you really want to have distinctive beers, you need two yeasts.

We keep a mainstay of five beers and one rotating handle. Due to the success of the beers so far, we're looking to adding one more handle. Our number one seller is called Buttface Amber Ale — when you see the logo of two rams butting heads, you'll understand the name. Our Hefeweizen, brewed German style, is number two, followed by our Red, an English bitter style. We also have a Honey Stout and Blewesberry (spelled with a "ewe" in it) blueberry weizen. The rotating special beer is left up to each individual brewer. Eventually, we'll move into selling cask-conditioned beer and offering beer to-go in growlers. And the Salem brewery will be the only one where we'll be distributing kegs.

We offer a diversified menu. Since we have twenty-five years in the restaurant business, the menus are solid. We know that in the nineties, casual dining restaurants are on top. Our research shows that the three major food groups for casual dining are pizza, burgers, and salads. We also offer steak, seafood, and pasta, so there's something for everybody.

We sell the major domestic beers as well. We thought it makes sense when you figure that A-B holds 43 percent of the market. Some people just want a Bud, and we didn't want to turn those people off. You have to get them in a comfort zone and then once they're in there we get them to try one of our beers.

We're looking at the ripe opportunities. Our plan for between now and the year 2000 is to add breweries to at least six more existing units, build nine brand new brewpubs, and where allowed to by law, start two or three microbreweries, one of which we plan for Alaska.

Transitions

Alaska's first-ever brewpubs opened during 1995 — one in Anchorage and one in Eagle River. There was a change in the state law last year that finally made operating Alaskan brewpubs feasible.

Seattle became more of a brewpub capital during 1995 as five more brewpubs or brewery-restaurants opened in or near the city last year.

Willamette Brewpub, Salem, Oregon, which had been struggling for a couple of years, closed in late 1995, the sole brewery closure in the region. Rock Bottom Restaurants purchased the company's assets in order to take its brewing equipment for use in another brewpub in a different city.

Siskyou Brewing Co. is the new name for Rogue River Brewing Co., Ashland, Oregon.

(See sidebar on page 17 for a complete listing of the region's 1995 openings and closings.)

Pacific

Contract-brewing company Pete's Brewing had yet another mind-boggling year. Its 91 percent growth brought it to 348,000-barrel sales, as its share of the total craft-brewing market surged from 7.2 percent to 9.2 percent. Pete's introduced its fourth year-round brand, the unfiltered Pete's Wicked Honey Wheat, plus its first summer seasonal, Pete's Wicked Summer Brew, an ale brewed with wheat malt and natural lemon flavor. The company switched its contract from Minnesota Brewing Co. to the Stroh Brewery facility in Minneapolis, Minnesota.

Sierra Nevada Brewing Co.'s sales rose to 200,000 barrels, achieving 28 percent growth for the year. Its share of the total craft-brewing market decreased from 6.2 percent to 5.3 percent.

Anchor Brewing Co. was flat for the year with 103,000 barrels in sales. Historically referred to as the "grandfather" or "godfather" of the microbrewing industry because it preceded the first micro by more than a decade, Anchor is truly the father of the U.S. craft-brewing movement, without question. No longer alone at the top, Anchor Brewing Co. President Fritz Maytag explains their philosophy of business.

Fritz Maytag, Anchor Brewing Co.

I don't feel comfortable talking about the future of this industry. We as a company have consciously decided to be very careful. I don't know where it's going. It's very flexible, fluid, and dynamic. I've always been terrified of not succeeding in the brewing business. It's extremely competitive and always has been. Now I'm scared for all new reasons.

Nor if I did know where it's going would I tell you — then you'd tell my competitors! Some think it's going for the moon, but we don't want to bet on that. We are what we've always been, small and creative. We've reached a size that is absolutely wonderful. I always wanted to be small and I like being small.

The rules are the same, but the players have developed some very bad habits in my opinion. These are the people whose goals are to make money, not to make beer. You get invaded by a lot of people who don't care, as long as they make money. Bless our lucky stars that it tends not to be the giant brewers. But instead, it's with some of the pretend breweries and the very aggressive new companies.

One of my concerns is your business at the Institute for Brewing Studies. What are you doing telling people about freshness dating? What about alcohol content? What about ingredient labeling? What about telling people which Anheuser-Busch brewery their beer comes from? Why are you trying to tell brewers they have to date their beer? We considered it a long time ago and decided it wasn't a good idea. If I refrigerate my beer all through distribution from the brewery to the consumer, do you know how long the beer will last?

We like to be very private about our marketing plans. We don't ever talk about it. If you ask about why we don't advertise it's because our beer is so good.

Our brands have always been at a low price point. In a competitive environment it may be more difficult for small breweries to be profitable. It's been a great pleasure to watch the price of Henry Weinhard's go down and down and down. It's like watching someone taking their mask off in stages. You can quote me on that. I've always had a grudge against them because they literally stole our truck design. They called the artists that worked for me to get them to help. It was flattering and then it was infuriating. Then they helped us tremendously by promoting the idea of a little brewery. It's an interesting dynamic. It was supposed to be a family thing and great quality and all. They used to say it was handmade. We had been saying that too, so I decided to take it off my label.

We make our beer and make a modest profit. Between brands like Michelob, Henry Weinhard's and Molson, it's a tough world out there. If I knew what to do, I wouldn't tell you — I'd run and tell my staff. We emphasize value, integrity, quality, distinctiveness, and personality. We've been doing it for thirty years.

We sell in forty-seven states. California is number one. Beyond that we wouldn't say. One of the nice things about not going public is we don't have to tell anybody how much we spend on sales support. We have two salespeople. They cover the whole country and Europe as well.

It's a company philosophy not to do discounting, but there are markets and individual situations where our distributors believe it's absolutely essential and in those cases we have been known to approve it. We believe in the opposite. We believe we already have a fabulous price. Our biggest problem has been people overpricing the beers because of the brewery's reputation. We can't control the price, of course. It's heartbreaking to have a realistic price and see it higher in remote areas. Our beers are coming down in price. It's good to see it coming down because of increased competition in the marketplace — one of the benefits to the consumer. Our beers are probably more competitive than they used to be.

We installed a new bottling line a year ago so that we can package Old Foghorn in 7-ounce bottles. We have fifty-four employees at the brewery.

I think the company's personality is very, very important. I don't believe in improving the image but in improving the reality and having an accurate reality. If you need to improve your image, work on the reality first. The reason that the whole microbrewing renaissance has succeeded is that the early pioneers were interested in making beer. People were in love with the idea of brewing beer. That's been a fantastic source of energy and has fueled public approval of our movement.

What Anchor stands for is the way our beer is made, our attitude, style, and philosopy. Our brewery has a theme. Our beers have a theme. It reminds me of what Winston Churchill said at a state dinner. When a woman asked what he thought of the dessert he said, "Madam, it's a pudding without a theme." We try to make a pudding with a theme.

Contract brewing company William and Scott/Rhino Chasers continued its growth trend with 29,000 barrels sold, posting a 32 percent increase. Arcata's Humboldt Brewery had a a great year too, joining the regional specialty brewery ranks in 1995 with 19,000-barrel sales for a 29 percent increase. Mendocino Brewing Co. also crossed the line selling 15,100 barrels for 11 percent growth. By the fall the company will be brewing at its new 100-barrel facility in Ukiah, California. The new brewery will expand Mendocino's capacity from its current 18,000-barrel level to an eventual 200,000 barrels.

Microbreweries

Karl Strauss' Old Columbia group, consisting of one microbrewery and two brewpubs, grew to 15,000-barrel total sales. St. Stan's Brewery was up 10 percent for the year with just under 14,000-barrel sales. St. Stan's added a new year-round brand, Whistle Stop Pale Ale. The veteran micro recently completed a new expansion, adding a new 60-barrel brewhouse, two 120-barrel fermenters and a high-speed bottler. St. Stan's capacity increased to 17,000 barrels with the capability for expansion to 50,000 barrels.

Mad River Brewing Co., Blue Lake, California, enjoyed a 42 percent increase last year with 8,800-barrel sales. Gordon Biersch sold 6,200 barrels produced in its draft-only Emeryville, California, facility. The Emeryville brewery was originally just a kegging facility for beer from its San Francisco brewpub. The company began fermenting beer there in January 1995, and the San Francisco brewery now supplies it with wort instead of finished beer.

Brewing Director Dan Gordon discusses Gorson Biersch's sale of a majority interest in the company and its plans for a new micro and more brewpubs.

Dan Gordon, Gordon Biersch Brewery Restaurants

I was contacted by Fertitta Enterprises for a project called Barley's Casino Brewery in Henderson, Nevada (a suburb of Las Vegas). Fertitta owns part of Station Casinos Inc., which operates several Las Vegas casinos. I got to meet the Fertittas and they expressed an interest in investing in Gordon Biersch.

We shut down the private placement we were working on to fund a bottling facility and new brewery restaurants, and Fertitta took it on. They invested new equity in the company and bought out some of our initial investors, to obtain a majority ownership. From an equity as well as an operations standpoint, Dean (Biersch) and I have the same position as before.

We're going full-blast ahead with all of our original plans. Our new microbrewery in San Jose will have bottled beer on the market in October. Initial capacity will be 100,000 barrels, expandable to 200,000. We're already at 10,000-barrel sales of draft beer alone, distributing in California and Hawaii. We're having a helluva time keeping up with the demand.

We discovered a real synergy between the outside accounts promoting the brewpubs and vice versa. We distribute two brands. Märzen is 80 percent of the total and Export is 20 percent. We have high-profile accounts at Candlestick Park and the Oakland Coliseum — the kind of thing a brewery-restaurant can't step into.

We'll sell our bottled beer initially in California, Nevada, and Hawaii, and later expand to Arizona and the Northwest.

In the brewpubs the ratio is 57 percent Märzen to 29 percent Export and 14 percent Dunkles (*sic*). This year we'll offer regular seasonals. We'll have Pilsener in late winter/early spring, maibock in spring, hefeweizen in summer, dunkel weizen in fall, and doublebock in winter.

We're a non-cookie-cutter place when it comes to menu development. The majority of the recipes are designed by the head chefs at the respective locations. For instance, the Hawaii location emphasizes Pacific Rim cuisine. With each one, the scenery, architecture, menu, and staff are all different. That's what makes it exciting. Wherever we are we try to hire as many locals as possible.

For us, a new brewpub costs about $2.5 million, not factoring in tenant improvement allowances we get from the landlords. We spend $600,000 on the brewery. I design it so one person can operate them. We're putting 30-barrel brewhouses in all of our locations. We have a large batch size and we double-batch everything into the fermenters.

For the restaurants we use Wachsmann Brautechnik brewhouses. Most have JVNW tanks, except one that has tanks from Liquid Assets. For our bottling brewery we have a Huppmann brewhouse we purchased used. Our grain handling equipment is Seeger, tankage is Mueller, and filtration is Velo and Seitz. We'll have a Krones bottler, filler, and labeler, as well as an IDD automatic two-lane keg filler. When purchasing fermenters I work with JVNW, Mueller, and Liquid Assets. I have a lot of faith in those three companies.

The key to successful expansion is having great people in the organization. What minimizes our turnover is stock options some of the key employees have, allowing them to participate in the growth, too. My side of the company has been fortunate, because the brewing department has lost only one brewer in seven years. It's a little addictive. You get a brewer on the machine at our place, train him in lager brewing, and he latches on to that production method and doesn't want to let go.

We plan just two brewpubs for 1996: one in Las Vegas, within the next seven months, and the other in the Los Angeles area. The plan for 1997 is a whole 'nother story. It will likely include one more again for both Las Vegas and Los Angeles. Barley's opened January 17th, located ten minutes from the Las Vegas airport. We set it up, but it's not a Gordon Biersch.

We don't advertise the brewery-restaurants. Our advertising is our big grain silo in front of the San Francisco restaurant and our other key locations. There's definitely visibility in having high-profile real estate alone.

For the draft business we spend about 21 percent of expenses on general marketing. We have painted trucks, we advertise in the Oakland A's and Giants' programs, hosted the NFL Pro-Bowl Superfest in Honolulu, and sponsor outrigger canoe races, jazz festivals, etc. Events are the key for us.

We have a sales staff of three. We hired Anastasy Tynan (*Brew Hawaii* brewspaper editor) three months ago in Hawaii and he's done a great job for us. We're already the number-one draft microbrew in Hawaii.

We don't do any discounting — quite the opposite, in fact. We're positioned as the most expensive beer in any given market. It's usually twenty-five cents to fifty cents more per glass at the accounts. People are willing to pay for quality. A lot of brewers don't understand that. Distributors talk them into pushing their prices down. The name of the game is standing behind your product quality. Our accounts can make more because they can charge more for it. We've never had an account claim that people weren't buying our beer because it's too expensive.

We do some distributor incentives — but that's a rarity. Last year we held a contest and the winners got a trip to the Pro Bowl. It worked very well for us. I don't want to say how many accounts it got us, but it was a lot. We're in Bud and Coors houses in California and just started with Southern Wine and Spirits in Nevada.

We don't feel any undue pressure to go public. It doesn't clutter our decision-making process. We're under no pressure to overexpand or to compromise any of our qualitative factors.

Everybody in this industry is riding high still. I think the forecast of an 18 to 20 percent marketshare for micros is going to happen. It may happen a little too fast. It's more of a problem in terms of adaptation for distributors than it is for the brewers. They're so oriented towards their major brands carrying all the weight. They have to open up a little bit and realize they can't prevent the inevitable.

Contract brewing company Owens Brewing Co. (formerly known as Buffalo Bill's) reported doubling its sales for a total of 6,000 barrels last year.

A number of California micros posted increases in 1995. North Coast Brewing Co., Fort Bragg, with its new bottling line fully operational, more than tripled its sales with just under 6,000 barrels. Sudwerk Privatbrauerei Hübsch, Davis, was up 14 percent with 5,400-barrel sales. Anderson Valley Brewing Co., Boonville, sold 5,000 barrels for an 11 percent increase. Anderson Valley added an India Pale Ale to its line last year. The company broke ground for a new brewery it hopes to have operational during 1996.

Riverside Brewing Co., Riverside, more than doubled its sales in its second calendar year with close to 5,000 barrels. Newcomer Carmel Brewing Co., Carmel, in business less than one year, sold 3,000 barrels. Covany Brewing Co., Grover Beach, sold 2,600 barrels in its first full year. Redwood Coast Brewing Co./Tied House (No. 3), Alameda, sold 2,300 barrels for 16 percent growth.

PACIFIC : 1995 OPENINGS AND CLOSINGS
STATES: California and Hawaii

Companies listed as opened include all those that began selling their own beers during the 1995 calendar year.

† Denotes microbrewery with on-site restaurant or pub.

‡ Also operates as brew-on-premise.

MICROBREWERIES (10)
California
AleSmith Brewing Co., San Diego
Bayhawk Ales/McCormick and Schmick's Pilsener Room, Irvine
BrewMaker's, Mountain View ‡
Carmel Brewing Co., Carmel
Coast Range Brewing Co., Gilroy
K. C. Brewing Co., San Leandro
Gordon Biersch (No. 6), Emeryville
Hawaii
Hawaiian Style Brewing, Makawao
Tradewinds Brewing Co., Wailuku
Kona Brewing Co., Kailua Kona

CONTRACT BREWING COMPANIES (3)
Danse-Skjold Brewing Co., Solvang, CA (St. Stans Brewery)
Humpback Brewing Co., Cerritos, CA (Minnesota Brewing Co.)
Wanker Beer, Newport Beach, CA (Pittsburgh Brewing Co.)

BREWPUBS (25)
California
AleHouse Rock Brewery & Broiler, Huntington Beach
Amber Waves Brewery Pub, Vacaville
Barley & Hopps, San Mateo
Brewski's Brewing Co., Hermosa Beach
Burlingame Station Brewing Co./Golden State Brewing Co., Burlingame
Carlsbad Brewery and Public House, Carlsbad
Del Mar Stuft Pizza and Microbrewery, San Diego
Dino and Luigi's Stuft Pizza, Sports Bar and Brewery, San Diego
Eel River Brewing Co., Fortuna
Elk Grove Brewing Co., Elk Grove
Faultline Brewing Co., Sunnyvale
Grizzly Bay Brewing Co., Suisun City
Joe-Joe's Brewing Co., Simi Valley
Mainline Brewing Co., Los Angeles
Moylan's Brewing Co., Novato
Newport Beach Brewing Co., Newport Beach
Parrotts Ferry Brewing Co., Columbia
Powerhouse Brewing Co., Sebastopol
Sacramento Brewing Co., Sacramento
Santa Barbara Brewing Co., Santa Barbara
Santa Monica Brewing Co., Santa Monica
Snowshoe Brewing Co., Arnold
Steelhead Brewing Co., Irvine
Sutter Brewing Co., Sacramento
Terrific Pacific Brewery & Grill, La Jolla

CLOSINGS (YEAR OF OPENING IN PARENTHESES)
1 Microbrewery
Bay Brewing Co./Devil Montain, Benicia, CA (1987)

5 Brewpubs
Live Soup, Santa Cruz, CA (1993)
Pacific Beach Brewhouse, Pacific Beach, CA (1991)
Rio Bravo Restaurant and Brewery, Santa Barbara, CA (1994)
Sunset Brewery and Fish House, Huntington Beach, CA (1994)
Pacific Tap and Grill, San Rafael, CA (1993)

United States — 1995 in Review

Contract brewing company Lake Tahoe Brewing Co. sold 2,300 barrels its second full year in business, posting a 95 percent gain.

Brewpubs

Number five in the nation and the largest in the region is Gordon Biersch Brewery Restaurant (No. 5), Honolulu, Hawaii, which sold 3,400 barrels in its first full year in business. The rest of the Pacific brewpub story takes place in California. Lost Coast Brewery, Eureka, continued its pattern of steady growth with 2,700 barrels sold for a 29 percent increase, boosted by increased distribution of bottled beers. Gordon Biersch Brewery Restaurant (No. 3), San Francisco, sold close to 2,600 barrels in 1995 for a 28 percent decrease due to its draft sales business being taken over by the company's new micro.

Fresno's Butterfield Brewing Co. sold 2,400 barrels for a 20 percent increase. Blind Pig Brewing Co., Temecula, did well for its first calendar year with 2,000-barrel sales. Further to the north, Stoddard's Brewhouse and Eatery in Sunnyvale achieved 1,800 barrels in its second full year, reflecting growth of 36 percent. Fullerton Hofbrau in Fullerton sold 1,700 barrels for 40 percent growth last year. Tied House Brewery and Cafe (No. 2) in San Jose was up 16 percent for the year with 1,600-barrel sales. Blue Water Brewing Co. in Tahoe City grew by 40 percent in its second calendar year with 1,400-barrel sales. Gordon Biersch Brewery Restaurant (No. 1) in Palo Alto sold just 1,300 barrels, a decline of 24 percent.

Transitions

- Of California's seven microbreweries opened during 1995, one, BrewMakers in Mountain View, doubles as a brew-on-premise. Oregon's Steelhead Brewing Co. built two new brewpubs in California — one in Irvine and the other in Burlingame. Of the state's twenty-five brewpub openings, eleven were in northern California, ten in southern California, three in the Bay Area, and one in the central region.
- Berkeley Mayor Shirley Dean's photo has appeared in a lot of brewspapers and beer magazines lately. Mayor Dean joined the photo-op for the groundbreaking of two new micros under construction in Berkeley: first, a new facility for Golden Pacific Brewing Co., and second, the fourth brewery for Hart Brewing Co., its first outside of Washington State.
- New brewpub Moylan's in Novato, California, is the second brewpub venture for Marin Brewing Co. owner Brendan Moylan.
- Harbor Lights Brewing Co. is the new name for the Heritage Brewing Co., Dana Point, California, which changed owners last year.
- The one microbrewery closure was Devil Mountain Brewing Co./Bay Brewing Co. which began as a brewpub in 1989. After losing its lease it moved to nearby Benicia and converted to a packaging microbrewery in 1990. Mark Feinberg, owner of the brewery since 1992, said new expensive wastewater assessments by the city of Benicia were the last straw, when added to factors of increased competition and lower profit margins.

(See sidebar on page 21 for a complete listing of the region's 1995 openings and closings.)

Mountain West

Contract brewing company Spanish Peaks Brewing Co., Bozeman, Montana, racked up another 83 percent growth in sales of its Black Dog ales for 53,000-barrel sales in 1995.

Rockies Brewing Co. led the way for another year in the Mountain West region, its 32,400-barrel sales marking a 24 percent gain. The brewery added a new fall seasonal packaged in 12-ounce bottles, Boulder Fall Fest. New Belgium Brewing Co. continued on its fast track with 31,800-barrel sales, adding up to a 68 percent increase. New Belgium spent much of the year building its new brewery, complete with an automated, 100-barrel Steinecker brewhouse, which rolled out its first kegs in December. The company began selling its Belgian-style ales in 12-ounce bottles for the first time in March 1996.

Microbreweries

Breckenridge Brewery, Denver, Colorado, also had a great year with 12,200-barrel sales in its second full year operating, adding up to a 44 percent increase. Breckenridge opened its third brewery and restaurant combination in Buffalo, New York. The Buffalo Breckenridge began serving its own ales during January 1996.

Schirf Brewing Co./Wasatch Brewery, Park City, Utah, added a second facility, Wasatch Brewery No. 2, in Salt Lake City. With the new brewery on line the sales of Wasatch beers expanded 36 percent for 11,500 barrels. Odell Brewing Co., Fort Collins, Colorado, sold 10,400 barrels for a 24 percent increase for its final year as a draft-only brewery. The veteran Colorado brewer planned to have its products in 12-ounce bottles by spring of 1996. Odell introduced a seasonal India Pale Ale brand during the fall.

Denver's Broadway Brewing Co., in its first full year of operation, sold 9,700 barrels of beers marketed by Denver's Wynkoop Brewing Co., Aspen's Flying Dog Brewing Co., and Crested Butte Brewery. In related news, contract brewing company Crested Butte Brewery reported a total of 9,000-barrel sales of brands produced by the combination of both Broadway Brewing and Dubuque Brewing and Bottling. Contract brewing company Alpine Brewing Co., Littleton, Colorado, sold 7,000 barrels of its Naked Aspen brand of beers.

H. C. Berger Brewing Co., Fort Collins, Colorado, introduced Chocolate Stout and a seasonal Rauchbier last year. The brewpub Oasis Brewery, Boulder, Colorado, added a microbrewery in Boulder simply called Oasis Brewery Annex. The new brewery sold 5,200 barrels after opening during summer 1995. Uinta Brewing Co., Salt Lake City, Utah, sold 4,500 barrels for its first calendar year in business. Coeur d'Alene Brewing Co./T. W. Fisher's, Coeur d'Alene, Idaho, bounced back in 1995 with 4,500-barrel sales for a 13 percent increase. Left Hand Brewing Co., Longmont, Colorado, sold 4,000 barrels during its first full year in business. The draft-only Tabernash Brewing Co., Denver, Colorado, doubled its output during its second calendar year, also selling 4,000 barrels.

Bayern Brewing Inc., Missoula, Montana, sold 3,600 barrels last year for a 64 percent gain. The combination microbrewery and brewpub Tommyknocker Brewery and Pub, Idaho Springs, Colorado, sold 2,900 barrels after opening in March 1995. Also doing well with less than one year under its belt is Great Northern Brewing Co., Whitefish, Montana, selling 2,800 barrels. Another micro-pub combo, Snake River Brewing Co./Jackson Hole Pub and Brewery, Jackson Hole, Wyoming, sold 2,600 barrels in its first calendar year. Selling the same amount was Eddie McStiff's Brewery, Moab, Utah. Eddie McStiff's built a brand new brewery last year and is now in a separate location from the Eddie McStiff's restaurant.

Great Divide Brewing Co., Denver, Colorado, sold 2,300 barrels for its first full year of operation. Irons Brewing Co., Lakewood, Colorado, tripled its sales with 2,200 barrels in 1995. The micro boosted sales through a combination of a new family of Iron-themed brands, such as Long Iron and Iron Heart, and brewing beer for contract brewing companies. The successful Table Rock Brewing Inc., Boise, Idaho, added a microbrewery under the same name, which sold 2,200 barrels last year. Bristol Brewing Co., Colorado Springs, Colorado, sold just under 2,200 barrels in its first calendar year.

Kessler Brewing Co., Helena, Montana, was looking for a buyer by the end of 1995. Kessler was off by 37 percent for the year with 2,000 barrels sold. Avery Brewing Co., Boulder, Colorado, sold 2,000 barrels in its first calendar year. Avery introduced 14'er Extra Special Bitter last year. Sun Valley Brewing Co., Hailey, Idaho, grew by 79 percent in its second calendar year in business with 1,900-barrel sales. Contract brewing company Reno Brewing Co., Reno, Nevada, sold 1,700 barrels in its first full year. Durango Brewing Co., Durango, Colorado, was up 19 percent for the year with 1,600-barrel sales.

Brewpubs

Wynkoop Brewing Co. sold 5,008 barrels in 1995, making it the number one brewpub in the country and the world. Founder John Hickenlooper explains how they made it happen.

John Hickenlooper, Wynkoop Brewing Co.

No one has harder-working, more talented, or more dedicated employees than the Wynkoop Brewing Co. It also doesn't hurt to have the main entrance to the nation's most popular baseball stadium two blocks from our front door. When we opened Wynkoop we never dreamed there would be a baseball stadium next door. As my grandfather says, I would rather be lucky than good.

Part of the appeal of being a really big brewpub is to have something for all people. People always say you can't be all things to all people. I say try and have something for everyone. We try to have a variety of prices for our meals, and to always keep eight to twelve beers on tap. We keep looking for ways to re-create ourselves and keep it fresh for the customers.

We had some grad students do a marketing survey for us recently and they found that in the restaurant more than 40 percent of our customers were over forty years old. That's a pretty broad demographic. The other thing that really helped, just by luck, is that we have a gold medal location at skid row prices. We could afford to own a large facility because we bought it back when the real estate wasn't worth very much. Not to deny that Kyle Carstens is one of the hardest-working brewers in show business, but we've had a lot of luck.

Out of the 5,000 barrels, only 400 barrels (8 percent) was sold to off-site accounts. Our largest brand, Railyard Ale (produced on-site), sold 2,450 barrels. One of the several things that helped us grow was building a banquet kitchen so we could do more banquets. In actuality, we doubled the size of our kitchen at a $350,000 investment. This also allowed us to do banquet-type parties in the pool hall. Keep in mind, our whole place is 36,000 square feet!

We've never done a capital call since we raised the $400,000 in the beginning. Ever since, it's all been cash flow and bank debt. Then the baseball stadium opened. Our summer months were up as high as 30 percent over the previous years. Those fans get thirsty, and we have a moral obligation to satisfy that thirst.

Ironically, because I'm an advocate for maintaining good quality housing in Lower Downtown Denver, I was quoted in the Denver papers saying that a baseball park was not appropriate for this area because it would be detrimental to housing.

With the other brewpubs we have help set up, our ownership varies anywhere from 15 to 50 percent. With all the new ventures, however, we'll be a majority partner. It will be more like a chain in that respect. We want to do more for the new ones, to give them more exposure, and in return we need to maintain control. We have six new brewpubs, in various stages of development, that we expect to open during 1996. They are: Racoon River Brewing Co., Des Moines, Iowa; Upstream Brewing Co., Omaha, Nebraska; Titletown Brewing Co., Green Bay, Wisconsin; Nail City Brewing Co., Wheeling, West Virginia; Savannah Brewing Co., Savannah, Georgia; and one more still to be determined.

We have used a lot of different companies for our brewing equipment. Right now we're working mostly with Specific Mechanical Systems. We did a bulk deal with them. Some are 8 1/2-barrel and some are 15-barrel breweries. They averaged a little over $200,000 per brewery.

The total capitalization for the six new ventures combined is over 7 million, including partners' money. We always try to find local investors to invest. We believe in that communal approach to opening brewpubs.

Wynkoop helped set up the first brewpub in Mexico, and likely in all of Latin America, last year. Called Pepe and Joe's, it opened in the resort town of Mazatlan in April 1995.

Rock Bottom Brewery in Denver was the number two brewpub for the nation, with more than 3,800-barrel sales for an increase of 13 percent. In fact, five Rock Bottom brewpubs are listed among the top twenty-five selling brewpubs in the United States. The other four are: Addison, Texas, at 3,100 barrels; Minneapolis, Minnesota, at 2,600 barrels; its Denver Chop House and Brewery at 2,600 barrels; and Portland, Oregon, at 2,300 barrels. When you add up all ten of their operations, which include eight Rock Bottoms plus Denver Chop House and the Walnut Brewery, the company sold close to 20,000 barrels in 1995! Director Tom Moxcey discusses the company's plans to get more people to hit Rock Bottom.

Tom Moxcey, Rock Bottom Restaurants

Rock Bottoms are first and foremost restaurants. We look to a profile to exceed customer expectations, with good food, good service, and great quaffable beer. All three of these ingredients have to be there. If you're missing one, you're in trouble. Also we like them to be easy for customers to get to, in good locations.

We've been fortunate because we've been able to put together a good formula of very successful brewpubs around the country. People like the food, the beer, and the atmosphere. But you never want to rest on your laurels. You treat people nicely and you'll do okay in the restaurant business.

We'll open four in 1996, in Indianapolis, Cincinnati, Seattle, and Bethesda, Maryland. While we have currently targeted four for 1997 (one of which will be another Chop House), I would expect that number to grow. We are not currently looking to franchise. We may consider joint venturing down the line but there are no plans for franchising this year. We don't have further plans to open Old Chicago restaurants with breweries in them. Old Chicago does well selling everybody else's beer.

We really believe that it's the people that make the difference. Great servers, great chefs, and a great team of brewers. I wouldn't say we think we're the most successful group in the world, but we've got great people working with us.

While the recipes for the main beers are generally the same from city to city, the names are almost always different. Our best selling beers include red ale, golden ale, bitter, and brown ale.

Advertising for the group is 3 percent of expenses, not counting any pre-opening expenses. We do promotions for charity events but very little print or radio.

The menu is eclectic, bistro-style variety, all chef-made, mostly from scratch, and an interesting selection of regional cooking. It's not all pub fare, but more bistro. The Chop House menu is more upscale, featuring more red meat, but still is eclectic with twists on familiar items. On the average, it has a little higher check than Rock Bottom.

Seasonal beers generate new interest for the customer, plus they allow the brewers to express themselves by creating something different. Specialty beers play a huge role. We have at least one at all times. And we have two cask-conditioned versions of our beers at every brewpub. There's a big variety of beers with that combination of regular beers, seasonals, and cask-conditioned.

While we have a number of restaurants, we don't think of it as a chain. We view them all as single restaurants. Every day we're faced with the challenge of building the business of the restaurant. But we have no grand corporate scheme. Each restaurant is responsible for continually building its own customer base.

Being a publicly held, Nasdaq-listed company is pretty simple: You do what you say you're going to do and it's great — otherwise, it's not so great. We can't affect why the Wall Street people do what they do. From our reporting aspects it's not terribly difficult. It takes time away from running the restaurants. Essentially if you think of it in terms of setting expectations and meeting them, it's the same as running any restaurant.

People like to be entertained and brewpubs offer a great opportunity for that. It's not an inelastic-demand cycle. I think that the brewpub business is really exciting. As long as brewpub owners remember they're in the restaurant business it'll be profitable. People like fresh, quality beer and you can't get it anywhere but from brewpubs.

Personally, I don't believe that the major players will be able to crack the shell. I think there's a mindset among young people and Generation X that big is not necessarily better. Small batch, locally made — that they can identify with. I think the brewpub and microbrewery business is perfectly positioned.

The original Breckenridge Brewery, Breckenridge, Colorado, sold 2,700 barrels for an 11 percent increase. And the original Oasis Brewery, Boulder, Colorado, declined 39 percent to just under 2,500 barrels, due to its passing on the company's wholesale business to its new Oasis Annex facility. Vail's Hubcap Brewery and

MOUNTAIN WEST: 1995 OPENINGS AND CLOSINGS
STATES: Arizona, Colorado, Idaho, Montana, Nevada, New Mexico, Utah, and Wyoming

Companies listed as opened include all those that began selling their own beers during the 1995 calendar year.

† Denotes microbrewery with on-site restaurant or pub.

‡ Also operates as brew-on-premise.

MICROBREWERIES (24)
Arizona
Oak Creek Brewing Co., Sedona
Colorado
Back Alley Brewing Co., Colorado Springs
Brouwer Brewery, Loveland
Colorado Brewing Co., Thornton
Coophouse Brewery, Broomfield
Eldorado Canyon Brewing Co., Broomfield
Mark's Brewing Co., Berthoud
Mile High Brewing Co., Denver
Oasis Brewery Annex, Boulder †
One Keg Brewhouse, Arvada
Only the Best Brewing Co., Divide
Palmer Lake Brewing Co., Palmer Lake
Peak to Peak, Rollinsville
Powers Brewing Co., Brighton
SandLot Brewery at Coors Field, Denver †
SKA Brewing Co., Durango
Tommyknocker Brewery and Pub, Idaho Springs †
Twisted Pine Brewing Co., Boulder
Idaho
Table Rock Brewing Co. (No. 2), Meridian

Montana
Big Sky Brewing Co., Missoula
Great Northern Brewing Co., Whitefish
Nevada
Ruby Mountain Brewing Co., Wells
New Mexico
Elephant Butte Brewery and Pizzeria, Elephant Butte †
Utah
Wasatch Brewing Co. (No. 2), Salt Lake City

CONTRACT BREWING COMPANIES (5)
Atlantis Brewing Co., Denver, CO (Lonetree Brewing Co.)
Cherry Creek Brewing Co., Denver, CO (Twisted Pine Brewing Co.)
Jamestown Brewing Co., Denver, CO (Minnesota Brewing Co.)
Pine Street Brewing Co., Louisville, CO (Lonetree Brewing Co.)
Two Angels Brewing Co., Englewood, CO (Lonetree Brewing Co.)

BREWPUBS (18)
Arizona
Copper Canyon Brewing and Ale House, Mesa
Colorado
Big Horn Brewing Co./C. B. Potts, Englewood
Denver Chop House and Brewery, Denver
Dimmer's Brewpub Inc., Fort Collins
Fleetside Pub and Brewery, Greeley
Main Street/Four Corners Brewing Co., Cortez

Ouray Brewing Co., Ouray
Overland Stage Stop Brewery, Longmont
Rockslide Brewery Restaurant, Grand Junction (opened 1994)
Sharkey's Brew Club, Colorado Springs ‡
Tivoli Brewery/(america!), Denver
Idaho
Star Garnet Brewing Co., Boise
Nevada
Brew Brothers/Eldorado Hotel and Casino, Reno
Utah
Desert Edge Brewery at the Pub/Desert Edge Brewing Co., Salt Lake City
Roosters 25th Street Brewing Co., Ogden
Wyoming
Bowmans Pub and Brewing Co., Laramie
Humphreys Bar and Grill, Gillette
Library Restaurant and Brewing Co., Laramie
Medicine Bow Brewing Co., Cheyenne

CLOSINGS (YEAR OF OPENING IN PARENTHESES)
1 Microbrewery
Bridger Brewing Co., Belgrade, MT (1993)

2 Brewpubs
Wild Wild West Brewery and Gambling Hall, Cripple Creek, CO (1992)
Gentle Ben's Brewing Co., Tucson, AZ (1992)

United States — 1995 in Review

Kitchen sold close to 1,900 barrels for a 10 percent increase.

Red Rock Brewing Co., Salt Lake City, Utah, sold 1,800 barrels in its first full year in business. Phantom Canyon Brewing Co., Colorado Springs, Colorado, sold 1,600 barrels in its second calendar year for a 16 percent gain. Coyote Springs Brewing Co., Phoenix, Arizona, sold 1,500 barrels for 11 percent growth for the year. Champion Brewing Co., Denver, Colorado, hired a new brewer midway through the year and finished up 12 percent over 1994 sales with 1,500 barrels.

Mountain Sun Pub and Brewery, Boulder, Colorado, posted a gain of 50 percent as it sold 1,200 barrels during its second calendar year. The brewpub also began limited distribution of 22-ounce bottles of its brands, including Colorado Kind Ale and Isadore's Java Porter. Beaver Street Brewery and Whistlestop Cafe, Flagstaff, Arizona, sold 1,100 barrels for its first full year brewing.

Transitions

- Four new brewpubs opened in Wyoming in 1995. Yeee-hah!
- Sharkey's Brew Club, Colorado Springs, Colorado, opened in January 1995 as the nation's first combination brew-on-premise and brewpub.
- You thought the Colorado market was crowded enough? Well, the *seventeen* new microbreweries that opened in 1995 didn't seem to think so. Nor did another five startup contract brewing companies.
- One of Colorado's new microbreweries, One-Keg Brewhouse in Arvada, takes a novel approach to the business. With no brands of its own, the brewery exclusively brews contract house brands for Denver-area restaurants.
- Fleetside Brewing Co., Greeley, Colorado, is the second Colorado venture from the folks at the successful CooperSmith's Pub and Brewery, Fort Collins.
- Remember Tivoli beer? Well, it's back in the form of Tivoli Brewery (located in Denver's original historic Tivoli brewery building that's now a shoppping mall). The brewery was set up in conjunction with a trendy nightclub called (america!).
- Another Colorado "first in the nation," the Wild Wild West Brewery and Gambling Hall in Cripple Creek closed its doors last year. Former head brewer Mark Sommer moved on to the nearby mountain town of Divide and set up his own micro called Only the Best Brewing Co.
- Gentle Ben's Brewing Co., Tucson, Arizona, closed because of a loss of lease and will reopen in a brand new site in 1996.

(See sidebar on page 25 for a complete listing of the region's 1995 openings and closings.)

North Central

Dubuque Brewing Co./Brandevor USA, Dubuque, Iowa, had another great year with over 25,000 barrels in sales for a 53 percent increase. Two more breweries from this region joined the ranks of regional specialty breweries: Boulevard Brewing and Summit Brewing. Boulevard Brewing Co., Kansas City, Missouri, sold 21,000 barrels, posting a 42 percent gain for the year. Boulevard President John McDonald discusses the company's approach.

John McDonald, Boulevard Brewing Co.

We pay a lot of attention to our home market and price our beers reasonably. Almost 75 percent of our sales are within fifty miles of the brewery. We're a local brewer first and then a regional brewer, and now we're in that transition phase of local to regional. We're trying to take it slow and develop our sales force.

We just expanded capacity to 40,000 barrels and we'll probably sell 30,000 barrels this year. We sell 60 percent draft. Our main markets are Missouri, Kansas, and Nebraska. We sell 85 to 90 percent in Missouri and Kansas combined. We've been in St. Louis for about a year. It's a huge metro area, but we feel it's important to get to that side of the state. We just opened up Oklahoma and Iowa. We're also starting to sell a little bit each in Chicago and Denver, on an experimental basis. Beyond that, we're not going to open up any new markets this year.

We've been kind of curious about Denver and Chicago, just to see what we can do in a more mature market where everything's there. We've avoided sending our beer to where everyone else is. Oklahoma is really promising. But it has a crazy system. In Oklahoma, 95 percent of sales is 3.2 beer. The wholesalers own the business and that's all they want to do. We thought our Ten-Penny, a newer, low-alcohol ale, would be ideal there. They said they didn't even want it because it would just muddy the waters. They see these beers as telling people that there are other things out there and to them that's a threat.

Boulevard Pale Ale is still our largest seller at 43 percent. But our draft-only unfiltered wheat beer, which was 34 percent in 1995, is just on fire and could possibly overtake Boulevard Pale Ale this year. Irish Ale is our largest selling beer when we have it available, which is only January through St. Patrick's Day. Porter is fairly small but growing every year. Ten-Penny, at only 2.7 percent alcohol, is also growing. It does well in Kansas where it's the only beer of its type that can go into a grocery store. They've allowed us to say it contains 2.7 percent alcohol by weight on the label, instead of 3.2. If you do 3.2 it's sort of the kiss of death. Low-alcohol beer with flavor is a category of beer that has a lot of potential.

We only make it in one strength. I think the big breweries' huge mistake is to make the same beer in two strengths. It just invites the question of how do you make a beer of two strengths? I said no, we're only going to make it one way. It's funny how American consumers think they're being cheated when you tell them the beer has less alcohol. If you look at the British bitters, they're all low alcohol and that's why an Englishman can drink five or six pints in a sitting.

Bob's 47 is the only lager beer we do. It's a Munich-style fall seasonal named after an old brewmaster in Kansas City who was a real friend of the brewery. We only make 300 barrels and they sell immediately. Last year we added our first new brand in a while, a Christmas beer called Nutcracker. It's a real high-gravity, nonspiced beer. We used a caramelized sugar adjunct, in the Belgian tradition, because wanted a big beer.

At the rate we're growing we'll be maxed out in capacity by the middle of next year. We're close to starting a new brewery project. Our plan is to have it as a second, larger facility and then use this brewery to make more esoteric and specialty products. We hope to come out with some lager beers.

Previous expansions were funded with bank debt. For the brewery we'll use both debt and a private placement. We'll get some money to make us look good to the banks.

We've always used beer wholesalers. Now we have two smaller wine and beer wholesalers — and that's a big concern of mine. We had a bad experience with a wine wholesaler that almost put us out of business. I think the right wine distributors can be great. But in a local market where you want to sell beer to a lot of people, you're better off with a beer wholesaler.

We have four salespeople now. One local, one who covers Kansas, one in St. Louis, and our vice president of sales and marketing who handles all the wholesalers in our region.

We spend 15 percent on sales support, which seems high, but we want to be in this for the long term. The key to success in this business is to make a great product and then really push it and sell it. There's too many beers out there that just assume they're going to sell. We do a lot of point-of-sale, we have metal signs and banners, and then there's truck logoing, which we like to get our wholesalers to do. Our greatest marketing tool is the brewery itself. We do lots of tours as well as public relations work such as donations for civic events.

We don't do post-offs or discounting. We decided we weren't going to post-off the beer we sent to Colorado. I hear there's a big problem there with that. That side of the business is something I don't look at too much. We do some distributor incentives, but we try to use beer education-type things instead of money. For example, one contest prize was a trip to the Oregon Brewers Festival. We've also done jackets with the brewery logo.

We sold our draft distributorship to a local wholesaler and part of the agreement was that they would give us their people for seminars on a quarterly basis. We're trying to help them be much more knowledgable about what they're selling.

We are constantly trying to make our beer better. We've spent as much money making our beer better as we have making more beer. We're experimenting with bottle conditioning for some of the beers and we're a month away from releasing it.

We're in it for the long haul. We think brewing is an honorable profession and we're proud of it. Contrary to what everybody thinks right now, I don't think brewing is a license to print money. Over periods of history brewing has always been a very tough business. A lot of people in the industry will do really well. The original idea of small breweries is really great. Small producers can fit in. There are going to be a lot of losers, though. The people that are going to really win are the American beer consumers. There's a lot of breweries making world class beers in this country and that's a good thing.

The veteran Summit Brewing Co., St. Paul, Minnesota, also enjoyed a year of 42 percent growth, with 19,900-barrel sales. President Mark Stutrud explains his company's approach of deep market penetration concentrating on a single urban market.

Mark Stutrud, Summit Brewing

Our growth was very conservative in the beginning, which had a lot to do with the conservative nature of the Midwest. In the past three to four years our growth has been stronger than it was in the previous five to six years. It's a combination of the quality and distinctiveness of the product and credibility in the marketplace. It takes time to establish credibility with wholesalers and retailers, as it does everywhere, but more so in this area.

Ninety percent of Summit Brewing's product is sold in the Twin Cities. In 1995 we were up 43 percent and during the previous three years averaged 36 to 38 percent. Growth during this time has been achieved in the same distribution area. About 4 percent of sales are in eastern North and South Dakota and Wisconsin, plus "a trickle" in Illinois. We will probably not significantly change our distribution area for the next three to five years.

We sell 60 percent draft. In 1995 our two year-round beers, Extra Pale Ale and Porter, accounted for 64 percent and 10 percent of sales respectively, and the five seasonals take up the rest of the balance. We made our late-winter seasonal, India Pale Ale, a year-round brand this year due to public demand. The other seasonals are Maibock, Hefeweizen, Alt, and Winter Ale, our biggest seller. The seasonals suffered due to capacity constraints at the brewery. Year to year we've gradually added more fermentation capacity. Now we're up to 35,000 barrels.

We've been using a classic two-vessel vintage 1938 brewhouse that limited us to three brews a day. We added a custom-fabricated mash vessel so we can do at least five to six brews a day, as a band-aid or stopgap until we get our new brewery up and running in late fall. The heart of the new facility is a 150-barrel brewhouse shipped from Germany last July. It will have twenty-eight 64-barrel fermenting tanks. We fund our expansions with cash, a little debt, and a little equity offered through privately held stock.

I'm looking forward to being able to brew once or twice a day instead of five or six times a day. We have five full-time brewers brewing 'round the clock. In most of 1996 we'll be able to fall back to a five-day work week but that will still be twenty-four hours a day. The brewery employs a total of fourteen people full-time plus ten part-time, primarily in packaging.

When asked if we're a microbrewery I reply that we're a tiny regional. In a lot of ways we're an urban brewery, because in terms of distribution, 90 percent of our beer doesn't go beyond a twenty-five-mile radius from the brewery. We have no ambition to distribute our beers nationally. I'd much rather operate a solid business and a sane one at the same time. We get calls from New York or other parts of the country and we're very up front in telling them that they won't see it, certainly not in this decade. We'll concentrate exclusively on the Upper Midwest. Going anywhere beyond Iowa or Michigan is not in our long-term business plan.

Two things come into play — volume and capacity. We'd rather operate a successful regional brewery at capacity than to have to be national and rely on contract brewing to fulfill demand. Maybe it's elitist to say to someone "If you're in Denver or New York you can't get it," but it's more in line with how Euoropean breweries operate. We feel that the character and nature of products we create determine our distribution area. If you're producing beer that's not microfiltered, ultrafiltered, or highly processed, the complexity of the flavor profile changes quickly, and you have a shorter shelf life.

To sum up our business philosophy, we're looking at very deep market penetration in a very local area as opposed to superficial penetration on a national level and having to drive our sales through expensive marketing efforts. Some people getting into contract brewing may not recognize the cost of getting product to the customer in a wholesale network.

We use exclusively beer wholesalers. A couple of outlying wholesalers may have started in wine or liquor, but they are beer wholesalers at this time. They handle draft product, so it's not just that we're a box in their portfolio. We focus aggressively on getting on-premise draft beer sales first and work on the off-premise retail level after that.

In Minnesota we have six-tenths of a percent marketshare. I don't think we're saturating the market but we have to be reasonable in terms of how many points we can acquire over the next fifty or sixty years. It's a very tough market and it's something we've had to build. I don't know of an easy draft beer market. We still have quite a bit of work to do because the maturation has yet to occur in this market.

We spend more on sales support on a per-barrel basis than you might think. We're probably spending more than some major brewers or contract brewers. It's as high as 10 percent or more. We focus almost exclusively on point-of-sale. We do no radio except underwriting of public radio. We have two salespeople plus one sales manager.

We do not do post-offs or discounting. Hell, no! We make a living out of selling beer, not by giving it away. Pricing policies have really eroded this industry terribly, especially with contract brewing companies using a large brewery but saying they're small. It really messes up the market. Retailers and wholesalers are used to that kind of strategy from major brewers, but for small brewers it's not smart or even viable or economically feasible. It's just a strategy to sell more beer.

In the future there's going to be a certain amount of consolidation among major breweries and consolidations among smaller breweries. Chains of brewpubs will slow down eventually. There will be strong regional breweries doing anywhere from 40,000 to 200,000 barrels, then some at 15,000 barrels or less, then the brewpubs and who knows what's going to happen with major breweries.

Traditional Regional Breweries

Miller subsidiary Jacob Leinenkugel Brewing Co. was up 19 percent for the year with 280,000 barrels sold. Although its flagship brand is still the American lager-style Leinenkugels, according to Scott Barnum of American Specialty and Craft Beer Co., the brewery has reached a point where the majority of its sales are specialty beers. Leinenkugel added three new specialty-type products including Honey Weiss in the summer, Autumn Gold lager, and its first ever ale, Auburn Ale, this past winter. The company added a second brewery in September when it purchased the G. Heileman Brewing Co.'s 70,000-barrel-capacity, draft-only Milwaukee brewery, formerly known as the Val Blatz brewery.

Barton Beers subsidiary Stevens Point Brewery sold 41,000 barrels for a 32 percent increase last year. Point's new craft-style beers included Point Pale Ale and an all-malt spiced winter ale. August Schell Brewing Co. continued to crank out new craft brews during the year, with Maifest Blonde Double Bock in spring and Blizzard Ale, a raspberry brown ale, in winter.

Cold Spring Brewery was sold last year to Beverage International of Northglenn, Colorado, formerly known as Pure Colorado Inc. The Minnesota brewery has also been building its business back up through contracting

NORTH CENTRAL: 1995 OPENINGS AND CLOSINGS
STATES: Illinois, Indiana, Kansas, Michigan, Minnesota, Missouri, Nebraska, North Dakota, Ohio, South Dakota, and Wisconsin

Companies listed as opened include all those that began selling their own beers during the 1995 calendar year.

† Denotes microbrewery with on-site restaurant or pub.

‡ Also operates as brew-on-premise.

* Ceased brewing, restaurant remains open.

MICROBREWERIES (12)
Illinois
Goose Island Beer Co., Chicago
Kansas
Pony Express Brewing Co., Olathe
Michigan
Boyne River Brewing Co., Boyne City
King Brewing Co., Pontiac
Motor City Brewing Works, Detroit
Michigan Brewing Co., Williamston †
Ohio
Barrelhouse Brewing Co., Cincinnati
Ringneck Brewing Co./The Brew Kettle Inc., Strongsville ‡
Wooden Pony Brewing Co., Mansfield
South Dakota
Black Hills Brewing Co., Deadwood
Wisconsin
Green Bay Brewing Co., Denmark
Remington Watson Smith Brewing Co., Waukesha

CONTRACT BREWING COMPANIES (8)
August Brewing Co., Detroit, MI (Stroh Brewery)
Bad Frog Brewery/Wauldron Corp., Rose City, MI (Frankenmuth Brewing Co.)
Barley Boys Brewery, Omaha, NE (Minnesota Brewing Co.)
Cross Plains Brewery, Cross Plains, WI (G. Heileman)
Nebraska Brewing Co., Omaha, NE (Cold Spring Brewing Co.)
Slopeside Brewing Co., Chicago, IL (Star Union Brewery Co.)
St. Croix Beer Co., Lakeland, MN (August Schell Brewing Co.)
State Street Brewing Co., Chicago, IL (Evansville Brewing Co.)

BREWPUBS (36)
Illinois
Pinch Penny Pub, Carbondale
Rock Bottom Brewery (No. 7), Chicago
Prairie Rock Brewing Co., Elgin
Indiana
Alcatraz Brewing Co., Indianapolis
Kansas
Barley's, Topeka
Blind Tiger, Topeka
Dave's Brewpub, Overland Park
Lazy Hound Restaurant & Brewery, Pittsburgh
Overland Park Brewing Co., Overland Park
Rock Bottom Brewery (No. 6), Overland Park
Michigan
Arbor Brewing Co., Ann Arbor
Big Buck Brewery and Steakhouse, Gaylord
Blue Coyote Brewing Co., Lansing
Great Baraboo Brewing Co., Clinton Township
Grizzly Peak Brewing Co., Ann Arbor
Hereford and Hops, Escanaba
Minnesota
Backwater Brewing Co., Winona
Clubhaus Brewpub, Rochester
Missouri
Ebbets Field, Springfield
Morgan Street Brewery, St. Louis
River Market Brewing Co., Kansas City
Trailhead Brewing Co., St. Charles

Ohio
Alessis Ristorante/Garretts Mill Brewing Co., Garrettsville
Firehouse Brewery and Restaurant, Cleveland Heights
Gottberg Brewpub/Gottberg Auto Co., Columbus
Maumee Bay Brewing Co., Toledo
Rock Bottom Brewery (No. 8), Cleveland
Wallaby Bob's Grill and Brewpub, Westlake
North Dakota
Old Broadway, Fargo
Rattlesnake Creek Brewery, Dickinson
South Dakota
Sioux Falls Brewing Co., Sioux Falls
Wisconsin
Angelic Brewing Co., Madison
Black River Brewery and Pub, La Crosse
Fox River Brewing Co./Fratello's Italian Cafe, Oshkosh
Railhouse Brewing Co./R Ales Inc., Marinette
South Shore Brewery, Ashland

CLOSINGS (YEAR OF OPENING IN PARENTHESES)

roughly a dozen different brands and selling its own craft-style brand, Cold Spring Pale Ale.

Microbreweries

Capital Brewery, Middleton, Wisconsin, sold 12,800 barrels in 1995 for an 8 percent increase. Capital introduced Razz, a raspberry wheat lager, last summer. Sprecher Brewing Co., Milwaukee, Wisconsin, had a great year with 12,000-barrel sales for a 33 percent gain. About 40 percent of Sprecher's total is draft beer brewed at Capital Brewery. Sprecher celebrated its tenth year in business by brewing a commemorative Belgian-style Brown Ale. Another pioneer, Kalamazoo Brewing Co., Kalamazoo, Michigan, celebrated its tenth year in business, with sales of 10,200 barrels, a 70 percent surge.

With its new brewery up and running, Great Lakes Brewing Co., Cleveland, Ohio, more than doubled its sales for a total of 8,000 barrels. Pony Express Brewing Co., a new microbrewery in Olathe, Kansas, just south of Kansas City, sold 4,800 barrels of draft ales during its roughly six months in business. Gray Brewing, Janesville, Wisconsin, an ale brewer in a lager-saturated market, sold 4,800 barrels in its first full year in business. In that same market area is New Glarus Brewing Co., a versatile brewery producing both lagers and ales, which sold 4,500 barrels in its second calendar year, ratcheting up 88 percent. New Glarus has added a number of new seasonal beers last year, including a Belgian Red Cherry Beer and a cider called Apple Jack Ale.

The folks at the Goose Island Brewing Co. brewpub joined forces with one of the partners behind Beer Across America and raised $2.5 million for a new 100,000-barrel-capacity JV Northwest brewery called Goose Island Beer Co. Besides 1,700 barrels it contract brewed at the aforementioned G. Heileman-Val Blatz brewery, Goose Island sold 4,000 barrels of its own beer it produced during the fourth quarter of 1995.

Crooked River Brewing Co., Cleveland, Ohio, sold 3,100 barrels during its first calendar year brewing. Veteran Millstream Brewing Co., Amana, Iowa, sold 2,200 barrels, posting a 10 percent gain. Ohio's Columbus Brewing had a good year with 46 percent growth for 2,000-barrel sales. Milwaukee's Lakefront Brewery sold the same amount for a 36 percent increase. Contract brewing company Signature Beer, St. Louis, Missouri, sold 2,000 barrels last year. Michigan's new microbrewery-brewpub combination, Big Buck Brewery and Steakhouse, sold 1,500 barrels in less than a year of operation.

Brewpubs

Main Street Brewery/Queen City Brewing Co., Cincinnati, Ohio, sold 2,200 barrels during its first full year of operation. St. Louis Brewery/The Taproom increased 32 percent for 2,200-barrel sales. Two brewpubs each sold just under 1,800 barrels during their first calendar year in business, Mickey Finn's Brewery, Libertyville, Illinois, and Great Dane Pub and Brewing Co., Madison, Wisconsin. Flat Branch Brewing Co., Columbia, Missouri, sold 1,500 for its first full year. Jones Street Brewery, Omaha, Nebraska, was down 16 percent for the year with 1,000-barrel sales.

Transitions

- New contract brewing company Bad Frog Brewery/Wauldron Corp. is generating lots of press and controversy with its "frog flipping the bird" label image. The brand's success is good news to Frankenmuth Brewery, Frankenmuth, Michigan, which produces the beer.
- Former employees of Detroit and Mackinac Brewery, Detroit, Michigan, purchased the idle microbrewery and renamed it Motor City Brewing Works.
- North Dakota's first brewpub opened in 1995 (as did its second).
- South Dakota's first microbrewery, Black Hills Brewing Co. in Deadwood, opened last year.

(See sidebar on page 29 for a complete listing of the region's 1995 openings and closings.)

Northeast

Boston Beer Co. continues as the craft-brewing industry's pacesetter. The contract brewing company sold 960,000 barrels for 34 percent growth during 1995. With the whole of the industry expanding by 51 percent, Boston Beer's share of this market declined for the first year, from 28.5 percent to 25.4 percent. Nonetheless, in an industry crowded with more than one thousand competitors, one out of every four beers consumed is an incredible feat.

Boston introduced three new brands in 1995. Scotch Ale is the newest brand available year-round. Cherry Wheat was introduced as a summer seasonal to replace Samuel Adams Wheat Beer, a German-style wheat brand that was not well understood in the market. Old Fezziwig is Samuel Adams entry into the ever-expanding posse of winter spiced ales that somehow magically appear on beer store and supermarket shelves the day after Thanksgiving.

According to a report in *Beer Marketer's Insights*, the flagship Boston Lager's percent share of the company's total sales has decreased each year for the last four years. *Insights* postulated that the company's strategy relies on the introduction of new brands each year for generating expansion of total sales.

Competing with Boston Beer on its home turf is Mass. Bay Brewing Co. In 1995 Mass. Bay's total sales reached 39,000 barrels for a gain of 68 percent. President Richard Doyle tells about the evolution of the company over the past several years.

Richard Doyle, Mass. Bay Brewing Co.

We've been averaging about 75 percent growth over the past three years. Recently we've been focusing primarily on product development and attention to our customer. We're less concerned about what other people are doing and more concerned about wholesaler relations, retailer relations, and concentrating on our customer.

There are a lot of new entrants in the industry. The biggest thing for us as a group is that we market responsibly and communicate the message that beer is a positive thing and can be part of an enjoyable lifestyle and existence.

Our best-selling beer is Harpoon India Pale Ale, representing one-third of our volume. The seasonals as a group are another one-third of our business. Our other three year-round products make up the balance: Harpoon Ale, Pilsener, and Alt. Alt was our summer seasonal and is now year-round.

In terms of brand management we've been taking a kind of a weed-and-seed approach. Harpoon Golden Lager was a successful product, but we liked our Harpoon Golden Pilsener better. It's difficult in a small company to market something effectively if you don't like the product. If there was a bucketful of beers at a company party, the lager was the one that wouldn't get drunk. So we didn't just introduce something new and leave the other one there — we pulled up the roots, and replaced the Lager with the Pilsener. It's a more traditional, hoppier lager. We felt you can't have both.

We're doing the same with our Alt, which is a full-bodied, darker Alt, and replacing our light product with that. We didn't want to just keep pushing things out there. We're trying to stick with our best products. The lager and the light, which were late eighties, early nineties products, were aimed at a less discerning drinker. That is no longer a direction that we are going in.

I'm just trying to do what's best for us, for who we are — in addition to what we can be more successful selling. You sell best what you feel strongly about. It's not like I was the brand manager for pretzels last month and now I'm the brand manager for Harpoon. That's not what we are. What we do has a personality to it. That's why we got in the business.

We sell forty-five-to-fifty-five draft-to-bottled. We brew the draft ourselves here at the brewery in Boston and the bottled beer is produced at F. X. Matt.

We just expanded the brewery, putting in a 60-barrel brewhouse. We have five 120-barrel fermenters currently installed. We are receiving six more 120s from Mueller next week and have two more scheduled to arrive in May. Also, we bought a new mill because with the larger system we saw more clearly that our extraction rates we were getting were not what we thought they should be. When you start going through a truckload of grain every week — two to three hundred pounds of grain every brew, four brews a day — your payback on a new mill is not four years but more like six months or nine months. The bigger batch sizes also adds greater consistency.

We sell 50 percent of our beer in Massachusetts, plus 5 or 6 percent each in New Hampshire, Connecticut, New York, New Jersey, and Maryland. Plus we sell about 2 or 3 percent each in Maine and Rhode Island. We didn't add any states last year. Our growth in the last three years has all been same-state growth. In 1996 we'll expand down the east coast and into the Midwest and Rockies as well.

We increasingly appreciate the benefits of beer distributors. You could write a book on all of the issues involved. A good wholesaler at one level of sales is not necessarily the greatest when you're selling three times that amount. And then it's not always easy to change distributors, especially with laws in certain states. Managing wholesaler relationships is very important.

Another chapter in that book is the pros and cons for people who have large brewery ownership. The best competitive situation for you in any market will be different If you're locked into brewery X or brewery Y's market, it can be good or it can be bad. In some of their markets they're the best and in some others they're the worst. One of the large breweries recently spent a lot of time upgrading its distributorships in a lot of markets. What does that say about how they used to be? Then there are the areas where they haven't upgraded them at all — you know those aren't markets you're going to do well in.

I'm not trying to say that the large brewers have total control. The wholesalers are sophisticated, independent-minded businesses. I mean that in a positive way.

Sales support historically has been 5 percent and is more than that now and will be more in the future. We have about sixteen sales people. We have a program of distributor incentives that we are implementing this year.

In different states we do different types of discounting. We do volume discounting in states where it is allowed. Then there are the one-case price states, where for a particular month every case you sell is at a given price. For those states, to do a price promotion you have to post-off that month at a given, predetermined volume. Whereas in states like Massachusetts, it's all dependent on volume. Retail pricing is fascinating — each state is a different situation.

We funded our expansion partly out of company funds and partly out of bank debt. As you develop a more reliable cash flow, banks are much more likely to lend. Plus, the market for used equipment is buoyant. As we've bought equipment we've always sold equipment simultaneously. It takes away some of the shock — basically funding a portion of the expansion. There's a very competitive market for used equipment.

I think there's going to be increased growth for the whole industry. You're going to see some companies successful in creating national brands, along with local and regional players doing well, and kind of a backlash against the national brands. And you're still going to see a lot of new entrants. Eventually, over time, there will be a lot of consolidation of regional and local companies.

In some markets craft brewers will have a 7 or 8 percent share. The bigger guys are going to get most of that while the regional and local ones will get a goodly amount. And there will be a flattening out of the boundless upside for small new entrants. There's also the probability that there are people not in the business yet that will be very successful. It's a very fluid situation.

Next in the Northeast region is Shipyard Brewery of Portland, Maine. Currently the fastest-growing craft brewer in the nation, Shipyard took off like a rocket, reaching an unprecedented 30,400 barrels sales in its first calendar year. Last fall Shipyard gained additional notoriety as the newest craft brewer to sign an agreement with the Miller Brewing Co. Shipyard's president, Fred Forsely, and brewmaster, Alan Pugsley, discuss the company's brief history and its future plans.

Fred Forsely and Alan Pugsley, Shipyard Brewery

FF: A variety of things have contributed to recent growth. The introduction of Old Thumper strong ale, now our second largest brand, had a lot do with it, together with the growth of the industry in the Northeast. The introduction of our Goat Island Light and Blue Fin Stout also contributed.

We're not necessarily stealing customers from other microbrew brands. But we're getting more drinkers from other beverage categories, people that used to mostly drink wine or imports or domestic beers.

The combination of our variety of beers as well as our flagship beer, Shipyard Export Ale, continued to grow. The population of breweries in New England has undergone major growth also, and with these new micros and brewpubs we saw a lot of our market areas opening up.

AP: Shipyard Export Ale is 50 percent of sales, Old Thumper is 15 to 17 percent, while Goat Island Light, Blue Fin Stout, Brown Ale, Mystic Seaport Pale Ale are about 7 percent each. Also, our seasonal Longfellow Winter Ale was 4 or 5 percent. We sell 30 percent draft.

Maine is our number one state with 45 percent of sales, followed by Massachusetts with 20 percent, New Hampshire with 15 percent, and the rest is more or less evenly divided between Connecticut, Vermont, Rhode Island, and New Jersey. This year we started selling in New York and Illinois, plus we'll open up more of New Jersey and the Mid-Atlantic region for the next two months.

We're working on a small, 20-barrel draft-only micro in the Orlando airport and we're adding a second 50-barrel brewhouse in Portland to bring capacity there up to 108,000 barrels.

FF: We've been going down the Eastern Seaboard. When we open the brewery in Orlando we'll be able to distribute draft product from the south northward.

We really feel there's a lot of room for growth in our existing markets. Some markets, like Connecticut, have a lot of untapped potential. The biggest problem is that you don't want to open new markets and then run out of beer. We want to also stay focused on growing our existing markets

As a total package we spend 10 to 13 percent for sales support. We have nine sales staff, primarily in New England. We use mainly beer distributors, and our new ones will be in the Miller network. We've done sales staff incentives for individual sales employees within the distributors' houses, but not for distributors themselves. In some markets we post-off, although in general we try not to do it.

AP: We're also adding a 300-barrel conditioning tank, a new Krones bottling line, a new automated Ameripac kegging line, and a significant amount of warehouse storage space.

Our new brewhouse will consist of two 50-barrel kettles, one 100-barrel mash tun, and one 100-barrel whirlpool. We're still keeping the integrity of the Peter Austin system of a single temperature mash, single-infusion mash tun and hop percolators.

FF: American Specialty & Craft Beer Group has been helping to fund the expansion. The partnership involved the Portland location and all our brands. However, Kennebunkport Brewing/Federal Jack's Brewpub, Alan's Peter Austin Projects, and Pugsley Brewing Projects International are not involved in the partnership.

It's an even fifty-fifty. We have full control over the product and everybody has certain rights. We've been able to work very well with them. They have truly helped us, especially in terms of distributor relationships and technical support, but they basically let us run our own operation.

This industry is one where you need to run the brewery as a small company, and American Specialty & Craft Beer Group allowed us to operate that way and continue to grow, without smothering it.

AP: We employ about thirty people at the brewery, not including sales staff, plus we use a temporary service for bottling.

We'll add new seasonals this year with India Pale Ale in spring, Wheat in summer, and Harvest Ale in the fall.

FF: I think we're helped a lot by Alan's strong brewing heritage and his still phenomenal ability to create world class products. He and I are a good team together — I stay out of the brewery and he assists in whatever marketing anlges we come up with. Hopefully the relationship with American Specialty will bring it to the next level.

I'm really excited by the number of brewpubs opening in the Northeast, which will allow the true microbrewers to grow stronger in this region. As the growth of that area happens, quality brewers can have a successful growth path long into the nineties and can have a strong future.

AP: I own Peter Austin in England and Fred and I are equal partners in Pugsley's Brewing Projects International. Pugsley's has two brewpubs we're finishing up on for which we have a long-term licensing and consulting arrangement, Alewife Restaurant and Brewery in Glastonbury, Connecticut, and Bank Street Brewing Co. in Stamford, Connecticut. We'll train and oversee the brewers on an ongoing basis, assist with raw materials costs, and do some cross marketing for all of the brewpubs. They'll have two Shipyard brands they brew themselves, under license, and four of their own brands.

We're confident that this will help the growth of the microbrewing industry in the Connecticut market. We signed up another brewpub partnership with the Brunswick Corporation in Edmonton, Canada, inside the biggest mall in the world. They have a 100,000-square-foot facility where they're planning a large multilane bowling alley together with billiards, a beer hall, and a dance hall to open by September.

Contract brewing company Dock Street Brewing Co. sold 25,000 barrels last year for a 25 percent increase. Dock Street redesigned the packaging for its three brands — Amber, Bohemian Pilsner, and Double Bock — with a stronger focus on each brands' central imagery. Catamount Brewing Co. sold 19,200 barrels in 1995 for a 16 percent gain. The company introduced one new brand called Catamount Pale Ale.

Old Dominion sold 18,500 barrels in 1995, posting a 31 percent increase. Pennsylvania Brewing Co. total sales added up to 18,500 barrels for a massive 92 percent increase. More than half of the company's sales are produced by its Pittsburgh microbrewery while the remainder is contract-brewed.

Traditional Regional Breweries

Sales at D. G. Yuengling & Son Inc., the nation's oldest brewery, have been accelerating at such a pace in recent years — fueled by the craft brewing's revival of interest in styles like porter and black-and-tan which Yuengling never stopped brewing — that President Richard Yuengling has been weighing the decision of building a new facility or contract-brewing somewhere else. Yuengling & Son sold 320,000 barrels in 1995 for a 16 percent gain.

F. X. Matt added two more seasonals to its Saranac line of craft-brews. Saranac Chocolate Amber was its spring release followed by Saranac Mountain Berry ale, brewed with raspberries and blackberries, for the summer.

The Lion Brewery added Raspberry Red Ale to its Brewery Hill line of craft-style beers.

Microbreweries

Long Trail Brewing Co. is the new name for the Mountain Brewers, Bridgewater Corners, Vermont. Concentrating on building its new brewery and related tasks like sourcing appropriate-sized used tanks, Long Trail was up slightly over 1994 with 14,500 barrels. Contract brewing company Brooklyn Brewery, Brooklyn, New York, also reached 14,500-barrel sales for a 20 percent gain. Brooklyn's new all-draft microbrewery in Brooklyn will release its first beers this spring. Head brewer Garret Oliver said the facility's primary purpose is for producing seasonal and specialty products such as German-style hefeweizen. Production of Brooklyn's already established brands will remain at F. X. Matt.

Wild Goose Brewery, Cambridge, Maryland, continued its steady course of growth with 14,300-barrel sales reflecting a 43 percent increase. Stoudt Brewery, Adamstown, Pennsylvania, aided by increased distribution and redesigned packaging for its 12-ounce contract-brewed products, jumped 60 percent to 13,600-barrel total sales. Of this total, 40 percent was the draft and bottled brands from its own brewery. D. L. Geary Brewing Co., Portland, Maine, sold just over 13,000 barrels with a 27 percent increase. Geary added its second year-round brand, Geary's London Porter.

Frederick Brewing Co., Frederick, Maryland, ramped up several notches with more than 10,000-barrel sales reflecting 74 percent growth. Otter Creek Brewing Co., Middlebury, Vermont, also hit 10,000 barrels, posting a 67 percent increase. The brewery built a new $2-million facility featuring a 40-barrel Century Manufacturing brewhouse and 200-bottle-per-minute SMB Technik bottling line.

Smuttynose Brewing Co., Portsmouth, New Hampshire, had an active first calendar year of operation with 6,000-barrel sales. Ipswich Brewing Co., Ipswich, Massachusetts, surged by 92 percent with 4,800-barrel sales. Also at the 4,800-barrel level for 1995 was Arrowhead Brewing Co., Chambersburg, Pennsylvania, achieving 41 percent growth.

Elm City Brewing Co. (formerly New Haven Brewing Co.) sold over 9,000 barrels, of which 4,500 was contract brewed at F. X. Matt's. By early 1996, Elm City abandoned its previous strategy of concentrating more on its middle-of-the-road brands and spending a huge amount of money marketing and advertising them. The brewery did an about-face, selling its top-of-the-line Krones bottler for much-needed cash, adding a brewpub on the building's second floor, and reemphasizing draft sales. The last change gave Elm City's wizard head brewer, Ron Page, free rein to brew specialties inspired by those developed during his homebrewing days, such as Chocolate Cherries Porter.

New England Brewing Co. made its long-awaited move into a combination microbrewery and brewpub set-up on the shore in Norwalk, Connecticut.

Oxford Brewing Co., Linthicum, Maryland, sold a total of 7,300 barrels for the year. Of that amount, 2,800 was contract-brewed at Dubuque Brewing Co. Oxford's recent growth has been driven by the success of its Raspberry Wheat brand, which last summer was averaging more than 70 percent of sales. Old Harbor Brewing Co. started brewing in its own facility in spring of 1995 and sold 3,800 barrels by year end.

Potomac River Brewing Co., Chantilly, Virginia, tripled sales in its second full year in business with 3,000 barrels. Steamship Brewing Co., Norfolk, Virginia, sold 2,800 with less than one full year in business. The draft-only Magic Hat Brewing Co. sold 2,700 barrels in its first calendar year. Bottled Magic Hat beers are contracted at Shipyard Brewery.

Contract brewing company Tun Tavern Brewing, Abington, Pennsylvania, sold 2,800 barrels during its first full business year. Gritty McDuff's sold slightly less than this amount for its first year contract brewing as well. It added a new brand, Gritty McDuff's Best Brown Ale, and moved its contract arrangement from D. L. Geary Brewing across town to Shipyard Brewery. A third contract brewing company, Old World Brewing Co., Staten Island, New York, increased 10 percent in 1995 with 2,300-barrel sales.

Atlantic Coast Brewing Co., Boston, Massachusetts, sold 2,000 barrels of its Tremont Ales in its first full year in business. Within a year after opening Lowell Brewing Co., Lowell, Massachusetts, completely reformulated its recipes and packaging after realizing that its initial brands were not distinctive enough for the competitive Massachusetts craft-brewing market. This appears to have worked in its favor, as Lowell sold 1,800 barrels during its first calendar year. Another Massachusetts micro, Wachusett Brewing in Westminster, sold 1,700 barrels in its first year.

Brimstone Brewing Co., Baltimore, Maryland, sold 1,500 barrels during its first calendar year. Certainly one of the more creative young breweries, Brimstone became the first microbrewery in the United States to brew an interpretation of German steinbeere, or "stone beer," that is produced by adding red-hot rocks to the wort. The rocks caramelize a significant amount of the malt sugars, which later contribute a caramellike flavor to the beer.

Brewpubs

Boston Beer Works, Boston, Massachusetts, held its status as the largest New England brewpub with 3,700-barrel sales for 13 percent over 1994. Baltimore Brewing Co. continued expansion of its wholesale draft business and also sold 3,700 barrels for a 42 percent gain. Long Island Brewing Co., Jericho, New York, had a fabulous first calendar year with 2,300-barrel sales. Mountain Valley Brewpub, Suffern, New York, began distributing its Ruffian brand ales in 22-ounce bottles, helping to grow its total sales by 64 percent to 2,300 barrels.

Gritty McDuff's Brewpub, aided by its contract-brewed six-packs with a map to the brewery on the bottom, increased its house beer sales by 30 percent for 2,200 barrels. Northampton Brewery/Brewster Court Bar, Northampton, Massachusetts, sold 1,300 barrels for a 22 percent gain. The West Virginia Brewing Co. in Morgantown, also sold 1,300 barrels which reflected a 28 percent gain. Troy Brewing Co. (formerly Brown and Moran Brewing Co., Troy, New York) sold 1,300 barrels for a 13 percent increase.

Stark Mill Brewery and Restaurant, Manchester, New Hampshire, sold 1,200 barrels during its first full year operating, as did Boston's Brew Moon. Newcomer Triumph Brewing Co., Princeton, New Jersey, opened during 1995 and sold just under 1,200 barrels. Old Towne Tavern and Brewery, Gaithersburg, Maryland, sold 1,100 barrels during its first calendar year.

Another 1995 opening, New York City's Carnegie Hill Brewing Co., sold 1,000 barrels.

Transitions

Delaware's first microbrewery, Rockford Brewing Co. in Wilmington, opened last year. So did Delaware's first brewub ... and second and third.

- Two new microbreweries opened in New Jersey, the first to operate since Vernon Valley Brewery (aka Clement's Brewing Co.) closed in 1992. The Garden State's first-ever brewpub also opened, followed by three more before the year's end.
- What do you do when the state where you want to open a microbrewery is already awash with fine

---

NORTHEAST: 1995 OPENINGS AND CLOSINGS
STATES: Connecticut, Delaware, Maine, Maryland, Massachusetts, New Hampshire, New Jersey, New York, Pennsylvania, Rhode Island, Vermont, Virginia, District of Columbia, and West Virginia

Companies listed as opened include all those that began selling their own beers during the 1995 calendar year.

† Denotes microbrewery with on-site restaurant or pub.

‡ Also operates as brew-on-premise.

MICROBREWERIES (23)
Delaware
Rockford Brewing Co., Wilmington
Maine
Allagash Brewing Co., Portland
Sheepscot Valley Brewing Co., Whitefield
Sea Dog Brewing Co. (No. 2), Bangor
Maryland
Mount Airy Brewing Co., Mount Airy †
Massachusetts
Cisco Brewers, Nantucket
Clamtown Brewery Inc., Old Newburyport
Old Harbor Brewing Co., Hudson
New Hampshire
Nutfield Brewing Co., Derry
Winnepesaukee Brewing and Soda Works, Laconia
New Jersey
Hoboken Brewing Co., Hoboken
Red Bank Brewery Co., Redbank
New York
DryTown Brewing Co., Treadwell
Middle Ages Brewing Co., Syracuse
Neptune Brewery, New York
Pennsylvania
Independence Brewing Co., Philadelphia
Lancaster Malt Brewing Co., Lancaster †
Ugly Dog Brewery Inc., West Chester
Weyerbacher Brewing Co., Easton
Yards Brewing Co., Philadelphia
Virginia
James River Brewing Co., Richmond
Steamship Brewing Co., Norfolk
Williamsville Brewery, Doswell

CONTRACT BREWING COMPANIES (6)
Fischer Brewing Co., Washington, D.C. (Stroh Brewery Co., North Carolina)
Johnstown Brewing Co., Johnstown, PA (Jones Brewing Co.)
Rock Creek Brewing Co, Richmond, VA (Whitetail Brewing Co.)
Starview Brewing Co., Mount Wolf, PA (Dubuque Brewing and Bottling)
Crooked Creek Brewery, Jamestown, PA (Straub Brewery/The Lion Inc.)
Kobor and White Brewing Co., Schuylerville, NY (The Lion Inc.)

BREWPUBS (37)
Maryland
Fordham Brewing Co./Ramshead Tavern, Annapolis
Delaware
Brandywine Brewing Co., Wilmington
Dogfish Head Brewing and Eats, Rehoboth Beach
Stewart's Brewing Co., Bear
Maine
Bear Brewing Co., Orono
Bray's Brewpub and Eatery, Naples
Gritty McDuffs (No. 2), Freeport
Maine Coast Brewing Co., Bar Harbor
Mass. Back Bay Brewing Co., Boston
Barrington Brewery and Restaurant, Great Barrington
Brewhouse at Danvers, Danvers
Cape Cod Brewhouse, Hyannis
Olde Salem Brewery, Salem
New Hampshire
Brewers Bier Haus, Merrimack
Stark Mill Brewing Co., Manchester
Woodstock Brewing Co., North Woodstock
New Jersey
Joe's Millhill Saloon and Restaurant, Trenton
Long Valley Pub and Brewery, Long Valley
Ship Inn, Milford
Triumph Brewing Co., Princeton
New York
Atlantic Brewing Co., Island Park
Bootleggers Pub and Brewery, Plattsburgh
Carnegie Hill Brewing Co., New York
Ellicottville Brewing Co., Ellicottville
Heartland Brewing Co., New York
Nacho Mama's Brewery, New York
Original Saratoga Springs Brewpub, Saratoga Springs
Parlor City Brewing Co., Binghamton
Rohrbach Brewing Co. (No. 2), Rochester
Pennsylvania
Barley Creek, Tannersville
Buckingham Mountain, Lahaska
Sly Fox Brewhouse and Eatery, Phoenixville
Valley Forge Brewing Co., Wayne
Queen City Brewing Co., Allentown
Rhode Island
Coddington Brewing Co., Middleton
Vermont
Brew House, Ludlow
Virginia
Cobblestone Pub and Brewery, Richmond

CLOSINGS (YEAR OF OPENING IN PARENTHESES)
1 Microbrewery
Old Salem Village Brewing Co., Danvers, MA (1994)
3 Brewpubs
Manhattan Brewing Co., NY (1984/1989)
Queen City Brewing Co., Allentown, PA (1995)
Winnipesaukee Brewing and Soda Works, Laconia, NH (1995)

Institute for Brewing Studies

examples of British-inspired ales? How about brewing Belgian-style instead? Great idea! As it turns out, in Maine the state's two new startup microbreweries in 1995 each had this same great idea. Rob Tod of Allagash Brewing Co. in Portland and Stephen Gorrill of Sheepscott Valley Brewing in Whitefield also have in common that they are one-man, draft-only operations. Fortunately the range of beers that could be considered Belgian-style is rather vast and the brands from the two breweries have more than a few differences, according to reports from those that have tried both.

- The phoenix rises again as New York City's twice-opened-and-closed Manhattan Brewing Co. reopened, this time with the successful Nacho Mama's restaurant groups at the helm. What else could they call it but Nacho Mama's Brewery.
- Rochester, New York's Rohrbach Brewing Co. opened its second brewpub, also in Rochester.
- Commonwealth Brewing Co., Boston, Massachusetts, opened its number two brewpub, Back Bay Brewing Co., also in Boston. Its third venture will open in New York City this spring in the Rockefeller Center, under the Commonwealth Brewing Co. name.
- Two years ago Blair Potts was president of New Haven Brewing Co. and Ron Page was assistant brewer at the Connecticut micro New England Brewing Co. Not long after Potts left New Haven to pursue his own project, New Haven hired Page to be its head brewer, shortly after which, New England hired Potts to be its vice president. Such activity begs the question, Which company got the draft picks to be named later?

(See sidebar on page 35 for a complete listing of the region's 1995 openings and closings.)

South

Abita Brewing Co. kept the lead position in the South with 30,500-barrel sales for a 38 percent gain in 1995. Jack Daniel's Brewery, a new contract brewing company with a whiskey pedigree, made a big splash with 21,400-barrel sales, 2,000 barrels of which were brewed at the company's Tennessee microbrewery. Celis Brewery sold 19,600 barrels for a 23 percent increase for the year. Under Miller's guidance Celis pulled out of many of its markets, however, they plan to return to many of those during 1996.

Contract brewing company Florida Beer Brands sold 9,000 barrels.

Microbreweries

Ybor City Brewing Co., Tampa, Florida, sold 7,000 barrels for its first calendar year in business. Atlanta Brewing Co., Atlanta, Georgia, sold 6,000 barrels in its first full year brewing. Birmingham Brewing Co., Birmingham, Alabama, sold 5,000 barrels, 18 percent fewer than in 1994. Atlanta's other micro, Marthasville Brewing Co., achieved 3,500-barrel sales during its inaugural calendar year.

Contract brewing company Old City Brewing Co., Austin, Texas, sold just under 2,600 barrels for a 14 percent gain for the year. Weeping Radish Brewery, Manteo, North Carolina, increased distribution of its German-style lagers, tipping the scales for classifying the company as a microbrewery rather than brewpub. Its newly expanded distribution helped boost sales 47 percent, to the 2,500-barrel level. Johnson Beer Co., Charlotte, North Carolina, sold 2,500 barrels after opening during 1995.

Saint Arnold Brewing Co., Houston, Texas, sold 2,400 barrels during its first full year in business. Miami Brewing Co., Miami, Florida, sold 1,800 barrels after it opened in 1995. Beach Brewing Co., Orlando, Florida, grew to 1,700 barrels, a 30 percent increase. Hill Country Brewing and Bottling Co., Austin, Texas, quadrupled sales with 1,600 barrels during its second full year in business.

Brewpubs

Georgia passed a brewpub law in March 1995. The Institute for Brewing Studies provided a lot of assistance with the effort. Association of Brewers President Charlie Papazian also helped, participating in a pro-brewpub legalization rally during 1994.

Boston-based the Brewhouse Inc. opened the first Georgia brewpub in December in Atlanta as John Harvard's Brewhouse (No. 2). The U.S. Border Brewery Cantina in Atlanta's suburb Alpharetta was competing for the "first in Georgia" honors and opened its doors prior to John Harvard's. However, it apparently failed to comply to the letter with the wishes of the state's licensing authorities and at press time still had not received permission to legally sell its beers to the public.

Copper Tank Brewing Co., Austin, Texas, was the largest selling brewpub in the South with just under 3,300-barrel sales for its first calendar year. Copper Tank did not have the restaurant side of the business operational until mid-1995. Rock Bottom Brewery (No. 5), Addison, Texas, was second largest with 3,100 barrels sold in less than a full year of operation.

Bricktown Brewing Co., Oklahoma City, Oklahoma, enjoyed 33 percent growth for 2,600 barrels sold in 1995. Rock Bottom Brewery (No. 3), Houston, Texas, sold 2,000 barrels during its first full year operating. Crescent City Brewhouse sold 2,000 barrels for a 14 percent gain over 1994. Meanwhile, the Southend Brewery and Smokehouse, Charlotte, North Carolina, sold 1,500 barrels after opening during 1995. Magic City Brewery, the second operation for the owners of Mobile's Port City Brewery, also opened in 1995, selling 1,300 barrels.

Ragtime Taproom, Atlantic Beach, Florida, decreased by 12 percent with 1,200-barrel sales. Two Houston brewpubs, Village Brewery and Houston Brewery, each sold 1,000 barrels during their first calendar year in business. Smoky Mountain Brewing Co., Knoxville, Tennessee, sold 1,000 barrels in its inaugural calendar year, as did Ozark Brewing Co., Fayetteville, Arkansas, in its first full year. Tulsa Brewing Co., Tulsa, Oklahoma, was off by 20 percent for the year with its 1,000-barrel sales.

Greenshields Pub and Brewery, Raleigh, North Carolina, added a Prospero bottling line in 1995 and now distributes several brands in six-packs of twelve-ounce bottles.

The successful Hops Grill and Bar chain added four more brewpubs in 1995, giving it fourteen brewpubs, all in Florida, by the year's end. Hops' corporate head brewer, John Schwarzen, came to the chain after a long career as a different type of corporate brewer, spending thirty-five years at Anheuser-Busch, preceded by three years at Falstaff. Schwarzen explained the chain's brewery operations philosophy.

John Schwarzen, Hops Grill and Bar Inc.

The main things Hops Grill and Bar emphasizes are great quality beers, great quality food, and good service. Excellent quality and good ingredients are high priorities.

We opened four brewpubs in 1995 and plan six to eight more this year. So far for 1996 we already opened Boynton Beach followed by St. Petersburg. We'll add at least two more in Florida this year, in Altamonte Springs, near Orlando, and Pampano Beach. We'll also begin venturing out of state, with new brewpubs in Bowling Green, Kentucky, and Cherry Creek in Denver, Colorado.

In 1997 we'll add probably another ten to twelve. Besides more for Florida, we'll likely open others in Kentucky, Colorado, and possibly Georgia or North Carolina. We've got a very aggressive plan.

We brew four beers at all the brewpubs: Clearwater Light, Lightning Bolt Gold Pilsener, Hammerhead Red Ale (with a caramel taste), and A1 Ale (a dark, creamy ale). There are no plans now to add others. We feel we have a good variety of beers — and we only have four taps. We do get some requests for heavier beers, but we design our beers for many, many people. We don't have anything else to fall back on if we don't get a favorable response to the beers we have.

The light beer sells the most, at 40 percent, the red is 35 percent, gold about 20 percent, and the rest is A1 Ale, our newest brand added a year and a half ago.

The new restaurants are partially franchised. They have limited partners, but the majority is owned by Hops Grill and Bar corporate. Before they can have ownership in a Hops, new partners are required to work all the different jobs within the restaurant, including in the kitchen and in the front area seating people. That's one important part of the corporate philosophy.

The menu features a full line of steaks, prime rib, fish, pastas, appetizers, soups, and desserts. It's designed to cater more to families. It's a different concept from other brewpubs, which are designed specifically for beer. We put an equally high priority on beer and food.

We advertise using billboards, television spots, and radio. We're not allowed to take beer off-premise and sell it, but we are allowed to give it to charities and things like that.

Most of our brewpubs each have one full-time head brewer, although some brewers cover two brewpubs. We have a form for them to follow for brewing each type of beer. We make sure that the set-up, follow-up, and sanitation is the same. I do periodic checks on temperatures, times, and paperwork.

We try to maintain our quality standards by checking and double checking the beers to make sure they're consistent. We do cross-tastings of all our beers. We try to get all of the brewers in here at one time, the first Monday of every month. I try to check all of the beers twice a month at least. Our northernmost brewpubs are in Jacksonville, and the southernmost are in Coral Springs and Boynton Beach (near Miami). I fly as much as drive to visit the brewpubs, especially for the middle-of-the-month checking of the beers.

I hire new brewing staff through recommendations — either homebrewers or people already working in the restaurant that have no brewing experience. Knowing their work habits are good, I usually give them a chance.

We have a three-month training period the brewer does on site. First, they watch the brewer do the job for

United States — 1995 in Review

SOUTH: 1995 OPENINGS AND CLOSINGS
STATES: Alabama, Arkansas, Florida, Georgia, Kentucky, Louisiana, Mississippi, North Carolina, Oklahoma, South Carolina, Tennessee, and Texas

Companies listed as opened include all those that began selling their own beers during the 1995 calendar year.
† Denotes microbrewery with on-site restaurant or pub.
‡ Also operates as brew-on-premise.

MICROBREWERIES (13)
Georgia
Blind Man Ales, Athens
Florida
Key West Overseas Brewery, Key West
Miami Brewing Co., Miami
Kentucky
Lexington Brewing Co., Lexington
Louisiana
Louisiana Brewing Co./Brasserie de la Louisiane, Beaux Bridge
North Carolina
Carolina Brewing Co., Holly Springs
Johnson Beer Co., Charlotte
Old Raleigh Brewing Co., Raleigh
South Carolina
Reedy River Brewing Co., Greer
Texas
Basin Brewing Ltd., Midland
Bosque Brewing Co., Waco
Old West Brewing Co. (No. 2), El Paso
St. Andrews Brewing Co., Dallas

CONTRACT BREWING COMPANIES (6)
Abbey Brewing Co., Miami Beach, FL (Key West Overseas Brewery)
Barley Field Brewing Co., Tulsa, OK (August Schell Brewing Co.)
Full Moon International, Maitland, FL (brewer unknown)
Pelican Brewing Co., New Orleans, LA (Abita Brewing Co.)
T. Pauls Beer Co., Tulsa, OK (Dubuque Brewing and Bottling)
Volunteer Beer, Knoxville, TN (Marthasville Brewing Co.)

BREWPUBS (57)
Alabama
Magic City Brewery, Birmingham
Montgomery Brewing Co., Montgomery
Poplar Head Mule Co. and Grill, Dothan
Mill Brewery, Bakery and Eatery, Birmingham

Florida
A1A Aleworks, St. Augustine
Buckhead Brewery and Grill, Tallahassee
Hops Grill and Bar in Ocala, Ocala
Hops Grill and Bar in Orlando, Orlando
Hops Grill and Bar in Coral Springs, Coral Springs
Hops Grill and Bar in Port Richey, Port Richey
New World Brewery, Tampa
South Pointe Seafood House, Miami Beach
Thai Orchid Restaurant (No. 2), Miami
Tortuga's, Jacksonville Beach
Windrose Brewpub, Naples
Georgia
John Harvard's Brewhouse, Atlanta
Kentucky
Kentucky Brewing Co. (Brewpub and Grill), Lexington
Lexington City Brewery, Lexington
Louisiana
Abita Brewpub, Abita Springs
North Carolina
Carolina Brewery, Chapel Hill
Front Street Brewery, Wilmington
Olde Hickory Brewing Co., Hickory
South End Brewery & Smokehouse, Charlotte
Oklahoma
Belle Isle Brewing Co., Oklahoma City
Pete's Place, Krebs
South Carolina
Blue Ridge Brewing Co., Greenville
Chicago Brew Pub, Greenville
Columbia Brewing Co., Columbia
Downtown Brewing Co., Greenville
Hunter Gatherer, Columbia
Liberty Steakhouse and Brewery at Broadway at the Beach, Myrtle Beach
Market Street Mill, Charleston
T-Bonz Grill, Mount Pleasant
Tennessee
Big River Grille and Brewing Works (No. 2), Nashville
Blackstone Restaurant and Brewery, Nashville
lack Horse Brewery, Clarksville
Calhoun's BBQ and Brewery, Knoxville
Mill Brewery, Bakery and Eatery, Knoxville
Mill Brewery, Bakery and Eatery, Nashville
Texas
Bank Draft Brewing Co., Houston
Hunperdinck's/Big Horn Brewing Co. of Texas, Arlington
Brazos Brewing Co., College Station
Cafe on the Square and Brewpub, San Marcos
Draught Horse Pub and Brewery, Austin
Galveston Brewery, Galveston
Hoffbrau Steaks Brewery, Dallas
Hoffbrau Steaks Brewery, Addison
Hub City Brewery, Lubbock
Jaxson's Restaurant and Brewing Co., El Paso
Joey's Inc., San Antonio
Katie Bloom's Irish Pub and Brewery, Austin
Padre Island Brewing Co., South Padre Island
Rock Bottom Brewery (No. 5), Addison
Routh Street Brewery, Dallas
Silk's Grill and Brewing Co., Amarillo
Strand Brewery, Galveston
TwoRows Restaurant & Brewery, Dallas

CLOSINGS (YEAR OF OPENING IN PARENTHESES)
8 Brewpubs
Bryan Brewing Co., Bryan, TX (1994)
Bull City Brewery and Cafe, Durham, NC (1993)
G. T. Vito's, Clearwater, FL (1994)
Boars Head Brewing/Stone House Brewery, Austin, TX (1994)
Armadillo Brewing Co., Austin, TX (1994)
Riverwalk Brewery, Fort Lauderdale, FL (1995)
Silo Brewpub and Restaurant, Louisville, KY (1992)
Spur Steakhouse and Saloon/Toisnot Brewing Co., Wilson, NC (1994)

a number of brews. Then they help out hands-on. Then for the last sequence of brews they do the whole job — brewing, in-line solutioning, cleaning the brewhouse, and paperwork — with the brewer watching over. By the time they're through with these three stages they should have gone through twenty brews. This will go on until we've opened up a location for the brewer-in-training to go to. Then it'll be his job to get to get the equipment in place, clean the area, and do test-brewing. And I oversee all of that.

Our equipment comes from the Pub Brewing Co. We've used them since the first one. We've made some changes along the way, and they have worked with us very well to make sure these changes are put in place.

All the breweries are almost identical to each other. The first two or three were gas-fired boilers, since then the rest use an electric boiler. The mash tun might be on one side or the other, but it's all right there in the same place.

If everything works right, we can get our brewing equipment in and fastened down with piping and wiring in place, and do solutioning and test-brewing all within about a week. We've got our own construction company called Cyprus Coast that does all our buildings. Having gone through fourteen already, they're familiar with what's going on.

I think the brewpub industry, at least for a while, has a great future — especially for the next four or five years. It has some of the big guys concerned. We're taking some of their sales from the low end. It's having a big impact on the beer industry. I relate it back to the way it was years ago before there were major brewers.

Transitions

- After its first brewpub opened in 1994, eight new brewpubs opened in South Carolina in 1995, including three in Greenville.
- Eighteen brewpubs opened in Texas during 1995!
- TwoRows Restaurant and Brewery in Dallas, Texas, and Bell Isle Brewing Co. in Oklahoma City, Oklahoma, were both opened by the company operating Tulsa Brewing Co. in Tulsa and Interurban Brewpub in Norman, Oklahoma.
- Florida's Thai Orchid Restaurant added a brewery to an existing sister operation, creating the company's second brewpub.
- Florida's Mill, Brewery, Bakery and Eatery chain reignited its momentum, adding one brewpub in Alabama and two in Tennessee.
- Big River Brewing Co., Chattanooga, Tennessee, opened its second Big River in Nashville in 1995 and plans its third for Orlando's Walt Disney World during 1996.
- Katie Bloom's Irish Pub and Brewery, Austin, Texas, took over the site formerly occupied by the failed Armadillo Brewing Co.

(See sidebar on page 38 for a complete listing of the region's 1995 openings and closings.)

Imports Increase Again

Sales of imports in the United States increased 7.4 percent for a total of 11,262,906 barrels, posting a fourth straight growth year for the category. Import marketshare increased to 5.7 percent, up from 5.3 percent in 1994. The growth of imports combined with the growth of craft-brewers gives a 2-million-barrel increase in the total volume of high-priced brands, and corresponding 1.3 percent total marketshare increase during 1995.

In general, Dutch and Mexican imports showed strong gains while Canadian brands were mostly down for the year.

Segment leader Heineken was up 12 percent with 2,468,000 barrels sold for its best year since its 1986 peak of 2,629,000 barrels. Corona Extra reclaimed its number two position with 26 percent growth. Corona's 1,487,000 barrels in 1995 was its best year since its 1987 high of 1,671,000 barrels. Molson Ice, after making a big splash in 1994, was off 11 percent with 1,065,000-barrel sales. Number four Beck's was up 5 percent with 645,000-barrel sales. Number five Molson Golden was down 1 percent with 445,000 barrels for the year.

The number five import brand in 1994, Labatt's Blue, fell to the number eight position in 1995 as it posted a 30 percent decrease in sales with 323,000 barrels. Also showing substantial volume losses were Molson Light (no. 18), down by 16 percent, and Molson Canadian (no. 19) down 14 percent.

The seventh largest import, Foster's, posted a 10 percent gain with 348,000 barrels in 1995. Number eleven, Labatt's Ice, was up 17 percent with 290,000-barrel sales. Also making double-digit gains for the year were Modelo Especial (no. 16), up 13 percent, Corona Light (no. 17), up 36 percent, and Carlsberg (no. 20), up 10 percent.

Large Brewers Losing Share?

The nation's largest breweries declined slightly last year. Overall sales of domestic beers in the United States decreased by 1.1 percent, while the total domestic consumption was off just 0.4 percent. If you subtract the combined total of craft-brewed beer sales and import sales, the resulting marketshare of large brewers (and traditional regional brewers) ends up at 92.3 percent for 1995, down from 93.4 percent in 1994. Thus it is clear that craft-brewers are gradually beginning to win marketshare away from the large brewers, as a tiny percent of the beer-drinking populous is trading up to fuller-flavored brands.

One new strategy by large brewers to win back share (besides others mentioned in this article) is to *replicate* successful craft-brands in their home regions. This appears to be the case in Oregon, where the number one draft craft-brew is Widmer Hefe-Weizen. Within the past year, two large brewery, American-style hefeweizens have appeared on the market in the Northwest, from Henry Weinhard's (G. Heileman) and Michelob (Anheuser-Busch).

It remains to be seen if this strategy actually wins share back, or just functions to expand the full-flavored beer market, as the other large brewery craft-style beers appear to have done. However, if successful, it could conceivably pave the way for other large-brewer knock-offs of established craft-beers such as Samuel Adams Lager or Sierra Nevada Pale Ale, for example. Consumers would likely stay loyal to the original brand, but that loyalty could be softened if the large brewers were to follow up with substantial price undercutting.

Ice beer appears to have peaked as a category and begun its slow descent into the brewing history books. Ice beer sales decreased by almost 25 percent compared to 1994. Remember dry beer?

All of the top six brewers were down in 1995. Anheuser-Busch Inc. was off 1.1 percent, Miller Brewing Co. by 0.4 percent, and Coors Brewing Co. by 1 percent. Decreasing by larger margins were Stroh Brewery Co. at 9 percent and G. Heileman Brewing Co. by 8.2 percent, while Pabst Brewing Co. was off just 1.2 percent.

The one success story among large brewers was Genesee, which increased by 3.9 percent for the year with a total of 1,870,000-barrel sales.

The big news in early 1996 was the purchase of G. Heileman Brewing Co. by Stroh Brewery Co. The single new Stroh-Heileman company puts number four brewer Stroh much closer to number three Coors in terms of total marketshare. It also consolidates two of the largest brewers of contract brands such as Samuel Adams and Pete's Wicked Ale.

The Forecast

The future still looks bright for continued success of all-malt beers and independent craft-brewing companies. This is not to mean that success will come easy. As several brewers have been quoted in this article emphasized, the beer business is a very tough business and the larger you grow the tougher it becomes. One possible key to expanding your market is to become creative in thinking up ways to create beer drinking occasions or beer-drinking-associated activities (such as beer dinners) that give people reasons to drink beer when they might otherwise instead opt for wine, coffee, carbonated sodas, or New Age drinks. You may also consider focusing your marketing more closely on why consumers should drink natural, fresh, local, craft-brewed beer instead of mass-produced beer or imports.

Several potential threats could negatively affect the craft-brewing industry's growth in the coming years:

1. A tax increase or the loss of the small brewer's excise tax differential. While the former seems unlikely in the current political climate, the latter — loss of the differential — could be sparked by the ironing out of the final details of international trade agreements such as GATT (the General Agreement on Tariffs and Trade).

2. A sudden downturn in the economy. Similar to number one, this would hit consumers where it hurts — in the pocketbook. If craft beers alone or if all beers together were to jump in price by 50 percent or 100 percent, American's tastes would certainly drift more towards the "popularly priced" mass-produced brands, for no other reason than the bottom-line difference in cost.

3. An accelerated trend of large breweries purchasing craft-brewers and then closing them down. The oft-cited "history repeats itself" scenario. This could only possibly occur if craft-brewers were so strapped for cash that they were only looking for a way out of the beer business. It's extremely difficult just imagining this scenario simply because the decline of the large domestic brewers coupled with the continually expanding success of the independent craft-brewers points to exactly the opposite of this happening.

Coors' CEO, Peter Coors, was quoted in an interview in *Modern Brewery Age* saying, "I don't know whether there's going to be any real mega brands in the future." While this is a startling admission coming from a Coors, it points to the simple physics of what happens when a consumer tries a more flavorful beer and enjoys it more than the less-flavorful brand he or she was drinking the previous week, or even the previous round.

The beer industry is slowly beginning a process of devolving to a point where it was a century ago when thousands of breweries served their local areas, and wherever you went people drank the local beers. While this may sound a little extreme, I am not suggesting that there won't be any national brands in the future. Rather, I propose that the national brands of the future will not be as important, as dominant, or as "mega" as they are today.

The craft-brewing industry's rate of growth will begin to slow down. This year, a 40 percent total increase for the year is more likely than any amount much above that. But this is not a market in which the bottom will all of a sudden fall out. This a multi-faceted, multi-layered group of human stories — of Horatio Algers, of Rube Goldbergs, of risk-takers, underdogs, non-conformists, of people who have decided to buck the overall trend and who are willing to stand up and yell out at the top of their lungs that the emperor is wearing no clothes, that people aren't buying beers anymore, they're buying marketing concepts, TV commercials, and ad campaigns. And consumers like to hear about these people overcoming the odds and want to help them succeed in their efforts to give their state, their county, a richer, fresher, and more flavorful beer.

If beer drinkers *truly* follow the advice of one currently popular TV commercial, which is to "be your own dog," then they won't consider buying the brand of the company that paid for the commercial. This is because the commercial, by its very nature of being widely broadcasted and often-repeated, is designed to foster the development of a "herd" mentality of masses of consumers marching in step with each other. While craft-beer consumers have always taken pride in being out of step with the mainstream, it is curious that some major brewers are promoting this spirit of independent-mindedness, especially for brands that do not always stand apart in terms of flavor profile.

Craft-brewing industry expansion still has at the very least another five if not, more likely, ten years of double-digit growth to come. Estimating conservatively, the industry will capture likely between 6 and 7 percent of the U.S. beer market by the year 2000.

— David Edgar
Director, Institute for Brewing Studies

3 Canadian Craft-Brewing: 1995 Industry in Review

The continued growth of the Canadian microbrewery industry remained front page business news throughout the year. New microbreweries opened at a good pace despite a sluggish economy. No fewer than fourteen new microbreweries and seven brewpubs opened across Canada during the past year, bringing the total of regional specialty brewers to twelve, microbreweries to thirty-seven, and brewpubs to fifty-two, for a grand total of 101 craft-brewing operations.

While these statistics had some beer industry analysts scratching their heads and wondering when the microbrewery phenomenon would level off and even disappear as they had so boldly predicted over ten years ago, the microbrewery segment of the beer market remained the only true growth area. Four microbreweries achieved regional specialty status at the end of the year as the result of increased production, namely: Brasserie McAuslan of Montreal, Québec; Creemore Springs Brewery Ltd. of Creemore, Ontario; the Great Lakes Brewing Co., a draft-only brewery in Etobicoke, Ontario; and Shaftebury Brewing Co., formerly of Vancouver, British Columbia, now located in sparkling new facilities in Delta, British Columbia.

Still, 1995 was not without its casualties as a large regional brewery, three microbreweries (including one that lasted less than six months), and a brewpub ceased operations, with some brewery equipment finding new homes south of the border.

John Labatt Ltd., Canada's second largest brewer, fell into foreign hands – namely the Belgian brewing giant, Interbrew SA – leaving the government-granted monopoly in Ontario, Brewers Retail, dominated by those same foreign beer powers.

Total microbrewery production for Canada in 1995 saw an overall increase of 26 percent, climbing from 590,838 hectoliters to 747,408 hectoliters. Regional specialty breweries saw the biggest rise with a 38 percent hike, and production rising from 427,271 hectoliters to 591,036 hectoliters. Microbreweries fell from 143,288 hectoliters to 128,282 hectoliters of production, a drop of 10 percent, but part of this change resulted from 82,720 hectoliters of production being transferred to the regional specialties segment. Brewpubs showed strong growth with a 34 percent advancement, leaping from 20,429 hectoliters to 27,515 hectoliters.

After several years of backsliding sales and little or no growth, brewpub production again surged forward, though the opening of several large-volume brewpubs did help to boost production numbers for 1995.

Still, a number of brewpubs have "maxed-out" for a given site with no space available for expansion, or existing municipal or provincial bylaws (for example, off license sales are not legal in some provinces such as Ontario) have prevented these brewpubs from seeking a larger segment of the beer market. It is therefore not cost effective to expand existing brewing facilities.

The Maritimes and Québec

Regional Specialty Breweries

Unibroue Inc. of Chambly, Québec, surged to a 36 percent gain, climbing from 28,000 hectoliters to 38,000 hectoliters. Les Brasseurs du Nord, Blainville,

Québec, in its first full year as a regional, posted a 20 percent rise, moving from 21,500 hectoliters to 25,835 hectoliters.

Brasserie McAuslan of Montreal pushed into regional specialty status at 18,720 hectoliters, up from 16,700 hectoliters, a 12 percent hike.

Peter McAuslan, Brasserie McAuslan
Montreal, Québec

When I started Brasserie McAuslan in 1989, I figured to do one brew a week and produce 5,000 hectoliters of beer by year's end. Having more than trebled that figure, it's very satisfying to have reached the benchmark of a regional specialty brewery.

We definitely are in the beer business for the long run.

The beer business is a lot more difficult now than when I started. McAuslan's was the only micro then. Today, Canadian beer sales are still flat. And there are more and more players. Big brewers are discounting heavily, making for tighter margins and more difficulty getting and keeping shelf space.

It's definitely a lot tougher business now, and we still don't have ease of access to other Canadian markets.

Still, I see growth on a continuing basis for the specialty beer segment. Though if there is an economic downturn, specialty brews will be extremely important to the survival of microbreweries.

While I still expect volume to grow, there is potential for contraction of the number of players.

As we are currently configured, McAuslan's can produce about 30,000 hectoliters annually, with space available for tankage to bring us to 45,000 hectoliters, which is the obvious next target. We'll be adding fermentation and maturation vessels as demand requires it.

Microbreweries

Brasserie Beauce Broue Inc. opened in St. Odilon near Québec City with a 25-hectoliter brewing system.

La Brasseurs de l'Anse came on stream with a 35-hectoliter Peter Austin brewery in Anse Saint-Jean. Believed to be the only microbrewery in Canada with a tunnel pasteurizer to facilitate export of its two products, Illegal and Blueberry Ale, to Paris, France, and to South America.

La Brasserie les Maskoutains de Saint-Hyacinthe, producers of Metayer, a red ale, opened in St. Hyacinthe, Québec, and following a short-lived run, quietly closed after less than six months in the marketplace.

Picaroons Brewing Co. opened at the close of the year in Fredericton, New Brunswick, becoming the first microbrewery operating on the East Coast, though at present Picaroons is operating more like a brewpub as it has draft lines running next door to Dolan's Pub, a 150-seat pub.

Les Brasseurs GMT climbed to the top of the microbrewery ranks with a healthy gain of 41 percent, jumping from 12,047 hectoliters to 17,000 hectoliters in 1995.

Production at the Brasal-Brasserie Allemande remained steady at 12,000 hectoliters in 1995.

Brewpubs

The Granite Brewery (No. 1) in Halifax, Nova Scotia, the only other operating small brewery on the East Coast, began work at an expansion site a few blocks down the street from its existing facility on Barrington Street. The Granite celebrated its tenth year of operation in 1995.

Vieux Copenhagen Brasseurs, a brewpub, flung open its doors in St. Saveur de Monts, Québec, with a 10-hectoliter full-mash brewery from Cask Brewing Systems and brewed up a storm with output of a whopping 2,500 hectoliters.

L'Inox, a Québec city brewpub, after almost ten years of brewing, finally made the conversion from malt extract to full mash.

L'Cervois of Montreal posted a 12 percent increase with production growing to 660 hectoliters, up from last year's 590 hectoliters.

Shawn Tordon, La Cervoise
Montreal, Québec

We installed a 1-hectoliter system from Stainless Steel Specialists of Laval, Québec, to do specialty recipes under what we call our Cuvee de la Marmite

---

THE MARITIMES AND QUEBEC: 1995 OPENINGS AND CLOSINGS
Provinces: New Brunswick, Nova Scotia, Northwest Territories, Yukon, and Quebec

Companies listed as opened include all those that began selling their own beers during the 1995 calendar year.

MICROBREWERIES (4)
New Brunswick
Picaroons Brewing Co., Fredericton
Quebec
Brasserie Beau Ce Broue, St. Odilon
La Brasserie des Mouskoutains de Saint-Hyacinthe, Saint-Hyacinthe
La Brasseurs de l' Anse, Anse Saint-Jean

BREWPUB (1)
Quebec
Vieux Copenhagen Brasseurs, St. Saveur des Monts

CLOSINGS (YEAR OF OPENING IN PARENTHESES)
1 Microbrewery
La Brasserie des Mouskoutains de Saint-Hyacinthe, Saint-Hyacinthe (1995)

banner, literally "from the cauldron," and that may account for some of the increased production, probably 50 hectoliters of specialty beers.

We brewed a blueberry wit beer, a strong honey/coriander ale, a chocolate stout, and a raspberry brown ale, just to name a few. The beers are ready in seven to ten days. We don't filter the specialty brews. If they are really good, the two kegs of specialty beers go in a week.

If our customers make a request for a different beer, we'll try to accommodate them. We'll brew just about anything.

I've been experimenting with making my own syrups for the specialty brews. They are much easier to handle and give a greater depth of flavor.

Of our regular beers, la Futel is our biggest seller. It used to be a true lager, but now I use a great ale yeast and ferment at a lower temperature to achieve the smoothness and roundness of a lager.

La Cervoise is really a bar that happens to brew beer. We don't have anything in Montreal on the scale of brewpubs in say, Boston, where they have plenty of space for sit-down meals as well as the brewery.

We've been doing beer tastings and that gets new people into la Cervoise. When new customers notice we make beer, they try them and like them and come back for more.

The specialty beer thing is a good hook. It keeps people returning to see what is on tap next at la Cervoise.

(See sidebar on page 43 for a complete listing of the region's 1995 openings and closings.)

Ontario

Regional Breweries

Sleeman Brewing and Malting Ltd., a large regional brewery in Guelph, Ontario, and Okanagan Spring Brewery Ltd., a sizeable regional specialty brewery located in Vernon, British Columbia, have joined forces under the Allied Strategies banner to better serve both domestic and international markets. Sleeman chalked up a 35 percent gain, moving from 98,500 hectoliters to 132,874 hectoliters.

Regional Specialty Breweries

Production at the Upper Canada Brewery of Toronto climbed from 60,000 hectoliters to 70,000 hectoliters, a rise of 17 percent, while Brick Brewing Co. Ltd. remained steady at 67,500 hectoliters in 1995.

Creemore Springs Brewery Ltd., in joining the regional specialty ranks, saw production climb by 9 percent to 18,000 hectoliters, up from 16,500 hectoliters.

Also achieving regional specialty status, though on a quieter note, was the Great Lakes Brewing Co. of Etobicoke with production of some 25,000 hectoliters of beer.

Howard Thompson, Creemore Springs Brewery Ltd.
Creemore, Ontario

I'm surprised that we have reached regional specialty status. I thought a regional would be more like 100,000 hectoliters of production, not the 18,000 hectoliters we produced in 1995.

We really haven't done anything different. We're still in the same building. We still produce a single product. We still self distribute to some four hundred bar accounts.

I think beer connoisseurs and regular beer drinkers have accepted Creemore Springs Premium Lager. Demand for our product will always be there.

We have a strong local market in the Collingwood and Barrie area, but yet we are close to the large urban market of Toronto.

The market is much more competitive now. There are a limited number of draft taps, and the bottle market has been flat for several years.

While there is increasing interest in microbrewery products, I expect a shake out soon. It's make it or break it time. There are a lot of good micros, but some can't survive.

We, however, at Creemore are still very optimistic about microbrewed beer. We've added three new 100-hectoliter fermenters, bringing our current site capacity to just under 25,000 hectoliters. We also added a 100-hectoliter water tank so we have more of the spring water we use for brewing on-site.

We haven't changed the way we do things at Creemore, and we wouldn't want to see Brewers Retail dissolved. Brewers Retail is an efficient system which deals with our product in a quality way. They have cold storage for the variety of microbrewery products on the market. I would not like to have to deal with the distribution systems in Québec or the United States.

Microbreweries

Europeanbeer (also known as Eurobeer) opened in Windsor with a 10-hectoliter system to produce lagers. F & M Breweries opened in Guelph with a custom-designed 16-hectoliter brewhouse and are currently brewing two products, MacLean's Pale Ale and StoneHammer™ Pilsner.

The Gold Crown Brewing Co. opened in Waterloo with a 16-hectoliter brewery from Criveller Co. of Niagara Falls.

Hometowne Breweries Ltd. of London ceased brewing and closed its doors during 1995.

Canada's Finest Beers of Wheatley also succumbed during the year, making Ontario the dubious leader in microbrewery closures for the past year.

And in related brewing news, MHD Canada Inc., suppliers of malt and hops to the microbrewing industry, also went into receivership.

Hart had a solid gain of 18 percent, moving from 5,500 hectoliters to 6,500 hectoliters, while Conners rang up a 14 percent increase, climbing from 13,130 hectoliters to 15,000 hectoliters.

Look for the Kawartha Lakes Brewing Co. to open in Peterborough in 1996.

Anetta Bulut, Great Lakes Brewing Co.
Etobicoke, Ontario

We just do one draft beer, Great Lakes Lager. We only sell to restaurants, pubs, and taverns. We have no retail sales and no retail store on-site at the brewery.

At the present time, we do not have a bottling line, but we plan to add one when we complete a six-story addition at our current site. We'll be putting in a 100-hectoliter brew kettle to replace the existing 40-hectoliter one.

We attained regional specialty size with zero advertising. It's strictly been word of mouth. We offered excellent service to our customers and a good quality beer.

We see ourselves as a true alternative to the Big Two. Great Lakes Lager is a fairly mainstream lager, but it was in response to demand from our customers. They wanted something different than what was coming from the Big Two, and we supplied it.

But, being frank, the one thing we are lacking is brand awareness. There's no real image associated with Great Lakes Brewing Co. We've been at this location for five years, and the brewery has been in existence for almost ten years. Perhaps over time things will evolve so that we create an image for ourselves.

To that end, we hope to change that with our second brand, Red Leaf Lager, 5 percent alcohol by volume, and the arrival of our new brewer, Peter Haupenthal, who wants to brew some different specialty beers, so there's the very real possibility of a lot of change at Great Lakes.

While it goes without saying the beer business is very competitive, I think there is quite a lot of room for a variety of beer choices.

Competition is definitely good for the consumer who is getting quality choices, though we are limited in what we can do on the pricing side of things.

The industry can only get better for microbreweries.

Brewpubs

Addington's opened its doors in the nation's capital, Ottawa, with an 8-barrel, full-mash brewery from Canadian Custom Stainless.

Major's Brew House also opened in Ottawa with an 8-hectoliter brewery.

On the downside, Quinn's on the Danforth in Toronto ceased brewing and closed.

The Port Arthur Brasserie and Brewpub in Thunder Bay recorded a 25 percent rise after several years of declining sales, while Denison's of Toronto nudged up by 3 percent. The Kingston Brewing Co., Ontario's first brewpub, slipped slightly, from 345 hectoliters to 306 hectoliters as it was poised to celebrate its tenth year of operation in April 1996.

Watch for the Olde Stone Brewing Co. to open a sixty seater in Peterborough.

Van Turner, The Kingston Brewing Co.
Kingston, Ontario

Surviving ten years in the brewpub business has been a real adventure, but the key was having a really good staff.

Along with having a well-trained staff, you have to make quality products to continue to attract good clientele.

Kingston is a good town for beer and food, but ten years ago we had to try to sell them on trying our beer. Now people come in to sample our beers and are outraged if someone in the party orders a Coors Light.

ONTARIO: 1995 OPENINGS AND CLOSINGS

Companies listed as opened include all those that began selling their own beers during the 1995 calendar year.

MICROBREWERIES (3)
F & M Breweries, Guelph
Europeanbeer, Windsor
Gold Crown Brewing Co., Waterloo

BREWPUBS (3)
Addingtons, Ottawa
Majors Brew House, Ottawa
The Feathers, Toronto (opened 1994)

CLOSINGS (YEAR OF OPENING IN PARENTHESES)

2 Microbreweries
Hometowne Brewies Ltd., London (1993)
Canada's Finest Beers, Wheatley

1 Brewpub
Quinn's on the Danforth, Toronto

Five years ago our Regal Lager was outselling Dragon's Breath Pale Ale sixty-to-forty, but today the cask-conditioned version of Dragon's Breath is fifty-to-fifty with the lager.

Having Dragon's Breath Pale Ale contract-brewed, one of Canada's first to do so, by Hart Brewing Co. Ltd. of Carelton Place, has helped get the Kingston Brewing Co. name out there. A lot of tourists come to the home of the Dragon to see and sample at the brewery where the recipe originated.

People aren't going out as often, but when they do they are treating themselves to premium products which use premium ingredients.

I think the prospects for brewpubs are strong. We're expanding. We've taken over upstairs and we're in the process of renovating to add another 60 seats, giving us 150 seats in winter and 250 seats in summer.

The new room, which will have a mural on the ceiling, stained glass windows, and a gas stove, will give us a lot more flexibility for parties and special functions.

(See sidebar on page 45 for a complete listing of the region's 1995 openings and closings.)

The West

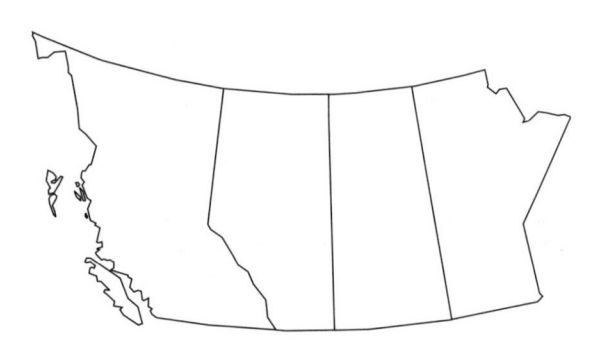

Regional Breweries

The Drummond Brewing Co., Alberta's largest independent brewery, voluntarily went into receivership, though the Tsingtao Brewery of China has plans to reopen the facility to brew its namesake brand.

Regional Specialty Breweries

The Shaftebury Brewing Co. of Vancouver, British Columbia, in achieving regional specialty status during 1995, posted a 38 percent increase, as production rose from 15,200 hectoliters to 21,000 hectoliters. The Shaftebury Brewing Co. Ltd. underwent a major overhaul, installing a new 100-hectoliter brewhouse with a mash/lauter tun and a brew kettle/whirlpool combination.

Big Rock of Calgary, Alberta, continued its growth pattern with a 14 percent increase, climbing from 105,000 hectoliters to 120,000 hectoliters. Granville Island, Vancouver, British Columbia, powered its way to a whopping 56 percent rise, jumping from 28,800 hectoliters to 45,000 hectoliters.

Okanagan Spring Brewery of Vernon, British Columbia, rang up a 37 percent increase, moving from 69,971 hectoliters to 95,981 hectoliters.

Paul Beaton, Shaftebury Brewing Co. Ltd.
Delta, British Columbia

Having just moved into a new brewery with a 105-hectoliter brew kettle with a potential yearly capacity of 30,000 hectoliters and space for expansion to 80,000 hectoliters, we were pleasantly surprised that our brewery has achieved regional specialty brewery status.

We literally ran out of space in Vancouver. The whole trend has been to microbrewery beers, and we've been riding the same wave. Certainly we run a good business, but public awareness has increased and there's a greater knowledge among beer consumers.

When we started in 1987, people thought we were coming from Mars. But now microbrewed beer is in vogue.

I see continued growth for three to five years, though there are a lot of players. There's more competition developed all the way round.

I figure the big brewers will want to get more involved, become a bigger factor. Even though net migration of people to British Columbia continues to rise and thus there are more customers, I believe the big brewers haven't fully addressed the issue of microbrewery success.

And there has to be some fall out. Microbreweries can't go on expanding like they have been.

Stefan Tobler, Okanagan Spring Brewery
Vernon, British Columbia

The Okanagan Spring Brewery, with a capacity of 125,000 hectoliters, is currently undergoing yet another expansion with the installation of a 160-hectoliter gas-fired brew kettle and five 1,000-hectoliter outdoor tanks.

Increased sales are due overall to more advertising, more marketing via radio, consumer tastings, and more advertising in pubs and restaurants.

Consumers want natural beers such as our current best-selling brand Okanagan Pale Ale. People want and like a great variety of beers, so we introduced Okanagan Brown Ale this year.

Though it's still a growing market, it gets tougher every time. We will not see such rapid double-digit growth like we've had in the past.

However, we expect to complete a deal by May 1996 with Sleeman Brewing and Malting of Guelph that will allow us to share marketing and distribution. Eventually we will brew each other's products for our respective markets, as well as for export.

That looks promising.

Microbreweries

The Fort Garry Brewing Co. opened in a suburb of Winnipeg with a 20-hectoliter system from Specific Mechanical Systems, becoming the first microbrewery in the province of Manitoba. The Alley Kat Brewing Co. opened in Edmonton, Alberta, with a 20-hectoliter brewing system from Specific Mechanical Systems.

The Bow Valley Brewing Co. began production in Canmore, Alberta, with a custom-designed 25-hectoliter brewing system.

The Banff Brewery Corporation of Calgary, Alberta, came on stream with a 30-hectoliter brewhouse from Newlands Services Inc., Clearbrook, British Columbia.

The Tin Whistle Brewing Co. Ltd. opened in Penticton, British Columbia, with a 20-hectoliter full-mash brewery from Ripley Stainless.

The Russell Brewing Co. opened in Surrey, British Columbia, with a 30-hectoliter brewhouse from Newlands Services and a draft-only policy of distribution.

The Storm Brewing Co. began brewing in Vancouver, British Columbia, with a 25-hectoliter decoction mash system created out of previously owned stainless steel equipment from nonrelated industries.

The Brew Brothers Brewing Co. Ltd. became a contract brewer with the launch of Black Pilsener, utilizing excess capacity at Great Western Brewing Co. in Saskatoon.

The Vancouver Island Brewing Co., Victoria, British Columbia, in rising from 12,000 hectoliters to 14,000 hectoliters, saw a 17 percent gain.

The Tree Brewing Co. Ltd. anticipates opening in Kelowna, British Columbia, during 1996.

Brewpubs

The Mission Bridge Brewing Co. opened in Calgary, Alberta, with a 15-hectoliter system from Specific Mechanical Systems to serve a 380-seat brewpub.

In Vancouver, British Columbia, the Steam Works Brewing Co., a sixty-five-seat brewpub, went full steam ahead with steam as the sole source of power for the brewery.

Brewsters continued its expansion program as it opened Brewsters Brewery and Restaurant (No. 5) in Regina, Saskatchewan, and Brewsters Brewery and Resaurant (No. 6) in Edmonton, Alberta.

Brewsters (No. 1) of Regina posted a 28 percent gain, climbing from 800 hectoliters to 1,020 hectoliters, while Brewsters (No. 2) of Calgary chalked up a 17 percent gain, climbing from 1,260 hectoliters to 1,470 hectoliters, and Brewsters (No. 3) in Moose Jaw saw a 10 percent rise.

The Saskatoon Brewing Co. of Saskatoon, Saskatchewan, recorded a 13 percent rise, moving from 1,700 hectoliters to 1,920 hectoliters.

Swans Brewpub/Buckerfield Brewery, Victoria, British Columbia, made an 8 percent climb in production to 1,350 hectoliters, up from 1,250 hectoliters. The Bushwakker Brewing Co. in Regina, Saskatchewan, nudged up from 880 hectoliters to 930 hectoliters, an increase of 6 percent.

On the downside, the Prairie Inn in Saanichton, British Columbia, ceased its brewing operations, but remains open as a neighborhood pub.

The Howe Sound Brewing Co., a brewpub and small hotel complex, is currently under construction in Squamish, British Columbia.

Barry Berderdall, Saskatoon Brewing Co./Cheers Roadhouse Inn
Saskatoon, Saskatchewan

The Saskatoon Brewing Co./Cheers Roadhouse Inn, having produced 1,920 hectoliters in 1995, is pushing the upper reaches of the legal limit of 2,000 hectoliters for brewpub production in Saskatchewan.

Thanks to our concentrated efforts, the province's 2,000-hectoliter limit is now under review, with a sliding scale of taxes being proposed as a way of dealing with the surge in sales.

We have no more storage space available. We've maxed out for this location using a 10-hectoliter system.

THE WEST: 1995 OPENINGS AND CLOSINGS
Provinces: Alberta, British Columbia, Manitoba, and Saskatchewan

Companies listed as opened include all those that began selling their own beers during the 1995 calendar year.

MICROBREWERIES (6)

Alberta
Alley Kat Brewing Co., Edmonton
Bow Valley Brewing Co., Canmore
Banff Brewing Co., Calgary

British Columbia
Steam Works Brewing Co., Vancouver
Tin Whistle Brewing Co., Penticton

Manitoba
Fort Garry Brewing Co., Winnipeg

BREWPUBS (3)

Alberta
Brewsters Brewery and Restaurant (No. 6), Edmonton

Mission Bridge Brewing Co., Calgary

Saskatchewan
Brewsters Brewing Co. and Restaurant (No. 5), Regina

General public awareness of brewpub beers is good in Saskatoon as there are now four brewpubs, and people are switching from the majors to our brands.

In the summer, Arctic Pilsner is our biggest seller, while in the winter Prairie Dark Ale gets the nod, though we have run out of some brands during the busy summer months.

We had a good response to our Belgian ale which had a trial run in December, and I think it will be joining our regular brews.

I think the prospects are good for continued growth in the microbrewing industry, but I don't know how far or how many. Still, projections look good.

In fact, we see it as a very positive situation. We'll open a second Cheers location in Saskatoon, which will have a 20-hectoliter brew kettle and be double the size of our existing location.

Cheers Two, already under construction, will also have twice the aging and storage capacity of the original.

We haven't come up with the final name for Cheers Two, but we are certainly looking forward to opening in three or four months.

(See sidebar on page 47 for a complete listing of the region's 1995 openings and closings.)

Large Breweries

Interbrew SA of Belgium completed the purchase of John Labatt Ltd. for a reported $2.7 billion. Combined production of Interbrew and Labatt is expected to exceed 36 million hectoliters and generate sales of some $3.9 billion.

Total production from the big brewers fell slightly, from 19,251,949 hectoliters to 19,239,159 hectoliters in 1995. A stubborn, stagnant economy, increased competition from imports and microbreweries, and an aging population were all contributing factors in the big brewers' sluggish results.

In the Maritimes, Nova Scotia saw production fall by just over 3 percent, from 568,639 hectoliters to 550,856 hectoliters. Prince Edward Island's production climbed from 80,971 hectoliters to 81,721 hectoliters, a gain of just under 1 percent. New Brunswick, dropped from 471,927 hectoliters to 470,455 hectoliters, a loss of 0.3 percent.

Newfoundland saw production losses of 4.8 percent, from 427,887 hectoliters to 407,494 hectoliters.

Production in Québec rose from 5,287,921 hectoliters to 5,372,313 hectoliters, a rise of 1.6 percent.

Large brewery beer production in Ontario was off by .6 percent, from 7,002,312 hectoliters to 6,960,524 hectoliters.

Beer production in Manitoba dropped by .5 percent, from 676,352 hectoliters to 673,168 hectoliters.

Saskatchewan's total for big brewery production rose by almost 2 percent, up from 539,158 hectoliters to 548,132 hectoliters.

Alberta beer production by the big brewers dropped from 1,598,242 hectoliters to 1,582,227 hectoliters, off by 1 percent.

British Columbia saw big brewery beer production fall slightly, from 2,531,911 hectoliters to 2,527,536 hectoliters.

Sales in the Yukon fell from 33,086 hectoliters to 32,325 hectoliters, a drop of just under 2 percent.

In the Northwest Territories, production fell by 3.5 percent, from 33,543 hectoliters to 32,409 hectoliters.

Imports

Imported beer consumption rose from 578,654 hectoliters to 658,549 hectoliters, a solid gain of 13 percent, bringing imports to just over 3 percent of the Canadian market.

— Robert Hughey
"Canadian Brew News" Editor for **The New Brewer**

4 Brewing Industry Statistics

Thanks to the help of breweries and the generosity of brewing industry research organizations, the Institute for Brewing Studies has compiled a broad range of industry statistics. Together, they paint a good picture of the actual volume of business done in North America.

One interesting paradox should be noted. Despite dramatically increased sales volume in each of the last six years, the craft-brewing industry in North America is still very small in relation to the overall brewing industry and is responsible for approximately 2 percent of overall beer consumption in the United States and approximately 2.6 percent in Canada.

To clearly illustrate the growth of the market we created the "Craft Brewing Index" (see pages 50 and 52), which depicts the combined total volume of beer sold by microbreweries, brewpubs, contract brewing companies, and regional specialty breweries (breweries that began as microbreweries but have since grown to regional size, such as Anchor Brewing Co. and Sierra Nevada Brewing Co.).

The different types of breweries listed in the Institute for Brewing Studies' individual estimated taxable removals charts are defined as follows.

Brewing Industry Definitions

Microbrewery: A brewery that produces less than 15,000 barrels (17,600 hectoliters) of beer per year. Microbreweries sell to the public by one or more of the following methods: the traditional three-tier system (brewer to wholesaler to retailer to consumer); the two-tier system (brewer acting as wholesaler to retailer to consumer); and in some cases, directly to the consumer through carry outs, on-site tap room, or brewery restaurant sales.

Brewpub: A restaurant-brewery that sells the majority of its beer on-site. The beer is brewed for sale and consumption in the adjacent restaurant and/or bar. The beer is often dispensed directly from the brewery's storage tanks. Where allowed by law, brewpubs often sell beer "to go" and/or distribute to off-site accounts. Note: For statistical purposes, brewpubs whose off-site beer sales grow to exceed 50 percent of total sales are recategorized as microbreweries.

Regional Brewery: A brewery with a capacity to brew between 15,000 and 500,000 barrels (17,600 and 586,700 hectoliters). Although its distribution may be regional (or greater) in scope, for categorization purposes "regional" refers to the brewery's size only.

Regional Specialty Brewery: A regional-scale brewery whose flagship (largest selling) brand is positioned as a "micro" or specialty beer.

Large Brewery: A company with sales of more than 500,000 barrels (586,700 hectoliters). Some large brewing companies operate a single brewing facility, while others may have more than a dozen.

Contract Brewing Company: A business that hires a brewery to produce its beer. The contract brewing company handles marketing, sales, and distribution of its beer, while generally leaving the brewing and packaging to its producer-brewery (which is also sometimes confusingly referred to as a contract brewer).

Beer and Brewery Statistics

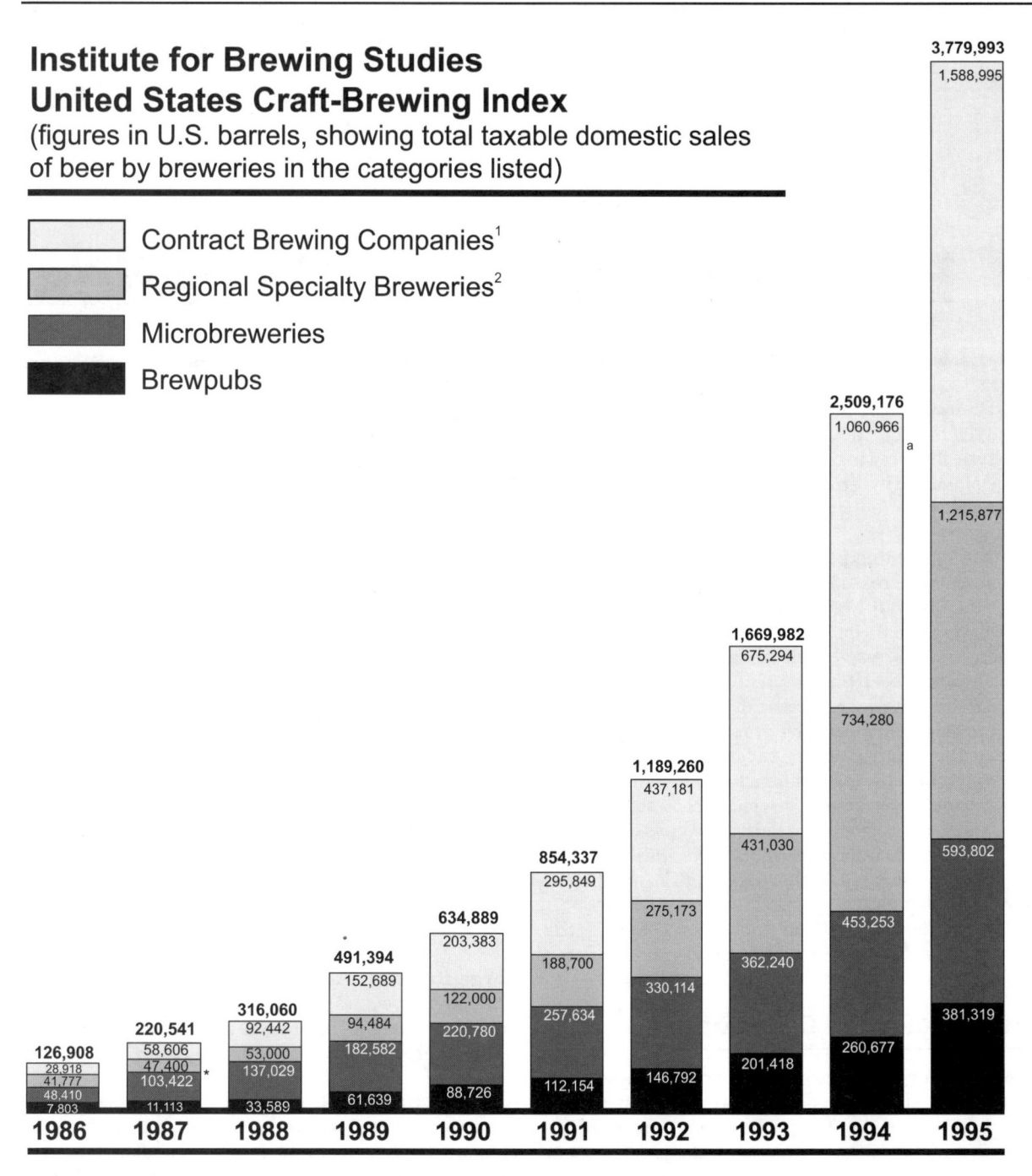

Institute for Brewing Studies
United States Craft-Brewing Index
(figures in U.S. barrels, showing total taxable domestic sales of beer by breweries in the categories listed)

- ☐ Contract Brewing Companies[1]
- ▫ Regional Specialty Breweries[2]
- ▪ Microbreweries
- ■ Brewpubs

Year	Total	Contract Brewing	Regional Specialty	Microbreweries	Brewpubs
1986	126,908	28,918	47,777	48,410	7,803
1987	220,541	58,606	47,400	103,422	11,113
1988	316,060	92,442	53,000	137,029	33,589
1989	491,394	152,689	94,484	182,582	61,639
1990	634,889	203,383	122,000	220,780	88,726
1991	854,337	295,849	188,700	257,634	112,154
1992	1,189,260	437,181	275,173	330,114	146,792
1993	1,669,982	675,294	431,030	362,240	201,418
1994	2,509,176	1,060,966	734,280	453,253	260,677
1995	3,779,993	1,588,995	1,215,877	593,802	381,319

* Estimate

a Adjusted from previous year's chart.

1 The total for contract brewing companies does not include amounts for companies whose flagship brands are either malt liquors or American-lager-style beers. The contract brewing companies' total also does not include barrels of beer brewed at microbreweries or regional specialty breweries (which is already accounted for in the totals for those breweries).

2 Regional specialty breweries are regional-size breweries that produce an "all-malt" or "specialty"-style beer for their flagship brand. Regional specialty breweries include the following companies: Anchor Brewing Co. (beginning 1985); Sierra Nevada Brewing Co. and Redhook Ale Brewery (beginning 1989); Widmer Brewing Co. and Full Sail Brewing Co. (beginning 1991); Hart Brewing Co. (beginning 1992); Rockies Brewing Co., Portland Brewing Co., and BridgePort Brewing Co. (beginning 1993); Abita Brewing Co., Deschutes Brewery, New Belgium Brewing Co., Nor'Wester Brewing Co., Dubuque Brewing & Bottling Co./Brandevor USA Inc., Catamount Brewing Co., and Celis Brewery (beginning 1994); Alaskan Brewing and Bottling Co., Boulevard Brewing Co., Humboldt Brewery, Mass. Bay Brewing Co., Mendocino Brewing Co., Old Dominion Brewing Co., Rogue Ales/Oregon Brewing Co., Shipyard Brewery, and Summit Brewing Co. (beginning 1995).

Note: Cumulative totals are compiled from brewers' reported figures and IBS' estimates.

Beer and Brewery Statistics

United States Microbrewery and Brewpub Openings

Key: Micros | Brewpubs | Total

Year	Micros	Brewpubs	Total
1986	11	10	21
1987	17	13	30
1988	11	44	55
1989	21	41	62
1990	17	34	51
1991	11	47	58
1992	20	39	59
1993 [a]	32	69	101
1994	66	102	168
1995	91	196	287

United States Microbrewery and Brewpub Closings

Key: Micros | Brewpubs | Total

Year	Micros	Brewpubs	Total
1986	2	2	4
1987	3	0	3
1988	1	4	5
1989	8	3	11
1990	5	9	14
1991	7	13	20
1992	7	7	14
1993	3	14	17
1994	2	6	8
1995	3	24	27

United States Regional Specialty Breweries, Microbreweries, and Brewpubs Operating

Key: Regional Specialty Breweries | Micros | Brewpubs | Total

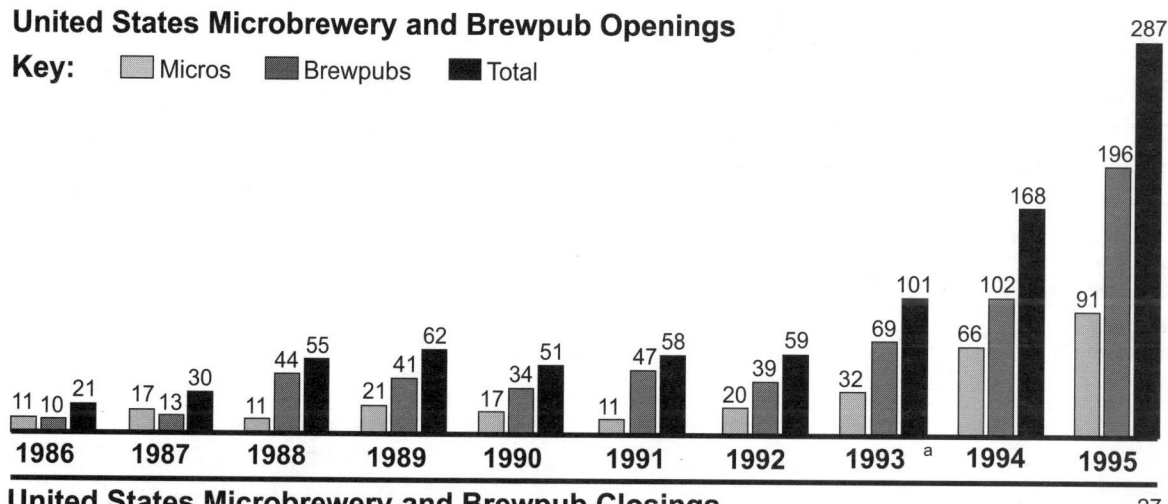

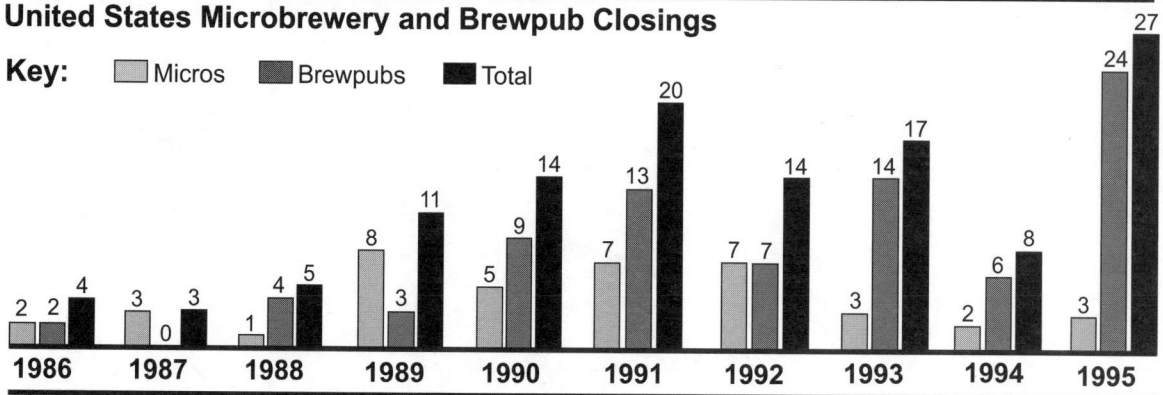

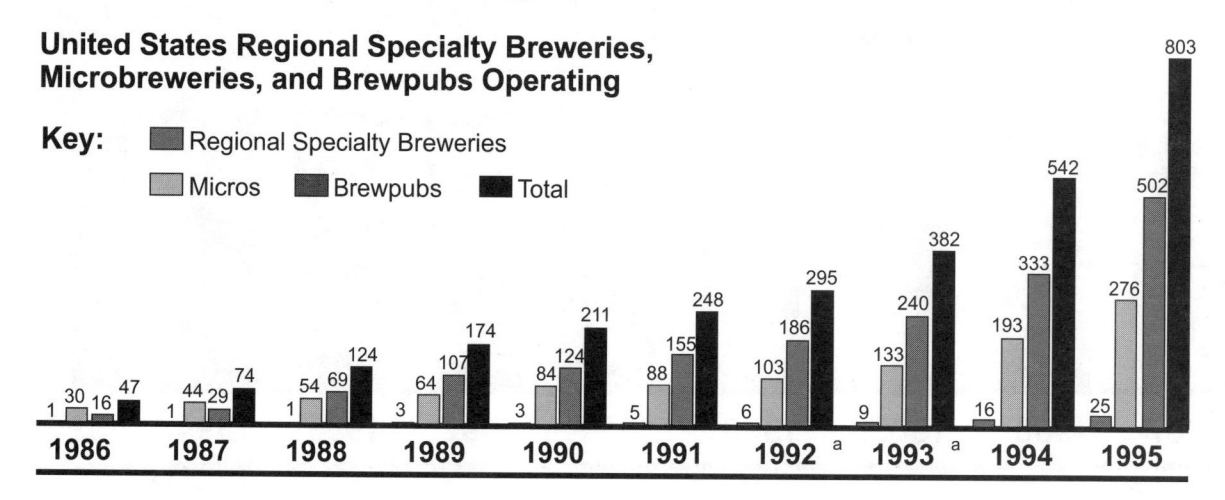

Year	Regional Specialty	Micros	Brewpubs	Total
1986	1	30	16	47
1987	1	44	29	74
1988	1	54	69	124
1989	3	64	107	174
1990	3	84	124	211
1991	5	88	155	248
1992 [a]	6	103	186	295
1993 [a]	9	133	240	382
1994	16	193	333	542
1995	25	276	502	803

a Adjusted from previous year's chart.

Note: The difference of brewpub or microbrewery openings and closings for one year added to the previous year's total operating does not always equal the subsequent year-end total because one to three brewpubs are subject to reclassification as microbreweries each year. The reclassification occurs when a brewpub reports selling more than 50 percent of its beer off-site.

Regional specialty breweries are regional-size breweries that produce an "all-malt" or "specialty"-style beer for their flagship brand. Regional specialty breweries include the following companies: Anchor Brewing Co. (beginning 1985); Sierra Nevada Brewing Co. and Redhook Ale Brewery (beginning 1989); Widmer Brewing Co. and Full Sail Brewing Co. (beginning 1991); Hart Brewing Co. (beginning 1992); Rockies Brewing Co., Portland Brewing Co., and BridgePort Brewing Co. (beginning 1993); Abita Brewing Co., Deschutes Brewery, New Belgium Brewing Co., Nor'Wester Brewing Co., Dubuque Brewing & Bottling Co./Brandevor USA Inc., Catamount Brewing Co., and Celis Brewery (beginning 1994). Alaskan Brewing and Bottling Co., Boulevard Brewing Co., Humboldt Brewery, Mass. Bay Brewing Co., Mendocino Brewing Co., Old Dominion Brewing Co., Rogue Ales/Oregon Brewing Co., Shipyard Brewery, and Summit Brewing Co. (beginning 1995). Cumulative totals are compiled from brewers' reported figures and IBS' estimates.

Beer and Brewery Statistics

Institute for Brewing Studies
Canadian Craft-Brewing Index (figures in hectoliters showing total taxable domestic sales of beer in the categories listed)

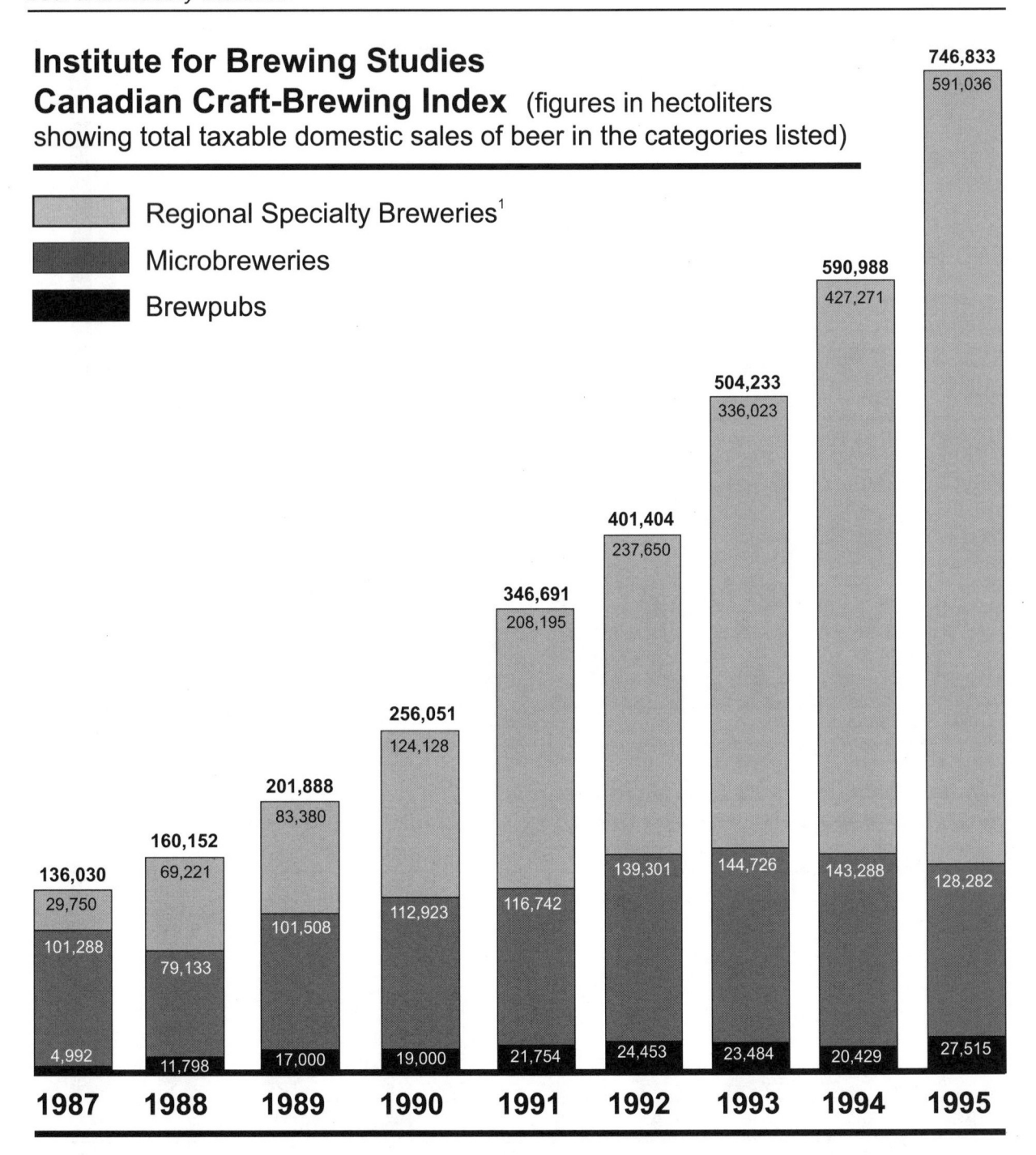

- Regional Specialty Breweries[1]
- Microbreweries
- Brewpubs

Year	Total	Regional Specialty	Microbreweries	Brewpubs
1987	136,030	—	101,288	4,992
		29,750		
1988	160,152	69,221	79,133	11,798
1989	201,888	83,380	101,508	17,000
1990	256,051	124,128	112,923	19,000
1991	346,691	208,195	116,742	21,754
1992	401,404	237,650	139,301	24,453
1993	504,233	336,023	144,726	23,484
1994	590,988	427,271	143,288	20,429
1995	746,833	591,036	128,282	27,515

1 Regional specialty breweries are regional-size breweries that produce an "all-malt" or "specialty"-style beer for their flagship brand. Regional specialty breweries' totals include the following companies: Brick Brewing Co. (beginning 1987); Upper Canada Brewing Co. and Big Rock Brewers Co. (beginning 1988); Okanagan Spring Brewery (beginning 1990); Algonquin Brewing Co. (beginning 1991); Granville Island Brewing Co. (beginning 1993); Les Brasseurs du Nord Inc. and Unibroue Inc. (beginning 1994). Creemore Springs Brewery, Great Lakes Brewing Co., Brasserie McAuslan, and Shaftebury Brewing Co. (beginning 1995).
Note: Cumulative totals are compiled from brewers' estimates as well as IBS' estimates.

Canadian Microbrewery and Brewpub Openings

Key: Micros | Brewpubs | Total

Year	Micros	Brewpubs	Total
1986	8	7	15
1987	8	7	15
1988	9	10	19
1989	7	16	23
1990	1	3	4
1991	4	11	15
1992	2	4	6
1993	8	6	14
1994 [a]	6	4	10
1995	15	6	21

Canadian Microbrewery and Brewpub Closings

Key: Micros | Brewpubs | Total

Year	Micros	Brewpubs	Total
1986	4	2	6
1987	2	1	3
1988	4	1	5
1989	5	2	7
1990	6	1	7
1991	5	7	12
1992	0	6	6
1993 [a]	2	4	6
1994	1	5	6
1995	3	2	5

Canadian Regional Specialty Breweries[1], Microbreweries, and Brewpubs Operating

Key: Regional Specialty Breweries | Micros | Brewpubs | Total

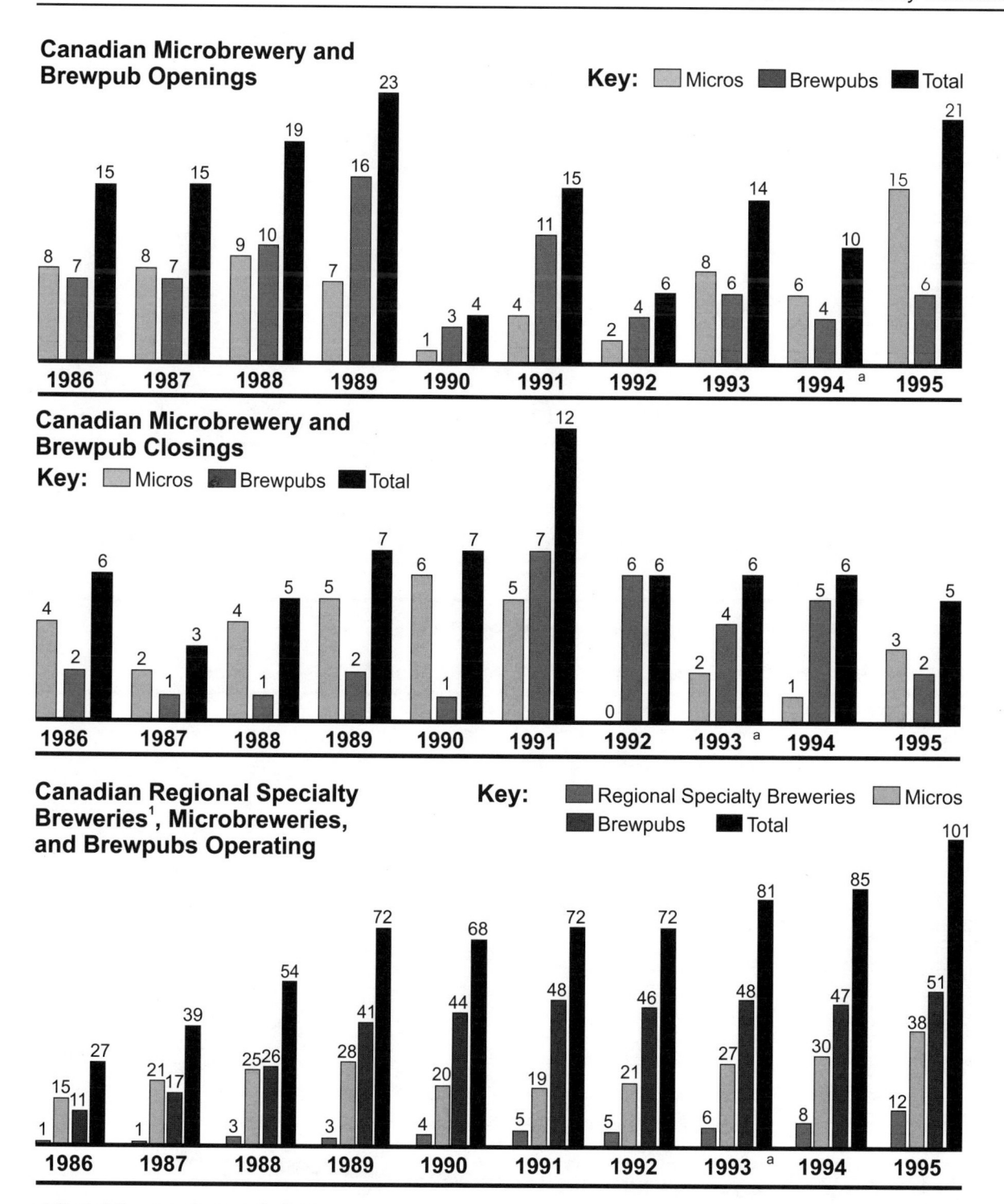

Year	Regional Specialty	Micros	Brewpubs	Total
1986	1	15	11	27
1987	1	21	17	39
1988	3	25	26	54
1989	3	28	41	72
1990	4	20	44	68
1991	5	19	48	72
1992	5	21	46	72
1993 [a]	6	27	48	81
1994	8	30	47	85
1995	12	38	51	101

a Adjusted from previous year's chart.

1 Regional specialty breweries are regional-size breweries that offer a "specialty" or "micro"-style beer as their flagship brand. Regional specialty breweries' totals include the following companies: Brick Brewing Co. (beginning 1985); Upper Canada Brewing Co. and Big Rock Brewing Co. (beginning 1988); Okanagan Spring Brewery (beginning 1990); Algonquin Brewing Co. (beginning 1991); Granville Island Brewing Co. (beginning 1993); Les Brasseurs du Nord Inc. and Unibroue Inc. (beginning 1994); Creemore Springs Brewery, Great Lakes Brewing Co., Brasserie McAuslan, and Shaftebury Brewing Co. (beginning 1995).

Beer and Brewery Statistics

Total United States and Canadian Craft-Brewing Industry Percentage Annual Growth

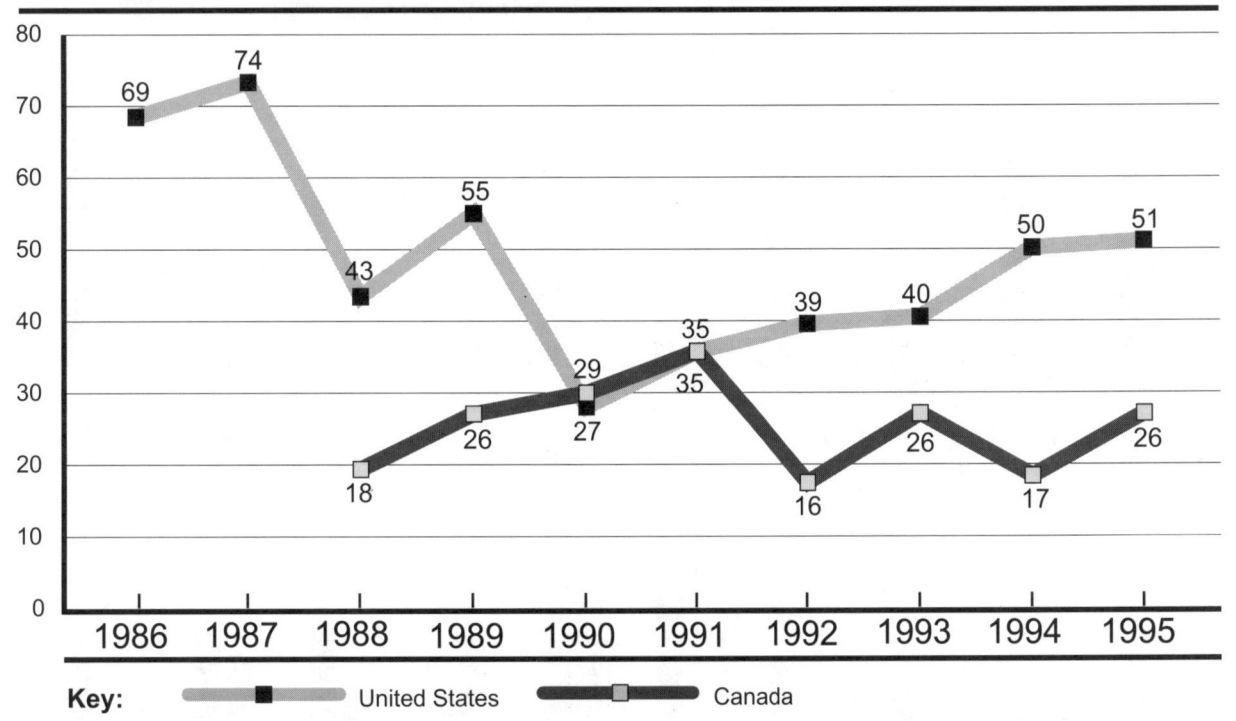

Year	United States	Canada
1986	69	—
1987	74	—
1988	43	18
1989	55	26
1990	29	27
1991	35	35
1992	39	16
1993	40	26
1994	50	17
1995	51	26

Total United States Craft-Brewing Industry Annual Dollar Volume ($ Millions)

Compiled by the Institute for Brewing Studies with assistance from Pete Slosberg, Pete's Brewing Co.

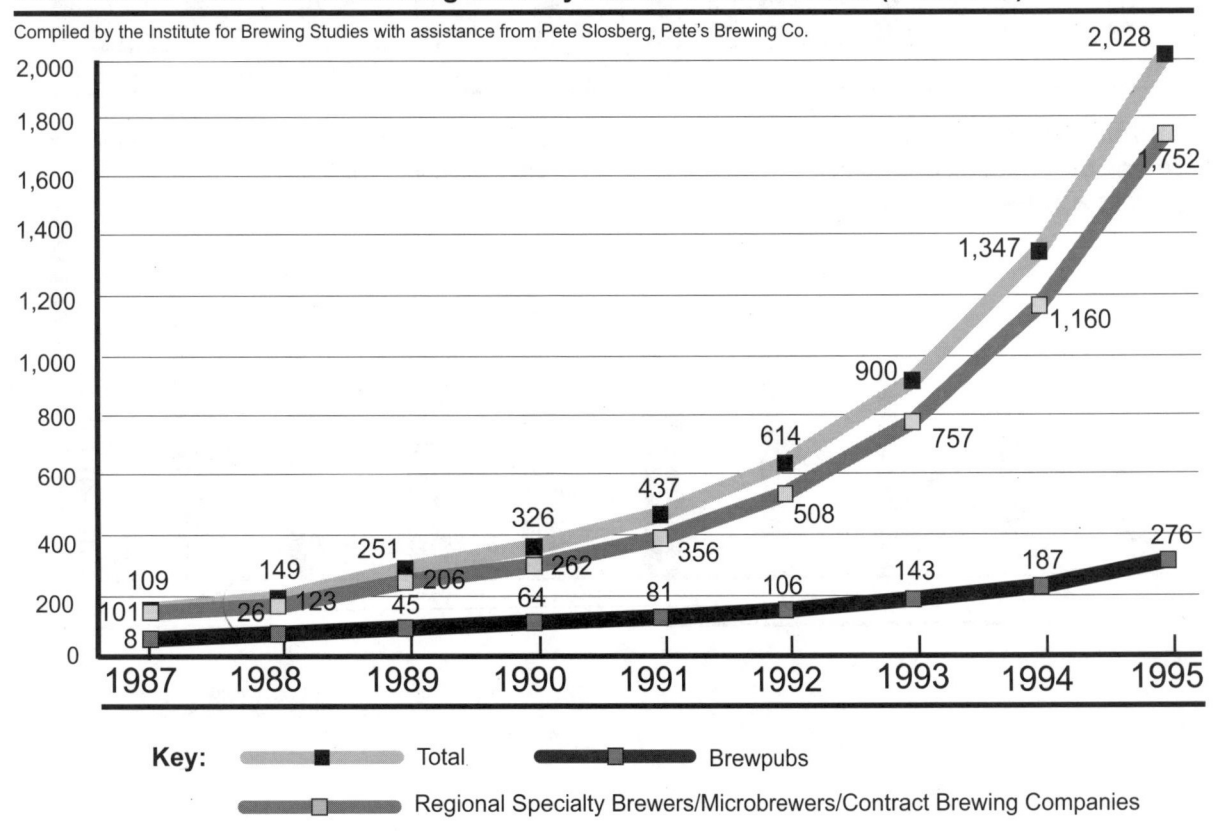

Year	Total	Regional Specialty Brewers/Microbrewers/Contract Brewing Companies	Brewpubs
1987	109	101	8
1988	149	123	26
1989	251	206	45
1990	326	262	64
1991	437	356	81
1992	614	508	106
1993	900	757	143
1994	1,347	1,160	187
1995	2,028	1,752	276

Top Fifty United States Craft-Brewing Companies in 1995

(Companies including regional specialty breweries, microbreweries, contract brewing companies, and brewpub chains whose flagship brand is an all-malt beer.)
Shipment amounts rounded to nearest 100 barrels.
* Denotes all or partially contract brewed by another company.
† Denotes more than one facility.
‡ Denotes percent of total craft brewing segment.
§ Includes total of Oregon Ale and Beer subsidiary (35,000 barrels).

Company	1995 Shipments	% Growth Over 1994	Market Share ‡	Share Change
1. Boston Beer Co.* §	948,000	34	25.1	-3.1
2. Pete's Brewing Co.*	347,800	91	9.2	+2.0
3. Sierra Nevada Brewing Co.	200,000	28	5.3	-0.9
4. Redhook Brewing Co.†	155,000	66	4.1	+0.4
5. Hart Brewing Co.†	123,100	70	3.3	+0.4
6. Anchor Brewing Co.	103,000	1	2.7	-1.4
7. Full Sail Brewing Co.†	71,500	36	1.9	-0.2
8. Widmer Brewing Co.†	69,200	40	1.8	-0.2
9. Portland Brewing Co.†	62,000	68	1.6	-0.1
10. Spanish Peaks Brewing Co.*	53,200	83	1.4	-0.2
11. Mass. Bay Brewing Co.*	39,000	63	1.0	0
12. Nor'Wester Brewery	32,900	96	0.9	+0.2
13. Rockies Brewing Co.	32,400	24	0.9	-0.1
14. New Belgium Brewing Co.	31,800	68	0.8	0
15. Deschutes Brewery†	31,600	60	0.8	0
16. Abita Brewing Co.	30,500	38	0.8	-0.1
17. William and Scott/Rhino Chasers*	29,000	32	0.8	N/A
18. Shipyard Brewing Co.	30,500	N/A	0.8	N/A
19. Rogue Ales/Oregon Brewing Co.	26,000	74	0.7	+0.1
20. Dubuque Brewing/Brandevor USA	25,200	53	0.7	+0.1
21. Dock Street Brewing Co.*	25,000	25	0.7	-0.1
22. Alaskan Brewing and Bottling Co.	21,800	56	0.6	0
23. Jack Daniels Brewery*	21,400	N/A	0.6	N/A
24. Boulevard Brewing Co.	21,000	42	0.6	0
25. Rock Bottom Restaurants †	19,900	133	0.5	N/A
26. Summit Brewing Co.	19,900	42	0.5	-0.1
27. Celis Brewery (subsidiary of Miller Brewing Co.)	19,600	23	0.5	-0.1
28. Catamount Brewing Co.	19,200	16	0.5	-0.2
29. BridgePort Brewing Co. (subsidiary of Gambrinus Importing Co.)	19,200	6	0.5	-0.2
30. Humboldt Brewing Co.	19,000	29	0.5	-0.1
31. Old Dominion Brewing Co.	18,600	31	0.4	-0.2
32. Pennsylvania Brewing Co.*	18,500	92	0.4	N/A
33. Gordon Biersch Breweries†	16,800	82	0.4	N/A
34. McMenamin's Breweries†	15,600	25	0.4	-0.1
35. Mendocino Brewing Co.	15,100	11	0.4	-0.1
36. Karl Strauss' Old Columbia Breweries†	15,000	N/A	0.4	N/A
37. Breckenridge Breweries†	14,900	37	0.4	N/A
38. Long Trail Brewing Co.	14,900	18	0.4	-0.2
39. Brooklyn Brewery*	14,500	20	0.3	N/A
40. Wild Goose Brewery	14,300	43	0.3	-0.1
41. Black Mountain Brewing Co.*	14,000	-22	0.3	-0.4
42. St. Stan's Brewery	13,800	10	0.3	-0.2
43. Stoudt's Brewery*	13,600	60	0.3	N/A
44. D. L. Geary Brewing Co.	13,100	27	0.3	-0.1
45. Capital Brewing Co.	12,800	8	0.3	-0.2
46. Frankenmuth Brewery	12,500	4	0.3	-0.2
47. Sprecher Brewing Co.*	12,000	33	0.3	N/A
48. Grant's Yakima Brewing & Malting Co. (subsidiary of UST Inc.)	11,500	0	0.3	-0.2
49. Schirf Brewing Co./Wasatch Brewery†	11,500	36	0.3	N/A
50. Odell Brewing Co.	10,400	24	0.2	N/A

United States Regional Breweries: Estimated Total Taxable Shipments

All figures are in U.S. barrels.

Totals, in many cases, are estimates reported to the Institute for Brewing Studies and may not reflect exact taxpaid amount.

£ Produces more than 25 percent for other companies.

O/C Denotes year opened or closed, if occurring between 1991 and 1995.

Company Name	O/C	1991	1992	1993	1994	1995	1992 % Growth	1993 % Growth	1994 % Growth	1995 % Growth
Evansville Brewing Co. (IN)		360,000	330,000	300,000	520,000	510,000	-8	-9	73	-2
D. G. Yuengling & Son Inc. (PA)		160,000	210,810	N/A	275,110	319,936	32	N/A	N/A	16
Jacob Leinenkugel Brewing Co. (subsidiary of Miller Brewing Co.) (WI)		156,900	166,800	193,000	235,300	280,000	6	16	22	19
Sierra Nevada Brewing Co. (CA)		45,000	68,039	104,325	155,942	200,000	51	53	49	28
Redhook Ale Brewery (WA)		33,000	49,000	73,000	93,577	155,000	48	49	28	66
Hart Brewing Co. (includes Thomas Kemper Brewing Co.) (WA)		11,350	17,681	39,200	72,416	123,100	56	122	85	70
Anchor Brewing Co. (CA)		70,200	82,653	92,000	102,462	103,000	18	11	11	1
Full Sail Brewing Co. (both facilities) (OR)		22,500	28,500	38,159	52,598	71,526	27	34	38	36
Widmer Brothers Brewing Co. (both facilities) (OR)		18,000	27,500	40,520	50,000	69,200	53	47	23	40
Jones Brewing Co. (PA)		55,852	N/A	100,000	75,000	65,000	N/A	N/A	-25	-13
Portland Brewing Co. (both facilities) (OR)		7,000	9,000	16,606	36,994	62,000	29	85	123	68
Joseph Huber Brewing Co. Inc. (WI)		100,000	134,500	80,000	79,700	60,000	35	-41	0	-25
Stevens Point Brewery Co. (subsidiary of Barton Beers) (WI)		32,000	27,200	N/A	31,000	41,000	-15	N/A	N/A	32
Nor'Wester Brewery (OR)	O-93			1,950	16,777	32,911			760	96
Rockies Brewing Co. (CO)		6,100	11,839	17,900	26,180	32,416	94	51	46	24
New Belgium Brewing Co. (CO)		220	993	5,837	18,951	31,770	351	488	225	68
Deschutes Brewing Co. (both facilities) (OR)		3,800	6,298	8,564	19,719	31,600	66	36	130	60
Abita Brewing Co. (both facilities) (LA)		6,500	10,900	15,000	22,080	30,500	68	38	47	38
Shipyard Brewery (ME)	O-94				9,800	30,456				211
Straub Brewery (PA)		26,000	26,300	N/A	27,000	29,500	1	N/A	N/A	9
Rogue Ales Brewery/Oregon Brewing Co. (OR)		3,500	5,500	8,620	14,900	26,000	57	57	73	74
Dubuque Brewing & Bottling Co./Brandevor USA (IA) £		6,000	N/A	10,500	16,500	25,185	N/A	N/A	57	53
Cold Spring Brewing Co. Inc. (MN) £		25,000	7,100	N/A	N/A	25,000	-72	N/A	N/A	N/A
Alaskan Brewing and Bottling Co. (AK)		6,000	7,000	10,000	14,000	21,775	17	43	40	56
Boulevard Brewing Co. (MO)		4,800	7,837	10,750	14,748	21,000	63	37	37	42
Summit Brewing Co. (MN)		5,800	7,400	10,500	14,000	19,866	28	42	33	42
Celis Brewery Inc. (TX)	O-92		6,000	10,000	16,000	19,600		67	60	23
Catamount Brewing Co. (VT)		9,000	11,800	13,000	16,500	19,200	31	10	27	16
BridgePort Brewing Co. (subsidiary of Gambrinus Importing Co.) (OR)		11,128	13,354	16,020	18,000	19,162	20	20	12	6
Humboldt Brewery (CA)		1,400	1,500	8,300	14,732	18,964	7	453	77	29
Old Dominion Brewing Co. (VA)		3,389	6,092	10,225	14,118	18,546	80	68	38	31
Mass. Bay Brewing Co. (MA)		N/A	5,000	6,450	7,920	18,000	N/A	29	23	127
Mendocino Brewing Co. (CA)		11,000	12,703	13,153	13,600	15,100	15	4	3	11
Florida Brewery Inc. (FL)		N/A	6,892	150,000	N/A	6,202	N/A	2,076	N/A	N/A
August Schell Brewing Co. (MN)		30,000	25,000	25,000	N/A	N/A	-17	0	N/A	N/A
Dixie Brewing Co., Inc. (LA)		N/A	N/A	N/A	N/A	N/A	N/A	N/A	N/A	N/A
Hudepohl-Schoenling Inc. (OH)		515,000	N/A	N/A	N/A	N/A	N/A	N/A	N/A	N/A
Lion Inc./Gibbons-Stegmaier (PA)		N/A	58,327	50,000	N/A	N/A	N/A	-14	N/A	N/A
Minnesota Brewing Co. (MN)	O-91	N/A	175,000	300,000	400,000	N/A	N/A	71	33	N/A
Spoetzl Brewery Inc. (subsidiary of Gambrinus Importing Co.) (TX)		45,900	51,806	72,976	N/A	N/A	13	41	N/A	N/A

United States Microbreweries: Estimated Total Taxable Shipments

All figures are in U.S. barrels.
Totals, in many cases, are estimates reported to the Institute for Brewing Studies and may not reflect exact taxpaid amount.
O/C Denotes year opened or closed if occurring between 1991 and 1995.
† Produces between 5 and 15 percent for other companies.
‡ Produces between 15 and 25 percent for other companies.
§ Produces between 25 and 50 percent for other companies.

Company Name	O/C	1991	1992	1993	1994	1995	1992 % Growth	1993 % Growth	1994 % Growth	1995 % Growth
Karl Strauss' Old Columbia Breweries (three facilities) (CA)		1,000	N/A	N/A	7,000	15,000	N/A	N/A	N/A	114
Long Trail Brewing Co. (formerly Mountain Brewers Inc.) (VT)		5,000	7,000	11,200	14,200	14,500	40	60	27	2
Wild Goose Brewery (MD)		3,300	4,000	6,500	10,000	14,300	21	63	54	43
St. Stans Brewery, Pub & Restaurant (CA)		5,000	6,000	7,000	12,600	13,800	20	17	80	10
D. L. Geary Brewing Co. Inc. (ME)		5,690	6,205	7,200	10,330	13,125	9	16	43	27
Capital Brewery Inc. (WI) §		4,500	5,000	10,071	11,869	12,824	11	101	18	8
Frankenmuth Brewery Inc. (MI)		8,400	10,000	11,950	12,000	12,520	19	20	0	4
Breckenridge Brewery, Denver (CO)	O-93			4,020	8,472	12,200			111	44
Yakima Brewing and Malting Co. Inc. (subsidiary of UST Inc.) (WA)		6,500	7,500	8,000	11,500	11,500	15	7	50	0
Schirf Brewing Co./ Wasatch Brewery (both facilities) (UT)		4,150	6,196	7,365	8,404	11,460	49	19	14	36
Pennsylvania Brewing Co./ Allegheny Brewery and Pub (PA)		2,500	3,000	3,000	4,850	10,500	20	0	62	116
Odell Brewing Co. (CO)		1,822	3,099	5,627	8,391	10,367	70	82	49	24
Kalamazoo Brewing Co. Inc. (MI)		1,100	1,500	3,085	6,022	10,250	36	106	95	70
Frederick Brewing Co. (MD)	O-93			327	5,832	10,143			1,683	74
Otter Creek Brewing Inc. (VT)	O-91	390	600	2,750	5,972	10,000	54	358	117	67
Broadway Brewing Co. (CO) †	O-94				3,000	9,720				224
Hale's Ales Ltd. (both facilities) (WA)		6,150	7,387	8,305	9,600	9,466	20	12	16	-1
Mad River Brewing Co. (CA)		1,200	2,250	3,500	6,200	8,800	88	56	77	42
Great Lakes Brewing Co. (OH)		1,200	1,625	2,754	3,831	8,000	35	69	39	109
Oldenberg Brewery/ Drawbridge Inn (KY)		7,300	9,100	9,750	7,837	7,530	25	7	-20	-4
Sprecher Brewing Co. (WI)		6,400	8,000	5,038	5,000	7,000	25	-37	-1	40
Ybor City Brewing Co. (FL)	O-94				N/A	7,000			N/A	N/A
Gordon Biersch Brewery (No. 6) (CA)	O-94				N/A	6,236			N/A	N/A
Pavichevich Brewing Co. (IL) †		6,200	6,200	6,800	6,100	6,000	0	10	-10	-2
Smuttynose Brewing Co. (NH)	O-94				850	6,000				606
Atlanta Brewing Co. (GA)	O-94				N/A	6,000			N/A	N/A
North Coast Brewing Co. (CA)		805	1,000	1,260	1,370	5,925	24	26	9	332
Stoudt's Brewery (PA)		2,100	3,200	3,500	5,200	5,800	52	9	49	12
Bohannon Brewing Co. (TN)		N/A	N/A	N/A	N/A	5,500	N/A	N/A	N/A	N/A
Sudwerk Privatbrauerei Hübsch (CA)		2,200	2,900	4,261	4,726	5,388	32	47	11	14
Edgefield Brewery (OR)		2,424	4,822	5,300	5,167	5,257	99	10	-3	2
Oasis Brewery Annex (CO)	O-95					5,200				
Anderson Valley Brewing Co. (CA)		1,840	2,350	3,300	4,555	5,050	28	40	38	11
Birmingham Brewing Co. (AL) ‡	O-92		2,000	4,000	6,101	5,000		100	53	-18
Riverside Brewing Co. (CA)	O-93			272	1,452	4,913			434	238
Arrowhead Brewing Co. (PA) †	O-91	300	1,600	2,375	3,400	4,800	433	48	43	41
Gray Brewing Co. (WI)	O-94				1,800	4,800				167
Ipswich Brewing Co. (MA)	O-92		N/A	887	2,500	4,800	N/A	N/A	182	92
Pony Express Brewing Co. (KS)	O-95					4,800				
Elm City Brewing Co. (CT)		3,805	4,200	N/A	N/A	4,646	10	N/A	N/A	N/A
Uinta Brewing Co. (UT)	O-94				2,130	4,542				113
New Glarus Brewing Co. (WI)	O-93			300	2,400	4,500			700	88

Beer and Brewery Statistics

Company Name	O/C	1991	1992	1993	1994	1995	1992 % Growth	1993 % Growth	1994 % Growth	1995 % Growth
Maritime Pacific Brewing Co. (WA)		700	1,800	2,950	3,789	4,490	157	64	28	19
Oxford Brewing Co. (MD)		3,000	3,100	N/A	N/A	4,480	3	N/A	N/A	N/A
Left Hand Brewing Co. (CO)	O-94				1,419	4,020				183
Casco Bay Brewing Co. (ME)	O-94				1,478	4,000				171
Goose Island Beer Co. (IL)	O-95					4,000				
Tabernash Brewing Co. (CO)	O-93			75	2,000	4,000			2,567	100
New England Brewing Co. (CT)		2,000	2,500	3,200	4,200	3,905	25	28	31	-7
Old Harbor Brewing Co. (MA)	O-93			N/A	N/A	3,800		N/A	N/A	N/A
Bayern Brewing Inc./ Iron Horse Brewpub (MT)		N/A	1,825	1,900	2,200	3,600	N/A	4	16	64
Marthasville Brewing Co. (GA)	O-94				N/A	3,500			N/A	N/A
Crooked River Brewing Co. (OH)	O-94				682	3,100				355
Carmel Brewing Co. (CA)	O-95					3,000				
Potomac River Brewing Co. (VA)	O-93			N/A	770	3,000		N/A	N/A	290
Tommyknocker Brewery Pub (CO)	O-95					2,928				
Great Northern Brewing (MT)	O-95					2,825				
Steamship Brewing Co. (VA)	O-95					2,800				
Magic Hat Brewing Co. (VT)	O-94				75	2,700				3,500
Covany Brewing Co. (CA)	O-94				580	2,623				352
Jack Daniel's Brewery (TN)	O-94				N/A	2,603			N/A	N/A
Eddie McStiff's Brewing Co. (UT)	O-91	356	659	1,010	1,810	2,600	85	53	79	44
Jackson Hole Pub & Brewery (WY)	O-94				N/A	2,600			N/A	N/A
Johnson Beer Co. (NC)	O-95					2,500				
Weeping Radish Restaurant & Brewery (both facilites) (NC) ‡		700	884	1,750	1,696	2,500	26	98	-3	47
Saint Arnold Brewing Co. (TX)	O-94				610	2,450				302
Tied House Cafe and Brewery (No. 3) (CA)	O-91	120	750	1,135	2,021	2,343	525	51	78	16
Cherryland Brewing Co. (WI)		750	300	350	500	2,300	-60	17	43	360
Great Divide Brewing Co. (CO)	O-94				282	2,300				716
Irons Brewing Co. (CO)	O-92		40	249	546	2,235		523	119	309
Millstream Brewing Co. (IA)		1,840	1,875	1,500	2,000	2,200	2	-20	33	10
Table Rock Brewing Co. (No. 2) (ID)	O-95					2,200				
Dallas County Brewing Co. Inc./Old Depot Pub (IA)	O-92		435	1,541	N/A	2,185		254	N/A	N/A
Bristol Brewing Co. (CO) †	O-94				700	2,165				209
Columbus Brewing Co. (OH)		700	650	850	1,400	2,050	-7	31	65	46
Lakefront Brewery (WI)		350	850	1,424	1,500	2,047	143	68	5	36
Pike Brewing Co. (WA)		1,600	2,000	1,900	2,000	2,045	25	-5	5	2
SandLot Brewery at Coors Field (CO)	O-95					2,010				
Atlantic Coast Brewing Co. (MA)	O-94				620	2,000				223
Avery Brewing Co. (CO)	O-94				793	2,000				152
Black Mountain Brewing Co. (AZ)		N/A	3,500	2,000	3,000	2,000	N/A	-43	50	-33
Fish Brewing Co. (WA)	O-93			200	1,200	2,000			500	67
Kessler Brewing Co. (MT)		1,300	1,389	2,500	3,200	2,000	7	80	28	-38
Bird Creek Brewery (AK)	O-91	29	378	393	1,000	1,990	1,203	4	154	99
Sugarloaf Brewing Co. (ME)	O-94				N/A	1,968			N/A	N/A
Sun Valley Brewing Co. (ID)	O-93			N/A	1,059	1,900		N/A	N/A	79
Lowell Brewing Co. (MA)	O-94				N/A	1,800			N/A	N/A
Miami Brewing Co. (FL)	O-95					1,800				
Star Brewing Co. (OR)	O-93			1,000	1,182	1,797			18	52
Beach Brewing Co. (FL)	O-92		328	750	1,350	1,750		129	80	30
Wachusett Brewing Co. (MA)	O-94				N/A	1,690			N/A	N/A
Durango Brewing Co. (CO)		320	700	950	1,350	1,600	119	36	42	19
Hill Country Brewing Co. (TX)	O-93			N/A	300	1,582		N/A	N/A	427
Michigan Brewery Inc./ Big Buck Brewery (MI)	O-95					1,514				
Brimstone Brewing Co. (MD)	O-94				N/A	1,500			N/A	N/A
Kennebunkport Brewing Co. (ME)	O-92		473	2,300	2,950	1,445		386	28	-51
Cardinal Brewing Co. (WV)	O-94				N/A	1,400			N/A	N/A

Beer and Brewery Statistics

Company Name	O/C	1991	1992	1993	1994	1995	1992 % Growth	1993 % Growth	1994 % Growth	1995 % Growth
Dilworth Brewing Co. (NC)	O-94				551	1,400				154
El Toro Brewing Co. (CA)	O-94				450	1,391				209
American River Brewing Co. (CA)	O-93			36	780	1,383			2,067	77
Lonetree Brewing Ltd. (CO)	O-93			247	530	1,340			115	153
Napa Valley Ale Works (CA)	O-94				382	1,324				247
Bayhawk Ales Inc. (CA)	O-95					1,300				
Estes Park Brewery (CO)	O-93			200	N/A	1,300			N/A	N/A
Wilmington Brewing Co. (NC)	O-94				N/A	1,300			N/A	N/A
Berkshire Brewing Co. (MA)	O-94				90	1,233				1,270
Atlantic Brewing Co. (ME)	O-91	N/A	200	N/A		1,200	N/A	N/A	N/A	N/A
Murphy's Creek Brewing Co. (CA)	O-93			N/A	885	1,200		N/A	N/A	36
Oak Creek Brewing Co. (AZ)	O-95					1,200				
Kona Brewing Co. (HI)	O-95					1,165				
Silver Plume Brewing Co. (CO)	O-94				700	1,094				56
Mac & Jack Brewery (WA)	O-94				N/A	1,093			N/A	N/A
Middle Ages Brewing Co. (NY)	O-95					1,090				
Rockford Brewing Co. (DE)	O-95					1,071				
Montana Brewing Co. (MT)	O-94				N/A	1,010			N/A	N/A
Highland Brewing Co. (NC)	O-94				N/A	1,000			N/A	N/A
Old Raleigh Brewing Co. (NC)	O-95					1,000				
Rock 'n' M Brewing Co. (MT)	O-94				N/A	1,000			N/A	N/A
Skagit River Brewing Co. (WA)	O-94				N/A	1,000			N/A	N/A
Snowy Mountain Brewing Co. (CO)	O-94				203	850				319
Bosque Brewing Co. (TX)	O-95					775				
Lagunitas Brewing Co. (CA)	O-94				N/A	760			N/A	N/A
Otto Brothers' Brewing Co. Inc. (WY)		290	415	625	766	739	43	51	23	-4
Lang Creek Brewery (MT)	O-94				545	709				30
Whitetail Brewing Inc. (PA)	O-94				105	700				567
Frio Brewing Co. (TX)	O-94				N/A	675			N/A	N/A
Neptune Brewer (NY)	O-95					650				
Hoboken Brewing Co. (NJ)	O-95					630				
Aviator Ales Brewery (WA)	O-95					623				
Yellow Rose Brewing Co. (TX)	O-94				N/A	600			N/A	N/A
Golden City Brewery (CO)	O-93			21	314	590			1,395	88
Big Sky Brewing Co. (MT)	O-95					575				
M. J. Barleyhoppers Brewery & Public House (ID)	O-91	N/A	420	N/A	163	567	N/A	N/A	N/A	248
Golden Prairie Brewing Co. (IL)	O-92		18	113	420	556		528	272	32
Lift Bridge Brewing Co. (OH)	O-94				69	556				706
Moonlight Brewing Co. (CA)	O-92		56	271	403	554		384	49	37
Oregon Trail Brewery (OR)	O-93			149	500	519			236	4
Ould Newbury Brewing Co. (MA)	O-93			225	300	465			33	55
Great Baraboo Brewing Co. (MI)	O-95					464				
Seattle Brewers (WA)	O-92		N/A	N/A	N/A	450	N/A	N/A	N/A	N/A
Midnight Sun Brewing Co. (AK)	O-95					445				
Yards Brewing Co. (PA)	O-95					437				
Roslyn Brewing Co. (WA)		360	320	354	411	415	-11	11	16	1
Whidbey Island Brewing Co. (WA)	O-95					410				
West Seattle Brewing Co./California & Alaskan St. Brewery (WA)	O-91	70	223	N/A	350	400	219	N/A	N/A	14
Kelley Creek Brewing Co. (WA)	O-94				N/A	370			N/A	N/A
Trade Winds Brewing Co. (HI)	O-95					360				
Thunder Mountain Brewery (ID)	O-93			N/A	121	350		N/A	N/A	189
Weyerbacher Brewing Co. Inc. (PA)	O-95					350				
El Dorado Brewing Co. (CA)	O-94				77	325			N/A	N/A
Pikes Peak Brewery (CO)	O-94				N/A	325			N/A	N/A
Boyne River Brewing Co. (MI)	O-95					300				
James River Brewing Co. (VA)	O-95					300				
Lake Titus Brewery (NY)	O-94				N/A	300			N/A	N/A
Northern Lights Brewing Co. (WA)	O-93			N/A	300	300		N/A	N/A	0

Beer and Brewery Statistics

Company Name	O/C	1991	1992	1993	1994	1995	1992 % Growth	1993 % Growth	1994 % Growth	1995 % Growth
Carolina Brewing Co. (NC)	O-95					270				
Andrew's Brewing Co. (ME)	O-93			97	182	267			88	47
Middlesex Brewing Co. (MA)	O-93			123	250	260			103	4
Humes Brewing Co. (CA)	O-93			N/A	200	255		N/A	N/A	28
Lake Superior Brewing Co. (MN)	O-94				N/A	250			N/A	N/A
Etna Brewing Co. (CA)		275	285	250	325	226	4	-12	30	-30
Bar Harbor Brewing (ME)		61	130	110	190	225	113	-15	73	18
Tapps Brewing Inc. (WA)	O-95					210				
Twisted Pine Brewing Co. (CO)	O-95					210				
King Brewing Co. (MI)	O-95					203				
Hair of the Dog Brewing Co (OR)	O-94				32	200				525
Russell Brewing Co. (NM)	O-92		21	40	170	184		90	325	8
Brew Makers (CA)	O-95					180				
Young's Brewing Co. (WA)	O-95					157				
Allagash Brewing Co. Inc. (ME)	O-95					150				
Lake Saint George Brewing Co. (ME)	O-93			22	120	150			445	25
La Belle Brewing Co. (WI)	O-94				N/A	131			N/A	N/A
Eldorado Canyon Brewing Co. (CO)	O-95					130				
Onalaska Brewing Co. (WA)	O-91	N/A	204	292	226	125	N/A	43	-23	-45
Beier Brewing Co. (ID)	O-92		16	N/A	N/A	125		N/A	N/A	N/A
Coophouse Brewery (CO)	O-95					120				
Mark's Brewing Co. (CO)	O-95					100				
Pacific Hop Exchange (CA)	O-94				68	100				47
SKA Brewing Co. (CO)	O-95					100				
Platte Bottom Brewery (CO)	O-95					65				
Remington Watson Smith Brewing Co. Inc. (WI)	O-95					55				
AleSmith Brewing Co. (CA)	O-95					52				
Eagle Brewing Co. (WA)	O-95					50				
Palmer Lake Brewing Co. (CO)	O-95					50				
Blind Man Ales (GA)	O-95					45				
Powers Brewing Co. (CO)	O-95					44				
Only the Best Brewing Co. Inc. (CO)	O-95					41				
Ellensburg Brewing Co. (WA)	O-95					40				
K. C. Brewing Co. (CA) †	O-95					35				
Brouwer Brewery (CO)	O-95					20				
Clamtown Brewery Inc. (MA)	O-95					10				
Ali'i Brewing Co. (HI)	O-94				N/A	N/A			N/A	N/A
Back Alley Brewing Co. (CO)	O-95					N/A				N/A
Bandon Brewing Co. (OR)	O-94				N/A	N/A			N/A	N/A
Barrelhouse Brewing Co. (OH)	O-95					N/A				N/A
Basin Brewing Ltd. (TX)	O-95					N/A				N/A
Black Hills Brewing Co. (SD)	O-95					N/A				N/A
Boston Beer Co. (MA)		N/A	N/A	N/A	N/A	N/A	N/A	N/A	N/A	N/A
Buchanon Brewing Corp. (WA)	O-95					N/A				N/A
Buffalo Brewing Co. (NY)		5,100	6,905	6,020	4,600	N/A	35	-13	-24	N/A
Captain City Brewing Co. (WA)	O-95					N/A				N/A
Chicago Brewing Co. (IL)		N/A	N/A	N/A	N/A	N/A	N/A	N/A	N/A	N/A
Cisco Brewers (MA)	O-95					N/A				N/A
Clipper City Brewing Co. (MD)	O-95					N/A				N/A
Coast Range Brewing Co. (CA)	O-95					N/A				N/A
Colorado Brewing Co. (CO)	O-95					N/A				N/A
Diamond Knot Brewing Co. (WA)	O-94				N/A	N/A			N/A	N/A
DryTown Brewing Co. (NY)	O-95					N/A				N/A
Duster's Microbrewery Co. (MI)	O-94				N/A	N/A			N/A	N/A
Ebenezer's (UT)	O-92		N/A	450	N/A	N/A	N/A	N/A	N/A	N/A
Elephant Butte Brewery & Pizzeria (NM)	O-95					N/A				N/A
Emerald Isle Brew Works (RI)	O-94				N/A	N/A			N/A	N/A
Essex Brewing Co. Ltd. (MA)	O-94				N/A	N/A			N/A	N/A

Beer and Brewery Statistics

Company Name	O/C	1991	1992	1993	1994	1995	1992 % Growth	1993 % Growth	1994 % Growth	1995 % Growth
Golden Pacific Brewing Co. (CA)		950	2,500	2,483	3,876	N/A	163	-1	56	N/A
Green Bay Brewing Co. (WI)	O-95					N/A				N/A
H. C. Berger Brewing Co. (CO)	O-92		612	2,060	N/A	N/A		237	N/A	N/A
Hangtown Brewery (CA)	O-92		N/A	N/A	N/A	N/A	N/A	N/A	N/A	N/A
Hawaiian Style Brewing Co. (HI)	O-95					N/A				N/A
Heritage Brewing Co. (CA)	O-94				N/A	N/A			N/A	N/A
Himmelberger Brewing Co. (MT)	O-94				N/A	N/A			N/A	N/A
Independence Brewing Co. (PA) †	O-94				N/A	N/A			N/A	N/A
Indianapolis Brewing Co. (IN)		1,600	2,100	3,000	4,200	N/A	31	43	40	N/A
James Page Brewing Co. (MN)		1,200	1,300	1,500	1,400	N/A	8	15	-7	N/A
Key West Overseas Brewery (FL)	O-95					N/A				N/A
Lancaster Malt Brewing Co. (PA)	O-95					N/A				N/A
Legend Brewery (VA)	O-94				1,200	N/A				N/A
Lexington Brewing Co. (KY)	O-95					N/A				N/A
Lind Brewing Co. (CA)		700	800	703	1,000	N/A	14	-12	42	N/A
Lone Wolfe Brewing Co. (CO)	O-93			N/A	N/A	N/A		N/A	N/A	N/A
Louisiana Brewing Co./ Brasserie de la Louisiane (LA)	O-95					N/A				N/A
Michigan Brewing Co. (MI)	O-95					N/A				N/A
Mile High Brewing Co. (CO)	O-95					N/A				N/A
Milestown Brewing Co./Golden Spur (MT)	O-92		N/A	N/A	N/A	N/A	N/A	N/A	N/A	N/A
Miracle Brewing Co. (KS)	O-92		145	290	450	N/A		100	55	N/A
Motor City Brewing Works (MI)	O-95					N/A				N/A
Mt. Hood Brewing Co. (OR)	O-92		380	N/A	1,075	N/A		N/A	N/A	N/A
Multnomah Brewery (OR)	O-93			N/A	235	N/A		N/A	N/A	N/A
Namaqua Brewing Co. (CO)	O-94				N/A	N/A			N/A	N/A
Nevada City Brewing Co. (CA)		800	470	520	694	N/A	-41	11	33	N/A
Nutfield Brewing Co. (NH)	O-95					N/A				N/A
Old River Brewing Co. (CA)	O-94				N/A	N/A			N/A	N/A
One Keg Brewhouse (CO)	O-95					N/A				N/A
Orchard Street Brewing Co. (WA)	O-95					N/A				N/A
Oregon Trader Brewing Co. (OR) ‡	O-94				N/A	N/A			N/A	N/A
Organ Mountain Brewing Co./ O'Ryans Tavern & Brewery (NM)	O-94				N/A	N/A			N/A	N/A
Palmetto Brewing (SC)	O-94				N/A	N/A			N/A	N/A
Peak to Peak Brewing (CO)	O-95					N/A				N/A
Raven Ridge Brewing Co. (AK)	O-94				N/A	N/A			N/A	N/A
Red Bank Brewery Co. (NJ)	O-95					N/A				N/A
Reedy River Brewing Co. (SC)	O-95					N/A				N/A
Republic Brewery (UST)	O-93			N/A	N/A	N/A		N/A	N/A	N/A
Rikenjaks Brewery (LA)	O-93			29	N/A	N/A			N/A	N/A
Ringneck Brewing Co./Brew Kettle (OH)	O-95					N/A				N/A
Rio Grande Brewing Co. (NM)	O-94				287	N/A				N/A
Ruby Mountain Brewing Co. (NV)	O-95					N/A				N/A
St. Andrew's Brewing Co. (TX)	O-95					N/A				N/A
Santa Fe Brewing Co. (NM)		N/A	550	N/A	N/A	N/A	N/A	N/A	N/A	N/A
Saxer Brewing Co. (OR)	O-93			5,000	9,524	N/A			90	N/A
Sea Dog Brewing Co. (No. 2) (ME)	O-95					N/A				N/A
Sheepscot Valley Brewing Co. (ME)	O-95					N/A				N/A
Smokey Mountain Brewery (NC)	O-93			N/A	1,000	N/A		N/A	N/A	N/A
Snake River Brewing/ Jackson Hole Pub and Brewery (WY)	O-94				1,116	N/A				N/A
Southern California Brewing Co. (CA)		3,500	3,000	N/A	N/A	N/A	-14	N/A	N/A	N/A
Star Union Brewing Co. (IL) ‡	O-94				N/A	N/A			N/A	N/A
Texas Brewing Co. (TX)		N/A	N/A	N/A	N/A	N/A	N/A	N/A	N/A	N/A
Thomas Kemper Brewing Co. (subsidiary of Hart Brewing Co.) (WA)		3,600	4,226	N/A	N/A	N/A	17	N/A	N/A	
Tradewinds Brewing Co. (HI)	O-95					N/A				N/A

Institute for Brewing Studies

Beer and Brewery Statistics

Company Name	O/C	1991	1992	1993	1994	1995	1992 % Growth	1993 % Growth	1994 % Growth	1995 % Growth
Tuscan Brewing Co. (CA)	O-93			N/A	N/A	N/A		N/A	N/A	N/A
Ugly Dog Brewery Inc. (PA)	O-95					N/A				N/A
Whitefish Brewing Co. (MT)	O-91	N/A	N/A	N/A	N/A	N/A	N/A	N/A	N/A	N/A
Williamsville Brewery (VA)	O-95					N/A				N/A
Wooden Pony Brewing Co. (OH)	O-95					N/A				N/A
Woodstock Brewing Co. (NY)	O-92		1,000	1,200	1,500	N/A		20	25	N/A
Olde Salem Village Brewery (MA)	O-94/C-95				N/A	480			N/A	N/A
Bay Brewing Co. Inc./ Devil Mountain Brewery (CA)	C-95	1,719	2,550	2,800	3,600	N/A	48	10	29	N/A
Bridger Brewing Co. (MT)	O-93/C-95			N/A	495	N/A		N/A	N/A	N/A
Winnepesaukee Brewing & Soda Works (NH)	O-95/C-95					N/A				N/A
Angeles Brewing Co. (CA)	C-94	1,100	2,200	N/A	N/A		100	N/A	N/A	N/A
Detroit & Mackinac Brewing Co. (MI)	O-92/C-94		450	1,423	1,934			216	36	N/A
Electric Dave Brewery (AZ)	C-93	330	350	N/A			6	N/A	N/A	
Frank Jones Brewing Co. Ltd. (NH)	O-92/C-93		N/A	N/A			N/A	N/A	N/A	
Monterey Brewing Co. (CA)	C-93	1,092	382	550			-65	44	-100	
Virginia Brewing Co. (VA)	C-93	3,900	2,000	N/A			-49	N/A	N/A	
Woodland Brewing Co. (CA)	C-93	600	N/A	N/A			N/A	N/A	N/A	
Charter Oak Brewing Co. (CT)	C-92	245	N/A				N/A	N/A		
Clement's Brewing Co. (NJ)	C-92	3,000	N/A				N/A	N/A		
Fox Classic Brewing Co. Inc. (WI)	O-91/C-92	1,000	N/A				N/A	N/A		
Los Angeles Brewing Co./ Eureka Restaurant and Brewery (CA)	C-92	N/A	N/A				N/A	N/A		
Manzano Mountain Brewing Co. (NM)	C-92	N/A	N/A				N/A	N/A		
Obispo Brewing Co. (CA)	C-91	N/A	N/A				N/A	N/A		
Yukon Brewing & Bottling Co. (AK)	O-91/C-91	500					N/A			

United States Brewpubs: Estimated Total Taxable Shipments

All figures are in U.S. barrels.
Totals, in many cases, are estimates reported to the Institute for Brewing Studies and may not reflect exact taxpaid amount.
O/C Denotes year opened or closed, if occurring between 1991 and 1995.
† Denotes brewpubs distributing less than 10 percent to off-site accounts.
‡ Denotes brewpubs distributing 10 to 25 percent to off-site accounts.
§ Denotes brewpubs distributing 25 to 50 percent to off-site accounts.

Company Name	O/C	1991	1992	1993	1994	1995	1992 % Growth	1993 % Growth	1994 % Growth	1995 % Growth
Wynkoop Brewing Co. (CO) †		2,200	2,450	4,250	4,538	5,008	11	73	7	10
Salt Lake Brewing Co. (both facilities) (UT)		1,300	1,605	1,915	2,020	4,039	23	19	5	100
Rock Bottom Brewery (No. 1) (CO)	O-91	N/A	2,496	3,048	3,746	3,854	N/A	22	23	3
Boston Beer Works (MA) †	O-92		2,354	3,319	3,327	3,750		41	0	13
Baltimore Brewing Co. (MD)		1,000	N/A	1,600	2,634	3,745	N/A	N/A	65	42
Gordon Biersch Brewery-Restaurant (No. 5) (HI)	O-94				562	3,395				504
Copper Tank Brewing Co. (No. 1) (TX)	O-94				1,554	3,263				110
Rock Bottom Brewery (No. 5) (TX)	O-95					3,100				
Spring Garden Brewing Co. (NC)	O-91	1,500	1,000	1,500	N/A	3,000	-33	50	N/A	N/A
Lost Coast Brewing Co. (CA) ‡		310	800	1,663	2,100	2,714	158	108	26	29
Breckenridge Brewery and Pub (CO)		N/A	2,750	2,223	2,427	2,700	N/A	-19	9	11
Marin Brewing Co. (CA) ‡		1,500	2,004	2,375	2,606	2,694	34	19	10	3
Bricktown Brewing Co. (OK)	O-92		310	1,320	2,000	2,650		326	52	33
Rock Bottom Brewery (No. 2) (MN)	O-93			N/A	2,735	2,600		N/A	N/A	-5
Gordon Biersch Brewery-Restaurant (No. 3) (CA)	O-92		2,742	2,770	3,588	2,572		1	30	-28

Beer and Brewery Statistics

Company Name	O/C	1991	1992	1993	1994	1995	1992 % Growth	1993 % Growth	1994 % Growth	1995 % Growth
Rubicon Brewing Co. (CA)		1,499	1,812	2,323	2,810	2,550	21	28	21	-9
Goose Island Brewing Co. (IL) †		2,200	2,040	2,400	2,550	2,500	-7	18	6	-2
Oasis Brewery and Restaurant (CO) †	O-91	N/A	1,435	2,657	4,009	2,464	N/A	85	51	-39
Butterfield Brewery (CA)		1,000	1,200	1,429	2,000	2,400	20	19	40	20
Denver Chop House & Brewery (CO)	O-95					2,400				
Cambridge Brewing Co. (MA) ‡		1,840	2,035	2,210	2,375	2,370	11	9	7	0
Long Island Brewing Co. (NY) †	O-94				N/A	2,340			N/A	N/A
Redwood Coast Brewing Co./Tied House Cafe and Brewery (No. 1) (CA) †		2,700	2,600	2,335	2,485	2,337	-4	-10	6	-6
Mountain Valley Brewpub (NY) ‡	O-92		N/A	1,000	1,400	2,300	N/A	N/A	40	64
Rock Bottom Brewery (No. 4) (OR) †	O-94				N/A	2,300			N/A	N/A
CooperSmith's Pub and Brewing (CO) ‡		1,331	1,700	2,300	2,350	2,250	28	35	2	-4
Main Street Brewery (OH)	O-94				N/A	2,240			N/A	N/A
Free State Brewing Co. (KS)		1,350	1,445	1,680	2,130	2,200	7	16	27	3
St. Louis Brewery/Taproom (MO)	O-91	N/A	880	1,254	1,669	2,200	N/A	43	33	32
Bardo Rodeo (VA)	O-93			N/A	N/A	2,100		N/A	N/A	N/A
Hoster Brewing Co. (OH)		850	1,325	1,703	1,998	2,073	56	29	17	4
Table Rock Brewpub and Grill (ID)	O-91	750	1,500	2,000	2,000	2,070	100	33	0	4
Westside Brewing Co. (NY) †	O-93			N/A	N/A	2,065		N/A	N/A	N/A
Crescent City Brewhouse (LA)	O-91	1,250	1,050	1,595	1,750	2,000	-16	52	10	14
Rock Bottom Brewery (No. 3) (TX)	O-95					2,000				
Blind Pig Brewing Co. (CA)	O-94				545	2,000				267
Walnut Brewery (CO) †		2,154	2,160	2,366	2,044	1,980	0	10	-14	-3
75th Street Brewery (KS) †	O-93			N/A	1,948	1,920		N/A	N/A	-1
Holy Cow! Casino, Cafe and Brewery (NV) ‡	O-93			915	1,821	1,910			99	5
Hubcap Brewery and Kitchen (CO) †	O-91	N/A	N/A	1,750	1,715	1,880	N/A	N/A	-2	10
Commonwealth Brewing Co. (MA) †		1,910	1,750	1,800	1,825	1,860	-8	3	1	2
Stoddard's Brewhouse and Eatery (CA) †	O-93			512	1,350	1,830			164	36
Red Rock Brewing Co. (UT)	O-94				1,250	1,800				44
Capitol City Brewing Co. (DC)	O-92		1,800	1,400	N/A	1,775		-22	N/A	N/A
Mickey Finn's Brewery (IL)	O-94				460	1,770				285
Gordon Biersch Brewery-Restaurant (No. 2) (CA)		2,257	1,947	1,798	1,841	1,761	-14	-8	2	-4
Great Dane Pub & Brewing Co. (WI)	O-94				415	1,761				324
Fullerton Hofbrau (CA) †		1,000	800	1,000	1,250	1,750	-20	25	25	40
Greenshields Brewery and Pub (NC)		1,000	1,176	1,193	1,298	1,741	18	1	9	34
Big Time Brewing Co. (WA) †		1,250	1,355	1,298	1,375	1,630	8	-4	6	19
Phantom Canyon Brewing Co. (CO) †	O-93			N/A	1,394	1,620		N/A	N/A	16
Tied House Cafe and Brewery (No. 2) (CA)	O-91	450	1,200	1,121	1,334	1,616	167	-7	19	21
Sunday River Brewing Co. (ME)	O-93			1,100	1,652	1,553			50	-6
Champion Brewing Co. (CO) †	O-91	N/A	1,119	N/A	1,383	1,550	N/A	N/A	N/A	12
Coyote Springs Brewing Co. and Cafe (AZ)		725	560	N/A	1,400	1,550	-23	N/A	N/A	11
Southend Brewery & Smokehouse (NC) †	O-95					1,550				
Flat Branch Brewing Co. (MO) †	O-94				1,216	1,530				26
Santa Cruz Brewing Co./Front Street Pub (CA) ‡		1,820	1,850	1,579	1,601	1,520	2	-15	1	-5
Steelhead Brewery & Cafe (No. 1) (OR) †	O-91	925	1,400	1,360	1,750	1,500	51	-3	29	-14
Twenty Tank Brewery (CA)		1,500	1,600	1,400	1,501	1,500	7	-13	7	0
Gordon Biersch Brewery-Restaurant (No. 4) (CA)	O-93			36	1,469	1,477			3,981	1
Birkebeiner Brewing Co. (WA) ‡	O-94				N/A	1,444			N/A	N/A
Yegua Creek (TX)	O-94				1,530	1,420				-7
Blue Water Brewing Co. (CA) ‡	O-93			N/A	1,000	1,400		N/A	N/A	40
Los Gatos Brewing Co. (CA) †	O-92		500	1,200	1,400	1,400		140	17	0

Beer and Brewery Statistics

Company Name	O/C	1991	1992	1993	1994	1995	1992 % Growth	1993 % Growth	1994 % Growth	1995 % Growth
Oliver Breweries Ltd./										
Wharf Rat at Camden Yards (MD)	O-93			820	1,300	1,400			59	8
River City Brewing Co. (CA)	O-93			N/A	1,373	1,394		N/A	N/A	2
Northampton Brewery/										
Brewster Court Bar and Grill (MA)		900	750	900	1,107	1,350	-17	20	23	22
Weinkeller Brewery (both facilities) (IL)		800	800	500	980	1,350	0	-38	96	38
West Virginia Brewing Co. (WV) ‡	O-92		150	N/A	1,028	1,320		N/A	N/A	28
Gordon Biersch										
Brewery-Restaurant (No. 1) (CA)		1,440	1,575	1,606	1,726	1,313	9	2	7	-24
Great Basin Brewing Co. (NV) †	O-93			140	N/A	1,300			N/A	N/A
Huntington Beach Beer Co. (CA)	O-92		N/A	1,150	1,214	1,300	N/A	N/A	6	7
Troy Brewing Co. (formerly										
Brown & Moran Brewing Co.) (NY) †	O-93			954	1,154	1,300			21	13
Magic City Brewery (AL)	O-95					1,290				
River City Brewing Co. (FL)	O-93					1,278				
Burlingame Station Brewing Co. (CA)	O-95					1,256				
Santa Rosa Bay Brewing Co. (FL)	O-93			1,500	N/A	1,250			N/A	N/A
Ragtime Taproom (FL)	O-91	316	1,600	1,500	1,400	1,238	406	-6	-7	-12
Gentle Ben's Brewing Co. (AZ)	O-91	N/A	850	1,100	1,219	1,220	N/A	29	11	0
Brew Moon (MA)	O-94				N/A	1,200			N/A	N/A
Hops Bistro and Brewery (No. 2) (CA)	O-92		N/A	1,254	N/A	1,200	N/A	N/A	N/A	N/A
Mountain Sun Pub and Brewery (CO) ‡	O-93			N/A	800	1,200		N/A	N/A	50
Portsmouth Brewery (NH)	O-91	700	1,043	1,123	1,200	1,200	49	8	7	0
Seabright Brewery (CA) †		1,200	1,200	1,200	1,300	1,200	0	0	8	-8
Stark Mill										
Brewery & Restaurant (NH) †	O-94				N/A	1,200			N/A	N/A
Hubcap Brewery										
and Kitchen (No. 2) (TX)	O-94				N/A	1,200			N/A	N/A
Leavenworth Brewery (WA) ‡	O-92		200	800	1,100	1,200		300	38	9
Truckee Brewing Co./										
Pizza Junction (CA)		N/A	650	800	1,100	1,200	N/A	23	38	9
Triumph Brewing Co. (NJ)	O-95					1,180				
Beaver Street										
Brewery & Whistlestop Cafe (AZ) †	O-94				1,000	1,150				15
Martha's Exchange (NH)	O-93			N/A	1,200	1,150		N/A	N/A	-4
Olde Towne Tavern & Brewery (MD)	O-94				700	1,150				64
Mishawaka Brewing Co. (IN) †	O-92		195	580	765	1,135		197	32	48
Assets Grill and Brewing Co. (NM) †	O-93			991	1,100	1,124			11	2
Grand Rapids Brewing Co. (MI)	O-93			N/A	1,200	1,100		N/A	N/A	-8
Newport Beach Brewing Co. (CA)	O-95					1,100				
Sioux Falls Brewing Co. (SD) ‡	O-95					1,100				
River City Brewing Co. (KS) †	O-93			825	1,000	1,050			21	5
Village Brewery (TX)	O-94				784	1,043				33
Black Diamond Brewing Co. (CA)	O-94				120	1,040				767
Houston Brewery (TX)	O-94				N/A	1,040			N/A	N/A
Steamboat Brewery and Tavern (CO) ‡	O-93			N/A	N/A	1,025		N/A	N/A	N/A
Jones Street Brewing Co. (NE)	O-92		253	956	1,210	1,021		278	27	-16
Belmont Brewing Co. (CA)		600	1,100	1,100	N/A	1,000	83	0	N/A	N/A
Carnegie Hill Brewing Co (NY)	O-95					1,000				
Ozark Brewing Co. (AR)	O-94				520	1,000				92
Santa Barbara Brewing Co. (CA) †	O-95					1,000				
Smoky Mountain Brewing Co. (TN)	O-94				N/A	1,000			N/A	N/A
Idle Spur Crested Butte										
Brewery and Restaurant (CO) †	O-91	600	1,000	1,100	N/A	1,000	67	10	N/A	N/A
Triple Rock Brewing (CA) †		1,500	1,500	N/A	933	1,000	0	N/A	N/A	7
Tulsa Brewing Co. (OK)	O-93			758	1,255	1,000			66	-20
Wild River Brewing & Pizza Co. (OR)		140	290	560	750	1,000	107	93	34	33
Fulton Pub and Brewery (OR)		954	997	960	945	986	5	-4	-2	4
Laguna Beach Brewing Co. (CA)	O-94				N/A	983			N/A	N/A
Oak Hills Brewpub (OR)		944	1,014	960	943	983	7	-5	-2	4

Beer and Brewery Statistics

Company Name	O/C	1991	1992	1993	1994	1995	1992 % Growth	1993 % Growth	1994 % Growth	1995 % Growth
Hartford Brewery Ltd. (CT)	O-91	250	775	853	1,000	975	210	10	17	-3
Wild River Brewing Co. (No. 2) (OR)	O-94				N/A	975			N/A	N/A
Big River Grill & Brewing Works (No. 1) (TN) †	O-93			N/A	1,036	968		N/A	N/A	-7
Empire Brewery & Grill (NY) †	O-94				N/A	962			N/A	N/A
Big River Grill & Brewing Works (No. 2) (TN)	O-95					948				
Blackstone Restaurant & Brewery (TN)	O-94				N/A	927			N/A	N/A
Downtown Joe's Brewing Co. (CA)		750	700	N/A	610	921	-7	N/A	N/A	51
Valley Forge Brewing Co. Restaurant & Pub (PA)	O-95					910				
Trinity Brewhouse (RI)	O-94				N/A	905			N/A	N/A
Bend Brewing Co. (OR) †	O-95					900				
Columbine Mill Brewery (CO)	O-94				N/A	900			N/A	N/A
Fremont Brewing Co. (CA) †		800	800	800	800	900	0	0	0	13
McCall Brewery Co. (ID) †	O-94				800	900				13
Pizza Port/ Solana Beach Brewery (CA) †	O-92		N/A	411	N/A	900	N/A	N/A	N/A	N/A
Sarasota Brewing Co. (No. 1) (FL)		600	1,500	N/A	N/A	900	150	N/A	N/A	N/A
South Baltimore Brewing Co./ Sisson's Restaurant (MD) ‡		500	700	750	875	900	40	7	17	3
Cornelius Pass Roadhouse and Brewery (OR)		493	475	500	617	889	-4	5	23	44
Port City Brewery (AL)	O-93			N/A	1,210	880		N/A	N/A	-27
Brewmaster's Pub (WI)		350	500	504	726	875	43	1	44	21
Golden Valley Brewery and Pub (OR) †	O-93			N/A	441	864		N/A	N/A	96
Lazlo's Brewery and Grill (NE)	O-91	750	1,000	1,000	950	859	33	0	-5	-10
Appleton Brewing Co. (WI)		300	431	487	496	857	44	13	2	73
Firehouse Brewing Co. (SD) †	O-91	N/A	800	850	840	854	N/A	6	-1	2
Barley's Brewing Co. (OH)	O-92		N/A	480	650	850	N/A	N/A	35	31
Bison Brewing Co. (CA) ‡		500	600	800	N/A	850	20	33	N/A	N/A
Bootleggers Brewing Co. (CA) ‡	O-94				350	850				143
Fort Spokane Brewery (WA) ‡		578	950	1,004	840	850	64	6	-16	1
Highland Pub and Brewery (OR)		899	888	900	819	850	-1	1	-9	4
Carolina Brewery (NC)	O-95					833				
Medicine Bow Brewing Co. (WY) ‡	O-95					828				
Santa Rosa Brewing Co. (CA) ‡		1,050	816	584	776	824	-22	-28	33	6
Rock Bottom Brewery (No. 6) (OH)	O-95					817				
Erie Brewing Co. (PA) †	O-94				N/A	808			N/A	N/A
Trailhead Brewing Co. (MO)	O-95					803				
Carver Brewing Co. (CO)		450	530	560	670	802	18	6	20	20
Fredericksburg Brewing Co. Inc. (TX)	O-94				N/A	800			N/A	N/A
Hops Grill and Bar (No. 1) (FL)		715	1,630	N/A	N/A	800	128	N/A	N/A	N/A
Hops Grill and Bar (No. 2) (FL)	O-91	N/A	N/A	N/A	N/A	800	N/A	N/A	N/A	N/A
Hops Grill and Bar (No. 3) (FL)	O-92		N/A	N/A	N/A	800	N/A	N/A	N/A	N/A
Hops Grill and Bar (No. 4) (FL)	O-92		N/A			800	N/A	N/A		
Hops Grill and Bar (No. 5) (FL)	O-93			N/A	N/A	800		N/A	N/A	N/A
Hops Grill and Bar (No. 6) (FL)	O-93			800	800	800			0	0
Hops Grill and Bar (No. 7) (FL)	O-94				800	800				0
Hops Grill and Bar (No. 8) (FL)	O-94				N/A	800				N/A
Hops Grill and Bar (No. 9) (FL)	O-94				N/A	800				N/A
Hops Grill and Bar (No. 10) (FL)	O-95					800				
Hops Grill and Bar (No. 11) (FL)	O-95					800				
Hops Grill and Bar (No. 12) (FL)	O-95					800				
Hops Grill and Bar (No. 13) (FL)	O-95					800				
Oregon Fields Brewing Co. (OR) †	O-94				150	800				433
Pacific Tap & Grill (CA) ‡	O-93			400	900	800			125	-11
McMenamin's on Murray (OR)		695	769	750	782	798	11	-2	4	2
Cherry Street Brewery (OK)	O-93			144	N/A	786			N/A	N/A
Hereford and Hops (MI)	O-95					775				

Beer and Brewery Statistics

Company Name	O/C	1991	1992	1993	1994	1995	1992 % Growth	1993 % Growth	1994 % Growth	1995 % Growth
McGuire's Irish Pub and Brewery (FL)		815	797	813	789	766	-2	2	-3	-3
Faultline Brewing Co. (CA)	O-95					750				
Old San Marcos Brewery and Grill (CA)	O-93			N/A	685	750		N/A	N/A	9
Philadelphia Brewing Co./ Samuel Adams Brewhouse (PA)		700	700	700	700	750	0	0	0	7
Bitter End Bistro & Brewery (TX)	O-94				N/A	750			N/A	N/A
Water Street Brewery (WI)		670	800	N/A	650	750	19	N/A	N/A	15
Rock Bottom Brewery (No. 7) (IL)	O-95					740				
Hillsdale Brewery and Public House (OR)		746	800	800	769	738	7	0	-4	-4
Prescott Brewing Co. (AZ)	O-94				600	735				23
Thompson Brewery and Public House (OR)		749	695	720	699	730	-7	4	-3	4
Calhoun's Restaurant & Brewery (TN)	O-94				N/A	724			N/A	N/A
Park Slope Brewing Co. (NY) †	O-94				230	721				213
Clubhaus Brewpub (NY)	O-95					720				
Dilworth Brewing Co. (NC)		650	900	1,200	1,029	720	38	33	-14	-30
Redondo Beach Brewing Co. (CA) †	O-93			400	960	720			140	-25
McMenamin's West Linn Pub and Brewery (OR)	O-92		98	770	728	717		686	-5	-2
McMenamin's on the Columbia (WA)	O-95					708				
Lighthouse Brew-Pub (OR)		682	590	620	612	704	-13	5	-1	15
Broad Ripple Brewing Co. (IN)	O-91	425	690	680	700	700	62	-1	3	0
Crane River Brewery & Cafe (NE)	O-92		217	685	641	700		216	-6	9
Interurban Brewpub/ Norman Brewing Co. (OK) †	O-94				337	700				108
Liberty St Brewing Co. (OH)	O-94				N/A	700			N/A	N/A
Lucky Labrador Brew Pub (OR)	O-94				150	700				367
Mill Creek Brewery & Restaurant (MO)	O-95					700				
Richbrau Brewery (VA)	O-93			400	N/A	700			N/A	N/A
Rohrbach Brewing Co. (No. 1) (NY)	O-92		320	650	650	700		103	0	8
Santa Clarita Brewing Co. (CA) †	O-94				750	700				-7
Sonoma Brewing Co. (CA) †	O-91	N/A	700	700	700	700	N/A	0	0	0
High St. Pub (OR)		675	693	730	662	689	3	5	-9	4
Blind Tiger Brewery (KS) †	O-95					686				
Burkhardts Brewing Co. (OH) †	O-91	252	378	N/A	N/A	684	50	N/A	N/A	N/A
Bloomington Brewing Co. (IN) ‡	O-94				N/A	670			N/A	N/A
Oaken Barrel Brewing Co. (IN) ‡	O-94				N/A	670			N/A	N/A
San Diego Brewing Co. (CA)	O-93			N/A	N/A	650		N/A	N/A	N/A
Gritty McDuff's (No. 2) (ME)	O-95					644				
Wallaby's Grill & Brewpub (OH) †	O-95					640				
Bosco's Pizza Kitchen and Brewery (No. 1) (TN)	O-92		25	590	614	616		2,260	4	0
Flying Dog Brewpub (CO)	O-91	550	800	870	760	607	45	9	-13	-20
Fitzpatrick's Brewing Co. (IA)		500	525	510	N/A	600	5	-3	N/A	N/A
Flagstaff Brewing Co. (AZ)	O-94				N/A	600			N/A	N/A
North Dakota/ Old Broadway Brewing (ND) †	O-95					600				
Padre Island Brewing Co. (TX)	O-95					600				
Sacramento Brewing Co. (CA) †	O-95					600				
Snowshoe Brewing Co. (CA)	O-95					600				
Shed Restaurant & Brewery (VT) ‡	O-94				N/A	600			N/A	N/A
Lafayette Brewing Co. (IN) †	O-93			N/A	511	575		N/A	N/A	13
Olde Salem Brewery (MA) †	O-95					575				
Seven Barrel Brewery (NH)	O-94				406	560				38
Mill Bakery, Brewery and Eatery (FL)		1,000	730	N/A	N/A	550	-27	N/A	N/A	N/A
B. F. Coleman Brewing Co./ Judge Baldwin's (CO) †	O-91	225	1,550	780	N/A	548	589	-50	N/A	N/A

Beer and Brewery Statistics

Company Name	O/C	1991	1992	1993	1994	1995	1992 % Growth	1993 % Growth	1994 % Growth	1995 % Growth
Eske's: A Brewpub (NM) †	O-92		43	450	450	520		947	0	16
Il Vicino Wood Oven Pizza (No. 1) (NM)	O-94				69	520				654
Crown City Brewery (CA)		350	360	484	502	518	3	34	4	3
Fordham Brewing Co./ Rams Head Tavern (MD)	O-95					500				
Hops Bistro & Brewery (No. 4) (AZ) †	O-95				N/A	500			N/A	N/A
Woodstock Brewing Co. (NH) ‡	O-95					500				
Cafe Pacifica Brewpub/ Sankt Gallen Brewery (CA)	O-93			N/A	N/A	495		N/A	N/A	N/A
Blue Ridge Brewing Co. (SC)	O-95					480				
Hilton Head Brewing Co. (SC)	O-94				N/A	464			N/A	N/A
Cascade Lakes Brewing Co. (OR)	O-95					460				
Brandywine Brewing Co. (DE)	O-95					450				
McMenamin's on Roy Street (WA)	O-95					438				
Buffalo Bill's Brewery (CA) †		300	330	300	350	432	10	-9	17	23
Desert Edge Brewing Co. (UT)	O-95					431				
Palm Springs Brewery/Brewmeisters (CA) ‡	O-94				300	430				43
Union Colony Brewery (CO) †	O-94				N/A	425			N/A	N/A
San Juan Brewing Co./ Front Street Ale House (WA)	O-93			N/A	354	412		N/A	N/A	16
Irish Times Pub & Brewery (FL)	O-91	400	N/A	400	N/A	408	N/A	N/A	N/A	N/A
Bandersnatch Brewpub (AZ)		500	850	N/A	N/A	400	70	N/A	N/A	N/A
Buffalo Brewpub (NY)		450	450	475	365	400	0	6	-23	10
Coddington Brewing Co. (RI)	O-95					400				
Lexington City Brewery (KY)	O-95					400				
Shannon Kelly's Brew Pub (MN)	O-94				N/A	400			N/A	N/A
Spencer's Restaurant & Brewhouse (OR) †	O-95					400				
Weidman's Old Fort Brew Pub/Weidman's Brewery (AR)	O-92		300	300	N/A	400		0	N/A	N/A
Pacific Coast Brewing Co. (CA) †		400	470	447	N/A	386	18	-5	N/A	N/A
Moylan's Brewing Co. (CA) †	O-95					384				
Little Apple Brewing Co. (KS)	O-93			225	N/A	380			N/A	N/A
Carlsbad Brewery & Public House (CA)	O-95					375				
Napa Valley Brewing Co./Calistoga Inn (CA)		400	329	330	350	375	-18	0	6	7
Umpqua Brewing Co. (OR) ‡	O-91	150	358	N/A	323	369	139	N/A	N/A	14
Hazel Dell Brewpub (WA)	O-93			198	439	365			122	-17
Front Street Brewery (IA)	O-92		N/A	333	379	364	N/A	N/A	14	-4
Boulder Creek Brewing Co. (CA)		355	1,190	N/A	370	363	235	N/A	N/A	-2
Blue Ridge Brewing Co. (VA)		450	400	375	400	360	-11	-6	7	-10
Mill Rose Brewing Co. (IL)	O-92		400	300	400	350		-25	33	-13
Shannon Pub (formerly Rochester Brewpub) (NY)		250	360	350	234	350	44	-3	-33	50
Ship Inn Inc. (NJ)	O-95					343				
Roosters 25th St. Brewing Co. (UT)	O-95					329				
Alcatraz Brewing Co. (IN) †	O-95					327				
El Dorado Brewing Co. (CA)	O-94				400	N/A				-19
Kelly's Caribbean Bar and Grill (FL)	O-93			258	950	318			268	-67
Columbia Brewing Co. (SC)	O-95					308				
San Andreas Brewing Co. (CA)		700	300	N/A	260	308	-57	N/A	N/A	18
Brewer's Bier Haus (NH)	O-95					300				
Callahan's Pub and Brewery (CA)		300	350	320	N/A	300	17	-9	N/A	N/A
Cottonwood Grille and Brewery (NC)	O-95					300				
Maine Coast Brewing (ME)	O-95					300				
Poplar Head Mule Co. Brewpub (AL)	O-95					300				
No Tomato Restaurant & Brewery (ME)	O-94				300	280				-7

Institute for Brewing Studies

Beer and Brewery Statistics

Company Name	O/C	1991	1992	1993	1994	1995	1992 % Growth	1993 % Growth	1994 % Growth	1995 % Growth
Rowland's Calumet Brewery and Brewpub (WI) †		80	101	147	240	270	26	46	63	13
Atlantic Brewing Co. (NY)	O-95					250				
Downtown Brewing Co. (SC)	O-95					250				
Latchis Grille and Windham Brewery (VT)	O-91	250	250	250	N/A	250	0	0	N/A	N/A
South Pointe Seafood House (FL)	O-95					250				
Star Garnet Brewing Co. (ID) ‡	O-95					250				
Dimmer's Brewub Inc. (CO) †	O-95					245				
Brew House of Danvers (MA)	O-95					239				
Stewart's Brewing Co. (DE)	O-95					239				
John Harvard's Brewhouse (No. 2)/The Brewhouse LLC (GA)	O-95					238				
Taylor Brewing Co. (IL)	O-94				N/A	237			N/A	N/A
Library Restaurant & Brewing Co. (WY)	O-95					227				
Olde Hickory Brewing Co. (NC)	O-95					225				
Black Horse Brewery (TN) ‡	O-95					220				
Treaty Grounds Brewpub (ID)	O-94				60	220				267
McMenamin's at Mill Creek (WA)	O-95					213				
Box Office Brewery (IL)	O-94				N/A	210			N/A	N/A
Amber Waves Brewery & Pub (CA)	O-95					204				
Black River Brewing Co./Brew House (VT) †	O-95					200				
Mt. Angel Brewing Co. (OR)	O-95					200				
Queen City Brewing Co. (PA)	O-95/C-95					200				
Silo Brew Pub & Restaurant (KY)	O-92/C-95		2,000	1,500	1,000	200		-25	-33	-80
Il Vicino Wood Oven Pizza (No. 2) (CO)	O-94				53	194				266
Six Arms Pub/ McMenamin's on Pike Street (WA)	O-95					193				
Shields Brewing Co. (CA) ‡		400	170	276	313	182	-58	62	13	-42
Routh Street Brewery (TX)	O-95					180				
Morgan Street Brewery (MO)	O-95					175				
Randy's Supper Club (WI)	O-94				120	171				43
South Shore Brewery (WI)	O-95					170				
Blue Pine Brewpub Co. (OR)	O-93			N/A	N/A	156		N/A	N/A	N/A
Cafe on the Square and Brewub (TX)	O-95					150				
Main Street Brewery/ Four Corners Brewing Co. (CO)	O-95					150				
Liberty Steakhouse & Brewery (SC)	O-95					143				
Thai Orchid Restaurant (No. 1) (FL)	O-93			N/A	N/A	140		N/A	N/A	N/A
Overland Stage Stop Brewery (CO)	O-95					120				
Preston Brewery/Embudo Station (NM)		200	173	83	85	120	-14	-52	2	41
Overland Park Brewing Co. (KS)	O-95					117				
Jaipur Restaurant and Brewpub (NE)	O-92		120	80	88	110		-33	10	25
Katie Bloom's Irish Pub & Brewery (TX)	O-95					110				
Jasper Murdock Ale House/Norwich Inn (VT)	O-93			34	81	103			138	27
Bank Draft Brewing Co. (TX)	O-95					100				
Mill Brewery, Bakery & Eatery (TN)	O-95					100				
Old Chicago Brewery & Pub (OR)	O-94				N/A	100			N/A	N/A
Philadelphia's (OR)	O-94				N/A	98			N/A	N/A
Hoppers Brooker Creek Grille and Tap Room (FL)	O-94				N/A	92			N/A	N/A
Traffic Jam and Snug (MI)	O-93			34	95	89			179	-6
Baked and Brewed in Telluride (CO) †	O-91	N/A	75	N/A	91	87	N/A	N/A	N/A	-4
Boardwalk Bistro (TX)	O-94				57	74				30
R. Ales Inc./ Rail House Brewing Co. (WI)	O-95					72				

Beer and Brewery Statistics

Company Name	O/C	1991	1992	1993	1994	1995	1992 % Growth	1993 % Growth	1994 % Growth	1995 % Growth
Wiltse's Brewpub & Family Restaurant (MI)	O-94				N/A	65			N/A	N/A
New World Brewery (FL)	O-95					63				
Rattlesnake Creek Brewery & Grill (ND)	O-95					60				
Joey's Inc. (TX)	O-95					58				
Galveston Brewery (TX)	O-95					40				
Regal Eagle Brewing Co./ North Slope Brewing Co. (AK)	O-95					40				
Gottberg Brew Pub (NE)	O-95					36				
Bosco's Nashville Brewing Co. (No. 2) (TN)	O-95					34				
Maumee Bay Brewing Co. (OH)	O-95					26				
Anacortes Brewhouse (WA) ‡	O-94				N/A	25			N/A	N/A
Parlor City Brewing Co. (NY)	O-95					25				
Ouray Brewing Co. (CO)	O-95					22				
Bootlegger's Pub & Brewery (NY)	O-95					13				
AleHouse Rock Brewery & Broiler (CA)	O-95					N/A				N/A
Alessis Risorante/ Garretts Mill Brewing Co. (OH)	O-95					N/A				N/A
Aleworks (FL)	O-95					N/A				N/A
Angelic Brewing Co. (WI)	O-95					N/A				N/A
Arbor Brewing Co. (MI)	O-95					N/A				N/A
Babe's (IA)	O-93			90	N/A	N/A			N/A	N/A
Backwater Brewing Co. (MN)	O-95					N/A				N/A
Bank Brewing Co. (OR)	O-95					N/A				N/A
Bare Bones Grill & Brewery (MD)	O-95					N/A				N/A
Barley & Hopps (CA)	O-95					N/A				N/A
Barley Creek (PA)	O-95					N/A				N/A
Barley's (KS)	O-95					N/A				N/A
Bear Brewing Co. (ME)	O-95					N/A				N/A
Belle Isle Brewing Co. (OK)	O-95					N/A				N/A
Berkshire Mountain Brewers (MA) †						N/A				N/A
Big Horn Brewing Co. of Texas/Humperdinck's (TX)	O-95					N/A				N/A
Big Horn Brewing Co./C.B. Potts (CO)	O-95					N/A				N/A
Big Horn Brewing Co./RAM Int'l. (OR)	O-95					N/A				N/A
Big Horse Brewpub (OR)	O-95					N/A				N/A
Black River Brewery & Pub (WI)	O-95					N/A				N/A
Black Rose Brewpub (WI)	O-95					N/A				N/A
Blue Cat Brewing Co. (IL)	O-94				N/A	N/A			N/A	N/A
Blue Coyote Brewing Co. (MI)	O-95					N/A				N/A
Bluegrass Brewing Co. (KY)	O-93			210	1,546	N/A			636	N/A
Boundary Bay Brewing Co. (WA)	O-95					N/A				N/A
Bowman's Pub & Brewing Co. (WY)	O-95					N/A				N/A
Bray's Brewpub & Eatery (ME)	O-95					N/A				N/A
Brazos Brewing Co. (TX)	O-95					N/A				N/A
Brew Brothers/ Eldorado Hotel & Casino (NV)	O-95					N/A				N/A
Brewbaker's Ale House & Deli (IL)	O-94				N/A	N/A			N/A	N/A
Brewery at 34 Depot St. (MA) †	O-94				N/A	N/A			N/A	N/A
Brewery at Lake Tahoe (CA)	O-92		N/A	300	N/A	N/A	N/A	N/A	N/A	N/A
Brewski's Brewing Co. (CA)	O-95					N/A				N/A
Buckhead Brewery (FL)	O-95					N/A				N/A
Buckingham Mountain Brewing Co. (PA)	O-95					N/A				N/A
C. J.'s Brewpub (WA)	O-95					N/A				N/A
Capitol City Brewing Co. (IL)	O-94				273	N/A				N/A
Carolina Mill Bakery, Brewery and Eatery (NC)		300	500	N/A	N/A	N/A	67	N/A	N/A	N/A
Carson Depot (NV)	O-93			N/A	N/A	N/A		N/A	N/A	N/A

Beer and Brewery Statistics

Company Name	O/C	1991	1992	1993	1994	1995	1992 % Growth	1993 % Growth	1994 % Growth	1995 % Growth
Cascade Microbrewery & Public Firehouse (OR)	O-95					N/A				N/A
Chapter House Brewpub (NY)		N/A	N/A	N/A	N/A	N/A	N/A	N/A	N/A	N/A
Chicago Brew Pub (SC)	O-95					N/A				N/A
Cobblestone Pub & Brewery (VA)	O-95					N/A				N/A
Copper Canyon Brewing & Ale House (AZ)	O-95					N/A				N/A
Cottonwood Grille & Microbrewery (formerly Tumbleweed Grille) (NC)	O-92		N/A	200	250	N/A	N/A	N/A	25	N/A
Cusack's Brewpub and Roaster (AK)	O-95					N/A				N/A
Dave's Brewpub (KS)	O-95					N/A				N/A
Del Mar Stuffed Pizza & Microbrewery (CA)	O-95					N/A				N/A
Dino & Luigi's Stuffed Pizza, Sports Bar & Brewery (CA)	O-95					N/A				N/A
Dock Street Brewing Co. Brewery and Restaurant (PA)		1,500	N/A	N/A	N/A	N/A	N/A	N/A	N/A	N/A
Dogfish Head Brewings & Eats (DE)	O-95					N/A				N/A
Draught Horse Pub & Brewery (TX)	O-95					N/A				N/A
Ebbet's Field (MO)	O-95					N/A				N/A
Eel River Brewing Co. (CA)	O-95					N/A				N/A
Ellicottville Brewing Co. (NY)	O-95					N/A				N/A
Engine House #9/Power Station (WA)	O-95					N/A				N/A
Eugene City Brewing Co./ West Brothers BBQ (OR) †	O-93			N/A	N/A	N/A		N/A	N/A	N/A
Fields Restaurant & Brewpub (OR)	O-95					N/A				N/A
Firehouse Brewery & Restaurant (OH)	O-95					N/A				N/A
Fleetside Pub & Brewing (CO) †	O-95					N/A				N/A
Fox River Brewing Co./ Fratellos Italian Cafe (WI)	O-95					N/A				N/A
Front Street Brewery (NC)	O-95					N/A				N/A
Galena Main Street Brewpub/ Kingston Inn Restaurant (IL)	O-93			N/A	N/A	N/A		N/A	N/A	N/A
Galveston Brewery (TX)	O-95					N/A				N/A
Gambrinus Brewing Co. (OH)	O-93			N/A	N/A	N/A		N/A	N/A	N/A
Grizzly Bay Brewing Co. (CA)	O-95					N/A				N/A
Harbor Lights Brewing Co. (formerly Heritage Brewing Co. [No. 1]) (CA)		1,050	1,150	1,100	N/A	N/A	10	-4	N/A	N/A
Harrison Hollow Brewhouse (ID) ‡	O-92		246	610	871	N/A			148	43	N/A
Heartland Brewing Co. (NY) †	O-95					N/A				N/A
Heavenly Daze (CO)	O-93			N/A	1,850	N/A		N/A	N/A	N/A
Highlands Brewery (FL)	O-94				N/A	N/A			N/A	N/A
Hoffbrau Steaks Brewery (TX)	O-95					N/A				N/A
Hogshead Brewpub (CA)		600	600	N/A	600	N/A	0	N/A	N/A	N/A
Hops Bistro & Brewery (No. 3) (AZ)	O-94				N/A	N/A			N/A	N/A
Hops Bistro and Brewery (No. 1) (AZ)		1,300	1,200	1,350	1,485	N/A	-8	13	10	N/A
Hub City Brewery (TX)	O-95					N/A				N/A
Humphrey's Bar & Grill (WY)	O-95					N/A				N/A
Hunter Gatherer (SC)	O-95					N/A				N/A
Issaquah Brewhouse/ Eagle River Brewing Co. (WA) †	O-95					N/A				N/A
Italian Oasis Restaurant & Brewery (NH)	O-94				N/A	N/A			N/A	N/A
Ithaca Brewing Co. (NY)	O-95					N/A				N/A
J & L Brewing Co./ T. J.'s Bar, Grill and Pub (CA)		290	364	202	N/A	N/A	26	-45	N/A	N/A
James Bay Brewery Restaurant (NY) ‡	O-94				N/A	N/A			N/A	N/A
Jaxson's Restaurant & Brewing Co. (TX)	O-95					N/A				N/A
Joe-Joe's Brewing Co. (CA)	O-95					N/A				N/A

Company Name	O/C	1991	1992	1993	1994	1995	1992 % Growth	1993 % Growth	1994 % Growth	1995 % Growth
Joe's Brewing Co. (IL)	O-91	N/A	160	N/A	N/A	N/A	N/A	N/A	N/A	N/A
Joe's Millhill Saloon & Restaurant (NJ)	O-95					N/A				N/A
John Harvard's Brewhouse (MA)	O-93			N/A	N/A	N/A		N/A	N/A	N/A
Karl Strauss Brewery Gardens (CA)	O-94				300	N/A				N/A
Kentucky Brewpub & Grill (KY)	O-95					N/A				N/A
La Conner Brewing Co. (WA)	O-95					N/A				N/A
La Jolla Brewing Co. (CA)		750	1,100	973	1,037	N/A	47	-12	7	N/A
Lazy Hound Restaurant & Brewery (KS)	O-95					N/A				N/A
Long Valley Pub & Brewery (NJ)	O-95					N/A				N/A
Mainline Brewing Co. (CA)	O-95					N/A				N/A
Manhattan Beach Brewing Co. (CA)	O-91	900	N/A	N/A	N/A	N/A	N/A	N/A	N/A	N/A
Market Street Mill (SC)	O-95					N/A				N/A
Market Street Pub (FL)		425	N/A	N/A	500	N/A	N/A	N/A	N/A	N/A
McNeill's Brewery (VT)		N/A	N/A	N/A	N/A	N/A	N/A	N/A	N/A	N/A
Mercury Café (CO)	O-94				N/A	N/A			N/A	N/A
Mill Bakery, Brewery & Eatery (AL)	O-95					N/A				N/A
Montgomery Brewing Co. (AL)	O-95					N/A				N/A
Mount Baker Brewing Co. (WA)	O-95					N/A				N/A
Nacho Mama's Brewery (NY)	O-95					N/A				N/A
Norman Brewing Co. (OK)	O-93			N/A	N/A	N/A		N/A	N/A	N/A
Ocean Ave. Brewing Co. (CA) †	O-94				N/A	N/A			N/A	N/A
Old Baldy Brewing Co. (CA)	O-94				168	N/A				N/A
Old Broadway Brewing (ND)	O-95					N/A				N/A
Old Colorado Brewing Inc. (CO)	C-92/O-93	330	N/A	N/A	100	N/A	N/A	N/A	N/A	N/A
Old West Brewing Co. (No. 2) (TX)	O-95					N/A				N/A
Original Saratosa Springs Brewpub (NY)	O-95					N/A				N/A
Pacific Northwest Brewing Co. (WA)		700	475	N/A	N/A	N/A	-32	N/A	N/A	N/A
Parrotts Ferry Brewing Co. (CA)	O-95					N/A				N/A
Pete's Place (OK)	O-95					N/A				N/A
Pinch Penny Pub (IL)	O-95					N/A				N/A
Power House Restaurant & Brewery (WA)	O-95					N/A				N/A
Powerhouse Brewing Co. (CA)	O-95					N/A				N/A
Prairie Rock Brewing Co. (IL)	O-95					N/A				N/A
Red, White & Brew (CA)	O-93			N/A	N/A	N/A		N/A	N/A	N/A
Rio Bravo Restaurant & Brewery (NM)	O-93			80	600	N/A			650	N/A
River Market Brewing Co. (MO)	O-95					N/A				N/A
R. J.'s Riptide Brewery (CA)	O-92		1,460	1,905	2,946	N/A		30	55	N/A
Rock Bottom Brewery (No. 8) (KS)	O-95					N/A				N/A
Rohrbach Brewing Co. (No. 2) (NY)	O-95					N/A				N/A
Royal Bavarian Brewhaus (OK)	O-94				N/A	N/A			N/A	N/A
San Francisco Brewing Co. (CA)		850	700	800	750	N/A	-18	14	-6	N/A
San Juan Brewing Co. (CO)	O-91	N/A	420	640	N/A	N/A	N/A	52	N/A	N/A
Santa Monica Brewing Co. (CA)	O-94				N/A	N/A			N/A	N/A
Sea Dog Brewing Co. (No. 1) (ME) †	O-93			N/A	1,400	N/A		N/A	N/A	N/A
Sharkey's Brew Club (CO)	O-95					N/A				N/A
Sherlock's Home (MN)		N/A	1,500	1,740	1,850	N/A	N/A	16	6	N/A
Siletz Brewing Co. (OR)	O-95					N/A				N/A
Silk's Grill and Brewing Co. (TX)	O-95					N/A				N/A
Siskyou Brewing Co. (formerly Rogue River Brewing Co.) (OR)		N/A	1,000	840	1,100	N/A	N/A	-16	31	N/A
SLO Brewing Co. Inc. (CA)		800	620	1,000	N/A	N/A	-23	61	N/A	N/A
Sly Fox Brewhouse & Eatery (PA)	O-95					N/A				N/A
South End Brewery & Smokehouse (NC)	O-95					N/A				N/A
Spanish Peaks Brewing Co. and Italian Cafe (MT)	O-91	N/A	950	900	742	N/A	N/A	-5	-18	N/A
Steelhead Brewery & Cafe (No. 2) (CA)	O-95					N/A				N/A
Strand Brewery (TX)	O-95					N/A				N/A

Beer and Brewery Statistics

Company Name	O/C	1991	1992	1993	1994	1995	1992 % Growth	1993 % Growth	1994 % Growth	1995 % Growth
Sutter Brewing Co. (CA)	O-95					N/A				N/A
Syracuse Suds Factory (NY)	O-93			150	N/A	N/A			N/A	N/A
T-Bonz Grill (SC)	O-95					N/A				N/A
Terrific Pacific Brewery & Grill (CA)	O-95					N/A				N/A
Thai Orchid Restaurant (No. 2) (FL)	O-95					N/A				N/A
Tivoli Brewery/(america!) (CO)	O-95					N/A				N/A
Tortuga's (FL)	O-95					N/A				N/A
Trader & Trapper (MN)	O-94				N/A	N/A			N/A	N/A
Tugboat Brewpub and Cafe (OR)	O-93				N/A	N/A			N/A	N/A
TwoRows Brewing Co. (TX)	O-94				N/A	N/A			N/A	N/A
Union Station Brewing (RI)	O-93			N/A	1,200	N/A		N/A	N/A	N/A
Vermont Pub and Brewery of Burlington (VT)		756	847	850	N/A	N/A	12	0	N/A	N/A
Vino's (AR)	O-93			N/A	N/A	N/A		N/A	N/A	N/A
Waterloo Brewing Co. (TX)	O-93			N/A	1,277	N/A		N/A	N/A	N/A
Weinkeller Brewpub (No. 2) (IL)	O-92		600	700	N/A	N/A		17	N/A	N/A
Westport Brewing Co. (MO)	O-95					N/A				N/A
Wild Bill's Brewing Co. (SD)	O-95					N/A				N/A
Windrose Brewpub (FL)	O-95					N/A				N/A
Winthrop Brewing Co. (WA)	O-93			N/A	N/A	N/A		N/A	N/A	N/A
Yorkville Brewery & Tavern (NY)	O-94				N/A	N/A			N/A	N/A
Zip City Brewing Co. (NY)	O-91	70	1,127	N/A	N/A	N/A	1,510	N/A	N/A	N/A
Adam's Rib Barbeque & Brewery (KS)	O-94/C-95				N/A	N/A			N/A	N/A
Armadillo Brewing Co. (TX)	O-94/C-95				N/A	N/A			N/A	N/A
Bryan Brewing Co. (TX)	O-94/C-95				N/A	N/A			N/A	N/A
Captain Tony's Pizza and Pasta Emporium (OH)	O-93/C-95			N/A	90	N/A		N/A	N/A	N/A
G. T. Vito's (FL)	O-94/C-95				N/A	N/A			N/A	N/A
J. D. Nick's (IL)	O-92/C-95		200	625	N/A	N/A		213	N/A	N/A
Johnny's Brewery and Cafe (NE)	O-93/C-95			126	N/A	N/A			N/A	N/A
Live Soup Brewery & Cafe (CA)	O-93/C-95			N/A	400	N/A		N/A	N/A	N/A
Melbourne's Brewing Co. (OH)	C-95	450	553	N/A	N/A	N/A	23	N/A	N/A	N/A
Rio Bravo Restaurant & Brewery (No. 2) (CA)	O-94/C-95				N/A	N/A			N/A	N/A
Riverwalk Brewery/ Boca Beer Works (FL)	C-95					N/A				N/A
Saddle Sore Brewing Co. (KS)	O-94/C-95				N/A	N/A			N/A	N/A
Sharky's Brewery and Grill (NE)	O-92/C-95		357	N/A	N/A	N/A		N/A	N/A	N/A
Spur Steakhouse and Ale/ Toisnot Brewing Co. (NC)	O-94/C-95				N/A	N/A			N/A	N/A
Stone House Brewery (TX)	O-94/C-95				N/A	N/A			N/A	N/A
Sunset Brewery and Fish House (CA)	C-95					N/A				N/A
Wild Wild West Gambling Hall and Brewery (CO)	O-92/C-95		N/A	N/A	N/A	N/A	N/A	N/A	N/A	N/A
Willamette Brew Pub (OR)	O-91/C-95	520	N/A	N/A	930	N/A	N/A	N/A	N/A	N/A
Bluff City Brewery & Grill/The Brewery (TN)	O-93/C-94			N/A	N/A			N/A	N/A	N/A
Brewhouse Grill, Manhattan Beach (CA)	O-92/C-94		50	N/A	N/A			N/A	N/A	N/A
Brewhouse Grill, Santa Barbara (CA)	C-94	800	720	N/A	N/A		-10	N/A	N/A	N/A
Loggerhead Brewing Co. (NC)	C-94	785	907	800	N/A		16	-12	N/A	N/A
Okie Girl Brewery (CA)	C-94	420	259	N/A	N/A		-38	N/A	N/A	N/A
Pacific Beach Brewhouse (CA)	O-91/C-94	550	675	950	N/A		23	41	N/A	N/A
River Walk Brewery/ Boca Beer Works (FL)	O-91/C-94	N/A	N/A	N/A	N/A		N/A	N/A	N/A	N/A
San Francisco Bar & Grill Brewpub (AZ)	C-94	N/A	80	N/A	N/A		N/A	N/A	N/A	N/A
Berghoff Brewery and Restaurant (IL)	O-91/C-93	2,000	N/A	N/A			N/A	N/A	N/A	
Chickery (OH)	O-91/C-93	N/A	1,000	N/A			N/A	N/A	N/A	
Gorky's Cafe and Brewery (CA)	C-93	1,500	1,800	N/A			20	N/A	N/A	

Company Name	O/C	1991	1992	1993	1994	1995	1992 % Growth	1993 % Growth	1994 % Growth	1995 % Growth
Kidder's Brew Pub (FL)	O-91/C-93	1,200	1,000	N/A			-17	N/A	N/A	
Lone Star Cantina and Brewery (VA)	C-93	N/A	N/A	N/A			N/A	N/A	N/A	
Red Kettle (CA)	O-91/C-93	125	900	N/A			620	N/A	N/A	
Roger's Zoo (OR)	C-93	N/A	N/A	N/A			N/A	N/A	N/A	
Sarasota Brewing Co. (No. 2) (FL)	O-91/C-93	N/A	400	N/A			N/A	N/A	N/A	
Winchester Brewing Co. (CA)	C-93	1,150	1,500	N/A			30	N/A	N/A	
Brown Street Brewery and Restaurant (CA)	C-92	110	N/A				N/A	N/A		
Meander Brewing Co. (OH)	O-91/C-92	500	N/A				N/A	N/A		
Mill Bakery, Brewery and Eatery (No. 4) (LA)	C-92	N/A	150				N/A	N/A		
Union Brewery Co. (NV)	C-92	10	N/A				N/A	N/A		
Manhattan Brewing Co. (NY)	C-91	N/A					N/A			

United States Contract Brewing Companies: Estimated Sales

All figures are in U.S. barrels.

Totals, in many cases, are estimates reported to the Institute for Brewing Studies and may not reflect exact taxpaid amount.

O/C Denotes year opened or closed, if occurring between 1991 and 1995.

reO Denotes year reopened, if occurring between 1991 and 1995.

‡ See U.S. Microbreweries Estimated Total Taxable Shipments table for subsequent years' figures.

[1] Indicates companies also doing business as a brewpub.

[2] Indicates companies also doing business as a microbrewery.

* Indicates figures adjusted to reflect domestic sales only.

Company Name	O/C	1991	1992	1993	1994	1995	1992 % Growth	1993 % Growth	1994 % Growth	1995 % Growth
Boston Beer Co. (MA)		163,000	273,000	445,000*	696,000*	913,000*	67	65	56	32
Pete's Brewing Co. (CA)		17,200	35,700	74,800	182,000	347,800	108	110	143	91
Spanish Peaks Brewery (MT)	O-93			N/A	29,028	53,215		N/A	N/A	83
Oregon Ale & Beer Co. (subsidiary of Boston Beer Co.) (OR)	O-94				N/A	35,000			N/A	N/A
William & Scott Co./Rhino Chasers (CA)		N/A	15,000	15,000	22,000	29,032	N/A	0	47	36
Dock Street Brewing Co.[1] (PA)		10,000	N/A	N/A	20,000	25,000	N/A	N/A	N/A	25
Mass. Bay Brewing Co. (MA)[2]		N/A	2,250	N/A	16,080	21,000	N/A	N/A	N/A	31
Jack Daniels Brewery[2] (TN)					N/A	18,812			N/A	N/A
Brooklyn Brewery (NY)		8,400	9,200	10,200	12,100	14,500	10	11	19	20
Black Mountain Brewing Co.[2] (AZ)	O-92		2,177	18,000	18,000	12,000		N/A	0	-33
Florida Beer Brands (FL)		N/A	653	N/A	N/A	9,145	N/A	N/A	N/A	N/A
Crested Butte Brewery & Pub[2] (CO)	O-93				N/A	9,000			N/A	N/A
Stoudt's Brewery (PA)		1,200	1,800	4,200	3,300	7,800	50	133	-21	136
Alpine Brewing Co. (CO)	O-94				N/A	7,000			N/A	N/A
Owens Brewing Co. (CA)	O-92	N/A	200	N/A	3,000	6,000	N/A	N/A	N/A	100
Sprecher Brewing Co.[2] (WI)	O-91	800	4,500	3,750	4,000	5,000	N/A	-17	7	25
Jet City Brewing Co. (WA)	O-93			N/A	4,460	4,650		N/A	N/A	4
Elm City Brewing[2] (CT)	O-95					4,500				
Oxford Brewing Co.[2] (MD)	O-95					2,800				
Tun Tavern Brewing Co. Inc. (PA)	O-94				N/A	2,800			N/A	N/A
Gritty McDuff's[1] (ME)	O-94				1,723	2,768				61
Old City Brewing Co. (TX)		2,000	2,250	N/A	2,250	2,575	13	N/A	N/A	14
Old World Brewing Co. (NY)	O-92		1,006	1,800	2,100	2,300		79	17	10
Lake Tahoe Brewing Co. (CA)	O-93			290	1,163	2,273			301	95
Old Peconic Brewing Co. Ltd. (NY)	O-93			N/A	N/A	2,250		N/A	N/A	N/A
Pike Brewing Co. (formerly Pike Place Brewery) (WA)	O-92		500	2,100	3,000	2,045		N/A	43	-32
Signature Beer Co. (MO)	O-92		300	500	N/A	2,000		67	N/A	N/A

Beer and Brewery Statistics

Company Name	O/C	1991	1992	1993	1994	1995	1992 % Growth	1993 % Growth	1994 % Growth	1995 % Growth
Commonwealth Brewing Co.[1] (MA)	O-92		300	1,831	1,920	1,906		N/A	5	-1
Post Road Brewing Co. (formerly Old Marlborough Brewing Co.) (MA)		1,108	1,650	N/A	2,537	1,762	49	N/A	N/A	-31
Goose Island Beer Co.[2] (IL)	O-94				N/A	1,750			N/A	N/A
Reno Brewing Co. (NV)	O-94				N/A	1,700			N/A	N/A
Sunday River Brewing Co.[1] (ME)	O-94				N/A	1,533			N/A	N/A
Blue Hen Beer Co. (DE)		200	N/A	N/A	2,700	1,500	N/A	N/A	N/A	-44
Tuppers Hop Pocket Ale (MD)	O-95					1,120				
High Point Brewing Co. (CO)	O-95					1,100				
Helenboch Brewery/ Friends Brewing Co. (GA)		700	550	800	800	1,000	-21	45	0	25
Pelican Brewing Co./Sazerac (LA)	O-95					586				
T.ROY Brewing Co. (CA)	O-94				200	550				175
Johnstown Brewing Co. (PA)	O-95					500				
San Andreas Brewing (CA)	O-94				600	500				-17
Redondo Beach Brewing[1] (CA)	O-95					450				
Cross Plains Brewery Inc. (WI)						400				
Nebraska Brewing Co. (NE)	O-95					400				
T.Paul's Beer Co. (OK)	O-95					400				
Frederick Brewing Co.[2] (MD)	O-93			450	N/A	320			N/A	N/A
Brimstone Brewing Co.[2] (MD)	O-94				N/A	300			N/A	N/A
Starview Brewing Co. Inc. (PA)	O-95					300				
Columbus Brewing Co.[2] (OH)	O-92		1,451	850	700	250		-41	-18	-64
Mill Bakery, Brewery and Eatery[1] (FL)		N/A	5,700	N/A	N/A	250	N/A	N/A	N/A	N/A
Oliver Breweries/ Wharf Rat at Camden Yards[1] (MD)	O-95					250				
Lexington Brewing Co. (KY)	O-95					200				
Slopeside Brewing Co. (IL)	O-95					200				
McGuire's Irish Pub and Brewery[1] (FL)	O-90	150	1,014	N/A	N/A	180	576	N/A	N/A	N/A
Atlantis Brewing Co. (CO)	O-95					179				
Faultline Brewing Co.[1] (CA)	O-95					130				
Pacific Hop Exchange[2] (CA)	O-93			N/A		125			N/A	N/A
Atlantic Brewing Co.[2] (ME)	O-95					100				
Buffalo Brewpub[1] (NY)	O-95					100				
Danse-Skjold Brewing Co. (CA)	O-95					100				
Dilworth Brewing Co.[2] (NC)	O-95					100				
Newport Beach Brewing Co.[1] (CA)	O-95					100				
Otto Brothers' Brewing Co.[2] (WY)	O-95					60				
Bodega Brew Pub Inc. (WI)	O-95					20				
Two Angels Brewing Co. (CO)	O-95					20				
American Beer Guy (CA)	C-91/ reO-95	N/A			N/A	N/A	N/A			N/A
Atlantic City Brewing Co. (NJ)		218	5,400	N/A	N/A	N/A	2,377	N/A	N/A	N/A
Bad Frog Brewing Co. (MI)	O-95					N/A				N/A
Barley Field Brewing Co. (OK)	O-95					N/A				N/A
Beverly Hills Beerhouse Co. (CA)	O-93			N/A	N/A	N/A		N/A	N/A	N/A
Brandevor (WA)		2,100	11,000	N/A	N/A	N/A	424	N/A	N/A	N/A
Brewery Atlantis (CA)	O-95					N/A				N/A
Brewski Brewing Co. (CA)	O-93			N/A	N/A	N/A		N/A	N/A	N/A
Cherryland Brewing Co.[2] (WI)		N/A	900	800	2,000	N/A	N/A	-11	150	N/A
Coastal Brewing Inc. (MA)		N/A	N/A	750	N/A	N/A	N/A	N/A	N/A	N/A
Dakota Brewing Co. (ND)		1,500	500	N/A	1,820	N/A	-67	N/A	N/A	N/A
Detroit & Mackinac Brewery Ltd. (MI)	O-94				1,116	N/A				N/A
El Dorado Brewing Co. (CA)	O-94				20	N/A				N/A
Fort Wayne Brewing Co. (IN)	O-93			103		N/A				N/A
Frontier Brewing Co. (IA)	O-93			N/A	275	N/A		N/A	N/A	N/A
Georgia Brewing Co. (GA)		880	1,100	2,500	8,500	N/A	25	127	240	N/A
Gilbert Robinson Inc. (MO)		N/A	N/A	N/A	N/A	N/A	N/A	N/A	N/A	N/A
Hazel Dell Brewpub (WA)	O-94				100	N/A				N/A
Heavenly Daze Brewery & Grill (CO)	O-94				663	N/A				N/A

Beer and Brewery Statistics

Company Name	O/C	1991	1992	1993	1994	1995	1992 % Growth	1993 % Growth	1994 % Growth	1995 % Growth
Heckler Brewing Co. (CA)	O-93			300	3,000	N/A			900	N/A
Hornell Brewing Co. (NY)	O-91	N/A	N/A	N/A	N/A	N/A	N/A	N/A	N/A	N/A
Hubcap Brewery (CO)	O-94				15	N/A				N/A
Huntington Beach Beer Co. (CA)	O-94				462	N/A				N/A
Kershenstine Diamond (MS)		4,717	N/A	N/A	N/A	N/A	N/A	N/A	N/A	N/A
La Jolla Brewing Co. (CA)	O-94				N/A	N/A			N/A	N/A
Lakefront Brewery Inc. (WI)	O-94				300	N/A				N/A
Maui Beer Co. (HI)	O-93			N/A	N/A	N/A		N/A	N/A	N/A
McKenzie River Corp. (CA)		10,000	N/A	N/A	N/A	N/A	N/A	N/A	N/A	N/A
Mid-Coast Brewing Inc. (WI)	O-91	2,000	2,000	2,700	N/A	N/A	0	35	N/A	N/A
Mt. Airey Brewing Co. (MD)	O-95					N/A				N/A
Napa Springs Malting and Beverage Co. (CA)	O-90	N/A	16	N/A	N/A	N/A	N/A	N/A	N/A	N/A
Neuweiler Brewing Co. Inc. (PA)	O-92		8,000	N/A	N/A	N/A		N/A	N/A	N/A
New Amsterdam Brewing Co. (NY)		N/A	N/A	N/A	N/A	N/A	N/A	N/A		
Newman Brewing Co. (NY)		1,221	N/A	N/A	N/A	N/A	N/A	N/A	N/A	N/A
Oertel Brewing Co. (KY)	O-92		430	N/A	N/A	N/A		-100		
Olde Heurich Brewing Co. (DC)		2,200	3,487	3,573	N/A	N/A	59	2	N/A	N/A
Pennsylvania Brewing Co. (PA)		6,000	4,000	4,000	4,800	N/A	-33	0	20	N/A
Preservation Ale (CA)	O-93			N/A	N/A	N/A			N/A	N/A
Rainbow Ridge Brewing Co. Inc. (GA)	O-95					N/A				N/A
Red Bell Brewing Co. (PA)	O-93			N/A	N/A	N/A			N/A	N/A
Riverosa Co. (NY)	O-93			3,000	2,375	N/A			-21	N/A
R. J.'s Ginseng Co. (IL)	O-92		N/A	N/A	1,200	N/A	N/A	N/A	N/A	N/A
SLO Brewing Co. (CA)	O-94				N/A	N/A			N/A	N/A
Smith and Reilly (WA)		N/A	N/A	N/A	N/A	N/A	N/A	N/A	N/A	N/A
Spring Street Brewing Co. (NY)	O-93			1,400	N/A	N/A			N/A	N/A
Stone Mountain Brewers (GA)	O-93			N/A	N/A	N/A			N/A	N/A
Telluride Beer Co. Inc. (CO)		1,580	N/A	1,000	N/A	N/A	N/A	N/A	N/A	N/A
Traverse Beverage Co. Ltd. (MI)	O-94				200	N/A				N/A
Tye Dye Brewing Co. (FL)	O-93			N/A	N/A	N/A			N/A	N/A
Woodstock Brewing & Bottling Co. (IL)	O-93			330	N/A	N/A			N/A	N/A
Yen Sum (CA)	O-92		N/A	N/A	300	N/A	N/A	N/A	N/A	N/A
Goldfinch Brewing Co. (NJ)	O-92/C-94		N/A	N/A	N/A			N/A	N/A	N/A
Olde Time Brewers Inc. (MA)	O-92/C-94		800	N/A	N/A			N/A	N/A	N/A
Walter Brewing Co. (WI)	O-91/C-94	N/A	N/A	N/A	N/A		N/A	N/A	N/A	
Aspen Beer Co. (CO)	C-93	N/A	400	N/A			N/A	N/A	N/A	
Saratoga Lager Brewing Co. (NJ)	O-91/C-93	N/A	N/A	N/A			N/A	N/A	N/A	
Ambier Brewing Inc. (WI)	C-92	N/A	N/A				N/A	N/A		
Braumeister Inc. (PA)	C-92	N/A	N/A				N/A	N/A		
Cleveland Brewing Co. (OH)	C-92	N/A	N/A				N/A	N/A		
Red Rock Beer Co. (AZ)	O-91/C-92	N/A	N/A				N/A	N/A		
Sun Valley Brewing Co. (ID)		1,000	N/A	‡			N/A	N/A	N/A	
Thousand Oaks Brewing Co. (CA)	C-92	N/A	N/A				N/A	N/A		
Vail Brewery Co. (CO)	C-92	346	N/A				N/A	N/A		
Connecticut Brewing Co. (CT)	C-91	N/A					N/A			
Hope Brewing Corp. (RI)	C-91	N/A					N/A			
Jersey Lager Beer Co. (NJ)	C-91	N/A					N/A			
Long Island Brewery Co. (NY)	C-91	N/A					N/A			
William Penn Brewing Co. (OR)	C-91	N/A					N/A			

Canadian Regional Breweries: Estimated Total Taxable Shipments

All figures are in hectoliters.
Totals, in many cases, are estimates reported to the Institute for Brewing Studies and may not reflect exact taxpaid amount.
O/C Denotes year opened or closed, if occurring between 1991 and 1995.
reO Denotes year reopened, if occurring between 1991 and 1995.
† Produces between 5 and 15 percent for other companies.

Company Name	O/C	1991	1992	1993	1994	1995	1992 % Growth	1993 % Growth	1994 % Growth	1995 % Growth
Pacific Western Brewing Co. (BC)		N/A	150,000	150,000	N/A	200,000	N/A	0	N/A	N/A
Sleeman Brewing & Malting Co. (ON) †		75,000	90,000	87,154	98,500	132,874	20	-3	13	35
Big Rock Brewery Ltd. (AB)		47,695	56,150	85,023	105,000	120,000	18	51	23	14
Okanagan Spring Brewery (BC)		34,000	50,000	65,000	69,971	95,481	47	30	8	36
Upper Canada Brewing Co. Ltd. (ON)		39,000	37,000	52,000	60,000	70,000	-5	41	15	17
Brick Brewing Co. Ltd. (ON)		42,000	44,500	51,000	67,500	67,500	6	15	32	0
Granville Island Brewing Co. (BC)		12,000	16,000	18,000	28,800	45,000	33	13	60	56
Unibroue Inc. (PQ)		2,600	12,000	N/A	28,000	38,000	362	N/A	N/A	36
Les Brasseurs du Nord Inc. (PQ)		9,300	14,000	17,204	21,500	25,835	51	23	25	20
Great Lakes Brewing Co. (ON)	C-91/ reO-91	500	5,000	N/A	N/A	25,000	900	N/A	N/A	N/A
Shaftebury Brewing Co. Ltd. (BC)		8,000	9,300	11,000	15,200	21,000	16	18	38	38
Brasserie McAuslan (PQ)		9,290	11,267	13,800	16,700	18,720	21	22	21	12
Creemore Springs Brewery Ltd. (ON)		10,500	11,700	13,000	16,500	18,000	11	11	27	9
Les Brasseurs G.M.T. (PQ)		6,240	N/A	N/A	12,047	17,000	N/A	N/A	N/A	41
Algonquin Brewery (ON)		45,500	45,000	65,000	46,500	N/A	-1	44	-28	N/A
Drummond Brewing Co. Ltd. (AB)		N/A	N/A	N/A	150,404	N/A	N/A	N/A	N/A	N/A
Great Western Brewing Co. (SK)		N/A	55,000	N/A	60,000	N/A	N/A	N/A	N/A	N/A
Lakeport Brewing Corp. (ON)	O-92		N/A	N/A	N/A	N/A	N/A	N/A	N/A	N/A
Northern Breweries Ltd. (ON)		N/A	N/A	N/A	N/A	N/A	N/A	N/A	N/A	N/A
Oland Breweries Ltd. (NS)		N/A	N/A	N/A	N/A	N/A	N/A	N/A	N/A	N/A

Canadian Microbreweries: Estimated Total Taxable Shipments

All figures are in hectoliters.
Totals, in many cases, are estimates reported to the Institute for Brewing Studies and may not reflect exact taxpaid amount.
O/C Denotes year opened or closed, if occurring between 1991 and 1995.
† Produces between 5 and 15 percent for other companies.

Company Name	O/C	1991	1992	1993	1994	1995	1992 % Growth	1993 % Growth	1994 % Growth	1995 % Growth
Conners Brewing Co. Ltd. (ON)		N/A	8,015	11,500	13,130	15,000	N/A	43	14	14
Vancouver Island Brewing Co. (BC)		N/A	14,000	12,000	12,000	14,000	N/A	-14	0	17
Brasal-Brasserie Allemande (PQ)		8,000	6,000	10,000	12,000	12,000	-25	67	20	0
Niagara Falls Brewing Co. (ON)		6,000	6,000	12,480	N/A	9,284	0	108	N/A	N/A
Whistler Brewing Co. (BC)		7,600	6,860	11,000	N/A	9,000	-10	60	N/A	N/A
Bowen Island Brewing Co. (BC)	O-94				N/A	6,500			N/A	N/A
Hart Breweries Ltd. (ON) †	O-91	480	2,509	4,024	5,500	6,500	423	60	37	18
Wellington County Brewery Ltd. (ON)		N/A	5,000	8,000	N/A	6,000	N/A	60	N/A	N/A
Amsterdam Brewing Co. (ON)		1,400	1,180	N/A	N/A	5,000	-16	N/A	N/A	N/A
Bear Brewing Co. (BC)	O-95					4,500				
Tall Ship Ale Co. (BC)	O-94				N/A	4,400			N/A	N/A
Nelson Brewing Co. (BC)	O-91	1,000	2,500	3,500	3,120	2,000	150	40	-11	-36
Banff Brewery Corp. (AB)	O-95					1,900				
Fort Garry Brewing Co. (MB)	O-95					1,758				
Bow Valley Brewing Co. (AB)	O-95					1,400				
Trafalgar Brewing Co. (ON)	O-93			N/A	1,040	1,000		N/A	N/A	-4

Beer and Brewery Statistics

Company Name	O/C	1991	1992	1993	1994	1995	1992 % Growth	1993 % Growth	1994 % Growth	1995 % Growth
Tin Whistle Brewing Co. (BC)	O-95					250				
Alley Kat Brewing Co. (AB)	O-95					N/A				N/A
Arctic Brewing Co. (NWT)	O-93			N/A	N/A	N/A		N/A	N/A	N/A
Beau Ce Broue (PQ)	O-95					N/A				N/A
La Brasserie Portneuvoise (PQ)	O-91	N/A	990	N/A	N/A	N/A	N/A	N/A	N/A	N/A
La Brasseurs de L'Anse Saint-Jean (PQ)	O-95					N/A				N/A
Copperhead Brewing Co. Ltd. (ON)	O-95					N/A				N/A
Elora Brewing Ltd./ Taylor & Bate Brewery (ON)		N/A	N/A	N/A	400	N/A	N/A	N/A	N/A	N/A
F & M Breweries Ltd. (ON)	O-95					N/A				N/A
Glatt Bros. Brewing Co. (ON)	O-93			N/A	2,000	N/A		N/A	N/A	N/A
Horseshoe Bay Brewing Co. Ltd. (BC)		N/A	N/A	960	N/A	N/A	N/A	N/A	N/A	N/A
Old Credit Brewing Co. (ON)	O-94				N/A	N/A			N/A	N/A
Picaroons Brewing Co. (NB)	O-95					N/A				N/A
Quinte Brewery (ON)	O-94				N/A	N/A			N/A	N/A
Robinson Brewing Co. (ON)	O-94				N/A	N/A			N/A	N/A
Russell Brewing Co. (BC)	O-95					N/A				N/A
Steamworks Brewing Co. (BC)	O-95					N/A				N/A
Storm Brewing Co. (BC)	O-95					N/A				N/A
Thames Valley Brewing Co. (ON)	O-92		160	1,138	N/A	N/A		611	N/A	N/A
Canada's Finest Beers Ltd. (ON)	O-93/C-95			N/A	N/A	N/A		N/A	N/A	N/A
Hometown Breweries Ltd. (ON)	O-93/C-95			N/A	N/A	N/A		N/A	N/A	N/A
Angel Brewing Co. (ON)	O-93/C-94			N/A				N/A	N/A	
Strathcona Brewing Co. Inc. (AB)	C-93	N/A	1,000	N/A			N/A	N/A		
Sunshine Coast Brewers Ltd. (BC)	C-92	N/A	N/A			N/A				

Canadian Brewpubs: Estimated Total Taxable Shipments

All figures are in hectoliters.
Totals, in many cases, are estimates reported to the Institute for Brewing Studies and may not reflect exact taxpaid amount.
O/C Denotes year opened or closed, if occurring between 1991 and 1995.
§ Produces between 25 and 50 percent for other companies.

Company Name	O/C	1991	1992	1993	1994	1995	1992 % Growth	1993 % Growth	1994 % Growth	1995 % Growth
Vieux Copenhagen Brasseurs (PQ)	O-95					2,500				
Saskatoon Brewing Co./ Cheers Roadhouse Inn (SK)	O-91	1,900	1,200	1,242	1,700	1,920	-37	4	37	13
Spinnakers Brewpub Inc. (BC)		1,550	1,500	N/A	N/A	1,550	-3	N/A	N/A	N/A
Brewsters Brewing Co. & Restaurant (No. 2) (AB)	O-91	100	1,100	1,500	1,260	1,410	1,000	36	-16	12
Swans Brewpub/ Buckerfield Brewery (BC)		1,475	1,400	1,500	1,250	1,350	-5	7	-17	8
Mission Bridge Brewing Co. (AB)	O-95					1,280				
Lion Brewery and Museum (ON)		1,152	1,350	1,200	1,200	1,200	17	-11	0	0
Brewsters Brewing Co. & Restaurant (No. 1) (SK)		580	600	600	800	1,020	3	0	33	28
Post-Production Bistro (ON)	O-95					1,000				
Denison's Brewing Co. & Restaurant/Growlers' Bar (ON)		1,250	978	900	918	941	-22	-8	2	3
Bushwakker Brewing Co. Ltd. (SK)	O-91	800	750	780	880	930	-6	4	13	6
Brewsters Brewing Co. & Restaurant (No. 4) (AB)	O-92		450	750	800	720		67	7	-10
Le Cheval Blanc (PQ)		600	600	585	550	700	0	-3	-6	27
La Cervoise (PQ)		630	700	595	590	660	11	-15	-1	12
Granite Brewery (No. 2) (ON)	O-91	550	650	700	580	580	18	8	-17	0

Institute for Brewing Studies

Beer and Brewery Statistics

Company Name	O/C	1991	1992	1993	1994	1995	1992 % Growth	1993 % Growth	1994 % Growth	1995 % Growth
Sailor Hagar's Brew Pub (ON)	O-94				400	550				38
Al Frisco's (ON)	O-94				N/A	500			N/A	N/A
Bar L'Inox (PQ)		450	520	500	500	500	16	-4	0	0
Brewsters Brewing Co. & Restaurant (No. 6) (AB)	O-95					480				
Brewsters Brewing Co. & Restaurant (No. 3) at the Cornerstone Inn (SK)	O-91	90	480	400	400	440	433	-17	0	10
Port Arthur Brasserie and Brewpub (ON)		485	360	400	320	400	-26	11	-20	25
CEEPS Barney's Ltd. (ON)	O-91	250	300	360	400	360	20	20	11	-10
Kingston Brewing Co. Ltd. (ON)		450	N/A	317	345	306	N/A	N/A	9	-11
Brewsters Brewing Co. & Restaurant (No. 5) (SK)	O-95					240				
Tracks Brewpub (ON)		170	140	N/A	226	180	-18	N/A	N/A	-20
Addington's (ON)	O-95					N/A				N/A
Barley Mill Brewpub (SK)		675	432	N/A	N/A	N/A	-36	N/A	N/A	N/A
Blue Anchor Brewery (ON)		170	N/A	200	N/A	N/A	N/A	N/A	-100	
Bonzzini's Brewpub (SK)	O-91	N/A	N/A	N/A	960	N/A	N/A	N/A	N/A	N/A
C. C.'s Brew Pub (ON)		360	N/A	N/A	N/A	N/A	N/A	N/A	N/A	N/A
Charley's Tavern (ON)		N/A	N/A	N/A	N/A	N/A	N/A	N/A	N/A	N/A
Chubby's Brewpub (SK)	O-94				N/A	N/A			N/A	N/A
Clark's Crossing Brewpub (SK)		300	800	N/A	550	N/A	167	N/A	N/A	N/A
Crocodile Club (PQ)		400	290	N/A	400	N/A	-28	N/A	N/A	N/A
Feathers (ON)	O-95					N/A				N/A
Fox and Hounds Brewpub (SK)		650	960	N/A	120	N/A	48	N/A	N/A	N/A
Golden Lion Brewing Co. (PQ) §		N/A	830	N/A	560	N/A	N/A	N/A	N/A	N/A
Granite Brewery (NS)		N/A	400	N/A	450	N/A	N/A	N/A	N/A	N/A
Heidelberg Restaurant and Brewery (ON)		N/A	107	180	N/A	N/A	N/A	68	N/A	N/A
James Gate (ON)	O-92		N/A	N/A	N/A	N/A	N/A	N/A	N/A	N/A
MacBradee's Brewing Co. (SK)	O-93			N/A	N/A	N/A		N/A	N/A	N/A
Major's Brew House (ON)	O-95					N/A				N/A
Master's Brasserie and Brewpub (ON)		512	N/A	N/A	N/A	N/A	N/A	N/A	N/A	N/A
Mon Village Brewery (PQ)		235	N/A	N/A	N/A	N/A	N/A	N/A	N/A	N/A
O'Toole's (ON)	O-93			N/A	150	N/A		N/A	N/A	N/A
Queen's Inn/Taylor and Bate Ltd. (ON)		N/A	40	N/A	N/A	N/A	N/A	N/A	N/A	N/A
La Taverne du Sergeant Recruiter (PQ)	O-94				150	N/A				N/A
Yale Town Brewing Co. (BC)	O-94				N/A	N/A			N/A	N/A
Last Straw (SK)	O-91	200	N/A	N/A	N/A	N/A	N/A	N/A	N/A	N/A
Prairie Inn Cottage Brewery (BC)	C-95	N/A	400	N/A	N/A	N/A	N/A	N/A	N/A	N/A
Quinn's on the Danforth (ON)	O-92/C-95		N/A	45	N/A	N/A	N/A	N/A	N/A	N/A
Lighthouse Brewpub/ Flying Dutchman Hotel (ON)	C-94	N/A	N/A	120	N/A		N/A	N/A	N/A	
Marconi's Steak and Pasta House Ltd. (ON)	C-94	N/A	N/A	N/A	N/A		N/A	N/A	N/A	
Spruce Goose Brewing Co. (ON)	O-91/C-94	100	N/A	80	N/A		N/A	N/A	N/A	
Union Station Brew Pub (ON)	C-94	N/A	N/A	N/A	N/A		N/A	N/A	N/A	
Brax 'n' Brew (ON)	C-93	300	100	N/A			-67	N/A		
Crocodile Club St. Laurent (PQ)	C-93	300	350	N/A			17	N/A		
Jolly Friar Brewpub and Dining Lounge (ON)	C-93	425	345	N/A			-19	N/A		
Rotterdam Brewing Co. (ON)	C-93	1,000	820	N/A			-18	N/A		
Tapsters Brewhouse and Restaurant (ON)	C-93		330	264	N/A			-20	N/A	
Vinifera Bar and Grill (ON)	O-92/C-93		N/A	550			N/A	N/A		
Boccalino Pasta Bistro (AB)	C-92	250	N/A				N/A			
Luxembourg Brewpub (No. 4) (ON)	O-91/C-92	100	N/A				N/A			
Madawaska Tavern (ON)	C-92	N/A	N/A				N/A			
Pepperwood Bistro (ON)	O-91/C-92	N/A	N/A				N/A			
Winchester Arms (ON)	C-92	N/A	N/A				N/A			

Large Brewers' Shipments 1990–1995

Barrels times 1,000

	1990	1991	1992	1993	1994	1995
Anheuser-Busch	86,499	86,037	86,846	87,306	*88,159	*87,539
Miller	43,500	43,556	42,145	**44,024	**45,200	**45,000
Coors	19,300	19,550	20,000	20,000	20,200	20,000
Stroh	16,200	14,800	14,000	12,610	11,850	10,780
Heileman	10,914	9,377	9,133	8,940	8,315	7,635
Pabst	6,700	6,600	6,900	7,000	6,630	6,550
Labatt USA	n/a	1,420	1,500	1,730	1,865	***2,275
Genesee	2,200	2,220	2,150	2,000	1,800	1,870
Barton	n/a	750	825	945	1,070	1,310
Top Brewers	**185,313**	**178,370**	**170,899**	**184,555**	**185,089**	**182,959**
All Others	4,854	****9,587	****17,825	5,175	5,711	6,536
Domestic Brewers	**190,167**	**187,957**	**188,724**	****188,530**	****188,500**	****187,370**
Imports	8,922	8,031	8,409	**9,348	**10,600	**11,450
Total	**199,089**	**195,988**	**197,133**	****197,778**	****199,100**	****198,820**

Notes:

1995 totals are estimates as of 3/1/96. Import data is complete through November, 1995. Domestic data is complete through September, 1995. Figures are subject to revision as additional data becomes available.

*Anheuser-Busch 1994 figure excludes 370,000 barrels of Kirin Ice contract brewed for Kirin, and an unknow, but similar, amount in 1995.

**Miller figure for 1995 includes 2.125 million barrels of Molson products; Miller figure for 1994 includes 2.3 million barrels of Molson products; Miller figure for 1993 includes 1.2 million barrels of Molson products. Those barrels included with Miller, Top Brewers, Imports, and Total, excluded from Domestic Brewers total to avoid double-counting.

***Includes 1,075,000 barrels brewed for Latrob.

****Figures reported are unusually high due to changes in "Top Brewers" for 1995 table.

Coors figures adjusted to show shipments for calendar years.

Domestic Brewers total equals taxpaid plus taxfree shipments, including non-alcohol and exports. All Others derived by subtracting major brewers from this figure. Resulting series hard to reconcile in some years. Few brewers report "official" totals.

All Others includes approximately 425,000 barrels of malt beverages used in wine and spirit coolers in 1991; 900,000 barrels in 1992; 1.5 million barrels in 1993; 1.7 million barrels in 1994; and an estimated 2 million barrels in 1995.

Compiled using figures courtesy of *Beer Marketer's Insights*.

Beer and Brewery Statistics

Large Brewers' Market Share 1990-1994

Percent of Total Beer Shipments*

	1990	1991	1992	1993	1994	1995
Anheuser-Busch	43.4	43.9	44.1	44.1	44.3	44.0
Miller	21.8	22.2	21.4	22.2	22.6	22.6
Coors	9.7	10.0	10.1	10.1	10.1	10.1
Stroh	8.1	7.6	7.1	6.4	5.9	5.4
Heileman	5.5	4.8	4.6	4.5	4.2	3.8
Pabst	3.4	3.4	3.5	3.5	3.3	3.3
Labatt USA	n/a	0.7	0.8	0.9	0.9	1.1
Genesee	1.1	1.1	1.1	1.0	0.9	0.9
Barton	n/a	0.4	0.4	0.5	0.5	0.7
Top Brewers	**93.0**	**94.1**	**93.1**	**93.2**	**92.7**	**91.9**
Imports	4.6	4.2	4.4	4.9	5.5	6.0
Others Domestic	2.4	2.6	3.4	3.5	3.9	4.5

***Note:** Anheuser-Busch figure for 1994 excludes 370,000 barrels contract brewed for Kirin, and an unknown, but similar, amount in 1995. Miller figure for 1995 includes 2.125 million barrels of Molson USA; Miller figure for 1994 includes 2.3 million barrels of Molson USA; Miller figure for 1993 includes 1.2 million barrels of Molson products. Because brewers include export shipments with total shipments, figures for major brewers and "Other Domestic" show share of total shipments, including domestic taxpaid, taxfree (exports and no-alcohol), imports, and malt coolers sold by vintners from 1991 to 1994. If export data and/or malt cooler shipments were excluded, some of the share figures might be slightly higher, others would remain unchanged. Figures for imports only show share of taxpaid plus imports to give a more accurate picture of import share in the United States. Because of these adjustments and rounding, totals do not add exactly to 100 percent.

Compiled using figures courtesy of *Beer Marketer's Insights*.

United States Imports: Sales
(In 31-Gallon Barrels)

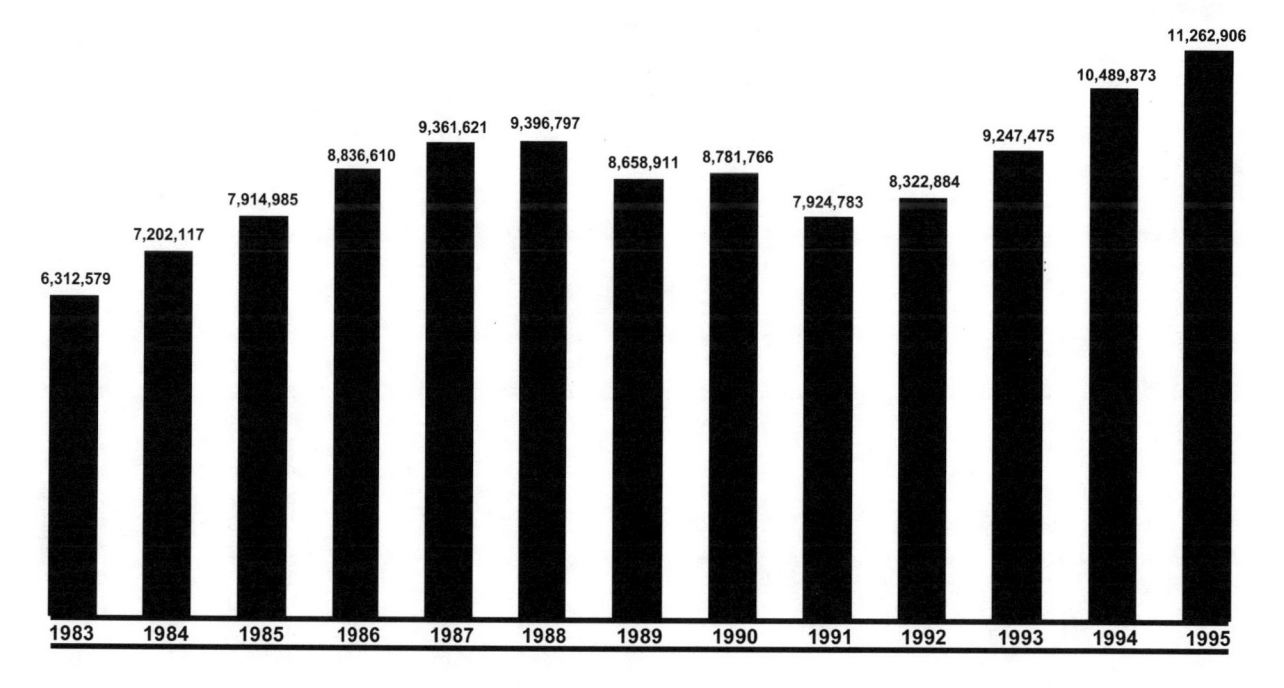

Year	Barrels
1983	6,312,579
1984	7,202,117
1985	7,914,985
1986	8,836,610
1987	9,361,621
1988	9,396,797
1989	8,658,911
1990	8,781,766
1991	7,924,783
1992	8,322,884
1993	9,247,475
1994	10,489,873
1995	11,262,906

Information provided by the Beer Institute, courtesy of the U.S. Department of Commerce.

Beer and Brewery Statistics

Leading Imported Beer Brands

In millions of gallons. Listed in order of estimated 1994 market share.
*Distributed by Heineken.

	1987	% of Market	1988	% of Market	1989	% of Market	1990	% of Market	1991	% of Market	1992	% of Market	1993	% of Market	1994	% of Market	1995	% of Market
Heineken	76.1	26.2	73.0	25.1	70.0	26.0	67.5	24.7	58.7	24.0	60.5	23.4	64.0	23.4	68.5	21.7	76.5	23.2
Corona Extra	51.8	17.8	48.0	16.5	36.9	13.7	28.1	10.3	26.0	10.6	29.5	11.4	31.5	11.5	36.7	11.7	46.1	14.0
Molson Ice	—	—	—	—	—	—	—	—	—	—	—	—	2.3	0.8	36.9	11.7	33.0	10.0
Becks	24.5	8.4	26.0	8.9	24.1	9.0	23.6	8.7	18.0	7.3	18.0	7.0	18.5	6.8	19.0	6.0	20.0	6.1
Foster's	7.2	2.5	9.0	3.1	6.6	2.5	6.4	2.3	7.2	2.9	7.9	3.1	8.2	3.0	9.8	3.1	16.8	3.3
Molson Golden	22.1	7.6	22.3	7.7	21.2	7.9	19.8	7.3	19.3	7.9	19.0	7.4	19.0	6.9	14.0	4.4	13.8	4.2
Amstel Light *	8.3	2.9	8.7	3.0	9.8	3.6	11.0	4.0	11.2	4.6	11.0	4.3	11.5	4.2	11.4	3.6	11.7	3.5
Labatt's Blue	11.2	3.9	12.4	4.3	13.1	4.9	13.6	5.0	13.3	5.4	13.3	5.2	13.9	5.1	14.3	4.5	10.0	3.0
Guinness	4.7	1.6	5.0	1.7	5.5	2.0	5.9	2.2	5.7	2.3	5.5	2.2	8.5	3.1	9.0	2.9	9.5	2.9
Labatt's Ice	—	—	—	—	—	—	—	—	—	—	—	—	1.9	0.7	7.7	2.4	9.0	2.7
Tecate	6.1	2.1	7.0	2.4	7.2	2.7	8.3	3.0	8.5	3.5	8.6	3.3	8.7	3.2	8.9	2.8	9.0	2.7
Bass Ale	4.0	1.4	5.0	1.7	5.0	1.9	5.6	2.1	5.5	2.2	5.5	2.1	7.7	2.8	8.5	2.7	8.7	2.6
Moosehead	13.3	4.6	13.0	4.5	11.0	4.1	9.7	3.6	8.0	3.3	7.0	2.7	8.0	2.9	7.8	2.5	7.6	2.3
Dos Equis	4.5	1.6	4.5	1.5	4.5	1.7	4.6	1.7	4.6	1.9	4.6	1.8	4.6	1.7	4.7	1.5	5.0	1.5
St. Pauli Girl	7.4	2.5	6.5	2.2	5.7	2.1	5.8	2.5	4.7	1.9	4.5	1.7	4.4	1.6	4.4	1.4	4.4	1.3
Modelo Especial	—	—	—	—	—	—	1.0	0.4	1.1	0.4	1.3	0.5	1.8	0.7	3.1	1.0	3.5	1.1
Corona Light	—	—	—	—	2.1	0.8	3.2	0.4	2.5	1.0	2.5	1.0	2.5	0.9	2.5	0.8	3.4	1.0
Molson Light	3.5	1.2	3.4	1.2	3.8	1.4	4.0	1.5	4.2	1.7	4.2	1.6	4.2	1.5	3.8	1.2	3.2	1.0
Sapporo	2.6	0.9	2.2	0.8	2.3	0.9	2.4	0.9	2.5	1.0	2.6	1.0	2.6	1.0	2.8	0.9	2.7	0.8
Molson Canadian	3.9	1.3	3.8	1.3	3.5	1.3	3.5	1.3	3.5	1.4	3.5	1.4	3.4	1.2	2.9	0.9	2.5	0.8
Carlsburg	—	—	—	—	—	—	1.8	0.9	1.8	0.7	1.8	0.7	1.8	0.7	2.0	0.6	2.2	0.7
Grolsch	2.3	0.8	2.6	0.9	2.8	1.0	2.5	0.9	2.2	0.9	2.2	0.9	2.2	0.8	2.4	0.8	2.1	0.6
Harp	1.6	0.6	1.7	0.6	1.8	0.7	2.0	0.7	2.0	0.8	2.0	0.8	2.0	0.7	2.0	0.6	2.0	0.6
Tsingtao	2.3	0.8	2.7	0.9	2.5	0.9	2.1	0.8	2.1	0.9	2.0	0.8	2.0	0.7	1.9	0.6	2.0	0.6
Molson Export	1.9	0.7	1.9	0.7	1.8	0.7	1.8	0.7	1.8	0.7	1.8	0.7	1.7	0.6	1.8	0.6	1.8	0.5
Pacifico	—	—	—	—	—	—	1.0	0.4	1.0	0.4	1.1	0.4	1.2	0.4	1.2	0.4	1.6	0.5
Warsteiner	—	—	—	—	—	—	—	—	—	—	—	—	1.5	0.5	1.7	0.5	1.6	0.5
Asahi	—	—	0.4	0.1	1.1	0.4	1.3	0.5	1.4	0.6	1.5	0.6	1.5	0.5	1.8	0.6	1.5	0.5
Kirin	2.2	0.8	2.3	0.8	1.4	0.5	1.2	0.4	1.0	0.4	1.1	0.4	1.2	0.4	1.4	0.4	1.5	0.5
Red Stripe	—	—	—	—	—	—	—	—	0.8	0.3	1.1	0.4	1.2	0.4	1.2	0.4	1.5	0.5
Tecate Light	—	—	—	—	—	—	—	—	—	—	—	—	1.3	0.5	1.3	0.4	1.5	0.5
Spaten	—	—	—	—	—	—	1.4	0.5	1.5	0.6	1.5	0.6	1.4	0.5	1.4	0.4	1.4	0.4
Labatt's Blue Light	0.9	0.3	1.7	0.6	1.7	0.6	2.1	0.8	2.2	0.9	2.2	0.9	2.3	0.8	2.4	0.8	1.3	0.4
Negra Modelo	—	—	—	—	—	—	0.3	0.1	0.5	0.2	0.7	0.3	0.9	0.3	1.0	0.3	1.3	0.4
Carta Blanca	1.4	0.5	1.2	0.4	1.0	0.4	0.8	0.3	1.0	0.4	1.1	0.4	1.1	0.4	1.1	0.3	1.1	0.3
Chihuahua	2.0	0.7	1.5	0.5	1.2	0.4	0.9	0.3	0.6	0.2	0.9	0.3	1.1	0.4	1.1	0.3	1.1	0.3
Old Vienna/O. V. Lt.	—	—	—	—	—	—	N/A	N/A	3.2	1.3	2.9	1.1	2.6	1.0	1.8	0.6	1.0	0.3
Watney's	1.4	0.5	1.5	0.5	1.6	0.6	1.8	0.7	1.8	0.7	1.8	0.7	1.8	0.7	1.8	0.6	1.0	0.3
Kirin Dry	—	—	—	—	1.0	0.4	0.9	0.3	0.8	0.3	0.8	0.3	0.8	0.3	0.8	0.3	0.8	0.2
Moretti	—	—	—	—	—	—	—	—	0.4	0.2	0.5	0.2	0.5	0.2	0.4	0.1	0.6	0.2
Murphy's Stout	—	—	—	—	—	—	—	—	—	—	0.1	0.0	0.2	0.1	0.4	0.1	0.6	0.2
Double Diamond	—	—	—	—	—	—	—	—	—	—	—	—	0.4	0.1	0.4	0.1	0.4	0.1
Labatt's "50" Ale	1.4	0.5	1.2	0.4	1.4	0.5	1.2	0.4	0.9	0.4	0.9	0.3	0.6	0.2	0.5	0.2	0.4	0.1
Kronenborg	—	—	—	—	—	—	—	—	—	—	—	—	—	—	0.4	0.1	0.4	0.1
Peroni	—	—	—	—	—	—	—	—	—	—	—	—	0.3	0.1	0.4	0.1	0.4	0.1
Bohemia	—	—	—	—	—	—	—	—	1.1	0.4	1.3	0.5	1.4	0.5	1.6	0.5	0.2	0.1
John Courage	—	—	—	—	—	—	—	—	—	—	—	—	—	—	0.4	0.1	0.2	0.1
Molson Special Dry	—	—	—	—	—	—	—	—	—	—	—	—	—	—	0.4	0.1	0.2	0.1
Sol	1.9	0.7	2.5	0.9	1.5	0.6	0.9	0.3	0.6	0.2	0.3	0.1	0.2	0.1	0.2	0.1	0.2	0.1
O'Keefe	1.3	0.4	1.3	0.4	1.3	0.5	1.1	0.4	0.8	0.3	0.7	0.3	0.6	0.2	0.3	0.1	0.1	0.1
Sapporo Giginjikomi	—	—	0.6	0.2	0.7	0.3	0.5	0.2	0.5	0.2	0.5	0.2	0.5	0.2	0.2	0.1	—	—
Steinlager	—	—	—	—	—	—	—	—	1.6	0.7	1.9	0.7	2.3	0.8	—	—	—	—
Others	31.7	6.2	32.7	6.2	29.7	5.0	25.3	9.2	8.8	4.0	16.5	6.4	11.5	4.5	8.0	3.7	6.1	4.4
Total	**290.3**	**100.0**	**291.3**	**100.0**	**269.2**	**100.0**	**272.8**	**100.0**	**244.9**	**100.0**	**254.2**	**100.0**	**273.6**	**100.0**	**320.4**	**102.6**	**334.5**	**102.3**

Reprinted courtesy of John C. Maxwell Jr., Wheat First Securities.

Beer and Brewery Statistics

1994 POPULATION AND MALT BEVERAGE CONSUMPTION

	State	Total Population (000)	Total Malt Beverage Consumption (000) Gallons	Total Per Capita Consumption (gallons)
1.	Alabama	4,219	88,408	21.0
2.	Alaska	606	14,943	24.7
3.	Arizona	4,075	110,775	27.2
4.	Arkansas	2,453	48,255	19.7
5.	California	31,431	633,314	20.1
6.	Colorado	3,656	84,462	23.1
7.	Connecticut	3,275	58,687	17.9
8.	Delaware	706	18,259	25.9
9.	District of Columbia	570	16,371	28.7
10.	Florida	13,953	360,419	25.8
11.	Georgia	7,055	152,539	21.4
12.	Hawaii	1,179	30,011	25.5
13.	Idaho	1,133	24,289	21.4
14.	Illinois	11,752	277,597	23.6
15.	Indiana	5,752	118,516	20.6
16.	Iowa	2,829	65,911	23.3
17.	Kansas	2,554	49,678	19.5
18.	Kentucky	3,827	74,967	19.6
19.	Louisiana	4,315	117,077	27.1
20.	Maine	1,240	25,178	20.3
21.	Maryland	5,006	96,383	19.3
22.	Massachusetts	6,041	129,346	21.4
23.	Michigan	9,496	207,374	21.8
24.	Minnesota	4,567	102,637	22.5
25.	Mississippi	2,669	65,257	24.5
26.	Missouri	5,278	127,830	24.2
27.	Montana	856	22,743	26.6
28.	Nebraska	1,623	40,045	24.7
29.	Nevada	1,457	51,203	35.1
30.	New Hampshire	1,137	35,198	31.0
31.	New Jersey	7,904	149,770	18.9
32.	New Mexico	1,654	41,971	25.4
33.	New York	18,169	324,105	17.8
34.	North Carolina	7,070	147,309	20.8
35.	North Dakota	638	16,476	25.8
36.	Ohio	11,102	255,390	23.0
37.	Oklahoma	3,258	66,504	20.4
38.	Oregon	3,086	68,372	22.2
39.	Pennsylvania	12,052	281,581	23.4
40.	Rhode Island	997	22,541	22.6
41.	South Carolina	3,664	90,604	24.7
42.	South Dakota	721	17,530	24.3
43.	Tennessee	5,175	111,033	21.5
44.	Texas	18,378	519,796	28.3
45.	Utah	1,908	24,558	12.9
46.	Vermont	580	13,523	23.3
47.	Virginia	6,552	141,893	21.7
48.	Washington	5,343	111,684	20.9
49.	West Virginia	1,822	39,211	21.5
50.	Wisconsin	5,082	143,951	28.3
51.	Wyoming	476	11,887	25.0
	Totals	260,341	5,847,361	22.5

Reprinted from *Brewers Almanac 1995*, courtesy of the Beer Institute.

Beer and Brewery Statistics

SEASONAL INDEX OF PRODUCTION AND WITHDRAWALS
For 1995

MONTH	PRODUCTION	PACKAGED WITHDRAWALS	DRAUGHT WITHDRAWALS	TOTAL TAXPAID WITHDRAWALS
January	95	89	87	89
February	93	88	86	88
March	106	103	101	102
April	104	100	102	101
May	111	111	105	109
June	113	115	113	114
July	109	112	114	112
August	108	111	114	111
September	95	98	103	100
October	97	97	100	98
November	86	89	89	89
December	83	87	86	87
Average	100	100	100	100

MALT BEVERAGE SALES BY STATES—For Calendar Year 1994
TAXABLE REMOVALS BY STATE AND COMBINATION GROUPINGS

STATE	TAXPAID SALES PACKAGED	TAXPAID KEG SALES	TOTAL TAXABLE SALES
California	17,596,023	1,896,580	19,492,603
Colorado	16,779,959	2,475,871	19,255,830
Florida	9,175,963	975,774	10,151,737
Minnesota	2,567,196	200,738	2,767,934
North Carolina	9,488,540	619,439	10,107,979
New Jersey	7,555,189	1,185,496	8,740,685
New York	9,130,428	1,582,843	10,713,271
Oregon	1,183,600	228,436	1,412,036
Pennsylvania	4,479,321	762,987	5,242,308
Texas	19,765,166	1,153,436	20,918,602
Virginia	10,633,908	1,765,095	12,399,003
Washington	2,534,418	327,287	2,861,705
Wisconsin	10,905,613	2,042,397	12,948,010
AZ, HA, IA, ID, MO, NE, MT, NV, NM	11,425,994	1,688,125	13,114,119
IN, MI, OH, IL	11,154,159	1,636,597	12,790,756
NH, RI, ME, MA, VT	2,707,311	443,401	3,150,712
TN, GA, KY, LA, MD, SC	13,025,491	584,274	13,609,765
Total	160,108,279	19,568,776	179,677,055

Reprinted from *Brewers Almanac 1995*, courtesy of the Beer Institute.

Beer and Brewery Statistics

PRODUCTION DRAUGHT AND PACKAGED SALES AND TOTAL TAXPAID WITHDRAWALS OF MALT BEVERAGES
For Calendar Years 1946-1994 (Quantities in 31 Gallon Barrels)

Calendar Year	Production	Packaged Sales	% of Total	Draught Sales	% of Total	Total Taxpaid Withdrawals
1946	83,312,516	53,010,253	66.6	26,530,243	33.4	79,540,496
1947	91,742,212	58,899,477	67.6	28,272,887	32.4	87,172,334
1948	88,125,320	58,699,355	69.0	26,367,959	31.0	85,067,314
1949	88,618,322	59,443,805	70.3	25,113,802	29.7	84,557,607
1950	88,178,356	59,487,521	71.8	23,342,616	28.2	82,830,137
1951	89,742,138	61,706,743	73.6	22,116,893	26.4	83,823,636
1952	90,489,824	63,359,469	74.7	21,477,011	25.3	84,836,480
1953	92,104,063	65,830,505	76.5	20,214,611	23.5	86,045,116
1954	88,940,268	63,927,035	76.7	19,377,986	23.3	83,305,021
1955	90,285,488	66,179,019	77.9	18,798,255	22.1	84,977,274
1956	90,338,445	67,087,002	78.9	17,921,154	21.1	85,008,156
1957	89,465,986	66,982,200	79.4	17,388,825	20.6	84,371,025
1958	90,120,512	67,168,341	79.6	17,256,368	20.4	84,424,709
1959	93,127,427	70,308,462	80.2	17,313,897	19.8	87,622,359
1960	93,415,363	70,955,595	80.7	16,957,244	19.3	87,912,839
1961	95,030,031	71,910,757	80.8	17,117,674	19.2	89,028,431
1962	96,831,989	74,128,498	81.3	17,068,659	18.7	91,197,157
1963	100,631,563	76,343,134	81.4	17,446,808	18.6	93,789,942
1964	105,897,968	80,685,951	81.8	17,958,041	18.2	98,643,992
1965	108,221,725	82,624,078	82.3	17,796,839	17.7	100,420,917
1966	113,037,193	86,531,831	83.0	17,730,210	17.0	104,262,041
1967	116,550,659	89,579,475	83.7	17,394,922	16.3	106,974,397
1968	122,407,762	94,007,957	84.4	17,407,741	15.6	111,415,698
1969	127,311,042	98,991,915	85.1	17,279,482	14.9	116,271,397
1970	133,123,267	104,619,875	85.9	17,240,131	14.1	121,860,006
1971	137,479,910	110,026,703	86.4	17,370,566	13.6	127,397,269
1972	141,336,930	114,219,578	86.7	17,589,085	13.3	131,808,663
1973	148,601,510	120,340,835	86.9	18,127,596	13.1	138,468,431
1974	156,147,443	127,277,705	87.5	18,236,377	12.5	145,464,082
1975	160,598,916	130,229,488	87.6	18,414,297	12.4	148,643,785
1976	163,656,955	132,125,154	87.9	18,262,233	12.1	150,387,387
1977	170,507,857	138,673,342	88.4	18,240,789	11.6	156,914,131
1978	179,656,544	144,585,652	88.9	18,120,235	11.1	162,705,887
1979	184,187,771	148,684,013	88.4	19,431,684	11.6	168,115,697
1980	194,086,267	152,346,481	87.9	21,020,539	12.1	173,367,020
1981	193,687,085	154,545,763	87.5	22,150,730	12.5	176,696,493
1982	194,349,406	153,606,164	87.0	22,968,671	13.0	176,574,835
1983	195,123,375	154,186,944	86.9	23,307,984	13.1	177,494,928
1984	193,021,392	152,640,123	86.9	22,839,376	13.1	175,479,499
1985	193,307,822	153,362,068	87.6	21,769,542	12.4	175,131,610
1986	196,498,984	157,422,686	88.1	21,298,341	11.9	178,721,027
1987	195,420,205	156,872,204	88.2	20,976,382	11.8	177,848,586
1988	198,024,766	157,934,409	88.6	20,299,638	11.4	178,234,047
1989	200,124,365	159,433,057	88.9	19,963,928	11.1	179,396,985
1990	203,658,410	163,998,656	88.9	20,475,177	11.1	184,473,833
1991	202,370,518	160,930,740	88.7	20,518,639	11.3	181,449,379
1992	202,107,376	159,809,506	88.4	21,014,744	11.6	180,824,250
1993r	202,638,598	160,337,440	88.6	20,563,370	11.4	180,900,810
1994*	202,100,000	160,108,279	89.1	19,568,776	10.9	179,677,055

Source: Treasury Department, Bureau of Alcohol, Tobacco and Firearms.
r-revised
*Subject to revision

13

Reprinted from *Brewers Almanac 1995*, courtesy of the Beer Institute.

Institute for Brewing Studies

Beer and Brewery Statistics

SHIPMENT OF MALT BEVERAGES BY GEOGRAPHICAL DIVISION
Calendar Years Ended December 31, 1985 - 1994

REGION	1985	1986	1987	1988	1989
New England (CT, ME, MA, NH, RI, VT)	9,956,483	10,057,162	10,141,240	10,164,403	9,886,378
Middle Atlantic (NJ, NY, PA)	26,630,870	26,607,014	26,994,351	26,960,825	26,258,680
East North Central (IL, IN, MI, OH, WI)	33,035,656	33,208,724	33,422,935	33,358,661	33,006,277
West North Central (IA, KS, MN, MO, NE, ND, SD)	12,938,355	13,052,380	13,115,616	12,999,661	13,024,642
South Atlantic (DE, DC, FL, GA, MD, NC, SC, VA, WV)	30,965,710	32,188,374	32,905,808	32,841,062	33,388,327
East South Central (AL, KY, MS, TN)	9,471,797	9,888,716	9,951,846	10,113,497	9,966,391
West South Central (AR, LA, OK, TX)	21,994,609	22,443,127	21,768,913	21,825,031	21,973,689
Mountain (AZ, CO, ID, MT, NV, NM, UT, WY)	10,733,568	11,004,216	10,964,711	10,995,965	11,173,993
Pacific (CA, OR, WA)	25,341,080	26,610,843	26,739,070	26,994,920	27,626,544
Total (Excluding Alaska & Hawaii)	181,068,128	185,060,556	186,004,490	186,254,025	186,304,921

REGION	1990	1991	1992	1993r	1994
New England (CT, ME, MA, NH, RI, VT)	9,873,379	9,488,668	9,188,757	9,140,144	9,176,561
Middle Atlantic (NJ, NY, PA,)	6,976,103	25,919,964	25,012,507	24,744,998	24,369,547
East North Central (IL, IN, MI, OH, WI)	33,707,871	32,870,080	32,193,240	32,263,771	32,349,316
West North Central (IA, KS, MN, MO, NE, ND, SD)	13,321,401	13,267,839	13,140,423	13,180,781	13,551,823
South Atlantic (DE, DC, FL, GA, MD, NC, SC, VA, WV)	34,197,388	33,371,883	33,787,411	34,041,123	34,289,890
East South Central (AL, KY, MS, TN)	10,371,348	10,299,376	10,519,801	10,708,757	10,956,950
West South Central (AR, LA, OK, TX)	22,694,561	22,633,788	23,514,598	23,642,187	24,246,170
Mountain (AZ, CO, ID, MT, NV, NM, UT, WY)	11,376,461	11,442,245	11,680,889	11,842,913	11,996,392
Pacific (CA, OR, WA)	28,560,762	27,490,733	27,135,089	26,651,916	26,237,779
Total (Excluding Alaska & Hawaii)	191,079,274	186,784,576	186,172,765	186,216,590	187,174,428

1994 CONSUMPTION AND PER CAPITA CONSUMPTION OF MALT BEVERAGES, DISTILLED SPIRITS AND WINES
By Region-In Gallons

Region	Total Population (000)	Malt Beverage Consumption (000)	Total Per Capita Consumption	Distilled Spirits Consumption (000)	Total Per Capita Consumption	Wine Consumption (000)	Total Per Capita Consumption
New England	13,270	284,473	21.44	22,949	1.73	35,448	2.67
Middle Atlantic	38,125	755,456	19.82	45,314	1.19	74,706	1.96
East North Central	43,184	1,002,829	23.22	56,479	1.31	61,680	1.43
W. North Central	18,210	420,107	23.07	22,380	1.23	20,317	1.12
South Atlantic	46,398	1,062,987	22.91	66,489	1.43	78,491	1.69
E. South Central	15,890	339,665	21.38	17,307	1.09	12,597	0.79
W. South Central	28,404	751,631	26.46	29,477	1.04	32,143	1.13
Mountain	15,214	371,888	24.44	22,769	1.50	27,584	1.81
Pacific*	39,860	813,371	20.41	50,877	1.28	109,971	2.76
U.S.	258,555	5,802,407	22.44	334,041	1.29	452,937	1.75

Source: The Beer Institute, DISCUS, Steve L. Barsby and Associates, and United States Department of Commerce.
Note: Due to rounding, components do not always add up to totals.

*Excludes Alaska and Hawaii

Reprinted from *Brewers Almanac 1995*, courtesy of the Beer Institute.

PER CAPITA CONSUMPTION OF MALT BEVERAGES
1984-1994 - Gallons

STATE	\multicolumn{11}{c}{TOTAL POPULATION}

STATE	1984	1985	1986	1987	1988	1989	1990	1991	1992	1993	1994*
Alabama	18.0	18.7	19.3	19.4	19.4	19.4	20.1	20.1	20.4	20.3	21.0
Alaska	28.4	27.4	27.7	26.7	26.2	25.9	26.6	25.3	25.7	23.3	24.7
Arizona	29.8	29.8	30.6	29.8	29.4	29.0	28.6	28.0	28.0	28.1	27.2
Arkansas	17.9	18.1	18.7	19.0	18.9	19.0	19.9	19.9	20.0	19.7	19.7
California	25.0	24.0	24.7	24.1	23.6	23.7	23.8	22.3	21.3	20.8	20.1
Colorado	25.7	25.2	25.5	24.8	24.2	23.9	24.2	23.5	23.7	23.5	23.1
Connecticut	20.3	20.8	20.6	21.1	20.7	19.8	19.8	18.7	18.3	17.9	17.9
Delaware	26.6	26.2	26.0	25.9	25.7	24.9	25.8	24.9	25.2	26.2	25.9
District of Columbia	29.2	26.9	27.9	27.2	26.8	26.9	26.7	26.9	30.4	28.9	28.7
Florida	29.0	29.1	29.5	29.6	28.3	28.2	28.0	27.0	26.7	26.1	25.8
Georgia	21.3	21.4	22.1	22.3	21.7	21.5	22.3	21.2	21.6	21.7	21.4
Hawaii	28.7	27.7	28.0	27.6	28.5	27.1	29.3	27.8	27.4	26.3	25.5
Idaho	23.2	22.3	22.5	22.0	21.1	21.6	22.9	22.2	22.6	21.8	21.4
Illinois	24.6	24.3	24.7	25.1	25.0	24.4	25.7	24.4	23.8	23.5	23.6
Indiana	22.0	22.0	22.1	21.9	21.9	21.5	22.4	21.6	20.7	20.5	20.6
Iowa	23.9	22.9	23.3	23.1	23.0	22.7	23.6	23.5	23.3	23.0	23.3
Kansas	20.7	20.1	19.9	19.7	19.3	19.4	19.7	20.0	19.2	19.4	19.5
Kentucky	18.5	18.9	19.2	19.0	19.1	18.3	20.1	19.4	19.0	19.3	19.6
Louisiana	23.8	23.0	23.7	24.3	24.6	24.4	26.4	26.1	26.7	26.5	27.1
Maine	22.1	22.2	22.4	22.6	22.9	21.8	22.1	21.5	20.8	20.6	20.3
Maryland	24.1	23.9	24.0	23.7	23.0	22.7	21.8	20.4	19.7	19.5	19.3
Massachusetts	24.4	22.4	24.6	24.4	24.3	23.6	23.0	21.9	21.2	21.1	21.4
Michigan	23.2	23.1	23.5	23.4	23.2	22.7	23.5	22.9	22.2	22.2	21.8
Minnesota	23.5	23.0	23.0	23.2	22.9	22.5	23.2	22.7	22.0	21.9	22.5
Mississippi	20.1	20.6	21.5	21.6	21.9	21.6	23.3	22.9	23.5	23.9	24.5
Missouri	23.7	23.7	24.2	24.2	23.6	23.6	24.3	23.9	23.7	23.6	24.2
Montana	29.4	27.8	27.4	27.2	27.6	27.2	27.8	28.0	27.7	26.2	26.6
Nebraska	25.4	24.6	24.5	24.8	24.3	24.1	25.2	24.6	24.2	24.3	24.7
Nevada	35.1	35.7	37.2	37.7	39.3	40.4	40.2	37.7	36.4	35.1	35.1
New Hampshire	35.6	35.7	34.7	34.7	34.1	33.3	32.9	32.9	32.2	32.4	31.0
New Jersey	21.5	21.4	21.5	21.5	20.9	20.5	21.0	19.9	19.5	19.4	18.9
New Mexico	28.3	28.7	27.9	27.8	27.2	27.9	27.2	27.1	26.7	26.4	25.4
New York	20.8	20.8	20.3	20.9	20.7	20.0	20.4	19.6	18.8	18.1	17.8
North Carolina	19.8	19.7	20.0	20.0	20.1	20.3	20.9	20.2	20.7	20.9	20.8
North Dakota	24.0	23.1	23.0	23.3	24.1	24.5	26.6	26.1	25.4	25.6	25.8
Ohio	24.9	24.2	23.4	23.9	23.7	23.9	23.9	23.6	23.0	23.0	23.0
Oklahoma	17.8	18.1	18.3	18.2	18.3	18.4	19.7	19.7	19.9	20.0	20.4
Oregon	22.6	22.1	22.5	22.6	22.6	22.5	23.4	22.7	22.9	22.2	22.2
Pennsylvania	24.9	24.9	25.2	25.1	25.3	24.6	25.8	24.6	23.5	23.7	23.4
Rhode Island	25.1	25.7	26.0	25.6	25.3	24.8	24.0	24.3	22.8	22.3	22.6
South Carolina	22.0	22.1	22.9	23.5	24.0	24.0	25.6	23.8	23.8	24.2	24.7
South Dakota	21.7	20.9	21.2	21.5	21.0	21.6	23.4	23.5	23.6	23.5	24.3
Tennessee	19.7	19.8	20.9	21.0	21.5	21.1	21.9	21.4	21.7	21.6	21.5
Texas	29.8	29.1	29.0	27.5	27.5	27.6	29.0	27.7	28.5	28.1	28.3
Utah	13.4	13.8	13.7	13.0	12.8	12.7	12.7	13.2	13.0	12.9	12.9
Vermont	26.3	26.6	27.6	27.8	27.0	26.0	26.1	25.0	23.9	23.7	23.3
Virginia	22.4	22.4	23.4	23.5	23.3	23.6	24.0	23.0	22.5	22.2	21.7
Washington	21.8	21.5	21.8	21.9	21.7	21.9	22.4	21.6	22.1	21.0	20.9
West Virginia	19.7	19.7	19.6	19.9	20.1	20.2	21.7	21.5	21.0	21.6	21.5
Wisconsin	32.9	32.1	32.7	31.5	31.0	30.2	30.5	29.0	28.1	28.3	28.3
Wyoming	26.3	26.0	24.5	24.5	23.6	23.0	25.1	24.7	24.7	24.3	25.0
Total	23.9	23.7	24.0	23.9	23.7	23.4	24.0	23.1	22.8	22.6	22.5

*Subject to revision.
r-revised

Reprinted from *Brewers Almanac 1995*, courtesy of the Beer Institute.

Beer and Brewery Statistics

PER CAPITA CONSUMPTION OF DISTILLED SPIRITS
1984 - 1994

STATE	TOTAL POPULATION										
	1984	1985	1986	1987	1988	1989	1990	1991	1992	1993r	1994*
Alabama (r)	1.32	1.28	1.23	1.18	1.17	1.15	1.20	1.15	1.14	1.10	1.06
Alaska (r)	2.79	2.74	2.29	2.31	2.20	2.22	2.24	2.04	1.95	1.68	1.95
Arizona (r)	2.14	1.86	1.78	1.72	1.68	1.67	1.60	1.41	1.54	1.50	1.39
Arkansas	1.22	1.12	0.92	1.01	1.03	1.10	1.18	1.12	1.27	1.14	0.95
California	2.07	1.97	1.85	1.78	1.72	1.67	1.68	1.43	1.43	1.30	1.28
Colorado (r)	2.15	2.05	1.81	1.78	1.74	1.61	1.44	1.67	1.58	1.69	1.64
Connecticut	2.41	2.41	2.31	2.25	2.15	1.97	1.92	1.73	1.75	1.62	1.57
Delaware (r)	2.57	2.55	2.42	2.37	2.32	2.19	2.26	1.86	1.89	1.86	1.89
Dist. of Columbia(r)	5.38	4.93	4.15	4.78	4.03	3.64	4.05	3.83	3.62	3.21	3.17
Florida (r	2.35	2.27	2.24	2.17	2.08	2.03	2.08	1.84	1.93	1.85	1.76
Georgia (r)	1.97	1.93	1.77	1.75	1.72	1.78	1.71	1.61	1.53	1.49	1.46
Hawaii	1.74	1.68	1.58	1.47	1.61	1.52	1.55	1.36	1.34	1.26	1.21
Idaho	1.28	1.18	1.12	1.06	1.07	1.03	1.08	1.05	1.06	1.05	1.02
Illinois	1.93	1.86	1.75	1.68	1.63	1.59	1.65	1.40	1.44	1.40	1.42
Indiana (r)	1.39	1.39	1.28	1.29	1.28	1.23	1.23	1.16	1.14	1.26	1.16
Iowa (r)	1.16	1.10	0.98	1.04	0.96	0.94	0.97	0.92	0.90	0.94	0.91
Kansas	1.21	1.22	1.14	1.08	1.08	1.04	1.03	1.10	1.05	1.00	0.94
Kentucky	1.30	1.28	1.17	1.16	1.15	1.12	1.14	1.11	1.15	1.09	1.07
Louisiana	1.74	1.60	1.45	1.40	1.39	1.34	1.47	1.38	1.40	1.42	1.41
Maine (r)	1.97	1.83	1.79	1.78	1.78	1.69	1.63	1.49	1.53	1.54	1.52
Maryland	2.32	2.26	2.13	2.10	1.98	1.93	1.88	1.73	1.67	1.56	1.49
Massachusetts	2.46	2.40	2.20	2.26	2.15	2.09	1.93	1.73	1.73	1.59	1.59
Michigan (r)	1.87	1.84	1.75	1.65	1.62	1.55	1.55	1.43	1.43	1.40	1.33
Minnesota	2.06	2.04	1.78	1.81	1.73	1.71	1.84	1.56	1.64	1.62	1.61
Mississippi	1.42	1.36	1.27	1.23	1.23	1.22	1.24	1.21	1.20	1.20	1.23
Missouri	1.27	1.35	1.37	1.40	1.32	1.27	1.22	1.22	1.26	1.18	1.18
Montana (r)	1.75	1.67	1.54	1.46	1.44	1.38	1.47	1.44	1.44	1.39	1.35
Nebraska (r)	1.45	1.43	1.29	1.26	1.24	1.20	1.23	1.17	1.19	1.14	1.11
Nevada (r)	4.65	4.40	4.12	4.01	3.89	3.73	3.77	3.20	3.17	3.40	3.28
New Hampshire (r)	4.58	4.36	4.05	3.90	3.79	3.89	3.85	3.82	3.80	4.08	3.69
New Jersey (r)	2.18	2.15	2.06	2.01	1.85	1.89	1.89	1.61	1.65	1.58	1.57
New Mexico	1.38	1.41	1.31	1.24	1.25	1.19	1.27	1.20	1.23	1.21	1.14
New York	2.05	1.94	1.82	1.78	1.71	1.61	1.51	1.35	1.33	1.23	1.19
North Carolina	1.53	1.50	1.45	1.40	1.34	1.29	1.29	1.20	1.18	1.12	1.09
North Dakota (r)	1.85	1.85	1.59	1.65	1.65	1.61	1.71	1.72	1.64	1.62	1.53
Ohio (r)	1.16	1.18	1.17	1.14	1.06	0.98	1.03	0.99	0.97	1.12	1.05
Oklahoma	1.41	1.29	1.17	1.09	1.06	1.01	1.07	1.04	1.06	1.04	0.98
Oregon	1.58	1.50	1.43	1.40	1.38	1.35	1.41	1.30	1.31	1.26	1.21
Pennsylvania	1.31	1.29	1.27	1.23	1.14	1.11	1.10	1.03	1.02	0.95	0.93
Rhode Island	2.06	2.07	1.87	1.88	1.93	1.72	1.64	1.43	1.40	1.38	1.32
South Carolina (r)	1.91	1.90	1.77	1.69	1.70	1.65	1.78	1.63	1.53	1.46	1.46
South Dakota	1.67	1.76	1.47	1.50	1.45	1.32	1.50	1.42	1.40	1.39	1.41
Tennessee	1.35	1.32	1.24	1.21	1.18	1.15	1.19	1.07	1.10	1.06	1.05
Texas	1.48	1.37	1.21	1.13	1.09	1.07	1.10	1.02	1.04	1.00	0.97
Utah	0.86	0.89	0.89	0.84	0.82	0.80	0.81	0.75	0.75	0.71	0.71
Vermont	2.24	2.13	2.03	1.93	1.82	1.71	1.66	1.60	1.51	1.44	1.38
Virginia (r)	1.58	1.52	1.45	1.39	1.33	1.28	1.23	1.15	1.12	1.07	1.01
Washington	1.75	1.68	1.59	1.54	1.49	1.46	1.46	1.41	1.39	1.34	1.28
West Virginia	0.85	0.81	0.81	0.79	0.79	0.74	0.83	0.86	0.82	0.80	0.77
Wisconsin	2.13	2.02	1.75	1.68	1.65	1.70	1.83	1.71	1.75	1.74	1.75
Wyoming	1.91	1.88	1.70	1.59	1.55	1.53	1.72	1.67	1.72	1.63	1.59
Total (r)	1.80	1.74	1.64	1.59	1.54	1.50	1.51	1.37	1.38	1.33	1.29

Source: Distilled Spirits Council of the U. S. and United States Deparment of Commerce
r - revised
*Subject to revision.

Reprinted from *Brewers Almanac 1995*, courtesy of the Beer Institute.

PER CAPITA CONSUMPTION OF WINE
1984 - 1994 - Gallons

STATE	1984	1985	1986	1987	1988	1989	1990	1991	1992	1993	1994
					TOTAL POPULATION						
Alabama	1.14	1.05	1.07	1.12	1.12	1.04	1.13	1.07	1.15	1.02	0.90
Alaska	3.30	3.29	3.21	3.06	2.80	2.64	2.66	2.44	2.39	1.93	2.29
Arizona	2.69	2.82	2.84	2.79	2.61	2.10	2.36	1.95	1.99	1.73	1.80
Arkansas	0.72	0.81	0.57	0.65	0.84	0.77	0.80	0.71	0.77	0.70	0.52
California	4.57	4.83	4.82	4.59	4.17	3.78	3.54	3.17	3.07	2.86	2.84
Colorado	2.75	3.09	2.85	2.62	2.37	2.28	1.90	2.07	2.34	2.11	2.16
Connecticut	3.19	3.22	3.27	3.28	3.19	2.96	2.80	2.63	2.77	2.61	2.71
Delaware	2.37	2.56	2.78	2.64	2.50	2.35	2.33	2.18	2.26	2.23	2.34
District of Columbia	7.14	6.71	6.60	6.42	6.26	5.55	5.02	4.05	4.65	4.78	4.90
Florida	2.58	2.65	2.74	2.93	2.63	2.47	2.48	2.20	2.18	2.06	2.17
Georgia	1.46	1.62	1.62	1.61	1.55	1.47	1.46	1.36	1.32	1.22	1.38
Hawaii	2.50	2.51	2.64	2.92	2.75	2.62	2.48	2.46	2.40	2.26	2.35
Idaho	1.83	2.14	1.21	2.22	2.13	1.80	1.93	1.86	1.87	1.71	2.13
Illinois	2.26	2.29	2.40	2.38	2.30	2.17	2.27	2.09	2.14	2.04	2.07
Indiana	1.27	1.35	1.42	1.38	1.29	1.19	1.23	1.18	1.25	1.18	1.24
Iowa	0.73	1.29	1.41	1.30	1.17	1.12	1.12	0.94	0.80	0.65	0.67
Kansas	0.92	0.98	1.02	1.01	0.92	0.82	0.81	0.78	0.85	0.82	0.79
Kentucky	0.77	0.83	0.85	0.81	0.76	0.68	0.73	0.67	0.69	0.64	0.69
Louisiana	1.72	1.61	1.52	1.43	1.41	1.39	1.40	1.27	1.35	1.29	1.29
Maine	1.99	2.14	2.33	2.42	2.29	2.09	2.11	1.96	1.79	1.75	1.69
Maryland	2.35	2.31	2.46	2.37	2.27	2.15	2.11	1.91	1.85	1.70	1.72
Massachusetts	3.25	3.25	3.38	3.28	3.20	2.99	2.88	2.72	2.95	2.72	2.80
Michigan	1.92	2.01	2.06	2.06	1.98	1.82	1.74	1.35	1.33	1.24	1.27
Minnesota	1.67	1.93	2.07	1.95	1.85	1.65	1.65	1.44	1.51	1.46	1.55
Mississippi	0.62	0.61	0.58	0.55	0.55	0.55	0.55	0.56	0.56	0.64	0.49
Missouri	1.57	1.61	1.72	1.70	1.56	1.39	1.38	1.33	1.31	1.24	1.21
Montana	1.92	1.98	2.05	2.01	1.92	1.76	1.77	1.67	1.60	1.49	1.55
Nebraska	1.24	1.32	1.40	1.35	1.32	1.17	1.22	1.05	1.09	1.07	1.10
Nevada	5.08	5.35	5.48	5.13	4.85	4.54	4.31	3.91	3.91	3.55	3.61
New Hampshire	3.71	3.31	3.26	3.13	3.03	3.12	3.03	3.01	3.22	3.32	2.99
New Jersey	3.47	3.51	3.57	3.41	3.22	3.17	3.07	2.71	2.78	2.60	2.74
New Mexico	1.88	2.10	2.10	2.09	1.95	1.62	1.65	1.55	1.51	1.32	1.13
New York	3.12	3.13	3.19	3.03	2.81	2.62	2.59	2.31	2.34	2.19	2.19
North Carolina	1.52	1.70	1.86	1.74	1.78	1.71	1.72	1.53	1.42	1.24	1.35
North Dakota	1.00	1.13	1.32	1.22	1.13	1.03	1.03	0.95	0.94	0.93	0.93
Ohio	1.53	1.57	1.57	1.46	1.47	1.38	1.33	1.15	1.05	0.97	1.00
Oklahoma	0.96	0.92	0.93	0.91	0.85	0.81	0.83	0.78	0.79	0.77	0.78
Oregon	3.25	3.41	3.39	3.28	3.20	2.88	2.88	2.70	2.84	2.65	2.54
Pennsylvania	1.39	1.31	1.31	1.26	1.19	1.16	1.19	1.05	1.12	1.04	1.10
Rhode Island	3.34	3.27	3.39	3.29	3.13	2.92	2.79	2.39	2.51	2.29	2.47
South Carolina	1.45	1.53	1.66	1.66	1.59	1.48	1.58	1.39	1.24	1.18	1.06
South Dakota	0.99	1.05	1.17	1.17	0.96	0.88	1.06	0.90	0.87	0.75	0.76
Tennessee	0.94	1.01	0.99	0.95	0.90	0.86	0.91	0.84	0.89	0.84	0.94
Texas	1.65	1.71	1.78	1.67	1.59	1.57	1.59	1.41	1.46	1.29	1.24
Utah	0.74	0.81	0.89	0.81	0.76	0.72	0.68	0.65	0.66	0.63	0.53
Vermont	3.04	3.43	3.65	3.60	3.45	3.21	3.00	2.87	2.75	2.66	2.90
Virginia	1.81	1.89	1.70	1.61	1.81	1.95	1.89	1.74	1.74	1.67	1.69
Washington	3.49	3.67	3.76	3.63	3.45	3.18	3.11	2.92	2.85	2.61	2.43
West Virginia	0.75	0.82	0.82	0.80	0.73	0.66	0.66	0.56	0.57	0.52	0.53
Wisconsin	1.89	1.97	2.10	2.19	2.03	1.89	1.87	1.67	1.52	1.37	1.39
Wyoming	1.29	1.42	1.51	1.42	1.36	1.29	1.32	1.21	1.21	1.13	0.93
Total	2.35	2.38	2.43	2.36	2.24	2.09	2.05	1.85	1.86	1.74	1.76

Source: Steve L. Barsby and Associates, Wine Institute of the U. S. and United States Department of Commerce.
r - revised.

Reprinted from *Brewers Almanac 1995*, courtesy of the Beer Institute.

Beer and Brewery Statistics

PRODUCTION AND WITHDRAWALS ADJUSTED FOR SEASONAL VARIATION
1990 - 1994 (Barrels)

	Barrels Produced	% of Chg. from Pr. Mo.	Barrels Packaged	% of Chg. from Pr. Mo.	Barrels Draught	% of Chg. from Pr. Mo.	Total Withdrawals	% of Chg. from Pr. Mo.
1990								
January	18,287,969	8.8	14,684,101	11.6	1,778,261	10.3	16,462,362	11.4
February	17,889,580	—2.2	14,031,364	—4.4	1,815,551	0.1	15,846,915	—3.7
March	16,949,697	—5.3	13,627,401	—2.9	1,683,667	—7.3	15,311,068	—3.4
April	16,330,868	—3.7	12,867,564	—5.6	1,672,710	—0.7	14,540,274	—5.0
May	15,876,660	—2.8	13,110,772	1.9	1,650,777	—1.3	14,761,549	1.5
June	16,296,854	2.6	12,902,209	—1.6	1,628,376	—1.4	14,530,585	—1.6
July	15,862,400	—2.7	13,222,861	2.5	1,648,970	1.3	14,871,831	2.3
August	16,926,874	6.7	13,640,027	3.2	1,731,277	5.0	15,371,304	3.4
September	17,109,752	1.1	13,459,620	—1.3	1,645,330	—5.0	15,104,950	—1.7
October	17,310,176	1.2	14,235,389	5.8	1,737,018	5.6	15,972,407	5.7
November	18,381,262	6.2	14,436,071	1.4	1,791,446	3.1	16,227,517	1.6
December	17,461,004	—5.0	14,549,970	0.8	1,769,506	—1.2	16,319,476	0.6
1991								
January	18,286,972	4.7	14,175,436	—2.6	1,794,379	1.4	15,969,815	—2.1
February	17,436,179	—4.7	13,777,081	—2.8	1,755,536	—2.2	15,532,617	—2.7
March	15,520,759	—11.0	12,623,083	—8.4	1,575,804	—10.2	14,198,887	—8.6
April	15,951,654	2.8	12,361,254	—2.1	1,651,652	4.8	14,012,906	—1.3
May	16,580,796	3.9	13,161,791	6.5	1,675,097	1.4	14,836,888	5.9
June	16,958,935	2.3	13,037,833	—0.9	1,672,637	—0.1	14,710,470	—0.9
July	17,139,281	1.1	13,939,807	6.9	1,701,130	1.7	15,640,937	6.3
August	16,780,823	—2.1	13,759,531	—1.3	1,736,776	2.1	15,496,307	—0.9
September	16,962,666	1.1	13,153,271	—4.4	1,681,892	—3.2	14,835,163	—4.3
October	17,347,946	2.3	13,857,846	5.4	1,847,705	9.9	15,705,551	5.9
November	17,023,734	—1.9	13,509,700	—2.5	1,696,557	—8.2	15,206,257	—3.2
December	16,840,367	—1.1	13,891,429	2.8	1,767,220	4.2	15,658,649	3.0
1992								
January	17,783,292	5.6	13,837,073	—0.4	1,903,271	7.7	15,740,344	0.5
February	17,887,550	0.6	13,835,560	—0.01	1,933,530	1.6	15,769,090	0.2
March	17,041,035	—4.7	13,330,987	—3.6	1,750,052	—9.5	15,081,039	—4.4
April	16,825,618	—1.3	13,084,071	—1.9	1,741,848	—0.5	14,825,919	—1.7
May	16,718,938	—0.6	12,986,735	—0.7	1,606,349	—7.8	14,593,084	—1.6
June	16,620,970	—0.6	13,353,479	2.8	1,726,345	7.5	15,079,824	3.3
July	16,234,358	—2.3	12,887,731	3.5	1,733,128	0.4	14,620,859	—3.0
August	15,807,932	—2.6	12,856,051	—0.2	1,653,649	—4.6	14,509,700	—0.8
September	16,371,113	3.2	12,684,819	—1.3	1,727,526	4.5	14,412,345	—0.7
October	17,000,984	4.2	13,119,930	3.4	1,776,554	2.8	14,896,484	3.4
November	16,977,962	—0.1	13,161,598	0.3	1,688,396	—5.0	14,849,994	—0.3
December	17,461,291	2.8	14,017,586	6.5	1,873,335	11.0	15,890,921	7.0
1993r								
January	16,880,470	—3.3	13,134,608	—6.3	1,701,875	—9.2	14,836,483	—6.6
February	17,540,286	3.9	13,659,661	4.0	1,814,890	6.6	15,474,551	4.3
March	16,301,082	—7.1	12,973,187	—5.0	1,732,339	—4.5	14,705,526	—5.0
April	16,173,891	—0.8	12,765,058	—1.6	1,752,950	1.2	14,518,008	—1.3
May	16,894,793	4.5	13,028,960	2.1	1,631,397	—6.9	14,660,357	1.0
June	16,955,337	0.4	13,693,437	5.1	1,712,916	5.0	15,406,353	5.1
July	16,544,871	—2.4	13,351,043	—2.5	1,643,326	—4.1	14,994,369	—2.7
August	16,830,455	1.7	13,036,648	—2.4	1,734,190	5.5	14,770,838	—1.5
September	16,997,621	1.0	13,691,856	5.0	1,760,439	1.5	15,452,295	4.6
October	16,873,350	—0.7	13,068,991	—4.5	1,591,760	—9.6	14,660,751	—5.1
November	17,348,538	2.8	13,649,475	4.4	1,718,810	8.0	15,368,285	4.8
December	17,716,178	2.1	14,522,842	6.4	1,777,780	3.4	16,300,622	6.1
1994								
January	17,272,912	—2.5	13,447,688	—7.4	1,617,595	—9.0	15,065,283	—7.6
February	16,095,088	—6.8	13,930,420	3.6	1,688,990	4.4	15,619,410	3.7
March	16,542,016	2.8	12,815,018	—8.0	1,677,358	—0.7	14,492,376	—7.2
April	16,464,317	—0.5	12,679,237	—1.1	1,568,266	—6.5	14,247,503	—1.7
May	17,252,119	4.8	12,965,839	2.3	1,597,797	1.9	14,563,636	2.2
June	17,148,417	—0.6	13,590,787	4.8	1,705,538	6.7	15,296,325	5.0
July	16,957,330	—1.1	13,204,780	—2.8	1,533,064	—10.1	14,737,844	—3.7
August	16,816,469	—0.8	13,490,245	2.2	1,641,490	7.1	15,131,735	2.7
September	16,413,395	—2.4	13,819,119	2.4	1,635,095	—0.4	15,454,214	2.1
October	16,659,171	1.5	12,703,837	—8.1	1,620,333	—0.9	14,324,170	—7.3
November	16,431,841	—1.4	13,728,035	8.1	1,642,675	1.4	15,370,710	7.3
December	16,904,066	2.9	14,064,371	2.4	1,660,301	1.1	15,724,672	2.3

(r) - revised

Reprinted from *Brewers Almanac 1995*, courtesy of the Beer Institute.

Beer and Brewery Statistics

COMPARATIVE PROFIT AND LOSS STATEMENT FOR BREWERIES* SUBMITTING BALANCE SHEETS
Calendar Years - Money Figures in Thousands of Dollars

	1987		1988		1989		1990		1991		1992	
	Ret. With Net Inc.	Ret. With No Net Inc.	Ret. With Net Inc.	Ret. With No Net Inc.	Ret. With Net Inc.	Ret. With No Net Inc.	Ret. With Net Inc.	Ret. With No Net Inc.	Ret. With Net Inc.	Ret. With No Net Inc.	Ret. With Net Inc.	Ret. With No Net Inc.
Number of returns	7	11	5	7	15	94	7	113	50	63	32	19
Gross sales [2]	11,445,681	4,170,447	12,105,979	2,880,705	14,582,849	993,436	16,578,833	481,074	18,199,682	163,583	17,237,840	1,898,169
Gross receipts from operations [3]												
Interest, rents, royalties, etc.	164,972	43,212	147,561	79,922	180,162	119,240	260,935	26	202,125	285	166,488	22,065
Dividends received	1,126	3,725	564	3,886	3,487	218	4,167	—	2,372	—	1,688	4
Other receipts [4]	153,034	91,892	200,139	50,762	200,397	101,063	268,824	1,738	164,385	848	196,040	14,759
Total receipts	11,764,813	4,309,276	12,454,293	3,015,275	14,966,895	1,213,957	17,112,759	482,838	18,568,564	164,716	17,602,056	1,934,997
Cost of goods sold [5]	6,457,118	2,282,520	6,798,923	1,539,047	8,119,912	581,677	9,270,881	342,812	9,797,491	127,269	8,998,870	1,145,061
Cost of operations [5]												
Compensation of officers	54,712	31,272	81,705	17,259	77,368	4,671	67,935	4,207	87,744	3,245	89,400	13,159
Rents paid on business property	88,114	33,924	84,603	25,101	88,441	11,482	108,481	8,228	110,105	332	99,882	7,053
Repairs [6]	168,980	42,336	186,531	37,613	210,243	3,206	257,713	1,001	257,877	145	255,112	1,691
Bad debts	40,836	7,671	2,945	672	2,408	182	11,685	39	3,084	154	4,296	3,776
Interest paid	199,469	178,016	207,347	261,533	304,241	279,711	534,796	12,288	346,709	8,080	304,763	46,568
Contributions or gifts [7]	19,276		15,572		10,670		22,038		11,231		16,623	
Depreciation, depletion and amortization	504,022	171,582	695,641	82,960	653,698	41,357	850,519	22,173	743,565	26,112	723,635	52,943
Advertising	813,464	262,715	866,700	294,266	720,965	132,576	831,247	9,596	802,145	2,159	797,021	153,329
Contributions under pension plans, etc. [8]	250,744	84,246	178,059	62,357	323,221	6,844	325,042	2,663	417,760	2,052	373,117	52,021
Loss (net) on sales of other than capital assets	20,905	238	768	—	309	5,947	—	263	4,647	842	1,110	76
Taxes other than Federal Income Taxes [9]	1,018,189	533,325	1,045,439	403,820	1,530,527	112,843	1,608,413	29,980	2,514,386	12,372	2,278,001	359,658
Other deductions [10]	1,211,073	833,871	1,389,866	549,056	1,982,904	93,406	2,018,325	70,014	2,224,281	10,669	2,287,357	108,930
Total deductions	10,846,902	4,461,716	11,464,099	3,274,184	14,024,907	1,273,897	15,907,075	503,264	17,321,025	193,431	16,229,187	1,944,265
Net profit (or loss) before Federal Income Taxes	917,911	(152,440)	990,194	(258,909)	941,988	(59,940)	1,205,684	(20,426)	1,247,539	(28,715)	1,372,869	(9,268)
Federal Income Taxes:												
Normal and Surtax	361,815	—	335,375	—	305,469	—	403,398	—	414,938	—	456,234	—
Declared Value Excess Profits Tax	—	—	—	—	—	—	—	—	—	—	—	—
Total Federal Income Taxes												
Net profit (or loss) after normal Federal Income Taxes [9]	556,096	(152,440)	654,819	(258,909)	636,519	(59,940)	802,286	(20,426)	832,601	(28,715)	916,635	(9,268)

Details may not add due to rounding.
Note: Figures in parentheses are negative amounts.
Source: U.S. Treasury Department, Internal Revenue Service, Source Book.
*Includes malt industry.

1 Includes returns of inactive corporations.
2 "Gross sales" consists of amounts received for goods, less returns and allowances, in transactions where inventories are an income-determining factor. "Gross sales" and "Gross receipts from operations" combined under the term "Business Receipts" in the Source Book.
3 "Gross receipts from operations" consists of amounts received from transactions in which inventories are not an income-determining factor.
4 "Other receipts" includes amounts not elsewhere reported on the return such as: Profit from sales other than the principal commodity in which the corporation deals; income from minor operations; bad debts, recovered; cash discount; income from claims, license rights, judgments and joint venture; net amount under operating agreements; net profit from commissaries; profit on dealing in futures; profit on prior years' collections (installment basis); profit on purchase of corporation's own bonds; recoveries of bonds, stocks and other securities; refunds for cancellation of contracts, for insurance, management expenses, processing taxes; income from sales of scrap, salvage, or waste; excess of net short-term capital gain over the long-term capital loss; excess of net long-term capital gain over net short-term capital loss; and net gain, sales other than capital assets.
5 Cost of goods sold and cost of operations excludes identifiable amounts of taxes, depreciation, depletion, amortization, advertising, and contributions under pension plans and other employee benefit plans included therein. Such items were transferred to their respective headings. Beginning with the year 1958, "Cost of goods sold" and "cost of sales and operations."
6 Amount shown as "Repairs" is the cost of incidental repairs, including labor and supplies, which do not add materially to the value of the property or appreciably prolong its life.
7 The deduction claimed for "Contributions or gifts" is limited to 5 per cent of the net income as computed without the benefit of this deduction.
8 Employee benefit plans (other than pension plans, etc.).
9 This item includes (1) Federal income and excess profits taxes, (2) estate, inheritance, legacy, succession and gift taxes, (3) income taxes paid to a foreign country or possession of the United States if any portion is claimed as a tax credit, (4) taxes assessed against local benefits, and (5) Federal taxes paid on tax-free covenant bonds, and (6) taxes reported in "cost of goods sold." Excludes 10 Included in "Other deductions" are (1) negative amounts reported under income, (2) losses by abandonment, fire, storm, shipwreck, or other casualty (including war losses), and theft, (3) salaries and wages not deducted elsewhere on the return, and (4) amounts not otherwise reported, such as: "Administrative, general, and office expenses; bonuses and commissions, delivery charges, freight and shipping expenses; payments in connection with lawsuits; research expenses; sales discount; selling costs; travel expenses; unrealized profits on installment sales.

Reprinted from *Brewers Almanac 1995*, courtesy of the Beer Institute.

Beer and Brewery Statistics

EMPLOYMENT, HOURS AND EARNINGS FOR PRODUCTION WORKERS IN THE MALT BEVERAGE,[1] ALL FOOD AND ALL MANUFACTURING INDUSTRIES
Calendar Years 1975-1994

	ESTIMATED NO. EMPLOYED (Thousands)			AVERAGE WEEKLY EARNINGS (Dollars)		
YEAR	MALT BEVERAGES	ALL FOOD	ALL MANUFACTURING	MALT BEVERAGES	ALL FOOD	ALL MANUFACTURING
1975	34.2	1,136	13,070	298.35	184.17	190.79
1976	32.8	1,164	13,625	337.82	199.89	209.32
1977	33.9	1,167	14,066	359.12	213.07	228.90
1978	34.5	1,147	14,610	391.53	230.84	249.27
1979	35.3	1,176	15,068	426.34	250.17	269.34
1980	33.4	1,175	14,223	470.88	272.34	288.62
1981	32.2	1,151	14,083	511.41	295.77	317.60
1982	30.4	1,127	12,782	564.14	311.66	330.65
1983	28.5	1,114	12,530	587.85	323.51	354.08
1984	27.4	1,124	13,310	649.30	333.52	373.63
1985	27.1	1,144	13,214	666.40	342.80	385.97
1986	26.3	1,131	12,877	692.68	350.00	396.01
1987	25.4	1,149	12,995	707.69	359.89	406.31
1988r	24.1	1,166	13,338	722.89	368.04	418.81
1989r	24.9	1,192	13,375	783.00	379.73	429.68
1990r	24.0	1,186	12,936	813.14	392.90	441.86
1991	22.9	1,210	12,447	826.23	401.13	455.03
1992	22.9	1,214	12,345	851.04	413.71	469.45
1993	23.5	1,205	12,143	846.00	424.50	486.86
1994	24.5	1,222	12,445	925.00	440.67	506.52
	AVERAGE WEEKLY HOURS			AVERAGE HOURLY EARNINGS		
1975	42.5	40.3	39.5	7.02	4.57	4.83
1976	43.2	40.3	40.1	7.82	4.96	5.22
1977	42.6	39.9	40.3	8.43	5.34	5.68
1978	42.1	39.8	40.4	9.30	5.80	6.17
1979	41.8	39.9	40.2	10.20	6.27	6.70
1980	43.2	39.7	39.7	10.90	6.86	7.27
1981	42.3	39.7	39.8	12.09	7.45	7.98
1982	42.9	39.5	38.9	13.15	7.89	8.50
1983	42.2	39.5	40.1	13.93	8.19	8.83
1984	40.3	39.8	40.7	15.10	8.38	9.18
1985	42.5	40.0	40.5	15.68	8.57	9.53
1986	42.6	40.0	40.7	16.26	8.75	9.73
1987	42.6	40.2	41.0	16.61	8.94	9.91
1988	42.8	40.4	41.1	16.89	9.11	10.17
1989	43.5	40.7	41.0	18.00	9.33	10.47
1990r	43.6	40.8	40.8	18.65	9.63	10.83
1991	43.1	40.6	40.7	19.17	9.88	11.18
1992	43.2	40.6	41.0	19.70	10.19	11.45
1993	42.3	40.7	41.4	20.00	10.43	11.76
1994	45.1	41.3	42.0	20.51	10.67	12.06

[1]This includes establishments primarily engaged in the manufacture of malt liquors.
Source: Bureau of Labor Statistics-U. S. Department of Labor.

Reprinted from *Brewers Almanac 1995*, courtesy of the Beer Institute.

MALT BEVERAGE SHIPMENTS BY STATE
Barrels per Month in 1994 with Percent Change from the Same Month in 1993

ALABAMA

PER CAPITA CONSUMPTION: 21.0 GALLONS

	PACKAGED	% CHANGE	DRAUGHT	% CHANGE	TOTAL	% CHANGE
JANUARY	204,378	13.0	5,774	14.1	210,152	13.0
FEBRUARY	227,954	8.2	6,076	11.7—	234,030	7.6
MARCH	245,732	12.4	7,892	6.2—	253,624	11.7
APRIL	225,151	2.2—	7,260	6.4	232,411	2.0—
MAY	243,901	4.0	6,987	7.6—	250,888	3.6
JUNE	298,974	14.5	8,859	15.6	307,833	14.5
JULY	238,700	5.4—	6,348	1.2	245,048	5.3—
AUGUST	238,036	2.5—	7,696	2.1	245,732	2.3—
SEPTEMBER	227,058	1.3—	6,972	6.1—	234,030	1.5—
OCTOBER	208,603	.9	6,475	8.6—	215,078	.6
NOVEMBER	217,971	7.5	6,178	11.2—	224,149	6.9
DECEMBER	193,171	.9	5,719	4.2	198,890	1.0
TOTAL	2,769,629	4.0	82,236	1.1—	2,851,865	3.8

ALASKA

PER CAPITA CONSUMPTION: 24.7 GALLONS

	TOTAL	% CHANGE
JANUARY	39,425	54.7
FEBRUARY	26,799	7.3—
MARCH	44,516	16.4
APRIL	31,743	23.8—
MAY	41,310	6.2—
JUNE	50,553	8.6—
JULY	68,043	40.3
AUGUST	52,211	87.6
SEPTEMBER	39,886	3.9—
OCTOBER	20,989	31.9—
NOVEMBER	34,375	60.9
DECEMBER	32,189	32.3—
TOTAL	482,039	6.8

ARIZONA

PER CAPITA CONSUMPTION: 27.2 GALLONS

	TOTAL	% CHANGE
JANUARY	290,000	19.1
FEBRUARY	295,000	11.5
MARCH	305,400	9.6—
APRIL	302,000	3.8—
MAY	357,600	2.3
JUNE	298,800	.7—
JULY	282,600	1.6—
AUGUST	316,700	4.0
SEPTEMBER	293,100	5.7—
OCTOBER	283,700	6.7—
NOVEMBER	281,000	1.0—
DECEMBER	267,500	1.3—
TOTAL	3,573,400	.1

The above and following state-by-state charts are reprinted from *Brewers Almanac 1994*, courtesy of the Beer Institute.

Beer and Brewery Statistics

ARKANSAS

PER CAPITA CONSUMPTION: 19.7 GALLONS

	PACKAGED	% CHANGE	DRAUGHT	% CHANGE	TOTAL	% CHANGE
JANUARY	120,858	9.4	5,842	4.9	126,700	9.1
FEBRUARY	122,111	14.6	5,089	2.1	127,200	14.1
MARCH	115,667	8.3—	5,933	9.3—	121,600	8.4—
APRIL	112,975	13.1—	4,625	21.4—	117,600	13.5—
MAY	138,281	17.7	5,319	5.2	143,600	17.2
JUNE	151,604	4.8	5,496	9.4—	157,100	4.3
JULY	139,983	2.1	4,817	6.1—	144,800	1.8
AUGUST	124,588	6.2—	4,712	19.7—	129,300	6.8—
SEPTEMBER	132,031	4.0	4,969	7.2—	137,000	3.6
OCTOBER	115,782	3.6—	5,218	7.0	121,000	3.2—
NOVEMBER	111,835	1.6	5,465	12.0	117,300	2.0
DECEMBER	109,956	5.9—	3,444	27.2—	113,400	6.7—
TOTAL	1,495,671	1.1	60,929	6.2—	1,556,600	.8

CALIFORNIA

PER CAPITA CONSUMPTION: 20.1 GALLONS

	TOTAL	% CHANGE
JANUARY	1,446,104	3.6—
FEBRUARY	1,640,146	20.4
MARCH	1,720,613	6.7—
APRIL	1,677,340	9.7—
MAY	1,827,780	9.3—
JUNE	2,079,107	.9—
JULY	1,795,300	1.4—
AUGUST	1,957,037	2.1—
SEPTEMBER	1,934,986	7.0
OCTOBER	1,578,247	.7
NOVEMBER	1,479,231	1.4—
DECEMBER	1,293,608	16.6—
TOTAL	20,429,499	2.4—

COLORADO

PER CAPITA CONSUMPTION: 23.1 GALLONS

	PACKAGED	% CHANGE	DRAUGHT	% CHANGE	TOTAL	% CHANGE
JANUARY	164,313	15.9	36,329	6.9	200,642	14.2
FEBRUARY	157,208	3.9	35,083	9.7—	192,291	1.1
MARCH	171,114	5.2—	40,683	3.6	211,797	3.6—
APRIL	182,594	7.4	36,318	16.5—	218,912	2.5
MAY	210,655	2.4—	39,560	3.9—	250,215	2.6—
JUNE	232,876	1.2—	45,296	81.9	278,172	6.7
JULY	213,620	2.9	42,459	4.9—	256,079	1.6
AUGUST	219,163	5.1	45,542	2.6	264,705	4.7
SEPTEMBER	186,325	5.5—	37,559	12.6—	223,884	6.8—
OCTOBER	168,194	4.3—	35,921	1.5—	204,115	3.8—
NOVEMBER	178,342	4.0	35,924	1.4—	214,266	3.0
DECEMBER	174,509	2.6—	35,000	6.6—	209,509	3.3—
TOTAL	2,258,913	1.1	465,674	.4	2,724,587	1.0

CONNECTICUT

PER CAPITA CONSUMPTION: 17.9 GALLONS

	PACKAGED	% CHANGE	DRAUGHT	% CHANGE	TOTAL	% CHANGE
JANUARY	96,324	2.4—	16,575	11.6—	112,899	3.9—
FEBRUARY	110,216	8.9	16,377	8.5—	126,593	6.3
MARCH	130,103	14.6	21,732	7.9	151,835	13.6
APRIL	132,896	6.0—	20,914	14.7—	153,810	7.2—
MAY	135,999	7.3—	25,142	7.7—	161,141	7.3—
JUNE	186,140	3.9	28,182	2.9—	214,322	2.9
JULY	145,031	3.2—	26,556	13.8—	171,587	5.0—
AUGUST	169,575	10.1	26,840	4.1—	196,415	7.9
SEPTEMBER	122,941	5.6—	25,546	4.0—	148,487	5.3—
OCTOBER	122,589	10.8—	19,963	21.6—	142,552	12.5—
NOVEMBER	136,373	31.1	19,505	2.9—	155,878	25.6
DECEMBER	137,155	2.0—	20,462	10.4—	157,617	3.2—
TOTAL	1,625,342	1.8	267,794	8.1—	1,893,136	.3

DELAWARE

PER CAPITA CONSUMPTION: 25.9 GALLONS

	TOTAL	% CHANGE
JANUARY	37,767	1.0—
FEBRUARY	31,286	5.6—
MARCH	44,674	11.6
APRIL	44,496	5.6—
MAY	58,120	4.1
JUNE	64,782	.1—
JULY	56,325	8.4—
AUGUST	60,580	1.0
SEPTEMBER	51,368	.1—
OCTOBER	42,567	.1—
NOVEMBER	44,106	2.1
DECEMBER	52,922	.7—
TOTAL	588,993	.4—

DISTRICT OF COLUMBIA

PER CAPITA CONSUMPTION: 28.7 GALLONS

	TOTAL	% CHANGE
JANUARY	36,600	9.6—
FEBRUARY	39,900	4.8—
MARCH	43,400	1.2
APRIL	41,000	5.1—
MAY	48,500	10.7—
JUNE	52,700	10.1—
JULY	50,500	.8
AUGUST	50,800	3.7
SEPTEMBER	47,600	.2—
OCTOBER	43,600	1.6—
NOVEMBER	38,500	1.3—
DECEMBER	35,000	1.5
TOTAL	528,100	3.3—

Beer and Brewery Statistics

FLORIDA

PER CAPITA CONSUMPTION: 25.8 GALLONS

	PACKAGED	% CHANGE	DRAUGHT	% CHANGE	TOTAL	% CHANGE
JANUARY	804,021	4.6	88,356	9.7—	892,377	3.0
FEBRUARY	830,040	.3—	106,687	6.6	936,727	.4
MARCH	924,618	3.6	128,096	1.6—	1,052,714	2.9
APRIL	871,327	4.3	105,825	5.1—	977,152	3.2
MAY	950,109	11.9	99,209	4.0	1,049,318	11.1
JUNE	896,432	3.7	104,067	1.0—	1,000,499	3.2
JULY	728,668	17.6—	89,735	4.0—	818,403	16.3—
AUGUST	920,637	3.0—	105,728	3.4	1,026,365	2.4—
SEPTEMBER	843,014	10.6	99,896	8.1—	942,910	8.2
OCTOBER	849,544	7.8	107,398	2.0	956,942	7.1
NOVEMBER	894,660	1.7	98,869	4.7—	993,529	1.0
DECEMBER	877,902	5.0—	101,590	6.7—	979,492	5.2—
TOTAL	10,390,972	1.6	1,235,456	2.1—	11,626,428	1.1

GEORGIA

PER CAPITA CONSUMPTION: 21.4 GALLONS

	PACKAGED	% CHANGE	DRAUGHT	% CHANGE	TOTAL	% CHANGE
JANUARY	397,864	13.0	21,000	9.7	418,864	12.9
FEBRUARY	363,372	9.8	20,266	.2	383,638	9.2
MARCH	395,853	3.1—	26,540	5.2—	422,393	3.2—
APRIL	350,858	.6	20,742	8.5—	371,600	.0
MAY	419,284	10.3	23,498	3.9	442,782	10.0
JUNE	429,898	1.4—	24,649	2.4	454,547	1.2—
JULY	401,692	1.7—	19,656	10.4—	421,348	2.1—
AUGUST	410,817	4.2	24,393	6.3	435,210	4.4
SEPTEMBER	386,647	1.2—	23,491	5.2—	410,138	1.5—
OCTOBER	363,380	7.9	22,732	5.3	386,112	7.8
NOVEMBER	334,475	4.9—	20,259	9.6—	354,734	5.2—
DECEMBER	336,964	10.2—	21,501	1.4	358,465	9.6—
TOTAL	4,591,104	1.7	268,727	1.1—	4,859,831	1.6

HAWAII

PER CAPITA CONSUMPTION: 25.5 GALLONS

	PACKAGED	% CHANGE	DRAUGHT	% CHANGE	TOTAL	% CHANGE
JANUARY	74,673	6.1	3,846	13.4	78,519	6.5
FEBRUARY	66,752	10.8—	3,786	6.9—	70,538	10.6—
MARCH	80,627	2.4	4,740	32.0	85,367	3.6
APRIL	75,149	8.4—	3,627	20.8—	78,776	9.1—
MAY	90,228	3.7—	3,647	9.7—	93,875	4.0—
JUNE	71,644	12.9—	3,846	5.9—	75,490	12.6—
JULY	75,003	6.1—	4,286	3.8	79,289	5.6—
AUGUST	75,791	4.2—	3,988	.1—	79,779	4.0—
SEPTEMBER	84,053	6.2	3,964	13.6—	88,017	5.1
OCTOBER	76,769	3.6—	3,634	1.2	80,403	3.4—
NOVEMBER	86,621	18.8	4,093	1.2—	90,714	17.7
DECEMBER	63,586	15.4—	3,743	26.6—	67,329	13.8—
TOTAL	920,896	2.8—	47,200	.1	968,096	2.7—

IDAHO

PER CAPITA CONSUMPTION: 21.4 GALLONS

	TOTAL	% CHANGE
JANUARY	58,600	4.5
FEBRUARY	54,500	.4—
MARCH	63,400	8.4
APRIL	63,400	6.8—
MAY	81,600	12.6
JUNE	78,000	7.0—
JULY	73,900	2.2
AUGUST	80,000	10.7
SEPTEMBER	62,000	.2—
OCTOBER	56,500	4.2—
NOVEMBER	58,600	1.5—
DECEMBER	53,000	1.0
TOTAL	783,500	1.6

ILLINOIS

PER CAPITA CONSUMPTION: 23.6 GALLONS

	TOTAL	% CHANGE
JANUARY	567,750	5.5
FEBRUARY	583,041	.7
MARCH	670,284	.4—
APRIL	755,961	2.5
MAY	832,977	.9—
JUNE	921,448	1.8
JULY	803,709	3.1—
AUGUST	871,457	.9
SEPTEMBER	760,315	3.3
OCTOBER	688,283	.0
NOVEMBER	685,731	.1
DECEMBER	813,799	.9
TOTAL	8,954,755	.8

INDIANA

PER CAPITA CONSUMPTION: 20.6 GALLONS

	PACKAGED	% CHANGE	DRAUGHT	% CHANGE	TOTAL	% CHANGE
JANUARY	230,810	4.4—	20,971	15.0—	251,781	5.4—
FEBRUARY	202,431	13.0	24,419	1.4	226,850	11.6
MARCH	329,567	5.7	24,584	16.1—	354,151	3.8
APRIL	286,067	5.4—	27,317	6.5—	313,384	5.5—
MAY	321,474	.7	30,721	.4	352,195	.6
JUNE	347,176	5.3	29,372	4.7—	376,548	4.5
JULY	335,078	7.7	29,668	.7—	364,746	7.0
AUGUST	352,937	5.4	32,056	5.7—	384,993	4.3
SEPTEMBER	292,928	3.5—	29,635	10.5—	322,563	4.2—
OCTOBER	257,762	4.1—	28,408	2.2	286,170	3.5—
NOVEMBER	284,020	9.2	25,886	10.9—	309,906	7.2
DECEMBER	258,817	1.8—	21,007	11.2—	279,824	2.6—
TOTAL	3,499,067	2.1	324,044	6.4—	3,823,111	1.4

Beer and Brewery Statistics

IOWA

PER CAPITA CONSUMPTION: 23.3 GALLONS

	PACKAGED	% CHANGE	DRAUGHT	% CHANGE	TOTAL	% CHANGE
JANUARY	137,397	21.0	30,493	1.0	167,890	16.8
FEBRUARY	116,832	5.2—	28,633	12.8—	145,465	6.8—
MARCH	139,664	3.0	34,289	3.9—	173,953	1.5
APRIL	139,354	.6—	33,180	11.4—	172,534	2.9—
MAY	147,364	5.1—	35,728	11.9—	183,092	6.5—
JUNE	194,250	28.1	40,468	2.5—	234,718	21.6
JULY	169,468	13.0	38,147	6.5—	207,615	8.8
AUGUST	153,129	1.0—	38,920	7.7—	192,049	2.5—
SEPTEMBER	139,924	.3—	34,337	13.7—	174,261	3.2—
OCTOBER	123,554	6.5—	33,850	1.7	157,404	4.8—
NOVEMBER	142,213	11.9	28,744	12.3—	170,957	7.0
DECEMBER	117,655	7.0—	28,581	7.3—	146,236	7.1—
TOTAL	1,720,804	4.3	405,370	7.4—	2,126,174	1.8

KANSAS

PER CAPITA CONSUMPTION: 19.5 GALLONS

	PACKAGED	% CHANGE	DRAUGHT	% CHANGE	TOTAL	% CHANGE
JANUARY	92,815	4.2—	15,785	8.3—	108,600	4.8—
FEBRUARY	102,487	21.4	15,513	11.8—	118,000	15.7
MARCH	111,628	5.4	18,872	2.7—	130,500	4.2
APRIL	120,050	3.7	18,550	11.6—	138,600	1.4
MAY	119,381	9.0—	18,319	4.5—	137,700	8.4—
JUNE	155,395	12.8	19,105	9.8—	174,500	9.8
JULY	125,400	7.9—	18,400	4.6—	143,800	7.5—
AUGUST	131,753	1.9	21,947	2.2	153,700	1.9
SEPTEMBER	112,371	4.2	19,329	9.4—	131,700	1.9
OCTOBER	108,502	1.5	19,198	4.4	127,700	1.9
NOVEMBER	98,861	12.9	16,439	10.6—	115,300	8.8
DECEMBER	106,085	1.7—	16,315	11.4—	122,400	3.1—
TOTAL	1,384,728	2.8	217,772	6.5—	1,602,500	1.4

KENTUCKY

PER CAPITA CONSUMPTION: 19.6 GALLONS

	TOTAL	% CHANGE
JANUARY	148,000	11.2—
FEBRUARY	167,000	3.7
MARCH	218,000	10.1
APRIL	189,000	.5
MAY	217,000	1.4
JUNE	243,000	2.8—
JULY	230,000	5.0
AUGUST	235,000	2.2
SEPTEMBER	203,300	1.1—
OCTOBER	179,000	4.1
NOVEMBER	195,000	12.1
DECEMBER	194,000	4.3
TOTAL	2,418,300	2.3

LOUISIANA

PER CAPITA CONSUMPTION: 27.1 GALLONS

	TOTAL	% CHANGE
JANUARY	286,167	4.8
FEBRUARY	286,464	.1
MARCH	324,303	1.5
APRIL	323,454	3.0
MAY	353,524	8.9
JUNE	337,931	1.1
JULY	305,280	8.1—
AUGUST	338,421	3.4
SEPTEMBER	317,415	2.6
OCTOBER	287,670	3.3—
NOVEMBER	289,515	7.1
DECEMBER	326,540	14.9
TOTAL	3,776,684	2.8

MAINE

PER CAPITA CONSUMPTION: 20.3 GALLONS

	TOTAL	% CHANGE
JANUARY	53,989	.1—
FEBRUARY	57,752	6.2
MARCH	67,713	2.9—
APRIL	63,551	8.0—
MAY	74,319	4.3—
JUNE	89,448	7.5
JULY	89,380	9.4—
AUGUST	86,461	18.6
SEPTEMBER	56,743	12.2—
OCTOBER	61,589	2.0
NOVEMBER	53,009	13.8—
DECEMBER	58,250	4.4
TOTAL	812,204	1.2—

MARYLAND

PER CAPITA CONSUMPTION: 19.3 GALLONS

	TOTAL	% CHANGE
JANUARY	180,572	11.0—
FEBRUARY	191,654	4.4
MARCH	265,585	10.4
APRIL	247,220	1.7—
MAY	293,275	3.6—
JUNE	327,307	3.1
JULY	292,915	6.4—
AUGUST	290,926	2.7—
SEPTEMBER	275,924	1.2
OCTOBER	228,158	1.8—
NOVEMBER	242,475	3.2
DECEMBER	273,102	.8—
TOTAL	3,109,113	.6—

Beer and Brewery Statistics

MASSACHUSETTS

PER CAPITA CONSUMPTION: 21.4 GALLONS

	TOTAL	% CHANGE
JANUARY	290,916	10.0
FEBRUARY	309,315	16.9
MARCH	333,012	.8
APRIL	320,306	4.3—
MAY	342,995	1.2
JUNE	424,346	7.0—
JULY	409,038	4.7
AUGUST	469,793	22.5
SEPTEMBER	298,001	14.6—
OCTOBER	282,574	11.4—
NOVEMBER	350,942	13.9
DECEMBER	341,201	3.9—
TOTAL	4,172,439	1.9

MICHIGAN

PER CAPITA CONSUMPTION: 21.8 GALLONS

	TOTAL	% CHANGE
JANUARY	415,141	7.4—
FEBRUARY	478,927	2.3
MARCH	557,184	1.2—
APRIL	546,940	6.0—
MAY	641,336	3.3
JUNE	683,998	5.7
JULY	617,911	3.0—
AUGUST	660,454	.5—
SEPTEMBER	526,931	8.8—
OCTOBER	516,744	4.8—
NOVEMBER	557,790	.3—
DECEMBER	486,115	.6
TOTAL	6,689,471	1.5—

MINNESOTA

PER CAPITA CONSUMPTION: 22.5 GALLONS

	TOTAL	% CHANGE
JANUARY	224,592	1.6
FEBRUARY	234,488	.2—
MARCH	283,378	20.3
APRIL	275,499	7.3—
MAY	307,469	.7
JUNE	360,423	14.1
JULY	339,808	13.2
AUGUST	295,621	2.7
SEPTEMBER	261,025	5.8—
OCTOBER	247,328	3.0
NOVEMBER	248,775	1.3
DECEMBER	232,456	.9—
TOTAL	3,310,862	3.6

MISSISSIPPI

PER CAPITA CONSUMPTION: 24.5 GALLONS

	PACKAGED	% CHANGE	DRAUGHT	% CHANGE	TOTAL	% CHANGE
JANUARY	151,507	3.6	5,092	91.6	156,599	5.2
FEBRUARY	163,289	6.6	4,755	31.8	168,044	7.1
MARCH	189,204	8.8	5,854	8.8	195,058	8.8
APRIL	163,407	3.5	5,845	45.0	169,252	4.5
MAY	190,389	10.4	5,593	26.3	195,982	10.8
JUNE	190,326	2.4—	6,135	28.8	196,461	1.7—
JULY	172,095	8.1—	5,149	29.9	177,244	7.4—
AUGUST	191,667	7.5	5,704	12.1	197,371	7.7
SEPTEMBER	170,537	3.3	4,058	4.8—	174,595	3.1
OCTOBER	160,850	5.6	5,284	13.8	166,134	5.9
NOVEMBER	147,285	.5—	4,202	16.3—	151,487	1.0—
DECEMBER	153,332	4.0—	3,515	9.6—	156,847	4.2—
TOTAL	2,043,888	2.7	61,186	18.3	2,105,074	3.1

MISSOURI

PER CAPITA CONSUMPTION: 24.2 GALLONS

	TOTAL	% CHANGE
JANUARY	322,334	12.4
FEBRUARY	310,488	7.4
MARCH	342,379	4.1
APRIL	323,074	4.6—
MAY	378,139	5.7
JUNE	411,396	10.6
JULY	381,532	.7
AUGUST	405,334	5.4
SEPTEMBER	352,288	3.2
OCTOBER	290,826	9.7—
NOVEMBER	313,284	5.5
DECEMBER	292,482	.2
TOTAL	4,123,556	3.4

MONTANA

PER CAPITA CONSUMPTION: 26.6 GALLONS

	PACKAGED	% CHANGE	DRAUGHT	% CHANGE	TOTAL	% CHANGE
JANUARY	41,502	10.1	8,096	8.9	49,598	9.9
FEBRUARY	42,277	2.1	7,155	16.5—	49,432	1.1—
MARCH	50,667	11.4	8,215	4.3	58,882	10.4
APRIL	51,451	3.7	8,376	18.5—	59,827	.1—
MAY	60,705	6.5—	8,359	21.5—	69,064	8.6—
JUNE	64,376	3.5—	8,860	27.0—	73,236	7.1—
JULY	66,525	16.0	9,438	4.8	75,963	14.5
AUGUST	62,366	8.1	9,565	7.7	71,931	8.0
SEPTEMBER	52,368	19.1	8,177	2.4—	60,545	15.6
OCTOBER	45,659	11.7—	8,051	2.9—	53,710	10.5—
NOVEMBER	48,979	5.9	7,280	3.1	56,259	5.5
DECEMBER	47,637	14.4	7,560	5.3	55,197	13.1
TOTAL	634,512	5.0	99,132	6.2—	733,644	3.3

Beer and Brewery Statistics

NEBRASKA

PER CAPITA CONSUMPTION: 24.7 GALLONS

	PACKAGED	% CHANGE	DRAUGHT	% CHANGE	TOTAL	% CHANGE
JANUARY	78,252	15.4	13,734	2.3—	91,986	12.4
FEBRUARY	75,108	2.3—	13,532	14.0—	88,640	4.3—
MARCH	89,330	10.4	17,512	9.7	106,842	10.3
APRIL	93,838	3.0	15,629	11.7—	109,467	.6
MAY	97,044	5.7—	16,357	11.2—	113,401	6.5—
JUNE	118,572	10.4	17,000	10.7—	135,572	7.2
JULY	111,399	14.1	16,282	1.3—	127,681	11.9
AUGUST	105,862	15.3	18,866	3.1	124,728	13.3
SEPTEMBER	88,797	3.9—	16,754	9.4—	105,551	4.8—
OCTOBER	77,580	6.2—	14,368	8.5—	91,948	6.6—
NOVEMBER	86,548	1.0—	15,162	2.0	101,710	.5—
DECEMBER	80,326	3.4—	13,916	4.9—	94,242	3.6—
TOTAL	1,102,656	3.8	189,112	5.2—	1,291,768	2.4

NEVADA

PER CAPITA CONSUMPTION: 35.1 GALLONS

	TOTAL	% CHANGE
JANUARY	124,700	15.5
FEBRUARY	130,200	10.3
MARCH	134,300	9.9
APRIL	146,300	3.1
MAY	149,300	2.8—
JUNE	161,400	7.2
JULY	141,000	5.6
AUGUST	154,300	3.1
SEPTEMBER	145,200	8.0
OCTOBER	122,500	3.9—
NOVEMBER	125,000	3.0—
DECEMBER	117,500	10.2
TOTAL	1,651,700	4.9

NEW HAMPSHIRE

PER CAPITA CONSUMPTION: 31.0 GALLONS

	TOTAL	% CHANGE
JANUARY	83,202	9.2
FEBRUARY	83,001	4.0—
MARCH	83,195	15.8—
APRIL	81,195	6.4—
MAY	99,044	8.1—
JUNE	136,801	14.7
JULY	118,004	2.2
AUGUST	124,927	5.9
SEPTEMBER	80,044	19.7—
OCTOBER	79,805	1.8—
NOVEMBER	91,622	.4
DECEMBER	74,594	20.3—
TOTAL	1,135,434	3.3—

NEW JERSEY

PER CAPITA CONSUMPTION: 18.9 GALLONS

	TOTAL	% CHANGE
JANUARY	260,000	4.6—
FEBRUARY	243,828	12.6—
MARCH	390,000	8.5
APRIL	358,857	3.3—
MAY	507,888	.0
JUNE	514,020	2.1—
JULY	485,000	.6—
AUGUST	494,431	2.2
SEPTEMBER	398,243	1.6—
OCTOBER	387,550	.6
NOVEMBER	398,627	4.0—
DECEMER	392,854	9.1—
TOTAL	4,831,298	1.9—

NEW MEXICO

PER CAPITA CONSUMPTION: 25.4 GALLONS

	PACKAGED	% CHANGE	DRAUGHT	% CHANGE	TOTAL	% CHANGE
JANUARY	82,424	12.8—	6,276	13.4	88,700	11.4—
FEBRUARY	98,930	8.3	5,770	29.4—	104,700	5.2
MARCH	94,609	.9—	7,491	7.4	102,100	.3—
APRIL	110,278	12.3	7,522	9.6—	117,800	10.6
MAY	120,317	13.6—	9,483	7.6	129,800	12.4—
JUNE	122,426	6.5	7,574	12.7—	130,000	5.2
JULY	115,092	11.0	6,308	15.8—	121,400	9.2
AUGUST	114,627	9.8—	7,773	6.3—	122,400	9.6—
SEPTEMBER	115,173	4.5	7,727	7.8—	122,900	3.6
OCTOBER	116,380	8.7	6,620	7.4	123,000	8.7
NOVEMBER	103,753	10.7—	6,747	3.6	110,500	9.9—
DECEMBER	75,270	12.9—	5,330	13.4—	80,600	13.0—
TOTAL	1,269,279	1.2—	84,621	5.4—	1,353,900	1.5—

NEW YORK

PER CAPITA CONSUMPTION: 17.8 GALLONS

	TOTAL	% CHANGE
JANUARY	600,000	3.2—
FEBRUARY	620,000	1.6
MARCH	850,000	3.7
APRIL	820,000	4.1—
MAY	940,000	2.1—
JUNE	1,125,000	4.2
JULY	1,100,000	2.2—
AUGUST	1,090,000	7.9
SEPTEMBER	870,000	7.5—
OCTOBER	780,000	6.0—
NOVEMBER	830,000	1.2—
DECEMBER	830,000	8.8—
TOTAL	10,455,000	1.4—

Beer and Brewery Statistics

NORTH CAROLINA

PER CAPITA CONSUMPTION: 20.8 GALLONS

	PACKAGED	% CHANGE	DRAUGHT	% CHANGE	TOTAL	% CHANGE
JANUARY	366,939	13.9	13,142	5.8—	380,081	13.1
FEBRUARY	350,665	3.9	15,507	5.6	366,172	4.0
MARCH	396,703	2.2	16,830	5.7—	413,533	1.8
APRIL	370,678	2.8	16,583	4.8—	387,261	2.5
MAY	423,447	14.0	16,913	1.4	440,360	13.5
JUNE	416,932	5.3—	17,026	11.6—	433,958	5.5—
JULY	436,383	2.0—	15,906	7.5—	452,289	2.2—
AUGUST	424,173	10.4	17,753	7.0—	441,926	9.6
SEPTEMBER	429,959	4.8	16,839	20.2	446,798	5.3
OCTOBER	357,013	1.8	17,560	15.4	374,573	2.4
NOVEMBER	293,523	10.9—	15,317	5.1—	308,840	10.6—
DECEMBER	293,044	13.4—	13,057	10.3—	306,101	13.3—
TOTAL	4,559,459	1.8	192,433	1.8—	4,751,892	1.7

NORTH DAKOTA

PER CAPITA CONSUMPTION: 25.8 GALLONS

	PACKAGED	% CHANGE	DRAUGHT	% CHANGE	TOTAL	% CHANGE
JANUARY	32,104	11.8	3,249	7.7—	35,353	9.6
FEBRUARY	33,422	3.7—	4,261	.3—	37,683	3.3—
MARCH	36,831	1.2—	5,351	11.2	42,182	.3
APRIL	36,894	.6—	4,685	3.4—	41,579	1.0—
MAY	45,963	6.3—	4,580	12.2—	50,543	6.8—
JUNE	53,572	4.6	5,242	8.0	58,814	4.9
JULY	47,193	6.5	5,835	7.8	53,028	6.7
AUGUST	48,038	25.1	4,862	12.7	52,900	23.8
SEPTEMBER	36,483	3.3—	4,575	.2—	41,058	3.0—
OCTOBER	33,129	10.6—	4,343	4.8—	37,472	9.9—
NOVEMBER	35,835	5.7—	4,477	7.8	40,312	4.4—
DECEMBER	36,393	2.3	4,150	4.3	40,543	2.5
TOTAL	475,857	1.4	55,610	2.0	531,467	1.5

OHIO

PER CAPITA CONSUMPTION: 23.0 GALLONS

	PACKAGED	% CHANGE	DRAUGHT	% CHANGE	TOTAL	% CHANGE
JANUARY	524,975	1.5	47,410	5.9—	572,385	.9
FEBRUARY	509,749	11.4—	50,152	9.0—	559,901	11.2—
MARCH	667,987	10.2	57,167	9.6—	725,154	8.3
APRIL	616,082	16.4	64,179	1.2	680,261	14.8
MAY	693,840	.6	72,884	2.8	766,724	.8
JUNE	715,194	1.5—	80,439	5.3—	795,633	1.9—
JULY	689,963	4.0—	75,213	7.6—	765,176	4.4—
AUGUST	725,799	7.9	79,365	5.3—	805,164	6.4
SEPTEMBER	599,530	6.1—	68,579	8.5—	668,109	6.3—
OCTOBER	554,254	7.3—	62,489	1.0—	616,743	6.7—
NOVEMBER	617,976	10.2	56,451	7.2—	674,427	8.5
DECEMBER	558,641	3.3—	50,081	7.5—	608,722	3.7—
TOTAL	7,473,990	.9	764,409	5.2—	8,238,399	.3

OKLAHOMA

PER CAPITA CONSUMPTION: 20.4 GALLONS

	PACKAGED	% CHANGE	DRAUGHT	% CHANGE	TOTAL	% CHANGE
JANUARY	150,194	16.0	12,128	1.7—	162,322	14.5
FEBRUARY	141,294	15.5	11,777	7.7—	153,071	13.3
MARCH	176,210	6.9	12,902	23.8—	189,112	4.1
APRIL	175,802	4.0	14,159	4.5—	189,961	3.4
MAY	179,382	7.1	13,469	8.3	192,851	7.2
JUNE	213,633	3.4	11,177	23.7—	224,810	1.6
JULY	189,708	.2	12,017	10.7—	201,725	.5—
AUGUST	175,193	2.5—	11,763	19.0—	186,956	3.8—
SEPTEMBER	167,137	3.1—	14,732	12.3—	181,869	3.9—
OCTOBER	143,248	.7—	12,263	2.4—	155,511	.9—
NOVEMBER	154,173	18.2	11,567	5.3—	165,740	16.2
DECEMBER	130,370	9.9—	10,979	15.5—	141,349	10.3—
TOTAL	1,996,344	3.9	148,933	10.5—	2,145,277	2.8

OREGON

PER CAPITA CONSUMPTION: 22.2 GALLONS

	PACKAGED	% CHANGE	DRAUGHT	% CHANGE	TOTAL	% CHANGE
JANUARY	119,240	8.2	29,749	7.9	148,989	8.1
FEBRUARY	122,347	.3	29,694	6.0	152,041	1.4
MARCH	151,916	1.1	37,009	2.3—	188,925	.4
APRIL	157,627	2.1	32,073	8.5—	189,700	.1
MAY	179,607	7.7	34,810	8.7	214,417	7.9
JUNE	173,486	3.1—	36,028	2.9—	209,514	3.1—
JULY	174,123	11.2—	35,629	2.3—	209,752	9.8—
AUGUST	194,180	21.6	38,948	4.5	233,128	18.3
SEPTEMBER	147,787	6.3	35,286	.4	183,073	5.1
OCTOBER	140,756	8.1	28,620	7.1—	169,376	5.1
NOVEMBER	131,687	5.7—	30,750	.7	162,437	4.6—
DECEMBER	115,175	10.2—	29,037	6.2—	144,212	9.4—
TOTAL	1,807,931	1.8	397,633	.3—	2,205,564	1.4

PENNSYLVANIA

PER CAPITA CONSUMPTION: 23.4 GALLONS

	PACKAGED	% CHANGE	DRAUGHT	% CHANGE	TOTAL	% CHANGE
JANUARY	455,892	5.8—	130,358	17.2—	586,250	8.6—
FEBRUARY	467,143	8.4—	127,797	13.0—	594,940	9.4—
MARCH	580,826	6.1	171,872	.2—	752,698	4.6
APRIL	554,936	4.2—	159,392	2.7—	714,328	3.9—
MAY	634,035	2.1	179,984	.8	814,019	1.8
JUNE	659,531	4.6—	200,168	2.1—	859,699	4.1—
JULY	637,451	2.8—	188,504	3.7—	825,955	3.0—
AUGUST	679,775	5.3	188,269	5.9—	868,044	2.6
SEPTEMBER	569,701	3.0—	167,140	7.8—	736,841	4.2—
OCTOBER	555,330	2.0—	164,971	3.3—	720,301	2.3—
NOVEMBER	724,116	23.0	161,397	1.1—	885,513	17.8
DECEMBER	568,646	9.4—	156,015	14.3—	724,661	10.5—
TOTAL	7,087,382	.3—	1,995,867	5.7—	9,083,249	1.5—

Beer and Brewery Statistics

RHODE ISLAND

PER CAPITA CONSUMPTION: 22.6 GALLONS

	PACKAGED	% CHANGE	DRAUGHT	% CHANGE	TOTAL	% CHANGE
JANUARY	51,364	42.5	6,941	12.5	58,305	38.1
FEBRUARY	47,927	16.4	8,027	38.4	55,954	19.2
MARCH	50,754	8.2—	6,395	28.7—	57,149	11.0—
APRIL	35,806	21.6—	5,749	30.3—	41,555	22.9—
MAY	50,140	15.2—	8,037	15.7	58,177	11.9—
JUNE	58,399	8.2—	7,360	25.7—	65,759	10.5—
JULY	63,130	8.9—	9,090	8.5—	72,220	8.9—
AUGUST	70,520	24.1	9,965	5.9	80,485	21.5
SEPTEMBER	55,174	12.2—	8,728	14.5—	63,902	12.5—
OCTOBER	50,817	2.2	7,879	14.0—	58,696	.3—
NOVEMBER	49,797	15.4	6,921	1.0—	56,718	13.1
DECEMBER	51,190	28.6	7,011	16.8	58,201	27.0
TOTAL	635,018	2.0	92,103	5.8—	727,121	1.0

SOUTH CAROLINA

PER CAPITA CONSUMPTION: 24.7 GALLONS

	PACKAGED	% CHANGE	DRAUGHT	% CHANGE	TOTAL	% CHANGE
JANUARY	209,080	6.9	7,920	1.3	217,000	6.6
FEBRUARY	216,403	4.2	8,797	5.5—	225,200	3.8
MARCH	260,583	10.8	11,717	1.7—	272,300	10.2
APRIL	229,149	7.6	9,851	13.2—	239,000	6.5
MAY	251,705	5.1	11,895	7.6	263,600	5.2
JUNE	262,392	.7	10,708	8.4—	273,100	.3
JULY	253,012	8.0—	8,688	20.2—	261,700	8.4—
AUGUST	256,427	5.7	10,773	2.2—	267,200	5.3
SEPTEMBER	243,968	3.3	9,231	11.4—	253,199	2.7
OCTOBER	214,664	2.6	9,337	1.7	224,001	2.5
NOVEMBER	197,564	1.0—	8,236	4.8—	205,800	1.2—
DECEMBER	212,926	1.4	7,674	11.9—	220,600	.9
TOTAL	2,807,873	3.1	114,827	5.9—	2,922,700	2.7

SOUTH DAKOTA

PER CAPITA CONSUMPTION: 24.3 GALLONS

	PACKAGED	% CHANGE	DRAUGHT	% CHANGE	TOTAL	% CHANGE
JANUARY	36,665	13.9	5,514	6.9	42,179	13.0
FEBRUARY	34,303	10.3	5,507	7.4—	39,810	7.5
MARCH	37,507	3.3	6,536	2.4	44,043	3.2
APRIL	35,859	.0	6,433	6.2	42,292	.9
MAY	45,161	.5	6,687	.4	51,848	.5
JUNE	55,939	19.1	6,752	14.1—	62,691	14.3
JULY	51,970	2.7	7,349	5.3—	59,319	1.6
AUGUST	45,933	.9	7,664	5.2	53,597	1.5
SEPTEMBER	38,665	11.4	6,151	14.4—	44,816	7.0
OCTOBER	38,598	1.3	5,951	1.9—	44,549	.9
NOVEMBER	34,161	6.6	5,510	2.3	39,671	6.0
DECEMBER	35,602	2.4—	5,079	9.1—	40,681	3.3—
TOTAL	490,363	5.5	75,133	2.9—	565,496	4.3

TENNESSEE

PER CAPITA CONSUMPTION: 21.5 GALLONS

	PACKAGED	% CHANGE	DRAUGHT	% CHANGE	TOTAL	% CHANGE
JANUARY	285,101	11.8	10,054	12.8—	295,155	10.8
FEBRUARY	265,658	6.3	11,239	4.2—	276,897	5.8
MARCH	282,665	7.1—	12,836	9.3—	295,501	7.2—
APRIL	282,010	6.4	13,304	2.5	295,314	6.2
MAY	314,113	10.6	15,033	9.3	329,146	10.5
JUNE	345,212	7.1	15,414	5.1	360,626	7.0
JULY	288,172	9.7—	11,434	15.9—	299,606	9.9—
AUGUST	316,830	4.1	15,008	11.7	331,838	4.4
SEPTEMBER	281,325	4.8—	12,974	17.7—	294,299	5.4—
OCTOBER	272,745	4.2	14,122	16.8	286,867	4.7
NOVEMBER	253,791	4.9—	11,371	13.5—	265,162	5.3—
DECEMBER	240,669	10.9—	10,631	6.3—	251,300	10.7—
TOTAL	3,428,291	.9	153,420	3.0—	3,581,711	.7

TEXAS

PER CAPITA CONSUMPTION: 28.3 GALLONS

	PACKAGED	% CHANGE	DRAUGHT	% CHANGE	TOTAL	% CHANGE
JANUARY	1,259,812	15.8	64,960	8.0	1,324,772	15.4
FEBRUARY	1,119,036	1.9—	67,942	4.0	1,186,978	1.6—
MARCH	1,351,154	1.8—	82,731	3.0	1,433,885	1.6—
APRIL	1,333,480	.6	79,956	4.1—	1,413,436	.3
MAY	1,490,960	9.3	73,832	2.9	1,564,792	9.0
JUNE	1,525,735	2.4	85,742	3.5	1,611,477	2.4
JULY	1,347,288	.6	66,413	11.4—	1,413,701	.1—
AUGUST	1,461,336	1.6	75,648	3.1	1,536,984	1.7
SEPTEMBER	1,317,378	4.1—	81,567	3.4	1,398,945	3.7—
OCTOBER	1,249,992	1.8—	77,040	7.7	1,327,032	1.3—
NOVEMBER	1,206,371	10.3	75,200	.2—	1,281,571	9.6
DECEMBER	1,218,866	5.5	55,170	9.2—	1,274,036	4.7
TOTAL	15,881,408	2.7	886,201	.9	16,767,609	2.6

UTAH

PER CAPITA CONSUMPTION: 12.9 GALLONS

	PACKAGED	% CHANGE	DRAUGHT	% CHANGE	TOTAL	% CHANGE
JANUARY	49,771	7.2	6,476	2.0	56,247	6.6
FEBRUARY	52,518	10.8	7,290	24.5—	59,808	4.8
MARCH	60,873	6.5	7,539	15.9	68,412	7.5
APRIL	58,557	1.5	5,586	4.5—	64,143	.9
MAY	59,976	2.2	6,036	9.1—	66,012	1.0
JUNE	73,106	2.3—	6,233	3.5—	79,339	2.4—
JULY	77,975	13.6	5,943	4.7	83,918	13.0
AUGUST	67,031	17.2	6,129	14.4—	73,160	13.7
SEPTEMBER	55,781	11.1—	6,764	4.8—	62,545	10.4—
OCTOBER	55,723	7.7—	5,963	12.3—	61,686	8.1—
NOVEMBER	51,969	10.0	5,921	15.5—	57,890	6.7
DECEMBER	52,302	1.6—	6,740	16.3—	59,042	3.5—
TOTAL	715,582	3.5	76,620	8.0—	792,202	2.3

Beer and Brewery Statistics

VERMONT

PER CAPITA CONSUMPTION: 23.3 GALLONS

	PACKAGED	% CHANGE	DRAUGHT	% CHANGE	TOTAL	% CHANGE
JANUARY	27,650	3.1—	3,419	11.9—	31,069	4.1—
FEBRUARY	28,128	.4	3,759	10.2—	31,887	1.0—
MARCH	30,149	7.9—	4,375	.6	34,524	7.1—
APRIL	32,239	.3	3,582	.4—	35,821	.2
MAY	33,042	6.0	3,454	1.9—	36,496	5.2
JUNE	40,307	6.1	4,440	20.1	44,747	7.4
JULY	41,275	4.2	3,274	21.7—	44,549	1.8
AUGUST	35,487	8.2—	3,858	5.4—	39,345	8.0—
SEPTEMBER	28,399	15.7—	3,974	8.5—	32,373	14.9—
OCTOBER	29,040	6.2	3,405	6.4	32,445	6.2
NOVEMBER	32,981	3.3	3,429	10.7—	36,410	1.8
DECEMBER	32,352	.4—	4,209	9.3	36,561	.6
TOTAL	391,049	.8—	45,178	3.4—	436,227	1.1—

VIRGINIA

PER CAPITA CONSUMPTION: 21.7 GALLONS

	TOTAL	% CHANGE
JANUARY	351,000	12.0
FEBRUARY	306,800	5.3—
MARCH	405,500	2.0
APRIL	367,500	6.2—
MAY	430,300	2.0
JUNE	423,100	5.0—
JULY	437,200	4.0—
AUGUST	428,000	.5
SEPTEMBER	412,000	2.0—
OCTOBER	343,300	.1—
NOVEMBER	346,000	1.5
DECEMBER	326,500	9.7—
TOTAL	4,577,200	1.4—

WASHINGTON

PER CAPITA CONSUMPTION: 20.9 GALLONS

	PACKAGED	% CHANGE	DRAUGHT	% CHANGE	TOTAL	% CHANGE
JANUARY	195,514	1.9	50,755	7.8	246,269	3.0
FEBRUARY	217,425	12.2	51,767	10.2	269,192	11.8
MARCH	242,944	3.4	61,294	6.2—	304,238	1.3
APRIL	263,255	2.2	53,448	13.2—	316,703	.8—
MAY	300,931	10.4	52,888	6.1—	353,819	7.6
JUNE	279,528	17.1—	55,079	3.2—	334,607	15.1—
JULY	301,062	8.6	53,216	10.4—	354,278	5.3
AUGUST	304,028	21.8	63,174	3.9	367,202	18.3
SEPTEMBER	245,384	2.3—	55,124	2.6—	300,508	2.3—
OCTOBER	217,617	2.4	50,176	5.3—	267,793	.9
NOVEMBER	199,111	3.4—	52,502	3.3—	251,613	3.4—
DECEMBER	188,615	4.4—	47,879	9.3—	236,494	5.5—
TOTAL	2,955,414	2.6	647,302	3.5—	3,602,716	1.4

WEST VIRGINIA

PER CAPITA CONSUMPTION: 21.5 GALLONS

	TOTAL	% CHANGE
JANUARY	90,400	6.2
FEBRUARY	99,500	1.5
MARCH	98,400	2.0
APRIL	101,000	4.5—
MAY	111,400	2.8
JUNE	122,100	1.9—
JULY	117,000	2.6—
AUGUST	121,400	1.8
SEPTEMBER	101,061	4.3—
OCTOBER	98,000	9.2—
NOVEMBER	103,000	9.0
DECEMBER	101,600	2.1—
TOTAL	1,264,861	.4—

WISCONSIN

PER CAPITA CONSUMPTION: 28.3 GALLONS

	TOTAL	% CHANGE
JANUARY	292,071	6.1—
FEBRUARY	336,546	3.7
MARCH	391,729	3.3
APRIL	398,423	3.7
MAY	432,440	4.9—
JUNE	477,546	.9—
JULY	455,258	10.9
AUGUST	450,187	5.8
SEPTEMBER	369,738	7.1—
OCTOBER	358,281	.7
NOVEMBER	355,323	2.4
DECEMBER	326,038	.1—
TOTAL	4,643,580	1.0

WYOMING

PER CAPITA CONSUMPTION: 25.0 GALLONS

	PACKAGED	% CHANGE	DRAUGHT	% CHANGE	TOTAL	% CHANGE
JANUARY	22,995	8.2	3,743	19.4	26,738	9.6
FEBRUARY	24,943	15.4	3,590	9.2—	28,533	11.6
MARCH	27,065	13.5	4,256	23.5	31,321	14.8
APRIL	22,628	.5	3,241	8.7—	25,869	.7—
MAY	30,828	4.0—	4,286	4.0	35,114	3.1—
JUNE	33,072	2.4	4,329	9.3—	37,401	.9
JULY	35,053	.9	4,903	.7	39,956	.9
AUGUST	33,712	11.9	4,452	11.8	38,164	11.9
SEPTEMBER	30,931	6.1	3,738	1.8—	34,669	5.2
OCTOBER	23,440	7.5—	3,136	3.4	26,576	6.4—
NOVEMBER	25,041	5.2	3,414	2.6	28,455	4.9
DECEMBER	24,590	3.6—	6,073	75.7	30,663	5.9
TOTAL	334,298	3.7	49,161	8.2	383,459	4.3

Beer and Brewery Statistics

Malt Beverage Consumption in the United States 1947-1995

	DOMESTIC TAX PAID SHIPMENTS	IMPORT SHIPMENTS	TOTAL APPARENT CONSUMPTION	ADULT* RESIDENT POPULATION	BARRELS PER ADULT	SERVINGS** PER ADULT	CHANGE IN TOTAL CONSUMPTION	CHANGE IN PER CAPITA CONSUMPTION
	(Thousands of Barrels)	*(Thousands of Barrels)*	*(Thousands of Barrels)*	*(Thousands of Persons)*	*(Units)*	*(Units)*	*(Percent)*	*(Percent)*
1947	87,172	109	87,281	100,539	0.8681	287.1	9.20	7.16
48	85,067	94	85,161	101,977	0.8351	276.1	-2.43	-3.80
49	84,557	79	84,636	103,250	0.8197	271.1	-0.62	-1.84
50	82,830	93	82,923	104,597	0.7928	262.1	-2.02	-3.29
51	83,824	115	83,939	105,160	0.7982	263.9	1.23	0.68
1952	84,836	123	84,959	105,902	0.8022	265.3	1.22	0.51
53	86,045	164	86,209	106,829	0.8070	266.8	1.47	0.59
54	83,305	183	83,488	107,991	0.7731	255.6	-3.16	-4.20
55	84,977	227	85,204	109,342	0.7792	257.7	2.06	0.79
56	85,008	249	85,257	110,548	0.7712	255.0	0.06	-1.03
1957	84,371	297	84,668	111,725	0.7578	250.6	-0.69	-1.74
58	84,425	333	84,758	112,833	0.7512	248.4	0.11	-0.88
59	87,622	384	88,006	114,090	0.7714	255.1	3.83	2.69
60	87,913	401	88,314	115,461	0.7649	252.9	0.35	-0.84
61	89,028	445	89,473	117,208	0.7634	252.4	1.31	-0.20
1962	91,197	503	91,700	118,655	0.7728	255.5	2.49	1.24
63	93,790	548	94,338	120,073	0.7857	259.8	2.88	1.66
64	98,644	668	99,312	121,468	0.8176	270.4	5.27	4.06
65	100,421	638	101,059	123,803	0.8163	269.9	1.76	-0.16
66	104,262	676	104,938	125,689	0.8349	276.1	3.84	2.28
1967	106,974	664	107,638	127,536	0.8440	279.1	2.57	1.09
68	111,416	774	112,190	129,511	0.8663	286.4	4.23	2.64
69	116,271	795	117,066	131,623	0.8894	294.1	4.35	2.67
70	121,860	890	122,750	134,226	0.9145	302.4	4.86	2.82
71	127,397	921	128,318	137,019	0.9365	309.7	4.54	2.41
1972	131,809	931	132,740	139,867	0.9490	313.8	3.45	1.34
73	138,468	1,132	139,600	142,597	0.9790	323.7	5.17	3.15
74	145,464	1,386	146,850	145,355	1.0103	334.1	5.19	3.20
75	148,644	1,679	150,323	148,299	1.0136	335.2	2.36	0.33
76	150,387	2,386	152,773	151,312	1.0097	333.9	1.63	-0.39
1977	156,914	2,546	159,460	154,299	1.0334	341.7	4.38	2.36
78	162,706	3,463	166,169	157,321	1.0562	349.3	4.21	2.21
79	168,116	4,443	172,559	160,464	1.0754	355.6	3.85	1.81
80	173,367	4,567	177,934	163,542	1.0880	359.8	3.11	1.17
81	176,696	5,221	181,917	166,253	1.0942	361.8	2.24	0.57
1982	176,578	5,754	182,332	168,852	1.0798	357.1	0.23	-1.31
83	177,495	6,314	183,809	171,226	1.0735	355.0	0.81	-0.59
84	175,479	7,203	182,682	173,345	1.0539	348.5	-0.61	-1.83
85	175,130	7,916	183,046	175,300	1.0442	345.3	0.20	-0.92
86	178,724	8,838	187,562	177,269	1.0581	349.9	2.47	1.33
1987	177,849	9,363	187,212	179,235	1.0445	345.4	-0.19	-1.28
88	178,234	9,398	187,632	181,253	1.0352	342.3	0.22	-0.89
89	179,397	8,660	188,057	183,363	1.0256	339.1	0.23	-0.93
90	184,474	8,783	193,257	185,246	1.0432	345.0	2.77	1.72
91 (1)	181,024	7,926	188,950	187,022	1.0103	334.1	-2.23	-3.16
1992 (2)	178,924	8,323	187,247	188,866	0.9914	327.8	-0.90	-1.87
93 (3)	178,901	9,247	188,148	190,684	0.9867	326.3	0.48	-0.48
94 (4)	176,872	10,490	187,362	192,316	0.9742	322.1	-0.42	-1.26
95 (5)	174,461	11,263	185,724	194,015	0.9573	316.5	-0.87	-1.74

* Eighteen years of age and older.
** Twelve ounce equivalent servings
(1) Excludes an estimated 425 thousand barrels of malt based coolers.
(2) Excludes an estimated 900 thousand barrels of malt based coolers.
(3) Excludes an estimated 1,500 thousand barrels of malt based coolers and 500 thousand barrels of Zima "clear malt beverage".
(4) Excludes an estimated 1,700 thousand barrels of malt based coolers and 1,240 thousand barrels of Zima "clear malt beverage".
(5) Excludes an estimated 1,800 thousand barrels of malt based coolers and 700 thousand barrels of Zima "clear malt beverage"

© Copyright 1996, R.S. Weinberg & Associates

BREWING INDUSTRY RESEARCH PROGRAM
R. S. WEINBERG & ASSOCIATES
May 24, 1996

Beer and Brewery Statistics

TOTAL MALT BEVERAGE CONSUMPTION 1947–1995

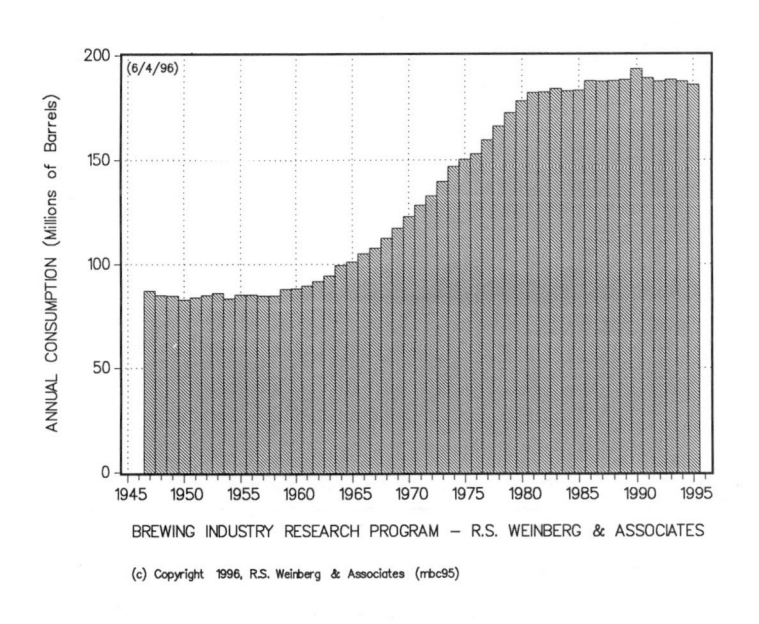

MALT BEVERAGE CONSUMPTION 1948–1995
ANNUAL PERCENTAGE CHANGE

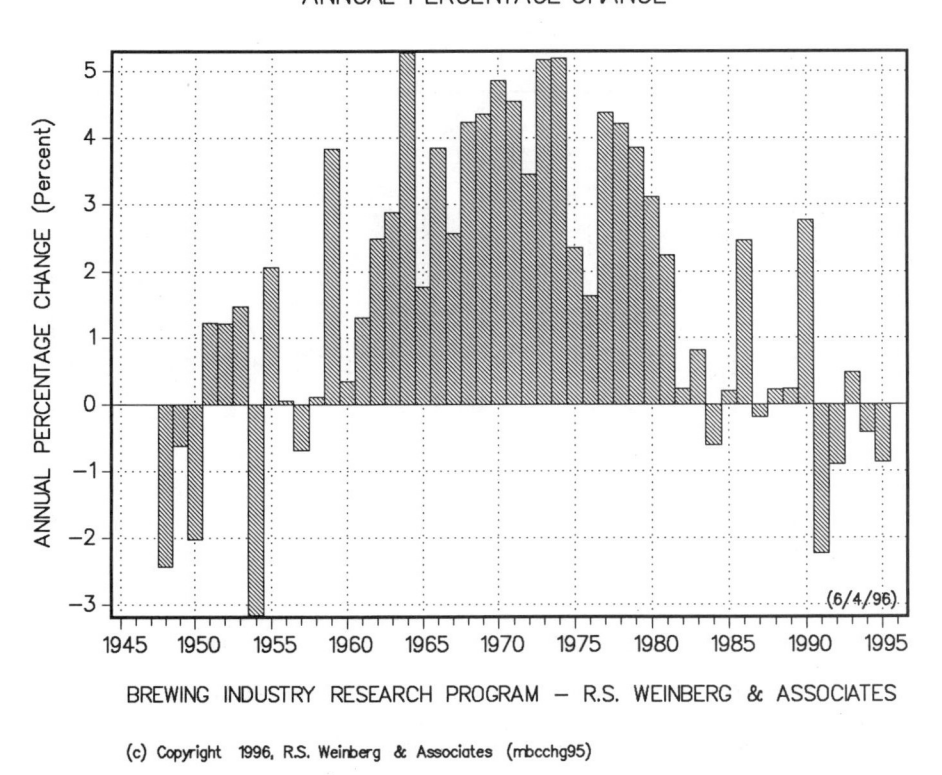

Institute for Brewing Studies — Page 111

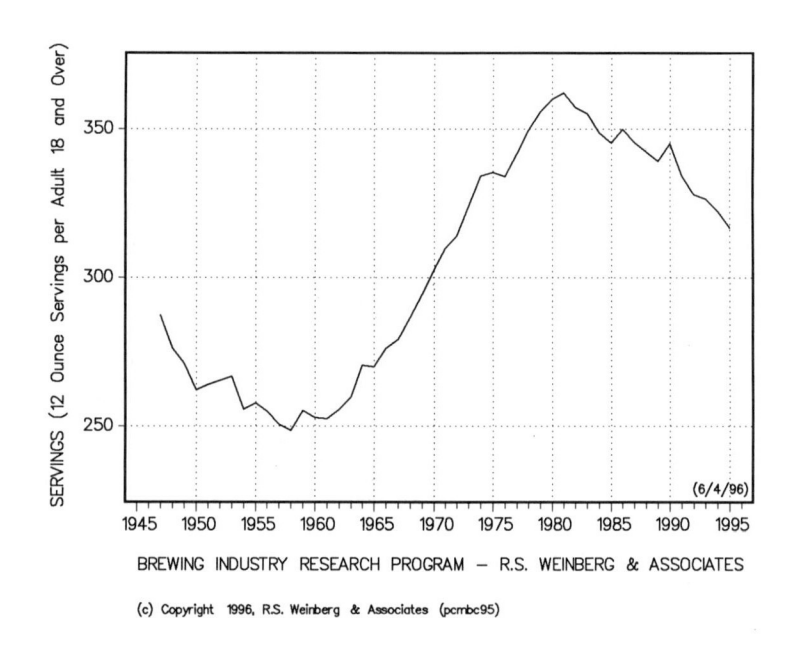

Beer and Brewery Statistics

ADULT PER CAPITA MALT BEVERAGE CONSUMPTION 1947–1995

BREWING INDUSTRY RESEARCH PROGRAM – R.S. WEINBERG & ASSOCIATES

(c) Copyright 1996, R.S. Weinberg & Associates (pcmbc95)

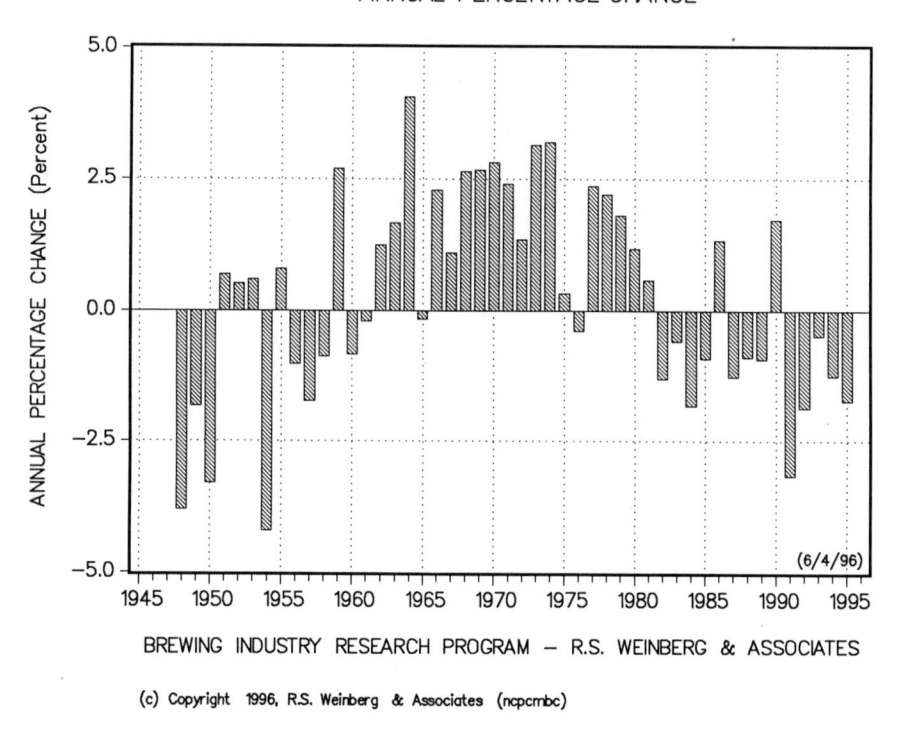

ADULT PER CAPITA MALT BEVERAGE CONSUMPTION 1948–1995
ANNUAL PERCENTAGE CHANGE

BREWING INDUSTRY RESEARCH PROGRAM – R.S. WEINBERG & ASSOCIATES

(c) Copyright 1996, R.S. Weinberg & Associates (ncpcmbc)

Beer and Brewery Statistics

Brewing Operations Ratios

Component	Actual Production of Beer			
	5,000 bbl. beer	15,000 bbl. beer	25,000 bbl. beer	50,000 bbl. beer
100% malt (raw barley weight)	275,870 lb. (328,300 lb.)	827,610 lb. (984,900 lb.)	1,379,350 lb. (1,641,500 lb.)	2,758,700 lb. (3,283,000 lb.)
75% malt (raw barley weight)	199,430 lb. (237,160 lb.)	598,290 lb. (711,480 lb.)	997,150 lb. (1,185,800 lb.)	1,994,300 lb. (2,371,600 lb.)
25% rice	66,640 lb.	199,920 lb.	333,200 lb.	666,400 lb.
Hops (20 IBU) (6.5%)	2,450 lb.	7,350 lb.	12,250 lb.	24,500 lb.
Yeast (pressed cake)	6,585 lb.	19,755 lb.	33,930 lb.	65,855 lb.
Spent yeast (pressed cake)	1,915 lb.	59,265 lb.	101,790 lb.	197,565 lb.
Water (entire process)	75,000 bbl.	225,000 bbl.	375,000 bbl.	750,000 bbl.
Brewhouse (60 bbl./brew)	98 brews, 1 line	294 brews, 1 line	490 brews, 1 line	980 brews, 1 line
Fermenting (7 days)	2 tanks, 135 bbl. ea.	4 tanks, 135 bbl. ea.	6 tanks, 135 bbl. ea.	11 tanks, 135 bbl. ea.
Aging (28 days)	5 tanks, 130 bbl. ea.	14 tanks, 130 bbl. ea.	22 tanks, 130 bbl. ea.	44 tanks, 130 bbl. ea.
Finishing (7 days)	2 tanks, 110 bbl. ea.	7 tanks, 110 bbl. ea.	12 tanks, 110 bbl. ea.	24 tanks, 110 bbl. ea.
Staff	2 skilled, 2 unskilled	2 skilled, 4 unskilled	2 skilled, 6 unskilled	2 skilled, 8 unskilled
Square footage	2,500 sq. ft.	7,500 sq. ft.	12,500 sq. ft.	25,000 sq. ft.

5 United States Breweries

With the resurgence of microbreweries and brewpubs, the number of companies making beer in the United States has grown from fewer than forty in 1980 to more than eight hundred today. From the large corporations that operate using 1,000-barrel-sized fermenters all the way down to backyard operations with homebrew-style glass carboy fermenters, every commercially licensed brewery is now listed in this single chapter of the *North American Brewers Resource Directory*.

The breweries are compiled in two ways. First is a state-by-state list with only a brewery's name, city, and state. This list separates the breweries into the following categories: large breweries (having annual sales greater than 500,000 barrels); regional breweries (having annual sales and/or capacity between 15,000 and 500,000 barrels); microbreweries (having annual sales less than 15,000 barrels); and brewpubs (restaurant-breweries with 50 percent or greater sales on site). Second is the directory listing of all breweries, also ordered alphabetically by state, complete with addresses, phone numbers, and personnel.

Note: Companies that sell a brand of beer but do not operate their own brewing facility are listed in chapter 7, "North American Contract Brewing Companies," page 199.

* Denotes Institute for Brewing Studies Brewery Member.
† Denotes brewery with on-site restaurant or pub.
‡ Denotes also operates brew-on-premise.

ALABAMA
MICROBREWERIES
Birmingham Brewing Co*
Birmingham, Alabama

BREWPUBS
Magic City Brewery
Birmingham, Alabama

Mill Brewery Bakery & Eatery
Birmingham, Alabama

**Montgomery Brewing Co/
Alabama Brewpubs LLC***
Montgomery, Alabama

**Poplar Head Mule Co
Brewpub and Grill**
Dothan, Alabama

Port City Brewery
Mobile, Alabama

ALASKA
REGIONAL BREWERIES
Alaskan Brewing and Bottling Co*
Juneau, Alaska

MICROBREWERIES
Bird Creek Brewery Inc
Anchorage, Alaska

Borealis Brewery
Anchorage, Alaska

Midnight Sun Brewing Co
Anchorage, Alaska

Railway Brewing Co†
Anchorage, Alaska

Raven Ridge Brewing Co*
Fairbanks, Alaska

BREWPUBS
Cusack's Brewpub and Roaster
Anchorage, Alaska

**Northern Lights
Brewing Co/Shannon's Cafe***
Anchorage, Alaska

**Regal Eagle Brewing Co/
North Slope Brewing Co**
Eagle River, Alaska

ARIZONA
MICROBREWERIES
Black Mountain Brewing Co*
Cave Creek, Arizona

Four Peaks Brewing Co*
Tempe, Arizona

McFarlane Brewing Co
Scottsdale, Arizona

Oak Creek Brewing Co*
Sedona, Arizona

Sonora Brewing Co
Phoenix, Arizona

BREWPUBS
Bandersnatch Brewpub
Tempe, Arizona

**Beaver Street
Brewery & Whistle Stop Cafe***
Flagstaff, Arizona

Copper Canyon Brewing Ale House†
Chandler, Arizona

**Coyote Springs
Brewing Co and Cafe***
Phoenix, Arizona

Flagstaff Brewing Co*
Flagstaff, Arizona

Gentle Bens Brewing Co
Tucson, Arizona

Hops Bistro and Brewery (No 1)
Scottsdale, Arizona

Hops Bistro and Brewery (No 3)
Phoenix, Arizona

Hops Bistro and Brewery (No 4)
Scottsdale, Arizona

Lawler Brewing Co
Scottsdale, Arizona

Prescott Brewing Co*
Prescott, Arizona

Tombstone Brewing Co‡
Tempe, Arizona

ARKANSAS
MICROBREWERIES
Weidman's Old Fort Brewery*
Fort Smith, Arkansas

BREWPUBS
Ozark Brewing Co*
Fayetteville, Arkansas

Vino's
Little Rock, Arkansas

CALIFORNIA — NORTHERN
LARGE BREWERIES
Anheuser-Busch Inc
Fairfield, California

REGIONAL BREWERIES
Humboldt Brewery†
Arcata, California

Mendocino Brewing Co*†
Hopland, California

Sierra Nevada Brewing Co*†
Chico, California

MICROBREWERIES
American River Brewing Co
Auburn, California

Anderson Valley Brewing Co*†
Boonville, California

Bear Republic Brewing Co*
Healdsburg, California

El Dorado Brewing Co*
Mount Aukum, California

Etna Brewing Co*
Etna, California

Hangtown Brewery Inc
Placerville, California

Humes Brewing Co Inc*
Glen Ellen, California

Mad River Brewing Co
Blue Lake, California

Moonlight Brewing Co
Fulton, California

Murphys Creek Brewing Co
Murphys, California

Napa Valley Ale Works*
Napa, California

Nevada City Brewing Co
Nevada City, California

North Coast Brewing*†
Fort Bragg, California

Pacific Hop Exchange
Novato, California

Sudwerk Privatbrauerei Hubsch*†
Davis, California

Truckee Brewing Co†
Truckee, California

Tuscan Brewery
Red Bluff, California

BREWPUBS
Amber Waves Brewery and Pub
Vacaville, California

Blue Water Brewing Co*
Tahoe City, California

Brewery at Lake Tahoe*
South Lake Tahoe, California

Carlsbad Brewery
and Public House
Carlsbad, California

Downtown Joe's
Brewery and Restaurant
Napa, California

Eel River Brewing Co*
Fortuna, California

Elk Grove Brewing Co Inc*
Elk Grove, California

Grizzly Bay Brewing Co
Suisun City, California

Hogshead Brewpub
Sacramento, California

Lost Coast Brewery & Cafe*
Eureka, California

Moylan's Brewing Co*
Novato, California

Napa Valley Brewing Co
Calistoga, California

Powerhouse Brewing Co
Sebastopol, California

Red White and Brew
Redding, California

River City Brewing Co*
Sacramento, California

Rubicon Brewing Co
Sacramento, California

Santa Rosa Brewing Co*
Santa Rosa, California

Sonoma Brewing Co*
Petaluma, California

Sutter Brewing Co Inc*
Sacramento, California

Third Street Ale Works
Santa Rosa, California

Valley of the Moon Brewery*
Sonoma, California

CALIFORNIA — BAY AREA
REGIONAL BREWERIES
Anchor Brewing Co*
San Francisco, California

MICROBREWERIES
Brew City*‡
San Francisco, California

BrewMakers/Venture Brewing Inc‡
Mountain View, California

Golden Pacific Brewing Co*
Emeryville, California

Gordon Biersch Brewery (No 1)*
Emeryville, California

Hop Town Brewing Co
Pleasanton, California

K C Brewing Co
San Leandro, California

Lagunitas Brewing Co*
Lagunitas, California

Lind Brewing Co
San Leandro, California

Pacific Brewing Co
San Rafael, California

Tied House Cafe
and Brewery (No 3)
Alameda, California

BREWPUBS
Barley & Hopps*
San Mateo, California

Bison Brewing Co*
Berkeley, California

Black Diamond Brewing Co*
Walnut Creek, California

Buffalo Bill's Brewery
Hayward, California

Burlingame Station Brewing
Co/Golden State Brewing Co
Burlingame, California

Cafe Pacifica/Sankt Gallen Brewery
San Francisco, California

Faultline Brewing Co Inc
Sunnyvale, California

Fremont Brewing Co
Fremont, California

Fullerton Hofbrau
Fullerton, California

Gordon Biersch
Brewery Restaurant (No. 1)*
Palo Alto, California

Gordon Biersch
Brewery Restaurant (No 2)*
San Jose, California

Gordon Biersch
Brewery Restaurant (No 3)*
San Francisco, California

United States Breweries

Los Gatos Brewing Co
Los Gatos, California

Marin Brewing Co*
Larkspur, California

Pacific Coast Brewing Co*
Oakland, California

Pleasanton Main St Brewin Co
Pleasanton, California

**Pyramid Alehouse
and Brewery at Berkeley**
Berkeley, California

**Redwood Coast Brewing Co/Tied
House Cafe and Brewery (No 1)***
Mountain View, California

San Francisco Brewing Co
San Francisco, California

Stoddard's Brewhouse & Eatery
Sunnyvale, California

Tied House Cafe and Brewery (No 2)
San Jose, California

Triple Rock Brewing*
Berkeley, California

Twenty Tank Brewery
San Francisco, California

CALIFORNIA — CENTRAL
REGIONAL BREWERIES
**St Stan's Brewery
Pub and Restaurant***†
Modesto, California

MICROBREWERIES
Carmel Brewing Co
Carmel, California

Coast Range Brewing Co*
Gilroy, California

Covany Brewing Co
Grover Beach, California

El Toro Brewing Co*
Morgan Hill, California

San Andreas Brewing Co†
Hollister, California

BREWPUBS
Boulder Creek Brewing Co
Boulder Creek, California

Butterfield Brewing Co*
Fresno, California

El Dorado Brewing Co*
Stockton, California

Mammoth Brewing Co
Mammoth Lakes, California

Parrots Ferry Brewing Co
Sonora, California

Sacramento Brewing Co*
Sacramento, California

**Santa Cruz Brewing
Co./Front Street Pub**
Santa Cruz, California

Seabright Brewery Inc*
Santa Cruz, California

Seaport Pub and Brewery
Stockton, California

SLO Brewing Co Inc *
San Luis Obispo, California

Snowshoe Brewing Co
Arnold, California

CALIFORNIA — SOUTHERN
LARGE BREWERIES
Anheuser-Busch Inc
Los Angeles, California

Miller Brewing Co*
Irwindale, California

MICROBREWERIES
AleSmith Brewing Co
San Diego, California

Bayhawk Ales Inc*
Irvine, California

Blind Pig Brewing Co
Temecula, California

California Brewing Co
El Segundo, California

Heritage Brewing Co*
Lake Elsinore, California

**Karl Strauss Breweries/
Associated Microbreweries***
San Diego, California

Newport Beach Brewing Co
Newport Beach, California

Old River Brew Co*
Bakersfield, California

Riverside Brewing Co*†
Riverside, California

Southern California Brewing Co
Torrance, California

BREWPUBS
**Ale House Rock
Brewery and Broiler***
Huntington Beach, California

B J's Brewery/Chicago Pizza Inc
Brea, California

Baja Brewing Co
San Diego, California

Belmont Brewing Co*
Long Beach, California

**Bootlegger's
Steakhouse & Brewery***
Shafter, California

**Brewmeisters/
Palm Springs Brewery Inc**
Palm Springs, California

Brewski's Brewing Co
El Segundo, California

Callahan's Pub and Brewery*
San Diego, California

Crown City Brewery
Pasadena, California

**Delmar Stuft
Pizza and Microbrewery**
San Diego, California

**Dino & Luigi's Stuft
Pizza Sports Bar and Brewery**
San Diego, California

Glencastle Brewing Co
Glendale, California

**Gordon Biersch
Brewery Restaurant (No 4)***
Pasadena, California

Harbor Lights Brewing Co*
Dana Point, California

Hops Bistro and Brewery (No 2)*
San Diego, California

Huntington Beach Beer Co*
Huntington Beach, California

Joe - Joe's Brewing Co
Simi Valley, California

Karl Strauss Brewery Gardens
San Diego, California

La Jolla Brewing Co
La Jolla, California

Laguna Beach Brewing Co*
Laguna Beach, California

Mainline Brewing Co
Los Angeles, California

Manhattan Beach Brewing Co
Manhattan Beach, California

Newport Beach Brewing Co
Newport Beach, California

Ocean Ave Brewing Co*
Laguna Beach, California

Old Baldy Brewing Co
Upland, California

Old Columbia Brewery
San Diego, California

R J's Riptide Brewery*
San Diego, California

Redondo Beach Brewing Co
Redondo Beach, California

San Diego Brewing Co*
San Diego, California

San Marcos Brewery and Grill*
San Marcos, California

Santa Barbara Brewing Co*
Santa Barbara, California

Santa Clarita Brewing Co
Santa Clarita, California

Santa Monica Brewing Co*
Culver City, California

Shields Brewing Co*
Ventura, California

Steelhead Brewery and Cafe
Irvine, California

Terrific Pacific Brewery and Grill
La Jolla, California

Westwood Brewing Co
Los Angeles, California

COLORADO

LARGE BREWERIES

Anheuser-Busch Inc
Fort Collins, Colorado

Coors Brewing Co*
Golden, Colorado

REGIONAL BREWERIES

Broadway Brewing Co*†
Denver, Colorado

New Belgium Brewing Co*
Fort Collins, Colorado

Rockies Brewing Co./Pub at Rockies*†
Boulder, Colorado

MICROBREWERIES

Avery Brewing Co*
Boulder, Colorado

Back Alley Brewing Co*
Colorado Springs, Colorado

Breckenridge Brewery Colorado*†
Denver, Colorado

Breckenridge Brewery Denver*†
Denver, Colorado

Bristol Brewing Co*
Colorado Springs, Colorado

Brouwer Brewery
Loveland, Colorado

Colorado Brewing Co
Thornton, Colorado

Coophouse Brewery
Broomfield, Colorado

Durango Brewing Co
Durango, Colorado

Eldorado Canyon Brewing Co
Broomfield, Colorado

Estes Park Brewery†
Estes Park, Colorado

Golden City Brewery*
Golden, Colorado

Great Divide Brewing Co*
Denver, Colorado

H C Berger Brewing Co*
Fort Collins, Colorado

Irons Brewing Co*
Lakewood, Colorado

**Judge Baldwin's Brewing Co/
B F Coleman Brewing Corp***
Colorado Springs, Colorado

Left Hand Brewing Co*
Longmont, Colorado

Lone Wolfe Brewing Co
Carbondale, Colorado

Lonetree Brewing Ltd
Denver, Colorado

Mark's Brewing Co
Berthoud, Colorado

Mile High Brewing Co*
Denver, Colorado

Namaqua Brewing Co*
Loveland, Colorado

Oasis Brewery Annex*
Boulder, Colorado

Odell Brewing Co*
Fort Collins, Colorado

One Keg Brewhouse
Arvada, Colorado

Only the Best Brewing Co Inc
Divide, Colorado

Palmer Lake Brewing Co
Palmer Lake, Colorado

Peak to Peak Brewing Co
Rollinsville, Colorado

Pikes Peak Brewery Inc*
Colorado Springs, Colorado

Platte Bottom Brewery*
Brighton, Colorado

**Powers Brewing Co/
Powers Colorado Brew***
Brighton, Colorado

**Rockslide Brewpub/
Snowy Mountain Brewpub***
Grand Junction, Colorado

**SandLot Brewery at
Coors Field/Coors Brewing Co**
Denver, Colorado

Silver Plume Brewing Co*
Silver Plume, Colorado

SKA Brewing Co
Durango, Colorado

Tabernash Brewing Co*
Denver, Colorado

Tivoli Brewery/(america!)†
Denver, Colorado

Tommyknocker Brewery & Pub*†
Idaho Springs, Colorado

Twisted Pine Brewing Co
Boulder, Colorado

BREWPUBS

Baked and Brewed in Telluride*
Telluride, Colorado

**Big Horn Brewing
Co of Colorado/C B Potts***
Englewood, Colorado

Breckenridge Brewery and Pub*†
Breckenridge, Colorado

Carver Brewing Co*
Durango, Colorado

Champion Brewing Co
Denver, Colorado

Columbine Mill Brewery Inc*
Littleton, Colorado

CooperSmith's Pub and Brewing*
Fort Collins, Colorado

**Crested Butte
Brewing Co/Idle Spur Restaurant***
Crested Butte, Colorado

Denver Chop House and Brewery
Denver, Colorado

Dimmer's Brew Pub Inc*
Fort Collins, Colorado

Fleetside Pub & Brewery
Greeley, Colorado

Flying Dog Brewpub*
Aspen, Colorado

Glenwood Canyon Brewing Co
Glenwood Springs, Colorado

Heavenly Daze Brewery & Grill*
Steamboat Springs, Colorado

Hubcap Brewery and Kitchen*
Vail, Colorado

Il Vicino Wood Oven Pizza (No 2)*
Salida, Colorado

**Main Street Brewery/
Four Corners Brewing Co**
Cortez, Colorado

Mercury Cafe*
Denver, Colorado

Mountain Sun Pub and Brewery
Boulder, Colorado

Oasis Brewery and Restaurant*
Boulder, Colorado

**Old Colorado
Brewing Co/Casa de Colorado**
Fort Collins, Colorado

Ouray Brewing Co
Ouray, Colorado

Overland Stage Stop Brewery
Longmont, Colorado

Phantom Canyon Brewing Co*
Colorado Springs, Colorado

Pumphouse Brewery
Longmont, Colorado

Rock Bottom Brewery
Denver, Colorado

San Juan Brewing Co*
Telluride, Colorado

Sharkey's Brew Club‡
Colorado Springs, Colorado

Smiling Moose Inc
Greeley, Colorado

Steamboat Brewery and Tavern*
Steamboat Springs, Colorado

Union Colony Brewery*
Greeley, Colorado

United States Breweries

Walnut Brewery*
Boulder, Colorado

Wynkoop Brewing Co*
Denver, Colorado

CONNECTICUT
MICROBREWERIES

Elm City Brewing Co/The Brewery*†
New Haven, Connecticut

Farmington River Brewing Co*
Bloomfield, Connecticut

Hammer and Nail Brewers
Oakville, Connecticut

Mystic River Brewing Co*
Mystic, Connecticut

New England Brewing Co/Brewhouse Restaurant*†
Norwalk, Connecticut

Quality Assured Brewing
New Haven, Connecticut

BREWPUBS

Brürm at Bar
New Haven, Connecticut

Hartford Brewery Ltd
Hartford, Connecticut

DELAWARE
MICROBREWERIES

Rockford Brewing Co
Wilminton, Delaware

BREWPUBS

Brandywine Brewing Co
Wilminton, Delaware

Dogfish Head Brewing and Eats
Rehoboth Beach, Delaware

Stewart's Brewing Co
Bear, Delaware

DISTRICT OF COLUMBIA
BREWPUBS

Capitol City Brewing Co*
Washington, District of Columbia

Capitol City Brewing Co (No 2)
Washington, District of Columbia

Dock Street Brewery and Restaurant (No 2)
Washington, District of Columbia

FLORIDA
LARGE BREWERIES

Anheuser-Busch Inc
Tampa, Florida

Anheuser-Busch Inc
Jacksonville, Florida

Stroh Brewery Co Tampa Plant*
Tampa, Florida

REGIONAL BREWERIES

Florida Brewery Inc*
Auburndale, Florida

MICROBREWERIES

Beach Brewing Co*
Orlando, Florida

Dunedin Brewery/Prospector Brewing Services*
Dunedin, Florida

Firehouse Brewing Co*
Miami, Florida

Key West Overseas Brewery
Key West, Florida

Miami Brewing Co*
Miami, Florida

Treasure Coast Brewing Co*
Stuart, Florida

Williamsville Brewery
Fernandina Beach, Florida

Ybor City Brewing Co
Tampa, Florida

BREWPUBS

A1A Aleworks
St Augustine, Florida

Blue Anchor Pub
Jacksonville, Florida

Buckhead Brewery and Grill
Tallahasee, Florida

Coasters
Melbourne, Florida

Don Gambrinu's Brewpub Inc*
Miami, Florida

Highlands Brewery
Sebring, Florida

Hoppers Brooker Creek Grille and Taproom
Palm Harbor, Florida

Hops Grill and Bar in Boynton Beach
Boynton Beach, Florida

Hops Grill and Bar in Bradenton
Bradenton, Florida

Hops Grill and Bar in Carrollwood
Tampa, Florida

Hops Grill and Bar in Clearwater
Clearwater, Florida

Hops Grill and Bar in Jacksonville
Jacksonville, Florida

Hops Grill and Bar in Lakeland
Lakeland, Florida

Hops Grill and Bar in N Tampa
Tampa, Florida

Hops Grill and Bar in Ocala
Ocala, Florida

Hops Grill and Bar in Orange Park
Orange Park, Florida

Hops Grill and Bar in Orlando
Orlando, Florida

Hops Grill and Bar in Palm Harbor
Palm Harbor, Florida

Hops Grill and Bar in Port Richey
Port Richey, Florida

Hops Grill and Bar in S Tampa
Tampa, Florida

Hops Grill and Bar in St Petersburg
St Petersburg, Florida

Irish Times Pub & Brewery
Palm Beach, Florida

Kelly's Caribbean Bar & Grill
Key West, Florida

Market Street Pub
Gainesville, Florida

McGuire's Irish Pub and Brewery*
Pensacola, Florida

Mill Brewery, Eatery, & Bakery
Fort Myers, Florida

Mill Brewery, Eatery, & Bakery
Winter Park, Florida

New World Brewery
Tampa, Florida

Ragtime Taproom
Atlantic Beach, Florida

River City Brewing Co*
Jacksonville, Florida

Santa Rosa Bay Brewing Co*
Fort Walton Beach, Florida

Sarasota Brewing Co*
Sarasota, Florida

South Pointe Seafood House and Brewing Co*
Miami Beach, Florida

Thai Orchid Restaurant
Coral Gables, Florida

Thai Orchid Restaurant/Thai Orchid USA Inc*
Miami, Florida

Tortuga's
Jacksonville Beach, Florida

Windrose Brew Pub
Naples, Florida

GEORGIA
LARGE BREWERIES

Anheuser-Busch Inc
Cartersville, Georgia

Miller Brewing Co*
Albany, Georgia

MICROBREWERIES

Atlanta Brewing Co*
Atlanta, Georgia

Blind Man Ales
Athens, Georgia

Dogwood Brewing Co
Atlanta, Georgia

Marthasville Brewing Co
Atlanta, Georgia

BREWPUBS
Athens Brewing Co
Athens, Georgia

Atlanta Beer Garden
Atlanta, Georgia

Buckhead Beer Co*
Atlanta, Georgia

John Harvard's Brewhouse
(No 2)/The Brew House LLC
Atlanta, Georgia

Phoenix Brewing Co
Atlanta, Georgia

US Border Brewery Cantina
Alpharetta, Georgia

HAWAII
MICROBREWERIES
Ali'i Brewing Co
Honolulu, Oahu, Hawaii

Great Hawaiian Brewing Co
Honolulu, Oahu, Hawaii

Kona Brewing Co
Kailua, Oahu, Hawaii

Maui Kine Brewery Ltd*
Kahului, Maui, Hawaii

Trade Winds Brewing Co
Wailuku, Maui, Hawaii

BREWPUBS
Gordon Biersch
Brewery and Restaurant (No 5)*
Honolulu, Oahu, Hawaii

Shark Tooth
Brewery and Steakhouse
Kahului, Maui, Hawaii

IDAHO
MICROBREWERIES
Beier Brewing Co
Boise, Idaho

Coeur D'Alene Brewing
Co./T W Fisher's Brewpub*†
Coeur D'Alene, Idaho

Eagle Brewing Co Inc*
Eagle, Idaho

McCall Brewing Co/Cerveceria Inc*
McCall, Idaho

M J Barleyhoppers
Brewery and Sports Pub*†
Lewiston, Idaho

Sun Valley Brewing Co*†
Hailey, Idaho

Table Rock Brewing Inc*
Meridian, Idaho

Thunder Mountain Brewery
Ketchum, Idaho

BREWPUBS
Gem State Brewing*
Caldwell, Idaho

Harrison Hollow Brewhouse
Boise, Idaho

Pend Oreille Brewing Co*
Sandpoint, Idaho

Star Garnet Brewing
Boise, Idaho

Table Rock Brewpub and Grill*
Boise, Idaho

Treaty Grounds Brewpub
Moscow, Idaho

Twin Falls Brewing
Co./Muggers Brewpub
Twin Falls, Idaho

ILLINOIS
LARGE BREWERIES
G Heileman Brewing Co Inc
Rosemont, Illinois

MICROBREWERIES
Americas Brewpub at Walter
Payton's Roundhouse Complex†
Aurora, Illinois

Chicago Brewing Co*
Chicago, Illinois

Flatlander's Brewing Co*
Lincolnshire, Illinois

Golden Prairie Brewing Co*
Chicago, Illinois

Goose Island Brewing Co (No 2)
Chicago, Illinois

Pavichevich Brewing Co*
Elmhurst, Illinois

Star Union Brewery Co*
Hennepin, Illinois

BREWPUBS
Blue Cat Brew Pub*
Rock Island, Illinois

Box Office Brewery*
Dekalb, Illinois

Capitol City Brewing Co
Springfield, Illinois

Galena Main Street Brewpub/
Kingston Inn Restaurant*
Galena, Illinois

Goose Island Brewing Co*
Chicago, Illinois

Joe's Brewing Co
Champaign, Illinois

Mickey Finn's Brewery/
Libertyville Brewing Co*
Libertyville, Illinois

Millrose Brewing Co*
South Barrington, Illinois

Pinch Penny Pub Inc*
Carbondale, Illinois

Prairie Rock Brewing Co
Elgin, Illinois

Rock Bottom Brewery (No 7)
Chicago, Illinois

Taylor Brewing Co
Naperville, Illinois

Weinkeller Brewery
Berwyn, Illinois

Weinkeller Brewpub (No 2)
Westmont, Illinois

INDIANA
LARGE BREWERIES
Evansville Brewing Co*
Evansville, Indiana

MICROBREWERIES
Indianapolis Brewing Co*
Indianapolis, Indiana

BREWPUBS
Alcatraz Brewing Co
Indianapolis, Indiana

Bloomington Brewing Co/
One World Enterprises*
Bloomington, Indiana

Broad Ripple Brewing Co*
Indianapolis, Indiana

Circle V Brewing Co*
Indianapolis, Indiana

Lafayette Brewing Co*
Lafayette, Indiana

Mishawaka Brewing Co*
Mishawaka, Indiana

Oaken Barrel Brewing Co
Greenwood, Indiana

IOWA
REGIONAL BREWERIES
Dubuque Brewing & Bottling Co*
Dubuque, Iowa

MICROBREWERIES
Millstream Brewing Co*
Amana, Iowa

BREWPUBS
Cedar Brewing Co*
Cedar Rapids, Iowa

Fitzpatrick's Brewing Co
Iowa City, Iowa

Front Street Brewery
Davenport, Iowa

KANSAS

MICROBREWERIES
Pony Express Brewing Co
Olathe, Kansas

BREWPUBS
Barley's
Topeka, Kansas

Blind Tiger
Brewery and Restaurant*
Topeka, Kansas

Dave's Brewpub
Overland Park, Kansas

Free State Brewing Co*
Lawrence, Kansas

Lazy Hound
Restaurant and Brewery*
Pittsburg, Kansas

Little Apple Brewing Co*
Manhattan, Kansas

Overland Park Brewing Co†
Overland Park, Kansas

River City Brewing Co*
Wichita, Kansas

Rock Bottom Brewery (No 6)
Overland Park, Kansas

Topeka City Brewing Co
Topeka, Kansas

KENTUCKY

MICROBREWERIES
Jack Daniel's Brewery
Louisville, Kentucky

Oldenberg Brewing Co*†
Fort Mitchell, Kentucky

BREWPUBS
Bluegrass Brewing Co*
Louisville, Kentucky

KBC Brewpub and
Grill/Kentucky Brewing Co
Lexington, Kentucky

Lexington City Brewery
Lexington, Kentucky

Louisiana Jack's/Silo Brewpub
Louisville, Kentucky

LOUISIANA

REGIONAL BREWERIES
Abita Brewing Co*
Abita Springs, Louisiana

Dixie Brewing Co Inc
New Orleans, Louisiana

MICROBREWERIES
Acadian Brewing Co LLC*
New Orleans, Louisiana

Louisiana Brewing Co/
Brasserie de la Louisiane*
Beaux Bridge, Louisiana

Rikenjaks Brewery
Jackson, Louisiana

BREWPUBS
Abita Brewpub*
Abita Springs, Louisiana

Crescent City Brewhouse*
New Orleans, Louisiana

MAINE

REGIONAL BREWERIES
Shipyard Brewing Co
Portland, Maine

MICROBREWERIES
Allagash Brewing Co Inc
Portland, Maine

Andrew's Brewing Co*
Lincolnville, Maine

Atlantic Brewing Co/
Lompoc Cafe Brewpub*
Bar Harbor, Maine

Bar Harbor Brewing
Bar Harbor, Maine

Casco Bay Brewing Co
Portland, Maine

D L Geary Brewing Co Inc*
Portland, Maine

Lake St George Brewing Co
Liberty, Maine

Maine Coast Brewing Co
Bar Harbor, Maine

Sea Dog Brewing Co (No 2)*
Bangor, Maine

Sheepscot Valley Brewing Co
Whitefield, Maine

Sugarloaf Brewing Co
Kingfield, Maine

BREWPUBS
Bear Brewing Co
Orono, Maine

Bray's Brewpub and Eatery
Naples, Maine

Gritty McDuff's*
Portland, Maine

Gritty McDuff's (No 2)
Freeport, Maine

Kennebunkport Brewing Co*
Kennebunk, Maine

No Tomatoes Restaurant/
Great Falls Brewing Co
Auburn, Maine

Sea Dog Brewing Co*
Camden, Maine

Stone Coast Brewing Co
South Portland, Maine

Sunday River Brewing Co*
Bethel, Maine

MARYLAND

LARGE BREWERIES
Carling National Brewing Co
Baltimore, Maryland

G Heileman Brewing Co Inc
Baltimore, Maryland

MICROBREWERIES
Baltimore Brewing Co*
Baltimore, Maryland

Brauhaus Schloss†
Ellicott City, Maryland

Brimstone Brewing Co*
Baltimore, Maryland

Clipper City Brewing Co LP
Baltimore, Maryland

Frederick Brewing Co*
Frederick, Maryland

Mount Airy Brewing Co/
Firehouse Pub and Restaurant†
Mount Airy, Maryland

Oxford Brewing Co
Linthicum, Maryland

Wild Goose Brewery
Cambridge, Maryland

BREWPUBS
Bare Bones Grill and Brewery
Ellicott City, Maryland

Duclaw Brewing Co
Forest Hill, Maryland

Fordham Brewing Co/
Ramshead Tavern
Annapolis, Maryland

Olde Towne Tavern & Brewery*
Gaithersburg, Maryland

Sisson's/South
Baltimore Brewing Co*
Baltimore, Maryland

Wharf Rat Camden
Yards/Oliver Breweries Ltd*
Baltimore, Maryland

MASSACHUSETTS

REGIONAL BREWERIES
Mass Bay Brewing Co*
Boston, Massachusetts

MICROBREWERIES
Atlantic Coast Brewing Co*
Boston, Massachusetts

Berkshire Brewing Co Inc
South Deerfield, Massachusetts

Boston Beer Co*
Boston, Marssachusetts

Cisco Brewers
Nantucket, Massachusetts

Clamtown Brewery Inc*
Ipswich, Massachusetts

Ipswich Brewing Co*
Ipswich, Massachusetts

Lowell Brewing Co*
Lowell, Massachusetts

Middlesex Brewing Co Inc
Wilmington, Massachusetts

Northampton Brewery/Brewster Court Bar & Grill*†
Northampton, Massachusetts

Old Harbor Brewing Co/The Pilgrim Brewery*
Hudson, Massachusetts

Ould Newbury Brewing Co*
Newbury, Massachusetts

Wachusett Brewing Co
Westminster, Massachusetts

BREWPUBS

Back Bay Brewing Co
Boston, Massachusetts

Barrington Brewery and Restaurant*
Great Barrington, Massachusetts

Blackstone Valley Brewing Co
Worcester, Massachusetts

Boston Beer Works*
Boston, Massachusetts

Brew House of Danvers*
Danvers, Massachusetts

Brew Moon Enterprises*
Boston, Massachusetts

Brew Moon (No 2)
Saugus, Massachusetts

Brewery at 34 Depot St/ Arrowhead Brewing Co*
Pittsfield, Massachusetts

Cambridge Brewing Co*
Cambridge, Massachusetts

Cape Cod Brew House/Nantucket Brewing Co*
Hyannis, Massachusetts

Commonwealth Brewing Co*
Boston, Massachusetts

John Harvard's Brew House/The Brew House LLC*
Cambridge, Massachusetts

Main Street Brewing Co*
Worcester, Massachusetts

Olde Salem Brewery
Salem, Massachusetts

Owen O'Learys Restaurant
Natick, Massachusetts

Watch City Brewing Co Inc*
Dover, Massachusetts

MICHIGAN

LARGE BREWERIES

Stroh Brewery Co*
Detroit, Michigan

MICROBREWERIES

Big Buck Brewery and Steakhouse†
Gaylord, Michigan

Boyne River Brewing Co
Boyne City, Michigan

Duster's Microbrewery*†
Lawton, Michigan

Frankenmuth Brewery Inc*
Frankenmuth, Michigan

Kalamazoo Brewing Co Inc*
Kalamazoo, Michigan

King Brewing Co
Pontiac, Michigan

Michigan Brewing Co*
Williamston, Michigan

Motor City Brewing Works Inc
Detroit, Michigan

Traverse Brewing Co Ltd*
Williamsburg, Michigan

BREWPUBS

Arbor Brewing Co*
Ann Arbor, Michigan

Blue Coyote Brewing Co*
Lansing, Michigan

Grand Rapids Brewing Co*
Grand Rapids, Michigan

Great Baraboo Brewing Co*
Clinton Township, Michigan

Grizzly Peak Brewing Co*
Ann Arbor, Michigan

Hereford and Hops*
Escanaba, Michigan

Jackson Brewing Co
Jackson, Michigan

Old Peninsula Brewpub
Kalamazoo, Michigan

Traffic Jam and Snug
Detroit, Michigan

Wiltse's Brew Pub and Family Restaurant*
Oscoda, Michigan

MINNESOTA

LARGE BREWERIES

Stroh Brewery Co St Paul Plant/Northern Plains Brewing Co*
St Paul, Minnesota

REGIONAL BREWERIES

August Schell Brewing Co
New Ulm, Minnesota

Cold Spring Brewing Co/ Beverage International Group Ltd
Cold Spring, Minnesota

Minnesota Brewing Co
St Paul, Minnesota

Summit Brewing Co*
St Paul, Minnesota

MICROBREWERIES

James Page Brewing Co*
Minneapolis, Minnesota

Lake Superior Brewing Co*
Duluth, Minnesota

BREWPUBS

Backwater Brewing Co
Winona, Minnesota

Clubhaus Brewpub
Rochester, Minnesota

Rock Bottom Brewery (No 2)*
Minneapolis, Minnesota

Shannon Kelly's Brewpub
St Paul, Minnesota

Sherlock's Home*
Minnetonka, Minnesota

Trader & Trapper
Moorhead, Minnesota

MISSOURI

LARGE BREWERIES

Anheuser-Busch Inc
St Louis, Missouri

REGIONAL BREWERIES

Boulevard Brewing Co*
Kansas City, Missouri

BREWPUBS

75th Street Brewery*
Kansas City, Missouri

Ebbets Field*
Springfield, Missouri

Flat Branch Brewing Co*
Columbia, Missouri

Mill Creek Brewery & Restaurant
Kansas City, Missouri

Morgan Street Brewery
St Louis, Missouri

River Market Brewing Co*
Kansas City, Missouri

Saint Louis Brewery/The Tap Room*
St Louis, Missouri

Trailhead Brewing Co*
St Charles, Missouri

Westport Brewing Co*
Kansas City, Missouri

MONTANA

MICROBREWERIES

Bayern Brewing Inc/ Iron Horse Brewpub*†
Missoula, Montana

Big Sky Brewing Co*
Missoula, Montana

Great Northern Brewing Co
Whitefish, Montana

United States Breweries

Himmelberger Brewing Co
Billings, Montana

Kessler Brewing Co*
Helena, Montana

Lang Creek Brewery*
Marion, Montana

Milestown Brewing Co./The Golden Spur†
Miles City, Montana

Montana Brewing Co*
Billings, Montana

Rock'n M Brewing Co*
Belgrade, Montana

Spanish Peaks Brewing Co*†
Bozeman, Montana

Whitefish Brewing Co
Whitefish, Montana

NEBRASKA
BREWPUBS
Crane River Brewpub & Cafe*
Lincoln, Nebraska

Gottberg Brew Pub/ Gottberg Auto Co*
Columbus, Nebraska

Jaipur Restaurant and Brewpub*
Omaha, Nebraska

Jones Street Brewery*
Omaha, Nebraska

Lazlo's Brewery and Grill*
Lincoln, Nebraska

NEVADA
MICROBREWERIES
Ruby Mountain Brewing Co Inc*
Wells, Nevada

BREWPUBS
Barley's Casino and Brewing Co
Henderson, Nevada

Brew Brothers/ Eldorado Hotel and Casino
Reno, Nevada

Carson Depot
Carson City, Nevada

Great Basin Brewing Co*
Sparks, Nevada

Holy Cow! Casino, Cafe & Brewery*
Las Vegas, Nevada

Union Brewery Co
Virginia City, Nevada

NEW HAMPSHIRE
LARGE BREWERIES
Anheuser-Busch Inc
Merrimack, New Hampshire

MICROBREWERIES
Nutfield Brewing Co*
Derry, New Hampshire

Smuttynose Brewing Co*
Portsmouth, New Hampshire

BREWPUBS
Brewer's Bier Haus
Merrimack, New Hampshire

Italian Oasis Restaurant & Brewery
Littleton, New Hampshire

Martha's Exchange
Nashua, New Hampshire

Portsmouth Brewery*
Portsmouth, New Hampshire

Seven Barrel Brewery
West Lebanon, New Hampshire

Stark Mill Brewery & Restaurant
Manchester, New Hampshire

Woodstock Brewing Co*
North Woodstock, New Hampshire

NEW JERSEY
LARGE BREWERIES
Anheuser-Busch Inc
Newark, New Jersey

MICROBREWERIES
Climax Brewing Co
Roselle Park, New Jersey

Hoboken Brewing Co
Hoboken, New Jersey

New Jersey Brewery LLC
Phillipsburg, New Jersey

Red Bank Brewery Co
Redbank, New Jersey

Thunder Bay Brewing Co
Englewood, New Jersey

BREWPUBS
Harvest Moon Brewery/ The Ales Co/Sullivan Brewing
Redbank, New Jersey

Joe's Millhill Saloon and Restaurant†
Trenton, New Jersey

Long Valley Pub & Brewery/Long Valley Brewing Co*
Long Valley, New Jersey

Ship Inn Inc*
Milford, New Jersey

Triumph Brewing Co/ Disch Brewing Co*
Princeton, New Jersey

NEW MEXICO
MICROBREWERIES
Alamogordo Brewing Co/ Kegs Brewery and Fine Dining†
Alamogordo, New Mexico

Elephant Butte Brewery and Pizzeria†
Elephant Butte, New Mexico

Old West Brewery
Deming, New Mexico

Rio Grande Brewing Co Inc
Albuquerque, New Mexico

Russell Brewing Co
Santa Fe, New Mexico

Santa Fe Brewing Co
Galisteo, New Mexico

BREWPUBS
Assets Grille/Southwest Brewing Co
Albuquerque, New Mexico

Embudo Station/Preston Brewery
Embudo, New Mexico

Eske's Brew Pub/ Sangre De Cristo Brewing Co*
Taos, New Mexico

Il Vicino Wood Oven Pizza*
Albuquerque, New Mexico

O'Ryan's Tavern & Brewery/Oregon Mtn Brewing Co*
Las Cruces, New Mexico

Rio Bravo Restaurant & Brewery*
Albuquerque, New Mexico

Wolf Canyon Brewing Co*
Santa Fe, New Mexico

NEW YORK
LARGE BREWERIES
Anheuser-Busch Inc
Baldwinsville, New York

Genesee Brewing Co/ Dundee's Brewery
Rochester, New York

REGIONAL BREWERIES
F X Matt Brewing Co*
Utica, New York

MICROBREWERIES
Buffalo Brewing Co†
Buffalo, New York

Drytown Brewing Co
Treadwell, New York

Lake City Brewing Co
Plattsburgh, New York

Lake Titus Brewery*
Malone, New York

Middle Ages Brewing Co Ltd*
Syracuse, New York

Neptune Brewery
New York, New York

Old Hampton Brewers Ltd
East Hampton, New York

United States Breweries

Saw Mill River Brewing Co
Yonkers, New York

Shea's Brewery
Rochester, New York

Woodstock Brewing Co*
Kingston, New York

BREWPUBS

Atlantic Brewing Co*
Island Park, New York

Bootleggers Pub and Brewery/
Christophers Restaurant Inc
Plattsburgh, New York

Breckenridge Brewery in Buffalo
Buffalo, New York

Carnegie Hill Brewing Co*
New York, New York

Chapter House Brewpub
Ithaca, New York

Ellicotville
Brewing Co/S&W Co LLC*
Ellicotville, New York

Empire Brewing Co*
Syracuse, New York

Gentleman Jims*
Poughkeepsie, New York

Heartland Brewing Co*
New York City, New York

Hyde Park Brewing Co*
Hyde Park, New York

James Bay Restaurant & Brewery*
Port Jefferson, New York

Long Island Brewing Co*
Jericho, New York

Mountain Valley Brewpub*
Suffern, New York

Nacho Mama's Brewery*
New York City, New York

Original Saratoga Springs Brewpub
Saratoga Springs, New York

Park Slope Brewing Co*
Brooklyn, New York

Parlor City Brewing Co
Binghamton, New York

Rochester Brewpub
Henrietta, New York

Rohrbach Brewing Co*
Rochester, New York

Rohrbach Brewing Co (No 2)
Rochester, New York

Shannon Pub
Snyder, New York

Syracuse Suds Factory
Syracuse, New York

Troy Brewing Co
Troy, New York

Westside Brewing Co*
New York, New York

Westchester Brewing Co
Pound Ridge, New York

Yorkville Brewery & Tavern*
New York, New York

Zip City Brewing Co*
New York, New York

NORTH CAROLINA
LARGE BREWERIES

Miller Brewing Co
Eden, North Carolina

Stroh Brewery Co*
Winston-Salem, North Carolina

MICROBREWERIES

Carolina Brewing Co
Holly Springs, North Carolina

Dilworth Micro Brewery*
Charlotte, North Carolina

Highland Brewing Co*
Asheville, North Carolina

Johnson Beer Co*
Charlotte, North Carolina

Old North State Brewing Co
Fuquay-Varina, North Carolina

Old Raleigh Brewing Co
Raleigh, North Carolina

Pinehurst Village Brewery*
Chapel Hill, North Carolina

Smokey Mountain Brewery
Waynesville, North Carolina

Spring Garden Brewing Co*†
Greensboro, North Carolina

Tomcat Brewing Co
Raleigh, North Carolina

Weeping Radish
Restaurant and Brewery*†
Manteo, North Carolina

Wilmington Brewing Co Inc*
Wilmington, North Carolina

BREWPUBS

Carolina Brewery*
Chapel Hill, North Carolina

Carolina Mill Bakery Brewery
Charlotte, North Carolina

Cottonwood Grille & Brewery
Boone, North Carolina

Dilworth Brewing Co*
Charlotte, North Carolina

Front Street Brewery*
Wilmington, North Carolina

Greenshields Brewery and Pub*
Raleigh, North Carolina

Olde Hickory Brewing Co
Hickory, North Carolina

Queen City Bakery and Brewery
Charlotte, North Carolina

Southend
Brewery and Smokehouse*
Charlotte, North Carolina

Weeping Radish Brewery (No 2)
Durham, North Carolina

NORTH DAKOTA
BREWPUBS

Great Northern Brewing Co
Fargo, North Dakota

Old Broadway
Fargo, North Dakota

Rattlesnake Creek Brewery
Dickinson, North Dakota

OHIO
LARGE BREWERIES

Anheuser-Busch Inc
Columbus, Ohio

Miller Brewing Co
Trenton, Ohio

REGIONAL BREWERIES

Hudepohl-Schoenling Brewing Co
Cincinnati, Ohio

MICROBREWERIES

All American Brewing Co
Dublin, Ohio

Barrel House Brewing Co
Cincinnati, Ohio

Columbus Brewing Co
Columbus, Ohio

Crooked River Brewing Co*
Cleveland, Ohio

Gambrinus Brewing Co
Columbus, Ohio

Great Lakes Brewing Co*†
Cleveland, Ohio

Lift Bridge Brewing Co*
Ashtabula, Ohio

Ringneck Brewing Co/
The Brew Kettle Inc*‡
Strongsville, Ohio

BREWPUBS

Alessis Ristorante/
Garretts Mill Brewing Co
Garrettsville, Ohio

Barley's Brewing Co
Columbus, Ohio

Burkhardt Brewing Co*
Uniontown, Ohio

Firehouse Brewery and Restaurant†
Cleveland Heights, Ohio

Hoster Brewing Co*
Columbus, Ohio

Liberty Street Brewing Co
Akron, Ohio

Institute for Brewing Studies

United States Breweries

Main Street Brewery/
Queen City Brewing Co*
Cincinnati, Ohio

Maumee Bay Brewing Co*
Toledo, Ohio

O'Hooleys Pub and Brewery
Athens, Ohio

Rock Bottom
Brewery (No 8) at Cleveland
Cleveland, Ohio

Wallaby's Grill & Brewpub*
Westlake, Ohio

Wooden Pony Brewing Co*
Mansfield, Ohio

OKLAHOMA

BREWPUBS

Belle Isle Brewing Co
Oklahoma City, Oklahoma

Bricktown Brewery*
Oklahoma City, Oklahoma

Cherry Street Brewery*
Tulsa, Oklahoma

Interurban Brewpub
Norman, Oklahoma

Norman Brewing Co
Norman, Oklahoma

Pete's Place
Krebs, Oklahoma

Royal Bavaria
Brewhaus and Restaurant
Moore, Oklahoma

Tulsa Brewing Co*
Tulsa, Oklahoma

OREGON

LARGE BREWERIES

Blitz-Weinhard Brewing Co
Portland, Oregon

REGIONAL BREWERIES

BridgePort Brewing Co*†
Portland, Oregon

Deschutes Brewery (No 2)*
Bend, Oregon

Nor'wester Brewery
and Public House*†
Portland, Oregon

Portland Brewing Co (No 2)*†
Portland, Oregon

Rogue Ales/Oregon Brewing Co*
Newport, Oregon

Widmer Brothers Brewing Co/
Widmer Brothers Gasthaus*†
Portland, Oregon

MICROBREWERIES

Bandon Brewing Co/
Bandon-by-the-Sea*
Bandon, Oregon

Blue Mountain Brewing
La Grande, Oregon

Deschutes Brewery
and Public House*†
Bend, Oregon

Edgefield Brewery/McMenamins*†
Troutdale, Oregon

Full Sail Brewing Co
(No 2)/Pilsener Room*†
Portland, Oregon

Hair of the Dog Brewing Co*
Portland, Oregon

Mount Hood Brewing Co*
Government Camp, Oregon

Multnomah Brewery
Portland, Oregon

Oregon Trader Brewing Co*†
Albany, Oregon

Oregon Trail Brewery
Corvallis, Oregon

Portland Brewing Co*
Portland, Oregon

Saxer Brewing*
Lake Oswego, Oregon

Star Brewing Co*
Portland, Oregon

Widmer Brothers Brewing Co/
B Moloch/Heathman Pub
Portland, Oregon

BREWPUBS

Bank Brewing Co
Coos Bay, Oregon

Bend Brewing Co
Bend, Oregon

Big Horn Brewing Co of
Oregon/RAM International
Salem, Oregon

Big Horse Brewpub
Hood River, Oregon

Blue Pine Brewpub Co
Grants Pass, Oregon

Cascade Lakes Brewing Co*
Redmond, Oregon

Cascade Microbrewery
and Public Firehouse
Salem, Oregon

Cornelius Pass Roadhouse
and Brewery/McMenamins*
Hillsboro, Oregon

Eugene City Brewing Co/
West Brothers Bar-B-Q
Eugene, Oregon

Field's Restaurant & Brewpub
Eugene, Oregon

Full Sail Brewing Co/WhiteCap
Brewpub and Tasting Room
Hood River, Oregon

Fulton Pub and
Brewery/McMenamins*
Portland, Oregon

Golden Valley Brewery & Pub*
McMinnville, Oregon

High Street Brewery
and Cafe/McMenamins*
Eugene, Oregon

Highland Pub and
Brewery/McMenamin's*
Gresham, Oregon

Hillsdale Brewery and
Public House/McMenamins*
Portland, Oregon

John Barleycorn's/McMenamins *
Tigard, Oregon

Lighthouse Brewery
and Public House/Mcmenamins*
Lincoln City, Oregon

Lucky Labrador Brew Pub
Portland, Oregon

Maroney Sausage Est/
Widmer Brothers Brewing Co
Portland, Oregon

McMenamins/Murray and Allen*
Beaverton, Oregon

McMenamins/West Linn Pub*
West Linn, Oregon

Mount Angel Brewing Co
Mount Angel, Oregon

Oak Hills Brewpub/McMenamins*
Portland, Oregon

Old Chicago Brewery & Pub
Portland, Oregon

Old Market Pub & Brewery
Portland, Oregon

Oregon Fields Brewing Co†
Eugene, Oregon

Osprey Ale Brewing Co
Medford, Oregon

Pacific City Brewing Co*
Pacific City, Oregon

Philadelphia's
Portland, Oregon

Rock Bottom Brewery (No 4)
Portland, Oregon

Siletz Brewing Co
Siletz, Oregon

Siskyo Brewing Co
Ashland, Oregon

Spencer's
Restaurant and Brewhouse
Springfield, Oregon

Steelhead Brewery & Cafe
Eugene, Oregon

United States Breweries

Thompson Brewpub/McMenamins*
Salem, Oregon

Tugboat Brewpub & Cafe*
Portland, Oregon

Umpqua Brewing Co
Roseburg, Oregon

**Wild Duck
Brewery and Restaurant***
Eugene, Oregon

Wild River Brewing and Pizza Co*
Cave Junction, Oregon

**Wild River Brewing
and Pizza Co (No 2)***
Grants Pass, Oregon

PENNSYLVANIA
LARGE BREWERIES

Latrobe Brewing Co*
Latrobe, Pennsylvania

Pittsburgh Brewing Co*
Pittsburgh, Pennsylvania

Stroh Brewery Co*
Lehigh Valley, Pennsylvania

REGIONAL BREWERIES

D G Yuengling & Son Inc
Pottsville, Pennsylvania

Jones Brewing Co
Smithton, Pennsylvania

**Lion Inc/
Gibbons-Stegmaier Brewery***
Wilkes-Barre, Pennsylvania

Straub Brewery
St Mary's, Pennsylvania

MICROBREWERIES

Arrowhead Brewing Co*
Chambersburg, Pennsylvania

Independence Brewing Co*
Philadelphia, Pennsylvania

Lancaster Malt Brewing Co*†
Lancaster, Pennsylvania

Manayunk Malt & Hops Co
Philadelphia, Pennsylvania

Red Bell Brewing Co
Philadelphia, Pennsylvania

Stoudt Brewery*
Adamstown, Pennsylvania

Ugly Dog Brewery Inc
West Chester, Pennsylvania

Victory Brewing Co†
Downingtown, Pennsylvania

Weyerbacher Brewing Co Inc*
Easton, Pennsylvania

Whitetail Brewing Inc*
York, Pennsylvania

Yards Brewing Co
Philadelphia, Pennsylvania

BREWPUBS

Barley Creek Brewing Co Inc
Tannersville, Pennsylvania

**Buckingham Mountain
Brewing Co/McGallen Brewing Co†**
Lahaska, Pennsylvania

**Dock St Brewing Co
Brewery and Restaurant***
Philadelphia, Pennsylvania

**Erie Brewing Co/
Hoppers Brewpub***
Erie, Pennsylvania

**Philadelphia Brewing Co/
Samuel Adams Brewhouse**
Philadelphia, Pennsylvania

Sly Fox Brewhouse & Eatery*
Phoenixville, Pennsylvania

**Valley Forge Brewing
Co/Restaurant and Pub***
Wayne, Pennsylvania

RHODE ISLAND
MICROBREWERIES

Emerald Isle Brew Works Ltd*
West Warwick, Rhode Island

BREWPUBS

Coddington Brewing Co
Middleton, Rhode Island

Trinity Beer Works Inc*
Providence, Rhode Island

**Union Station Brewing/
The Brew House LLC**
Providence, Rhode Island

SOUTH CAROLINA
MICROBREWERIES

Appalachian Ale Works
Moore, South Carolina

Palmetto Brewing Co*
Charleston, South Carolina

Reedy River Brewing Co*
Greenville, South Carolina

Southeastern Brewing Co
White Rock, South Carolina

BREWPUBS

Blue Ridge Brewing Co*
Greenville, South Carolina

Chicago Brew Pub
Greenville, South Carolina

Columbia Brewing Co*
Columbia, South Carolina

Downtown Brewing Co
Greenville, South Carolina

Hilton Head Brewing Co*
Hilton Head Island, South Carolina

Hunter Gatherer
Columbia, South Carolina

**Liberty Steakhouse and
Brewery at Broadway at the Beach**
Myrtle Beach, South Carolina

Market Street Mill
Charleston, South Carolina

T-Bonz Gill & Grill*
Mount Pleasant, South Carolina

Vista Brewing Co
Columbia, South Carolina

SOUTH DAKOTA
MICROBREWERIES

Black Hills Brewing Co*
Deadwood, South Dakota

BREWPUBS

Firehouse Brewing Co
Rapid City, South Dakota

Sioux Falls Brewing*
Sioux Falls, South Dakota

Wild Bill's Brewing Co
Sioux Falls, South Dakota

TENNESSEE
LARGE BREWERIES

Coors Brewing Co*
Memphis, Tennessee

MICROBREWERIES

**Bohannon Brewing Co/Market
Street Brewery and Public House*†**
Nashville, Tennessee

BREWPUBS

**Big River Grille and
Brewing Works (No 1)***
Chattanooga, Tennessee

**Big River Grille and
Brewing Works (No 2)***
Nashville, Tennessee

**Black Horse Brewery/
Franklin St Pub Corp**
Clarksville, Tennessee

**Blackstone
Restaurant and Brewery***
Nashville, Tennessee

**Bosco's Pizza
Kitchen and Brewery (No 1)***
Germantown, Tennessee

**Bosco's Nashville
Brewing Co (No 2)***
Nashville, Tennessee

Calhoun's BBQ and Brewery*
Knoxville, Tennessee

Mill Brewery, Eatery, & Bakery*
Knoxville, Tennessee

TEXAS

LARGE BREWERIES

Anheuser-Busch Inc
Houston, Texas

**G Heileman Brewing Co Inc/
Lone Star Brewing Co**
San Antonio, Texas

Miller Brewing Co*
Fort Worth, Texas

**Pearl Brewing Co/
Pabst Brewing Co**
San Antonio, Texas

Stroh Brewery Co*
Longview, Texas

REGIONAL BREWERIES

Celis Brewery Inc*
Austin, Texas

Spoetzl Brewery Inc
Shiner, Texas

MICROBREWERIES

Basin Brewing Ltd
Midland, Texas

Bosque Brewing Co*
Waco, Texas

Frio Brewing Co*
San Antonio, Texas

**Hill Country
Brewing and Bottling Co***
Austin, Texas

Main Street Brewing Co
Dallas, Texas

Old West Brewery (No 2)
El Paso, Texas

Saint Andrew's Brewing Co
Dallas, Texas

Saint Arnold Brewing Co*
Houston, Texas

Strand Brewing Co*
Galveston, Texas

Yellow Rose Brewing Co*
San Antonio, Texas

BREWPUBS

**Bank Draft Brewing Co/
Vaulted Ales Inc***
Houston, Texas

**Big Horn Brewing Co
of Texas/Humperdincks**
Arlington, Texas

Bitter End Brewery*
Austin, Texas

Boardwalk Bistro
San Antonio, Texas

Bradley's Restaurant and Brewery
Webster, Texas

Brazos Brewing Co*
College Station, Texas

Cafe on the Square and Brewpub
San Marcos, Texas

**Copper Tank Brewing Co (No 1)/
Austin Microbrewers LLC**
Austin, Texas

**Copper Tank Brewing Co (No 2)/
Austin Microbrewers LLC**
Dallas, Texas

Draught Horse Pub and Brewery
Austin, Texas

Fredericksburg Brewing Co Inc*
Fredericksburg, Texas

Galveston Brewery
Galveston, Texas

Harp & Star Brewing Co
Humble, Texas

Hierman's Hofbrau
Midland, Texas

Hoffbrau Steaks Brewery (No 1)*
Addison, Texas

Hoffbrau Steaks Brewery (No 2)*
Dallas, Texas

Houston Brewery*
Houston, Texas

Hub City Brewery
Lubbock, Texas

Hubcap Brewery & Kitchen (No 2)
Dallas, Texas

**Jaxson's
Restaurant and Brewing Co**
El Paso, Texas

Joey's Inc*
San Antonio, Texas

**Katie Bloom's
Irish Pub and Brewery**
Austin, Texas

Padre Island Brewing Co
South Padre Island, Texas

Panther City Brewery & Cafe
Fort Worth, Texas

Rock Bottom Brewery (No 3)*
Houston, Texas

Rock Bottom Brewery (No 5)*
Addison, Texas

Routh Street Brewery*
Dallas, Texas

Silk's Grill and Brewing Co
Amarillo, Texas

TwoRows Restaurant and Brewery*
Dallas, Texas

Village Brewery*
Houston, Texas

Waterloo Brewing Co*
Austin, Texas

Yegua Creek Brewing Co*
Dallas, Texas

UTAH

MICROBREWERIES

Eddie McStiff's Brewing Co*†
Moab, Utah

**Schirf Brewing Co/
Wasatch Brewpub*†**
Park City, Utah

Uinta Brewing Co*†
Salt Lake City, Utah

**Wasatch Brewing Co
(No 2)/Schirf Brewing Co*†**
Salt Lake City, Utah

BREWPUBS

**Desert Edge Brewery at the
Pub/Desert Edge Brewing Co**
Salt Lake City, Utah

Naisbitt's Brewery
Riverdale, Utah

Red Rock Brewing Co*
Salt Lake City, Utah

Roosters 25th St Brewing Co
Ogden, Utah

**Salt Lake Brewing Co/
Squatters Pub***
Salt Lake City, Utah

Salt Lake Brewing Co/Fuggles*
Salt Lake City, Utah

VERMONT

REGIONAL BREWERIES

Catamount Brewing Co*
White River Jct, Vermont

MICROBREWERIES

Bennington Brewers Ltd
Bennington, Vermont

Long Trail Brewing Co
Bridgewater Corners, Vermont

Magic Hat Brewing Co*
Burlington, Vermont

Otter Creek Brewing Inc*
Middlebury, Vermont

BREWPUBS

Black River Brew House
Ludlow, Vermont

Champion Billiards and Cafe
Arlington, Vermont

**Latchis Grille
and Windham Brewery**
Brattleboro, Vermont

**Madison Brewing Co
Pub and Restaurant**
Bennington, Vermont

McNeill's Brewery
Brattleboro, Vermont

**Norwich Inn/
Jasper Murdocks Ale House***
Norwich, Vermont

Shed Restaurant and Brewery*
Stowe, Vermont

Vermont Pub and Brewery
Burlington, Vermont

VIRGINIA

LARGE BREWERIES

Anheuser-Busch Inc
Williamsburg, Virginia

Coors Brewing Co*
Elkton, Virginia

REGIONAL BREWERIES

Old Dominion Brewing Co*
Ashburn, Virginia

MICROBREWERIES

James River Brewing Co*
Richmond, Virginia

Legend Brewing Co*
Richmond, Virginia

Oxford Brewing Co*
Falls Church, Virginia

Potomac River Brewing Co*
Chantilly, Virginia

Steamship Brewing Co
Norfolk, Virginia

Williamsville Brewery*
Doswell, Virginia

BREWPUBS

Bardo Rodeo*
Arlington, Virginia

Blue and Gold Brewing Co
Arlington, Virginia

Blue Ridge Brewing Co*
Charlottesville, Virginia

Cobblestone Pub and Brewery
Richmond, Virginia

Richbrau Brewing Co*
Richmond, Virginia

Virginia Beverage Co*
Alexandria, Virginia

WASHINGTON

LARGE BREWERIES

Pabst Brewing Co
Tumwater, Washington

Rainier Brewing Co Inc
Seattle, Washington

REGIONAL BREWERIES

Hart Brewing Co Inc*
Seattle, Washington

Redhook Ale Brewery*†
Seattle, Washington

Redhook Ale Brewery (No 2)*†
Woodinville, Washington

MICROBREWERIES

Aviator Ales Brewery/
Seattle Brewing Co
Woodinville, Washington

Buchanan Brewing Corp
Oroville, Washington

Captain City Brewing Inc
Coupeville, Washington

Chuckanut Bay Brewing Co*‡
Bellingham, Washington

Diamond Knot Brewery
Mukilteo, Washington

Ellensburg Brewing Co
Ellensburg, Washington

Fish Brewing Co/Fishbowl Pub*†
Olympia, Washington

Grant's Yakima Brewing Co*
Yakima, Washington

Hale's Ales Ltd (No 1)
Kirkland, Washington

Hale's Ales Ltd (No 2)
Spokane, Washington

Hale's Ales Ltd (No 3)†
Seattle, Washington

Kelley Creek Brewing Co
Bonney Lake, Washington

Mac & Jack's Brewery Inc*
Redmond, Washington

Maritime Pacific Brewing*
Seattle, Washington

Meheen Brewing Co*
Pasco, Washington

Northern Lights Brewing Co
Airway Heights, Washington

Onalaska Brewing Co
Onalaska, Washington

Orchard Street Brewing Co†
Bellingham, Washington

Pike Brewing Co/Merchant du Vin*
Seattle, Washington

Roslyn Brewing Co
Roslyn, Washington

Seattle Brewers
Seattle, Washington

Skagit River Brewing Co*
Mount Vernon, Washington

Tapps Brewing Co
Sumner, Washington

Whatcom Brewery
Ferndale, Washington

Whidbey Island Brewing Co*
Langley, Washington

Young's Brewing Co/
Northwest Sausage and Deli†
Centralia, Washington

BREWPUBS

Anacortes Brewhouse *
Anacortes, Washington

Bentley's Brewhouse Restaurant*
Point Roberts, Washington

Big Time Brewing Co
Seattle, Washington

Birkebeiner Brewing Co*
Spokane, Washington

Boundary Bay Brewing
Bellingham, Washington

C J's Brewpub Inc
Vancouver, Washington

Eagle Brewing Co
Mukilteo, Washington

Engine House #9
Tacoma, Washington

Fort Spokane Brewery
Spokane, Washington

Front Street Ale House/
San Juan Brewing Co*
Friday Harbor, Washington

Glacier Peak Brewing Co*
Everett, Washington

Grant's Brewery Pub*
Yakima, Washington

Hazel Dell Brewpub
Vancouver, Washington

Issaquah Brewhouse/
Eagle River Brewing Co
Issaquah, Washington

La Conner Brewing Co
La Conner, Washington

Leavenworth Brewery*
Leavenworth, Washington

McMenamins/Columbia*
Vancouver, Washington

McMenamins/Mill Creek*
Mill Creek, Washington

McMenamins/Roy Street*
Seattle, Washington

McMenamins/Six Arms Pub*
Seattle, Washington

Mount Baker Brewing Co
Bellingham, Washington

Pacific Northwest Brewing Co
Seattle, Washington

Power House
Restaurant and Brewery
Puallup, Washington

West Seattle Brewing Co
Seattle, Washington

Winthrop Brewing Co
Winthrop, Washington

WEST VIRGINIA

MICROBREWERIES
Cardinal Brewing*
Charleston, West Virginia

BREWPUBS
Brewbakers
Huntington, West Virginia

West Virginia Brewing Co*
Morgantown, West Virginia

WISCONSIN

LARGE BREWERIES
G Heileman Brewing Co
La Crosse, Wisconsin

Miller Brewing Co*
Milwaukee, Wisconsin

Pabst Brewing Co
Milwaukee, Wisconsin

REGIONAL BREWERIES
Jacob Leinenkugel Brewing Co*
Chippewa Falls, Wisconsin

Jacob Leinenkugel
Brewing Co (No 2)*
Milwaukee, Wisconsin

Joseph Huber Brewing Co
Monroe, Wisconsin

Stevens Point Brewery Co*
Stevens Point, Wisconsin

MICROBREWERIES
Capital Brewing Co
Middleton, Wisconsin

Cherryland Brewing Co
Sturgeon Bay, Wisconsin

Egan Brewing Co
Green Bay, Wisconsin

Gray Brewing Co*
Janesville, Wisconsin

Green Bay Brewing Co
Denmark, Wisconsin

LaBelle Brewing Co Inc*
Oconomonowoc, Wisconsin

Lakefront Brewery Inc*
Milwaukee, Wisconsin

New Glarus Brewing Co
New Glarus, Wisconsin

Remington Watson
Smith Brewing Co Inc
Waukesha, Wisconsin

Sprecher Brewing Co*
Glendale, Wisconsin

Wisconsin Brewing Co
Wauwatosa, Wisconsin

BREWPUBS
Angelic Brewing Co*
Madison, Wisconsin

Appleton Brewing Co/Adler Brau*
Appleton, Wisconsin

B T McClintick Brewing Co
Janesville, Wisconsin

Black River Brewery and Pub*
La Crosse, Wisconsin

Black Rose Brewpub
LaCrosse, Wisconsin

Bodega Brewpub
La Crosse, Wisconsin

Brewery Creek Brewing Co
Mineral Point, Wisconsin

Brewmaster's Pub
Kenosha, Wisconsin

Fox River Brewing Co/
Fratello's Italian Cafe†
Oshkosh, Wisconsin

Great Dane Pub & Brewing Co*
Madison, Wisconsin

J T Whitney's
Brewpub and Eatery/Kicks*
Madison, Wisconsin

Railhouse
Restaurant and Brewery/R Ales Inc*
Marinette, Wisconsin

Randy's Restaurant/
Fun Hunter's Brewery*
Whitewater, Wisconsin

Rowland's Calumet Brewery
Chilton, Wisconsin

South Shore Brewery*
Ashland, Wisconsin

Water Street Brewery*
Milwaukee, Wisconsin

WYOMING

MICROBREWERIES
Otto Brothers' Brewing Co*
Jackson, Wyoming

Snake River Brewing Co/
Jackson Hole Pub and Brewery*†
Jackson, Wyoming

BREWPUBS
Bootleggers Brewery/
Sunshine Valley Brewing Co
Casper, Wyoming

Bowman's Pub & Brewing Co*
Laramie, Wyoming

Humphreys Bar & Grill
Gillette, Wyoming

Library
Restaurant and Brewing Co*
Laramie, Wyoming

Medicine Bow Brewing Co
Cheyenne, Wyoming

U.S. Territories and Possessions

MARSHALL ISLANDS

MICROBREWERIES
Marshall's Best Micro Brewery
Majuro, Marshall Islands

Republic Brewery
Majuro, Marshall Islands

PUERTO RICO

LARGE BREWERIES
Cerveceria India Inc
Mayaguez, Puerto Rico

MICROBREWERIES
La Villa De Torrimar
Guaynabo, Puerto Rico

ALABAMA

Birmingham Brewing Co
3118 Third Ave S
Birmingham, AL 35233-3006
(205) 326-6677; FAX (205) 326-6601
Founded: June 19, 1992
Capacity: 6,000 bbl
Sales Mgr.: Marshall Hogan
Head Brewer: Steve Betts
Treas.: Carolyn Hogan
Pres.: Ben Hogan
Contact: Ben Hogan

Magic City Brewery
1241 29th St S/Suite 3
Birmingham, AL 35205
(205) 328-2739; FAX (205) 328-1539
Founded: March 11, 1995
Contact: Brad Fournier

Mill Brewery, Eatery, & Bakery
2035 20th St S
Birmingham, AL 35205
(205) 939-3001
Founded: Aug. 1, 1995
Contact: John Wycliffe

**Montgomery Brewing Co/
Alabama Brewpubs LLC**
12 W Jefferson St
Montgomery, AL 36104
(334) 834-BREW
Founded: Oct. 22, 1995
Capacity: 1,000 bbl
Contact: Barry Morton

**Poplar Head Mule
Co Brewpub and Grill**
PO Box 398/155 S St Andrew St
Dothan, AL 36302
(334) 793-5665; FAX (334) 793-1101
Founded: Aug. 15, 1995
Capacity: 700 bbl
Head Brewer: Scott Saunders
Contact: W. Terry Bullard

Port City Brewery
225 Dauphin St
Mobile, AL 36602-2717
(334) 438-2739; FAX (332) 438-3612
Founded: Nov. 5, 1993
Capacity: 1,500 bbl
Co-Owner: Mike Wojciechowski
Co-Owner: Bill Casto
Gen. Mgr./Owner: Sam Casto
Head Brewer: Todd Hicks
Asst. Brewer: Ed Nelson
Contact: Todd Hicks

ALASKA

**Alaskan Brewing
and Bottling Co**
5429 Shaune Dr
Juneau, AK 99801-9540
(907) 780-5866; FAX (907) 780-4514
Founded: Dec. 28, 1986
Capacity: 48,000 bbl
Head Brewer: Dayton Canaday
Brewmistress: Marcy Larson
Brewmaster/Sales Mgr.: Geoffrey Larson
Sales Mgr.: Ed Cesarone
Contact: Marci Larson

Bird Creek Brewery Inc
310 E 76th Ave/Unit B
Anchorage, AK 99518-2840
(907) 344-2473; FAX (907) 522-2739
Founded: Dec. 21, 1991
Capacity: 5,000 bbl
Head Brewer: Bill Haliday
Owner: Ike Kelly
Contact: Ike Kelly

Borealis Brewery
PO Box 112402/349 E Shipcreek
Anchorage, AK 99501
(907) 566-6071
Founded: April 1, 1996
Capacity: 1,000 bbl
Head Brewer: Gary Pattison
Contact: S. J. Klein

**Cusack's
Brewpub and Roaster**
598 W Northern Lights Blvd
Anchorage, AK 99503
(907) 561-5200; FAX (907) 563-8217
Founded: Oct. 14, 1995
Head Brewer: Laurence Livingston
Sales Mgr.: Cathy Janigo
Asst. Brewer: Bryn Perkins
General Mgr.: Jerry Gibson
Contact: Laurence Livingston

Midnight Sun Brewing Co
7329 Arctic Blvd
Anchorage, AK 99518-2156
(907) 344-1179; FAX (907) 344-6656
beer@alaska.net
http://www.alaska.net/~beer/beer.html
Founded: May 15, 1995
Capacity: 1,500 bbl
Head Brewer: Ray Hodge
Pres.: Mark Staples
Contact: Ray Hodge

**Northern Lights
Brewing Co/Shannon's Cafe**
3301 C St
Anchorage, AK 99503-3935
(907) 563-8700
Contact: David Heier

Railway Brewing Co
421 W First Ave
Anchorage, AK 99501
(907) 277-1914
Founded: April 1, 1996
Capacity: 750 bbl
Head Brewer: Richard Sassara
Brewpub Mgr.: J. Brooke Corkery
Marketing Dir.: Mary Sassara
Contact: Richard Sassara

Raven Ridge Brewing Co
PO Box 81395
5690 Supply Rd/Bay 4
Fairbanks, AK 99708-1395
(907) 457-BREW; FAX (907) 455-6252
Founded: May 25, 1994
Capacity: 1,000 bbl
Pres./Brewmaster: Hal Tippens
Contact: Hal Tippens

**Regal Eagle Brewing Co/
North Slope Brewing Co**
11501 Old Glen Hwy
Eagle River, AK 99577
(907) 694-9120
Founded: Sept. 15, 1995
Capacity: 80 bbl
Head Brewer: Ken Pajak
Sales Mgr./Owner: George Malekos
Owner: Susan Malekos
Contact: Ken Pajak

ARIZONA

Bandersnatch Brewpub
125 E Fifth St
Tempe, AZ 85281-3701
(602) 966-4438
Founded: Jan. 1, 1987
Capacity: 850 bbl
Head Brewer: Joe Bob Grisham
Pres.: Joe Mocca
Contact: Joe Mocca

**Beaver Street
Brewery & Whistle Stop Cafe**
11 S Beaver St
Flagstaff, AZ 86001-5501
(520) 779-0079; FAX (520) 779-0029
Founded: March 3, 1994
Capacity: 1,200 bbl

United States Breweries (Arizona–Arkansas)

Owner/Brewer: Evan Hanseth
Contact: Evan Hanseth

Black Mountain Brewing Co
PO Box 1940
Cave Creek, AZ 85331-1940
(602) 253-6293; FAX (602) 488-2609
Founded: Dec. 1, 1989
Capacity: 4,000 bbl
Head Brewer: Scott Chilleen
Pres.: Ed Chilleen
Sales Mgr./Gen. Mgr.: Dick Chilleen
Mktg. Dir.: John Hellweg
Contact: Ed Chilleen

Copper Canyon Brewing Ale House
5945 W Ray Rd/Suite 13
Chandler, AZ 85226
(602) 940-7677
Founded: Dec. 25, 1995
Capacity: 1,200 bbl
Sales Mgr.: Bill Mondragon
Head Brewer: Jerry L. Gantt
Contact: Doug Snyder

Coyote Springs Brewing Co and Cafe
4883 N 20th St
Phoenix, AZ 85016-4707
(602) 468-0403; FAX (602) 468-1645
Founded: Aug. 11, 1992
Capacity: 1,650 bbl
Head Brewer: Brian W. Miller
Pres.: Bill Garrard
Contact: Bill Garrard

Flagstaff Brewing Co
16 E Route 66
Flagstaff, AZ 86001-5755
(520) 773-1442; FAX (520) 773-7772
thorset@infomagic.com
Founded: July 18, 1994
Capacity: 1,250 bbl
Head Brewer: Jeff Thorsett
General Mgr.: Al Henes
Contact: Jeff Thorsett

Four Peaks Brewing Co
1340 E Eighth St
Tempe, AZ 85281
(602) 303-9967; FAX (602) 303-9964
Founded: Jan. 1, 1996
Capacity: 2,000 bbl
Asst. Brewer: Andy Ingram
Head Brewer: Clark Nelson
Sales Mgr.: Jim Scusell
Principle Contact: David Roberts
Sales: John Hostak
Contact: David Roberts

Gentle Ben's Brewing Co
865 E University Blvd
Tucson, AZ 85719-4828
(602) 624-4177; FAX (602) 323-1193
Pres./Head Brewer: Dennis Arnold
Contact: Dennis Arnold

Hops Bistro and Brewery (No 1)
7000 E Camelback Rd/Suite 100
Scottsdale, AZ 85251-1229
(602) 945-4677; FAX (602) 423-9755
Founded: Jan. 1, 1990
Capacity: 1,300 bbl
Sales Mgr.: Russell Veenema
General Mgr.: Robert Gabrick
Owner/Pres.: Lessing Stern
Head Brewer: Sean McLin
Contact: Russ Veenema

Hops Bistro and Brewery (No 3)
2584 E Camelback Rd
Phoenix, AZ 85016-4204
(602) 468-0500; FAX (602) 468-0188
Contact: James Salter

Hops Bistro and Brewery (No 4)
8668 E Shea Blvd
Scottsdale, AZ 85260-6614
(602) 998-7777
Founded: Nov. 1, 1994
Head Brewer: James Salter
Contact: James Salter

Lawler Brewing Co
11375 E Sahuaro Dr
Scottsdale, AZ 85259
(602) 314-9405
Founded: June 1, 1996
Contact: Tim Lawler

McFarlane Brewing Co
5921 E Evans
Scottsdale, AZ 85254
(602) 914-9190
Founded: April 15, 1996
Capacity: 4,700 bbl
Head Brewer: Peter M. McFarlane
Sales Mgr./Business Contact: Stephen J. McFarlane
Contact: Peter M. McFarlane

Oak Creek Brewing Co
2050 Yavapai Dr
Sedona, AZ 86336
(520) 204-1300; FAX (520) 204-1361
Founded: Feb. 22, 1995
Capacity: 2,000 bbl

Head Brewer: Fred Kraus
Sales Mgr.: Bob Powers
Treas.: Rita Kraus
Contact: Fred Kraus

Prescott Brewing Co
130 W Gurley/Suite A
Prescott, AZ 86301-3602
(520) 771-2795; FAX (520) 771-1115
Founded: Aug. 1, 1994
Capacity: 750 bbl
Pres./Head Brewer: John Nielsen
General Mgr.: Dave Jacobson
Buisness Mgr.: Roxane Nielsen
Contact: John Nielsen

Sonora Brewing Co
3601 N 36th Ave
Phoenix, AZ 85019
(602) 484-7775; FAX (602) 906-3793
Founded: April 1, 1996
Contact: John Watt

Tombstone Brewing Co
710 E Gilbert Dr
Tempe, AZ 85281
(602) 967-2337
climba514@aol.com
Founded: Jan. 15, 1996
Contact: Nathan Hoffman

ARKANSAS

Ozark Brewing Co
430 W Dickson St
Fayetteville, AR 72701-5107
(501) 521-2739; FAX (501) 442-0077
Founded: May 30, 1994
Capacity: 2,200 bbl
Executive Chef: Parker Lee IV
General Mgr.: Tim Ryan
Proprietor/Head Brewer: John Gilliam, Jr.
Contact: John Gilliam

Vino's
923 W Seventh St
Little Rock, AR 72201-4005
(501) 375-8466
Founded: June 1, 1993
Capacity: 350 bbl
Owner: Henry Lee
Head Brewer: Mark Crossley
Contact: Mark Crossley

Weidman's Old Fort Brewery
422 N Third St
Fort Smith, AR 72901-1410
(501) 782-9898; FAX (501) 782-0258
Founded: Aug. 6, 1992

Capacity: 1,500 bbl
Sales Mgr.: Terry Weidman
VP: Peggy Weidman
Pres.: Bill Weidman
Head Brewer: Daniel Weidman
Contact: Daniel Weidman

CALIFORNIA

Ale House Rock Brewery and Broiler
8082 Adams Ave
Huntington Beach, CA 92648
(714) 374-0811; FAX (714) 374-0810
Founded: Sept. 13, 1995
Capacity: 1,500 bbl
Head Brewer/Co-Owner: Jim Fisher
Co-Owner: Peter Russo
Contact: Jim Fisher

AleSmith Brewing Co
9368 Cabot Dr
San Diego, CA 92126
(619) 549-9888; FAX (619) 552-9235
Founded: Sept. 1, 1995
Capacity: 2,300 bbl
Head Brewer: Skip Vergilio
Partner: Ted Newcomb
Contact: Ted Newcomb

Amber Waves Brewery and Pub
600 Orange Dr
Vacaville, CA 95687
(707) 452-8600; FAX (707) 453-8260
Founded: Aug. 2, 1995
Capacity: 1,620 bbl
Head Brewer: Russell Ware
Sales Mgr.: Jerry Ware
Contact: Jerry Ware

American River Brewing Co
100 Borland Ave
Auburn, CA 95603-4922
(916) 889-0841; FAX (916) 889-0841
Founded: Oct. 1, 1993
Capacity: 5,000 bbl
Head Brewer/Sales Mgr.: Don Smith
Treas.: John Mehlhaff
Pres./General Mgr.: James Fair
Contact: James Fair

Anchor Brewing Co
1705 Mariposa St
San Francisco, CA 94107-2334
(415) 863-8350; FAX (415) 552-7094
Capacity: 102,000 bbl
Public Affairs: Philip Rogers
Pres.: Fritz Maytag

General Mgr.: Gordon MacDermott
Production Mgr.: Mark Carpenter
Head Brewer: Mike Lee

Anderson Valley Brewing Co
14081 Hwy 128
Boonville, CA 95415
(707) 895-2337; FAX (707) 895-2353
http://catalog.com/avbc/home.html
Founded: Dec. 26, 1987
Capacity: 4,700 bbl
Head Brewer: Loren Allen
Co-Owner: Kimberly Allen
Co-Owner/Pres.: Kenneth Allen
Sales Mgr.: Loren Allen
Contact: Loren Allen

Anheuser-Busch Inc
PO Box 2113
Los Angeles, CA 90051
(818) 989-5300
Capacity: 11,600,000 bbl
Plant Mgr.: Gary P. Lee
Resident Brewmaster: Dennis E. Whelan
Contact: Gary P. Lee

Anheuser-Busch Inc
PO Box AB/3101 Busch Dr
Fairfield, CA 94533
(707) 429-2000
Capacity: 4,100,000 bbl
Plant Mgr.: Wayne P. Senalik
Resident Brewmaster: Gary Eckman
Contact: Wayne P. Senalik

B J's Brewery/ Chicago Pizza Inc
600 Brea Mall Dr
Brea, CA 92621
(714) 990-2095
Founded: April 1, 1996
Contact: Alex Puchner

Baja Brewing Co
203 Fifth Ave
San Diego, CA 90007
(619) 231-9279
Founded: March 1, 1996
Contact: Stuart Gildred

Barley & Hopps
201 S B St
San Mateo, CA 94401
(415) 348-7808; FAX (415) 348-8789
Founded: March 22, 1995
Contact: R. J. Trent

Bayhawk Ales Inc
2000 Main St/Suite A
Irvine, CA 92714
(714) 442-7565; FAX (714) 442-7566
Founded: Feb. 1, 1995
Capacity: 10,000 bbl
General Mgr.: David Voorhies
Brewer: Joe Scagliotti
Head Brewer: Jon Newman
Contact: David Voorhies

Bear Republic Brewing Co
345 Healdsburg Ave
Healdsburg, CA 95448
(707) 433-2337; FAX (707) 433-2337
Founded: Jan. 25, 1996
Contact: Richard Norgrove

Belmont Brewing Co
25 39th Pl
Long Beach, CA 90803-2806
(310) 433-3891; FAX (310) 434-0604
Founded: June 16, 1990
Capacity: 800 bbl
Pres.: David Lott
Head Brewer/Sales Mgr.: Malcolm McDonald
Contact: David Lott

Bison Brewing Co
2598 Telegraph Ave
Berkeley, CA 94704-2920
(510) 841-7734
Founded: Jan. 1, 1989
Capacity: 900 bbl
Pub. Mgr.: Daniel Rogers
Head Brewer: Scott Meyer
Contact: Daniel Rogers

Black Diamond Brewing Co
2330 N Main St
Walnut Creek, CA 94596-3523
(510) 943-2330
Contact: Johnnie Koeller

Blind Pig Brewing Co
42387 Avenida Alvarado/Suite 108
Temecula, CA 92590-3467
(909) 695-4646; FAX (909) 695-4648
Founded: July 1, 1994
Capacity: 3,600 bbl
Head Brewer: Vinnie Cilurzo
Sales Mgr.: David Stovall
Contact: Vinnie Cilurzo

Blue Water Brewing Co
PO Box 5622
Tahoe City, CA 96145-5622
(916) 581-2583; FAX (916) 581-1607

United States Breweries (California)

Founded: March 20, 1994
Capacity: 2,000 bbl
VP Brewery Operations: Phillip Millbrand
CEO: Chris Loughlin
Sales Mgr./Head Brewer: Phillip Millbrand
Contact: Phillip Milbrand

Bootlegger's Steakhouse & Brewery
PO Box 1475
Shafter, CA 93263-1475
(805) 322-2464; FAX (805) 322-2461
Founded: May 15, 1994
Contact: Ralph Fruguglietti

Boulder Creek Brewing Co
13040 Hwy 9
Boulder Creek, CA 95006-9118
(408) 338-7882
Founded: Oct. 11, 1990
Capacity: 430 bbl
Head Brewer: Peter Catizone
Co-Owner: Nancy Long
Co-Owner: Steve Wyman
Contact: Steve Wyman

Brew City
2198 Filbert St
San Francisco, CA 94123-3413
(415) 929-2255; FAX (415) 929-2256
omholt@haas.berkeley.edu
Founded: Dec. 1, 1994
Contact: Clark Omholt

Brewery at Lake Tahoe
3542 Lake Tahoe Blvd
South Lake Tahoe, CA 96150-8900
(916) 544-2739; FAX (916) 544-7359
Pres.: Russell Penn
Head Brewer: Mike Doane
Contact: Russell Penn

BrewMakers/ Venture Brewing Inc
1020 N Rengstorff Ave
Mountain View, CA 94043
(415) 969-6253; FAX (415) 969-7700
Founded: Sept. 1, 1995
Sales Mgr.: Tim Cloonan
Head Brewer: Stuart Glaun
Contact: Tim Cloonan

Brewmeisters/ Palm Springs Brewery Inc
369 N Palm Canyon
Palm Springs, CA 92262
(619) 327-2739; FAX (619) 327-2337
psbrew@aol.com

Founded: March 4, 1994
Capacity: 1,200 bbl
Pres.: Andrew Neiderman
Sales Mgr.: Victor Yaskanich
VP: Eugene Andrews
Sec.: Gerald Orseck
Head Brewer: Erik Neiderman
Sales Mgr.: Richard Kasofsky
Contact: Erik Neiderman

Brewski's Brewing Co
142 Arena St
El Segundo, CA 90245
(310) 322-1000; FAX (310) 322-6700
Founded: Aug. 1, 1995
Pres./Head Brewer: Sandy Saemann
Contact: Steve Hogan

Buffalo Bill's Brewery
1082 B St
Hayward, CA 94541-4108
(510) 886-9823; FAX (510) 886-8157
http://www.and.com/bb/bb.html
Founded: Sept. 9, 1993
Capacity: 600 bbl
Owner/Head Brewer: Geoff Harries
Contact: Geoff Harries

Burlingame Station Brewing Co/Golden State Brewing Co
333 California Dr
Burlingame, CA 94010
(415) 344-6050; FAX (415) 344-6097
Founded: March 8, 1995
Capacity: 2,500 bbl
General Mgr.: Domingo Garcia
Head Brewer: Curt Anderson
Contact: Curt Anderson

Butterfield Brewing Co
777 E Olive Ave
Fresno, CA 93728-3350
(209) 264-5521
Founded: March 1, 1989
Capacity: 3,000 bbl
Head Brewer: Kevin Cox
Owner/Pres./Sales Mgr.: Jeff Wolpert
Contact: Jeff Wolpert

Cafe Pacifica/ Sankt Gallen Brewery
333 Bush St
San Francisco, CA 94104-2806
(415) 296-8203; FAX (415) 296-9348
Founded: April 1, 1993
Pres./Head Brewer: Kozo Iwamoto
Sales Mgr.: Noriko Akita
Contact: Kozo Iwamoto

California Brewing Co
142 Arena St/Suite B
El Segundo, CA 90245
Contact: Steve Hogan

Callahan's Pub and Brewery
8280-A Mira Mesa Blvd
San Diego, CA 92126
(619) 578-7892; FAX (619) 578-7962
Founded: June 1, 1990
Capacity: 400 bbl
Co-Owner/Head Brewer: Scott Stamp
Co-Owner/Sales Mgr.: Lee Doxtader
General Mgr.: Larry Marshall
Contact: Scott Stamp

Carlsbad Brewery and Public House
571 Carlsbad Village Dr
Carlsbad, CA 92008
(619) 434-4212
Founded: July 22, 1995
Capacity: 1,600 bbl
Partner Brewer: Brett Redmayne-Titley
Head Brewer: Vince Marsaglia
Contact: Vince Marsaglia

Carmel Brewing Co
225 The Crossroads/Suite 121
Carmel, CA 93923-8600
(408) 771-2537; FAX (408) 771-0651
Founded: Feb. 28, 1995
Capacity: 15,000 bbl
Head Brewer/Owner: Paul Tarantino
Sales Mgr.: Angela Mussio
Contact: Paul Tarantino

Coast Range Brewing Co
7050 Monterey St
Gilroy, CA 95020
(408) 842-1000; FAX (408) 842-1025
Founded: Feb. 28, 1995
Capacity: 3,000 bbl
Owner: Ron Erskine
Head Brewer: Peter Licht
VP/Sales Mgr.: Paul Borrelli
Head Brewer: Peter Licht
Contact: Ron Erskine

Covany Brewing Co
359 Grand Ave
Grover Beach, CA 93433-1940
(805) 489-4042
Contact: David Covany

Crown City Brewery
300 S Raymond Ave
Pasadena, CA 91105-2620
(818) 577-5548; FAX (818) 577-5590

Founded: July 5, 1988
Capacity: 550 bbl
Sales Mgr.: Dennis Hartman
Gen. Partner: John Robinson
Gen. Partner: Dennis Hartman
Gen. Partner: Mike Lanzarotta
Head Brewer: Jay Baum
Contact: Mike Lanzarotta

Delmar Stuft Pizza and Microbrewery
12840 Carmel Country Rd
San Diego, CA 92130
(619) 481-7883
Founded: Sept. 10, 1995
Contact: John Garvey

Dino & Luigi's Stuft Pizza Sports Bar and Brewery
10155 Rancho Carmel Dr
San Diego, CA 92128
(619) 592-7883
Founded: Oct. 15, 1995
Contact: John Stewart

Downtown Joe's Brewery and Restaurant
902 Main St
Napa, CA 94559-3045
(707) 258-2337; FAX (707) 258-2740
Founded: Jan. 1, 1994
Capacity: 1,200 bbl
Co-Owner: Joe Peatman
Co-Owner: Joe Ruffino
Brewmaster: Brian Hunt
Brewer: Lance McLaughlin
Asst. Brewer: Rik Graham
Contact: Brian Hunt

Eel River Brewing Co
1777 Alamarway
Fortuna, CA 95540
(707) 725-2739
Founded: Dec. 4, 1995
Contact: Ted and Margaret Vivatson

El Dorado Brewing Co
PO Box 3
Mount Aukum, CA 95656-0003
(916) 620-4253; FAX (916) 620-4259
Contact: Jim Boyer

El Dorado Brewing Co
PO Box 4037
Stockton, CA 95204-0022
(209) 948-2537; FAX (209) 948-4924
Founded: June 1, 1994
Capacity: 900 bbl
Head Brewer: Blake Bonmen

El Toro Brewing Co
17370 Hill Rd
Morgan Hill, CA 95037-9704
(408) 778-2739
Founded: April 1, 1994
Capacity: 4,000 bbl
Head Brewer/Sales Mgr.: H. Geno Acevedo
Contact: H. Acevedo

Elk Grove Brewing Co Inc
9085 Elk Grove Blvd
Elk Grove, CA 95624
(916) 685-2537
Founded: Nov. 6, 1995
Contact: Dave Ogden

Etna Brewing Co
PO Box 757
Etna, CA 96027-0757
(916) 467-5277
Founded: June 1, 1990
Capacity: 750 bbl
Sec.: Brenda Hurlimann
VP: Vernon Smith
Pres./Head Brewer/Sales Mgr.: Andrew Hurlimann
Asst. Brewer: Luke Hurlimann
Contact: Andrew Hurlimann

Faultline Brewing Co Inc
1235 Oakmead Pkwy
Sunnyvale, CA 94086
(408) 736-2739; FAX (408) 736-2752
faultlineb@aol.com
http://www.flbc.copm
Founded: Dec. 2, 1994
General Mgr.: Mark Perry
Pres.: Steve Geiszler
Head Brewer: Greg Friday
Contact: Mark Perry

Fremont Brewing Co
3350 Stevenson Blvd
Fremont, CA 94538-2328
(510) 651-5510
FBC@SineWave.com
http://www.SineWave.com/FBC/
Founded: Jan. 11, 1994
Capacity: 2,000 bbl
VP Oper./Sales Mgr.: David Lawler
Pres.: Thomas Lawler
Head Brewer: Richard Webster
Contact: David Lawler

Fullerton Hofbrau
323 N State College Blvd
Fullerton, CA 92631-4205
(714) 870-7400; FAX (714) 870-1135
Founded: June 29, 1990
Capacity: 2,000 bbl
General Mgr./Sales Mgr.: Ron Raboin
Head Brewer: Axel Buerk
Contact: Gunther Buerk

Glencastle Brewing Co
214 N Brand
Glendale, CA 91206
(818) 240-4832
Founded: March 15, 1996
Owner: Dwight Lee
Contact: Brett Pugh

Golden Pacific Brewing Co
5515 Doyle St
Emeryville, CA 94608-2510
(510) 655-3322; FAX (510) 655-3364
Founded: Jan. 1, 1987
Capacity: 7,000 bbl
Senior Brewer: Alec Moss
Production Mgr.: Mark Witty
Pres.: David Harnden
Distribution Mgr.: Juerg Spoerry
Senior Brewer: Matt Hubych
Contact: David Harnden

Gordon Biersch Brewery (No 1)
4240 Hollis St
Emeryville, CA 94608-3533
(415) 323-7723; FAX (415) 323-6129
Founded: June 1, 1988
Capacity: 1,650 bbl
Head Brewer: Jason Drotar
Brewing Dir.: Dan Gordon
Contact: Dan Gordon

Gordon Biersch Brewery Restaurant (No 1)
640 Emerson St
Palo Alto, CA 94301-1609
(415) 323-7723
Contact: Tom Davis

Gordon Biersch Brewery Restaurant (No 2)
33 E San Fernando St
San Jose, CA 95113-2508
(408) 294-6785; FAX (408) 294-4052
Founded: Jan. 1, 1990
Capacity: 2,200 bbl
Contact: Dean Biersch

Gordon Biersch Brewery Restaurant (No 3)
2 Harrison St
San Francisco, CA 94105-1672
(415) 243-8246; FAX (415) 243-9214
Founded: Jan. 1, 1992
Contact: John Berardino

United States Breweries (California)

Gordon Biersch Brewery Restaurant (No 4)
41 Hugus Alley
Pasadena, CA 91103-3644
(818) 449-0052; FAX (818) 449-0067
Founded: Dec. 14, 1994
Capacity: 2,500 bbl
Head Brewer: Michael Doherty
Brewery/Sales Mgr.: Michael Doherty
Contact: Michael Doherty

Grizzly Bay Brewing Co
325 Main St
Suisun City, CA 94585
(707) 434-8031
Founded: Aug. 4, 1995
Capacity: 750 bbl
Pres.: Tom Costello
VP/Head Brewer: Kevin McGee
Sales Mgr.: Maike Costello
Asst. Brewer: Kent McGee
Contact: Kevin McGee

Hangtown Brewery Inc
560-A Placerville Dr
Placerville, CA 95667
(916) 621-3999; FAX (916) 621-2157
75322.2101@compuserve.com
Founded: Dec. 1, 1992
Capacity: 2,160 bbl
Brewer: David Coody
Sales Mgr.: Larry Coody
Corp. Sec.: Matthew Chitiea
Contact: Larry Coody

Harbor Lights Brewing Co
24921 Dana Point Harbor Dr
Dana Point, CA 92629
(714) 240-2060; FAX (714) 240-4694
Founded: Feb. 1, 1995
Head Brewer: Joe Hitchman
Owner: Dave Littlefield
Contact: Dave Littlefield

Heritage Brewing Co
571-C Crane St
Lake Elsinore, CA 92530
(909) 245-1752
Founded: Jan. 1, 1994
Capacity: 10,000 bbl
Head Brewer: Mark Mericle
Contact: John Stoner

Hogshead Brewpub
114 J St
Sacramento, CA 95814-2207
(916) 443-2739
Founded: Oct. 1, 1985
Contact: Phil Salmon

Hop Town Brewing Co
3015 Hopyard Rd/Suite E
Pleasanton, CA 94588
(510) 426-1450; FAX (510) 426-9191
Founded: Feb. 26, 1996
Capacity: 1,000 bbl
Primary Contact: Mark Garetz
Head Brewer: Scott James
Contact: Mark Garetz

Hops Bistro and Brewery (No 2)
University Town Ctr/Suite H29
4353 La Jolla Village Dr
San Diego, CA 92122-1259
(619) 587-6677; FAX (619) 587-6739
Founded: Sept. 24, 1992
Capacity: 1,500 bbl
General Mgr.: Justin Hurd
Head Brewer: Ike Manchester
Sales Mgr.: Aug. Heuss
Contact: Justin Hurd

Humboldt Brewery
856 10th St
Arcata, CA 95521-9016
(707) 826-1734; FAX (707) 826-2045
Founded: Jan. 1, 1987
Capacity: 35,000 bbl
Head Brewer: Steve Parkes
Co-Owner/Dist.: Vince Celotto
Owner/Sales: Mario Celotto
Contact: Steve Parkes

Humes Brewing Co Inc
2775 Cavedale Rd
Glen Ellen, CA 95442
(707) 935-0723; FAX (707) 935-1683
Founded: Dec. 27, 1993
Capacity: 624 bbl
Sales Mgr.: Rusty Schwartz
Owner/Head Brewer: Peter Humes
Contact: Peter Humes

Huntington Beach Beer Co
201 Main St/Suite E
Huntington Beach, CA 92648-8110
(714) 960-5343
Founded: Oct. 20, 1992
Capacity: 1,500 bbl
Pres.: Peter Andriet
Head Brewer: Robert Brandt
General Mgr.: Sharon Andriet
Contact: Peter Andriet

Joe-Joe's Brewing Co
1397 Los Angeles Ave
Simi Valley, CA 93065
(805) 522-7725
Founded: March 17, 1995
Contact: Joe Tremonti

K C Brewing Co
14278 Doolittle Dr
San Leandro, CA 94577
(510) 352-1401
Founded: Aug. 29, 1995
Capacity: 1,300 bbl
Head Brewer: Ken Lindstrom
Co-Owner: Chrysan Lindstrom
Co-Owner: Gary Lindstrom
Contact: Ken Lindstrom

Karl Strauss Breweries/ Associated Microbreweries
2785 Kurtz/Suite 5
San Diego, CA 92110
(619) 491-0218; FAX (619) 297-4678
Founded: Feb. 1, 1991
Capacity: 15,000 bbl
Head Brewer: Marty Johnson
CFO: Mathew Rattner
CEO: Christopher Cramer
Brewery Oper. Mgr.: Charles Isaac
Sales Mgr.: Guy Sciacca
Contact: Christopher Cramer

Karl Strauss Brewery Gardens
9675 Scranton Rd
San Diego, CA 92121-1761
(619) 587-2739
Founded: Jan. 3, 1994
Capacity: 100 bbl
Head Brewer: Charles Isaac
Contact: Chris Cramer

La Jolla Brewing Co
7536 Fay Ave
La Jolla, CA 92037-4839
(619) 456-2739
Founded: Oct. 13, 1990
Capacity: 988 bbl
Partner: Mike Green
Partner: Mike Long
Partner: Jon Atwater
Head Brewer: Jon Atwater
Contact: Wade Lemaster

Laguna Beach Brewing Co
422 S Coast Hwy
Laguna Beach, CA 92651-2404
(714) 499-2337
Founded: Dec. 22, 1994
Capacity: 1,500 bbl
Pres.: Charles Matter
VP: Peter Andriet
Head Brewer/VP: Alex Puchner
Contact: Alex Puchner

United States Breweries (California)

Lagunitas Brewing Co
PO Box 456
Lagunitas, CA 94938-0456
(415) 488-1601; FAX (415) 454-1979
Founded: Feb. 1, 1994
Contact: Tony Magee

Lind Brewing Co
1933 Davis St/Suite 177
San Leandro, CA 94577-1200
(510) 562-0866
Founded: Sept. 1, 1989
Capacity: 1,000 bbl
Head Brewer: Roger Lind
Contact: Roger Lind

Los Gatos Brewing Co
130-G N Santa Cruz Ave
Los Gatos, CA 95030
(408) 395-9929; FAX (408) 395-2769
Founded: Oct. 5, 1992
Capacity: 1,400 bbl
Chef: Jim Stump
Owner: Andrew Pavicich
General Mgr.: Jennifer Colasuonno
Head Brewer: Jeff Alexander
Contact: Jeff Alexander

Lost Coast Brewery & Cafe
617 Fourth St
Eureka, CA 95501-1013
(707) 445-4480; FAX (707) 445-4483
http://realbeer.com/lostcoast/
Founded: Jan. 1, 1990
Capacity: 4,000 bbl
Pres./Head Brewer: Barbara Groom
Sec./Treas.: Wendy Pound
Sales Mgr.: Ray West
Contact: Wendy Pound

Mad River Brewing Co
PO Box 767
Blue Lake, CA 95525-0787
(707) 668-4151; FAX (707) 668-4297
Founded: Dec. 14, 1990
Capacity: 15,000 bbl
Sales Mgr.: John Campbell
Head Brewer: Bryan Bohannan
Treas.: Chris Frolking
Sec.: Greg Blomstrom
Pres./Gen. Mgr.: Robert Smith
Contact: Robert Smith

Mainline Brewing Co
1056 Westwood Blvd
Los Angeles, CA 90024
(310) 443-5401; FAX (310) 209-7499
Founded: July 1, 1995
Contact: Tom Anderson

Mammoth Brewing Co
18 Main St
Mammoth Lakes, CA 93546
(619) 934-2555
Founded: Jan. 12, 1996
Owner: Sam Walker
Contact: Sam Walker

Manhattan Beach Brewing Co
124 Manhattan Beach Blvd
Manhattan Beach, CA 90266-5432
(310) 798-2744
Contact: David Zislis

Marin Brewing Co
1809 Larkspur Landing Cir
Larkspur, CA 94939-1801
(415) 898-9640; FAX (415) 897-6063
moylan1@aol.com
http://and.com/mbc/
Founded: April 1, 1989
Capacity: 2,375 bbl
Head Brewer: Grant Johnston
Gen. Partner: Craig Tasley
Gen. Partner/Head Brewer: Brendan Moylan
Brewer: Arne Johnson
Brewer: Dave Zimmerman
Contact: Brendan Moylan

Mendocino Brewing Co
PO Box 400
Hopland, CA 95449-0400
(707) 744-1015; FAX (707) 744-1910
Founded: Aug. 14, 1983
Capacity: 18,000 bbl
Mktg. Dir.: Michael Lovett
Maintenance Mgr.: John Scahill
Pres./CEO: Michael Laybourn
VP/CFO: Norman Franks
Master Brewer: Donald Barkley
Head Brewer: Kit Schweitzer
Contact: Michael Laybourn

Miller Brewing Co
15801 E First St
Irwindale, CA 91706-2036
(818) 969-6811
Capacity: 5,000,000 bbl
Plant Mgr.: Edward L. Beers
Oper. Mgr.: Gene R. Bosse
Brewing Mgr.: Robert E. LaSota
Contact: Edward L. Beers

Moonlight Brewing Co
PO Box 316
Fulton, CA 95439-0316
(707) 528-2537
Founded: Sept. 1, 1992
Capacity: 1,500 bbl
Sole Proprietor/Brewmaster: Brian Hunt
Asst. Brewer: Lance McLaughlin
Contact: Brian Hunt

Moylan's Brewing Co
15 Rowland Way
Novato, CA 94945
(415) 898-4677; FAX (415) 897-0100
Brendan@Moylans.com
http://realbeer/Moylans
Founded: Aug. 20, 1995
Capacity: 3,500 bbl
Owner/Brewmaster: Brendan Moylan
Brewmaster: Paddy Giffen
Asst. Brewer: Craig Stager
General Mgr.: Eric Reimer
Contact: Brendan Moylan

Murphys Creek Brewing Co
PO Box 1076
Murphys, CA 95247-1076
(209) 736-2739
Founded: April 1, 1993
Capacity: 3,000 bbl
Brewmaster: Micah Millspaw
Sales Mgr.: Kelly Blanc
Pres.: Dan Ayala
Contact: Micah Millspaw

Napa Valley Ale Works
PO Box 5268/110 Camino Oruga
Napa, CA 94558
(707) 257-8381; FAX (707) 257-2436
Brewer: Elaine St. Clair
General Mgr.: Dwayne Mathews
Contact: Dwayne Mathews

Napa Valley Brewing Co
Calistoga Inn
1250 Lincoln Ave
Calistoga, CA 94515-1741
(707) 942-4101
Founded: Nov. 1, 1987
Capacity: 400 bbl
Owner: Ken Nilsson
Contact: Ken Nilsson

Nevada City Brewing Co
75 Bost Ave
Nevada City, CA 95959-3049
(916) 265-2446
Founded: Dec. 9, 1986
Capacity: 2,000 bbl
Sales Mgr.: Robert Barth
Head Brewer: Keith Downing
Pres./Head Brewer: Gene Downing
Contact: Gene Downing

United States Breweries (California)

Newport Beach Brewing Co
2920 Newport Blvd
Newport Beach, CA 92663
(714) 675-8449
Founded: May 1, 1995
Capacity: 2,000 bbl
Pres.: Orazio Salamone
VP: Tamara Madlock
Sec./Treas.: Peter Andriet
Head Brewer: Julius Hummer
Operations Mgr.: Shawn Needleman
Contact: Orazio Salamone

North Coast Brewing
444 N Main St
Fort Bragg, CA 95437-3216
(707) 964-2739; FAX (707) 964-8768
http://www.SLIP.NET//~ESCHRIG/NCBC.HTM
Founded: Aug. 1, 1988
Pres./Brewmaster: Mark Reudrich
Contact: Mark Ruedrich

Ocean Ave Brewing Co
237 Ocean Ave
Laguna Beach, CA 92651
(714) 497-3381; FAX (714) 497-9371
Founded: Dec. 9, 1994
Capacity: 1,500 bbl
Head Brewer: Jonathan Thomas
Contact: Jonathan Thomas

Old Baldy Brewing Co
271 N Second Ave
Upland, CA 91786-6003
(909) 946-1750; FAX (909) 920-9292
Founded: Sept. 23, 1994
Capacity: 1,500 bbl
Head Brewer: William Romero Jr.
Head Brewer/Sales Mgr.: Art Lydick
Contact: William Romero

Old Columbia Brewery
1157 Columbia St
San Diego, CA 92101-3511
(619) 491-0218; FAX (619) 297-4678
http://go-explore.com/ads/ca/so/kstrauss/home.htm
Head Brewer: Martin Johnson
Sales Mgr.: Guy Sciacca
Contact: Christopher W. Cramer

Old River Brew Co
8524 Old River Rd
Bakersfield, CA 93311-9733
(805) 398-0454; FAX (805) 832-8620
Founded: March 24, 1993
Capacity: 520 bbl

Head Brewer/Sales Mgr.: Craig Scharpenberg
Contact: Craig Scharpenberg

Pacific Brewing Co
812 Fourth St
San Rafael, CA 94901-3224
(415) 457-9167; FAX (415) 457-2299
Founded: July 1, 1993
Capacity: 2,250 bbl
Dir. of Operations: Keith Burrall II
Head Brewer: Jeff Held
Sales Mgr.: Keith Burrall II
Contact: Keith Burrall II

Pacific Coast Brewing Co
906 Washington St
Oakland, CA 94607-4032
(510) 836-2739; FAX (510) 836-1987
oaklanda@hooked.net
http://members.gnn.com/paccoast/index.htm/index.htm
Founded: Oct. 1, 1988
Capacity: 431 bbl
Public Relations: John Campau
General Mgr.: Steve Wolf
Brewmaster: Don Gortemiller
Head Brewer: Steve Sites
Contact: Don Gortemiller

Pacific Hop Exchange
158 Hamilton Dr/Suite A1
Novato, CA 94949-5630
(415) 884-2820; FAX (415) 884-2820
hopexchg@aol.com
http://www.wco.com./~wwmnsmrtr
Founded: April 21, 1993
Capacity: 3,500 bbl
VP: Zach Shaw
VP: Thomas Wheelan
Pres./CFO: Robert Ankrum
Head Brewer/VP: Warren Stief
Contact: Robert Ankrum

Parrots Ferry Brewing Co
22265 Parrotts Ferry Rd
Sonora, CA 95370
(209) 532-3089
Founded: Oct. 14, 1995
Owner: Bill Coffey
Contact: Bill Ritzman

**Pizza Port
Solana Beach Brewery**
135 N Hwy 101
Solana Beach, CA 92075-1128
(619) 481-7332; FAX (619) 481-7448
Founded: Oct. 9, 1992
Capacity: 1,000 bbl

Treas./Head Brewer: Vince Marsaglia
CEO: Gina Marsaglia
Sales Mgr.: Eddie Glassett
Contact: Gina Marsaglia

Pleasanton Main St Brewing Co
830 Main St
Pleasanton, CA 94566
(510) 462-8218
Founded: Feb. 3, 1996
Contact: Terry Yee

Powerhouse Brewing Co
268 Petaluma Ave
Sebastopol, CA 95472
(707) 829-9171
Founded: Dec. 22, 1995
Head Brewer: Donald Thornton
Sales Mgr./VP: Bill Bradt
Executive Chef: Sam Begler
Contact: Kathy Weir

**Pyramid Alehouse
and Brewery at Berkeley**
901 Gilman St
Berkeley, CA 94710
Founded: April 1, 1996
Capacity: 80,000 bbl
Contact: George Arnold

R J's Riptide Brewery
310 Fifth Ave
San Diego, CA 92101-6936
(619) 231-7700
Founded: Feb. 11, 1992
Capacity: 3,000 bbl
Head Brewer: B Antrim
Sales Mgr.: Mike Costanzo
Contact: R. J. Silber

Red White and Brew
2181 Hilltop Dr
Redding, CA 96002-0522
(916) 222-5891
http://www.symgrp.com/brew
Founded: June 1, 1993
Contact: Bill Ward

Redondo Beach Brewing Co
1814 S Catalina Ave
Redondo Beach, CA 90277-5505
(310) 316-8477
Founded: June 1, 1993
Pres.: Michael Zislis
Head Brewer: Michael Zislis
Contact: Michael Zislis

United States Breweries (California)

Redwood Coast Brewing Co/Tied House Cafe and Brewery (No 1)
PO Box 1028/954 Villa St
Mountain View, CA 94041-1236
(415) 965-2739; FAX (415) 965-0748
Founded: Jan. 1, 1988
Capacity: 3,600 bbl
Pres.: Louis Jemison
VP: Dr. Andreas Heller
Head Brewer: Dr. Andreas Heller
Contact: Andreas Heller

River City Brewing Co
545 Downtown Plaza/Suite 1115
Sacramento, CA 95814-3332
(916) 447-2750; FAX (916) 448-7153
Founded: Nov. 23, 1993
Capacity: 1,800 bbl
Owner: Manuel Pereira
Head Brewer: Luke Dimichele
Contact: Luke Dimichele

Riverside Brewing Co
3397 Seventh St
Riverside, CA 92501-3302
(909) 682-5465; FAX (909) 682-5487
http://riversidebrewing.co/riverside
Founded: June 1, 1993
Capacity: 25,000 bbl
Head Brewer: Daniel Kahn
Pres./Sales Mgr.: John Barnicoat
Asst. Brewer: Sean Tucker
Contact: Daniel Kahn

Rubicon Brewing Co
2004 Capitol Ave
Sacramento, CA 95814-4215
(916) 448-7032
Founded: Nov. 1, 1987
Capacity: 4,320 bbl
Head Brewer: Scott Cramlet
Owner: Ed Brown
Contact: Scott Cramlet

Sacramento Brewing Co
2713 El Paseo Lane
Sacramento, CA 95821
(916) 485-4677; FAX (916) 485-3041
Founded: June 8, 1995
Capacity: 1,500 bbl
Chairman/Head Brewer: Sam Petersen
Pres.: Joe Lee
VP: Jeri Petersen
VP: Jan Lee
Contact: Sam Petersen

San Andreas Brewing Co
737 San Benito St
Hollister, CA 95023-3916
(408) 637-7074; FAX (408) 637-6170
Founded: Oct. 1, 1988
Capacity: 500 bbl
Pres./Head Brewer/Sales Mgr.: Bill Millar
Contact: Bill Millar

San Diego Brewing Co
10450 Friars Rd/Suite L
San Diego, CA 92120-2311
(619) 284-2739; FAX (619) 284-0428
Founded: Aug. 7, 1993
Capacity: 700 bbl
Co-Owner/Pres.: Lee Doxtader
Co-Owner/Head Brewer: Scott Stamp
Head Brewer: Charles Hudais
Contact: Scott Stamp

San Francisco Brewing Co
155 Columbus Ave
San Francisco, CA 94133-5114
(415) 434-3344; FAX (415) 434-2433
http://www.sfbrewing.com
Founded: Jan. 16, 1986
Capacity: 800 bbl
Brewmaster/Gen. Partner: Allan Paul
Head Brewer: Steve Haderle
Contact: Allan Paul

San Marcos Brewery and Grill
1080 W Old San Marcos Blvd
San Marcos, CA 92069
(619) 471-0050
Founded: Sept. 15, 1993
Capacity: 1,000 bbl
General Mgr.: Bill Maxfield
VP: Lee Garich
Pres./Head Brewer: David Nutley
Contact: David Nutley

Santa Barbara Brewing Co
501 State St
Santa Barbara, CA 93101
(805) 730-1040; FAX (805) 730-3317
Founded: Aug. 21, 1995
Capacity: 1,000 bbl
Head Brewer: Larry Kreider
Sales Mgr.: Larry Kreider
Contact: Larry Kreider

Santa Clarita Brewing Co
20655 Soledad Canyon Rd/Suite 1
Santa Clarita, CA 91351-2472
(805) 259-9608
Founded: Jan. 14, 1994

Co-Owner: Sheila Van Leeuwen
Co-Owner/Sales Mgr.: Mark Van Leeuwen
Head Brewer: Mark Van Leeuwen
Contact: Mark Van Leeuwen

Santa Cruz Brewing Co/Front Street Pub
516 Front St
Santa Cruz, CA 95060-4506
(408) 429-8838; FAX (408) 429-8915
Founded: May 1, 1986
Capacity: 1,850 bbl
Contact: Gerald J. Turgeon
Brewmaster: Scotty Morgan
Head Brewer: Jim Smith
Sales Mgr.: Carlin Schelstraete
Contact: Gerald Turgeon

Santa Monica Brewing Co
5041 Coolidge Ave
Culver City, CA 90230-5122
(213) 852-4643
Founded: Nov. 1, 1994
Contact: Andrea Harsayni

Santa Rosa Brewing Co
458 B St
Santa Rosa, CA 95401-6355
(707) 544-4677
http://and.com/srbc/srbc.html
Founded: April 15, 1993
Capacity: 1,200 bbl
Owner: Diana McCullough
Owner: Frank McCullough
Owner: Kevin McCullough
Head Brewer: Tim O'Day
Contact: Frank McCullough

Seabright Brewery Inc
519 Seabright Ave/Suite 107
Santa Cruz, CA 95062-3482
(408) 426-2739; FAX (408) 426-2760
cranmer@hooked.net
Founded: May 14, 1988
Capacity: 1,300 bbl
Pres./Partner/Sales Mgr.: Keith Cranmer
VP/Partner: Charlie Meehan
Head Brewer: Will Turner

Seaport Pub & Brewery
678 Grider Way
Stockton, CA 95209
(209) 474-7678
Founded: Nov. 1, 1995
Headbrewer: Dennis Michniuk
Contact: Dennis Michniuk

United States Breweries (California)

Shields Brewing Co
24 E Santa Clara St
Ventura, CA 93001-2714
(805) 643-1807; FAX (805) 643-1807
Capacity: 1,000 bbl
Co-Owner/Head Brewer: Robert Shields
Co-Owner/Sales Mgr.: Trudy Shields
Contact: Robert Shields

Sierra Nevada Brewing Co
1075 E 20th St
Chico, CA 95928-6722
(916) 893-3520; FAX (916) 893-1275
Founded: Jan. 1, 1981
Capacity: 270,000 bbl
Head Brewer: Steve Dresler
Plant Mgr.: Bob Aug.
Pres.: Ken Grossman
Sales Mgr.: Steve Harrison
VP: Paul Camusi
Contact: Steve Harrison

SLO Brewing Co Inc
1119 Garden St
San Luis Obispo, CA 93401-3525
(805) 546-8573
brewhoffa@aol.com
Founded: Sept. 17, 1988
Capacity: 1,500 bbl
Pres.: Michael Hoffman
Head Brewer: David Kane
Business/Sales Mgr.: Ken Jaeques
Contact: Michael Hoffman

Snowshoe Brewing Co
2050 Hwy 4
Arnold, CA 95223
(209) 795-2272
Founded: July 20, 1995
Head Brewer: Bob Blass
Contact: Jeff Yarnell

Sonoma Brewing Co
50 E Washington St
Petaluma, CA 94952-3115
(707) 765-9694
Founded: Dec. 7, 1991
Capacity: 700
Chef: Bernadette Burrell
Head Brewer: Peter Burrell
Contact: Peter Burrell

Southern California Brewing Co
833 W Torrance Blvd
Torrance, CA 90502-1735
(310) 329-8881; FAX (310) 516-7989
Founded: July 1, 1987
Capacity: 10,000 bbl

Sales Mgr.: Felix Duhovic
Head Brewer: Curtis Womach
VP: Ray Mathys
Pres.: William Van Liere
Contact: Bill Van Liere

St Stan's Brewery Pub and Restaurant
821 L St
Modesto, CA 95354-0837
(209) 524-2337; FAX (209) 524-4827
Founded: July 1, 1984
Capacity: 45,000 bbl
Sales Mgr.: Russ Torres
Production Mgr.: Eric Kellner
Brewmaster/CEO: Garith Helm
CFO: Romy Angle
Contact: Garith Helm

Steelhead Brewing Co
4175 Campus Dr
Irvine, CA 92715
(714) 856-2227; FAX (714) 509-6407
Founded: Sept. 21, 1995
Capacity: 1,700 bbl
Head Brewer: Mike Key
Contact: Robbie Acher

Stoddard's Brewhouse & Eatery
111 S Murphy Ave
Sunnyvale, CA 94086-6113
(408) 733-7824; FAX (408) 733-8969
http://www.losgatos.ca.us/stoddards.html
Founded: April 1, 1993
Capacity: 2,600 bbl
Head Brewer: Robert Stoddard
Contact: Robert Stoddard

Sudwerk Privatbrauerei Hubsch
2001 Second St
Davis, CA 95616
(916) 756-2739; FAX (916) 753-0590
Founded: April 10, 1990
Capacity: 2,000 bbl
Stockholder: Dean Unger
Stockholder: Ron Broward
Brewer/Sales Mgr.: Dave Morrow
Packaging Mgr./Head Brewer: David Sipes
Contact: Ron Broward

Sutter Brewing Co Inc
6300 Folsom Blvd
Sacramento, CA 95819
(800) 273-9488
Founded: March 1, 1995
Capacity: 2,500 bbl

Head Brewer: Jeff Blake
Contact: Kevin Standlield

Terrific Pacific Brewery and Grill
PO Box 2703
La Jolla, CA 92038-2703
(619) 270-3596
Founded: May 1, 1995
Capacity: 1,000 bbl
VP: Valerie Duband
Pres.: William Sussman
Brewmaster: Didier Husson
Contact: William Sussman

Third Street Ale Works
610 Third St
Santa Rosa, CA 95402
(707) 523-3060; FAX (707) 523-3063
Founded: March 8, 1996
Capacity: 2,000 bbl
Principle Contact: Christopher Hagan
Head Brewer: Grant Johnston
Contact: Grant Johnston

Tied House Cafe and Brewery (No 2)
PO Box 90400
San Jose, CA 95109-3400
(408) 295-2739
http://realbeer.com/tiedhouse/
Contact: Andreas Heller

Tied House Cafe and Brewery (No 3)
Pacific Marina Village
Alameda, CA 94501
(510) 521-4321; FAX (510) 521-4890
tiedzu@netcom.com
http://www.realbeer.com/tiedhouse
Founded: Dec. 19, 1991
Capacity: 4,500 bbl
Head Brewer: Scott Phillips
Sales Mgr.: Michael Nicholas
Brewmaster: Dr. Andreas Heller
Contact: Dr. Andreas Heller

Triple Rock Brewing
1920 Shattuck Ave
Berkeley, CA 94704-1022
(510) 843-4677; FAX (510) 843-2856
http://and.com/3rock/3rock.html
Founded: March 1, 1986
Capacity: 1,500 bbl
Head Brewer: Sandy Savage
VP: John Martin
VP/VP Brewing Oper.: Reid Martin
Contact: Reid Martin

Truckee Brewing Co
PO Box 2348
Truckee, CA 96160
(916) 587-5406; FAX (916) 589-5406
Founded: Jan. 1, 1985
Capacity: 1,600 bbl
Co-Owner/Head Brewer: Jean-Luc GiBassier
Co-Owner: Steve Downing
Contact: Jean-Luc GiBassier

Tuscan Brewery
25009 Kauffman Ave
Red Bluff, CA 96080-8924
(916) 527-7048; FAX (916) 529-9318
Capacity: 300 bbl
Pres./Sales Mgr.: Val Theis
Head Brewer: Jim Hudson
Contact: Val Theis

Twenty Tank Brewery
316 11th St
San Francisco, CA 94103-4314
(415) 255-9455; FAX (415) 255-6325
http://and.com/20tank/20.html
Founded: Sept. 7, 1990
Capacity: 2,000 bbl
Head Brewer: Chris Sheehan
Mktg. Mgr.: Elinore Boeke
Contact: John Martin

Uhlig Brewing Co
1510 Vista Club/Suite 306
Santa Clara, CA 95054
(408) 980-1028
Contact: Gordon Uhlig

Valley of the Moon Brewery
442 E Napa St
Sonoma, CA 95476-6725
(707) 935-3664
Contact: Alec McTaggart

Westwood Brewing Co
1097 Glendon Ave
Los Angeles, CA 90024
(310) 209-2739
Founded: Jan. 9, 1996
Contact: Ben Madden

COLORADO

Anheuser-Busch Inc
2351 Busch Dr
Fort Collins, CO 80524
(970) 490-4500
Capacity: 6,100,000 bbl

Plant Mgr.: Steve McDaniel
Resident Brewmaster: Martin Watz
Contact: Steve McDaniel

Avery Brewing Co
5763 Arapahoe Ave/Suite E
Boulder, CO 80301
(303) 440-4324; FAX (303) 786-8790
Founded: March 1, 1994
Capacity: 3,500 bbl
Pres./Head Brewer: Adam Avery
CEO: Larry Avery
Sec.: Steve Wagner
Sales Mgr.: Angela Avery
Contact: Adam Avery

Back Alley Brewing Co
3200 N Stone Ave
Colorado Springs, CO 80907
(719) 520-1980; FAX (719) 592-9570
aadallen@cris.com
http://www.webpost.com/backalley/home.htm
Founded: Sept. 29, 1995
Capacity: 1,500 bbl
Head Brewer: Aaron Allen
Sales Mgr.: Bob Catalano
Contact: Aaron Allen

Baked and Brewed in Telluride
PO Box 575/127 S Fir
Telluride, CO 81435-0575
(970) 728-4705; FAX (970) 728-6324
Founded: Dec. 6, 1991
Capacity: 150 bbl
Owner/Head Brewer: Jerry Green
Sales Mgr./Asst. Brewer: Dylan Sloan
Contact: Jerry Greene

Big Horn Brewing Co of Colorado/C B Potts
6575 Greenwood Plaza Blvd
Englewood, CO 80112
(303) 770-1982; FAX (303) 770-1932
Founded: Dec. 12, 1995
Capacity: 1,800 bbl
Head Brewer: Jeff Nickel
Asst. Brewer: Rob Parela
Contact: David Hollow

Breckenridge Brewery Colorado
471 Kalamath St
Denver, CO 80204
(303) 297-2341
Head Brewer: J. Todd Usry
Contact: J. Todd Usry

Breckenridge Brewery Denver
2220 Blake St
Denver, CO 80205-2013
(303) 297-3644; FAX (303) 297-2341
Founded: Dec. 4, 1992
Capacity: 16,000 bbl
Sales Mgr.: Trevor Smith
Sales Mgr.: Matt Patterson
Managing Gen. Partner: Richard Squire
Head Brewer: J. Todd Usry
Operations Mgr.: Robert Eilert
Distribution Mgr.: Caty Hayes
Contact: J. Todd Usry

Breckenridge Brewery and Pub
PO Box 75/600 Main St
Breckenridge, CO 80424-0075
(970) 453-1550; FAX (970) 453-0928
brewery@brecknex.com
Founded: Jan. 1, 1990
Capacity: 3,600 bbl
Master Brewer/Sales Mgr: Michael Reed
Contact: Michael Reed

Bristol Brewing Co
4740 Forge Rd/Suite 108
Colorado Springs, CO 80907-3558
(719) 535-2824; FAX (719) 535-2749
Founded: June 10, 1994
Capacity: 3,200 bbl
Owner/Gen. Mgr.: Mike Bristol
Contact: Mike Bristol

Broadway Brewing Co
2441 Broadway
Denver, CO 80205-2116
(303) 292-5027; FAX (303) 296-0164
Founded: June 1, 1994
Capacity: 24,000 bbl
Head Brewer: Scott W. Turnnidge
Dir. Sales/Mktg.: Lori Tullberg-Kelly
General Mgr.: Mike Magle
Contact: Scott Turnnidge

Brouwer Brewery
7229 E County Rd 18
Loveland, CO 80537-8819
(970) 669-8492
Founded: Sept. 1, 1995
Capacity: 150 bbl
Head Brewer: Carl Brouwer
Sales Mgr.: Jana Brouwer
Contact: Carl Brouwer

United States Breweries (Colorado)

Carver Brewing Co
1022 Main Ave
Durango, CO 81301-5124
(970) 259-2545; FAX (970) 385-7268
Founded: Dec. 31, 1988
Capacity: 1,000 bbl
Head Brewer: Chris Tough
Owner: Bill Carver
Contact: Bill Carver

Champion Brewing Co
1400 Larimer/Suite 300
Denver, CO 80202-1705
(303) 534-5444; FAX (303) 534-5490
Founded: Nov. 1, 1991
Capacity: 1,500 bbl
Head Brewer: Jason Dawdy
Contact: Jason Dawdy

Colorado Brewing Co
12160 Pennsylvania St
Thornton, CO 80241
(303) 457-1770; FAX (303) 457-1716
Founded: Dec. 3, 1995
Capacity: 1,500 bbl
Head Brewer/Sales Mgr.: Steven P. Klover
Contact: Susan Klover

Columbine Mill Brewery Inc
5798 S Rapp St
Littleton, CO 80120-1929
(303) 347-1488; FAX (303) 795-9104
TheColMill@aol.com
http://www.mount.com/mww/mill
Founded: Dec. 20, 1994
Capacity: 6,500 bbl
Co-Owner: Patricia Girolamo
Co-Owner: Pasquale Girolamo
Head Brewer: Sean Halloran
Contact: Pasquale Girolamo

CooperSmith's Pub and Brewery
Five Old Town Sq
Fort Collins, CO 80524-2463
(970) 498-0483; FAX (303) 498-0471
brewtron@aol.com
http://www.fortnet.org/~cooper
Founded: Nov. 4, 1989
Capacity: 2,500 bbl
Head Brewer: Dwight Hall
Chef: Theo Otte
General Mgr.: Mark Sluss
Pres.: Scott Smith
Contact: Brad Page

Coophouse Brewery
2400 Industrial Ln/Suite 350
Broomfield, CO 80020-1662
(303) 466-3777; FAX (303) 439-9891
Founded: March 1, 1996
Capacity: 900 bbl
Sales Mgr.: Brian Cooper
Head Brewer: John Allshouse
Production Mgr.: Glenn Eiles
Contact: John Allshouse

Coors Brewing Co
Golden, CO 80401
(303) 279-6565; FAX (303) 277-6834
Capacity: 25,000,000 bbl
Research Scientist: Keith Villa
Research Associate: David Bright
Contact: Steve Gress

Crested Butte Brewing Co
PO Box 1089
Crested Butte, CO 81224-1089
(970) 349-5026; FAX (970) 349-2737
Founded: Feb. 21, 1991
Capacity: 1,000 bbl
Owner/Sales Mgr.: Gary Garcia
General Mgr.: Joe Garcia
Head Brewer: Ted Bosler
Asst. Brewer: Wykoff Ashton
Contact: Gary Garcia

Denver Chop House and Brewery
1735 19th/Suite 100
Denver, CO 80202
(303) 296-0800; FAX (303) 296-2800
Founded: March 24, 1995
Contact: Carol Schaver

Dimmer's Brew Pub Inc
306 Alpert Ave
Fort Collins, CO 80525-1002
(970) 490-2477; FAX (970) 416-7583
Founded: July 24, 1995
Contact: Steve Dim

Durango Brewing Co
3000 Main Ave
Durango, CO 81301-4245
(970) 247-3396; FAX (970) 247-3396
Founded: May 1, 1990
Capacity: 2,000 bbl
Head Brewer: Archie Byers
Contact: Steve McClaran

Eldorado Canyon Brewing Co
6901 W 117th Ave/Suite A-6
Broomfield, CO 80020
(303) 439-9506; FAX (303) 460-1947
Founded: July 15, 1995
Capacity: 5,000 bbl
Sales Mgr.: Victor Przedelski
Pres./Head Brewer: Sean Phillips
Contact: Sean Philips

Estes Park Brewery
PO Box 2161/470 Prospect Dr
Estes Park, CO 80517-2161
(970) 586-5421; FAX (970) 586-0651
Capacity: 6,000 bbl
Contact: Eric Bratrud

Fleetside Pub & Brewery
721 10th St
Greeley, CO 80631
(970) 346-1122; FAX (970) 304-0703
brewtron@aol.com
Founded: July 30, 1995
Capacity: 2,500 bbl
Head Brewer: Jim Weatherwax
Brewmaster: Brad Page
Pres.: Scott Smith
Chef: Patrick Gonzales
General Mgr.: Erin Devitt
Contact: Jim Weatherwax

Flying Dog Brewpub
424 E Cooper
Aspen, CO 81611-1832
(970) 925-7464
Founded: July 1, 1991
Capacity: 1,500 bbl
Owner: George Stranahan
General Mgr.: Jonathan Fightlin
General Mgr.: Deborah Fightlin
Head Brewer: Dennis A. Miller
Contact: Dennis Miller

Glenwood Canyon Brewing Co
402 Seventh St
Glenwood Springs, CO 81601
(970) 945-6565, ext. 129; FAX (970) 945-2204
Founded: March 15, 1996
Contact: Bill Carver

Golden City Brewery
920 12th St
Golden, CO 80401-1114
(303) 279-8092
Founded: Nov. 1, 1993
Capacity: 1,200 bbl
Pres.: Janine M. Sturdavant
Brewmaster: Charlie Sturdavant
Head Brewer: Aaron Fleet
Sales Mgr.: Jeff Wilson
Contact: Charlie Sturdavant

Great Divide Brewing Co
2201 Arapahoe St
Denver, CO 80205-2512
(303) 296-9460; FAX (303) 296-9464
Founded: June 24, 1994
Capacity: 4,500 bbl
Head Brewer/Pres.: Brian M. Dunn
VP/Sales Mgr.: Tara Leigh Dunn
Senior Brewer: Mason Thomas
Brewer: Chris Dunn
Contact: Brian Dunn

H C Berger Brewing Co
1900 E Lincoln Ave
Fort Collins, CO 80524-2750
(970) 493-9044; FAX (970) 493-9044
Founded: June 1, 1992
Capacity: 8,840 bbl
Head Brewer: Jesse Angell
Co-Owner/Gen. Mgr.: Karen Jones
Co-Owner/Brewmaster: Sandy Jones
Contact: Sandy Jones

Heavenly Daze Brewery & Grill
PO Box 776308/1860 Ski Time Sq
Steamboat Springs, CO 80477-9018
(970) 879-8080; FAX (970) 879-0443
Founded: Jan. 2, 1993
Capacity: 2,000 bbl
Brewer: Andy Stern

Hubcap Brewery and Kitchen
143 E Meadow Dr
Vail, CO 81658
(970) 476-5757; FAX (303) 476-9170
Founded: Jan. 28, 1991
Capacity: 1,870 bbl
Owner: Dean Liotta
General Mgr.: Brian LeFebvre
Head Brewer: Tony Parker
Brewer: J. R. Rulapaugh
Asst. Brewer: Dan Seidel
Contact: Tony Parker

Il Vicino
Wood Oven Pizza (No 2)
136 E Second St
Salida, CO 81201-2115
(719) 539-5219; FAX (719) 539-2918
Founded: Aug. 1, 1994
Capacity: 750 bbl
Pres./General Mgr./Head Brewer: Tom Hennessy
Sec./Treas.: Greg Atkin
VP: Tom White
VP: Rick Post
Head Brewer: Dean Rouleau
Contact: Tom Hennessy

Irons Brewing Co
12354 W Alameda Pkwy/Unit E
Lakewood, CO 80228-2844
(303) 985-2337; FAX (303) 985-1634
Founded: Sept. 10, 1992
Capacity: 10,000 bbl
Brewmaster: David Martin
VP: Adrian R. Tucker
Pres.: Matt A. Handel
Sales Mgr.: Matt Handel
Contact: Adrian Tucker

Judge Baldwin's Brewing Co/
B F Coleman Brewing Corp
2015 N El Paso St
Colorado Springs, CO 80907-7104
(719) 578-5658
Founded: May 11, 1991
Capacity: 640 bbl
Pres.: Greg Kelley
Head Brewer: Greg Kelly
Contact: Greg Kelley

Left Hand Brewing Co
1265 Boston Ave
Longmont, CO 80501-5809
(303) 772-0258; FAX (303) 772-0258
Founded: Jan. 20, 1994
Capacity: 10,000 bbl
VP/Head Brewer: Dick Doore
Pres./Sales Mgr.: Eric Wallace
Contact: Eric Wallace

Lone Wolfe Brewing Co
0898 Hwy 133/Suite 102
Carbondale, CO 81623-1542
(970) 963-8777
Founded: Sept. 21, 1993
Capacity: 720 bbl
Owner/Sales Mgr.: Donald J. Wolfe, Jr.
Head Brewer: Donald J. Wolfe, Jr.
Contact: Donald Wolfe

Lonetree Brewing Ltd
375 E 55th Ave
Denver, CO 80216-1702
(303) 297-3832; FAX (303) 297-3832
Founded: April 1, 1993
Capacity: 5,000 bbl
Sec./Head Brewer: Ken Piel
Sales Mgr.: Ken Piel
Contact: Ken Piel

Main Street Brewery/
Four Corners Brewing Co
21 E Main
Cortez, CO 81321
(970) 564-9112
Founded: Aug. 18, 1995
Capacity: 10,661 bbl

Sales Mgr.: Rudolf Baeumel
Head Brewer: Mike Morgan
Contact: Mike Morgan

Mark's Brewing Co
PO Box 225
225 Bunyan Ave/Suite B
Berthoud, CO 80513-0225
(970) 532-3015
Founded: March 16, 1995
Capacity: 800 bbl
Head Brewer/Sales Mgr.: Mark Beck
Contact: Mark Beck

Mercury Cafe
2199 California St
Denver, CO 80205-2821
(303) 294-9258
Contact: Marilyn Megenity

Mile High Brewing Co
2401 Blake St
Denver, CO 80205
(303) 299-0148; FAX (303) 299-9192
Founded: Aug. 28, 1995
Capacity: 28,000 bbl
Head Brewer: Mark Thompson
Asst. Brewer: Traye Veillon
Sales/General Mgr.: Ron Smith
Contact: Mark Thompson

Mountain Sun
Pub and Brewery
1535 Pearl St
Boulder, CO 80302-5408
(303) 546-0886
Founded: Sept. 29, 1993
Capacity: 1,800 bbl
Head Brewer: Jack Harris
VP: Ian Blackford
Pres.: Kevin Daly
Contact: Kevin Daly

Namaqua Brewing Co
128 E Fourth St
Loveland, CO 80537-5502
(970) 667-8227; FAX (970) 635-9288
Contact: Gary Weeks

New Belgium Brewing Co
500 Linden St
Fort Collins, CO 80524
(970) 221-0524; FAX (970) 221-0535
nbb123@aol.com
Founded: June 28, 1991
Capacity: 85,000 bbl

Owner/Head Brewer: Jeffrey Lebesch
Owner/Sales Mgr.: Kim Jordan
Owner/Production Mgr.: Brian Callahan
Contact: Jeffrey Lebesch

Oasis Brewery and Restaurant
1095 Canyon
Boulder, CO 80302-5119
(303) 449-0363
Capacity: 5,000 bbl
Pres.: George Hanna
Head Brewer: Bill Sherwood
Sales Mgr.: Tom Lane

Oasis Brewery Annex
3201 Walnut
Boulder, CO 80301
(303) 449-0363; FAX (303) 449-0263
Founded: April 1, 1995
Capacity: 6,000 bbl
Head Brewer: Bill Sherwood
Contact: Bill Sherwood

Odell Brewing Co
800 E Lincoln Ave
Fort Collins, CO 80524-2507
(970) 498-9070; FAX (970) 498-0706
Founded: Nov. 18, 1989
Capacity: 22,000 bbl
Sec./Treas./Sales Mgr.: Wynne Odell
VP: Corkie Odell
Pres./Head Brewer/Sales Mgr.: Doug Odell
Contact: Doug Odell

Old Colorado Brewing Co/ Casa de Colorado
320 Link Lane
Fort Collins, CO 80524-2790
(975) 493-2739
Founded: April 1, 1989
Capacity: 500 bbl
Head Brewer: Joe Neckel
Brewmaster: Al Colby
Contact: Joe Neckel

One Keg Brewhouse
5891 Nolan
Arvada, CO 80003
(303) 423-1534; FAX (303) 423-8743
Founded: Nov. 1, 1995
Capacity: 5,000 bbl
CEO: Don Marable
Pres./CFO: Steve DeBaetes
Head Brewer: Tim Armstrong
Contact: Tim Armstrong

Only the Best Brewing Co Inc
PO Box 727/170 Weaverville Rd
Divide, CO 80814
(719) 687-3461
Founded: Aug. 1, 1995
Capacity: 400 bbl
Head Brewer/Sales Mgr.: Mark Sommer
Contact: Mark Sommer

Ouray Brewing Co
522 Main St
Ouray, CO 81427
(970) 325-4265; FAX (970) 325-0450
Founded: Oct. 31, 1995
Contact: Mark Conkle

Overland Stage Stop Brewery
526 Main St
Longmont, CO 80501
(303) 772-3734
Founded: Sept. 20, 1995
Capacity: 780 bbl
Head Brewer: Andrew Schwartz
Contact: Geoffrey Sewell

Palmer Lake Brewing Co
PO Box 653
Palmer Lake, CO 80133
(719) 331-3221
Founded: July 27, 1995
Capacity: 600 bbl
Head Brewer: Kurt Schoen
Sales Mgr.: Sallie Schoen
Contact: Kurt Schoen

Peak to Peak Brewing Co
17384 Hwy 119
Rollinsville, CO 80474
(303) 642-BEER; FAX (303) 642-BEER
Founded: Dec. 6, 1995
Contact: Robert Baile

Phantom Canyon Brewing Co
2 E Pikes Peak
Colorado Springs, CO 80903
(719) 635-2800; FAX (719) 635-9930
Founded: Dec. 15, 1993
Capacity: 2,500 bbl
Sec./Treas.: Joel Collins
Pres.: John Hickenlooper
VP/Head Brewer: Erik Jefferts
Contact: Erik Jefferts

Pikes Peak Brewery Inc
2547 Weston Rd
Colorado Springs, CO 80910-1022
(719) 391-8866
Founded: May 20, 1993
Capacity: 840 bbl

Pres.: Jack Wallick
VP: Vivian Wallick
Contact: Jack Wallick

Platte Bottom Brewery
780 N Ninth/Suite 5
Brighton, CO 80601
(303) 659-7554
Founded: Dec. 15, 1994
Head Brewer: Jack Bruner
Contact: Jack Bruner

Powers Brewing Co/ Powers Colorado Brew
1885 August Lane
Brighton, CO 80601
(303) 659-9114
Founded: Sept. 15, 1995
Capacity: 1,000 bbl
Contact: Kenneth Powers

Pumphouse Brewery
540 Main St
Longmont, CO 80501
(303) 702-0881
Founded: May 18, 1996
Contact: Craig Taylor

Rock Bottom Brewery
1001 16th St/Suite A-100
Denver, CO 80265
(303) 534-7616; FAX (303) 534-2129
Founded: Dec. 1, 1991
Capacity: 5,100 bbl
General Mgr.: Larry Moss
Co-Owner: Diane Greenlee
Co-Owner: Gina Day
Brewmaster: Mark Youngquist
Head Brewer: Steven Miller
Contact: Steven Miller

Rockies Brewing Co/ Pub at Rockies
2880 Wilderness Pl
Boulder, CO 80301-2258
(303) 444-8448; FAX (303) 444-4796
Founded: Feb. 1, 1979
Capacity: 50,000 bbl
Sales Mgr.: Pat Meyer
Pres.: Gina Day
Head Brewer: David Zuckerman
Purchasing: Jeff Bynum
General Mgr.: Jeff Brown
Contact: David Zuckerman

Rockslide Brewpub/ Snowy Mountain Brewpub
405 Main St
Grand Junction, CO 81501-2511
(970) 241-9311

Founded: Nov. 7, 1994
Capacity: 1,000 bbl
Head Brewer: Clint Peterson
Contact: Maureen Howard

San Juan Brewing Co
PO Box 1989
Telluride, CO 81435-1989
(970) 728-4587
Contact: James Loo

SandLot Brewery at Coors Field/Coors Brewing Co
2145 Blake St
Denver, CO 80205-2010
(303) 298-1587; FAX (303) 298-1594
sandbrew@aol.com
Founded: March 31, 1995
Capacity: 4,000 bbl
Head Brewer: Wayne Waananen
Brewer: John Legnard
Contact: Wayne Waananen

Sharkey's Brew Club
3231 Shelton Circle
Colorado Springs, CO 80906
(719) 632-2337
mikem@usa.net
http://iglobal.net/iwc/sharkeys
Founded: Jan. 12, 1995
Capacity: 720 bbl
Head Brewer: Sterling Largin
Contact: Sterling Largin

Silver Plume Brewing Co
PO Box 1028/458 Main
Silver Plume, CO 80476
(970) 569-3040
Contact: Eric Pierson

SKA Brewing Co
545 Turner Dr
Durango, CO 81301
(970) 247-5792; FAX (970) 247-5792
Founded: Sept. 27, 1995
Capacity: 1,000 bbl
Pres./Head Brewer: David Thibodeau
Head Brewer/Sec./Treas.: Bill Graham
Contact: Bill Graham

Smiling Moose Inc
295 E 29th St/Suite 200
Greeley, CO 80538-2728
(970) 493-2029
Contact: Theresa Riemenschneider

Steamboat Brewery and Tavern
PO Box 775748/435 Lincoln Ave
Steamboat Springs, CO 80477
(970) 879-2233; FAX (970) 879-4401
Founded: June 24, 1993
Capacity: 1,200 bbl
Head Brewer: David Brereton
Chef: Joel Kunkel
General Mgr.: Joe Walker
Brewer: Charlie Noble
Contact: David Brereton

Tabernash Brewing Co
205 Denargo Market
Denver, CO 80216-5032
(303) 293-2337; FAX (303) 293-2253
Founded: Nov. 15, 1993
Capacity: 12,000 bbl
Brewmaster: Eric Warner
Sales Mgr.: George Barela
Customer Service/Special Events: Jeff Mendel
Quality Control Scientist: Mark Lupa
Cellar Master: Joe Barfield
Contact: Jeff Mendel

Tivoli Brewery/(america!)
900 Auraria Pkwy
Denver, CO 80202
(303) 534-2556
Founded: Dec. 23, 1995
Contact: Joe Michael

Tommyknocker Brewery & Pub
PO Box 3188/1401 Miner St
Idaho Springs, CO 80452
(303) 567-2688; FAX (303) 567-4575
Founded: April 21, 1995
Capacity: 6,000 bbl
Head Brewer/Pres.: Tim Lenahan
Head Brewer: Charlie Sturdavant
Sales/Mktg.: Tom Martinez
Contact: Larry Nemhich

Twisted Pine Brewing Co
3280 Valmont Rd
Boulder, CO 80301
(303) 786-9270
Founded: June 1, 1995
Contact: Gordon Knight

Union Colony Brewery
1412 Eighth Ave
Greeley, CO 80631-4604
(970) 356-4116; FAX (303) 356-8783
Founded: Nov. 13, 1994
Capacity: 1,000 bbl

Head Brewer: Karl-Heinz Dukstein
Dir. Brewery Operations: Kristopher Oyler
Sales Mgr.: Brian McEachron
Contact: Lary Oyler

Walnut Brewery
1123 Walnut St
Boulder, CO 80302-5116
(303) 447-1345; FAX (303) 447-0068
Founded: May 1, 1990
Capacity: 2,184 bbl
General Mgr.: Susan Ralston
Head Brewer: Roy Emmons
Contact: Roy Emmons

Wynkoop Brewing Co
1634 18th St
Denver, CO 80202-1212
(303) 297-2700; FAX (303) 297-2958
dbrad666@gnn.com
http://members.gnn.com/dbrad666/wynkoop/index.html
Founded: Oct. 18, 1988
Capacity: 5,500 bbl
Dir. Mktg.: Matt McAleer
Pres.: Jim Caruso
Brewmaster: Kyle Carstens
Chef: John Dickinson
Contact: Kyle Carstens

CONNECTICUT

Brürm at Bar
254 Crown St
New Haven, CT 06511
(203) 495-8924; FAX (203) 498-0916
Founded: Feb. 17, 1996
Capacity: 1,500 bbl
Head Brewer: Jeff Shannon
Contact: Randy Hoder

Elm City Brewing Co/The Brewery
458 Grand Ave
New Haven, CT 06513-3842
(203) 772-2739
Founded: Oct. 10, 1989
Contact: Peter Poanessa

Farmington River Brewing Co
462 Tunxis Ave
Bloomfield, CT 06002-1127
Founded: Feb. 6, 1996
Contact: Bill Hodkin

United States Breweries (Connecticut–Florida)

Hammer and Nail Brewers
900 Main St
Oakville, CT 06779
(860) 274-5911
Founded: Feb. 28, 1996
Contact: Pete Hammer

Hartford Brewery Ltd
35 Pearl St
Hartford, CT 06103-2306
(203) 246-2337; FAX (203) 246-2337
Founded: Aug. 15, 1991
Capacity: 1,100 bbl
Pres./Sales Mgr.: Philip Hopkins
VP/Head Brewer: Les Sinnock
Contact: Philip Hopkins

Mystic River Brewing Co
76 New London Rd
Mystic, CT 06355-2252
(860) 536-6566; FAX (860) 885-0865
Capacity: 20 bbl
Contact: Ralph Bergman

New England Brewing Co/ Brewhouse Restaurant
13 Marshall St
Norwalk, CT 06854-2203
(203) 866-1339; FAX (203) 838-7168
Founded: Feb. 1, 1990
Capacity: 14,000 bbl
Pres.: Marcia King
Head Brewer: Ralph Wittkopp
Sales Mgr.: Joni Flaherty
Contact: Marcia King

Quality Assured Brewing
19 Burns St
New Haven, CT 06511-1301
(203) 772-2739
Founded: Oct. 10, 1989
Capacity: 6,000 bbl
Contact: Mike Gettings

DELAWARE

Brandywine Brewing Co
3801 Kennett Pike
Bldg E/Suite 220
Wilmington, DE 19807
(302) 655-8000; FAX (302) 655-8144
Founded: Aug. 15, 1995
Capacity: 800 bbl
Head Brewer: Jay B. Fisher
Pres.: David W. Dietz
Asst. Brewer: Bart Kramlick
Contact: Jay Fisher

Dogfish Head Brewing and Eats
320 Rehoboth Ave
Rehoboth Beach, DE 19971
(302) 226-2739; FAX (302) 226-2517
http://overlord.dmv.com/dogfish
Founded: June 28, 1995
Capacity: 200 bbl
General Mgr.: John Rishko
Head Brewer: Sam Calagione
Contact: John Rishko

Rockford Brewing Co
15 James Ct
Wilmington, DE 19801
(302) 575-1640; FAX (302) 575-1640
Founded: June 1, 1995
Capacity: 4,800 bbl
Asst. Brewer: Jack Conaty
Head Brewer: Charles Garbini
Sales Mgr.: Loretta Haugh
Contact: Marty Haugh

Stewart's Brewing Co
219 Governor's Sq/Rts 40-47
Bear, DE 19701
(302) 836-2739; FAX (302) 836-8065
Founded: July 27, 1995
Contact: Al Stewart

DISTRICT OF COLUMBIA

Capitol City Brewing Co
1100 New York Ave NW
Washington, DC 20005-3918
(202) 628-2222; FAX (202) 628-3332
Founded: Oct. 7, 1992
Capacity: 1,800 hL
Brewmaster: Bill Foster
Man. Gen. Partner: David Von Storch
Head Brewer: Chris Frashier
Contact: Bill Foster

Capitol City Brewing Co (No 2)
2 Massachusetts Ave/Postal Sq
Washington, DC 20001
(202) 842-2337
Founded: April 15, 1996
Head Brewer: Bill Madden
Contact: David Von Stork

Dock Street Brewery and Restaurant (No 2)
Warner Building
1299 Pennsylvania Ave NW
Washington, DC 20004
(202) 639-0403
Founded: Jan. 12, 1996
Capacity: 1,500 bbl
Head Brewer: Nick Funnel
Dir. Public Relations: Rosemarie Certo
Pres.: Jeffrey Ware
Contact: Nick Funnel

FLORIDA

A1A Aleworks
1 King St
St Augustine, FL 32084
(904) 829-2977
Founded: May 1, 1995
Capacity: 1,200 bbl
Contact: Amy Morton

Anheuser-Busch Inc
PO Box 18017 AMF
Jacksonville, FL 32229
(904) 751-0700
Capacity: 7,200,000 bbl
Plant Mgr.: John Wilchek
Resident Brewmaster: Tom Walter
Contact: John Wilchek

Anheuser-Busch Inc
PO Box 9245
Tampa, FL 33674
(813) 988-4111
Founded: May 1, 1959
Capacity: 2,700,000 bbl
Plant Mgr.: Renaul Abel
Resident Brewmaster: Rudi Hernandez
Contact: Renaul Abel

Beach Brewing Co
5905 S Kirkman Rd
Orlando, FL 32819-7925
(407) 345-8802; FAX (407) 345-0351
Founded: June 1, 1992
Capacity: 4,000 bbl
Pres./Sales Mgr.: Angela Ranson
VP/Head Brewer: Brian Baldasano
Contact: Brian Baldasano

Blue Anchor Pub
10550-2 Old St Augustine Rd
Jacksonville, FL 32257
(904) 262-1592
Founded: April 1, 1996
Capacity: 400 bbl
Contact: Frank Gregory

Buckhead Brewery and Grill
1900 Capitol Cir NE
Tallahasee, FL 32308
(904) 894-0987; FAX (904) 942-4947
Founded: Aug. 15, 1995
Capacity: 1,000 bbl

United States Breweries (Florida)

Head Brewer/Brewery Mgr.: Gary Essex
Asst. Brewer: Jonathan Zangwill
Contact: Gary Essex

Coasters
971-A E Eaugallic Blvd
Melbourne, FL 32927
(407) 779-2739
Founded: March 1, 1996
Contact: Derrell Doll

Don Gambrinu's Brewpub Inc
7335 NW 35th St
Miami, FL 33122-1268
(305) 477-7605; FAX (305) 477-2959
Founded: Jan. 1, 1996
Contact: Jaime Delgadillo

Dunedin Brewery/ Prospector Brewing Services
PO Box 2832
Dunedin, FL 34697
(813) 734-9515; FAX (813) 734-9666
Founded: Feb. 1, 1996
Capacity: 280 bbl
Contact: Michael Bryant

Firehouse Brewing Co
7902 NW 64th St
Miami, FL 33166-2722
(305) 718-9620
Founded: April 30, 1996
Contact: Christopher Schalk

Florida Brewery Inc
202 Gandy Rd
Auburndale, FL 33823-2701
(813) 965-1825
Contact: Jim Boggs

Highlands Brewery
623 US Hwy 27 S
Sebring, FL 33870
(813) 471-6200
Founded: April 1, 1996
Head Brewer: John Chappell
Contact: John Chappell

Hoppers Brooker Creek Grille and Taproom
36221 E Lake Rd
Palm Harbor, FL 34685
(813) 786-2966
Founded: Sept. 6, 1994
Capacity: 100 bbl
Head Brewer: John Doble
Sales Mgr.: Carson Kohlmetz
Contact: Wes Short

Hops Grill and Bar in Bradenton
4502 14th St W
Bradenton, FL 33207-1428
(813) 756-1069; FAX (813) 756-9342
Founded: Oct. 11, 1993
Capacity: 800 bbl
Head Brewer: Wesley Chastain
Sales Mgr.: Ben Hachey

Hops Grill and Bar in Boynton Beach
545 N Congress Ave
Boynton Beach, FL 33425
(407) 731-3313
Founded: Feb. 12, 1996
Contact: John Schwarzen

Hops Grill and Bar in Carrollwood
14303 N Dale Mabry Hwy
Tampa, FL 33618
(813) 264-0522; FAX (813) 962-7162

Hops Grill and Bar in Clearwater
18825 US Hwy 19 N
Clearwater, FL 34624-3122
(813) 531-5300
Founded: Nov. 20, 1989
Capacity: 800 bbl
Contact: Dave Mason

Hops Grill and Bar in Jacksonville
9826 San Jose Blvd
Jacksonville, FL 32257-5438
(904) 886-0296
Founded: March 7, 1994
Capacity: 800 bbl
Head Brewer: Tim Shackton
Contact: Tim Shackton

Hops Grill and Bar in Lakeland
4820 S Florida Ave
Lakeland, FL 33813-2181
(813) 647-9117
Founded: Dec. 13, 1993
Capacity: 800 bbl

Hops Grill and Bar in N Tampa
11241 E Fowler Ave
Tampa, FL 33612
(813) 632-0717; FAX (813) 632-0436

Hops Grill and Bar in Ocala
2505 SW College Rd
Ocala, FL 34474
(904) 873-6976

Founded: May 8, 1995
Contact: Dave Mason

Hops Grill and Bar in Orange Park
1780 Wells Rd
Orange Park, FL 32073-2321
(904) 278-7273
Founded: Sept. 19, 1994
Capacity: 92 bbl
Head Brewer: Tim Shackton
Contact: Tim Shackton

Hops Grill and Bar in Orlando
848 San Lake Rd
Orlando, FL 32809
(407) 240-9116
Founded: April 10, 1995
Contact: Dave Mason

Hops Grill and Bar in Palm Harbor
33086 US Hwy 19 N
Palm Harbor, FL 33684-3122
(813) 789-5678
Founded: May 18, 1992
Capacity: 400 bbl
Head Brewer: Ed Bullen

Hops Grill and Bar in Port Richey
10042 US Hwy 19 N
Port Richey, FL 34668
(813) 862-5913; FAX (813) 861-0752

Hops Grill and Bar in S Tampa
327 N Dale Mabry Hwy
Tampa, FL 33609-1238
(813) 871-3600; FAX (813) 876-9883
Founded: Nov. 9, 1992
Capacity: 800 bbl
Principal Contact: David Mason
Head Brewer: David Richter
Contact: David Mason

Hops Grill and Bar in St Petersburg
8305 Tyrone Rd
St Petersburg, FL 33709
(813) 845-4442
Founded: March 18, 1996

Irish Times Pub & Brewery
9920 Alternate A-1-A/Suite 810
Palm Beach, FL 33410
(407) 624-1504; FAX (407) 624-0761
Founded: Jan. 1, 1990
Capacity: 400 bbl

United States Breweries (Florida)

Sales Mgr.: Richard Meyer
Pres.: Alan Craig
Contact: Fran Andrelevich

Kelly's Caribbean Bar & Grill
301 Whitehead St
Key West, FL 33040-6542
(305) 293-8484
Founded: Jan. 1, 1993
Contact: Fred Tilman

Key West Overseas Brewery
1107 Key Plaza/Suite 299
Key West, FL 33040
(305) 295-0327; FAX (305) 295-0565
Founded: June 16, 1995
Head Brewer: Donn Chunn
Sales Mgr.: Bill Bohmfalk
Contact: Joseph Lambert

Market Street Pub
120 SW First Ave
Gainesville, FL 32601-6243
(904) 377-2927
Contact: Edmund Cooper

McGuire's Irish Pub and Brewery
600 E Gregory St
Pensacola, FL 32501-4153
(904) 433-6789; FAX (904) 434-8364
Founded: March 3, 1989
Capacity: 1,250 bbl
Co-Owner: Molly Martin
Co-Owner: McGuire Martin
Head Brewer: Steve Fried
Asst. Brewer: Daryn Morain
Contact: Martin McGuire

Miami Brewing Co
9292 NW 101st
Miami, FL 33178
(305) 888-6505; FAX (305) 888-8868
Founded: Aug. 16, 1995
Capacity: 10,000 bbl
Pres.: Rick Durkin
Head Brewer: Andy Rathmann
Brewer: Mark Safrik
Sales Mgr.: Louis Lopez
Contact: Rick Durkin

Mill Brewery, Eatery, & Bakery
330 W Fairbanks Ave
Winter Park, FL 32789-5093
(407) 644-1544; FAX (407) 674-3982
Founded: May 1, 1990
Capacity: 1,000 bbl

Sales Mgr.: Les Callahan
Head Brewer: John Stuart
Pres.: Paul Smith
Contact: John Stuart

Mill Brewery, Eatery, & Bakery
11491 S Cleveland Ave
Fort Myers, FL 33907-2875
(813) 939-2739

New World Brewery
3317 W Sevilla Cir
Tampa, FL 33629
(813) 248-4969
Founded: May 5, 1995
Capacity: 150 bbl
Head Brewer: Steve Bird
Contact: Steve Bird

Ragtime Taproom
207 Atlantic Blvd
Atlantic Beach, FL 32233-5273
Founded: Oct. 1, 1991
Capacity: 1,600 bbl
Partner: William Morton
Partner: Thomas Morton
Head Brewer: Scott Morton
Contact: Scott Morton

River City Brewing Co
835 Museum Cir
Jacksonville, FL 32207
(904) 398-2299; FAX (904) 398-2099
Founded: Dec. 22, 1993
Capacity: 2,300 bbl
Head Brewer: Steve Sullivan
Contact: Jim Lee

Santa Rosa Bay Brewing Co
54 Miracle Strip Pkwy
Fort Walton Beach, FL 32548
(904) 664-2739
Owner: Ted Bass
Head Brewer: Ted Bass
Contact: Ted Bass

Sarasota Brewing Co
6607 Gateway Ave
Sarasota, FL 34231-5805
(813) 925-2337; FAX (813) 922-5283
Founded: Sept. 28, 1989
Capacity: 2,000 bbl
Sales Mgr.: Tim Speicher
Head Brewer: Ed Canty
Contact: Ed Canty

South Pointe Seafood House and Brewing Co
1 Washington Ave
Miami Beach, FL 33139
(305) 673-1708; FAX (305) 673-5943
Founded: June 5, 1995
Capacity: 1,200 bbl
Owner: Arthur Forgette
General Mgr.: Randy Baird
Head Brewer: Jeff Nelson
Contact: Jeffrey Nelson

Stroh Brewery Co Tampa Plant
11111 30th St
Tampa, FL 33612-6496
(813) 972-8500
Capacity: 1,700,000 bbl
Plant Mgr.: Otto Wiesneth
Master Brewer: D. Barker
Packaging Mgr.: M. Cooke
Contact: Otto Wiesneth

Thai Orchid Restaurant
317 Miracle Mile
Coral Gables, FL 33134-5819
(305) 443-6364
Contact: John Boyle

Thai Orchid Restaurant/ Thai Orchid USA Inc
9565 Sunset Dr
Miami, FL 33173
(305) 279-8583; FAX (305) 665-8439
Founded: Nov. 24, 1992
Capacity: 90 bbl
Brewer: John Boyle
Contact: John Boyle

Tortuga's
200 N First St
Jacksonville Beach, FL 32250
(904) 249-7007
Founded: Sept. 1, 1995
Contact: Jim Burns

Treasure Coast Brewing Co
2851 Monroe St
Stuart, FL 34994
(407) 781-1120
Founded: Feb. 1, 1996
Contact: Paul Buttrose

Williamsville Brewery
128 N Second St
Fernandina Beach, FL 32035
(904) 277-8944; FAX (904) 277-8968
Founded: Feb. 28, 1996
Capacity: 8,000 bbl
Head Brewer: Jim Deboet
Contact: Dick Wilson

Windrose Brew Pub
1933 Davis Blvd
Naples, FL 33942
(813) 793-3383
Founded: April 1, 1995
Head Brewer: Keith Williams
Contact: Keith Williams

Ybor City Brewing Co
2205 N 20th St
Tampa, FL 33605-3919
(813) 242-9222; FAX (813) 248-2130
Founded: Nov. 15, 1994
Capacity: 15,000 bbl
Operations Mgr.: Humberto E. Lopez
Pres.: Humberto J. Perez
Scott Sadis
Head Brewer: David J. Evans
Contact: Dean Giancola

GEORGIA

Anheuser-Busch Inc
PO Box 200248/100 Busch Dr
Cartersville, GA 30120-6456
(404) 382-7347
Capacity: 6,800,000 bbl
Plant Mgr.: Nick Dalba
Resident Brewmaster: Paul A. Cobet
Contact: Nick Dalba

Athens Brewing Co
312 E Washington St
Athens, GA 30601
(706) 549-0027; FAX (706) 549-0013
Founded: March 10, 1996
Head Brewer: Brian Nummer

Atlanta Beer Garden
3013 Peachtree Rd
Atlanta, GA 30305
(404) 261-9898; FAX (404) 261-0283
Founded: April 10, 1996
Head Brewer: David Hull
Sales Mgr.: Brad Hitt
Contact: Boyd Barrow

Atlanta Brewing Co
1219 Williams St NW
Atlanta, GA 30309-2811
(404) 892-4436; FAX (404) 897-1411
Founded: July 1, 1994
Capacity: 10,000 bbl
Pres./Founder: Gregory F. Kelly
Head Brewer/Dir. Operations: David Hagemes
Contact: Gregory Kelly

Blind Man Ales
PO Box 649
Athens, GA 30603
(706) 613-7070
Founded: Sept. 8, 1995
Capacity: 215 bbl
Head Brewer: John Gayer
Sales Manager: Bob Tibbs
Contact: John Gayer

Buckhead Beer Co
PO Box 550007
Atlanta, GA 30355
(404) 841-9754
Founded: April 1, 1996
Contact: Dave Thomas

Dogwood Brewing Co
1222 Logan Cir
Atlanta, GA 30318
(404) 367-0500; FAX (404) 367-0505
Founded: April 10, 1996
Head Brewer: Joe Schaar
Contact: Crawford Moran

John Harvard's Brewhouse (No 2)/The Brew House LLC
3041 Peachtree Rd NE
Atlanta, GA 30305
(404) 816-BREW; FAX (404) 816-5377
Founded: Dec. 13, 1995
Capacity: 2,750 bbl
Head Brewer: Rolfe Saundersreed
Asst. Brewer: Nate Heck
Executive Chef: Casey Hally
Sous Chef: James Dillon
Sous Chef: Doug Jontos
Contact: Steve Papero

Marthasville Brewing Co
829 Courtenay Dr NE
Atlanta, GA 30306-3424
(404) 713-0333; FAX (404) 699-9937
Head Brewer: Doug Hubbard
Sales Mgr.: Mike Gerard
Contact: Doug Hubbard

Miller Brewing Co
405 Cordele Rd
Albany, GA 31708-6601
(912) 888-3000; FAX (912) 431-9247
Capacity: 8,000,000 bbl
Plant Mgr.: Adam W. Martin
Brewing Mgr.: Lewis Jefer
Admin. Services Mgr.: Peter J. Konecny
Contact: Adam Martin

Phoenix Brewing Co
5600 Roswell/Suite 21
Atlanta, GA 30342
(404) 843-2739; FAX (404) 843-2044
Founded: Feb. 15, 1996
Pres.: Warren Bruno
Treas.: Sandra Spoon
Sec.: Loren Sprouse
VP Head Brewer: Glen Sprouse
Contact: Glen Sprouse

US Border Brewery Cantina
12460 Crabapple Rd/Suite 601
Alpharetta, GA 30201
(770) 772-4400; FAX (770) 772-4219
Founded: Jan. 30, 1996
Capacity: 700 bbl
Head Brewer: David Hull
General Mgr.: Eddie Baldwin
Contact: David Hull

HAWAII

Ali'i Brewing Co
500 Alakawa/Suite 220
Honolulu, Oahu, HI 96817
(808) 841-4883; FAX (808) 949-6096
aliibrew@pixi.com
http://www.pixi.com/~aliibrew
Founded: Oct. 28, 1994
Capacity: 5,000 bbl
Head Brewer/Pres.: Frank Wenzl
Brewer: Scott Spicola
Brewer: Greg Yount
Sales Mgr.: Frank Wenzl
Contact: Frank Wenzl

Gordon Biersch Brewery and Restaurant (No 5)
Aloha Towers/Suite 1123
101 Ala Moana Blvd
Honolulu, Oahu, HI 96813-4803
(808) 599-4877
Founded: Nov. 19, 1994
Capacity: 3,000 bbl
Co-Owner: Dan Gordon
Co-Owner: Dean Biersch
Contact: Tom Davis

Kona Brewing Co
75-5629 Kuakini Hwy
Kailua, Oahu, HI 96740
(808) 334-1133; FAX (808) 334-1884
Founded: March 1, 1995
Contact: Mark Lazich

Maui Kine Brewery Ltd
444 Hana Hwy "F"
Kahului, Maui, HI 96732
(808) 573-2374
Founded: April 1, 1996
Contact: Debra Irby

Shark Tooth Brewery and Steakhouse
PO Box 1151
Kahului, Maui, HI 96753
(808) 874-4986
Founded: Dec. 22, 1995
Contact: Mark Ehrets

Trade Winds Brewing Co
850 Kolu
Wailuku, Maui, HI 96793
(808) 244-6631; FAX (808) 244-7797
Founded: Oct. 10, 1995
Capacity: 300 bbl
Contact: Jim Fishwild

IDAHO

Beier Brewing Co
202 E 37th St/Suite 13
Boise, ID 83714-6470
(208) 338-5133
Founded: Aug. 11, 1992
Capacity: 1,800 bbl
Sales Mgr.: Peggy Beier
Head Brewer: Gerry Beier
Contact: Peggy Beier

Coeur D'Alene Brewing Co/ T W Fisher's Brewpub
204 N Second St
Coeur D'Alene, ID 83814-2804
(208) 664-2739; FAX (208) 664-4749
Founded: Nov. 1, 1987
Capacity: 4,500 bbl
Pres.: Thomas W. Fisher
Sales Mgr.: Chris Bolka
Head Brewer: Laurie Krauss
Contact: T.W. Fisher

Eagle Brewing Co Inc
PO Box 538
134 Silverwood Way
Eagle, ID 83616
(208) 866-5143
Contact: Bradley Giles

Gem State Brewing
704 Arthur
Caldwell, ID 83605
(208) 454-9944
Founded: April 1, 1996
Contact: Vincent Wright

Harrison Hollow Brewhouse
2455 Harrison Hollow
Boise, ID 83702-0962
(208) 343-6820
Founded: May 12, 1992
Capacity: 1,400 bbl
VP: Mike Eddy
Pres./Gen. Mgr.: Dave Kent
Head Brewer: Jim Fishwild
Brewer: Chris Compton
Production Mgr.: Ben Brownell
Brewery Asst.: Robert Flannery
Brewery Asst.: Brooke Bell
Contact: Jim Fishwild

McCall Brewing Co/ Cerveceria Inc
PO Box 1677/807 N Third St
McCall, ID 83638-1677
(208) 634-2333; FAX (208) 634-4005
Founded: Jan. 1, 1994
Pres.: John S. Borkoski
VP: Matt Hunter
Sec.: Kathy Borkoski
Head Brewer: Brad Willis
Contact: John Borkoski

M J Barleyhoppers Brewery and Sports Pub
621 21st Street
Lewiston, ID 83501-1461
(208) 746-5300; FAX (208) 799-1000
Founded: Aug. 1, 1994
Capacity: 1,456 bbl
Brewmaster: Mark Miller
Contact: Mark Miller

Pend Oreille Brewing Co
PO Box 1903
Sandpoint, ID 83864
(208) 263-7837; FAX (208) 263-7837
Founded: Jan. 15, 1996
Contact: Chris Campbell

Star Garnet Brewing
6017 W State St/Trlr 5
Boise, ID 83703-2760
(208) 388-8501
Founded: May 1, 1995
Capacity: 525 bbl
Head Brewer: DeWain Hughes
Contact: Craig Simon

Sun Valley Brewing Co
PO Box 389/202 Main St
Hailey, ID 83333-0389
(208) 788-5777; FAX (208) 788-6319
Founded: Nov. 30, 1993
Capacity: 8,000 bbl
Pres.: Michael J. Kraynick
Sec./Treas./Brewmaster: Gordon Gammell
Sales Mgr.: Michael Kraynick
Packaging Mgr.: Daniel Sparks
Sales Rep.: Paul "P. K." King
Contact: Gordon Gammell

Table Rock Brewing Inc
3550 E Commercial Ct
Meridian, ID 83702
(208) 884-8000; FAX (208) 884-8002
Founded: June 15, 1995
Capacity: 16,000 bbl
Head Brewer: Terry Dennis
Head Brewer: Dave Stevens
Contact: Terry Dennis

Table Rock Brewpub and Grill
705 W Fulton
Boise, ID 83702
(208) 342-0944; FAX (208) 344-3670
Founded: March 9, 1991
Capacity: 2,100 bbl
Brewer: Bob McSherry
Brewer: Dave Stevens
Co-Owner: Peg Fitzgerald
Co-Owner: Mike Fitzgerald
Head Brewer: Terry Dennis
Contact: Mike Fitzgerald

Thunder Mountain Brewery
PO Box 10145
Ketchum, ID 83340
(203) 726-1832
Contact: Eric Hochendoner

Treaty Grounds Brewpub
2124 W Pullman Rd
Moscow, ID 83843-4011
(208) 882-3807
Founded: May 20, 1994
Capacity: 220 bbl
Head Brewer: Jess Caudill
Pres.: Orville Barnes
General Mgr.: Joe Frankel
Contact: Joe Frankel

Twin Falls Brewing Co/ Muggers Brewpub
516 Second St S/Suite 1
Twin Falls, ID 83301
(208) 733-8159; FAX (208) 734-8075
Founded: Jan. 15, 1996
Capacity: 500 bbl
Contact: Rick Beus

ILLINOIS

Americas Brewpub at Walter Payton's Roundhouse
205 N Broadway
Aurora, IL 60507
(708) 264-BREW
Founded: March 20, 1996
Contact: Tom Sweeney

Blue Cat Brew Pub
113 18th St
Rock Island, IL 61201-8708
(309) 788-8247; FAX (309) 788-8270
Founded: March 2, 1994
Capacity: 965 bbl
Pres./Head Brewer: Dan Cleaveland
Sec./Office Mgr.: Martha Cleaveland
General Mgr.: David Smigo
Contact: Dan Cleaveland

Box Office Brewery
145 N Third St
Dekalb, IL 60115
(815) 748-2739; FAX (815) 748-3254
Founded: Jan. 14, 1994
Capacity: 500 bbl
Head Brewer: Mike Rybinski
Owner: David Blitzblau
Contact: Mike Rybinski

Capitol City Brewing Co
107 W Cook St
Springfield, IL 62704-2571
(217) 753-5725; FAX (217) 753-4478
Founded: Jan. 22, 1994
Capacity: 1,000 bbl
Pres.: Scott Boys
Head Brewer: Tom Goldstein
Sales Mgr./Asst. Brewer: William Goldstein
Owner: Bud Hunter
Contact: Tom Goldstein

Chicago Brewing Co
1830 N Besly Ct
Chicago, IL 60622-1210
(312) 252-2739
Founded: July 5, 1990
Capacity: 30,000 bbl
Pres.: Stephen J. Dinehart
Sr. VP Oper.: Craig Dinehart
Sr. VP Sales/Mktg.: Jennifer W. Dinehart
Public Relations Mgr.: Keith Dinehart
Contact: Stephen Dinehart

Flatlander's Brewing Co
PO Box 536
Lincolnshire, IL 60069-0536
(847) 821-1234; FAX (312) 665-0725
Founded: May 1, 1996
Contact: Rick Westervelt

G Heileman Brewing Co Inc Corporate Headquarters
9399 W Higgins Rd/Suite 700
Rosemont, IL 60018
(708) 292-2100; FAX (708) 292-6870
Chairman/CEO: Thomas J. Rattigan
Exec. VP/CAO: Michael B. Evans
Exec. VP Finance/Treas.: Daniel J. Schmid, Jr.
Contact: Thomas J. Rattigan

Galena Main Street Brewpub/ Kingston Inn Restaurant
629 Franklin St
Galena, IL 61036-1505

Golden Prairie Brewing Co
2536 N Elston Ave
Chicago, IL 60647-2030
(312) 862-0106; FAX (312) 477-9582
Founded: Oct. 21, 1992
Capacity: 2,500 bbl
VP Mktg.: Laura S. Elliott
Pres.: David E. Bouhl
Brewmaster: Ted Furman
Head Brewer: Greg Browne
Contact: Ted Furman

Goose Island Brewing Co
1800 N Clybourn Ave
Chicago, IL 60614-4941
(312) 915-0071; FAX (312) 337-0172
Founded: May 19, 1988
Capacity: 2,500 bbl
Head Brewer: Greg Hall
Pres.: John Hall
Brewer: Miguel Migiutama
Asst Brewer: Purcell Young
Contact: John Hall

Goose Island Brewing Co (No 2)
1800 W Fulton
Chicago, IL 60612
(312) 226-1119; FAX (312) 733-1692
Founded: Nov. 1, 1995
Contact: Greg Hall

Joe's Brewing Co
706 S Fifth St
Champaign, IL 61820-5604
(217) 384-1790
Founded: Jan. 31, 1992
Capacity: 1,000 bbl

Head Brewer: Bill Morgan
Contact: Bill Morgan

Mickey Finn's Brewery/ Libertyville Brewing Co
412 N Milwaukee Ave
Libertyville, IL 60048-2248
(708) 362-6688; FAX (708) 362-3121
Founded: Aug. 24, 1994
Capacity: 2,000 bbl
Pres.: Patrick Elmquest
Head Brewer: Christopher Swersey
Sales Mgr./Treas.: Bill Sugars
General Mgr.: Pam Kopacz
Contact: Bill Sugars

Millrose Brewing Co
45 S Barrington Rd
South Barrington, IL 60010-9508
(708) 382-7673
Founded: Oct. 1, 1991
Capacity: 600 bbl
General Mgr.: Ron Ager
Head Brewer: Tom Sweeney
Contact: Ron Ager

Pavichevich Brewing Co
383 Romans Rd
Elmhurst, IL 60126-2035
(708) 617-5252; FAX (708) 617-5259
Founded: March 13, 1989
Capacity: 20,000 bbl
Pres./CEO: Ken Pavichevich
Head Brewer: George Vlamis
Contact: Ken Pavichevich

Pinch Penny Pub Inc
700 E Grand
Carbondale, IL 62901
(618) 549-3348
Founded: April 1, 1995
Contact: Ann Fotios Karayiannis

Prairie Rock Brewing Co
127 S Grove
Elgin, IL 60120
(708) 622-8888; FAX (708) 622-9587
Founded: Oct. 30, 1995
Capacity: 2,200 bbl
Head Brewer: Brian Miller
Principal: Joe Elias
Principal: Mike Origer
Contact: Brian Miller

Rock Bottom Brewery (No 7)
1 W Grand Ave
Chicago, IL 60611
(312) 755-9339; FAX (312) 755-0164
Founded: Oct. 26, 1995
Contact: Mark Petchenik

United States Breweries (Illinois–Iowa)

Star Union Brewery Co
RR 1 Route 26/PO Box 282
Hennepin, IL 61327-0282
(815) 925-7400; FAX (815) 925-7401
Head Brewer: Dave Urnikis
Sales Mgr.: John Redshaw
Contact: John Redshaw

Taylor Brewing Co
200 E Fifth Ave
Naperville, IL 60563-3100
(708) 717-8000; FAX (708) 717-8069
Founded: April 15, 1994
Capacity: 237 bbl
Owner: Glenn Taylor
Head Brewer: Ed Bronson
General Mgr.: Gary Taylor
Contact: Glenn Taylor

Weinkeller Brewery
6417 Roosevelt Rd
Berwyn, IL 60402-1166
(708) 749-2276; FAX (708) 749-7129
Founded: July 1, 1988
Capacity: 1,500 bbl
Head Brewer: Patrick Wilke
Pres.: Udo Harttung
Contact: Udo Harttung

Weinkeller Brewpub (No 2)
651 Westmont Dr
Westmont, IL 60559-1239
(708) 789-2236; FAX (708) 789-2368
Founded: Feb. 28, 1992
Capacity: 750 bbl
Sec.: Marguerite Harttung
Pres.: Udo Harttung
Head Brewer: Udo Harttung
Contact: Udo Harttung

INDIANA

Alcatraz Brewing Co
49 W Maryland
Indianapolis, IN 46204
(317) 488-1230; FAX (317) 488-1231
Founded: Oct. 29, 1995
Capacity: 1,500 bbl
Head Brewer: Drew Goldberg
Sales Mgr.: Ted Sexton
Contact: Michael Merriman

**Bloomington Brewing Co/
One World Enterprises**
PO Box 6955
Bloomington, IN 47407-6955
(812) 339-2256; FAX (812) 333-3100
jeff@bloomington.com
http://bbc.bloomington.com
Founded: Oct. 10, 1994
Capacity: 1,100 bbl
Pres.: Jeff Mease
Dir. Mktg.: Jeff Hamlin
Contact: Jeff Mease

Broad Ripple Brewing Co
840 E 65th St
Indianapolis, IN 46220-1674
(317) 253-2739
Founded: Feb. 15, 1991
Capacity: 700 bbl
Head Brewer: Kevin Matalucci
Owner/Sales Mgr.: John Hill
Contact: John Hill

Circle V Brewing Co
10212 Leeward Dr
Indianapolis, IN 46250
(317) 577-0153; FAX (317) 595-0253
Founded: April 22, 1996
Capacity: 1,200 bbl
Pres./Treas.: Curtis D. Grelle
VP/Sec.: Mark Vojnovich
Contact: Curtis Grelle

Evansville Brewing Co
1301 Lloyd Expressway
Evansville, IN 47710
(812) 425-7101; FAX (812) 425-7150
Founded: Sept. 1, 1988
Capacity: 1,200,000 bbl
Head Brewer: Ken Griffiths
Pres.: Mark S. Mattingly
COO: John F. Stone
Contact: John F. Stone

Indianapolis Brewing Co
3250 N Post Rd/Suite 285
Indianapolis, IN 46226-6541
(317) 898-1235; FAX (317) 899-8965
Founded: March 1, 1989
Capacity: 3,500 bbl
Pres.: Tom Peters
Sales Mgr.: Kim Renfro
Contact: Tom Peters

Lafayette Brewing Co
622 Main
Lafayette, IN 47901-1451
(317) 742-2591
Founded: Sept. 17, 1993
Capacity: 700 bbl
Restaurant Gen. Mgr.: Nancy Emig
Pres.: Joe Emig Jr.
Head Brewer/Sec./Treas.: Greg Emig
Contact: Greg Emig

Mishawaka Brewing Co
3703 N Main St
Mishawaka, IN 46545-3111
(219) 256-9994
Founded: Oct. 17, 1991
Capacity: 1,400 bbl
Co-Owner: John Foster
Co-Owner/Head Brewer: Thomas Schmidt
Brewer: Rick Schmidt
Contact: Thomas Schmidt

Oaken Barrel Brewing Co
50 Airport Pkwy
Greenwood, IN 46143-1438
(317) 887-2287; FAX (317) 887-2446
Founded: July 1, 1994
Capacity: 1,000 bbl
Dir. Business Operations: Bill Fulton
Restaurant Operations: Kwang Casey
Head Brewer: Brook Belli
Contact: Brook Belli

IOWA

Cedar Brewing Co
500 Blairs Ferry Rd NE
Cedar Rapids, IA 52402
(319) 378-9090
spsbeer@netins.net
http://www.netins.net/showcase/spsbeer/cbc
Contact: Rob Copenhaver

**Dubuque
Brewing & Bottling Co**
E Fourth St Extension
Dubuque, IA 52001
(319) 583-2042; FAX (319) 583-0009
Founded: April 15, 1991
Capacity: 50,000 bbl
Mktg.: Keith Johnson
VP/General Mgr.: Ronald McCarl
Pres./CEO: Robert Imeson
Sales Mgr.: Rob Nelson
Contact: Ron McCarl

Fitzpatrick's Brewing Co
PO Box 2263
Iowa City, IA 52244-2263
(319) 356-6900
Founded: Jan. 1, 1990
Capacity: 800 bbl

Pres./Head Brewer/Sales Mgr.: Gary Fitzpatrick
Contact: Gary Fitzpatrick

Front Street Brewery
208 E River Dr
Davenport, IA 52801-1609
(319) 322-1569; FAX (319) 322-3483
Capacity: 1,000 bbl
Sales Mgr.: Jinnie Ash
Head Brewer: Steve Zuidima
Contact: Jennie Ash

Millstream Brewing Co
PO Box 284
Amana, IA 52203-0284
(319) 622-3672; FAX (319) 622-6516
Founded: Dec. 19, 1985
Capacity: 2,300 bbl
Head Brewer: Larry Schantz
Pres.: Carroll Zuber
VP: James Roemig
Sec.: Dennis Roemig
Sales Mgr.: Steve Martin
Asst. Brewer: Thane Vomacha
Contact: James Roemig

KANSAS

Barley's
801 S Kansas Ave
Topeka, KS 66612
(913) 357-5300
Founded: Nov. 1, 1995
Contact: Steve Burdett

**Blind Tiger
Brewery and Restaurant**
417 SW 37th
Topeka, KS 66611
(913) 267-2739; FAX (913) 267-7527
Founded: May 29, 1995
Capacity: 2,184 bbl
Head Brewer: John Anschutz
Sales Mgr.: Mike Owens
Asst. Brewer: Kevin Eichelberger
Contact: John Anschutz

Dave's Brewpub
10635 Floyd
Overland Park, KS 66212
(913) 385-0003; FAX (913) 385-0003
Founded: June 1, 1995
Head Brewer: David Cattle
Sales Mgr.: Mike Watson
Contact: David Cattle

Free State Brewing Co
636 Massachusetts
Lawrence, KS 66044-2236
(913) 843-4555; FAX (913) 843-2543
Founded: Feb. 23, 1989
Capacity: 3,500 bbl
Head Brewer: Steve Bradt
Pres.: Chuck Magerl
Contact: Chuck Magerl

**Lazy Hound
Restaurant and Brewery**
111 N Pine
Pittsburg, KS 66762
(316) 231-2739
Founded: June 5, 1995
Capacity: 500 bbl
Head Brewer: Kevin Cates
Contact: Kevin Cates

Little Apple Brewing Co
1110 Westloop
Manhattan, KS 66502
(913) 539-5500; FAX (919) 537-4736
Founded: Oct. 29, 1993
Capacity: 638 bbl
Head Brewer: Robert Moline
Contact: Robert Moline

Overland Park Brewing Co
9083 Metcalf
Overland Park, KS 66212
(913) 385-BREW; FAX (913) 385-1153
Founded: July 21, 1995
Contact: Dan Carter

Pony Express Brewing Co
311 N Burch
Olathe, KS 66061
(913) 782-6699; FAX (913) 782-4321
Founded: Sept. 23, 1995
Capacity: 8,500 bbl
Head Brewer: Artie Tafoya
Pres.: Joe Effertz
Head Brewer: Bill McGrainer
Sales Mgr.: Stephanie Pack
Distribution Mgr.: Brian Neville
Contact: Artie Tafoya

River City Brewing Co
150 N Mosley St
Wichita, KS 67202-2804
(316) 263-2739; FAX (316) 263-2739
Founded: March 24, 1993
Capacity: 1,000 bbl
Head Brewer: Chris Magerkurth
Co-Owner: Carol Griffin
Co-Owner: William Shea
Pres.: Monte Griffin
Contact: Monte Griffin

Rock Bottom Brewery (No 6)
11721 Metcalf Ave
Overland Park, KS 66210
(913) 663-2422; FAX (913) 663-1694
Founded: Nov. 13, 1995

Topeka City Brewing Co
801 S Kansas Ave
Topeka, KS 66612
(913) 357-5300
Founded: Oct. 1, 1995
Head Brewer: Steve Burdett
Contact Steve Burdett

KENTUCKY

Bluegrass Brewing Co
3929 Shelbyville Rd
Louisville, KY 40207-3120
(502) 899-7070; FAX (502) 899-7051
Founded: Nov. 1, 1993
Capacity: 2,100 bbl
Pres./Sales Mgr.: Patrick Hagan
Head Brewer: David R. Pierce
Contact: Patrick Hagan

Jack Daniel's Brewery
4360 Brownsboro Rd/Suite 100
Louisville, KY 40207
(502) 891-8034; FAX (502) 891-8059
Founded: Nov. 28, 1994
Capacity: 2,400 bbl
Head Brewer: Martin Winslow
Sales Mgr.: John Gomatos
Primary Contact: John Barret
Contact: John Barrett

**Jack Daniel's
Corporate Headquarters**
110 21st Ave S
Nashville, TN 37203-2416
(615) 327-1557

**KBC Brewpub and Grill/
Kentucky Brewing Co**
122 W Maxwell
Lexington, KY 40508
(606) 233-7821; FAX (606) 255-1711
Founded: Sept. 8, 1995
Pres./Partner: Philip Talbert
Bar Mgr./Partner: Larry Ellington
General Mgr./Partner: Steve Laird
Chef/Partner: Steve Garth
Asst. Mgr.: Kim Tackett
Brewmaster: David Pierce
Contact: Philip Talbert

United States Breweries (Kentucky–Maine)

Lexington City Brewery
1050 S Broadway
Lexington, KY 40504
(606) 259-2739; FAX (310) 260-1932
Founded: Nov. 10, 1995
Capacity: 1,500 bbl
Head Brewer: Brad Fournier
VP Development: Sam Casto
VP Operations: Jim Brennan
Contact: Mark Reckard

Louisiana Jack's/Silo Brewpub
630 Barret Ave
Louisville, KY 40204-1142
(502) 589-2739; FAX (502) 584-4375
Founded: Jan. 1, 1996
Capacity: 2,500 bbl
Head Brewer: Eileen Martin
General Mgr.: John Bollinger
Asst. Brewer: Matthew Gould
Contact: John Bollinger

Oldenberg Brewing Co
400 Buttermilk Pike
Fort Mitchell, KY 41017
(606) 341-7223; FAX (606) 341-0580
http://realbeer.com/oldenberg
Founded: Oct. 15, 1987
Capacity: 12,500 bbl
Sales Mgr.: Frank Cento
Head Brewer: Ken Schierberg
Pres.: Dave Heidrich
Contact: Dave Heidrich

LOUISIANA

Abita Brewing Co
PO Box 762
Abita Springs, LA 70420-0762
(504) 898-3544; FAX (504) 898-3546
abitabeer@aol.com
Founded: July 4, 1986
Capacity: 35,000 bbl
Sales Mgr.: Robert Primes
Head Brewer: Brooks Hamaker
Pres./Head Brewer: Jim Patton
Contact: Jim Patton

Abita Brewpub
PO Box 762
Abita Springs, LA 70420-0762
(504) 892-5837; FAX (504) 892-9565
Founded: July 1, 1995
Capacity: 600 bbl
Contact: Kathleen Patton

Acadian Brewing Co LLC
201 N Carrollton Ave
New Orleans, LA 70119
(504) 488-8274
Founded: Feb. 9, 1996
Capacity: 5,000 bbl
Head Brewer: Doug Lindley
Contact: James Cronin

Crescent City Brewhouse
527 Decatur St
New Orleans, LA 70130-1027
(504) 522-0571; FAX (504) 522-0577
Founded: Jan. 31, 1991
Capacity: 2,500 bbl
Asst. Brewmaster: Thomas Lenz
General Mgr.: Philip Gilberti
Pres.: Christian Eisenbeiss
VP/Brewmaster: Wolfram Koehler
Sales Mgr.: Christine Miller
Contact: Wolfram Koehler

Dixie Brewing Co Inc
2401 Tulane Ave
New Orleans, LA 70119-6796
(504) 822-8711; FAX (504) 827-0410
Founded: Oct. 31, 1987
Capacity: 300,000 bbl
Pres.: Kendra Bruno
Chairman/CEO: Joseph Bruno
Head Brewer: Kevin Stuart
Dir. of Sales: Stephen Armstrong
Contact: Kendra Elliott Bruno

**Louisiana Brewing Co/
Brasserie de la Louisiane**
1058 O'Neal Dr
Beaux Bridge, LA 70517
(318) 332-2155; FAX (318) 332-2305
Founded: Sept. 1, 1995
Capacity: 4,600 bbl
Pres./Head Brewer: Ed Boudreaux
Sec./Treas./VP: George Harris
General Operations Mgr: George Harris
Contact: George Harris

Rikenjaks Brewery
9916 Hwy 421
Jackson, LA 70748
(504) 634-2785; FAX (504) 634-5726
Founded: Aug. 1, 1993
Capacity: 7,500 bbl
Pres./Sales Mgr.: Theda Little
Head Brewer: Richard Nyberg

MAINE

Allagash Brewing Co Inc
100 Industrial Way
Portland, ME 04103-1042
(207) 878-5385; FAX (207) 878-5385
Founded: June 30, 1995
Capacity: 1,500 bbl
Contact: Rob Tod

Andrew's Brewing Co
RFD 1 Box 4975
Lincolnville, ME 04849
(207) 763-3305
Founded: Jan. 1, 1993
Capacity: 500 bbl
Pres./Head Brewer: Andrew Hazen
Contact: Andrew Hazen

**Atlantic Brewing Co/
Lompoc Cafe Brewpub**
30 Rodick St
Bar Harbor, ME 04609-1868
(207) 288-9392; FAX (207) 288-3589
Founded: June 1, 1991
Capacity: 1,200 bbl
Asst. Brewer: Shawn Duncan
Sales Mgr.: Tim Smith
Head Brewer: Roger Normand
Brewer: Bryce Cough
Contact: Doug Maffucci

Bar Harbor Brewing
HC 30 Box 61
Bar Harbor, ME 04609-9802
(207) 288-4592
Founded: July 18, 1990
Capacity: 320 bbl
CEO/CFO/Sales Mgr.: Suzi Foster
Owner/Head Brewer: Tod Foster
Contact: Suzi Foster

Bear Brewing Co
36 Main St
Orono, ME 04473
(207) 866-2739
Founded: Sept. 1, 1995
Contact: Milos Blagojevic

Bray's Brewpub and Eatery
PO Box 548/Junction Route 302 and 35
Naples, ME 04055
(207) 693-6806
Founded: Dec. 22, 1995
Pres./Head Brewer: Michael G. Bray
VP/Treas.: Michele A. Windsor
Contact: Michele Windsor

Casco Bay Brewing Co
57 Industrial Way
Portland, ME 04103-1071
(207) 797-2020; FAX (207) 797-2020
http://www.maine.com/brew/cbb/cbb-comp.htm
Founded: July 29, 1994
Capacity: 8,000 bbl
Pres./Brewer: Michael LaCharite
Exec. VP/Treas.: Robert Wade
Contact: Mike LaCharite

D L Geary Brewing Co Inc
38 Evergreen Dr
Portland, ME 04103-1066
(207) 878-2337; FAX (207) 878-2388
dgeary1047@aol.com
Founded: Dec. 1, 1986
Capacity: 25,000 bbl
Sales Mgr.: David Kesel
Pres./Head Brewer: David Geary
Treas.: Karen Geary
Prod. Mgr.: Stephen Spear
Contact: David Geary

Gritty McDuff's
369 Fore St
Portland, ME 04101-5010
(207) 772-2739; FAX (207) 772-6204
Founded: Dec. 21, 1988
Capacity: 1,700 bbl
Head Brewer: Ed Stebbins
Sales Mgr.: Richard Pfeffer
General Mgr.: Linda Mehlhorn
Contact: Ed Stebbins

Gritty McDuff's (No 2)
Lower Main St
Freeport, ME 04032
(207) 865-4321; FAX (207) 772-6204
Founded: July 21, 1995
Capacity: 2,000 bbl
Co-Owner: Ed Stebbins
Head Brewer: William Stebbins
Co-Owner: Richard Pfeffer
General Mgr.: John Soule
Contact: Ed Stebbins

Kennebunkport Brewing Co
8 Western Ave/Unit 6
Kennebunk, ME 04093
(207) 967-4311; FAX (207) 967-4903
Founded: June 15, 1992
Capacity: 3,500 bbl
Owner: Fred Forsley
Sales Mgr.: Bruce Forsley
Owner/Head Brewer: Alan Pugsley
First Asst. Brewer: Jim Sanders
Asst. Brewer: Justin Ramos
Contact: Fred Forsley

Lake St George Brewing Co
RR 1 Box 2505
Liberty, ME 04949-9738
(207) 589-4180
Founded: June 29, 1993
Capacity: 650 bbl
Treas.: Kellon Thames
Head Brewer: Dan McGovern
Contact: Dan McGovern

Maine Coast Brewing Co
21A Cottage St
Bar Harbor, ME 04609
(207) 288-4914; FAX (207) 288-9964
Founded: May 19, 1995
Capacity: 800 bbl
Taproom Mgr.: Dan St. Germain
Head Brewer: Nate Hills
Contact: Tom St. Germain

No Tomatoes Restaurant/ Great Falls Brewing Co
36 Court St
Auburn, ME 04210-5902
(207) 784-3919
Founded: March 1, 1994
Contact: Charlie Harrick

Sea Dog Brewing Co
PO Box 1055
Camden, ME 04843-1055
(207) 236-6863
Founded: May 17, 1993
Capacity: 1,750 bbl
Pres.: Pete Camplin
Brewmaster: Dennis Hansen
Head Brewer: Kai Adams
Contact: Pete Camplin

Sea Dog Brewing Co (No 2)
26 Front St
Bangor, ME 04401
(207) 947-8009; FAX (207) 947-8720
Founded: March 17, 1995
Capacity: 20,000 bbl
Pres./Brewmaster: Pete Camplin
Brewmaster: Dennis Hansen
Sales Mgr.: Pete McArdle
Head Brewer: Travis Audet
Operations Mgr.: Angie Stidams
Packaging Mgr.: Ralph Gagner
Contact: Pete Camplin

Sheepscot Valley Brewing Co
RR 1 Box 88
Whitefield, ME 04353
(207) 549-5530
Founded: May 1, 1995
Contact: Steve Gorrill

Shipyard Brewing Co
86 Newbury St
Portland, ME 04101-4219
(207) 761-0807; FAX (207) 775-5567
http://shipyard.com/shipyard
Founded: May 1, 1994
Capacity: 54,000 bbl
Pres.: Fred M. Forsley
Brewmaster: Alan J. Pugsley
Head Brewer: Paul Hendry
Sales Mgr.: Bruce Forsley
Contact: Fred Forsley

Stone Coast Brewing Co
11 Oak St/Suite 3
South Portland, ME 04106
(207) 741-2495
Founded: Jan. 30, 1996
Co-Owner: Grant Wilson
Contact: Pete Leavitt

Sugarloaf Brewing Co
RR 1 Box 2268
Kingfield, ME 04947-9758
(207) 237-2211; FAX (207) 237-3028
Founded: June 29, 1994
Capacity: 5,200 bbl
Pres.: Richard Leeman
VP: Jim Mcmanus
Head Brewer: Jeff Hinckley

Sunday River Brewing Co
1 Sunday River Rd
Bethel, ME 04217-4623
(207) 824-4253; FAX (207) 824-3380
Founded: Jan. 6, 1993
Capacity: 1,600 bbl
Head Brewer: Peter Leavitt
Owner: Grant Wilson
Contact: Hans Trupp

MARYLAND

Baltimore Brewing Co
104 Albemarle St
Baltimore, MD 21202-4457
(410) 837-5000; FAX (410) 837-5024
Founded: Dec. 8, 1989
Capacity: 8,000 bbl
Pres./Head Brewer: Theo De Groen
Contact: Theo De Groen

Bare Bones Grill and Brewery
9150 Baltimore National Pike
Ellicott City, MD 21043
(410) 461-0770
Founded: Feb. 1, 1996
Contact: Derrick Reese

Brauhaus Schloss
Talbot Stone House Inn
8308-8316 Main St
Ellicott City, MD 21043
(410) 203-9666
Founded: March 1, 1996
Head Brewer: Ryan Morris
Contact: Martin Virga

Brimstone Brewing Co
3701 Dillon St
Baltimore, MD 21224-5244
(410) 342-1363; FAX (410) 342-6454
Founded: Oct. 1, 1994
Capacity: 1,500 bbl
Head Brewer: Marc Tewey
Contact: Marc Tewey

Carling National Brewing Co
4501 Hollins Ferry Rd
Baltimore, MD 21227
(608) 785-3336; FAX (608) 785-3323
Contact: George Arnold

Clipper City Brewing Co LP
4615 Hollins Ferry Rd/Suite B
Baltimore, MD 21227
(410) 247-7822; FAX (410) 247-7829
Founded: Jan. 1, 1996
Capacity: 900 bbl
Brewmaster: Tom Flores
Contact: Hugh Sisson

Duclaw Brewing Co
2034 Tiffany Terr
Forest Hill, MD 21050
(410) 879-1485; FAX (410) 879-0882
Founded: April 1, 1996
Capacity: 1,900 bbl
Contact: Dave Benfield

Fordham Brewing Co/ Ramshead Tavern
33 West St
Annapolis, MD 21401
(410) 268-4545; FAX (410) 626-1044
Founded: Sept. 1, 1995
Capacity: 2,300 hl
Head Brewer: Allen Young
Sales Mgr.: Paula Muehlhauser
Pres.: Bill Muehlhauser
General Mgr.: Wayne Friata
Asst. Brewer: Mark Pavkov
Contact: Allen Young

Frederick Brewing Co
PO Box 3664/103 S Carroll St
Frederick, MD 21705-3664
(301) 694-7899; FAX (301) 694-2971
Founded: Nov. 14, 1993
Capacity: 12,500 bbl
Master Brewer/VP Brewing Op.: Steve Nordahl
COO/Pres.: Marjorie McGinnis
CEO/Chairman: Kevin Brannon
Head Brewer: John Pinkerton
VP Sales: Steven Nuszcz
VP Finance/Admin.: Craig O'Connor
Packaging Mgr.: Ken Mason
QA Mgr.: Ben Straight
Contact: Kevin Brannon

G Heileman Brewing Co Inc
4501 Hollins Ferry Rd
Baltimore, MD 21227
(301) 247-1600
Brewery Mgr.: David McFarland
Admin. Mgr.: Robert T. Lathroum
Brewmaster: John M. Houseman
Contact: David McFarland

Mount Airy Brewing Co/ Firehouse Pub and Restaurant
233 Main St
Mount Airy, MD 21771
(410) 795-5557
Founded: Oct. 30, 1995
Contact: Reid Allison

Olde Towne Tavern & Brewery
3 Russell Ave/Suite F
Gaithersburg, MD 20877-2961
(301) 948-4200; FAX (301) 840-9702
Founded: June 15, 1994
Capacity: 1,500 bbl
Brewmaster: Joseph J. Kalish
Asst. Brewer: George Humbert
Contact: Joseph Kalish

Sisson's/ South Baltimore Brewing Co
36 E Cross St
Baltimore, MD 21230-4036
(410) 539-2093; FAX (410) 539-2109
sissons@aol.com
Founded: Sept. 1, 1989
Capacity: 1,080 bbl
Head Brewer: John Ellis
Contact: John Callanan

Wharf Rat Camden Yards/ Oliver Breweries Ltd
206 W Pratt St
Baltimore, MD 21201
(410) 244-8900; FAX (410) 659-1676
Founded: Feb. 2, 1993
Capacity: 5,000 bbl
Head Brewer: Harold Faircloth
Sales Mgr.: Bill Oliver
Contact: Carole Oliver

Wild Goose Brewery
20 Washington St
Cambridge, MD 21613-2802
(410) 221-1121; FAX (410) 221-1123
Founded: Oct. 1, 1989
Capacity: 40,000 bbl
Head Brewer: Alan Pugsley
Pres./Chairman: Jim Lutz
Head Brewer: Mark Seack
Sales Mgr.: Chris Minnick
Contact: Jim Lutz

MASSACHUSETTS

Atlantic Coast Brewing Co
50 Terminal St
Boston, MA 02129-1973
(617) 242-6464; FAX (617) 242-7273
arevelio@linx.dac.neu.edu
Founded: March 1, 1994
Capacity: 4,200 bbl
VP/Head Brewer: Chris Lohring
Pres./Head Brewer/Sales Mgr.: Alex Reveliotty
Contact: Alex Reveliotty

Back Bay Brewing Co
755 Boylston St
Boston, MA 02114
(617) 424-8300
Founded: Dec. 19, 1995
Capacity: 1,000 bbl
Head Brewer: Tod Mott
General Mgr.: Jack Di Caccia
Owner: Joe Quattrocchi
Owner: Lisa Quattrocchi
Contact: Tod Mott

Barrington Brewery and Restaurant
420 Stockbridge Rd
Great Barrington, MA 01230
(413) 528-8282; FAX (413) 528-1272
Founded: May 23, 1995
Capacity: 700 bbl
Head Brewer: Andrew Mankin
Contact: Andrew Mankin

Berkshire Brewing Co Inc
12 Railroad/Suite 96
South Deerfield, MA 01373-1034
(413) 665-6600
Contact: Chris Lalli

United States Breweries (Massachusetts)

Boston Beer Co
30 Germania St
Boston, MA 02130-2312
(617) 368-5000; FAX (617) 368-5183
http://alumni.caltech.edu/~randy/samadams/samadams.html
Founded: Nov. 1, 1987
Head Brewer: James Koch
Sales Mgr.: Rhonda Kallman
Contact: James Koch

Boston Beer Works
61 Brookline Ave
Boston, MA 02215-3406
(617) 536-2337; FAX (617) 536-3325
Founded: April 10, 1992
Capacity: 4,000 bbl
VP Brewery Operations: Steve Slesar
Kitchen Mgr.: Russell Cornelisson
Pres.: Joe Slesar
Co-General Mgr.: Don Pinnell
Co-General Mgr.: John Surdek
Head Brewer: Bryan House
Head Chef: Bob Willis
Asst. General Mgr.: Eric White
Asst. General Mgr.: Kevan Butler
Contact: Steve Slesar

Brew House of Danvers
65 Newbury St
Danvers, MA 01923
(508) 777-6666; FAX (508) 777-7892
brewmaster@digiworld.com
http://www.digiworld.com/brewhousedanvers
Founded: Oct. 4, 1995
Head Brewer: Fred Wesemann
Contact: Dennis Sherman

Brew Moon (No 2)
Route 1 N
Saugus, MA 01916
(617) 941-BREW
Founded: Jan. 8, 1996
Head Brewer: Tony Vierra
Asst Brewer: Dan Cahill
Contact: Daniel Feiner

Brew Moon Enterprises
Cityplace/115 Stuart St
Boston, MA 02116-5609
(617) 742-5225; FAX (617) 742-6620
Capacity: 2,000 bbl
Head Brewer: Tony Vieira
Contact: Daniel Feiner

Brewery at 34 Depot St/ Arrowhead Brewing Co
PO Box 4107/34 Depot St
Pittsfield, MA 01201-5130
(413) 442-2072
Founded: July 20, 1994
Capacity: 1,000 bbl
Head Brewer: Michael Merrill
Contact: Paul Fortini

Cambridge Brewing Co
1 Kendall Sq/Bldg 100
Cambridge, MA 02139-1562
(617) 494-1994; FAX (617) 494-8958
http://www.cambrew.com
Founded: May 1, 1989
Capacity: 2,500 bbl
Head Brewer: Darryl Goss
Sales Mgr.: Philip Bannatyne
Contact: Philip Bannatyne

Cape Cod Brew House/ Nantucket Brewing Co
720 Main St
Hyannis, MA 02601
(508) 775-4110; FAX (508) 775-5006
Founded: May 1, 1995
Capacity: 1,020 bbl
Sales Mgr.: Bob Melley
Head Brewer: Blair Potts
Contact: Blair Potts

Cisco Brewers
PO Box 2928/5 Bartlett Farm Rd
Nantucket, MA 02584
(508) 325-5929
brewers@nantucket.net
Founded: July 15, 1995
Capacity: 400 bbl
Head Brewer: Randy Hudson
Sales Mgr.: Wendy Hudson
Contact: Randy Hudson

Clamtown Brewery Inc
PO Box 319
Ipswich, MA 01938
(508) 465-9965; FAX (508) 465-9965
Founded: Dec. 1, 1995
Capacity: 500 bbl
Head Brewer: Edward Frost
Contact: Edward Frost

Commonwealth Brewing Co
Boston Hops
85 Merrimac St
Boston, MA 02114-4715
(617) 523-8383; FAX (617) 528-1037
Founded: Aug. 1, 1986
Capacity: 1,800 bbl
Head Brewer: Jeff Charnick

VP: Lisa Quattrocchi
General Mgr.: Bill Goodwin
Executive Chef: Glenn Jordan
Pres.: Joe Quattrocchi
Contact: Tod Mott

Ipswich Brewing Co
23 Hayward St
Ipswich, MA 01938-2000
(508) 356-3329; FAX (508) 356-8826
http://www.ipswich.com
Founded: Aug. 30, 1992
Capacity: 11,000 bbl
Pres.: James Beauvais
Treas./Mktg. Dir.: Paul Sylva
Head Brewer: Jeff Geudreau
Contact: James Beauvais

John Harvard's Brewhouse
33 Dunster St
Cambridge, MA 02318
(617) 868-3585; FAX (617) 868-4341
Founded: Aug. 28, 1993
Head Brewer: Brian Sanford
General Mgr.: Christine Didiuk
Executive Chef: Frank L'Hereux
Brewer: Gwen Lloyd
Contact: Brian Sanford

Lowell Brewing Co
199 Cabot St
Lowell, MA 01854
(508) 937-1200; FAX (508) 937-1212
Founded: March 1, 1994
Capacity: 4,000 bbl
Head Brewer: Paul McErlean
Contact: Marty Finnigan

Main Street Brewing Co
244 Main St
Worcester, MA 01608
(508) 753-6700; FAX (508) 755-1704
Founded: March 11, 1996
Contact: Dana Fischer

Mass Bay Brewing Co
306 Northern Ave
Boston, MA 02210-2324
(617) 574-9551; FAX (617) 574-9551
Founded: June 2, 1986
Capacity: 40,000 bbl
Head Brewer: Alan Marzi
VP/Sales Mgr.: Mark Sampson
Mktg. Dir.: Nicholas Godfrey
Pres.: Richard Doyle
Treas.: Warren Dibble
Contact: Richard Doyle

United States Breweries (Massachusetts–Michigan)

Middlesex Brewing Co Inc
844 Woburn St
Wilmington, MA 01887
(508) 657-8100; FAX (508) 657-8100
Founded: May 1, 1993
Capacity: 3,000 bbl
Head Brewer: Brian Friguliette
Contact: Brian Friguliette

**Northampton Brewery/
Brewster Court Bar & Grill**
PO Box 791
Northampton, MA 01061-0791
(413) 584-9903; FAX (413) 584-9972
Founded: Aug. 10, 1987
Capacity: 1,800 bbl
Head Brewer: Chris O'Connor
Partner: Janet O. Egelston
Partner: Peter R. Egelston
Contact: Janet Egelston

**Old Harbor Brewing Co/
The Pilgrim Brewery**
577 Main St
Hudson, MA 01749
(508) 562-6992; FAX (508) 562-7920
yost@marcam.com
http://www.webmart.com/icc/
pilgrim.html
Founded: March 25, 1995
Capacity: 8,000 bbl
Principle/Sales Mgr.: Lou Amorati
Principle: John Munro
Sales Coord.: Kathleen Angiulo
Head Brewer: Ed Yost
Head Brewer: John Munro
Transportation Engineer: David Adams
Contact: Lou Amorati

Olde Salem Brewery
278 Derby St
Salem, MA 01970
(508) 741-7088; FAX (508) 741-7632
Founded: June 1, 1995
Capacity: 2,000 bbl
General Mgr.: Joe Pickle
Head Brewer: Gregg Norris
Sales Mgr./Asst. Brewer: Scott Houghton
Contact: John Athanatopoulos

Ould Newbury Brewing Co
227 High Rd
Newbury, MA 01951-2216
(508) 462-1980
onbc@shore.net
http://www.shore.net/~onbc/oldnbury/ontop.htm
Founded: Sept. 1, 1992
Capacity: 2,500 bbl

Pres. Mktg. and Sales: Pam Rolfe
Head Brewer/VP: Joe Rolfe
Sales Mgr.: Graydon Lockard
Sales: Rob Denuccio
Sales: Alan Mons
Contact: Joe Rolfe

Owen O'Learys Restaurant
50 Turnpike Rd
Natick, MA 01745
(508) 650-0792
Founded: April 28, 1996
Contact: Kevin Gill

Paper City Brewing Co
108 Cabot St
Holyoke, MA 01040
(413) 536-2608
Founded: April 1, 1996
Contact: Jay Hebert

Wachusett Brewing Co
175 State Rd E
Westminster, MA 01473-0417
(508) 874-9965; FAX (508) 874-0784
Founded: Dec. 19, 1994
Head Brewer: Peter Quinn
Pres./Gen. Mgr./Sales Mgr.: Ned LaFortune
Plant Engineer/Treas.: Kevin Buckler
Contact: Ned LaFortune

Watch City Brewing Co Inc
PO Box 754
Dover, MA 02030
(508) 785-1505; FAX (508) 785-2127
Founded: March 13, 1996
Head Brewer: Stephen Lincoln
Head Mgr.: Frank McLaughlin
Gen. Mgr./Owner: Jocelyn Fryer
Contact: Jocelyn Fryer

MICHIGAN

Arbor Brewing Co
114 E Washington
Ann Arbor, MI 48104
(313) 213-1393; FAX (313) 213-2835
abrew@ic.net
http://www.ic.net/arborbrew
Founded: July 12, 1995
CFO: Rene Greff
Contact: Matt Greff

**Big Buck
Brewery and Steakhouse**
PO Box 1203
Gaylord, MI 49735
(517) 732-5781; FAX (517) 732-3990

http://www.bigbuck.com
Founded: May 27, 1995
Capacity: 5,000
Sales Mgr./Head Brewer: Scott A. Graham
Contact: Scott Graham

Blue Coyote Brewing Co
113 Pere Marquette
Lansing, MI 48912
(517) 485-2583; FAX (517) 485-8937
Founded: Sept. 24, 1995
Capacity: 2,000 bbl
Head Brewer: Alan Pagliere
Sales Mgr.: Mike O'Leary
Contact: Harry Hepler

Boyne River Brewing Co
419 E Main St
Boyne City, MI 49712
(616) 582-5588
Founded: July 1, 1995
Capacity: 700 bbl
Head Brewer: Scott Hill
Contact: Scott Hill

Duster's Micro-brewery
114 N Main St
Lawton, MI 49065
(616) 624-3771; FAX (616) 624-7392
Founded: April 1, 1994
Head Brewer/Sales Mgr.: Phil Balog
Contact: Phil Balog

Frankenmuth Brewery Inc
425 S Main St
Frankenmuth, MI 48734-1615
(517) 652-6183; FAX (517) 652-3882
Founded: May 1, 1988
Capacity: 50,000 bbl
Pres.: Randall Heine
Head Brewer: Fred M. Scheer
Sales Mgr.: William L. Lopo
Special Projects Dir.: Tarkton Heine
General Mgr.: Brian Greenlee
Contact: Tarkton Heine

Grand Rapids Brewing Co
3689 28th St
Grand Rapids, MI 49512-1605
(616) 285-5970; FAX (616) 957-0812
Founded: Nov. 1, 1993
Capacity: 1,000 bbl
Chairman: Robert Kowalewski
Pres. Schelde Enterprise: Howard Schelde
Mgr.: John Rapezzi
Mgr.: Tom McCormack
Mgr.: Harley Pebbles
Mgr.: Jeff Taylor

Head Brewer: Mark Stehl
Contact: Mark Stehl

Great Baraboo Brewing Co
36907 Utica Rd
Clinton Township, MI 48035
(810) 772-9720
Founded: May 1, 1995
Contact: David Tamulevich

Grizzly Peak Brewing Co
120 W Washington St
Ann Arbor, MI 48104-1325
(313) 741-7325; FAX (313) 741-5976
Founded: Aug. 17, 1995
Capacity: 1,800 bbl
Pres.: Jon A. Carlson
Head Brewer: Gregory J. Burke
General Mgr.: Scott Joling
Chef: Paul Mawhinney
Asst. Brewer: Ron Jeffries
Contact: Scott Joling

Hereford and Hops
624 Ludington St
Escanaba, MI 49829
(906) 786-1945; FAX (906) 789-4238
http://www.visit-usa.com/mi/delta/brewpub.htm
Founded: Dec. 12, 1994
Co-Owner/Head Brewer: Donald Moody
Co-Owner: Jack Mellinger
Co-Owner: Sharon Mellinger
Co-Owner: Becky Moody
Contact: Donald Moody

Kalamazoo Brewing Co Inc
355 E Kalamazoo Ave
Kalamazoo, MI 49007-3807
(616) 382-2332; FAX (616) 382-3820
Founded: Sept. 19, 1985
Capacity: 22,000 bbl
Pres.: Larry Bell
Head Brewer: Steve Buszka
Sales Mgr.: Fred Bueltmann
Contact: Larry Bell

King Brewing Co
985 Oakland Ave
Pontiac, MI 48340
(810) 745-5900; FAX (810) 745-0160
kingbrewco@aol.com
Founded: Aug. 15, 1995
Sales Mgr.: Jeff Gibbs
Head Brewer: Scott King
Contact: Scott King

Michigan Brewing Co
2582 M-52
Williamston, MI 48895
(517) 521-3600; FAX (517) 521-3229
Founded: Jan. 1, 1996
Capacity: 4,500 bbl
Contact: Robert Mason

Motor City Brewing Works Inc
470 W Canfield St
Detroit, MI 48201-1220
(301) 832-2700
Founded: Jan. 1, 1995
Capacity: 1,500 bbl
Pres.: John Linardos
Head Brewer: Steven Rouse
Contact: Steven Rouse

Old Peninsula Brewpub
200 E Michigan Ave
Kalamazoo, MI 49007
(616) 343-BREW
Founded: March 15, 1996
Capacity: 765 bbl
Head Brewer: Greg "Ganzo" Horner
Contact: Steve Blinn

Stroh Brewery Co Corporate Headquarters
300 River Pl
Detroit, MI 48207-4291
(313) 446-2000; FAX (313) 446-2730
Founded: Jan. 1, 1949
Capacity: 15,000,000 bbl
Sr. VP/Customer Mktg. and Admin.: Joseph Franzem
Pres./CEO: William L. Henry
Chairman: Peter W. Stroh
Dir. Public Relations: Lacey Logan
VP Brewing: Joseph D. Hertich
Contact: Lacey Logan

Traffic Jam and Snug
4268 Second Ave
Detroit, MI 48201-1706
(313) 831-1265; FAX (313) 831-4022
Founded: Feb. 10, 1993
Capacity: 250 bbl
Pres./Head Brewer: Ben Edwards
Contact: Ben Edwards

Traverse Brewing Co Ltd
PO Box 158
Williamsburg, MI 49690-0158
(616) 264-9343
Founded: Jan. 3, 1996
Contact: John Edstrom

Wiltse's Brew Pub and Family Restaurant
5606 N F-41
Oscoda, MI 48750
(517) 739-2231; FAX (517) 739-6930
Founded: Dec. 2, 1994
Capacity: 200 bbl
Head Brewer: Dean Wiltse
Contact: Dean Wiltse

MINNESOTA

August Schell Brewing Co
PO Box 128
New Ulm, MN 56073-0128
(507) 354-5528; FAX (507) 359-9919
Founded: Jan. 1, 1960
Capacity: 50,000 bbl
Sales Mgr.: Kelly Kuehl
Pres./Head Brewer: Ted Marti
Contact: Ted Marti

Backwater Brewing Co
1429 W Service Dr
Winona, MN 55987
(507) 452-2103; FAX (507) 454-3133
Founded: June 1, 1995
Capacity: 2 bbl
Head Brewer: Chris Gardner
Owner: Geoff Gardner
Contact: Geoff Gardner

Clubhaus Brewpub
7 Second St SW
Rochester, MN 55902
(507) 252-0400
Founded: January 13, 1995
Owner: Peter Henderson
Head Brewer: Todd Eracek
Contact: Peter Henderson

Cold Spring Brewing Co/Beverage International Group Ltd
219 N Red River Rd
Cold Spring, MN 56320
(612) 685-8686; FAX (612) 685-8318
Founded: Jan. 1, 1974
Capacity: 100,000 bbl
Sales Mgr.: Al May
Head Brewer: Mike Kneip
VP: Jeffery Burger
Pres.: James Stegura
Contact: James Stegura

James Page Brewing Co
1300 Quincy St NE
Minneapolis, MN 55413-1574
(612) 331-2833; FAX (612) 781-8529

jiminmpls@aol.com
Founded: Oct. 1, 1987
Capacity: 5,000 bbl
Head Brewer: Ron Flett
Pres.: James Page
Contact: James Page

Lake Superior Brewing Co
600 E Superior St
Duluth, MN 55802
(218) 720-3491; FAX (218) 722-8826
Founded: Dec. 9, 1994
Capacity: 1,250 bbl
Head Brewer: Bob Dromeshauser
Contact: Bob Dromeshauser

Minnesota Brewing Co
882 Seventh St W
St Paul, MN 55102-3641
(612) 228-9173; FAX (612) 290-8211
Founded: Dec. 1, 1991
Capacity: 600,000 bbl
Pres.: R. McMahon
Head Brewer: Sig Plagems
Sales Mgr.: Mike Dougherty
Contact: Sig Plagems

Rock Bottom Brewery (No 2)
825 Hennepin Ave
Minneapolis, MN 55402
(612) 332-2739; FAX (612) 332-1508
Founded: Dec. 18, 1993
Capacity: 2,500 bbl
Co-Owner: Diane Greenlee
Co-Owner: Frank Day
General Mgr.: Neil Harfert
Head Brewer: Rick Hammond
Contact: Rick Hammond

Shannon Kelly's Brewpub
395 Wabasha St N
St Paul, MN 55102-1305
(612) 292-0905
Founded: Nov. 21, 1994
Capacity: 5,000 bbl
Head Brewer: Jamie McGovern
Contact: Jamie McGovern

Sherlock's Home
11000 Red Cir Dr
Minnetonka, MN 55343-9120
(612) 931-0203
Contact: Bill Burdick

Stroh Brewery
Co St Paul Plant/
Northern Plains Brewing Co
707 E Minnehaha Ave
St Paul, MN 55106
(612) 778-3100

Capacity: 3,500,000 bbl
Plant Mgr.: J. A. Glynn
Master Brewer: J. Thorner
Packaging Mgr.: T. Carstens
Contact: J. A. Glynn

Summit Brewing Co
2264 University Ave W
St Paul, MN 55114-1801
(612) 645-5029; FAX (612) 645-5139
Founded: Sept. 25, 1986
Capacity: 35,000 bbl
Operations Mgr.: Christopher Seitz
Pres./Head Brewer: Mark Stutrud
Sales Mgr.: Jeffrey Spaeth
Production Mgr.: Jon Lindberg
Contact: Mark Stutrud

Trader & Trapper
617 Center Ave
Moorhead, MN 56560-1923
(218) 236-0202; FAX (218) 233-4433
Founded: Dec. 15, 1994
Capacity: 750 bbl
Head Brewer: Doug Frey
Pres.: Paul Quarve
Contact: Paul Quarve

MISSOURI

75th Street Brewery
520 75th St
Kansas City, MO 64114
(816) 523-4677; FAX (816) 523-3228
Founded: Aug. 16, 1993
Capacity: 2,200 bbl
Head Brewer: Tom Ricker
Sales Mgr.: Chris Sutton
General Mgr.: James Westphal
Contact: James Taylor

Anheuser-Busch Inc
PO Box 1828/Bechtold Station
St Louis, MO 63118-0828
(314) 577-2000
Founded: Jan. 1, 1952
Capacity: 94,900,000 bbl
Pres./CEO: August A. Busch III
VP Brewing: Gerhardt Kraemer
VP Sales: James Hunter
Contact:

Boulevard Brewing Co
2501 Southwest Blvd
Kansas City, MO 64108-2345
(816) 474-7095; FAX (816) 474-1722
Founded: Nov. 17, 1989
Capacity: 35,000 bbl
VP Sales/Mktg.: Bob Sullivan

Head Brewer: William R. Cherry
Pres.: John McDonald
General Mgr.: Mary Harrison
Contact: John McDonald

Ebbets Field
1027 E Walnut
Springfield, MO 65806
(417) 865-5050
Founded: March 17, 1995
Capacity: 350 bbl
Head Brewer: David Lamb
Co-Owner: Nick Russo
Co-Owner: Steve West
Co-Owner: Annette West
Contact: David Lamb

Flat Branch Brewing Co
115 S Fifth St
Columbia, MO 65201-4230
(314) 499-0400
tsmith@socketis.net
http://flatbranch.datastorm.com:8000
Founded: April 18, 1994
Capacity: 2,000 bbl
Head Brewer: Paul Hoffman
Pres.: Tom Smith
Business Mgr.: Jim Smith
Operations Coord.: Lance Wood
Contact: Paul Hoffman

Mill Creek
Brewery & Restaurant
4050 Pennsylvania Ave/Suite 115
Kansas City, MO 64111
(816) 931-4499; FAX (816) 931-8603
Founded: Jan. 15, 1994
Capacity: 500 bbl
Head Brewer: John Jordan
Head Brewer: Lance Leirheisen
Sales Mgr.: Annie Kingsland
Asst. Brewer: Barry Pennell
Contact: Kyle Kelly

Morgan Street Brewery
721 N Second St
St Louis, MO 63102
(314) 231-9970; FAX (314) 231-2469
Founded: Nov. 1, 1995
Head Brewer: Lance Lierheimer
Pres.: Dennis Harper
VP: Randy Harper
Sec.: Steve Owings
Contact: Lance Lierheimer

River Market Brewing Co
500 Walnut
Kansas City, MO 64106
(816) 471-6300; FAX (816) 471-5562
http://users.aol.com/RvrMarket/index

Founded: April 1, 1995
Capacity: 400 bbl
Pres./Head Brewer: Steve Palmer
General Mgr.: Angelo Gangai
Contact: Steve Palmer

Saint Louis Brewery/ The Tap Room
2100 Locust St
St Louis, MO 63103-1616
(314) 241-2337; FAX (314) 241-8101
schlaflybeers@oui.com
Founded: Dec. 26, 1991
Capacity: 2,300 bbl
General Mgr.: Tom Flood
Asst. Brewer/QC: Sara Choler
CFO: Ed Gordon
Pres.: Tom Schlafly
Head Brewer: Stephen Hale
Sales Mgr.: Paul Jensen
Asst. Brewer: James Ottolini
Sales Mgr.: Tom Sweeney
Contact: Stephen Hale

Trailhead Brewing Co
PO Box 879/921 S Riverside Dr
St Charles, MO 63302-0879
(314) 946-2739; FAX (314) 946-1297
Founded: June 28, 1995
Capacity: 2,500 bbl
Head Brewer: Dr. John Witte
Owner: Robert Kirkwood, Jr.
Brewer: Terry Watson
Sales Mgr: Yvonne Briese
Contact: John Witte

Westport Brewing Co
4057 Pennsylvania Ave
Kansas City, MO 64111-3021
(816) 931-2739
Founded: Nov. 15, 1994
Capacity: 2,500 bbl
Contact: John Ross

MONTANA

Bayern Brewing Inc/ Iron Horse Brewpub
2600 S Third St W/Suite E
Missoula, MT 59801
(406) 721-1482; FAX (406) 549-6444
Founded: Aug. 1, 1987
Capacity: 2,300 bbl
Sec./Treas.: Bill Baldassin
Brewmaster: Juergen Knoeller
Contact: Juergen Knoeller

Big Sky Brewing Co
120-A Hickory St
Missoula, MT 59802
(406) 549-2777; FAX (406) 549-1919
mqtv@ism.net
http://www.graphi.com/bigskybrew.html
Founded: July 3, 1995
Capacity: 5,400 bbl
Head Brewer: Neal Leathers
Sales Mgr.: Brad Robinson
Contact: Neal Leathers

Great Northern Brewing Co
10 Central Ave
Whitefish, MT 59937
(406) 863-1000; FAX (406) 863-1001
Founded: Feb. 3, 1995
Capacity: 5,000 bbl
Head Brewer: David Jerke
Sales Mgr.: Nancie Bailey
Production Mgr.: Dan Rasmussen
Dir. of Operations: Peter Kobelt
Contact: Peter Kobelt

Himmelberger Brewing Co
PO Box 22272
Billings, MT 59104-2272
(406) 252-1200
Capacity: 180 bbl
Head Brewer/Sales Mgr.: Dennis Himmelberger
Contact: Dennis Himmelberger

Kessler Brewing Co
1439 N Harris St
Helena, MT 59601-3022
(406) 449-6214; FAX (406) 449-8119
Founded: Jan. 1, 1984
Capacity: 6,000 bbl
Head Brewer: Steve Shellhardt
VP: Roger Pasch
Contact: Roger Pasch

Lang Creek Brewery
655 Lang Creek Rd
Marion, MT 59925-9717
(406) 858-2200; FAX (406) 858-2200
http://www.teleport.com/~ediehl/langcrk/
Founded: Jan. 14, 1994
Capacity: 1,800 bbl
Co-Owner: John Campbell
Co-Owner/Office Mgr.: Sandra Campbell
Head Brewer: Carl Liebig
Sales Mgr.: Dsoug Wilkey
Contact: John Campbell

Milestown Brewing Co/ The Golden Spur
1014 S Haynes Ave
Miles City, MT 59301-5726
(406) 232-3898; FAX (406) 232-7806
Founded: April 29, 1992
Capacity: 400 bbl
Co-Owner/Brewer: Larry Grant
Co-Owner/Brewer: Ernest Sonny
Contact: Larry Grant

Montana Brewing Co
N 113 Broadway Ave
Billings, MT 59101-2043
(406) 252-9200
Founded: Dec. 2, 1994
Capacity: 900 bbl
Head Brewer: Tom Runge
Asst. Brewer: Mark Hastings
Sales Mgr.: Dan Konen
Contact: Mike Schmechel

Rock'n M Brewing Co
401 E Main St
Belgrade, MT 59714-3852
(406) 388-2007; FAX (406) 388-1443
Founded: Aug. 4, 1994
Capacity: 2,000 bbl
Head Brewer: Jeff Archer
Sales Mgr.: John Dinneny
Primary Contact: Jennifer Ballard
Contact: Jennifer Ballard

Spanish Peaks Brewing Co
PO Box 3644/120 N 19th Ave
Bozeman, MT 59772-3644
(406) 585-2296; FAX (406) 585-2483
chug@montana.avicom.net
http://www.avicom.net/spb.html
Founded: Dec. 15, 1991
Capacity: 1,000 bbl
Head Brewer: Todd Scott
Pres.: Mark Taverniti
Contact: Mark Taverniti

Whitefish Brewing Co
PO Box 1949
Whitefish, MT 59937-1949
(417) 862-2684; FAX (417) 862-2684
Founded: July 1, 1991
Capacity: 2,100 bbl
Head Brewer: Gary Hutchinson
Sales Mgr.: Kirk Dietrich
Contact: Gary Hutchinson

United States Breweries (Nebraska–New Hampshire)

NEBRASKA

Crane River Brewpub & Cafe
200 N 11th
Lincoln, NE 68508-1406
(402) 476-7477
Founded: Oct. 16, 1992
Capacity: 2,200 bbl
General Mgr.: Linda Vescio
VP/Head Brewer: Kristina Tiebel
Contact: Kristina Tiebel

Gottberg Brew Pub/ Gottberg Auto Co
PO Box 605
Columbus, NE 68602-0602
(402) 562-6488
Founded: Nov. 20, 1995
Capacity: 880 bbl
Head Brewer: Ron Willis
Contact: Ron Willis

Jaipur Restaurant and Brewpub
10922 Elm St
Omaha, NE 68114-4822
(402) 392-7331
Founded: March 20, 1992
Capacity: 100 bbl
Head Brewer: Mark Herse
Contact: Gary Herse

Jones Street Brewery
PO Box 3451
Omaha, NE 68103
(402) 344-3858; FAX (402) 344-3362
deano@well.com
Founded: Oct. 15, 1992
Capacity: 3,500 bbl
Pres./Sales Mgr.: Dean J. Dobmeier
Head Brewer: Dean J. Dobmeier
Contact: Dean J. Dobmeier

Lazlo's Brewery and Grill
710 P St
Lincoln, NE 68508-1326
(402) 474-2337
Founded: March 20, 1991
Capacity: 1,500 bbl
VP: Jay Jarvis
Pres.: Brian Boles
Head Brewer: Rich Chapin
VP: Scott Boles
Contact: Scott Boles

NEVADA

Barley's Casino and Brewing Co
4500 E Sunset Rd
Henderson, NV 89014
(702) 458-2739
Founded: Jan. 18, 1996
Contact: Michael Fergusson

Brew Brothers/ Eldorado Hotel and Casino
Fourth and Virginia
Reno, NV 89501
(702) 786-2100
Founded: July 28, 1995
Capacity: 1,800 bbl
Head Brewer: Darren Whitcher
Contact: Billy Morris

Carson Depot
111 E Telegraph St
Carson City, NV 89701-4208
(702) 884-4546
Founded: Nov. 15, 1993
Contact: Al Gasper

Great Basin Brewing Co
846 Victorian Ave
Sparks, NV 89431-5077
(702) 355-7711
Founded: Dec. 10, 1993
Capacity: 1,500 bbl
Controller: Camille Prenn
Brewmaster: Eric McClary
General Mgr.: Tom Young
Brewmaster: Tom Young
Contact: Tom Young

Holy Cow! Casino, Cafe & Brewery
2423 Las Vegas Blvd S
Las Vegas, NV 89104-2530
(702) 732-2697; FAX (702) 732-1413
Founded: May 1, 1992
Capacity: 2,200 bbl
Head Brewer: Dan Rogers
Proprietor: Tom Wiesner
Brewery and Sales Mgr.: Tom Almquist
Asst. Brewer: Mark Cohen
Contact: Tom Almquist

Ruby Mountain Brewing Co Inc
HC 60 Box 100/Clover Valley
Wells, NV 89835-9802
(702) 752-2337; FAX (702) 752-3697
jvolk@sierra.net
Founded: April 15, 1995
Capacity: 1,000 bbl
Head Brewer: Steve Safford
Sales Mgr.: Maggie Safford
Contact: Steve Safford

Union Brewery Co
PO Box 685
Virginia City, NV 89440-0685
(702) 847-0328
Founded: Jan. 1, 1987
Capacity: 100 bbl
Contact: Julie Hoover

NEW HAMPSHIRE

Anheuser-Busch Inc
PO Box 610/221 Daniel Webster Hwy
Merrimack, NH 03054
(603) 889-6631
Capacity: 3,200,000 bbl
Plant Mgr.: Rodney Hanson, Jr.
Resident Brewmaster: David J. Hollows
Contact: Rodney Hanson Jr.

Brewer's Bier Haus
4 Continental Blvd
Merrimack, NH 03054
(603) 424-0888; FAX (603) 424-6142
Founded: Sept. 5, 1995
Capacity: 2,000 bbl
Head Brewer: Phil Markowski
Contact: Karin Baker

Italian Oasis Restaurant & Brewery
127 Main St
Littleton, NH 03561
(603) 444-6995
Founded: Aug. 2, 1994
Capacity: 312 bbl
Co-Owner/Head Brewer: John Morello
Co-Owner: Wayne Morello
Co-Owner: Lisa Morello
Contact: John Morello

Martha's Exchange
185 Main
Nashua, NH 03060-2701
(603) 883-8781; FAX (603) 883-2541
http://www.Destek.Net/Marthas
Founded: Sept. 15, 1993
Capacity: 1,200 bbl
Treas.: William J. Fokas
Pres.: Christopher J. Fokas
Head Brewer: Dean Jones
Contact: Christopher J. Fokas

Nutfield Brewing Co
22 Manchester Rd/Route 28
Derry, NH 03038-3005
(603) 434-9678; FAX (603) 434-1042
http://www.nutfield.com
Founded: June 29, 1995
Capacity: 7,700 bbl
Head Brewer: Bruce Wheeler
Sales Mgr.: Jim Killeen
Contact: Jim Killeen

Portsmouth Brewery
56 Market St
Portsmouth, NH 03801-3705
(603) 431-1115; FAX (603) 431-3610
Founded: June 1, 1991
Capacity: 2,500 bbl
Head Brewer: Sean Nevish
Contact: Peter Egelston

Seven Barrel Brewery
Route 12A at I-89 NH Exit 20
West Lebanon, NH 03784
(802) 865-0500; FAX (802) 658-4112
Founded: April 20, 1994
Capacity: 700 bbl
Head Brewer: Paul White
General Mgr.: Handsome Mick
Brewmaster: Greg Noonan
Contact: Greg Noonan

Smuttynose Brewing Co
225 Heritage Ave
Portsmouth, NH 03801-5610
(603) 436-4026; FAX (603) 431-3610
Founded: July 1, 1994
Capacity: 10,000 bbl
Pres.: Peter Egelston
VP/Gen. Mgr.: Paul Murphy
Head Brewer: Chuck Doughty
Sales Mgr.: Bruce Batura
Asst. Brewer: Dan Packard
Contact: Paul Murphy

Stark Mill Brewery & Restaurant
500 Commercial St
Manchester, NH 03101
(603) 622-0000; FAX (603) 623-8820
Founded: Nov. 1, 1994
Capacity: 1,200 bbl
Head Brewer: J. B. Smith
Contact: Peter Telge

Woodstock Brewing Co
PO Box 118
North Woodstock, NH 03262
(603) 745-3951; FAX (603) 745-3701
Founded: March 1, 1995
Capacity: 500 bbl
Owner: Scott Rice
Head Brewer: Butch Chase
Head Brewer: Sue Markum Cassy
Contact: Scott Rice

NEW JERSEY

Anheuser-Busch Inc
200 US Hwy 1
Newark, NJ 07101-0879
(201) 645-7700
Capacity: 9,900,000 bbl
Plant Mgr.: James Lukaszewicz
Resident Brewmaster: Hans T. Stallmann
Contact: James Lukaszewicz

Climax Brewing Co
Roselle Park, NJ 08900
(908) 620-9585
Contact: Dave Hoffman

Harvest Moon Brewery/ The Ales Co/Sullivan Brewing
146 Bodman Pl/Suite 400
Redbank, NJ 07701
(908) 747-5568; FAX (908) 747-0736
Founded: Feb. 23, 1996
Capacity: 800 bbl
VP: Michael Sullivan
Head Brewer: Scott Falk
Contact: Kristen Sullivan

Hoboken Brewing Co
1125 Hudson St
Hoboken, NJ 07030
(201) 792-2337; FAX (201) 659-2900
Founded: Sept. 4, 1995
Capacity: 6,000 bbl
Head Brewer: Michael Gilmore
Contact: Mitchell Dell Aquila

Joe's Millhill Saloon and Restaurant
300 S Broad St
Trenton, NJ 08608
(609) 394-7222
Founded: May 1, 1995
Contact: Andrew Schuessler

Long Valley Pub & Brewery/ Long Valley Brewing Co
PO Box 368
Long Valley, NJ 07853
(908) 876-1122; FAX (908) 876-5212
Founded: Oct. 6, 1995
Capacity: 2,000 bbl
Head Brewer: Norman Grisewood
Head Brewer: Geoff Price
Contact: Tim Yarrington

New Jersey Brewery LLC
201 Broad St
Phillipsburg, NJ 08865
(908) 213-1900; FAX (908) 213-1905
Founded: April 1, 1996
Capacity: 3,000 bbl
Manager/CEO: Joel Napolitan
Contact: Joel Napolitan

Red Bank Brewery Co
111 Oakland St
Redbank, NJ 07701
(908) 842-2970
Founded: Dec. 30, 1995
Capacity: 3,000 bbl
Brewer: Sean Hamilton
Brewer: Larry Kennedy
Head Brewer: Jay Misson-Sigplagens
Head Brewer: Guy Hagner
Head Brewer: Phil Gagne
Contact: Tom Clark

Ship Inn Inc
61 Bridge St
Milford, NJ 08848-0497
(908) 995-0188; FAX (908) 806-3782
Founded: Jan. 1, 1995
Capacity: 900 bbl
Principal Contact: Ann Hall
Principal Contact: David Hall
Head Brewer: Timothy Hall
Contact: Ann Hall

Thunder Bay Brewing Co
412 Tenafly Rd
Englewood, NJ 07631
(201) 568-5336; FAX (201) 568-3028
Founded: March 30, 1996
Contact: Chuck Schroeder

Triumph Brewing Co/ Disch Brewing Co
138 Nassau St
Princeton, NJ 08542
(609) 924-7855; FAX (609) 924-7857
Founded: March 14, 1995
Capacity: 2,000 bbl
Pres.: Raymond Disch
VP: Erica Disch
VP: Adam Rechnitz
Head Brewer: Adam Rechnitz
Head Brewer: Jon Holland
Contact: Raymond Disch

NEW MEXICO

**Alamogordo Brewing Co/
Kegs Brewery and Fine Dining**
817 Scenic Dr
Alamogordo, NM 88310
(505) 434-4156
Founded: March 15, 1996
Capacity: 2,000 bbl
Sales Mgr.: Dwight Hartman
Owner: Gary Shewan
Contact: Rebecca Gladstone

**Assets Grille/
Southwest Brewing Co**
6910 Montgomery St NE
Albuquerque, NM 87109-1424
(505) 889-6400; FAX (505) 856-6465
assets@indirect.com
http://www.indirect.com/www/assets
Founded: May 15, 1993
Capacity: 1,200 bbl
General Mgr.: Ray Hornfleck
Contact: Mark Matheson

**Elephant Butte
Brewery and Pizzeria**
PO Box 1419
Elephant Butte, NM 87935
(505) 744-5734; FAX (505) 244-9132
wenit@aol.com
Founded: June 30, 1995
Contact: David Robbins

**Embudo Station/
Preston Brewery**
PO Box 154
Embudo, NM 87531-0154
(505) 852-4707
Founded: Jan. 1, 1992
Capacity: 84 bbl
Head Brewer: Brandon Santos
Pres.: Preston Cox
Contact: Preston Cox

**Eske's Brew Pub/
Sangre De Cristo Brewing Co**
106 Des Georges Lane
Taos, NM 87571
(505) 758-1517
Founded: Aug. 6, 1992
Capacity: 475 bbl
Exec. Brewer/Sales Mgr.: Steve Eskeback
Head Brewer: Bill Bockbrader
Contact: Steve Eskeback

Il Vicino Wood Oven Pizza
3403 Central Ave NE
Albuquerque, NM 87106-1431
(505) 266-7855; FAX (505) 265-5133
Founded: May 1, 1994
Capacity: 520 bbl
Head Brewer: Brady McKeown
Sales Mgr.: Ror McKeown
Sales Mgr.: Tom Hennessy
General Mgr.: Ken Brock
Contact: Brady McKeown

**O'Ryan's Tavern & Brewery/
Oregon Mtn Brewing Co**
700 S Telshor Blvd
Las Cruces, NM 88011-4669
(505) 552-8191; FAX (505) 523-0051
Founded: Oct. 7, 1994
Capacity: 630 bbl
Brewmaster: Dave Million
Brewery Operations Mgr.: John Ritter
Contact: John Ritter

Old West Brewery
PO Box 1180
Deming, NM 88001
(505) 524-2408; FAX (505) 546-7905
Founded: July 1, 1994
Head Brewer: Rick Sharp
Contact: Herve Lescombes

**Rio Bravo
Restaurant & Brewery**
515 Central Ave NW
Albuquerque, NM 87102-3113
(505) 242-6800; FAX (505) 242-9492
Founded: Nov. 13, 1993
Capacity: 1,100 bbl
Head Brewer: Brad Kraus
Contact: Dave Richards

Rio Grande Brewing Co Inc
3760 Hawkins St NE
Albuquerque, NM 87109-4511
(505) 343-0903
Founded: May 15, 1994
Capacity: 1,500 bbl
CEO: Scott Moore
Head Brewer: Tom Hart
Sales Mgr.: Matt Shappell
Contact: Scott Moore

Russell Brewing Co
1242 Siler Rd
Santa Fe, NM 87505-3191
(505) 438-3138
Founded: Sept. 4, 1992
Capacity: 50 bbl
Sales Mgr.: Chrissy Mccousland
Owner: Robert Russell
Head Brewer: Robert Russell
Contact: Robert Russell

Santa Fe Brewing Co
PO Box 83
Flying M Ranch
Galisteo, NM 87504-0083
(505) 988-2340
Founded: June 1, 1988
Capacity: 1,000 bbl
Pres.: Mike Levis
Contact: Mike Levis

Wolf Canyon Brewing Co
PO Box 22717
Santa Fe, NM 87502-2717
(505) 982-3101
Founded: April 1, 1996
Capacity: 500 bbl
Head Brewer: Brad Kraus
Contact: Chuck Nashan

NEW YORK

Anheuser-Busch Inc
PO Box 200/2885 Belgium Rd
Baldwinsville, NY 13027
(315) 635-4000
Capacity: 8,200,000 bbl
Plant Mgr.: William Ohlendorf
Resident Brewmaster: James Misthos
Contact: William Ohlendorf

Atlantic Brewing Co
4556 Austin Blvd
Island Park, NY 11558
(516) 432-BREW; FAX (516) 432-0089
Founded: Oct. 5, 1995
Capacity: 312 bbl
Head Brewer: Jim Bovich
Contact: Warren G. Whitman

**Bootleggers Pub and Brewery/
Christophers Restaurant Inc**
411 Cornelia St/Route 3
Plattsburgh, NY 12901
(518) 561-6222; FAX (518) 563-1562
Founded: Dec. 24, 1995
Owner: Terry Meron
Head Brewer: Rick Lemarsh
Head Brewer: Mike O'Connor
Head Brewer/Owner: James Murray
Contact: Terry Meron

United States Breweries (New York)

Breckenridge Brewery in Buffalo
621-623 Main St
Buffalo, NY 14203
(716) 856-2739
Founded: Jan. 26, 1996
Capacity: 6,000 bbl
Primary Contact: Doug Mackinnon
Head Brewer: Rick Whitehouse
Contact: Rick Whitehouse

Buffalo Brewing Co
1830 Abbott Rd/Abbott Sq
Buffalo, NY 14218-3236
(716) 828-0004; FAX (716) 824-7472
Founded: July 2, 1990
Capacity: 10,000
Head Brewer: Jim O'Connor
Sales Mgr.: Fred Lang
Pres.: Kevin Townsell
Contact: Kevin Townsell

Carnegie Hill Brewing Co
1600 Third Ave at 90th St
New York, NY 10128
(212) 369-0808; FAX (212) 369-8514
uptownale@aol.com
Founded: July 12, 1995
Capacity: 1,100 bbl
Pres.: Kevin O'Shea
VP: Colman McCarthy
Treas.: Stephen Ryan
Sec.: Chris Logan
VP: John Armstrong
Head Brewer: Bill Mulligan
Asst. Brewer: Alex Gowe
Contact: Bill Mulligan

Chapter House Brewpub
400 Stewart Ave
Ithaca, NY 14850-4559
(607) 277-9782; FAX (607) 277-9782
Capacity: 832 bbl
Head Brewer: J. Clement
Contact: Fiona Hoey

Drytown Brewing Co
PO Box 258
Treadwell, NY 13846
(607) 431-2337; FAX (607) 432-2439
Founded: July 20, 1995
Capacity: 3,500 bbl
Head Brewer: Harold Leitenberger
Sales Mgr.: Paul Robinson
Pres.: Ken Walter
Contact: Harold Leitenberger

Ellicotville Brewing Co/S&W Co LLC
28-A Monroe St
Ellicotville, NY 14731
(716) 699-2537
Founded: Sept. 23, 1995
Capacity: 1,000 bbl
Head Brewer: Phin Demink
Contact: Peter Kreinheder

Empire Brewing Co
120 Walton St
Syracuse, NY 13202
(315) 475-2337; FAX (315) 475-4413
Founded: Nov. 13, 1994
Capacity: 1,400 bbl
Head Brewer: David Hartmann
Sales Mgr./Mktg.: Mike Hodgdon
Pres.: David Katleski
Contact: David Hartmann

F X Matt Brewing Co
811 Edward St
Utica, NY 13502-4001
(315) 732-3181; FAX (315) 732-4296
Founded: Jan. 1, 1988
Brewmaster/Chairman: F. X. Matt II
Pres.: Nicholas O. Matt
Mktg. and Sales Dir.: Fred Matt
Contact: Marie McNamara

Genesee Brewing Co/Dundee's Brewery
PO Box 762/445 Saint Paul St
Rochester, NY 14605-0762
(716) 546-1030; FAX (716) 546-5011
Founded: April 1, 1933
Capacity: 3,500,000 bbl
Pres./CEO/Chairman: John L. Wehle, Jr.
Exec. VP Sales/Mktg.: Charles Wehle
Exec. VP/COO: Robert N. Latella
Head Brewer: Gart Geminn
Contact: Mark Holdren

Gentleman Jims
522 Dutchess Turnpike
Poughkeepsie, NY 12603
(914) 485-5467
Founded: April 4, 1996
Contact: Jim Fahey

Heartland Brewing Co
35 Union Sq W
New York City, NY 10003
(212) 645-3400
Founded: Jan. 1, 1995
Contact: Jim Migliorini

Hyde Park Brewing Co
514 Albany Post Rd
Hyde Park, NY 12538
(914) 229-8277
Founded: April 15, 1996
Contact: Joey LoBianco

James Bay Restaurant & Brewery
154 W Broadway
Port Jefferson, NY 11777-1314
(516) 928-2525; FAX (516) 928-4414
Capacity: 1,500 bbl
Head Brewer/Sales Mgr.: Jeffrey Smith
Contact: Jeffrey Smith

Lake City Brewing Co
20 and 22 City Hall Pl
Plattsburgh, NY 12946
(518) 566-7000; FAX (518) 523-7088
rkane@cencom.net
Founded: Feb. 14, 1996
Head Brewer: Tony Hurst
Sales Mgr.: Joe Lanless
Contact: Robert Kane

Lake Titus Brewery
HCR 1 Box 58-B
Malone, NY 12953
(518) 483-2337
Founded: Oct. 17, 1994
Capacity: 400 bbl
Pres./Co-Brewer: Fred Ruvola
Sec./Treas./Co-Brewer: Jerry Ida
Contact: Fred Ruvola

Long Island Brewing Co
111 Jericho Tpke
Jericho, NY 11753
(516) 897-3622; FAX (516) 897-2625
brewer@LIBC.com
http://www.libc.com
Founded: Dec. 1, 1994
Capacity: 2,600 bbl
Pres.: Thane P. Gevas
VP: David A. Glicker
Head Brewer/Sales Mgr.: Mark Burford
Contact: David Glicker

Middle Ages Brewing Co Ltd
PO Box 1164
Syracuse, NY 13201
(315) 476-4250; FAX (315) 476-4264
Founded: May 30, 1995
Capacity: 6,240 bbl
Head Brewer/Owner: Marc Rubenstein
Pres./Owner: Mary Rubenstein
Sales Mgr.: Joseph Colucci
Contact: Mary Rubenstein

United States Breweries (New York)

Mountain Valley Brewpub
122 Orange Ave
Suffern, NY 10901-5409
(914) 357-0101; FAX (914) 357-1088
Founded: Oct. 26, 1992
Capacity: 7,000 bbl
Head Brewer: Jay Misson
Asst. Brewer: John Eecle
Asst. Brewer: Scott Suter
Contact: Lon Lauterio

Nacho Mama's Brewery
42-42 Thompson St
New York City, NY 10013
(212) 925-8966; FAX (212) 925-4607
Founded: Nov. 24, 1995
Contact: Joshua Mandel

Neptune Brewery
448 W 16th St
New York, NY 10011
(212) 229-2129; FAX (212) 366-1934
Founded: June 15, 1995
Capacity: 5,000 bbl
Head Brewer: Paul Levitt
Sales Mgr.: Anne Clark
Contact: Paul Levitt

Old Hampton Brewers Ltd
PO Box 2700
East Hampton, NY 11937
(516) 329-5870; FAX (516) 329-5870
Founded: March 1, 1996
Capacity: 1,800 bbl
Pres.: Page E. Martin
Sec./Treas.: E. Sayre Wiseman
Contact: Page E. Martin

Original Saratoga Springs Brewpub
14 Phila St
Saratoga Springs, NY 12866
(518) 583-3209
Founded: Nov. 25, 1995
Capacity: 3,000 bbl
Asst. Brewer: Matt Furman
Contact: David Terella

Park Slope Brewing Co
356 Sixth Ave
Brooklyn, NY 11215-3403
(718) 788-1756; FAX (718) 788-1758
Founded: Aug. 6, 1994
Capacity: 720 bbl
General Mgr.: Eugene Kaleniak
Head Brewer: Steve Deptula
Contact: Steve Deptula

Parlor City Brewing Co
4 W State St
Binghamton, NY 13901
(607) 772-6900
Founded: Dec. 18, 1995
Contact: David Dellacorino

Rochester Brewpub
800 Jefferson Rd
Henrietta, NY 14623
(716) 272-1550; FAX (716) 424-2173
Founded: April 1, 1988
Capacity: 330 bbl
Owner: Kevin Townsell
Head Brewer: Jeff Snell
Contact: Kevin Townsell

Rohrbach Brewing Co
315 Gregory St
Rochester, NY 14620-1305
(716) 244-5680
Founded: May 1, 1992
Capacity: 600 bbl
Head Brewer: David Schlosser
Pres.: John Urlaub
Contact: John Urlaub

Rohrbach Brewing Co (No 2)
3859 Buffalo Rd
Rochester, NY 14620
Founded: Aug. 1, 1995
Contact: John Urlaub

Saw Mill River Brewing Co
201-C Saw Mill River Rd
Yonkers, NY 10701
(914) 963-4106
Founded: Jan. 1, 1996
Contact: Charles Ewen

Shannon Pub
5050 Main St
Snyder, NY 14226
(716) 839-0002; FAX (716) 839-2042
Founded: April 1, 1995
Capacity: 500 bbl
Head Brewer: Keith Morgan
Contact: Kevin Townsell

Shea's Brewery
445 St Paul St
Rochester, NY 14605
(716) 546-1030; FAX (716) 546-5011
Contact: Mark Holdren

Syracuse Suds Factory
210-216 W Water St
Syracuse, NY 13202
(315) 471-2253; FAX (315) 471-1519
Founded: Feb. 1, 1993
Capacity: 100 bbl
Owner: Al Smith
Head Brewer: Norm Soine
Sales Mgr.: Patty Sheriden
Contact: Al Smith

Troy Brewing Co
417-419 River St
Troy, NY 12180
(518) 273-2337; FAX (518) 273-4834
Founded: Feb. 26, 1993
Capacity: 1,400 bbl
VP/Restaurant Mgr.: Peter Lindley
Pres.: Garrett Brown
Head Brewer: Michael Duerr
Head Chef: Duayne Carrington
Contact: Garrett Brown

Westchester Brewing Co
156 Honey Hollow Rd
Pound Ridge, NY 10576
(914) 763-6280
Contact: Benn Lewis

Westside Brewing Co
340 Amsterdam Ave
New York, NY 10024-6977
(212) 721-2161
Head Brewer: William Kingsbury
Contact: Steve Lagan

Woodstock Brewing Co
PO Box 1000-W/20 St James St
Kingston, NY 12401-4534
(914) 331-2810; FAX (914) 331-2950
Founded: Feb. 1, 1992
Capacity: 10,000 bbl
Pres./Gen. Mgr./Head Brewer: Nat Collins
Sales Mgr.: Nancy Baker
Contact: Nat Collins

Yorkville Brewery & Tavern
1359 First Ave
New York, NY 10021-4403
(212) 517-2739; FAX (212) 517-2005
uptownale@aol.com
Founded: Oct. 25, 1994
Capacity: 1,800 bbl
Head Brewer: Bill Mulligan
Co-Owner: Stephen Ryan
Co-Owner: John Armstrong
Co-Owner: Chris Logan
Co-Owner: Colman McCarthy
Asst. Brewer: Alex Crowe
Asst. Brewer: John Baldy
Contact: Stephen Ryan

Zip City Brewing Co
3 W 18th St
New York, NY 10011-4610
(212) 366-6333; FAX (212) 366-6454
74722.2202@compuserve.com
Founded: Nov. 21, 1991
Capacity: 2,300 bbl
Pres.: Kirby Shyer
Head Brewer: Allan Duvall
Contact: Kirby Shyer

NORTH CAROLINA

Carolina Brewery
PO Box 8/460 W Franklin St
Chapel Hill, NC 27514-0008
(919) 942-1800; FAX (919) 942-1809
ricepatye@aol.com
Founded: Feb. 9, 1995
Contact: Chris Rice

Carolina Brewing Co
140 Thomas Mill Rd
Holly Springs, NC 27540
(919) 557-2337; FAX (919) 557-2338
Founded: July 1, 1995
Capacity: 8,000 bbl
Head Brewer: John Shuck
Contact: Greg Shuck

Carolina Mill Bakery Brewery
122 W Woodlawn Rd
Charlotte, NC 28217-2120
(704) 525-2530; FAX (704) 525-5561
Head Brewer: Jason McKnight
Sales Mgr.: Vince Ditmore
Contact: Jason McKnight

Cottonwood Grille & Brewery
473 Blowing Rock Rd
Boone, NC 28607
(704) 264-7111
baughmankr@conrad.appstate.edu
Founded: Feb. 1, 1992
Capacity: 300 bbl
Operations Mgr.: Brian Lee
CEO: Bart Conway
Head Brewer: Kinney Baughman
Contact: Kinney Baughman

Dilworth Brewing Co
1301 East Blvd
Charlotte, NC 28203
(704) 522-0311; FAX (704) 332-1165
Founded: March 1, 1986
Capacity: 1,200 bbl
Head Brewer: James Muck
Contact: John Begley

Dilworth Micro Brewery
655-R Presley Rd
Charlotte, NC 28217
(704) 522-0311; FAX (704) 332-1165
Founded: April 1, 1989
Capacity: 2,000 bbl
Head Brewer: James Muck
Sales Mgr.: John Begley
Contact: John Begley

Front Street Brewery
9 N Front St
Wilmington, NC 28401
(910) 251-1935; FAX (910) 256-9239
Founded: June 1, 1995
Capacity: 600 bbl
Head Brewer: Don Lynch
Contact: John McLatchy

Greenshields Brewery and Pub
214 E Martin St
Raleigh, NC 27601-1863
(919) 829-0214; FAX (919) 828-1013
Founded: July 6, 1989
Capacity: 6,000 bbl
Tres.: Katherine Hemric
Sec.: Martha Greenshields
Pres.: Gary Greenshields
Head Brewer: Thomas Kunzmann
Contact: Gary Greenshields

Highland Brewing Co
PO Box 2351
Asheville, NC 28802-2351
(704) 255-8240; FAX (704) 687-0166
Founded: Dec. 15, 1994
Capacity: 3,000 bbl
Head Brewer/Co-Owner: John McDermott
Co-Owner: Oscar Wong
Head Brewer: John Lyda
Sales Mgr.: John McDermitt
Contact: John McDermott

Johnson Beer Co
2210 South Blvd
Charlotte, NC 28203
(704) 339-0340; FAX (704) 339-0360
jcbbeer@aol.com
Founded: March 1, 1995
Capacity: 10,000 bbl
Head Brewer: Timothy Johnson
Sales Mgr.: Susan Johnson
Contact: Susan Johnson

Miller Brewing Co
PO Box 3327/863 E Meadow Rd
Eden, NC 27288-2099
(919) 627-2100

Capacity: 8,000,000 bbl
Plant Mgr.: James M. Daly, Jr.
Oper. Mgr.: Leornard D. McCumber, Jr.
Brewing Mgr.: I. Patricia Henry
Contact: James M. Daly

Old North State Brewing Co
4329 Basal Creek Lane
Fuquay-Varina, NC 27526
(919) 557-7321
Founded: April 30, 1996
Contact: Michael James

Old Raleigh Brewing Co
2810-5F Yonkers Rd
Raleigh, NC 27604
(919) 833-7644; FAX (919) 832-9914
Founded: June 1, 1995
Capacity: 1,000 bbl
Head Brewer: Ed Meeks
Contact: Mark Mosley

Olde Hickory Brewing Co
2828 Hwy 70 W
Hickory, NC 28602
(704) 323-8753; FAX (704) 327-3292
slyerly@aol.com
Founded: Jan. 2, 1995
Capacity: 700 bbl
Owner/Sales Mgr.: Jason Yates
Head Brewer: Steven Lyerly
Contact: Steven Lyerly

Pinehurst Village Brewery
3914 Sweeten Creek Rd
Chapel Hill, NC 27514
(910) 295-4545; FAX (910) 295-0341
Founded: April 1, 1996
Capacity: 5,000 bbl
Head Brewer: Jim Hearl
Sales Mgr.: Tom Horley
Contact: Jim Hearl

Queen City Bakery and Brewery
122 W Woodlawn Rd
Charlotte, NC 28217
Founded: March 15, 1996

Smokey Mountain Brewery
92 Stamey Cove Rd
Waynesville, NC 28786
(704) 648-8354
Founded: March 22, 1993
Capacity: 1,200 bbl
Contact: Rich Prochaska

United States Breweries (North Carolina–Ohio)

Southend Brewery and Smokehouse
2100 South Blvd
Charlotte, NC 28203
(704) 358-4677; FAX (704) 358-9960
southend@interserv.com
Founded: April 1, 1995
Capacity: 2,500 bbl
Head Brewer: Pat Johnson
Brewer: Larry Drago
Sales Mgr.: Joe Ryan
Contact: Joe Ryan00

Spring Garden Brewing Co
5804 Hunt's Club Rd
Greensboro, NC 27410-4119
(910) 299-3649; FAX (910) 292-8156
Founded: March 1, 1994
Capacity: 2,500 bbl
Head Brewer: Christian Boos
Pres.: Bill Sherrill
Contact: Bill Sherrill

Stroh Brewery Co
4791 Schlitz Ave
PO Drawer T/Salem Station
Winston-Salem, NC 27108-0410
(919) 788-6710
Capacity: 5,500,000 bbl
Plant Mgr.: W. R. Abt
Packaging Mgr.: T. F. Ganas
Contact: W. R. Abt

Tomcat Brewing Co
1249 Wicker Dr
Raleigh, NC 27604
(919) 834-9200; FAX (919) 834-8040
tomcatales@aol.com
Founded: March 22, 1996
Capacity: 7,500 bbl
Pres.: Thomas Tomlinson
Brewing Dir.: Daniel Thomasson
Contact: Thomas Tomlinson

Weeping Radish Restaurant and Brewery
PO Box 1471/Hwy 64 E
Manteo, NC 27954-1471
(919) 473-1880; FAX (919) 473-5030
Founded: July 1, 1986
Capacity: 2,700 bbl
Head Brewer: Paul Hummer
Head Brewer: Andy Duck
Sec./Business Mgr.: Bonnie Duvall
Pres./Sales Mgr.: Uli Bennewitz
Contact: Bonnie Dunall

Weeping Radish Brewery (No 2)
115 N Duke St
Durham, NC 27701-2010
(919) 688-2739
Founded: Jan. 1, 1988
Capacity: 2,600 bbl
Contact: Paul Hummer

Wilmington Brewing Co Inc
111 Bryan Rd
Wilmington, NC 28412-7033
(910) 791-2337; FAX (910) 791-0186
Founded: Dec. 1, 1994
Capacity: 3,000 bbl
Pres./Sales Mgr.: Tom Dergay
Head Brewer: Melinda Woods
Dir. Public Relations: Pam Suhre
Brewer: Jeff Williams
Contact: Thomas Dergay

NORTH DAKOTA

Great Northern Brewing Co
425 Broadway
Fargo, ND 58102
(701) 235-9707; FAX (701) 235-5087
Founded: Nov. 18, 1995
Contact: Ray Taylor

Old Broadway
16 Broadway/Suite 212
Fargo, ND 58102
(701) 237-6161; FAX (701) 237-3395
Founded: Feb. 1, 1995
Capacity: 700 bbl
Head Brewer: Michael Johnston
Sales Mgr.: Warren Ackley
Contact: Michael Johnston

Rattlesnake Creek Brewery
PO Box 1475
Dickinson, ND 58602
(701) 225-9518; FAX (701) 225-9518
Founded: Dec. 13, 1995
Owner: Kirk Martinez
Head Brewer: Joel Anderson
Contact: Joel Anderson

OHIO

Alessis Ristorante/ Garretts Mill Brewing Co
8148 Main St
Garrettsville, OH 44231
(216) 527-5849
Founded: Aug. 1, 1995
Capacity: 300 bbl
Head Brewer: Tom Divis

All American Brewing Co
6528 Riverside Dr
Dublin, OH 43017
(614) 889-1199
Founded: Nov. 1, 1994
Contact: Scott Francis

Anheuser-Busch Inc
700 E Schrock Rd
Columbus, OH 43229
(614) 888-6644
Capacity: 6,900,000 bbl
Plant Mgr.: Ronald Morgan
Resident Brewmaster: C. Goetsch
Contact: Ronald Morgan

Barley's Brewing Co
467 N High St
Columbus, OH 43215-2007
(614) 228-2537
Founded: Nov. 20, 1992
Head Brewer: Scott Francis
Contact: Scott Francis

Barrel House Brewing Co
22 E 12th St
Cincinnati, OH 45210
(513) 421-2337; FAX (513) 421-8478
http://www.barrelhouse.com
Founded: June 30, 1995
Head Brewer: Rick J. DeBar
VP: Mike Cromer
Pres.: David Rich
Contact: Rick DeBar

Burkhardt Brewing Co
3700 Massillon Rd
Uniontown, OH 44685-9589
(216) 896-9200; FAX (216) 896-4012
Sales Mgr.: Jennifer Heinbuch
Head Brewer: Thomas Burkhardt
Contact: Thomas Burkhardt

Columbus Brewing Co
476 S Front St
Columbus, OH 43215-5627
(614) 224-3626; FAX (614) 241-2080
Founded: Jan. 1, 1989
Capacity: 1,950 bbl
Brewmaster: Ben Pridgeon
Brewer: Matt Lewis
Contact: Ben Pridgeon

Crooked River Brewing Co
1101 Center St
Cleveland, OH 44113-2405
(216) 771-2337; FAX (216) 771-7990
Founded: Aug. 17, 1994
Capacity: 10,000 bbl
Pres./Brewmaster: Stephen Danckers
Sales and Mktg. Dir.: Stuart Sheridan
Contact: Stephan Danckers

**Firehouse
Brewery and Restaurant**
3216 Silsby Rd
Cleveland Heights, OH 44118
(216) 397-3232
Founded: Jan. 1, 1996
Capacity: 2,800 bbl
Head Brewer: Henryk Orlik
Primary Contact: Nick Gantam
Contact: Nick Gautam

Gambrinus Brewing Co
1152 S Front St
Columbus, OH 43206-3405
(614) 444-7769; FAX (614) 444-6662
dfoster@aol.com
Founded: Oct. 1, 1993
Capacity: 2,000 bbl
Hallis: Mike Venrick
Treas.: Wayne Logan
VP Sales: Wayne Foster
VP Operations: Lee Spangler
Brewmaster/Pres.: David Foster
Contact: David Foster

Great Lakes Brewing Co
2516 Market St
Cleveland, OH 44113-3434
(216) 771-4404; FAX (216) 771-4466
Founded: Sept. 1, 1988
Capacity: 13,000 bbl
Principal Contact: Daniel Conway
Brewmaster: Andrew Tveekrem
Master Brewer: Thaine Johnson
Contact: Daniel Conway

Hoster Brewing Co
550 S High St
Columbus, OH 43215-5607
(614) 228-6066; FAX (614) 228-0102
Founded: Nov. 11, 1990
Capacity: 4,000 bbl
Brewmaster: Victor Ecimovich
Head Brewer: Vince Falcone
Sales Mgr.: John Weixel
Contact: Victor Ecimovich

**Hudepohl-Schoenling
Brewing Co**
1625 Central Pkwy
Cincinnati, OH 45214-2423
(513) 241-4344; FAX (513) 241-2190
Founded: Dec. 31, 1985
Mktg. Dir.: Kathleen Lichtendahl
Pres.: Kenneth Lichtendahl
Head Brewer: John Piening
Sales Mgr.: R. J. Bozsan
Contact: Kenneth Lichtendahl

Liberty Street Brewing Co
1238 Weathervane Lane
Akron, OH 44313
(216) 869-2337; FAX (216) 869-2328
Founded: Dec. 20, 1994
Capacity: 1,600 bbl
Brewmaster: Tim Rastetter
Co-Owner: Chuck Graybill
Co-Owner: Rory O'Neill
Contact: Tim Rastetter

Lift Bridge Brewing Co
PO Box 2856/1119 Lake Ave
Ashtabula, OH 44004-2929
(216) 964-6200; FAX (216) 998-0285
Founded: Dec. 9, 1990
Capacity: 1,200 bbl
Head Brewer: Daniel L. Madden
Sales Mgr.: Kenneth Frisbie
Contact: Dan Madden

**Main Street Brewery/
Queen City Brewing Co**
1203 Main St
Cincinnati, OH 45210-2311
(513) 665-4677; FAX (513) 665-7842
Founded: Nov. 28, 1994
Capacity: 2,300 bbl
Head Brewer: Toby Hunt
Brewer: Vince Bryant
Brewer: Jim Elkus
Contact: Jim Elkus

Maumee Bay Brewing Co
27 Broadway
Toledo, OH 43602
(419) 241-1253; FAX (419) 243-9256
Founded: Nov. 15, 1995
Capacity: 1,600 bbl
Head Brewer: Norman A. Dixon
Sales Mgr.: Debra West
Asst. Brewer: Ric Herrold
Contact: Norman A. Dixon

Miller Brewing Co
2525 Wayne Madison Rd
PO Box 2165
Trenton, OH 45067
(513) 896-9200
Capacity: 7,500,000 bbl
Plant Mgr.: Dennis B. Puffer
Oper. Mgr.: William P. McIntyre
Brewing Mgr.: F. Ed Novess
Contact: Dennis B. Puffer

O'Hooleys Pub and Brewery
24 W Union St
Athens, OH 45701
(614) 592-9686; FAX (614) 594-2358
Founded: April 1, 1996
Head Brewer: Terry Hawbaker
Contact: Jim Prouty

**Ringneck Brewing Co/
The Brew Kettle Inc**
15143 Pearl Rd
Strongsville, OH 44136
(216) 846-4677; FAX (216) 846-4675
Founded: Dec. 23, 1995
Capacity: 3,000 bbl
Pres.: J. Chris McKim
VP: James A. McKim
Sec./Treas.: Pamela C. McKim
Contact: J. Chris McKim

**Rock Bottom
Brewery (No 8) at Cleveland**
2000 Sycamore St/Suite 260
Cleveland, OH 44113
(216) 623-1555; FAX (216) 623-1551
brewer6362@aol.com
Founded: Sept. 17, 1995
Capacity: 2,500 bbl
Head Brewer: Steven Miller
Contact: Steven Miller

Wallaby's Grill & Brewpub
30005 Clemens Rd
Westlake, OH 44145
(216) 808-1700
Founded: May 15, 1995
Capacity: 1,000 bbl
CEO: Nicholas Alexakos
Sec.: James Alexakos
Head Brewer: Joseph Marunowski
Asst. Brewer: Brad Unruh
Contact: Joseph Marunowski

Western Reserve Brewing Co
5074 W Streetsboro Rd
Richfield, OH 44286
(216) 659-4884
Contact: Dave Sutula

United States Breweries (Ohio–Oregon)

Wooden Pony Brewing Co
37 E Fourth St
Mansfield, OH 44902
(419) 524-2739; FAX (419) 524-2729
kiplikm@erinet.com
http://www.erinet.com/woodpony
Founded: Feb. 19, 1996
Head Brewer/Sales Mgr.: Larry Horwitz
Contact: Don Welch

OKLAHOMA

Belle Isle Brewing Co
50 Penn Pl
Oklahoma City, OK 73118
(405) 840-1911; FAX (405) 840-4488
Founded: Aug. 28, 1995
Head Brewer: Jack Sparks
Contact: Neal Harden

Bricktown Brewery
Mull Corporation
6403 N Grand Blvd/Suite 200
Oklahoma City, OK 73116
(405) 843-0006; FAX (405) 842-6416
Founded: Oct. 18, 1992
Capacity: 4,000 bbl
CEO: Tom McLain
Contact: Tom McLain

Cherry Street Brewery
PO Box 52217
Tulsa, OK 74152-0217
(918) 582-2739; FAX (918) 582-3299
Founded: Dec. 7, 1993
Head Brewer: Chris Cauthon
Sales Mgr.: Kristin Ferguson
Pres.: Roy Thomason
Contact: Kristin Ferguson

Interurban Brewpub
115 W Main St
Norman, OK 73069-1308
(405) 364-7942
Founded: June 17, 1994
Capacity: 1,200 bbl
Head Brewer: Randy Palmer
Sales Mgr.: Robert Lavender
Contact: Robert Ross

Norman Brewing Co
102 W Main St
Norman, OK 73069-1307
(405) 360-5726
Founded: Dec. 15, 1993
VP: Lisa Hooper
Pres.: Jack Hooper
Sec.: Todd Reed

Head Brewer: Brian Smittle
Contact: Brian Smittle

Pete's Place
PO Box 66/120 SW Eighth St
Krebs, OK 74554
(918) 423-2042; FAX (918) 423-7859
Founded: Nov. 1, 1995
Capacity: 500 bbl
Head Brewer: Michael Lalli
Contact: Joe Prichard

Royal Bavaria Brewhaus and Restaurant
3401 S Sooner Rd
Moore, OK 73160
(405) 799-7666; FAX (405) 799-7689
Capacity: 10,000 bbl
Head Brewer: Roger Steely
Contact: Jorg Kuhne

Tulsa Brewing Co
7227 S Memorial Dr
Tulsa, OK 74133-2943
(918) 459-2739
Founded: Aug. 11, 1993
Capacity: 2,200 bbl
Co-Owner: Kenny Tolbert
Co-Owner/Head Brewer: Mike Brotzman
Contact: Mike Brotzman

OREGON

Bandon Brewing Co/ Bandon-by-the-Sea
PO Box 1270/55347 Melton Rd
Bandon, OR 97411-1270
(503) 347-5007; FAX (503) 347-4827
Founded: Aug. 20, 1994
Capacity: 1,800 bbl
Head Brewer: Bob Hawkins
Contact: Bob Hawkins

Bank Brewing Co
201 Central Ave
Coos Bay, OR 97420
(503) 267-0963
Founded: Sept. 1, 1995
Contact: Michael Maas

Bend Brewing Co
PO Box 1340/1019 Brook St
Bend, OR 97709
(503) 383-1599
Founded: Feb. 5, 1995
Capacity: 1,800 bbl
Head Brewer: Scott Salsbury
Contact: Scott Salsbury

Big Horn Brewing Co of Oregon
515 12th St SE
Salem, OR 97301
(503) 363-1904; FAX (503) 375-9327
Founded: Sept. 15, 1995
Capacity: 1,400 bbl
Head Brewer: Tim Chamberlain
Contact: David Hollow

Big Horse Brewpub
115 State St
Hood River, OR 97031
(503) 386-4411; FAX (509) 365-4422
Founded: April 1, 1995
Capacity: 416 bbl
Head Brewer: Randy Orzeck
Sales Mgr.: Susan Orzeck
Contact: Randy Orzeck

Blitz-Weinhard Brewing Co
1133 W Burnside St
Portland, OR 97209-2909
(503) 222-4351

Blue Mountain Brewing
1610 Jefferson Ave
La Grande, OR 97850
(503) 963-5426; FAX (503) 963-5227
Founded: Feb. 29, 1996
Head Brewer: Roy Skendzel
Contact: Rene Skendzel

Blue Pine Brewpub Co
PO Box 471/422 SW Fifth St
Grants Pass, OR 97526-2802
(503) 476-0760
Founded: Sept. 16, 1993
Brewer: Richard Armstrong
Head Brewer: Jerry Elder
Contact: Richard Armstrong

BridgePort Brewing Co
1313 NW Marshall St
Portland, OR 97209-2806
(503) 241-7179; FAX (503) 241-0625
Founded: Nov. 4, 1984
Capacity: 30,000 bbl
Head Brewer: William Lundeen
General Mgr.: Wayne Anderson
Packaging Mgr.: Neal Dickey
Shipping: Carolyn Johnston
Contact: Paula Fasano
Subsidiary of Gambrinus Importing Co.

Cascade Lakes Brewing Co
2141 SW First St
Redmond, OR 97756-9608
(503) 923-3110

Founded: Nov. 20, 1994
Capacity: 4,000 bbl
Head Brewer/Gen. Mgr.: Dave Gazeley
Sales Mgr./Asst. Gen. Mgr.: Steve Gazeley
Sec/Treas.: Danielle Gazeley
Contact: Steve Gazeley

Cascade Microbrewery and Public Firehouse
3529 Fairview Industrial Dr SE
Salem, OR 97302
(503) 378-0737; FAX (503) 315-7330
Founded: Aug. 7, 1995
Contact: Tim Maroney

Cornelius Pass Roadhouse and Brewery/McMenamins
4045 NW Cornelius Pass Rd
Hillsboro, OR 97124-9367
(503) 640-6174; FAX (503) 640-2930
Founded: July 1, 1986
Contact: Bart Hance

Deschutes Brewery and Public House
901 SW Simpson Ave
Bend, OR 97702-3118
(503) 385-8606; FAX (503) 383-4505
Founded: Aug. 15, 1993
Capacity: 46,000 bbl
Sales Mgr.: John Bryant
Head Brewer: Bill Pengelly
Brewery Operations: Tim Gossack
Packaging: Ron Allen
Pres.: Gary Fish
Contact: Gary Fish

Deschutes Brewery (No 2)
1044 Bond St NW
Bend, OR 97701-2002
(503) 382-9242; FAX (503) 383-4505
Founded: June 28, 1988
Capacity: 4,000 bbl
Head Brewer: Mark Vickery
Pres.: Gary Fish
Restaurant Gen. Mgr.: Bill Panton
Contact: Gary Fish

Edgefield Brewery/McMenamins
2126 SW Halsey St
Troutdale, OR 97060-1026
(503) 667-4352; FAX (503) 665-8295
http://McMenamin.com/~edge/index
Founded: Jan. 1, 1991
Capacity: 5,000 bbl
Head Brewer: Eric Lengvenis
Brewery Mgr.: Mike Altman
Contact: Mike Altman

Eugene City Brewing Co/West Brothers Bar-B-Q
844 Olive St
Eugene, OR 97401-2935
(503) 345-8489; FAX (503) 345-4026
Founded: July 1, 1993
Capacity: 1,200 bbl
Co-Owner: Mike West
Co-Owner: Jim West
Co-Owner: Phil West
Head Brewer: Tim Barr
Contact: Tim Barr

Field's Restaurant & Brewpub
1290 Oak St
Eugene, OR 97401
(503) 345-8584; FAX (503) 465-1325
dps@rio.com
http://www.rio.com/nfields
Founded: Oct. 25, 1995
Capacity: 1,200 bbl
Head Brewer: David Sohigian
Contact: John Kieran

Full Sail Brewing Co (No 2)/Pilsener Room at Riverplace
0307 SW Montgomery
Portland, OR 97201-5125
(503) 222-5343; FAX (503) 222-3771
Founded: April 1, 1993
Capacity: 5,000 bbl
Brewmaster: John Harris
Brewer: Peter Kruger
Brewer: Chris Morton
Contact: John Harris

Full Sail Brewing Co/WhiteCap Brewpub and Tasting Room
506 Columbia St
Hood River, OR 97031-2000
(503) 386-2247; FAX (503) 386-7316
Founded: Sept. 1, 1987
Capacity: 100,000 bbl
Head Brewer: John Harris
Asst. Brewer: Jim Kelter
Asst. Brewer: Greg Knutson
Sales/Mktg. Dir.: Jerome Chicvara
General Mgr.: Irene Firmat
Exec. Brewmaster: James Emmerson
Sales Mgr.: Greg Herman
Contact: Irene Firmat

Fulton Pub and Brewery/McMenamins
618 SW Nebraska St
Portland, OR 97201-3556
(503) 246-4363
Founded: July 2, 1988
Capacity: 1,100 bbl

Owner: Mike McManamin
Head Brewer: Daniel Rothman
Sales Mgr.: Ed Lawrence
Contact: Todd Meister

Golden Valley Brewery & Pub
980 E Fourth St
McMinnville, OR 97128-4308
(503) 472-2739; FAX (503) 434-8523
Founded: Dec. 20, 1993
Capacity: 1,000 bbl
Head Brewer: John R. Eliassen
Owner: Peter Kircher
VP: Celia Kircher
Contact: Peter Kircher

Hair of the Dog Brewing Co
4509 SE 23rd Ave
Portland, OR 97202-4771
(503) 232-6585; FAX (503) 234-6687
doug@teleport.com
http://www.teleport.com/~doug/
Founded: Aug. 23, 1993
Capacity: 300 bbl
Brewer/Sales Mgr.: Doug Henderson
Brewer: Alan Sprints
Contact: Doug Henderson

High Street Brewery and Cafe/McMenamins
1243 High St
Eugene, OR 97401-3207
(503) 345-4913; FAX (503) 686-4320
Contact: Steve Van Rossem

Highland Pub and Brewery/McMenamin's
4225 SE 182nd Ave
Gresham, OR 97030-5082
(503) 665-3015
Founded: June 1, 1988
Capacity: 1,000 bbl
Pub Mgr.: Mike Laschiver
Head Brewer: Tom Reeder
Brewery Mgr.: Keith Mackie
Contact: Ty Reeder

Hillsdale Brewery and Public House/McMenamins
1505 SW Sunset Blvd
Portland, OR 97201-2625
(503) 293-1735
Founded: Oct. 1, 1985
Capacity: 925 bbl
Head Brewer: Michael Altman
General Mgr.: Chris Wilson
Contact: Mike Hogan

United States Breweries (Oregon)

John Barleycorn's/McMenamins
14610 SW Sequoia
Tigard, OR 97209
(503) 684-2688
Founded: March 14, 1996
Capacity: 600 bbl
Contact: Todd Meister

Lighthouse Brewery and Public House/Mcmenamins
4157 N Hwy 101
Lincoln City, OR 97367
(503) 994-9678; FAX (503) 994-9401
Founded: July 1, 1986
Capacity: 780 bbl
Head Brewer: Keith Mackie
Contact: Kevin Tillotsen

Lucky Labrador Brew Pub
915 SE Hawthorne
Portland, OR 97214-3545
(503) 236-3555
http://www.delta-9.com/LuckyLab
Founded: Oct. 15, 1994
Capacity: 700 bbl
Head Brewer: Alex Stiles
Contact: Gary Geist

Maroney Sausage Est/ Widmer Brothers Brewing Co
One Center Ct/Suite 120
Portland, OR 97227
(503) 281-2437
Founded: April 1, 1996
Contact: Rob Widmer

McMenamins/Murray and Allen
6179 SW Murray Blvd
Beaverton, OR 97005-4421
(503) 526-9618
Founded: Jan. 1, 1990
Capacity: 720 bbl
Pres.: Mike McMenamin
Head Brewer: Thomas Keins
Sales Mgr.: Keith Mackie
Contact: Doug Goding

McMenamins/West Linn Pub
2090 SW Eighth Ave
West Linn, OR 97068-4612
(503) 656-2935
Founded: Nov. 4, 1992
Capacity: 850 bbl
General Mgr.: Bob Bednarek
Head Brewer: Daniel Rothman
Contact: Rob Vallance

Mount Angel Brewing Co
PO Box 377/210 Monroe St
Mount Angel, OR 97362
(503) 845-9624; FAX (503) 845-9891
Founded: July 30, 1995
Sales Mgr.: Joe Rapport
Head Brewer: Curt Gouverneur
Pres.: Randy Traeger
Contact: Curtis Gouverneur

Mount Hood Brewing Co
PO Box 56
87304 E Govt Camp Loop
Government Camp, OR 97028
(503) 272-0102
Founded: Oct. 8, 1992
Capacity: 3,200 bbl
Brewmaster/Operations Mgr.: Jon Graber
Pres.: Kevin Kohnstamm
Contact: Jon Graber

Multnomah Brewery
1603 SE Pardee St
Portland, OR 97202-4733
(503) 236-3106
Contact: Jeff Hendryx

Nor'wester Brewery and Public House
66 SE Morrison St
Portland, OR 97214-2110
(503) 232-9771; FAX (503) 232-2363
norwester.com
http://www.Norwester.com
Founded: Nov. 20, 1995
Capacity: 39,000 bbl
General Mgr.: Karlin Conklin
Pres.: Jim Berneau
Head Brewer: Andrew Fratianni
Sales Dir.: Kevin Chambers
Production Mgr.: Allan Castagne
Contact: Karlin Conklin

Oak Hills Brewpub/McMenamins
14740 NW Cornell Rd/Suite 80
Portland, OR 97229-5400
(503) 645-0117
Contact: Jeff Kennelly

Old Chicago Brewery & Pub
11211 SE 82nd
Portland, OR 97266
(503) 786-5009; FAX (503) 786-5158
Founded: Dec. 25, 1994
Capacity: 200 bbl
Head Brewer: Debbie Svoboda
Restaurant Mgr.: Matt Oquita
Contact: Matt Oquita

Old Market Pub & Brewery
6959 SW Garden Home Rd
Portland, OR 97223-9543
(503) 244-0450
Founded: April 13, 1994
Contact: Shelly Bigley

Oregon Fields Brewing Co
1290 Oak St
Eugene, OR 97401-3542
(503) 345-6599; FAX (503) 465-1325
dps@rio.com
http://surf.rio.com/~fields/fields.html
Founded: Oct. 22, 1994
Capacity: 1,000 bbl
Head Brewer: David Sohigian
Comptroller: Kristy Running
Asst. Brewer: Scott Thompson
Head Chef: Frank Beber
General Mgr.: John Kieran
Contact: David Sohigian

Oregon Trader Brewing Co
PO Box 447/140 Hill St
Albany, OR 97321-0128
(503) 928-1931; FAX (503) 928-1931
Founded: Oct. 10, 1993
Capacity: 1,200 bbl
Sales Mgr.: Jerry Mathern
Head Brewer: Eric Munger
Contact: Jerry Mathern

Oregon Trail Brewery
341 SW Second St
Corvallis, OR 97333-4640
(503) 758-3527
Capacity: 1,200 bbl
Head Brewer: Jerry Bockmore
Contact: Dave Wills

Osprey Ale Brewing Co
404 E Main
Medford, OR 97525
(503) 855-9826
Founded: April 1, 1996
Contact: Larry Bruce

Pacific City Brewing Co
PO Box 189
Pacific City, OR 97135
(503) 965-7779; FAX (503) 965-7778
pelpub@aol.com
Founded: April 15, 1996
Capacity: 1,000 bbl
Head Brewer: Darron Welch
Contact: Darron Welch

United States Breweries (Oregon)

Philadelphia's
6410 SE Milwaukie Ave
Portland, OR 97202
(503) 239-8544
Contact: Andy Armstrong

Portland Brewing Co
2730 NW 31st Ave
Portland, OR 97210-1781
(503) 226-7623; FAX (503) 226-2702
Founded: Feb. 1, 1986
Capacity: 2,000 bbl
Head Brewer: Chris Harley
Contact: Fred Bowman

Portland Brewing Co (No 2)
2730 NW 31st Ave
Portland, OR 97210-1718
(503) 226-7623; FAX (503) 226-2702
Founded: Feb. 15, 1986
Capacity: 105,000 bbl
Sales Mgr.: Mark Carver
Head Brewer: Matt Munoz
VP Mktg.: Gene Clark
Pres.: Tony Adams
VP: Fred Bowman
Contact: Fred Bowman

Rock Bottom Brewery (No 4)
206 SW Morrison St
Portland, OR 97204
(503) 796-2739; FAX (503) 796-1051
Founded: Dec. 19, 1994
Capacity: 3,000 bbl
Head Brewer: Matt Sage
General Mgr.: Gregg Schillinger
Brewer: David Myers
Brewer: Deb Svboda
Contact: Gregg Schillinger

**Rogue Ales/
Oregon Brewing Co**
2320 OSU Dr
Newport, OR 97365
(541) 867-3660; FAX (541) 867-3260
rogue@pstat.com
http://realbeer.com/rogue/
Founded: Oct. 1, 1988
Capacity: 32,000 bbl
Sales Mgr.: Jim Cline
Sec.: Jeff Schultz
VP: Steve Lovin
Pres.: Jack Joyce
Head Brewer: John Maier
Contact: Jack Joyce

Saxer Brewing
PO Box 2298
Lake Oswego, OR 97035-0663
(503) 694-9524; FAX (503) 699-9527
Founded: April 1, 1993
Capacity: 20,000 bbl
Pres.: Steve Goebel
VP Mktg./Sales: Tom Zimmerman
Head Brewer: Tony Gomes
Sales Mgr.: Bill Benowicz
Contact: Kerry Gilbert

Siletz Brewing Co
PO Box 241/243 Gaither
Siletz, OR 97380
(541) 444-7256; FAX (541) 444-2160
Founded: Oct. 31, 1995
Contact: Tony Dilley

Siskyo Brewing Co
31-B Water St
Ashland, OR 97520
(503) 488-5061
Founded: Jan. 15, 1996
Head Brewer: Tod Kemp
Contact: Jack Joyce

**Spencer's
Restaurant and Brewhouse**
980 Kruse Way
Springfield, OR 97477
(503) 726-1726; FAX (503) 744-9358
Founded: May 18, 1995
Head Brewer: Anders Johansen
Owner: David Andrews
Asst. Brewer: Gary Nance
Contact: Anders Johansen

Star Brewing Co
5231 NE Martin Luther
King Junior Blvd
Portland, OR 97211-3235
(503) 282-6003; FAX (503) 282-6003
Founded: April 1, 1993
Capacity: 3,500 bbl
Treas.: Vicky Wenzel
Pres./Head Brewer: Scott Wenzel
Sales Mgr.: Rob Stone
Contact: Scott Wenzel

Steelhead Brewery & Cafe
199 E Fifth Ave
Eugene, OR 97401-8715
(503) 686-2739
Founded: Jan. 22, 1991
Capacity: 1,700 bbl
General Mgr.: Jeff Passerotti
Head Brewer: Teri Fahrendorf
Contact: Jeff Passerotti

**Thompson
Brewpub/McMenamins**
3575 Liberty Rd S
Salem, OR 97302-5621
(503) 371-2945; FAX (503) 371-2945
Founded: Jan. 11, 1990
Capacity: 800 bbl
Sales Mgr.: Mark Yelton
Head Brewer: David Lederfine
Contact: David Lederfine

Tugboat Brewpub & Cafe
711 SW Ankeny St
Portland, OR 97205-3703
(503) 226-2508
Contact: Terry Nelson

Umpqua Brewing Co
328 Jackson St
Roseburg, OR 97470-3473
(503) 672-0452; FAX (503) 672-0660
Founded: March 27, 1991
Capacity: 3,000 bbl
Pres./Owner: Michael Murphy
Sales Mgr./Head Brewer: Michael Murphy
Contact: Michael Murphy

**Widmer Brothers Brewing
Co/Widmer Brothers Gasthaus**
929 N Russell St
Portland, OR 97227-1733
(503) 281-2437; FAX (503) 281-1496
Founded: Jan. 1, 1985
Capacity: 335,000 bbl
Head Brewer: Sebastian Pastore
CFO: Mike Nicholls
VP: Rob Widmer
Pres.: Kurt Widmer
Sales Mgr.: Jim L. Ford
Contact: Kurt Widmer

**Widmer Brothers Brewing Co
B Moloch/Heathman Pub**
923 SW Ninth Ave
Portland, OR 97205-2401
(503) 221-0631; FAX (503) 231-1496
Founded: May 1, 1988
Capacity: 2,700 bbl
Head Brewer: Jim Powell
Contact: Jim Powell

**Wild Duck
Brewery and Restaurant**
169 W Sixth St
Eugene, OR 97401
(503) 485-3825

Founded: Feb. 1, 1996
Capacity: 2,160 bbl
Sales Mgr./Contact: Pat McCallum
Head Brewer: Glen Falconer
Contact: Bob Jensen

Wild River
Brewing and Pizza Co
144 Kenrose Lane
Cave Junction, OR 97523-9651
(503) 592-3556; FAX (503) 471-9390
Founded: July 1, 1990
Capacity: 1,000 bbl
Owner: Bertha Miller
Head Brewer: Hubert Smith
Owner: Jerry Miller
Contact: Hubert Smith

Wild River
Brewing and Pizza Co (No 2)
595 NE East St
Grants Pass, OR 97526-1944
(503) 471-7487; FAX (503) 471-9390
Founded: Dec. 15, 1994
Capacity: 1,500 bbl
Head Brewer: Hubert Smith
Owner: Jerry Miller
Owner: Bertha Miller
Contact: Hubert Smith

PENNSYLVANIA

Arrowhead Brewing Co
1667 Orchard Dr
Chambersburg, PA 17201-9206
(717) 264-0101
Founded: Dec. 16, 1991
Capacity: 6,000 bbl
Sec./CFO: Cynthia Mead
Pres./Head Brewer/CEO: Francis Mead
Contact: Francis Mead

Barley Creek Brewing Co Inc
RR 1/Box 185
Sullivan Trail/Camelback Rd
Tannersville, PA 18372
(717) 629-9399; FAX (717) 595-2649
Founded: Dec. 17, 1995
Capacity: 2,500 bbl
Head Brewer: Luca Evans
Sales Mgr.: Trip Ruvane
Contact: Joseph "Trip" Ruvane

Buckingham
Mountain Brewing Co/
McGallen Brewing Co
PO Box 500
Lahaska, PA 18931
(215) 794-0440
Founded: Sept. 20, 1995
Head Brewer: Jack Owen
Contact: Donna McGowan

D G Yuengling & Son Inc
Fifth and Manhantongo
Pottsville, PA 17901
(717) 622-4141
Founded: Jan. 1, 1929
Capacity: 170,000 bbl
Contact: George Smith

Dock St Brewing Co
Brewery and Restaurant
2 Logan Sq
Philadelphia, PA 19103-2707
(215) 496-0413; FAX (215) 668-1837
Founded: Oct. 15, 1990
Capacity: 2,080 bbl
Head Brewer: Nicholas D. Funnell
Dir. of Public Relations: Rosemarie Certo
Pres.: Jeffrey Ware
Sales Mgr. Eastern Regions: Andrew O'Rourke
Contact: Nick Funnel

Erie Brewing Co/
Hoppers Brewpub
123 W 14th St
Erie, PA 16501-1717
(814) 452-2787; FAX (814) 459-7488
Founded: Nov. 10, 1994
Capacity: 2,000 bbl
Head Brewer: Brian Hollinger
Pres.: Jim Williams
VP: Jason Williams
Contact: Brian Hollinger

Independence Brewing Co
1000 E Comley St
Philadelphia, PA 19149
(215) 537-2337; FAX (215) 537-4677
Founded: April 26, 1995
Capacity: 12,500 bbl
Head Brewer: William Moore
Sales Mgr.: Dave Masterson
Asst. Brewer/Sales Mgr.: Gregory Letter
Contact: Bob Connor

Jones Brewing Co
PO Box 746
Smithton, PA 15479-0746
(412) 872-2337; FAX (412) 872-6538
Founded: Jan. 1, 2007
Capacity: 70,000 bbl
Head Brewer: Greg King
Pres./Treas./Sales Mgr.: Gabriel Podlucky, Jr.
VP/Sec.: Sandra M. Podlucky
Sales Mgr.: Rob Caruso
Contact: Gabriel Podlucky

Lancaster Malt Brewing Co
302-304 N Plum St
Lancaster, PA 17602
(717) 391-6258; FAX (717) 391-6015
Founded: April 18, 1995
Capacity: 8,000 bbl
Master Brewer: Christian Heim
Sales Mgr.: Bob Grote
Contact: Mike Oehrlein

Latrobe Brewing Co
PO Box 350
Latrobe, PA 15650-0350
(412) 537-5545; FAX (412) 537-4035
Founded: June 1, 1939
Capacity: 1,500,000 bbl
Brewmaster: Mike Fitzpatrick
VP Operations: Al Spinelli

Lion Inc/
Gibbons-Stegmaier Brewery
700 N Pennsylvania Ave
Wilkes-Barre, PA 18703-2451
(717) 823-8801; FAX (717) 823-6686
Head Brewer: Leo Orlandini
Pres.: Charles E. Lawson
Contact: Charles Lawson

Manayunk Malt & Hops Co
PO Box 41086
Philadelphia, PA 19127
(800) 625-8467; FAX (215) 487-0652
Founded: May 27, 1994
Capacity: 300 bbl
Contact: Stephen Rosati

Philadelphia Brewing Co/
Samuel Adams Brewhouse
1516 Sansom St/Second Floor
Philadelphia, PA 19102-2804
(215) 563-2326; FAX (215) 567-0476
Founded: Nov. 28, 1989
Capacity: 1,000 bbl
Pres.: Judi Mink
Head Brewer: William Reed
Contact: William Reed

Pittsburgh Brewing Co
3340 Liberty Ave
Pittsburgh, PA 15201-1321
(412) 682-7400; FAX (412) 682-2379
Capacity: 1,250,000 bbl
Head Brewer: Mike Carota
Marketing Mgr.: Tim McAleer
Contact: Mike Carrotta

Red Bell Brewing Co
PO Box 2168
Philadelphia, PA 19103-0168
(215) 822-7117
Founded: April 30, 1996
Contact: Jim Bell

Sly Fox Brewhouse & Eatery
Route 113 Pikeland Village Sq
Phoenixville, PA 19460
(610) 935-4540; FAX (610) 935-4541
Founded: Dec. 20, 1995
Contact: Pete Giannopoulos

Stoudt Brewery
PO Box 880
Adamstown, PA 19501-0880
(717) 484-4386; FAX (717) 484-4182
Founded: June 17, 1987
Capacity: 10,000 bbl
Pres.: Carol Stoudt
Sales Mgr.: Kevin Chrusciel
Brewer: Kevin Sondey
Brewer: John Smulowitz
Salesperson: Robert Rudgers
Salesperson: Floyd Craft
Salesperson: Tyrone Irby
Contact: Carol Stoudt

Straub Brewery
303 Sorg St
St. Mary's, PA 15857-1537
(814) 834-2875; FAX (814) 834-7628
Founded: Jan. 1, 1972
Capacity: 33,000 bbl
CEO: Thomas J. Straub
Pres.: Daniel A. Straub
VP Sales and Mktg.: Terry L. Straub
Head Brewer: Thomas J. Straub
Sales Mgr.: Terry L. Straub
Contact: Dan Straub

Stroh Brewery Co
Lehigh Valley Plant
PO Box 25013
Lehigh Valley, PA 18002-5013
(215) 395-6811
Plant Mgr.: T. P. Knabe
Master Brewer: Dan Melideo
Packaging Mgr.: E. Ybarra
Contact: T. P. Knabe

Ugly Dog Brewery Inc
PO Box 3526
West Chester, PA 19381
(610) 430-8060; FAX (610) 431-4800
Founded: Nov. 1, 1995
Contact: Cliff Short

Valley Forge Brewing Co Restaurant and Pub
267 E Swedesford Rd
Wayne, PA 19087
(610) 687-8700; FAX (610) 687-8549
Founded: May 1, 1995
Capacity: 1,300 bbl
Head Brewer: Matt Revier
Contact: David Biles

Victory Brewing Co
420 Acorn Lane
Downingtown, PA 19335
(610) 873-0881
Founded: Feb. 15, 1996
Head Brewer: Ron Barchet
Contact: Bill Covaleski

Weyerbacher Brewing Co Inc
20 S Sixth St
Easton, PA 18042
(610) 559-5561; FAX (610) 559-7564
Founded: Sept. 30, 1995
Capacity: 3,000 bbl
Contact: Daniel Weirback

Whitetail Brewing Inc
1600 Pennsylvania Ave
York, PA 17404-1754
(717) 843-6520; FAX (717) 854-9333
Founded: Nov. 7, 1994
Capacity: 2,100 bbl
Head Brewer/Sales Mgr.: Wade Keech
Contact: Wade Keech

Yards Brewing Co
219 Krams Ave
Philadelphia, PA 19127
(215) 482-9109
yardsbrew@aol.com
Founded: May 18, 1995
Capacity: 1,000 bbl
Head Brewer/Co-Owner: Tom Kehoe
Co-Owner/Head Brewer: John Bovit
Contact: Tom Kehoe

RHODE ISLAND

Coddington Brewing Co
210 Coddington Hwy
Middleton, RI 02842
(401) 847-6690
Founded: June 21, 1995
Head Brewer: Forrest Williams
Contact: Forrest Williams

Emerald Isle Brew Works Ltd
11 Bank St
West Warwick, RI 02893-4801
(401) 821-3149; FAX (401) 822-5077
Founded: July 1, 1994
Capacity: 200 bbl
Sales Mgr.: Marilyn McConnell
Head Brewer: Raymond McConnell
Contact: Raymond McConnell

Trinity Beer Works Inc
186 Fountain St
Providence, RI 02903
(401) 453-2337; FAX (401) 861-2498
Founded: Dec. 7, 1994
Capacity: 1,500 bbl
Head Brewer: Kurt Musselman
Contact: Joshua Miller

**Union Station Brewing/
The Brew House LLC**
100 Fountain St
Providence, RI 02903-1845
(401) 274-9300; FAX (401) 274-9302
Founded: Dec. 1, 1993
Capacity: 1,500 bbl
Co-Owner/Sales Mgr.: Joe Gately
Co-Owner: Frank Hennessey
Head Brewer: Rolfe Saunders Reed
General Mgr.: Andy Cook
Brewer: Gregg Motta
Head Brewer: Norm Allaire
Head Chef: Joe Protano
Contact: Joe Gately

SOUTH CAROLINA

Appalachian Ale Works
4776 Anderson Mill Rd
Moore, SC 29369
(803) 574-0716
Founded: April 15, 1996
Capacity: 200 bbl
Head Brewer/Sales Mgr.: Kerry Henderson
Contact: Kerry Henderson

Blue Ridge Brewing Co
PO Box 4677
Greenville, SC 29608-3648
(803) 232-4677; FAX (803) 232-4677
Founded: June 26, 1995
Head Brewer: Charles Lloyd
Contact: Bob Hiller

Chicago Brew Pub
1145 Woodruff Rd
Greenville, SC 29607
(803) 297-3222; FAX (803) 297-6500

Founded: Feb. 27, 1995
Head Brewer: Jim Blume
Contact: Jim Blume

Columbia Brewing Co
931 Senate St
Columbia, SC 29201
(803) 254-2739; FAX (803) 254-4547
Founded: Oct. 18, 1995
Capacity: 1,500 bbl
Contact: Martin Herbkersman

Downtown Brewing Co
18 E North/Suite 100
Greenville, SC
(864) 242-2293; FAX (864) 271-2944
Founded: Oct. 12, 1995
Capacity: 250 bbl
Pres.: Todd King
Dir. of Operations: Larry Grosshams
Head Brewer: Ben Pierson
Contact: Ben Pierson

Hilton Head Brewing Co
7-C Greenwood Dr
Hilton Head Island, SC 29928
(803) 785-2739; FAX (803) 785-8711
Founded: Dec. 15, 1994
Capacity: 2,000 bbl
Head Brewer: Joseph F. Ziegler
Contact: Tony Arcuri

Hunter Gatherer
900 Main St
Columbia, SC 29201
(803) 748-0540
Founded: Oct. 5, 1995
Contact: Kevin Varner

Liberty Steakhouse and Brewery at Broadway at the Beach
1321 Celebrity Cir
Myrtle Beach, SC 29577
(803) 626-4677; FAX (803) 626-2001
Founded: Nov. 7, 1995
Contact: Josh Quigley

Market Street Mill
99 S Market St
Charleston, SC 29401
(803) 722-6100
Founded: June 29, 1995
Contact: Eric Crotty

Palmetto Brewing Co
289 Huger St
Charleston, SC 29403-4522
(803) 937-0903

Founded: May 15, 1994
Capacity: 4,000 bbl
Pres./Sales Mgr.: Louis Bruce
VP/Sales Mgr.: Ed Falkenstein
Head Brewer: Louis Bruce
Head Brewer: Ed Falkenstein
Contact: Louis Bruce

Reedy River Brewing Co
PO Box 5205
Greenville, SC 29606
(864) 948-1400; FAX (864) 879-3768
Founded: Nov. 11, 1995
Capacity: 3,000 bbl
Pres.: Jim Malone
Head Brewer: Dave Bracken
VP: Chuck Rockwell
Contact: Chuck Rockwell

Southeastern Brewing Co
PO Box 720
White Rock, SC 29177
(803) 799-2337
Founded: March 1, 1996
Contact: John Denise

T-Bonz Gill & Grill
1116 Monaco Dr
Mount Pleasant, SC 29464-9035
(803) 769-5852; FAX (803) 856-2444
Founded: May 6, 1995
Capacity: 500 bbl
Head Brewer: Josh Quigley
Contact: Josh Quigley

Vista Brewing Co
936 Gervais St
Columbia, SC 29901
(803) 799-2739
Founded: Jan. 17, 1996
Brewmaster: Jonas Rambert
Contact: I. Barton Dumas

SOUTH DAKOTA

Black Hills Brewing Co
47 Lincoln
Deadwood, SD 57732
(605) 578-2876; FAX (605) 578-2876
Founded: April 15, 1995
Capacity: 400 bbl
Head Brewer: Karl M. Emanuel
Sales Mgr.: Rose McCarty Emanuel
Contact: Karl Emanuel

Firehouse Brewing Co
610 Main St
Rapid City, SD 57701-2736
(605) 348-1915; FAX (605) 341-7898

Founded: Nov. 29, 1991
Capacity: 950 bbl
Pres.: Mark Polenz
Head Brewer: Christopher Jochimsen
Contact: Mark Polenz

Sioux Falls Brewing
PO Box 1304
431 N Phillips Ave/Suite 100
Sioux Falls, SD 57102-0112
(605) 332-4847; FAX (605) 332-4314
Founded: Feb. 23, 1995
Capacity: 1,800 bbl
Chairman: Dean L. Stalheim
Pres./Gen. Mgr.: Mike Pospischil
VP/Head Brewer: Dan Zaayer
Contact: Dean Stalheim

Wild Bill's Brewing Co
1401 E Sioux St
Sioux Falls, SD 57103-2206
(605) 336-3320; FAX (605) 336-3322
Contact: Mike Brzica

TENNESSEE

Big River Grille and Brewing Works (No 1)
222 Broad St
Chattanooga, TN 37402-1009
(423) 267-2739; FAX (423) 266-1199
Founded: Sept. 6, 1993
Capacity: 1,200 bbl
VP/Head Brewer: Rob Gentry
Pres.: Tim Hennen

Big River Grille and Brewing Works (No 2)
111 Broadway
Nashville, TN 37201
(615) 251-4677; FAX (615) 742-3500
Founded: Jan. 1, 1995
Capacity: 1,300 bbl
VP/Head Brewer: Rob Gentry
Pres.: Tim Hennen
Contact: Rob Gentry

Black Horse Brewery/ Franklin St Pub Corp
134 Franklin St
Clarksville, TN 37040
(615) 552-9499
Founded: Aug. 1, 1995
Asst. Brewer: Jeff Smith
Contact: Michael Salyer

**Blackstone
Restaurant and Brewery**
3100 West End Ave/Suite 110
Nashville, TN 37203-1320
(615) 327-9969; FAX (615) 292-4834
Founded: Dec. 31, 1994
Capacity: 1,500 bbl
Partner: Stephanie Weins
Partner: Kent Taylor
Head Brewer: Dave Miller
Contact: Dave Miller

**Bohannon Brewing Co/
Market Street Brewery
and Public House**
134 Second Ave N
Nashville, TN 37201-1902
(615) 242-8223; FAX (615) 242-9851
Founded: May 15, 1989
Sec.: R. Mathews, Jr.
VP: J. Bohannon, Jr.
Pres.: Lindsay Bohannon
Head Brewer: Greg Davis
VP: Buster Williamson
Contact: Lindsay Bohannon

**Bosco's Pizza
Kitchen and Brewery (No 1)**
7615 W Farmington/Suite 30
Germantown, TN 38138-2820
(901) 756-7310; FAX (901) 755-3161
Founded: Dec. 28, 1992
Capacity: 910 bbl
VP: John Kinzel
Sec.: Jim Hooper
Pres./Mgr.: Jerry Feinstone
Head Brewer/VP: Chuck Skypeck
Contact: Chuck Skypeck

**Bosco's
Nashville Brewing Co (No 2)**
1805 21st Ave S
Nashville, TN 37212
(615) 385-0050; FAX (615) 385-0170
Founded: Jan. 18, 1996
Capacity: 1,533 bbl
Pres.: Jerry Fewstowe
VP/Head Brewer: Chuck Skypeck
Mgr.: Jim Hooper
Contact: Chuck Skypeck

Calhoun's BBQ and Brewery
6515 Kingston Pike
Knoxville, TN 37919
(423) 522-3500; FAX (423) 522-8526
Founded: Jan. 10, 1995
Capacity: 1,500 bbl
Head Brewer: Marty Velas

Coors Brewing Co
Memphis Brewery
5151 E Raines Rd
Memphis, TN 38118
(901) 325-2000
Capacity: 5,000,000 bbl
Plant Mgr.: Donald P. Brown
Contact: Donald P. Brown

**Mill Brewery,
Eatery, and Bakery**
4429 Kingston Pike
Knoxville, TN 37919
(615) 588-0080; FAX (423) 588-4050
Founded: Sept. 1, 1995
Capacity: 300 bbl
Head Brewer: Roy Milner
Contact: Dean Owens

TEXAS

Anheuser-Busch Inc
775 Gellhorn Dr
Houston, TX 77029-1405
(713) 675-2311
Capacity: 9,300,000 bbl
Plant Mgr.: R. H. Rathert
Resident Brewmaster: Paul E. Anderson
Contact: R. H. Rathert

**Bank Draft
Brewing Co/Vaulted Ales Inc**
2424 Dunstan/Suite 150
Houston, TX 77005
(713) 522-MALT; FAX (713) 522-3495
Founded: Aug. 23, 1995
Asst. Brewer: Scott Littlewood
VP/Mktg: Lauri Littlewood
Head Brewer: Jeff Humphreys
Contact: Scott Littlewood

Basin Brewing Ltd
904 W Florida
Midland, TX 79701
(915) 683-0014; FAX (915) 682-4823
Founded: Sept. 1, 1995
Capacity: 5,000 bbl
Head Brewer/Sales Mgr.: Paul T. Fry
Contact: Paul Fry

**Big Horn Brewing
Co of Texas/Humperdinks**
705 Six Flags Dr
Arlington, TX 76010
(817) 640-8553; FAX (817) 652-9185
Founded: Dec. 10, 1995
Capacity: 1,200 bbl
Contact: David Hollow

Bitter End Brewery
311 Colorado St
Austin, TX 78701-3924
(512) 478-2337; FAX (512) 478-2462
Founded: Feb. 10, 1994
Capacity: 1,800 bbl
Mgr.: Alan Unruh
Mgr.: Ryan Fulmer
Head Brewer: Tim Schwartz
Contact: Tim Schwartz

Boardwalk Bistro
4011 Broadway
San Antonio, TX 78209-6313
(210) 824-0100
Founded: March 1, 1994
Capacity: 125 bbl
Head Brewer: Adam Brogley
Sales Mgr./Proprietor: Barbara Hunt
Contact: Adam Brogley

Bosque Brewing Co
300 S Sixth St
Waco, TX 76701
(817) 772-0519
Founded: July 1, 1995
Contact: Kendall Garrison

**Bradley's
Restaurant and Brewery**
515 W Bay Area Blvd
Webster, TX 77598
(713) 332-8488
Founded: Jan. 26, 1996
Contact: Gary Heine

Brazos Brewing Co
PO Box 9369
College Station, TX 77842
(409) 693-4148; FAX (409) 696-0351
bam1587@zeus.tamu.edu
Founded: May 7, 1995
Capacity: 1,000 bbl
Head Brewer: Brian Clark
Pres.: Jere Blackwelder
Sec.: Bruce McDonald
Contact: Jere Blackwelder

**Cafe on the
Square and Brewpub**
126 N LBJ
San Marcos, TX 78666
(512) 353-9289
Founded: Feb. 4, 1995
Capacity: 180 bbl
Sales Mgr./Head Brewer: Gary Moore
Brewer: Paul Kuttner
Sales Mgr.: Gary Moore
Brewer: Webb Branen
Contact: Gary Moore

United States Breweries (Texas)

Celis Brewery Inc
2431 Forbes Dr
Austin, TX 78754-5148
(512) 835-0884; FAX (512) 835-0130
Founded: May 1, 1992
Capacity: 15,000 bbl
Pres.: Christine Celis
Head Brewer: Peter Camps
Contact: Peter Camps
Subsidiary of American Specialty and Craft Beer Co.

**Copper Tank
Brewing Co (No 1)/
Austin Microbrewers LLC**
504 Trinity St
Austin, TX 78701-3714
(512) 478-8444; FAX (512) 478-1832
Founded: June 21, 1994
Capacity: 3,100 bbl
Brewer: Bill Miller
Brewery Mgr.: Davis Tucker
Contact: Davis Tucker

**Copper Tank
Brewing Co (No 2)/
Austin Microbrewers LLC**
2600 Main St
Dallas, TX 75226
(214) 744-2739
Founded: Jan. 25, 1996
Head Brewer: Pat Carroll
Contact: Davis Tucker

**Draught Horse
Pub and Brewery**
4112 Medical Pkwy
Austin, TX 78756
(512) 452-6258; FAX (512) 499-0275
Founded: Feb. 1, 1995
Capacity: 700 bbl
Sales Mgr.: Josh Wilson
Head Brewer: Alice Heimer
Contact: Dan Moran

**Fredericksburg
Brewing Co Inc**
245 E Main St
Fredericksburg, TX 78624-4114
(210) 997-1646; FAX (210) 997-8026
Founded: Sept. 9, 1994
Capacity: 800 bbl
Pres./Gen. Mgr.: John Davies
Sales Mgr./Mktg. Dir.: Dick Estenson
Head Brewer: Adam J. Haughey
Contact: John Davies

Frio Brewing Co
1905 N St Mary's
San Antonio, TX 78212
(210) 225-8222; FAX (210) 225-8222
http://www.tristero.com/frio/
Founded: Aug. 10, 1994
Capacity: 7,000 bbl
Head Brewer: Larry Cash
Contact: David Strain

**G Heileman Brewing Co Inc/
Lone Star Brewing Co**
600 Lone Star Blvd
San Antonio, TX 78204
(210) 270-9488; FAX (210) 270-9430
Capacity: 1,400,000 bbl
Brewery Mgr.: Richard Anderson
Admin. Mgr.: John H. Belter
Brewmaster: Kenneth Lee
Contact: Richard Anderson

Galveston Brewery
2521 Mechanic
Galveston, TX 77550
(713) 331-6671
Founded: Dec. 1, 1995
Head Brewer: Steve Roberts
Contact: Steve Roberts

Harp & Star Brewing Co
1404 Fm 1960/Bypass Rd E
Humble, TX 77338-3910
(713) 446-0730
Contact: Richard Coggins

Hierman's Hofbrau
3303 N Midkiff/Suite 160
Midland, TX 79705
(915) 699-2337
Founded: Feb. 14, 1996
Capacity: 400 bbl
Head Brewer: John Heard
Primary Contact: Tom Herman
Contact: Tom Herman

**Hill Country
Brewing and Bottling Co**
730 Shady Lane
Austin, TX 78702-5006
(512) 385-9111
Founded: Oct. 1, 1993
Capacity: 7,500 bbl
Pres./Head Brewer: Mike McHone
Contact: Mike McHone

**Hoffbrau Steaks
Brewery (No 1)**
4180 Beltline Rd
Addison, TX 75244
(214) 392-1161; FAX (214) 661-2638
Founded: Feb. 15, 1995
Capacity: 1,000 bbl
Pres.: Randy Dishonh
Dir. Restaurant Operations: Matt Hanifen
Brewmaster: Steven Sandidge
Senior Brewer: John Morrison
Contact: Steven Sandidge

**Hoffbrau Steaks
Brewery (No 2)**
3205 Knox St
Dallas, TX 75244
(214) 559-2680; FAX (214) 520-9415
Founded: Sept. 19, 1995
Capacity: 1,000 bbl
Brewmaster: Steven Sandidge
Sales Mgr.: Matt Hanifen
Senior Brewer: Tim Deemer
Contact: Steven Sandidge

Houston Brewery
1207 Missouri St
Houston, TX 77006-2710
(713) 953-0101; FAX (713) 266-2537
Contact: Michael Holiday

Hub City Brewery
1807 Ave H
Lubbock, TX 79408
Founded: March 1, 1995
Contact: Kent Snead

**Hubcap Brewery
& Kitchen (No 2)**
1701 N Market St/Suite 130
Dallas, TX 75202-1841
(214) 651-0808; FAX (214) 651-0808
Founded: March 1, 1994
Capacity: 1,200 bbl
Head Brewer: Jose Olivares
Sales Mgr.: Rey Cardino
Contact: Patrick Carroll

**Jaxson's Restaurant and
Brewing Co**
1135 Airway
El Paso, TX 79925
(915) 778-9696; FAX (915) 778-6476
Founded: Sept. 20, 1995
Contact: Don Morrill

Joey's Inc
2417 N St Mary's
San Antonio, TX 78212
(210) 733-9573; FAX (210) 733-7618
Founded: Feb. 14, 1995
Capacity: 500 bbl
Head Brewer: Charles E. Jordan
Pres.: Joey Villarreal
Contact: Joey Villarreal

United States Breweries (Texas)

**Katie Bloom's
Irish Pub and Brewery**
419 E Sixth St
Austin, TX 78701
(512) 472-2528; FAX (512) 472-2541
Founded: Oct. 30, 1995
Capacity: 1,200 bbl
Owner: Gerard Kehoe
General Mgr.: Aileen Hurst
Contact: Ric Haughton

Main Street Brewing Co
2656 Main St
Dallas, TX 75226
(214) 939-2337; FAX (214) 939-9339
Founded: Feb. 1, 1996
Capacity: 2,000 bbl
Partner: George Corey
Head Brewer/Partner: Greg Correard
Contact: George Corey

Miller Brewing Co
7001 S Freeway
Fort Worth, TX 76134-4099
(817) 551-3300
Capacity: 7,500,000 bbl
Plant Mgr.: James R. Grandinetti
Oper. Mgr.: Washington A. Johnson
Brewing Mgr.: Richard A. Sherman
Contact: James R. Grandinetti

Old West Brewery (No 2)
5411 N Mesa
El Paso, TX 79913
Founded: Aug. 15, 1995
Contact: Scott Lynch

Padre Island Brewing Co
PO Box 3837
South Padre Island, TX 78597
(210) 761-9585; FAX (210) 761-9569
Founded: July 21, 1995
Capacity: 1,200 bbl
Head Brewer: Markkus Haggenmiller
Contact: Tony Benson

Panther City Brewery & Cafe
2513 Rodeo Plaza
Fort Worth, TX 75099
(817) 626-9500
Founded: March 12, 1996

**Pearl Brewing Co/
Pabst Brewing Co**
PO Box 1661/312 Pearl Pkwy
San Antonio, TX 78296-1661
(210) 226-0231; FAX (210) 226-2512
Founded: Jan. 1, 1986
Capacity: 1,500,000 bbl
Chairman: Lutz E. Issleib

Head Brewer: John Riley
Sales Mgr.: John C. Kratz
Plant Mgr.: Eddie Mueller
VP Export Sales/Dir.: Gary Damveld
VP Finance: John Schliess
Contact: Lutz Issleib

Rock Bottom Brewery (No 3)
6111 Richmond Ave
Houston, TX 77057-6209
(713) 974-2739; FAX (713) 789-8500
Contact: Kevin Marley

Rock Bottom Brewery (No 5)
4050 Beltline Rd
Addison, TX 75240
(214) 404-7456; FAX (214) 404-7454
Founded: May 20, 1995
Capacity: 3,600 bbl
Head Brewer: John Oliphant
Contact: Ky Belk

Routh Street Brewery
3011 Routh St
Dallas, TX 75201
(214) 922-8835; FAX (214) 922-0196
Founded: Sept. 28, 1995
Capacity: 1,500 bbl
Proprietor: Gary Brown
Head Brewer: Al Kinchen
Restaurant Mgr.: Ann Spicer
Asst. Brewer: Bob Calhoun
Contact: Al Kinchen

Saint Andrew's Brewing Co
703 McKinney Ave/Suite 002
Dallas, TX 75202
(214) 220-2023; FAX (214) 220-3772
Founded: June 1, 1995
Capacity: 12,000 bbl
Head Brewer/Pres.: James C. Wisniewski
VP: Joe Contreras
Sales Mgr.: Joe Contreras
Contact: Joe Contreras

Saint Arnold Brewing Co
2522 Fairway Park Dr
Houston, TX 77092-7607
(713) 686-9494; FAX (713) 686-9474
brewery@saintarnold.com
http://www.saintarnold.com
Founded: June 9, 1994
Capacity: 4,500 bbl
Founder/Head Brewer: Brock Wagner
Founder/Sales Mgr.: Kevin Bartol
Contact: Brock Wagner

Silk's Grill and Brewing Co
3705 Olsen
Amarillo, TX 79109
(806) 353-2622
Founded: Aug. 1, 1995
Contact: Gary Grant

Spoetzl Brewery Inc
PO Box 368
Shiner, TX 77984-0368
(512) 594-3852
Head Brewer: John J. Hysner
Contact: Carlos Alvarez
Subsidiary of Gambrinus Importing Co.

Strand Brewing Co
101 23rd St
Galveston, TX 77550
(409) 763-4500; FAX (409) 763-4467
Founded: May 22, 1995
Capacity: 1,700 bbl
Head Brewer: Michael Griggs
Sales Mgr.: Frank Petronella
Contact: Michael Griggs

Stroh Brewery Co
Longview Plant
1400 W Cotton St
Longview, TX 75604
(903) 753-0371
Capacity: 3,800,000 bbl
Plant Mgr.: R. A. Arendt
Master Brewer: M. P. Daveloose
Contact: R. A. Arendt

**TwoRows
Restaurant and Brewery**
5500 Greenville Ave
Dallas, TX 75243-4611
(214) 696-2739; FAX (214) 696-2232
Founded: May 1, 1995
Capacity: 3,100 bbl
Head Brewer: Mike Kraft
Sales Mgr.: Baine Brooks
Contact: Mike Brotzman

Village Brewery
2415 Dunstan Rd
Houston, TX 77005-2520
(713) 524-4677; FAX (713) 524-5054
Founded: April 15, 1994
Capacity: 2,000 bbl
Head Brewer: Bryan Pearson
Sales Mgr.: Rosemary Crawford
Owner: Raju Lulla
Contact: Bryan Pearson

Waterloo Brewing Co
401 Guadalupe St
Austin, TX 78701-2921
(512) 477-1836; FAX (512) 477-1837
Founded: Dec. 1, 1993
Capacity: 2,500 bbl
Sales Mgr.: Valarie Menzel
Co-Owner: Susan Forrester
Co-Owner: Billy Forrester
Head Brewer: Steve Anderson
Contact: Bill Forrester

Yegua Creek Brewing Co
2920 N Henderson Ave
Dallas, TX 75206-6403
(214) 824-2739; FAX (214) 821-0648
yeguacreek@aol.com
http://www.wn.com/biz/ycbc.html
Founded: Jan. 24, 1994
Capacity: 2,600 bbl
Head Brewer/Sales Mgr.: Rob Cromie
General Partner: Toby O'Brien
Contact: Toby O'Brien

Yellow Rose Brewing Co
17201 San Pedro Ave
San Antonio, TX 78232-1403
(210) 496-6669; FAX (210) 496-6678
Founded: Nov. 1, 1994
Capacity: 1,800 bbl
Head Brewer: Glen Fritz
Sales Mgr.: Carolyn Flanary
Sales Mgr.: John Monroe
Asst. Brewer: Warren Windsor
Contact: Glen Fritz

UTAH

Desert Edge Brewery at the Pub/Desert Edge Brewing Co
273 Trolley Sq
Salt Lake City, UT 84102
(801) 521-8917; FAX (801) 521-8839
pkrug@aol.com
Founded: June 8, 1995
Capacity: 1,400 bbl
Pres.: Scott Hale
VP: Royal Tyler
Head Brewer: Peter Kruger
Contact: Peter Kruger

Eddie McStiff's Brewing Co
57 S Main St
Moab, UT 84532-2502
(801) 259-4282; FAX (801) 259-3022
Founded: March 16, 1991
Capacity: 2,300 bbl

Head Brewer: Darwin Barker
Owner: Steve Patterson
Contact: Steve Patterson

Naisbitt's Brewery
4286 Riverdale Rd
Riverdale, UT 84405-3512
(801) 394-0302; FAX (801) 394-3640
Founded: Oct. 22, 1992
Capacity: 3,000 bbl
Owner/Mgr.: Brad Naisbitt
Owner: Jed Naisbitt
Head Brewer: David Gunn
Sales Mgr.: Craig Knight
Asst. Brewer: Steve LaRue
Contact: Brad Naisbitt

Red Rock Brewing Co
254 S 200 W
Salt Lake City, UT 84101-1801
(801) 521-7446; FAX (801) 521-0908
Founded: March 15, 1994
Capacity: 3,000 bbl
Brewery Oper. Mgr.: Brent Smith
Head Brewer: Eric Dunlap
Contact: Brent Smith

Roosters 25th St Brewing Co
253 Historic 25th St
Ogden, UT 84401
(801) 476-1969
Founded: April 7, 1995
Capacity: 700 bbl
Pres.: Judy Imlay
Head Chef: Pete Buttschardt
General Mgr.: Kym Buttschardt
Head Brewer: Steve Kirkland
Contact: Steve Kirkland

Salt Lake Brewing Co Corporate Office
375 W Second S
Salt Lake City, UT 84101-1211
(801) 364-3062; FAX (801) 359-5426

Salt Lake Brewing Co/Fuggles
367 W 200 S
Salt Lake City, UT 84101
(801) 363-7000; FAX (801) 359-5426
Founded: Dec. 1, 1994
Capacity: 6,000 bbl
Co-owner: Jeff Polychronis
Co-owner: Peter Cole
Head Brewer: Dan Burick
Contact: Jeff Polychronis

Salt Lake Brewing Co/Squatters Pub
375 W 200 S/Suite 201
Salt Lake City, UT 84101-1211
(801) 363-2739; FAX (801) 575-7139
Founded: Sept. 1, 1989
Capacity: 6,000 bbl
Head Brewer: Jennifer Tally
Contact: Jeff Polychronis

Schirf Brewing Co/Wasatch Brewpub
PO Box 459
Park City, UT 84060-0459
(801) 645-9500; FAX (801) 649-4999
Founded: Oct. 23, 1986
Capacity: 15,000 bbl
Head Brewer: Dan Graves
VP: Paul Brown
Dir. of Brewing: Michael Mankoschewski
Pres./Sales Mgr.: Gregory Schirf
Contact: Greg Schirf

Schirf Brewing Co/Wasatch Brewing Co (No 2)
1763 S 300 W
Salt Lake City, UT 84115
(801) 466-8855; FAX (801) 484-6665
Founded: Oct. 15, 1994
Capacity: 15,000 bbl
Head Brewer: Michael Mankoschewski
Sales Mgr.: Greg Schirf
Contact: Greg Schirf

Uinta Brewing Co
389 W 1700 S
Salt Lake City, UT 84115-5100
(801) 467-0909
Founded: March 1, 1994
Capacity: 10,000 bbl
Co-Owner/Head Brewer: Will Hamill
Co-Owner/Brewer/Sales Mgr.: Del Vance
Contact: Will Hamill

VERMONT

Bennington Brewers Ltd
PO Box 4172
Bennington, VT 05201
(802) 447-7836
Founded: April 1, 1996
Capacity: 2,880 bbl
Pres./Head Brewer: Frank Murray
Contact: Frank Murray

Black River Brew House
PO Box 404
Ludlow, VT 05149-0404
(802) 228-3100
Founded: April 1, 1995
Capacity: 200 bbl
Head Brewer/Sales Mgr.: Tom Coleman
Contact: Tom Coleman

Catamount Brewing Co
PO Box 457
White River Jct, VT 05001-0457
(802) 296-2248; FAX (802) 296-2420
Founded: Feb. 1, 1987
Capacity: 20,000 bbl
VP/Sales Mgr.: Philip Gentile
Head Brewer: Stephen Mason
Contact: Stephen Mason

Latchis Grille and Windham Brewery
Six Flat St
Brattleboro, VT 05301-3248
(802) 254-4747
Founded: July 1, 1991
Capacity: 250 bbl
Head Brewer: Dan Young
Contact: Dan Young

Long Trail Brewing Co
PO Box 168/Route 4
Bridgewater Corners, VT 05035-0168
(802) 672-5011; FAX (802) 672-5012
Capacity: 15,000 bbl
Pres.: Andy Pherson
Contact: Andy Pherson

Madison Brewing Co/ Pub and Restaurant
3 Stonehedge Dr
Bennington, VT 05201
(802) 442-9612; FAX (802) 447-3351
Founded: Jan. 1, 1996
Capacity: 1,400 bbl
Head Brewer: Mark Madison
Contact: Michael Madison

Magic Hat Brewing Co
180 Flynn Ave
Burlington, VT 05401-5482
(802) 658-2739; FAX (802) 658-5788
magichatvt@aol.com
Founded: Nov. 1, 1994
Capacity: 6,000 bbl
Pres.: Alan Newman
Contact: Bob Johnson

McNeill's Brewery
90 Elliot St
Brattleboro, VT 05301-3208
(802) 254-2553
Contact: Ray McNeill

Norwich Inn/ Jasper Murdocks Ale House
PO Box 908/325 Main St
Norwich, VT 05055-0908
(802) 649-1143; FAX (802) 649-2909
Founded: May 23, 1993
Capacity: 200 bbl
Head Brewer: Timothy F. Wilson
Contact: Timothy F. Wilson

Otter Creek Brewing Inc
85 Exchange St
Middlebury, VT 05753-1106
(802) 388-0727; FAX (802) 388-1645
Founded: March 12, 1991
Capacity: 40,000 bbl
VP/Sec.: Ginger Dowling Miller
Pres./Brewmaster: Lawrence Miller II
Cellarmaster: Tom Brande
VP/Mktg.: David Ebner
Plant Mgr.: Gerry Trielo
Contact: Lawrence Miller

Shed Restaurant and Brewery
1859 Mountain Rd
Stowe, VT 05672-4751
(802) 253-9311; FAX (802) 253-9694
Founded: Dec. 11, 1994
Capacity: 1,820 bbl
Head Brewer: Chris Ericson
Sales Mgr.: Ken Strong
Contact: Ken Strong

Vermont Pub and Brewery
144 College St
Burlington, VT 05401-8416
(802) 865-0500; FAX (802) 865-4112
Founded: Nov. 11, 1988
Capacity: 1,100 bbl
Sales Mgr.: Nancy Noonan
Brewer: Glenn Walter
Head Brewer: Gregory Noonan
Contact: Nancy Noonan

VIRGINIA

Anheuser-Busch Inc
PO Drawer U
Williamsburg, VA 23187-3713
(804) 253-3600
Capacity: 9,200,000 bbl
Plant Mgr.: John L. Carmichael
Resident Brewmaster: Ronald Lukoschek
Contact: John L. Carmichael

Bardo Rodeo
2000 Wilson Blvd
Arlington, VA 22201
(703) 527-9399; FAX (703) 516-4705
Founded: March 1, 1993
Capacity: 3,000 bbl
Pres.: Bill Stewart
Head Brewer: Shawn Ryan
Sales Mgr.: Graham Stewart
Contact: Bill Stewart

Blue and Gold Brewing Co
3100 Clarendon Blvd
Arlington, VA 22201
(703) 908-4995
Founded: Feb. 1, 1996
Capacity: 2,000 bbl
Asst. Brewer: Dan Hackley
Contact: Daniel Litwin

Blue Ridge Brewing Co
709 W Main St
Charlottesville, VA 22903-4570
(804) 977-0017
Founded: June 2, 1987
Capacity: 500 bbl
Pres.: Paul D. Summers III
VP: A. Burks Summers II
Head Brewer: A. Burks Summers II
Contact: A. Burks Summers

Champion Billiards and Cafe
200 Wilson Blvd
Arlington, VA 22201
(703) 527-1852
Founded: April 1, 1996
Contact: Bill Stewart

Cobblestone Pub and Brewery
110 N 18th St
Richmond, VA 23223
(804) 644-2739; FAX (804) 344-3610
Founded: June 15, 1995
Asst. Head Brewer: Peter Barclay
Contact: Brad Beatty

Coors Brewing Co
PO Box 25/Route 340 S
Elkton, VA 22827
(703) 289-6000
Plant Mgr.: Maurice Bryan
Contact: Maurice Bryan

James River Brewing Co
104 Shockoe Slip/Suite 3A
Richmond, VA 23219
(804) 342-6094; FAX (804) 342-6093
Founded: Sept. 15, 1995
Capacity: 1,000 bbl
Head Brewer/Contact: James Zobel
Stockholder: H. C. Berger
Contact: James Zobel

Legend Brewing Co
321 W Seventh St
Richmond, VA 23224-2307
(804) 232-8871; FAX (804) 231-3417
76460.1104@compuserve.com
Founded: Jan. 15, 1994
Capacity: 3,000 bbl
Sales Mgr.: Bob Barker
Pres.: Thomas Martin
Contact: Thomas Martin

Old Dominion Brewing Co
44633 Guilford Dr
Ashburn, VA 22011-6001
(703) 689-1225; FAX (703) 729-6717
Founded: May 15, 1990
Capacity: 25,000 bbl
Head Brewer: Rob Mullin
Sec.: Deborah Dawson
Dir.: Bud Hensgen
Pres.: Jerry Bailey
Sales Mgr.: Mike Graham
Contact: Jerry Bailey

Oxford Brewing Co
PO Box 2652
611-G Hammonds Ferry Rd
Falls Church, VA 22042
(410) 789-0003; FAX (410) 789-0005
Founded: Jan. 1, 1992
Capacity: 6,000 bbl
Owner: Marianne O'Brien
Contact: Marianne O'Brien

Potomac River Brewing Co
1414-A Parke Long Ct
Chantilly, VA 22021
(703) 631-5430; FAX (703) 631-6024
Founded: Oct. 11, 1993
Capacity: 5,000 bbl
Pres.: Jerry Russell
Head Brewer: Chris Schwartz
Contact: Jerry Russell

Richbrau Brewing Co
1214 E Cary St
Richmond, VA 23219
(804) 644-3018; FAX (804) 783-2106
Founded: July 19, 1993

Head Brewer: Mark Cardwell
Sales Mgr.: Pete Taubini
Contact: Mike Byrne

Steamship Brewing Co
415 W 24th St
Norfolk, VA 23517
(804) 623-3430; FAX (804) 623-3430
Founded: May 22, 1995
Capacity: 12,000 bbl
Head Brewer: Lee Scanlon
Sales Mgr.: Mark Scanlon
Contact: Lee Scanlon

Virginia Beverage Co
607 King St
Alexandria, VA 22314
(703) 684-5397
Founded: Feb. 6, 1996
Head Brewer: Alan Beal
Contact: Melton McGuire

Williamsville Brewery
1600 Theme Park Rd
Doswell, VA 23047
(804) 752-5886; FAX (804) 550-0556
Founded: May 1, 1995
Capacity: 7,000 bbl
Pres.: Robert Cabaniss
VP: James B. Cabaniss
Contact: Robert Cabaniss

WASHINGTON

Anacortes Brewhouse
320 Commercial Ave
Anacortes, WA 98221-1517
(360) 293-3666; FAX (360) 293-3666
Capacity: 1,500 bbl
Head Brewer: Paul Wusik
Contact: Linda Spicher

Aviator Ales Brewery/ Seattle Brewing Co
14655 Woodinville
Redmond Rd NE
Woodinville, WA 98072
(206) 485-5432; FAX (206) 487-0847
Founded: Sept. 1, 1995
Capacity: 25,000 bbl
General Mgr.: Dusty Wyant
Brewmaster: Will Kemper
Head Brewer: Brendan Smith
Washington Sales Rep.: Neil Blower
Office Mgr.: Joan Schaffner
Contact: Dusty Wyant

Bentley's Brewhouse Restaurant
PO Box 387
Point Roberts, WA 98281
(604) 273-5327; FAX (604) 278-7902
Founded: Jan. 1, 1996
Contact: John Ostaf

Big Time Brewing Co
4133 University Way NE
Seattle, WA 98105-6213
(206) 545-4509
Founded: Dec. 1, 1988
Capacity: 1,700 bbl
Head Brewer: Dick Cantwell
General Mgr.: Armon Jones
Owner: Reid Martin
Contact: Reid Martin

Birkebeiner Brewing Co
35 W Main St
Spokane, WA 99201
(509) 458-0854; FAX (509) 747-3911
birkebrew@aol.com
Founded: May 20, 1994
Capacity: 3,300 bbl
Head Brewer: Tom Taylor
Contact: James Gimurtu

Boundary Bay Brewing
PO Box 2446
Bellingham, WA 98227-2446
(206) 784-9362
Founded: March 1, 1995
Contact: Edward Bennett

Buchanan Brewing Corp
PO Box BB
Oroville, WA 98844
(509) 476-2889
Founded: Dec. 20, 1995
Contact: Alice Hittinger

C J's Brewpub Inc
11500 NE 76th St/Orchards Plaza
Vancouver, WA 98662
(360) 253-5859
Founded: April 30, 1995
Capacity: 96 bbl
Owner: Connie Michaels
Contact: Connie Michaels

Captains City Brewing Inc
23 Front St
Coupeville, WA 98239
(360) 678-9080
Founded: Nov. 1, 1995
Capacity: 500 bbl
Head Brewer/Sales Mgr.: Kevin Locke
Contact: Kevin Locke

Chuckanut Bay Brewing Co
709 W Orchard Dr/Suite 5
Bellingham, WA 98225
(360) 734-4223; FAX (360) 676-7502
Founded: April 1, 1995
Capacity: 1,000 bbl
Contact: Bill Bliss

Diamond Knot Brewery
4505 84th St SW
Mukilteo, WA 98275-1557
(206) 355-3446
74457.1317@compuserve.com
http://ourworld.compuserve.com/home-pages/diamondknot
Founded: Oct. 15, 1994
Capacity: 312 bbl
Head Brewer: Brian Sollenberger
Sales Mgr./Brewer: Bob Maphet
Contact: Brian Sollenberger

Eagle Brewing Co
625 Fourth St
Mukilteo, WA 98275
(206) 348-8088; FAX (206) 348-5320
Founded: Dec. 15, 1995
Capacity: 160 bbl
Head Brewer: Brian Sullivan
Contact: Brian Sullivan

Ellensburg Brewing Co
505 N Railroad
Ellensburg, WA 98926
(509) 649-3294
Founded: March 2, 1995
Capacity: 300 bbl
Head Brewer: Jerry Thompson
Sales Mgr: Mary Anderson
Contact: Jerry Thompson

Engine House #9/
The Power Station
611 N Pine St
Tacoma, WA 98406
(206) 272-3435
Founded: April 1, 1995
Capacity: 1,820 bbl
Head Brewer: Karl Ockert
Contact: Dusty Trail

Fish Brewing Co/
Fishbowl Pub
515 Jefferson St SE
Olympia, WA 98501-1467
(360) 943-3650; FAX (360) 943-6480
Founded: Oct. 1, 1993
Capacity: 4,000 bbl
VP/Gen. Mgr.: Mary Horton
Pres./Sales Mgr.: Crayne Horton
Head Brewer: Tom Chase
Sales Rep.: Andy Clarke
Asst. Brewer: Eric Chase
Customer Trainer: Scott Miller
Contact: Crayne Horton

Fort Spokane Brewery
401 W Spokane Falls Blvd
Spokane, WA 99201-0215
(509) 838-3809
Founded: June 2, 1989
Capacity: 850 bbl
Treas.: Gary Schroeder
Sales Mgr.: Carl Siler
Head Brewer: Brian Johnson
Contact: Brian Johnson

Front Street Ale House/
San Juan Brewing Co
Box 849/1 Front St
Friday Harbor, WA 98250
(360) 378-2337; FAX (360) 378-5555
Founded: May 24, 1993
Capacity: 2,000 bbl
Head Brewer/Sales Mgr.: Oren Combs
Contact: Ron Tekatch

Glacier Peak Brewing Co
2929 Colby Ave
Everett, WA 98201-4010
(206) 258-1797; FAX (206) 259-2911
Founded: Feb. 12, 1996
Pres.: James Jones
VP: Tom Bannister
VP/Head Brewer: Tom Munoz
Contact: Tom Munoz

Grant's Brewery Pub
32 N Front St
Yakima, WA 98901-2610
(509) 575-1900

Grant's Yakima Brewing Co
PO Box 9158
Yakima, WA 98909-0158
(509) 575-1900; FAX (509) 457-6782
http://www.grants.com
Founded: Jan. 7, 1982
Capacity: 50,000 bbl
Brewmaster: Herbert Grant
VP: Gary Huggard
Contact: Herbert Grant
  Subsidiary of Stimson Lane/UST Inc.

Hale's Ales Ltd (No 1)
109 Central Way
Kirkland, WA 98033-6107
(206) 827-4359
Founded: July 4, 1983
Pres.: Michael Hale
VP/Head Brewer: Phil O'Brien
Spokane Mgr.: David Metzger
Head Brewer: Jason Eckert
Sales Mgr.: Bill Preib
Operations: J Kipling
Contact: Phil O'Brien

Hale's Ales Ltd (No 2)
5634 E Commerce Ave
Spokane, WA 99212-1307
(509) 534-7553; FAX (509) 534-0159
Founded: Feb. 1, 1991
Capacity: 5,200 bbl
VP: Phil O'Brien
Brewer: David Metzger
Pres.: Michael Hale
Contact: David Metzger

Hale's Ales Ltd (No 3)
4301 Leary Way NW
Seattle, WA 98107
(206) 706-1544; FAX (206) 706-1572
Founded: Dec. 4, 1995
Contact: Jay Kipling

Hart Brewing Co Inc
91 S Royal Brogham Way
Seattle, WA 98134
(206) 682-8322; FAX (206) 682-8420
pyramid@HartBrew.com
http://www.HartBrew.com
Founded: Sept. 1, 1984
Capacity: 75,000 bbl
VP Sales: Brian Larson
Brewery Mgr.: Clay Biberdorf
Plant Engineer: Wayne Davis
VP Operations: Jack Schaller
CEO: George Hancock
Head Brewer: Ellis Owens
Plant Engineer: Paul Smithburg
Contact: George Hancock

Hazel Dell Brewpub
902 SE 121st Ave
Vancouver, WA 98684-6109
(206) 576-0996
Founded: June 1, 1993

Issaquah Brewhouse/
Eagle River Brewing Co
35 W Sunset Way/Suite C
Issaquah, WA 98027
(206) 557-1911
Founded: June 17, 1995
Capacity: 1,000 bbl
Head Brewer: Ron Oldfield
Contact: Ron Oldfield

United States Breweries (Washington)

Kelley Creek Brewing Co
20123 Old Buckley Hwy
Bonney Lake, WA 98390
(206) 862-5969
Founded: Dec. 1, 1993
Capacity: 1,000 bbl
Head Brewer/Sales Mgr./Pres.: Doug Cartwright

La Conner Brewing Co
PO Box 1396
La Conner, WA 98257
(360) 466-1415
Founded: Sept. 1, 1995
Contact: Scott Abrahamson

Leavenworth Brewery
PO Box 477/636 Front St
Leavenworth, WA 98826-1323
(509) 548-4545; FAX (509) 548-4830
Founded: Sept. 25, 1992
Capacity: 700 bbl
Head Brewer: Dennis Holland
Pres.: Scott Hansen
Contact: Scott Hansen

Mac & Jack's Brewery Inc
22845 NE Eighth St/Suite 285
Redmond, WA 98053-7299
(206) 868-4778; FAX (206) 869-0214
Contact: Malcolm MacRankin

Maritime Pacific Brewing
PO Box 17812
Seattle, WA 98107-1812
(206) 782-6181; FAX (206) 782-0718
Founded: Sept. 21, 1990
Capacity: 9,000 bbl
Pres./Owner: George Hancock
Head Brewer: Joe Curilla
Sales Mgr.: Todd Carden
Contact: George Hancock

McMenamins/Columbia
1801 SE Columbia River Rd
Vancouver, WA 98661
(360) 695-9033; FAX (360) 695-8881
Founded: Jan. 4, 1995
Capacity: 750 bbl
Head Brewer: Doug Robertson
Contact: Doug Robertson

McMenamins/Mill Creek
13300 Bothell
Everett Hwy/Suite 304
Mill Creek, WA 98012
(206) 316-9817; FAX (206) 316-9819
Contact: James Roberts

McMenamins/Roy Street
200 Roy St/Suite 105
Seattle, WA 98109
(206) 285-4339; FAX (206) 285-4931
Founded: March 15, 1995
Head Brewer: Lee Medoff
Contact: Tom Cunningham

McMenamins/Six Arms Pub
300 E Pike St
Seattle, WA 98122
(206) 223-1698; FAX (206) 223-1086
Contact: Lee Medoff

Meheen Brewing Co
415 W Columbia St
Pasco, WA 99301-5636
(509) 547-7029; FAX (509) 547-0939
Contact: Dave Meheen

Mount Baker Brewing Co
1408 Cornwall Ave
Bellingham, WA 98225
(360) 671-2031; FAX (360) 671-8631
Founded: May 1, 1995
Capacity: 1,000 bbl
Pres./Head Brewer: W. Burke Eilers
VP: Rob Corner
Sales Mgr.: Keith Armstrong
Head Brewer: Anne Doubek
Contact: W. Burke Eilers

Northern Lights Brewing Co
PO Box 40/1701 S Lawson
Airway Heights, WA 99001-0040
(509) 244-4909
Founded: Dec. 1, 1993
Capacity: 500 bbl
Owner/Sales Mgr.: Mark H. Irvin
Brewmaster: Mark H. Irvin
Contact: Mark Irvin

Onalaska Brewing Co
248 Burchett Rd
Onalaska, WA 98570-9405
(206) 978-4253
davansu@aol.com
Founded: Nov. 1, 1991
Capacity: 300 bbl
Pres./Head Brewer: David Moorehead
Sales Mgr.: Rocky Kolberg
Contact: David Moorehead

Orchard Street Brewing Co
709 W Orchard Dr/Suite 1
Bellingham, WA 98225
(360) 647-1614; FAX (360) 647-0293
Founded: March 24, 1995
Capacity: 5,000 bbl
Head Brewer: Christian Krogstad

Restaurant Mgr.: Frank Milliard
Asst. Brewer: Jeff Jantsch
Contact: Christian Krogstad

Pabst Brewing Co
PO Box 947
Tumwater, WA 98507
(206) 754-5000
Capacity: 4,500,000 bbl
Plant Mgr.: F. Haag
Operations Mgr.: Larry Sidor
Plant Eng.: Donald E. Eckloff
Contact: Roger Haag

Pacific Northwest Brewing Co
322 Occidental Ave S
Seattle, WA 98104-2840
(206) 621-7002
Founded: Jan. 1, 1989
Contact: Richard Wrigley

**Pike Brewing Co/
Merchant du Vin**
1432 Western Ave
Seattle, WA 98101-2017
(206) 622-3373; FAX (206) 622-6648
info@mdv.com
Founded: Oct. 3, 1989
Capacity: 2,400 bbl
Head Brewer: Algernon (Fal) Allen
Sales Mgr.: Steve Sensor
Co-Owner: Tom Leavitt
Co-Owner: Charles Finkel
Co-Owner: Roseann Finkel
Contact: Algernon Allen

**Power House
Restaurant and Brewery**
454 E Main St
Puallup, WA 98371
(206) 845-1370
Founded: Aug. 7, 1995
Capacity: 1,800 bbl
Contact: Karl Ockert

Rainier Brewing Co Inc
3100 Airport Way S
Seattle, WA 98124
(206) 622-2600; FAX (206) 386-8619
Brewery Mgr.: Steve Sarich
Contact: Steve Sarich

Redhook Ale Brewery
3400 Phinney Ave N
Seattle, WA 98103-8624
(206) 548-8000; FAX (206) 548-1305
http://www.halcyon.com/rh/rh.html
Founded: Jan. 1, 1982
Capacity: 300,000 bbl
VP Sales: Sandy Monblat

VP Brewing: Alan Triplett
VP Mktg.: Pamela Hinckley
EVP/COO: David Mickelson
Pres./CEO: Paul Shipman
EVP/CFO: Brad Berg
Contact: David Mickelson

Redhook Ale Brewery (No 2)
14300 NE 145th St
Woodinville, WA 98072
(206) 483-3232; FAX (206) 481-4010
http://www.halcyon.com/rh/rh.html
Founded: June 15, 1994
Capacity: 230,000 bbl
Head Brewer: Dan Landell
VP Sales: Sandy Montblatt
Production Mgr.: Doug MacNair
General Mgr.: Dave Mickelson
VP Mktg.: P. Hinckley
Contact: Al Triplett

Roslyn Brewing Co
PO Box 24
Roslyn, WA 98941-0024
(509) 649-2232
Founded: May 18, 1990
Capacity: 500 bbl
Head Brewer: Dino Enrico
Buisness Mgr.: Lea Beardsley
Contact: Roger Beardsley

Seattle Brewers
530 S Holden St
Seattle, WA 98108-4362
(206) 762-7421
Founded: Nov. 25, 1992
Capacity: 800 bbl
Head Brewer: Jerry Ceis
Pres./Sales Mgr.: Jerry Ceis
Contact: Jerry Ceis

Skagit River Brewing Co
404 S Third St
Mount Vernon, WA 98273-3824
(206) 336-2884; FAX (206) 336-2976
skagitbrew@aol.com
Founded: Dec. 13, 1994
Capacity: 2,500 bbl
Pres./Head Brewer: Charlie Sullivan
VP Mktg./Distribution: Scott Price
Operations Mgr.: Cindy Sullivan
Contact: Charlie Sullivan

Tapps Brewing Co
PO Box 849/15625 Main St
Sumner, WA 98390
(206) 863-8438; FAX (206) 863-0882
Founded: Aug. 15, 1995
Capacity: 8,000 bbl

Principal: Jay Fuchs
Principal: Douglas Taylor
Head Brewer: Stacy Tyler
Contact: Jay Fuchs

West Seattle Brewing Co
4720 California Ave SW
Seattle, WA 98116-4413
(206) 938-2476
Founded: Oct. 25, 1991
Capacity: 900 bbl
Brewmaster: Charles McElevey
General Mgr.: Gene Danielson
Head Brewer: Aaron Tate
Sales Mgr.: Buck Jones
Contact: Gene Danielson

Whatcom Brewery
PO Box 427
Ferndale, WA 98248
(360) 380-6969
Founded: Dec. 24, 1994
Capacity: 500 bbl
Head Brewer: John Hudson
Sales Mgr.: Lloyd Zimmerman
Accountant: Molly Zimmerman
Security: Saki Zimmerman
Senior Transport/Eng.: Harlin Hovander
Contact: Lloyd Zimmerman

Whidbey Island Brewing Co
630-B Second St
Langley, WA 98260
(360) 221-8373
Founded: Nov. 5, 1992
Capacity: 1,000 bbl
Head Brewer: Jim Grimes
Sales Mgr.: Rocco Gianni
Contact: James Grimes

Winthrop Brewing Co
PO Box 112
155 Riverside Ave (brewery)
Winthrop, WA 98862-0112
(509) 996-3183
Founded: July 15, 1993
Capacity: 1,000 bbl
Partner/Head Brewer/Sales Mgr.: Dan Yingling
Partner/General Mgr.: Paul Brown
Contact: Paul Brown

**Young's Brewing Co/
Northwest Sausage and Deli**
5945 Prather Rd
Centralia, WA 98531
(360) 736-7760; FAX (360) 736-7791
Founded: Nov. 1, 1994
Capacity: 750 bbl

Owner/Head Brewer: Richard Young
Asst. Brewer: Ezra Cox
Contact: Richard Young

WEST VIRGINIA

Brewbakers
857 Third Ave
Huntington, WV 25701
(304) 525-BREW
Founded: March 25, 1996
Contact: Ron Smith

Cardinal Brewing
PO Box 29
Charleston, WV 25321-0029
(304) 344-2900; FAX (304) 344-2900
Founded: July 4, 1994
Capacity: 5,000 bbl
Head Brewer: Joe Spratt
Sales Mgr.: Mark Saber
Contact: Will Slicer

West Virginia Brewing Co
1291 University Ave
Morgantown, WV 26505
(304) 296-2739
Founded: Oct. 16, 1992
Capacity: 1,800 bbl
Pres.: Glen Larew
Head Brewer: Charles "Buddy" Unangst
Brewer: Ned Strauser
Sales Mgr.: Doug Shelton

WISCONSIN

Angelic Brewing Co
322 W Johnson
Madison, WI 53703
(608) 257-2708; FAX (608) 257-2058
Founded: Feb. 18, 1995
Capacity: 1,600 bbl
Head Brewer: Dean Coffey
Sales Mgr.: Tom Woodford
Owner: Ralph Stayer
Contact: Ralph Stayer

**Appleton
Brewing Co/Adler Brau**
1004 S Olde Oneida
Appleton, WI 54915-1399
(414) 735-0507; FAX (414) 731-0800
Capacity: 1,400 bbl
Owner/Head Brewer: John Jungers
Sales Mgr./Asst. Brewer: Kip Damrow
Contact: John Jungers

United States Breweries (Wisconsin)

B T McClintick Brewing Co
1706 Mole Ave
Janesville, WI 53545
(608) 784-5729
Founded: Jan. 15, 1996
Contact: Tony McClintick

Black River Brewery and Pub
PO Box 2842
La Crosse, WI 54601
(608) 784-2739
Founded: March 13, 1995
Capacity: 960 bbl
Head Brewer: Blaise Strenn
General Mgr.: Lynda Jicha
Contact: Tom Jicha

Black Rose Brewpub
713 S Second St
LaCrosse, WI 54602
(608) 796-2337
Founded: May 1, 1995
Contact: Larry Mcmahen

Bodega Brewpub
122 S Fourth St
La Crosse, WI 54601
(608) 782-0677
Founded: May 1, 1996
Contact: Jeff Hotsun

Brewery Creek Brewing Co
PO Box 163/23 Commerce St
Mineral Point, WI 53565
Contact: Jeff Donaghue

Brewmaster's Pub
4017 80th St
Kenosha, WI 53142-4955
(414) 694-9050; FAX (414) 694-9271
brewq@aol.com
Founded: Feb. 18, 1988
Capacity: 800 bbl
Pres.: Jerry Rezny
Head Brewer: Shawn Quigley
Brewer: David J. Norton
Brewer: James Johnson
Contact: Jerry Rezny

Capital Brewing Co
7734 Terrace Ave
Middleton, WI 53562-3163
(608) 836-7100; FAX (608) 931-9155
Founded: June 1, 1986
Capacity: 17,500 bbl
VP/Head Brewer: Kirby Nelson
Pres.: Rich Lingk
Contact: Kirby Nelson

Cherryland Brewing Co
341 N Third Ave
Sturgeon Bay, WI 54235-2401
(414) 743-1945; FAX (414) 743-2860
Founded: May 1, 1988
Capacity: 5,000 bbl
Sales Mgr.: Robin Laak
Pres.: Thomas Alberts
VP/Head Brewer: Mark Feld
Contact: Mark Feld

Egan Brewing Co
PO Box 12500
Green Bay, WI 54397-2500
(414) 339-2705
Founded: April 1, 1996
Contact: Dan Gohr

Fox River Brewing Co/ Fratello's Italian Cafe
1501 Arboretum Dr
Oshkosh, WI 54901
(414) 232-2337
Founded: Dec. 15, 1995
Capacity: 1,800 bbl
Head Brewer: Alan Bunde
Sales Mgr.: Mickey West
Operations Mgr.: Jay P. Supple
Contact: Jay Supple

G Heileman Brewing Co
100 Harborview Plaza
La Crosse, WI 54601-4051
(608) 785-1000; FAX (608) 785-3323
Brewery Mgr.: Mike Newstrom
Head Brewer: John Snyder
Sales Mgr.: Tom Koehler
VP Brewing: Hans Reuther

Gray Brewing Co
2424 W Court St
Janesville, WI 53545-3307
(608) 754-5150; FAX (608) 752-0821
Founded: Jan. 1, 1994
Head Brewer: Keith Wayne
VP/Sale Mgr.: Fred Gray
Pres.: Robert Gray
Contact: Keith Wayne

Great Dane Pub & Brewing Co
123 E Doty St
Madison, WI 53703-3319
(608) 284-0000; FAX (608) 284-0990
Founded: Nov. 14, 1994
Head Brewer: Rob LoBreglio
Sales Mgr.: Ted Peterson
Pres./Treas.: Eliot Butler
VP/Sec.: Rob LoBreglio
Contact: Eliot Butler

Green Bay Brewing Co
5312 Steve's Cheese Rd
Denmark, WI 54208
(414) 863-6777; FAX (414) 863-6794
wtressler@aol.com
Founded: Nov. 9, 1995
Capacity: 1,700 bbl
Pres./Head Brewer: Bill Tressler
VP/Sales Mgr.: Michelle Tressler
Contact: Bill Tressler

J T Whitney's Brewpub and Eatery/Kicks
674 S Whitney Way
Madison, WI 53711-1035
(608) 274-1776; FAX (608) 274-0676
JTsbrewin@aol.com
Founded: Feb. 14, 1996
Capacity: 1,000 bbl
Head Brewer: Richard Becker
Contact: David Bookstaff

Jacob Leinenkugel Brewing Co
PO Box 368/1-3 Jefferson Ave
Chippewa Falls, WI 54729-0368
(715) 723-5558; FAX (715) 723-7158
Founded: July 1, 1967
Capacity: 250,000 bbl
Admin. Mgr.: Chuck Strehl
Plant Mgr.: Pete Dawson
Pres.: Jake Leinenkugel
Brewmaster: Dale Buhrow
Sales Mgr.: Dick Leinenkugel
Contact: Pete Dawson
Subsidiary of Miller Brewing Co.

Jacob Leinenkugel Brewing Co (No 2)
1514 N 10th St
Milwaukee, WI 53205
(414) 931-4345
Founded: Nov. 1, 1995
Contact: Pete Dawson
Subsidiary of Miller Brewing Co.

Joseph Huber Brewing Co
PO Box 277/1208 14th Ave
Monroe, WI 53566-2055
(608) 325-3191; FAX (608) 325-3198
Founded: Jan. 1, 1948
Sales Mgr.: Michael J. Huber
Head Brewer: Hans G. Kestler
VP/Treas.: Steve Preston
Pres.: Dave Dukelow
Contact: Hans G. Kestler

LaBelle Brewing Co Inc
PO Box 304/750 E Wisconsin Ave
Oconomonowoc, WI 53066
(414) 569-1957
Founded: Dec. 15, 1994
Capacity: 130 bbl
Pres.: Benjamin Gay
Contact: Benjamin Gay

Lakefront Brewery Inc
818-A E Chambers St
Milwaukee, WI 53212
(414) 372-8800; FAX (414) 372-4400
Founded: Dec. 2, 1987
Capacity: 3,000 bbl
Head Brewer/Sales Mgr.: Gary Versteegh
VP: Dorothy Candlish
Pres.: Russell Klisch
Contact: Russell Klisch

Miller Brewing Co
Comm Dept/Bldg 66/Fourth Floor
3939 W Highland Blvd
Milwaukee, WI 53208-2816
(414) 931-2000; FAX (414) 931-6352
mgdtaproom@mgdtaproom.com
http://www.mgdtaproom.com
Founded: Sept. 1, 1955
Capacity: 49,500,000 bbl
Corporate Publications Editor: Jeffry Waalkes
Senior Staff Brewer: Gary Luthen
Chairman and CEO: Jack McDonough
Senior VP Operations: Virgis Colbert
VP Brewing/Research: David Ryder
VP Marketing: Neil Harrison
VP Sales: Chris Moore
VP Corporate Affairs: Patti McKeithan
Contact: Jeffrey Waalkes

New Glarus Brewing Co
PO Box 759/Cty Rd W Hwy 69
New Glarus, WI 53574
(608) 527-5850; FAX (608) 527-5855
Founded: Nov. 1, 1993
Capacity: 5,000 bbl
Pres.: Deborah Carey
Brewer: Dan Carey
Contact: Deborah Carey

Pabst Brewing Co
917 W Juneau Ave
Milwaukee, WI 53233-1428
(414) 223-3500
Capacity: 10,000,000 bbl

Railhouse Restaurant and Brewery/R Ales Inc
W1130 Old Peshtigo Rd
Marinette, WI 54143
(715) 735-9800
Founded: June 25, 1995
Capacity: 200 bbl
Contact: Rick Sauer

Randy's Restaurant / Fun Hunter's Brewery
841 E Milwaukee St
Whitewater, WI 53190-2126
(414) 473-8000; FAX (414) 473-7030
rcruse@eagle.idnet.com
Founded: Feb. 1, 1994
Capacity: 350 bbl
Pres./Head Brewer: Randolph C. Cruse
Contact: Randolph C. Cruse

Remington Watson Smith Brewing Co Inc
223 Maple Ave
Waukesha, WI 53186
(414) 896-7766
idc@execpc.com
Founded: July 1, 1995
Capacity: 1,500 bbl
Head Brewer: Scott Watson Donald
Sales Mgr./Pres.: Brett Remington
Contact: Brett Remington

Rowland's Calumet Brewery
25 N Madison
Chilton, WI 53014-1451
(414) 849-2534
Founded: Sept. 15, 1990
Capacity: 270 bbl
VP/Sec.: Bonita Rowland
Pres./Head Brewer: Robert Rowland
Contact: Robert Rowland

South Shore Brewery
400 Third Ave W
Ashland, WI 54806
(715) 682-9199
Founded: June 10, 1995
Capacity: 460 bbl
Sales Mgr./Owner: Mark Gutteter
Head Brewer: Eugene "Bo" Belanger
Contact: Eugene "Bo" Belanger

Sprecher Brewing Co
701 W Glendale Ave
Glendale, WI 53209-6500
(414) 964-2739; FAX (414) 964-2462
Founded: Jan. 1, 1986
Capacity: 35,000 bbl
Brewmaster/Pres.: Randy Sprecher
Head Brewer: Craig Burke
Sales Mgr.: Will Mrotek
Contact: Randal Sprecher

Stevens Point Brewery Co
2617 Water St
Stevens Point, WI 54481-5248
(715) 344-9310; FAX (715) 344-8897
Founded: Jan. 1, 1987
Capacity: 70,000 bbl
Pres./CEO: James Ryan
Brewmaster: John Zappa
Contact: James Ryan
Subsidiary of Barton Beers Inc

Water Street Brewery
1101 N Water St
Milwaukee, WI 53202-3107
(414) 272-1195; FAX (414) 271-0406
roakless@aol.com
Founded: Nov. 1, 1987
Capacity: 750 bbl
Head Brewer: Robert Hansen
VP: Rick Schmidt
Contact: Rick Schmidt
Subsidiary of Barton Beers Inc

Wisconsin Brewing Co
1064 N 63rd St
Wauwatosa, WI 53213
(414) 443-9278; FAX (414) 443-1271
Founded: April 1, 1996
Capacity: 3,000 bbl
Head Brewer: Gary Versteegh
Contact: Mark May

WYOMING

Bootleggers Brewery/ Sunshine Valley Brewing Co
256 S Center
Casper, WY 82601
Founded: April 1, 1996
Contact: Neal Neumiller

Bowman's Pub & Brewing Co
320 S Second St
Laramie, WY 82070
(307) 742-3349
Founded: Nov. 20, 1995
Capacity: 1,440 hL
Head Brewer: Jeff Ogden
Pres.: Mike Bowman
Sales Mgr.: Ed Turk
Contact: Jeff Ogden

Humphreys Bar & Grill
408 W Juniper
Gillette, WY 82718
(307) 682-0100

United States Breweries (Wyoming–U.S. Territories and Possessions)

Founded: April 1, 1995
Contact: Charlie Douglas

Library Restaurant and Brewing Co
1622 Grand Ave
Laramie, WY 82070
(307) 742-0500
Founded: April 21, 1995
Capacity: 640 bbl
Head Brewer: Jade Miller
Sales Mgr.: Dwight Rowell
Contact: Dwight Rowell

Medicine Bow Brewing Co
115 E 17th St
Cheyenne, WY 82001
(307) 778-2739; FAX (307) 632-2887
Founded: March 28, 1995
Contact: Brett Boreing

Otto Brothers' Brewing Co
PO Box 4177
Jackson, WY 83001-4177
(307) 733-9000; FAX (307) 733-2745
Founded: June 14, 1989
Capacity: 3,000 bbl
VP/Sales Mgr.: Don Frank
VP: Ernie Otto
Pres./Head Brewer: Charlie Otto
Contact: Charlie Otto

Snake River Brewing Co/ Jackson Hole Pub and Brewery
PO Box 3319
Jackson, WY 83001-3319
(307) 739-2337; FAX (307) 739-2296
Founded: March 25, 1994
Capacity: 1,755 bbl
Owner: Albert Upsher
Head Brewer: Chip Holland
Sales Mgr.: Paula DiPaola
Contact: Chip Holland

U.S. TERRITORIES AND POSSESSIONS

MARSHALL ISLANDS

Republic Brewery
PO Box 477
Majuro, MH 96960-0477
(692) 625-5325; FAX (692) 625-3664
Founded: March 1, 1993
Capacity: 15,000 hL
Head Brewer/Sales Mgr.: Paul Fullerton
Contact: Harry Doulatram

PUERTO RICO

Cerveceria India Inc
PO Box 1690
Mayaguez, PR 00681-1690
(809) 834-1000; FAX (809) 265-7740
Founded: Jan. 1, 1938
Capacity: 700,000 bbl
Chairman/Board: Grace Valdes
Head Brewer: Carlos Latoni
Contact: Grace Valdes

La Villa De Torrimar
94 Calle Reina Catalina
Guaynabo, PR 00969-3274
(809) 731-8187

6 Canadian Breweries

The rise of microbreweries and brewpubs is truly a North American phenomenon. In certain parts of Canada, such as Québec, microbrewed brands have been more successful than many of their United States counterparts in capturing local market share. However, small Canadian breweries face an uphill battle due to the country's excessive taxation of beer.

The Canadian craft-brewing industry has demonstrated renewed vigor during the last three years. After a three-year period (1990 through 1992), during which the combined number of craft-brewery closures equaled that of openings, the industry total increased by nine, four, and sixteen in 1993, 1994, and 1995, respectively.

Every Canadian brewing company is listed in this single chapter of the *North American Brewers Resource Directory*. The breweries are compiled in two ways. First is a province-by-province list with each brewery's name, city, and province. This list separates the breweries into the following categories: large breweries (having annual sales of greater than 587,600 hectoliters); regional breweries (having annual sales and/or capacity of between 17,600 and 587,600 hectoliters); microbreweries (having annual sales of less than 17,600 hectoliters); and brewpubs (restaurant-breweries with 50 percent or greater sales on-site). Second is the directory listing of all breweries, in alphabetical order by province, complete with addresses, phone numbers, and personnel.

---

* Denotes Institute for Brewing Studies Brewery Member.
† Denotes brewery with on-site restaurant or pub.
‡ Denotes brew-on-premise/microbrewery/brewpub.

ALBERTA

LARGE BREWERIES
Labatt's Alberta Brewery
Edmonton, Alberta

Molson Breweries/Western Div/ Alberta Region/Edmonton Plant
Edmonton, Alberta

REGIONAL BREWERIES
Big Rock Brewery Ltd*
Calgary, Alberta

MICROBREWERIES
Alley Kat Brewing Co
Edmonton, Alberta

Banff Brewery Corp
Calgary, Alberta

Bow Valley Brewing Co
Canmore, Alberta

BREWPUBS
Brewsters Brewing Co and Restaurant (No 2)
Calgary, Alberta

Brewsters Brewing Co and Restaurant (No 4)
Calgary, Alberta

Brewsters Brewing Co and Restaurant (No 6)
Edmonton, Alberta

Mission Bridge Brewing Co
Calgary, Alberta

BRITISH COLUMBIA

LARGE BREWERIES
Labatt's Breweries of British Columbia
Creston, British Columbia

Labatt's Breweries/ British Columbia
New Westminster, British Columbia

REGIONAL BREWERIES
Granville Island Brewing Co
Vancouver, British Columbia

Molson Breweries/Western Division
Vancouver, British Columbia

Okanagan Spring Brewery
Vernon, British Columbia

Pacific Western Brewing Co
Prince George, British Columbia

Shaftebury Brewing Co Ltd
Vancouver, British Columbia

MICROBREWERIES
Bayou Brewing Co Ltd
Richmond, British Columbia

Bear Brewing Co
Kamloops, British Columbia

Bowen Island Brewing Co
Bowen Island, British Columbia

Horseshoe Bay Brewing Co Ltd
Horseshoe Bay, British Columbia

Mount Begbie Brewing Co Ltd*
Revelstoke, British Columbia

Nelson Brewing Co
Nelson, British Columbia

Russell Brewing Co
Surrey, British Columbia

Storm Brewing Ltd
Vancouver, British Columbia

Canadian Breweries

Tall Ship Ale Co
Squamish, British Columbia

Tin Whistle Brewing Co
Penticton, Victoria, British Columbia

Tree Brewing Co Ltd*
Kelowna, British Columbia

Vancouver Island Brewing Co
Victoria, British Columbia

Whistler Brewing Co*
Whistler, British Columbia

BREWPUBS
Howe Sound Brewing Co Ltd
North Vancouver, British Columbia

Sailor Hagar's Brewpub
North Vancouver, British Columbia

Spinnakers Brewpub Inc*
Victoria, British Columbia

Steam Works Brewing Co*
Vancouver, British Columbia

Swans*
Victoria, British Columbia

Yale Town Brewing Co
Vancouver, British Columbia

MANITOBA
LARGE BREWERIES
Labatt's Manitoba Brewery
Winnipeg, Manitoba

Molson Breweries/Western Div/
Manitoba Region/Winnipeg Plant
Winnipeg, Manitoba

MICROBREWERIES
Fort Garry Brewing Co Ltd
Winnipeg, Manitoba

NEW BRUNSWICK
LARGE BREWERIES
Moosehead Breweries Ltd
St John, New Brunswick

MICROBREWERIES
Picaroons Brewing Co†
Fredericton, New Brunswick

NEWFOUNDLAND
LARGE BREWERIES
Labatt's Newfoundland Brewery
St John's, Newfoundland

Molson Breweries/ Atlantic
Region/St. John's Plant
St John's, Newfoundland

NORTHWEST TERRITORIES
MICROBREWERIES
Arctic Brewing Co*
Yellowknife, Northwest Territories

NOVA SCOTIA
LARGE BREWERIES
Oland Breweries Ltd
Halifax, Nova Scotia

MICROBREWERIES
Keith's Brewery
Halifax, Nova Scotia

BREWPUBS
Granite Brewery
Halifax, Nova Scotia

Heather Motel and Brewpub
Stellarton, Nova Scotia

Paddy's Pub and Brewery
Kentville, Nova Scotia

ONTARIO
LARGE BREWERIES
Labatt's Ontario Breweries
London, Ontario

Labatt's Breweries of Canada
Toronto, Ontario

Labatt's Ontario Breweries
Etobicoke, Ontario

Molson Breweries/Ontario Div
North York, Ontario

Molson Breweries/
Ontario Div/Etobicoke Plant
Toronto, Ontario

REGIONAL BREWERIES
Algonquin Brewery
Formosa, Ontario

Brick Brewing Co Ltd*
Waterloo, Ontario

Creemore Springs Brewery Ltd*
Creemore, Ontario

Lakeport Brewing Corp
Hamilton, Ontario

Molson Breweries/
Ontario Div/ Barrie Plant
Barrie, Ontario

Northern Breweries Ltd
Sault Ste Marie, Ontario

Northern Breweries Ltd
Sudbury, Ontario

Northern Breweries Ltd
Thunder Bay, Ontario

Sleeman Brewing & Malting Co
Guelph, Ontario

Upper Canada Brewing Co
Toronto, Ontario

MICROBREWERIES
Amsterdam Brewing Co
Toronto, Ontario

Conners Brewery*
St Catharines, Ontario

Copperhead Brewing Co Ltd
Nepean, Ontario

Elora Brewery Ltd/ Taylor & Bate
Elora, Ontario

F & M Breweries Ltd
Guelph, Ontario

Glatt Bros Brewing Co
London, Ontario

Gold Crown Brewing Co
Waterloo, Ontario

Great Lakes Brewing Co*
Etobicoke, Ontario

Hart Brewing Co Ltd*
Carleton Place, Ontario

Hometowne Breweries Ltd
London, Ontario

Kawartha Lakes Brewing Co
Peterborough, Ontario

Magnotta Brewery Ltd
Scarborough, Ontario

Niagara Falls Brewing Co*
Niagara Falls, Ontario

Old Credit Brewing Co
Port Credit, Ontario

Quinte Brewery
Belleville, Ontario

Thames Valley Brewing Co
London, Ontario

Trafalgar Brewing Co
Oakville, Ontario

Wellington County Brewery Ltd*
Guelph, Ontario

BREWPUBS
Addingtons
Ottawa, Ontario

Al Frisco's
Toronto, Ontario

Blue Anchor Brewery
Orillia, Ontario

C C's Brew Pub
Mississauga, Ontario

CEEPS Barney's Ltd
London, Ontario

Cellar Tap
Sault Ste Marie, Ontario

Charley's Tavern
Windsor, Ontario

Denison's Brewing Co
Toronto, Ontario

Feathers
Toronto, Ontario

Granite Brewery (No 2)*
Toronto, Ontario

Heidelberg
Restaurant and Brewery
Heidelberg, Ontario

Canadian Breweries

James Gate
Toronto, Ontario

Kingston Brewing Company Ltd
Kingston, Ontario

Lion Brewery and Museum
Waterloo, Ontario

Major's Brew House
Ottawa, Ontario

Master's Brasserie and Brewpub
Ottawa, Ontario

Olde Stone Brewing Co
Peterborough, Ontario

Pepperwood Bistro
Burlington, Ontario

Port Arthur Brasserie and Brewpub
Thunder Bay, Ontario

Post-Production Bistro/O'Toole's
Toronto, Ontario

Robinson Brewing Co
Mississavga, Ontario

Rotterdam Brewing Co
Toronto, Ontario

Tapsters Brewhouse and Restaurant
Mississauga, Ontario

Tracks Brewpub
Brampton, Ontario

QUÉBEC
LARGE BREWERIES
La Brasserie Labatt's Limitee
LaSalle, Québec

Molson Breweries/Québec Div/ La Brasserie Molson O'Keefe
East Montreal, Québec

REGIONAL BREWERIES
Brasserie McAuslan
Montreal, Québec

Les Brasseurs du Nord Inc*
Blainville, Québec

Unibroue Inc
Chambly, Québec

MICROBREWERIES
Brasal-Brasserie Allemande
Lasalle, Québec

Brasseries Beauce Broue Inc
St Odilon, Québec

La Brasserie Portneuvoise
St Casimir, Québec

La Brasseurs de L'Anse
Anse St Jean, Québec

Les Brasseurs GMT
Montreal, Québec

BREWPUBS
Golden Lion Pub and Brewing Co*
Lennoxville, Québec

L'Inox
Québec City, Québec

La Cervoise
Montreal, Québec

La Taverne Du Sergeant
Montreal, Québec

Le Cheval Blanc
Montreal, Québec

Mon Village Brewery
Hudson, Québec

Vieux Copenhagen Brasseurs
St-Sauver Des Monts, Québec

SASKATCHEWAN
REGIONAL BREWERIES
Great Western Brewing Co
Saskatoon, Saskatchewan

Molson Breweries/Western Div/ Saskatchewan Region/Regina Plant
Regina, Saskatchewan

BREWPUBS
Barley Mill Brewing Co
Regina, Saskatchewan

Bonzzini's Brewpub
Regina, Saskatchewan

Brewsters Brewing Co and Restaurant (No 5)
Regina, Saskatchewan

Brewsters Brewing Co and Restaurant*
Regina, Saskatchewan

Brewsters Brewing Co and Restaurant/Cornerstone Inn (No 3)
Moose Jaw, Saskatchewan

Bushwakker Brewing Co Ltd*
Regina, Saskatchewan

Checkers Brewpub/ MacBradee's Brewing Co
Swift Current, Saskatchewan

Cheers Brew Pub & Restaurant
Saskatoon, Saskatchewan

Chubby's Brew Pub & Sports Bar
Humboldt, Saskatchewan

Clark's Crossing Brewpub
Saskatoon, Saskatchewan

Fox & Hounds Brewpub
Saskatoon, Saskatchewan

Last Straw
Regina, Saskatchewan

Saskatoon Brewing Co/ Cheers Roadhouse Inn
Saskatoon, Saskatchewan

ALBERTA

Alley Kat Brewing Co
9929 60th Ave
Edmonton, AB T6E 0C7
(403) 436-8922; FAX (403) 430-7363
Founded: March 1, 1995
Capacity: 3,500 hL
Head Brewer: Neil Herbst
Sales Mgr.: Richard Cholon
Contact: Richard Cholon

Big Rock Brewery Ltd
6403 35th St SE
Calgary, AB T2E 1N2
(403) 279-2917; FAX (403) 236-7523
Founded: Sept. 1, 1985
Capacity: 120,000 hL
Pres.: Ed McNally
Brewmaster: Bernd Pieper
Sales Mgr.: Brian Rowland
Contact: David Farran

Bow Valley Brewing Co
PO Box 3308
Canmore, AB T0L 0M0
(403) 678-2739; FAX (403) 678-8813
Founded: Jan. 30, 1995
Capacity: 7,500 hL
Head Brewer: Gordon Demaniuk
Pres./Sales Mgr.: Hugh Hancock
Pkg./Maint. Supervisor: Anthony Bankum
Contact: Gordon Demaniuk

Brewsters Brewing Co and Restaurant (No 2)
834 11th Ave SW
Calgary, AB T2R 0E5
(403) 263-2739; FAX (403) 265-2620
Founded: July 1, 1991
Capacity: 2,600 hL
Head Brewer: Clifford Auckland
Sec. Treas.: Marty Lanigan
VP: Laurie Lanigan
Pres.: Michael Lanigan
Contact: Clifford Auckland

Brewsters Brewing Co and Restaurant (No 4)
176-755 Lake Bonavista Dr SE
Calgary, AB T2J 0N3
(408) 225-2739; FAX (408) 225-2792
Head Brewer: Clifford Aukland

Brewsters Brewing Co and Restaurant (No 6)
11620 104th Ave
Edmonton, AB T5K 2T7
(403) 482-4677
Founded: Sept. 1, 1995
Capacity: 2,080 hL
Contact: Robert Walsh

Labatt's Alberta Brewery
PO Box 1818/4415 Calgary Tr
Edmonton, AB T5J 2N9
(403) 436-6060; FAX (403) 462-0099
http://www.labatt.com
Capacity: 639,150 bbl
Pres. Western Region: Robert A. Binnedyk
Sales Mgr.: G. Croft
Controller: Daren Hawrich
Contact: Robert Binnedyk

Mission Bridge Brewing Co
2417 Fourth St SW
Calgary, AB T2S 1X5
(403) 228-0071
Founded: Feb. 14, 1995
Contact: Mike Tymchuk

Molson Breweries/Western Div/Alberta Region/Edmonton Plant
10449 121st St
Edmonton, AB T5N 1L3
(403) 482-1786; FAX (403) 482-5799
Capacity: 700,000 hL
Plant Mgr.: Jeffrey Banister
Head Brewer: Dave Small
Asst. Brewer: Doug Gallagher
Area Pkg. Mgr.: Gerry Clayton
Eng. Mgr.: Brian Cole
Quality Control Mgr.: Ian Jones
Plant Controller: Doug Mohns
Contact: Jeffrey Banister

BRITISH COLUMBIA

Bayou Brewing Co Ltd
12751 Bathgate Way
Richmond, BC V6V 1Y5
(604) 270-9965
Contact: Masumi Gates

Bear Brewing Co
975-B Notre Dame Dr
Kamloops, BC V2C 5P8
(604) 851-2543; FAX (604) 851-9953
Founded: Jan. 1, 1995
Capacity: 7,000 hL
Head Brewer: David Beardsell
Sales Mgr.: Brian Keast
Contact: David Beardsell

Bowen Island Brewing Co
595 Artisan Lane
Bowen Island, BC V09 1G0
(604) 947-0822; FAX (604) 947-0899
Founded: June 17, 1994
Capacity: 10,000 bbl
Head Brewer: Don Bradley
Contact: Don Bradley

Granville Island Brewing Co
1285 W Broadway/Suite 214
Vancouver, BC V6H 3X8
(604) 738-9463; FAX (604) 738-0182
Founded: Jan. 1, 1984
Capacity: 80,000 bbl
Pres.: Ian Tostenson
VP Operations: Nick Bennett
Mktg. Mgr.: Jennifer Brash
Head Brewer: Joe Goetz
Sales Mgr.: Andrew Philip

Happy Valley Brewing Co
PO Box 1517
Summerland, BC V0H 1Z0
(604) 494-9314
Contact: Ronald Jackson

Horseshoe Bay Brewing Co Ltd
6695 Nelson Ave
Horseshoe Bay, BC V7W 2B2
(604) 921-8112; FAX (604) 658-4994
Founded: April 1, 1982
Capacity: 2,252 hL
Pres./Sales Mgr.: Cameron Allen
Head Brewer: Dean Ashdown
Contact: Cameron Allen

Howe Sound Brewing Co Ltd
3454 St George Ave
North Vancouver, BC V7N 1V8
(604) 598-6123
Contact: Stephen Shard

Labatt's Breweries/ British Columbia
PO Box 1950/1220 Erickson
Creston, BC V0B 1G0
(604) 428-9344; FAX (604) 428-3433
http://www.labatt.com
Plant Mgr.: J. Clark
Head Brewer: Kevin Hryclik
Pkg. Mgr.: F. Wioka
Contact: J. Clark

Labatt's Breweries/ British Columbia
210 Brunette Ave
New Westminster, BC V3L 4Z2
(604) 521-1844; FAX (604) 521-6848

http://www.labatt.com
Capacity: 748,231 hL
Plant Mgr.: C. Lemire
General Mgr.: Robert J. Kemble
Master Brewer: B. Donnelly
Contact: C. Lemire

Molson Breweries/ Western Division
604 W Broadway/Suite 1100
Vancouver, BC V5Z 4C2
(604) 664-1786; FAX (604) 664-1900
VP Sales: Scott Ellis
VP Operations: Ernie Liedtke
VP Distribution: Rob Boguski
VP Finance: Wayne Wood
VP Public Affairs: John Winter
VP Human Resources: Dale Scriven
Contact: Blair Shier

Molson Breweries/Western Div/B C Region/Vancouver Plant
1550 Burrard St
Vancouver, BC V6J 3G5
(604) 664-1786; FAX (604) 664-1900
Capacity:
Plant Mgr.: Joe Naassan
Head Brewer: Armand Thompson
Area Pkg. Mgr.: Barry McCartney
Engineering Mgr.: Tom Saunders
Quality Control Mgr.: Don Hadden
Plant Controller: Barry DeVito
Contact: Joe Naassan

Mount Begbie Brewing Co Ltd
PO Box 2995
Revelstoke, BC V0E 2S0
(604) 837-2756; FAX (604) 837-3082
Founded: April 1, 1996
Contact: Bart Larson

Nelson Brewing Co
512 Latimer St
Nelson, BC V1L 4T9
(604) 352-3582; FAX (604) 352-3466
Founded: April 1, 1991
Capacity: 7,280 hL
Treas.: Rick Dietrick
Sec.: Tim Pollock
Pres./Head Brewer: Patrick Glenny
Sales Mgr.: Tim Pollock
Contact: Paddy Glenny

Okanagan Spring Brewery
2101 27A Ave
Vernon, BC V1T 1T5
(604) 542-2337; FAX (604) 542-7780
brewmaster@okspring.com
http://www.okspring.com

Founded: Dec. 1, 1985
Capacity: 125,000 bbl
Sales Mgr.: Buko Von Krosigk
General Mgr.: Jakob Tobler
Head Brewer: Stefan Tobler
Contact: Stefan Tobler

Pacific Western Brewing Co
641 N Nechako Rd
Prince George, BC V2K 2M4
(604) 562-1131; FAX (604) 562-0799
Founded: Jan. 1, 1990
Capacity: 200,000 hL
Sales Mgr.: Mike Haney
Head Brewer: Kelly Olson
Packaging Mgr.: Jim Hubbard
Plant Mgr.: Thomas LeBoe
Pres.: Kazuko Komatsu
Contact: Kazuko Komatsu

Russell Brewing Co
20213018 80th Ave
Surrey, BC V3W 3A8
(604) 599-1190
Founded: June 26, 1995
Head Brewer: Mark Russell
Contact: Mark Russell

Sailor Hagar's Brewpub
221 W First St
North Vancouver, BC V7B 1M3
(604) 984-3087; FAX (604) 984-2990
ariedlin@direct.ca
Founded: May 25, 1994
Capacity: 800 hL
Pres.: Allan Riedlinger
Head Brewer: Gary Lohin
Sales Mgr.: Brian Riedlinger
Contact: Allan Riedlinger

Shaftebury Brewing Co Ltd
1973 Pandora St
Vancouver, BC V5L 5B2
(604) 255-4550; FAX (604) 255-8213
Founded: Aug. 19, 1987
Capacity: 15,000 hL
Sales Mgr.: Timothy Wittig
Head Brewer: Brent Duncan
Pres.: Paul Beaton
Contact: Paul Beaton

Spinnakers Brewpub Inc
308 Catherine St
Victoria, BC V9A 3S8
(604) 384-6613
Founded: May 15, 1984
Capacity: 1,800 hL
Contact: Paul Hadfield

Steam Works Brewing Co
375 Water St
Vancouver, BC V6B 5C6
(604) 689-2739
Head Brewer: Shirley Warren
Contact: Eli Gershkovitch

Storm Brewing Ltd
310 Commercial Dr
Vancouver, BC V5L 3V6
(604) 255-9119; FAX (604) 255-7276
Founded: June 1, 1995
Capacity: 130,000 hL
Contact: James Walton

Swans
Buckerfield Brewery
506 Pandora
Victoria, BC V8W 1N6
(604) 361-3310; FAX (604) 361-3491
Founded: April 1, 1989
Capacity: 1,800 hL
Head Brewer: Chris Johnson
Contact: Chris Johnson

Tall Ship Ale Co
39002 Discovery Way/Unit E
Squamish, BC V0N 3G0
(604) 892-5696; FAX (604) 892-5696
Founded: June 28, 1994
Capacity: 5,000 bbl
Contact: Bill Herdman

Tin Whistle Brewing Co
954 W Eckhardt Ave
Penticton, Victoria, BC V2A 2C1
(604) 770-1122; FAX (604) 770-1122
Founded: Oct. 8, 1995
Capacity: 960 hL
Head Brewer: Richard Grierson
Sales Mgr.: Lawrie Lock
Contact: Richard Grierson

Tree Brewing Co Ltd
806 Coronation Ave
Kelowna, BC V1Y 7A3
(604) 860-8836; FAX (604) 860-8839
treebrewing@awimc_com
Founded: April 15, 1996
Capacity: 4,000 L
Sales/Distribution: David Willoughby
Brewmaster: Ken Belall
Pres./General Mgr.: Geoff Twyman
Mktg/Admin.: Sara Hooker
VP Mktg: Malcolm Skinner
Contact: Geoff Twyman

Vancouver Island Brewing Co
2330 Government St
Victoria, BC V8T 5G5
(604) 361-0007; FAX (604) 360-0336
ken.wilmhurst@cyberstore.ca
Founded: Oct. 1, 1986
Capacity: 25,000 hL
Head Brewer: Ross Elliot
Pres.: Barry Fisher
Contact: Barry Fisher

Whistler Brewing Co
1209 Alpha Lake Rd
Whistler, BC V01 1B1
(604) 932-6185; FAX (604) 932-7293
Founded: Oct. 1, 1989
Capacity: 23,000 bbl
Sales Mgr.: Glen Lee
Prod. Mgr./Head Brewer: Brad Wheeler
Pres.: Trevor Khoe
Contact: Brad Wheeler

Yale Town Brewing Co
1110 Hamilton St
Vancouver, BC V6B 2S2
(604) 688-0039; FAX (604) 681-2749
Founded: Dec. 22, 1994
Co-Owner/General Mgr.: Fraser Boyer
Co-Owner: Mark James
Head Brewer: Iain Hill
Contact: Fraser Boyer

MANITOBA

Fort Garry Brewing Co Ltd
1249 Clarence/Unit 13
Winnipeg, MB R3T 1T4
(204) 475-8995
Founded: Jan. 16, 1995
Capacity: 4,000 L
Head Brewer: Gary De Pape
Sales Mgr: Jeep Woolley
Contact: Richard Hoeschen

Labatt's Manitoba Brewery
PO Box 776/1600 Notre Dame/Suite A
Winnipeg, MB R3C 2N3
(204) 697-5100; FAX (204) 632-9088
http://www.labatt.com
Founded: Jan. 1, 1947
Capacity: 538,600 hL
Brewery Mgr.: Glen Kilback
Sales Mgr.: Mike Hogan
Contact: Glen Kilback

Molson Breweries/Western Div/Manitoba Region/Winnipeg Plant
77 Redwood Ave/Second Floor
Winnipeg, MB R2W 5J5
(204) 586-8011; FAX (204) 586-4883
Capacity: 500,000 hL
Plant Mgr.: Peter Walker
Engineering Mgr.: Jim Suggitt
Head Brewer: Alister Archibald
Plant Controller: Bob Mondor
Contact: Peter Walker

NEW BRUNSWICK

Moosehead Breweries Ltd
PO Box 3100 Station B
89 Main St
St John, NB E2M 3H2
(506) 635-7000; FAX (506) 635-7029
Capacity: 1,350,000 hL
Chairman/CEO: Philip W. Oland
Contact: Philip W. Oland

Picaroons Brewing Co
349 King St
Fredericton, NB E3B 1B2
(506) 455-2537; FAX (506) 459-5115
Founded: Oct. 19, 1995
Capacity: 2,000 hL
Head Brewer: Andrew Hashey
Sales Mgr.: Seqan Dunbar
Contact: Shawn Dunbar

NEWFOUNDLAND

Labatt's Newfoundland Brewery
PO Box 7160
St John's, NF A1E 3Y4
(709) 579-0121; FAX (709) 579-2018
http://www.labatt.com
Capacity: 225,000 hL
Provincial Gen. Mgr.: G. Burke
Provincial Sales Mgr.: G. Manning
Head Brewer: P. Bursey
Contact: G. Burke

Molson Breweries/Atlantic Region/St John's Plant
PO Box 5308/Circular Rd
St John's, NF A1C 5W1
(709) 726-1786; FAX (709) 726-2382
Capacity: 250,000 hL
General Mgr.: Jules A. Yetman
Plant Mgr.: Justin Conway
Head Brewer: Boob Reddy
Area Pkg. Supervisor: Gary Glass
Area Pkg. Supervisor: Carl LeGrow
Engineering Supervisor: Bill Hunt
Whse. Supervisor: Jack Rolls
Whse. Supervisor: George Hynes
Quality Control Mgr.: Les Maunder
Plant Controller: Edgar Parsons
Contact: Jules A. Yetman

NORTHWEST TERRITORIES

Arctic Brewing Co
3502 Wiley Rd
Yellowknife, NT X1A 2L5
(403) 920-2739; FAX (403) 920-2337
Capacity: 2,880 hL
Head Brewer: Victor MacIntosh
Brewer: Tim Noble
Mktg. Dir.: Barb Knight
Contact: Calvin Kuch

NOVA SCOTIA

Granite Brewery
1222 Barrington Rd
Halifax, NS B3J 2L4
(902) 422-4954; FAX (902) 423-2793
http://www.interlog.com/~granite
Founded: April 1, 1985
Capacity: 832 hL
Sales Mgr: Nadine Halliday
Head Brewer: Kevin Keefe
Contact: Kevin Keefe

Heather Motel and Brewpub
N Foord St
Stellarton, NS B0K 1F0
(902) 752-8401

Keith's Brewery
3055 Agricola St
Halifax, NS B3K 4G2
(902) 455-1474

Oland Breweries Ltd
3055 Agricola St
Halifax, NS B3K 4G2
(902) 453-1867; FAX (902) 453-3847
Capacity: 600,000 hL
Pres./General Mgr.: P. C. Carter
Contact: P. C. Carter

Paddy's Pub and Brewery
42 Aberdeen St
Kentville, NS B09 B9Z
(902) 678-3199

ONTARIO

Addingtons
575 Bank St
Ottawa, ON K1S 5L7
(613) 236-1641
Founded: Aug. 25, 1995
Contact: Jeff Kane

Al Frisco's
133 John St
Toronto, ON M5V 2Z4
(416) 595-8201; FAX (416) 595-5064
Founded: March 1, 1994
Capacity: 1,400 hL
Head Brewer: Michael Duggan
Sales Mgr.: Rick Colli
Contact: Michael Duggan

Algonquin Brewery
1 Old Brewery Lane
Formosa, ON N0G 1W0
(519) 367-2995; FAX (519) 367-5414
Founded: June 1, 1989
Capacity: 100,000 hL
Sales Mgr.: Leo Maroussi
Head Brewer: Jack Massey
Pres.: Evan Hayter
VP Sales and Mktg.: Drew Knox
Contact: Drew Knox

Amsterdam Brewing Co
600 King St W
Toronto, ON M5V 1M6
(416) 504-1040; FAX (416) 504-1043
Founded: April 18, 1988
Capacity: 5,000 hL
Head Brewer: Joel Manning
Pres.: Roel Bramer
Contact: Joel Manning

Blue Anchor Brewery
47 West St SE
Orillia, ON L3V 5G5
(705) 325-7735
Capacity: 170 hL
Pres.: Rick Neil
Contact: Rick Neil

Brick Brewing Co Ltd
181 King St S
Waterloo, ON N2J 1P7
(519) 576-9100; FAX (519) 576-0470
Founded: Dec. 18, 1984
Capacity: 87,000 hL
Pres.: James Brickman
Head Brewer: Bill Barnes
Sales Mgr.: Fred Gallagher
VP Operations: Mike Ostner
Dir. of Quality Control: Steven Smith
VP Finance: Paul Chadder
Contact: James Brickman

C C's Brew Pub
6981 Mill Creek Dr/Unit 1
Mississauga, ON L5N 6B8
(905) 542-0136
Head Brewer: Murray Voakes
Contact: Murray Voakes

CEEPS Barney's Ltd
671 Richmond St
London, ON N6A 3G7
(519) 432-1425
Founded: Jan. 1, 1991
Capacity: 500 hL
Head Brewer: Charles MacLean
Contact: Rick Tatersall

Cellar Tap
320 Bay St
Sault Ste Marie, ON P6A 1X1
(705) 946-2867
Founded: Dec. 15, 1994
Contact: Ms. Scholsteal

Charley's Tavern
4715 Tecumseh Rd E
Windsor, ON N8T 1B6
(519) 945-5512
Contact: Gord O'Keefe

Conners Brewery
227 Bunting Rd
St Catharines, ON L2M 3Y2
(905) 988-9363; FAX (905) 988-1621
Founded: March 1, 1991
Capacity: 20,000 hL
Sales Mgr.: John Mertens
Consulting Brewmaster: Doug Morrow
Pres.: Glen Dalzell
VP Finance: Marc Bedard
Packaging and Plant Services Mgr: Dan Unkerskov
Brewing and Quality Assurance Mgr.: Jamie MacNaughton
Contact: Glen Dalzell

Copperhead Brewing Co Ltd
174 Colonnade Rd S
Nepean, ON K2E 7J5
(613) 226-8340; FAX (613) 727-0426
info@copperhead-brewing.com
http://www.copperhead-brewing.com
Founded: Jan. 1, 1992
Partner: Brian Nixon
Head Brewer: Bill McGarry
Sales Mgr.: Laurie Howland

Creemore Springs Brewery Ltd
PO Box 369
Creemore, ON L0M 1G0
(705) 466-2531; FAX (705) 466-3306
Founded: Aug. 15, 1987
Capacity: 17,900 hL
VP/Head Brewer: Gordon Fuller
VP/Brewery Mgr.: Kurtis Zeng
VP/Sales Mgr.: Howard Thompson
Pres.: John Wiggins
Sr. VP/Special Projects: Russell E. Thornton
Contact: Howard Thompson

Denison's Brewing Co
75 Victoria St
Toronto, ON M5C 2B1
(416) 360-5877; FAX (416) 360-5909
Founded: Jan. 11, 1989
Capacity: 2,000 bbl
General Mgr.: Ed Kusins
Pres./Head Brewer: Michael Hancock
Contact: Michael Hancock

Elora Brewery Ltd/ Taylor & Bate
55 Mill St W
Elora, ON N0B 1F0
(519) 846-2965
Founded: Sept. 5, 1993
Crozier Taylor
Head Brewer: Doug Warden
Sales Mgr: Brad Fornell
Contact: Crozier Taylor

F & M Breweries Ltd
355 Elmira Rd/Suite 135
Guelph, ON N1K 1S5
(519) 763-1155; FAX (519) 763-1525
fortnum@wat.hookup.net or
smits@wat.hookup.net
http://www.pints.com/pints/index.html
Founded: May 1, 1995
Capacity: 3,000 hL
Head Brewer: Richard Fortnum
Head Brewer: Charles Maclean
Administrator: Antonia Smits
Sales Mgr.: Terry Debono
Contact: Richard Fortnum

Feathers
962 Kingston Rd
Toronto, ON M4E 1S7
(416) 694-0443
Founded: Dec. 1, 1994
Contact: Ian Innis

Canadian Breweries (Ontario)

Glatt Bros Brewing Co
151 Thompson Rd
London, ON N5Z 2Y7
(519) 668-6204; FAX (519) 668-1385
Founded: Dec. 1, 1993
Head Brewer/Sec./Treas.: John Glatt
Pres./Sales Mgr.: Paul Glatt
Contact: Paul Glatt

Gold Crown Brewing Co
71 King St N
Waterloo, ON N2J 2X2
(519) 886-2071; FAX (519) 886-0761
Founded: Dec. 8, 1995
Capacity: 50 hL
Head Brewer: Kelly Adlys
Sales Mgr.: David Adlys
Advertising Mgr.: Crystal Adlys
Contact: Kelly Adlys

Granite Brewery (No 2)
245 Eglinton Ave E
Toronto, ON M4P 3B7
(416) 322-0723; FAX (416) 322-0117
granite@interlog.com
http://www.interlog.com/~granite
Founded: Aug. 12, 1991
Capacity: 1,400 hL
Proprietor: Kevin Keefe
Head Brewer/Sales Mgr.: Ron Keefe
Contact: Ron Keefe

Great Lakes Brewing Co
30 Queen Elizabeth Blvd
Etobicoke, ON M8Z 1L8
(416) 255-4510; FAX (416) 255-4907
Founded: Jan. 1, 1992
Capacity:
General Mgr.: Anetta Bulut
Head Brewer: Bruce Cornish
Pres.: Peter Built
VP: Peter Built, Jr.
Contact: Anetta Bulut

Hart Brewing Co Ltd
1 Brewery Lane
175 Industrial Ave
Carleton Place, ON K7C 3V7
(613) 253-4278; FAX (613) 253-3705
Founded: Oct. 1, 1994
Capacity: 15,000 hL
Head Brewer: Keith Hart
Pres./Brewery Mgr.: Lorne Hart
CEO/General Mgr.: Jon Hatchell
Contact: Jon Hatchell

Heidelberg Restaurant and Brewery
PO Box 116/2 King St
Heidelberg, ON NOB 1YO
(519) 699-4413
Contact: Howard MacMillan

Hometowne Breweries Ltd
1 Adelaide St N
London, ON N6B 3P8
(519) 432-1344
Founded: Aug. 1, 1993
Capacity: 4,000 hL
Head Brewer: Joe Caccamo
Sales Mgr.: Ron Knull
Contact: Brian Abraham

James Gate
1661 Bloor St W
Toronto, ON M6P 1A6
(416) 530-4034
Contact: Robert Costello

Kawartha Lakes Brewing Co
687 Rye St/Unit 5
Peterborough, ON K9J 6X1
(705) 741-1819
Founded: April 1, 1996
Contact: Andrew Cousins

Kingston Brewing Co Ltd
34 Clarence St
Kingston, ON K7L 1W9
(613) 542-4978; FAX (613) 541-1218
Founded: April 25, 1986
Capacity: 430 hL
Business Mgr.: Van Turner
Head Brewer: Roger Eccleston
Contact: Van Turner

Labatt's Ontario Breweries
PO Box 5050/150 Simcoe St
London, ON N6A 4M3
(519) 676-5050; FAX (519) 667-7422
http://www.labatt.com
Capacity: 2,000,000 hL
Brewery Mgr.: Les Sparling
Brewmaster: Mark Hantiuk
Pkg. Mgr.: Ed Miziolek
Sales Mgr.: Doug Elliott
Contact: Les Sparling

Labatt's Breweries of Canada
181 Bay St/Suite 200
Toronto, ON M5J 2T3
(416) 361-5050; FAX (416) 361-5200
http://www.labatt.com
Pres.: H. Powell
Contact: H Powell

Labatt's Ontario Breweries
Box 5050/Station A
50 Resources Rd
Etobicoke, ON M9N 3N7
(416) 248-0751
http://www.labatt.com
Capacity: 1,720,000 hL
Pres./General Mgr.: H. Powell
Head Brewer: B. White
Dir. Finance: F. Heinemann
Contact: H. Powell

Lakeport Brewing Corp
201 Burlington St E
Hamilton, ON L8L 4H2
(905) 523-4200; FAX (905) 523-1422
Capacity: 600,000 bbl
VP Finance and Administration: Vince Lubertino
VP Operations: Adam Foye
VP Sales: Russ Hutchings

Lion Brewery and Museum
Huether Hotel/59 King St N
Waterloo, ON N2J 2X2
(519) 886-3350
Founded: June 3, 1987
Head Brewer: Kelly Adlys
Sales Mgr.: Kelly Adlys
Contact: Kelly Adlys

Magnotta Brewery Ltd
1760 Midland Ave
Scarborough, ON M1P 3G2
(416) 701-9463
Founded: April 1, 1996
Contact: Gabe Magnotta

Major's Brew House
453 Sussex Dr
Ottawa, ON K1N 6Z4
(613) 789-7405
Founded: Feb. 15, 1995
Contact: Omar Quadar

Master's Brasserie and Brewpub
330 Queen St
Ottawa, ON K1R 5A5
(613) 594-3688
Founded: Jan. 20, 1988
Capacity: 840 hL
Sec.: Tom Barton
Treas.: Tom Barton
Head Brewer: Tom Barton

Molson Breweries
175 Bloor St E/North Tower
Toronto, ON M4W 3S4
(416) 975-1786; FAX (416) 975-4088

Founded: Jan. 7, 1986
Capacity: 8,063,000 hL
Sr. VP Brewing: Walter Hogg
Pres./CEO: John Barnett
Pres./Québec: Andre Tranchemontagne
Pres./Ontario and Atlantic: David Perkins
Pres./West: Blair Shier
Sr. VP Finance/CFO: Hugh C. Atkin
Sr. VP Corporate Affairs: A. Barry Joslin
Contact: John Barnett

Molson Breweries/ Ontario Div/North York Plant
4100 Yonge St/Second Fl
North York, ON M2P 2E6
(416) 226-1786; FAX (416) 512-3800
Pres.: David Perkins
VP Mktg: David W. Minnett
VP Sales: Roy Hryn
VP Distribution: John Aitken
VP Finance: John Amodeo
VP Public Affairs: John Hay
VP Human Resources: Keith Gilbert
Contact: David Perkins

Molson Breweries/ Ontario Div/Etobicoke Plant
1 Carlingview Dr
Toronto, ON M9W 5E5
(416) 675-1786; FAX (416) 675-2199
Capacity: 2,987,700 hL
Plant Mgr.: Ronald K. Kitamura
Head Brewer: Ian Douglas
Area Pkg. Mgr.: Chris Nunes
Area Pkg. Mgr.: Daniel Pelland
Plant Eng.: Steve McLaughlin
Warehouse Mgr.: Jack Keeling
Quality Control Mgr.: Al Coutts
Plant Mgr.: Lorna Scott
Contact: Ronald K. Kitamura

Molson Breweries/ Ontario Div/Barrie Plant
1 Big Bay Point Rd
Barrie, ON L4M 4V3
(416) 361-1407; FAX (416) 721-7296
Capacity: 2,130,500 bbl
Plant Mgr.: Pierre Ferland
Head Brewer: Barry Heisz
Area Pkg. Mgr.: Dan Beasoleil
Area Pkg. Mgr.: Bruce Thompson
Warehouse Mgr.: Steve Ropp
Quality Control Mgr.: Paul Dore
Plant Controller: Jim Cruikshank
Contact: Pierre Ferland

Niagara Falls Brewing Co
6863 Lundy's Lane
Niagara Falls, ON L2G 1V7
(905) 374-1166; FAX (416) 374-2930
Founded: July 22, 1989
Capacity: 14,000 hL
Head Brewer: Harvey Hurlbutt
VP: Frank Marotta
Pres.: Mario Criveller
Sales Mgr./Gen. Mgr.: Claude Corriveau
Contact: Wally Moroz

Northern Breweries Ltd
154 N Algoma St
Thunder Bay, ON P7B 5E7
(807) 345-6518
Capacity: 60,000 bbl
Plant Mgr.: G. Vondrasek
Contact: G. Vondrasek

Northern Breweries Ltd
503 Bay St
Sault Ste Marie, ON P6A 5L9
(705) 254-7373; FAX (705) 254-4482
didier@soonet.com
Capacity: 310,000 hL
Head Brewer: Robert Shami
VP/Sec. Treas.: Barry Didier
Contact: R. E. Eaket

Northern Breweries Ltd
185 Lorne St
Sudbury, ON P3E 4P8
(705) 675-7561; FAX (705) 675-2926
Capacity: 130,000 bbl
Plant Mgr./Master Brewer: Jim Kaminski
Contact: Jim Kaminski

Old Credit Brewing Co
6 Queen St W
Port Credit, ON K5H 1R4
(905) 271-9888
Founded: Sept. 1, 1994
Capacity: 416 hL
Head Brewer: Orrin Besko
Contact: Orrin Besko

Olde Stone Brewing Co
380 George St N
Peterborough, ON K9H 3R3
(705) 745-0495
Founded: April 1, 1996
Contact: Scott Wood

Pepperwood Bistro
1455 Lakeshore Rd
Burlington, ON L7S 2J1
(905) 333-6999; FAX (905) 333-6858
dwood@canrem.com
Capacity: 100 bbl
Head Brewer/Sales Mgr.: David Wood
Contact: David Wood

Port Arthur Brasserie and Brewpub
901 Red River Rd
Thunder Bay, ON P7B 1K3
(807) 767-4415; FAX (807) 767-4140
Founded: Jan. 1, 1988
Capacity: 360 bbl
Head Brewer: John Tilbury
General Mgr.: Traci Calder
Contact: Fraser Dougall

Post-Production Bistro/O'Toole's
1189 King St W
Toronto, ON M6K 3C5
(416) 534-3666; FAX (416) 534-3257
Contact: William Stewart

Quinte Brewery
150 Sidney St
Belleville, ON K8P 5EZ
(613) 968-2739; FAX (613) 969-9934
Contact: Ron Powell

Robinson Brewing Co
2390 Cawthra Rd/Suite 3
Mississavga, ON L5A 2X1
(905) 270-0040; FAX (905) 273-4383
Contact: Michael

Rotterdam Brewing Co
600 King W
Toronto, ON M5V 1M6
(416) 868-6882
Contact: Gary Hoyer

Sleeman Brewing & Malting Co
551 Clair Rd W
Guelph, ON N1H 6H9
(519) 822-1834; FAX (519) 822-0430
Founded: Sept. 1, 1988
Capacity: 225,000 hL
Sales Mgr.: Nick Porcellato
VP: Doug Berchtold
VP: Kevin Meens
VP: Al Brash
Head Brewer: Al Brash
Pres./CEO: John Sleeman
Contact: Al Brash

Canadian Breweries (Ontario–Québec)

Tapsters Brewhouse and Restaurant
100 Britania Rd E
Mississauga, ON L4Z 2G1
(416) 890-8909
Founded: Jan. 1, 1987
Capacity: 400 hL
Contact: Derrick Grimaldi

Thames Valley Brewing Co
1764 Oxford St
London, ON N5V 3R6
(519) 457-2023
Founded: Sept. 19, 1992
Capacity: 6,000 hL
Head Brewer: Joe Caccamo
Sales Mgr.: Sandy Munro
Contact: Joe Caccamo

Tracks Brewpub
60 Queen St E
Brampton, ON L6V 1A9
(905) 453-3063
Founded: Jan. 1, 1988
Capacity: 170 hL
Co-Owner: Chris Minos
Co-Owner: Jimmy Floris
Head Brewer: John Lippert
Contact: Chris Minos

Trafalgar Brewing Co
760 Pacific Rd/Unit 9
Oakville, ON L6L 6M5
(905) 847-3378; FAX (905) 845-2246
Founded: Dec. 15, 1993
Capacity: 15,000 hL
Sales Mgr.: Brent Popek
Head Brewer: George Hengsthan
General Mgr.: M. Arnold
Pres.: N. Arnold
Contact: George Hengstman

Upper Canada Brewing Co
2 Atlantic Ave
Toronto, ON M6K 1X8
(416) 534-9281; FAX (416) 534-6998
Founded: Aug. 5, 1985
Capacity: 72,000 hL
VP Sales: Greg Cromwell
Pres.: Frank Heaps
VP Production./Brewmaster: Dr. Richard Rench
Exec. VP: Terry Smith
Contact: Frank Heaps

Wellington County Brewery Ltd
950 Woodlawn Rd W
Guelph, ON N1K 1B8
(519) 837-2337; FAX (519) 837-3142
ironduke@sentex.net
http://www.sentex.net/wellington
Founded: Oct. 1, 1985
Capacity: 8,000 hL
Head Brewer: Michael Stirrup
Office Mgr.: Faith Laird
Pres.: Philip R. Gosling
Sales Mgr.: Jake McKay
Contact: Faith Laird

QUÉBEC

Brasal-Brasserie Allemande
8477 Cordner
Lasalle, PQ H8N 2X2
(514) 365-5050; FAX (514) 365-2954
Founded: Sept. 1, 1989
Capacity: 20,000 hL
Head Brewer: Harald Sowade
Distributing Mgr.: Daniel Boileau
Mgr. Dir.: Etan Jagermann
Pres.: Marcel Jagermann
Contact: Etan Jagermann

Brasserie McAuslan
4850 Rue St Ambroise
Bureau 100
Montreal, PQ H4C 3N8
(514) 939-3060; FAX (514) 939-6136
Founded: Feb. 9, 1989
Capacity: 35,000 bbl
Sales Mgr.: Georges Treskine
Head Brewer: Ellen Bounsall
Pres.: Peter McAuslan
Distribution Dir.: Cynthia Montgomery
Contact: Peter McAuslan

Brasseries Beauce Broue Inc
295 Industrial St
St Odilon, PQ G0S 3A0
(418) 464-2768; FAX (418) 464-4560
Founded: Feb. 21, 1995
Capacity: 5,500 hL
General Mgr.: Raymond Parent
Pres./Co-Owner: Clement Cliche
Head Brewer: Serge Campeau
Distributor/Sales Mgr.: Pascal Schoune
Sec.: Tina Lauzon
Contact: Raymond Parent

Golden Lion Pub and Brewing Co
PO Box 474/2 College St
Lennoxville, PQ J1M 1Z6
(819) 562-4589; FAX (819) 346-4533
Founded: July 1, 1986
Capacity: 1,000 hL
Sales Mgr.: Stephen Groves
Head Brewer: W. S. Groves
Second Brewer: Terry Drew
Contact: Stan Groves

L'Inox
37 Rue St Andre
Québec City, PQ G1K 8T3
(418) 692-2877
Founded: Dec. 10, 1987
Capacity: 500 hL
Partner: Roger Roy
Partner/Head Brewer: Pierre Turgeon
Partner: Andre Jean
Contact: Andre Jean

La Brasserie Labatt's Limitee
50 Labatt St
LaSalle, PQ H8R 3E7
(514) 366-5050; FAX (514) 364-8005
Capacity: 1,960,060 bbl
Pres.: M. Boisvert
VP Finance: M. Portelance
VP Operations: A. Lessard
Contact: M. Boisvert

La Brasserie Portneuvoise
225 Hardy St
St Casimir, PQ G0A 3L0
(418) 339-3242
Owner: Hercule Trottier
Contact: Hercule Trottier

La Brasseurs de L'Anse
182-170 Rd
Anse St Jean, PQ G0V 1J0
(418) 272-3045
Founded: Jan. 1, 1995
Contact: Sylvain Boudreault

La Cervoise
4457 Blvd St Laurent
Montreal, PQ H2W 1Z8
(514) 843-6586
Capacity: 800 hL
Asst. Brewer: Luc Montpetit
Head Brewer: Shawn Tordon
Pres.: Jean Pierre Trepanier
Contact: Jean Pierre Trepanier

La Taverne du Sergeant
Recrute/4650 St Lawrence Blvd
Montreal, PQ H2T 1R2
(514) 287-1412
Founded: Oct. 15, 1993
Capacity: 500 hL
Co-Proprietor: Louis Andre Joyal
Co-Proprietor: Louis Regimbald
Co-Proprietor: Philippe Calendre

Head Brewer: Stephane Durocher
Head Brewer: Pascal Theriault
Contact: Louis Andrejoyal

Le Cheval Blanc
809 Ontario St
Montreal, PQ H2L 1P1
(514) 522-0211
Contact: Jerome Denys

Les Brasseurs du Nord Inc
875 Michele-Bohec
Blainville, PQ J7C 5J6
(514) 979-8400; FAX (514) 979-3733
Founded: June 1, 1988
Capacity: 35,000 hL
Sales Mgr.: Jean Morin
General Dir.: Bernard Morin
Pres./Head Brewer: Laura Urtnowski
Contact: Laura Urtnowski

Les Brasseurs GMT
5585 Rue de la Roche
Montreal, PQ H2J 3K3
(514) 274-4941; FAX (514) 274-6138
Founded: March 1, 1988
Capacity: 35,000 bbl
General Mgr.: Normand Guerin
Head Brewer: Andre Lafreniere
Sales Mgr.: Claude Allaire
Contact: Normand Guerin

Molson Breweries/Québec Div/La Brasserie Molson O'Keefe
1555 Notre Dame St
East Montreal, PQ H2L 2R5
(514) 521-1786; FAX (514) 598-6968
Capacity: 770,000 hL
Pres.: Andre Tranchemontagne
VP Mktg.: Gerry Frappier
VP Sales: Mike Robitaille
VP Public Affairs: Alban Asselin
VP Human Resources: Roger Carpentier
VP/Plant Mgr.: Robert Presseau
VP Finance: Robert Cholette
VP Distribution: Mario Halle
Plant Controller: Danny Berthelet
Contact: Andre Tranchemontagne

Mon Village Brewery
PO Box 794/2750 Cote St
Hudson, PQ J0P 1H0
(514) 458-7006
Founded: March 1, 1987
Contact: David Crockart

Unibroue Inc
80 des Carrieres
Chambly, PQ J3L 2H6
(514) 658-7658; FAX (514) 658-9195
Founded: Jan. 1, 1991
Capacity: 125,000 bbl
Head Brewer: Gino Vantiechem
Pres./Sales Mgr.: Andre Dion
Contact: Andre Dion

Vieux Copenhagen Brasseurs
220 A Chemin du Lac Millette/
Carrefour des Trois Villages
St-Sauver des Monts, PQ J0R 1R3
(514) 227-7777
Founded: June 18, 1995
Contact: Paul Fountotous

SASKATCHEWAN

Barley Mill Brewing Co
6807 Rochdale Blvd
Regina, SK S4X 2Z2
(306) 949-1500; FAX (306) 949-0006
Capacity: 756 hL
Co-Owner: Kevin McCutcheon
Co-Owner/Sales Mgr.: Perry Dunn
Head Brewer: Perry Dunn
Co-Owner: Dave Dunn
Contact: Perry Dunn

Bonzzini's Brewpub
4634 Albert St S
Regina, SK S4S 6B4
(306) 586-3553
Contact: Perry Dunn

Brewsters Brewing Co and Restaurant (No 5)
480 McCarthy Boulevard N
Regina, SK S4R 7M2
(306) 522-2739
Founded: Sept. 18, 1995
Capacity: 1,560 hL
Head Brewer: Mike Gamblin
Contact: Mike Gamblin

Brewsters Brewing Co and Restaurant/ Cornerstone Inn (No 3)
8 Main St N
Moose Jaw, SK S6H 3J6
(306) 694-5580; FAX (306) 565-3384
Capacity: 520 bbl
Head Brewer: Stan Gerlach
General Mgr.: Vic Dormuth
Brewer: Matthew Heisler
Contact: Laurie Lanigan

Brewsters Brewing Co and Restaurant
1832 Victoria Ave E
Regina, SK S4N 7K3
(306) 761-1500; FAX (306) 565-3384
Founded: May 17, 1989
Capacity: 1,560 hL
Head Brewer: Michael Gamblin
Sec.: Marty A. Lanigan
Pres.: Michael H. Lanigan
VP/Head Brewer: Laurie G. Lanigan
Manager: Stan Gerlach
Contact: Michael Gamblin

Bushwakker Brewing Co Ltd
2206 Dewdney Ave
Regina, SK S4R 1H3
(306) 359-7276; FAX (306) 359-7750
bush.info@eagle.wbm.ca
http://www.wbm.ca/users/broberts
Founded: Jan. 25, 1991
Capacity: 2,000 hL
Head Brewer: Scott Robertson
Gen. Mgr./Sales Mgr.: Elaine Robertson
Owner: Bev Robertson
Contact: Bev Robertson

Checkers Brewpub/ MacBradee's Brewing Co
240 Central Ave N/Suite 2
Swift Current, SK S9H 0L2
(306) 778-9110; FAX (306) 773-9800
Founded: Jan. 2, 1996
Capacity: 1,872 bbl
Pres.: Randy Ludwar
Head Brewer/Sales Mgr.: Chad Thompson
Contact: Randy Ludwar

Cheers Brew Pub & Restaurant
32-2105 Eighth St E
Saskatoon, SK S7K 5M8
(306) 955-7500; FAX (306) 955-8144
Capacity: 2,130 bbl
Owner/Pres.: Russ Turner
Brewer: Randy Uytterhagen
General Mgr.: Ross Meredith
Contact: Russ Turner

Chubby's Brew Pub & Sports Bar
PO Box 1650
Humboldt, SK S0K 2A0
(306) 682-2110
Founded: June 15, 1994
Head Brewer: Larry Couchene
Contact: Larry Courchene

Canadian Breweries (Saskatchewan)

Clark's Crossing Brewpub
3030 Diefenbaker
Saskatoon, SK S7L 7K2
(306) 384-6633
Founded: Jan. 1, 1990
Head Brewer: Peter Kufeldt
Contact: Pete Kufeldt

Fox & Hounds Brewpub
7 Asisniboine Dr
Saskatoon, SK S7K 4C1
(306) 664-2233; FAX (306) 664-2237
Capacity: 450 hL
General Mgr.: John Cunningham
Head Brewer: Peter Kufeldt
Contact: Pete Kufeldt

Great Western Brewing Co
519 Second Ave N
Saskatoon, SK S7K 2C6
(306) 653-4653; FAX (306) 653-2166
Founded: Jan. 1, 1990
Capacity: 80,000 bbl
Sales Mgr.: Jack Whyte
Finance Mgr.: Dean Orosz
Pres./CEO: Ron Waldman
Head Brewer: Gib Henderson
Contact: Gib Henderson

Last Straw
127 Albert St N
Regina, SK S4R 8C7
(306) 545-1911
Contact: Mike Taschuk

Molson Breweries/Western Div/Saskatchewan Region/Regina Plant
1300 Dewdney Ave
Regina, SK S4R 1G4
(306) 359-1786; FAX (306) 757-3011
Capacity: 255,660 bbl
Plant Mgr.: John Hood
Head Brewer: Kerry Scarsbrook
Area Pkg. Mgr.: Peter J. Kirychuk
Engineering Mgr.: Bruce Alexander
Quality Control Mgr.: Anita Fuller
Plant Controller: George Gross
Contact: John Hood

Saskatoon Brewing Co./ Cheers Roadhouse Inn
2105 Grosvenor Park/Suite 32
Saskatoon, SK S7H 2T5
(306) 955-7500; FAX (306) 955-8144
Founded: Jan. 15, 1991
Capacity: 2,340 hL
Pres.: Russ Turner
Head Brewer: Randy Uytterhagen
Contact: Randy Uytterhagen

7 North American Contract Brewing Companies

Contract brewing companies are an important segment of the craft-brewing industry. These are businesses that hire or "rent" a brewery to produce their beer. Whether or not they operate their own brewing facility (as many of them do, in addition to contracting), contract brewing companies play just as significant a role as microbreweries and brewpubs in helping craft-brewed beer gain greater recognition and wider acceptance among North American beer drinkers.

In addition, contract brewing companies benefit the entire brewing industry by utilizing the excess capacity available at many regional breweries, microbreweries, and large breweries alike.

The companies are compiled in two ways. First is a state-by-state list with only the company name, city, and state. Second is the directory listing of all companies, in alphabetical order, complete with addresses, phone numbers, and personnel. In addition, each company's listing also includes the name of the brewery (or breweries) that makes their beer.

---

* Denotes Institute for Brewing Studies Brewery Member.
[1] Also does business as a brewpub.
[2] Also does business as a microbrewery.

UNITED STATES CONTRACT BREWING COMPANIES

ARIZONA
Black Mountain Brewing Co[2]
Cave Creek, Arizona

CALIFORNIA
American Beerguy Inc[1]
Suasalito, California

Beverly Hills Beerhouse Co
Brisbane, California

Bohemian Brewery
Torrance, California

Brewery Atlantis
San Francisco, California

Danse-Skjold Brewing Co
Solvang, California

Heckler Brewing Co*
Tahoe City, California

Hoppy Brewing Co*
San Jose, California

Humpback Brewing Co
Cerritos, California

Lake Tahoe Brewing Co Inc*
Tahoe City, California

McKenzie River Partners*
San Francisco, California

Owen's Brewing Co[1]
Hayward, California

Pete's Brewing Co*
Palo Alto, California

Preservation Ale
Orinda, California

San Andreas Brewing Co[2]
Hollister, California

Wanker Beer Inc
Newport Beach, California

William & Scott Brewing Co/Rhino Chasers*
Huntington Beach, California

Yen Sum
Sonoma, California

COLORADO
Alpine Brewing Co/ Naked Aspen Beer Co
Littleton, Colorado

Atlantis Brewing Co
Denver, Colorado

Beartooth Brewing Co*
Boulder, Colorado

Big Nose Brewing Co*
Denver, Colorado

Blue Moon Brewing Co
Denver, Colorado

Cherry Creek Brewing Co*
Denver, Colorado

High Point Brewing Corp
Denver, Colorado

Jamestown Brewing Co
Denver, Colorado

Pine Street Brewing Co
Louisville, Colorado

Red Ass Brewing Co*
Fort Collins, Colorado

San Juan Brewing Co*[1]
Telluride, Colorado

Snow Dog Brewing Corp
Avon, Colorado

Telluride Beer Co
Denver, Colorado

Two Angels Beer Co
Englewood, Colorado

North American Contract Brewing Companies

CONNECTICUT
Elm City Brewing Co[2]
New Haven, Connecticut

DELAWARE
Blue Hen Beer Co*
Newark, Delaware

DISTRICT OF COLUMBIA
Fischer Brewing Co Inc
Washington, District of Columbia

Olde Heurich Brewing Co*
Washington, District of Columbia

FLORIDA
Abbey Brewing Co*
Miami Beach, Florida

Florida Beer Brands
Orlando, Florida

Full Moon International Inc./ Lake Highland Brewing Co.*
Maitland, Florida

McGuire's Irish Pub and Brewery*[1]
Pensacola, Florida

Mill Bakery, Brewery & Eatery[1]
Winter Park, Florida

Old Florida Brewing Corp[2]
Oakland Park, Florida

Seagrams Beverage Co
Tampa, Florida

GEORGIA
David & Mark Brewing Co
Atlanta, Georgia

Friends Brewing Co
Atlanta, Georgia

Rainbow Ridge Brewing Co
Marietta, Georgia

Stone Mountain Brewers
Marietta, Georgia

Wild Boar Brewing Co
Atlanta, Georgia

HAWAII
Maui Beer Co
Kula, Hawaii

ILLINOIS
Mississippi Delta Microbrewery
West Frankfurt, Illinois

R J's Gingseng
Chicago, Illinois

Slopeside Brewing Co
Chicago, Illinois

State Street Brewing*
Chicago, Illinois

INDIANA
Fort Wayne Brewing Co
Fort Wayne, Indiana

IOWA
Frontier Brewing Co
Norway, Iowa

KENTUCKY
Lexington Brewing Co
Lexington, Kentucky

Oertel Brewing Co
Louisville, Kentucky

LOUISIANA
Abita Brewing Co*
Abita Springs, Louisiana

Sazerac Co Inc/
Pelican Brewing Co
New Orleans, Louisiana

MAINE
Gritty McDuff's*[1]
Portland, Maine

Sunday River Brewing Co*[1]
Bethel, Maine

MARYLAND
Brimstone Brewing Co*[2]
Baltimore, Maryland

Oxford Brewing Co*[2]
Linthicum Heights, Maryland

Tuppers Hop Pocket Ale
Bethesda, Maryland

MASSACHUSETTS
Boston Beer Co*
Boston, Massachusetts

Coastal Brewing Inc
Duxbury, Massachusetts

Commonwealth Brewing Co*[1]
Boston, Massachusetts

Dornbusch Brewing Co Inc*
Ipswich, Massachusetts

Mass Bay Brewing Co[2]
Boston, Massachusetts

Old Marlborough Brewing Co
Framingham, Massachusetts

MICHIGAN
August Brewing Co
Detroit, Michigan

Bad Frog
Brewery Co/Wauldron Corp
Rose City, Michigan

Detroit & Mackinac Brewery Ltd
Detroit, Michigan

Franklin Street Brewing Co
Detroit, Michigan

MINNESOTA
St Croix Beer Co*
Lakeland, Minnesota

MISSISSIPPI
Kershenstine Diamond
Europa, Mississippi

MISSOURI
Gilbert Robinson Inc
Kansas City, Missouri

Signature Beer Co*
St Louis, Missouri

MONTANA
Spanish Peaks Brewery*[2]
Bozeman, Montana

NEBRASKA
Barley Boys Brewery Inc
Omaha, Nebraska

Nebraska Brewing Co
Omaha, Nebraska

NEVADA
Reno Brewing Co*
Reno, Nevada

NEW JERSEY
Atlantic City Brewing Co
Brigantine, New Jersey

Gold Coast Brewing Co
Westfield, New Jersey

Hoboken Brewing Co[2]
Hoboken, New Jersey

NEW YORK
Brooklyn Brewery*
Brooklyn, New York

Hornell Brewing Co
Brooklyn, New York

Kobor and White Brewery Inc
Schuylerville, New York

New Amsterdam Brewing Co
New York, New York

Old Peconic Brewing Co Ltd*
Shelter Island, New York

Old World Brewing Co*
Staten Island, New York

Riverosa Co
New York, New York

Spring Street Brewing Co*[1]
New York, New York

NORTH CAROLINA
Gate City Brewing Co
Greensboro, North Carolina

NORTH DAKOTA
Dakota Brewing Co
Grand Forks, North Dakota

OHIO
Columbus Brewing Co[2]
Columbus, Ohio

Mad Monk Brewing Co Ltd*
Cincinnati, Ohio

OKLAHOMA
Barley Field Brewing Co
Tulsa, Oklahoma

T Pauls Beer Co
Tulsa, Oklahoma

OREGON
Oregon Ale and Beer Co*
Lake Oswego, Oregon

Yamhill Brewing Co LLC
Portland, Oregon

PENNSYLVANIA
Braumeister Ltd
Drexel Hill, Pennsylvania

Crooked Creek Brewery
Jamestown, Pennsylvania

Dock Street Brewing Co*[1]
Bala Cynwyd, Pennsylvania

Fredimo Bottlers Inc*
Wayne, Pennsylvania

Johnstown Brewing Co*
Johnstown, Pennsylvania

Manayunk Malt & Hops Co[2]
Philadelphia, Pennsylvania

Neuweiler Brewing Co Inc*
Bethlehem, Pennsylvania

Pennsylvania Brewing Co*[2]
Pittsburgh, Pennsylvania

Starview Brewing Co
Mount Wolf, Pennsylvania

Stoudt Brewery*[1]
Adamstown, Pennsylvania

Tun Tavern Brewing Co Inc
Abington, Pennsylvania

Whitetail Brewing Inc[2]
York, Pennsylvania

SOUTH DAKOTA
Wild Bill's Brewing Co[1]
Sioux Falls, South Dakota

TENNESSEE
Eastern Rivers Brewing Co*
Chattanooga, Tennessee

Volunteer Beer Inc*
Knoxville, Tennessee

TEXAS
Old City Brewing Co
Austin, Texas

Salado Creek Brewing Co
San Antonio, Texas

Tye Dye Brewing Co
Dallas, Texas

VIRGINIA
Rock Creek Brewing Co
Richmond, Virginia

WASHINGTON
Jet City Brewing Co
Seattle, Washingtion

**Pike Brewing Co/
Merchant du Vin*[2]**
Seattle, Washingtion

Smith & Reilly
Vancouver, Washingtion

WISCONSIN
B T McClintick Brewing Co
Janesville, Wisconsin

Cherryland Brewing Co[1]
Sturgeon Bay, Wisconsin

Cross Plains Brewery Inc
Cross Plains, Wisconsin

Mid-Coast Brewing
Oshkosh, Wisconsin

CANADIAN CONTRACT BREWING COMPANIES

ALBERTA
Banff Brewery Corp[2]
Calgary, Alberta

ONTARIO
Lakeside Brewery and Wine Inc
Scarborough, Ontario

UNITED STATES CONTRACT BREWING COMPANIES

ARIZONA

Black Mountain Brewing Co
PO Box 1940
Cave Creek, AZ 85331-1940
(602) 253-6293; FAX (602) 488-2609
Founded: Dec. 1, 1989
Head Brewer: Scott Chilleen
Pres.: Ed Chilleen
Sales Mgr./Gen. Mgr.: Dick Chilleen
Mktg. Dir.: John Hellweg
Contact: Ed Chilleen
Beer produced at Evansville Brewery, Black Mountain Brewing Co., Cold Spring Brewing Co.

CALIFORNIA

American Beerguy Inc
46 Varda Landing
Suasalito, CA 94965
(415) 332-7421; FAX (415) 332-5924
Contact: D. Tony Nguyen

Beverly Hills Beerhouse Co
PO Box 654
Brisbane, CA 94005-0654
(310) 328-5010
Founded: Sept. 15, 1993
Contact: Wolfgang Morandell
Beer produced at August Schell Brewing Co.

Bohemian Brewery
23883 Madison St
Torrance, CA 90505
Contact: Jean Pugh

Brewery Atlantis
1969 Hayes St
San Francisco, CA 94117
(415) 378-3243
atlantis@hooked.net
http://www.hooked.net/users/mcpdirt/atl5.html
Contact: Matt Petrik

Danse-Skjold Brewing Co
PO Box 1113
Solvang, CA 93464
(805) 668-4626; FAX (805) 688-3629
Founded: Aug. 1, 1995
Partner: Ron Nielsen
Partner: Allan Jones
Contact: Ron Nielsen
Beer produced at St. Stan's Brewery

Heckler Brewing Co
PO Box 947/175 Mackinan
Tahoe City, CA 96145-0947
(916) 583-2728; FAX (916) 583-1642
Founded: Sept. 1, 1993
Pres.: Keith Hilken, Jr.
Head Brewer: Keith Hilken
Sales Mgr.: Rob Wells
Contact: Keith Hilken
Beer produced at August Schell Brewing Co.

Hoppy Brewing Co
355 Shadow Run Dr
San Jose, CA 95110-3548
(408) 294-6861; FAX (408) 294-9320
anyone@hoppy.com
http://www.hoppy.com/
Founded: July 15, 1994
Head Brewer: Troy Paski
Restauranteur: Tony Hernandez
Contact: Troy Paski

Humpback Brewing Co
17101 Valleyview Ave
Cerritos, CA 90703
(310) 926-7662; FAX (310) 921-3950
Founded: July 1, 1995
Sales Mgr.: Ken Kribel
Contact: Ken Kribel
Beer produced at Minnesota Brewing Co.

Lake Tahoe Brewing Co Inc
PO Box 7608
Tahoe City, CA 96145-7608
(916) 581-5822; FAX (916) 581-5827
Founded: Aug. 28, 1993
Sales Mgr.: Rob Curt
Brewer: Everette Charles
Pres.: Rob Curtis
CFO: Eric Bledsoe
Contact: Eric Bledsoe
Beer produced at Golden Pacific Brewing Co.

McKenzie River Partners
117 Greenwich
San Francisco, CA 94111
(415) 732-1000; FAX (415) 732-1001
Founded: June 15, 1987
Contact: Minott Wessinger

Owens Brewing Co
PO Box 510
Hayward, CA 94541-0510
(510) 538-9500; FAX (510) 538-7644
http://www.ambrew.com
Founded: Oct. 1, 1992
Pres.: Bill Owens
Contact: Bill Owens
Beer produced at Dubuque Brewing Co.

Pete's Brewing Co
514 High St
Palo Alto, CA 94301-1623
(415) 328-7383; FAX (415) 327-3675
Founded: Dec. 1, 1986
Brewmaster: Pat Couteaux
VP Sales: David Bozzini
Pres.: Mark Bozzini
Founder: Pete Slosberg
Public Relations: Kristin Seuell
Contact: Mark Bozzini
Beer produced at Stroh Brewing Co. (St. Paul, MN)

Preservation Ale
5 Tappan Ct
Orinda, CA 94563-1308
(510) 254-7396
Contact: Dale Grabman

San Andreas Brewing Co
737 San Benito St
Hollister, CA 95023-3916
(408) 637-7074; FAX (408) 637-6170
Founded: Oct. 1, 1988
Pres./Head Brewer/Sales Mgr.: Bill Millar
Contact: Bill Millar
Beer produced at August Schell Brewing Co.

Wanker Beer Inc
PO Box 8894
Newport Beach, CA 92658
(714) 724-9191; FAX (714) 724-9849
Founded: Sept. 1, 1995
Principle Contact: Fred Van Urk
Contact: Fred Van Urk

William & Scott Brewing Co/Rhino Chasers
2130 Main St/Suite 250
Huntington Beach, CA 92648
(714) 374-3222; FAX (714) 374-3232
webmail@rhinochasers.com
http://www.rhinochasers.com
Pres.: John Lennon
Chairperson/CEO: Scott Griffiths
Head Brewer: Marty Velas
Contact: Diana Chock
Beer produced at Minnesota Brewing Co.

COLORADO

**Alpine Brewing Co/
Naked Aspen Beer Co**
4 Whiteoak Dr
Littleton, CO 80127
(303) 933-1921; FAX (303) 933-1921
Founded: Dec. 1, 1994
Contact: Tom Sorenson

Atlantis Brewing Co
PO Box 370664
Denver, CO 80237
(303) 369-2808; FAX (303) 369-2808
atlantis@ales.com
http://rainbow.rmii.com/~jhicks/ales/
Founded: April 20, 1995
Head Brewer/Sales Mgr.: Jay Hicks
Contact: Jay Hicks
Beer produced at Lonetree Brewing Ltd.

Beartooth Brewing Co
PO Box 6100/1113 Spruce St
Boulder, CO 80302
(303) 444-6993; FAX (303) 938-5005
Contact: Aldo Stanton
Beer produced at Minnesota Brewing Co.

Big Nose Brewing Co
511 16th St/Suite 310
Denver, CO 80202-4228
(303) 893-6725
Contact: Debbie Snow
Beer produced at Lonetree Brewing Ltd.

Blue Moon Brewing Co
2145 Blake St
Denver, CO 80205
Contact: Keith Villa
*Subsidiary of Coors Brewing Co.
Beer produced at F. X. Matt Brewing Co.*

Cherry Creek Brewing Co
1065 S Elisabeth St
Denver, CO 80209
(303) 733-5622
Founded: Nov. 23, 1995
Sales Mgr.: Brian Brieske
Head Brewer: Dan Ricketts
Contact: Brian Brieske
Beer produced at Twisted Pine Brewing Co.

High Point Brewing Corp
4910 Fox St/Unit E
Denver, CO 80216
(303) 297-8568
Contact: Monty Bruce

Jamestown Brewing Co
1390 S Colorado Blvd
Denver, CO 80222
(303) 757-5155; FAX (303) 757-4811
Founded: April 15, 1995
Contact: Tom Campbell
Beer produced at Minnesota Brewing Co.

Pine Street Brewing Co
1006 Pine St
Louisville, CO 80027
(303) 666-5232
Founded: Feb. 1, 1995
Co.-Owner: Brad Talbert
Co.-Owner: Tim Norbeerg
Contact: Brad Talbert
Beer produced at Lonetree Brewing Ltd.

Red Ass Brewing Co
4825 Crest Rd
Fort Collins, CO 80526
(970) 204-1366; FAX (970) 204-4291
Contact: Maggie Kunze
Beer produced at Cold Spring Brewery

San Juan Brewing Co
PO Box 1989
Telluride, CO 81435-1989
(970) 728-4587
Contact: James Loo

Snow Dog Brewing Corp
PO Box 5570
Avon, CO 81620
(970) 845-5020; FAX (970) 845-5098
Founded: Nov. 1, 1993
Sales Mgr.: Jim Dellarosa
Head Brewer: Kenneth Piel
Contact: Jerry Jones
Beer produced at Lonetree Brewing Ltd.

Telluride Beer Co
PO Box 371623
Denver, CO 80237
(813) 961-7090; FAX (813) 961-8663
Founded: Aug. 31, 1995
Sales Mgr.: Steve Patterson
Contact: Stan Birkin
Beer produced at Joseph Huber Brewing Co.

Two Angels Beer Co
8223 S Quebec/Suite 107
Englewood, CO 80112
(303) 773-8277
Founded: Dec. 1, 1995
Brewer: John Shaver
Brewer: Fred Frazier
Contact: Fred Frazier
Beer produced at Lonetree Brewing Ltd.

CONNECTICUT

Elm City Brewing Co
458 Grand Ave
New Haven, CT 06513-3842
(203) 772-2739
Founded: Oct. 10, 1989

DELAWARE

Blue Hen Beer Co
PO Box 7077
Newark, DE 19714-7077
(302) 737-8375; FAX (302) 737-8375
http://realbeer.com/bluehen
Founded: May 10, 1990
Sec./Treas.: John Wisniewski
Pres.: Jeff Johnson
VP: Kurt Kohl
Contact: Jeff Johnson
Beer produced at the Lion Inc./Gibbons-Stegmaier Brewery

DISTRICT OF COLUMBIA

Fischer Brewing Co Inc
1342 G St NW/Suite 200
Washington, DC 20005
(202) 783-3333; FAX (202) 783-2938
Founded: Aug. 1, 1995
Contact: Benson Fischer

Olde Heurich Brewing Co
1111 34th St NW
Washington, DC 20007-3204
(202) 333-2313; FAX (202) 333-9198
lager@oldeheurich.com
Founded: June 1, 1986
Head Brewer: Joseph L. Owades
Pres./Sales Mgr.: Gary F. Heurich
Contact: Gary Heurich
Beer produced at F. X. Matt Brewing

FLORIDA

Abbey Brewing Co
1115 16th St
Miami Beach, FL 33139
(305) 538-8110
Founded: July 1, 1995
Contact: Richard Dispenzieri
Beer produced at Key West Overseas Brewery

Florida Beer Brands
PO Box 561357
Orlando, FL 32805
(407) 423-3929; FAX (407) 423-2257
Founded: Nov. 1, 1988
Sec.: M. Burrer
VP: D. O. Beusse
Pres./Sales Mgr.: William P. Burrer
Contact: William Burrer
Beer produced at August Schell Brewing Co.

**Full Moon International Inc/
Lake Highland Brewing Co**
101 Southhall Lane/Suite 400
Maitland, FL 32751
(407) 894-6109
Founded: July 1, 1995
Head Brewer: John Zappa
Pres.: George A. Williston
Contact: George A. Williston
Beer produced at Stevens Point Brewery

**McGuire's
Irish Pub and Brewery**
600 E Gregory St
Pensacola, FL 32501-4153
(904) 433-6789; FAX (904) 434-8364
Founded: July 1, 1991
VP/General Mgr.: Dave Heidrich
Contact: Dave Heidrich
Beer produced at Oldenberg Brewery

Mill Brewery, Eatery, & Bakery
330 W Fairbanks Ave
Winter Park, FL 32789-5093
(407) 644-1544; FAX (407) 674-3982
Founded: May 1, 1990
Contact: John Stewart

Old Florida Brewing Corp
4525 NE Sixth Ave
Oakland Park, FL 33334
(305) 772-5544
Founded: April 1, 1996
Contact: Richard Powers

Seagrams Beverage Co
5430 Bay Center Dr
Tampa, FL 33609-3492
(813) 286-3822; FAX (813) 286-3449
VP South/Central Region Mgr.: David A. Clay
Contact: David A. Clay

GEORGIA

David & Mark Brewing Co
359 Clifton Rd NE
Atlanta, GA 30307-2101
(404) 373-9121
Contact: David Verzello

Friends Brewing Co
PO Box 29464
Atlanta, GA 30359
(770) 986-8505; FAX (770) 590-1770
Founded: Sept. 1, 1989
VP/Sales Mgr.: Rick Roberts
Brewmaster: Jon Downing
Contact: Dow Scoggins
Beer produced at August Schell Brewing Co.

Rainbow Ridge Brewing Co
3852 W Clinton Ct
Marietta, GA 30062
(770) 565-4466; FAX (770) 565-4466
Founded: Aug. 2, 1994
Head Brewer: Kenneth Griffiths
Sales Mgr.: Steven L. Bender
Contact: William Anderson

Stone Mountain Brewers
803 Powder Springs Rd
Marietta, GA 30064-3649
(770) 421-1158; FAX (770) 421-1158
claude@mindspring.com
Founded: Jan. 3, 1993
Head Brewer: Claude Smith
Sales Mgr.: Scott Bohnenkamp
Contact: Claude Smith

**Wild Boar
Brewing Co/Georgia Brewing**
PO Box 8239
Atlanta, GA 30306-0239
(404) 633-0924; FAX (404) 633-1029
Contact: Rob Nelson
Beer produced at Dubuque Brewing and Bottling Co.

HAWAII

Maui Beer Co
PO Box 486
Kula, HI 96790-0486
(808) 661-4157; FAX (808) 669-9065
Founded: April 1, 1994
Founder: Paula Thompson
Beer produced at Blitz-Weinhard Brewing Co.

ILLINOIS

**Mississippi
Delta Microbrewery**
RR 4/Box 2798
West Frankfurt, IL 62896
(618) 932-2739; FAX (618) 937-1941
Contact: Michael Le Vault
Beer produced at Capital Brewing Co.

R J's Ginseng
PO Box 10437
Chicago, IL 60610-0437
Contact: Thomas Swane

Slopeside Brewing Co
3445 N Elaine Pl/Suite 1N
Chicago, IL 60657
(312) 665-2077; FAX (312) 296-9674
Founded: Aug. 9, 1995
Head Brewer: Kris Youngsteadt
Contact: Jay Schwartz
Beer produced at Star Union Brewing Co.

State Street Brewing
PO Box 28-8560
11038 S State St
Chicago, IL 60628-8560
(708) 794-0074; FAX (708) 794-0081
Founded: Oct. 1, 1995
Contact: Steven Cahillane

INDIANA

Fort Wayne Brewing Co
2020 Florida Dr
Fort Wayne, IN 46805-4510
(219) 248-0135
Contact: Jim McIntyre

IOWA

Frontier Brewing Co
Frontier Herbs
PO Box 299
Norway, IA 52318-0299
(800) 729-5422; FAX (319) 227-7966
Founded: Jan. 1, 1994
Sales Mgr.: Steve Bosking
Contact: Steve Bosking
Beer produced at Evansville Brewing Co.

KENTUCKY

Lexington Brewing Co
401 Cross St
Lexington, KY 40508-2806
(606) 252-6004; FAX (606) 259-2736
Founded: May 1, 1995
Head Brewer: Lynton L. Register
Sales Mgr.: George M. Van Mouy
Contact: William Ambrose

Oertel Brewing Co
1332 Story Ave
Louisville, KY 40206-1734
(502) 585-1800
Contact: David Barhorst

LOUISIANA

Abita Brewing Co
PO Box 762
Abita Springs, LA 70420-0762
(504) 892-5837; FAX (504) 892-9565
Founded: Jan. 1, 1986
Contact: Jim Patton
Beer produced at Pittsburgh Brewing Co., Blitz Weinhard Brewing Co., Stroh Brewery Co.

Pelican Brewing Co/Sazerac Co
PO Box 52821
New Orleans, LA 70121
(504) 841-3431
Founded: July 1, 1995
Head Brewer: Jim Patton
National Sales Mgr.: Jerry Barber
Brand Mgr.: Chris Hoffman
Contact: Christopher Hoffman
Beer produced at Abita Brewing Co.

MAINE

Gritty McDuff's
369 Fore St
Portland, ME 04101-4026
(207) 772-2739; FAX (207) 772-6204
Grittys@maine.com
Founded: July 1, 1988
Head Brewer: Ed Stebbins
Sales Mgr.: Richard Pfeffer
Contact: Ed Stebbins
Beer produced at Shipyard Brewery

Sunday River Brewing Co
1 Sunday River Rd
Bethel, ME 04217-4623
(207) 824-4253; FAX (207) 824-3380
Founded: January 6, 1993
Head Brewer: Peter Leavitt
Owner: Grant Wilson
Contact: Hans Trupp
Beer Produced at Shipyard Brewery

MARYLAND

Brimstone Brewing Co
3701 Dillon St
Baltimore, MD 21224-5244
(410) 342-1363; FAX (410) 342-6454
Contact: Marc Tewey

Oxford Brewing Co
611-G Hammonds Ferry Rd
Linthicum Heights, MD 21090
(410) 789-0003
Founded: July 1, 1992
Owner: Marianne O'Brien
General Mgr.: Mike Jaeger
Contact: Marianne O'Brien
Beer produced at Dubuque Brewing and Bottling Co.

Tuppers Hop Pocket Ale
6404 Redwing Rd
Bethesda, MD 20817
(301) 229-2027
Founded: March 1, 1995
Co.-Owner: Bob Tupper
Co.-Owner: Ellie Tupper
Contact: Bob Tupper
Beer produced at Old Dominion Brewing Co.

MASSACHUSETTS

Boston Beer Co
30 Germania St
Boston, MA 02130-2312
(617) 368-5000; FAX (617) 482-5527
http://alumni.caltech.edu/~randy/samadams/samadams.html
Founded: Dec. 7, 1984
Pres./Head Brewer: James Koch
Sales Mgr.: Rhonda Kallman
Prod. Mgr.: David Grinnell
Contact: James Koch
Beer produced at Blitz-Weinhard, Genesee, Hudepohl-Schoenling, and Stroh Breery (Lehigh Valley, PA)

Coastal Brewing Inc
PO Box 1179
Duxbury, MA 02331
(617) 837-2491
Founded: Jan. 1, 1986
Sales Mgr: Christine Whitney
Contact: Christine Whitney
Beer produced at F. X. Matt Brewing Co.

Commonwealth Brewing Co
Boston Hops
85 Merrimac St
Boston, MA 02114-4715
(617) 523-8383; FAX (617) 528-1037
Founded: Aug. 1, 1986
Head Brewer: Jeff Charnick
VP: Lisa Quattrocchi
General Mgr.: Bill Goodwin
Exec. Chef: Glenn Jordan
Pres.: Joe Quattrocchi
Contact: Tod Mott
Beer produced at Catamount Brewing Co.

Dornbusch Brewing Co Inc
31 Mitchell Rd
Ipswich, MA 01938
(508) 356-0093
Founded: May 26, 1995
Head Brewer/Pres.: Horst Dornbusch
Sales Mgr./Treas.: Gordon Gibson
Contact: Horst Dornbusch
Beer produced at Ipswich Brewing Co., Smuttynose Brewing Co.

Mass Bay Brewing Co
306 Northern Ave
Boston, MA 02210-2324
(617) 574-9551; FAX (617) 261-3849
Founded: June 2, 1987
Contact: Richard Doyle
Beer produced at F. X. Matt Brewing Co.

Old Marlborough Brewing Co
PO Box 1157
Framingham, MA 01701-0206
(617) 924-6959; FAX (508) 879-6521
Founded: July 1, 1989
Treas.: Kevin P. Moran
Pres.: Austin J. Moran, Jr.
Contact: Austin Moran
Beer produced at Catamount Brewing Co.

MICHIGAN

August Brewing Co
743 Bearbien/Suite 342
Detroit, MI 48226
(313) 963-0373
Founded: Nov. 1, 1995
Contact: Pete Stenger
Beer produced at Stroh Brewing Co.

Bad Frog Brewery Co./Wauldron Corp
PO Box 310
Rose City, MI 48654
(517) 685-2990; FAX (517) 685-2922
http://realbeer.com/badfrog/
Founded: Sept. 29, 1995
Beer produced at Frankenmuth Brewery

Detroit & Mackinac Brewery Ltd
15414 Mack Ave
Detroit, MI 48224-3351
(313) 881-2337
Founded: May 30, 1992
Microbiologist: Steven Rouse
Gen. Superintendent: John J. Linardos
Contact: Priscilla Burns
Beer produced at Oldenberg Brewery

Franklin Street Brewing Co
1560 Franklin St
Detroit, MI 48207
(313) 568-0390; FAX (313) 568-0202
Founded: March 17, 1991
Contact: Ginny Vincent
Beer produced at Frankenmuth Brewery

MINNESOTA

St Croix Beer Co
1051 Quixote Ave N
Lakeland, MN 55043-9617
(612) 436-7610; FAX (612) 642-1239
saintcroix@aol.com
Contact: Karl Bremer
Beer produced at August Schell Brewing Co.

MISSISSIPPI

Kershenstine Diamond
Dept AAB/401 Industrial Rd
Europa, MS 39744-2598
(601) 258-2049; FAX (601) 258-2002
Founded: July 8, 1988
Sec.: A. K. Alexis
Pres.: Tim Kershenstine
Contact: Tim Kershenstine
Beer produced at Dubuque Brewing and Bottling Co.

MISSOURI

Gilbert Robinson Inc
PO Box 16000
Kansas City, MO 64112-0800
Beer produced at Dubuque Brewing and Bottling Co.

Signature Beer Co
2737 Hereford St
St Louis, MO 63139-1055
(314) 772-5911; FAX (314) 772-6092
Founded: Feb. 24, 1992
Owner/Sales Mgr.: Tony Caradonna
Head Brewer: Ken Schierberg
Head Brewer: Mike Kaneip
Contact: Tony Caradonna
Beer produced at Oldenberg Brewery/Drawbridge Inn, Cold Spring Brewing Co.

MONTANA

Spanish Peaks Brewery
PO Box 3644
Bozeman, MT 59772-3644
(406) 585-2296; FAX (406) 585-2483
Founded: Jan. 1, 1992
Pres.: Mark Taverniti
Head Brewer: Todd Scott
Contact: Todd Scott
Beer produced at August Schell Brewing Co., G. Heileman

NEBRASKA

Barley Boys Brewery Inc
8931 J St
Omaha, NE 68127
(402) 593-1289; FAX (402) 593-1375
Contact: Steve Nasr
Beer produced at Minnesota Brewing Co.

Nebraska Brewing Co
13417 B St
Omaha, NE 68144
(402) 330-3588; FAX (402) 330-3588
7115.3331@compuserve.com
Founded: April 1, 1995
Pres.: Dave Begley
Contact: Dave Begley
Beer produced at Cold Spring Brewing

NEVADA

Reno Brewing Co
PO Box 5045
Reno, NV 89513
(702) 322-2739; FAX (702) 322-2434
kirk@reno-brewing.reno.nv.us
http://www.Renobrew.com
Founded: Sept. 1, 1994
Head Brewer/Pres./General Mgr.: Kirk Ellern
VP Mktg.: Davie Pierson
Contact: Kirk Ellern
Beer produced at Cold Spring Brewing

NEW JERSEY

Atlantic City Brewing Co
PO Box 1021
Brigantine, NJ 08203-7021
(609) 641-7884
Co.-Owner: Joseph Colavito
Co.-Owner: James Colavito
Co.-Owner: Donald Gallo
Co.-Owner: Michael Gallo
Contact: Michael Gallo

Gold Coast Brewing Co
37 Elm St
Westfield, NJ 07090-2179
(908) 233-5222; FAX (908) 233-4805
Head Brewer: Dave Hoffman
Contact: Dave Hoffman
Beer produced at Arrowhead Brewing Co.

Hoboken Brewing Co
1125 Hudson St
Hoboken, NJ 07030
(201) 792-2337; FAX (201) 659-2900
Founded: Sept. 4, 1995
Head Brewer: Michael Gilmore
Contact: Mitchell Dell Aquila

NEW YORK

Brooklyn Brewery
118 N 11th St
Brooklyn, NY 11211-1914
(718) 486-7422; FAX (718) 486-7440
Founded: March 30, 1988
Pres.: Steve Hindy
CEO: Thomas D. Potter
Head Brewer: William Moeller
Head Brewer: Garrett Oliver
National Sales Mgr.: Ed Raun
New York Sales Mgr.: Jim Munson
Suburban Sales Mgr.: Mike Vitale
Contact: Stephen Hindy
Beer produced at F. X. Matt Brewing Co.

Hornell Brewing Co
4501 Glenwood Rd
Brooklyn, NY 11203-6587
(516) 327-0002

Kobor and White Brewery Inc
220 Stonebridge Rd
Schuylerville, NY 12871
(518) 695-4210; FAX (518) 695-3462
tig22@aol.com
Founded: March 1, 1995
Contact: Peter Kobor
Beer produced at the Lion Brewery Inc.

New Amsterdam Brewing Co
275 Park Ave S
New York, NY 10010-6125
(212) 473-1900; FAX (212) 473-2956
Head Brewer: J. MacLoughlin
Pres.: Joe Tighe
Contact: Joe Tighe
Beer produced at F. X. Matt Brewing Co.

Old Peconic Brewing Co Ltd
PO Box 2027
Shelter Island, NY 11964-2027
(516) 749-8823; FAX (516) 749-4331
Founded: April 1, 1993
Sales Mgr.: Tom Riggio
Executive VP: Bliss Morehead
Pres.: Michael Zisser
Contact: Michael Zisser
Beer produced at Wild Goose Brewery

Old World Brewing Co
2070 Victory Blvd
Staten Island, NY 10314-3526
(718) 370-0551; FAX (718) 370-0558
Founded: Feb. 1, 1992
VP: Karen Pennacchio
Pres.: Sal Pennacchio
Contact: Sal Pennacchio
Beer produced at Stevens Point Brewery Co.

Riverosa Co
101 W 75th St Unit 5B
New York, NY 10023-1812
(212) 721-4566; FAX (212) 721-2679
Founded: July 1, 1993
Pres.: Mark Butler
Contact: Mark Butler
Beer produced at Frankenmuth Brewery

Spring Street Brewing Co
113 University Pl/Suite 11B
New York, NY 10003-4527
(212) 226-9110; FAX (212) 226-8935
witbeer@interport.net
http://www.interport.net:80/witbeer/index.html
Founded: June 1, 1993
Pres.: Andrew Klein
Head Brewer: Herm Hegger
Sales Mgr.: Margaritte Malfy
Contact: Andrew Klein
Beer produced at Minnesota Brewing Co.

NORTH CAROLINA

Gate City Brewing Co
2006 W Vandalia Rd
Greensboro, NC 27407-7618
(910) 299-2739; FAX (910) 299-9059
Founded: Aug. 15, 1994
Pres.: Gary Vickers
Head Brewer: Wendell Grisim
Contact: Gary Vickers
Beer produced at Tomcat Brewery

NORTH DAKOTA

Dakota Brewing Co
PO Box 5786
Grand Forks, ND 58206-5786
(701) 775-0187
Founded: July 1, 1990
VP: Judd McKinnon
Pres.: Philip Omdahl
Contact: Philip Omdahl

OHIO

Columbus Brewing Co
476 S Front St
Columbus, OH 43215-5627
(614) 224-3626; FAX (614) 241-2080
Founded: Jan. 1, 1989
Brewmaster: Ben W. Pridgeon
Contact: Ben Pridgeon
Beer produced at Columbus Brewing Co., F. X. Matt Brewing Co.

Mad Monk Brewing Co Ltd
49 Central Ave
Cincinnati, OH 45202
(513) 421-9999
monkismad@aol.com
Founded: April 15, 1996
Contact: Matthew Folan
Beer produced at Oldenberg Brewing Co.

OKLAHOMA

Barley Field Brewing Co
1143 E 33rd Pl
Tulsa, OK 74105
(918) 749-8171; FAX (918) 749-3536
Founded: July 3, 1995
Recipe Formulator: Davis Redding
Contact: Charles Culbreath
Beer produced at August Schell Brewing Co.

T Pauls Beer Co
5327 E Fifth St
Tulsa, OK 74112
(918) 835-7285; FAX (918) 835-7285
Founded: January 23, 1995
Head Brewer: T. Paul Eagleton
Sales Mgr.: Rick Bahlinger
Contact: T. Paul Eagleton
Beer produced at Dubuque Brewing and Bottling Co.

OREGON

Oregon Ale and Beer Co
5875 Lakeview Blvd
Lake Oswego, OR 97035-7058
(503) 968-7706; FAX (503) 624-9018
oregonale@aol.com
Founded: Aug. 1, 1995
Head Brewer: Gregg LeBlanc
Sales Mgr.: Duke Maines
Contact: Gregg LeBlanc
Beer produced at Saxer Brewing Co., G. Heileman
Subsidiary of Boston Beer Co.

Yamhill Brewing Co LLC
909 SE Yamhill
Portland, OR 97214
(503) 234-0440; FAX (503) 238-3770

(503) 234-0440; FAX (503) 238-3770

Founded: April 15, 1996
General Mgr.: Tim Glenn
Administrator: Rick Rivera
Sales: Steve Woolard
Brewmaster: Jerry Bockmore
Contact: Tim Glenn

PENNSYLVANIA

Crooked Creek Brewery
PO Box 545
Jamestown, PA 16134
(412) 932-3006
Founded: June 23, 1995
Contact: Debbie Lewis
Beer produced at Straub Brewing Co.

Dock Street Brewing Co
225 E City Line Ave/Suite 110
Bala Cynwyd, PA 19004
(610) 668-1480; FAX (610) 668-1837
Founded: Oct. 1, 1985
Public Relations Dir.: Rosemarie Certo
Pres.: Jeffrey Ware
Head Brewer: William Moellen
Sales Mgr.: Andrew O'Rourke
Contact: Jeffrey Ware
Beer produced at F. X. Matt Brewing Co.

Fredimo Bottlers Inc
PO Box 806
Wayne, PA 19087
(610) 975-9866; FAX (610) 975-9730
Founded: April 1, 1996
Pres./CEO: Okon W. Akpan
Head Brewer: Mike Carota
Contact: Okon Akpan
Beer produced at Pittsburgh Brewing Co.

Johnstown Brewing Co
134 Gazebo Park
Johnstown, PA 15901
(814) 479-4426; FAX (814) 479-2387
Founded: March 15, 1995
Pres./Brewing: Daniel Thomas
Pres./Corporate: Michael Kane
Treas.: Richard Mayer
Contact: Daniel Thomas
Beer produced at Jones Brewing Co.

Manayunk Malt & Hops Co
PO Box 41086
Philadelphia, PA 19127
(800) 625-8467; FAX (215) 487-0652
Founded: May 27, 1994

Contact: Stephen Rosati
Beer produced at Jones Brewing Co.

Neuweiler Brewing Co Inc
51 W Washington Ave/SuiteT-210
Bethlehem, PA 18018-2433
(610) 954-0503; FAX (610) 954-0823
Founded: Nov. 7, 1991
Pres.: Barry J. Szmodis
Contact: Barry J. Szmodis
Beer produced at the Lion Inc.

Pennsylvania Brewing Co
Penn Brewery
Troy Hill Rd and Vinial St
Pittsburgh, PA 15212-5100
(412) 237-9400; FAX (412) 237-9406
Founded: June 1, 1986
Sales Mgr.: Tom Auchter
Brewmaster: Alexander Deml
Pres.: Thomas Pastorius
Contact: Thomas Pastorius
Beer produced at F. X. Matt Brewing Co.

Starview Brewing Co
51 Codorus Furnace Rd
Mount Wolf, PA 17347
(717) 266-5091; FAX (717) 266-0833
Founded: June 16, 1995
Pres./Head Brewer: Mike Knaub
Sales Mgr.: Mike Knaub
Head Brewer: Ron McCarl
Contact: Mike Knaub
Beer produced at Dubuque Brewing and Bottling Co.

Stoudt Brewery
PO Box 880
Adamstown, PA 19501-0880
(717) 484-4387; FAX (717) 484-4182
Founded: June 28, 1987
Pres./Sales Mgr.: Carol Stoudt
Contact: Carol Stoudt
Beer produced at the Lion Inc.

Tun Tavern/Tun Tavern Brewing Co Inc
947 Old York Rd
Abington, PA 19001
(215) 887-8819; FAX (215) 887-8818
Founded: Dec. 22, 1994
Contact: Montgomery Dahm
Beer produced at the Lion Inc.

SOUTH DAKOTA

Wild Bill's Brewing Co
1401 E Sioux St

Sioux Falls, SD 57103-2206
(605) 336-3320; FAX (605) 336-3322

Contact: Mike Brzica
Beer produced at Dubuque Brewing and Bottling Co.

TENNESSEE

Eastern Rivers Brewing Co
7011 Shallowford Rd/Suite 203
Chattanooga, TN 37421
(423) 344-0751; FAX (423) 855-6965
Founded: April 14, 1996
Contact: Thomas Mann
Beer produced at Oldenburg Brewing Co., Birmingham Brewing Co.

Volunteer Beer Inc
2706 E Magnolia Ave
Knoxville, TN 37914
(423) 637-8242
Contact: David Ewan

TEXAS

Old City Brewing Co
603 W 13th St/Suite 1A-345
Austin, TX 78701-1731
(512) 448-4844
Founded: April 1, 1988
Head Brewer: Davis Tucker
Sales Mgr.: Frank Perry
Contact: Davis Tucker
Beer produced at August Schell Brewing Co.

Salado Creek Brewing Co
PO Box 1839
San Antonio, TX 78296
(210) 224-5319
Founded: Feb. 12, 1996
Head Brewer: Wolfgang Heff
Contact: Ken Baumann
Beer Produced at Pearl Brewing Co.

Tye Dye Brewing Co
3626 N Hall St/Suite 916
Dallas, TX 75219-5107
(214) 522-7874; FAX (214) 522-1125
Contact: Michael Whiteside

VIRGINIA

Rock Creek Brewing Co
2500 E Cary St/Suite 522
Richmond, VA 23223

WASHINGTON

Jet City Brewing Co
PO Box 3554
Seattle, WA 98124-3554
(206) 392-5991; FAX (206) 392-6003
Founded: Aug. 1, 1993
Pres./Sales Mgr.: Jeff Leggett
Head Brewer: Jeff Leggett
Contact: Jeff Leggett
Beer produced at Jet City Brewing Co., Rainier Brewing Co.

**Pike Brewing Co./
Merchant du Vin**
1432 Western Ave
Seattle, WA 98101-2017
(206) 622-3373; FAX (206) 622-6648
info@mdv.com
Founded: Oct. 3, 1989
Head Brewer: Algernon (Fal) Allen
Sales Mgr.: Steve Sensor
Co.-Owner: Tom Leavitt
Co.-Owner: Charles Finkel
Co.-Owner: Roseann Finkel
Contact: Algernon Allen
Beer produced at Minnesota Brewing Co.

Smith & Reilly
3107 NE 65th St
Vancouver, WA 98663-1483
Sales Mgr.: Mick Rehn
Contact: Tom Brady

WISCONSIN

B T McClintick Brewing Co
1706 Mole Ave
Janesville, WI 53545
(608) 754-5729
Founded: Jan. 15, 1996
Contact: Tony McClintic

Cherryland Brewing Co
341 N Third Ave
Sturgeon Bay, WI 54235-2401
(414) 742-1945; FAX (414) 743-2860
Founded: June 1, 1988
Sales Mgr.: Robin Laak
Pres./Treas.: Thomas Alberts
VP/Head Brewer: Mark Feld
Contact: Mark Feld
Beer produced at Dubuque Brewing and Bottling Co.

Cross Plains Brewery Inc
2109 Hickory St
Cross Plains, WI 53528
(608) 798-3911; FAX (608) 798-3926
Founded: May 4, 1995
Contact: Wayne Esser
Beer produced at G Heileman Brewing

Mid-Coast Brewing
35 Wisconsin St
Oshkosh, WI 54901-3566
Founder: Jeff Fulbright
Contact: Jeff Fulbright
Beer produced at Stevens Point Brewery Co.

CANADIAN CONTRACT BREWING COMPANIES

ALBERTA

Banff Brewery Corp
3833 29th St NE
Calgary, AB T1Y 6B5
(403) 250-3883; FAX (403) 250-8589
Founded: Jan. 6, 1995
Brewmaster: Alexander Diehm
Contact: Alan Barrie

ONTARIO

**Lakeside
Brewery and Wine Inc**
1210 Kingston Rd
Scarborough, ON M1N 1N8
(416) 694-1835
Contact: Simon Cowe

8 Mexican Breweries

One of the next frontiers for craft brewing lies south of the border. Already one United States chain helped build a brewpub in Mazatlan, and others are certain to follow. Mexico has a rich history of brewing that reaches beyond the obvious popular brands to include full-flavored beers such as the Vienna-lager-style beer, Dos Equis, and the Christmas seasonal, Noche Buena.

There are no laws for or against brewpubs in the country. Having contacts in the area where you are considering a brewery venture reduces the chances that you will face opposition. Keep in mind, though that you'll be a pioneer like those few who started the North American craft-beer revolution fifteen years ago, and you'll face physical constraints such as an inability to acquire the right types and quantities of malts and hops. This problem will also extend to replacing and servicing equipment and parts for the brewery.

There will likely be a growing demand for craft beers and especially brewpubs in Mexican resort towns like Mazatlan that cater to American and European tourists. However, with the present economic realities throughout the rest of the country, this potential demand will not translate to a craft-brewing boom in Mexico like we have witnessed in the United States and Canada.

Due to limited responses from our surveys of Mexican breweries, some of the information contained herein may be out of date. Nonetheless, we provide this chapter as our first attempt to cover the Mexican beer industry, and we look forward to receiving helpful constructive feedback from those who live in or travel to Mexico.

BAJA CALIFORNIA (SUR)
LARGE BREWERIES
Cerveceria Cuauhtemoc
Baja, Baja California (Sur)

CHIHUAHUA
LARGE BREWERIES
Cerveceria Cuauhtemoc
Cuidad Juarez, Chihuahua

COAHUILA DE ZARAGOZA
LARGE BREWERIES
Cerveceria Modelo De Torreon
Torreon, Coahuila de Zaragoza

DISTRITO FEDERAL
LARGE BREWERIES
Cerveceria Modelo
Mexico City, Distrito Federal

JALISCO
LARGE BREWERIES
Cerveceria Cuauhtemoc
Guadalajara, Jalisco

Cerveceria Moctezuma
Guadalajara, Jalisco

Cerveceria Modelo de Guadalajara
Guadalajara, Jalisco

NUEVO LEON
LARGE BREWERIES
Cerveceria Cuauhtemoc
Monterrey, Nuevo Leon

Cerveceria Moctezuma
Monterrey, Nuevo Leon

OAXACA
LARGE BREWERIES
Cia Cervecera del Tropico
Tuxtepec, Oaxaca

SINALOA
LARGE BREWERIES
Cerveceria Cuauhtemoc
Culiacan, Sinaloa

Cerveceria Del Pacifico
Mazatlan, Sinaloa

BREWPUBS
Pepe and Joes
Mazatlan, Sinaloa

SONORA
LARGE BREWERIES
Cerveceria Cuauhtemoc
Sonora, Sonora

Cerveceria Cuauhtemoc
Nogales, Sonora

Cerveceria Modelo del Noroeste
Cuid Obregon, Sonora

TOLUCA
LARGE BREWERIES
Cerveceria Cuauhtemoc Toluca
Toluca, Mexico

VERACRUZ-LLAVE
LARGE BREWERIES
Cerveceria Moctezuma
Orizaba, Veracruz-Llave

YUCATAN
LARGE BREWERIES
Cerveceria Yucateca
Merida, Yucatan

Cerveceria Yucateca
Yucatan, Yucatan

Mexican Breweries

BAJA CALIFORNIA (SUR)

Cerveceria Cuauhtemoc
Calle Ferrocarril/Tecate
Baja California (Sur)
4-11-11/4-12-18
Contact: Felix Viveros Melo

CHIHUAHUA

Cerveceria Cuauhtemoc
Ave Reforma 1774/Ap Post 94
Ciudad Juarez, Chihuahua
2-00-14,2-00-13
Contact: Jose Molina

COAHUILA DE ZARAGOZA

Cerveceria Modelo de Torreon
Ave Bravo Ote Y Saltillo 400
Torreon, Coahuila de Zaragoza, 27040
3-51-50
Contact: Manuel Alvarez Loyo

DISTRITO FEDERAL

Cerveceria Modelo
Calle de Lago Alberto 156
Mexico City, Distrito Federal 11320
5-45-60-60
Contact: Salvador Lee

JALISCO

Cerveceria Cuauhtemoc
Avenida Vallarta No 3539
Guadalajara, Jalisco
Contact: Jorge Padilla

Cerveceria Moctezuma
Lazaro Cardenas No 975
Zona Industrial
Guadalajara, Jalisco
12-06-75
Contact: Pablo F. Calva Reyna

Cerveceria Modelo de Guadalajara
Calzado Mariano Otero No 663
Guadalejara, Jalisco
36-12-39-40
Contact: Francisco Barberena

NUEVO LEON

Cerveceria Cuauhtemoc
Ave Universidad Nte 2202/Ap106
Monterrey, Nuevo Leon
75-22-00
Contact: Carlos M. Torres

Cerveceria Moctezuma
Ave Colon Edison/Ap 223
Monterrey, Nuevo Leon
46-25-00
Contact: Alfredo Castillo

OAXACA

Cia Cervecera del Tropico
Car Tuxtepec-Oaxaca Km 2
Col Yucal
Tuxtepec, Oaxaca
287-5-04-80
Contact: Roberto Jiminez

SINALOA

Cerveceria Cuauhtemoc
Apartado Postal 244
Culiacan, Sinaloa
2-22-22
Contact: Luis Aguilar

Cerveceria del Pacifico
Calz Gabriel Leyva Melchor Oca
Ap 42
Mazatlan, Sinaloa 82000
678-2-79-00
Contact: Abel Rodriguez Rivas

Pepe and Joes
Mazatlan, Sinaloa
84-16-66; FAX 84-24-69
Contact: Rogelio Fontes

SONORA

Cerveceria Cuauhtemoc
Ap 335
Navojoa, Sonora 85800
Contact: Carlos Reyes Esquivel

Cerveceria Cuauhtemoc
Ocampo Y Ferrocarril
Nogales, Sonora
Contact: Ramon Martin

Cerveceria Modelo del Noroeste
Carretare Federal No 15
Km 1849
Cuidad Obregon, Sinora 85000
641-4-16-66
Contact: Peter Gokus

TOLUCA

Cerveceria Cuauhtemoc
Ap 187, Toluca
6-16-00, 6-11-30
Contact: Gustavo A Ballesteros

VERACRUZ-LLAVE

Cerveceria Moctezuma
Sur 10 Y/Poniente No 15
Orizaba, Veracruz-Llave
Contact: Javier Buccio

YUCATAN

Cerveceria Yucateca
Calle 14 No 70
Col Chuminopolis
Merida, Yucatan
992-7-19-00
Contact: Arturo Ponce Canton

9 Caribbean Breweries

Craft brewing is well on its way in the diverse and multinational community collectively known as the Caribbean, or the West Indies. New breweries have started on islands such as Bermuda, St. Maarten, and Grand Cayman.

Fulfilling your fantasy of building your micro on a tropical island will be no small challenge, compounded by problems caused by distance from suppliers, high year-round atmospheric and water temperatures, and unpredictable variations in both cost and availability of even reasonably good brewing water. (And don't forget hurricane season ...)

Most of the older, traditional breweries of the Caribbean region are similar in size to American microbreweries and regional breweries. Furthermore, they are primarily local breweries, likely due to the high shipping costs and international tariffs which factor into interisland trade. While many existing breweries are independent, some have ties to major brewing companies such as Guinness and Heineken.

Most of the island-brewed products are either pale Pilsener-style lagers stylistically similar to Jamaica's Red Stripe or Barbados' Banks brand, or else they are hearty stouts. There is not much that falls in between pale lagers and stouts, in terms of beer styles. Therefore, the markets may be ready now, especially in resort areas, to support a modest-sized microbrewery or brewpub that is prepared to offer island drinkers some fresh alternatives.

As with Mexico, partnering with someone local may be the only real way to build a successful brewery in a Caribbean nation. Also, as with Mexico, your target customers are mostly likely the tourists, and this means substantial seasonal variations

As this is the first time we present Caribbean breweries in the *BRD*, there may be some omissions. Nonetheless, we provide this chapter in our effort to cover the Caribbean beer industry, and we look forward to receiving helpful constructive feedback from those of you who live in or travel through the Caribbean region.

BARBADOS
LARGE BREWERIES
Banks Barbados Breweries Ltd
St Michael, Barbados

BERMUDA
MICROBREWERIES
Bermuda Triangle Brewing Ltd
Hamilton, Bermuda

North Rock Brewing
Hamilton, Bermuda

CAYMAN ISLANDS
LARGE BREWERIES
Banks DIH Ltd
Georgetown, Cayman Islands

REGIONAL BREWERIES
Buccaneer Brewery Ltd
Georgetown, Cayman Islands

MICROBREWERIES
Stingray Brewery Ltd
Grand Cayman, Cayman Islands

CUBA
REGIONAL BREWERIES
Cerveceria Modelo
La Habana, Cuba

Compania Cerveceria de las Antillas
La Habana, Cuba

Compania Cerveceria International
La Habana, Cuba

Tropical Brewery
Marianao, Cuba

DOMINICAN REPUBLIC
LARGE BREWERIES
Cerveceria Nacional Dominicana
Santo Domingo, Dominican Republic

REGIONAL BREWERIES
Cerveceria Bohemia
Santo Domingo, Dominican Republic

Cerveceria Vegana
La Vega, Dominican Republic

GRENADA
REGIONAL BREWERIES
Grenada Breweries Ltd
St George's, Grewnada

Institute for Brewing Studies

Caribbean Breweries

GUADELOUPE
LARGE BREWERIES
Sagba
Guadeloupe

REGIONAL BREWERIES
Brasserie du Corsaire
Baie-Mahault, Gaudeloupe

GUYANA
REGIONAL BREWERIES
Banks Brewing Co
Georgetown, Guyana

HAITI
LARGE BREWERIES
Brasserie Nationale d'Haiti
Port-au-Prince, Haiti

JAMAICA
LARGE BREWERIES
Desnoes & Geddes Ltd
Kingston 11, Jamaica

Guinness Jamaica Ltd
Spanish Town, Jamaica

MARTINIQUE
LARGE BREWERIES
Brasserie Lorraine
Fort-de-France, Martinique

NETHERLANDS ANTILLES
LARGE BREWERIES
Antilliaanse Brouwerij
Curacao, Netherlands Antilles

Antilliaanse Brouwerij
Willemstad, Netherlands Antilles

Grandes Brasseries Antillaises
Guadelope, Netherlands Antilles

MICROBREWERIES
St Maarten Breweries
St Maarten, Netherlands Antilles

ST KITTS AND NEVIS
LARGE BREWERIES
St Kitts Breweries Ltd
Basseterre, St Kitts and Nevis

TRINIDAD AND TOBAGO
LARGE BREWERIES
Caribbean Development Co Ltd
Trinidad and Tobago

National Brewing Co Ltd
Port of Spain, Trinidad and Tobago

Brewing Equipment by JVNW

JV NORTHWEST, INC.

Rock Bottom Brewery, Portland, Oregon

CRAFT BREWING

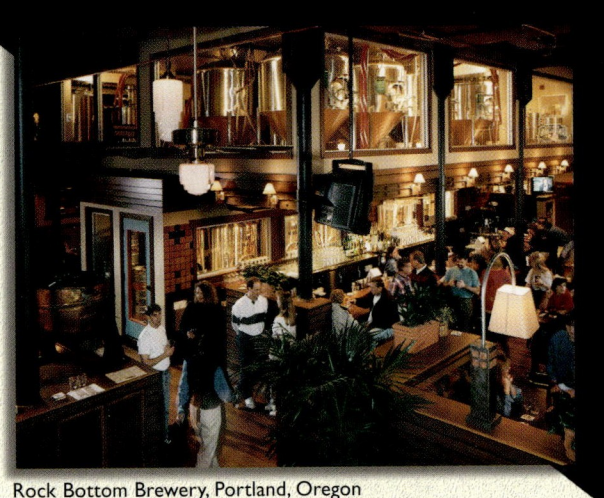

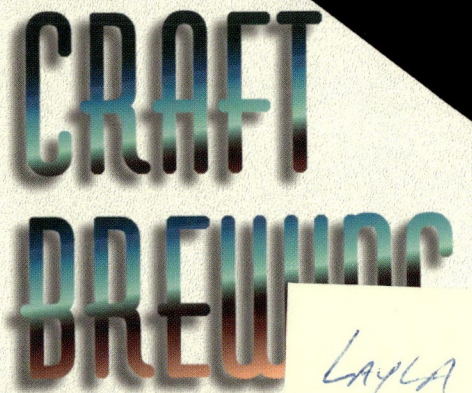

JVNW's new Shadowless Manway provides a smooth cleanable t...

Deschutes Brewing Co., Bend, Oregon

JVNW is an equipment manufacturing company which recognizes the specific needs of the microbrewery segment of the brewing industry. Our products range from individual pieces of equipment to complete turn-key systems. We can simplify for you, the complexities of the overall brewing process. Our services include brewery sizing, equipment layout, professional installation, system testing, technical assistance, and follow-up support.

JV Northwest • 28120 SW Boberg Rd. • Wilsonville • Oregon • 97070 • Phone (503) 682-2596 • Fax (503) 682-8060

ASME CODED FACILITY

Brewing Equipment

JVNW Adjustable Tank Pressure - Vacuum Relief Valve
The Ultimate Tank Pressure Valve for the Craft Brewing Industry

Pressure Arm Manifolds (PAM)

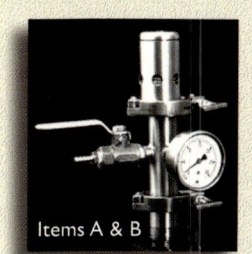

A. 2" x 2" TC Spool
- pressure gauge
- $3/8$" ball valve X hose barb or quick release
- clamps & gaskets

B. $1^{1}/_{2}$" x 2" TC Spool
- pressure gauge
- $3/8$" ball valve X hose barb or quick release
- clamps & gaskets

C. $1^{1}/_{2}$" x 2" TC Tree
- pressure gauge
- $3/8$" ball valve X hose barb or quick release
- clamps & gaskets

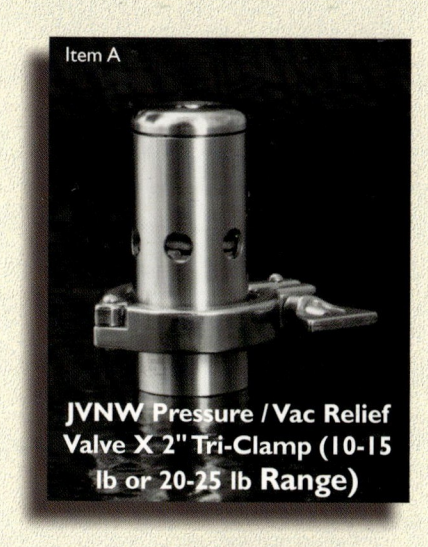

Items A & B

Item C

Item A

JVNW Pressure / Vac Relief Valve X 2" Tri-Clamp (10-15 lb or 20-25 lb Range)

Pressure can be dangerous... vacuum is just plain costly.

The pressure that fermentation creates inside a brewing tank can be dangerous. Protect your investment and your employees. These valves are sanitary and cleanable, allow adjustable pressure control, and are made in the U.S.A. But above all...they are dependable. In fact, we warranty them against defect for life...your life.

JV Northwest • 28120 S.W. Boberg Rd. • Wilsonville, Oregon 97070 • (503) 682-2596

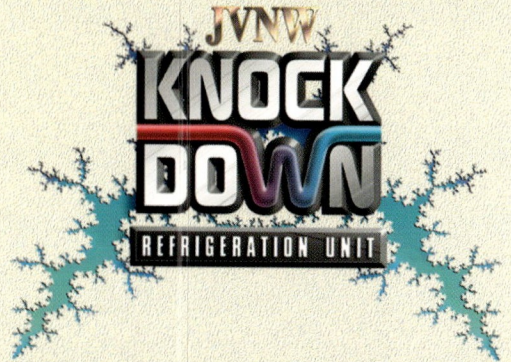

JVNW Knock Down Refrigeration Unit

JVNW Glycol Chiller Systems
1.5 to 120 HP
12,000 BTU/hr to 1,175,600 BTU/hr
The Ultimate Chiller Unit for the Craft Brewing Industry

8hp Air Cooled unit pictured. Water cooled models also available.

- Center Baffle Fiber Glass Glycol Storage Tank
- Stainless Steel Glycol Recirculating Pump
- Stainless Steel Glycol Process Pump
- U.L. Listed High Efficiency Evaporator Chiller Barrels
- U.L. Listed Electrical Enclosure with:
  - All Pump Motor Starters
  - Compressor Contactors
  - All System Fusing
  - Main Electrical Disconnect
- All Chilled Water Piping in Type "L" Copper Tubing
- All Glycol & Low Pressure Refrigeration Piping insulated.

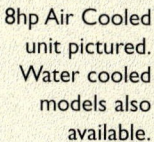

- All Refrigeration Components & Piping Factory Installed.
- Refrigeration System Evacuated to 500 Microns before Charging
- Chiller Factory Charged with Refrigerant and Test Run.
- Process Water & Water Cooled Condenser Connections located on exterior of Packaged Chiller System.
- Packaged Chiller Skinned with Removable Panels for easy Service Access.

JV Northwest • 28120 S.W. Boberg Rd. • Wilsonville, Oregon 97070 • (503) 682-2596

BARBADOS

Banks
Barbados Breweries Ltd
PO Box 507C, Wildey
St Michael, Barbados
Contact: C. Edghill

BERMUDA

Bermuda Triangle Brewing Ltd
PO Box HM 1686
Hamilton, HM GX Bermuda
(441) 238-2430; FAX (441) 238-1759
beerman@ibl.bm
Founded: Sept. 12, 1994
Capacity: 6,000 bbl
Contact: Paul Mason

North Rock Brewing
PO Box HM 555
Hamilton, HM CX Bermuda
(809) 292-0437; FAX (809) 236-4380
Contact: David Littlejohn

CAYMAN ISLANDS

Banks DIH Ltd
PO Box 10194/Thirst Park
Georgetown, Cayman Islands
Contact: W. Griffith

Buccaneer Brewery Ltd
PO Box 1608 Gt
George Town, Cayman Islands
(809) 949-8762; FAX (809) 949-8764
Contact: Bill Messer

Stingray Brewery Ltd
PO Box 32329
Seven Mile Beach
Grand Cayman, Cayman Islands
(809) 947-6002; FAX (809) 947-6003
Founded: March 15, 1996
Contact: Huig Zuiderent

CUBA

Cerveceria Modelo
KI 18
Carretera Central, Cotorro
La Habana, Cuba

Compania
Cerveceria de las Antillas
Edificia Ene, Dpto 705 Vedado
La Habana, Cuba

Compania
Cerveceria International
La Polar Apartado 1147
Puentes Grandes
La Habana, Cuba

Tropical Brewery
Nueva Fabrica de Hielo S A
PO Box 2817
Marianao, Cuba

DOMINICAN REPUBLIC

Cerveceria Bohemia
S A Apartado 2470
Santo Domingo, Dominican Republic
Contact: Jose Leon

Cerveceria Nacional
Dominicana
Carretera Sanchez
Apartado Postal 1086
Santo Domingo, Dominican Republic
(809) 535-5555
Contact: M. Lightbourne De Rodriguez

Cerveceria Vegana
Avenida General Juan Rodriquez
Ap 125
La Vega, Dominican Republic
(809) 573-3151; FAX (809) 573-4242
Contact: Desmond Miller

GRENADA

Grenada Breweries Ltd
Grand Anse
PO Box 202/12 Young St
St George's, Grenada
(809) 444-4248; FAX (809) 444-4842
Contact: C. F. Toppin

GUADELOUPE

Brasserie du Corsaire
Rue Thomas Edison
21 Jarry
97122 BAIE-MAHAULT, Guadeloupe
(00590) 2672-28; FAX (00590) 2680-91
Contact: Laurent Despointes

Sagba
ZI de Jerry/97122 Baie Mahault
Guadeloupe

GUYANA

Banks Brewing Co Ltd
PO Box 10194/Thirst Park
Georgetown, Guyana
592-2-62491-8

HAITI

Brasserie Nationale d'Haiti
PO Box 1334
Ave Haile Selassie
Port-au-Prince, Haiti
6-1528

JAMAICA

Desnoes & Geddes Ltd
PO Box 190/214 Spanish Town Rd
Kingston 11, Jamaica
(809) 923-9291; FAX (809) 923-8599
Contact: P. H. Geddes

Guinness Jamaica Ltd
Central Village Brewery
PO Box 620
Spanish Town, Jamaica
Contact: R. Dempster

MARTINIQUE

Brasserie Lorraine
Union/97232 Lamétin Martinique
Fort-de-France, Martinique
79-19-55
Contact: Paul Meertens

NETHERLANDS ANTILLES

Antilliaanse Brouwerij
PO Box 465
Rijkseenheid
Willemstad, Netherlands Antilles
612-944; FAX 612-035
Contact: M. A. Pourier

Grandes
Brasseries Antillaises
ZI de Jarry
Baie Mahault
Guadelope, 97122 Netherlands Antilles

St Maarten Breweries
PO Box 1122
St Maarten, Netherlands Antilles
5995-25153
Contact: Robin Back

ST KITTS AND NEVIS

St Kitts Breweries Ltd
PO Box 45
Basseterre, St Kitts and Nevis
2616-7-8-9
Contact: Calvin Cable

TRINIDAD AND TOBAGO

Caribbean Development Co Ltd
Eastern Main Rd/Champs Fleurs
PO Box 1287
Trinidad and Tobago
662-2231-7
Contact: Timothy Nafziger

National Brewing Co Ltd
PO Box 1131
Port of Spain, Trinidad and Tobago
662-5586-7-9
Contact: H. C. Habbershaw

10 Brewing Equipment Manufacturers and Suppliers

There are a myriad of options for setting up a small-scale brewery. They range from designing and fabricating your own system to purchasing a new, complete brewing system. Buying tanks from another industry, such as dairy, and converting them to brewing vessels is another route. The amount of tried-and-true used equipment available is gradually increasing as successful small breweries purchase new and bigger vessels and put their smaller ones up for sale. There are also a few brewhouses for sale as a result of microbrewery or brewpub failures. However, due to the tremendous growth of the industry, the number of interested buyers is also increasing. Used equipment, thus, is not easy to find.

When choosing equipment, it is very important to know the style of beer you plan to make. A lager brewery, for example, will require twice as much cellar tankage as an ale brewery. Knowing the dimensions of your building is another key factor in acquiring the right brewing vessels. In addition, having a well-written business plan and skilled engineering on your side are crucial to sizing your equipment.

The best way to learn is to talk to other brewers about their equipment and the company from which they purchased it. Are they happy with it? Did they receive quality service? Does the company provide good follow-up support or do they ignore you once they cash your check? You are considering spending a large sum of money. Ask companies for references and check them. If you are uncertain of a company's track record, you may be well advised to withhold a percentage of payment until the delivery of the equipment, in its entirety, by a scheduled date agreed upon in advance by both parties.

Research every option. Don't make a purchase without first getting several bids from different companies.

In this chapter, you will find the most comprehensive list to date of manufacturers and suppliers who cater to the small brewing industry.

Disclaimer: *Companies are allowed to list in the* Brewers Resource Directory *free of charge. They are not screened. A listing in this book does not, in any way, constitute an endorsement of the company, or its products or services, by the Institute for Brewing Studies.*

A. Gusmer Inc.
Jack Ehmann, VP Sales
Charles Tannert, VP Technical Services
27 North Ave. E.
Cranford, NJ 07016
(908) 272-9400; FAX (908) 272-8735

A. Handtmann Armaturenfabrik GmbH & Co. KG
Wolfgang Klawitter, Sales Mgr.
Birkenallee 25-29
Biberach, 88400
Germany
07351/342-0; FAX 07351/342-480

Handtmann is your competent partner for: fittings; valves; CIP installations; control systems; project works and multimicro systems — deepbed filters for fine/sterile filtration directly in front of the filling lines assuring quality and high biological safety low filter material costs fast payback and easy modular expansion from 25 to 400 hL/h.

A. O. Wilson Process Equipment Ltd.
Graham Wilson, Equipment Mgr.
PO Box 820
Bolton, ON L7E 5T5
Canada
(416) 857-1511; FAX (416) 857-0325

Brewing Equipment Manufacturers and Suppliers

A. Ziemann Gmbh
H. Haller, Sales Mgr.
P.B. 1160
Ludwigsburg, D-71611
Germany
07141-4080; FAX 07141-408335

AAA Metal Fabrication Inc.
Ron Krol, Pres.
1002 Hostetler
The Dalles, OR 97058
(503) 298-8313; FAX (503) 298-2508
http://www.gorge.net/business/aaametal/
   Manufacturer of all brewhouse vessels. Sizes from seven-barrel up. Direct fired or low-pressure steam kettles, mash and/or lauter vessels, fermenters, bright beer, and hot/cold liquor tanks built to your specifications — or let us help you design your brew house.

Abec Filtration Systems Inc.
Peter M. Abec, Pres.
10-1 County Line Rd.
Somerville, NJ 08876
(902) 575-0700; FAX (902) 575-0770
AFSINC@aol.com

Accurate Metering Systems Inc.
Bob Elliott
Don Arndtsen
1651 Wickening Rd.
Schaumburg, IL 60173
(708) 882-0690; FAX (708) 882-2695

Advanced Bottling UK Ltd
Peter Kerr, Dir.
The Old Rocket Site, Misson Springs
Doncaster, S Yorks DN10 GET
England
00-44-1302-772882; FAX 00-44-1302-772882

AFTEK Inc.
Ed Marchetti, VP
Liz Cooper, Office Mgr.
740 Driving Park Ave.
Rochester, NY 14613
(716) 458-7550; FAX (716) 458-7476
   Full line distributor of filtration equipment for the brewing industry.

Albert Handtmann Armaturenfabrik GmbH & Co. KG
Wolfgang Klawitter, Sales Mgr.
Birkenallee 25-29
Biberach, 88400
Germany
07351/342-0; FAX 07351/342-480
   Single-use/reuse cleaning installations, manual or automatic operation, from concept to completion.

Albert Handtmann Armaturenfabrik GmbH & Co. KG
Michael Feische, Sales Mgr.
Birkenallee 25-29
Biberach, 88400
Germany
07351/342-0; FAX 07351/342-480
   MultiMicro System. Deepbed filter for fine and sterile filtration of beer.

Alfa Laval Brewery Systems
Alan F. Dowie, Business Mgr.
200 S. Park Blvd.
Greenwood, IN 46143
(317) 889-5100; FAX (317) 889-4620
   Alfa Laval manufactures a comprehensive range of process equipment: high-speed centrifugal clarifiers, heat exchangers, flow equipment, automation, etc. We also assemble these components into modular systems for: yeast dosing, water deaeration, carbonation, high gravity blending, pasteurization, and external wort boiling. All units are pre-assembled and fully tested. We have reference plants in most of the world's major brewing companies.

Alfa Laval Brewery Systems/Separation
Dave Steger, Brewery Product Mgr.
101 Milner Ave.
Scarborough, ON M1S 4S6
Canada
(416) 299-6101; FAX (416) 299-5864

Alfa Laval S. A. DE C. V.
Juan Carlos Trujillo
Recursos Petroleros No. 7 Frac. Ind. La Loma
Tial., Edo. de Mexico, 54060
Mexico
(5) 398-87-30 or (5) 398-87-00; FAX (5) 398-9710

Alumasc
Derek Swanson, Sales Dir.
Steve Hart, International Sales Mgr.
Station Rd., Burton Latimer
Kettering, Northhamptonshire NN15 5JP
United Kingdom
44-1536-383-828; FAX 44-1536-420-147

Manufacturer of stainless-steel and plastic faucets, and American half barrels (stainless steel and aluminum). Other products available: dispense towers and pressure relief regulators.

Amazon Filters Ltd.
Jeff Kirby, Sales Mgr.
Albany Park Estate, Frimley Rd.
Camberley, Surrey GLL15 2PL
United Kingdom
1276-670600; FAX 1276-670101

AMBEC
Brian Wallace, Mgr.
H. Sevilla, Sales
50 Crwynns Mills Ct.
Owings Mills, MD 21117
(410) 363-9599; FAX (410) 363-3821

Packaging and process solutions.

Anchor Glass Container
Lee Farlander, VP Mktg. and New Product Development
Jim Gorski, Mktg. Mgr. Beer
4343 Anchor Plaza Pkwy.
Tampa, FL 33634
(813) 882-7756; FAX (813) 882-7773

APV Inc.
John G. Brunning, Sales and Mktg.
John H. Bergmann
9525 W. Bryn Mawr Ave.
Rosemont, IL 60018
(708) 678-4300; FAX (708) 678-4407

Aquionics Inc.
Marc J. Scanlon, Sales Eng.
PO Box 18395/21 Kenton Lands Rd.
Erlanger, KY 41018
(606) 341-0710; FAX (606) 341-2302

Ultraviolet light disinfection and microbial control of water used in brewing. Applications include plant makeup, post carbon, dilution, deaerated, etc., using a single lamp approach.

Arc Machines Inc.
Richard Shilline, VP Sales
10280 Glendaks Blvd.
Pacoima, CA 91331
(818) 896-9556; FAX (818) 890-3724

Atelier Zillich
Dipl. — Kfm. Peter Zillich,
Monatshausen
D 82327 Tutzing,
Germany
08158/8201; FAX 08158/1670

Automatic Equipment Mfg.
Sandy Eggert
PO Box P
Pender, NE 68047
(402) 385-3051; FAX (402) 385-3360

AZCO INC.
Robert Helein, VP Business Development
Meg Murphy, Mgr. Fabricat Sales
PO Box 567/AZCO Building, Hwy. 41
Appleton, WI 54912-0567
(414) 734-5791; FAX (414) 734-7432

B & J Machinery Inc.
James F. English, VP Sales
PO Box 62067
Cincinnati, OH 45262
(513) 771-7374; FAX (513) 771-3820

Bottling equipment — rinsers, fillers, crowners, cappers, pasteurizers, labelers. Production rates 50 to 800 b.p.m. New and rebuilt. Trade name executive/PE, executive/AROL, executive/Gherri.

Bavarian Brewery Technologies
Lewis Harsanyi, Pres.
Otto, Sales Mgr.
5041 Coolidge Ave.
Culver City, CA 90230
(310) 391-1091

Beraplan Härter GmbH
Allen Young, North American Consultant
Wolfgang Roth, Brewmaster
33 West St.
Annapolis, MD 21401
(410) 268-4545; FAX (410) 626-1044

Beraplan engineers "state-of-the-art" turnkey brewing systems, with outputs from 65 hL to 100 hL. When second best won't do, Beraplan does it.

BIRKO Corp.
Dana Johnson, Mgr. Con-Tact-It Systems
Fred Holzbauer, Chemist
9152 Yosemite St.
Henderson, CO 80640
(800) 525-0476; FAX (303) 289-1190

Cleaning and sanitizing products and systems for every size brewery or pub. Featuring environmentally friendly, metallurgically correct, and safety conscious chemical and application designs that ABOVE ALL don't flavor the brew. Nationwide distribution, offices and warehouses in principal cities. Convenient packages, reasonable prices. "By Brewers, for Brewers!"

Bloodhound Sensors Ltd.
Ed Ruck-Keene, Man. Dir.
Dr. Tim Gibson, Electronic Nose Development Mgr.
175 Woodhouse Lane
Leeds, Yorkshire LS2 3AR
United Kingdom
(44) 113-233-3444; FAX (44) 113-234-3811

Bohemian Breweries Inc.
Jean Pugh
Michael Lislis
23883 Madison St.
Torrance, CA 90505
(310) 375-2739; FAX (310) 373-6097

Bohemian Brewery Importers
Jean Pugh, VP Sales and Mktg.
Michael Lislis, Pres./CEO
710 Silver Spur Rd., Suite193
Rolling Hills Estate, CA 90274
(310) 544-1037; FAX (310) 541-2667

Brauhaus Systems Caspary
Scott Stephen
C/O Marabout Trading of America
110 Pleasant St., Suite 301
Marlborough, MA 01752
(888) 481-5777 or (508) 481-5777; FAX (508) 481-0617

Bratney Equipment Co./ Ken Bratney Co.
Bruce Bratney, VP
George Manset, Sales Eng.
13400 N.E. 20th St., Suite 49
Bellevue, WA 98005
(206) 747-6352; FAX (206) 641-8782

Bratney Equipment Co. provides equipment, design, and installation for special handling of dry malt grain in today's microbreweries. Conveyors, storage bins, scales, and solutions!

Brew Store
Gary Deathe
Dean Thrasher
114 Lakeshore Rd. E.
Oakville, ON L6J 6N2
(905) 845-2120; FAX (905) 845-1104
brewstor@hookup.net

The Brew Store is the manufacturer of quality on-premise brewing equipment. Their advantages range from having company-owned stores for over five years to suppling many similar BOP locations; literally coast to coast. Full training and recipe files included. Most importantly they know what it takes to be profitable.

Brewers & Bottlers Equipment Corp.
Bernard Z. Greenberg, Pres.
PO Box 67
Indian Rocks Beach, FL 34635-0067
(813) 593-2638; FAX (813) 596-4752

Bruce Brewing System — Brewery Builders
Bruce White, Brewer/Owner
PO Box 61251
Denver, CO 80206
(303) 778-8574; FAX (303) 778-0665

Manufacturer and designer of great brewing equipment — vessels that look and operate like a dream. Single tanks or whole breweries. Try equipment designed and built by brewers for brewers. Services and training also available. Custom design encouraged! Call today.

Buhler (Canada) Inc.
Peter Moeller, Sales/Prod. Mgr.
16 Esna Park Dr., Unit 8
Markham, ON L3R 5X1
Canada
(905) 940-6910; FAX (905) 940-3298

CAE Screen Plates
Mike Kupin, Prod. Mgr.
72 Queen
Lennoxville, Quebec J1M 2C3
Canada
(819) 562-4754; FAX (819) 562-6064

False bottom screen-lanter; drilled, sloted, or punched screen plates and screen cylinders.

Brewing Equipment Manufacturers and Suffixes

Picture the future of Microbrewing

The MonoBloc Advantage

Designed by Brewers For Brewers

The MonoBloc Turnkey Brewhouse combines today's advanced brewing technology with European beauty and craftsmanship, setting new standards for brewing and serving the finest handcrafted ales and lagers.

We know. As owners of a successful string of brewpubs, our requirements in a brewhouse are the same as yours: Uncompromising quality; efficiency of production; rapid return on investment.

Contact us for complete details to secure your future today!

Complete Customer & Product Support INCLUDED

310.375.BREW (2739)

Bohemian Breweries
Breweries superior by design

Torrance, CA 90505   Fax 310.373.6097

BREW SCHOOL
Knowledge...And Experience

Therefore, students will work with a state-of-the-art, completely functional brewery installed on the premises, immediately put training into action. This practical experience—along with the take-home course materials—will ensure that the knowledge you acquire will be fully and completely integrated into your own operations.

Call Today
310.375.2739
for complete information

Handwritten note (3/5/1997):

- Tony Taylor — vice president
  - James Brown
- Bo's Pontiac
- 15 Barrel System   Will send info
- National statistics
- 9600 Sq ft Rest = 350 seats.
- $8000/seat/yr. i.e. 2-8 Million/yr. income

* Not direct-fire brewery
* Steam operated 100%
* ~ 200,000
* 95% of Beer sold is not Ale
* Budweiser/Coors etc. are not ale but other side of spectrum.
* Much of the equip. is Valve sanitary & purks only
* Made by Granger

Course Director — Marty Velas
Beer Styles & History — Michael Jackson 
Beer Formulation — Dr. Joseph Owades 
Yeast Management — David Logsdon 
Filtration — Tom Anders 
Brewery Operations — Dr. Paul Farnsworth 

Institute for Brewing Studies

Cargocaire Engineering Co.
Davis McDougall, National Sales Mgr.
PO Box 640/79 Monroe St.
Amesbury, MA 01913-0640
(508) 388-0600; FAX (508) 388-4556
cargo@munters.com
http://www.munters.com/users/cargo

Munters Cargocaire is an engineering firm that designs and manufactures dry desiccant dehumidification systems. Since 1939, these systems have helped to prevent corrosion, reduce housekeeping issues, and improve worker safety. Using a desiccant impregnated HoneyCombe rotor, our units contain only four moving parts for reduced maintenance time.

Carlson Filtration Ltd.
Phil Brown, International Sales Mgr.
Butts Mill
Barnoldswick, Lancashire BB8 5HP
United Kingdom
(0) 1282-812271; FAX (0) 1282-816404

Cask Brewing Systems
Peter Love, Pres.
5925 12th St. S.E., Suite 225
Calgary, AB T2H 2M3
Canada

Cask Brewing Systems Inc., manufacturers and suppliers of brewing equipment and ingredients. For consistent quality product and service you can depend on Cask Brewing Systems Inc. for all your brewing requirements.

Brew Pubs,
Brew on Premise facilities
Brewing ingredients

Cask Brewing Sytems Inc.
No. 255, 5925 12th St. S.E., Calgary, Alberta T2H 2M3
Ph. (403) 640-4677 Fax (403) 640-4680

(403) 640-4677; FAX (403) 640-4680
caskbru@ibm.net or info@cask.com
http://www.cask.com

Cask Brewing Systems specializes in the sale, supply, and servicing of complete brew-on-premise's systems. The company provides a full range of services from initial planning, and layout to installation, brewing training, and on-going service and support. Cask Brewing also provides recipe development and a full range of brewing ingredients. With over sixty installations operating in the United States, Canada, and Australia, Cask Brewing is the leading supplier of brew-on-premise systems worldwide.

CDC Inc.
Pam Shirbish, Sales
John Cross, Pres.
40610 Balch Park Rd.
Springville, CA 93265
(209) 539-2293; FAX (209) 539-3146

Celite Corp., c/o World Minerals Inc.
George Christoferson, Mktg. Mgr.
Andy Masters, Dir. Special Projects
PO Box 519/137 W. Central Ave.
Lompoc, CA 93438
(800) 342-8667; FAX (805) 735-5699

Centrico Inc.
100 Fairway Ct.
Northuale, NJ 07647
(201) 767-3900; FAX (201) 767-3416

Centrico Inc. is the exclusive marketer for Westfalia Centrifuges in North America. Now a member of the GEA Group which includes Niro Inc., Tughenhagen, and Damrow, we offer the latest technology backed by an extensive after sales service and parts organization.

Century Mfg. Inc.
Charles Kerns, Pres.
Estill Eversole, General Mgr.
PO Box 33/4858 Rte. 35
West Alexandria, OH 45381
(513) 839-4397; FAX (513) 839-4022

Manufacturer of ten- to fifty-barrel brewing systems of superior quality in a reasonable amount of time, Century Mfg. Inc. is proud to be the eastern United States' largest manufacturer of micro/pub-brewing systems.

It Won't Take Forever
Just Century

Holy Cow! Cafe • Brewery
Las Vegas' First Brew Pub

Handwritten note:
2/17/96
Charles KERN 15 Barrel
Suggested Visiting
* Bavarian Toledo

- Consulting • Brewery Design
- Site Evaluation
- Installation
- Technical Assistance
- Follow-Up Support

& Micros

We Contain the Finest…Guaranteed

CENTURY MANUFACTURING

For the best custom built stainless steel tanks, equipment, technical support and service the way you like it, write or call us today.
Century Manufacturing • PO Box 33 • West Alexandria, Ohio 45381 • (513) 839-4397

Ceramem Separations
Pieris O'Donnell, Dir. Mktg. and Sales
20 Clematis Ave.
Waltham, MA 02154
(617) 899-0467; FAX (617) 899-1227

Manufacturer of ceramic, crossflow-membrane modules and systems for beer recovery from tank bottoms, decant-beer clarification, and cold filtration.

Chemdet Inc.
Phillip Joachim, Pres.
Michael Evans, Regional Sales Mgr.
50 Sintsink Dr. E.
Port Washington, NY 11050
(516) 883-1510 or (800) 645-1510; FAX (516) 883-2044

Chemgrate Corp.
Joanne Turic, Mktg. Mgr.
19240 144th Ave. N.E.
Woodinville, WA 98072
(206) 483-9797; FAX (206) 481-3622

Chester-Jensen Co. Inc.
Tom Pakradooni, VP Sales
James F. Donovan, Pres.
PO Box 908
Chester, PA 19016
(610) 876-6276; FAX (610) 876-0485

Chrislan Ceramics Inc.
Al Laninga, Dir. Mktg. and Finance
1650 Broadway St., Suite 101
Port Coquitlam, BC V3L 2M8
Canada
(604) 941-7557; FAX (604) 941-5661

Chrislan Ceramics manufactures ceramic tap handles for the brewery industry. Numerous shapes are available, or we can help you design an exclusive shape that will be unique to your marketing plans. We are one of the only ceramic tap handle manufacturers that kiln fires a decoration on your handle in house. This gives you tremendous flexability in the design of one of the most valuable marketing tools you have.

Criveller Co.
Bruno Criveller, Owner
6935 Oakwood Dr.
Niagra Falls, ON L2E 6S5
Canada
(905) 357-2930; FAX (905) 374-2930

Cross Distributing Co. Inc.
John Cross, Owner
Pamela Shirbish, Sales Dir.
40610 Balch Park Rd.
Springville, CA 93265
(209) 539-2293; FAX (209) 539-3146

Custom Brew Beer Systems
Mark Hamelin, Pres.
36 Keefer Ct., Suite 5
Hamilton, ON L8E 4V4
Canada
(905) 573-0655 or (800) 363-4119; FAX (905) 573-2322

Pioneers in the brew-on-premise's equipment industry. Sales, installation, and training available for complete packages or individual components. Custom designs and fabrications.

Dairy Engineering Co.
Mike Hlatki, Sales Engineer
Randy Hirsh, Sales Engineer
5783 N. Sheridan
Arvada, CO 80002
(303) 423-2332; FAX (303) 423-0740
info@dairyeng.com
http://www.dairyeng.com

Dairy Engineering is a service oriented and price conscious company serving the sanitary industries since 1981. We specialize in stainless-steel processing equipment including pumps, valves, fittings, tanks, etc. We keep a very large stock of new and used equipment and have a reputation among brewers for fast, reliable service.

DCI Inc.
Steve Stonestrom, VP Mktg.
PO Box 1227/600 N. 54th Ave.
St. Cloud, MN 56302
(612) 252-8200; FAX (612) 252-0866

Dicalite/Grefco Inc.
Walt Pevlakovich, Technical Mgr.
Glenn Jones, VP
3435 W. Lomita Blvd.
Torrance, CA 90505
(310) 517-0700; FAX (310) 517-0794

Diversey Corp.
John Muuse, Dir. of Brewing and Beverages
Dave Zoochi, Oper. Mgr. Brewing
12025 Tech Center Dr.
Livonia, MI 48150
(313) 281-0930

Diversey Inc.
Mike Salisbury, Business Dev./Mgr. Brewing
2645 Royal Windsor Dr.
Mississauga, ON L5J 1L1
Canada
(905) 822-3511; FAX (905) 822-3797

The company offers a complete line of sanitation programs specifically for the brewing industry. Services include implementation of state-of-the-art cleaners, sanitizers, and systems for conveyor track treatment, water treatment, cip, and environmental cleaning.

DME Brewing Services
Barry MacLeod, VP Mktg. and Sales
Kelly Dunne, Mktg. and Sales
PO Box 553
Charlottetown, PE C1A 7L1
Canada
(902) 628-6900; FAX (902) 628-1313
ksampson@cycor.ca
http://www.cycor.ca/DME/

DME Brewing Services designs and manufactures standard and custom brewery equipment for the craft-brewing industry. We provide complete breweries as well as beer engines, cask ale packages, cellar tanks, and keg washers. Our regional representatives provide face-to-face consultation in installation, site inspection, operations, beer formulations, technical brewing, and on-going support.

Drinktec USA Ltd.
Nicolas Haase, Sales and Mktg. Mgr.
JoAnn Seeger, Office Mgr.
100 Railroad Dr., Suite B
Ivyland, PA 18974
(215) 953-9335; FAX (215) 953-8636
drinktec@aol.com

Serving the beverage industry worldwide; equipment, parts, systems, expendable supplies, promotional articles. A member of BrauHaase International Management Group.

DuBois
Dan McElroy, Product Line Mgr.
Chris Horstman, Mktg. Specialist
255 E. Fifth St.
Cincinnati, OH 45202
(800) 543-4906; FAX (513) 762-6601

DuBois is the specialty chemical supplier of choice for the brewing industry. We have over seven hundred field service representatives who specialize in the areas of cleaning, sanitizing, cooling tower and boiler treatments, lubricants, and waste water treatment to provide local care and service with global strength.

Edwards Engineering Corp.
Vincent W. Dardo, Sales Mgr.
Jorge Molato, Sales Eng.
101 Alexander Ave
Pompton Plains, NJ 07444
(201) 835-2800; FAX (201) 835-3222

Electro-Steam Generator Corp.
Jack Harlin, Acct. Mgr.
1000 Bernard St.
Alexandria, VA 22314
(800) 634-8177 or (703) 549-0664; FAX (703) 836-2581

Electro-Steam Generator Corp. manufacturers all-electric steam generators. Ninety-eight percent efficiency. Point-of-use placement. No flames, fuel, fumes, or firegrade walls. Lower insurance. No boiler chemicals. One to 72 BHP. ASHE, National Board of PVI, ETL, UL, and CSA.

Elliott Bay Metal Fabricating Inc.
Chris Michaelsen, Pres.
Greg Bujak, Brewing Consultant
PO Box 777
Monroe, WA 98272
(206) 788-5297; FAX (206) 844-2209

Elliott Bay crafts the finest stainless steel brewing systems from one to fourteen barrels. We provide full service from installation to brewing your first batches. We are commited to making your operation a top-of-the-line brew system putting out the best brews while keeping control of costs.

Enerfab Inc.
Jeff Raasch, Sr. VP Sales and Mktg.
4955 Spring Grove Ave.
Cincinnati, OH 45232
(513) 641-0500; FAX (513) 242-6833

Enerfab is a fabricator of brewhouse femative and storage tanks. Enerfab also has the ability to custom design, engineer, fabricate, and build total process systems.

England Worthside Ltd.
Chris Brearley, Mktg. Mgr.
Hope Mills S. Street
Keighley, West Yorkshire BD 21 1AG
United Kingdom
01535-606876; FAX 01535-610052

Major British manufacturer of traditional beer fonts and handpull units. Customization service available.

Brewing Equipment Manufacturers and Suppliers

Ertel Engineering Co.
William Kearney, Sales Mgr.
PO Box 3358
Kingston, NY 12401
(914) 331-4552; FAX (914) 339-1063

Falco Stainless Steel Equipment Ltd.
Angelo Penta, G.M.
Louis Penta
125 B St. Joseph
Lachine, PQ H8S 2L2
Canada
(514) 634-3541; FAX (514) 636-0350

Figgie
John Mojonnier, Technical Mktg. Mgr.
PO Box 118008
Charleston, SC 29411
FAX (803) 553-3033

Filter Equipment Co. Inc.
Scott Groh, Sales Mgr.
Steve Groh
PO Box 1452/1440 HWY 34
Wall, NJ 07719
(800) 445-9775; FAX (800) 777-3477

We offer filter pads, presses, cartridges, and parts for all types of beverage filtration.

Filtrine Manufacturing Co.
Peter Hansel, Pres.
Alan Wall, Sales Mgr.
Elm St.
Harrisville, NH 03450
(603) 827-3321; FAX (603) 827-3081
filtrine@top.monad.net

First Fabrics Inc.
James Bohm, Pres.
Frank Weaver, VP
4927 N. Damen Ave.
Chicago, IL 60625
(312) 271-0336

Flo-Pac Corp.
LeRoy J. Schwartz, VP Advertising
700 N. Washington Ave., Suite 400
Minneapolis, MN 55401
(612) 332-6240

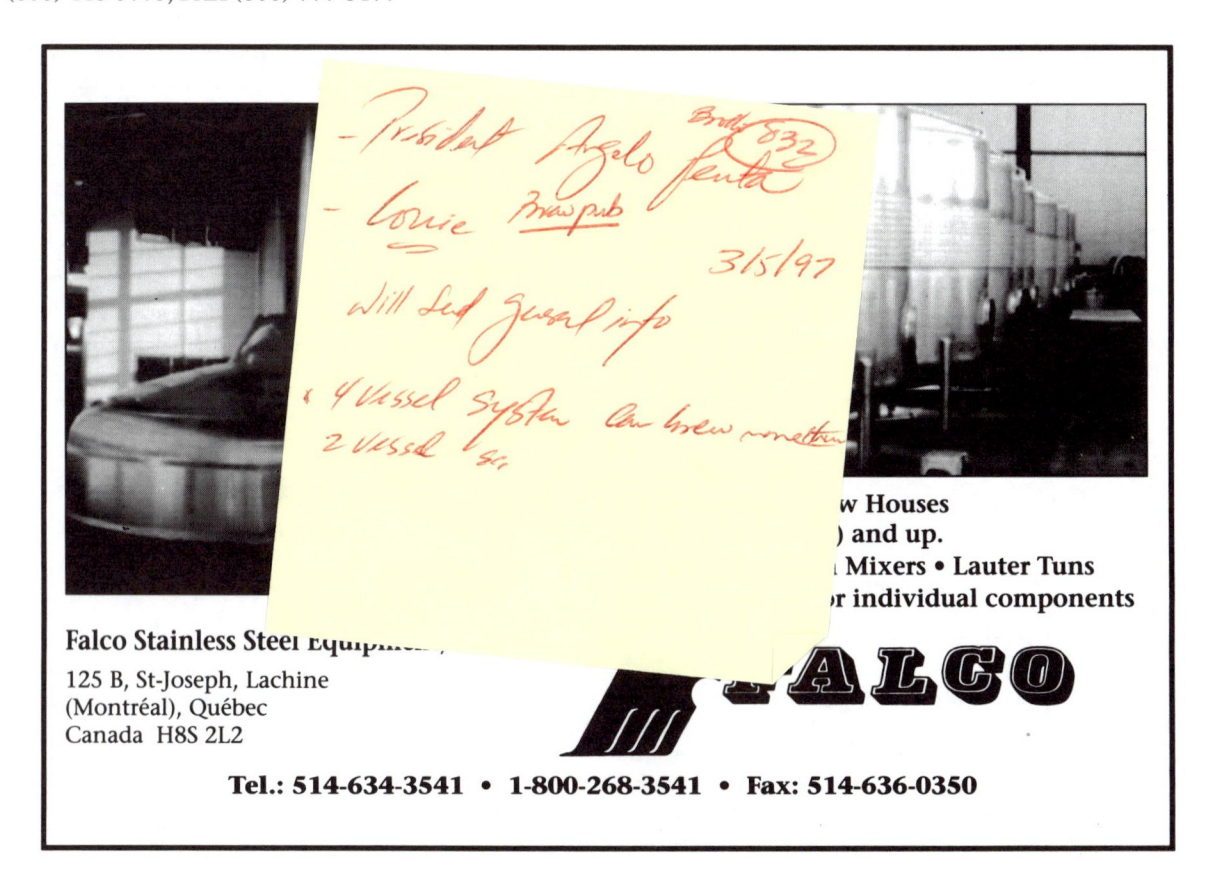

Falco Stainless Steel Equipment
125 B, St-Joseph, Lachine
(Montréal), Québec
Canada H8S 2L2

Tel.: 514-634-3541 • 1-800-268-3541 • Fax: 514-636-0350

Foxboro Co.
D. Gilmore, Dir. Corp. Communications
33 Commercial St.
Foxboro, MA 02035-2099
(508) 543-8750; FAX (508) 549-4433
http://www.foxboro.com

Foxx Equipment Co.
955 Decatur St., Unit B
Denver, CO 80204
(800) 525-2484; FAX (303) 893-3028

Frick/Reco Division, York International Corp.
Glenn Fair, Mktg. Mgr.
Sam Sanchez, Parts Mgr.
5680 E. Houston St.
San Antonio, TX 78220
(210) 661-9191; FAX (210) 662-6591

Friesen of Iowa Inc.
Garry Friesen, Pres.
2897 Expansion Blvd.
Storm Lake, IA 50588
(800) 437-2234 or (712) 732-1780; FAX (712) 732-1028

Manufacturer of fully welded, smooth walled, hopper bottom bulk bins. Friesen bins are custom made to your specifications and are ideal for your grain storage needs. They can be painted to match your decor and with application of your logo or decals, the bins can be a functional billboard.

G & D Chillers Inc.
Dan Smith, Pres.
Ray Tatum, VP
3498 W. First St.., Suite 7
Eugene, OR 97402
(800) 555-0973; FAX (541) 345-3903

G & H Products Corp
Mark Ream, Brewery Application Mgr.
Susan Govea, Mktg. Coordinator
7600 57th Ave.
Kenosha, WI 53142
(800) 558-4060; FAX (414) 694-2907

G & H Products Corp., part of the worldwide Alfa Laval Group, manufactures a wide range of brewing equipment, including sanitary pumps, valves, tank cleaning equipment, fittings, and flow meters. State-of-the-art technology is used to develop our line of quality equipment.

G. W. Kent Inc.
Randall Reichwage
3667 Morgan Rd.
Ann Arbor, MI 48108
(313) 572-1300; FAX (313) 572-0097

G. W. Kent Inc. is the exclusive North American importer of Durst Malz German two-row malts.

Gafco-Worldwide, Inc.
Frank E. May, Pres.
Eduardo Rosado, Latin American Sales Dir.
6302 Harrison Ave., Suite 5
Cincinnati, OH 45247
(513) 574-2257; FAX (513) 574-2362

GWW Inc. is an import/export management company with twenty-nine years experience in international sourding, centralized purchasing, and contract manufacturing for bottling and brewery needs. We service large and small companies providing machinery, spare parts, components, and turnkey operations.

Gamajet Cleaning Systems Inc.
Victor Sheronas, Pres.
Robert Delaney, Chairman
2421 Yellow Springs Rd. Unit 1
Malvern, PA 19355
(800) BUY-JETS; FAX (610) 408-9945

General Filtration, Division of Lee Chemicals Ltd.
Ed Bridge, Mktg. Mgr.
1119 Yonge St.
Toronto, ON M4W 2L7
Canada
(416) 924-9349; FAX (416) 960-8750

Gimson Engineering Limited
Paul Sergent, General Mgr.
David Frost, Managing Dir.
41 Boston Rd.
Leicester, LE4 1AW
United Kingdom
00-44-116-2368-688; FAX 00-44-116-2363-663

Goodall Rubber Co.
Darice Keyes, Advertising Administrator
Grovers Mill Rd, Suite 203
Lawrenceville, NJ 08648
(800) GOODALL; FAX (609) 799-4232

Grain Systems Inc.
Gene Wiseman, VP Sales
Burl Shuler, Chief Eng.
1004 E. Illinois St.
Assumption, IL 62510
(217) 226-4421; FAX (217) 226-4420

Guardian Labs
H. Roberts, Pres.
S. Duckett, Sales Mgr.
PO Box 28591
St. Louis, MO 63146
(800) 255-4429; FAX (314) 367-6669

Gulfstream Brewing Product
Phil Hunt, Owner
6331-A Woodville Hwy.
Tallahassee, FL 32311
(904) 421-6902

Haffmans B. V.
J.A.E. Visser, Mktg. Mgr.
Marinus Dammeweg 30
NL-5928 PW Venlo,
Netherlands
(77) 3873232; FAX (77) 3825982
Postbus 3150, 5902 RD Venlo

Haffmans B. V., worldwide supplier of: CO_2 recovery systems, OG-measurement and carbonating systems, and a variety of quality control–instrumentation such as CO_2-measurement on- and off-line, hazemeters, foam stability testers, PU measurement, keg monitoring, and malt modification analysers.

Heavy Duty Products Inc.
John Cressman
Rance Tupling
1261 Industrial Rd.
Cambridge, ON N3H 4W3
Canada
(519) 653-4222 or (800) 563-8247; FAX (519) 653-4220

Hilge/Shanley Pump
Jim Shanley, Prod. Mgr.
2525 S. Clearbrook Dr.
Arlington Heights, IL 60005
(708) 439-9200; FAX (708) 439-9388

Exclusive distributor of Hilge products, offering complete line of stainless-steel sanitary pumps. With more than 130 years of experience, Hilge is the market leader in all aspects of brewery pumping.

Hoover Materials Handling Group Inc./ SABCO Industries/Sav-a-Barrel Corp.
Rick Henzler, Sales Mgr.
4511 South Ave.
Toledo, OH 43615-6418
(419) 531-5347

American manufacturer of high quality new straight-sided, single entry kegs. Preferred by large and small brewers alike for their heavy duty characteristics and dependable performance.

Hopfen und Malz GmbH
Hermann Hörterer, Brewmaster
Hans Schilp, Brewmaster
Schloßstr. 8
82269 Kaltenberg,
Germany
08193-9330; FAX 08193-933123

Hopfen und Malz GmbH, as a subsidiary of Kaltenberg Brewery, provides innovative and modern turnkey pub- and minibreweries, backed by the experience of a well-established Bavarian brewery.

IDD Process & Packaging Inc.
Jeff Gunn, Pres.
Tom Thilert, Sales Dir.
646 Flinn Ave
Moorpark, CA 93021
(800) 621-4144 or (805) 529-9890; FAX (805) 529-9282
idd2jeff@aol

Brewery process and packaging system design and manufacturing engineers. This includes turnkey brewpub and microbreweries, kegging systems, tank valves, yeast propagation and management systems, deaeration, filtration and pasteurization systems, hops (leaf, pellet, and extract), cleaners, sanitizers, brewing and fermenting aids. Full service formula and systems brewery engineering and consultation.

Indcon Design Ltd.
Harold Kluthe, Mktg. and Sales
Barrie Miller, Head Designer
10459 178th St., Suite 101
Edmonton, Alberta T5S 1R5
Canada
(403) 444-7184; FAX (403) 481-4931

Suppliers of stainless-steel, brass, plastic dispense faucets for the draft-beer industry. Other products available: dispense towers, pressure regulators, stainless-steel and aluminum beer kegs.

Industrial Filter & Pump Mfg. Co.
E.H. King, VP Sales
5900 Ogden Ave.
Cicero, IL 60650
(708) 656-7800; FAX (708) 656-7806

Innozyme Ltd.
Jon Caplan, Pres.
PO Box 68, Station "H"
Montreal, PQ H3G 2K5
Canada
(514) 369-3078; FAX (514) 369-3079

International Brewing & Manufacturing Inc.
Jai Chaudhuri
Paul Holborn
6989 Corte Santa Fe
San Diego, CA 92121
(619) 550-0955; FAX (619) 550-0960

Ion Exchange Prod. Inc.
Irving Reichstein, CEO
4834 S. Halsted St.
Chicago, IL 60609-4418
(312) 254-1300; FAX (312) 847-7243

ISP (International Specialty Products)
Rolf D. Schmidt, Sr. Sales Eng./Beverage Specialist
1919 S. Highland Ave., Suite 124-D
Lombard, IL 60148
(800) 323-2272 or (708) 932-4022; FAX (708) 495-0245

J. E. Siebel Sons' Co.
Ron Siebel, Pres.
Tim Stover, Technical Sales
4055 W. Peterson Ave.
Chicago, IL 60646
(312) 279-0966; FAX (312) 463-4962

Supplies: Purple Snake beer hose, kettle coagulants, yeast nutrients, fining agents, microbiological media, water treatment salts, chillproofing, enzyme systems, and foam stabilizers. Distributor: Crosby & Baker.

J. V. Northwest Inc.
Jeri Riha, Mktg.
28120 S.W. Boberg Rd.
Wilsonville, OR 97070
(503) 682-2596; FAX (503) 682-8060

J. V. Northwest is a leading manufacturer of seven-to-one-hundred-barrel brewing systems. Our Northwest location is a testing ground for brewing innovation. J. V. vessels feature no-shadow manways, back-up safety systems, variable sizing of all brewing vessels. Brewers and engineers are on staff. Efficient and quick brewery installations. Large parts department. An ASME coded facility.

JACO Equipment Corp.
Maurice Osterman, Pres.
3116 Main St.
Buffalo, NY 14214
(716) 836-3755; FAX (716) 836-3576

The oldest U.S. dealer offering used brewery equipment. Individual items and complete breweries available.

Jet Carboy & Bottle Washer Co.
Michael Anton, Pres.
Angela Fall,
3301 Veterans Dr.
Traverse City, MI 49684
(616) 935-4555; FAX (616) 941-2334

Manufacturer of "Jet" carboy and bottle washers that attach to laundry or kitchen faucets to easily clean out bottles. Washers carry a lifetime guarantee. Established 1973.

Keg Club
Richard Wagner, VP Sales
Rod Senior, Pres.
620 19th St., Suite 300
Niagara Falls, NY 14301-2226
(519) 751-1201; FAX (519) 753-2305

Kenerik/Golden Gate
Joe Toby, Pres.
4179 Front St.
Goodwood, ON L0C 1A0
Canada
(905) 642-1925; FAX (905) 642-1925

KHS Machines Inc.
Albert A. Burns, Jr., Pres.
1350 Industrial Ave., Suite G
Petaluma, CA 94952
(707) 763-4844; FAX (707) 763-6997

KLR Machines Inc.
Jurgen Koch, Pres.
David J. Reagan, VP
47 W. Steuben St.
Bath, NY 14810
(607) 776-4193; FAX (607) 776-9044

Brewing Equipment Manufacturers and Suppliers

Kramer Stainless Systems
Michael Kramer, Pres.
PO Box 315
Quakertown, PA 18951
(610) 346-8919; FAX (610) 346-8919

Krones Inc.
Konie Brenneman, Mktg. Mgr.
9600 S. 58th St.
Franklin, WI 53132
(414) 421-5650; FAX (414) 421-2222

L. C. Thomsen Inc.
Jeff Stevens, Sales Mgr.
Mike Dyutka, Customer Service Mgr.
1303 43rd St.
Kenosha, WI 53140
(414) 652-3662; FAX (414) 652-3526

Manufacturing quality stainless steel flow equipment for the dairy, food, and beverage industry for sixty years. L. C. Thomsen Inc. offers a full line of pumps, valves, filters and strainers, tanks, tubing, and all related fittings needed for the brewing industry. L. C. Thomsen Inc. serves all domestic and foreign markets.

Lazar & Co.
Wayne Lazar, Pres.
404 Mendocino Ave., Suite 200
Santa Rosa, CA 95401
(707) 577-0835; FAX (707) 575-4094

Maas Brewing Systems
Steve Maas, Pres.
Pete Maas, VP Manufacturing
1645 Washington Ave.
Louisville, CO 80027
(303) 604-0545

MacLean Brewery Equipment Ltd.
Charles MacLean, Pres.
Antonia Smits
175 Arthur St. N.
Guelph, ON N1E 4V6
Canada
(519) 824-1455; FAX (519) 824-1455

Mangel, Scheuermann & Oeters Inc.
Bernard E. Black, Pres.
Gertrude Terraschke, VP
1957 Pioneer Rd., Bldg. B
Huntingdon Valley, PA 19006-2503
(215) 674-5500; FAX (215) 441-0458

Suppliers of cleaning devices for tanks and kegs, all brewery hardware, valves, fittings, pumps, carbonation and aeration devices, laboratory testing equipment, bungs, brewer's hose, Grundy tanks, combination manifolds, and all Grundy spares.

Marcon Wine & Filters
Dr. Giuseppe Marcon, Pres.
Maria Marcon, Sec.
1428 Speers Rd., Suite 9
Oakville, ON L6L 5M1
Canada
(906) 825-8847; FAX (905) 825-8404

Macron Filters produces filters for homebrewers, pilot breweries, microbreweries, winemakers, wineries, and laboratories. All models can use pads or reusable membranes. D. E. plates available. Manufacturer of four-week wine kits.

Mechanical Welding Service
Steve Maontua, Owner
PO Box 340
Woodbine, MD 21797
(800) 791-7088 or (410) 795-9147; FAX (410) 489-4827

Mechanical Welding Service is a stainless sanitary pipe/tubing installation contractor. We have piped numerous microbreweries and brewpubs in the eastern United States and Canada. Associated services are tank alterations and repairs, mobile service, and shop fabrication of stainless-steel and aluminum.

Meyer Supply Inc.
Jim Wamser, Pres.
3470 Hampton Ave., Suite 102B
St. Louis, MO 63139
(800) 325-8818

MicroPure Filtration
Robert A. Pollmann, VP/General Mgr.
Marcy Pollman, Sales Admin.
7879 Forest Hills Rd.
Rockford, IL 61111
(800) 654-7873; FAX (815) 962-7360

Solid, secure filtration solutions for sterile air, gas, liquid, and steam applications. Environmentally friendly while saving production costs. On-line automatic samplers for product sampling.

Millipore Corp.
David Stack, Mktg. Mgr.
Michel Pailhes
80 Ashby Rd.
Bedford, MA 01730
(800) 645-5476; FAX (617) 533-8873
david_stack@millipore.com
http://www.millipore.com

Bräuhaus
Die Gaststättenbrauerei

System Caspary

To brew professional beer...

...join the Professionals

„ Bräuhaus "
System Caspary

For more information please call

(888) 481-5777

Scott Stephen
Marabout Trading of America
110 Pleasant Street, Marlborough, MA 01752. Fax: (508) 481-0617

Field Of Dreams

DME systems are designed by Engineers and Brewers. Specialists in custom building out-of-the-ordinary systems. All DME systems are safe, efficient and flexible and are backed by a brewing [...] over they face-to-face, personal service. A representative is always close by. We stay on the scene until your system flows the way it should.

Turnkey services. Business planning. Beer formulation. Equipment fabrication and installation. Plus post-sale follow up. DME is outstanding in every field. Tell us your brewing plans and dreams. We can make them come true.

DME Brewing Services

Join our family of fine brewers.

P.O. Box 553, West Royalty Industrial Park, Charlottetown, PEI, Canada C1A 7L1   Telephone (902) 628-6900   Facsimile (902) 628-1313

SHAFTEBURY * CARMEL * QUEEN CITY * RIVERSIDE * PONY EXPRESS * BARLEY'S * ROYAL OAK * 75TH STREET * BIG RIVER * WESTWOOD * BLACKHORSE * VALLEY FORGE * BLACK SWAMP * TAP STREET * BLOOMINGTON * T-BONZ

WE COULD BUILD ORDINARY LOOKING BREWERIES

... BUT MOST FOLKS SEEM TO PREFER THESE

SPECIFIC MECHANICAL SYSTEMS LTD.

Manufacturers of Over 150 Breweries Worldwide

6848 KIRKPATRICK CRES., VICTORIA, B.C. V8M 1Z9 TEL: (604) 652-2111 FAX: (604) 652-6010
WEB SITE: http://www.commercial.net/vault/specific EMAIL: specific@commercial.net

Side left: EDDY McSTIFF'S * COPPER CANYON * SMILING MOOSE * FLEETSIDE * COLUMBINE MILL * SHERLOCK'S * GETTYSBREW * COOPER SMITH'S * FLAT BRANCH * FLOSSMOOR * RANDY'S FUNHUNTER'S * ALLEY KAT * FOUNDER'S HILL * TAKAYAMA * LEFT HAND * COEUR D'ALENE

Side right: PORT CITY * MAGIC CITY * LAZLO'S * O'GRADY'S * PETE'S PLACE * LAWRENCEVILLE * HEAVENLY DAZE * PHANTOM CANYON * NORMAN * GLENWOOD SPRINGS * MISSION BRIDGE * SOUTHEND * RIVER MARKET * SAILOR HAGAR'S * TERRIFIC PACIFIC * WATERING HOLE * SAN JUAN

BLUE STAR * TEXAS CATTLE * BOWMAN * HUNTINGTON * BREWSTERS * LAGUNA BEACH * NEWPORT BEACH * CARVER'S * RAILWAY * QUEEN CITY * MAD BOAR * LIBERTY * MICKEY FINNS * LEXINGTON CITY

Quench Your Thirst
with Brewers Publications.

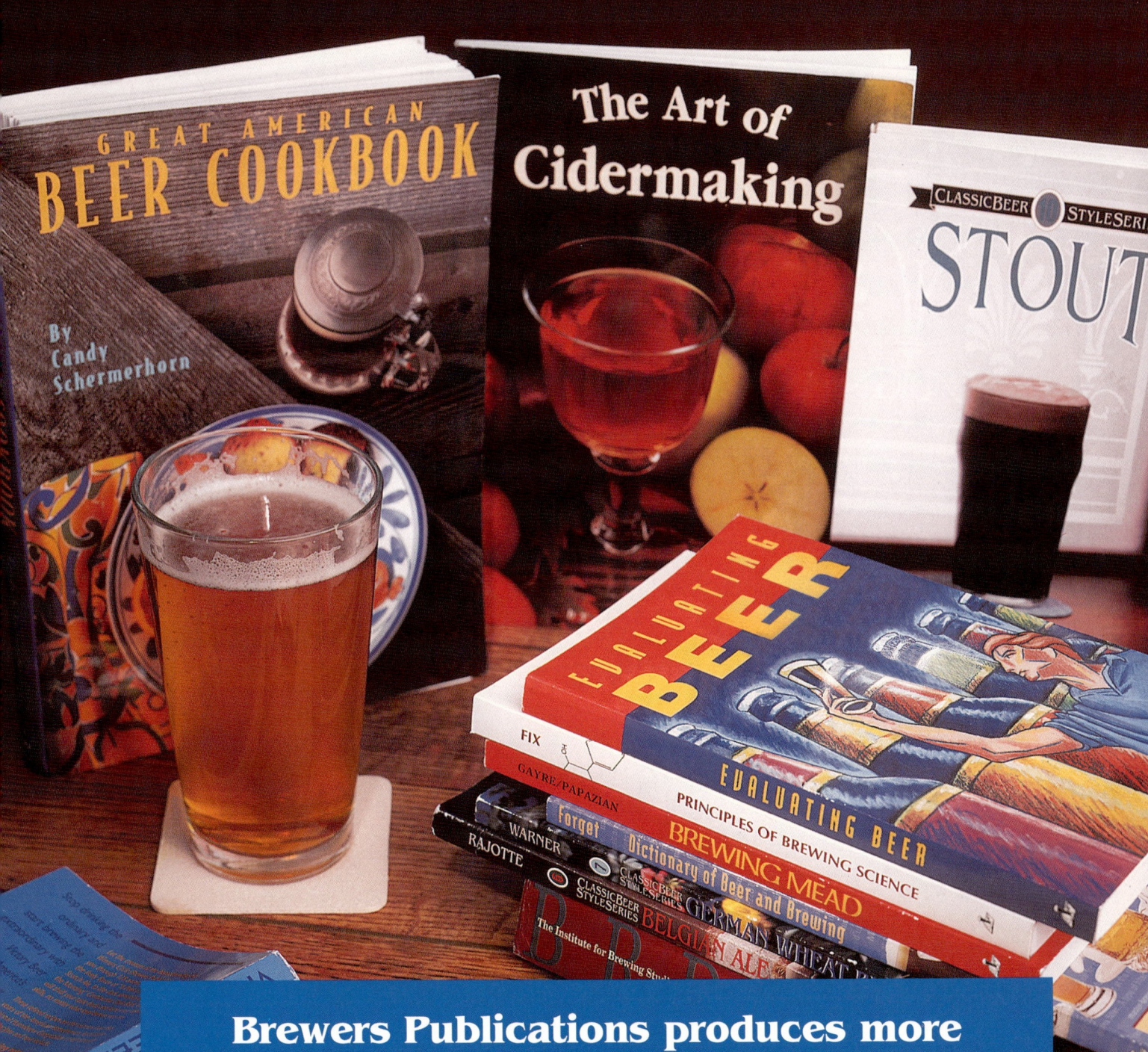

Brewers Publications produces more than books, it creates resources.

For more information or a catalog of available titles, contact Brewers Publications at (303) 447-0816, FAX (303) 447-2825, orders@aob.org or http://www.aob.org/aob.

Milllipore offers a full range of filter-based products to assess the microbiological quality of beer beverages and the cleanliness of equipment used to process them. From Millipore's Samplers and Swab Test Kits to disposable monitor systems, simple, cost-effective products are offered for routine in-plant quality assurance programs.

Monitek Technologies Inc.
Tim Day, Sales Mgr.
Frank Vetrokel, Pres.
1495 Zephyr Ave.
Hayward, CA 94544
(510) 471-8300 or (800) 458-4454; FAX (510) 471-8647

Monitek is a leading company in the liquid monitorinal industry. The company offers a full line of liquid monitoring products for the measurement of clarity (turbidity), suspended solids content, color, pH, and conductivity. Monitek has been a leading instrumentation supplier to the brewing industry for twenty-five years.

NDA Engineering Group
Dave Potter, Process Engineering
709 TE Rapa Rd.
Hamilton,
New Zealand
078492979; FAX 078492971

National Chemicals Inc.
Dr. L. Charles Landman, Jr., Gen. Mgr.
PO Box 32/105 Liberty St.
Winona, MN 55987
(800) 533-0027; FAX (507) 454-5641

Manufacturer of detergents, sanitizers and disinfectants, and related cleaners for public eating and drinking establishments, brewing and draught systems in microbreweries, brewpubs, and homebrewing operations.

New World Brewing Systems Inc.
7183 123rd Circle N.
Largo, FL 34643
(800) 520-5777 or (813) 535-5777; FAX (813) 535-0350

BREWING SYSTEM INNOVATORS

New World Brewing Systems, Inc. is the leader in brewing system technology. We manufacture the highest quality, cost effective equipment for the micro-brewing industry. With our fine craftsmanship of custom fabricated systems and our uncommonly quick delivery on standard fermenters and serving tanks, we'll create a micro-brewery or brew-pub system to meet your specifications. We work with you providing design, installation and on-site brewmaster training. We're there where you need us . . . when you need us.

We don't imitate, we innovate!

7183 123RD CIRCLE N ▪ LARGO, FL 34643
(813) 535-5777 ▪ FAX (813) 535-0350
TOLL FREE 1-800-520-5777

Brewing Equipment Manufacturers and Suppliers

Newlands Services Inc.
Brad McQuhae, Technical Dir.
Barry Benson, Senior Brewer
#202-31136 Peardonville Rd.
Abbotsford, BC V2T 6K7
Canada
(604) 855-4890; FAX (604) 855-8826

NSI, a fully-integrated brewing service company complete with staff brewers, designers, engineers, fabricators, and quality assurance personnel. International in all aspects of brewing for systems 5 to 250 barrels. Systems and equipment designed to suit clients requirements and budgets.

Nigrelli Systems Inc.
16024 CTH X
Kiel, WI 53042
(414) 693-3161; FAX (414) 693-3245

Orbisphere Laboratories
Bill Miller, VP
70 Kinderkamack Rd.
Emerson, NJ 07630
(201) 265-4900; FAX (201) 265-5899

Manufacturer of dissolved oxygen, dissolved carbon dioxide, and dissolved nitrogren analyzers for in-line and package measurements.

Outterson Brewing Services Inc.
Donald Outterson, Pres.
7747 Woodstone Dr.
Cincinnati, OH 45244-2855
(513) 474-9385; FAX (513) 474-9384

Paar Scientific (Export) Ltd.
Mike Stevens, Export Mgr.
594 Kingston Rd., Raynes Park
London, SW20 8DN
United Kingdom
81-5408553; FAX 81-5438727

Paar offers a wide range of density measuring equipment for both laboratory and in-line use covering a variety of applications including alcohol and OG measurements.

Paguag GmbH & Co., Hose Division
W. Fassbeuder, Prod. Mgr.
P. Kosmehl, General Mgr.
Am Gatherhof 41
Dusseldorf, 40472
Germany
011-49-2116505-362; FAX 011-49-2116505-459

Pall Corp.
Sara Rictbroek, PR Specialist
25 Harbor Park Dr.
Port Washington, NY 11050
(516) 484-3600 or (800) 289-PALL; FAX (516) 484-3637
custsvc@pall.com

Pall manufactures: D. E. trap filters; filters for sterile fertilization of CO_2; air final beer polishing; polishing water used for bottle/keg washing.

Pall Ultrafine Filtration Co.
Donna Aloisio, Sales Mgr.
2200 Northern Blvd.
East Hills, NY 11548
(516) 484-5400; FAX (516) 484-5228

D. E. trap filters; filters for sterile fertilization of CO_2, and air; final beer polishing and polishing water used for bottle/keg washing.

Parker Hannifin Corp., Process Filtration Division
Susan Hiland, Mktg. Service Specialist
James E. Schmitz, Mkt. Sales Mgr.
PO Box 1300/1515 W. South St.
Lebanon, IN 46052
(317) 482-3900; FAX (317) 482-8413

Paul Mueller Co.
Michael R. Bither, Sales Engineer
PO Box 828
Springfield, MO 65801-0828
(800) MUELLER; FAX (417) 831-3528

Paul Mueller Company is a manufacturer of high-quality stainless-steel brewing equipment. With approximatley one million square feet under one roof, we are recognized for highly engineered and skillfully crafted stainless-steel custom and standard brewing vessels.

Paul Zaft Copper Works
Fred Zaft, Owner
9554 Vancouver Lane
Windsor, CA 95492
(707) 836-0425

Perlick Corp.
Joe Restivo, Sales Specialist
8300 W. Good Hope Rd.
Milwaukee, WI 53223-0098
(414) 353-7060; FAX (414) 353-7069

Manufacturer of stainless-steel sanitary fittings and fabrication for process piping and tanks. Also, remote beer systems, back bars, underbar workboards, and beverage coolers.

Pico-Brewing Systems Inc.
Mike O'Brien, Mktg. Dir.
8383 Geddes Rd.
Ypsilanti, MI 48198
(313) 482-8565; FAX (313) 485-BREW

Pierre Rajotte
Pierre Rajotte, Owner
PO Box 734
Mont Royal, QC H3P 3G4
Canada
(514) 739-9424; FAX (514) 739-2717

Turnkey two and four-barrel brewery. Training, recipe formulation, setting up included. Yeast propagation: training and equipment. Brew-on-premises mashing equipment. Steam-heated step infusion combination mash-brew kettle twenty-five-barrel. Serving tanks. All vessels can be ASME certified. More than twenty breweries presently operating coast to coast.

Polar Ware Co.
Tammy Hittman, Mkt. Development Supervisor
Jerry Balthus, VP Mktg. and Sales
2806 N. 15th St.
Sheboygan, WI 53083
(414) 458-3561; FAX (414) 458-2205

Port Jackson Mfg.
Dennis Gogg
Taylor Thompson
25 S. Pine St.
Kingston, NY 12401
(914) 331-0237; FAX (914) 331-3471
portjack@aol.com

Power Flame Inc.
Tom Tubman
PO Box 974/2001 South 21st St.
Parsons, KS 67357
(316) 421-0480; FAX (316) 421-0948

Price-Schonstrom Inc.
Dave Hellerud, Sales Mgr.
Doug Price, Pres.
35 Elm St.
Walkerton, ON N0G 2V0
Canada
(519) 881-0262; FAX (519) 881-3573

Price-Schonstrom Inc. is a leading international supplier of microbrewery, brewpub, and brew-on-premise systems. We have been extensively involved in the design, fabrication, installation, and commissioning of brewing systems since 1985. Being an ASME-coded facility our customers are assured of the highest quality standards in the industry.

Profamo Analytical Services Inc.
K. Nimptsch, Pres.
1805 Dawson Ave.
Dorval, PQ HQ5 1Z2
Canada
(514) 636-4918; FAX (514) 631-6315

PROGINOX Inc.
Michel Neault, Eng.
8090 Saguenay
Brossard, PQ J4X 1H7
Canada
(514) 466-8779; FAX (514) 466-2806

Prolong Systems Inc.
Dan Tekorius
Sy Manaitis
23939 SW Gage Rd.
Wilsonville, OR 97070
(503) 638-1414; FAX (503) 638-5252
aras@teleport.com

Prolong Systems Inc. is a designer and builder of on-site nitrogen generating systems for brewing and dispensing industries. Prolong's Ni-Gen Systems utilize hollow fiber membrane technology wich allows unlimited production of nitrogen at low cost. Let Prolong show you the benefits of on-site produced nitrogen over purchased CO_2 and CO_2/N blends.

Prosser/Enpo (Sellers)
Mike Kemp, Prod. Mgr.
420 Third St.
Piqua, OH 45356
(513) 773-2442

Pugsley's Brewing Projects International/Shipyard Brewing
Alan J. Pugsley, Pres.
Chris Dowe, Brewery Consultant
PO Box 11604
Portland, ME 04104
(207) 871-1121/(207) 761-0807; FAX (207) 871-1122

Pugsley's Brewing Projects offers qualified investors and restaurateurs the opportunity to share in Shipyard Brewing Co. and Alan Pugsley's success by establishing a brewpub or microbeer pub based on a proven successful formula. Pugsley provides prospectors "partners" with first class equipment, brewer training, and world class beer formulations from Pugsley.

R-P Products
Jim Embrey, Inside Sales
Norman Beckwith, Mgr. National and Customer Service
PO Box 388/407 Jefferson St
Three Rivers, MI 49093
(616) 273-1512; FAX (616) 273-1812

Rapids Wholesale Equipment Co.
Joe Schmitt
Joe Dodds
PO Box 396/1011 Second Ave. S.W.
Cedar Rapids, IA 52406
(319) 364-5186; FAX (319) 364-2111

Rapids has a full line of restaurant/brewpub equipment and supplies from knives and forks to walk-in cooler systems. Call for your catalog.

Read Systems, Inc.
Thomas W. Read, Pres.
PO Box 530443
Birmingham, AL 35253
(205) 939-4334; FAX (205) 939-4332

Refrigeration Service 6
David A. Payne, Owner/Eng.
1830 Sutton Ave.
Cincinnati, OH 45230
(513) 231-9700; FAX (513) 752-5726

Remcor Products Co
Darla Schibur, Sales
Tom Best, Sales Mgr.
500 Regency Dr.
Glendale Heights, IL 60139
(800) 551-4423; FAX (708) 980-8511

RLS Equipment Co. Inc.
Robert E. Stollenwerk, VP
PO Box 282/1017 White Horse Pike
Egg Harbor City, NJ 08215
(609) 965-0074 or (800) 527-0197 (West Coast); FAX (609) 965-2509

Roskamp Champion
Linda Kruckenberg, Asst. Sales Mgr.
2975 Airline Circle
Waterloo, IA 50703
(800) 366-2563 or (319)232-8444; FAX (319) 232-2773

Manufacturers of malt mills in configurations of two-, four-, or six-roll mills. Roskamp malt mills are designed with single point roll adjustment, spring loaded solid to the shaft rolls, V-belt drive for quiet efficient operation to provide you with uniform particle size.

SABCO Industries/Sav-a-Barrel Corp.
Rick Henzler, Sales Mgr.
4511 South Ave.
Toledo, OH 43615-6418
(419) 531-5347

Salvadore Machinery Corp.
Michael Salvadore, Pres.
945 Eddy St.
Providence, RI 02905
(401) 941-1950; FAX (401) 781-5840

Santa Rosa Stainless Steel
Rod Ferronato, Pres.
Jeff Humes, Consultant
PO Box 518/1400 Airport Blvd.
Santa Rosa, CA 95402
(707) 544-7777; FAX (707) 544-6316

Sasib Beverage & Food North America Inc.
George Freeman, VP Sales and Mktg.
John Mojonnier, Technical Mktg. Mgr.
PO Box 118008
Charleston, SC 29423
(803) 572-6640; FAX (803) 553-3033

Schafer Container Systems
Reinhold Holzemer
PO Box 1120
D-57272 Neunkirchen,
Germany
(+49) 2735-787-525; FAX (+49) 2735-787-493

The Schafer PLUS KEG (20, 30, 50l), junior PLUS KEG (10, 15, 20l) and the soft drink KEG (10, 15, 20l) are made of a combination of stainless-steel liner and PU jacket. Transparency in logistics is provided due to character coding datix PLUS. The Schafer SUDEX KEG (20l, 30l, 50l, 7.75 gallons, and 15.5 gallons) is a classic stainless-steel KEG.

Brewing Equipment Manufacturers and Suppliers

Custom equipment for better beer.

Left: Two-vessel brewhouse, with 50-barrel knockout wort capacity.

Inset: Mash/lauter tun with specially designed rakes and plows for efficient lautering.

Brewers leading the renaissance of full-flavored beers in America are now looking to Santa Rosa Stainless Steel for custom brewhouse equipment.

Our team can provide anything from a single uni-tank to the layout and equipment for a complete turnkey system, of 25 to 125-barrel brew capacity. The key is designing the equipment to meet your specific requirements for brewing great beer.

We can help in laying out your facility, specifying equipment, installation, start-up and training, and ongoing technical support. Santa Rosa Stainless Steel is ASME-certified for the manufacture of pressurized fermentation, lagering and bright beer tanks.

Call or write for more information, or a free estimate.

Santa Rosa Stainless Steel

1400 Airport Boulevard • P. O. Box 518
Santa Rosa, California 95402
(707) 544-SRSS • FAX 707-544-6316

Institute for Brewing Studies

Brewing Equipment Manufacturers and Suppliers

Schenk Filter Systems Inc.
John Herrguth, Sales Mgr.
235 Montgomery Ct., Suite 804
San Francisco, CA 94104
(415) 392-0331; FAX (415) 392-0337
schenkusa@aol.com

Schlueter MFG
James Schlueter
5419 Munysville Rd.
Brown's Valley, CA 95918
(916) 743-2957

Scott Laboratories Inc.
Tom Anders, VP
Bruce Scott, Pres.
2220 Pine View Way
Petaluma, CA 94954
(707) 765-6666; FAX (707) 765-6674

VELO plate and frame and diatomaceous earth filter systems, SEITZ filter sheets, LALLEMAND-UVAFERM active dry brewers yeast, BRAUEREI-TECHNIK STABIFIX silica gel stabilizer, CoMAC keg-filling systems.

Scott Laboratories Ltd.
1845 Sandstone Manor, Unit 14
Pickering, ON L1W 3X9
Canada

VELO plate and frame and diatomaceous earth filter systems, SEITZ filter sheets, LALLEMAND-UVAFERM active dry brewers yeast, BRAUEREI-TECHNIK STABIFIX silica gel stabilizer, CoMAC keg-filling systems.

Shanley Pump
Jim Shanley, Prod. Mgr.
2525 S. Clearbrook Dr.
Arlington Heights, IL 60005
(708) 439-9200; FAX (708) 439-9388

Exclusive distributor of Hilge Products, offering complete line of stainless-steel sanitary pumps. With more than 130 years of experience, Hilge is the market leader in all aspects of brewery pumping.

SMB Technik
Larry Langbehn, U.S. Mktg. Mgr.
5400 Alpine Rd.
Santa Rosa, CA 95404
(707) 539-3826; FAX (707) 538-4502

Clarity. Quality. Reliability. For nearly 50 years Schenk Filterbau has been recognized as the leader in designing high quality filtration systems around the world. So whether you need a single filter sheet or a completely engineered filter system, Schenk can help you meet your filtration challenges. Please contact us at our new San Francisco location so that we can assist you in all of your filtration needs.

SCHENK FILTER SYSTEMS -THE CLEAR CHOICE.

SCHENK FILTER SYSTEMS

Schenk Filter Systems, Inc. 235 Montgomery Street Suite 804 San Francisco CA 94104 Phone 415.392.0331 Fax 415.392.0337 E-mail Schenk USA@aol.com

SMB Technik manufactures high-quality German built rinsers, fillers, and crowners for the brewing industry. Speed of machinery ranges from 10 to 250 b.p.m. Long-tube (low oxygen pickup) or short-tube filler configurations available. Complete bottling line installations available.

Sonoco Engraph Label Group
Thomas Coker, Mktg. Mgr.
Jim Prendergast, VP Sales
8800 South Blvd.
Charlotte, NC 28273
(704) 554-5796; FAX (704) 554-8122

Sound Brewing Systems Inc.
Vince Cottone, Pres.
11223 Palatine Ave. N.
Seattle, WA 98133
(206) 362-2668; FAX (206) 368-3961
soundbrew@prostar.com

Brewpub and production brewery start-ups, seven to seventy plus barrels; plant/equipment design and installation; product formulation, training, and business planning. Sole U.S. agents for Ripley Stainless Ltd., British Columbia, Canada.

Spartanburg Steel Products Inc.
Linda E. Chadwick, Cust. Service Rep.
Bill Horthrop, VP Sales
PO Box 6428/1290 New Cut Rd.
Spartanburg, SC 29304
(803) 585-5211 or (800) 334-6318; FAX (803) 583-5641

Spartanburg Steel Products offers a complete line of straight-sided, single-opening beer kegs in both stainless-steel and polyurethane-ended varieties.

Specific Mechanical Systems Ltd.
Blaine Clemston, Sales Mgr.
Ray Freeman, Sales
6840 Oldfield Rd.
Saanichton, BC V8M 2A3
Canada
(604) 652-2111; FAX (604) 652-6010

We are one of North America's leading microbrewing and pubbrewing equipment manufacturers in business for ten years. We design, build, and install brewing systems designed to your specific needs. Our experienced staff will provide assistance and support at all phases of developement and production.

Stab: Fix Brauerer — Technik GmbH
Tom Anders
Martin Vagners
2220 Pine View Way
Petaluma, CA 94955-4559
(707) 765-6666; FAX (707) 765-6674

Velo plate and frame and diatomaceous earth filter systems, SEITZ filter sheets, LALLEMAND-UVAFERM active dry brewers yeast, BRAUEREI-TECHNIK STAB-IFIX, and xerogel/hydrogels are available.

Stainless Steel Containment Systems Inc.
Jeffrey Balck
500 N. Washington St., Suite 301
Alexandria, VA 22314
(703) 836-4003; FAX (703) 836-4005

Stainless Steel Specialist Inc.
Yvon Labonne, Pres.
Normand Tanguay, VP
509-B
Boisbriand, PQ J7G 2B7
Canada
(514) 979-6733; FAX (514) 979-6733

Brewing experience for over sixteen years.

Steensen U.S.A. Inc.
Theodor Petersen, Pres.
Mary Peterson, VP
959 Melvin Rd.
Annapolis, MD 21403
(410) 269-6585; FAX (410) 263-3110
EAH15A@prodigy.com

Serve beer or wine with a German handcrafted Mayolika ceramic fountain. Suitable for all bar systems. Hand-painted ceramics with top quality brass units available for one to six taps. Ten stock designs (shipment usually within forty-eight hours). Or customize a unit with your own colors or logo. Call for a free brochure.

Stonhard Inc.
Colleen Miele, Mktg. Coordinator
One Park Ave.
Maple Shade, NJ 08052
(609) 779-7500; FAX (609) 321-7525

Stord Inc.
Bonnie Bailley, Exec. Sec.
309 Regional Road S.
Greensboro, NC 27409
(910) 668-7727; FAX (910) 668-0537

Strahman Valves Inc.
Dennis E. Gallagher, Assistant Sales Mgr.
3 Vreeland Rd.
Florham Park, NJ 07932
(201) 377-4900; FAX (201) 822-1819

Superb Gas Products Co.
Marisa Lucash, Sales
48 Empire Dr.
Belleville, IL 62220
(618) 234-6169; FAX (618) 234-5218

Sussman Electric Boilers
Louise Mound, Sales Admin.
Charles Monteverdi, Sr. VP
43-20 34th St.
Long Island City, NY 11101
(718) 937-4500; FAX (718) 937-4676

Team Industries Inc.
John M. Kreisle, VP
PO Box 350/1200 Maloney Rd.
Kaukauna, WI 54130
(414) 766-7977; FAX (414) 766-0486

Tel-Tru Manufacturing Co.
Annette Coderre, Sales Mgr.
408 St. Paul St.
Rochester, NY 14605
(800) 232-5335; FAX (716) 232-3857
tel-tru@industry.net
http://www.industry.net/tel-tru

Terriss Consolidated Industries
S. Bodnovich
PO Box 110/807 Summerfield Ave.
Asbury Park, NJ 07712
(908) 988-0909; FAX (908) 502-0526

Toby Jug Bop System
Joe Toby, Pres.
4179 Front St.
Goodwood, ON L0C 1A0
Canada
(905) 642-1925; FAX (905) 642-1925

   Incorporating the experiences of twenty-two different Bops in Canada and complete filtration, carbonation, bottle and vessel washing machines, Toby-Limited provides turnkey beer and wine systems. Including design, start-up, training, and back-up. Bop systems includes both computerized point-of-purchase sales and invoicing, and custom label manufacturing.

Tosca Limited
John Frey, VP
PO Box 8127/1032 Bay Beach Rd.
Green Bay, WI 54308
(414) 465-8534; FAX (414) 465-9198

Total Brewing International Ltd.
Martin Soden, Man. Dir.
Unit 3C Trow Way Diglis
Worcester, WR5 3BX
United Kingdom
905-613-027 exts. 133, 134, 145; FAX 905-209-77

Tuchenhagen North America Inc.
Knuth Loranzen, Components Mgr.
Bernie Thompson, VP Technical Service
PO Box 1458
Fond du Lac, WI 54936-1458
(414) 922-3500; FAX (414) 922-9690

Unipath Co., Oxiod Division
Gerald Moore, Pres.
Larry Margindale, Prod. Mgr.
PO Box 691
Ogdensburg, NY 13669
(613) 226-1318; FAX (613) 226-3728

VAFAC Inc. (Virginia Food and Craft)
Philip H. Pryor, Pres.
212 Freedom Ct.
Fredericksburg, VA 22408
(540) 898-3202; FAX (540) 898-8442

Vendome Copper & Brass Works Inc.
Philip N. Hambrick, Mgr. Projects and Engineering
729 E. Franklin St.
Louisville, KY 40202
(502) 587-1930; FAX (502) 589-0639

Vinotheque
Russ Nicol, Pres.
2142 Trans Canada Hwy.
Dorval, PQ H9H 2T2
Canada
(514) 684-1331; FAX (514) 684-4241

W. M. Sprinkman Corp.
Brain Sprinkman, Project Coordinator
Chad Sprinkman, Project Coordinator
PO Box 3901/4234 Courtney St.
Franksville, WI 53126
(800) 816-1610
bsprink@execpc.com
http://www.execpc.com/~bsprink

W. M. Sprinkman has been in the food/beverage industry since 1929. Our experience has allowed us to take a fresh look at the craft-brewing industry. W. M. Sprinkman's high volume of purchasing new and used tanks, tubing, valves, pumps, etc. has allowed us to pass those savings on to the customer.

W. W. Reichert,
Bavarian Brewhouse Inc.
Rex Reichert, Pres.
Holgenburg 4
D-73728 Esslingen, 73728
Germany
(711) 357-333; FAX (711) 350-8343

Waukesha Fluid Handling
Gordon Hurst, VP Sales
Tony Mazza, National Sales Mgr.
611 Sugar Creek Rd.
Delavan, WI 53115
(414) 728-1900; FAX (414) 728-4320

Wilson Brewing Systems Ltd.
A. Ross Wilson, Pres.
R. Graham Wilson, Mgr.
PO Box 820
Bolton, ON L7E 5T5
Canada
(905) 857-1511; FAX (905) 857-0325

Wittemann Co. Inc.
Daniel Gruber, Regional Sales Mgr.
Joesph Gruber, Regional Sales Mgr.
2 Commerce Blvd.
Palm Coast, FL 32164-3126
(904) 445-4200; FAX (904) 445-7042

YSI Inc.
Richard Spencer, Mktg. Communications Mgr.
PO Box 279
Yellow Springs, OH 45387
(800) 765-4974 or (513) 767-7241; FAX (513) 767-9353
info@YSI.com

Zahm and Nagel Co. Inc.
Gary Koch, Pres.
David Koch, Sales
74 Jewett Ave.
Buffalo, NY 14214-2497
(716) 833-1532 or (800) 216-1542; FAX (716) 833-0834

11 Packaging Equipment Manufacturers and Suppliers

Draft or bottled? Bottled or canned? Maybe all three? Twelve-ounce or twenty-two-ounce bottles? Or something different?

The type of package you choose for your beer determines a lot about how and where you will sell it, as well as who will buy it. If you're a purist and you want your beer tasted at its peak of freshness, then draft-only may be the route to go. Conversely, if you're looking for maximum brand recognition, twelve-ounce bottles with four-color printed six-pack carriers may be the best method, despite being much more expensive than simply filling half-barrel kegs.

Packaging in cans may help get your product on a commercial airline. Cans, however, also carry a stigma that most craft brewers would prefer to avoid.

One package currently popular with both brewers and consumers is the twenty-two-ounce bottle. The higher per-ounce price that the market currently bears gives the brewer a higher profit margin. Twenty-two-ounce bottles also hold the perfect amount for customers to share your product with a friend. Many beer and package stores now devote special sections to twenty-two-ounce microbrews. Those that don't, however, may end up stocking your brand along with other oversize packages, such as the forty-ounce "king" malt liquors.

A half-gallon jug can be the ideal vehicle for customers who want fresh beer from your brewpub to enjoy at home. A five-liter can is also good for this and can keep beer fresh for a longer period of time. On the other hand, the cans are not currently recyclable.

These are some of the pros and cons that you need to weigh while trying to decide how best to present your product to customers.

Brewing good beer presents its own set of problems for a small business owner; packaging that beer adds an entirely new set of challenges.

Concerning draft-only, achieving the desired flavor profile and maintaining it consistently are the primary tasks brewers face. When bottling the beer, you add to the process a new variable known as shelf life. Shelf life, or product stability, is often the greatest challenge — and sometimes the biggest handicap — for small breweries. It doesn't matter how much malt or hops you put in your beer; if it goes bad while sitting on a retailer's shelf two months after it left the brewery, it's still bad beer — "full-flavored" won't make it any better.

The large and regional breweries owe much of their success to their expertise in packaged-beer stability. Their greater sophistication in filtration, pasteurization, and quality assurance is why many entrepreneurs opt for contract brewing with a regional or large brewery, rather than package their product themselves.

If you open a new brewery, your goal may be to introduce draft and bottled products simultaneously. While this is ambitious and admirable (if you succeed), it may not be the most sensible approach when launching a new company.

As you can see, the issue of packaging presents many variables for you to consider. This edition of the *Brewers Resource Directory* lists separately companies that specialize in packaging equipment and supplies. These companies can help you make the right decisions about packaging and presenting your product.

Advanced Bottling U.K. Ltd.
Peter Kerr, Dir.
The Old Rocket Site, Misson Springs
Doncaster, S Yorks DN10 GET
England
44-302-772882; FAX 44-302-772882

Aidpac International Ltd.
Victor Kent, Man.Dir.
Reg Hill, Technical Dir.
Eltric Rd.
Worcester, WR3 7NU
England
44-905-755666; FAX 44-905-754214

Packaging Equipment Manufacturers and Suppliers

Alvey Inc.
Steve Williams, Mktg./Communications Mgr.
9301 Olive Blvd.
St. Louis, MO 63132
(314) 993-4700

Alyn D. Snedigar
9035 W. Burdick Ave.
Milwaukee, WI 53227
(414) 541-8453
   Consultant for layout and installation of bottling lines, rinsers, fillers, cappers, labelers, and packers. Twenty-five years experience, trained on equipment and processors such as the Continental and Anqulus Seamers, H & K, Meyer and Cemco liquid fillers; Mayer Krones and Mayer ALFA Labelers; J.N.J., R. A. Jones, Mead and Illinois Food Packaging Equipment.

APM Inc.
Shahbaz Sohrobi, VP Sales
Louise Goanies, Customer Service
441 Industrial Way
Benicia, CA 94510
(800) 487-7555; FAX (707) 745-0371

B & J Machinery Inc.
James F. English, VP Sales
PO Box 62067
Cincinnati, OH 45262
(513) 771-7374; FAX (513) 771-3820
   Bottling equipment — rinsers, fillers, crowners, cappers, pasteurizers, labelers. Production rates 50 to 800 b.p.m.. New and rebuilt. Trade name executive/PE, executive/AROL, executive/Gherri.

Beers of the World Packaging Co.
Patrick J. McShane, Pres.
PO Box 2182
Morristown, NJ 07962-2182
(201) 538-1519; FAX (201) 993-5548

Brewers & Bottlers Equipment Corp.
Bernard Z. Greenberg, Pres.
PO Box 67
Indian Rocks Beach, FL 34635-0067
(813) 593-2638; FAX (813) 596-4752

Burch Bottle & Packaging
George Ide, Sales
811 10th St.
Watervliet, NY 12189
(518) 273-1845; FAX (518) 273-1846

Busse Inc.
Thomas Young, Pres.
124 N. Columbus St.
Randolph, WI 53956
(314) 993-4700

Cambridge Inc.
Gordy E. Jones, Mgr. Sales Administrator
PO Box 399
Cambridge, MD 21613
(301) 228-3000

Cargocaire Engineering Co.
Davis McDougall, National Sales Mgr.
PO Box 640/79 Monroe St.
Amesbury, MA 01913-0640
(508) 388-0600; FAX (508) 388-4556
cargo@munters.com
http://www.munters.com/users/cargo
   Munters Cargocaire is an engineering firm that designs and manufactures dry desiccant dehumidification systems. Since 1939, these systems have helped to prevent corrosion, reduce housekeeping issues, and improve worker safety. Using a desiccant impregnated HoneyCombe rotor, our units contain only four moving parts for reduced maintenance time.

Criveller Co.
Bruno Criveller, Owner
6935 Oakwood Dr.
Niagra Falls, ON L2E 6S5
Canada
(905) 357-2930; FAX (905) 374-2930

D & F Engineering Inc.
Tom Carpenter, Owner
3300 Union Ave. S.E.
Grand Rapids, MI 49548
(616) 245-8077; FAX (616) 245-8077

DATOGRAF Apparatebau GmbH & Co.
Joachim Mogler, Geschaftsfuhrer
Austrabe 34-36
74076 Heilbronn
Germany
49-7131-98600; FAX 49-7131-162154

Diversified Packaging Products Inc.
James S. McCrea, Pres.
1265 Pine Hill Dr.
Annapolis, MD 21401
(410) 974-4411; FAX (410) 974-4415

Packaging Equipment Manufacturers and Suppliers

Drinktec USA Ltd.
Nicolas Haase, Sales and Mktg. Mgr.
JoAnn Seeger, Office Mgr.
100 Railroad Dr., Suite B
Ivyland, PA 18974
(215) 953-9335; FAX (215) 953-8636
drinktec@aol.com

Serving the beverage industry worldwide; equipment, parts, systems, expendable supplies, promotional articles. A member of BrauHaase International Management Group.

E. Z.CAP
Doug Arkell
4224 Chippewa Rd. N.W.
Calgary, AB T2L1A3
Canada
(403) 282-5972; FAX (403) 282-5972

Manufacturers and distributors of the unique FLIP TOP amber glass bottles. Available in 500 milliliter/16-ounce size. Early 1996 available in 1 liter/32-ounce size.

ENCORE!
Peter Heylin, Sales Mgr.
John First, Sales Mgr.
860 S. 19th St.
Richmond, CA 94804
(510) 234-5670

Epsen Hillmer Graphics Co.
Dirk Duling, VP Mktg.
Craig Curran, VP Sales and Mktg.
511 N. 20th St.
Omaha, NE 68102
(402) 342-7000

Printers of litho rotary letterpress and UV flexo labels. Paper, metallized, and film substrates available for glue-applied or pressure-sensitive application.

EUROSOURCE Inc.
Frederic Petit, CEO
Eric Corticchiato, Pres.
2351 Northwest Hwy., Suite 3285
Dallas, TX 75220
(214) 357-4688; FAX (214) 357-5280

EUROSOURCE Inc. is the exclusive American representitive of Maisonneuve Keg and M & F Keg Technik. Maisonneuve is a leading manufacturer of stainless kegs and casks. Sizes range from 20 liters to 15.5 gallons. M & F is a German manufacturer of keg cleaning and filling machines from manual to fully automated lines.

Filter Equipment Co. Inc.
Scott Groh, Sales Mgr.
Steve Groh
PO Box 1452/1440 Hwy. 34
Wall, NJ 07719
(800) 445-9775; FAX (800) 777-3477

We offer filter pads, presses, cartridges, and parts for all types of beverage filtration.

Filtrine Manufacturing Co.
Peter Hansel, Pres.
Alan Wall, Sales Mgr.
Elm St.
Harrisville, NH 03450
(603) 827-3321; FAX (603) 827-3081
filtrine@top.monad.net

GEA Ecoflex, Division of NIRO Inc.
Rolf Dickhoff
9165 Rumsey Rd.
Columbia, MD 21045
(410) 997-6685; FAX (410) 997-5021

GEA ECOFLEX

$Q = UA\Delta T$

"The Cool Option"
- Free-flow, wide-gap design handles products with high viscosity materials and those with particulate
- Unique self-centering, lock-in gasket requiring no special glue or tools
- Constructed to be cleaned in place
- Fully assembled and pressure-tested prior to shipment to the customer

GEA ECOFLEX
Division of NIRO, Inc.
9165 Rumsey Road, Columbia, MD 21045
Tel. 410-997-6685 • Fax 410-997-5021

G. W. Kent Inc.
Randall Reichwage
3667 Morgan Rd.
Ann Arbor, MI 48108
(313) 572-1300; FAX (313) 572-0097

G. W. Kent Inc. is the exclusive North American importer of Durst Malz German two-row malts.

Gafco-Worldwide, Inc.
Frank E. May, Pres.
Eduardo Rosado, Latin American Sales Dir.
6302 Harrison Ave., Suite 5
Cincinnati, OH 45247
(513) 574-2257; FAX (513) 574-2362

GWW Inc. is an import/export management company with twenty-nine years experience in International sourding, centralized purchasing, and contract manufacturing for bottling and brewery needs. We service large and small companies providing machinery, spare parts, components, and turnkey operations.

Gamse Lithographing Co.
Pat Hennegan, VP
7413 Pulaski Hwy.
Baltimore, MD 21237
(410) 866-4700; FAX (410) 866-5672

Gamse Manufactures paper, metallized, and pressure-sensitive labels, both cut and stack and roll-fed. Our labels can be embossed, stamped, or printed on holographic substrates. Stocks used are resistant to water. Our customer base includes over fifty small breweries.

Heavy Duty Products Inc.
John Cressman
Rance Tupling
1261 Industrial Rd.
Cambridge, ON N3H 4W3
Canada
(519) 653-4222 or (800) 563-8247; FAX (519) 653-4220

Hedwin Corporation
Ray Carlson, Mktg. Mgr.
Ann Jones, Sales Service Mgr.
1600 Roland Heights Ave.
Baltimore, MD 21211
(800) 638-1012 or (410) 467-8209; FAX (410) 889-5189

Cubitainer the original flexible poly container in a box. With both cost saving and environment friendly design advantages, Cubitainer Combination Package provides safe, easy, convenient shelf dispensing. Cubitainer has been selected as the container of choice by leading manufacturers in a wide variety of industries. Available in a range of sizes.

Heuft USA Inc.
Ken Fay, Sales Mgr.
Carl Bonnan, VP Sales Mktg.
5157 Thatcher Rd.
Dowmers Grove, IL 60515
(708) 968-9011; FAX (708) 968-8767

Heuft manufactures a complete line of inspection and rejection equipment for the brewing trades. Our budget-priced line offers modular inspection capabilities including fill height, closure inspection, label inspection, and pressure check technologies. Possibilities include as many as three inspection bridges on one machine. Our inspectors never rest.

Hilge/Shanley Pump
Jim Shanley, Prod. Mgr.
2525 S. Clearbrook Dr.
Arlington Heights, IL 60005
(708) 439-9200; FAX (708) 439-9388

Exclusive distributor of Hilge products, offering complete line of stainless-steel sanitary pumps. With more than 130 years of experience, Hilge is the market leader in all aspects of brewery pumping.

Hopfen und Malz GmbH
Hermann Hörterer, Brewmaster
Hans Schilp, Brewmaster
Schloßstr. 8
82269 Kaltenberg
Germany
08193-9330; FAX 08193-933123

Hopfen und Malz GmbH, a subsidiary of Kaltenberg Brewery, provides innovative and modern turnkey pub- and minibreweries, backed by the experience of a well-established Bavarian brewery.

Huber Verpackungen
Walter Fegert, Sales Dir.
PO Box 1240
Oehringen, D-74602
Germany
07941-66-0; FAX 07941-66-302

IDD Process & Packaging Inc.
Jeff Gunn, Pres.
Tom Thilert, Sales Dir.
646 Flinn Ave.
Moorpark, CA 93021
(800) 621-4144 or (805) 529-9890; FAX (805) 529-9282
idd2jeff@aol

Brewery process and packaging system design and manufacturing engineers. This includes turnkey brewpub and microbreweries, kegging systems, tank valves, yeast propagation and management systems, deaeration, filtration and pasteurization systems, hops (leaf,

Packaging Equipment Manufacturers and Suppliers

pellet, and extract), cleaners, sanitizers, brewing and fermenting aids. Full service formula and systems brewery engineering and consultation.

Indcon Design Ltd.
Harold Kluthe, Mktg. and Sales
Barrie Miller, Head Designer
10459 178th St., Suite 101
Edmonton, AB T5S 1R5
Canada
(403) 444-7184; FAX (403) 481-4931

Suppliers of stainless-steel, brass, plastic dispense faucets for the draft beer industry. Other products available: dispense towers, pressure regulators, stainless-steel and aluminum beer kegs.

Industrial Dynamics Co. Ltd. — Manufacturers of Filtec Inspection Systems
Mktg. Department
2927 Lomita Blvd.
Torrance, CA 90505
(310) 325-5633; FAX (310) 530-1000

Inland Printing Co./Inland Label
Dan Pretasky, VP Sales
Roman Artz, Sales Representative
PO Box 1268/2009 West Ave. S.
La Crosse, WI 54601
(608) 788-5800; FAX (608) 787-5870

Industry leader for supplying paper or metalized labels to brewers. Also, we print point-of-sale items including table tents, shelf or channel strips, static stickers, posters, case cards, counter cards, neck hangers, etc. We are your label and POS experts.

Kal Grafx
Victoria Page, Mktg. Dir.
4617 E. Parts Ave. S.E.
Kentwood, MI 49512
(616) 554-5400 or (800) 321-0076; FAX (616) 554-4090

Kenerik/Golden Gate
Joe Toby, Pres.
4179 Front St.
Goodwood, ON L0C 1A0
Canada
(905) 642-1925; FAX (905) 642-1925

With over twenty-five years manufacturing experience, K/G G provides expandable bottling lines from twelve through forty-eight bottles per minute. Featuring double pre-evacuation, and long-tube filling to provide big-beery finish, along with rinsers, labelers, and crowners. The "Kegger" system completes the packaging of beer, with keg washing and filling.

Lawson Mardon Packaging
Marc Robitaille, Account Mgr./Mktg. Specialist
(East Coast)
Art Bernard (West Coast)
2277 Autoroute des Laurentides
Laval, PQ H7S 1Z6
Canada
(514) 334-9120 (East Coast) or (514) 510-9952 (West Coast); FAX (514) 681-7195 (East Coast)

"We help outstanding brands stand out"™. For more information contact: Art Bernard (510) 972-0777 (West Coast) or Marc Robitatile (514) 334-9120 (East Coast).

Malnove Corp.
Wayne N. Platt, Sales
34 Arrowhead Lane
Bethlehem, CT 06751
(203) 266-5242; FAX (203) 266-5243

Manufacturer of quality, printed six-pack basket carriers.

Maryland Wire Belts Inc.
LeeAnn Brannock, Domestic Mktg.
Joy Loeffler, Export Mgr.
PO Box 67/1959 Church Creek Rd.
Church Creek, MD 21622
(800) 677-2358; FAX (410) 228-1647

Meheen Manufacturing
Dave Meheen, Pres.
Pat Collins, VP
415 W. Columbia St.
Pasco, WA 99301
(509) 547-7029; FAX (509) 547-0939

Manufacturer of state-of-the-art computer automated long-tube bottle filling and crowning machinery with production rates of 1,200 bottles per hour. Includes clean place and sanitize in place features. Other products provided include tank management systems, keg filling systems, and labeling machines.

Micro Matic U.S.A. Inc.
Barry Broughton, Divisional Sales Mgr.
Carol Rusk
19791 Bahama St.
Northridge, CA 91324
(818) 882-8012; FAX (818) 341-9501
Keg spear/dispense head manufacturer.

Packaging Equipment Manufacturers and Suppliers

MicroPure Filtration
Robert A. Pollmann, VP/General Mgr.
Marcy Pollman, Sales Administrator
7879 Forest Hills Rd.
Rockford, IL 61111
(800) 654-7873; FAX (815) 962-7360

Solid, secure filtration solutions for sterile air, gas, liquid and steam applications. Environmentally friendly while saving production costs. On-line automatic samplers for product sampling.

MSK Covertech Inc.
Guido Oswald, Pres.
4710 JVL Industrial Park Dr.
Marietta, GA 30066
(404) 928-1099; FAX (404) 928-3849

Nuttings Lake Publishing
Catherine Zuk, Office Mgr.
Rolf Zuk, Owner
PO Box 203/604 Middlesex Tpk.
Nutting Lake, MA 01865
(800) 232-LABEL

Owens-Brockway
Mark Rennels, Beer Product Mgr.
One Seagate
Toledo, OH 43666
(419) 247-2958; FAX (419) 247-2058

Pacific Coast Container
Kent Skibbie, Account Mgr.
11010 N.E. 37th Cir., Suite 110
Vancouver, WA 98682
(360) 892-3451; FAX (360) 892-4955

Party Pig/Quoin
401 Violet St.
Golden, CO 80401
(303) 279-8731; FAX (303) 278-0833

Pneumatic Scale
Richard O'Donnell, Sales Mgr.
Mike McLaughlin, Mgr. of Tech. Sales
10 Ascot Pkwy.
Cuyahoga Falls, OH 44223
(216) 923-0491; FAX (216) 923-8720

FILLING AND CAPPING MONOBLOCK
MULTIMA

Available with long fill tubes for low oxygen pick up

True monoblock construction for superior bottling handling

Sizes with maximum speeds of 50 to 300 bpm

Complete bottling line installation

German engineering and quality

SMB Technik, Inc.
5400 Alpine Road
Santa Rosa, CA 95404
Tel: (707) 539-3826
Fax: (707) 538-4502

R. A. Jones & Co. Inc.
Mr. N. Jack Fox, Product Mgr.
Arthur H. Trefry, Industrial Mgr.
2701 Cresent Springs Rd.
Covington, KY 41017
(606) 341-0400; FAX (606) 341-0519

Salvadore Machinery Corp.
Michael Salvadore, Pres.
945 Eddy St.
Providence, RI 02905
(401) 941-1950; FAX (401) 781-5840

SMB Technik
Larry Langbehn, U.S. Mktg. Mgr.
5400 Alpine Rd.
Santa Rosa, CA 95404
(707) 539-3826; FAX (707) 538-4502

SMB Technik manufactures high quality German built rinsers, fillers, and crowners for the brewing industry. Speed of machinery ranges from 10 to 250 b.p.m. Long tube (low oxygen pickup) or short-tube filler configurations available. Complete bottling line installations available.

Sonoco Engraph Label Group
Thomas Coker, Mktg. Mgr.
Jim Prendergast, VP Sales
8800 South Blvd.
Charlotte, NC 28273
(704) 554-5796; FAX (704) 554-8122

Spartanburg Steel Products Inc.
Linda E. Chadwick, Cust. Service Rep.
Bill Horthrop, VP Sales
PO Box 6428/1290 New Cut Rd.
Spartanburg, SC 29304
(803) 585-5211 or (800) 334-6318; FAX (803) 583-5641

Spartanburg Steel Products offers a complete line of straight-sided, single-opening beer kegs in both stainless-steel and polyurethane-ended varieties.

Spear Inc.
Dan Muenzer, Dir. of Mktg.
Tom Sargent, National Sales Mgr.
5510 Courseview Dr.
Mason, OH 45040
(513) 459-1100 or (800) 627-7327; FAX (513) 459-1362

Spear is the world's leading manufacturer of clear pressure-sensitive film labels and application equipment. Featuring screen and combination printing, the Spear system provides superior shelf impact and premium image. This allows beer marketers to differentiate their products and raise price points. All with a label durable enough to withstand pasteurization and ice chests.

Stainless Steel Containment Systems Inc.
Jeffrey Balck
500 N. Washington St., Suite 301
Alexandria, VA 22314
(703) 836-4003; FAX (703) 836-4005

Standard Box Corp.
Frank Pattison, N.E. Division Mgr.
Charles Ruble III, Pres.
PO Box 505718/28-38 Gerrish Ave.
Chelsea, MA 02150
(617) 884-4200; FAX (617) 884-5722

Manufacturers and designers of four-pack, six-pack, twelve-pack, and wraps. Using the highest-quality materials for offset printing for eye-catching beer carriers. Design assistance available

Standard Paper Box Corp.
Frank Pattison, N.W. Division Mgr.
Charles Ruble III, Pres.
PO Box 289
Medina, WA 98039
(206) 454-6100; FAX (206) 450-9574

Over seventy years serving one hundred micro-/macro-breweries with superior strenght, high-quality graphics. Two-, three-, four-, and six-pack; 12-, 16-, 22-ounce cartons for bottles and cans. Large combination runs, quality pricing, custom-design engineering, and machinery services available. New package development — a specialty. Customers onshore and offshore and across the United States.

Thielmann Container Systems
Jeff Balck, Sales Mgr.
R. Wurm, Mgr.
500 N. Washington St.
Alexandria, VA 22314
(703) 836-4003; FAX (703) 836-4005

Manufacturer of stainless-steel beer kegs, beverage containers, and yeast propogation tanks. Also specializing in aseptic packaging, bulk draft systems, party kegs, mini-kegs, and five-gallon kegs.

Twinpak Inc.
Martin Lochran, Mktg. Mgr.
Brian Walsh, Dir. Sales and Mktg.
910 Central Pkwy. W.
Mississauga, ON L5C 2V5
Canada
(905) 275-1592; FAX (905) 275-1061

Canada's largest supplier of PET plastic bottles coast to coast. Currently investigating a commercially viable alternative to glass packaging for the brewing industry.

Bottles and Glasses are Just Part of our Package.

Packaging Equipment

CALIFORNIA GLASS COMPANY

155 98th Avenue Oakland, CA 94603
(510) 635-7700
Fax (510) 635-4288

PACIFIC COAST CONTAINER, INC.

Vancouver Commerce Park
11010 N.E. 37th Circle, Unit 110
Vancouver, WA 98682
(360) 892-3451   (800) 326-8971
Fax (360) 892-4955

CARLEN COMPANY, L.L.C.

6834 S. University Blvd.
Littleton, CO 80122
(303) 694-0919
Fax (303) 694-0859

COLUMBIA PACKAGING

#3 20306 Dewdney Trunk Rd.
Maple Ridge, BC V2X 3E2
Canada
(604) 465-7694
Fax (604) 465-1702

The Ultimate Package.

"I read it in *The New Brewer.*"

ROCKIES BREWING COMPANY

Rockies Brewing Company enjoys the distinction of being the oldest operating microbrewery in the United States. This great tradition in microbrewing began in 1979. Based in Boulder, Colo., Rockies takes great pride in producing original beers.

**Gina Day, President
Rockies Brewing Co.,
Boulder, Colo.**

> "*The New Brewer* covers it all. The educational and technical articles are great and very relevant to what we're doing at the Rockies on a day-to-day basis. I also count on the *The New Brewer* to give me the scoop on who's who and who's doing what in the industry."

Industry leaders like Gina Day know that only *The New Brewer* provides the inside information craft brewers from coast to coast depend on. Each issue is packed with vital statistics for business planning, the latest in brewing techniques, alternative technologies, beer recipes, legislative alerts, marketing and distribution ideas — everything you need to succeed in today's competitive market.

Whether you're an established brewery or just in the planning stages, our in-depth coverage will give you information you can put to work immediately. After all, your business is our business.

See for yourself. Subscribe to *The New Brewer* today!

Please complete the following information. We'll rush subscription information your way!

NAME _____
TITLE _____
COMPANY _____
ADDRESS _____
CITY _____
STATE/PROVINCE _____ ZIP/POSTAL CODE _____
COUNTRY _____ TELEPHONE _____

Please return this coupon to: Institute for Brewing Studies, PO Box 1510, Boulder, CO 80306-1510, U.S.A. For faster service contact: (303) 447-0816; FAX (303) 447-2825; orders@aob.org or http://www.aob.org/aob

BRD

The **New Brewer** • YOUR INSIDER'S VIEW TO THE CRAFT-BREWING INDUSTRY

Packaging Equipment

Union Camp Corporation
J. D. Majesky, Mgr. Business Development
53 Forest Ave.
Old Greenwich, CT 06870
(203) 698-0468; FAX (203) 698-2424

Videojet Systems International Inc.
Theresa Rossin, Mktg. Communication Specialist
Harlene Henry, Global Communications
1500 Mittel Blvd.
Wood Dale, IL 60191-1073
(708) 860-7300; FAX (708) 616-3657

Vitro Packaging Inc.
John Althaus, Mktg. Mgr.
16051 Addison Rd., Suite 300
Dallas, TX 75284
(800) 766-0600; FAX (214) 960-1076

A glass packaging supplier to the United States and Canada. Stock line of twelve-, sixteen-, and twenty-two-ounce glass containers with several label and carton options available.

Volckening Inc.
Henry Schneider, Customer Service Mgr.
6700 Third Ave.
Brooklyn, NY 11220
(718) 836-4000 or (800) 221-0876; FAX (718) 748-2811

Wine Bottle & Packaging Inc.
Haim Kalev, Pres.
Ed Humphrey, VP Sales and Mktg.
100 Jutland Rd.
Etobicoke, ON M8Z 2H1
Canada
(800) 387-5314; FAX (416) 255-6043

Suppliers of domestic and imported glass and PET. bottles throughout Canada and the United States.

Zumbiel Packaging
Charles Mace, Dir. Mktg./Sales
Myrna Miller, Customer Service Representative
1743 Cleneay Ave.
Cincinnati, OH 45212
(513) 351-7050; FAX (513) 841-1060

Full-service paperboard packaging supplier to the beer industry. Structural and graphic design, Rotogravace, flexographic, and offset printing processes. Turnkey equipment systems for can and bottle packaging. Industry leader in four-, six-, and eight-pack bottle basket carriers.

12 Restaurant and Pub Equipment Suppliers

With more than five hundred brewpubs now in North America, plus the dozens of microbreweries that have on-site pubs and restaurants, it is clear that the restaurant trade plays a major role in today's craft-brewing renaissance. In fact, several of the United States' most successful specialty brewers have added taverns and full-scale restaurants onto their brewery sites, both as a marketing tool — to help promote their beers — and as a significant source of additional revenue.

Before embarking on a brewpub venture, it is crucial to understand that a brewpub is a restaurant first and brewery second. If you don't like the restaurant business, don't even think of opening a brewpub. In the United States, brewpubs derive a greater amount of gross revenue from food sales than from beer sales. Of course, it is vital that the beers have character and be clean and consistent — a constant challenge in itself. However, one of the most important lessons brewpub owners have learned is that a greater percentage of people will return to your brewpub if they felt the food was outstanding than if they loved the beer.

While many brewery-equipment suppliers are experienced in providing and setting up pubs and restaurants, others are less qualified in this area. Recognizing the importance of restaurants in the craft-brewing industry, we have included this chapter of companies that specialize in supplying products and services for restaurants and pubs — everything from equipment and supplies to design and consulting services.

AJEX USA INC.
Martin E. Schuster, Jr., Pres.
Dean Howell, Sales Mgr.
7100 Broadway, Suite 5S
Denver, CO 80221-0103
(303) 427-4104 or (800) 394-7416; FAX (303) 427-1869

Alan Courtenay Ltd.
Alan Courtenay, Man. Dir.
Marie C. Rauzy, Export Exec.
12 Fleetsbridge Business Centre, Upton Rd.
Poole, Dorset BH17 7AF
United Kingdom
44-202-666-383; FAX 44-202-666-384

Alumasc
Derek Swanson, Sales Dir.
Steve Hart, International Sales Mgr.
Station Rd./Burton Latimer
Kettering, Northhamptonshire NN15 5JP
United Kingdom
44-1536-383-828; FAX 44-1536-420-147

Manufacturer of stainless-steel and plastic faucets, and American half barrels (stainless steel and aluminum). Other products available: dispense towers and pressure relief regulators.

Arrow Neon
Jim Grier
139 Walnut Rd.
Boerne, TX 78006
(800) 451-NEON; FAX (210) 537-5209

Banner Equipment Co.
Michael Tannhauser, VP Sales
3816 N. Carnation St.
Franklin Park, IL 60131
(800) 621-4625; FAX (708) 678-1540

Banner manufactures' draft beer tapping, dispensing, and long draw refrigerated systems (over five hundred feet). Banner manufactures the industry's largest selection of draft towers. Banner is the exclusive North American distributor of beer engines and FOBS manufactured by Homark (U.K.), also for stout and traditional pub-style faucets (ales, lagers) manufactured by Alumasc (U.K.).

Beer-Guano™
John W. Ljepava
3897 Hitchcock Rd.
Concord, CA 94518
(510) 689-2731

Flow-meter design beer inventory control system. Tracks beer flow ounce by ounce. National Sanitation Foundation approved, 1992.

Bohemian Brewery Importers
Jean Pugh, VP Sales and Mktg.
Michael Lislis, Pres./CEO
710 Silver Spur Rd., Suite193
Rolling Hills Estate, CA 90274
(310) 544-1037; FAX (310) 541-2667

Brown Manufacturing Co.
W. B. James, Pres.
C. Evans, Mgr.
PO Box 12945
Newport News, VA 23612-2945
(804) 873-6975; FAX (804) 873-6977

California Glass Co.
Don Grivois, Acct. Mgr.
155 98th Ave.
Oakland, CA 94603
(510) 635-7700

Cargocaire Engineering Co.
Davis McDougall, National Sales Mgr.
PO Box 640/79 Monroe St.
Amesbury, MA 01913-0640
(508) 388-0600; FAX (508) 388-4556
cargo@munters.com
http://www.munters.com/users/cargo

Munters Cargocaire is an engineering firm that designs and manufactures dry desiccant dehumidification systems. Since 1939, these systems have helped to prevent corrosion, reduce housekeeping issues, and improve worker safety. Using a desiccant impregnated HoneyCombe rotor, our units contain only four moving parts for reduced maintenance time.

Chrislan Ceramics Inc.
Al Laninga, Dir. Mktg. and Finance
1650 Broadway St., Suite 101
Port Coquitlam, BC V3L 2M8
Canada
(604) 941-7557; FAX (604) 941-5661

Chrislan Ceramics manufactures ceramic tap handles for the brewery industry. Numerous shapes are available, or we can help you design an exclusive shape that will be unique to your marketing plans. We are one of the only ceramic tap handle manufacturers that kiln fires a decoration on your handle in house. This gives you tremendous flexibility in the design of one of the most valuable marketing tools you have.

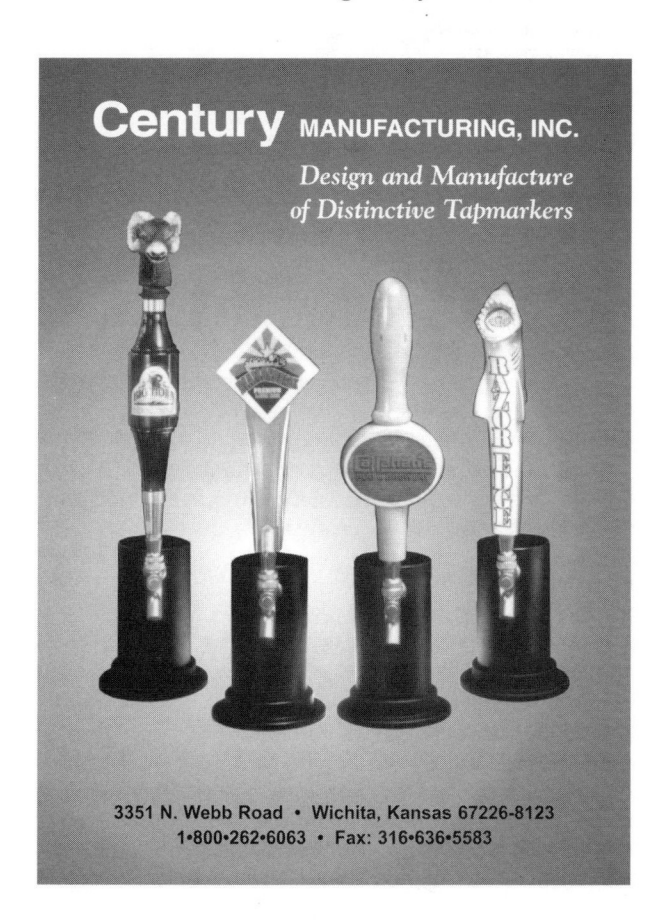

Century MANUFACTURING, INC.

Design and Manufacture of Distinctive Tapmarkers

3351 N. Webb Road • Wichita, Kansas 67226-8123
1•800•262•6063 • Fax: 316•636•5583

Restaurant and Pub Equipment Suppliers

Criveller Co.
Bruno Criveller, Owner
6935 Oakwood Dr.
Niagra Falls, ON L2E 6S5
Canada
(905) 357-2930; FAX (905) 374-2930

Custom Deco Inc.
Todd Lincoln, Sales Mgr. Special Markets
Lisa Dieringer, Customer Service Mgr.
1343 Miami St.
Toledo, OH 43605
(419) 698-2900; FAX (419) 698-9928

Detroit Stool & Chair Mfg. Inc.
Patrick Lesperance, Sales Mgr.
T. J. (Jim) Lesperance, Consultant
50979 Powell Rd.
Plymouth, MI 48170
(800) 424-5140; FAX (313) 455-1257

Dorette Co.
Tom Hagan, Pres.
Jack Teeden, VP
80 Fountain St.
Pawtucket, RI 02860
(401) 723-1690; FAX (401) 728-8430

Draft Service Inc.
John H. Soler, Pres.
Dennis Miller, Sales Mgr.
1208 Hanover Ave.
Allentown, PA 18103
(800) 345-3020; FAX (610) 432-9958

Draft Service is a wholesale distributor of beer dispensing equipment and supplies. We provide a wide variety of draft beer towers, glycol power packs, beer housing, and other necessary items for a complete beer system. Expert technical assistance is available from our professional sales associates.

Drinktec USA Ltd.
Nicolas Haase, Sales and Mktg. Mgr.
JoAnn Seeger, Office Mgr.
100 Railroad Dr., Suite B
Ivyland, PA 18974
(215) 953-9335; FAX (215) 953-8636
drinktec@aol.com

Serving the beverage industry worldwide; equipment, parts, systems, expendable supplies, promotional articles. A member of BrauHaase International Management Group.

Electro-Steam Generator Corp.
Jack Harlin, Acct. Mgr.
1000 Bernard St.
Alexandria, VA 22314
(800) 634-8177 or (703) 549-0664; FAX (703) 836-2581

Electro-Steam Generator Corp. manufacturers all-electric steam generators. Ninety-eight percent efficiency. Point-of-use placement. No flames, fuel, fumes, or firegrade walls. Lower insurance. No boiler chemicals. One to seventy-two BHP. ASHE, National Board of PVI, ETL, UL, and CSA.

Elliott Bay Metal Fabricating Inc.
Chris Michaelsen, Pres.
Greg Bujak, Brewing Consultant
PO Box 777
Monroe, WA 98272
(206) 788-5297; FAX (206) 844-2209

Elliott Bay crafts the finest stainless-steel brewing systems from one to fourteen barrels. We provide full service from installation to brewing your first batches. We are commited to making your operation a top-of-the-line brew system, putting out the best brews while keeping control of costs.

Europe 1992 Connection
Ulrich Kostuch, Pres.
1966 Davids View W.
West Bend, WI 53095
(414) 338-9898; FAX (414) 335-2700

Friesen of Iowa Inc.
Garry Friesen, Pres.
2897 Expansion Blvd.
Storm Lake, IA 50588
(800) 437-2234 or (712) 732-1780; FAX (712) 732-1028

Manufacturer of fully welded, smooth walled, hopper bottom bulk bins. Friesen bins are custom made to your specifications and are ideal for your grain storage needs. They can be painted to match your decor and with application of your logo or decals, the bins can be a functional billboard.

German Glass & Gift Imports Inc.
Heinz M. Scherzer, Pres.
PO Box 663/W200 N10320 Lannon Rd.
Germantown, WI 53022
(414) 253-0226; FAX (414) 253-0155

Specializing in logo glasses for the brewing industry. Quality German wheat beer glasses, Pilsener glasses, and beer boots.

Gilbert Insect Light Traps
David Gilbert, Pres.
Tony King, VP Sales
5611 Krueger Dr.
Jonesboro, AR 72401
(800) 643-0400; FAX (501) 932-5609

Homark Group Ltd.
N. J. Cherowbrier, Sales and Mktg. Mgr.
R. W. Corbett, Dir. Sales and Mktg.
Pottery Rd., Parkstone
Poole, Dorset BH14 8RB
United Kingdom
01202-734000; FAX 01202-737526

Manufacturers of traditional beer handpull engines and cellar equipment such as "solent" profit gaurd/FOB detector, check valves, cask aspirators, and non-return valves. Also manufacturers point-of-sale and customized dispense fonts. All facilities are in-house from concept design to production.

Home on the Range PhotoTops
Jared Resnick, Sales Dir.
Nathan Beavman, Mktg. Dir.
6819 Morrow Mill Rd.
Chapel Hill, NC 27516
(800) 449-8677; FAX (919) 968-7959

JTECH Inc.
Randy McDermott, Dir. Corporate Mktg.
Jay Tully, VP Sales
6413 Congress Ave., Suite 150
Boca Raton, FL 33487
(800) 321-6221; FAX (305) 784-9888

JTECH is the world leader in waiters and customers paging systems. Used in hundreds of microbrews, brewpubs, and mini breweries throughout the United States and Canada. Call (800) 321-6221 for a list of users and references.

Lazar & Co.
Wayne Lazar, Pres.
404 Mendocino Ave., Suite 200
Santa Rosa, CA 95401
(707) 577-0835; FAX (707) 575-4094

Liquid Assets Brewing Systems
Andy Bernadett, VP Sales
Don Goodenough, Pres.
980 B Airway Ct.
Santa Rosa, CA 95403
(800) 730-1030; FAX (707) 527-9306
http://www.indirect.com/www/assets

LABS offers state-of-the-art microbrewery and brewpub equipment and consulting. They provide a complete high-tech equipment package along with all of the necessary services, supplies, and training. They successfully operate a brewpub with sales in excess of $2.5 million.

LABS is an ASME-rated fabrication facility.

Liquidtech Inc.
Doug Holloman, Pres.
Sharon Mowry, VP
1330 Zuni St., Unit F
Denver, CO 80204
(303) 436-9322; FAX (303) 436-9323

Specializing in installation and service of bulk CO_2 systems for microbreweries and brewpubs. Authorized dealer/installer of Perlick draft-beer systems.

Louie's Custom Tap Handles
Louie Marino, Owner
PO Box 2065
Metairie, LA 70004
(504) 831-2026

We duplicate your glass bottle in fine woods. After staining, your labels and crown are put in place. A plasticlike coating is then applied. Brass fittings are used for mounting to make tap handles of distinction. Call us for price quotes and additional information.

McCloud Pest Control
Jim Ludden, VP Oper.
Patricia Hottel, Dir. Technical Services
1012 W. Lunt Ave.
Scheumburg, IL 60193
(708) 893-3900; FAX (708) 893-8815

Multiplex Company Inc.
Joe Viola, Sales Mgr. Beer Systems
Mike Andrews, Prod. Specialist Beer Systems
250 Old Ballwin Rd.
Ballwin, MO 63021
(800) 787-8880; FAX (800) 787-4313

Manufacturer of draught-beer dispensing equipment. Product line includes remote glycol systems; dispensing towers in brass, stainless, ceramic, and wood; custom dispensers and drain tray fabrication; air/nitrogen separation systems; gas blenders; and custom beer distribution panels.

Restaurant and Pub Equipment Suppliers

MVE Inc.
Paul Ploostek, Sales and Mktg. Mgr.
Gary Sedivy, National Acct. and Sales
8011 34th Ave. S.
Bloomington, MN 55425
(800) 247-4446 or (612) 853-9600; FAX (612) 853-9661

World-leading manufacturer of bulk CO_2 systems for brewing and fountain beverage applications with over 75,000 systems installed worldwide. Our systems are available in many different sizes for customization to meet your flow requirements. Bulk CO_2 is designed to replace high pressure, CO_2 cylinders and provide your operation with improved convience, beverage quality, safety, and savings.

National Chemicals Inc.
Dr. L. Charles Landman, Jr., General Mgr.
PO Box 32/105 Liberty St.
Winona, MN 55987
(800) 533-0027; FAX (507) 454-5641

Manufacturer of detergents, sanitizers/disinfectants, and related cleaners for public eating and drinking establishments, brewing and draught systems in microbreweries, brewpubs, and homebrewing operations.

Nielsen's Equipment & Design Inc.
Don Zytkoskee, Pres.
Len J. Groschen, VP
6318 Lakeland Ave. N.
Minneapolis, MN 55428
(612) 536-9919; FAX (612) 536-1239

Nightwing Enterprises Inc.
Milton C. Watkins Jr., Pres.
Joyanne La Maine, Office Mgr.
PO Box 3280/25 N. Depot St.
Binghamton, NY 13902
(607) 723-5886 or (800) 836-YARD; FAX (607) 723-3871

Perlick Corp.
Joe Restivo, Sales Specialist
8300 W. Good Hope Rd.
Milwaukee, WI 53223-0098
(414) 353-7060; FAX (414) 353-7069

Manufacturer of stainless-steel sanitary fittings and fabrication for process piping and tanks. Also, remote beer systems, back bars, underbar workboards, and beverage coolers.

MVE...THE Brewmaster's Choice For Bulk CO_2.

- High flow with no electricity required
- Eliminates CO_2 runouts and hassles of changing out high pressure cylinders
- Low pressure system ensures safe work environment
- Increase your production efficiency
- Reduces CO_2 usage up to 30%
- *Plus many more benefits. For more information on how an MVE Bulk CO_2 System can benefit your brewery, please call us at 800-247-4446.*

MVE Carbo-Max 600 HIGH FLOW
Actual Height = 68 in.
Actual Diameter = 24 in.

MVE, Inc.
Two Appletree Square, Suite #100 • 8011 34th Avenue South
Bloomington, MN 55425-1636
Phone 800-247-4446 •612-853-9600 •Fax 612-853-9661

Prolong Systems Inc.
Dan Tekorius
Sy Manaitis
23939 S.W. Gage Rd.
Wilsonville, OR 97070
(503) 638-1414; FAX (503) 638-5252
aras@teleport.com

Prolong Systems Inc. is a designer and builder of on-site nitrogen generating systems for brewing and dispensing industries. Prolong's Ni-Gen Systems utilize hollow fiber membrane technology wich allows unlimited production of nitrogen at low cost. Let Prolong show you the benefits of on-site produced nitrogen over purchased CO_2 and CO_2/N blends.

Rapids Wholesale Equipment Co.
Joe Schmitt
Joe Dodds
PO Box 396/1011 Second Ave. S.W.
Cedar Rapids, IA 52406
(319) 364-5186; FAX (319) 364-2111

Rapids has a full line of restaurant/brewpub equipment and supplies from knives and forks to walk-in cooler systems. Call for your catalog.

Refrigeration Service 6
David A. Payne, Owner/Eng.
1830 Sutton Ave.
Cincinnati, OH 45230
(513) 231-9700; FAX (513) 752-5726

Sonoco Engraph Label Group
Thomas Coker, Mktg. Mgr.
Jim Prendergast, VP Sales
8800 South Blvd.
Charlotte, NC 28273
(704) 554-5796; FAX (704) 554-8122

Specialist Joinery Fittings
Judith Clinton, Mktg. Exec.
1489 Webster St. Suite 108
San Francisco, CA 94115
(415) 292-4807; FAX (415) 922-3654

Summit Commercial
Steve Ross, VP
Alan Cohen, Mktg. Mgr.
1435 Watson Ave.
Bronx, NY 10472
(718) 893-3900; FAX (718) 842-3093

Thunder Bay Brewing Co. Inc.
Chuck Schroeder, Pres.
Louis Farrell, Exec. VP/Head Brewer
412 Tenafly Rd.
Englewood, NJ 07631
(201) 568-5336; FAX (201) 568-3028

W. W. Reichert, Bavarian Brewhouse Inc.
Rex Reichert, Pres.
Holgenburg 4
D-73728 Esslingen, 73728
Germany
(711) 357-333; FAX (711) 350-8343

Wilson Brewing Systems Ltd.
A. Ross Wilson, Pres.
R. Graham Wilson, Mgr.
PO Box 820
Bolton, ON L7E 5T5
(905) 857-1511; FAX (905) 857-0325

13 Brewing Consultants

When building a brewery, expanding an existing facility, or designing a new beer, experience counts. That's where brewing consultants enter the picture. A consultant with the appropriate background and attitude can prevent frustration and save time and money on a project.

While your fellow brewer might be more than eager to share knowledge gained in the school of hard knocks, paid consultants can be worth every cent of their fee. (You know the saying: Free advice is worth the price you pay for it.) Of course, as with most professionals, consultants may have personal biases regarding equipment, methods, and beer styles.

The best way to select a consultant is to get references and check them carefully. Interview several consultants and look for like-mindedness to determine which one possesses a philosophy about brewing and budget that matches yours.

Equally important is finding a knowledgeable, compatible brewer. In some cases, the brewer may also act as your consultant, if he or she possesses the adequate background. Finding a trained brewer can be difficult though, as demand continues to increase.

The Institute for Brewing Studies keeps a file of brewmasters currently seeking employment. This information is available to IBS members for free upon request and to non-members for $75. To obtain this information or if you would like to add your résumé to the brewer file, contact Brewmaster for Hire at Institute for Brewing Studies, PO Box 1679, Boulder, CO 80306-1679, USA; (303) 447-0816; FAX (303) 447-2825.

Aero Resources Inc.
John J. MacLeod, Pres.
Kenneth H. Campbell
287 Lacewood Dr., Box 266, Unit 103
Halifax, NS B3M 3Y7
Canada
(902) 873-3843; FAX (902) 873-3843

Beverage Consult International Inc.
Finn B. Knudsen, Pres.
Evergreen Plaza/4602 Plettner Lane, Suite 2E
Evergreen, CO 80439-7300
(303) 674-2251; FAX (303) 727-6555

Consulting in all technical and management aspects of brewing. Engineering solutions to condensation control in buildings.

Bill Owens, Consultant
Bill Owen
PO Box 510
Hayward, CA 94543-0510
(510) 538-9500 (A.M. only); FAX (510) 538-7644
Ambrew@Ambrew.com
http://www.Ambrew.com

The Society of Beer from the Wood celebrates all breweries that use wooden mash tuns, fermentation tanks, or lagering vessels in the manufacturing of beer. The goal of the society is to preserve this traditional way of brewing. Members of the society believe that beer touched by wood is softer and easier to drink.

Bohemian Brewery Importers
Jean Pugh, VP Sales and Mktg.
Michael Lislis, Pres./CEO
710 Silver Spur Rd., Suite 193
Rolling Hills Estate, CA 90274
(310) 544-1037; FAX (310) 541-2667

CBS Insurance
Spencer H. Nicoll, CIC, AAI
Matt A. Coleman, CPCU
PO Box 1900/15 S Weber
Colorado Springs, CO 80901
(719) 634-8807; FAX (719) 634-8909

Cemcorp Ltd., Consulting Engineers
Michael A. Coulter, P.E., Managing Dir.
2170 Stanfield Rd.
Mississauga, ON L4Y 1R5
Canada
(905) 566-7227; FAX (905) 566-7228

Specializing in brewery process and equipment design services including conceptual studies, engineering specifications, complete plans and drawings, procurement, and construction management services.

CM Supply and Consulting
Charles McElevey, Owner
4341 S.W. Concord St.
Seattle, WA 98136
(206) 932-6877

Charles, a Weihenstephan graduate, has thirty-two years in commercial brewing and thirteen years as a consultant for micro- and pubbreweries. Services include business plans, design, product formulations, start-ups, and training. (Formerly production assistance.)

D.R.B. & Associates
Douglas R. Babcook, Pres.
RR 3 Box 3270
Collingwood, ON L9Y 3Z2
Canada
(705) 444-1042; FAX (705) 444-0932

Diversified Management Servicies Ltd.
Marty Post, Managing Consultant
Randee Gunn, Business Consultant
730 17th St., Suite 620
Denver, CO 80202
(303) 534-3626; FAX (303) 534-3516

DME Brewing Services
Barry MacLeod, VP Mktg. and Sales
Kelly Dunne, Mktg. and Sales
PO Box 553
Charlottetown, PE C1A 7L1
Canada
(902) 628-6900; FAX (902) 628-1313
ksampson@cycor.ca
http://www.cycor.ca/DME/

DME Brewing Services designs and manufactures standard and custom brewery equipment for the craft-brewing industry. We provide complete breweries as well as beer engines, cask ale packages, cellar tanks, and keg washers. Our regional representatives provide face-to-face consultation in installation, site inspection, operations, beer formulations, technical brewing, and on-going support.

DMS Group
Dennis M. Sherman, Pres.
17 Highland Terrace
North Andover, MA 01845-5249
(508) 689-7433; FAX (508) 689-7433
DMS@digiworld.com
http://www.digiworld.com/brewhousedanvers

The DMS Group is engaged in the development of brewpubs, brew restaurants, and microbreweries. The company's services include conversions, start-ups, joint ventures, and capital acquisition. DMS is in the game and looking for action! Call and explore the possibilities.

Ed Tringali & Associates
Ed Tringali, Pres.
931 N. 35th St., Suite 1
Seattle, WA 98103
(206) 547-8374; FAX (206) 547-8374
bc003@scn.org

We get new breweries up and running fast with a high quality product. Interpret bids and save clients money. Provide GABF winning recipes, pitching quantities of yeast, and physically help brew. We can even find and train brewers. Each project opens with excellent beer. With several Asian start-ups, we are international.

First Key Industrial Corp.
Jim L. Clarke, Pres.
Ray G. Moore, Chief Financial Officer
210-4320 Viking Way
Richmond, BC V6V 2L4
Canada
604-273-8884; FAX 604-273-1481
102044.3207@compuserve.com

Whether projects are limited to single areas of focus or involve the convergence of strategy, operations, finance, marketing and engineering, First Key's objective is to help clients with the business opportunities and technical issues that will enhance their competitive positions, profitability, and future in the brewing world.

Brewing Consultants

Global Brewing Services Inc.
Chris Dowe
Mike Hall
70 Stanford St.
South Portland, ME 04106
(207) 799-6697; FAX (207) 799-6600
http://www.maine.com/cdowe

Goggins & Whalen Insurance Agency Inc.
Peter J. Whalen, Pres.
Shirley Dean
PO Box 478/71 King St.
Northampton, MA 01061
(800) 235-0355

Hopfen und Malz GmbH
Hermann Hörterer, Brewmaster
Hans Schilp, Brewmaster
Schloßstr. 8
82269 Kaltenberg,
Germany
08193-9330; FAX 08193-933123

Hopfen und Malz GmbH, as a subsidiary of Kaltenberg Brewery, provides innovative and modern turnkey pub- and minibreweries, backed by the experience of a well-established Bavarian brewery.

IDD Process & Packaging Inc.
Jeff Gunn, Pres.
Tom Thilert, Sales Dir.
646 Flinn Ave.
Moorpark, CA 93021
(800) 621-4144 or (805) 529-9890; FAX (805) 529-9282
414 Ridgeview Ct., Arnold, MD 21012
idd2jeff@aol

Brewery process and packaging system design and manufacturing engineers. This includes turnkey brewpub and microbreweries, kegging systems, tank valves, yeast propagation and management systems, deaeration, filtration and pasteurization systems, hops (leaf, pellet, and extract), cleaners, sanitizers, brewing and fermenting aids. Full-service formula and systems brewery engineering and consultation.

Insurance Associates of Northern California
Dick Monroe, CEO
Frank Rogers, VP
2735 N. Main St.
Walnut Creek, CA 94596
(510) 934-0505; FAX (510) 977-1591

James R. Van Liere Structural Engineer
James R. Van Liere
2359 Van Gordon St.
Lakewood, CO 80215
(303) 232-2330; FAX (303) 232-2330
73441.541@compuserve.com

Jenkins/Athens Insurance Services
Mark A. Niebuar, CPCU/VP
PO Box 5668
Concord, CA 94524
(510) 798-3334

Independently owned and opperated for over fifty years, providing professional commercial risk management and insurance services to clients nationally and internationally.

John H. Bergmann Associates Ltd.
John H. Bergmann
100 Railroad Dr.
Warminster, PA 18974
(215) 953-8781; FAX (215) 953-8748

Joseph L. Owades & Co.
Joseph Owades, Ph.D.
3097 Wood Valley Rd.
Sonoma, CA 95476
(707) 935-1919; FAX (707) 935-1750

KMS Consultants
Karl M. Strauss, Certified Management Consultant
8515 N. Manor Lane
Milwaukee, WI 53217
(414) 352-1746; FAX (414) 352-1023

International consulting to breweries of all sizes. Specialty: Assisting with small-brewery design, brand formulation, and start-up.

Law Offices of Earle D. Bellamy II, P.C.
Earle D. Bellamy II ("Chip")
730 17th St., Suite 620
Denver, CO 80202

Offering legal assistance to brewers with brewery start-up, licensing, financing, label approval, and trademarks. Also experience dealing with federal and state agancies and regulations governing the sale and marketing of malt beverages. Extensive experience working with brewers in their dealings with distributors and with distribution issues.

Lax & Noll
Jerome Noll, Managing Partner
Robert Lax, Managing Partner
551 Fifth Ave.
New York, NY 10176
(212) 818-9150; FAX (212) 682-9040
LAXNOLL@pipeline.com

Lazar & Co.
Wayne Lazar, Pres.
404 Mendocino Ave., Suite 200
Santa Rosa, CA 95401
(707) 577-0835; FAX (707) 575-4094

Lewis Twice Consultancy
Michael J. Lewis, Ph.D., F.I. Brew/Managing Partner
Ashton S. Lewis, Msc./Partner
731 Lake Terrace Cir.
Davis, CA 95616
(916) 756-4302 or 759-8081

Principals Michael Lewis and Ashton Lewis teach and consult about all aspects of brewing science and technical brewery design. They specialize in new brewery ventures, product developement, equipment design, brewery evaluation, problem solving, and research and development. Custom brewing at their seven-barrel research and education brewery is also available.

Long-Kesh Funding
Mark Eldridge, Finance Consultant
PO Box 70/816 Depot St.
Brasher Falls, NY 13613
(315) 389-5007; FAX (315) 265-3102

Martin Velas
Martin Velas, Brewing Consultant
10901 Nestle Ave.
Northridge, CA 91326
(818) 831-3705 or (818) 596-1206; FAX (818) 368-7395

Matter Co.
Terry R. Soloman, Co-Owner
95 Mamaroneck Ave., Suite 114
White Plains, NY 10601
(914) 633-2973; FAX (914) 681-2924

Micro Brew Express — Beer-of-the-Month Club
Craig Wesley, Pres.
2246 Calle Del Mundo
Santa Clara, CA 95054
(408) 748-9090; FAX (408) 748-9099

MicroPure Filtration
Robert A. Pollmann, VP/General Mgr.
Marcy Pollman, Sales Admin.
7879 Forest Hills Rd.
Rockford, IL 61111
(800) 654-7873; FAX (815) 962-7360

Solid, secure filtration solutions for sterile air, gas, liquid and steam applications. Environmentally friendly while saving production costs. On-line automatic samplers for product sampling.

Noel/Greaves Inc.
Greg Hoes
Stephen Smith
3100 Monticello, Suite 300
Dallas, TX 75205
(214) 443-3100; FAX (214) 443-3900

For over forty years, with its network of more than fifty insurance companies, Noel/Greaves Inc. has assisted its clients in managing risks and attaining cost-effective insurance programs. Let us craft a risk management program for your microbrewery or brewpub.

OUTTERSON BREWING SERVICES INCORPORATED

specializes in turnkey brewing systems for brewpubs and microbreweries. Each system is carefully designed and built with the finest stainless steel, valves and fittings. We also troubleshoot existing systems, analyzing operational, product or equipment problems. If you need a new recipe, we can target a beer to your particular clientele or formulate a special occasion brew. We can also locate specific new or used equipment and supplies worldwide.

- Brewery Equipment • Bottling Lines
- International Specialty Grains • System Design
- Site Evaluation • Feasibility Studies • Sourcing
- Product Formulation/Pilot Brews • Training
- Installation & Testing • Technical Support
- Licensing & Bookkeeping Forms Assistance
- Advertising & Graphic Design Service

Contact Donald Outterson, President
(513) 474-9385
Fax (513) 474-9384
7747 Woodstone Drive • Cincinnati, Ohio 45244-2855

Brewing Consultants

Norman R. Soine — Consulting Brewing Chemist
Norman Soine, Consultant
PO Box 257
Plainville, NY 13137
(315) 638-4978

Outterson Brewing Services Inc.
Donald Outterson, Pres.
7747 Woodstone Dr.
Cincinnati, OH 45244-2855
(513) 474-9385; FAX (513) 474-9384

Pacific Rim Consulting Group
Barbara Winde
Sandy Schafer
PO Box 13310
Mill Creek, WA 98082
(800) 789-7498 or (206) 486-2618; FAX (206) 486-2618

Consulting services focusing on the pub operation. Offering a full range of services for the front and back of the house, including project coordination, management, human resources, kitchen design, menu developement, vendor sourcing, accounting, bookkeeping systems, and hands-on staff training.

Would you like to have *your* beer exported to Europe?

In Europe, premium beers, specialty ales and imported beers have made surprising gains over the last 3 years.

VERA FOODS S.A. of Paris, France (the beverage company) and **S & M** of Barcelona, Spain (the brewer) have joined forces to offer a new range of services for American craft beers in Europe.

- Gain direct access to decision makers for Europe's retailers.
- Gain approval for volume sales in the New Europe.
- Access contract services in Europe for beer or soft drinks.
- Access distribution networks.

If you are a microbrewer, help change the image of North American beers in Europe. Contact Vera Foods in Paris about our STARTER PLAN for entering the European market.

Contact: Mr. S. Randle
Vera Foods S.A.
42 Avenue Montaigne
75008 Paris, France
011-33-1-53-67-54-93
011-33-1-53-67-53-53 (fax)
verafoods@earthlink.net
www.spainbeercompany.com
U.S.A.:
213-243-8544
213-938-5056 (fax)

PROGINOX Inc.
Michel Neault, Engineer
8090 Saguenay
Brossard, PQ J4X 1H7
Canada
(514) 466-8779; FAX (514) 466-2806

Pugsley's Brewing Projects International/Shipyard Brewing
Alan J. Pugsley, Pres.
Chris Dowe, Brewery Consultant
PO Box 11604
Portland, ME 04104
(207) 871-1121 or (207) 761-0807; FAX (207) 871-1122

Pugsley's Brewing Projects offers qualified investors and restaurantreurs the oppertunity to share in Shipyard Brewing Co. Alan Pugsley's sucess by establishing a brewpub or microbeer pub based on a proven successful formula. Pugsley provides prospective "partners" with first class equipment, brewer training and world class beer formulations from Pugsley.

Robert J. Ryan Inc.
Robert J. Ryan Jr., VP
PO Box 3995/95 Schwenk Dr.
Kingston, NY 12401
(800) 724-7463; FAX (914) 331-0006

Salvadore Machinery Corp.
Michael Salvadore, Pres.
945 Eddy St.
Providence, RI 02905
(401) 941-1950; FAX (401) 781-5840

Schumacher & Associates
Ferdinand M. (Fred) Schumacher
PO Box 318
Frankenmuth, MI 48734
(517) 652-6535; FAX (517) 652-6535

Siebel Institute of Technology
Bill Siebel, Pres.
Jim Helmke, Sr. Brewing Consultant
4055 W. Peterson Ave.
Chicago, IL 60646-6001
(312) 279-0966; FAX (312) 463-7688

Founded in 1872, we provide worldwide consulting to breweries of all sizes. We specialize in brand formulations, independent review of brewery design, plant audits, and technical problem solving.

Sonoco Engraph Label Group
Thomas Coker, Mktg. Mgr.
Jim Prendergast, VP Sales
8800 South Blvd.
Charlotte, NC 28273
(704) 554-5796; FAX (704) 554-8122

Sound Brewing Systems Inc.
Vince Cottone, Pres.
11223 Palatine Ave. N.
Seattle, WA 98133
(206) 362-2668; FAX (206) 368-3961
soundbrew@prostar.com

    Brewpub and production brewery start-ups, seven to seventy-plus barrels; plant/equipment design and installation; product formulation, training and business planning. Sole U.S. agents for Ripley Stainless Ltd., British Columbia, Canada.

Spider Roll Brewing LLC
Kyle Carstens or C. S. Derrick, Mgrs.
3327 Alcott Rd.
Denver, CO 80211
(303) 455-6692

Summit Products Inc.
Rao Palamand, VP/Beverage Dir.
12660 Lamplighter Sq.
St. Louis, MO 63128
(314) 842-3837

U-Brew Inc.
Daron Kirchmeier, Pres.
8260 S.W. Nimbus Ave.
Beaverton, OR 97008
(503) 644-UBRU (8278); FAX (503) 626-9646
UBREW1@aol.com
http://public.navisoft.com/pub/ubrew.htm

VAFAC Inc. (Virginia Food and Craft)
Philip H. Pryor, Pres.
212 Freedom Ct.
Fredericksburg, VA 22408
(540) 898-3202; FAX (540) 898-8442

Vera Foods
Mr. S. Randle
42nd Ave. Mantaigne
75008 Paris
France
(213) 243-8544; FAX (213) 938-5056 or
11-33-1-53-67-54-93; FAX 11-33-53-67-53-53
verafoods@earthlink.net
http://www.spainbeercompany.com

WMS Inc.
H. Richard Werth
15973 S.W. Westminster Dr.
Portland, OR 97224
(503) 590-4400; FAX (503) 590-4499

Wyeast Laboratories
David W. Logsdon, Pres./Brewer
Teri Byrne, Cust. Service
PO Box 425
Mount Hood, OR 97041
(503) 354-1335; FAX (503) 354-3449

14 Marketing, Point-of-Sale, and Merchandise Suppliers and Consultants

The final steps in putting a product on the market are packaging, logo or label design, and promotion. With the increased number of competing brands on the market, package design and presentation can make the difference between a product that moves and one that doesn't.

Besides a striking label and colorful six-pack carrier, a bottled brand may benefit from other devices for attracting greater consumer attention. These include six-pack inserts, bottle neck ringers, cardboard point-of-sale displays, and shelf talkers.

For draft beer, a unique tap handle is a great way to make your beer stand out from the others. If you can afford them, silkscreened mirrors and neon signs are great for getting extra attention for your beer, but are not usually necessary.

Paper point-of-sale materials — especially posters, coasters, and table tents — are the most cost-effective mechanisms for selling your beer. The poster must have sufficient space for a bar or retail store to write in a price special. A beer wholesaler or distributor can be the best source for advice on what types of marketing pieces retailers and on-premise accounts need to sell more of your beer.

Of course, no beer brand or brewing company is complete without its own T-shirt and other logo-emblazoned merchandise. Caps, sweatshirts, glassware, beer trays, keyrings, etc. are all popular with consumers. The more people like your product (and/or your logo), the more they'll pay for items that help you advertise it. Microbreweries, brewpubs, and contract brewing companies alike have found that merchandise doesn't just help spread the word about your beer, it can also be a significant source of additional revenue.

Conversely, you may want to ignore potential merchandise profits in favor of the pure marketing value of getting your logoed goods on customers' bodies by selling your items for only a break-even price (or just above). Your company may ultimately derive greater benefit from the increased exposure to your brands (or brewpub) caused by the larger number of people volunteering to be your "walking billboards."

This chapter lists marketing consultants, design studios, printing houses, and merchandise suppliers. While your beer may already look great, these companies are interested in making it look better!

Acrylic Designs Inc.
Thomas A. Davidson, Sales and Mktg. Mgr.
100 River St.
Springfield, VT 05156
(802) 885-8579; FAX (802) 885-8581

Designers and manufacturers of promotional products including table tents, bottle glorifiers, condiment dispensers, wall signs, and bar lamps. Best value for your marketing dollar.

Action Graphics
Mark Hess, Owner
1778 Highland Ave.
Las Cruces, NM 88005
(505) 527-1046

Custom labels, logos, POS designs, table tents, fliers, and more!

Ad-Mat Coasters U.S.A. Inc.
Jack DeGatis, Sales Mgr.
PO Box 3724
Johnson City, TN 37602
(800) 844-MATS; FAX (423) 434-2210

Allen-Morrison Sales Co.
Lisa S. Ramsey, National Sales and Mktg. Mgr.
Renee H. Draney, Account Exec.
300 Rutherford St.
Lynchburg, VA 24501
(804) 846-8461; FAX (804) 845-0898

American Coaster Co.
Sue Belford, Sales Administrator
3685 Lockport Rd.
Sanborn, NY 14132
(716) 731-9193; FAX (716) 731-4138

Arrow Neon
Jim Grier
139 Walnut Rd.
Boerne, TX 78006
(800) 451-NEON; FAX (210) 537-5209

ASA Beverage Brokers Inc.
1736 S. Hiawassee Rd., Suite 33
Orlando, FL 32835
(407) 293-4515; FAX (407) 293-0555

Atelier Zillich
Dipl. - Kfm. Peter Zillich
Monatshausen
D 82327 Tutzing
Germany
08158/8201; FAX 08158/1670

AVVA Technologies
David Komonoski, VP Sales
Kelly Compton, Design Mgr.
6025 12th St. S.E., Suite 5
Calgary, AB T2H 2K1
Canada
(800) 665-3749; FAX (403) 252-5580

AVVA designs and manufactures unique neon edge-lit illuminated signs. AVVA's products offer unique visual appeal, five-year lamp gaurantees, and extreme durability. Computer controlled manufacturing ensures accurate reproduction of even the most intricate detail. Location-specific costumization easily and inexpensively available for every sign.

Tap Into This...

Sharp looks from Crisa at even sharper price points! Our pint or 16 oz. mixing glass (far left) and 5-1/2 oz. sampler glasses (inset) are standouts in a Five Star line that includes handblown mugs, pressed mugs, pilsners, yards, half-yards and feet of ale!

To tap into these, contact your foodservice distributor for information or call Crisa at 1-800-643-9093.

Crisa
FIVE STAR TOTAL TABLETOP

1 - 800 - 643 - 9093

Marketing, Point-of-Sale, and Merchandise Suppliers and Consultants

Beer Business Services
Jane Chamberlain, Pres.
Ken Vermes, VP
454 Las Gallinas, Suite 136
San Rafael, CA 94903
(415) 479-8767
75601.1364@compuserve.com

Beer Business Services specializes in marketing, beer regulatory compliance, and computer services for the brewing industry. From label approvals to promotions, BBS can assist you.

Beer Gear
Clark Turner, Pres.
PO Box 90460
San Diego, CA 92169
(619) 581-9440 or (800) 582-9440; FAX (619) 581-9443

Specializing in custom decorated clothing and glassware. We represent Rastal, top quality European drinking glasses and steins. We screen print and embroider T-shirts, sweats, pub towels, polo shirts, caps, aprons, and more.

Beeraphernalia Co.
Adam Ekstein, Pres.
325 Huntington Ave, Suite 89
Boston, MA 02115
(617) 262-1356; FAX (617) 262-1356

The Beeraphernalia Company provides promotion and merchandise. Promote your brewery by offering hats, T-shirts, mugs, etc. For sale in the Beeraphernalia color catalog. Distribution of the catalogs will take place in liquor stores at the point-of-sale. Wholesale merchandise available, glassware and bar stools with your logo emblazoned.

Beers of the World Packaging Co.
Patrick J. McShane, Pres.
PO Box 2182
Morristown, NJ 07962-2182
(201) 538-1519; FAX (201) 993-5548

BIXIE COASTERS
Mike Jakubowski, Sales Mgr.
Smitty Thomas, VP Sales
4061 BlueRidge Industrial Pkwy.
Norcross, CA 30071
(800) 264-BIXI (7404); FAX (770) 623-4745

Boelter Companies
Steve Dindorf
Jay O'Connor
Quentin Shafer, Account Exec.
Rick Boelter, Account Exec.
11100 W. Silver Spring Rd.
Milwaukee, WI 53225
(800) BEER-CUP; FAX (800) 5 FAX-CUP

For twenty-five years, the Boelter Companies has been servicing the brewing industry with various promotional utility products, such as cups, coasters, glassware, taps, neons, paper POS, and many others. Exceptional customer service and competitive pricing set us apart in the industry. Please call for more information, samples, and a quote!

Bolin Agency
Jack A. Silverman, VP/Account Mgr.
2318 Park Ave.
Minneapolis, MN 55402
(612) 872-1200; FAX (612) 872-7056

Beer and beverage brand development consultants. Over 30 brands developed. Integrated marketing, graphic design and advertising services.

Capabilities (in-house): research, product naming, legal search, label and package design, marketing plans, distributor sell sheets, POP materials and promotions, advertisings and media services, and extensive Macintosh desktop production facility.

Brew Tee's
Jon Chamoff
Ted Chapin
202 U.S. Rte. 1, Suite 357
Falmouth, ME 04105
(207) 829-9903 or (800) 585-TEES; FAX (207) 829-4305

The finest quality, screen-printed T-shirts available; embroidery service; outstanding conceptual art department.

Brown-Miller Communications
Greg Belloni, Account Exec.
Ken Freeze, Account Exec.
1330 Arnold Dr., Suite 242
Martinez, CA 94553
(800) 710-9333; FAX (510) 370-9811
bmc@dnai.com
http://www.dnai.com/~bmc

Carlson's Brewery Research
Randy Carlson, Owner
PO Box 758
Walker, MN 56484
(218) 547-1830

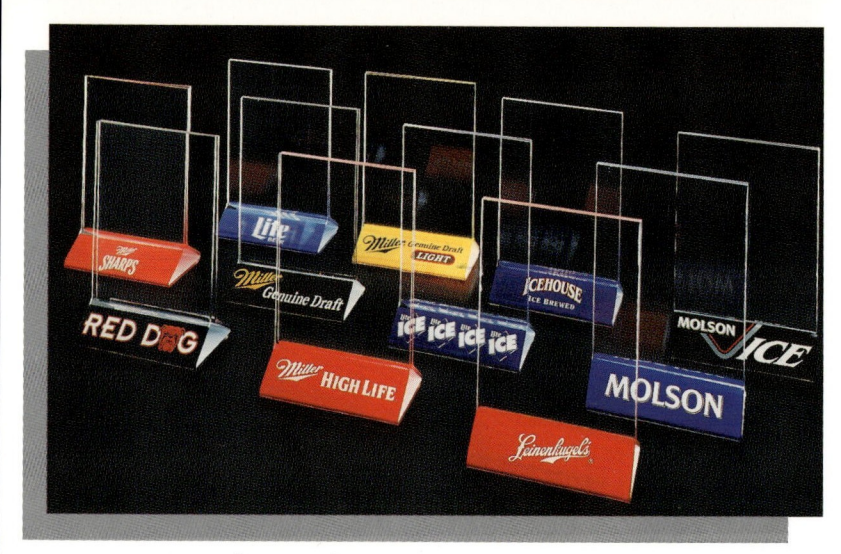

Printed Acrylic Menu Card Holders

Card Holders - *Bottom Load*

Custom Displays

Winged Acrylic Display Card Holders

Palmer®
Promotional Products
A Division Of PDI
23540 Reynolds Ct.
Clinton Township, MI 48036
Fax (800) 573-4329

800-444-1912
Ext. 11

Tap Knobs

Marketing

I·C LIGHT

Poly Banners - 3' x 5'

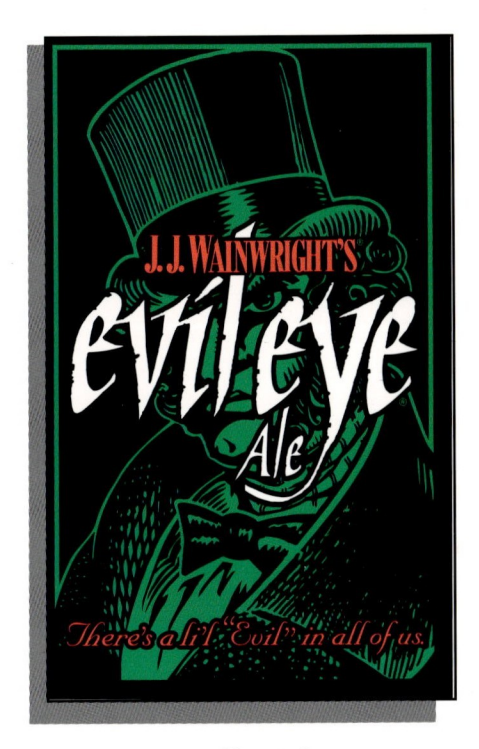

IRON CITY

J.J. Wainwright's Evil Eye Ale
There's a li'l "Evil" in all of us.

Wall Tacker

Luminated Write On Board

BECK'S
AMERICA'S NUMBER ONE IMPORTED GERMAN BEER

DRAFT $1.25
Bottle $2.00

FROM CONCEPT TO CONCLUSION

Palmer Promotional Products is your starting point for creation of cost effective advertising programs. We take your program from concept to conclusion, designing and manufacturing award winning displays that are proven winners throughout the brewery industry. Our approach utilizes a recipe that any brewer would love, it starts with low cost products and services that make the initial order easy. Call now!

Other products and services not outlined in this ad including the following:

Products:
- Illuminated Lightboxes
- Wallmount Clocks
- Mirrors
- Edge Lits
- Wearables
- Back Bar Displays
- Translites
- Counter Mats
- Bottle Glorifiers
- Napkin Holders

Services:
- Laser Cutting
- Silk Screening
- Hot Stamping
- Computerized Fulfillment
- Engraving and Etching
- Design and Layout
- Vacuum Forming
- Injection Molding
- Blow Molding
- Fabrication
- Printing
- Die Cutting

Palmer®
Promotional Products

800-444-1912 Ext. 11

Graphics Supplied By Media Associates

Chrislan Ceramics Inc.
Al Laninga, Dir. Mktg. and Finance
1650 Broadway St., Suite 101
Port Coquitlam, BC V3L 2M8
Canada
(604) 941-7557; FAX (604) 941-5661

Chrislan Ceramics manufactures ceramic tap handles for the brewery industry. Numerous shapes are available, or we can help you design an exclusive shape that will be unique to your marketing plans. We are one of the only ceramic tap handle manufacturers that kiln fires a decoration on your handle in house. This gives you tremendous flexibility in the design of one of the most valuable marketing tools you have.

Ciao! Travel
Bill Snider, Dir.
2707 Congress St., Suite 1F
San Diego, CA 92110
(619) 297-8112 or (800) 942-2426; FAX (619) 297-8112

Crystalite Corp.
Michael C. Sammartino, Pres.
David C. Sammartino, VP
17 Industrial Dr.
Smithfield, RI 02917
(401) 231-1111; FAX (401) 231-9470

Dale W. Woys & Associates
Dale W. Woys, Dir.
PO Box 2440/2014 N. Saginaw Rd., Suite 110
Midland, MI 48640
(517) 662-9000; FAX (517) 662-9000

Davis and Small Oldtime Sign & Photo Co.
Tom Davis, Pres.
Margaret Riggs, Customer Service
500 La Mesa Dr.
Mount Pleasant, SC 29464
(800) 849-5082; FAX (803) 881-8990

Diversified Management Servicies Ltd.
Marty Post, Managing Consultant
Randee Gunn, Business Consultant
730 17th St., Suite 620
Denver, CO 80202
(303) 534-3626; FAX (303) 534-3516

Etched Images
Stu McFarland, Owner
David Lincoln, Owner
1758 Industrial Way, Suite 121
Napa Valley, CA 94558
(707) 252-5450; FAX (707) 252-2666
72163.567@compuserve.com

A distinctive first impression, a memento for valued clients, a unique sales incentive — your company name/logo etched in glass is all this and more.

Foxboro Co.
D. Gilmore, Dir. Corp. Comm.
33 Commercial St.
Foxboro, MA 02035-2099
(508) 543-8750; FAX (508) 549-4433
http://www.foxboro.com

General Press Corp.
Kevin Conroy, Customer Service
Box 316 Allegheny Dr.
Natrona Heights, PA 15065
(412) 224-3500

Glasses, Mugs & Steins
Peter Kroll, Owner
PO Box 207
Sun Prairie, WI 53590
(608) 837-4818; FAX (608) 825-4205

Grandstand Sportswear
Jerry Kenefake
Chris Piper
315 N.E. Industrial Lane
Lawrence, KS
(913) 843-8888; FAX (913) 843-3777

Graphic Nature
Mike Ferney, Mktg. Dir.
PO Box 422
Brattleboro, VT 05302
(802) 254-6253; FAX (802) 257-4022
ferney@sover.net

Handy Button Machine Co. of New York Inc.
Marc Baritz, Mktg. Dir.
PO Box 658/50-05 47th Ave.
Woodside, NY 11377-0658
(718) 446-1900; FAX (718) 446-8662

Marketing, Point-of-Sale, and Merchandise Suppliers and Consultants

High Range Graphics
Jan Stuessi, Pres.
Tim Tasker, Sales Rep.
PO Box 3302/365 N. Glenwood
Jackson, WY 83001
(307) 733-8723; FAX (307) 733-0999

The screen printed image on your T-shirts needs to be as good as your beer. HRG is commited to unmatched quality, service, and attention to detail. Our satisfied customers can recommend us. Our design team can finish creative new art or update exisiting designs to provide maximum marketing potential.

Inland Printing Co./Inland Label
Dan Pretasky, VP Sales
Roman Artz, Sales Rep.
PO Box 1268/2009 West Ave. S.
La Crosse, WI 54601
(608) 788-5800; FAX (608) 787-5870

Industry leader for supplying paper or metalized labels to brewers. Also, we print point-of-sale items including tabletents, shelf or channel strips, static stickers, posters, case cards, counter cards, neck hangers, etc. We are your label and P.O.S. experts.

Integrated Restaurant Software
Richard Adler
Peter Pouzzano
1402 Bergen Rd.
Fort Lee, NJ 07024
(201) 461-9096; FAX (201) 947-3870

ISO — Insurance Services of San Francisco
Kenneth Johnson, Acct. Exec.
100 Pine St.
San Francisco, CA 94111
(800) 782-9400; FAX (415) 397-5530

Johnson Litho Graphics of Eau Claire Ltd.
Tom Lienhardt, Sales/Mktg.
2219 Galloway St.
Eau Claire, WI 54703
(715) 832-3211; FAX (715) 832-5120

Lazar & Co.
Wayne Lazar, Pres.
404 Mendocino Ave., Suite 200
Santa Rosa, CA 95401
(707) 577-0835; FAX (707) 575-4094

McCormick Distribution and Marketing
Tom McCormick, Pres.
PO Box 1281
Meadow Vista, CA 95722
(916) 878-1214; FAX (916) 878-9215
mdmcbeer@aol.com

Tom McCormick has been involved in the sales and distribution of craft beers for over ten years. Services provided include distribution and market expansion, self-distribution, package design, POS programs, marketing plans, and much more. Increase sales in this ever increasingly competitive market by calling for more information.

Menasha Corp.
Kim E. Dresselhaus, Field Sales Mgr.
Dave Lodle, Customer Service Mgr.
8085 220th St. W.
Lakeville, MN 55044
(612) 469-4451; FAX (612) 469-1068

Micro Brew Express — Beer-of-the-Month Club
Craig Wesley, Pres.
2246 Calle Del Mundo
Santa Clara, CA 95054
(408) 748-9090; FAX (408) 748-9099

Momentum Management
Randy Bryson, Pres.
1720 Willow Creek Cir., Suite 510
Eugene, OR 97402
(503) 485-3907; FAX (503) 485-7372

North Country Smokehouse
Michael Satzow, Pres.
PO Box 1415
Claremont, NH 03743
(800) 258-4304; FAX (603) 543-3016
ncsmokes@cyberportal

Quality manufacturer of Irish bangors, aiydouille, chicken apple sausage, black forest hams, smoked turkey, applewood smoked bacon, Montreal smoked meats. Specializing in mono development for the brewpub industry. Free recipes utilizing our loan products available upon request.

O'Herin Enterprises
Charles O'Herin
PO Box 7002
Tacoma, WA 98407
(206) 761-0443; FAX (206) 761-0443
cmoherin@wolfenet.com

Omniart
Fred Becht
122 N. York Rd., Suite 207
Elmhurst, IL 60126
(708) 530-0040; FAX (708) 530-0047

Phoenixx Ltd.
R. G. Bailey, Pres.
PO Box 1855
New London, NH 03257
(603) 526-2226

Photo Marketing Products Co.
Duane Walsh, Owner
Bill Mathe, Mktg. Dir.
4605 London Rd.
Eau Claire, WI 54701
(715) 835-9310 or (800) 433-3882; FAX (715) 835-3664

Pin Center
Lynn Becker, Owner
Starla Becker, Co-Owner
2408 Las Verdes St.
Las Vegas, NV 89102
(800) 553-9490; FAX (702) 227-6644

R. M. Yates Co. Inc.
Robert Yates, Pres.
4452 Warner Rd.
Cleveland, OH 44105-5958
(216) 441-0900; FAX (216) 441-5608

RASTAL GmbH & Co. KG
Robert Pilaar
Beer Gear, Clark Turner, U.S. representative
(800) 582-9440 or (619) 581-9440
Lindenstraße 12-18, Postfach 1354
Höhr-Grenzhausen, 56203
Germany
(011) 49-26-24/16-220; FAX (011) 49-26-24/16-107

Rixie Paper Products
Kent Adicks, VP Oper.
Jack De Gatis, Special Accts. Mgr.
PO Box 478/10 Quinter St.
Pottstown, PA 19464
(610) 323-9220; FAX (610) 323-6146

Service Training Systems
Robert Welcher, Pres.
360 W. Fifth Ave.
Columbus, OH 43201
(800) 859-7201; FAX (614) 421-1777

Sonoco Engraph Label Group
Thomas Coker, Mktg. Mgr.
Jim Prendergast, VP Sales
8800 South Blvd.
Charlotte, NC 28273
(704) 554-5796; FAX (704) 554-8122

Stout Marketing
Theo Spack Jr., Mktg. Dir.
Richard Slaughter, Sales Mgr.
5425 W. Florissant Ave.
St. Louis, MO 63136
(800) 325-8530; FAX (314) 385-9412

Sun International Trading Ltd.
Ken Armke, Mgr. Giftware
PO Box 2556/3700 Hwy. 421 N.
Wilmington, NC 28402
(800) 325-4880; FAX (910) 343-3388
gift@sun-intl.com

Sun International Trading Ltd. offers stock and custom glassware and steins for the micro- and pub-brewer. Sun International is also an excellent source for genuine European-made growlers.

Swancock Designworks
Judy Babcock
52 Baxter Rd.
Hollis, NH 03049
(603) 465-2015

Valu-Wear
Harry Horne, Sales Mgr.
Lance Dunn, Pres.
815 Seymour St.
Monroe, NC 28110
(800) 277-0031; FAX (800) 309-4778

Vintage F/X
Brian Nase, Pres.
PO Box 7338
Audubon, PA 19407
(800) 851-9463; FAX (610) 631-1592

Walker & Lee Advertising/Design
Kevin Lee, Partner
Anne Walker, Partner
1728 16th St., Suite 202
Boulder, CO 80302
(303) 444-4924; FAX (303) 938-8383

Label/carrier design, advertising, POS, and promotions. W&L has more than twenty years direct experience in the brewing industry with regional and national brewers.

Marketing, Point-of-Sale, and Merchandise Suppliers and Consultants

Winstanley Associates
Carolyn Hapeman, Account Exec.
Nathan Winstanley, Pres.
114 Main St.
Lenoy, MA 01240
(413) 637-9887; FAX (413) 637-2045
Info@isw.com

Winter People
Clay Bonton, Sales & Mktg.
Dale Bouton, Pres.
PO Box 45A/5 Cumberland Rd.
Cumberland, ME 04021
(207) 829-3745; FAX (207) 829-3572
  Full service embroidery, silk screen, and logo design.

Wordenglass & Electricity Inc.
Tim Demmond, National Acct. Mgr.
Jeff Kinsley, National Acct. Mgr.
5600 Collingwood Dr.
Kalamazoo, MI 49004
(616) 345-5005; FAX (616) 345-9670

World Division U.S.A.
Francois Louis, Sr. VP
Marc Parker
11929 Denton Dr.
Dallas, TX 75234
(214) 241-2612; FAX (214) 241-8807
  World Division manufactures banners, flags, pennants, and signage. Our flexibility allows us to produce small runs as well as large ones. Our printing capabilities enable us to make small pieces (9" x 12") as well as large ones (4' x 40' long banners).

Wright Metal Signs Ltd.
Jason Butcher, VP Sales
Lee McCutcheon, Sales Rep.
PO Box 130/2272 Hwy. 6
Freelton, ON L0R 1K0
Canada
(800) 808-9669; FAX (800) 472-5476
  Designer and manufacturer of metal beer signs, screen printed and color, die cut and embossed. Our ability to produce small runs and two-week lead time make us friends to brewers of all sizes. Call one of our knowledgeable sales reps for free samples and to answer all your questions.

15 Malt Suppliers

Malted barley is the primary grain for making beer, although wheat is common, and rice and corn are used in some products. The starches in barley convert to fermentable sugars during the malting process. The extract from the malted barley gives beer its flavor, body, head, and color. Selecting the barley malt, or "malt" as it is commonly referred to, is therefore one of the most important tasks in assuring that the beer you brew has the flavor profile you seek.

If you decide to brew using malt extract, be aware that barley syrup is a different product than malt extract. Also, understand that food-grade malt extract is inferior to brewing-grade malt extract.

Until recently, getting maltsters to supply their products in small quantities was one of the many problems facing small-scale brewers. Fortunately, this situation has changed with the increased number of microbreweries and brewpubs.

Whether your needs are for grain malts or malt syrup, the following companies are sensitive to the requirements of small-scale breweries and are more than happy to work with you. When selecting a maltster, apply the same rule as with any other aspect of your brewery: Check the references. Can the maltster provide the best product for your beer style? Is he or she quick to respond to your order? The more information you can gather, the better chance you have of picking the best maltster for your business and product.

When buying malt, it is also important to ask for an analysis. This will provide you with information on potential extract yield, an important factor in cost-effective brewing. Also, like any agricultural crop, barley is sensitive to weather, fertilizers, and handling. Within a particular barley type, there may be differences from season to season that can affect your brew. A good maltster should provide you with the information to make a sound purchase of the kinds of malts your products require.

ADM Malting
Dr. Bruce Sebree, Technical Dir.
Jim Revell, VP Admin.
4666 Faries Pkwy., Box 1470
Decatur, IL 62525
(217) 424-5200; FAX (217) 424-5447
62854730/s=sebree@eln.attmail.com

Alexander's Sun Country Malt Products
Thomas Alexander
18678 N. Hwy. 99
Acampo, CA 95220
(209) 334-9112; FAX (209) 334-1311

Alexander's Sun Country Malt Products is a supplier of: specialty malt extract (pale, amber, wheat, and dark); custom processed malt extracts; grains from around the world; and custom packaged malt products (drums, pails, and cans).

Aspera/Jaenicke & Co. LLC
Katrin A. Jaenicke
Harold Schwarz
PO Box 1940
Yakima, WA 98907
(509) 457-6808; FAX (509) 457-1187

Beeston Malt Co.
John Sutcliffe, Sales Dir.
Elliot Industrial Estate
Arbroath, Angus DD11 2NJ
Scotland, United Kingdom
01241-870431; FAX 01241-874251

Malt Suppliers

Bioriginal Food and Science Corp.
David Powell, Representative
411 Downey Rd., Suite 1
Saskatoon, SK S7N 4L8
Canada
(306) 469-4437

Bioriginal malt barley and malt extracts are organically cultivated and processed in strict compliance with the exacting standards of the Organic Crop Improvement Association (O.C.I.A.) International, the globally recognized third-party organic certification agency. Bioriginal's malt products are made with the renowned Saskatchewan Harrington two-row barley.

Brewing Products (U.K.) Ltd.
Les Shield, Dir.
Doug Duthie, Export Mgr.
The Malt Extract Factory
Kirkliston, Scotland EH28 9DR
United Kingdom
011 (44) 31 333 3261; FAX 011 (44) 31 333 1394

Briess Malting Co.
Mary Anne Gruber, Dir. Brewing Services
Roger Briess, Pres.
29 S. Columbia St.
Chilton, WI 53014
(414) 849-7711; FAX (414) 849-4277
(212) 247-0780; FAX (212) 333-5170

Briess Malting Co. manufactures whole kernel and preground (Brewer's Grist) malts, pregelatinized brewing flakes, and CBW (Concentrated Brewers Wort) in both liquid and dry powder forms. All malts, extracts, and flakes are available to pub- and microbreweries in small or large lots. Pilot brewing services available. Call today for more information!

Canada Malting Co. Ltd.
Keith Potter, Pres.
Jeff Parks, Coordinator Logistics and Customer Service
21 Four Seasons Pl., Suite 325
Toronto, ON M9B 6J8
Canada
(416) 620-7575; FAX (416) 620-5004

THE BEESTON MALTING COMPANY

A division of

MORAY FIRTH MALTINGS

Scottish Floor Malts of Unhurried Precision

Pipkin Pale • Maris Otter • Halcyon Pale • Amber • Brown • Caramalt • Wheat • Pale Crystal • Crystal • Dark Crystal • Pale Chocolate • Chocolate • Black • Roasted Barley

Other Malts available upon request

Imported By

Consolidated Beverages   (800) 368-9363

Canada Malting is Canada's leading producer and distributor of malted grain since 1902, supplying top quality Pilsen and specialty malts in both bags and bulk lots. Convenient distribution centers in Montreal, Toronto, Calgary, and Vancouver service both domestic and export customers.

Cask Brewing Systems
Peter Love, Pres.
5925 12th St. S.E., Suite 225
Calgary, AB T2H 2M3
Canada
(403) 640-4677; FAX (403) 640-4680
caskbru@ibm.net or info@cask.com
http://www.cask.com

Cask Brewing Systems is the exclusive North American distributor of Edme Ltd. bulk malt extracts. With over one hundred years of production experience, Edme now operates the world's newest state-of-the-art malt extract plant. We carry a full range of bulk extract: lager, MEQ, ale, dark ale, wheat, and stout.

Consolidated Beverages America Ltd.
Ron Gamble
PO Box 714
Medina, WA 98039-0714
(800) 368-9363; FAX (206) 635-9364
conbev@halcyon.com
http://www.halcyon.com/conbev/coopers.htm

Since 1984 Consolidated Beverages and its affiliates have represented Coopers Malt Extract for the North American market. Produced in Australia by Coopers Brewery, Coopers Home Brew Kits are unmatched in worldwide sales. In 1994 Consolidated began importing grain from Beeston Malting Company, a subsidiary of Moray Firth Malting of Scotland. Beeston offers a wide variety of pale, specialty, and floor malts that can be blended to meet your specifications.

Crisp Malt
William Crisp
32 Ayrault St.
Newport, RI 02840
(401) 846-6925; FAX (401) 846-4209

Two-row and British malt. Ranging from floor-made pale malts to chocolate — best service and quality.

Quality, Service & Integrity to the Brewing Industry Since 1876

BRIESS = MALT

WHOLE KERNEL & PREGROUND MALTS
- PALE (BREWERS) MALT
- CARAMEL MALT
- MUNICH (HIGH-DRIED)
- SPECIAL ROAST MALT
- WHEAT (WEIZEN) MALT
- BLACK (STOUT) BARLEY
- CARAPILS® (DEXTRINE)
- ROASTED BARLEY
- VICTORY MALT
- BLACK (PATENT) MALT
- CHOCOLATE MALT
- RYE (ROGGEN) MALT
- VIENNA MALT

CBW® (CONCENTRATED BREWERS WORT®)
- BREWERS GOLD (LIQUID & DRY)
- BAVARIAN WEIZEN (LIQUID & DRY)
- PORTER (LIQUID ONLY)
- SPARKLING AMBER (LIQUID & DRY)
- TRADITIONAL DARK (LIQUID & DRY)
- PURE MALT COLOR (LIQUID & DRY)

PREGELATINIZED BREWER'S FLAKES
- FLAKED BARLEY
- FLAKED RICE
- FLAKED CORN
- FLAKED RYE
- FLAKED OATS
- FLAKED WHEAT

BRIESS ALSO OFFERS PILOT BREWING SERVICES!

Briess Malting Company
29 SOUTH COLUMBIA ST. ■ CHILTON, WI 53014-0226
TEL: (414) 849-7711 ■ FAX: (414) 849-4277

Malt Suppliers

Crosby and Baker
Robert P. Makuch, Brewery Products Mgr.
Seth Schneider, General Mgr.
999 Main Rd.
Westport, MA 02790
(800) 999-2440; FAX (508) 636-4170

CZ Tech
Leon Meuch
333 S. Cross St.
Wheaton, IL 60187
(708) 668-7886; FAX (708) 668-5076
73073.2625@compuserve.com

DCV ULTRAMALT
James A. Doncheck, Exec. VP
Keith Gretenhart, VP Sales and Technical Services
1035 S. Seventh St.
Manitowoc, WI 54220
(414) 682-MALT; FAX (414) 684-5519

ULTRAMALT® is a novel specialty malt containing high levels of malt and beer flavor precursors used for producing super premium specialty beers or full-flavored, lower-calorie, nonalcoholic, and lower alcohol beers.

Edme Ltd.
James Hibbins, Buisness Delv. Mgr.
Mistley
Manningtree, Essex CO11 1HG
United Kingdom
(206) 393-725; FAX (206) 393-6699
edme@dial.pipex.com
http://www.ip7.co.uk/edme

F. H. Steinbart Co.
John DeBenedetti, Gen. Mgr.
Fred Czuba, Wholesale Mgr.
234 S.E. 12th Ave.
Portland, OR 97214
(503) 232-8793; FAX (503) 238-1649

G. W. Kent Inc.
Randall Reichwage
3667 Morgan Rd.
Ann Arbor, MI 48108
(313) 572-1300; FAX (313) 572-0097

G.W. Kent Inc. is the exclusive North American importer of Durst Malz German two-row malts.

Gambrinus Malting Corp.
Robert Liedl, General Mgr.
R.R. No. 3, C-86, Palisades
Armstrong, BC V0E 1B0
Canada
(604) 546-8911; FAX (604) 546-8798

Gambrinus Malting uses only the plumpest two-row barley to meet the pale and specialty malt needs of the small- to medium-sized brewery. We are producers of low-protein, pale malt, Munich malt, wheat malt, afte pale malt, ESB pale malt, honey malt, and custom-made malts upon request. We distribute black and caramel malt from Weyermann maltings of Germany.

Glatt Bros. Brewing Co.
Paul Glatt, Pres.
John Glatt, Sec./Treas.
151 Thompson Rd.
London, ON NS2 247
Canada
(519) 668-1385; FAX (519) 668-1385

Grain Millers Inc.
David S. Ritchie, Dir. Brewing Services
Darren Schubert, Dir. Sales & Mktg.
625 W. Fourth St.
Eugene, OR 97402
(503) 687-8000; FAX (503) 687-2155
eugene!gmieug!dave@gmil.attmail.com
http://www.rio.com/~gmisales/gmihome.html

Proud suppliers to the world's Great Brewers

Canada Malting
MONTREAL, TORONTO, THUNDER BAY, WINNIPEG, CALGARY AND VANCOUVER

Great Western Malting Co.
Lee Ann Stewart, Sales Specialist
Bernie Duenwald, Cust. Service
PO Box 1529/1701 Industrial Way
Vancouver, WA 98668-1529
(800) 426-1654; FAX (306) 696-8354

Great Western Malting Co. supplies domestic two-row and specialty malts in fifty-pound sacks and in bulk. We also carry a full line of the Hugh Baird U.K. specialty products in twenty-five kilo sacks. We have warehouses throughout the United States for prompt delivery.

Hugh Baird & Sons Ltd.
R. E. Martin, Export Dir.
Diana Montgomerie
Station Maltings
Witham, Essex R416 2AP
England
44-1376-513566; FAX 44-1376-518171

J. M. Swank Co.
Laurie Rath, Mktg. Asst.
Mark Lobb, Prod. Mktg. Mgr.
PO Box 365
North Liberty, IA 52317
(319) 626-3683 or (800) 593-6375; FAX (319) 626-3662

Malt & Hop Distributors of Canada Inc.
David Boal, Pres.
Andre Kuttis, Customer Service Mgr.
1250-B Reid St., Unit 2
Richmond Hill, ON L4B 1G3
Canada
(905) 881-9074; FAX (905) 881-9074

Malt Products Corp.
Joe Hickenbottom, VP
88 Market St.
Saddle Brook, NJ 07663
(800) 526-0180 or (201) 845-4420; FAX (201) 845-0028

Leading supplier of all types and varieties of domestic and imported malt extracts, liquid and dry. Serving the microbreweries, brewpubs and brew-on-premises units. Also provides various brewing adjuncts and grains.

COOPERS BREWERY
AUSTRALIA'S FINEST

Available in:
Unhopped: *Light, Amber and Dark.*
Hopped: *Lager, Draught, Real Ale, Stout, Bitter, Classic Old Dark Ale.*
Coopers yeast is also available.

For more information and a distributor near you call: 1-800-368-9363.

Malt Suppliers

Malteries Franco-Belges
Bruno Cothenet
33 Rue Du Louvre
Paris, 75002
France
33-1-44-88-16-21; FAX 33-1-44-88-16-28

Malteries Franco-Belges is part of the Soufflet Group, the world's largest malt exporter and the only French producer of caramel and roasted malts. Ninety percent of the countries producing beer use our different malts, proving our ability to supply materials adapted to every kind of beer.

MHD Canada Inc.
David Boal, Dir. of Oper.
1250 Reid St., Suite 2
Richmond Hill, ON L4B 1G3
Canada
(800) 643-6258; FAX (905) 881-9074

Munton and Fison PLC
A. J. Janes, Mktg. Mgr.
Cedars Maltings
Stowmarket, Suffolk IP14 2AG
United Kingdom
(01449) 612401; FAX (01449) 677800

Pauls Malt Ltd.
Andrew J. Crane, Export Mgr.
PO Box 54 Kentford
Newmarket, Suffolk CB8 7QU
0638-751100; FAX 0638-751160

Suppliers of quality U.K. malts to breweries and distilleries throughout the world. Product range: Pilsen, ale, mild, crystal, caramel, brown, chocolate, black, and peated malts.

Premier Malt Products Inc.
Susan E. Graydon, Sales and Mktg. Mgr.
M. Stuart Andreas, Pres.
PO Box 36359
Grosse Pointe, MI 48236
(800) 521-1057 or (313) 822-2200; FAX (313) 822-9511

Schreier Malting Co.
Tom Testwuide Jr., Specialty Malt Prod. Mgr.
Keith Gretenhart, VP Sales and Technical Services
PO Box 59
Sheboygan, WI 53082-0059
(800) 669-MALT; FAX (414) 458-9034

Sonoco Engraph Label Group
Thomas Coker, Mktg. Mgr.
Jim Prendergast, VP Sales
8800 South Blvd.
Charlotte, NC 28273
(704) 554-5796; FAX (704) 554-8122

Specialty Products International Ltd.
Leigh P. Beadle, Pres.
PO Box 784
Chapel Hill, NC 27514
(919) 929-4277; FAX (919) 929-8848

We are a domestic producer of the world's lightest malt extract. We produce malt extract only for the brewpub, microbrewery, and home brewing industries, in pails, drums, and cans. We supply dried yeast fully tested by us for freshness, viability, and purity. We advise on extremely inexpensive brewpub design.

Sunrise Milling
Andy Didion
210 Grell Lane
Johnson Creek, WI 53038
(414) 699-2771; FAX (414) 699-3622

United Canadian Malt Ltd.
J. M. Smith
843 Park St. S.
Peterborough, ON K9J 3V1
Canada
(705) 876-9110; FAX (705) 876-9118

Premier Malt Products, Inc.
Specialists in Malt Extract for Craft-Breweries

For more information contact:

Susan Graydon
Premier Malt Products
P. O. Box 36359
Grosse Point, MI 48236

Call Toll Free:
1-800-521-1057
In Michigan: 313-822-2200

Malt Suppliers

VAFAC Inc. (Virginia Food and Craft)
Philip H. Pryor, Pres.
212 Freedom Ct.
Fredericksburg, VA 22408
(540) 898-3202; FAX (540) 898-8442

Weyermann, Heinz GmbH
Sabine Weyermann, Pres./Sales Mgr.
Thomas Kraus-Weyermann, Managing Dir./Sales Mgr.
Brennerstrasse 17 - 19
Bamberg, 96052
Germany
01149-951/93220-33; FAX 01149-951/35604

Weyermann is a family run malting company, which produces an enormous range of specialty malt made out of only Bavarian-grown two-row barley. We ship all over the world, in twenty-pound containers, bulk, or in fifty-pound bags, to brewpubs, microbreweries, and macrobreweries. Just give us a call; we do speak English!

16 Hop Suppliers

Hops are important for the bitterness, flavor, and aroma of beer. The timing, quantity of hops added, and the quality of the hops are key factors in achieving distinct characteristics in a brew. Hops are grown primarily in the western United States, Belgium, Germany, Slovenia, Czech Republic, United Kingdom, and New Zealand.

In the past, buying less than a two-hundred-pound bale of hops was a problem for micro- and pubbrewers. Today, however, hop suppliers — like those listed in this chapter — routinely sell smaller quantities of whole hops, hop pellets, and hop extracts.

A cautionary note for buying hops: Know the seasonal variance, as hops can become scarce toward the end of their season. Furthermore, the same variety of hops from the same growing area will vary in quality and brewing value from year to year (or even field to field). To ensure consistent beers, request a certified analysis of the hops you want to purchase from your hop supplier.

It is also important to be aware of natural (or unnatural) forces affecting the hop crop. The United States' drought in 1988 reduced the available quantities of certain hops. Likewise, the Soviet nuclear accident at Chernobyl in 1986 affected some European hops, making them scarce for a while. Fortunately, a knowledgeable hop supplier can advise you on market conditions and the best hops for your beer.

Beverage Consult International Inc.
Finn B. Knudsen, Pres.
Evergreen Plaza/4602 Plettner Lane, Suite 2E
Evergreen, CO 80439-7300
(303) 674-2251; FAX (303) 727-6555

Consulting in all technical and management aspects of brewing. Engineering solutions to condensation control in buildings.

Crosby and Baker
Robert P. Makuch, Brewery Products Mgr.
Seth Schneider, General Mgr.
999 Main Rd.
Westport, MA 02790
(800) 999-2440; FAX (508) 636-4170

F. H. Steinbart Co.
John DeBenedetti, Gen. Mgr.
Fred Czuba, Wholesale Mgr.
234 S.E. 12th Ave.
Portland, OR 97214
(503) 232-8793; FAX (503) 238-1649

Freshops
36180 Kings Valley Hwy.
Philomath, OR 97370
(503) 929-2736

Fromm, Mayer-Bass Inc.
Linda Haywood, Microbrewery Sales
Rosemarie Bach-Jaenicke, VP/Gen. Mgr.
PO Box 2889/402 E. Yakima Ave., Suite 1070
Yakima, WA 98907
(509) 248-4084 or (800) FMB-HOPS; FAX (509) 453-6656

Established in Germany in 1845, Fromm, Mayer-Bass Inc. has kept pace into the 1990s by supplying the world's breweries with quality hop products. From the microbrewer to the largest brewer, Fromm, Mayer-Bass Inc. is pleased to be a part of this exciting industry.

G. W. Kent Inc.
Randall Reichwage
3667 Morgan Rd.
Ann Arbor, MI 48108
(313) 572-1300; FAX (313) 572-0097

G. W. Kent Inc. is the exclusive North American importer of Durst Malz German two-row malts.

German Agricultural Marketing Board — CMA
Margaret C. Eckert, Dir. Trade Relations
950 Third Ave., Ninth Floor
New York, NY 10022
(212) 753-5900; FAX (212) 826-3278

Glatt Bros. Brewing Co.
Paul Glatt, Pres.
John Glatt, Sec./Treas.
151 Thompson Rd.
London, ON NS2 247
Canada
(519) 668-1385; FAX (519) 668-1385

Hop Growers of America Inc.
Sean McGree, Exec. Dir.
PO Box 9218
Yakima, WA 98909
(509) 248-7043; FAX (509) 248-7044

Hoptech
Mark Garetz, Owner
3015 Hopyard Rd., Suite E
Pleasanton, CA 94588
(510) 426-1450; FAX (510) 426-9191
mgaretz@hoptech.com
http://www.hoptech.com

Hopunion USA Inc.
Ralph Olson and Greg Lewis
PO Box 9697
Yakima, WA 98909
(509) 457-3200; FAX (509) 453-1551

IDD Process & Packaging Inc.
Jeff Gunn, Pres.
Tom Thilert, Sales Dir.
646 Flinn Ave.
Moorpark, CA 93021
(800) 621-4144 or (805) 529-9890; FAX (805) 529-9282
idd2jeff@aol.com

Brewery process and packaging system design and manufacturing engineers. This includes turnkey brewpub and microbreweries, kegging systems, tank valves, yeast propagation and management systems, deaeration, filtration and pasteurization systems, hops (leaf, pellet, and extract), cleaners, sanitizers, brewing and fermenting aids. Full-service formula and systems brewery engineering and consultation.

J. M. Swank Co.
Laurie Rath, Mktg. Asst.
Mark Lobb, Prod. Mktg. Mgr.
PO Box 365
North Liberty, IA 52317
(319) 626-3683 or (800) 593-6375; FAX (319) 626-3662

Jaenicke Inc.
Albert Jaenicke
Harold Schwarz
PO Box 2008
Yakima, WA 98907
(509) 457-6808; FAX (509) 457-1187

John I. Haas Inc.
Kim Ehrman
John Gorman
1112 N. 16th Ave.
Yakima, WA 98902
(509) 248-4188 or (800) 289-4677; FAX (509) 452-1863

GROWER • DEALER • PROCESSOR

HOPUNION

- **HOPS**
- **HOP PELLETS**
- **HOP EXTRACTS**

The "MICROBREW INDUSTRY SPECIALISTS"

HOPUNION USA INC.
1(509) 457-3200

P.O. BOX 9697
YAKIMA WA 98909 USA

Hop Suppliers

Lupofresh Inc.
John Mueller, Mgr.
Harold Doerge, Pres.
PO Box 36/214 Ivy Rd.
Wapato, WA 98951
(509) 877-2194; FAX (509) 877-4032

Lupofresh Limited
A. H. Davis, Dir.
138 Alexandra Rd.
Wimbledon, London SW19 7JX
United Kingdom
0180-947-8551; FAX 0181-879-0589

International hop merchants supplying the finest aroma and bittering hops and hop extracts. We specialize in the growing and marketing of the traditional English varieties of Fuggles and Goldings, and the dual purpose varieties Northdown and Challenger, plus all the new English varieties such as First Gold and Pheonix.

MHD Canada Inc.
David Boal, Dir. of Oper.
1250 Reid St., Suite 2
Richmond Hill, ON L4B 1G3
Canada
(800) 643-6258; FAX (905) 881-9074

Hopsteiner

Extracts • Powder • Pellets
Hops • HopFarming

Serving the entire brewing industry with the finest hops and hop products

655 Madison Ave., New York, NY 10021
Phone 212-838-8900. Cable Address: "Hopsteiner" New York.
Teletype: 710-581-2274 FAX: 212-593-4238

S. S. Steiner, Inc.

Morris Hanbury Jackson Le May Ltd.
W. McEwan-Cargill, Chief Exec.
J. R. Smith, Office Sales Mgr.
Nettlestead Oast, Paddock Wood
Tonbridge, Kent TN12 6DA
United Kingdom
(44) 892-835155; FAX (44) 892-836003

Specializing in custom packaging for the microbrewery/brewpub. Suppliers of leaf hops, pellets, whole hop plugs, domestic, English, and European varieties. Hop production/buying consultants.

Morris Hanbury USA Inc.
Gerard W. Ch. Lemmens, Exec. VP
Rebecca Bassett, Administrative Asst.
PO Box 1548/402 E. Yakima Ave.
Yakima, WA 98907
(509) 457-6699; FAX (509) 452-9468

Morris Hanbury has been Hop Merchants since 1773, specializing in custom packaging for the microbreweries and brewpubs. The company is a supplier of leaf hops, hop pellets and whole hop plugs in U.S.A., England, and European varieties. Hop production and buying consultation is also available.

New Zealand Hop Marketing Board
Tom Inglis, Board Chairman
Mieke Van Drunen, Board Secretary
PO Box 3205, Richmond
Nelson
New Zealand
(64) 03-544-1151; FAX (64) 03-544-6007

New Zealand Hop Marketing Board, American Region
Finn Knudsen, Pres.
Tom Inglis, Chairman
Evergreen Plaza/4602 Plettner Lane, Suite 2D
Evergreen, CO 80439-7300
(303) 674-2251; FAX (303) 727-6555

Leaf hops, pellets, hop extracts, and other hop products pesticide free from New Zealand.

S. S. Steiner Inc.
Martin Ungewitter, VP
Scott Harris
655 Madison Ave.
New York, NY 10021
(212) 838-8900; FAX (212) 593-4238 or (509) 457-4368

Steiner is a full-service worldwide grower, processor, and dealer in hops and hop products.

Hop Suppliers

Sonoco Engraph Label Group
Thomas Coker, Mktg. Mgr.
Jim Prendergast, VP Sales
8800 South Blvd.
Charlotte, NC 28273
(704) 554-5796; FAX (704) 554-8122

Wigan Richardson International Ltd.
Chris Barker, Dir.
Chris Daws, Mgr.
National Westminster Bank Chambers/Church Rd.,
Paddock Wood
Tonbridge, Kent TN12 6EP
United Kingdom
(189) 283-2235; FAX (189) 283-6008
   International hop merchant. Suppliers of traditional English aroma hops and hop pellets (Type 90, Plugs), hop oils, extracts, emulsions.

17 Yeast Suppliers and Laboratories

Yeast is the fermentation agent in beer which, upon metabolizing the sugars from the wort, produces alcohol. In addition, yeast affects the flavor, aroma, body, and carbonation level of a beer.

You can obtain yeast in both dry and liquid forms from a number of different suppliers. Some breweries have successfully recultured and reused particularly hardy yeasts for hundreds of generations. However, breweries should not reuse other yeasts more than once or twice. (A bad or contaminated yeast slurry can ruin a batch of beer, potentially costing you thousands of dollars.)

While you can switch the brand of malt or hops you use and keep a very similar, if not identical, flavor profile, using a different yeast strain guarantees you a different beer.

Yeast is a living microbiological organism. Variations in temperature, pitching rate, or ingredients used could affect its performance. A thorough understanding of your yeast and knowledge of the conditions under which it performs best are essential for creating a high-quality, consistent beer.

Listed here are companies that have laboratory facilities to propagate various yeast strains. These companies generally prefer to supply yeast in small quantities.

Center for Brewing Studies
Dr. Joseph Owades, Dir.
3097 Wood Valley Rd.
Sonoma, CA 95476
(707) 935-1919; FAX (707) 935-1750

Consolidated Beverages America Ltd.
Ron Gamble
PO Box 714
Medina, WA 98039-0714
(800) 368-9363; FAX (206) 635-9364
conbev@halcyon.com
http://www.halcyon.com/conbev/coopers.htm

Since 1984 Consolidated Beverages and its affiliates have represented Coopers Malt Extract for the North American market. Produced in Australia by Coopers Brewery, Coopers Home Brew Kits are unmatched in worldwide sales. In 1994 Consolidated began importing grain from Beeston Malting Company, a subsidiary of Moray Firth Malting of Scotland. Beeston offers a wide variety of pale, specialty, and floor malts that can be blended to meet your specifications.

ETS Laboratories
Gordon Burns, Pres.
Rebecca Newman, Dir.
899 Adams St., Suite A
St. Helena, CA 94574
(707) 963-4806; FAX (707) 963-1054

ETS provides prompt, accurate, and cost-effective analytical services to the brewing industry.

G. W. Kent Inc.
Randall Reichwage
3667 Morgan Rd.
Ann Arbor, MI 48108
(313) 572-1300; FAX (313) 572-0097

G. W. Kent Inc. is the exclusive North American importer of Durst Malz German two-row malts.

Glatt Bros. Brewing Co.
Paul Glatt, Pres.
John Glatt, Sec./Treas.
151 Thompson Rd.
London, ON NS2 247
Canada
(519) 668-1385; FAX (519) 668-1385

J. M. Swank Co.
Laurie Rath, Mktg. Asst.
Mark Lobb, Prod. Mktg. Mgr.
PO Box 365
North Liberty, IA 52317
(319) 626-3683 or (800) 593-6375; FAX (319) 626-3662

Lallemand Inc.
Gordan Specht
Clayton Cone, Tech. Dir.
PO Box 5512
Petaluma, CA 94955-5512
(415) 492-0642; FAX (415) 492-0642

Lallemand, a specialty active dried yeast producer, offers four exceptionally clean active dried ale yeast. These strains have been selected and isolated from commercial breweries. All four easy-to-use top-fermenting strains may be used in home brewing, brew on premise, and in breweries to ferment a variety of ales.

Scott Laboratories Inc.
Tom Anders, VP
Bruce Scott, Pres.
2220 Pine View Way
Petaluma, CA 94954
(707) 765-6666; FAX (707) 765-6674

VELO plate and frame and diatomaceous earth filter systems, SEITZ filter sheets, LALLEMAND-UVAFERM active dry brewers yeast, BRAUEREI-TECHNIK STABIFIX silica gel stabilizer, CoMAC keg-filling systems.

Scott Laboratories Ltd.
1845 Sandstone Manor, Unit 14
Pickering, ON L1W 3X9
Canada

VELO plate and frame and diatomaceous earth filter systems, SEITZ filter sheets, LALLEMAND-UVAFERM active dry brewers yeast, BRAUEREI-TECHNIK STABIFIX silica gel stabilizer, CoMAC keg-filling systems.

Siebel Institute of Technology
Ilse Shelton, VP Laboratory Services
Dr. Joe Power, VP
4055 W. Peterson Ave.
Chicago, IL 60646-6001
(312) 279-0966; FAX (312) 463-7688

Offering complete laboratory services, including microbiological, chemical, and physical tests as well as descriptive flavor evaluations of beer and ingredients. Also supply liquid yeast from our yeast bank containing numerous different strains.

Sonoco Engraph Label Group
Thomas Coker, Mktg. Mgr.
Jim Prendergast, VP Sales
8800 South Blvd.
Charlotte, NC 28273
(704) 554-5796; FAX (704) 554-8122

StabiFix Brauerer — Technik GmbH
Tom Anders
Martin Vagners
2220 Pine View Way
Petaluma, CA 94955-4559
(707) 765-6666; FAX (707) 765-6674

Wyeast Laboratories
David W. Logsdon, Pres./Brewer
Teri Byrne, Cust. Service
PO Box 425
Mount Hood, OR 97041
(503) 354-1335; FAX (503) 354-3449

Yeast Culture Kit Co.
Martin Schiller, Owner
11450 Schuylkill Rd.
Rockville, MD 20852
(800) 742-2110; FAX (301) 231-8211

18 Miscellaneous Ingredient and Material Suppliers

Aspera/Jaenicke & Co. LLC
Katrin A. Jaenicke
Harold Schwarz
PO Box 1940
Yakima, WA 98907
(509) 457-6808; FAX (509) 457-1187

fla-vor \fla-vŏr\ n: distinctive taste: characteristic quality.
california brands flavors
\'kal-ǒ-fŏr-nyǒ 'brands\
n: an exceptional flavor company, native to the state of california, principle purveyor of fruit, herb and spice flavors to **micro breweries.**

California Brands Flavors, Inc.
411 Pendleton Way. Oakland. CA 94621
Tel. 510.562-2371 FAX 510.562-1279

Bioriginal Food and Science Corp.
David Powell, Representative
411 Downey Rd., Suite 1
Saskatoon, SK S7N 4L8
Canada
(306) 469-4437

Bioriginal malt barley and malt extracts are organically cultivated and processed in strict compliance with the exacting standards of the Organic Crop Improvement Association (O.C.I.A.) International, the globally recognized third-party organic certification agency. Bioriginal's malt products are made with the renowned Saskatchewan Harrington two-row barley.

California Brands Flavors Inc.
Chaim Gur-Arieh, Pres.
Avonne J. Ruiz, Executive Asst.
411 Pendleton Way
Oakland, CA 94612
(510) 562-2371; FAX (510) 562-1279

California Brands has been supplying flavors to microbreweries since the industry evolved. Working together with microbreweries, we formulated a line of natural flavors designed for flavoring beer and other malt-based beverages. We have the expertise and state-of-the-art knowledge for compounding flavors. Further, our thorough understanding of the process involved in brewing enables us to adjust our flavor formulations to be compatible with beer.

Canadian Liquid Air Ltd.
Donald Fraser
3004 54th Ave. S.E.
Calgary, AB T2C 0A7
Canada
(403) 777-4700; FAX (403) 777-4727

Miscellaneous Ingredient and Material Suppliers

Crosby and Baker
Robert P. Makuch, Brewery Products Mgr.
Seth Schneider, General Mgr.
999 Main Rd.
Westport, MA 02790
(800) 999-2440; FAX (508) 636-4170

Crystalite Corp.
Michael C. Sammartino, Pres.
David C. Sammartino, VP
17 Industrial Dr.
Smithfield, RI 02917
(401) 231-1111; FAX (401) 231-9470

Dayton Superior Corp.
Jan Hawkins
John A. Gill
402 S. First St.
Oregon, IL 61061
(800) 745-3707; FAX (815) 732-2866

Drinktec USA Ltd.
Nicolas Haase, Sales and Mktg. Mgr.
JoAnn Seeger, Office Mgr.
100 Railroad Dr., Suite B
Ivyland, PA 18974
(215) 953-9335; FAX (215) 953-8636
drinktec@aol.com

   Serving the beverage industry worldwide; equipment, parts, systems, expendable supplies, promotional articles. A member of BrauHaase International Management Group.

Edgar A. Weber & Co.
S. Turyna, Sales Admin.
R. P. Passaglia, VP
549 Palwaukee Dr.
Wheeling, IL 60090
(800) 558-9078; FAX (708) 215-2073

Equipment Enterprises Inc.
Alan J. McGinley, Sales
1875 Graves Rd.
Norcross, GA 30093
(800) 221-3681; FAX (770) 368-0587

Europe 1992 Connection
Ulrich Kostuch, Pres.
1966 Davids View W.
West Bend, WI 53095
(414) 338-9898; FAX (414) 335-2700

Want great stuff? It's as easy as 1, 2, 3 down.

At Crosby and Baker, we carry a full line of the finest ingredients and supplies for your microbrewery or brewpub...like

**Brewing Aids from
J. E. Siebel Sons Co.**

Crosby & Baker—craft brewing excellence made easier by a great vendor.

CROSBY & BAKER LTD
We Serve the Brewer

Wholesale Brewing Supplies
Westport, MA • Atlanta, GA
1-800-999-2440

Miscellaneous Ingredient and Material Suppliers

Five Star Products and Services LLC
Charles Talley
6731 E. 50th St.
Commerce City, CO 80022
(800) 782-7019 or (303) 287-0186; FAX (303) 287-0391
http://www.fivestaraf.com

General Filtration, Division of Lee Chemicals Ltd.
Ed Bridge, Mktg. Mgr.
1119 Yonge St.
Toronto, ON M4W 2L7
Canada
(416) 924-9349; FAX (416) 960-8750

Grace Davison
Barry Rappe, Mktg. Mgr.
Michael Rosenberg, Dir. Mktg.
PO Box 2117
Baltimore, MD 21203-2117
(410) 659-9041; FAX (410) 659-9213

Grain Millers Inc.
David S. Ritchie, Dir. Brewing Services
Darren Schubert, Dir. Sales and Marketing
625 W. Fourth St.
Eugene, OR 97402
(503) 687-8000; FAX (503) 687-2155
eugene!gmieug!dave@gmil.attmail.com
http://www.rio.com/~gmisales/gmihome.html

Heinrich Ceramic Decal Inc.
Michael Foley, VP Sales
Jada Lugo, Dir. Customer Relations
150 Goddard Memorial Dr.
Worcester, MA 01603
(508) 797-4800; FAX (508) 799-9365

American manufacturer of high-quality custom water-slide and heat-release decals for the glass and ceramic decorating industry.

Hoptech
Mark Garetz, Owner
3015 Hopyard Rd., Suite E
Pleasanton, CA 94588
(510) 426-1450; FAX (510) 426-9191
mgaretz@hoptech.com
http://www.hoptech.com

Simply The Best Brewery Cleaning Products

The new star of Five Star Affiliates' product line is **PBW**. This revolutionary cleaner has achieved excellent commercial acceptance.

Its unique formulation of buffers and mild alkalies means it is safe on hands, and performs better than caustic cleaners.

The revolutionary benefits of **PBW**:

- Environmentally friendly
- Safe to handle
- Non-hazardous & Non-corrosive
- Effective at cold temperatures
- Safe on all surfaces
- Excellent hard water tolerance
- Replaces caustic soda cleaners
- Removes beerstone, protein soil and staining

PBW is just one of the revolutionary products being developed by Five Star chemists.

Five Star seeks to become your partner in creating, implementing and managing your cleaning and sanitizing program. Working **with** you to better serve all of your cleaning and equipment needs.

For information call **800-782-7019** or 303-287-0186

Five Star Products and Services, LLC.

"Simply The Best"
Brewery Cleaning Products

Maintain a Five Star seal of excellence by utilizing our full line of cleaning and equipment products

Miscellaneous Ingredient and Material Suppliers

VELO plate and frame diatomaceons parth filter systems, Seitz filter sheets, LALLEMAJO-UUAFERM active dry brewers yeast, BRAUEREI-TECHNIK STABIFIX silica gel stabilizers, CoMAC keg-filling systems.

IDD Process & Packaging Inc.
Jeff Gunn, Pres.
Tom Thilert, Sales Dir.
646 Flinn Ave
Moorpark, CA 93021
(800) 621-4144 or (805) 529-9890; FAX (805) 529-9282
idd2jeff@aol

Brewery process and packaging system design and manufacturing engineers. This includes turnkey brewpub and microbreweries, kegging systems, tank valves, yeast propagation and management systems, deaeration, filtration and pasteurization systems, hops (leaf, pellet, and extract), cleaners, sanitizers, brewing and fermenting aids. Full-service formula and systems brewery engineering and consultation.

Ion Exchange Prod. Inc.
Irving Reichstein, CEO
4834 S. Halsted St.
Chicago, IL 60609-4418
(312) 254-1300; FAX (312) 847-7243

ISP (International Specialty Products)
Rolf D. Schmidt, Sr. Sales Eng./Beverage Specialist
1919 S. Highland Ave., Suite 124-D
Lombard, IL 60148
(800) 323-2272 or (708) 932-4022; FAX (708) 495-0245

James Vickers & Co. Ltd.
M. Grace, Bus. Development Dir.
Dallow St.
Burton Upon Trent, DE14 2PLO
United Kingdom
01283-563268; FAX 01283-511472

Le Vintage Collection (Designer Labels)
Larry Bossy, Owner
2745 Pierre De Froment
Carignan, PQ J3L 4A7
Canada
(514) 658-3664; FAX (514) 658-3664

Loeffler Chemical Corp.
Dirk Loeffler, Tech. Dir.
Tim Reilly, Sales Mgr.
5700 Bucknell Dr.
Atlanta, GA 30336
(404) 629-0999; FAX (404) 620-0690

Acid and alkaline cleaners, chlorinated/alkaline cleaners/disinfectants, beerstone removers, bottle cleaning additives, conveyor belt lubricants, defoamers, peracetic acid, disinfectants/sanitizers, special products, automated conveyor belt lubrication systems, automated bottle washer dispensing systems, water treatment products, conductivity control systems, metering pumps.

Northwestern Extract Co.
William Peter, Pres.
Raymond Koeppen, VP
3590 N. 126th St.
Brookfield, WI 53005
(800) 466-3034; FAX (414) 781-0660

Oregon Fruit Products Co.
Bryan Brown or Sara Barlew
PO Box 5283
Salem, OR 97304
(503) 581-6211; FAX (503) 581-4413

Oregon Fruit Products Co. manufactures aseptic real fruit puree in forty-two-pound bag-in-box for brewers making fruit beer or mead. All our fruit purees are 100 percent real fruit, with no additives, extracts, or flavors added.

Outterson Brewing Services Inc.
Donald Outterson, Pres.
7747 Woodstone Dr.
Cincinnati, OH 45244-2855
(513) 474-9385; FAX (513) 474-9384

PQ Corp.
Mark Phipps, Industry Mgr.
Adam Brozzetti, Buisness Mgr.
PO Box 840
Valley Forge, PA 19482
(610) 651-4440; FAX (610) 215-9124

PQ Corporation is the world's largest supplier of silica-based specialty adsorbents for the brewing industry. A range of products is offered for the stabilization of all beer types, improving shelf life. PQ offers technical assistance from experienced staff brewers. Represented in the craft-brewing industry by A. Gusmer Company.

Miscellaneous Ingredient and Material Suppliers

PepperWorks
Frani Bentley, Production Mgr.
Joann Geist, General Mgr.
303 Industrial Way, Suite 7
Fallbrook, CA 92028
(800) 551-5094; FAX (619) 723-2227
winery@winery.com
http://www.winery.com/winery-bin/prod-inv?1005

Unique salt and pepper shakers handcrafted from richly grained eastern maple, dark and light finish. Long- or short-necked replicas of twelve-ounce beer bottles. Stainless steel shaker caps. Personalize your own labels or choose from PepperWorks wide selection. Cost is $19.95 a set. No minimum order. Allow two weeks for delivery.

Prime Time Printing
Joseph A. Mendonca
William Fossa
52 Conant St.
Danvers, MA 01923
(800) 886-Beer
acacio@aol.com

Custom printed bottles, glasses, and mugs. Label is printed directly on the bottle and fused to the glass. Image is washable, chip and scratch resistant. No paper label mess. We print quantities from four cases to multiple pallets. Call for a brochure.

Rascher & Betzold Inc.
J. I. Smith, Sales Mgr.
5410 N. Damen Ave.
Chicago, IL 60625
(312) 275-7300; FAX (312) 275-7304

Roller Coat Products
Sheila M. Duckett
Hess M. Robert
333 N. Euclid Ave.
St. Louis, MO 63108
(800) 255-4429; FAX (314) 367-6669

Sea Moss Inc.
Jim Vantangoli, Brewery Sales Mgr.
Paul L. Vantangoli, Dir.
30 Prospect St.
Kingston, MA 02364
(617) 585-2050; FAX (617) 585-2255

Serving brewers since 1936. No additives. Sea Moss brand Irish moss flakes, sun bleached, machine dehydrated, highest quality, lowest prices, large inventory, fast/rush service. Proudly harvesting in the U.S.A. Free samples. International accounts welcome.

Silbrico Corp.
Stephen Toedt, Prod. Mgr.
Rick Willis, Mktg. Mgr.
6300 River Rd.
Hodgkins, IL 60525
(800) 323-4287; FAX (708) 354-6698

Sonoco Engraph Label Group
Thomas Coker, Mktg. Mgr.
Jim Prendergast, VP Sales
8800 South Blvd.
Charlotte, NC 28273
(704) 554-5796; FAX (704) 554-8122

Waymatic
Wanda Barker, Mktg. and Sales
PO Box 5320
South Fulton, TN 38257
(901) 479-1741; FAX (901) 479-0008

Weyermann, Heinz GmbH
Sabine Weyermann, Pres./Sales Mgr.
Thomas Kraus-Weyermann, Managing Dir./Sales Mgr.
Brennerstrasse 17 - 19
Bamberg, 96052
Germany
011-49-951/93220-33; FAX 011-49-951/35604

Our product "SINAMAR" is naturally produced in accordance with the "German Reinheitsgebot" and gives your beer, cakes, bread, and beverages more taste and color.

19 Control Agencies, Laws, and Regulations

Prior to 1935 and the repeal of Prohibition, no federal government agency existed to oversee the alcoholic beverage industry. Congress recognized that an illegitimate industry existed during Prohibition and, as a result, passed the Federal Alcohol Administration (FAA) Act, administered by the Bureau of Alcohol, Tobacco, and Firearms (ATF).

ATF oversees permit registration and revenue collection, monitors the taxable removals of all breweries, and requires every new brewery to file a Brewer's Notice. The requirements of the federal law apply only to the extent that the state law imposes similar requirements. ATF has five regional offices, listed on page 286 to 288.

Each state has its own alcohol beverage control agency (although not necessarily referred to as such) and, as a result, its own set of laws governing the manufacture and distribution of beer, licensing and zoning of breweries, and other factors affecting the operation of a brewery. The states administer brewery operation regulations more closely than the federal government does.

With the brewing revolution currently sweeping North America, states are redefining and restructuring their laws dealing with brewing and breweries. Each year the number of brewpubs in the United States increases by 15 to 25 percent. While most states have new laws allowing breweries to sell their products directly to the consumer, two states still prohibit pubbrewing — Mississippi and Montana.

The Canadian system of licensing and regulating alcoholic beverage industries is somewhat similar to that of the United States. The national government implements certain provisions, particularly pertaining to distribution. Each province has its own liquor control agency which oversees licensing and regulation of its alcoholic-beverage manufacturers.

The more you treat your local regulators with courtesy and respect for their authority, the less likely they will interfere with your plans for operating your brewery. Experienced brewers throughout the United States and Canada have found it helps to develop a good relationship with the people who monitor their breweries' production. This affords direct access when a brewer needs answers or clarifications of procedures.

Lastly, we cannot over emphasize the importance of good, consistent record keeping in the brewery. It is a safe bet that, sooner or later, the ATF will audit you.

With this year's edition, we include all of the information regarding brewpub laws, license fees, and regulations for each state's (or province's) regulatory agency. Furthermore, we list for every state (and province) whether microbreweries have permission to self-distribute, and if brewpubs have permission to: (1) sell to a distributor or wholesaler; (2) sell to retailers; (3) sell beer to go; (4) sell draft beer to go; (5) sell guest beer; (6) sell guest wine; and (7) offer a full bar.

Disclaimer: *Institute for Brewing Studies and Brewers Publications cannot be held responsible for errors or inaccuracies which this following chapter may contain. We updated the information January 1996. As laws and regulations are always subject to change, make sure to check with the appropriate federal, state, or provincial agency office regarding any questions or uncertainties you may have. We believe our information is as accurate as possible and would appreciate notification either of errors discovered here or changes enacted during 1996 affecting brewers.*

Control Agencies, Laws, and Regulations

Bureau of Alcohol, Tobacco, and Firearms

Headquarters
ATF Headquarters
650 Massachusetts Ave.
Washington, DC 20226
(202) 927-8700; FAX (202) 927-8876
Industry Compliance: (202) 927-8100

North Atlantic District
Covering: Connecticut, Delaware, District of Columbia, Maine, Maryland, Massachusetts, New Hampshire, New Jersey, New York, Pennsylvania, Rhode Island, and Vermont

District Headquarters
Bruce Weininger, District Dir.
6 World Trade Center
6th Floor
New York, NY 10048
(212) 264-2328

Philadelphia Technical Services
Bob Hart, ATF
Curtis Center, Suite 875
Independence Square West
Philadelphia, PA 19106
(215) 597-4107

Area Offices:
Baltimore Area Office
31 Hopkins Plaza, Room 938
Baltimore, MD 21201
(410) 962-3200

Boston Area Office
10 Cauuseway St., Room 795
Boston, MA 02222
(617) 565-7073

Buffalo Area Office
111 W. Huron St., Room 219
Buffalo, NY 14202
(716) 846-4048

Hartford Area Office
450 Main St., Room 403
Hartford, CT 06103
(203) 240-3400

Lansdale Area Office
Century Plaza Building
100 W. Main St., Suite 300-B
Lansdale, PA 19446
(215) 362-1840

New York Area Office
6 World Trade Center, Room 626
New York, NY 10048
(212) 264-4650

Parsippany Area Office
120 Littleton Rd., Room 305
Parsippany, NJ 07054
(201) 334-7058

Pittsburg Area Office
Federal Building, Room 2126
1000 Liberty Ave.
Pittsburg, PA 15222
(412) 644-2919

Midwest District
Covering: Illinois, Indiana, Kentucky, Michigan, Minnesota, North Dakota, Ohio, South Dakota, West Virgina, and Wisconsin

District Headquarters
Wayne Moran, District Dir.
300 S. Riverside Plaza, Suite 310
Chicago, IL 60606-6616
(312) 353-1967

Cincinnati Technical Services
Norris Alford, ATF (Acting)
550 Main St.
Cincinnati, OH 45202
(513) 684-3334

Area Offices:
Chicago Area Office
1 S. 450 Summit Ave., Suite 225
Oakbrook Terrace, IL 60181
(708) 268-1282

Cincinnati Area Office
St. Paul Builking, Suite 301
801-B W. Eighth St.
Cincinnati, OH 45203
(513) 684-3351

Cleveland Area Office
Plaza South 1, Suite 110
7251 Engle Rd.
Middleburg Heights, OH 44130
(216) 522-3374

Detroit Area Office
Arboretum Building, Suite 195
34505 W. Twelve Mile Rd.
Farmington Hills, MI 48331
(313) 226-4736

Frankfort Area Office
330 W. Broadway, Room 124
Frankfort, KY 40601-1229
(502) 223-3350

Louisville Area Office
510 W. Broadway, Suite 704
Louisville, KY 40202
(502) 582-5217

Milwaukee Area Office
1000 N. Water St., Suite 1710
Milwaukee, WI 53202
(414) 297-3991

St. Paul Area Office
Minnesota World Center
30 E. Seventh St., Suite 1840
St. Paul, MN 55101
(612) 290-3496

Control Agencies, Laws, and Regulations

Southeast District
Covering: Alabama, Florida, Georgia, Mississippi, North Carolina, Puerto Rico, South Carolina, Tennessee, Virgin Islands, and Virginia

District Headquarters
Larry J. Moore, District Dir.
2600 Century Parkway, N.E.
Atlanta, GA 30345
(404) 679-5010

Atlanta Technical Services
Myrna Huntley, ATF
2600 Century Parkway, N.E.
Atlanta, GA 30345
(404) 679-5080

Area Offices
Atlanta Area Office
2600 Century Parkway, N.E.
Atlanta, GA 30345
(404) 679-5130

Birmingham Area Office
600 Beacon Pkwy. W., Suite 730
Birmingham, AL 35209
(205) 290-7189

Charlotte Area Office
4530 Park Rd., Suite 441
Charlotte, NC 28209
(704) 344-6127

Miami Area Office
5205 N.W. 84th Ave., Suite 104
Miami, FL 33166
(305) 592-9967

Puerto Rico Area Office
U.S. Courthouse Federal Building
Carlos Chardon, Room 659
Hato Rey, PR 00918
(809) 766-5584

Richmond Area Office
804 Moorefield Park Dr., Suite 201-CO
Richmond, VA 23236
(804) 771-2877

Tampa Area Office
550 Reo St., Suite 303
Tampa, FL 33609
(813) 288-1252

Southwest District
Covering: Arizona, Arkansas, Colorado, Iowa, Kansas, Louisiana, Missouri, Nebraska, New Mexico, Oklahoma, and Texas

District Headquarters
David Royalty, District Dir.
1114 Commerce St.
7th Floor
Dallas, TX 75242
(214) 767-2280

Dallas Technical Services
Claude Maraist, ATF
1114 Commerce St.
7th Floor
Dallas, TX 75242
(214) 767-2281

Area Offices:
Albuquerque Area Office
201 Third St., Suite 1555
Albuquerque, NM 87103
(505) 766-1984

Dallas Area Office
1100 Commerce St., Room 13C22
Dallas, TX 75242
(214) 767-9461

Denver Area Office
8 W. Dry Creek Circle, Room 210
Littleton, CO 80120
(303) 843-4144

Des Moines Area Office
210 Walnut, Room 703
Des Moines, IA 50309
(515) 284-4857

Houston Area Office
515 N. Sam Houston Pkwy. E.
Suite 400
Houston, TX 77060
(713) 931-0291

Kansas City Area Office
2600 Grand Ave., Suite 280
Kansas City, MO 64108
(816) 221-4036

Lubbock Area Office
1205 Texas Ave., Room 616-D
Lubbock, TX 79401
(806) 798-1030

New Orleans Area Office
111 Veterans Memorial Blvd.
Suite 1216
Metairie, LA 70005
(504) 589-7113

Oklahoma City Area Office
200 N.W. Fifth St., Room 103
Oklahoma City, OK 73102
(405) 231-3571

Omaha Area Office
106 S. 15th St., Room 700
Omaha, NE 68101
(402) 221-3571

St. Louis Area Office
815 Olive St., Room 310
St. Louis, MO 63101
(314) 539-2251

San Antonio Area Office
8610 Broadway, Suite 410
San Antonio, TX 78217
(210) 805-2777

Shreveport Area Office
401 Edwards St., Suite 1105
Shreveport, LA 71101
(318) 226-5435

Western District
Covering: Alaska, California, Guam, Hawaii, Idaho, Montana, Nevada, Oregon, Utah, Washington, and Wyoming

District Headquarters
Vikki Renneckar, District Dir.
221 Main St.
11th Floor
San Francisco, CA 94105
(415) 744-7013

San Francisco Technical Services
Gloria Bieniek, ATF
221 Main St.
11th Floor
San Francisco, CA 94105
(415) 744-9419

Area Offices:
Sacramento Area Office
801 K St., Suite 921
Sacramento, CA 95814-3518
(916) 498-5095; FAX (916) 496-5088

San Francisco Area Office
221 Main St., Suite 1340
San Francisco, CA 94105-1992
(415) 744-9458; FAX (415) 744-7800

Los Angeles Area Office
350 S. Figueroa St., Suite 800
Los Angeles, CA 90071-1303
(213) 894-4815; FAX (213) 894-3176

San Jose Area Office
55 S. Market St., Suite 440
San Jose, CA 95113-2324
(408) 291-7464; FAX (408) 291-6474

Santa Ana Area Office
600 W. Santa Ana Blvd., Suite 510
Santa Ana, CA 92701-4534
(714) 836-2946; FAX (714) 836-2431

Seattle Area Office
915 Second Ave., Suite 842
Seattle, WA 98174
(206) 220-6456; FAX (206) 220-6459

Portland Area Office
9828 E. Burnside, Suite 210
Portland, OR 97216-2330
(503) 231-2331; FAX (503) 231-2356

Post of Duty Phone Numbers:

Fresno:
(209) 487-5093; FAX (209) 487-5983

San Diego:
(619) 557-7079; FAX (619) 557-6804

Santa Rosa:
(707) 576-0184; FAX (707) 525-8538

Van Nuys:
(818) 904-6494

Anchorage:
(907) 271-5701; FAX (907) 271-5704

Boise:
(208) 334-1321; FAX (208) 334-9501

Modesto:
(209) 522-6925

Napa:
(707) 224-7801

Oakland:
(510) 637-3441; FAX (510) 637-3449

United States

Alabama
Charles Baugh, Lieutenant, Enforcement Division
Alabama Alcoholic Beverage Control Board
PO Box 1151
Montgomery, AL 36101
(334) 271-3840; FAX (334) 244-1815
Alternate Contact: Freddy D. Day

Microbreweries
Is there a specific microbrewery law?	n/a
Are microbreweries allowed to:	
sell directly to retailers?	No
sell directly to consumers?	n/a
Production ceiling:	n/a
License fees:	n/a

Brewpubs
Are brewpubs legal?	Yes
Is there a specific brewpub law?	Yes
Date of legalization:	5/7/92
Are brewpubs allowed to:	
sell to a distributor/wholesaler?	No
sell to retailers?	No
sell beer to go?	No
sell draft beer to go?	No
sell guest beer?	Yes
sell guest wine?	n/a
offer a full bar?	Yes
Production ceiling:	10,000 barrels
License fees:	$1,000 annually

Regulatory Information
Does a "Franchise Law" requiring suppliers to form exclusive contracts with distributors exist? n/a

Additional Notes
A brewpub must be located in a historic building in a wet county or municipality where beer was brewed for public consumption prior to Prohibition, and contain and operate a restaurant with a seating capacity of at least eighty.

Local approval and licensing are required. Alabama does not distinguish between brewpubs and microbreweries.

Alaska
Patrick Sharrock, Dir.
Alcoholic Beverage Control Board
550 W. Seventh Ave., Suite 350
Anchorage, AK 99501
(907) 277-8638; FAX (907) 272-9412
Alternate Contact: Bill Roche, Enforcement Supervisor
(907) 277-8638

Microbreweries
Is there a specific microbrewery law?	No
Are microbreweries allowed to:	
sell directly to retailers?	Yes
sell directly to consumers?	Yes
Production ceiling:	n/a
License fees:	$1,000 bi-annually

Brewpubs
Are brewpubs legal?	Yes
Is there a specific brewpub law?	Yes
Date of legalization:	6/16/88

Description:
Brewpub licenses may be issued to the holders of beverage dispensary (full service, on-premises liquor licenses) licenses.

Are brewpubs allowed to:	
sell to a distributor/wholesaler?	No
sell to retailers?	No
sell beer to go?	No
sell draft beer to go?	No
sell guest beer?	Yes
sell guest wine?	Yes
offer a full bar?	Yes
Production ceiling:	516 barrels
License fees:	$500 bi-annually

Regulatory Information
Does a "Franchise Law" requiring suppliers to form exclusive contracts with distributors exist? No
Size restrictions for malt beverage containers:
1/6 gallon and 1/10 gallon prohibited

Additional Notes
To operate a brewpub, a beverage dispensary license is required in addition to the brewpub license, which cannot be transferred independently of the dispensary license.

Arizona
Howard Adams, Dir.
Department of Liquor Licenses and Control
800 W. Washington St., Suite 500
Phoenix, AZ 85007
(602) 542-5141; FAX (602) 542-5707
Alternate Contact: Ron Herman or Norman Perkins, Investigators

Microbreweries
Is there a specific microbrewery law? Yes
Description:
"Domestic microbrewery" means a place within this state where a person engages in the business of manufacturing or producing at least 10,000 gallons but less than 310,000 gallons of beer annually.

Control Agencies, Laws, and Regulations

Are microbreweries allowed to:
    sell directly to retailers?   Yes
    sell directly to consumers?   Yes
Production ceiling: 310,000 barrels
License fees: $600 per year

Brewpubs
Are brewpubs legal?   Yes
Is there a specific brewpub law?   No
Date of legalization: 4/1/87
Description:
    "In-state producer's license" only. Must purchase additional licenses to sell guest wine and spirits.
Are brewpubs allowed to:
    sell to a distributor/wholesaler?   Yes
    sell to retailers?   Yes
    sell beer to go?   Yes
    sell draft beer to go?   Yes
    sell guest beer?   Yes
    sell guest wine?   n/a
    offer a full bar?   Yes
Production ceiling: 10,000 gallons or 323 barrels
License fees: $300

Regulatory Information
Does a "Franchise Law" requiring suppliers to form exclusive contracts with distributors exist?   No

Additional Notes
An Arizona pubbrewer must have a brewing license, plus one of three different retail licenses for either a restaurant, bar, or beer and wine. In the case of a restaurant, brewpub food must account for 40 percent of sales. The barrelage ceiling is not enforced for brewpubs maintaining an "In-State Producer's License."

Arkansas
Robert S. Moore Jr., Dir.
Alcohol Beverage Control Division
100 Main St., Suite 503
Little Rock, AR 72201-1535
(501) 682-1105; FAX (501) 682-2221
Alternate Contact: Don Bennett, Staff Attorney

Microbreweries
Is there a specific microbrewery law?   No
Are microbreweries allowed to:
    sell directly to retailers?   Undetermined, none exist
    sell directly to consumers?   n/a
Production ceiling: n/a
License fees: n/a

Brewpubs
Are brewpubs legal?   Yes
Is there a specific brewpub law?   Yes
Date of legalization: 3/19/91
Description:
    Recent ammendments have been added to the 1991 act.
Are brewpubs allowed to:
    sell to a distributor/wholesaler?   No
    sell to retailers?   No
    sell beer to go?   Yes
    sell draft beer to go?   Yes
    sell guest beer?   Yes
    sell guest wine?   Yes
    offer a full bar?   Yes
Production ceiling: 5,000 barrels
License fees: $750
Additional selling restrictions:
    May only sell wine with additional permit. May only sell beer or malt liquor to go that is made by the brewpub/microbrewery-restaurant.

Regulatory Information
Does a "Franchise Law" requiring suppliers to form exclusive contracts with distributors exist?   Yes
Description:
    Three-tier monopoly system
Container labeling requirements:
    See ABC Reg. 2.17 and ABC Reg. 2.17.1 (Supp.)

Additional Notes
Act 611 created a microbrewery-restaurant license which entitles the holder to brew and sell beer, whether brewed on the premises or not. Additional licenses can be obtained to sell wine or other spirits, if allowed by local regulations.

The brewpub must be in wet territory and operate as a limited exception to the state's three-tier system. Now you may brew malt liquor (5% ABW to 21% ABW) per ACA 3-5-1201, et seq. (Supp.); 2.53; 2.55; 2.57; 2.58; 2.59; and 2.60 (Supp.).

California
Donald D. Decious, Chief of Bus. Practices
California Department of Alcoholic Beverage Control
3810 Rosin Ct., Suite 150
Sacramento, CA 95834
(916) 263-6845; FAX (916) 263-6912
http://www.abc.ca.gov
Alternate Contact: David Wright, Asst. Chief of Bus. Practices
(916) 263-6846

Microbreweries

Is there a specific microbrewery law?   *No*
Are microbreweries allowed to:
    sell directly to retailers?   *Yes*
    sell directly to consumers?   *Yes*
Production ceiling: *n/a*
License fees: *$244 annually*

Brewpubs

Are brewpubs legal?   *Yes*
Is there a specific brewpub law?   *No*
Date of legalization: *n/a*
Are brewpubs allowed to:
    sell to a distributor/wholesaler?   *Yes*
    sell to retailers?   *Yes*
    sell beer to go?   *Yes*
    sell draft beer to go?   *Yes*
    sell guest beer?   *Yes*
    sell guest wine?   *Yes*
    offer a full bar?   *See Notes*
Production ceiling: *60,000 barrels*
License fees:

Type 23 small beer manufacturer—$224; other fees with other agencies. Check with California Small Brewers Association.

Additional selling restrictions:

May sell only beer they produce to retailers and to consumers for off-premises consumption.

Regulatory Information

Does a "Franchise Law" requiring suppliers to form exclusive contracts with distributors exist?   *No*
Retail-level packaging restrictions:

Not more than 52 gallons

Container labeling requirements:

Draught beer and packaged beer sold in California, except for export, shall not exceed an alcoholic content of 4 percent by weight; provided, however, that bottled or canned ale, porter, brown, stout, or malt liquor may exceed such alcoholic content if it bears a label which correctly designates the contents as such ale, porter, brown, stout, or malt liquor. All bottles or cans containing ale, porter, brown, stout, or malt liquor of an alcoholic content of 4 percent or less by weight must have firmly affixed thereto in type of not less than one-sixteenth inch in height a notice specifically certifying that the alcoholic content of the beverages in the package is not greater than 4 percent by weight. Only ale, porter, brown, stout, and malt liquor in packages bearing such labels may be sold by on-sale beer licensees.

Additional Notes

In a limited number of cases, distilled spirits can be served on the same premises as a brewpub so long as the brewpub and the general on-sale premises are physically divided by a barrier of some kind. Decisions are made on a case-by-case basis. Contact the California Small Brewers Association for details.

Colorado

David Reitz, Dir.
Liquor Enforcement Division
1375 Sherman St., Room 600
Denver, CO 80261
(303) 866-3741; FAX (303) 866-4541
Alternate Contact: Laura Smith, Investigator
(303) 866-3741

Microbreweries

Is there a specific microbrewery law?   *No*
Are microbreweries allowed to:
    sell directly to retailers?   *Yes*
    sell directly to consumers?   *Yes*
Distribution restrictions:

May sell directly to retailers and consumers only if they have a malt liquor distibutor's license in addition to a manufacter's license.

Production ceiling: *n/a*
License fees:

$275, manufacturer's license; $525, wholesalers license

Brewpubs

Are brewpubs legal?   *Yes*
Is there a specific brewpub law?   *Yes*
Date of legalization: *4/23/96*
Description:

"Brewpub" means a retail establishment that manufactures not more than 60,000 barrels of malt liquor on its premises each year. Fifteen percent of total gross revenue must be from the sale of food.

Are brewpubs allowed to:
    sell to a distributor/wholesaler?   *Yes*
    sell to retailers?   *Yes*
    sell beer to go?   *Yes*
    sell draft beer to go?   *Yes*
    sell guest beer?   *Yes*
    sell guest wine?   *Yes*
    offer a full bar?   *Yes*
Production ceiling: *60,000 barrels*
License fees:

$300, brewpub license; $275, retail license; $325, local municipality license

Additional selling restrictions:
Effective January 1997, "brewpub" licensees will no longer be able to hold a wholesaler's license. However, brewpub licensees will be allowed to self-distribute up to 9,677 barrels per year.

Regulatory Information
Does a "Franchise Law" requiring suppliers to form exclusive contracts with distributors exist? Yes
Description:
One territory (defined by supplier) per wholesaler.
Container labeling requirements:
Special labeling for 3.2% beer (fermented malt beverage) only.

Connecticut
Gerald Langlais, Dir.
Liquor Control Commission
165 Capital Ave., Room 556
Hartford, CT 06106
(860) 566-5207; FAX (860) 566-6060

Microbreweries
Is there a specific microbrewery law?	n/a
Are microbreweries allowed to:	
sell directly to retailers?	Yes
sell directly to consumers?	No
Production ceiling:	n/a
License fees:	n/a

Brewpubs
Are brewpubs legal?	Yes
Is there a specific brewpub law?	Yes
Date of legalization:	1989
Are brewpubs allowed to:	
sell to a distributor/wholesaler?	No
sell to retailers?	No
sell beer to go?	No
sell draft beer to go?	Yes
sell guest beer?	Yes
sell guest wine?	Yes
offer a full bar?	Yes
Production ceiling:	None
License fees:	$240

Regulatory Information
Does a "Franchise Law" requiring suppliers to form exclusive contracts with distributors exist? Yes
Deposit requirements: 5¢ deposit

Additional Notes
A special manufacturer's license allows for on-premise production and consumption of beer. Recent rulings allow a brewpub to sell other spirits with the appropriate license.

Delaware
Donald J. Bowman, Dir.
Delaware Alcoholic Beverage Control Commission
820 N. French St.
Wilmington, DE 19801
(302) 577-3200; FAX (302) 577-3204
Alternate Contact: Mary Ann D. Heesters, Deputy Dir.

Microbreweries
Is there a specific microbrewery law?	Yes
Are microbreweries allowed to:	
sell directly to retailers?	Yes
sell directly to consumers?	Yes
Production ceiling:	25,000 barrels
License fees:	$1,000

Brewpubs
Are brewpubs legal?	Yes
Is there a specific brewpub law?	Yes
Date of legalization:	6/26/91
Are brewpubs allowed to:	
sell to a distributor/wholesaler?	No
sell to retailers?	No
sell beer to go?	No
sell draft beer to go?	No
sell guest beer?	Yes
sell guest wine?	n/a
offer a full bar?	Yes
Production ceiling:	2,000 barrels
License fees:	$1,000

Regulatory Information
Does a "Franchise Law" requiring suppliers to form exclusive contracts with distributors exist? Yes
Description:
Rule 46, need a contract submitted between supplier and distributor.
Size restrictions for malt beverage containers:
Follows BATF regulations
Deposit requirements:
5¢ for bottles

Additional Notes
An additional license is required to sell spirits other than beer manufactured on-premises. Service of complete meals in a licensed restaurant is required.

District of Columbia
Paul E. Waters, Program Mgr.
Alcoholic Beverage Control Board
614 H St. N.W., Room 807
Washington, DC 20001
(202) 727-7378; FAX (202) 727-7027
Alternate Contact: Geneivieve Lyons, Chief Investigator
(202) 727-7375

Microbreweries
Is there a specific microbrewery law?	n/a
Are microbreweries allowed to:	
sell directly to retailers?	No
sell directly to consumers?	n/a
Production ceiling:	n/a
License fees:	n/a

Brewpubs
Are brewpubs legal?	Yes
Is there a specific brewpub law?	Yes
Date of legalization:	7/24/91

Description:
Brewpubs must be part of an ABC restaurant or tavern.

Are brewpubs allowed to:	
sell to a distributor/wholesaler?	No
sell to retailers?	No
sell beer to go?	No
sell draft beer to go?	No
sell guest beer?	Yes
sell guest wine?	Yes
offer a full bar?	Yes
Production ceiling:	n/a
License fees:	$3,000

Regulatory Information
Does a "Franchise Law" requiring suppliers to form exclusive contracts with distributors exist?   n/a

Additional Notes
Act 9-77 legalized brewpubs in a limited area. The brewpub-legal section includes D.C.'s new downtown and the central business districts, but does not include the Georgetown or DuPont Circle areas.

Florida
John J. Harris, Dir.
Florida Division of Alcohol, Beverages, and Tobacco
1940 N. Monroe St.
Tallahassee, FL 32399-1020
(904) 488-8288; FAX (904) 488-9264
Alternate Contact: Bob Kronmiller, Cheif of Bureau of Auditing, Tax Collection, Licensing, and Records
(904) 487-4338

Microbreweries
Is there a specific microbrewery law?	No
Are microbreweries allowed to:	
sell directly to retailers?	No
sell directly to consumers?	No

Distribution restrictions:
Must sell to distributors who have territorial agreements and franchise agreement 5503.021 and 5503.022

Production ceiling:	None

License fees:
$3,000 annual fine for each manufacturing plant.

Brewpubs
Are brewpubs legal?	Yes
Is there a specific brewpub law?	Yes
Date of legalization:	7/1/87
Are brewpubs allowed to:	
sell to a distributor/wholesaler?	No
sell to retailers?	No
sell beer to go?	No
sell draft beer to go?	No
sell guest beer?	Yes
sell guest wine?	Yes
offer a full bar?	Yes
Production ceiling:	5,000 barrels

License fees:
$500 plus retail license fee depending on type of license needed

Additional selling restrictions:
Beer must be brewed at single location where it is sold to consumers. Cannot remove from premises except for shows and gifts.

Regulatory Information
Does a "Franchise Law" requiring suppliers to form exclusive contracts with distributors exist?   Yes

Description:
A manufacturer shall not cause a distributor to resign from an agreement or cancel, terminate, fail to renew, or refuse to continue under agreement unless the manufacturer has complied with all of the following: (a) Has satisfied the applicable notice requirements of subsection (9) (90 days written). (b) Has acted in good faith. (c) Has good cause for the cancellation, termination, nonrenewal, discontinuance, or forced resignation.

Size restrictions for malt beverage containers:
8-, 12-, 16-, and 32-ounce containers and kegs

Container labeling requirements:
The word "Florida" or "FL" must be on each container, except kegs; no other state's name is permitted except addresses of manufacturers.

Georgia
Chet Bryant, Dir.
Alcohol and Tobacco Tax Unit
PO Box 38368/270 Washington St. S.W.
Atlanta, GA 30334
(404) 656-4252; FAX (404) 657-6880
Alternate Contact: Herman Oliver, Conferee
(404) 656-4262

Microbreweries
Is there a specific microbrewery law?	No
Are microbreweries allowed to:	
sell directly to retailers?	No
sell directly to consumers?	No
Production ceiling:	n/a
License fees:	$1,000

Brewpubs
Are brewpubs legal?	Yes
Is there a specific brewpub law?	Yes
Date of legalization:	7/1/96
Are brewpubs allowed to:	
sell to a distributor/wholesaler?	No
sell to retailers?	No
sell beer to go?	No
sell draft beer to go?	No
sell guest beer?	Yes
sell guest wine?	Yes
offer a full bar?	Yes
Production ceiling:	5,000 barrels
License fees:	$1,000

Additional selling restrictions:
Brewpubs shall file annually with the State Revenue commissioner a bond or an irrovocable bank letter of credit acceptable to the Commissioner, in the amount of $20,000.

Regulatory Information
Does a "Franchise Law" requiring suppliers to form exclusive contracts with distributors exist?   Yes
Description:
Manufacturer must designate sales territories for each of its brands or labels sold in Georgia and shall name one licensed wholesaler as exclusive distributor in such territories.
Container labeling requirements:
Must be BATF approved and approved by the GA Alcohol and Tobacco Tax Unit.

Hawaii
John Rybczyk, Liquor Control Administrator
Liquor Commission of the City and County of Honolulu
711 Kapiolani Blvd., Sixth Floor, Suite 600
Honolulu, HI 96813
(808) 523-4458; FAX (808) 591-2700
Alternate Contact: John A. Carroll, Chief Investigator
(808) 527-5399

Microbreweries
Is there a specific microbrewery law?	No
Are microbreweries allowed to:	
sell directly to retailers?	No
sell directly to consumers?	Yes, draught only
Production ceiling:	n/a
License fees:	

$1,500 or 0.75% of gross sales, whichever is higher, not to exceed $25,000

Brewpubs
Are brewpubs legal?	Yes
Is there a specific brewpub law?	Yes
Date of legalization:	7/1/94
Are brewpubs allowed to:	
sell to a distributor/wholesaler?	Yes
sell to retailers?	No
sell beer to go?	No
sell draft beer to go?	No
sell guest beer?	Yes
sell guest wine?	Yes
offer a full bar?	Yes
Production ceiling:	5,000 barrels
License fees:	

$1,800 per year or .0075 % of gross sales

Regulatory Information
Does a "Franchise Law" requiring suppliers to form exclusive contracts with distributors exist?   No
Container labeling requirements:
A label stating the name of the manufacturer or, in lieu thereof, if the manufacturer does business under another name, stating such name, and stating the kind and quantity of liquor contained therein. All such labels shall conform in all respects to the then existing federal laws and regulations regarding such lables.

Idaho
John Gould, Bureau Chief
Alcohol Beverage Control Division
PO Box 700
Meridian, ID 83680-0700
(208) 884-7060

Microbreweries

Is there a specific microbrewery law?   Yes
Description:
    Sec. 23-1003 (3) Idaho brewpub license
Are microbreweries allowed to:
    sell directly to retailers?   Yes
    sell directly to consumers?   Yes
Production ceiling: 30,000 barrels
License fees: $50

Brewpubs

Are brewpubs legal?   Yes
Is there a specific brewpub law?   Yes
Date of legalization: 1/1/87
Description:
    May sell at brewery and one remote location.
Are brewpubs allowed to:
    sell to a distributor/wholesaler?   Yes
    sell to retailers?   Yes
    sell beer to go?   Yes
    sell draft beer to go?   Yes
    sell guest beer?   Yes
    sell guest wine?   n/a
    offer a full bar?   No
Production ceiling: 30,000 barrels
License fees: $50 to $500
Additional selling restrictions:
    Brewpubs may purchase a retail beer, wine, and liquor by the drink license in Idaho.

Regulatory Information

Does a "Franchise Law" requiring suppliers to form exclusive contracts with distributors exist?   Yes
Description: *Sec. 23-1003 (b)*
Deposit requirements: *Deposit may be charged*

Additional Notes

To act as a wholesaler or sell beer to go, the brewer must obtain additional licenses. Only the highest fee of any of the licenses held is collected. An alcohol beverage code book is available for $6.

Illinois

Arabel Alva Rosales, Exec. Dir.
Illinois Liquor Control Commission
100 W. Randolph, Suite 5-300
Chicago, IL 60601
(312) 814-2206; FAX (312) 814-2241
Alternate Contact: John R. Stanton, Chief of Legal Counsel
(312) 814-2206

Microbreweries

Is there a specific microbrewery law?   No
Are microbreweries allowed to:
    sell directly to retailers?   Yes
    sell directly to consumers?   n/a
Production ceiling: n/a
License fees: n/a

Brewpubs

Are brewpubs legal?   Yes
Is there a specific brewpub law?   Yes
Date of legalization: 1993
Description:
    A brewpub license shall allow the licensee to manufacture beer only on the premises specified in the license, to make sales of the beer manufactured on the premises to importing distributors, distributors, and to non-licensees for use and consumption, to store the beer upon the premises, and to sell and offer for sale at retail.
Are brewpubs allowed to:
    sell to a distributor/wholesaler?   Yes
    sell to retailers?   No
    sell beer to go?   Yes
    sell draft beer to go?   Yes
    sell guest beer?   Yes
    sell guest wine?   n/a
    offer a full bar?   Yes
Production ceiling: n/a
License fees: $1,050

Regulatory Information

Does a "Franchise Law" requiring suppliers to form exclusive contracts with distributors exist?   No
Retail-level packaging restrictions:
    Check with each local municipality — locals have discretion
Container labeling requirements:
    Adhere to federal regulations

Additional Notes

By obtaining the brewpub license, a brewpub licensee can sell beer retail for on- or off-premise consumption, or both. Draft to go must be in an appropriate container.

Indiana

Patricia Hebenstreit, Exec. Sec.
Indiana Alcoholic Beverage Commission
302 W. Washington, Room E114
Indianapolis, IN 46204
(317) 232-2472; FAX (317) 233-6114
Alternate Contact: Don Okey, Industry Liaison
(317) 232-2463

Microbreweries

Is there a specific microbrewery law?	Yes
Description:	IC 7.1-3-2-7
Are microbreweries allowed to:	
sell directly to retailers?	Yes
sell directly to consumers?	Yes
Production ceiling:	20,000 barrels
License fees:	$500 per year

Brewpubs

Are brewpubs legal?	Yes
Is there a specific brewpub law?	Yes
Date of legalization:	3/17/93
Are brewpubs allowed to:	
sell to a distributor/wholesaler?	Yes
sell to retailers?	Yes
sell beer to go?	Yes
sell draft beer to go?	Yes
sell guest beer?	Yes
sell guest wine?	n/a
offer a full bar?	Yes
Production ceiling:	20,000 barrels
License fees:	$500

Regulatory Information

Does a "Franchise Law" requiring suppliers to form exclusive contracts with distributors exist? **No**

Container labeling requirements:

All producers must register with the commission all brands, labels, and trademarks used or proposed to be used in the state. IC 7.1-2-3-17 and 905 IAC 1-23-1.

Additional Notes

Separate ownership of adjacent brewing and pub operations is no longer necessary, and transfer from brewery to pub in bulk containers or by continuous flow system is allowed. House bill 1502 amends various sections of 7.1-4.

Iowa

Jack Nystrom, Dir.
Alcoholic Beverage Division
1918 S.E. Hulsizer Ave.
Ankeny, IA 50021
(515) 281-7430; FAX (515) 281-7372
Alternate Contact: Judy K. Seib, Chief of Licensing, Regulation, and Auditing
(515) 281-7432

Microbreweries

Is there a specific microbrewery law?	n/a
Are microbreweries allowed to:	
sell directly to retailers?	No
sell directly to consumers?	n/a
Production ceiling:	n/a
License fees:	n/a

Brewpubs

Are brewpubs legal?	Yes
Is there a specific brewpub law?	Yes
Date of legalization:	1/1/92

Description:

From Iowa code section 123, 130: A person who holds a special Class A (manufacturer/retail for on-premises consumption or to sell to wholesalers for off-premises consumption) permit for the same location at which the person holds a Class C (retail for off-premises consumption only) liquor control license or Class B (retail for on- or off-premises consumption) beer permit may manufacture and sell beer to be consumed on the premises and may sell beer to a Class A permittee for resale purposes.

Are brewpubs allowed to:	
sell to a distributor/wholesaler?	Yes
sell to retailers?	No
sell beer to go?	No
sell draft beer to go?	No
sell guest beer?	Yes
sell guest wine?	n/a
offer a full bar?	Yes
Production ceiling:	n/a

License fees:

$250 plus $5.89 per barrel plus an on-site fee.

Regulatory Information

Does a "Franchise Law" requiring suppliers to form exclusive contracts with distributors exist? **No**

Deposit requirements:

Not more than 5¢ per container.

Container labeling requirements:

Labels approved by the BATF are accepted by Iowa. Additional 5¢ refund required by Department of Natural Resources.

Additional Notes

Iowa issues a special Class A beer (brewpub) permit to holders of any of three on-premises licenses. This allows retail sales for both on- and off-premises consumption, but the pub must be on premises.

Iowa also allows native breweries to manufacture on-premises. These manufacturers can only sell beer to go or at wholesale into the three-tier system.

Kansas
Bernie Norwood, Dir. of the Kansas Department of Revenue
Alcoholic Beverage Control Division
4 Townsite Plaza/200 E. Sixth St., Suite 210
Topeka, KS 66603-3512
(913) 296-3946; FAX (913) 296-0922
Alternate Contact: Jim Conant, Chief Admin. Officer

Microbreweries
Is there a specific microbrewery law?	Yes
Are microbreweries allowed to:	
sell directly to retailers?	No
sell directly to consumers?	Yes
Production ceiling:	15,000 barrels
License fees:	

$250 annually plus registration fee ($50 new/$10 renewal)

Brewpubs
Are brewpubs legal?	Yes
Is there a specific brewpub law?	n/a
Date of legalization:	4/1/87

Description:
Microbreweries may also hold on-premises licenses and thereby operate as a brewpub.

Are brewpubs allowed to:	
sell to a distributor/wholesaler?	Yes
sell to retailers?	No
sell beer to go?	Yes
sell draft beer to go?	Yes
sell guest beer?	Yes
sell guest wine?	n/a
offer a full bar?	Yes
Production ceiling:	15,000 barrels
License fees:	See microbrewery information

Regulatory Information
Does a "Franchise Law" requiring suppliers to form exclusive contracts with distributors exist? Yes
Description:
Distribution rights are exclusive in designated geographic areas.
Container labeling requirements:
Federal size and labeling requirements are followed.

Additional Notes
Beer produced by brewpubs or microbreweries must be made with at least 50 percent Kansas-grown grain unless a written waiver is obtained from the licensing commission. No distinction is made between brewpubs and microbreweries (microbreweries may also hold an on-premises license and thereby operate as a "brewpub").

Kentucky
Donald B. Grugin, Commissioner
Department of Alcoholic Beverage Control
123 Walnut St.
Frankfort, KY 40601
(502) 573-4850; FAX (502) 573-5672
Alternate Contact: Revonda Duncan, Asst. Malt Beverage Administrator

Microbreweries
Is there a specific microbrewery law?	n/a
Are microbreweries allowed to:	
sell directly to retailers?	Yes
sell directly to consumers?	n/a
Production ceiling:	n/a
License fees:	n/a

Brewpubs
Are brewpubs legal?	Yes
Is there a specific brewpub law?	Yes
Date of legalization:	1/24/84
Are brewpubs allowed to:	
sell to a distributor/wholesaler?	Yes
sell to retailers?	No
sell beer to go?	Yes
sell draft beer to go?	No
sell guest beer?	Yes
sell guest wine?	n/a
offer a full bar?	Yes
Production ceiling:	12,500 barrels
License fees:	$250

Regulatory Information
Does a "Franchise Law" requiring suppliers to form exclusive contracts with distributors exist? n/a

Additional Notes
Brewpubs must be located in wet territory and are subject to licensing and regulation by local authorities as well as by the state ABC.

Louisiana
Terry E. Pitre, Commissioner
Louisiana Alcoholic Beverage Control
PO Box 66404/1885 Wooddale Blvd.
Baton Rouge, LA 70896
(504) 925-4041; FAX (504) 925-3975
Alternate Contact: Bob Roshto
(504) 925-4068

Microbreweries
Is there a specific microbrewery law?	n/a
Are microbreweries allowed to:	
sell directly to retailers?	No
sell directly to consumers?	n/a
Production ceiling:	n/a
License fees:	n/a

Brewpubs
Are brewpubs legal?	Yes
Is there a specific brewpub law?	Yes
Date of legalization:	10/5/89
Are brewpubs allowed to:	
sell to a distributor/wholesaler?	No
sell to retailers?	No
sell beer to go?	Yes
sell draft beer to go?	No
sell guest beer?	Yes
sell guest wine?	n/a
offer a full bar?	Yes
Production ceiling:	12,500 barrels
License fees:	$530

Regulatory Information
Does a "Franchise Law" requiring suppliers to form exclusive contracts with distributors exist?   n/a

Additional Notes
A microbrewer permit must be held with a retailer's Class A permit to establish a brewpub. The alcohol content of the beer produced cannot exceed 6 percent by volume (4.7 percent by weight.).

Maine
David Campbell, Dir.
Bureau of Alcoholic Beverages and Lottery Operations
State House, Station 8
Augusta, ME 04333
(207) 287-3721; FAX (207) 287-4049
Alternate Contact: Jeff Austin, Dir. of Bureau of Public Safety, Malt and Wine Division
(207) 287-3572

Microbreweries
Is there a specific microbrewery law?	n/a
Are microbreweries allowed to:	
sell directly to retailers?	Yes
sell directly to consumers?	n/a
Production ceiling:	n/a
License fees:	n/a

Brewpubs
Are brewpubs legal?	Yes
Is there a specific brewpub law?	No
Date of legalization:	n/a
Are brewpubs allowed to:	
sell to a distributor/wholesaler?	Yes
sell to retailers?	Yes
sell beer to go?	Yes
sell draft beer to go?	No
sell guest beer?	Yes
sell guest wine?	n/a
offer a full bar?	Yes
Production ceiling:	1,613 barrels
License fees:	$50 on-premises license

Regulatory Information
Does a "Franchise Law" requiring suppliers to form exclusive contracts with distributors exist?   n/a

Additional Notes
Brewpubs in Maine are issued a small Maine brewery license which must be held with any of several on-premises licenses to create a brewpub. Although small Maine brewers are allowed to sell to distributors/wholesalers or directly to retailers, large breweries are not allowed to self-distribute.

Maryland
Dr. Charles Ehart, Administrator, Comptroller of the Treasury
Alcohol and Tobacco Tax Unit
PO Box 2999
Annapolis, MD 21404-2999
(410) 974-3311; FAX (410) 974-3201
Alternate Contact: Daniel Adams, Asst. Administrator
(410) 974-3313

Microbreweries
Is there a specific microbrewery law?   Yes
Description:
    A holder of a Class 7 microbrewery license may brew and bottle malt beverages at a single location and sell to customers for consumption on premises. Off-sale privilege authorizes sale and delivery to any state-licensed wholesaler or to individuals from outside states who are authorized to recieve brewed beverages in their home state.

Are microbreweries allowed to:	
sell directly to retailers?	No
sell directly to consumers?	Yes
Production ceiling:	10,000 barrels
License fees:	

$500, plus retail license of $1,000 to $3,000 depending on county

Brewpubs
Are brewpubs legal?	Yes
Is there a specific brewpub law?	Yes
Date of legalization:	1/1/89

Are brewpubs allowed to:
sell to a distributor/wholesaler?	No
sell to retailers?	No
sell beer to go?	Yes
sell draft beer to go?	Yes
sell guest beer?	Yes
sell guest wine?	Yes
offer a full bar?	Yes
Production ceiling:	2,000 barrels

License fees:

$500, plus retail license of $1,000 to $3,000 depending on county

Additional selling restrictions:

The Class 6 pubbrewery license is void if the restaurant ceases to be operated as a restaurant, or the holder's Class B beer, wine and liquor (on-sale) license is revoked or transferred to a different location.

Regulatory Information
Does a "Franchise Law" requiring suppliers to form exclusive contracts with distributors exist?   Yes
Description:

Law allows for exclusive sales territories by brand.

Size restrictions for malt beverage containers:

Minimum legal size is 6.33-ounce container.

Container labeling requirements:

Adheres to federal label requirements.

Additional Notes
Pubbrewery license available in Ann Arundel, Baltimore, Carroll (13th election district), Cecil, Charles, Frederick, Harford, Washington, Worcester counties and cities of Baltimore, Annapolis, and Gaithersburg. Microbrewery license available in Allegany, Anne Arundel, Baltimore, Carroll (13th election district), Charles, Dorchester, Howard, Prince George's counties and the cities of Baltimore and Annapolis.

Individual counties maintain particular amendments to state legislation.

Massachusetts
Stuart Krusell, Chairman
Alcoholic Beverage Control Commission
Leverett Saltonstall Building, Government Center,
100 Cambridge St., Room 2204
Boston, MA 02202
(617) 727-3040; FAX (617) 727-1258
Alternate Contact: Janet DeCarlo or William Kelley

Microbreweries
Is there a specific microbrewery law?	No

Are microbreweries allowed to:
sell directly to retailers?	Yes
sell directly to consumers?	Yes
Production ceiling:	n/a
License fees:	n/a

Brewpubs
Are brewpubs legal?	Yes
Is there a specific brewpub law?	Yes
Date of legalization:	12/30/82

Are brewpubs allowed to:
sell to a distributor/wholesaler?	Yes
sell to retailers?	Yes, up to 50,000 gallons (1,613 barrels)
sell beer to go?	Yes
sell draft beer to go?	No
sell guest beer?	No
sell guest wine?	Yes
offer a full bar?	No
Production ceiling:	n/a

License fees:

$22 for less than 5,000 barrels annually; $44 for 5,000 to 20,000 barrels annually; maximum $111 per year

Regulatory Information
Does a "Franchise Law" requiring suppliers to form exclusive contracts with distributors exist?   Yes
Description:

There is a franchise law, but it does not require an exclusive contract.

Deposit requirements:

5¢ per can/bottle, $20 per keg

Additional Notes
A farm brewery license may be procured by those who grow cereal grains or hops for the purpose of producing malt beverages. All sales must be made on the brewery premises. Chapter 138 of Massachusetts code pertains to alcoholic beverages.

Michigan
Asha Shah, Business Mgr.
Michigan Liquor Control Commission
PO Box 30005/7150 Harris Dr.
Lansing, MI 48909
(517) 322-1345; FAX (517) 322-6137
Alternate Contact: Rick Perkins, Dir. of Licensing
(517) 322-1420

Microbreweries

Is there a specific microbrewery law?	n/a
Are microbreweries allowed to:	
sell directly to retailers?	No
sell directly to consumers?	n/a
Production ceiling:	n/a
License fees:	n/a

Brewpubs

Are brewpubs legal?	Yes
Is there a specific brewpub law?	Yes
Date of legalization:	12/18/92
Are brewpubs allowed to:	
sell to a distributor/wholesaler?	No
sell to retailers?	No
sell beer to go?	No
sell draft beer to go?	No
sell guest beer?	Yes
sell guest wine?	n/a
offer a full bar?	Yes
Production ceiling:	2,000 barrels

License fees:

$100 annually plus A, B, or C license fee ($250 to $850); microbreweries pay up to $1,000 annually plus $50 per vehicle used for deliveries to licensed retailers.

Regulatory Information

Does a "Franchise Law" requiring suppliers to form exclusive contracts with distributors exist?   n/a

Additional Notes

A brewpub license is issued in conjunction with an on-premises license to sell by the glass and requires that 25 percent of revenue come from food and non-alcoholic beverages. No one may have an interest in more than one brewpub. Microbreweries have a higher production ceiling (20,000 barrels) and are allowed to self-distribute, but they must pay higher licensing fees.

Minnesota

Fred C. Petersen, Dir.
Department of Public Safety, Liquor Control Division
444 Cedar St./100-L Townsquare
St. Paul, MN 55101
(612) 296-6159; FAX (612) 297-5259
Alternate Contact: Lisa Kreter, Wholesale Licensing Mgr.
(612) 296-6939

Microbreweries

Is there a specific microbrewery law?	Yes

Description:

Brewers who manufacture fewer than 2,000 barrels of malt liquor per year.

Are microbreweries allowed to:	
sell directly to retailers?	Yes
sell directly to consumers?	No
Production ceiling:	2,000 barrels
License fees:	$150 per year

Brewpubs

Are brewpubs legal?	Yes
Is there a specific brewpub law?	Yes
Date of legalization:	11/30/87
Are brewpubs allowed to:	
sell to a distributor/wholesaler?	No
sell to retailers?	No
sell beer to go?	No
sell draft beer to go?	No
sell guest beer?	Yes
sell guest wine?	Yes
offer a full bar?	Yes
Production ceiling:	3,500 barrels
License fees:	$500 plus retail license fee

Additional selling restrictions:

The entire production of malt liquor is soley for consumption on tap at the licensed premises. Brands brewed must be registered by Brand Registration.

Regulatory Information

Does a "Franchise Law" requiring suppliers to form exclusive contracts with distributors exist?   Yes
Description: Civil law chapter 325B.01-17
Size restrictions for malt beverage containers: Yes
Container labeling requirements:

Products containing more than 0.5% alcohol by volume and not more than 3.2% by weight must list "contains not more than 3.2% alcohol by weight" on the label.

Additional Notes

Minnesota does not recognize microbreweries specifically. Brewpubs are a unique exception to an otherwise strict three-tier system.

Mississippi

Edward Buelow, Chairman of State Tax Commission
State Tax Commission
PO Box 1033
Jackson, MS 39215
(601) 359-1100; FAX (601) 359-1033
Alternate Contact: Kathy Waterbury, Dir. of Miscellaneous Beverages
(601) 359-1137

Microbreweries
Is there a specific microbrewery law? No
Are microbreweries allowed to:
    sell directly to retailers? No
    sell directly to consumers? No
Distribution restrictions:
May only sell to licensed wholesalers. May not have any relationship (other than supplier) to wholesaler or retailer.
Production ceiling: n/a
License fees: $1,00 per year

Brewpubs
Are brewpubs legal? No
Is there a specific brewpub law? No
Date of legalization: n/a
Are brewpubs allowed to:
    sell to a distributor/wholesaler? n/a
    sell to retailers? n/a
    sell beer to go? n/a
    sell draft beer to go? n/a
    sell guest beer? n/a
    sell guest wine? n/a
    offer a full bar? n/a
Production ceiling: n/a
License fees: n/a

Regulatory Information
Does a "Franchise Law" requiring suppliers to form exclusive contracts with distributors exist? Yes
Description:
Manufacturers must designate distributors. It is unlawful for distributors to sell outside of their territory.
Retail-level packaging restrictions:
No statewide restrictions. May be certain restrictions at local government level.

Additional Notes
Under Mississippi law, brewpubs are illegal. A strict three-tier system exists.

Missouri
Ruby L. Bonner, State Supervisor
Division of Liquor Control
PO Box 837/301 W. High St.
Jefferson City, MO 65101
(314) 751-2333; FAX (314) 526-4540
Alternate Contact: Mike Schler, Chief Auditor
(314) 751-2333

Microbreweries
Is there a specific microbrewery law? Yes
Description: Section 311.195
Are microbreweries allowed to:
    sell directly to retailers? No
    sell directly to consumers? Yes
Production ceiling: 10,000 barrels
License fees:
$5 per 100 barrels or fraction thereof, maximum fee $250

Brewpubs
Are brewpubs legal? Yes
Is there a specific brewpub law? Yes
Date of legalization: 8/28/90
Are brewpubs allowed to:
    sell to a distributor/wholesaler? Yes
    sell to retailers? No
    sell beer to go? Yes
    sell draft beer to go? No
    sell guest beer? Yes
    sell guest wine? Yes
    offer a full bar? Yes
Production ceiling: 2,500 barrels
License fees: *$5 per 100 barrels, maximum $250*

Regulatory Information
Does a "Franchise Law" requiring suppliers to form exclusive contracts with distributors exist? Yes
Description:
Brewer authorizes wholesaler to distribute brand or brands to specific geographical area. This exclusive agreement will be in written form and submitted to supervisor of liquor control.
Retail-level packaging restrictions:
Packaged sales must consist of a minimum of three 12-ounce containers.
Container labeling requirements:
Adheres to federal ATF labeling requirements, adding only that the name and address of the manufacturer be included. Additional packaging and labeling requirements are discribed in Regulation No. 70-2.060.

Additional Notes
House bill 1180 allows a brewer producing less than 2,500 barrels per year (the state's legal definition of a microbrewer) to obtain an on- and/or off-premises retail license. Brewpubs and microbrewery owners may not have any interest, directly or indirectly, in a wholesaler's license.

Montana

Denise C. King, Audit Mgr.
Department of Revenue, Liquor Division
PO Box 1712/2517 Airport Rd.
Helena, MT 59624
(406) 444-0723; FAX (406) 444-0750
Alternate Contact: Diana Koon, Chief-License of Bureau
(406) 444-0711

Microbreweries
Is there a specific microbrewery law? *No*
Are microbreweries allowed to:
    sell directly to retailers? *Yes*
    sell directly to consumers? *Yes**
Distribution restrictions:
    Must produce less than 60,000 barrels per year to sell to consumers.
Production ceiling: *n/a*
License fees: *$500*

Brewpubs
Are brewpubs legal? *No*
Is there a specific brewpub law? *No*
Date of legalization: *n/a*
Are brewpubs allowed to:
    sell to a distributor/wholesaler? *n/a*
    sell to retailers? *n/a*
    sell beer to go? *n/a*
    sell draft beer to go? *n/a*
    sell guest beer? *n/a*
    sell guest wine? *n/a*
    offer a full bar? *n/a*
Production ceiling: *n/a*
License fees:
    On-premises license fees are: $200 for beer; $300 for beer and wine; $400 to $2,000 (depending on locale) for all beverage; and $500 for manufacturer.

Regulatory Information
Does a "Franchise Law" requiring suppliers to form exclusive contracts with distributors exist? *n/a*
Container labeling requirements:
    Addheres to federal regulations

*Additional Notes
Brewers may distribute on a wholesale basis and retail packaged beer for off-premises consumption, but pubbreweries are illegal. While, for instance, Bayern Brewing/Iron Horse Pub is a brewpub-type situation, the brewery and restaurant are owned by separate parties.

Nebraska

Forrest Chapman, Dir.
Nebraska Liquor Control Commission
PO Box 95046/Statehouse Station
Lincoln, NE 68509-5046
(402) 471-2571; FAX (402) 471-2814
Alternate Contact: Jerry Van Ackeren, Wholesale Compliance and Audit Mgr. of Revenue Division

Microbreweries
Is there a specific microbrewery law? *No*
Are microbreweries allowed to:
    sell directly to retailers? *No*
    sell directly to consumers? *n/a*
Production ceiling: *n/a*
License fees: *n/a*

Brewpubs
Are brewpubs legal? *Yes*
Is there a specific brewpub law? *Yes*
Date of legalization: *7/9/88*
Are brewpubs allowed to:
    sell to a distributor/wholesaler? *No*
    sell to retailers? *No*
    sell beer to go? *Yes, not to exceed 10 percent of sales*
    sell draft beer to go? *Yes*
    sell guest beer? *Yes*
    sell guest wine? *n/a*
    offer a full bar? *Yes*
Production ceiling: *5,000 barrels*
License fees: *$250*

Regulatory Information
Does a "Franchise Law" requiring suppliers to form exclusive contracts with distributors exist? *Yes*

Additional Notes
A brewpub license allows for on- or off-premises consumption of beer. The off-premises portion cannot exceed 50 percent of sales. Another license is required to serve wine or other spirits.

Nevada

Michael Pitlock, Dir.
Nevada Department of Taxation
Capital Complex
Carson City, NV 89710-0003
(702) 687-4820 or (702) 687-4892; FAX (702) 687-5981
Alternate Contact: Carmen Shipman, Tax Examiner
(702) 687-6481

Microbreweries
Is there a specific microbrewery law? *n/a*
Are microbreweries allowed to:
    sell directly to retailers? *No*
    sell directly to consumers? *n/a*
Production ceiling: *n/a*
License fees: *n/a*

Brewpubs
Are brewpubs legal? *Yes*
Is there a specific brewpub law? *Yes*
Date of legalization: *2/7/91*
Are brewpubs allowed to:
    sell to a distributor/wholesaler? *Yes*
    sell to retailers? *No*
    sell beer to go? *Yes*
    sell draft beer to go? *Yes*
    sell guest beer? *Yes*
    sell guest wine? *n/a*
    offer a full bar? *Yes*
Production ceiling:
    5,000 to 10,000 barrels depending on location
License fees: *$75 plus local fees*

Regulatory Information
Does a "Franchise Law" requiring suppliers to form exclusive contracts with distributors exist? *Yes*
Description:
    Unless otherwise specified by contract between the supplier and wholesaler, a supplier shall not grant more than one franchise to a wholesaler for any brand of alcoholic beverage in a marketing area.
Container labeling requirements:
    Adheres to federal regulations

Additional Notes
    Local regulations determine what other alcoholic beverages can be sold. In a county whose population is more than 400,000 a person may operate a brewpub in any redevelopment area or historic district established in that county; in any retail liquor store; or in any other area in the county designated by the Board of County Commissioners. A person who operates one or more brewpubs may not manufacture more than 10,000 barrels of malt beverages for all the brewpubs he operates in that county in any calendar year.
    In a county whose population is less than 400,000, a person may operate a brewpub in any redevelopment area or any historic district established in that county and may not manufacture more than 5,000 barrels of malt beverages in any calendar year. In any retail liquor store and in any other area of the county designated by the Board of County Commissioners for the operation of brewpubs.

New Hampshire
David Austin, Chief of Enforcement
State Liquor Commission
PO Box 503/Storrs St.
Concord, NH 03302-0503
(603) 271-3755; FAX (603) 271-1107
Alternate Contact: Ivan Bass, Examiner

Microbreweries
Is there a specific microbrewery law? *No*
Description:
    All breweries which do not meet the brewpub definition are considered the same, regardless of volume.
Are microbreweries allowed to:
    sell directly to retailers? *No*
    sell directly to consumers? *Yes (six pack)*
Production ceiling: *n/a*
License fees:
    $1,692 as manufacturer;vendor license also required to sell to NH wholesalers

Brewpubs
Are brewpubs legal? *Yes*
Is there a specific brewpub law? *Yes*
Date of legalization: *1/1/95*
Are brewpubs allowed to:
    sell to a distributor/wholesaler? *Yes*
    sell to retailers? *No*
    sell beer to go? *Yes, 180 ounces per person per day*
    sell draft beer to go? *No*
    sell guest beer? *Yes*
    sell guest wine? *Yes*
    offer a full bar? *Yes*
Production ceiling: *2,500 barrels*
License fees: *$1,692 for brewpubs*

Regulatory Information
Does a "Franchise Law" requiring suppliers to form exclusive contracts with distributors exist? *Yes*
Description:
    Exclusive territories for wholesalers.

New Jersey
John G. Holl, Dir.
Division of Alcoholic Beverage Control
140 E. Front St., CN 087
Trenton, NJ 08625
(609) 984-2830; FAX (609) 633-6078
Alternate Contact: Gerald Griffin, Deputy Attorney General in Charge
(609) 984-2598

Microbreweries

Is there a specific microbrewery law?   Yes
Description:
   NJSA 33: 1-10 1b "limited brewery license"
Are microbreweries allowed to:
   sell directly to retailers?   Yes
   sell directly to consumers?   No
Production ceiling: 300,000 barrels
License fees:
   $1,000 for up to 50,000 31-fluid-gallon barrels, $2,000 for 50,000 to 100,000 31-fluid-gallon barrels, $4,000 for 100,000 to 300,000 31-fluid-gallon barrels, $6,000 for over 300,000 31-fluid-gallon barrels.

Brewpubs

Are brewpubs legal?   Yes
Is there a specific brewpub law?   Yes
Date of legalization: 7/30/93
Description:
   Restricted brewery license issued only to entities holding "plenary retail consumption" license operating a restaurant pricipally used for the purpose of providing meals to its customers and having adequate kitchen and dining room facilities. The licensed restaurant must immediately adjoin to the premises licensed as a restricted brewery. Beer sales are restricted solely to the adjoining restaurant.
Are brewpubs allowed to:
   sell to a distributor/wholesaler?   No
   sell to retailers?   Yes
   sell beer to go?   No
   sell draft beer to go?   No
   sell guest beer?   No
   sell guest wine?   No
   offer a full bar?   No

Production ceiling: 3,000 barrels
License fees:
   $1,000 for first 1,000 barrels plus $500 per 1,000 barrels produced up to 3,000 barrels
Additional selling restrictions:
   "Brewpubs" may sell to their adjacent restaurant. This restaurant may sell beer, wine, and distilled spirits, as well as the beer brewed in the "brewpub."

Regulatory Information

Does a "Franchise Law" requiring suppliers to form exclusive contracts with distributors exist?   No
Size restrictions for malt beverage containers:
   Same as ATF
Deposit requirements:
   Regulation proposed for adoption: Beer that sells less than 3,000 barrels in New Jersey may have labels that contain deposit information from other states. Beer that sells more than 3,000 barrels in New Jersey may not have deposit information on its labels from other states.
Container labeling requirements:
   Same as ATF

Additional Notes

Brewpubs can only sell their own beer to its adjacent restaurant regularly and principally used for the purpose of providing meals.

New Mexico

Marianne Woodard, Dir.
Alcohol and Gaming Division
PO Box 25101/725 Saint Michael's Dr.
Sante Fe, NM 87504-5101
(505) 827-7066; FAX (505) 827-7168
Alternate Contact: Terri Gonzales, Mgr. of Licensing

Microbreweries

Is there a specific microbrewery law?   Yes
Description:
   A "small brewer" means any person who owns or operates a business for the manufacture of beer, but does not manufacture more than 200,000 barrels annually. Section 60-6A-22(C).
Are microbreweries allowed to:
   sell directly to retailers?   No
   sell directly to consumers?   Yes
Production ceiling: 200,000 barrels per year
License fees: $750 per year

Brewpubs

Are brewpubs legal?   Yes
Is there a specific brewpub law?   Yes
Date of legalization: 1/1/85
Are brewpubs allowed to:
   sell to a distributor/wholesaler?   Yes
   sell to retailers?   No
   sell beer to go?   Yes, packaged beer only
   sell draft beer to go?   No
   sell guest beer?   No
   sell guest wine?   No
   offer a full bar?   No
Production ceiling: 200,000 barrels per year
License fees: $750

Regulatory Information
Does a "Franchise Law" requiring suppliers to form exclusive contracts with distributors exist? n/a

Additional Notes
New Mexico law permits the operation of a pub-brewery with a small brewer's license in a local option district.

New York
Anthony J. Casale, Chairman
State Liquor Authority/Division of Alcoholic Beverage Control
84 Holland Ave.
Albany, NY 12208
(518) 474-4696; FAX (518) 473-2286
Alternate Contact: Maris C. Hart, Public Information Officer
(518) 474-4696

Microbreweries
Is there a specific microbrewery law?	Yes
Are microbreweries allowed to:	
sell directly to retailers?	Yes
sell directly to consumers?	Yes, with additional license
Production ceiling:	60,000 barrels
License fees:	$1,512.50 per year

Brewpubs
Are brewpubs legal?	Yes
Is there a specific brewpub law?	No
Date of legalization:	n/a
Are brewpubs allowed to:	
sell to a distributor/wholesaler?	Yes
sell to retailers?	Yes
sell beer to go?	Yes
sell draft beer to go?	Maybe
sell guest beer?	Yes
sell guest wine?	Depends on license
offer a full bar?	Yes
Production ceiling:	60,000 barrels per year

License fees:
Brewers license $3,125 annually, $200 filing fee; restaurant with all-beverage license $2,200 to $5,200, depending on the municipality

Regulatory Information
Does a "Franchise Law" requiring suppliers to form exclusive contracts with distributors exist? No
Size restrictions for malt beverage containers:
Adheres to federal restrictions

Deposit requirements: 5¢ deposit
Container labeling requirements:
$150 fee for beer label registration. Label must conform to "Federal Alcohol Administration Act" regulations.

North Carolina
Marvin L. Speight Jr., Chairman
Alcoholic Beverage Commission
PO Box 26687
Raleigh, NC 27611
(919) 779-0700; FAX (919) 662-1946
Alternate Contact: Lisa Nelson, Product Compliance Analyst

Microbreweries
Is there a specific microbrewery law?	n/a
Are microbreweries allowed to:	
sell directly to retailers?	No
sell directly to consumers?	n/a
Production ceiling:	n/a
License fees:	n/a

Brewpubs
Are brewpubs legal?	Yes
Is there a specific brewpub law?	Yes
Date of legalization:	n/a
Are brewpubs allowed to:	
sell to a distributor/wholesaler?	Yes
sell to retailers?	No
sell beer to go?	Yes, not to exceed 10 percent of sales
sell draft beer to go?	No
sell guest beer?	Yes
sell guest wine?	n/a
offer a full bar?	Yes
Production ceiling:	10,000 barrels

License fees:
Brewery permit $150 one-time; on-premises permit $200 one-time; brewers license $500 annually; retail license $100 annually; wholesale license $150 annually plus $25 annually for each driver and sales man.

Regulatory Information
Does a "Franchise Law" requiring suppliers to form exclusive contracts with distributors exist? n/a

Additional Notes
A manufacturer's license allows the manufacture and sale of beer to licensed wholesalers. A retail license allows on- or off-premises consumption. A wholesale license allows sale directly to licensed retailers.

North Dakota

Kathi Gilmore, State Treasurer
Office of State Treasurer
Capitol Building, Third Floor/600 E. Boulevard Ave.
Bismarck, ND 58505-0600
(701) 328-2643; FAX (701) 328-3002
Alternate Contact: Carol M. Siegert, Deputy Treas.
(701) 328-2643

Microbreweries
Is there a specific microbrewery law?   n/a
Description:
   Same as "brewpub" law
Are microbreweries allowed to:
   sell directly to retailers?   No
   sell directly to consumers?   Yes
Production ceiling: *10,000 barrels*
License fees: *$500*

Brewpubs
Are brewpubs legal?   Yes
Is there a specific brewpub law?   Yes
Date of legalization: *1/7/90, revised 1995*
Description:
   A microbrew pub may manufacture on the licensed premises, store, transport, sell to wholesale malt beverage licensees, and export no more than 10,000 barrels of malt beverages annually; sell malt beverages manufactured on the licensed premises; and sell alcoholic beverages regardless of source to consumers for consumption on the microbrew pub's licensed premises. A microbrew pub may not engage in any wholesaling activities. All sales and delivery of malt beverages to any other retail licensed premises may be made only through a wholesale malt beverage licensee.
Are brewpubs allowed to:
   sell to a distributor/wholesaler?   Yes
   sell to retailers?   No
   sell beer to go?   Yes
   sell draft beer to go?   Yes
   sell guest beer?   Yes
   sell guest wine?   Yes
   offer a full bar?   Yes
Production ceiling: *10,000 barrels*
License fees:
   $500 annual manufacturer's license; $25,000 manufacturer's bond; $50,000 bond for liquor sales

Regulatory Information
Does a "Franchise Law" requiring suppliers to form exclusive contracts with distributors exist?   No
Size restrictions for malt beverage containers:
   NDCC-5-02-07.2
Container labeling requirements:
   Brand registration required

Additional Notes
Recent ammendments establish no distinction between microbrewery and brewpub.

Ohio

Michael Akrouche, Dir.
Department of Liquor Control
2323 W. Fifth Ave.
Columbus, OH 43204-3692
(614) 644-2360; FAX (614) 644-2480
Alternate Contact: Dan Cesner, Deputy Chief of Beer and Wine Division
(614) 644-2407

Microbreweries
Is there a specific microbrewery law?   No
Are microbreweries allowed to:
   sell directly to retailers?   Yes
   sell directly to consumers?   Yes
Production ceiling: n/a
License fees: *$3,125 per year*

Brewpubs
Are brewpubs legal?   Yes
Is there a specific brewpub law?   No
Date of legalization: n/a
Are brewpubs allowed to:
   sell to a distributor/wholesaler?   Yes
   sell to retailers?   Yes
   sell beer to go?   Yes
   sell draft beer to go?   No
   sell guest beer?   Yes
   sell guest wine?   Yes
   offer a full bar?   Yes
Production ceiling: n/a
License fees: *$3,125 per year*
Additional selling restrictions:
   Brewpubs must also have a brewery permit costing $3,125.

Regulatory Information
Does a "Franchise Law" requiring suppliers to form exclusive contracts with distributors exist? Yes
Size restrictions for malt beverage containers:
Not larger than 5-1/6 gallons.
Container labeling requirements:
Must include name of brewery.

Additional Notes
A manufacturer's license allows the brewer to sell to licensed wholesalers, retailers, and to the consumer for consumption off the brewery's premises. An on-premises license may be obtained for a location adjacent to the brewery only.

Oklahoma
Russ Nordstrom, Dir. of Registration Division
**Registration Tax Division/
Oklahoma Tax Commission**
2501 Lincoln Blvd.
Oklahoma City, OK 73194
(405) 521-4328; FAX (405) 521-3826
Alternate Contact: Shera Neasbitt, Beverage Auditor
(405) 521-4437

Microbreweries
Is there a specific microbrewery law? No
Are microbreweries allowed to:
    sell directly to retailers? Yes
    sell directly to consumers? No
Distribution restrictions:
Must hold a wholesaler's license to sell to retailers.
Production ceiling: n/a
License fees:
Manufacturers' licenses are $500 annually

Brewpubs
Are brewpubs legal? Yes
Is there a specific brewpub law? Yes
Date of legalization: 4/13/92
Are brewpubs allowed to:
    sell to a distributor/wholesaler? No
    sell to retailers? No
    sell beer to go? No
    sell draft beer to go? No
    sell guest beer? Yes
    sell guest wine? Yes
    offer a full bar? Yes
Production ceiling: 5,000 barrels
License fees: $450 for three years
Additional selling restrictions:
Requires additional licenses to sell guest beer, wine, and a full bar.

Regulatory Information
Does a "Franchise Law" requiring suppliers to form exclusive contracts with distributors exist? Yes
Description:
Exclusive territorial arrangements for wholesalers distributors exist.

Additional Notes
Brewpubs can produce beer of no more than 3.2 percent alcohol by weight (4.1 percent alcohol by volume). As of November 1, 1995, beer of 3.2 percent by weight is referred to as "low point" beer.

Oregon
W. Eugene Hallman, Chairman
Oregon Liquor Control Commission
PO Box 22297/9079 S.E. McLoughlin Blvd.
Portland, OR 97222-7355
(503) 872-5200; FAX (503) 872-5260
Alternate Contact: Paul Williamson, Beer and Wine Section
(503) 872-5071

Microbreweries
Is there a specific microbrewery law? No
Description:
The term "microbrewery" is not recognized in statutes; however, breweries producing less than 200,000 barrels have limited retail privileges.
Are microbreweries allowed to:
    sell directly to retailers? Yes
    sell directly to consumers? Yes
Distribution restrictions:
Off-premises sales is limited to a minimum of 5 gallons.
Production ceiling: 200,000 barrels per year
License fees: $500

Brewpubs
Are brewpubs legal? Yes
Is there a specific brewpub law? Yes
Date of legalization: 6/12/85
Are brewpubs allowed to:
    sell to a distributor/wholesaler? Yes
    sell to retailers? No
    sell beer to go? Yes
    sell draft beer to go? Yes
    sell guest beer? Yes
    sell guest wine? Yes
    offer a full bar? No
Production ceiling: 60,000 barrels
License fees: $250

Control Agencies, Laws, and Regulations

Regulatory Information
Does a "Franchise Law" requiring suppliers to form exclusive contracts with distributors exist? Yes
Deposit requirements: 5¢ container deposit

Pennsylvania
James A. Goodman, Chairman
Pennsylvania Liquor Control Board
Capital and Forester Streets, Room 518
Harrisburg, PA 17124-0001
(717) 787-7114; FAX (717) 772-3714
Alternate Contact: Mike Plumley, Assistant Counsel
(717) 783-9454

Microbreweries
Is there a specific microbrewery law? n/a
Are microbreweries allowed to:
    sell directly to retailers? No
    sell directly to consumers? n/a
Production ceiling: n/a
License fees: n/a

Brewpubs
Are brewpubs legal? Yes
Is there a specific brewpub law? Yes
Date of legalization: 6/29/87
Are brewpubs allowed to:
    sell to a distributor/wholesaler? Yes
    sell to retailers? Yes
    sell beer to go? Yes
    sell draft beer to go? Yes
    sell guest beer? No
    sell guest wine? n/a
    offer a full bar? No
Production ceiling: 2,500 barrels
License fees:
    $730 annual renewal, $1,425 one-time cost; transfer cost $650 person to person (same location), $550 place to place (new location), $700 double transfer

Regulatory Information
Does a "Franchise Law" requiring suppliers to form exclusive contracts with distributors exist? n/a

Additional Notes
Pennsylvania requires Liquor Control Board approval for sale of items other than food or beer. It appears this approval has never been given for wine or other spirits.

Rhode Island
Joseph Gallucci, Administrator
Liquor Control Administration
233 Richmond St.
Providence, RI 02903
(401) 277-2562; FAX (401) 277-6029
Alternate Contact: Ann Cote, Supervisor of Importation
(401) 277-2562

Microbreweries
Is there a specific microbrewery law? n/a
Are microbreweries allowed to:
    sell directly to retailers? No
    sell directly to consumers? n/a
Production ceiling: n/a
License fees: n/a

Brewpubs
Are brewpubs legal? Yes
Is there a specific brewpub law? Yes
Date of legalization: 1/1/92
Are brewpubs allowed to:
    sell to a distributor/wholesaler? No
    sell to retailers? No
    sell beer to go? No
    sell draft beer to go? No
    sell guest beer? Yes
    sell guest wine? n/a
    offer a full bar? Yes
Production ceiling: None
License fees:
    Manufacturer's license is $100 annually. Local license varies, pending legislation would set a $1,000 standard across state.

Regulatory Information
Does a "Franchise Law" requiring suppliers to form exclusive contracts with distributors exist? n/a

Additional Notes
A brewpub must include a restaurant. A license will not be granted within 200 feet of a school or church, and within this same zone a majority of landowners can block the license. Licensees cannot reside out of state or have an interest in an out-of-state brewing operation.

South Carolina
Patricia Stites, Supervisor, ABL Division
South Carolina Department of Revenue
PO Box 125
Columbia, SC 29214
(803) 734-0470; FAX (803) 734-1401

Control Agencies, Laws, and Regulations

Microbreweries
Is there a specific microbrewery law?	Yes
Are microbreweries allowed to:	
sell directly to retailers?	No
sell directly to consumers?	No
Production ceiling:	n/a
License fees:	n/a

Brewpubs
Are brewpubs legal?	Yes
Is there a specific brewpub law?	Yes
Date of legalization:	7/1/94
Are brewpubs allowed to:	
sell to a distributor/wholesaler?	No
sell to retailers?	No
sell beer to go?	Yes
sell draft beer to go?	Yes
sell guest beer?	Yes
sell guest wine?	Yes
offer a full bar?	Yes
Production ceiling:	2,000 barrels
License fees:	Bi-annual: $2,000

Additional selling restrictions:

Brewpub beer manufacturing and sales must be approved by Department of Health and Environmental Control.

Regulatory Information
Does a "Franchise Law" requiring suppliers to form exclusive contracts with distributors exist? Yes

Description:

Registered producers cannot terminate agreements existing prior to 5/1/74 without just cause and written, sixty-day notice. Wholesalers cannot refuse to sell to licensed retail dealers within geographical regions covered by franchise agreements and cannot warehouse beer to be sold in South Carolina outside of the state.

Additional Notes
Brewpubs are allowed to offer a full bar with the following stipulations: A separate license to sell spirits must be obtained, and the brewpub must be primarily engaged in the production and sale of food.

South Dakota
Jim Schade, Dir. of Property and Special Taxes
Department of Revenue
700 Governors Dr.
Pierre, SD 57501-2291
(605) 773-3311; FAX (605) 773-6729
Alternate Contact: Carol Logan, Mgr. of Revenue Section
(605) 773-3311

Microbreweries
Is there a specific microbrewery law?	n/a
Are microbreweries allowed to:	
sell directly to retailers?	Yes
sell directly to consumers?	n/a
Production ceiling:	n/a
License fees:	n/a

Brewpubs
Are brewpubs legal?	Yes
Is there a specific brewpub law?	No
Date of legalization:	1991
Are brewpubs allowed to:	
sell to a distributor/wholesaler?	Yes
sell to retailers?	Yes
sell beer to go?	Yes
sell draft beer to go?	Maybe
sell guest beer?	Yes
sell guest wine?	n/a
offer a full bar?	Yes, if licensed for such
Production ceiling:	n/a
License fees:	

Manufacturer $500 annually, $150 package to go, $250 on- or off-site retailer license

Regulatory Information
Does a "Franchise Law" requiring suppliers to form exclusive contracts with distributors exist? n/a

Additional Notes
A brewpub is created by obtaining a manufacturer's license (which carries wholesale privileges) and a retail license to sell on- or off-premises. There is no prohibition on obtaining other dispensing licenses, fees of which are set by local agencies.

Beer to go must be properly packaged.

Tennessee
Eddie McCormack, Dir.
**Office of Audit and Examination,
Department of Revenue**
500 Deaderick St./801 Andrew Jackson Building, Sixth Floor
Nashville, TN 37242-1099
(615) 741-3501; FAX (615) 741-5319
Alternate Contact: Thomas R. Bain, Tax Counsel
(615) 741-2348

Microbreweries
Is there a specific microbrewery law?	No
Are microbreweries allowed to:	
sell directly to retailers?	No
sell directly to consumers?	n/a
Production ceiling:	n/a
License fees:	n/a

Brewpubs

Are brewpubs legal?	Yes
Is there a specific brewpub law?	Yes
Date of legalization:	6/1/91

Description:
   Beer manufacturer may operate as a beer retailer, either at a manufacturer's location or a contiguous site, for consumption on- or off-premises subject to statutory restrictions.

Are brewpubs allowed to:

sell to a distributor/wholesaler?	Yes
sell to retailers?	Yes*
sell beer to go?	Yes
sell draft beer to go?	Yes
sell guest beer?	Yes
sell guest wine?	n/a
offer a full bar?	n/a
Production ceiling:	5,000 barrels
License fees:	$40 plus local fee

*Additional selling restrictions:
   Beer manufacturer operating as a retailer is prohibited from selling beer directly to retailers located in a county other than a county in which the manufacturer is located.

Regulatory Information

Does a "Franchise Law" requiring suppliers to form exclusive contracts with distributors exist?   Yes

Description:
   Every manufacturer or importer of beer must designate sales territories for each of its brands sold in Tennessee and shall name one licensed beer wholesaler in each territory who, within such territory, shall be the exclusive wholesaler for the brand or brands.

Size restrictions for malt beverage containers:
   Only sizes permitted on Tennessee civilian market are: 7 ounce, 8 ounce, 10 ounce, 11 ounce, 12 ounce, 16 ounce, 24 ounce, 32 ounce, 38.43 ounce, 64 ounce (sold on military bases only), 2¼ gallon (tapper), 7¾ gallon (¼ barrel), 15½ gallon (1 barrel). Imported malt beverages are sold lawfully in containers that hold not less than 11.25 ounces nor more than 11.5 ounces. Also imported malt beverages are sold lawfully in containers holding not less than 13 gallons nor more than 14 gallons (or 49 to 53 liters).

Container labeling requirements:
   Imported malt beverage label cannot include the word "beer" or "ale."

*Additional Notes

Beer manufacturers operating as retailers must be located in a county with a population exceeding 75,000.

Texas

Doyne Bailey, Administrator
Texas Alcoholic Beverage Commission
5806 Mesa Dr.
Austin, TX 78731
(512) 458-2500; FAX (512) 206-3274
Alternate Contact: Randy Yarbrough, Asst. Admin.
(512) 458-2500

Microbreweries

Is there a specific microbrewery law?	No

Are microbreweries allowed to:

sell directly to retailers?	Yes
sell directly to consumers?	No
Production ceiling:	75,000 barrels
License fees:	$787 per year

Brewpubs

Are brewpubs legal?	Yes
Is there a specific brewpub law?	Yes
Date of legalization:	9/1/93

Description:
   See Sec. 74.01

Are brewpubs allowed to:

sell to a distributor/wholesaler?	No
sell to retailers?	No
sell beer to go?	Yes, kegs only
sell draft beer to go?	No or yes*
sell guest beer?	Yes
sell guest wine?	Yes
offer a full bar?	Yes
Production ceiling:	5,000 barrels

License fees:
   $500 plus other license cost; $3,000 mixed beverage to $150 beer and wine on-premises

Additional selling restrictions:
   Brewpubs must also hold a beer retailer's license, wine and beer retailer's permit, or a mixed beverage permit. Alcoholic beverages may not be removed from the premises of a mixed beverage permit holder.

Regulatory Information

Does a "Franchise Law" requiring suppliers to form exclusive contracts with distributors exist?   Yes

Description:
   Territorial agreement between manufacturer and distributor.

Size restrictions for malt beverage containers:
   The 7-, 8-, 12-, 16-, 24-, and 32-ounce containers and partial kegs are legal.

Container labeling requirements:
   See Sec. 45.83-845.91

Control Agencies, Laws, and Regulations

Additional Notes
Brewpubs must be located in wet areas. The brewpub license is issued in conjunction with a retail license. Owners are restricted from having interests in wholesaling or manufacturing alcohol, but are allowed to own multiple brewpubs. State laws allow a brewpub licensee to offer other producer's products, without charge, for the purpose of "beer tasting, competition, or review."

Utah
Kenneth Wynn, Dir.
State of Utah Alcoholic Beverage Control
PO Box 30408/1625 S. 900 W.
Salt Lake City, UT 84130-0408
(801) 977-6800; FAX (801) 977-6888
Alternate Contact: Earl Dorius, Compliance Mgr.

Microbreweries
Is there a specific microbrewery law?	n/a
Are microbreweries allowed to:	
sell directly to retailers?	Yes
sell directly to consumers?	n/a
Production ceiling:	n/a
License fees:	n/a

Brewpubs
Are brewpubs legal?	Yes
Is there a specific brewpub law?	Yes
Date of legalization:	2/1/88
Are brewpubs allowed to:	
sell to a distributor/wholesaler?	Yes
sell to retailers?	Yes
sell beer to go?	Yes
sell draft beer to go?	Yes
sell guest beer?	Yes
sell guest wine?	n/a
offer a full bar?	Yes
Production ceiling:	n/a

License fees:
$1,000 plus on-premises retail ($100 beer to $750 club); $300 to $1,000 one-time processing fee

Regulatory Information
Does a "Franchise Law" requiring suppliers to form exclusive contracts with distributors exist?   n/a

Additional Notes
The brewer is forbidden to sell packaged beer directly to the final consumer, but growlers are allowed. The beer must contain no more than 3.2 percent alcohol by weight (4 percent alcohol by volume).

Vermont
Norris Hoyt, Commissioner
Vermont Department of Liquor Control
Green Mountain Dr., Drawer 20
Montpelier, VT 05620-4501
(802) 828-2345; FAX (802) 828-2803
Alternate Contact: Albert R. Elwell, Dir. of Enforcement and Licensing
(802) 828-2339

Microbreweries
Is there a specific microbrewery law?	No
Are microbreweries allowed to:	
sell directly to retailers?	No
sell directly to consumers?	No
Production ceiling:	n/a
License fees:	$100 per year

Brewpubs
Are brewpubs legal?	Yes
Is there a specific brewpub law?	No
Date of legalization:	5/1/88
Are brewpubs allowed to:	
sell to a distributor/wholesaler?	Yes
sell to retailers?	No
sell beer to go?	Yes
sell draft beer to go?	Yes
sell guest beer?	Yes
sell guest wine?	Yes
offer a full bar?	No
Production ceiling:	n/a

License fees:
$150 manufacturer, $750 bottler; retail licenses vary from $50 to $400

Regulatory Information
Does a "Franchise Law" requiring suppliers to form exclusive contracts with distributors exist?   Yes
Description: *Exclusive territories*
Deposit requirements: 5¢ deposit
Container labeling requirements:
   Vermont's 5¢ deposit indication is required on containers.

Additional Notes
Manufacturing and retailing licenses must be obtained.

Virginia

Catherine H. Giordano, Chairperson
Virginia Department of Alcoholic Beverage Control
PO Box 27491
Richmond, VA 23261-7491
(804) 367-0649; FAX (804) 367-2054
Alternate Contact: Carl Hayden, Special Agent in Charge

Microbreweries
Is there a specific microbrewery law?	n/a
Are microbreweries allowed to:	
sell directly to retailers?	No
sell directly to consumers?	n/a
Production ceiling:	n/a
License fees:	n/a

Brewpubs
Are brewpubs legal?	Yes
Is there a specific brewpub law?	No
Date of legalization:	n/a
Are brewpubs allowed to:	
sell to a distributor/wholesaler?	No
sell to retailers?	No
sell beer to go?	Yes
sell draft beer to go?	Yes
sell guest beer?	Yes
sell guest wine?	n/a
offer a full bar?	Yes
Production ceiling:	n/a

License fees:
  $180 plus manufacturer's fees; $1,500 for fewer than 10,000 barrels; fee doubles after 10,000 barrels

Regulatory Information
Does a "Franchise Law" requiring suppliers to form exclusive contracts with distributors exist?   n/a

Additional Notes
The pub must be on the premises or immediately adjacent to the premises of the brewery. For the brewpub to be within the law, it is absolutely necessary for the establishment to have full food-service facilities as well.

Washington

Mike Murphy, Acting Chairman
Washington State Liquor Control Board
PO Box 43075/1025 E. Union
Olympia, WA 98504-3075
(360) 753-6263; FAX (360) 664-9689
Alternate Contact: Rich Raico, Supervisor of Manufacturing, Industry, and Wholesaling
(360) 664-2249

Microbreweries
Is there a specific microbrewery law?	No
Are microbreweries allowed to:	
sell directly to retailers?	Yes
sell directly to consumers?	Yes
Production ceiling:	n/a

License fees:
  $50 per 1,000 barrels; $2,000 maximum annually

Brewpubs
Are brewpubs legal?	Yes
Is there a specific brewpub law?	Yes
Date of legalization:	n/a

Description:
  A brewery in Washington state may add additional retail classes of license on the same property. This may include a full service bar and restaurant.

Are brewpubs allowed to:	
sell to a distributor/wholesaler?	Yes
sell to retailers?	Yes
sell beer to go?	Yes
sell draft beer to go?	Yes
sell guest beer?	Yes*
sell guest wine?	Yes*
offer a full bar?	Yes*
Production ceiling:	n/a

License fees:
  $50 per 1,000 barrels; $2,000 maximum annually

*Additional selling restrictions:
  Additional license classes are required.

Regulatory Information
Does a "Franchise Law" requiring suppliers to form exclusive contracts with distributors exist?   No
Size restrictions for malt beverage containers:
  Defined in WAC 314-20-030
Retail-level packaging restrictions:
  RCW 66.24.320, RCW 66.24.330, RCW 66.24.360
Container labeling requirements:
  RCW 66.28.120, WAC 314-20-020, WAC 314-20-030

Additional Notes
The consumer must provide his own container for beer to go (see RCW 66.24.320 and RCW 66.24.330). Licensed breweries in Washington State have the privilege of acting as a beer wholesaler and Class B and E retailer for product of their own production only. A Washington State brewery may also be licensed as a beer and/or wine retailer on the brewery premises pursuant to chapter RCW 66.24.

West Virginia
Rick Atkinson, Commissioner
Alcoholic Beverage Control Commission, Enforcement Division
322 70th St. S.E.
Charleston, WV 25304
(304) 558-2481; FAX (304) 558-0081
Alternate Contact: Ron Moates, Deputy Commissioner

Microbreweries
Is there a specific microbrewery law?	No
Are microbreweries allowed to:	
sell directly to retailers?	No
sell directly to consumers?	No
Production ceiling:	n/a
Licesnse fees:	n.a

Brewpubs
Are brewpubs legal?	Yes
Is there a specific brewpub law?	Yes
Date of legalization:	3/9/91

Description:
Brewpub shall mean a place of manufacture of "non-intoxicating" beer owned by the resident brewer subject to federal regulations and guidelines, a portion of which premises are designated for retail sales.

Are brewpubs allowed to:
sell to a distributor/wholesaler?	Yes
sell to retailers?	Yes
sell beer to go?	Yes
sell draft beer to go?	Yes
sell guest beer?	Yes
sell guest wine?	Yes
offer a full bar?	Yes
Production ceiling:	n/a
License fees:	$1,000 plus $5,000 to $10,000 bond

Regulatory Information
Does a "Franchise Law" requiring suppliers to form exclusive contracts with distributors exist? **Yes**

Description:
Suppliers must sign franchise agreements with distributors and offer all their products to those distributors.

Size restrictions for malt beverage containers:
No restrictions, but most receive approval from agency.

Container labeling requirements:
Labels must be approved through agency. No labels can be approved indicating contents are brewed for a certain distribution or retailer.

Additional Notes
House bill 2764 created a brewpub license that allows on-site consumption and other retailing privileges but not distribution. This bill also authorizes a resident brewer to sell to consumers from a location other than the brewery in 1/8-barrel quantities or higher, as well as allowing distributor privileges. The law seeks to eliminate any overlap between brewery and brewpub, but distribution by brewpubs may be allowed.

Wisconsin
Jim Jenkins, Chief of Alcohol and Tobacco Enforcement
Wisconsin Department of Revenue
PO Box 8910
Madison, WI 53708-8910
(608) 266-3969; FAX (608) 264-9920
jenkij@mail.state.wi.us
Alternate Contact: Roger Johnson, Asst. Chief
(608) 266-6757

Microbreweries
Is there a specific microbrewery law?	No

Description:
Small breweies receive a tax break on the first 50,000 barrels if producing less than 300,000 barrels per year.

Are microbreweries allowed to:
sell directly to retailers?	Yes
sell directly to consumers?	No

Distribution restrictions:
May sell to retailers if brewery holds a wholesale beer permit/license.

Production ceiling:	n/a
License fees:	n/a

Brewpubs
Are brewpubs legal?	Yes
Is there a specific brewpub law?	No
Date of legalization:	n/a

Are brewpubs allowed to:
sell to a distributor/wholesaler?	Yes
sell to retailers?	Yes
sell beer to go?	Yes
sell draft beer to go?	No
sell guest beer?	Yes
sell guest wine?	Yes
offer a full bar?	Yes
Production ceiling:	None

License fees:
Class B license for just beer is $100 annually; full bar is $50 to $500.

Additional selling restrictions:
May sell to wholesalers and retailers if brewery holds a wholesale beer permit/license.

Regulatory Information
Does a "Franchise Law" requiring suppliers to form exclusive contracts with distributors exist? **No**
Container labeling requirements:
In accordance with federal regulations

Additional Notes
Wisconsin allows brewers to obtain licenses to sell at any level in the distribution system. Class A licenses authorize package stores, and Class B licenses authorize the sale of beer only. Brewers are limited to two Class B licenses — one on brewery premises and one on property owned by the brewery or a subsidiary. A brewery with a wholesale beer license/permit cannot obtain a Class A beer license unless held before May 5, 1994.

Wyoming
Tom Lopez, Dir.
Wyoming Liquor Commission
1520 E. Fifth St.
Cheyenne, WY 82002
(307) 777-7120; FAX (307) 777-6255
Alternate Contact: Tom Montoya, Agent
(307) 777-6453

Microbreweries
Is there a specific microbrewery law?	n/a
Are microbreweries allowed to:	
sell directly to retailers?	No
sell directly to consumers?	n/a
Production ceiling:	n/a
License fees:	n/a

Brewpubs
Are brewpubs legal?	Yes
Is there a specific brewpub law?	Yes
Date of legalization:	2/25/92
Are brewpubs allowed to:	
sell to a distributor/wholesaler?	Yes
sell to retailers?	No
sell beer to go?	Yes
sell draft beer to go?	Yes
sell guest beer?	Yes
sell guest wine?	n/a
offer a full bar?	Yes
Production ceiling:	15,000 barrels

License fees:
Microbrewery licenses are $300 to $500 at pleasure of local authorizing entity.

Regulatory Information
Does a "Franchise Law" requiring suppliers to form exclusive contracts with distributors exist? **n/a**

Additional Notes
A microbrewery license allows the brewing of malt beverages. All other licenses (retail, on-site, consumption, etc.) are granted by, and at the pleasure of, local licensing authorities.

United States Territories

Puerto Rico
Rafael Caraballo, Dir.
Department of the Treasury, Bureau of Alchoholic Beverages and Taxes
PO Box S4515
San Juan, PR 00905
(809) 721-5245/721-5246; FAX (809) 722-6749
Alternate Contact: Jose M. Hernandez, Asst. to the Dir.

Microbreweries
Is there a specific microbrewery law?	No
Are microbreweries allowed to:	
sell directly to retailers?	No
sell directly to consumers?	No
Production ceiling:	Not allowed
License fees:	Not allowed

Brewpubs
Are brewpubs legal?	No
Is there a specific brewpub law?	No
Date of legalization:	n/a
Are brewpubs allowed to:	
sell to a distributor/wholesaler?	No
sell to retailers?	No
sell beer to go?	No
sell draft beer to go?	No
sell guest beer?	No
sell guest wine?	No
offer a full bar?	No
Production ceiling:	n/a
License fees:	n/a

Regulatory Information
Does a "Franchise Law" requiring suppliers to form exclusive contracts with distributors exist? **yes**
Description:
Any specific brand is restricted to a sole importer.
Size restrictions for malt beverage containers:
7-ounce and 12-ounce
Container labeling requirements:
Same as BATF including name of importer or manufacturer, alcohol content, and volume of content in milliliters.

Additional Notes
Brewpubs and microbreweries are not legal.

Control Agencies, Laws, and Regulations

United States Virgin Islands
Gary Spraure, Exececutive Dir.
Alcohol Control Board
#1 Sub Base, Room 205
St. Thomas, USVI 00801
(809) 774-3130; FAX (809) 776-0675
Alternate Contact: Knolah Nicholls

Microbreweries
Is there a specific microbrewery law?	n/a
Are microbreweries allowed to:	
sell directly to retailers?	Yes
sell directly to consumers?	n/a
Production ceiling:	n/a
License fees:	n/a

Brewpubs
Are brewpubs legal?	Yes
Is there a specific brewpub law?	No
Date of legalization:	n/a
Are brewpubs allowed to:	
sell to a distributor/wholesaler?	Yes
sell to retailers?	Yes
sell beer to go?	Yes
sell draft beer to go?	Yes
sell guest beer?	Yes
sell guest wine?	n/a
offer a full bar?	Yes
Production ceiling:	n/a
License fees:	Manufacturer $800; on-site $250

Regulatory Information
Does a "Franchise Law" requiring suppliers to form exclusive contracts with distributors exist? n/a

Canada

Alberta
Roy Bricker, Dir. of Corp. Development
Alberta Gaming and Liquor Commission
50 Corriveau Ave.
St. Albert, AB T8N 3T5
Canada
(403) 447-8820; FAX (403) 447-8916

Microbreweries
Is there a specific microbrewery law?	No
Are microbreweries allowed to:	
sell directly to retailers?	Yes
sell directly to consumers?	Yes, off-premises sales only

Distribution restrictions:
Microbrewery not defined. Have the same benefits as a large brewer.
Production ceiling: n/a
License fees:
$2,000 first year, then based on sales to the Commission ($0–$1 million sales, $500; $1 million–$5 million sales, $2,000; $5 million–$10 million sales, $3,000; etc.)

Brewpubs
Are brewpubs legal?	Yes
Is there a specific brewpub law?	Yes
Date of legalization:	1/1/80

Description:
Liquor Administration regulation provides for the establishment of brewpubs by Class A liquor license (operators of restaurants or lounges).
Are brewpubs allowed to:
sell to a distributor/wholesaler?	No
sell to retailers?	No
sell beer to go?	Yes
sell draft beer to go?	Yes
sell guest beer?	Yes
sell guest wine?	Yes
offer a full bar?	Yes
Production ceiling:	5,000 hectoliters

License fees:
Class E (manufacturer) — $500; Class A (liquor) — $200; Class D (off-sales) — $100
Additional selling restrictions:
Can only sell beer they manufacture for off-premises consumption.

Regulatory Information
Does a "Franchise Law" requiring suppliers to form exclusive contracts with distributors exist? n/a
Deposit requirements:
10¢ up to one-liter container, 20¢ over one-liter container
Container labeling requirements:
Must include alcohol content by volume, manufacturer's name and address, name of product, and metric quantity. Label must be bilingual (French and English).

Additional Notes
The Class A license allows the sale of liquor in a restaurant setting. The Class E manufacturer's license authorizes the brewing operation, and will be granted to a Class A licensee if the brewery and pub are in the same building. A brewpub must hold a Class D license to sell beer for off-premises consumption.

British Columbia

Mark Fukuhara, Mgr. of Retail Accounting
British Columbia Liquor Distribution Branch
2625 Rupert St.
Vancouver, BC V5M 3T5
Canada
(604) 252-3000; FAX (604) 252-3464
Alternate Contact: Bob Llougheed, Liquor Control and Licensing Branch
(604) 387-1254

Microbreweries

Is there a specific microbrewery law?	n/a
Are microbreweries allowed to:	
sell directly to retailers?	No
sell directly to consumers?	n/a
Production ceiling:	n/a
License fees:	n/a

Brewpubs

Are brewpubs legal?	Yes
Is there a specific brewpub law?	No
Date of legalization:	n/a
Are brewpubs allowed to:	
sell to a distributor/wholesaler?	No
sell to retailers?	No
sell beer to go?	Yes
sell draft beer to go?	No
sell guest beer?	Yes
sell guest wine?	n/a
offer a full bar?	Yes
Production ceiling:	None

License fees:
    $500 application fee; $1,000 minimum annually; .5¢ per imperial gallon produced

Regulatory Information

Does a "Franchise Law" requiring suppliers to form exclusive contracts with distributors exist?   n/a

Additional Notes

A brewpub can only sell to its associated on-premises retail licensee.

Manitoba

Al Ahoff, VP Finance and Licensing
Manitoba Liquor Control Commission
PO Box 1023
Winnipeg, MB R3C 2X1
Canada
(204) 474-5512; FAX (204) 475-7287
Alternate Contact: Kathi Semmidtke, Asst. to VP Finance and Licensing
(204) 474-5513

Microbreweries

Is there a specific microbrewery law?	No

Description:
    By policy a microbrewery is one producing 15,000 hectoliters or less annually.

Are microbreweries allowed to:	
sell directly to retailers?	No
sell directly to consumers?	Yes

Distribution restrictions:
    Must arrange for pick up of all empty containers

Production ceiling:	15,000 hectoliters
License fees:	No

Brewpubs

Are brewpubs legal?	Yes
Is there a specific brewpub law?	No
Date of legalization:	n/a
Are brewpubs allowed to:	
sell to a distributor/wholesaler?	No
sell to retailers?	No
sell beer to go?	Yes
sell draft beer to go?	Yes
sell guest beer?	Yes
sell guest wine?	No
offer a full bar?	Yes
Production ceiling:	n/a

License fees:
    Dining room — $200; cocktail lounge — $200; hotel beverage — $165; retail (package) — $110

Additional selling restrictions:
    Off-sale must be in a recycleable, deposit refundable container.

Regulatory Information

Does a "Franchise Law" requiring suppliers to form exclusive contracts with distributors exist?   No

Deposit requirements:
    10¢ per container up to 2 liters, 20¢ above 2 liters, no deposit for on-premises kegs

Retail-level packaging restrictions:
    Must be retained in package from supplier (6-packs, 12-packs, 24-packs). Six-packs may not be sold as six singles.

Container labeling requirements:
    Federal law requires English and French container size and percentage alcohol by volume. Beer in excess of 5.5 percent ABV requires adjective such as strong beer/ale or malt liquor.

New Brunswick
Roger Landry, Pres.
New Brunswick Liquor Corp.
PO Box 20787
Fredericton, NB E3B 5B8
Canada
(506) 452-6520; FAX (506) 452-9890
Alternate Contact: Gary Von Richter, Products and Purchasing Mgr.
(506) 452-6826

Microbreweries
Is there a specific microbrewery law?	No
Are microbreweries allowed to:	
sell directly to retailers?	No
sell directly to consumers?	Yes (as an agent of NBLC)
Production ceiling:	n/a
License fees:	n/a

Brewpubs
Are brewpubs legal?	Yes
Is there a specific brewpub law?	No
Date of legalization:	n/a
Are brewpubs allowed to:	
sell to a distributor/wholesaler?	No
sell to retailers?	No
sell beer to go?	No
sell draft beer to go?	No
sell guest beer?	Yes
sell guest wine?	n/a
offer a full bar?	Yes
Production ceiling:	n/a
License fees:	$800

Regulatory Information
Does a "Franchise Law" requiring suppliers to form exclusive contracts with distributors exist?   No
Deposit requirements:
    $1 per dozen for returnable/refillable packaging; 10¢ deposit for non-returnables with a 5¢ redemption
Container labeling requirements:
    Federal legislation applies

Newfoundland
Eugene Healey, Dir. of Enforcement
Newfoundland Liquor Corp.
PO Box 8750, Station A
St. John's, NF A1B 3V1
Canada
(709) 724-1161; FAX (709) 753-8625

Microbreweries
Is there a specific microbrewery law?	No
Are microbreweries allowed to:	
sell directly to retailers?	No
sell directly to consumers?	No
Production ceiling:	n/a
Licesne fees:	n/a

Brewpubs
Are brewpubs legal?	Yes
Is there a specific brewpub law?	No
Date of legalization:	n/a
Are brewpubs allowed to:	
sell to a distributor/wholesaler?	Yes
sell to retailers?	No
sell beer to go?	No
sell draft beer to go?	No
sell guest beer?	Yes
sell guest wine?	No
offer a full bar?	Yes
Production ceiling:	n/a
License fees:	$800

Regulatory Information
Does a "Franchise Law" requiring suppliers to form exclusive contracts with distributors exist?   No
Deposit requirements: 10¢ per bottle
Retail-level packaging restrictions:
    Retail sales are resticted to 6-pack, 12-pack, and 24-pack.

Additional Notes
    Newfoundland does not prohibit a brewery from obtaining an on-site retail license.

Northern Territories
Ron Courtoreille, Gen. Mgr.
Northwest Territories Liquor Commission
PO Box 1130
Hay River, NT X0E 0R0
Canada
(403) 874-2100; FAX (403) 874-2180

Microbreweries
Is there a specific microbrewery law?	n/a
Are microbreweries allowed to:	
sell directly to retailers?	Yes
sell directly to consumers?	n/a
Production ceiling:	n/a
License fees:	n/a

Control Agencies, Laws, and Regulations

Brewpubs
Are brewpubs legal?	Yes
Is there a specific brewpub law?	Yes
Date of legalization:	1993
Are brewpubs allowed to:	
sell to a distributor/wholesaler?	Yes
sell to retailers?	Yes
sell beer to go?	Yes
sell draft beer to go?	Yes
sell guest beer?	Yes
sell guest wine?	n/a
offer a full bar?	Yes
Production ceiling:	n/a

License fees:
$500 brewery; $400 off-sale; $200 pub

Regulatory Information
Does a "Franchise Law" requiring suppliers to form exclusive contracts with distributors exist?   n/a

Additional Notes
Territorial law requires paper transfer of beer from brewery to Liquor Commission to pub in order to assess taxes and control production.

Nova Scotia
Gary Findlay, General Mgr.
Nova Scotia Liquor Commission
PO Box 8720, Station A
Halifax, NS B3K 5M4
Canada
(902) 450-5802; FAX (902) 450-5225
Alternate Contact: Roy Weagle, Executive Dir. of Corporate Services
(902) 450-5901

Microbreweries
Is there a specific microbrewery law?	n/a
Are microbreweries allowed to:	
sell directly to retailers?	No
sell directly to consumers?	n/a
Production ceiling:	n/a
License fees:	n/a

Brewpubs
Are brewpubs legal?	Yes
Is there a specific brewpub law?	No
Date of legalization:	n/a
Are brewpubs allowed to:	
sell to a distributor/wholesaler?	Yes
sell to retailers?	No
sell beer to go?	No
sell draft beer to go?	No
sell guest beer?	Yes
sell guest wine?	n/a
offer a full bar?	Yes
Production ceiling:	2,000 hectoliters
License fees:	$500 brewery, $500 pub

Regulatory Information
Does a "Franchise Law" requiring suppliers to form exclusive contracts with distributors exist?   n/a

Ontario
Wayne Jackson, Mgr. of Manufacturers and Agent Licensing
Liquor License Board of Ontario
55 Lakeshore Blvd. E.
Toronto, ON M5E 1A4
Canada
(416) 326-0450; FAX (416) 326-5555
llbo@mccr.onramp.ca and http://www.llbo.on.ca
Alternate Contact: Lorna Rankine, Mgr. of customer service
(416) 326-0420

Microbreweries
Is there a specific microbrewery law?	No
Are microbreweries allowed to:	
sell directly to retailers?	No
sell directly to consumers?	Yes
Production ceiling:	n/a

License fees:
$1,575 plus $105 for each retail store annually

Brewpubs
Are brewpubs legal?	Yes
Is there a specific brewpub law?	Yes
Date of legalization:	2/01/86
Are brewpubs allowed to:	
sell to a distributor/wholesaler?	No
sell to retailers?	No
sell beer to go?	No
sell draft beer to go?	No
sell guest beer?	Yes*
sell guest wine?	No
offer a full bar?	Yes
Production ceiling:	None

License fees:
New license application fee $815; issuing fee $240; advertising fee for obtaining license from $150 to $1,000

Regulatory Information
Does a "Franchise Law" requiring suppliers to form exclusive contracts with distributors exist?   n/a

Control Agencies, Laws, and Regulations

*Additional Notes
You must have a sale license, which allows sale of any spirits.

Prince Edward Island
Ken Hicks, Dir. of Licensing
Prince Edward Island Liquor Control Commission
3 Garfield St.
Charlottetown, PE C1A 7M4
Canada
(902) 368-5710; FAX (902) 368-5735

Microbreweries
Is there a specific microbrewery law?	No
Are microbreweries allowed to:	
sell directly to retailers?	No
sell directly to consumers?	n/a
Production ceiling:	n/a
License fees:	n/a

Brewpubs
Are brewpubs legal?	No
Is there a specific brewpub law?	No
Date of legalization:	n/a
Are brewpubs allowed to:	
sell to a distributor/wholesaler?	n/a
sell to retailers?	n/a
sell beer to go?	n/a
sell draft beer to go?	n/a
sell guest beer?	n/a
sell guest wine?	n/a
offer a full bar?	n/a
Production ceiling:	n/a
License fees:	n/a

Regulatory Information
Does a "Franchise Law" requiring suppliers to form exclusive contracts with distributors exist?   n/a

Québec
Gilles Joliecoeur, Chief Counsel
Societe des Alcools du Quebec
905 Delorimier Ave.
Montreal, PQ H2K 3V9
Canada
(514) 873-3795; FAX (514) 873-6788
Alternate Contact: La Regie Des Alcools de Courses des Juex
(514) 873-3577

Microbreweries
Is there a specific microbrewery law?	n/a
Are microbreweries allowed to:	
sell directly to retailers?	No
sell directly to consumers?	n/a
Production ceiling:	n/a
License fees:	n/a

Brewpubs
Are brewpubs legal?	Yes
Is there a specific brewpub law?	No
Date of legalization:	n/a
Are brewpubs allowed to:	
sell to a distributor/wholesaler?	Yes
sell to retailers?	No
sell beer to go?	No
sell draft beer to go?	No
sell guest beer?	Yes
sell guest wine?	n/a
offer a full bar?	Yes
Production ceiling:	n/a
License fees:	
Manufacturer $250; on-site pub $348	

Regulatory Information
Does a "Franchise Law" requiring suppliers to form exclusive contracts with distributors exist?   n/a

Additional Notes
Brewpubs can package their beer for sale, but only through the Québec liquor store system.

Saskatchewan
Brian Poole, Assistant Mgr. of License Administration Branch
Saskatchewan Liquor and Gaming Authority
PO Box 5054/2500 Victoria Ave.
Regina, SK S4P 3M3
Canada
(306) 787-5225; FAX (306) 787-8981

Microbreweries
Is there a specific microbrewery law?	No
Are microbreweries allowed to:	
sell directly to retailers?	No
sell directly to consumers?	n/a
Production ceiling:	n/a
License fees:	n/a

Brewpubs
Are brewpubs legal?	Yes
Is there a specific brewpub law?	No
Date of legalization:	n/a

Control Agencies, Laws, and Regulations

Are brewpubs allowed to:
sell to a distributor/wholesaler?	No
sell to retailers?	No
sell beer to go?	Yes
sell draft beer to go?	Yes
sell guest beer?	Yes
sell guest wine?	Yes
offer a full bar?	Yes

Production ceiling: 2,000 hectoliters
License fees:
Tavern permit is $200 annually ($200 application fee); manufacturer permit is $500 ($200 application fee).

Regulatory Information
Does a "Franchise Law" requiring suppliers to form exclusive contracts with distributors exist? No

Additional Notes
A brewpub must have a manufacturer's permit and a tavern permit.

Yukon Territory
Jeannine McGregor, Mgr. of Licensing and Development
Yukon Liquor Corp.
9031 Quartz Rd.
Whitehorse, YT Y1A 4P9
Canada
(403) 667-8926; FAX (403) 668-7806
Alternate Contact: Rhonda McPhail, Licensing Development Officer
(403) 667-5241

Microbreweries
Is there a specific microbrewery law? No
Are microbreweries allowed to:
sell directly to retailers?	No
sell directly to consumers?	n/a

Production ceiling: n/a
License fees: n/a

Brewpubs
Are brewpubs legal? Yes
Is there a specific brewpub law? No
Date of legalization: n/a
Are brewpubs allowed to:
sell to a distributor/wholesaler?	Yes
sell to retailers?	No
sell beer to go?	Yes
sell draft beer to go?	No
sell guest beer?	Yes
sell guest wine?	No
offer a full bar?	No

Production ceiling: n/a
License fees:
Cocktail lounge based on seating, $612 maximum; brewers $720

Regulatory Information
Does a "Franchise Law" requiring suppliers to form exclusive contracts with distributors exist? n/a

Additional Notes
Liquor act allows for breweries and brewpubs, but none exist. Any operation starting up would be required to observe federal legislation regarding packaging and labelling.

Control Agencies, Laws, and Regulations

Maximum and Minimum Alcohol Content Limits by State

The maximum and minimum permissible alcoholic contents for beverages sold in the various states based on the latest data compiled by the Beer Institute.

State	Maximum Permissible Alcoholic Content	Minimum Alcoholic Content
Alabama	4% by weight; 5% by volume	0.5% by volume
Alaska	No limit	1% by volume
Arizona	No limit	0.5% by volume
Arkansas	5% by weight for most malt beverages	No minimum
California	4% by weight for beer; no limit for ale	0.5% by volume
Colorado	3.2% by weight, except for malt liquor	0.5% by weight
Connecticut	No limit	0.5% by volume
Delaware	No limit	0.5% by volume
District of Columbia	No limit	0.5% by volume
Florida	Beer with more than 6.243% by volume is considered "intoxicating liquors"	No minimum
Georgia	6% by volume	No minimum
Hawaii	No limit	0.5% by volume
Idaho	6% by weight; beer exceeding 4% alcohol by weight is taxed as wine	No minimum
Illinois	Some areas may limit to 4% by weight	0.5% by volume
Indiana	No limit	No minimum
Iowa	5% by weight in nonstate stores	0.5% by volume
Kansas	3.2% by weight except for liquor store package sales	No minimum
Kentucky	Some areas may limit to 3.2% by weight	0.1% by volume
Louisiana	6% by volume in most areas; 3.2% by weight in dry areas	No minimum
Maine	No limit	0.5% by volume
Maryland	No limit	0.5% by volume
Massachusetts	12% by weight	0.5% by volume
Michigan	No limit	0.5% by volume
Minnesota	0.2% by weight; if over 3.2% higher license and tax fees	0.5% by volume
Mississippi	4% by weight	No minimum
Missouri	3.2% by weight, except for malt liquor (greater than 3.2%); 5% by weight	0.5% by volume
Montana	7% by weight	0.5% by volume
Nebraska	No limit	No minimum
Nevada	No limit	0.5% by volume
New Hampshire	6% by volume	"Beverage" and "cider" 0.5% by volume
New Jersey	No limit	0.5% by volume
New Mexico	No limit	0.5% by volume
New York	No limit	0.5% by volume
North Carolina	6% by weight	0.5% by volume
North Dakota	No limit	0.5% by volume
Ohio	6% by weight	0.5% by weight
Oklahoma	3.2% by weight except for liquor store package sales	0.5% by volume
Oregon	4% by weight for beer; 14% by weight for other malt beverages	0.5% by volume
Pennsylvania	No limit	0.5% by weight
Rhode Island	No limit	0.5% by volume
South Carolina	0.5% by weight	No minimum
South Dakota	3.2% by weight for "low point" beer; 6% by weight for "high point"	0.5% by weight
Tennessee	5% by weight for most malt beverages	No minimum
Texas	4% by weight for "beer"; greater than 4% classified as ale or malt liquor	0.5% by volume
Utah	3.2% by weight in nonstate stores	0.5% by volume
Vermont	6% by volume in nonstate stores	1% by volume
Virginia	No limit	0.5% by volume
Washington	8% by weight in nonstate stores	0.5% by volume
West Virginia	4.2% by weight; 6% by volume	No minimum
Wisconsin	5% by weight for most malt beverages	0.5% by volume
Wyoming	No limit	0.5% by volume

In order to accommodate the differences in state regulations, most national brands are brewed in two strengths, one at 3.2 percent, the other as high as 5.0 percent alcohol by weight.

Information furnished by the Beer Institute.

Control Agencies, Laws, and Regulations

COMPLIANCE MATTERS 95-1

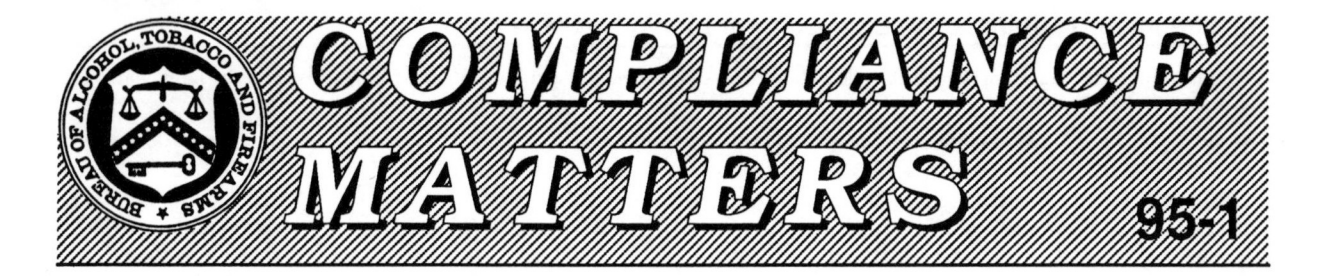

COMPLIANCE MATTERS 95-1 is a special edition intended to provide members of the alcoholic beverage and tobacco industries with detailed information regarding the recent restructuring of the Bureau of Alcohol, Tobacco and Firearms (ATF).

In addition, this edition describes changes in work assignments and personnel within the new Alcohol and Tobacco Programs Division. Please disregard pages 7-10 of COMPLIANCE MATTERS 94-1 and use this issue to answer questions dealing with organizational structure and work assignments.

ATF RESTRUCTURING

ATF recently restructured its organization. This restructuring will allow ATF to more efficiently utilize current technology and apply it to its operations, improve training for ATF employees, and increase its ability to provide oversight of operations through expanded internal controls. The restructuring will improve efficiency and allow ATF to better serve the public, regulated industries and law enforcement agencies nationwide. The new ATF management structure took effect October 2, 1994.

ATF's regulatory and criminal enforcement operations throughout the United States are now unified under Charles R. Thomson, Associate Director for Enforcement. Five Deputy Associate Directors oversee criminal and regulatory enforcement activities in Headquarters and the field.

As part of the restructuring, the Office of Compliance Operations was renamed the Office of Regulatory Enforcement and divided into two areas of responsibility, "Programs" and "Field Operations," under the authority, respectively, of the Deputy Associate Director, Regulatory Enforcement Programs, and the Deputy Associate Director, Regulatory Enforcement Field Operations.

Reprinted courtesy of the BATF.

Control Agencies, Laws, and Regulations

Regulatory Enforcement Field Changes

The term "region," which was used in the former Compliance Operations, has been replaced by the term "district" in the restructured Regulatory Enforcement.

The position of Regional Director has been renamed District Director. The position of Chief, Field Operations, has been renamed Assistant District Director. The position of Area Supervisor was not renamed. The District Director is the primary Regulatory Enforcement representative for the District and reports to the Deputy Associate Director, Regulatory Enforcement Field Operations.

The Regulatory Enforcement Technical Services offices no longer report to the District Directors (previously Regional Directors). They report to the Deputy Associate Director, Regulatory Enforcement Programs, through the new Chief, Industry Compliance Division.

In addition, responsibility for Regulatory Enforcement activities for the State of **Arizona** was transferred from the Western District to the Southwest District and responsibility for Regulatory Enforcement activities for the State of **Wyoming** was transferred from the Southwest District to the Western District.

Regulatory Enforcement Headquarters Changes

In Headquarters, the Revenue Programs Division and the Industry Compliance Division were combined into the Alcohol and Tobacco Programs Division. Within the Alcohol and Tobacco Programs Division, the Wine and Beer Branch and the Distilled Spirits and Tobacco Branch were consolidated into the Wine, Beer and Spirits Regulations Branch.

In addition, a new division, the Industry Compliance Division, was created, incorporating the Tax Compliance Branch, the five District Technical Services, and the Tax Processing Center.

The restructuring of ATF was an internal matter intended to improve ATF operations and should not affect industry members or members of the public. All requests for information, submissions of tax returns, reports, claims, etc., should continue to be submitted to the same office and in the same manner as they were prior to the restructuring.

Reprinted courtesy of the BATF.

Institute for Brewing Studies

Control Agencies, Laws, and Regulations

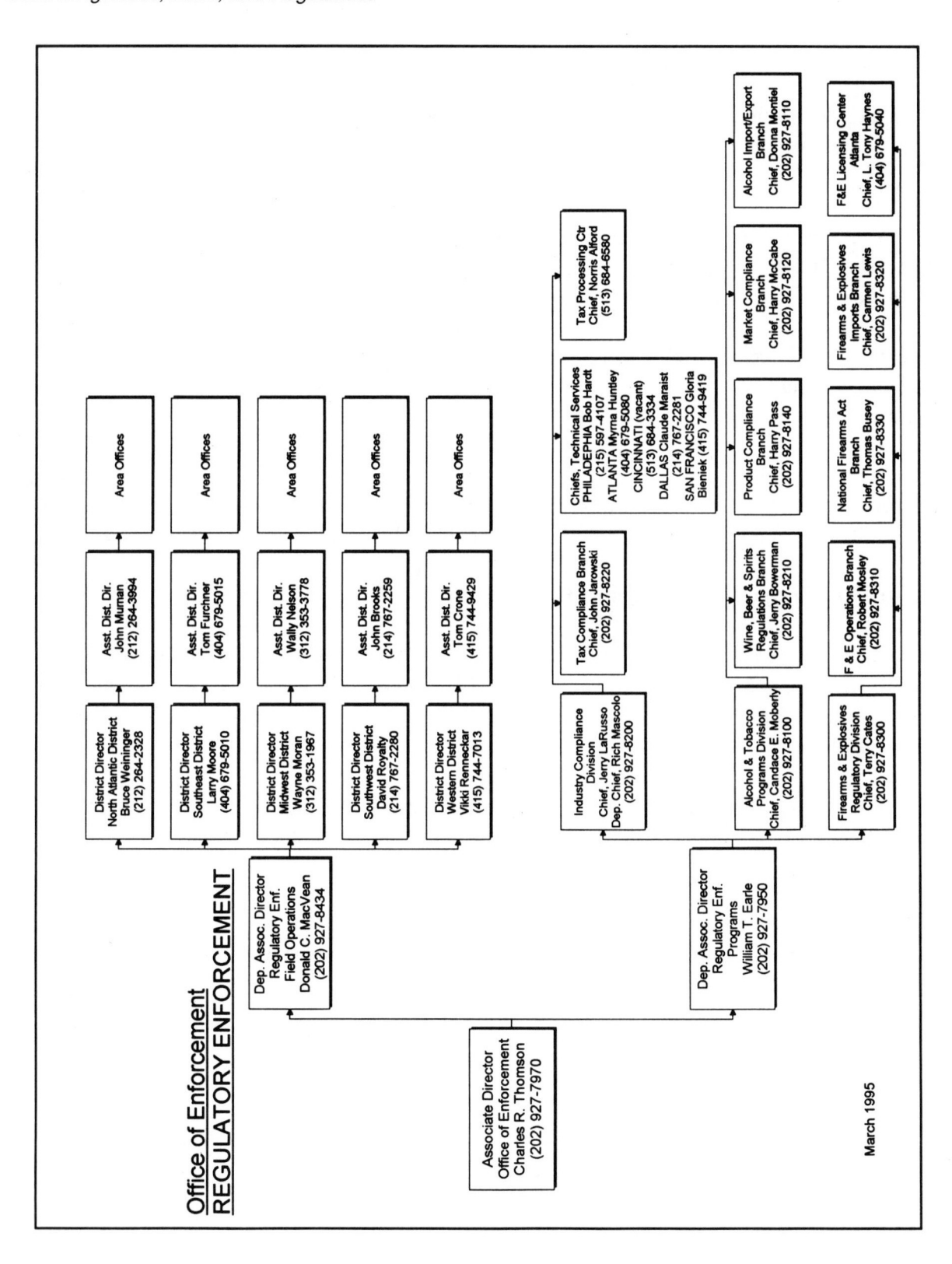

Office of Enforcement
REGULATORY ENFORCEMENT

Associate Director
Office of Enforcement
Charles R. Thomson
(202) 927-7970

Dep. Assoc. Director Regulatory Enf. Field Operations
Donald C. MacVean
(202) 927-8434

Dep. Assoc. Director Regulatory Enf. Programs
William T. Earle
(202) 927-7950

Field Operations

- **District Director, North Atlantic District** — Bruce Weininger (212) 264-2328
  - Asst. Dist. Dir. John Muman (212) 264-3994 → Area Offices
- **District Director, Southeast District** — Larry Moore (404) 679-5010
  - Asst. Dist. Dir. Tom Furchner (404) 679-5015 → Area Offices
- **District Director, Midwest District** — Wayne Moran (312) 353-1967
  - Asst. Dist. Dir. Wally Nelson (312) 353-3778 → Area Offices
- **District Director, Southwest District** — David Royalty (214) 767-2280
  - Asst. Dist. Dir. John Brooks (214) 767-2259 → Area Offices
- **District Director, Western District** — Vikki Rennecker (415) 744-7013
  - Asst. Dist. Dir. Tom Crone (415) 744-9429 → Area Offices

Programs

Industry Compliance Division
Chief, Jerry LaRusso
Dep. Chief, Rich Mascolo
(202) 927-8200

- Tax Compliance Branch — Chief, John Jarowski (202) 927-8220
  - Tax Processing Ctr — Chief, Norris Afford (513) 684-6580
- Chiefs, Technical Services
  - PHILADELPHIA Bob Hardt (215) 597-4107
  - ATLANTA Myrna Huntley (404) 679-5080
  - CINCINNATI (vacant) (513) 684-3334
  - DALLAS Claude Maraist (214) 767-2281
  - SAN FRANCISCO Gloria Bieniek (415) 744-9419

Alcohol & Tobacco Programs Division
Chief, Candace E. Moberly
(202) 927-8100

- Wine, Beer & Spirits Regulations Branch — Chief, Jerry Bowerman (202) 927-8210
- Product Compliance Branch — Chief, Harry Pass (202) 927-8140
- Market Compliance Branch — Chief, Harry McCabe (202) 927-8120
- Alcohol Import/Export Branch — Chief, Donna Montiel (202) 927-8110

Firearms & Explosives Regulatory Division
Chief, Terry Cates
(202) 927-8300

- F & E Operations Branch — Chief, Robert Mosley (202) 927-8310
- National Firearms Act Branch — Chief, Thomas Busey (202) 927-8330
- Firearms & Explosives Imports Branch — Chief, Carmen Lewis (202) 927-8320
- F&E Licensing Center Atlanta — Chief, L. Tony Haynes (404) 679-5040

March 1995

Reprinted courtesy of the BATF.

Control Agencies, Laws, and Regulations

PHONE TIPS

Calling about a label, formula, laboratory analysis, advertising, import/export information? Here are some helpful steps which will assist us in handling your calls more efficiently.

STEP I - Refer to pages 6 & 7 of this issue of Compliance Matters and determine the Branch or Section you need to call and the person with whom you need to speak.

EXAMPLES:

You are **THE ABC DISTRIBUTING COMPANY INC.**, an importer and a producer of domestic distilled spirits, doing business as **KONDO COMPANY**. Your organization wishes to use one of the services listed below or to find information regarding the importation of Austrian wine.

a) The importation of Austrian Wine into the United States.
   Where - Import/Export Branch   Who - John Colozzi

b) The status of a label you mailed in.
   Where - Labeling Section   Who - Shelia Smith-Harrod

c) The status of a formula you submitted.
   Where - Formula & Processing Section   Who - Wanda Williams

d) To ask a question concerning advertisments.
   Where - Market Compliance Branch   Who - Any Specialist
                                          (indicated by an *)

STEP II

If you are unable to determine where or to whom you should direct your call by using the Alcohol and Tobacco Programs Division Phone Guide, please be prepared to provide the following information to the person who receives your call:

1) Your name
2) Your telephone number
3) The name which appears on your basic permit
4) The reason for your call: label, formula, rejected label, rejected formula, import information, advertisement, statistical information, consumer complaints, label rejections, etc.
5) If you submitted a formula, label, or a letterhead request, how was it delivered?

   a) Front desk___ if so by whom _____
   b) Federal express____   Mail In____   Fax____

6) Date(s) Submitted_____

7) Applicant Serial #'s   Formula Serial #'s
   _____   _____
   _____   _____

8) A specific question(s) you may have regarding labeling, formulas, lab analysis, advertising, import/export information, etc:
   _____
   _____

Reprinted courtesy of the BATF.

Institute for Brewing Studies

Control Agencies, Laws, and Regulations

INTERNET REMINDER

Internet users can access ATF through the NSFNET network which is managed by the National Science Foundation. The domain address ATF.USTREAS.GOV can be used to access this system.

If you have any questions regarding access to ATF issuances via Internet, please contact Michael Breen, Technology Planning Staff, at (202) 927-8388.

If you have any ideas or items of interest you would like to submit for consideration in a future issue of **COMPLIANCE MATTERS** or if you have any questions concerning articles contained in this publication please contact:

>Bureau of Alcohol, Tobacco & Firearms
>COMPLIANCE MATTERS Coordinator
>Angela Shanks
>Room 5000
>650 Massachusetts Avenue, NW
>Washington, DC 20226

Reprinted courtesy of the BATF.

Control Agencies, Laws, and Regulations

CHANGES IN POLICIES AND PROCEDURES REGARDING LABELS AND ADVERTISEMENTS

ATF is in the process of re-evaluating many of its policies and procedures regarding the labeling of alcoholic beverages. Our goal is to reduce the regulatory burden on industry and expedite our processing of Certificates of Label Approval (COLAs) while still accomplishing our mission and enforcing the laws and regulations regarding labeling. While this re-evaluation is a long-term process, we have already made the following policy and procedural changes which we believe will make significant contributions to meeting this goal. We will discuss many of these changes in greater depth in a future ATF Ruling. Please note that Item 9 applies to advertisements as well as labels.

1) We have re-interpreted the phrase "direct conjunction", a phrase which appears in several places in the regulations. In the future, where the regulations give us the flexibility to do so, we will accept two items of information on an alcoholic beverage label as being in direct conjunction if (a) they are on the same label, (b) they are likely to be seen simultaneously by a customer or consumer looking at the label, and (c) they are of sufficient size and are printed in colors which contrast with the background sufficiently to make them legible to a customer or consumer reading the label.

2) We will no longer stamp a qualification requiring legibility and contrast on COLAs for legible black and white labels. However, the absence of this stamp does not relieve industry members of the responsibility of ensuring that all labels are legible and have adequate contrast.

3) We will no longer require submission of color labels for malt beverages. However, industry members are cautioned that they must still satisfy legibility and contrast requirements for all labels.

4) To expedite the processing of labels, we have disbanded the label review board and have eliminated automatic second review of labels for journeyman employees.

5) We will no longer require lists of ingredients or statements of process for products claiming to be natural. However, industry members making such claims should maintain these documents to produce to ATF, if requested.

6) For distilled spirits, we will not reject or qualify COLAs if a proof statement (optional information) is not in parentheses or brackets.

7) We will no longer require a letter of authorization before approving labels which depict or refer to famous people, places or organizations. However, we note that our approval of a COLA does not relieve industry members from acquiring such authorization where appropriate. Moreover, industry members making such claims should maintain these documents to produce to ATF, if requested.

8) For personalized labels, we will no longer require that additional documentation for slogans, salutations or graphics be submitted and approved; the submitter will only need to indicate in item 12 "Personalized label". However, we will qualify approved labels of

Reprinted courtesy of the BATF.

this sort by noting that approval of the COLA does not permit any personalizing information which discusses either the alcoholic beverage or characteristics of the alcoholic beverage.

9) We will not automatically consider deceptive or misleading each depiction of or reference to athletes, athletic activities or events, or motor vehicles used in alcoholic beverage labeling or advertising. We recognize that some such depictions or references may appear on labels and in advertisements without being deceptive or misleading. Each such depiction or reference will be reviewed on a case-by-case basis to determine whether it is deceptive or misleading. However, we will not approve applications for labels found to be misleading or deceptive and will initiate appropriate action against such labels and advertisements if they appear in the marketplace. This is discussed in greater detail in Industry Circular 95-2.

The following are examples of labels or advertisements considered to be <u>unacceptable</u>:

(a) any label or advertisement which states that consumption of the alcoholic beverage will enhance athletic prowess, performance at athletic activities or events, health or conditioning;

(b) any label or advertisement which depicts any individual (famous athlete or otherwise) consuming or about to consume an alcoholic beverage prior to or during an athletic activity or event;

(c) any label or advertisement depicting consumption of an alcoholic beverage while the party consuming the beverage is seated in, about to enter, operating, or about to operate automobiles or other machinery.

USE OF THE WORD "ORGANIC"

"Organic" is not currently defined by regulation. As additional information, however, truthful, accurate and specific organic claims are permissible. These claims are generally limited to a description of the commodity used to make the product (e.g., "organically grown grapes" or "organically grown barley"). A description of the alcoholic beverage itself as organic, (e.g., "organic wine") is not permissible as there is no standard of identity for such a product.

Organic claims must be documented to ensure that the additional information is truthful and accurate. The documentation must accompany each application for approval of a label containing an organic claim. Certification from an accredited or recognized certifying agency or State or foreign government is considered appropriate documentation. We consult with the Department of Agriculture (USDA) to determine whether a certifying agency is accredited or recognized. The USDA is the agency responsible for drafting regulations implementing the Organic Food Act of 1990 and maintains a list of U.S. and international certifying authorities.

Reprinted courtesy of the BATF.

Control Agencies, Laws, and Regulations

CUSTOMER SERVICE STANDARDS

In Compliance Matters, issue 94-3, the Labeling Section, Product Compliance Branch, published its customer service standards. We noted our commitment to courtesy, professionalism and confidentiality. We also established target turnaround times for the processing of the various documents we receive and indicated that we would notify our customers if we were unable to meet the target turnaround times. The turnaround times are:

Certificates of Label Approval - 9 calendar days
Informal comments on proposed labels - 15 calendar days
Correspondence - 21 calendar days

We regularly encounter label submissions and correspondence which raise issues requiring lengthier review times. Some of the situations which may affect our ability to meet our turnaround times are new products and new marketing techniques which industry develops and the difficult questions industry sometimes raise about policies and interpretations of laws and regulations. However, we are working to ensure that all submissions are processed as quickly as possible.

Our statistics on meeting these customer service standards for October 1, 1994 - March 31, 1995 are as follows:

<u>Formal Label Applications</u>
Received: 28,589
Completed in 9 or fewer days: 25,546 (89.4%)
Completed in over 9 days or
   still in process: 3,043 (10.6%)

<u>Informal Label Applications:</u>
Received: 178
Completed in 15 or fewer days: 154 (86.5%)
Completed in over 15 days or
   still in process: 24 (13.5%)

<u>General Correspondence:</u>
Received: 123
Completed in 21 or fewer days: 107 (87.0%)
Completed in over 21 days or
   still in process: 16 (13.0%)

We met our customer service standards almost 90% of the time during this period. We are committed to raising this percentage in the future. We will continue to examine our policies and procedures to find ways to improve our processing time and remove unnecessary burdens from industry. Some of the results of this examination can be found in the article entitled "Changes in Policies and Procedures Regarding Labeling and Advertising", which also appears in this issue of Compliance Matters.

Although we had success in meeting our target turnaround times for the items noted above, we have not yet fully implemented our plan to send out notifications when we would not meet the target turnaround times. We have been working to clarify requirements and to develop tracking and reporting systems to

Reprinted courtesy of the BATF.

Control Agencies, Laws, and Regulations

meet this commitment. We expect to have this fully implemented by October 1, 1995, with increasing numbers of notifications in the interim.

We are also currently working on a number of new initiatives which will enhance service to our customers. We are developing both a customer survey and a customer complaint system which will provide us with feedback on our performance and assist us in improving operations. We are continuing to work on development of new ADP applications which will help us better process and track our work and provide customers with better access to the information they need. As part of the Administration's Regulatory Reform Initiative, we are reviewing all of our regulations to identify obsolete or unnecessarily burdensome requirements. We are also reviewing the many comments we received regarding our regulations from industry members. As noted previously, we have already changed a number of policies and procedures in an effort to remove unnecessary burdens from industry and to improve processing times.

The Formula and Processing Section is developing customer service standards for the processing of formulas and statements of process. We plan to issue these in 1996.

REMINDER: COLA REQUIREMENTS FOR CHANGES IN PRODUCER, FORMULA, OR LOCATION OF PRODUCTION FOR IMPORTED PRODUCTS

Importers are required to submit an application for a new certificate of label approval (COLA), a list of ingredients, the method of manufacture and a sample, if necessary, when there is a change in a producer or formula for an imported alcoholic beverage product.

If a foreign producer changes the place(s) of manufacture for a product which is to be imported into the United States, the importer must provide ATF's Product Compliance Branch, Formula and Processing Section, with a statement on the producer's letterhead. The statement must note that the product is produced in the same manner and with the same ingredients as the product previously approved and it must include a list of ingredients and method of manufacture. The statement must be signed and dated by an officer of the producing company.

UPDATE: PRE-IMPORT APPROVALS

In Compliance Matters **94-2**, the "PRE-IMPORT SUPPLEMENTAL" sheet was introduced to help alcoholic beverage importers streamline the pre-import approval process. In an effort to improve this process, we are requesting that the following information be provided:

1) The foreign producers should include their name and complete address [the city/province of region/country] where the product will be produced. Please provide a separate address if there are multiple plant locations, in the same or different countries, where the product will be produced.

2) The alcoholic beverage importers are asked to include their vendor codes on all correspondence submitted in conjunction with the pre-import approval process. The vendor code is a four digit numeric identifier assigned by ATF. If you have not been assigned a vendor code, please include a copy of your basic permit and indicate that you would like to have one assigned.

Reprinted courtesy of the BATF.

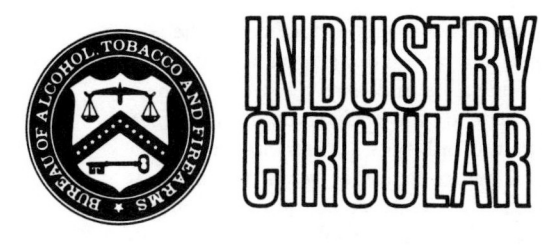

DEPARTMENT OF THE TREASURY
Bureau of Alcohol, Tobacco and Firearms
Washington, D. C. 20226
Number: 95-2   Date: 6-16-95

ATHLETES, ATHLETIC ACTIVITIES OR EVENTS AND MOTOR VEHICLES IN LABELING AND ADVERTISING OF ALCOHOLIC BEVERAGES

Distilled Spirits Plants, Bonded Wineries, Breweries, Importers, and Others Concerned:

Purpose. The purpose of this circular is to advise industry members of a forthcoming ATF ruling relating to the depiction of athletes, athletic activities or events and motor vehicles in the labeling and advertising of alcoholic beverages. This circular and the forthcoming ruling provide guidelines and clarification which industry members can use in developing labels and advertisements which will comply with legal and regulatory requirements. The pertinent portions of the ruling read substantially as follows:

Background. In recent years, ATF has received numerous inquiries regarding the appearance of or reference to athletes, athletic activities or events, and motor vehicles on labels and in advertisements of alcoholic beverages. In particular, concern has surfaced as to the circumstances in which these depictions are permissible.

In particular, there has been significant discussion about the extent to which depictions of or references to athletes, athletic activities or athletic events mislead consumers of alcoholic beverages to believe that consumption of these products will increase their athletic prowess. There has also been discussion about the extent to which depictions of or references to motor vehicles may mislead consumers to believe that it is safe to operate a motor vehicle after consuming alcoholic beverages. ATF policy significantly limits the extent to which these sorts of depictions and references are permissible on labels and advertisements.

ATF Policy. ATF continues to enforce the provisions of the FAA Act and its implementing regulations which prohibit misleading labels and advertisements. However, we recognize that, in recent years, there have been changes in the levels of consumer awareness, changes in industry marketing techniques, and other changes in the marketplace. For example, in recent years, consumers have become much more aware of the effects of alcohol consumption, not only through the efforts of numerous consumer groups, but also through the efforts of both industry and Congress. Furthermore, with the enactment of the health warning statement Congress has attempted to remind the public about health hazards that may be associated with consumption or abuse of alcoholic beverages. These changes and the limitations in our statutory and regulatory authority provide the bases for changes in ATF policy regarding the depictions of or references to athletes, athletic activities or events, or motor vehicles in alcoholic beverage labeling and advertising.

ATF will not automatically consider deceptive or misleading each depiction of or reference to athletes, athletic activities or events, or motor vehicles used in alcoholic beverage labeling or advertising. ATF recognizes that some such depictions or references may appear on labels and in advertisements without being deceptive or misleading. Each such depiction or reference will be reviewed on a case-by-case basis to determine whether it is deceptive or misleading.

Reprinted courtesy of the BATF.

Control Agencies, Laws, and Regulations

In reviewing labels and advertisements, ATF will base its conclusions on the totality of the message conveyed by the label or advertisement. ATF will not prohibit the mere appearance of athletes in labels or advertisements; rather, ATF will examine labels and advertisements in their entirety to determine whether the message conveyed in relation to the appearance of the athlete is deceptive or misleading. ATF is particularly sensitive to the influence athletes are known to have on youth as role models. This is particularly the case where active or recently retired athletes are concerned. Athletes, as role models, set a standard of conduct commonly emulated by youth who aspire to gain talent, success, and/or fame on a level comparable to the athlete's. ATF is concerned that the appearance of an athlete in a label or advertisement not convey a misleading impression to youth.

ATF recognizes that younger people (i.e., those below the legal age for purchase of alcoholic beverages) may be more susceptible to being misled by certain types of labels or advertisements than mature adults. In reviewing labels and advertisements containing references to athletes, athletic activities or events, or motor vehicles, ATF will be especially sensitive to whether such labels and advertisements would be likely to deceive or mislead youth to conclude or believe that consumption of an alcoholic beverage will increase their athletic prowess, enable them to perform at a level comparable to that of a famous athlete or, conversely, likely deceive or mislead youth to believe that such consumption will not inhibit athletic performance. ATF will be equally sensitive to labels and advertisements that would be likely to deceive or mislead youth to conclude or believe that consumption of an alcoholic beverage will enable them to safely operate a motor vehicle or other machinery or equipment.

ATF will not approve applications for labels found to be misleading or deceptive and will initiate appropriate action against such labels and advertisements if they appear in the marketplace.

Examples. With the following examples, we have attempted to more clearly address what we consider both impermissible and permissible labeling and advertising conduct insofar as such conduct falls within the confines of our statutory authority. ATF considers the following examples of labels or advertisements to be unacceptable:

(1) any label or advertisement which states that consumption of the alcoholic beverage will enhance athletic prowess, performance at athletic activities or events, health or conditioning;

(2) any label or advertisement which depicts any individual (famous athlete or otherwise) consuming or about to consume an alcoholic beverage prior to or during an athletic activity or event;

(3) any label or advertisement depicting consumption of an alcoholic beverage while the party consuming the beverage is seated in, about to enter, operating, or about to operate automobiles or other machinery.

Conversely, ATF considers the following examples of labels or advertisements to be acceptable as a general matter, provided they satisfy the criteria discussed above and are not otherwise in violation of applicable laws and regulations:

(1) depictions of or references to athletes, including famous athletes, whether in motion or not and whether in uniform or not;

(2) depictions of or references to motor vehicles or other machinery or equipment, whether in motion or not, whether occupied by a driver or not;

(3) team logos;

Reprinted courtesy of the BATF.

(4) schedules of athletic events; or

(5) depictions of, references to or commemorations of specific events (e.g., an automobile race), specific cars or other equipment, such as hockey sticks, footballs, golf clubs, and the like, on alcoholic beverage labels or advertisements.

For a comprehensive discussion regarding these issues and the history giving rise to this Industry Circular and analogous ruling, please refer to the ruling, which is available upon request.

Inquiries. Inquiries concerning this circular should refer to its number and be addressed to: Chief, Alcohol and Tobacco Programs Division, Bureau of Alcohol, Tobacco and Firearms, 650 Massachusetts Avenue, NW, Washington, DC 20226.

John W. Magaw
Director

Reprinted courtesy of the BATF.

20 State Excise Taxes

As a service to people interested in entering the craft-brewing industry, we have compiled information on the excise tax laws of all fifty states and the District of Columbia. For greater detail we suggest consulting the *State Tax Guide: All States* (Commerce Clearing House Inc., 4025 W. Peterson Ave., Chicago, IL 60646). Additionally, individual state control agencies are good sources of information. Chapter 17 of this publication provides a directory of these agencies.

State Excise Taxes

METHODS OF TAX COLLECTION, BY STATE
JULY 1, 1995

STATE	RATE	METHOD OF PAYMENT	BY WHOM PAID
Alabama	5¢ per fluid oz. or fraction. 1.625¢ per 4 fluid ounces (replaces local taxes).	Monthly reports. Monthly reports.	Wholesaler. Wholesaler.
Alaska	35¢ a gallon.	Monthly reports	Brewer or wholesaler.
Arizona	16¢ a gallon.	Monthly reports.	Wholesaler.
Arkansas	Beer 5% or less-$7.75 a barrel of 32 gallons. Malt liquor 20¢ gallon.	Monthly reports.	Wholesaler.
California	$6.20 a barrel. (7/15/91)	Monthly reports.	California brewers & importers.
Colorado	8¢ a gallon.	Monthly reports.	Colorado brewrs & wholesalers.
Connecticut	$6.00 a barrel; $3.00 per 1/2 barrel; $1.50 per 1/4 barrel; less than 1/4 barrel 20¢ per wine gallon. (4/1/89)	Monthly reports.	Conn. brewers & wholesalers.
Delaware	$4.85 a barrel. (9/13/90)	Monthly payment.	Importer (wholesaler).
District of Columbia	$2.79 a barrel. (6/1/89)	Monthly reports.	D.C. wholesalers/manufacturers.
Florida	Draught-48¢ gallon. Packaged-6¢ pint or fraction. 4¢ surcharge per 12 ounces. (7/1/90)	Monthly reports.	Florida brewers, wholesalers, vendors.
Georgia	Draught-$10.00 a barrel. Packaged 4 1/2¢ per 12 ounces and proportionally.	Monthly reports.	Georgia wholesalers.
Hawaii	81¢ cooler beverages; 50¢ draught beer; 89¢ beer other than draught. (See page 80.)	Monthly reports.	Hawaii brewers & wholesalers.
Idaho	$4.65 a barrel.	Monthly reports.	Wholesaler.
Illinois	7¢ a gallon.	Monthly reports	Illinois brewers & importing distributors.
Indiana	11 1/2¢ per gallon.	Monthly reports. (Stamps on reciprocal basis.)	Brewer liable for tax on sale or gift, or withdrawal for sale or gift of beer by him to a person within the state, & wholesaler liable for tax on beer received from brewer located outside of state. (6/1/84)
Iowa	$5.89 a barrel.	Monthly reports.	Iowa brewers & wholesalers.
Kansas	18¢ a gallon.	Monthly reports.	Brewer or wholesaler importer by agreement.
Kentucky	$2.50 a barrel. 9% gross receipts tax.	Monthly reports. Monthly reports.	Brewer. Distributors.
Louisiana	$10.00 a barrel. Parishes & municipalities also may impose excise tax not exceeding $1.50 a barrel.	Monthly reports.	Louisiana brewers or wholesaler.
Maine	35¢ a gallon.	To Liquor Commission with import order or by monthly reports.	Wholesaler (may post bond and pay monthly).
Maryland	9¢ a gallon.	Monthly reports.	Brewer; non-resident dealer, wholesaler.
Massachusetts	$3.30 a barrel.	Monthly reports.	Massachusetts brewers, farm brewers, wholesalers & importers.
Michigan	$6.30 a barrel.	Mid-month estimate & monthly report.	Michigan brewers or wholesalers.
Minnesota	3.2 - $2.40 a barrel. Over 3.2 - $4.60 a barrel.	Monthly reports (before 18th).	Brewer or importer.
Mississippi	42.68¢ per gallon.	Monthly reports.	Wholesaler or distributor.
Missouri	$1.86 a barrel.	Monthly reports.	Brewer, out-of-state solicitor, wholesale dealer.

Continued on Next Page.

Institute for Brewing Studies

State Excise Taxes

METHODS OF TAX COLLECTION, BY STATE
July 1, 1995

STATE	RATE	METHOD OF PAYMENT	BY WHOM PAID
Montana	$4.30 a barrel.	Monthly reports.	Montana brewers & wholesalers.
Nebraska	23¢ per gallon.	Monthly reports.	Brewers & distributors.
Nevada	9¢ a gallon.	Monthly reports.	Nevada importers.
New Hampshire	30¢ a gallon (7/1/91).	Monthly reports.	New Hampshire wholesalers.
New Jersey	12¢ a gallon.	Bi-monthly reports. Monthly reports.	N. J. brewers & wholesalers. Wholesalers.
New Mexico	41¢ a gallon	Monthly reports.	Wholesaler.
New York	21¢ a gallon (6/1/90); 16¢ a gallon effective 1/1/96.	Monthly reports.	N. Y. brewers & importers.
North Carolina	$15.00 a barrel, 6 oz., 2 1/2¢; 7 oz., 3¢; 12 oz., 5¢; 16 oz., 6 2/3¢, quart, 13 1/3¢; others at 0.42¢ an ounce.	Monthly reports.	Wholesalers & importers.
North Dakota	8¢ a gallon in bulk. 16¢ a gallon packaged.	Monthly reports.	Wholesaler.
Ohio	$5.58 on draught beer. In cans & bottles .14¢ per oz. on 12 oz. or less; .84¢ per 6 oz. on over 12 oz. containers.	Monthly advance payments and monthly reports.	Brewer.
Oklahoma	$12.50 a barrel (beer). $11.25 a barrel (nonintox. beer).	Monthly reports.	Oklahoma brewers or Class B wholesalers.
Oregon	$2.60 a barrel.	Monthly reports.	Oregon brewers importing distributor.
Pennsylvania	$2.48 a barrel. 2/3¢ per 8 oz. or fraction and 1¢ per 16 oz. or fraction.	Monthly reports.	Brewer.
Rhode Island	$3.00 a barrel. (7/1/89)	R. I. beer: Monthly reports. Out-of-state beer: With purchase order placed with Liquor Control Administration.	Brewer, on Rhode Island beer. Wholesaler, on out-of-state beer.
South Carolina	6/10¢ per ounce.	Estimated monthly reports.	Wholesaler.
South Dakota	$8.50 a barrel.	Bi-monthly reports.	Wholesaler.
Tennessee	$3.90 a barrel. Also 17% of wholesale price, for counties & municipalities.	Monthly reports.	Wholesaler. Wholesaler pays 17% tax.
Texas	$6.00 a barrel on 4% alcohol by weight. 19.8¢ a gallon over 4%.	4%: Monthly reports. Over 4%: Monthly reports or stamps.	4%: Texas brewers & importers. Over 4%: Brewer (or Texas importer).
Utah	$11.00 a barrel.	Monthly reports.	Utah brewers & wholesalers.
Vermont	26 1/2¢ a gallon.	Monthly reports.	Vermont bottler & wholesaler.
Virginia	25.65¢ per gallon. 2¢ per 7 oz., 2.65¢ up to 12 oz., 2.22 mills per oz. in containers over 12 oz.	Monthly reports.	Virginia brewer, bottler, or wholesaler.
Washington	$7.17 per barrel, effective 7/1/95-6/30/97; $9.56 effective 7/1/97.	Monthly reports.	Brewers & beer wholesalers. Importer for foreign beer.
West Virginia	$5.50 a barrel.	Monthly reports on est. sales purchased by 10th, and filing of amended receipts by 25th.	In-state brewer and distributor or nonresident brewer (behalf of distributor).
Wisconsin	$2.00 a barrel.	Monthly reports.	Wisconsin brewers & wholesalers.
Wyoming	2¢ a gallon.	Monthly reports.	Wholesaler.

Reprinted from *Brewers Almanac 1995*, courtesy of the Beer Institute.

21 Brewing Associations

As with any industry, the brewing industry and the allied trades can benefit from the support of trade associations. These brewing associations aid the industry by compiling and providing information for participants, the media, and the general public; holding conferences and seminars; promoting the industry and its products to the public; and acting as a networking service to put people with specific needs in contact with those who can fill those needs.

This chapter contains listings of associations that are specifically for brewers or those involved in the brewing industry. These associations are located in the United States, Canada, and Europe, and all can provide a wealth of information.

United States

American Breweriana Association Inc.
Stan Galloway, Exec. Dir.
Brad Baker, Pres.
PO Box 11157
Pueblo, CO 81001
(719) 544-9267

Association of brewery historians and collectors of beer advertising and memorabilia. Publishes bimonthly *American Breweriana Journal* and has lending library and exchange services. Annual dues $20.

American Homebrewers Association® Inc.
Karen Barela, Pres.
PO Box 1679
Boulder, CO 80306-1679
(303) 447-0816; FAX (303) 447-2825
aha@aob.org
http://www.aob.org/aob

The American Homebrewers Association® is the world's largest homebrewing association, with more than 24,500 members internationally. A division of the Association of Brewers, the AHA is an eighteen-year-old nonprofit organization dedicated to the collection and dissemination of information about the art and science of homebrewing. The American Homebrewers Association publishes *Zymurgy*® magazine, presents the annual AHA National Homebrewers Conference, and organizes the National Homebrewing Competition, which recieved more than 3,000 entries in 1996. The AHA also offers guidence for homebrew competition organizers, distributes educational materials for beer judges and enthusiasts, and provides support for more than 600 homebrew clubs around the world.

American Malting Barley Association Inc.
Michael P. Davis, Pres.
735 N. Water St., Suite 908
Milwaukee, WI 53202
(414) 272-4640

American Society of Brewing Chemists
Steven C. Nelson, Exec. Officer
3340 Pilot Knob Rd.
St. Paul, MN 55121
(612) 454-7250

Association of Brewers
Charlie Papazian, Pres.
Cathy Ewing, VP
PO Box 1679
Boulder, CO 80306-1679
(303) 447-0816; FAX (303) 447-2825
info@aob.org
http://www.aob.org

Brewing Associations

The Association of Brewers (AOB) is a nonprofit, educational association dedicated to educating consumers about quality beer and brewing. Founded in 1978, the AOB has three divisions, each representing various facets of the business of brewing: the American Homebrewers Association, the Institute for Brewing Studies, and Brewers Publications. The AOB also organizes and presents the International Beer Marketers Symposium^{SM} for the global brewing community and the World Beer Cup^{SM} international beer competition. The Association of Brewers has an affiliate, Brewing Matters, responsible for the Great American Beer Festival^{SM}.

BCI Industries Inc.
Charles (Chuck) Young, General Mgr.
Bobby Allen, Pres.
6400 Hwy. 51 Box 396
Brighton, TN 38011
(901) 476-8000; FAX (901) 476-4811

Beer Institute
Ray McGrath, Pres.
122 C St. N.W., Suite 750
Washington, DC 20001
(202) 737-2337; FAX (202) 737-7004

The Beer Institute represents more than 90 percent of the domestic brewers and suppliers to the industry. Its most recent edition of the *Brewer's Almanac* contains a valuable collection of brewing statistics and excise tax information. Cost is $160 per year for non-members.

Beer Institute
Ray McGrath, Pres.
1225 Eye St. N.W., Suite 825
Washington, DC 20005
(202) 737-2337; FAX (202) 737-7004

Beman and Beverage Systems Inc.
Brian Beman, Pres.
3501 Basswood Cir.
Prior Lake, MN 55372
(612) 447-7632; FAX (612) 447-7632

Specializing in the design and sales of remote dispensing systems for draft beer, liquor, juice, wine, and soda products. Custom systems available for brewpubs.

Brewers' Association of America
Henry B. King, Exec. Dir.
Patricia King, Office Administrator
PO Box 876
Belmar, NJ 07719
(908) 280-9153; FAX (908) 681-1891

Brewing Matters
Cathy Ewing, Pres.
Marcia Schirmer, VP and Festival Dir.
PO Box 4619
Boulder, CO 80306-4619
(303) 447-0816; FAX (303) 447-2825
info@aob.org
http://www.aob.org/aob/gabf.html

Brewing Matters is an affiliate of the Association of Brewers (AOB) established primarily to oversee and organize the Great American Beer Festival^{SM}, the largest beer festival in the United States. Like the AOB, Brewing Matters is a nonprofit organization dedicated to educating the public about beer, brewing, and the responsible consumption of beer as an alcohol-containing beverage. The Great American Beer Festival is the premiere beer tasting event in North America. The medals awarded by the Festival's Professional Panel Blind Tasting in more than thirty beer style catagories are recognized around the world as a symbol of excellence and dedication to quality brewing. The Festival celebrates its fifteenth anniversary in 1996, and expects to host more than 350 American breweries serving some 1,350 different beers over three nights at Currigan Hall in downtown Denver.

California Small Brewers Association
Bob Judd, Dir.
1330 21st St., Suite 201
Sacramento, CA 95814
(916) 444-8333; FAX (916) 444-3314

Filter Equipment Co. Inc.
Scott Groh, Sales Mgr.
Steve Groh
PO Box 1452/1440 Hwy. 34
Wall, NJ 07719
(800) 445-9775; FAX (800) 777-3477

We offer filter pads, presses, cartridges, and parts for all types of beverage filtration.

Hohensteins Inc.
Karl Hohenstein, VP
2330 Ventura Dr.
Woodburg, MN 55125
(612) 735-4978; FAX (612) 735-4987

Beer wholesalers covering the entire Twin City metropolitan area, including the cities of St. Paul and Minneapolis, Minnesota. Specializing in microbrews and imported beers.

Institute for Brewing Studies
David Edgar, Dir.
PO Box 1679
Boulder, CO 80306-1679
(303) 447-0816; FAX (303) 447-2825
ibs@aob.org
http://www.aob.org/aob

The Institute for Brewing Studies is the professional brewing organization of the Association of Brewers and publishes *The New Brewer*, a magazine specifically addressing the needs of the serious, small-scale commercial brewer. This magazine contains the most current information on technological developments, legislation, equipment, and product design, as well as excellent articles on financing and marketing. Institute services include the Brewmaster for Hire program, the Brewpub Legislation packet, the *Alcohol Issues Alert* binder, the Select Clippings Service, the PR/Media Kit, and the quarterly-updated *North American Brewery List*. Institute staff helps members locate brewing data, conduct research, and answer regulatory questions. The Institute also sponsors the annual National Craft-Brewers Conference and Trade Show. Membership is open to those interested or involved in the commercial brewing industry. Fees vary according to class of membership and include a subscription to *The New Brewer*. This publication also is available separately for $55 per year ($65 international).

MicroPure Filtration
Robert A. Pollmann, VP/General Mgr.
Marcy Pollman, Sales Admin.
7879 Forest Hills Rd.
Rockford, IL 61111
(800) 654-7873; FAX (815) 962-7360

Solid, secure filtration solutions for sterile air, gas, liquid, and steam applications. Environmentally friendly while saving production costs. On-line automatic samplers for product sampling.

Mid-Atlantic Assoc. of Craft Breweries
Bud Hensgen, Exec. Dir.
1327 N. Vermont St.
Arlington, VA 22201
(703) 527-1441; FAX (705) 527-5689
102546.3166@compuserve.com

National Beer Wholesalers Association
Gary Galanis, Dir. Public Affairs
1100 S. Washington St.
Alexandria, VA 22314
(703) 578-4300; FAX (703) 931-3216

Oregon Brewers Guild
Mike Sherwood, Dir.
510 N.W. Third St.
Portland, OR 97209
(503) 295-1862; FAX (503) 226-4895
beer@teleport.com
http://www.oregonbeer.com/~beer

Sonoco Engraph Label Group
Thomas Coker, Mktg. Mgr.
Jim Prendergast, VP Sales
8800 South Blvd.
Charlotte, NC 28273
(704) 554-5796; FAX (704) 554-8122

Africa

Kgalagadi Brewers
N. Mandela Dr.
Gaberone
Botswana

Nobra
Douala, Bp 2280
Cameroon
45-05-03

Soc Anonyme des Brasseries de Cote-d' Ivoire
25 Blvd. de Marseille
Abidjan, BP 1855
Ivory Coast
33-10-53

Soc Malienne de Boissons
Gazeuses
Rue Moussa Travele, Barnako
Mali

Societe Nationale des Brasseurs
Zi Route De Porto Dovd
Cotonou, BP 135
Benin

UCB
Douala, Bp 638
Cameroon
42-62-18

Brewing Associations

Asia

Brewers Association of Japan
Shows Building 2-8-18, Kyobashi, Chuo-Ku
Tokyo
Japan
03-561-8386; FAX 03-561-8380

Brewing Society of Japan
6-30, Takinogawa 2-chrome
Kita-Ku, Tokyo 114
Japan
910-3853

Japan Microbrewers Association
Sadat Yamanaka, Pres.
Nobuo Yoshikawa
1-1-19 Motoakasaka, Minato-ku
Tokyo, 107
Japan
03-3423-0404; FAX 03-3423-4628

Australia

Australian Associated Brewers
159 Latrobe St.
Melborne, Victoria 300
Australia

Brewers Assoc. New South Wales
95 York St.
Sydney
Australia
02-290-1422; FAX 02-262-2658

Institute of Brewing
Brookly Park/PO Box 229
Brookly Park, SA 5032
Australia

Canada

Brewers Association of Canada
H. Collins, VP-Corporate and Public Affairs
155 Queen St., Suite 1200
Ottawa, ON K1P 6L1
Canada
(613) 232-9601; FAX (613) 232-2283

Campaign for Real Ale (CAMRA)
John Rowling
1440 Ocean
Victoria, BC V8P 5K7
(604) 595-7728

Europe

Allied Brewery Traders' Association
M. J. Rayner, CEO
F. Bristow, Membership Sec.
85 Tettenhall Rd.
Wolverhampton, West Midlands WV3 9NE
United Kingdom
44-902-22303; FAX 44-902-712066

Association des Brasseurs de France (ABF)
25 Boulavard Malesherbes
Paris, F-75008
France
01-42-66-29-27; FAX 01-42-66-29-27

Assoc. dos Technicos de Cerveja
Av Almirante Reis 115
Lisbon Codex, P-1197
Portugal
01-355-8841; FAX 01-538-405

Association of Belgium Brewers
Grad Palace 10
Brussels, B-1000
Belgium
02-511-49-87; FAX 02-511-32-59

Association of Swiss Brewmasters
C/O Brauerei Adler
Schwanden, CH-8762
Switzerland
058-81-11-08; FAX 058-81-12-97

Basin Ve Halkele Iliskiler
Tekel Genel Mudurlugu
Mudurlugu
Unkanpani, Istanbul
Turkey

Brewers' Guild
P. J. Ogie, Pres.
8 Ely Pl.
London, EC1N 7HR
Great Britian

Brewers' Society
42 Portman Sq.
London
Great Britian
01-486-4831

Brewing Industry Council
Scheibenpogenstr 15
Linz, A-4020
Austria
0732-43394

Brewing Research
Foundation International
Nutfield
Surrey, RH1 4HY
Great Britian

Campaign for Real Ale (CAMRA)
Stephen Cox, Campaigns Mgr.
Iain Loe, Research Mgr.
34 Alma Rd.
St. Albans, Hertfordshire AL1 3BW
United Kingdom
01727-867201; FAX 01727-867670

Chambre Syndicale
de la Malterie Francaise
22 Rue Lavoisier
Paris, F-75008
France
01-42-66-28-74

Deutscher Brauer-Bund E.V.
Annaberger Str. 28
Postfach 20 04 52, Bonn 53134
Germany
02-28-959-060; FAX 02-28-959-0618

European Brewery Convention (EBC)
M. Jan Winjngaarden, Sec. General
PO Box 510
2380 BB Zoeterwoude
Netherlands
31-71-5456047 or 31-71-5456614; FAX 31-71-5410013

Independent Family
Brewers of Britain (IFBB)
Weymouth Ave.
Dorchester, Dorset DT1 1QT
Great Britiain

Incorporated Brewers' Guild
W. D. J. Carling, Gen. Sec.
8 Ely Pl., Holborn Circus
London
Great Britian

Institute of Brewing
F. Bolton, Pubs Mgr.
33 Clarges St.
London, W1Y 8EE
United Kingdom
(0) 1-499-8144; FAX (0) 1-499-1156

Institute of Brewing
Peter Istead
2 Hugenot Pl.
Wansworth Common, London SW18 2EN
Great Britian

Koospol
Leninova 178
6 Prague, CS-160 67
Czechoslovakia

Magyar Sorgyart Szovetsege
Magodi Ut 17
Budapest, H-1106
Hungary
157-13-18; FAX 127-08-37

De Objective Bierproevers
Postbus 32
5 Berchem, B-2600
Belgium

Small Independent
Brewers Association
2 Balfour Rd.
London, N5 2HB
Great Britian
071-359-8323; FAX 071-354-3962

Svenska Olframjandet
Box 16244
Stockholm, S-103 25
Sweden
08-669-36-30

Swiss Brewers Association
Bahnhofplatz 9
Zurich, 8023
Switzerland
01-201-2611

Verband Schweiz Brauerien
Postfach
Basel, CH-4001
Switzerland
061-261-07-57; FAX 061-261-07-52

Brewing Associations

Worshipful Company of Brewers
Brewers Hall
Aldermanbury Square
London, EC2V 7HR
Great Britian
071-606-1301

Mexico

Beer Manufacturers Association
Chapultapec Morales
Oracio 1556
Mexico City, Distrito Federal 11570
Mexico
5-520-6283

South America

Asociacion Latinosmericana
Jose-Maria De Romana
De Fabricantes De Cerveza
161 San Isidro, Lima 1642
Peru

22 Brewing Schools and Courses

The rapid proliferation of microbreweries and brewpubs in North America has led to a great demand for trained brewers. England, Scotland, Germany, and Belgium are still home to the most famous brewing schools. However, courses and degree programs providing quality instruction on brewing and running a brewery are available in the United States. This chapter lists United States, Asian, and European institutions offering courses.

The more knowledge you have, the better prepared you will be to deal with the unexpected in the brewhouse. Generally, a background in chemistry, chemical engineering, food science, or microbiology provides a good base from which to learn the intricacies of turning malts, yeast, hops, and water into a quality brew. Furthermore, learning to make beer at home is helpful, at least for understanding the basic dynamics of the brewing process.

There is no substitute for professional experience, especially in light of the wide variety of available equipment and beer styles. Obviously, hands-on experience in a microbrewery or brewpub provides a great deal of knowledge in the field. Many skilled brewers in this growing industry learned the trade through apprenticeships with one or more breweries in North America and Europe. Apprenticeships, however, are not commonly available in North America.

Whether it is one class or a certificate/degree program, attending brewing school can only enrich your understanding of both the art and the science of making beer. If you are an experienced brewer, you already know all of the steps necessary for making good beer in a professional environment. If this is the case, a good brewing class (or several classes) will help you learn more about why all of those steps are necessary.

Ultimately, the more education you have, the better off you are. Many a veteran brewmaster will attest to the fact that even after decades of experience, they still continuously learn new things about the craft of brewing.

Whatever your level of expertise, the ingredients for success in the brewhouse, or any business for that matter, are curiosity, attention to detail, and an open mind. With these, any course work from the following organizations will stand you in good stead for your brewing venture.

United States

AJEX USA INC.
Martin E. Schuster Jr., Pres.
Dean Howell, Sales Mgr.
7100 Broadway, Suite 5S
Denver, CO 80221-0103
(303) 427-4104 or (800) 394-7416; FAX (303) 427-1869

American Brewers Guild
Maria Tebbutt, Dir. of Operations
Bruce Winner, Pres.
1107 Kennedy Pl., Suite 3
Davis, CA 95616
(916) 753-0497; FAX (916) 753-0176
abgbrew@mother.com
http://www.mother.com/abg

The American Brewers Guild offers comprehensive technical training for the brewing industries. The Director of Academic Programs is Michael Lewis, Ph.D., Professor Emeritus of Brewing Science, University of California, Davis. Courses include six-month master brewers program, ten-week apprenticeship, and short courses in our state-of-the-art classroom, laboratory, and seven-barrel brewery.

Brewing Schools and Courses

American School for Malting & Brewing Science & Technology
Debbie Roberts
University Extension, University of California
Davis, CA 95616-8727
(916) 757-8899; FAX (916) 757-8634
droberts@unexmail.ucdavis.edu

The American School presents practical, intensive courses for professionals from major breweries, microbreweries, and brewpubs. Principal instructor Michael Lewis, Ph.D., is a professor at UC–Davis, the only university in the United States that offers a degree specialization in brewing science.

Weekend and weeklong courses focus on brewing science and technology, brewery operations and management, and practical applications. Subjects covered include quality assurance, sensory evaluation, and sanitation and microbiology. The nine-month Master Brewers Program prepares participants for associate membership in the Institute of Brewing in London. Call for a complete catalog of courses.

Bohemian Brewery Importers
Jean Pugh, VP Sales and Mktg.
Michael Lislis, Pres./CEO
710 Silver Spur Rd., Suite193
Rolling Hills Estate, CA 90274
(310) 544-1037; FAX (310) 541-2667

California State University Stanislaus
University Extended Education
801 W. Monte Vista Ave.
Turlock, CA 95382
(209) 667-3111 or (209) 529-0602; FAX (209) 667-3299

Center for Brewing Studies
Dr. Joseph Owades, Dir.
3097 Wood Valley Rd.
Sonoma, CA 95476
(707) 935-1919; FAX (707) 935-1750

Siebel Institute of Technology
Bill Siebel, Pres.
Dave Radzanowski, VP Educational Services
4055 W. Peterson Ave.
Chicago, IL 60646-6001
(312) 279-0966; FAX (312) 463-7688

Founded in 1872, we offer seven regular courses with more than twenty sessions each year. The resident faculty has experience exceeding four hundred years in all areas of brewing technology

Sonoco Engraph Label Group
Thomas Coker, Mktg. Mgr.
Jim Prendergast, VP Sales
8800 South Blvd.
Charlotte, NC 28273
(704) 554-5796; FAX (704) 554-8122

Asia

National Research Institute of Brewing
2-6-30, Takinogawa
Kita-ku, Tokyo
Japan

Europe

Academy of Sciences USSR
Baltijskaya Ul., 14
A-219 Moscow
Russia

Brewlab
Dr. K. R. Thomas
Life Sciences Bldg., Univ. of Sunderland, Chester Rd.
Sunderland, SR1 3SD
United Kingdom
(+191) 515-2535; FAX (+191) 515-2531

Brewlab provides introductory and advanced brewing courses. Brewery placements give working experience in British breweries. Specialist courses cover taste training, marketing, history, and microbiology.

British School of Brewing
University of Birmingham
Dept. of Biochemistry
Edgbaston, Birmingham
Great Britian

Catholic University of Leuven Laboratory of Brewing Science
Prof. D. Iserentant, Assistant Professor
Kardinaal Mercierlaan 92
Heverlee, B-3030
Belgium
32 67 21 12 55

Doemens School
Mr. Centgraf, Dir.
Stefanus St. 8
8032 Graefelfing, Munich
Germany

Heriot-Watt University International Centre for Brewing and Distilling
Prof. G. Stewart
Riccarton
Edinburgh, Scotland EH14 4AS
United Kingdom
44-131-451-3184; FAX 44-131-449-7459
bbsggs@bonaly.hw.ac.uk
http://www.hw.ac.uk/

The centre is the only institute that offers, in English, an honors (BSc) degree, a post-graduate diploma, and a master's degree in brewing and distilling.

23 Brewing Books and Journals

As the craft-brewing industry grows, there are more publications catering to this market. The small-scale brewer can best find information through associations, like the Institute for Brewing Studies, and their related books and journals.

This chapter lists many publications currently available, which cover a wide variety of topics. It is divided into three sections: books, journals, and regional beer journals.

Books

The Art of Cidermaking
by Paul Correnty
Published by Brewers Publications, 1995
PO Box 1679
Boulder, CO 80306-1679
(303) 447-0816; FAX (303) 447-2825
orders@aob.org
http://www.aob.org/aob
7 x 10, 86 pp., four-color soft cover, illustrations, b & w photos
$9.95
ISBN Number: 0-937381-42-X

With more than three hundred years of tradition and spellbinding lore, cidermaking is experiencing a resurgence in America. In *The Art of Cidermaking*, award-winning cidermaker Paul Correnty takes you on a fascinating journey through the diverse history and delicate art of making this luscious drink.

Beer Across America
A Guide to Brewpubs and Microbreweries
by Marty Nachel
Published by Storey Publishing, 1995
Schoolhouse Rd.
Pownal, VT 05261
(802) 823-5200; FAX (802) 823-5819
storey@storey.com
http://www.storey.com
7 x 10
$14.95
ISBN Number: 0-88266-902-8

Beer and Brewing, Volume 10
Transcripts of the 1990 National Conference on Quality Beer and Brewing
by Tracy Loysen, Editor
Published by Brewers Publications, 1990
PO Box 1679
Boulder, CO 80306-1679
(303) 447-0816; FAX (303) 447-2825
orders@aob.org
http://www.aob.org
5 1/2 x 8 1/2, 199 pp., three-color soft cover, illustrations, b & w photos
$20.95; $18.95 (AHA members)
ISBN Number: 0-937381-21-7

This volume offers something for all brewers — beginning to advanced. Chapters include: "Beer Blending a la Judy," "Food and Beer," "The Microbrewery and Brewpub Phenomenon," "Making Quality Homebrew," "The Flavorful World of Malt," "Experimenting with Munich Malt," "Honey! Let It Be Mead," "Simplified Quality Control," "Essentials of Step-Infusion Mashing," "Home Lab Culturing," "A Great System for Draft Beer," and more.

Beer and Brewing, Volume 8
Transcripts of the 1988 National Conference on Quality Beer and Brewing
by Virginia Thomas, Editor
Published by Brewers Publications, 1988
PO Box 1679
Boulder, CO 80306-1679
(303) 447-0816; FAX (303) 447-2825
orders@aob.org
http://www.aob.org/aob
5 1/2 x 8 1/2, 229 pp., three-color soft cover, b & w photos
$21.95; $18.95 (AHA members)
ISBN Number: 0-937381-11-X

    Brewing experts from all over the world discuss meadmaking, brewpubs in Austria and Bavaria, flavor recognition, improving your record keeping, hop flavor, developing an aroma-identification kit, and more.

Beer Directory
An International Guide
by Heather Wood
Published by Storey Publishing, 1995
Schoolhouse Rd.
Pownal, VT 05261
(802) 823-5200; FAX (802) 823-5819
storey@storey.com
http://www.storey.com
6 x 9
$12.95
ISBN Number: 0-88266-903-6

Beer Drinker's Guide to Australia and New Zealand
by James R. Robertson
Published by Bosak Publishing Inc.
4764 Galicia Way
Oceanside, CA 92056
(619) 940-4447; FAX (619) 940-0549
80 pp. plus cover, 4 1/2 x 9
$9.95

Beer Drinker's Guide to Southern Germany
by James R. Robertson
Published by Bosak Publishing Inc.
4764 Galicia Way
Oceanside, CA 92056
(619) 940-4447; FAX (619) 940-0549
96 pages plus cover, 4 1/2 x 9
$9.95

Beer Enthusiastis' Guide
Tasting and Judging Brews from Around the World
by Gregg Smith
Published by Storey Publishing, 1995
Schoolhouse Rd.
Pownal, VT 05261
(802) 823-5200; FAX (802) 823-5819
storey@storey.com
http://www.storey.com
6 x 9
$12.95
ISBN Number: 0-88266-838-2

Beer Industry Update
Published by Jerry Steinman
51 Virginia Ave.
West Nyack, NY 10994
(914) 358-7751; FAX (914) 358-7860
$675

The Beer Log
by James R. Robertson
Published by Bosak Publishing Inc.
4764 Galicia Way
Oceanside, CA 92056
(619) 940-4447; FAX (619) 940-0549
10 3/4 x 11 1/2
$37.50

The Beer Log
(Soft cover version, includes 1993 Update)
by James R. Robertson
Published by Bosak Publishing Inc.
4764 Galicia Way
Oceanside, CA 92056
(619) 940-4447; FAX (619) 940-0549
384 pp., 8 1/2 x 11
$39.75

'94 Beer Log Update
by James R. Robertson
Published by Bosak Publishing Inc.
4764 Galicia Way
Oceanside, CA 92056
(619) 940-4447; FAX (619) 940-0549
222 pp. (punched for loose leaf binder), 8 1/2 x 11
$16

Brewing Books and Journals

'93 Beer Log Update
by James R. Robertson
Published by Bosak Publishing Inc.
4764 Galicia Way
Oceanside, CA 92056
(619) 940-4447; FAX (619) 940-0549
192 pp. (punched for loose leaf binder), 8 1/2 x 11
$16

The Beer Lover's Rating Guide
by Bob Klien
Published by Workman Publishing Co., 1995
708 Broadway
New York, NY 10003
(212) 254-5900; FAX (212) 254-8098
3 3/4 x 7 1/4
$9.95
ISBN Number: 1-56305-682-8

Beer Packaging
by Harold Broderick, Editor
Published by Master Brewers Association of the Americas (MBAA)
2421 N. Mayfair Rd., Suite 310
Wauwatosa, WI 53226
(414) 774-8558; FAX (414) 774-8556
$55

The Beer Drinker's Guide to Munich
Third Edition
by Larry Hawthorne
Published by Freizeit Publishers, 1995
47-475 Hui Io St.
Kaneohe, HI 96744
(808) 239-8643; FAX (808) 438-8318
72242.2152@compuserve.com
8 1/2 x 6 1/2, 208 pp.
$11.95
First edition 1991, second edition 1992
ISBN Number: 0-9628555-0-2

Belgian Ale
by Pierre Rajotte
Published by Brewers Publications, 1992
PO Box 1679
Boulder, CO 80306-1679
(303) 447-0816; FAX (303) 447-2825
orders@aob.org
http://www.aob.org/aob
5 1/2 x 8 1/2, 176 pp., four-color soft cover, illustrations, b & w photos
$11.95
ISBN Number: 0-937381-31-4

Belgian Ale is the sixth title in the Classic Beer Style Series. Pierre Rajotte takes readers through Belgium's rich history that spawned more than six hundred brands of beer. Rajotte teaches the importance of sugar, Belgian hops, and top-fermenting yeasts in the Belgian ale tradition. After reading *Belgian Ale*, you'll be ready to brew your own Belgian-style, high-gravity beer.

The Biotechnology of Malting and Brewing
Cambridge Studies in Biotechnology 1
by J. S. Hough
Published by Cambridge University Press, 1985
32 E. 57th St.
New York, NY 10022
168 pp., illustrations, hard cover
$39.50

Bock
by Darryl Richman
Published by Brewers Publications, 1994
PO Box 1679
Boulder, CO 80306-1679
(303) 447-0816; FAX (303) 447-2825
orders@aob.org
http://www.aob.org/aob
5 1/2 x 8 1/2, 174 pp., four-color soft cover, illustrations, b & w photos
$11.95
ISBN Number: 0-937381-39-X

The ninth title in the Classic Beer Style Series, *Bock* provides historical insight into the development of this beer style. This exceptional guide gives the reader a thorough understanding of the style and includes multiple recipes and brewing instructions.

Brew Free or Die!
Beer and Brewing, Volume 11
Transcripts of the 1991 National Conference on Quality Beer and Brewing
by Tracy Loysen, Editor
Published by Brewers Publications, 1991
PO Box 1679
Boulder, CO 80306-1679
(303) 447-0816; FAX (303) 447-2825
orders@aob.org
http://www.aob.org/aob
5 1/2 x 8 1/2, 240 pp., three-color soft cover, illustrations, b & w photos
$21.95; $18.95 (AHA member)
ISBN Number: 0-937381-26-8

Chapters include: "Water Workshop," "Yeast and Its Importance to Homebrewing," "From Apples to Hard Cider," "Brewing on the Edge," "Scratch Brewing the Belgian Way," "All-Grain Brewing Using the Triple-Bucket System," "Computer Brewing," "Building an All-Grain Brewing System," "The Brewgal Gourmet — Cooking with Beer," and "Currents in the Neo-Prohibition Movement."

The Brewpub Manual™
by Bill Owens of Buffalo Bill's Brewery
Published by American Brewer Inc.
PO Box 510
Hayward, CA 94543-0510
(510) 538-9500 (a.m. only please) or (800) 646-2701
orders by VISA; FAX (510) 538-7644
ambrew@ambrew.com
http://www.ambrew.com/
8 x 10
$150

Pro-forma operating statement, P & L balance sheet, time line, and business organization. Manual shows how to enter the brewpub business.

Brewery Operations, Volume 6
Transcripts of the 1989 National Microbrewers Conference
by Virginia Thomas, Editor
Published by Brewers Publications, 1990
PO Box 1679
Boulder, CO 80306-1679
(303) 447-0816; FAX (303) 447-2825
orders@aob.org
http://www.aob.org/aob
5 1/2 x 8 1/2, 217 pp., three-color soft cover, illustrations, b & w photos
$25.95; $19.50 (IBS members)
ISBN Number: 0-937381-16-0

Twenty-one talks by brewing professionals given at the 1989 Microbrewers Conference in San Francisco provide the latest information on quality-assurance systems, brewery effluent, yeast management, package design, legislative issues, and more.

Brewery Operations, Volume 7
Transcripts of the 1990 National Microbrewers Conference
by Virginia Thomas, Editor
Published by Brewers Publications, 1991
PO Box 1679
Boulder, CO 80306-1679
(303) 447-0816; FAX (303) 447-2825
orders@aob.org
http://www.aob.org/aob
5 1/2 x 8 1/2, 229 pp., three-color soft cover, illustrations, b & w photos
$25.95; $19.50 (IBS members)
ISBN Number: 0-937381-23-3

The 1990 National Microbrewers Conference featured eighteen presentations that combined specialized information for the small brewer on the technical, practical, and business aspects of running a brewery. All of that valuable information is collected in this volume. Chapters include: "Microbrewery Design and Performance," "Current Legal Issues," "Strategic Planning for Contract Brewing," "Trademark Licensing and Premium Promotion," and more.

Brewery Planner
A Guide to Opening Your Own Small Brewery
by Jeff Mendel and Elizabeth Gold, Editors
Published by Brewers Publications, 1991
PO Box 1679
Boulder, CO 80306-1679
(303) 447-0816; FAX (303) 447-2825
orders@aob.org
http://www.aob.org/aob
8 1/2 x 11, 191 pp., one-color soft cover
$80; $60 (IBS members)
ISBN Number: 0-937381-25-X

Designed as a useful guide, the *Brewery Planner* is a collection of articles by industry experts that covers everything needed to turn a beginning brewer into a successful professional. Chapters include tips on opening a brewpub, microbrewery, and contract brewery; funding; licensing; quality control; formulating beer recipes; marketing and promoting your brewery and your beer; and more.

Handbook of Brewing
by William A. Hardwick
Published by Marcel Dekker Inc., 1994
270 Madison Ave.
New York, NY 10016
(212) 696-9000; FAX (212) 685-4540
7 x 10
$195
ISBN Number: 0-8247-8908-3

Brewing
by Michael J. Lewis and Tom W. Young
Published by Chapman & Hall
1107 Kennedy Pl., Suite 3
Davis, CA 95616
(916) 753-0497 or (800) 636-1331; FAX (916) 753-0176
abgbrew@mother.com
http://www.mother.com/abg
ISBN Number: 0-412-26420-X

Brewing Books and Journals

Brewing is the microbrewer's essential guide to brewing science and its relationship to brewing technology. A useful guide for students and an invaluable companion for professional brewers. Brewing details basic chemistry and microbiology; the use of barley, hops, and yeast; malting mashing; beer quality; flavor; packaging; and dispensing.

Brewing Quality Beers
The Home Brewer's Essential Guidebook
by Bryon Burch
Published by Joby Burch, 1993
PO Box 512
Fulton, CA 95439
(707) 544-2520; FAX (707) 544-5739
5 1/2 x 8 1/2
$5.95
Second edition
ISBN Number: 0-9604284-2-9

Brewing Mead
Wassail! In Mazers of Mead
by Lt. Colonel Robert Gayre with Charlie Papazian
Published by Brewers Publications, 1986
PO Box 1679
Boulder, CO 80306-1679
(303) 447-0816; FAX (303) 447-2825
orders@aob.org
http://www.aob.org/aob
5 1/2 x 8 1/2, 202 pp., four-color soft cover, illustrations
$11.95
ISBN Number: 0-937381-00-4

Delve into the past of this rare drink through poetry, myth, and history. The final chapter describes how to brew your own with Charlie Papazian's easy instructions.

Brewing Science, Volumes 1–3
by J.R.A. Pollock, Editor
Published by Academic Press Inc.
1250 Sixth Ave.
San Diego, CA 92101
Vol. 1 (1979) $165
Vol. 2 (1981) $165
Vol. 3 (1987) $161

Brewing under Adversity: Brewery Operations, Volume 8
Transcripts of the 1991 National Microbrewers Conference
by Virginia Thomas, Editor
Published by Brewers Publications, 1992
PO Box 1679
Boulder, CO 80306-1679
(303) 447-0816; FAX (303) 447-2825
orders@aob.org
http://www.aob.org/aob
5 1/2 x 8 1/2, 248 pp., three-color soft cover, b & w photos
$25.95; $19.50 (IBS members)
ISBN Number: 0-937381-29-2

The nineteen chapters include: "Brewing under Adversity," "Achieving Stability Using Membrane Filtration," "Angels and Vultures: The Search for Financing," "Tapping into History," "Operating Multiple Units," "Dynamics of Marketing Packaged Beer vs. Draft Beer," and "Industry Under Attack."

Brewing the World's Great Beers
A Step-by-Step Guide
by Dave Miller
Published by Storey Publishing, 1995
Schoolhouse Rd.
Pownal, VT 05261
(802) 823-5200; FAX (802) 823-5819
storey@storey.com
http://www.storey.com
6 x 9
$12.95
ISBN Number: 0-88266-775-0

California Brewin
Published by RedBrick Press, 1993
PO Box 1895
Sonoma, CA 95476-1895
(707) 996-2774
$11.95

Continental Pilsener
by David Miller
Published by Brewers Publications, 1990
PO Box 1679
Boulder, CO 80306-1679
(303) 447-0816; FAX (303) 447-2825
orders@aob.org
http://www.aob.org/aob
5 1/2 x 8 1/2, 101 pp., four-color soft cover, b & w photos
$11.95
ISBN Number: 0-937381-20-9

The second title in the Classic Beer Style Series, *Continental Pilsener* takes readers into the world of the father of all lagers. The recipes provided are designed to work for both beginners and microbrewers. Each country's version of this style, various ingredients used, and the different stages of brewing are all outlined.

The Dictionary of Beer and Brewing
The Most Complete Collection of Brewing Terms Written in English
Compiled by Carl Forget
Published by Brewers Publications, 1988
PO Box 1679
Boulder, CO 80306-1679
(303) 447-0816; FAX (303) 447-2825
orders@aob.org
http://www.aob.org/aob
6 x 9, 186 pp., four-color soft cover
$19.95
ISBN Number: 0-937381-10-1

The dictionary includes 1,929 essential definitions, including brewing processes, ingredients, beer types and styles, abbreviations, arcane terms, and conversion tables.

The Essentials of Beer Style
A Catalog of Classic Beer Styles for Brewers & Beer Enthusiasts
by Fred Eckhardt
Published by Fred Eckhardt Associates Inc.
PO Box 546
Portland, OR 97207
4 1/4 x 7 1/4, 224 pp., soft cover
$14.95

Evaluating Beer
by Elizabeth Gold, Managing Editor
Published by Brewers Publications, 1993
PO Box 1679
Boulder, CO 80306-1679
(303) 447-0816; FAX (303) 447-2825
orders@aob.org
http://www.aob.org/aob
5 1/2 x 8 1/2, 244 pp., four-color soft cover, illustrations, b & w photos
$19.95
ISBN Number: 0-937381-37-3

Thirteen beer-industry experts share their secrets and expertise in this unique and exciting book. *Evaluating Beer* will teach you easy-to-understand steps to be a pro at evaluating the beer you taste or the beer you make. This comprehensive collection meets the needs of beer enthusiasts, homebrewers, and professional brewers alike.

50 Great Homebrewing Tips
Practical Brewing Tips and Techniques to Help Beginning Homebrewers Brew the Perfect Pint!
by David Weisberg
Published by Lampman Brewing Publications, 1995
PO Box 684
Peterborough, NH 03458
(603) 827-3432; FAX (603) 827-3502
dwbrewer@aol.com
4 3/4 x 7 1/4
$9.95
ISBN Number: 0-9642746-2-0

German Wheat Beer
by Eric Warner
Published by Brewers Publications, 1992
PO Box 1679
Boulder, CO 80306-1679
(303) 447-0816; FAX (303) 447-2825
orders@aob.org
http://www.aob.org/aob
5 1/2 x 8 1/2, 161 pp., four-color soft cover, b & w photos
$11.95
ISBN Number: 0-937381-34-9

Eric Warner, graduate of the prestigious Weihenstephan school of brewing in Germany and brewmaster at Colorado's Tabernash Brewing Company, guides you through the history, tradition, and profiles of wheat beer in this thoroughly researched book. Warner has earned national recognition for his brewing ability. His German-style weizen took first place in the wheat beer category at the American Homebrewers Association 1992 National Homebrew Competition, and his Tabernash Weiss won the gold medal in the wheat beer category at the 1994 Great American Beer Festival. From history and profiles of original wheat beer recipes to modern recipes and techniques fit for home or microbrewery use, Warner's *German Wheat Beer* answers all the questions.

Good Beer Guide 1996
by Jeff Evans
Published by CAMRA, 1995
230 Hatfield Rd.
St. Albans, Hertsfordshire AL1 4LW
United Kingdom
01 727-867201; FAX 01 727-867670
100614.1313@compuserve.com
546 pp., soft cover
£9.99
ISBN Number: 1-85249-008X

Great American Beer Cookbook
by Candy Schermerhorn
Published by Brewers Publications, 1993
PO Box 1679
Boulder, CO 80306-1679
(303) 447-0816; FAX (303) 447-2825
orders@aob.org
http://www.aob.org/aob

Brewing Books and Journals

7 x 10, 291 pp., enclosed wire-o-bound, four-color cover, four-color photos
$24.95
ISBN Number: 0-937381-38-1

Television personality and cooking instructor Candy Schermerhorn combines the best of specialty beers and cooking with more than two hundred recipes for every occasion and appetite. All recipes use traditional beer styles to enhance flavor potential, giving food an added culinary dimension. This collection is for the casual cook, brewpub owner, culinary hobbyist, and beer enthusiast. Foreword was written by Michael Jackson.

Great Cooking with Beer
Published by RedBrick Press, 1989
PO Box 1895
Sonoma, CA 95476-1895
(707) 996-2774
$10.95 paperback, $16.95 hard cover

The Home Brewers Companion
by Charlie Papazian
Published by Avon Books
Department FP, 1350 Avenue of the Americas
New York, NY 10019
(800) 238-0658; FAX (212) 261-6895
5 1/4 x 8, 400 pp., illustrations, soft cover
$11

This new volume from the "guru of home brew" (Beverage Communicator) gives an in-depth discussion of all aspects of the brewing process. Designed to complement *The New Complete Joy of Home Brewing*, this book includes new recipes, a complete taste-evaluation program, and a guide to world beer styles as well as information addressing the most commonly encountered concerns of the homebrewer, from water quality to mashing your own grains, and much, much more.

Homebrew Favorites
A Coast-to-Coast Collection of More than 240 Beer Recipes
by Karl F. Lutzen and Mark Stevens
Published by Storey Publishing, 1995
Schoolhouse Rd.
Pownal, VT 05261
(802) 823-5200; FAX (802) 823-5819
storey@storey.com
http://www.storey.com
6 x 9
$12.95
ISBN Number: 0-88266-613-4

Dave Miller's Homebrewing Guide
Everything You Need to Know to Make Great Tasting Beer
by Dave Miller
Published by Storey Publishing, 1995
Schoolhouse Rd.
Pownal, VT 05261
(802) 823-5200; FAX (802) 823-5819
storey@storey.com
http://www.storey.com
6 x 9
$14.95
ISBN Number: 0-88266-905-2

Hops
by R. A. Neve
Published by Chapman and Hall
2-6 Boundary Row
London, SE1 8HN
United Kingdom
6 x 9, 266 pp., illustrations, hard cover, first edition
$59.95

How to Build a Small Brewery
Draft Beer in Ten Days
by Bill Owens
Published by *American Brewer* Magazine
PO Box 510
Hayward, CA 94543-0510
(510) 538-9500 (a.m. only please); FAX (510) 538-7644
ambrew@ambrew.com
http://www.ambrew.com/
Full mash, homebrewing.
$20

How to Open a Brewpub or Microbrewery
by Bruce Winner, Scott Smith, Ashton Lewis
Published by American Brewers Guild
1107 Kennedy Pl., Suite 3
Davis, CA 95616
(916) 753-0497; FAX (916) 753-0176
abgbrew@mother.com
http://www.mother.com/abg
ISBN Number: 0-9647668-0-9

How to Open a Brewpub or Microbrewery is everything you need to know to successfully open your brewery in one easy-to-follow book. The book takes you from feasibility analysis to buisness plan; through financing to brewery operations (grain to glass) and brew house design, regulatory compliance and marketing to achieve success.

Import INSIGHTS
Published by Jerry Steinman
51 Virginia Ave.
West Nyack, NY 10994
(914) 358-7751; FAX (914) 358-7860
$550

An Introduction to Brewing Science and Technology, Parts I, II and III
by C. Rainbow and G.E.S. Float, Editors
Published by the Institute of Brewing, 1981
33 Clarges St.
London, W1Y 8EE
United Kingdom
01-499-8144
$75

Just Brew It!
Beer and Brewing, Volume 12
Transcripts of the 1992 National Conference on Quality Beer and Brewing
by Tracy Loysen, Editor
Published by Brewers Publications, 1992
PO Box 1679
Boulder, CO 80306-1679
(303) 447-0816; FAX (303) 447-2825
orders@aob.org
http://www.aob.org/aob
5 1/2 x 8 1/2, 269 pp., three-color soft cover, illustrations, b & w photos
$21.95; $18.95 (AHA members)
ISBN Number: 0-937381-33-0

The conference transcripts feature fifteen information-packed chapters for all levels of brewers. Chapters include: "The Legend of Wild and Dirty Rose," "Beer and Brewing in the 21st Century," "Cooking with Beer," "Improving Extract Beers," "Recipe Formulation," "Breaking Out of Beginning Brewing," "Breathing New Life into Your Homebrew Club," "Just Brew It — With a Wort Chiller," "Beer Filtration for Homebrewers," "Oxygen: Friend or Foe?," "Brewing Lambic Beers Traditionally and at Home," "Setting Up Your Home Draft System," "Bock Talk," and "Evaluation of Pitching Yeast."

Lambic
by Jean-Xavier Guinard
Published by Brewers Publications, 1990
PO Box 1679
Boulder, CO 80306-1679
(303) 447-0816; FAX (303) 447-2825
orders@aob.org
http://www.aob.org/aob
5 1/2 x 8 1/2, 169 pp., four-color soft cover, b & w photos
$11.95
ISBN Number: 0-937381-22-5

The third title in the Classic Beer Style Series, *Lambic* completely examines this exotic and elusive style. Origins, brewing techniques, recipes, and the only printed directory of the lambic breweries of Belgium make this book a useful collector's item.

Malting and Brewing Science, Volumes 1 and 2
Second Edition, 1982
by D. E. Briggs, J. S. Hough, R. Stevens, and T. W. Young
Published by Chapman and Hall Ltd.
11 New Fetter Lane
London, EC4P 4EE
United Kingdom
Vol. 1, 387 pp.; Vol. 2, 533 pp.
$95 per volume
$160 set

New Brewing Lager Beer
by Gregory J. Noonan
Published by Brewers Publications, 1996
PO Box 1679
Boulder, CO 80306-1679
(303) 447-0816; FAX (303) 447-2825
orders@aob.org
http://www.aob.org/aob
5 1/2 x 8 1/2, 387 pp., four-color soft cover, illustrations
$14.95
ISBN Number: 0-937381-46-2

New Brewing Lager Beer has been completely revised and expanded to include more on craft-brewing techniques and more information specific to ale brewing. Author Greg Noonan guides you through an advanced discussion on how to produce high-quality beer every time you brew.

The New Complete Joy of Home Brewing, Second Edition
by Charlie Papazian
Published by Avon Books
Department FP, 1350 Avenue of the Americas
New York, NY 10019
(800) 238-0658; FAX (212) 261-6895
5 1/4 x 8, 416 pp., illustrations, soft cover
$11.00

Penthouse called this book "indispensable — the bible for homebrewers," and it is. Written in a bright, engaging style, *The New Complete Joy of Homebrewing* has all the tips a novice needs, covers more complex recipes for the intermediate brewer, and shows the experienced brewer how to perfect a variety of beers from Pilsener to stout. There is truly something here to please every palate.

Oktoberfest, Vienna, Märzen
by George and Laurie Fix
Published by Brewers Publications, 1992
PO Box 1679
Boulder, CO 80306-1679
(303) 447-0816; FAX (303) 447-2825
orders@aob.org
http://www.aob.org/aob
5 1/2 x 8 1/2, 117 pp., four-color soft cover, illustrations, b & w photos
$11.95
ISBN Number: 0-937381-27-6

Oktoberfest, Viena, Märzen by George and Laurie Fix, can help brewers of all levels perfect their technique and knowledge of these challenging, smooth, and malty styles. George Fix, Ph.D., chairman of mathematics at the University of Texas in Arlington, is an avid homebrewer and author of the *Principles of Brewing Science*. Laurie Fix is a well-known, long-time homebrewer.

On Tap
A Field Guide to North American Brewpubs and Craft Breweries
by Steve Johnson
Published by On Tap Publications
PO Box 71
Clemson, SC 29633
(803) 654-3360; FAX (803) 654-3360
$12.95

Also *On Tap: The Newsletter*, published bi-monthly as a supplement to the book.

On Tap
The Guide to Brewpubs — U.S. East of the Mississippi and Canada
by Steve Johnson
Published by WBR Publications
PO Box 71
Clemson, SC 29633
(803) 654-3360
5 1/2 x 8 1/2, 281 pp.
$14.50
ISBN Number: 0-9629368-6-3

On Tap
The Guide to Brewpubs — U.S. West of the Mississippi
by Steve Johnson
Published by WBR Publications
PO Box 71
Clemson, SC 29633
(803) 654-3360
5 1/2 x 8 1/2, 284 pp.
$14.50

Pale Ale
by Terry Foster, Ph.D.
Published by Brewers Publications, 1990
PO Box 1679
Boulder, CO 80306-1679
(303) 447-0816; FAX (303) 447-2825
orders@aob.org
http://www.aob.org/aob
5 1/2 x 8 1/2, 140 pp., four-color soft cover, illustrations, b & w photos
$11.95
ISBN Number: 0-937381-18-7

The first title in the Classic Beer Styles Series, *Pale Ale* is a technical masterpiece on the world's most popular ale style. Written by a British expatriate and renowned expert on British beers, this book covers history, character, flavor, brewing methods, ingredients, and commercial examples of pale ale — all explained in the author's engaging style.

Porter
by Terry Foster, Ph.D.
Published by Brewers Publications, 1992
PO Box 1679
Boulder, CO 80306-1679
(303) 447-0816; FAX (303) 447-2825
orders@aob.org
http://www.aob.org/aob
5 1/2 x 8 1/2, 142 pp., four-color soft cover, illustrations, b & w photos
$11.95
ISBN Number: 0-937381-28-4

The beer that George Washington brewed was almost lost as a beer style, but is now enjoying a revival led by the homebrewers and microbrewers of the United States. In Canada and England, porter has also enjoyed a resurgence. Foster's *Porter* is a colorful book that recounts the history of porter and helps brewers of all levels brew this full-bodied beer. Foster is a British expatriate and a renowned expert on British beers.

The Practical Brewer
(To be updated & republished in 1996)
by Harold Broderick, Editor
Published by Master Brewers Association of the Americas (MBAA), 1977
2421 N. Mayfair Rd., Suite 310
Wauwatosa, WI 53226
(414) 774-8558; FAX (414) 774-8556
5 1/2 x 8 1/2, 475 pp., hard cover
$40

Principles of Brewing Science
by George Fix, Ph.D.
Published by Brewers Publications, 1989
PO Box 1679
Boulder, CO 80306-1679
(303) 447-0816; FAX (303) 447-2825
orders@aob.org
http://www.aob.org/aob
5 1/2 x 8 1/2, 250 pp., two-color soft cover, illustrations
$29.95
ISBN Number: 0-937381-17-9

Principles of Brewing Science explains the fundamental chemical and biochemical processes involved in the creation of beer. This technical book covers water, malt, grains, hops, enzymes, yeast, carbohydrates, bacteria, and proteins. Appendix includes an overview of elementary chemistry. Fully indexed.

The Private Brewer's Guide
To the Art of Brewing Ale & Porter of 1822
Published by ZymoScribe, 1995
1 Evergreen Dr.
Woodbridge, CT 06525-1025
(203) 393-2176; FAX (203) 393-3257
weber@ksis.com
$19.95

Quality Brewing, Share the Experience: Brewery Operations, Volume 9
Transcripts of the 1992 National Microbrewers Conference
by Virginia Thomas, Editor
Published by Brewers Publications, 1992
PO Box 1679
Boulder, CO 80306-1679
(303) 447-0816; FAX (303) 447-2825
orders@aob.org
http://www.aob.org/aob
5 1/2 x 8 1/2, 330 pp., three-color soft cover, b & w photos
$25.95; $19.50 (IBS members)
ISBN Number: 0-937381-32-2

The 1992 Microbrewers Conference featured thirty-one presentations packed with valuable brewing information, industry statistics, marketing strategies, resource management tips, environmental brewing practices, legislative updates, and much more.

Scotch Ale
by Gregory J. Noonan
Published by Brewers Publications, 1993
PO Box 1679
Boulder, CO 80306-1679
(303) 447-0816; FAX (303) 447-2825
orders@aob.org
http://www.aob.org/aob
5 1/2 x 8 1/2, 197 pp., four-color soft cover, illustrations, b & w photos
$11.95
ISBN Number: 0-937381-35-7

Discover the history of this legendary ale and learn how to brew it at home or in your professional brewery with Greg Noonan's easy directions. Noonan's insight into yeast, hops, malts, water, and brewing conditions will help you get the results you demand in your next batch of Scotch ale.

Secret Life of Beer
Legends, Lore, and Little Known Facts
by Alan Eames
Published by Storey Publishing, 1995
Schoolhouse Rd.
Pownal, VT 05261
(802) 823-5200; FAX (802) 823-5819
storey@storey.com
http://www.storey.com
6 x 6
$9.95
ISBN Number: 0-88266-807-2

Guidelines for marrying beer and food, insight on selecting appropriate beers for every occasion, beer-based recipes — all delivered with Beaumont's unique North American perspective.

Star Spangled Beer
A Guide to America's New Microbreweries and Brewpubs
Published by RedBrick Press, 1987
PO Box 1895
Sonoma, CA 95476-1895
(707) 996-2774
$13.95

Brewing Books and Journals

Stout
by Michael J. Lewis, Ph.D.
Published by Brewers Publications, 1996
PO Box 1679
Boulder, CO 80306-1679
(303) 447-0816; FAX (303) 447-2825
orders@aob.org
http://www.aob.org/aob
5½ x 8½, 192 pp., four-color soft cover, illustrations, b & w photos
$11.95
ISBN Number: 0-937381-44-6

The tenth title in Brewers Publications' critically acclaimed Classic Beer Style Series, *Stout* details the historical developement of this rich brew, describes the sensory profiles of different stout styles, and compares several commercial interpretations. Michael Lewis, former director of the brewing program at the University of California–Davis, provides a variety of recipes to help homebrewers and professional brewers create their own unforgettable stouts.

A Taste for Beer
by Stephen Beaumont
Published by Storey Publishing, 1995
Schoolhouse Rd.
Pownal, VT 05261
(802) 823-5200; FAX (802) 823-5819
storey@storey.com
http://www.storey.com
7 x 10
$14.95
ISBN Number: 0-88266-907-9

Guidelines for marrying beer and food, insight on selecting appropriate beers for every occasion, beer-based recipes — all delivered with Beaumont's unique North American perspective.

A Textbook of Brewing
by Jean DeClerck
Published by Siebel Institute of Technology, 1994
4055 W. Peterson Ave.
Chicago, IL 60646
(312) 463-3400; FAX (312) 463-7688
8 3/8 x 9 1/2 x 3
$89 (+ $6 s/h in U.S.; $12 in other countries)

This is a classic two-volume set containing 1,235 pages that offers a comprehensive and relevant treatise to any brewer. It is of particular value to those in small breweries where an all-around knowledge of the brewing operation is essential for each member of the organization.

Victory Beer Recipes
America's Best Homebrew
Compiled by the American Homebrewers Association
Published by Brewers Publications, 1994
PO Box 1679
Boulder, CO 80306-1679
(303) 447-0816; FAX (303) 447-2825
orders@aob.org
http://www.aob.org/aob
5 1/2 x 8 1/2, 228 pp., four-color soft cover, illustrations, b & w photos
$11.95; $10.15 (AHA members)
ISBN Number: 0-937381-41-1

From the creators of the homebrewing hit *Winners Circle* comes *Victory Beer Recipes*. Brew and enjoy 128 award-winning recipes from the American Homebrewers Association's National Homebrew Competitions from 1989 to 1993.

Winners Circle
10 Years of Award-Winning Homebrew Recipes
by Tracy Loysen, Charlie Papazian, and Marjie Raizman, Editors
Published by Brewers Publications, 1989
PO Box 1679
Boulder, CO 80306-1679
(303) 447-0816; FAX (303) 447-2825
orders@aob.org
http://www.aob.org/aob
5 1/2 x 8 1/2, 199 pp., four-color soft cover, illustrations
$11.95; $9.95 (AHA members)
ISBN Number: 0-937381-14-4

Winners Circle contains 126 original, award-winning homebrew recipes selected from the winners of the AHA National Homebrew Competition. This homebrew helper includes recipes for twenty-one major styles of lager, ale, and mead. Recipes range from extract to all-grain.

Yeast Technology
by Gerald Reed and Tilak W. Nagodawithana
Published by Van Nostrand Reinhold
115 Fifth Ave.
New York, NY 10003
6 x 9, 454 pp., illustrations, hard cover, second edition
$62.95

Journals

All About Beer Magazine
America's Foremost Beer Publication
by Daniel Bradford, Editor
Published by Daniel Bradfrod
1627 Marion Ave.
Durham, NC 27705
(919) 490-0589; FAX (919) 490-0865
allabtbeer@aol.com
8 1/2 x 11
$4.25 each

    All About Beer Magazine, founded in 1978, is the nation's leading consumer beer magazine. Dedicated to educating the beer lover about beer — trends, styles, history, culture, industry — *All About Beer Magazine* delivers a consistent package of entertaining and informative material. A beer festival in print.

American Brewer
The Business of Beer™
by Bill Tressler, Editor
Published by Owens Publications
PO Box 510
Hayward, CA 94543-0510
(800) 646-2701; FAX (510) 538-7644
ambrew@ambrew.com
Business magazine for micro- and pubbrewing
U.S. $22 per year, $30 per 2 years; Canada $25 per year

American Breweriana Journal
Magazine of Brewery History & Advertising
by Bob Pirie, Editor
Published by American Breweriana Association Inc.
PO Box 11157
Pueblo, CO 81001
(719) 544-9267
breweriana@aol.com
8 1/2 x 11, pp. 52
$20 per year (includes membership in the Association)
ISBN Number: 0748-8343

Beer Magazine
"A Thirst Quenching Experience"
by Mario Deer, Editor
Published by Mario Deer
102 Burlington Crossing
Ottawa, ON K1T 3K5
Canada
(613) 737-3715; FAX (613) 737-3715
$4.50

Beer Statistics News
Published by Jerry Steinman
51 Virginia Ave.
West Nyack, NY 10994
(914) 358-7751; FAX (914) 358-7860
$297 for twenty-four issues per year.

Beer: The Magazine
by Jim Dorsch, Editor
Published by Beer, the Magazine Inc.
PO Box 717
Hayward, CA 94543-0717
(800) 646-2701; FAX (510) 538-7644
ambrew@ambrew.com
http://www.ambrew.com/
Business magazine for micro- and pubbrewing.
Sample $5; $22 per year

Beer Travelers
A Guide to Good Beer Bars in the U.S.
by Stan Hieronymus, Editor
Published by Stan Hieronymus
PO Box 187
Washington, IL 61571
(309) 745-8643; FAX (309) 745-5134
beertrav@aol.com
8 1/2 x 11
$15 for twelve issues

Beverage Industry
by John N. Frank, Editor
Published by Stagnito Publishing Company
1935 Shermer Rd., Suite 100
Northbrook, IL 60062
(708) 205-5660; FAX (708) 205-5680

Beverage World
by Larry Jabbonsky, Editor
Published by Jerry Keller
150 Great Neck Rd.
Great Neck, NY 11021
(516) 829-9210; FAX (516) 829-5414

Brauwelt International
Professional English Language Brewing Journal
by Dr. Karl-Ullrich Heyse, Editor
Published by Verlag Hans Carl Getränke-Fachverlag
Andernacher Str. 33a
Nuremberg, Bavaria 90411
Germany
(0) 911-95285-0; FAX (0) 911-95285-48
210/297mm, DIN A4, five issues per year
DM 95, — + postal charge each year

Brewing Books and Journals

BREW
The How-To Homebrew Beer Magazine
by Craig Bystrynski, Editor
Published by Niche Publications Inc.
216 F St., Suite 160
Davis, CA 95616
(916) 758-4596; FAX (916) 758-7477
8 1/8 x 10 7/8
$29.95 per year (twelve issues)

Brew Hawaii
Beer and Food Guide
by Anastasy Tynan, Editor
Published by Hawaiian Homebrewers Association
41-610 Nonokio St.
Waimanalo, HI 96795
(808) 259-6884; FAX (808) 259-6755
brew@lava.com
11 x 16
$10 per year (bimonthly)

Brewers Bulletin
by Marge Collins, Editor
Published by Marge Collins
PO Box 906
Woodstock, IL 60098
(815) 338-9330
$40 domestic/U.S., $50 international

Brewers Digest/Annual Buyers Guide & Brewery Directory
by Dori Whitney, Editor
Published by Ammark Publishing Co.
4049 W. Peterson Ave.
Chicago, IL 60646
(312) 463-3400
8 1/4 x 11 1/4
$25 per year; $40 per two years; $55 per three years; $40 per year international (monthly)

Brewer's Guardian
Incorporating International Brewer and Distiller
by Graham Large, Editor; Heidi Urban, Ad. Mgr.
Published by Hampton Publishing Ltd.
97 Station Rd.
Hampton, Middlesex TW12 2BD
United Kingdom
(44) 81-941 7750; FAX (44) 81-941 7721
A4
U.S. subscription £85 (air mail) (monthly)

1996 Brewers' Market Guide
The Art and Science of Small-Scale Brewing
by Stephen A. Mallery, Editor
Published by New Wine Press Inc.
PO Box 3222/1127 Lincoln St.
Eugene, OR 97403
(800) 427-2993; FAX (541) 687-8534
btcirc@aol.com
http://brewingtechniques.com/brewingtechniques
8 1/2 x 11
$9.95

Brewing & Distilling International
by Bruce Stevens, Editor
Published by Brewery Traders Publications
63 Burton Rd.
Burton Upon Trent, Staffs DE14 3DP
United Kingdom
01283-566784; FAX 01283-510674
A4 295mm x 210mm
£75 oversea airmail per year (twelve issues)

Europe's biggest-circulation, English-language journal posted globally to brewery and distillery executives in eighty-two countries every month.

BrewingTechniques
The Art and Science of Small-Scale Brewing
by Stephen A. Mallery, Editor
Published by New Wine Press Inc.
PO Box 3222/1127 Lincoln St.
Eugene, OR 97403
(800) 427-2993; FAX (541) 687-8534
btcirc@aol.com
http://brewingtechniques.com/brewingtechniques
8 1/2 x 11
$6.50 per issue; U.S. $33 per year (U.S. funds only)

The industry's premier technical magazine for craft brewers, *BrewingTechniques* offers in-depth articles ranging from brewing methods to troubleshooting, beer styles, and beer and brewing history. Practical, peer-reviewed, and carefully edited, it includes national and regional advertising and free product information through the reader service program. An unparalleled value.

Cerevisia
Belgian Journal of Brewing and Biotechnology
by Jacques Vander Stricht, Editor
Published by Belgian Brewing Schools — Belgium
11 Groene Dreef
St. Martens-Latem, 9830
Belgium
00-32-09-2825695; FAX 00-32-09-2829139
DIN A4
3.00 BEF (postage included); quarterly journal

Ferment
by J. S. Pierce, Editor
Published by the Institute of Brewing
33 Clarges St.
London, W1Y 8EE
United Kingdom
0171-499-8144; FAX 0171-499-1156
Six issues per year
£115

Homebrew Today
U.K.'s Only Consumer Newspaper for the Home Beer & Wine Enthusiast
by Evelyn Barrett, Editor
Published by Evelyn Barrett, Homebrew Publications
304 Northridge Way
Hemel Hempstead, Herts HP1 2AB
United Kingdom
0442-67228; FAX 0442-67228
£10

Journal of the American Society of Brewing Chemists
Newsletter of the American Society of Brewing Chemists
by Linda Kadler, Editor
Published by the American Society of Brewing Chemists
3340 Pilot Knob Rd.
St. Paul, MN 55121
(612) 454-7250; FAX (612) 454-0766
$80 per year

Journal of the Institute of Brewing
by J. S. Pierce, Editor
Published by the Institute of Brewing
33 Clarges St.
London, W1Y 8EE
United Kingdom
(44) 071-499-8144; FAX (44) 071-499-1156
£190

The MBAA Technical Quarterly
by John T. McCabe
Published by Master Brewers Association of the Americas
2421 N. Mayfair Rd., Suite 310
Wauwatosa, WI 53226
(414) 774-8558; FAX (414) 774-8556
$60 per year

Malt Advocate
by John Hansell, Editor
Published by John Hansell
3416 Oak Hill Rd.
Emmaus, PA 18049
(610) 967-1083; FAX (610) 965-2995
maltman999@aol.com (or)
75022.2401@compuserve.com
http://maltadvocate.com/maltadvocate
8 1/2 x 11
$3.50 (quarterly)

The *Malt Advocate* is dedicated to the discerning consumption of beer and whiskey. Regular columns include single malt scotch, bourbon, beer styles, pairing beer with food, vintage beers, homebrewing, our acclaimed buyer's guide, and other pleasures in life (i.e., cheese, coffee, chocolate).

Modern Brewery Age
by Peter V.K. Reid, Editor
Published by Business Journals Inc.
50 Day St.
Norwalk, CT 06854
(203) 853-6015
Weekly newspaper and bimonthly magazine.
$80 per year

The New Brewer
The Magazine for Micro- and Pubbrewers
by Virginia Thomas, Publisher and Editor-in-Chief
Published by Institute for Brewing Studies
PO Box 1679
Boulder, CO 80306-1679
(303) 447-0816; FAX (303) 447-2825
orders@aob.org
http://www.aob.org/aob
8 1/2 x 11, magazine, 100 pp. per issue, published bimonthly
U.S. $55 per year; $65 per year international subscriptions (U.S. funds)

The New Brewer is the bimonthly publication of the Institute for Brewing Studies. This magazine specifically addresses the needs of craft brewers with informational articles on brewing technology, beer recipes, legislation, equipment selection, brewery marketing, and management.

On Premise Magazine
by Steven Brist, Publisher
Published by the Tavern League of Wisconsin
PO Box 170
Madison, WI 53701
(608) 251-1133; FAX (608) 251-1303

Brewing Books and Journals

The Pint Post
The Official Magazine of the Microbrew Appreciation Society
by Larry Baush, Editor
Published by Microbrew Appreciation Society
12345 Lake City Way N.E., Suite 159
Seattle, WA 98125
(206) 527-7331; FAX (206) 523-1539
8 1/2 x 11, 28 pp.
$1 (quarterly)

Suds 'N' Stuff
by Sandra Powers, Editor
Published by Bosak Publishing Inc.
4764 Galicia Way
Oceanside, CA 92056
(619) 724-4447; FAX (619) 940-0549
8 x 10 7/8
$10 per year

What's Brewing
Newspaper of CAMRA, (the Campaign for Real Ale)
by Roger Protz, Editor
Published by CAMRA
34 Alma Rd.
St. Albans, Hertfordshire AL1 3BW
United Kingdom
(44) 01727-867201; FAX (44) 01727-848795
£14 p.a. Sterling (twelve issues)

Zymurgy®
For the Homebrewer and Beer Lover
by Dena Nishek, Editor
Published by American Homebrewers Association®
PO Box 1679
Boulder, CO 80306-1679
(303) 447-0816; FAX (303) 447-2825
orders@aob.org
http://www.aob.org/aob
8 1/2 x 11, 100+ pp. per issue, magazine
U.S. $33, Canada $38, International $51 per year

The magazine of the American Homebrewers Association, **Zymurgy**, is published quarterly with an annual Special Issue devoted to thoroughly covering one brewing topic. **Zymurgy**, appeals to those who brew their own beer and are interested in beer style variety and beer culture. Regular columns include tips for beginning brewers, cooking with beer, tips and gadgets, reviews of brewing products and beermaking kits, homebrew club news, and award-winning recipes. Peer-reviewed feature articles cover practical information for brewers of all levels including original research projects and beer style profiles.

Zymurgy Special Issues

Zymurgy: All-Grain Special Issue
For the Homebrewer and Beer Lover
Vol. 8, No. 4
by Dena Nishek, Editor
Published by American Homebrewers Association
PO Box 1679
Boulder, CO 80306-1679
(303) 447-0816; FAX (303) 447-2825
orders@aob.org
http://www.aob.org/aob
8 1/2 x 11, 80 pp., magazine
$8.50

This eighty-page compendium on all-grain brewing took more than a year to produce. Since its publication in 1985, it has become a classic reference for all-grain brewers. It covers the important aspects of recipe formulation, ingredients, equipment theory, and philosophy of grain brewing in understandable accurate terms.

Zymurgy: Troubleshooting Special Issue
For the Homebrewer and Beer Lover
Vol. 10, No. 4
by Dena Nishek, Editor
Published by American Homebrewers Association
PO Box 1679
Boulder, CO 80306-1679
(303) 447-0816; FAX (303) 447-2825
orders@aob.org
http://www.aob.org/aob
8 1/2 x 11, 64 pp., magazine
$8.50

Even if you brew near-perfect beer every time, you'll be able to fine-tune your product with this comprehensive guide to brewing problems and their solutions. The Troubleshooter's Chart is worth its weight in beer — a guide to identifying common flavor flaws, their origin and correction. Also: "Guide to Beer Flavor Descriptors," "Tasting Techniques," "Flavor Profiling," and more.

Zymurgy: Yeast Special Issue
For the Homebrewer and Beer Lover
Vol. 12, No. 4
by Dena Nishek, Editor
Published by American Homebrewers Association
PO Box 1679
Boulder, CO 80306-1679
(303) 447-0816; FAX (303) 447-2825

orders@aob.org
http://www.aob.org/aob
8 1/2 x 11, 80 pp., magazine
$8.50

This landmark *Zymurgy* issue contains all the latest information and techniques regarding yeast. Subjects include: test results on commercial brands, culturing yeast from bottle-conditioned beers, matching yeasts to beer styles, and much more.

Zymurgy: Hops and Beer Special Issue
For the Homebrewer and Beer Lover
Vol. 13, No. 4
by Dena Nishek, Editor
Published by American Homebrewers Association
PO Box 1679
Boulder, CO 80306-1679
(303) 447-0816; FAX (303) 447-2825
orders@aob.org
http://www.aob.org/aob
8 1/2 x 11, 80 pp., magazine
$8.50

This Special Issue offers essential technical information. Hops and Beer is the definitive guide to the mysterious vine that grew "wild among willows." Includes growing hops, use of hop oils, calculating hop bitterness, history, hop varieties and assessment, twenty-three winning recipes from the 1990 AHA National Competition, and lots more.

Zymurgy: Traditional Beer Styles Special Issue
For the Homebrewer and Beer Lover
Vol. 14, No. 4
by Dena Nishek, Editor
Published by American Homebrewers Association
PO Box 1679
Boulder, CO 80306-1679
(303) 447-0816; FAX (303) 447-2825
orders@aob.org
http://www.aob.org/aob
8 1/2 x 11, 92 pp., magazine
$8.50

Each of the twenty-six chapters is written by an expert in that particular category, and an amazing total of seventy-two beer styles are covered. Introductions by Charlie Papazian and Michael Jackson begin this thorough treatment.

Zymurgy: The Brewing Process Gadgets and Equipment Special Issue
For the Homebrewer and Beer Lover
Vol. 15, No. 4
by Dena Nishek, Editor
Published by American Homebrewers Association
PO Box 1679
Boulder, CO 80306-1679
(303) 447-0816; FAX (303) 447-2825
orders@aob.org
http://www.aob.org/aob
8 1/2 x 11, 120 pp., magazine
$9.50

The 1992 Special Issue, *The Brewing Process: Gadgets and Equipment*, describes some of the latest and most inventive brewing equipment available. Each article is written by an expert homebrewer, many by the equipment inventors themselves. In addition to the information on equipment, twenty-six award-winning homebrew recipes make this Special Issue a valuable resource.

Zymurgy: Special Ingredients and Indigenous Beer
For the Homebrewer and Beer Lover
Vol. 17, No. 4
by Dena Nishek, Editor
Published by American Homebrewers Association
PO Box 1679
Boulder, CO 80306-1679
(303) 447-0816; FAX (303) 447-2825
orders@aob.org
http://www.aob.org/aob
8 1/2 x 11, 136 pp., magazine
$9.50

This special issue features seventy-six recipes of indigenous beers from around the world (Scotland, Finland, Lithuania, Egypt, Africa, and Mexico just to name a few), as well as exotic herb and spice beers, fruit and vegetable beers, information on unique brewing grains and award-winning beers from the 1994 AHA National Homebrew Competition. More than thirty authors, several professional brewers, contributed to this creative collection. An issue no brewer or beer lover should be without.

Zymurgy: The Great Grain Issue
For the Homebrewer and Beer Lover
Vol. 18, No. 4
by Dena Nishek, Editor
Published by the American Homebrewers Association
PO Box 1679
Boulder, CO 80306-1679
(303) 447-0816; orders@aob.org; FAX (303) 447-2825

Brewing Books and Journals

orders@aob.org
http://www.aob.org/aob
5 1/2 x 8 1/2, 130+ pp., magazine
$9.50

The Great Grain Issue explores the philosophy, principles, practices, and products associated with using grain in homebrew. A collection of articles from twenty-two renowned homebrewers, this Special Issue is designed to appeal to all levels of brewers and beer enthusiasts. The magazine is divided into three sections: "Grain, The Heart of Beer" is a reference section featuring a comprehensive list of available grains and glossary terms; "Principles and Practice" is the bulk of the magazine and includes a practical how-to-section and various flavor experiments; and "Gears and Systems" provides an overview of brewing supplies and equipment.

Zymurgy: Why We Brew
For the Homebrewer and Beer Lover
Vol. 19, No. 4
by Dena Nishek, Editor
Published by the American Homebrewers Association
PO Box 1679
Boulder, CO 80306-1679
(303) 447-0816; FAX (303) 447-2825
orders@aob.org
http://www.aob.org/aob
5 1/2 x 8 1/2, 132 pp., magazine
$9.50

This Special Issue dives into the psyches of a full range of homebrewers. From astronauts and CEOs, to rock stars and models, the homebrewer profile is as varied as homebrew itself. Articles focus on the inspiration behind the infactuation, favorite recipes, personalized brewing set-ups, and more. *Why We Brew* also includes the winning recipes from the AHA 1996 National Homebrew Competition. Available in October 1996.

Videos

Beer and Ale
A Video Guide
by Timothy J. Lorang
Published by St. Clair Production Co.
624 NW 86th St.
Seattle, WA 98117
(206) 783-8001; FAX (206) 632-2553
tlorang@u.washington.edu
4 x 7 1/2
$19.95
ISBN Number: 1-882949-06-4

Trade Periodicals

Alcohol Issues INSIGHTS
Published by Benjamin Steinman
51 Virginia Ave.
West Nyack, NY 10994
(914) 358-7751; FAX (914) 358-7860
$230

Beer Marketer's Insights
Published by Jerry Steinman
51 Virginia Ave.
West Nyack, NY 10994
(914) 358-7751; FAX (914) 358-7860
$360 for 23 issues per year

Beverage Alcohol Market Report
by Perry Luntz, Editor
Published by Perry Luntz
160 E. 48th St.
New York, NY 10017
(212) 371-5237
8 1/2 x 11
$175 ; $195 (international)
Mondays

Brauindustrie
Brewing Industry
by Manfred Kaiser, Editor
Published by Verlag W. Sachon GMBH and Company
Schloss Mindelburg
Mindelheim, 87714
Germany
(01149) 8261-999-0; FAX (01149) 8261-999-132
DM 93, (annual subscription)
ISBN Number: 00341 7115

Brewing and Beverage Industry International
by Manfred Kaiser, Editor
Published by Verlag W. Sachon GMBH and Company
Schloss Mindelburg
Mindelheim, 87714
Germany
(01149) 8261-999-0; FAX (01149) 8261-999-132
DM 93, (annual subscription)

Regional Beer Journals

Ale Street News
by Tony Forder, Editor
Published by Tony Forder and Jack Babin
PO Box 1125
Maywood, NJ 07607
(800) 351-ALES; FAX (201) 368-9101
alestreet@aol.com
10 x 16, 64 to 80 pages
$16.95 per year

    This journal has the best writers in the buisness, and the largest circulation (100,000) in the buisness. This tabloid format brewspaper is the biggest bang for the buck in the East Coast market. Coverage: New York, New Jersey, Pennsylvania, District of Columbia, Maryland, Virginia, North Carolina, and New England.

Alephenalia Beer News
by Charles Finkel
Published by Alephenalia Publications
140 Lakeside Ave., Suite 300
Seattle, WA 98122
(206) 322-5022; FAX (206) 322-5185
info@mdv-beer.com
8 1/2 x 11
Free

BarleyCorn
Published by George Rivers
PO Box 2328
Falls Church, VA 22042
(703) 573-8970
$15 per year (eight issues)

Celebrator Beer News
by Thomas E. Dalldorf, Editor
Published by Thomas E. Dalldorf
PO Box 375
Hayward, CA 94543
(510) 670-0121; FAX (510) 670-0639
cbeernews@aol.com
http://celebrator.com/celebrator/
$14.95 for six issues

    Celebrator Beer News is a sixty-four-page, four-color tabloid dedicated to "craft-brewed" beer and brewery information. The 45,000-plus circulation is distributed primarily on the West Coast and has national distribution.

Midwest Beer Notes
All the Brews That's Fit to Print
by Mike Urseth, Editor
Published by Mike Urseth
339 Sixth Ave.
Clayton, WI 54004
(715) 948-2990; FAX (715) 948-2981
11 3/8 x 14
$12.95 for eight issues

The Northwest Beer Journal
The Largest Beer Newspaper in the NW!
by Randle V. Nilson
Published by Randle V. Nilson
PO Box 972
Port Orchard, WA 98366
(206) 272-1252
beerjourn@aol.com

Rocky Mountain Brews
All the Brews That's Fit to Drink
by A.J. Feldmann, Editor
Published by Jim Parker
251 Jefferson
Fort Collins, CO 80524
(303) 224-2524; FAX (303) 224-2524
$15 per year

    Rocky Mountain Brews is a monthly tabloid dedicated to the enjoyment and brewing of fine beer. While emphasizing the brewing scene in the Rocky Mountain region, the *Brews* reports on any important story concerning the beer world from anywhere on the globe.

Southern Draft Brew News
All the News About Brews
by Sara Doersam, Editor
Published by Phil & Sara Doersam
702 Sailfish Rd.
Winter Springs, FL 32708
(407) 327-9451 or (800) 206-7179; FAX (407) 327-3206
brewnews@aol.com
http://realbeer.com/sodraft/
14-inch tabloid paper
$17 per year or $32 for two years

    The Southeast's bible on the latest beer and brewing news has a circulation of 40,000, with each issue containing lively and interesting articles and industry advertising. This bimonthly brewspaper serves a valuable readership

Brewing Books and Journals

Southwest Brewing News
Published by Bill Metzger and Joe Barfield
11405 Evening Star Dr.
Austin, TX 78739
(512) 282-4935; FAX (512) 282-4936

Yankee Brew News™
New England's Beeriodical since 1989™
by Brett Peruzzi, Editor; Ken Spolsino, Gen. Mgr.
Published by Yankee Brew News Inc.
Donald S. Gosselin, Pres. & CEO
PO Box 520250
Winthrop, MA 02152-0005
(617) 361-6106; FAX (617) 361-0408
$14.95 (U.S.) six issues

Yankee Brew News™, New England's Bimonthly Beeriodical™ reaches an average 60,000 beer enthusiasts in America's hottest beer market. Subscribers are found in twenty-seven states, Canada, and the United Kingdom.

24 Brewing Libraries

Scattered throughout the United States and Canada are brewing libraries, and many of these are associated with major brewing companies. It may be possible to arrange an interlibrary loan to a local university or public library. Except where noted, brewing libraries are open to the public. If it is possible for you to visit one of these libraries, you can peruse many brewing books and journals that otherwise might not be available to you.

United States

Anheuser-Busch Corporate Library
One Busch Pl.
St. Louis, MO 63118
(314) 577-2669; FAX (314) 577-2006

Beer Institute
122 C St. N.W., Suite 750
Washington, DC 20001
(202) 737-2337; FAX (202) 737-7004

The Beer Institute represents more than 90 percent of the domestic brewers and suppliers to the industry. Its most recent edition of the Brewer's Almanac contains a valuable collection of brewing statistics and excise tax information. Cost is $160 per year for non-members.

Bohemian Brewery Importers
Jean Pugh, VP Sales and Mktg.
Michael Lislis, Pres./CEO
710 Silver Spur Rd., Suite193
Rolling Hills Estate, CA 90274
(310) 544-1037; FAX (310) 541-2667

Bureau of Alcohol, Tobacco and Firearms
Sumer A. Duger, Ph.D., Chief, Alcohol and Tobacco Laboratory
1401 Research Blvd.
Rockville, MD 20850
(301) 413-5227; FAX (301) 413-9463

Carlson's Brewery Research
Randy Carlson, Owner
PO Box 758
Walker, MN 56484
(218) 547-1830

Coors Brewing Co. Technical Library
Steve Boss, Librarian
12th & Ford Streets BC520
Golden, CO 80401-1295
(303) 277-3506; FAX (303) 277-2805

Siebel Institute of Technology
Bill Siebel, Pres.
Dave Radzanowski, VP Educational Services
4055 W. Peterson Ave.
Chicago, IL 60646-6001
(312) 279-0966; FAX (312) 463-7688

Large brewing technical library founded in 1872 with resources primarily available to students, writers and laboratory and consulting clients. Contact the Institute for an appointment.

Sonoco Engraph Label Group
Thomas Coker, Mktg. Mgr.
Jim Prendergast, VP Sales
8800 South Blvd.
Charlotte, NC 28273
(704) 554-5796; FAX (704) 554-8122

Canada

Molson Breweries
Sandy Lloyd, Librarian
33 Carlingview Dr.
Etobicoke, ON M9W 5E4
Canada
(416) 798-1786; FAX (416) 798-8930

Seagram Co. Ltd.
225 LaFleur Ave.
LaSalle, PQ H8R 3H2
Canada
(514) 366-2410; FAX (514) 366-3721

25 Association of Brewers' Beer Style Guidelines

By Charlie Papazian

Introduction by James Spence and Charlie Papazian

Since 1979, the Association of Brewers has provided beer style descriptions as a reference for brewers and beer competition organizers. The task of creating a realistic set of guidelines is always complex. The beer style guidelines developed for the Association of Brewers use sources from the commercial brewing industry, beer analyses, and consultations with beer industry experts as resources for information.

The Association of Brewers' beer style guidelines have, as much as possible, historical significance or a high profile in the current commercial beer market. Often, the historical significance is not clear, or a new beer in a current market may only be a passing fad, and thus, quickly forgotten. Another factor considered is that current commercial examples do not always fit well into the historical record, and instead represent a modern reincarnation of the style. Our decision to include a particular historical beer style takes into consideration the style's brewing traditions and the need to preserve those traditions in today's market. The more a beer style has withstood the test of time and marketplace and consumer acceptance, the more likely it is to be included in the Association of Brewers' style guidelines.

The availability of commercial examples plays a large role in whether or not a beer style "makes the list." It is important to consider that not every historical or commercial beer style can be included, nor is every commercial beer representative of the historical tradition (i.e., a brewery labeling a brand as a particular style does not always indicate a fair representation of that style).

Please note that almost all of these beer style guidelines have been cross referenced with data from commercially available beers representative of the style. The data referenced for this purpose has been Professor Anton Piendl's comprehensive work published in the German *Brauindustrie* magazine through the years 1982 through 1994, from the series "Biere Aus Aller Welt."

If you have suggestions for adding or changing a style guideline, write to us, making sure to include reasons and documentation for why you think the style should be included.

Beer Style Guidelines

Categories/Styles Listed

Type	Origin	Style	Substyle	Page
Ales				
	British Origin			
		Classic English-Style Pale Ale		370
		India Pale Ale		370
		Traditional English-Style Bitter	English Ordinary Bitter	370
			English (Special) Best Bitter	370
			English (Extra Special) Strong Bitter	370
		Scottish-Style Ales	Scottish Light Ale	371
			Scottish Heavy Ale	371
			Scottish Export Ale	371
		English-Style Mild Ale	English-Style Light Mild Ale	371
			English-Style Dark Mild Ale	371
		English-Style Brown Ale		372
		Strong Ale	English Old Ale/English Strong Ale	372
			Strong Scotch Ale	372
			Imperial Stout	372
			Other Strong Ales	372
		Barley Wine-Style Ale		372
		Porter	Robust Porter	373
			Brown Porter	373
		Specialty Stouts	Sweet Stout	373
			Oatmeal Stout	373
	Irish Origin			
		Dry Stouts	Classic Irish-Style Dry Stout	373
			Foreign-Style Stout	374
		Porter		See British Origin
	North American Origin			
		American-Style Pale Ale		374
		American-Style Amber Ale		374
		Golden Ale/Canadian-Style Ale		374
		American-Style Brown Ale		374
		Specialty Stouts		See British Origin
		Porter		See British Origin
	German Origin			
		German-Style Kölsch/Köln-Style Kölsch		374
		German-Style Brown Ale/Düsseldorf-Style Altbier		375
		Berliner-Style Weisse (Wheat)		375
		South German-Style Weizen/Weissbier		375
		South German-Style Dunkel Weizen/Dunkel Weissbier		375
		South German-Style Weizenbock/Weissbock		375
	Belgian and French Origin			
		Belgian-Style Flanders/Oud Bruin Ales		376
		Belgian-Style Abbey Ale	Belgian Dubbel	376
			Belgian Tripel	376
		Belgian-Style Pale Ale		376
		Belgian Strong Ale		376
		Belgian-Style White (or Wit)/Belgian-Style Wheat		377
		Belgian-Style Lambic	Belgian-Style Lambic	377
			Belgian-Style Gueuze lambic	377
			Belgian-Style Fruit Lambic	377
		French Biére de Garde		377
Lager Beers				
	European-Germanic Origin			
		European-Style All-Malt Pilsener	German-Style Pilsener	377
			Bohemian-Style Pilsener	378

Beer Style Guidelines

Categories/Styles Listed

Type	Origin	Style	Substyle	Page
Lager Beers				
	European-Germanic Origin			
		European-Style Pilsener		378
		European Low-Alcohol Lager/German Licht(bier)		378
		Münchner-Style Helles		378
		Dortmunder European-Style Export		378
		Vienna-Style Lager		378
		German-Style Märzen/Oktoberfest		379
		European-Style Dark/Münchner Dunkels		379
		German-Style Bock Beer	Traditional Bock	379
			German-Style Helles Bock/Mai Bock	379
		German-Style Strong Doppelbock		379
		German-Style Eisbock		380
		Schwarzbier		380
	North American Origin			
		American Lager		380
		American-Style Light Lager		380
		American-Style Premium Lager		380
		Dry Lager		380
		American Ice lager		380
		American Malt Liquor		381
		American-Style Amber		381
		American Dark Lager		381
	Other Origins			
		Tropical-Style Light Lager		381
		Dry Lager (Japanese)		See North American Origin
Hybrid/Mixed Styles				
	Other Origin			
		American Lager/Ale or Cream Ale		381
		American Wheat Ale or Lager		381
		Unusual Beers (Ales or Lagers)	Fruit Beers	382
			Vegetable Beers	382
			Herb and Spice Beers	382
			Specialty	382
		Smoke-Flavored Beer (Ales or Lagers)	Bamber-Style Rauchbier Lager	382
			Smoked-flavored Beer (Ales or Lager)	382
		Non-Alcoholic Malt Beverage		382

1996–97 Guidelines to Beer Styles
By Charlie Papazian© 1993, 1994, 1995, 1996

ALES

BRITISH ORIGIN

Classic English-Style Pale Ale
Classic English pale ales are golden to copper colored and display English-variety hop character. High hop bitterness, flavor, and aroma should be evident. This medium-bodied pale ale has low to medium malt flavor and aroma. Low caramel character is allowable. Fruity-ester flavors and aromas are moderate to strong. Chill haze is allowable at cold temperatures. Diacetyl (butterscotch character) should be at very low levels or not perceived.
Original Gravity (°Plato):
1.044–1.056 (11–14 °Plato)
Apparent Extract/Final Gravity (°Plato):
1.008–1.016 (2–4 °Plato)
Alcohol by Weight (Volume):
3.5–4.2% (4.5–5.5%)
Bitterness (IBU): 20–40
Color SRM (EBC): 4–11 (10–25 EBC)

India Pale Ale
India pale ales are characterized by intense hop bitterness with a high alcohol content. A high hopping rate and the use of water with high mineral content results in a crisp, dry beer. This golden to deep copper-colored ale has a full, flowery hop aroma and may have a strong hop flavor (in addition to the hop bitterness). India pale ales possess medium maltiness and body. Fruity-ester flavors and aromas are moderate to very strong. Chill haze is allowable at cold temperatures.
Original Gravity (°Plato):
1.050–1.070 (12.5–17.5 °Plato)
Apparent Extract/Final Gravity (°Plato):
1.012–1.018 (3–4.5 °Plato)
Alcohol by Weight (Volume):
4–6% (5–7.5%)
Bitterness (IBU): 40–60
Color SRM (EBC): 8–14 (16–35 EBC)

Traditional English-Style Bitter
In general, English bitters range from golden to copper in color and are well attenuated. Hop flavor and aroma character may be evident at the brewers discretion. Mild carbonation traditionally characterize draft-cask versions, but in bottled versions, a slight increase in carbon dioxide content is acceptable. Fruity-ester character and very low diacetyl (butterscotch) character are acceptable in aroma and flavor. Chill haze is allowable at cold temperatures.

Subcategory: English Ordinary Bitter
Ordinary bitter is gold to copper colored with medium bitterness, light to medium body, and low to medium residual malt sweetness. Hop flavor and aroma character may be evident at the brewers discretion. Mild carbonation traditionally characterize draft-cask versions, but in bottled versions, a slight increase in carbon dioxide content is acceptable. Fruity-ester character and very low diacetyl (butterscotch) character are acceptable in aroma and flavor, but should be minimized in this form of bitter. Chill haze is allowable at cold temperatures.
Original Gravity (°Plato):
1.033–1.038 (8–9.5 °Plato)
Apparent Extract/Final Gravity (°Plato):
1.006–1.012 (1.5–3 °Plato)
Alcohol by Weight (Volume):
2.4–3.0% (3–3.7%)
Bitterness (IBU): 20–35
Color SRM (EBC): 8–12 (16–30 EBC)

Subcategory: English (Special) Best Bitter
Special bitter is more robust than ordinary bitter. It has medium body and medium residual malt sweetness. It is gold to copper colored with medium bitterness. Hop flavor and aroma character may be evident at the brewers discretion. Mild carbonation traditionally characterize draft-cask versions, but in bottled versions, a slight increase in carbon dioxide content is acceptable. Fruity-ester character and very low diacetyl (butterscotch) character are acceptable in aroma and flavor. Chill haze is allowable at cold temperatures.
Original Gravity (°Plato):
1.038–1.045 (9.5–11 °Plato)
Apparent Extract/Final Gravity (°Plato):
1.006–1.012 (1.5–3 °Plato)
Alcohol by Weight (Volume):
3.3–3.8% (4.1–4.8%)
Bitterness (IBU): 28–46
Color SRM (EBC): 12–14 (30–35 EBC)

Subcategory: English (Extra Special) Strong Bitter
Extra special bitter possesses medium to strong hop qualities in aroma, flavor, and bitterness. The residual malt sweetness of this richly flavored, full-bodied bitter is more pronounced than in other bitters. It is gold to copper colored with medium bitterness. Mild carbonation traditionally characterize draft-cask versions, but in bottled versions, a slight increase in carbon dioxide content is acceptable. Fruity-ester character and very low diacetyl (butterscotch) character are acceptable in aroma and flavor. Chill haze is allowable at cold temperatures.

Original Gravity (°Plato):
1.046–1.060 (11.5–15 °Plato)
Apparent Extract/Final Gravity (°Plato):
1.010–1.016 (2.5–4°Plato)
Alcohol by Weight (Volume):
3.8–4.6% (4.8–5.8%)
Bitterness (IBU): 30–55
Color SRM (EBC): 12–14 (30–35 EBC)

Scottish-Style Ales

In general Scottish-Style ales are characterized by a rounded flavor profile. Scottish ales are malty, caramellike, soft, and chewy. Hop rates are low. Yeast characters such as diacetyl (butterscotch) and sulfuriness are acceptable at very low levels. Scottish ales range from golden-amber to deep brown in color and may possess a faint smoky character. Bottled versions of this traditional draft beer may contain higher amounts of carbon dioxide than is typical for draft versions. Chill haze is acceptable at low temperatures.

Subcategory: Scottish Light Ale

Scottish light ales are light bodied. Little-bitterness is perceived and hop flavor or aroma should not be perceived. Despite its lightness Scotttish light ale will still have a low degree of malty, caramellike, soft and chewy character. Yeast characters such as diacetyl (butterscotch) and sulfuriness are acceptable at very low levels. The color will range from golden-amber to deep brown in color and may possess a faint smoky character. Bottled versions of this traditional draft beer may contain higher amounts of carbon dioxide than is typical for draft versions. Chill haze is acceptable at low temperatures.
Original Gravity (°Plato):
1.030–1.035 (7.5–9 °Plato)
Apparent Extract/Final Gravity (°Plato):
1.006–1.012 (1.5–3 °Plato)
Alcohol by Weight (Volume):
2.2–2.8% (2.83–5%)
Bitterness (IBU): 9–20
Color SRM (EBC): 8–17 (16–40 EBC)

Subcategory: Scottish Heavy Ale

Scottish heavy ale is moderate in strength and dominated by a smooth, sweet maltiness balanced with low, but perceptible, hop bitterness. Hop flavor or aroma should not be perceived. Scottish heavy ale will have a medium degree of malty, caramellike, soft and chewy character in flavor and mouthfeel. It has medium body, and fruity esters are very low, if evident. Yeast characters such as diacetyl (butterscotch) and sulfuriness are acceptable at very low levels. The color will range from golden-amber to deep brown in color and may possess a faint smoky character. Bottled versions of this traditional draft beer may contain higher amounts of carbon dioxide than is typical for draft versions. Chill haze is acceptable at low temperatures.
Original Gravity (°Plato):
1.035–1.040 (9–10 °Plato)
Apparent Extract/Final Gravity (°Plato):
1.0010–1.014 (2.5–3.5°Plato)
Alcohol by Weight (Volume):
2.8–3.2% (3.5–4%)
Bitterness (IBU): 12–20
Color SRM (EBC): 10–19 (20–75 EBC)

Subcategory: Scottish Export Ale

The overriding character of Scottish Export Ale is sweet, caramellike, and malty. Its bitterness is perceived as low to medium. Hop flavor or aroma should not be perceived. It has medium body. Fruity-ester character may be apparent. Yeast characters such as diacetyl (butterscotch) and sulfuriness are acceptable at very low levels. The color will range from golden-amber to deep brown in color and may possess a faint smoky character. Bottled versions of this traditional draft beer may contain higher amounts of carbon dioxide than is typical for draft versions. Chill haze is acceptable at low temperatures.
Original Gravity (°Plato):
1.040–1.050 (10–12.5 °Plato)
Apparent Extract/Final Gravity (°Plato):
1.010–1.018 (2.5–4.5°Plato)
Alcohol by Weight (Volume):
3.2–3.6% (4.0–4.5%)
Bitterness (IBU): 15–25
Color SRM (EBC): 10–19 (20–75 EBC)
English-Style Mild Ale

Subcategory: English-Style Light Mild Ale

English light mild ales range from light amber to light brown in color. Malty sweet tones dominate the flavor profile with little hop bitterness or flavor. Hop aroma can be light. Very low diacetyl flavors may be appropriate in this low-alcohol beer. Fruity-ester level is very low. Chill haze is allowable at cold temperatures.
Original Gravity (°Plato):
1.030–1.038 (7.5–9.5 °Plato)
Apparent Extract/Final Gravity (°Plato):
1.004–1.008 (1–2 °Plato)
Alcohol by Weight (Volume):
2.7–3.2% (3.2–4.0%)
Bitterness (IBU): 10–24
Color SRM (EBC): 8–17 (16–40 EBC)

Subcategory: English-Style Dark Mild Ale

English dark mild ales range from deep copper to dark brown (often with a red tint) in color. Malty sweet, caramel, licorice and roast malt tones dominate

the flavor and aroma profile with very little hop flavor or aroma. Very low diacetyl flavors may be appropriate in this low-alcohol beer. Fruity-ester level is very low.
Original Gravity (°Plato):
1.030–1.038 (7.5–9.5 °Plato)
Apparent Extract/Final Gravity (°Plato):
1.004–1.008 (1–2 °Plato)
Alcohol by Weight (Volume):
2.7–3.2% (3.2–4.0%)
Bitterness (IBU): 10–24
Color SRM (EBC): 17–34 (40–135 EBC)

English-Style Brown Ale

English brown ales range from deep copper to brown in color. They have a medium body and a dry to sweet maltiness with very little hop flavor or aroma. Fruity-ester flavors are appropriate. Diacetyl should be very low, if evident. Chill haze is allowable at cold temperatures.
Original Gravity (°Plato):
1.040–1.050 (10–12.5 °Plato)
Apparent Extract/Final Gravity (°Plato):
1.008–1.014 (2–3.5 °Plato)
Alcohol by Weight (Volume):
3.3–4.7% (4–5.5%)
Bitterness (IBU): 15–25
Color SRM (EBC): 15–22 (35–90 EBC)

Strong Ale

Subcategory: English Old Ale/English Strong Ale

Amber to copper to mid-range brown in color, English strong ales are medium to full bodied with a malty sweetness. Hop aroma and flavor can vary from none to medium in character intensity. Fruity-ester flavors and aromas should contribute to the character of this ale. Bitterness should be evident and balanced with malt and/or caramellike sweetness. Alcohol types can be varied and complex. Chill haze is acceptable at low temperatures.
Original Gravity (°Plato):
1.055–1.075 (14–19 °Plato)
Apparent Extract/Final Gravity (°Plato):
1.008–1.020 (2–5°Plato)
Alcohol by Weight (Volume):
4.8–6.4% (6.0–8.0%)
Bitterness (IBU): 30–40
Color SRM (EBC): 10–16 (20–35 EBC)

Subcategory: Strong Scotch Ale

Scotch ales are overwhelmingly malty and full-bodied. Perception of hop bitterness is very low. Hop flavor and aroma are very low or nonexistent. Color ranges from deep copper to brown. The clean alcohol flavor balances the rich and dominant sweet maltiness in flavor and aroma. A caramel character is often a part of the profile. Fruity esters are generally at medium aromatic and flavor levels. A peaty/smoky character may be evident at low levels. Low diacetyl levels are acceptable. Chill haze is allowable at cold temperatures.
Original Gravity (°Plato):
1.072–1.085 (18–21 °Plato)
Apparent Extract/Final Gravity (°Plato):
1.016–1.028 (4–7 °Plato)
Alcohol by Weight (Volume):
5.2–6.7% (6.2–8%)
Bitterness (IBU): 25–35
Color SRM (EBC): 10–25 (20–100 EBC)

Subcategory: Imperial Stout

Dark copper to very black, Imperial stouts typically have a high alcohol content. The extremely rich malty flavor and aroma is balanced with assertive hopping and fruity-ester characteristics. Perceived bitterness can be moderate and balanced with the malt character or very high in the darker versions. Roasted malt astringency and bitterness can be moderately perceived but should not overwhelm the overall character. Hop aroma can be subtle to overwhelmingly floral. Diacetyl (butterscotch) levels should be very low.
Original Gravity (°Plato):
1.075–1.090 (19–22.5 °Plato)
Apparent Extract/Final Gravity (°Plato):
1.020–1.030 (4–7.5 °Plato)
Alcohol by Weight (Volume):
5.5–7% (7–9%)
Bitterness (IBU): 50–80
Color SRM (EBC): 20+ (80+ EBC)

Subcategory: Other Strong Ales

Any style of beer can be made stronger than the classic style guidelines. The goal should be to reach a balance between the style's character and the additional alcohol. See this guide for specifics on the style being made stronger and identify the style created appropriately (for example: double alt, triple bock, or quadruple Pilsener).

Barley Wine-Style Ale

Barley wines range from tawny copper to dark brown in color and have a full body and high residual malty sweetness. Complexity of alcohols and fruity-ester characters are often high and counterbalanced by the perception of low to assertive bitterness and extraordinary alcohol content. Hop aroma and flavor may be minimal to very high. Diacetyl should be very low. A caramel and vinous aroma and flavor are part of the character. Chill haze is allowable at cold temperatures.

Original Gravity (°Plato):
1.090–1.120 (22.5–30.0 °Plato)
Apparent Extract/Final Gravity (°Plato):
1.024–1.032 (6–8 °Plato)
Alcohol by Weight (Volume):
6.7–9.6% (8.4–12%)
Bitterness (IBU): 50–100
Color SRM (EBC): 14–22 (35–90 EBC)

Porter

Subcategory: Robust Porter

Robust porters are black in color and have a roast malt flavor but no roast barley flavor. These porters have a sharp bitterness of black malt without a highly burnt/charcoal flavor. Robust porters range from medium to full in body and have a malty sweetness. Hop bitterness is medium to high, with hop aroma and flavor ranging from negligible to medium. Fruity esters should be evident, balanced with roast malt and hop bitterness.
Original Gravity (°Plato):
1.045–1.060 (11–15 °Plato)
Apparent Extract/Final Gravity (°Plato):
1.008–1.016 (2–4 °Plato)
Alcohol by Weight (Volume):
4.0–5.2% (5.0–6.5%)
Bitterness (IBU): 25–40
Color SRM (EBC): 30+ (120+EBC)

Subcategory: Brown Porter

Brown porters are mid to dark brown (may have red tint) in color. No roast barley or strong burnt malt character should be perceived. Low to medium malt sweetness is acceptable along with medium hop bitterness. This is a light- to medium-bodied beer. Fruity esters are acceptable. Hop flavor and aroma may vary from being negligible to medium in character.
Original Gravity (°Plato):
1.045–1.060 (11–15 °Plato)
Apparent Extract/Final Gravity (°Plato):
1.008–1.016 (2–4 °Plato)
Alcohol by Weight (Volume):
3.5–4.7% (4.5–6.0%)
Bitterness (IBU): 20–30
Color SRM (EBC): 20–35 (80–135 EBC)

Specialty Stouts

Subcategory: Sweet Stout

Sweet stouts, also referred to as cream stouts, have less roasted bitter flavor and a full-bodied mouthfeel. The style can be given more body with milk sugar (lactose) before bottling. Malt sweetness, chocolate, and caramel flavor should dominate the flavor profile. Hops should balance sweetness without contributing apparent flavor or aroma.
Original Gravity (°Plato):
1.045–1.056 (11–14 °Plato)
Apparent Extract/Final Gravity (°Plato):
1.012–1.020 (3–5 °Plato)
Alcohol by Weight (Volume):
2.5–5% (3–6%)
Bitterness (IBU): 15–25
Color SRM (EBC): 40+ (150+ EBC)

Subcategory: Oatmeal Stout

Oatmeal stouts typically include oatmeal in their grist, resulting in a pleasant, full flavor and smooth profile that is rich without being grainy. A roasted malt character which is caramellike and chocolatelike should be evident, smooth and not bitter. Bitterness is moderate — not high. Hop flavor and aroma is optional but should not overpower the overall balance if present. This is a medium- to full-bodied beer, with minimal fruity esters.
Original Gravity (°Plato):
1.038–1.056 (9.5–14 °Plato)
Apparent Extract/Final Gravity (°Plato):
1.008–1.020 (2–5 °Plato)
Alcohol by Weight (Volume):
3.0–4.8% (3.8–6%)
Bitterness (IBU): 20–40
Color SRM (EBC): 20+ (80+ EBC)

IRISH ORIGIN

Dry Stouts

Subcategory: Classic Irish-Style Dry Stout

Dry stouts have an initial malt and caramel flavor profile with a distinctive dry-roasted bitterness in the finish. Dry stouts achieve a dry roasted character through the use of roasted barley. Some slight acidity may be perceived but is not necessary. Hop aroma and flavor should not be perceived. Dry stouts have medium body. Fruity esters are minimal and overshadowed by malt, high hop bitterness, and roasted barley character. Diacetyl (butterscotch) should be very low or not perceived. Head retention and rich character should be part of its visual character.
Original Gravity (°Plato):
1.038–1.048 (9.5–12 °Plato)
Apparent Extract/Final Gravity (°Plato):
1.008–1.014 (2–3.5 °Plato)
Alcohol by Weight (Volume):
3.2–4.2% (3.8–5%)
Bitterness (IBU): 30–40
Color (SRM): 40+ (150+ EBC)

Subcategory: Foreign-Style Stout

As with classic dry stouts, foreign-style stouts have an initial malt sweetness and caramel flavor with a distinctive dry-roasted bitterness in the finish. Some slight acidity is permissible and a medium- to full-bodied mouthfeel is appropriate. Bitterness may be high but the perception is often compromised by malt fullness and sweetness. Hop aroma and flavor should not be perceived. The perception of fruity esters is low. Diacetyl (butterscotch) should be negligible or not perceived. Head retention is excellent.

Original Gravity (°Plato):
1.052–1.072 (13–18 °Plato)
Apparent Extract/Final Gravity (°Plato):
1.008–1.020 (2–5 °Plato)
Alcohol by Weight (Volume):
4.8–6% (6–7.5%)
Bitterness (IBU): 30–60
Color (SRM): 40+ (150+ EBC)

Porter
See British Origins

NORTH AMERICAN ORIGIN

American-Style Pale Ale

American pale ales range from golden to light copper colored. The style is characterized by American-variety hops used to produce high hop bitterness, flavor, and aroma. American pale ales have medium body and low to medium maltiness. Low caramel character is allowable. Fruity-ester flavor and aroma should be moderate to strong. Diacetyl should be absent or present at very low levels. Chill haze is allowable at cold temperatures.

Original Gravity (°Plato):
1.044–1.056 (11–14 °Plato)
Apparent Extract/Final Gravity (°Plato):
1.008–1.016 (2–4 °Plato)
Alcohol by Weight (Volume):
3.5–4.3% (4.5–5.5%)
Bitterness (IBU): 20–40
Color SRM (EBC): 4–11 (10–25 EBC)

American-Style Amber Ale

American amber ales range from light copper to light brown in color. Amber ales are characterized by American-variety hops used to produce high hop bitterness, flavor, and aroma. Amber ales have medium to high maltiness with medium to low caramel character. They should have medium body. The style may have low levels of fruity-ester flavor and aroma. Diacetyl should be absent or barely perceived. Chill haze is allowable at cold temperatures.

Original Gravity (°Plato):
1.044–1.056 (11–14 °Plato)
Apparent Extract/Final Gravity (°Plato):
1.006–1.016 (1.5–4 °Plato)
Alcohol by Weight (Volume):
3.5–4.3% (4.5–5.5%)
Bitterness (IBU): 20–40
Color SRM (EBC): 11–18 (25–45 EBC)

Golden Ale Canadian-Style Ale

Golden ales and Canadian-style ales are straw to golden blonde in color. They closely approximate a lager in its crisp, dry palate, low (but noticeable) hop floral aroma, light body, and light malt sweetness. Perceived bitterness is low to medium. Fruity esters may be perceived but do not predominate. Chill haze should be absent.

Original Gravity (°Plato):
1.045–1.056 (11–14 °Plato)
Apparent Extract/Final Gravity (°Plato):
1.008–1.016 (2–4 °Plato)
Alcohol by Weight (Volume):
3.2–4% (4–5%)
Bitterness (IBU): 15–30
Color SRM (EBC): 3–10 (7–20 EBC)

American-Style Brown Ale

American brown ales range from deep copper to brown in color. Roasted malt caramellike and chocolate-like characters should be of medium intensity in both flavor and aroma. American brown ales have an evident hop aroma, medium to high hop bitterness, and a medium body. Estery and fruity-ester characters should be subdued; diacetyl should not be perceived. Chill haze is allowable at cold temperatures.

Original Gravity (°Plato):
1.040–1.055 (10–14 °Plato)
Apparent Extract/Final Gravity (°Plato):
1.010–1.018 (2.5–4.5 °Plato)
Alcohol by Weight (Volume):
3.3–4.7% (4–5.9%)
Bitterness (IBU): 25–60
Color SRM (EBC): 15–22 (35–90 EBC)

Specialty Stouts
Also see British Origin

Porter
Also see British Origin

GERMAN ORIGIN

German-Style Kölsch/Köln-Style Kölsch

Kölsch is warm fermented and aged at cold temperatures (German ale or alt-style beer). Kölsch is characterized by a golden color and a slightly dry, winy, and

subtly sweet palate. Caramel character should not be evident. The body is light. This beer has low hop flavor and aroma with medium bitterness. Wheat can be used in brewing this beer that is fermented using ale or lager yeasts. Fruity esters should be minimally perceived, if at all. Chill haze should be absent or minimal.
Original Gravity (°Plato):
1.042–1.046 (10.5–11.5 °Plato)
Apparent Extract/Final Gravity (°Plato):
1.006–1.010 (1.5–2.5 °Plato)
Alcohol by Weight (Volume):
3.8–4.1% (4.4–5%)
Bitterness (IBU): 20–30
Color SRM (EBC): 3.5–5 (8–14 EBC)

German-style Brown Ale/Düsseldorf-Style Altbier

Copper to brown in color, this German ale may be highly hopped (although the 25 to 35 IBU range is more normal for the majority of altbiers from Düsseldorf) and has a medium body and malty flavor. A variety of malts, including wheat, may be used. Hop character may be low to high in the flavor and aroma. The overall impression is clean, crisp, and flavorful. Fruity esters should be low. No diacetyl or chill haze should be perceived.
Original Gravity (°Plato):
1.044–1.048 (11–12 °Plato)
Apparent Extract/Final Gravity (°Plato):
1.008–1.014 (2–3.5 °Plato)
Alcohol by Weight (Volume):
3.6–4% (4.3–5%)
Bitterness (IBU): 25–48
Color SRM (EBC): 11–19 (25–65 EBC)

Berliner-Style Weisse (Wheat)

This is very pale in color and the lightest of all the German wheat beers. The unique combination of a yeast and lactic acid bacteria fermentation yields a beer that is acidic, highly attenuated, and very light bodied. The carbonation of a Berliner weisse is high, and hop rates are very low. Hop character should not be perceived. Fruity esters will be evident. No diacetyl should be perceived.
Original Gravity (°Plato):
1.028–1.032 (7–8 °Plato)
Apparent Extract/Final Gravity (°Plato):
1.004–1.006 (1–1.5 °Plato)
Alcohol by Weight (Volume):
2.2–2.7% (2.8–3.4%)
Bitterness (IBU): 3–6
Color SRM (EBC): 2–4 (5–10 EBC)

South German-Style Weizen/Weissbier

The aroma and flavor of a weissbier is decidedly fruity and phenolic. The phenolic characteristics are often described as clove- or nutmeglike and can be smoky or even vanillalike. These beers are made with at least 50 percent malted wheat, and hop rates are quite low. Hop flavor and aroma is absent. Weissbier is well attenuated and very highly carbonated, yet its relatively high starting gravity and alcohol content make it a medium- to full-bodied beer. The color is very pale to deep golden. Bananalike esters are often present. If yeast is present, the beer will appropriately have yeast flavor and a characteristically fuller mouthfeel. If this is served with yeast, the beer may be appropriately very cloudy. No diacetyl should be perceived.
Original Gravity (°Plato):
1.046–1.056 (11.5–14 °Plato)
Apparent Extract/Final Gravity (°Plato):
1.008–1.016 (2–4 °Plato)
Alcohol by Weight (Volume):
3.9–4.4% (4.9–5.5%)
Bitterness (IBU): 10–15
Color SRM (EBC): 3–9 (8–16 EBC)

South German-Style Dunkel Weizen/Dunkel Weissbier

This beer style is characterized by a distinct sweet maltiness and a chocolatelike character from roasted malt. Estery and phenolic elements of this weissbier still prevail. Color can range from copper-brown to dark brown. Dunkel weissbier is well attenuated and very highly carbonated and hop bitterness is low. Hop flavor and aroma are absent. Usually dark barley malts are used in conjunction with dark cara or color malts, and the percentage of wheat malt is at least 50 percent. If this is served with yeast, the beer may be appropriately very cloudy. No diacetyl should be perceived.
Original Gravity (°Plato):
1.048–1.056 (12–14 °Plato)
Apparent Extract/Final Gravity (°Plato):
1.008–1.016 (2–4 °Plato)
Alcohol by Weight (Volume):
3.8–4.3% (4.8–5.4%)
Bitterness (IBU): 10–15
Color SRM (EBC): 16–23 (35–95 EBC)

South German-Style Weizenbock/Weissbock

This style can be either pale or dark (golden to dark brown in color) and has a high starting gravity and alcohol content. The malty sweetness of a weizenbock is balanced with a clovelike phenolic and fruity-estery banana element to produce a well-rounded aroma and flavor. As is true with all German wheat beers, hop bitterness is low and carbonation is high.

Beer Style Guidelines

Hop flavor and aroma is absent. It has a medium to full body. If dark, a mild roast malt character should emerge in flavor and to a lesser degree in the aroma. If this is served with yeast the beer may be appropriately very cloudy. No diacetyl should be perceived.
Original Gravity (°Plato):
1.066–1.080 (16–20 °Plato)
Apparent Extract/Final Gravity (°Plato):
1.0016–1.028 (4–7 °Plato)
Alcohol by Weight (Volume):
5.5–7.5% (6.9–9.3%)
Bitterness (IBU): 10–15
Color SRM (EBC): 5–30 (14–120 EBC)

BELGIAN ORIGIN

Belgian-Style Flanders/Oud Bruin Ales

A light- to medium-bodied deep copper to brown ale characterized by a slight vinegar or lactic sourness and spiciness. A fruity-estery character is apparent with no hop flavor or aroma. Flanders brown ales have low to medium bitterness. Very small quantities of diacetyl are acceptable. Roasted malt character in aroma and flavor is acceptable at low levels. Chill haze is acceptable at low serving temperatures. Some versions may be more highly carbonated and when bottle conditioned may appear cloudy (yeast) when served.
Original Gravity (°Plato):
1.044–1.056 (11–14 °Plato)
Apparent Extract/Final Gravity (°Plato):
1.008–1.016 (2–4 °Plato)
Alcohol by Weight (Volume):
3.8–4.4% (4.8–5.2%)
Bitterness (IBU): 15–25
Color SRM (EBC): 12–18 (30–50 EBC)

Belgian-Style Abbey Ale

Subcategory: Belgian Dubbel

This medium- to full-bodied, dark amber to brown-colored ale has a malty sweetness and nutty, chocolate-like and roast malt aroma. A faint hop aroma is acceptable. Dubbels are also characterized by low bitterness and no hop flavor. Very small quantities of diacetyl are acceptable. Fruity esters (especially banana) are appropriate at low levels. Head retention is dense and mousselike. Chill haze is acceptable at low serving temperatures.
Original Gravity (°Plato):
1.050–1.070 (12.5–17.5 °Plato)
Apparent Extract/Final Gravity (°Plato):
1.012–1.016 (3–4°Plato)
Alcohol by Weight (Volume):
4.8–6.0% (6.0–7.5%)
Bitterness (IBU): 18–25
Color SRM (EBC): 10–14 (20–35 EBC)

Subcategory: Belgian Tripel

Tripels are often characterized by a spicy, phenolic-clove flavor. A banana fruity ester is also common. These pale/light-colored ales usually finish sweet. The beer is characteristically medium to full bodied with a neutral hop/malt balance. Its sweetness will come from very pale malts. There should not be character from any roasted or dark malts. Low hop flavor is okay. Alcohol strength and flavor should be perceived as evident. Head retention is dense and mousselike. Chill haze is acceptable at low serving temperatures.
Original Gravity (°Plato):
1.060–1.096 (17.5–24 °Plato)
Apparent Extract/Final Gravity (°Plato):
1.016–1.024 (4–6 °Plato)
Alcohol by Weight (Volume):
5.6–8.0% (7.0–10.0%)
Bitterness (IBU): 20–25
Color SRM (EBC): 3.5–5.5 (8–15 EBC)

Belgian-Style Pale Ale

Belgian-style pale ales are characterized by low, but noticeable, hop bitterness, flavor, and aroma. Light to medium body and low malt aroma are typical. They are golden to deep amber in color. Noble-type hops are commonly used. Low to medium fruity esters are evident in aroma and flavor. Low caramel or toasted malt flavor is okay. Diacetyl should not be perceived. Chill haze is allowable at cold temperatures.
Original Gravity (°Plato):
1.044–1.054 (11–13.5 °Plato)
Apparent Extract/Final Gravity (°Plato):
1.008–1.014 (2–3.5 °Plato)
Alcohol by Weight (Volume):
3.2–5.0% (4.0–6.0%)
Bitterness (IBU): 20–30
Color SRM (EBC): 3.5–12 (8–30 EBC)

Belgian Strong Ale

Belgian strong ales are often vinous, with darker styles typically colored with dark candy sugar. The perception of hop bitterness can vary from low to high, while hop aroma and flavor is very low. These beers are highly attenuated and have a highly alcoholic character — being medium bodied rather than full bodied. The intensity of malt character should be low to medium. Very little or no diacetyl is perceived. Chill haze is allowable at cold temperatures.
Original Gravity (°Plato):
1.064–1.096 (16–24 °Plato)
Apparent Extract/Final Gravity (°Plato):
1.012–1.024 (3–6 °Plato)
Alcohol by Weight (Volume):
5.6–8.8% (7.0–11.0%)
Bitterness (IBU): 20–50
Color SRM (EBC): 3.5–20 (8–80 EBC)

Belgian-Style White (or Wit)/Belgian-Style Wheat

Belgian white ales are brewed using unmalted and/or malted wheat and malted barley and can be spiced with coriander and orange peel. These very pale beers are often bottle conditioned and served cloudy. The style is further characterized by the use of noble-type hops to achieve a low to medium bitterness and hop flavor. This dry beer has low to medium body, no diacetyl, and a low fruity-ester level.
Original Gravity (°Plato):
1.044–1.050 (11–12.5 °Plato)
Apparent Extract/Final Gravity (°Plato):
1.006–1.010 (1.5–2.5 °Plato)
Alcohol by Weight (Volume):
3.8–4.4% (4.8–5.2%)
Bitterness (IBU): 15–25
Color SRM (EBC): 2–4 (5–10 EBC)

Belgian-Style Lambic

Subcategory: Belgian-Style Lambic

Unblended, naturally fermented lambic is intensely estery, sour, and acetic flavored. Low in carbon dioxide, these hazy beers are brewed with unmalted wheat and malted barley. They are very low in hop bitterness. Cloudiness is acceptable. These beers are quite dry and light bodied.
Original Gravity (°Plato):
1.044–1.056 (11–14 °Plato)
Apparent Extract/Final Gravity (°Plato):
1.000–1.010 (0–2.5 °Plato)
Alcohol by Weight (Volume):
4–5% (5–6%)
Bitterness (IBU): 11–23
Color SRM (EBC): 6–13 (15–33 EBC)

Subcategory: Belgian-Style Gueuze Lambic

Old lambic is blended with newly fermenting young lambic to create this special style of lambic. These unflavored blended and secondary fermented lambic beers may be very dry or mildly sweet and are characterized by intensely fruity-estery, sour, and acidic flavors. These pale beers are brewed with unmalted wheat, malted barley, and stale, aged hops. They are very low in hop bitterness. Cloudiness is acceptable. These beers are quite dry and light bodied.
Original Gravity (°Plato):
1.044–1.056 (11–14 °Plato)
Apparent Extract/Final Gravity (°Plato):
1.000–1.010 (0–2.5 °Plato)
Alcohol by Weight (Volume):
4.0–5.0% (5.0–6.0%)
Bitterness (IBU): 11–23
Color SRM (EBC): 6–13 (15–33 EBC)

Subcategory: Belgian-Style Fruit Lambic

These beers, also known by the names framboise, kriek, peche, cassis, etc., are characterized by fruit flavors and aromas. The intense color reflects the choice of fruit. Sourness predominates the flavor profile. These flavored lambic beers may be very dry or mildly sweet and range from a dry to a full bodied mouthfeel.
Original Gravity (°Plato):
1.040–1.072 (10–17.5 °Plato)
Apparent Extract/Final Gravity (°Plato):
1.008–1.016 (2–4 °Plato)
Alcohol by Weight (Volume):
4.0–5.5% (5.0–7.0%)
Bitterness (IBU): 15–21
Color SRM (EBC): N/A (Light color takes on hue of fruit.)

French-Style Biére de Garde

Beers in this category are golden to deep copper/light brown colored. They are light to medium in body. The beer is characterized by a malty, often toasted, aroma, slight malt sweetness, and medium hop bitterness. Noble-type hop aromas and flavors should be low to medium. Fruity esters can be light to medium in intensity. Earthy, cellarlike, musty aromas are okay. Diacetyl should not be perceived but chill haze is okay. Often bottle conditioned with some yeast character.
Original Gravity (°Plato):
1.060–1.080 (15–20 °Plato)
Apparent Extract/Final Gravity (°Plato):
1.012–1.024 (3–6 °Plato)
Alcohol by Weight (Volume):
3.5–6.3% (4.5–8%)
Bitterness (IBU): 25–30
Color SRM (EBC): 8–12 (16–30 EBC)

LAGER BEERS

EUROPEAN-GERMANIC ORIGIN

European-Style All-Malt Pilsener

Subcategory: German-Style Pilsener

A classic German Pilsener is very light straw/golden in color and well hopped. Hop bitterness is high. Noble-type hop aroma and flavor is moderate and quite obvious. It is a well-attenuated, medium-bodied beer, but a malty residual sweetness can be perceived in aroma and flavor. Fruity esters and diacetyl should not be perceived. There should be no chill haze. Its head should be dense and rich.

Beer Style Guidelines

Original Gravity (°Plato):
1.044–1.050 (11–12.5 °Plato)
Apparent Extract/Final Gravity (°Plato):
1.006–1.012 (1.5–3 °Plato)
Alcohol by Weight (Volume):
3.6–4.2% (4–5%)
Bitterness (IBU): 30–40
Color (SRM): 3–4 (7–10 EBC)

Subcategory: Bohemian-Style Pilsener

Pilseners in this subcategory are are slightly more medium bodied, and their color can be as dark as light amber. This style balances moderate bitterness and noble-type hop aroma and flavor with a malty, slightly sweet, medium body. Diacetyl may be perceived in very low amounts. There should be no chill haze. Its head should be dense and rich.

Original Gravity (°Plato):
1.044–1.056 (11–14 °Plato)
Apparent Extract/Final Gravity (°Plato):
1.014–1.020 (3.5–5 °Plato)
Alcohol by Weight (Volume):
3.2–4% (4–5%)
Bitterness (IBU): 35–45
Color (SRM): 3–5 (7–14 EBC)

European-Style Pilsener

European Pilseners are straw/golden in color and well-attenuated beers. This medium-bodied beer is often brewed with rice, corn, wheat, or other grain or sugar adjuncts making up part of the mash. Hop bitterness is low to medium. Hop flavor and aroma is low. Residual malt sweetness is low; it does not predominate but may be perceived. Fruity esters and diacetyl should not be perceived. There should be no chill haze.

Original Gravity (°Plato):
1.044–1.050 (11–12.5 °Plato)
Apparent Extract/Final Gravity (°Plato)
1.008–1.010 (2–2.5 °Plato)
Alcohol by Weight (Volume):
3.6–4.2% (4–5%)
Bitterness (IBU): 17–30
Color (SRM): 3–4 (7–10 EBC)

European Low-Alcohol Lager/German Leicht(bier)

These beers are very light in body and color. Malt sweetness is perceived at low to medium levels while hop bitterness character is perceived at medium levels. Hop flavor and aroma may be low to medium. These beers should be clean with no perceived fruity esters or diacetyl. Chill haze is not acceptable.

Original Gravity (°Plato):
1.026–1.032 (6.5–8 °Plato)
Apparent Extract/Final Gravity (°Plato):
1.006–1.010 (1.5–2.5 °Plato)
Alcohol by Weight (Volume):
2.0–2.6% (2.5–3.3%)
Bitterness (IBU): 17–28
Color (SRM): 2–4 (5–9 EBC)

Münchner-Style Helles

This beer has a relatively low bitterness. It is a medium-bodied, malt-emphasized beer; however, certain versions can approach a balance of hop character and maltiness. There should not be any caramel character. Color is light straw to golden. Fruity esters and diacetyl should not be perceived.

Original Gravity (°Plato):
1.044–1.050 (11–13 °Plato)
Apparent Extract/Final Gravity (°Plato):
1.008–1.012 (2–3 °Plato)
Alcohol by Weight (Volume):
3.8–4.4% (4.5–5.5%)
Bitterness (IBU): 18–25
Color (SRM): 3–5 (7–14 EBC)

Dortmunder/European-Style Export

Dortmunder has medium hop bitterness. Hop flavor and aroma are perceptible but low. Sweet malt flavor can be low and should not be caramellike. The color of this style is light straw to deep golden. The body will be medium bodied. Fruity esters, chill haze, and diacetyl should not be perceived.

Original Gravity (°Plato):
1.048–1.056 (12–14 °Plato)
Apparent Extract/Final Gravity (°Plato):
1.010–1.014 (2.5–3.5 °Plato)
Alcohol by Weight (Volume):
4–4.8% (5–6%)
Bitterness (IBU): 23–29
Color (SRM): 3–5 (8–13 EBC)

Vienna-Style Lager

Beers in this category are reddish brown or copper colored. They are light to medium in body. The beer is characterized by malty aroma and slight malt sweetness. The malt aroma and flavor may have a toasted character. Hop bitterness is clean and crisp. Noble-type hop aromas and flavors should be low to medium. Fruity esters, diacetyl, and chill haze should not be perceived.

Original Gravity (°Plato):
1.048–1.056 (12–14 °Plato)
Apparent Extract/Final Gravity (°Plato):
1.012–1.018 (3–4.5 °Plato)
Alcohol by Weight (Volume):
3.8–4.3% (4.8–5.4%)
Bitterness (IBU): 22–28
Color SRM (EBC): 8–12 (16–30 EBC)

German-Style Märzen/Oktoberfest

Märzens are characterized by a medium body and broad range of color. Oktoberfests can range from golden to reddish brown. Sweet maltiness should dominate slightly over a clean, hop bitterness. Malt character should be toasted rather than strongly caramel. Hop aroma and flavor should be low but notable. Fruity esters are minimal, if perceived at all. Diacetyl and chill haze should not be perceived.

Original Gravity (°Plato):
1.050–1.056 (12.5–14 °Plato)
Apparent Extract/Final Gravity (°Plato):
1.012–1.0120 (3–5 °Plato)
Alcohol by Weight (Volume):
4–4.7% (5.3–5.9%)
Bitterness (IBU): 18–25
Color (SRM): 4–15 (10–35 EBC)

European-Style Dark/Münchner Dunkel

These light brown to dark brown beers have a pronounced malty aroma and flavor that dominates over the clean, crisp, moderate hop bitterness. A classic Münchner Dunkel should have a chocolatelike, roast malt, breadlike aroma that comes from the use of Munich dark malt. Chocolate or roast malts can be used, but the percentage used should be minimal. Noble-type hop flavor and aroma should be low but perceptible. Diacetyl is acceptable at very low levels. Fruity esters and chill haze should not be perceived.

Original Gravity (°Plato):
1.052–1.056 (13–14 °Plato)
Apparent Extract/Final Gravity (°Plato):
1.014–1.018 (3.5–4.5 °Plato)
Alcohol by Weight (Volume):
3.8–4.2% (4.5–5%)
Bitterness (IBU): 16–25
Color (SRM): 17–20 (40–80 EBC)

German-Style Schwarzbier

These very dark brown to almost black beers have a roasted malt character without the associated bitterness. Malt flavor and aroma is low in sweetness. Hop bitterness is low to medium in character. Noble-type hop flavor and aroma should be low but perceptible. There should be no fruty esters. Diacetyl is acceptable at very low levels.

Original Gravity (°Plato):
10.44–1.052 (11–13 °Plato)
Apparent Extract/Final Gravity (°Plato):
1.012–1.016 (3–4 °Plato)
Alcohol by Weight (Volume):
3–3.9% (3.8–5%)
Bitterness (IBU): 22–30
Color (SRM): 25–30 (100–120 EBC)

German-Style Bock Beer

Subcategory: Traditional Bock

Traditional bocks are made with all malt and are strong, malty, medium- to full-bodied, bottom-fermented beers with moderate hop bitterness that should increase proportionately with the starting gravity. Hop flavor should be low and hop aroma should be very low. Bocks can range in color from deep copper to dark brown. Fruity esters may be perceived at low levels.

Original Gravity (°Plato):
1.066–1.074 (16.5–18.5 °Plato)
Apparent Extract/Final Gravity (°Plato):
1.018–1.024 (4.5–6 °Plato)
Alcohol by Weight (Volume):
5–6% (6–7.5%)
Bitterness (IBU): 20–30
Color SRM (EBC): 20–30 (80–120 EBC)

Subcategory:
German-Style Helles Bock/Maibock

The German word "helles" means light colored, and as such, a helles bock is light straw to deep golden in color. Maibocks are also light-colored bocks. The malty character should come through in the aroma and flavor. Body is medium to full. Hop bitterness should be low while noble-type hop aroma and flavor may be at low to medium levels. Bitterness increases with gravity. Fruity esters should be minimal. Diacetyl levels should be very low. Chill haze should not be perceived.

Original Gravity (°Plato):
1.066–1.068 (16.5–17 °Plato)
Apparent Extract/Final Gravity (°Plato):
1.012–1.020 (3–5 °Plato)
Alcohol by Weight (Volume):
5–6% (6–7.5%)
Bitterness (IBU): 20–35
Color SRM (EBC): 4–10 (10–20 EBC)

German-Style Strong Doppelbock

Malty sweetness is dominant but should not be cloying. Doppelbocks are full bodied and deep amber to dark brown in color. Astringency from roast malts is absent. Alcoholic strength is high, and hop rates increase with gravity. Hop bitterness and flavor should be low while hop aroma absent. Fruity esters are commonly perceived but at low to moderate levels.

Original Gravity (°Plato):
1.074–1.080 (18.5–20 °Plato)
Apparent Extract/Final Gravity (°Plato):
1.020–1.028 (5–7 °Plato)
Alcohol by Weight (Volume):
5.2–6.2% (6.5–8%)
Bitterness (IBU): 17–27
Color SRM (EBC): 12–30 (30–120 EBC)

Beer Style Guidelines

German-Style Strong Eisbock

A stronger version of doppelbock. Malt character can be very sweet. The body is very full and deep copper to almost black in color. Alcoholic strength is very high. Hop bitterness is subdued. Hop flavor and aroma are absent. Fruity esters may be evident but not overpowering. Typically these beers are brewed by freezing a doppelbock and removing resulting ice to increase alcohol content.
Original Gravity (°Plato):
1.092–1.116 (23–29 °Plato)
Apparent Extract/Final Gravity (°Plato):
N/A
Alcohol by Weight (Volume):
6.8–11.3% (8.6–14.4%)
Bitterness (IBU): 26–33
Color (SRM): 18–50 (42–200 EBC)

NORTH AMERICAN ORIGIN

American Lager

Light in body and color, American lagers are very clean and crisp and aggressively carbonated. Malt sweetness is absent. Corn, rice, or other grain or sugar adjuncts are often used. Hop aroma is absent. Hop bitterness is slight and hop flavor is mild or negligible. Chill haze, fruity esters, and diacetyl should be absent.
Original Gravity (°Plato):
1.040–1.046 (10–11.5 °Plato)
Apparent Extract/Final Gravity (°Plato):
1.006–1.010 (1.5–2.5 °Plato)
Alcohol by Weight (Volume):
3.2–3.8% (3.8–4.5%)
Bitterness (IBU): 5–17
Color (SRM): 2–4 (5–10 EBC)

American-Style Light Lager

According to the United States' FDA regulations, when used in reference to caloric content, "light" beers must have at least 25 percent fewer calories than the "regular" version of that beer. Such beers must have certain analysis data printed on the package label. These beers are extremely light colored, light in body, and high in carbonation. Flavor is mild and bitterness is very low. Chill haze, fruity esters, and diacetyl should be absent.
Original Gravity (°Plato):
1.024–1.040 (6–10 °Plato)
Apparent Extract/Final Gravity (°Plato):
1.002–1.008 (.5–2 °Plato)
Alcohol by Weight (Volume):
2.8–3.5% (3.5–4.4%)
Bitterness (IBU): 8–15
Color (SRM): 2–4 (5–10 EBC)

American-Style Premium Lager

Similar to the American lager, this style is a more flavorful, medium-bodied beer and may contain few or no adjuncts at all. Color may be light straw to golden. Alcohol content and bitterness may also be greater. Hop aroma and flavor is low or negligible. Chill haze, fruity esters, and diacetyl should be absent. NOTE: Some beers marketed as "premium" (based on price) may not fit this definition.
Original Gravity (°Plato):
1.046–1.050 (11.5–12.5 °Plato)
Apparent Extract/Final Gravity (°Plato):
1.010–1.014 (2.5–3.5 °Plato)
Alcohol by Weight (Volume):
3.6–4% (4.3–5%)
Bitterness (IBU): 13–23
Color (SRM): 2–8 (5–16 EBC)

Dry Lager

This straw-colored lager lacks sweetness and is reminiscent of an American-style light lager. However, its starting gravity and alcoholic strength are greater. Hop rates are low, and carbonation is high. Chill haze, fruity esters, and diacetyl should be absent.
Original Gravity (°Plato):
1.040–1.050 (10–12.5 °Plato)
Apparent Extract/Final Gravity (°Plato):
1.004–1.008 (1–2 °Plato)
Alcohol by Weight (Volume):
3.6–4.5% (4.3–5.5%)
Bitterness (IBU): 15–23
Color (SRM): 2–4 (5–10 EBC)

American Ice Lager

This style is slightly higher in alcohol than most other light-colored, American-style lagers. Its body is low to medium and has a low residual malt sweetness. It has few or no adjuncts. Color is very pale to golden. Hop bitterness is low but certainly perceptible. Hop aroma and flavor is low. Chill haze, fruity esters, and diacetyl should not be perceived. Typically these beers are chilled before filtration so that ice crysals (which may or may not be removed) are formed. This can contribute to a higher alcohol content (up to 0.5% more).
Original Gravity (°Plato):
1.040–1.060 (10–15 °Plato)
Apparent Extract/Final Gravity (°Plato):
1.006–1.014 (1.5–3.5 °Plato)
Alcohol by Weight (Volume):
3.8–5% (4.6–6%)
Bitterness (IBU): 7–20
Color (SRM): 2–8 (5–16 EBC)

American Malt Liquor

High in starting gravity and alcoholic strength, this style is somewhat diverse. Some American malt liquors are just slightly stronger than American lagers, while others approach bock strength. Some residual sweetness is perceived. Hop rates are very low, contributing little bitterness and virtually no hop aroma or flavor. Chill haze, diacetyl, and fruity esters should not be perceived.
Original Gravity (°Plato):
1.050–1.060 (12.5–15 °Plato)
Apparent Extract/Final Gravity (°Plato):
1.004–1.010 (1–2.5 °Plato)
Alcohol by Weight (Volume):
5–6% (6.25–7.5%)
Bitterness (IBU): 12–23
Color (SRM): 2–5 (4–8 EBC)

American-Style Amber Lager

American-Style amber lagers are amber, reddish brown, or copper colored. They are medium bodied. There is a noticeable degree of caramel-type malt character in flavor and often in aroma. This is a broad category in which the hop bitterness, flavor, and aroma may be accentuated or may only be present at relatively low levels, yet noticeable. Fruity esters, diacetyl, and chill haze should be absent.
Original Gravity (°Plato):
1.042–1.056 (10.5–14 °Plato)
Apparent Extract/Final Gravity (°Plato):
1.010–1.018 (2.5–4.5 °Plato)
Alcohol by Weight (Volume):
3.8–4.3% (4.8–5.4%)
Bitterness (IBU): 20–30
Color SRM (EBC): 6–12 (15–30 EBC)

American Dark Lager

This beer's malt aroma and flavor is low but notable. Its color ranges from a very deep copper to a medium brown color. Its body is light. Non-malt adjuncts are often used, and hop rates are low. Hop bitterness flavor and aroma are low. Carbonation is high. Fruity esters, diacetyl, and chill haze should not be perceived.
Original Gravity (°Plato):
1.040–1.050 (10–12.5 °Plato)
Apparent Extract/Final Gravity (°Plato):
1.008–1.012 (2–3 °Plato)
Alcohol by Weight (Volume):
3.2–4.4% (4–5.5%)
Bitterness (IBU): 14–20
Color (SRM): 10–20 (20–80 EBC)

OTHER ORIGIN

Tropical-Style Light Lager

Tropical light lagers are very light in color and light bodied. They have no hop flavor or aroma, and hop bitterness is negligible to moderately perceived. Sugar adjuncts are often used to lighten the body and flavor, sometimes contributing to a slight applelike fruity ester. Sugar, corn, rice, and other cereal grains are used as an adjunct. Chill haze and diacetyl should be absent. Fruity esters should be very low.
Original Gravity (°Plato):
1.032–1.046 (8–11.5 °Plato)
Apparent Extract/Final Gravity (°Plato):
1.004–1.010 (1–2.5 °Plato)
Alcohol by Weight (Volume):
2.0–4.5% (2.5–5.6%)
Bitterness (IBU): 9–25
Color (SRM): 2–4 (6–10 EBC)

Dry Beer (Japanese)
See North American Origin

Hybrid/Mixed Styles

American Lager/Ale or Cream Ale

A mild, pale, light-bodied ale, made using a warm fermentation (top or bottom) and cold lagering or by blending top- and bottom-fermented beers. Hop bitterness and flavor is very low. Hop aroma is often absent. Sometimes referred to as cream ales, these beers are crisp and refreshing. A fruity or estery aroma may be perceived. Diacetyl and chill haze should not perceived.
Original Gravity (°Plato):
1.044–1.056 (11–14 °Plato)
Apparent Extract/Final Gravity (°Plato):
1.004–1.010 (1–2.5 °Plato)
Alcohol by Weight (Volume):
3.4–4.5% (4.2–5.6%)
Bitterness (IBU): 10–22
Color (SRM): 2–5 (4–14 EBC)

American Wheat Ale or Lager

This beer can be made using either an ale or lager yeast. Brewed with 30 to 50 percent wheat, hop rates may be low to medium. A fruity-estery aroma and flavor is typical but at low levels; however, phenolic, clovelike characteristics should not be perceived. Color is usually golden to light amber, and the body should be light to medium in character. Diacetyl should be at very low levels.

Beer Style Guidelines

Original Gravity (°Plato):
1.030–1.050 (9.5–12.5 °Plato)
Apparent Extract/Final Gravity (°Plato):
1.004–1.018 (1–4.5 °Plato)
Alcohol by Weight (Volume):
2.8–3.6% (3.5–4.5%)
Bitterness (IBU): 5–17
Color (SRM): 2–8 (4–16 EBC)

Unusual Beers (Ales or Lagers)

Subcategory: Fruit Beers

Fruit beers are any beers using fruit as an adjunct in either primary or secondary fermentation, providing obvious, yet harmonious, fruit qualities. Fruit qualities should not be overpowered by hop character. If a fruit (such as juniper berry) has an herbal or spice quality, it is more appropriate to consider it in the herb and spice beers catagory.
Original Gravity (°Plato):
1.030–1.110 (7.5–27.5 °Plato)
Apparent Extract/Final Gravity (°Plato):
1.006–1.030 (1.5–7.5 °Plato)
Alcohol by Weight (Volume):
2–9.5% (2.5–12%)
Bitterness (IBU): 5–70
Color (SRM): 5–50 (14–200 EBC)

Subcategory: Vegetable Beers

Vegetable beers are any beers using vegetables as an adjunct in either primary or secondary fermentation, providing obvious, yet harmonious, qualities. Vegetable qualities should not be overpowered by hop character. If a vegetable (such as chile pepper) has an herbal or spice quality it should be classified as herb/spice beer catagory.
Original Gravity (°Plato):
1.030–1.110 (7.5–27.5 °Plato)
Apparent Extract/Final Gravity (°Plato):
1.006–1.030 (1.5–7.5 °Plato)
Alcohol by Weight (Volume):
2–9.5% (2.5–12%)
Bitterness (IBU): 5–70
Color (SRM): 5–50 (14–200 EBC)

Subcategory: Herb and Spice Beers

Herb beers use herbs or spices (derived from roots, seeds, fruits, vegetable, flowers, etc.) other than hops to create a distinct character. Under hopping allows the spice or herb to contribute to the flavor profile.
Original Gravity (°Plato):
1.030–1.110 (7.5–27.5 °Plato)
Apparent Extract/Final Gravity (°Plato):
1.006–1.030 (1.5–7.5 °Plato)
Alcohol by Weight (Volume):
2–9.5% (2.5–12%)
Bitterness (IBU): 5–70
Color (SRM): 5–50 (14–200 EBC)

Subcategory: Specialty

These beers are brewed using unusual fermentables other than, or in addition to, malted barley. For example, maple syrup, potatoes, or honey would be considered unusual. Rice, corn, or wheat are not considered unusual.
Original Gravity (°Plato):
1.030–1.110 (7.5–27.5 °Plato)
Apparent Extract/Final Gravity (°Plato):
1.006–1.030 (1.5–7.5 °Plato)
Alcohol by Weight (Volume):
2–9.5% (2.5–12%)
Bitterness (IBU): 0–100
Color (SRM): 1–100 (3–400 EBC)

Smoke-Flavored Beers (Ales or Lagers)

Subcategory: Bamberg-Style Rauchbier Lager

Rauchbier should have smoky characters prevalent in the aroma and flavor. The beer is generally toasted malty sweet and full bodied with low to medium hop bitterness. Noble-type hop flavor is low but perceptible. Low noble-type hop aroma is optional. The aroma should strike a balance between malt, hop, and smoke. Fruity esters, diacetyl, and chill haze should not be perceived.
Original Gravity (°Plato):
1.048–1.052 (12–13 °Plato)
Apparent Extract/Final Gravity (°Plato):
1.012–1.016 (3–4 °Plato)
Alcohol by Weight (Volume):
6–4% (4.3–4.8%)
Bitterness (IBU): 20–30
Color (SRM): 10–20 (20–80 EBC)

Subcategory: Smoke-Flavored Beer (Lager or Ale)

Any style of beer can be smoked; the goal is to reach a balance between the style's character and the smoky properties.

Non-Alcoholic Malt Beverages

Non-alcoholic (NA) malt beverages should emulate the character of a previously listed category/subcategory designation but without the alcohol (less than 0.5 percent).

Bibliography of Resources

The following books, magazines, and consultants were used to compile these style guidelines along with personal knowledge. The guidelines have continually evolved through annual revisions recommended by colleagues worldwide.

Eckhardt, Fred. *Essentials of Beer Style.* Portland, Ore.: Fred Eckhardt Associates, 1989.
Fix, Dr. George. *Vienna, Märzen, Oktoberfest.* Boulder, Colo.: Brewers Publications, 1992.
Foster, Terry. *Pale Ale.* Boulder, Colo.: Brewers Publications, 1990.
Foster, Terry. *Porter.* Boulder, Colo.: Brewers Publications, 1991.
Guinard, Jean Xavier. *Lambic.* Boulder, Colo.: Brewers Publications, 1990.
Jackson, Michael. *Simon and Schuster's Pocket Guide to Beer.* New York: Simon and Schuster, 1991.
Jackson, Michael. *World Guide to Beer.* Philadelphia: Running Press, 1989.
Jackson, Michael. *The Beer Companion.* Philadelphia: Running Press, 1993.
Kieninger, Dr. Helmut. "The Influence on Beermaking." In *Best of Beer and Brewing*. Volumes 1–5. Boulder, Colo.: Brewers Publications, 1987.
Miller, Dave. *Continental Pilsener.* Boulder, Colo.: Brewers Publications, 1990.
Narziss, L. "Types of Beer." *Brauwelt International II / 1991.*
New Brewer, The. 1983–1994. Boulder, Colo.: Institute for Brewing Studies.
Noonan, Greg. *Scotch Ale.* Boulder, Colo.: Brewers Publications, 1993.
Piendl, Professor Anton. *Brauindustrie* magazine, 1982–1994. From the series "Biere Aus Aller Welt." Schloss Mindelburg, Germany. **Note: All styles in this guideline have been cross referenced with technical beer data compiled by Professor Piendl.**
Rajotte, Pierre. *Belgian Ales.* Boulder, Colo.: Brewers Publications, 1992.
Richman, Daryll. *Bock.* Boulder, Colo.: Brewers Publications, 1994.
Warner, Eric. *German Wheat Beer.* Boulder, Colo.: Brewers Publications, 1992.
Zymurgy®. Boulder, Colo.: American Homebrewers Association®, 1979–1995.

Other Resources

J. E. Siebel and Sons, Chicago, Ill.
Siebel Institute of Technology, Chicago, Ill.
American Homebrewers Association® National Competition Committee
James Spence, National Homebrew Competition Director, American Homebrewers Association, Boulder, Colo.
Karen Barela, President, American Homebrewers Association, Boulder, Colo.
Pete Slosberg, Petes Brewing Co., Palo Alto, Calif.
Jeanne and Glenn Colon-Bonet, co-directors of Great American Beer Festival Professional Blind Panel Judging
Fred Scheer, Brewmaster, Pabst Brewing Co., Milwaukee, Wis.
Finn B. Knudsen, President, Beverage Consult International Inc., Evergreen, Colo.
Keith Thomas, Campaign for Real Ale (CAMRA), St. Albans, U.K.
Mark Dorber, British Guild of Beer Writers, and White Horse on Parson's Green, London, U.K.
Tom Thomlinson, past director of Great American Beer Festival Professional Blind Panel Judging.
Gary Luther, Senior Brewing Staff, Miller Brewing Co., Milwaukee, Wis.
Poul Sigsgaard, Scandanavian School of Brewing, Copenhagen, Denmark.
Dr. James Murray, Brewing Research Foundation International (BRFI), Nutfield, U.K.
Members of Great American Beer Festival Professional Tasting Panel.
Personal travels, tastings, and evaluations of beer and brewing experience, 1974 to 1994.

Equipment Index

Adhesives
Pacific Coast Container, 245
Sun International Trading Ltd., 265

Advertising/Novelties, Signs
Ad-Mat Coasters U.S.A. Inc., 260
Allen-Morrison Sales Company, 261
AVVA Technologies, 261
Beer Gear, 262
Beeraphernalia Company, 262
Bolin Agency, 262
Crystalite Corp., 262, 281
Davis and Small Oldtime Sign & Photo Company, 263
General Press Corp., 263
Heuft U.S.A. Inc., 243
PepperWorks, 284
Stout Marketing, 265
Valu-Wear, 265
Walker & Lee Advertising/Design, 265
Winter People, 266
World Division U.S.A., 266
Wright Metal Signs Ltd., 266

Air Conditioning Equipment
Cargocaire Engineering Company, 222, 241, 249
Frick/Reco Division, York International Corp., 227

Air Pollution Control Equipment
Cargocaire Engineering Company, 222, 241, 249

Analyzing/Inspection Equipment
A. Gusmer Inc., 217
Alfa Laval S. A. DE C. V., 218
Beer-Guano, 249
Bloodhound Sensors Ltd., 220
Centrico Inc., 222
ETS Laboratories, 278
Gafco-Worldwide Inc., 227, 243
Haffmans B. V., 228
Heuft U.S.A. Inc., 243
Industrial Dynamics Company Ltd.—Manufacturers of Filtec Inspection Systems, 244
Krones Inc., 32, 34, 230
MicroPure Filtration, 230, 245, 257, 339
Millipore Corp., 230
Monitek Technologies Inc., 231
Orbisphere Laboratories, 232
Paar Scientific (Export) Ltd., 232
Tel-Tru Manufacturing Company, 238
Tuchenhagen North America Inc., 238
YSI Inc., 239
Zahm and Nagel Company Inc., 239

Antioxidants
James Vickers & Company Ltd., 283

Bar/Pub Supplies
Acrylic Designs Inc., 260
Alan Courtenay Ltd., 248
Alumasc, 219, 249
American Coaster Company, 261
Atelier Zillich, 219, 261
Banner Equipment Company, 249
Beer Gear, 262
Beer-Guano, 249
Boelter Companies, 262
Brown Manufacturing Company, 249
CDC Inc., 222
Chrislan Ceramics Inc., 224, 249, 263
Cross Distributing Company Inc., 224
DATOGRAF Apparatebau GmbH & Company, 241
Davis and Small Oldtime Sign & Photo Company, 263
Diversey Inc., 225
Dorette Company, 250
Draft Service Inc., 250
Drinktec U.S.A. Ltd., 225, 242, 250, 281
Elliott Bay Metal Fabricating Inc., 225, 250
England Worthside Ltd., 225
Europe 1992 Connection, 250, 281
F. H. Steinbart Company, 270, 274

First Fabrics Inc., 226
Flo-Pac Corp., 226
German Glass & Gift Imports Inc., 250
Homark Group Ltd., 251
IDD Process & Packaging Inc., 228, 243, 256, 275, 283
Liquidtech Inc., 251
Multiplex Company Inc., 251
National Chemicals Inc., 231, 252
Nightwing Enterprises Inc., 252
Perlick Corp., 232, 252
Port Jackson Mfg., 233
Rapids Wholesale Equipment Company, 234, 253
Rixie Paper Products, 265
Specialist Joinery Fittings, 253
Summit Commercial, 253
Total Brewing International Ltd., 238
VAFAC Inc. (Virginia Food and Craft), 238, 259, 273
Wright Metal Signs Ltd., 266

Batch/Blend Systems
Alfa Laval Brewery Systems, 218
Alfa Laval Brewery Systems/Separation, 218
Alfa Laval S. A. DE C. V., 218
AMBEC, 219
Dairy Engineering Company, 224
Drinktec U.S.A. Ltd., 225, 242, 250, 281
Haffmans B. V., 228
IDD Process & Packaging Inc., 228, 243, 256, 275, 283
Krones Inc., 32, 34, 230
Price-Schonstrom Inc., 233
Team Industries Inc., 238
Tuchenhagen North America Inc., 238
VAFAC Inc. (Virginia Food and Craft), 238, 259, 273
Waukesha Fluid Handling, 239

Beer Hose
A. Gusmer Inc., 217
A. O. Wilson Process Equipment Ltd., 217
AJEX U.S.A. INC., 248, 343
Banner Equipment Company, 249
CDC Inc., 222
CM Supply and Consulting, 255
Dairy Engineering Company, 224
Draft Service Inc., 250
Foxx Equipment Company, 227
Goodall Rubber Company, 227
Hopfen und Malz GmbH, 228, 243, 256
Mangel, Scheuermann & Oeters Inc., 230
Perlick Corp., 232, 252
Rapids Wholesale Equipment Company, 234, 253
Sound Brewing Systems Inc., 237, 259
VAFAC Inc. (Virginia Food and Craft), 238, 259, 273
Wilson Brewing Systems Ltd., 239

Beerstone Remover
Draft Service Inc., 250
Loeffler Chemical Corp., 283
Mangel, Scheuermann & Oeters Inc., 230
Rapids Wholesale Equipment Company, 234, 253

Boilers/Steam Generators
Electro-Steam Generator Corp., 225, 250
Power Flame Inc., 233
Superb Gas Products Company, 238
Sussman Electric Boilers, 238

Bottle Cartoning Equipment
Brewers & Bottlers Equipment Corp., 220, 241
Gafco-Worldwide Inc., 227, 243
IDD Process & Packaging Inc., 228, 243, 256, 275, 283
Kenerik/Golden Gate, 229, 244
KHS Machines Inc., 229
Krones Inc., 32, 34, 230
Nigrelli Systems Inc., 232
Outterson Brewing Services Inc., 232, 258, 283
R. A. Jones & Company Inc., 246
Salvadore Machinery Corp., 234, 246, 258
Standard Box Corp., 246
Zumbiel Packaging, 247

Bottle Washing Machinery
B & J Machinery Inc., 219, 241
Brew Store, 220
Brewers & Bottlers Equipment Corp., 220, 241
Criveller Company, 45, 224, 241, 250
Gafco-Worldwide Inc., 227, 243
Heavy Duty Products Inc., 228, 243
IDD Process & Packaging Inc., 228, 243, 256, 275, 283
Innozyme Ltd., 229
Kenerik/Golden Gate, 229, 244
KHS Machines Inc., 229
Krones Inc., 32, 34, 230
Outterson Brewing Services Inc., 232, 258, 283
Pneumatic Scale, 245
RLS Equipment Company Inc., 234
Salvadore Machinery Corp., 234, 246, 258
Sasib Beverage & Food North America Inc., 234
SMB Technik, 34, 236, 246
VAFAC Inc. (Virginia Food and Craft), 238, 259, 273

Bottles
Anchor Glass Container, 219
APM Inc., 241
Burch Bottle & Packaging, 241
California Glass Company, 249
Custom Deco Inc., 250
E. Z. CAP, 242
ENCORE!, 242
Europe 1992 Connection, 250, 281

Equipment Index

G. W. Kent Inc., 227, 243, 270, 275, 278
Owens-Brockway, 245
Pacific Coast Container, 245
Prime Time Printing, 284
Twinpak Inc., 246
Vinotheque, 238
Vitro Packaging Inc., 247
Wilson Brewing Systems Ltd., 239
Wine Bottle & Packaging Inc., 247

Bottling Lines/Fillers
A. Gusmer Inc., 217
A. O. Wilson Process Equipment Ltd., 217
Advanced Bottling U.K. Ltd., 218, 240
Aidpac International Ltd., 240
Alvey Inc., 241
AMBEC, 219
B & J Machinery Inc., 219, 241
Bohemian Brewery Importers, 220, 249, 254, 344, 365
Brew Store, 220
Brewers & Bottlers Equipment Corp., 220, 241
Busse Inc., 241
CM Supply and Consulting, 255
Criveller Company, 45, 224, 241, 250
Drinktec U.S.A. Ltd., 225, 242, 250, 281
Figgie, 226
Gafco-Worldwide Inc., 227, 243
Heavy Duty Products Inc., 228, 243
Hopfen und Malz GmbH, 228, 243, 256
IDD Process & Packaging Inc., 228, 243, 256, 275, 283
JACO Equipment Corp., 229
Kenerik/Golden Gate, 229, 244
KHS Machines Inc., 229
Krones Inc., 32, 34, 230
Meheen Manufacturing, 244
Outterson Brewing Services Inc., 232, 258, 283
RLS Equipment Company Inc., 234
Salvadore Machinery Corp., 234, 246, 258
Sasib Beverage & Food North America Inc., 234
SMB Technik, 34, 236, 246
Sound Brewing Systems Inc., 237, 259
Volckening Inc., 247
Wilson Brewing Systems Ltd., 239

Brew on Premises Systems
A. O. Wilson Process Equipment Ltd., 217
Advanced Bottling U.K. Ltd., 218, 240
Bohemian Brewery Importers, 220, 249, 254, 344, 365
Brew Store, 220
Brewers & Bottlers Equipment Corp., 220, 241
Cask Brewing Systems, 43, 222, 269
Criveller Company, 45, 224, 241, 250
Custom Brew Beer Systems, 224
DME Brewing Services, 225, 255
Draft Service Inc., 250

Elliott Bay Metal Fabricating Inc., 225, 250
Glatt Bros. Brewing Company, 194, 270, 275, 278
Heavy Duty Products Inc., 228, 243
IDD Process & Packaging Inc., 228, 243, 256, 275, 283
International Brewing & Manufacturing Inc., 229
Kenerik/Golden Gate, 229, 244
Maas Brewing Systems, 230
Mangel, Scheuermann & Oeters Inc., 230
Newlands Services Inc., 47, 232
Outterson Brewing Services Inc., 232, 258, 283
Pierre Rajotte, 233
Price-Schonstrom Inc., 233
Schlueter MFG, 236
Stainless Steel Specialist Inc., 237, 243
Sussman Electric Boilers, 238
Team Industries Inc., 238
Thunder Bay Brewing Company Inc., 161, 253
Toby Jug Bop System, 238
Total Brewing International Ltd., 238
U-Brew Inc., 259
VAFAC Inc. (Virginia Food and Craft), 238, 259, 273
Vinotheque, 238
Wilson Brewing Systems Ltd., 239

Breweriana
Davis and Small Oldtime Sign & Photo Company, 263
Winter People, 266

Brewhouse Equipment
A. Gusmer Inc., 217
A. O. Wilson Process Equipment Ltd., 217
Advanced Bottling U.K. Ltd., 218, 240
Alfa Laval Brewery Systems, 218
Alfa Laval Brewery Systems/Separation, 218
Alfa Laval S. A. DE C. V., 218
APV Inc., 219
Atelier Zillich, 219, 261
Automatic Equipment Mfg., 219
Bavarian Brewery Technologies, 219
Beraplan Härter GmbH, 219
Bohemian Breweries Inc., 220
Bohemian Brewery Importers, 220, 249, 254, 344, 365
Brauhaus Systems Caspary, 220
Brewers & Bottlers Equipment Corp., 220, 241
Bruce Brewing System—Brewery Builders, 220
CAE Screen Plates, 220
CDC Inc., 222
Centrico Inc., 222
Century Mfg. Inc., 34, 222
Chester-Jensen Company Inc., 224
Chrislan Ceramics Inc., 224, 249, 263
CM Supply and Consulting, 255
Criveller Company, 45, 224, 241, 250
Cross Distributing Company Inc., 224
Custom Brew Beer Systems, 224

Equipment Index

Dairy Engineering Company, 224
DME Brewing Services, 225, 255
Dorette Company, 250
Drinktec U.S.A. Ltd., 225, 242, 250, 281
Electro-Steam Generator Corp., 225, 250
Elliott Bay Metal Fabricating Inc., 225, 250
Enerfab Inc., 225
Falco Stainless Steel Equipment Ltd., 226
Gafco-Worldwide Inc., 227, 243
Global Brewing Services Inc., 256
Grain Systems Inc., 228
Heavy Duty Products Inc., 228, 243
Hilge/Shanley Pump, 228, 243
Hopfen und Malz GmbH, 228, 243, 256
IDD Process & Packaging Inc., 228, 243, 256, 275, 283
International Brewing & Manufacturing Inc., 229
J. V. Northwest Inc., 14, 20, 30, 229
JACO Equipment Corp., 229
Kramer Stainless Systems, 230
Krones Inc., 32, 34, 230
Lewis Twice Consultancy, 257
Liquid Assets Brewing Systems, 20, 251
MacLean Brewery Equipment Ltd., 230
Mangel, Scheuermann & Oeters Inc., 230
Newlands Services Inc., 47, 232
Outterson Brewing Services Inc., 232, 258, 283
Paar Scientific (Export) Ltd., 232
Paul Mueller Company, 232
Paul Zaft Copper Works, 232
Pierre Rajotte, 233
Price-Schonstrom Inc., 233
PROGINOX Inc., 233, 258
Prolong Systems Inc., 233, 253
Pugsleys Brewing Projects International/Shipyard Brewing, 33, 233, 258
Santa Rosa Stainless Steel, 234
Schlueter MFG, 236
Shanley Pump, 236
Sound Brewing Systems Inc., 237, 259
Specific Mechanical Systems Ltd., 24, 47, 237
Stainless Steel Specialist Inc., 237, 243
Steinecker Brewhouse, 22
Sussman Electric Boilers, 238
Total Brewing International Ltd., 238
VAFAC Inc. (Virginia Food and Craft), 238, 259, 273
Vendome Copper & Brass Works Inc., 238
W. M. Sprinkman Corp., 239
W. W. Reichert, Bavarian Brewhouse Inc., 239, 253
Wilson Brewing Systems Ltd., 239
Wittemann Company Inc., 239

Brewing Instruction/Classes
Bohemian Breweries Inc., 220
Global Brewing Services Inc., 256
Newlands Services Inc., 47, 232
Pierre Rajotte, 233

Brushes
A. Gusmer Inc., 217
AJEX U.S.A. INC., 248, 343
Gafco-Worldwide Inc., 227, 243
Rapids Wholesale Equipment Company, 234, 253
Volckening Inc., 247

Bulk CO$_2$
Frick/Reco Division, York International Corp., 227
MVE Inc., 252
Zahm and Nagel Company Inc., 239

Bung Extractors
A. Gusmer Inc., 217
Mangel, Scheuermann & Oeters Inc., 230

Bungs
A. Gusmer Inc., 217
A. Handtmann Armaturenfabrik GmbH & Company KG, 217, 218
APM Inc., 241
Drinktec U.S.A. Ltd., 225, 242, 250, 281
Gafco-Worldwide Inc., 227, 243
Mangel, Scheuermann & Oeters Inc., 230
Outterson Brewing Services Inc., 232, 258, 283

Carbonating Equipment
A. Gusmer Inc., 217
A. O. Wilson Process Equipment Ltd., 217
Accurate Metering Systems Inc., 218
Advanced Bottling U.K. Ltd., 218, 240
Aidpac International Ltd., 240
Alfa Laval Brewery Systems, 218
Alfa Laval Brewery Systems/Separation, 218
Alfa Laval S. A. DE C. V., 218
AMBEC, 219
APV Inc., 219
Brew Store, 220
Brewers & Bottlers Equipment Corp., 220, 241
Canadian Liquid Air Ltd., 280
CDC Inc., 222
CM Supply and Consulting, 255
Criveller Company, 45, 224, 241, 250
Cross Distributing Company Inc., 224
Custom Brew Beer Systems, 224
Drinktec U.S.A. Ltd., 225, 242, 250, 281
England Worthside Ltd., 225
Figgie, 226
Foxx Equipment Company, 227
Gafco-Worldwide Inc., 227, 243
Gulfstream Brewing Product, 228
Haffmans B. V., 228

Equipment Index

Heavy Duty Products Inc., 228, 243
IDD Process & Packaging Inc., 228, 243, 256, 275, 283
J. V. Northwest Inc., 14, 20, 30, 229
Kenerik/Golden Gate, 229, 244
Krones Inc., 32, 34, 230
Liquidtech Inc., 251
Mangel, Scheuermann & Oeters Inc., 230
Meyer Supply Inc., 230
Outterson Brewing Services Inc., 232, 258, 283
Rapids Wholesale Equipment Company, 234, 253
Sasib Beverage & Food North America Inc., 234
Schlueter MFG, 236
Sound Brewing Systems Inc., 237, 259
Terriss Consolidated Industries, 238
Tuchenhagen North America Inc., 238
Vinotheque, 238
Wilson Brewing Systems Ltd., 239
Wittemann Company Inc., 239
Zahm and Nagel Company Inc., 239

Case Boxes
CZ Tech, 270
Menasha Corp., 264
Pacific Coast Container, 245

Case Packers
B & J Machinery Inc., 219, 241
Brewers & Bottlers Equipment Corp., 220, 241
Gafco-Worldwide Inc., 227, 243
IDD Process & Packaging Inc., 228, 243, 256, 275, 283
Kenerik/Golden Gate, 229, 244
KHS Machines Inc., 229
Krones Inc., 32, 34, 230
Nigrelli Systems Inc., 232
Outterson Brewing Services Inc., 232, 258, 283
Pneumatic Scale, 245
Sasib Beverage & Food North America Inc., 234
Sound Brewing Systems Inc., 237, 259

Chillproofing Compounds/Stabilizers
A. Gusmer Inc., 217
Aquanautics Inc., 219
CM Supply and Consulting, 255
Criveller Company, 45, 224, 241, 250
Drinktec U.S.A. Ltd., 225, 242, 250, 281
Europe 1992 Connection, 250, 281
G. W. Kent Inc., 227, 243, 270, 275, 278
Grace Davison, 282
Haffmans B. V., 228
Hopfen und Malz GmbH, 228, 243, 256
IDD Process & Packaging Inc., 228, 243, 256, 275, 283
ISP (International Specialty Products), 229, 283
J. E. Siebel Sons' Company, 229
James Vickers & Company Ltd., 283
PQ Corp., 283

Schenk Filter Systems Inc., 236
Scott Laboratories Inc., 236, 279
Stabifix Brauerei-Technik GMBH & Company OHG, 237, 279

CIP Equipment/Spray Balls
A. Handtmann Armaturenfabrik GmbH & Company KG, 217, 218
A. O. Wilson Process Equipment Ltd., 217
AMBEC, 219
Bavarian Brewery Technologies, 219
Bruce Brewing System—Brewery Builders, 220
CDC Inc., 222
CM Supply and Consulting, 255
Dairy Engineering Company, 224
Drinktec U.S.A. Ltd., 225, 242, 250, 281
DuBois, 225
Falco Stainless Steel Equipment Ltd., 226
G & H Products Corp., 227
Gamajet Cleaning Systems Inc., 227
IDD Process & Packaging Inc., 228, 243, 256, 275, 283
L. C. Thomsen Inc., 230
Mangel, Scheuermann & Oeters Inc., 230
Newlands Services Inc., 47, 232
Sasib Beverage & Food North America Inc., 234
Sound Brewing Systems Inc., 237, 259
Thielmann Container Systems, 246
Tuchenhagen North America Inc., 238
W. M. Sprinkman Corp., 239
Wilson Brewing Systems Ltd., 239

Cleaning Equipment
A. Handtmann Armaturenfabrik GmbH & Company KG, 217, 218
A. O. Wilson Process Equipment Ltd., 217
AJEX U.S.A. INC., 248, 343
Albert Handtmann Armaturenfabrik GmbH & Company KG, 217, 218
Alfa Laval Brewery Systems, 218
Alfa Laval Brewery Systems/Separation, 218
Alfa Laval S. A. DE C. V., 218
APV Inc., 219
Buhler (Canada) Inc., 220
Chemdet Inc., 224
Criveller Company, 45, 224, 241, 250
Cross Distributing Company Inc., 224
Custom Brew Beer Systems, 224
Diversey Inc., 225
Drinktec U.S.A. Ltd., 225, 242, 250, 281
DuBois, 225
Electro-Steam Generator Corp., 225, 250
Foxx Equipment Company, 227
Gafco-Worldwide Inc., 227, 243
Gamajet Cleaning Systems Inc., 227
Heavy Duty Products Inc., 228, 243

IDD Process & Packaging Inc., 228, 243, 256, 275, 283
J. V. Northwest Inc., 14, 20, 30, 229
Jet Carboy & Bottle Washer Company, 229
Kenerik/Golden Gate, 229, 244
Krones Inc., 32, 34, 230
Mangel, Scheuermann & Oeters Inc., 230
Meyer Supply Inc., 230
Micro Matic U.S.A. Inc., 244
Outterson Brewing Services Inc., 232, 258, 283
Prosser/Enpo (Sellers), 233
Rapids Wholesale Equipment Company, 234, 253
Strahman Valves Inc., 238
Sussman Electric Boilers, 238
Thielmann Container Systems, 246
Tuchenhagen North America Inc., 238
Vendome Copper & Brass Works Inc., 238
Volckening Inc., 247

Cleaning/Sanitizing Chemicals
AJEX U.S.A. INC., 248, 343
BIRKO Corp., 220
Chemdet Inc., 224
Diversey Inc., 225
Draft Service Inc., 250
DuBois, 225
Europe 1992 Connection, 250, 281
Foxx Equipment Company, 227
Glatt Bros. Brewing Company, 194, 270, 275, 278
Guardian Labs, 228
IDD Process & Packaging Inc., 228, 243, 256, 275, 283
Loeffler Chemical Corp., 283
Meyer Supply Inc., 230
National Chemicals Inc., 231, 252
Rapids Wholesale Equipment Company, 234, 253
Rascher & Betzold Inc., 284
Vinotheque, 238

Coasters
Ad-Mat Coasters U.S.A. Inc., 260
First Fabrics Inc., 226

CO$_2$ Recovery Systems
Frick/Reco Division, York International Corp., 227
Haffmans B. V., 228

Coders and Accessories
Gafco-Worldwide Inc., 227, 243
Videojet Systems International Inc., 247

Computer Software
Beer Business Services, 262
Integrated Restaurant Software, 264

Cooling/Chilling Equipment
Advanced Bottling U.K. Ltd., 218, 240
AMBEC, 219
Bavarian Brewery Technologies, 219
Beverage Consult International Inc., 254, 274
Brew Store, 220
Bruce Brewing System—Brewery Builders, 220
CDC Inc., 222
Century Mfg. Inc., 34, 222
Chester-Jensen Company Inc., 224
Dairy Engineering Company, 224
Drinktec U.S.A. Ltd., 225, 242, 250, 281
Edwards Engineering Corp., 225
Filtrine Manufacturing Company, 226, 242
Foxx Equipment Company, 227
Frick/Reco Division, York International Corp., 227
G & D Chillers Inc., 227
Gafco-Worldwide Inc., 227, 243
Port Jackson Mfg., 233
Rapids Wholesale Equipment Company, 234, 253
Remcor Products Co, 237
Sound Brewing Systems Inc., 237, 259
Wilson Brewing Systems Ltd., 239

Consulting (Beer/Brewery)
Aero Resources Inc., 254
Beman and Beverage Systems Inc., 338
Beverage Consult International Inc., 254, 274
Bruce Brewing System—Brewery Builders, 220
CBS Insurance, 255
CM Supply and Consulting, 255
Davis and Small Oldtime Sign & Photo Company, 263
Elliott Bay Metal Fabricating Inc., 225, 250
Global Brewing Services Inc., 256
IDD Process & Packaging Inc., 228, 243, 256, 275, 283
Japan Microbrewers Association, 340
Newlands Services Inc., 47, 232
Schenk Filter Systems Inc., 236
Sound Brewing Systems Inc., 237, 259
VAFAC Inc. (Virginia Food and Craft), 238, 259, 273
W. M. Sprinkman Corp., 239
W. W. Reichert, Bavarian Brewhouse Inc., 239, 253

Consulting (Engineering)
A. Handtmann Armaturenfabrik GmbH & Company KG, 217, 218
Alyn D. Snedigar, 241
CM Supply and Consulting, 255
Elliott Bay Metal Fabricating Inc., 225, 250
James R. Van Liere; Structural Engineer, 256
Newlands Services Inc., 47, 232
W. M. Sprinkman Corp., 239
W. W. Reichert, Bavarian Brewhouse Inc., 239, 253

Equipment Index

Control Systems
A. Handtmann Armaturenfabrik GmbH & Company KG, 217, 218
A. O. Wilson Process Equipment Ltd., 217
Accurate Metering Systems Inc., 218
Alfa Laval Brewery Systems, 218
Alfa Laval Brewery Systems/Separation, 218
Alfa Laval S. A. DE C. V., 218
Alvey Inc., 241
AMBEC, 219
APV Inc., 219
Beer-Guano, 249
Beman and Beverage Systems Inc., 338
Busse Inc., 241
Custom Brew Beer Systems, 224
Dairy Engineering Company, 224
Diversey Inc., 225
Drinktec U.S.A. Ltd., 225, 242, 250, 281
Foxboro Company, 227, 263
Haffmans B. V., 228
Heavy Duty Products Inc., 228, 243
IDD Process & Packaging Inc., 228, 243, 256, 275, 283
Integrated Restaurant Software, 264
Mangel, Scheuermann & Oeters Inc., 230
Meheen Manufacturing, 244
Meyer Supply Inc., 230
Outterson Brewing Services Inc., 232, 258, 283
Paar Scientific (Export) Ltd., 232
Schenk Filter Systems Inc., 236
Sound Brewing Systems Inc., 237, 259
Tuchenhagen North America Inc., 238
VAFAC Inc. (Virginia Food and Craft), 238, 259, 273
W. M. Sprinkman Corp., 239

Conveyors (Mechanical)
Alvey Inc., 241
AMBEC, 219
AZCO Inc., 219
Bratney Equipment Company/Ken Bratney Company, 220
Brewers & Bottlers Equipment Corp., 220, 241
Buhler (Canada) Inc., 220
Busse Inc., 241
Criveller Company, 45, 224, 241, 250
Elliott Bay Metal Fabricating Inc., 225, 250
Gafco-Worldwide Inc., 227, 243
Grain Systems Inc., 228
Heavy Duty Products Inc., 228, 243
IDD Process & Packaging Inc., 228, 243, 256, 275, 283
Kenerik/Golden Gate, 229, 244
KHS Machines Inc., 229
Krones Inc., 32, 34, 230
Maryland Wire Belts Inc., 244
Meyer Supply Inc., 230
MSK Covertech Inc., 245

Pneumatic Scale, 245
Read Systems Inc., 234
Salvadore Machinery Corp., 234, 246, 258
VAFAC Inc. (Virginia Food and Craft), 238, 259, 273

Conveyors (Pneumatic)
Bratney Equipment Company/Ken Bratney Company, 220
Buhler (Canada) Inc., 220
Gafco-Worldwide Inc., 227, 243
Pneumatic Scale, 245

Corrosion Inhibitors
Loeffler Chemical Corp., 283

Crowns
APM Inc., 241
California Glass Company, 249
G. W. Kent Inc., 227, 243, 270, 275, 278
Northwestern Extract Company, 283
Outterson Brewing Services Inc., 232, 258, 283
Pacific Coast Container, 245
Vinotheque, 238

Dispensing Equipment
AJEX U.S.A. INC., 248, 343
Alan Courtenay Ltd., 248
Alumasc, 219, 249
Banner Equipment Company, 249
Beer-Guano, 249
Beman and Beverage Systems Inc., 338
Chrislan Ceramics Inc., 224, 249, 263
DATOGRAF Apparatebau GmbH & Company, 241
DME Brewing Services, 225, 255
Dorette Company, 250
Draft Service Inc., 250
Drinktec U.S.A. Ltd., 225, 242, 250, 281
England Worthside Ltd., 225
Foxx Equipment Company, 227
Hedwin Corp., 243
Homark Group Ltd., 251
Huber Verpackungen, 243
IDD Process & Packaging Inc., 228, 243, 256, 275, 283
Keg Club, 229
Liquidtech Inc., 251
MacLean Brewery Equipment Ltd., 230
Micro Matic U.S.A. Inc., 244
Multiplex Company Inc., 251
Outterson Brewing Services Inc., 232, 258, 283
Party Pig/Quoin, 245
Perlick Corp., 232, 252
Port Jackson Mfg., 233
Prolong Systems Inc., 233, 253
Rapids Wholesale Equipment Company, 234, 253
Sound Brewing Systems Inc., 237, 259
Steensen U.S.A. Inc., 237

Summit Commercial, 253
Total Brewing International Ltd., 238

Draft ant To-Go Packaging
Aidpac International Ltd., 240
AJEX U.S.A. INC., 248, 343
AMBEC, 219
Drinktec U.S.A. Ltd., 225, 242, 250, 281
Keg Club, 229
O'Herin Enterprises, 264
Party Pig/Quoin, 245
Thielmann Container Systems, 246
Wilson Brewing Systems Ltd., 239

Dust Collection Systems
Aidpac International Ltd., 240
Buhler (Canada) Inc., 220
Grain Millers Inc., 270, 282

Enzymes
A. Gusmer Inc., 217
Aidpac International Ltd., 240
G. W. Kent Inc., 227, 243, 270, 275, 278
James Vickers & Company Ltd., 283

Filter Aids/Accessories
A. Gusmer Inc., 217
A. O. Wilson Process Equipment Ltd., 217
Abec Filtration Systems Inc., 218
AFTEK Inc., 218
Cambridge Inc., 241
Carlson Filtration Ltd., 222
Celite Corp., c/o World Minerals Inc., 222
Criveller Company, 45, 224, 241, 250
Custom Brew Beer Systems, 224
Dicalite/Grefco Inc., 224
Drinktec U.S.A. Ltd., 225, 242, 250, 281
Ertel Engineering Company, 226
Filter Equipment Company Inc., 226, 242, 338
G. W. Kent Inc., 227, 243, 270, 275, 278
General Filtration, Division of Lee Chemicals Ltd., 227, 282
Heavy Duty Products Inc., 228, 243
IDD Process & Packaging Inc., 228, 243, 256, 275, 283
ISP (International Specialty Products), 229, 283
J. E. Siebel Sons' Company, 229
J. V. Northwest Inc., 14, 20, 30, 229
JACO Equipment Corp., 229
James Vickers & Company Ltd., 283
KLR Machines Inc., 229
Marcon Wine & Filters, 230
Meyer Supply Inc., 230
MicroPure Filtration, 230, 245, 257, 339
Pall Ultrafine Filtration Company, 232
Parker Hannifin Corp., Process Filtration Div., 232

RLS Equipment Company Inc., 234
Schenk Filter Systems Inc., 236
Scott Laboratories Inc., 236, 279
Silbrico Corp., 284
Stabifix Brauerei-Technik GMBH & Company OHG, 237, 279
Terriss Consolidated Industries, 238
VAFAC Inc. (Virginia Food and Craft), 238, 259, 273

Filters (Air)
AFTEK Inc., 218
CM Supply and Consulting, 255
Dairy Engineering Company, 224
Filter Equipment Company Inc., 226, 242, 338
L. C. Thomsen Inc., 230
MicroPure Filtration, 230, 245, 257, 339
Millipore Corp., 230
Pall Corp., 232

Filters (Beer)
A. Gusmer Inc., 217
A. Handtmann Armaturenfabrik GmbH & Company KG, 217, 218
A. O. Wilson Process Equipment Ltd., 217
Abec Filtration Systems Inc., 218
AFTEK Inc., 218
Albert Handtmann Armaturenfabrik GmbH & Company KG, 217, 218
Amazon Filters Ltd., 219
APV Inc., 219
Bavarian Brewery Technologies, 219
Beraplan Härter GmbH, 219
Brew Store, 220
Brewers & Bottlers Equipment Corp., 220, 241
Carlson Filtration Ltd., 222
CDC Inc., 222
Century Mfg. Inc., 34, 222
Ceramem Separations, 224
CM Supply and Consulting, 255
Criveller Company, 45, 224, 241, 250
Cross Distributing Company Inc., 224
Dairy Engineering Company, 224
Drinktec U.S.A. Ltd., 225, 242, 250, 281
Ertel Engineering Company, 226
Falco Stainless Steel Equipment Ltd., 226
Filter Equipment Company Inc., 226, 242, 338
Foxx Equipment Company, 227
G. W. Kent Inc., 227, 243, 270, 275, 278
General Filtration, Division of Lee Chemicals Ltd., 227, 282
Heavy Duty Products Inc., 228, 243
IDD Process & Packaging Inc., 228, 243, 256, 275, 283
Industrial Filter & Pump Mfg. Company, 229
ISP (International Specialty Products), 229, 283
KHS Machines Inc., 229

Equipment Index

KLR Machines Inc., 229
L. C. Thomsen Inc., 230
Mangel, Scheuermann & Oeters Inc., 230
Marcon Wine & Filters, 230
MicroPure Filtration, 230, 245, 257, 339
Millipore Corp., 230
Newlands Services Inc., 47, 232
Outterson Brewing Services Inc., 232, 258, 283
Pall Corp., 232
Pall Ultrafine Filtration Company, 232
Parker Hannifin Corp., Process Filtration Div., 232
RLS Equipment Company Inc., 234
Schenk Filter Systems Inc., 236
Schlueter MFG, 236
Scott Laboratories Inc., 236, 279
Sound Brewing Systems Inc., 237, 259
Stabifix Brauerei-Technik GMBH & Company OHG, 237, 279
Stabifix Brauerei-Technik GMBH & Company OHG, 237, 279
Steinecker Brewhouse, 22
VAFAC Inc. (Virginia Food and Craft), 238, 259, 273
Vinotheque, 238
W. W. Reichert, Bavarian Brewhouse Inc., 239, 253
Wilson Brewing Systems Ltd., 239

Filters (Water)

Abec Filtration Systems Inc., 218
AFTEK Inc., 218
Amazon Filters Ltd., 219
Carlson Filtration Ltd., 222
Equipment Enterprises Inc., 281
Ertel Engineering Company, 226
Filter Equipment Company Inc., 226, 242, 338
Filtrine Manufacturing Company, 226, 242
Foxx Equipment Company, 227
General Filtration, Division of Lee Chemicals Ltd., 227, 282
IDD Process & Packaging Inc., 228, 243, 256, 275, 283
Industrial Filter & Pump Mfg. Company, 229
L. C. Thomsen Inc., 230
Mangel, Scheuermann & Oeters Inc., 230
MicroPure Filtration, 230, 245, 257, 339
Millipore Corp., 230
Multiplex Company Inc., 251
Outterson Brewing Services Inc., 232, 258, 283
Pall Corp., 232
Pall Ultrafine Filtration Company, 232
Parker Hannifin Corp., Process Filtration Div., 232
R-P Products, 234
Schenk Filter Systems Inc., 236
Scott Laboratories Inc., 236, 279
Stabifix Brauerei-Technik GMBH & Company OHG, 237, 279

Fittings

A. Gusmer Inc., 217
A. O. Wilson Process Equipment Ltd., 217
Alfa Laval Brewery Systems, 218
Alfa Laval Brewery Systems/Separation, 218
Alfa Laval S. A. DE C. V., 218
APV Inc., 219
AZCO Inc., 219
Banner Equipment Company, 249
CDC Inc., 222
CM Supply and Consulting, 255
Dairy Engineering Company, 224
Drinktec U.S.A. Ltd., 225, 242, 250, 281
England Worthside Ltd., 225
Falco Stainless Steel Equipment Ltd., 226
Foxx Equipment Company, 227
G & H Products Corp., 227
Heavy Duty Products Inc., 228, 243
IDD Process & Packaging Inc., 228, 243, 256, 275, 283
J. V. Northwest Inc., 14, 20, 30, 229
Mangel, Scheuermann & Oeters Inc., 230
Micro Matic U.S.A. Inc., 244
Outterson Brewing Services Inc., 232, 258, 283
Sound Brewing Systems Inc., 237, 259
Team Industries Inc., 238
Terriss Consolidated Industries, 238
Tuchenhagen North America Inc., 238
Waukesha Fluid Handling, 239
Wilson Brewing Systems Ltd., 239

Finings

CM Supply and Consulting, 255
Dairy Engineering Company, 224
Gafco-Worldwide Inc., 227, 243
James Vickers & Company Ltd., 283
Mangel, Scheuermann & Oeters Inc., 230
Sea Moss Inc., 284

Flavorings and Colorings

California Brands Flavors Inc., 280
Hoptech, 275, 282
Mangel, Scheuermann & Oeters Inc., 230
Northwestern Extract Company, 283
Edgar A. Weber & Company, 281

Floor and Wall Coatings

Chemgrate Corp., 224
Dayton Superior Corp., 281
Guardian Labs, 228
Roller Coat Products, 284
Specialist Joinery Fittings, 253
Stonhard Inc., 237

Equipment Index

Flow Meters
Accurate Metering Systems Inc., 218
Alfa Laval Brewery Systems, 218
Alfa Laval Brewery Systems/Separation, 218
Alfa Laval S. A. DE C. V., 218
Beer-Guano, 249
Beman and Beverage Systems Inc., 338
Beverage Consult International Inc., 254, 274
Dairy Engineering Company, 224
Drinktec U.S.A. Ltd., 225, 242, 250, 281
Foxboro Company, 227, 263
G & H Products Corp., 227
Gafco-Worldwide Inc., 227, 243
Heavy Duty Products Inc., 228, 243
Hopfen und Malz GmbH, 228, 243, 256
IDD Process & Packaging Inc., 228, 243, 256, 275, 283
J. V. Northwest Inc., 14, 20, 30, 229
Mangel, Scheuermann & Oeters Inc., 230
Meyer Supply Inc., 230
Monitek Technologies Inc., 231
Outterson Brewing Services Inc., 232, 258, 283
Salvadore Machinery Corp., 234, 246, 258

Fruit
Oregon Fruit Products Company, 283

Gauges
Beeraphernalia Company, 262
CDC Inc., 222
CM Supply and Consulting, 255
Dairy Engineering Company, 224
Draft Service Inc., 250
Drinktec U.S.A. Ltd., 225, 242, 250, 281
Foxx Equipment Company, 227
G & H Products Corp., 227
Gafco-Worldwide Inc., 227, 243
L. C. Thomsen Inc., 230
Mangel, Scheuermann & Oeters Inc., 230
Rapids Wholesale Equipment Company, 234, 253
Sound Brewing Systems Inc., 237, 259
Strahman Valves Inc., 238
Tel-Tru Manufacturing Company, 238
Wilson Brewing Systems Ltd., 239

Glassware
A. Gusmer Inc., 217
Aidpac International Ltd., 240
Chrislan Ceramics Inc., 224, 249, 263
Drinktec U.S.A. Ltd., 225, 242, 250, 281
Glasses, Mugs & Steins, 263
Nightwing Enterprises Inc., 252
Pacific Coast Container, 245
R. M. Yates Company Inc., 265
Rapids Wholesale Equipment Company, 234, 253
Sun International Trading Ltd., 265

Grain Handling Equipment
A. Gusmer Inc., 217
Bavarian Brewery Technologies, 219
Bratney Equipment Company/Ken Bratney Company, 220
Buhler (Canada) Inc., 220
CDC Inc., 222
CM Supply and Consulting, 255
Enerfab Inc., 225
Grain Millers Inc., 270, 282
Grain Systems Inc., 228
Heavy Duty Products Inc., 228, 243
J. V. Northwest Inc., 14, 20, 30, 229
Newlands Services Inc., 47, 232
Outterson Brewing Services Inc., 232, 258, 283
Read Systems Inc., 234
Sound Brewing Systems Inc., 237, 259
VAFAC Inc. (Virginia Food and Craft), 238, 259, 273

Grain Mills
A. Gusmer Inc., 217
A. O. Wilson Process Equipment Ltd., 217
Advanced Bottling U.K. Ltd., 218, 240
Automatic Equipment Mfg., 219
Bavarian Brewery Technologies, 219
Beraplan Härter GmbH, 219
Bratney Equipment Company/Ken Bratney Company, 220
Brewers & Bottlers Equipment Corp., 220, 241
Buhler (Canada) Inc., 220
CDC Inc., 222
CM Supply and Consulting, 255
Cross Distributing Company Inc., 224
Falco Stainless Steel Equipment Ltd., 226
Grain Millers Inc., 270, 282
Heavy Duty Products Inc., 228, 243
IDD Process & Packaging Inc., 228, 243, 256, 275, 283
J. V. Northwest Inc., 14, 20, 30, 229
Krones Inc., 32, 34, 230
Maas Brewing Systems, 230
Mangel, Scheuermann & Oeters Inc., 230
Newlands Services Inc., 47, 232
Outterson Brewing Services Inc., 232, 258, 283
Pugsleys Brewing Projects International/Shipyard Brewing, 33, 233, 258
Read Systems Inc., 234
Roskamp Champion
Schlueter MFG, 236
Sound Brewing Systems Inc., 237, 259
Steinecker Brewhouse, 22
VAFAC Inc. (Virginia Food and Craft), 238, 259, 273
W. W. Reichert, Bavarian Brewhouse Inc., 239, 253

Equipment Index

Heat Exchangers
A. O. Wilson Process Equipment Ltd., 217
Alfa Laval Brewery Systems, 218
Alfa Laval Brewery Systems/Separation, 218
Alfa Laval S. A. DE C. V., 218
APV Inc., 219
AZCO Inc., 219
Bavarian Brewery Technologies, 219
Brew Store, 220
Brewers & Bottlers Equipment Corp., 220, 241
Bruce Brewing System—Brewery Builders, 220
CDC Inc., 222
Century Mfg. Inc., 34, 222
Chester-Jensen Company Inc., 224
CM Supply and Consulting, 255
Cross Distributing Company Inc., 224
Custom Brew Beer Systems, 224
Dairy Engineering Company, 224
Drinktec U.S.A. Ltd., 225, 242, 250, 281
Electro-Steam Generator Corp., 225, 250
Frick/Reco Division, York International Corp., 227
Gafco-Worldwide Inc., 227, 243
Heavy Duty Products Inc., 228, 243
Hopfen und Malz GmbH, 228, 243, 256
IDD Process & Packaging Inc., 228, 243, 256, 275, 283
J. V. Northwest Inc., 14, 20, 30, 229
Maas Brewing Systems, 230
Mangel, Scheuermann & Oeters Inc., 230
Outterson Brewing Services Inc., 232, 258, 283
Paul Mueller Company, 232
Port Jackson Mfg., 233
Pugsleys Brewing Projects International/Shipyard Brewing, 33, 233, 258
RLS Equipment Company Inc., 234
Salvadore Machinery Corp., 234, 246, 258
Schlueter MFG, 236
Sound Brewing Systems Inc., 237, 259
Total Brewing International Ltd., 238
Tuchenhagen North America Inc., 238
VAFAC Inc. (Virginia Food and Craft), 238, 259, 273
Vendome Copper & Brass Works Inc., 238
W. M. Sprinkman Corp., 239
Wilson Brewing Systems Ltd., 239

Hop Extract
Beverage Consult International Inc., 254, 274
Hoptech, 275, 282
IDD Process & Packaging Inc., 228, 243, 256, 275, 283
Jaenicke Inc., 275
Lupofresh Inc., 276
Lupofresh Limited, 276
Morris Hanbury Jackson Le May Ltd.
S. S. Steiner Inc., 276

Hops
Aidpac International Ltd., 240
Beverage Consult International Inc., 254, 274
Hoptech, 275, 282
IDD Process & Packaging Inc., 228, 243, 256, 275, 283
Jaenicke Inc., 275
Lupofresh Inc., 276
Lupofresh Limited, 276
Morris Hanbury Jackson Le May Ltd., 276
New Zealand Hop Marketing Board, 276
S. S. Steiner Inc., 276
Wigan Richardson International Ltd., 277

Hoses
A. Gusmer Inc., 217
A. O. Wilson Process Equipment Ltd., 217
AJEX U.S.A. INC., 248, 343
CDC Inc., 222
CM Supply and Consulting, 255
Cross Distributing Company Inc., 224
Dairy Engineering Company, 224
Draft Service Inc., 250
Drinktec U.S.A. Ltd., 225, 242, 250, 281
Foxx Equipment Company, 227
Gafco-Worldwide Inc., 227, 243
Goodall Rubber Company, 227
Heavy Duty Products Inc., 228, 243
Hopfen und Malz GmbH, 228, 243, 256
IDD Process & Packaging Inc., 228, 243, 256, 275, 283
J. E. Siebel Sons' Company, 229
J. V. Northwest Inc., 14, 20, 30, 229
L. C. Thomsen Inc., 230
Maas Brewing Systems, 230
Mangel, Scheuermann & Oeters Inc., 230
Meyer Supply Inc., 230
Outterson Brewing Services Inc., 232, 258, 283
Paguag GmbH & Company, Hose Division, 232
RLS Equipment Company Inc., 234
Sound Brewing Systems Inc., 237, 259
Strahman Valves Inc., 238
Terriss Consolidated Industries, 238
Wilson Brewing Systems Ltd., 239

Indicators (Fluid Level)
BIXIE COASTERS, 262
Drinktec U.S.A. Ltd., 225, 242, 250, 281
Wilson Brewing Systems Ltd., 239

Insurance
CBS Insurance, 255
Insurance Associates of Northern California, 256
Noel/Greaves Inc., 257
Robert J. Ryan Inc., 258

Equipment Index

Jockey Boxes
Aidpac International Ltd., 240
Draft Service Inc., 250
Foxx Equipment Company, 227
Perlick Corp., 232, 252
Port Jackson Mfg., 233
Rapids Wholesale Equipment Company, 234, 253

Keg and Bulk Draft Packaging
A. O. Wilson Process Equipment Ltd., 217
Aidpac International Ltd., 240
Alumasc, 219, 249
AMBEC, 219
BCI Industries Inc., 338
Brewers & Bottlers Equipment Corp., 220, 241
CM Supply and Consulting, 255
D & F Engineering Inc., 241
DATOGRAF Apparatebau GmbH & Company, 241
DME Brewing Services, 225, 255
Drinktec U.S.A. Ltd., 225, 242, 250, 281
EUROSOURCE Inc., 242
G. W. Kent Inc., 227, 243, 270, 275, 278
Hedwin Corp., 243
Hoover Materials Handling Group Inc., 228
Hopfen und Malz GmbH, 228, 243, 256
Huber Verpackungen, 243
IDD Process & Packaging Inc., 228, 243, 256, 275, 283
Indcon Design Ltd., 228, 244
JACO Equipment Corp., 229
Keg Club, 229
Kenerik/Golden Gate, 229, 244
KHS Machines Inc., 229
Mangel, Scheuermann & Oeters Inc., 230
Micro Matic U.S.A. Inc., 244
Outterson Brewing Services Inc., 232, 258, 283
Party Pig/Quoin, 245
Prolong Systems Inc., 233, 253
SABCO Industries/Sav-A-Barrel Corp., 228, 234
Schafer Container Systems, 234
Scott Laboratories Inc., 236, 279
Sound Brewing Systems Inc., 237, 259
Spartanburg Steel Products Inc., 237, 246
Stabifix Brauerei-Technik GMBH & Company OHG, 237, 279
Stainless Steel Containment Systems Inc., 237, 246
Thielmann Container Systems, 246
Tosca Limited, 238
WAYMATIC, 284

Keg Handling, Storage, and Retrieving
AMBEC, 219
KHS Machines Inc., 229
Rapids Wholesale Equipment Company, 234, 253
Scott Laboratories Inc., 236, 279

Stabifix Brauerei-Technik GMBH & Company OHG, 237, 279
Stainless Steel Containment Systems Inc., 237, 246
W. W. Reichert, Bavarian Brewhouse Inc., 239, 253

Keg Repair
BCI Industries Inc., 338
Hoover Materials Handling Group Inc., 228
IDD Process & Packaging Inc., 228, 243, 256, 275, 283
SABCO Industries/Sav-A-Barrel Corp., 228, 234
W. W. Reichert, Bavarian Brewhouse Inc., 239, 253

Keg Washers
A. Gusmer Inc., 217
A. O. Wilson Process Equipment Ltd., 217
AAA Metal Fabrication Inc., 218
AMBEC, 219
APV Inc., 219
Bohemian Brewery Importers, 220, 249, 254, 344, 365
Brew Store, 220
Brewers & Bottlers Equipment Corp., 220, 241
Bruce Brewing System—Brewery Builders, 220
CDC Inc., 222
Chemdet Inc., 224
CM Supply and Consulting, 255
Criveller Company, 45, 224, 241, 250
Cross Distributing Company Inc., 224
DATOGRAF Apparatebau GmbH & Company, 241
DME Brewing Services, 225, 255
Drinktec U.S.A. Ltd., 225, 242, 250, 281
Elliott Bay Metal Fabricating Inc., 225, 250
EUROSOURCE Inc., 242
Falco Stainless Steel Equipment Ltd., 226
Gafco-Worldwide Inc., 227, 243
Heavy Duty Products Inc., 228, 243
IDD Process & Packaging Inc., 228, 243, 256, 275, 283
Indcon Design Ltd., 228, 244
J. V. Northwest Inc., 14, 20, 30, 229
Kenerik/Golden Gate, 229, 244
KHS Machines Inc., 229
MacLean Brewery Equipment Ltd., 230
Mangel, Scheuermann & Oeters Inc., 230
Outterson Brewing Services Inc., 232, 258, 283
Price-Schonstrom Inc., 233
Scott Laboratories Inc., 236, 279
Sound Brewing Systems Inc., 237, 259
Stabifix Brauerei-Technik GMBH & Company OHG, 237, 279
Sussman Electric Boilers, 238
Tuchenhagen North America Inc., 238
VAFAC Inc. (Virginia Food and Craft), 238, 259, 273
Wilson Brewing Systems Ltd., 239

Lab Equipment/Supplies
A. Gusmer Inc., 217

Equipment Index

Aidpac International Ltd., 240
Alan Courtenay Ltd., 248
Beverage Consult International Inc., 254, 274
Bloodhound Sensors Ltd., 220
CM Supply and Consulting, 255
Electro-Steam Generator Corp., 225, 250
ETS Laboratories, 278
Gafco-Worldwide Inc., 227, 243
Gilbert Insect Light Traps, 251
Mangel, Scheuermann & Oeters Inc., 230
Meyer Supply Inc., 230
Millipore Corp., 230
Monitek Technologies Inc., 231
Outterson Brewing Services Inc., 232, 258, 283
Paar Scientific (Export) Ltd., 232
Profamo Analytical Services Inc., 233
Rascher & Betzold Inc., 284
Sussman Electric Boilers, 238
Terriss Consolidated Industries, 238
Unipath Company, Oxiod Division, 238
Yeast Culture Kit Company, 279

Label Design
Action Graphics, 260
Alan Courtenay Ltd., 248
Anchor Glass Container, 219
Bolin Agency, 262
CZ Tech, 270
Epsen Hillmer Graphics Company, 242
Gafco-Worldwide Inc., 227, 243
Gamse Lithographing Company, 243
General Press Corp., 263
Graphic Nature, 263
High Range Graphics, 264
Kal Grafx, 244
Le Vintage Collection (Designer Labels), 283
Maas Brewing Systems, 230
Nuttings Lake Publishing, 245
Omniart, 265
Outterson Brewing Services Inc., 232, 258, 283
PepperWorks, 284
Rixie Paper Products, 265
Spear Inc., 246
Swancock Designworks, 265
Vitro Packaging Inc., 247
Walker & Lee Advertising/Design, 265

Label Machinery
A. O. Wilson Process Equipment Ltd., 217
Advanced Bottling U.K. Ltd., 218, 240
B & J Machinery Inc., 219, 241
Brewers & Bottlers Equipment Corp., 220, 241
Criveller Company, 45, 224, 241, 250
Custom Deco Inc., 250
Figgie, 226

Gafco-Worldwide Inc., 227, 243
Heavy Duty Products Inc., 228, 243
IDD Process & Packaging Inc., 228, 243, 256, 275, 283
JACO Equipment Corp., 229
Kal Grafx, 244
Kenerik/Golden Gate, 229, 244
KHS Machines Inc., 229
Krones Inc., 32, 34, 230
Meheen Manufacturing, 244
Outterson Brewing Services Inc., 232, 258, 283
Rixie Paper Products, 265
Sasib Beverage & Food North America Inc., 234
Sonoco Engraph Label Group, 237, 246, 253, 259, 265, 272, 277, 279, 284, 339, 34
Sound Brewing Systems Inc., 237, 259
Spear Inc., 246

Labels
CZ Tech, 270
Epsen Hillmer Graphics Company, 242
Gamse Lithographing Company, 243
General Press Corp., 263
Inland Printing Company/Inland Label, 244, 264
Kal Grafx, 244
Nuttings Lake Publishing, 245
PepperWorks, 284
Sonoco Engraph Label Group, 237, 246, 253, 259, 265, 272, 277, 279, 284, 339, 34
Spear Inc., 246
Vitro Packaging Inc., 247

Lubricants
DuBois, 225
Loeffler Chemical Corp., 283

Malt and Specialty Malts
Alexander's Sun Country Malt Products, 267
Bioriginal Food and Science Corp., 268, 280
Brew Store, 220
Briess Malting Company, 268
Consolidated Beverages America Ltd., 269, 278
Edme Ltd., 270
G. W. Kent Inc., 227, 243, 270, 275, 278
Gambrinus Malting Corp., 270
Grain Millers Inc., 270, 282
Great Western Malting Company, 271
Malteries Franco-Belges, 272
Munton and Fison PLC, 272
Northwestern Extract Company, 283
Outterson Brewing Services Inc., 232, 258, 283
United Canadian Malt Ltd., 272
VAFAC Inc. (Virginia Food and Craft), 238, 259, 273
WEYERMANN, Heinz GmbH, 273, 284

Malt (Extract)
A. Gusmer Inc., 217
Alexander's Sun Country Malt Products, 267
Aspera/Jaenicke & Company L.L.C., 267, 280
Bioriginal Food and Science Corp., 268, 280
Brew Store, 220
Briess Malting Company, 268
Cask Brewing Systems, 43, 222, 269
Consolidated Beverages America Ltd., 269, 278
CZ Tech, 270
Edme Ltd., 270
G. W. Kent Inc., 227, 243, 270, 275, 278
Grain Millers Inc., 270, 282
Munton and Fison PLC, 272
Northwestern Extract Company, 283
Specialty Products International Ltd., 272
United Canadian Malt Ltd., 272
WEYERMANN, Heinz GmbH, 273, 284

Malt (Specialty Malt)
Alexander's Sun Country Malt Products, 267
Bioriginal Food and Science Corp., 268, 280
Brew Store, 220
Briess Malting Company, 268
Edme Ltd., 270
G. W. Kent Inc., 227, 243, 270, 275, 278
Grain Millers Inc., 270, 282
Great Western Malting Company, 271
Malteries Franco-Belges, 272
Munton and Fison PLC, 272
Northwestern Extract Company, 283
United Canadian Malt Ltd., 272
WEYERMANN, Heinz GmbH, 273, 284

Malt Mills
A. Gusmer Inc., 217
Bavarian Brewery Technologies, 219
Bratney Equipment Company/Ken Bratney Company, 220
Buhler (Canada) Inc., 220
CDC Inc., 222
Century Mfg. Inc., 34, 222
Consolidated Beverages America Ltd., 269, 278
Grain Millers Inc., 270, 282
Newlands Services Inc., 47, 232
VAFAC Inc. (Virginia Food and Craft), 238, 259, 273
Wilson Brewing Systems Ltd., 239

Malt Storage
Grain Systems Inc., 228
Read Systems Inc., 234

Malthouse Equipment/Malting Units
A. Gusmer Inc., 217
Beraplan Härter GmbH, 219

Buhler (Canada) Inc., 220
Heavy Duty Products Inc., 228, 243
IDD Process & Packaging Inc., 228, 243, 256, 275, 283
Total Brewing International Ltd., 238
Winter People, 266

Marketing Services
Aero Resources Inc., 254
Beer Gear, 262
Beeraphernalia Company, 262
Bolin Agency, 262
Ciao! Travel, 263
Dale W. Woys & Associates, 263
Kramer Stainless Systems, 230
Newlands Services Inc., 47, 232
Sound Brewing Systems Inc., 237, 259
Walker & Lee Advertising/Design, 265
Winstanley Associates, 266

Mashing/Lautering Equipment
A. Gusmer Inc., 217
A. O. Wilson Process Equipment Ltd., 217
AAA Metal Fabrication Inc., 218
Beraplan Härter GmbH, 219
Brauhaus Systems Caspary, 220
Brew Store, 220
Brewers & Bottlers Equipment Corp., 220, 241
Bruce Brewing System—Brewery Builders, 220
CDC Inc., 222
Century Mfg. Inc., 34, 222
CM Supply and Consulting, 255
Criveller Company, 45, 224, 241, 250
DME Brewing Services, 225, 255
Drinktec U.S.A. Ltd., 225, 242, 250, 281
Elliott Bay Metal Fabricating Inc., 225, 250
Enerfab Inc., 225
Falco Stainless Steel Equipment Ltd., 226
Heavy Duty Products Inc., 228, 243
IDD Process & Packaging Inc., 228, 243, 256, 275, 283
J. V. Northwest Inc., 14, 20, 30, 229
Liquid Assets Brewing Systems, 20, 251
Maas Brewing Systems, 230
MacLean Brewery Equipment Ltd., 230
Mangel, Scheuermann & Oeters Inc., 230
Outterson Brewing Services Inc., 232, 258, 283
Paul Mueller Company, 232
Pierre Rajotte, 233
Price-Schonstrom Inc., 233
PROGINOX Inc., 233, 258
Schlueter MFG, 236
Sound Brewing Systems Inc., 237, 259
Stainless Steel Specialist Inc., 237, 243
Team Industries Inc., 238
Total Brewing International Ltd., 238
VAFAC Inc. (Virginia Food and Craft), 238, 259, 273

Equipment Index

W. M. Sprinkman Corp., 239
Wilson Brewing Systems Ltd., 239

Meters (Flow)
Accurate Metering Systems Inc., 218
Beman and Beverage Systems Inc., 338
Beverage Consult International Inc., 254, 274
Dairy Engineering Company, 224
Drinktec U.S.A. Ltd., 225, 242, 250, 281
G & H Products Corp., 227
Gafco-Worldwide Inc., 227, 243
Loeffler Chemical Corp., 283
Mangel, Scheuermann & Oeters Inc., 230

Meters (pH)
Equipment Enterprises Inc., 281
Loeffler Chemical Corp., 283
Tuchenhagen North America Inc., 238

Neon Signs
Arrow Neon, 248, 261
AVVA Technologies, 261
Wordenglass & Electricity Inc., 266

Nitrogen
Prolong Systems Inc., 233, 253

Organic Products
Bioriginal Food and Science Corp., 268, 280

Packaging Equipment
A. O. Wilson Process Equipment Ltd., 217
Advanced Bottling U.K. Ltd., 218, 240
Aidpac International Ltd., 240
vAlvey Inc., 241
Brewers & Bottlers Equipment Corp., 220, 241
Busse Inc., 241
Criveller Company, 45, 224, 241, 250
DATOGRAF Apparatebau GmbH & Company, 241
Drinktec U.S.A. Ltd., 225, 242, 250, 281
Figgie, 226
First Fabrics Inc., 226
Gafco-Worldwide Inc., 227, 243
Heavy Duty Products Inc., 228, 243
Hedwin Corp., 243
Heuft U.S.A. Inc., 243
Huber Verpackungen, 243
IDD Process & Packaging Inc., 228, 243, 256, 275, 283
Industrial Dynamics Company Ltd.—Manufacturers of Filtec Inspection Systems, 244
JACO Equipment Corp., 229
JTECH Inc., 251
Kenerik/Golden Gate, 229, 244
KHS Machines Inc., 229
Krones Inc., 32, 34, 230

Malnove Corp., 244
Meyer Supply Inc., 230
MSK Covertech Inc., 245
Nigrelli Systems Inc., 232
Outterson Brewing Services Inc., 232, 258, 283
Pneumatic Scale, 245
R. A. Jones & Company Inc., 246
Rixie Paper Products, 265
Salvadore Machinery Corp., 234, 246, 258
Sonoco Engraph Label Group, 237, 246, 253, 259, 265, 272, 277, 279, 284, 339, 34
Sound Brewing Systems Inc., 237, 259
Stainless Steel Containment Systems Inc., 237, 246
Standard Box Corp., 246
Standard Paper Box Corp., 246
Thielmann Container Systems, 246
Union Camp Corp., 247
Volckening Inc., 247
Zumbiel Packaging, 247

Packaging Supplies
Acrylic Designs Inc., 260
Anchor Glass Container, 219
APM Inc., 241
Aquanautics Inc., 219
California Glass Company, 249
Diversified Packaging Products Inc., 241
First Fabrics Inc., 226
Hopfen und Malz GmbH, 228, 243, 256
Huber Verpackungen, 243
Lawson Mardon Packaging, 244
Malnove Corp., 244
Menasha Corp., 264
Meyer Supply Inc., 230
Outterson Brewing Services Inc., 232, 258, 283
Pacific Coast Container, 245
Rixie Paper Products, 265
Scott Laboratories Inc., 236, 279
Sonoco Engraph Label Group, 237, 246, 253, 259, 265, 272, 277, 279, 284, 339, 34
Stabifix Brauerei-Technik GMBH & Company OHG, 237, 279
Standard Box Corp., 246
Standard Paper Box Corp., 246
Union Camp Corp., 247
Walker & Lee Advertising/Design, 265
Wine Bottle & Packaging Inc., 247
Zumbiel Packaging, 247

Pallet Loaders and Unloaders
Gafco-Worldwide Inc., 227, 243
Indcon Design Ltd., 228, 244
Krones Inc., 32, 34, 230
Stainless Steel Containment Systems Inc., 237, 246
Union Camp Corp., 247

Pasteurizers
Advanced Bottling U.K. Ltd., 218, 240
Alfa Laval Brewery Systems/Separation, 218
AMBEC, 219
Chester-Jensen Company Inc., 224
Dairy Engineering Company, 224
Drinktec U.S.A. Ltd., 225, 242, 250, 281
Gafco-Worldwide Inc., 227, 243
IDD Process & Packaging Inc., 228, 243, 256, 275, 283
Krones Inc., 32, 34, 230
Pneumatic Scale, 245
Sasib Beverage & Food North America Inc., 234
Scott Laboratories Inc., 236, 279
Sound Brewing Systems Inc., 237, 259
Stabifix Brauerei-Technik GMBH & Company OHG, 237, 279
Tuchenhagen North America Inc., 238

Pest Control
Gilbert Insect Light Traps, 251
McCloud Pest Control, 251

Pilot Brewing Systems
Briess Malting Company, 268
Hoover Materials Handling Group, 228
SABCO Industries/Sav-A-Barrel Corp., 228, 234

Piping and Tubing
A. Gusmer Inc., 217
A. Handtmann Armaturenfabrik GmbH & Company KG, 217, 218
A. O. Wilson Process Equipment Ltd., 217
AJEX U.S.A. INC., 248, 343
Alfa Laval Brewery Systems, 218
Alfa Laval S. A. DE C. V., 218
AZCO Inc., 219
Bruce Brewing System—Brewery Builders, 220
CDC Inc., 222
Century Mfg. Inc., 34, 222
CM Supply and Consulting, 255
Criveller Company, 45, 224, 241, 250
Cross Distributing Company Inc., 224
Dairy Engineering Company, 224
Drinktec U.S.A. Ltd., 225, 242, 250, 281
Enerfab Inc., 225
England Worthside Ltd., 225
Falco Stainless Steel Equipment Ltd., 226
Foxx Equipment Company, 227
Heavy Duty Products Inc., 228, 243
Hopfen und Malz GmbH, 228, 243, 256
IDD Process & Packaging Inc., 228, 243, 256, 275, 283
J. V. Northwest Inc., 14, 20, 30, 229
L. C. Thomsen Inc., 230
Maas Brewing Systems, 230
Mangel, Scheuermann & Oeters Inc., 230

Mechanical Welding Service, 230
Meyer Supply Inc., 230
Outterson Brewing Services Inc., 232, 258, 283
RLS Equipment Company Inc., 234
Sound Brewing Systems Inc., 237, 259
Stainless Steel Specialist Inc., 237, 243
Team Industries Inc., 238
Terriss Consolidated Industries, 238
Total Brewing International Ltd., 238
W. M. Sprinkman Corp., 239
Wilson Brewing Systems Ltd., 239

Plastic Tanks
Advanced Bottling U.K. Ltd., 218, 240
Aidpac International Ltd., 240
Filter Equipment Company Inc., 226, 242, 338
Heavy Duty Products Inc., 228, 243
Meyer Supply Inc., 230
Salvadore Machinery Corp., 234, 246, 258

Print Services
Alan Courtenay Ltd., 248
American Coaster Company, 261
Bolin Agency, 262
California Glass Company, 249
Dale W. Woys & Associates, 263
Diversified Packaging Products Inc., 241
Dorette Company, 250
General Press Corp., 263
Grandstand Sportswear, 263
Heinrich Ceramic Decal Inc., 282
Maas Brewing Systems, 230
Omniart, 265
Outterson Brewing Services Inc., 232, 258, 283
PepperWorks, 284
Photo Marketing Products Company, 265
Rixie Paper Products, 265
Standard Box Corp., 246
Standard Paper Box Corp., 246
Walker & Lee Advertising/Design, 265

Propagation Tanks
Thielmann Container Systems, 246

Pumps
A. Gusmer Inc., 217
A. O. Wilson Process Equipment Ltd., 217
Advanced Bottling U.K. Ltd., 218, 240
AJEX U.S.A. INC., 248, 343
Alan Courtenay Ltd., 248
Alfa Laval Brewery Systems, 218
Alfa Laval Brewery Systems/Separation, 218
Alfa Laval S. A. DE C. V., 218
APV Inc., 219
CDC Inc., 222

Equipment Index

Century Mfg. Inc., 34, 222
CM Supply and Consulting, 255
Criveller Company, 45, 224, 241, 250
Cross Distributing Company Inc., 224
Dairy Engineering Company, 224
Drinktec U.S.A. Ltd., 225, 242, 250, 281
England Worthside Ltd., 225
Foxx Equipment Company, 227
G & H Products Corp., 227
G. W. Kent Inc., 227, 243, 270, 275, 278
Heavy Duty Products Inc., 228, 243
Hilge/Shanley Pump, 236, 228, 243
Homark Group Ltd., 251
Hopfen und Malz GmbH, 228, 243, 256
Huber Verpackungen, 243
IDD Process & Packaging Inc., 228, 243, 256, 275, 283
J. V. Northwest Inc., 14, 20, 30, 229
L. C. Thomsen Inc., 230
Mangel, Scheuermann & Oeters Inc., 230
Meyer Supply Inc., 230
Outterson Brewing Services Inc., 232, 258, 283
Rapids Wholesale Equipment Company, 234, 253
RLS Equipment Company Inc., 234
Salvadore Machinery Corp., 234, 246, 258
Schenk Filter Systems Inc., 236
Shanley Pump, 236
Sound Brewing Systems Inc., 237, 259
Terriss Consolidated Industries, 238
Total Brewing International Ltd., 238
Tuchenhagen North America Inc., 238
VAFAC Inc. (Virginia Food and Craft), 238, 259, 273
W. M. Sprinkman Corp., 239
Waukesha Fluid Handling, 239
Wilson Brewing Systems Ltd., 239
Yeast Culture Kit Company, 279

Refrigeration Equipment/Supplies
AJEX U.S.A. INC., 248, 343
Banner Equipment Company, 249
Bruce Brewing System—Brewery Builders, 220
Century Mfg. Inc., 34, 222
Cross Distributing Company Inc., 224
Draft Service Inc., 250
Drinktec U.S.A. Ltd., 225, 242, 250, 281
England Worthside Ltd., 225
Foxx Equipment Company, 227
Frick/Reco Division, York International Corp., 227
Heavy Duty Products Inc., 228, 243
IDD Process & Packaging Inc., 228, 243, 256, 275, 283
J. V. Northwest Inc., 14, 20, 30, 229
Keg Club, 229
Multiplex Company Inc., 251
Outterson Brewing Services Inc., 232, 258, 283
Perlick Corp., 232, 252
Port Jackson Mfg., 233

Rapids Wholesale Equipment Company, 234, 253
Refrigeration Service 6
Sound Brewing Systems Inc., 237, 259
Summit Commercial, 253
VAFAC Inc. (Virginia Food and Craft), 238, 259, 273

Restaurant Equipment/Supplies
American Coaster Company, 261
Banner Equipment Company, 249
Beer-Guano, 249
Chrislan Ceramics Inc., 224, 249, 263
Detroit Stool & Chair Mfg. Inc., 250
Dorette Company, 250
Draft Service Inc., 250
Drinktec U.S.A. Ltd., 225, 242, 250, 281
Electro-Steam Generator Corp., 225, 250
Gilbert Insect Light Traps, 251
Home on the Range PhotoTops, 251
JTECH Inc., 251
Liquid Assets Brewing Systems, 20, 251
Liquidtech Inc., 251
Multiplex Company Inc., 251
Outterson Brewing Services Inc., 232, 258, 283
PepperWorks, 284
Perlick Corp., 232, 252
Port Jackson Mfg., 233
Rapids Wholesale Equipment Company, 234, 253
Refrigeration Service 6
Specialist Joinery Fittings, 253
Steensen U.S.A. Inc., 237
Summit Commercial, 253

Regulators (Pressure)
AJEX U.S.A. INC., 248, 343
Draft Service Inc., 250
Gimson Engineering Limited, 227
L. C. Thomsen Inc., 230
Multiplex Company Inc., 251
Perlick Corp., 232, 252
Rapids Wholesale Equipment Company, 234, 253
Sound Brewing Systems Inc., 237, 259

Safety Equipment
A. Handtmann Armaturenfabrik GmbH & Company KG, 217, 218
Tuchenhagen North America Inc., 238

Sanitary Equipment/Supplies
A. O. Wilson Process Equipment Ltd., 217
Alfa Laval Brewery Systems, 218
Alfa Laval Brewery Systems/Separation, 218
Alfa Laval S. A. DE C. V., 218
Aquionics Inc., 219
Chemdet Inc., 224
Dairy Engineering Company, 224

Electro-Steam Generator Corp., 225, 250
Europe 1992 Connection, 250, 281
First Fabrics Inc., 226
Flo-Pac Corp., 226
Gilbert Insect Light Traps, 251
IDD Process & Packaging Inc., 228, 243, 256, 275, 283
L. C. Thomsen Inc., 230
Mangel, Scheuermann & Oeters Inc., 230
Meyer Supply Inc., 230
Millipore Corp., 230
National Chemicals Inc., 231, 252
Outterson Brewing Services Inc., 232, 258, 283
Pall Ultrafine Filtration Company, 232
Prosser/Enpo (Sellers), 233
Sound Brewing Systems Inc., 237, 259
Stainless Steel Specialist Inc., 237, 243
Steinecker Brewhouse, 22
Terriss Consolidated Industries, 238
Tuchenhagen North America Inc., 238

Six-pack Carriers
Bolin Agency, 262
Malnove Corp., 244
Standard Box Corp., 246
Union Camp Corp., 247
Walker & Lee Advertising/Design, 265
Zumbiel Packaging, 247

Specialty Glassware/Steins
Aidpac International Ltd., 240
Drinktec U.S.A. Ltd., 225, 242, 250, 281
Grandstand Sportswear, 263
R. M. Yates Company Inc., 265
Sun International Trading Ltd., 265

Spent Grains Handling Equipment
A. Gusmer Inc., 217
Bratney Equipment Company/Ken Bratney Company, 220
Grain Millers Inc., 270, 282
Grain Systems Inc., 228
Sound Brewing Systems Inc., 237, 259
Stord Inc., 237
VAFAC Inc. (Virginia Food and Craft), 238, 259, 273

Stainless Steel Fabricators
A. Gusmer Inc., 217
A. Handtmann Armaturenfabrik GmbH & Company KG, 217, 218
A. O. Wilson Process Equipment Ltd., 217
AAA Metal Fabrication Inc., 218
AMBEC, 219
APV Inc., 219
AZCO Inc., 219
Bavarian Brewery Technologies, 219

Beraplan Härter GmbH, 219
Bruce Brewing System—Brewery Builders, 220
CAE Screen Plates, 220
CDC Inc., 222
Century Mfg. Inc., 34, 222
Chester-Jensen Company Inc., 224
Criveller Company, 45, 224, 241, 250
Cross Distributing Company Inc., 224
Custom Brew Beer Systems, 224
Dairy Engineering Company, 224
DCI Inc., 224
DME Brewing Services, 225, 255
Elliott Bay Metal Fabricating Inc., 225, 250
Enerfab Inc., 225
Falco Stainless Steel Equipment Ltd., 226
Heavy Duty Products Inc., 228, 243
IDD Process & Packaging Inc., 228, 243, 256, 275, 283
International Brewing & Manufacturing Inc., 229
J. V. Northwest Inc., 14, 20, 30, 229
JACO Equipment Corp., 229
Kramer Stainless Systems, 230
L. C. Thomsen Inc., 230
Liquid Assets Brewing Systems, 20, 251
Maas Brewing Systems, 230
Mangel, Scheuermann & Oeters Inc., 230
Mechanical Welding Service, 230
Meheen Manufacturing, 244
Meyer Supply Inc., 230
Newlands Services Inc., 47, 232
Outterson Brewing Services Inc., 232, 258, 283
Paul Mueller Company, 232
Perlick Corp., 232, 252
Pierre Rajotte, 233
Price-Schonstrom Inc., 233
PROGINOX Inc., 233, 258
Rapids Wholesale Equipment Company, 234, 253
Salvadore Machinery Corp., 234, 246, 258
Santa Rosa Stainless Steel, 234
Schlueter MFG, 236
Sound Brewing Systems Inc., 237, 259
Specific Mechanical Systems Ltd., 24, 47, 237
Stainless Steel Containment Systems Inc., 237, 246
Stainless Steel Specialist Inc., 237, 243
Steinecker Brewhouse, 22
Team Industries Inc., 238
Terriss Consolidated Industries, 238
Total Brewing International Ltd., 238
Tuchenhagen North America Inc., 238
VAFAC Inc. (Virginia Food and Craft), 238, 259, 273
Vendome Copper & Brass Works Inc., 238
W. M. Sprinkman Corp., 239
Wilson Brewing Systems Ltd., 239

Equipment Index

Standard/Custom Design Equipment
A. O. Wilson Process Equipment Ltd., 217
Alvey Inc., 241
Bavarian Brewery Technologies, 219
Beraplan Härter GmbH, 219
Brauhaus Systems Caspary, 220
Bruce Brewing System—Brewery Builders, 220
Busse Inc., 241
Century Mfg. Inc., 34, 222
CM Supply and Consulting, 255
Cross Distributing Company Inc., 224
Custom Brew Beer Systems, 224
Dairy Engineering Company, 224
Drinktec U.S.A. Ltd., 225, 242, 250, 281
Elliott Bay Metal Fabricating Inc., 225, 250
Grain Systems Inc., 228
Heavy Duty Products Inc., 228, 243
Heinrich Ceramic Decal Inc., 282
Heuft U.S.A. Inc., 243
Hopfen und Malz GmbH, 228, 243, 256
IDD Process & Packaging Inc., 228, 243, 256, 275, 283
International Brewing & Manufacturing Inc., 229
J. V. Northwest Inc., 14, 20, 30, 229
Lewis Twice Consultancy, 257
Liquid Assets Brewing Systems, 20, 251
Maas Brewing Systems, 230
MacLean Brewery Equipment Ltd., 230
Meyer Supply Inc., 230
Newlands Services Inc., 47, 232
Nigrelli Systems Inc., 232
Outterson Brewing Services Inc., 232, 258, 283
PepperWorks, 284
Port Jackson Mfg., 233
Price-Schonstrom Inc., 233
PROGINOX Inc., 233, 258
Prolong Systems Inc., 233, 253
Sound Brewing Systems Inc., 237, 259
Specific Mechanical Systems Ltd., 24, 47, 237
Stainless Steel Specialist Inc., 237, 243
Standard Box Corp., 246
Standard Paper Box Corp., 246
Steensen U.S.A. Inc., 237
Steinecker Brewhouse, 22
Terriss Consolidated Industries, 238
Total Brewing International Ltd., 238
Tuchenhagen North America Inc., 238
VAFAC Inc. (Virginia Food and Craft), 238, 259, 273
W. W. Reichert, Bavarian Brewhouse Inc., 239, 253

T-shirts/Hats, Etc.
Beer Gear, 262
Beeraphernalia Company, 262
Brew Tee's, 262
Consolidated Beverages America Ltd., 269, 278
First Fabrics Inc., 226
Grandstand Sportswear, 263
Graphic Nature, 263
High Range Graphics, 264
PepperWorks, 284
Walker & Lee Advertising/Design, 265
Winter People, 266

Table Tents/Posters/Point-of-Sale
Acrylic Designs Inc., 260
Ad-Mat Coasters U.S.A. Inc., 260
Atelier Zillich, 219, 261
AVVA Technologies, 261
Beer Gear, 262
Beeraphernalia Company, 262
Davis and Small Oldtime Sign & Photo Company, 263
First Fabrics Inc., 226
General Press Corp., 263
Grandstand Sportswear, 263
Heinrich Ceramic Decal Inc., 282
High Range Graphics, 264
Inland Printing Company/Inland Label, 244, 264
O'Herin Enterprises, 264
Stout Marketing, 265
Union Camp Corp., 247
Walker & Lee Advertising/Design, 265
World Division U.S.A., 266
Wright Metal Signs Ltd., 266

Tank and Valve Fittings
A. Handtmann Armaturenfabrik GmbH & Company KG, 217, 218
A. O. Wilson Process Equipment Ltd., 217
Advanced Bottling U.K. Ltd., 218, 240
Bavarian Brewery Technologies, 219
CDC Inc., 222
Century Mfg. Inc., 34, 222
CM Supply and Consulting, 255
Dairy Engineering Company, 224
Drinktec U.S.A. Ltd., 225, 242, 250, 281
Falco Stainless Steel Equipment Ltd., 226
G & H Products Corp., 227
Gafco-Worldwide Inc., 227, 243
IDD Process & Packaging Inc., 228, 243, 256, 275, 283
L. C. Thomsen Inc., 230
Mangel, Scheuermann & Oeters Inc., 230
Newlands Services Inc., 47, 232
Pugsleys Brewing Projects International, 33, 233, 258
RLS Equipment Company Inc., 234
Sound Brewing Systems Inc., 237, 259
Strahman Valves Inc., 238
Tuchenhagen North America Inc., 238
VAFAC Inc. (Virginia Food and Craft), 238, 259, 273
W. M. Sprinkman Corp., 239
W. W. Reichert, Bavarian Brewhouse Inc., 239, 253
Wilson Brewing Systems Ltd., 239

Equipment Index

Tanks
A. O. Wilson Process Equipment Ltd., 217
AAA Metal Fabrication Inc., 218
Advanced Bottling U.K. Ltd., 218, 240
Bavarian Brewery Technologies, 219
CDC Inc., 222
Century Mfg. Inc., 34, 222
CM Supply and Consulting, 255
Dairy Engineering Company, 224
Drinktec U.S.A. Ltd., 225, 242, 250, 281
Elliott Bay Metal Fabricating Inc., 225, 250
Enerfab Inc., 225
Falco Stainless Steel Equipment Ltd., 226
Friesen of Iowa Inc., 227, 250
G. W. Kent Inc., 227, 243, 270, 275, 278
Gafco-Worldwide Inc., 227, 243
IDD Process & Packaging Inc., 228, 243, 256, 275, 283
Kramer Stainless Systems, 230
L. C. Thomsen Inc., 230
Liquid Assets Brewing Systems, 20, 251
Mangel, Scheuermann & Oeters Inc., 230
Newlands Services Inc., 47, 232
Paul Mueller Company, 232
Pierre Rajotte, 233
RLS Equipment Company Inc., 234
Santa Rosa Stainless Steel, 234
Sound Brewing Systems Inc., 237, 259
VAFAC Inc. (Virginia Food and Craft), 238, 259, 273
W. M. Sprinkman Corp., 239
W. W. Reichert, Bavarian Brewhouse Inc., 239, 253
Wilson Brewing Systems Ltd., 239

Tap Handles
CDC Inc., 222
Crystalite Corp., 262, 281
Louie's Custom Tap Handles, 251
Walker & Lee Advertising/Design, 265

Turnkey Brewing Systems
A. O. Wilson Process Equipment Ltd., 217
Alvey Inc., 241
APV Inc., 219
Bavarian Brewery Technologies, 219
Beraplan Härter GmbH, 219
Bohemian Breweries Inc., 220
Bohemian Brewery Importers, 220, 249, 254, 344, 365
Brauhaus Systems Caspary, 220
Brew Store, 220
Brewers & Bottlers Equipment Corp., 220, 241
Bruce Brewing System—Brewery Builders, 220
Busse Inc., 241
Cask Brewing Systems, 43, 222, 269
CDC Inc., 222
Century Mfg. Inc., 34, 222
CM Supply and Consulting, 255
Criveller Company, 45, 224, 241, 250
Cross Distributing Company Inc., 224
Custom Brew Beer Systems, 224
DME Brewing Services, 225, 255
Drinktec U.S.A. Ltd., 225, 242, 250, 281
Elliott Bay Metal Fabricating Inc., 225, 250
Enerfab Inc., 225
Falco Stainless Steel Equipment Ltd., 226
Gafco-Worldwide Inc., 227, 243
Global Brewing Services Inc., 256
Heavy Duty Products Inc., 228, 243
Hopfen und Malz GmbH, 228, 243, 256
IDD Process & Packaging Inc., 228, 243, 256, 275, 283
International Brewing & Manufacturing Inc., 229
J. V. Northwest Inc., 14, 20, 30, 229
Kramer Stainless Systems, 230
Liquid Assets Brewing Systems, 20, 251
Maas Brewing Systems, 230
MacLean Brewery Equipment Ltd., 230
Mangel, Scheuermann & Oeters Inc., 230
Newlands Services Inc., 47, 232
Nigrelli Systems Inc., 232
Outterson Brewing Services Inc., 232, 258, 283
Pico-Brewing Systems Inc., 233
Pierre Rajotte, 233
Price-Schonstrom Inc., 233
PROGINOX Inc., 233, 258
Pugsleys Brewing Projects International/Shipyard Brewing, 33, 233, 258
Schlueter MFG, 236
Sound Brewing Systems Inc., 237, 259
Specific Mechanical Systems Ltd., 24, 47, 237
Stainless Steel Specialist Inc., 237, 243
Steinecker Brewhouse, 22
Sussman Electric Boilers, 238
Team Industries Inc., 238
Thunder Bay Brewing Company Inc., 161, 253
Total Brewing International Ltd., 238
Tuchenhagen North America Inc., 238
VAFAC Inc. (Virginia Food and Craft), 238, 259, 273
Vendome Copper & Brass Works Inc., 238
W. M. Sprinkman Corp., 239
W. W. Reichert, Bavarian Brewhouse Inc., 239, 253

Used Equipment
Advanced Bottling U.K. Ltd., 218, 240
Beer Business Services, 262
CDC Inc., 222
Centrico Inc., 222
CM Supply and Consulting, 255
Cross Distributing Company Inc., 224
Falco Stainless Steel Equipment Ltd., 226
Gafco-Worldwide Inc., 227, 243
Heavy Duty Products Inc., 228, 243
JACO Equipment Corp., 229

Equipment Index

KHS Machines Inc., 229
Mangel, Scheuermann & Oeters Inc., 230
Outterson Brewing Services Inc., 232, 258, 283
RLS Equipment Company Inc., 234
Salvadore Machinery Corp., 234, 246, 258
Schumacher & Associates, 258
Sound Brewing Systems Inc., 237, 259
Total Brewing International Ltd., 238
VAFAC Inc. (Virginia Food and Craft), 238, 259, 273
W. M. Sprinkman Corp., 239
W. W. Reichert, Bavarian Brewhouse Inc., 239, 253

Valves
A. Gusmer Inc., 217
A. Handtmann Armaturenfabrik GmbH & Company KG, 217, 218
A. O. Wilson Process Equipment Ltd., 217
Advanced Bottling U.K. Ltd., 218, 240
Alfa Laval Brewery Systems/Separation, 218
APV Inc., 219
CDC Inc., 222
Century Mfg. Inc., 34, 222
CM Supply and Consulting, 255
Criveller Company, 45, 224, 241, 250
Cross Distributing Company Inc., 224
Drinktec U.S.A. Ltd., 225, 242, 250, 281
Falco Stainless Steel Equipment Ltd., 226
Foxboro Company, 227, 263
G & H Products Corp., 227
Gafco-Worldwide Inc., 227, 243
Heavy Duty Products Inc., 228, 243
Homark Group Ltd., 251
IDD Process & Packaging Inc., 228, 243, 256, 275, 283
J. V. Northwest Inc., 14, 20, 30, 229
L. C. Thomsen Inc., 230
Mangel, Scheuermann & Oeters Inc., 230
Meyer Supply Inc., 230
Micro Matic U.S.A. Inc., 244
Outterson Brewing Services Inc., 232, 258, 283
Perlick Corp., 232, 252
Rapids Wholesale Equipment Company, 234, 253
RLS Equipment Company Inc., 234
Sound Brewing Systems Inc., 237, 259
Strahman Valves Inc., 238
Terriss Consolidated Industries, 238
Tuchenhagen North America Inc., 238
VAFAC Inc. (Virginia Food and Craft), 238, 259, 273
W. M. Sprinkman Corp., 239
Waukesha Fluid Handling, 239
Wilson Brewing Systems Ltd., 239
Zahm and Nagel Company Inc., 239

Waste Treatment/Disposal Systems
AFTEK Inc., 218
Centrico Inc., 222
DuBois, 225
Grain Systems Inc., 228
Schenk Filter Systems Inc., 236
Stainless Steel Containment Systems Inc., 237, 246
Stord Inc., 237
Waukesha Fluid Handling, 239
YSI Inc., 239

Water Analysis Equipment
Millipore Corp., 230
YSI Inc., 239

Water Treating Equipment/Materials
AFTEK Inc., 218
Aquionics Inc., 219
DuBois, 225
England Worthside Ltd., 225
Equipment Enterprises Inc., 281
Industrial Filter & Pump Mfg. Company, 229
Ion Exchange Prod. Inc., 229, 283
Loeffler Chemical Corp., 283
Monitek Technologies Inc., 231
Multiplex Company Inc., 251
Schenk Filter Systems Inc., 236
Team Industries Inc., 238

Welding
Arc Machines Inc., 219

Wort Chillers
A. O. Wilson Process Equipment Ltd., 217
Advanced Bottling U.K. Ltd., 218, 240
Aidpac International Ltd., 240
Alfa Laval Brewery Systems, 218
Alfa Laval Brewery Systems/Separation, 218
Alfa Laval S. A. DE C. V., 218
APV Inc., 219
Bavarian Brewery Technologies, 219
Brew Store, 220
CDC Inc., 222
Chester-Jensen Company Inc., 224
CM Supply and Consulting, 255
Cross Distributing Company Inc., 224
Custom Brew Beer Systems, 224
Dairy Engineering Company, 224
Drinktec U.S.A. Ltd., 225, 242, 250, 281
Heavy Duty Products Inc., 228, 243
IDD Process & Packaging Inc., 228, 243, 256, 275, 283
J. V. Northwest Inc., 14, 20, 30, 229
Mangel, Scheuermann & Oeters Inc., 230
Newlands Services Inc., 47, 232
Outterson Brewing Services Inc., 232, 258, 283
Paul Mueller Company, 232
Pugsleys Brewing Projects International/Shipyard Brewing, 33, 233, 258

Schlueter MFG, 236
Sound Brewing Systems Inc., 237, 259
Total Brewing International Ltd., 238
Tuchenhagen North America Inc., 238
VAFAC Inc. (Virginia Food and Craft), 238, 259, 273
Wilson Brewing Systems Ltd., 239
Wittemann Company Inc., 239

Yeast
Aidpac International Ltd., 240
Consolidated Beverages America Ltd., 269, 278
Edme Ltd., 270
G. W. Kent Inc., 227, 243, 270, 275, 278
Lallemand Inc., 279
Scott Laboratories Inc., 236, 279
Specialty Products International Ltd., 272
Stabifix Brauerei-Technik GMBH & Company OHG, 237, 279
Yeast Culture Kit Company, 279

Index

A

AAA Metal Fabrication Inc., 218
A-B. *See* Anheuser-Busch
Abbey Brewing Company, 204
Abec Filtration Systems Inc., 218
Abita Brewing Company, 11, 36, 152, 205
Abita Brewpub, 152
Academy of Sciences USSR, 344
Acadian Brewing Company LLC, 152
Accurate Metering Systems Inc., 218
Acrylic Designs Inc., 260
Action Graphics, 260
Addingtons, 45, 193
Ad-Mat Coasters U.S.A. Inc., 260
ADM Malting, 267
Advanced Bottling U.K. Ltd., 218, 240
Aero Resources Inc., 254
AFTEK Inc., 218
A. Gusmer Inc., 217
Aidpac International Ltd., 240
AJEX U.S.A. INC., 248, 343
Alabama Alcoholic Beverage Control Board, 289
Alan Courtenay Ltd., 248
Alaskan Brewing and Bottling Company, 13-14, 129
Alberta Gaming and Liquor Commission, 315
Albert Handtmann Armaturenfabrik GmbH & Company KG, 217, 218
Alcatraz Brewing Company, 10, 150
Alcohol and Gaming Division (New Mexico), 304
Alcohol and Tobacco Tax Unit (Georgia), 294
Alcohol and Tobacco Tax Unit (Maryland), 298
Alcohol Beverage Control Division (Arkansas), 290
Alcohol Beverage Control Division (Idaho), 294
Alcohol content, maximum/minimum (by state), 321 (table)
Alcohol Control Board (Virgin Islands), 315
Alcoholic Beverage Commission (North Carolina), 305
Alcoholic Beverage Control Board (Alaska), 289
Alcoholic Beverage Control Board (District of Columbia), 293
Alcoholic Beverage Control Commission (Massachusetts), 299
Alcoholic Beverage Control Commission, Enforcement Division (West Virginia), 313
Alcoholic Beverage Control Division (Kansas), 297
Alcoholic Beverage Division (Iowa), 296
Alcohol Issues INSIGHTS (video), 362
Ale House Rock Brewery and Broiler, 131
Alephenalia Beer News, 363
Ales, guidelines for, 370-377
AleSmith Brewing Company, 131
Alessis Ristorante/Garretts Mill Brewing Company, 166
Ale Street News, 363
Alewife Restaurant and Brewery, 33
Alexander's Sun Country Malt Products, 267
Alfa Laval Brewery Systems, 218
Alfa Laval Brewery Systems/Separation, 218
Alfa Laval S. A. DE C. V., 218
Al Frisco's, 193
Algonquin Brewery, 193
Ali'i Brewing Company, 147
All About Beer Magazine, 357
Allagash Brewing Company Inc., 36, 152
All American Brewing Company, 166
Allen-Morrison Sales Company, 261
Alley Kat Brewing Company, 47, 190
Allied Brewery Traders' Association, 340
Allied Strategies, 44
Alpine Brewing Company/Naked Aspen Brewing Company, 23, 203
Alumasc, 219, 248
Alvey Inc., 241
Alyn D. Snedigar, 241
Amazon Filters Ltd., 219
AMBEC, 219
Amber Waves Brewery and Pub, 131
American Beerguy Inc., 202
American Brewer, 357
American Breweriana Association Inc., 337

American Breweriana Journal, 357
American Brewers Guild, 343
American Coaster Company, 261
American Dark Lager, guidelines for, 381
American Homebrewers Association Inc., 13, 337
American Ice Lager, guidelines for, 380
American Lager, guidelines for, 380
American Lager/Ale, guidelines for, 381
American Malting Barley Association Inc., 337
American Malt Liquor, guidelines for, 381
American Originals, 10
American River Brewing Company, 131
American School for Malting & Brewing Science & Technology, 344
American Society of Brewing Chemists, 337
American Specialty & Craft Beer Group, 10, 32-33
American-Style Amber Ale, guidelines for, 374
American-Style Amber Lager, guidelines for, 381
American-Style Brown Ale, guidelines for, 374
American-Style Light Lager, guidelines for, 380
American-Style Pale Ale, guidelines for, 374
American-Style Premium Lager, guidelines for, 380
American Wheat Ale/Lager, guidelines for, 381
Americas Brewpub at Walter Payton's Roadhouse, 149
Amsterdam Brewing Company, 193
Anacortes Brewhouse, 180
Anchor Brewing Company, 12, 18-19, 131
Anchor Glass Container, 219
Anderson Valley Brewing Company, 21, 131
Andrew's Brewing Company, 152
Angelic Brewing Company, 183
Anheuser-Busch (A-B), 10, 13, 14, 18, 19, 40; California, 131; Colorado, 139; Florida, 144; Georgia, 147; Missouri, 158; New Hampshire, 160; New Jersey, 161; New York, 162; Ohio, 166; Texas, 175; Virginia, 179
Anheuser-Busch Corporate Library, 365
Antilliaanse Brouwerij, 215
A1A Aleworks, 144
A. O. Wilson Process Equipment Ltd., 217
APM Inc., 241
Appalachian Ale Works, 173
Appleton Brewing Company/Adler Brau, 183
APV Inc., 219
Aquionics Inc., 219
Arbor Brewing Company, 156
Arc Machines Inc., 219
Arctic Brewing Company, 192
Armadillo Brewing Company, 39
Arrowhead Brewing Company, 34, 172
Arrow Neon, 248, 261
Art of Cidermaking, The (Correnty), 346
ASA Beverage Brokers Inc., 261
Asociacion Latinosmericana, 342
Aspera/Jaenicke & Company LLC, 267, 280
Assets Grille/Southwest Brewing Company, 162
Assoc. dos Technicos de Cerveja, 340
Association des Brasseurs de France (ABF), 340
Association of Belgium Brewers, 340
Association of Brewers, 337
Atelier Zillich, 219, 261
Athens Brewing Company, 147
Atlanta Beer Garden, 147
Atlanta Brewing Company, 36, 147
Atlantic Brewing Company, 162
Atlantic Brewing Company/Lompoc Cafe Brewpub, 152
Atlantic City Brewing Company, 206
Atlantic Coast Brewing Company, 11, 34, 154
Atlantis Brewing Company, 203
Augsburger, 10
August Brewing Company, 29, 206
August Schell Brewing Company, 157
Australian Associated Brewers, 340
Automatic Equipment Mfg., 219
Avery Brewing Company, 23, 139
Aviator Ales Brewery/Seattle Brewing Company, 12, 180
AVVA Technologies, 261
AZCO Inc., 219
A. Ziemann GmbH, 218

B

Back Alley Brewing Company, 139
Back Bay Brewing Company, 11, 36, 154
Backwater Brewing Company, 157
Bad Frog Brewery/Wauldron Corp., 30, 206
Baja Brewing Company, 131
Baked and Brewed in Telluride, 139
Baltimore Brewing Company, 34, 153
Bamberg-Style Rauchbier Lager, guidelines for, 382
Bandersnatch Brewpub, 129
B. & J. Machinery Inc., 219, 241
Bandon Brewing Company/Bandon-by-the-Sea, 168
Banff Brewery Corp., 47, 209
Bank Brewing Company, 168
Bank Draft Brewing Company/Vaulted Ales Inc., 175
Banks Barbados Breweries Ltd., 215
Banks Brewing Company Ltd., 215
Banks DIH Ltd., 215
Bank Street Brewing Company, 33
Banner Equipment Company, 249
Bardo Rodeo, 179
Bare Bones Grill and Brewery, 153
Bar Harbor Brewing, 152
Barley & Hopps, 131
Barley Boys Brewery Inc., 206
BarleyCorn, 363
Barley Creek Brewing Company Inc. 172
Barley Field Brewing Company, 207

Index

Barley Mill Brewing Company, 197
Barley's Brewing Company, 20, 151, 166
Barley's Casino and Brewing Company, 20, 160
Barley Wine-Style Ale, guidelines for, 372
Barnum, Scott, 10; on Leinenkugel, 29
Barrel House Brewing Company, 166
Barrington Brewery and Restaurant, 154
Barton Beers, 29
Basin Brewing Ltd., 175
Basin Ve Halkele Iliskiler, 340
BATF. *See* Bureau of Alcohol, Tobacco, and Firearms
Bavarian Brewery Technologies, 219
Bayern Brewing Inc./Iron Horse Brewpub, 23, 159
Bayhawk Ales, 12, 131
Bayou Brewing Company Ltd., 190
BCI Industries Inc., 338
Beach Brewing Company, 36, 144
Bear Brewing Company, 152, 190
Bear Republic Brewing Company, 131
Beartooth Brewing Company, 203
Beaton, Paul: on Shaftebury Brewing, 46
Beaver Street Brewery and Whistlestop Cafe, 26, 129
Beer Across America, 30
Beer Across America (Nachel), 346
Beer and Ale (video), 362
Beer and Beer Brewing, Volume 8 (Thomas), 347
Beer and Beer Brewing, Volume 10 (Loysen), 346
Beeraphernalia Company, 262
Beer Business Services, 262
Beer Directory (Wood), 347
Beer Drinker's Guide to Australia and New Zealand (Robertson), 347
Beer Drinker's Guide to Munich, The (Hawthorne), 348
Beer Drinker's Guide to Southern Germany (Robertson), 347
Beer Enthusiasts' Guide (Smith), 347
Beer Gear, 262
Beer-Guano, 249
Beer Industry Update (Steinman), 347
Beer Institute, 338, 365
Beer Log, The (Robertson), 347
Beer Lover's Rating Guide, The (Klien), 348
Beer Magazine, 357
Beer Manufacturers Association, 342
Beer Marketer's Insights, 9, 31
Beer Marketer's Insights (video), 362
Beer Packaging (Broderick), 348
Beers of the World Packaging Company, 241, 262
Beer Statistics News, 357
Beer: The Magazine, 357
Beer Travelers, 357
Beeston Malt Company, 267
Beier Brewing Company, 148
Belgian Ale (Rajotte), 348

Belgian Dubbel, guidelines for, 376
Belgian Strong Ale, guidelines for, 376
Belgian-Style Abbey Ale, guidelines for, 376
Belgian-Style Flanders Ale, guidelines for, 376
Belgian-Style Fruit Lambic, guidelines for, 377
Belgian-Style Gueuze Lambic, guidelines for, 377
Belgian-Style Lambic, guidelines for, 377
Belgian-Style Pale Ale, guidelines for, 376
Belgian-Style Wheat/White, guidelines for, 377
Belgian Tripel, guidelines for, 376
Belle Isle Brewing Company, 39, 168
Belmont Brewing Company, 131
Beman and Beverage Systems Inc., 338
Bend Brewing Company, 168
Bennington Brewers Ltd., 178
Bentley's Brewhouse Restaurant, 180
Benzinger Winery, 11
Beraplan Härter GmbH, 219
Berderdall, Barry: on Saskatoon Brewing/Cheers, 47-48
Berkshire Brewing Company Inc., 154
Berliner-Style Weisse (Wheat), guidelines for, 375
Bermuda Triangle Brewing Ltd., 215
Bernau, Jim: on Nor'Wester, 12-13
Beverage Alcohol Market Report (video), 362
Beverage Consult International Inc., 254, 274
Beverage Industry, 357
Beverage International Group Ltd., 29, 157
Beverage World, 357
Beverly Hills Beerhouse Company, 202
Biersch, Dean, 20
Big Buck Brewery and Steakhouse, 30, 156
Big Horn Brewing Company of Colorado/C. B. & Potts, 17, 139
Big Horn Brewing Company of Oregon, 168
Big Horn Brewing Company of Texas/Humperdinks, 17, 175
Big Horse Brewpub, 168
Big Nose Brewing Company, 203
Big River Brewing Company, 39
Big River Grille and Brewing Works (No. 1), 174
Big River Grille and Brewing Works (No. 2), 174
Big Rock Brewery Ltd., 46, 190
Big Sky Brewing Company, 159
Big Time Brewing Company, 15, 180
Bill Owens, Consultant, 254
Bioriginal Food and Science Corp., 268, 280
Biotechnology of Malting and Brewing, The (Hough), 348
Bird Creek Brewery Inc., 15, 129
Birkebeiner Brewing Company, 15, 180
BIRKO Corp., 220
Birmingham Brewing Company, 36, 129
Bison Brewing Company, 131
Bitter End Brewery, 175

BIXIE COASTERS, 262
B. J.'s Brewery/Chicago Pizza Inc., 131
Black Diamond Brewing Company, 131
Black Hills Brewing Company, 30, 174
Black Horse Brewery/Franklin Street Pub Corp., 174
Black Mountain Brewing Company, 130, 202
Black River Brewery and Pub, 184
Black River Brew House, 179
Black Rose Brewpub, 184
Blackstone Restaurant and Brewery, 175
Blind Man Ales, 147
Blind Pig Brewing Company, 22, 131
Blind Tiger Brewery and Restaurant, 151
Blitz-Weinhard Brewing Company, 12, 168
Bloodhound Sensors Ltd., 220
Bloomington Brewing Company/One World
    Enterprises, 150
Blue Anchor Brewery, 193
Blue Anchor Pub, 144
Blue and Gold Brewing Company, 179
Blue Cat Brew Pub, 149
Blue Coyote Brewing Company, 156
Bluegrass Brewing Company, 151
Blue Hen Beer Company, 203
Blue Moon Brewing Company, 10, 203
Blue Mountain Brewing, 168
Blue Pine Brewpub Company, 168
Blue Ridge Brewing Company, 173, 179
Blue Water Brewing Company, 22, 131
Boardwalk Bistro, 175
Bock (Richman), 348
Bodega Brewpub, 184
Boelter Companies, 262
Bohannon Brewing Company/Market Street Brewery
    and Public House, 175
Bohemian Breweries Inc., 220
Bohemian Brewery, 202
Bohemian Brewery Importers, 220, 249, 254, 344, 365
Bohemian-Style Pilsener, 33; guidelines for, 378
Bolin Agency, 262
Bonzzini's Brewpub, 197
Bootleggers Brewery/Sunshine Valley Brewing
    Company, 185
Bootleggers Pub and Brewery/Christophers
    Restaurant Inc., 162
Bootlegger's Steakhouse & Brewery, 132
Borealis Brewery, 129
Bosco's Nashville Brewing Company (No. 2), 175
Bosco's Pizza Kitchen and Brewery (No. 1), 175
Bosque Brewing Company, 175
Boston Beer Company, 8, 11, 12, 30-31, 155, 205
Boston Beer Works, 34, 155
Boulder Creek Brewing Company, 132
Boulevard Brewing Company, 26-27, 158
Boundary Bay Brewing, 180

Bovit, Jon, 11
Bowen Island Brewing Company, 190
Bowman's Pub & Brewing Company, 185
Bow Valley Brewing Company, 47, 190
Box Office Brewery, 149
Boyne River Brewing Company, 156
Bradley's Restaurant and Brewery, 175
Brandywine Brewing Company, 144
Brasal-Brasserie Allemande, 43, 196
Brasserie Beauce Broue Inc., 43
Brasserie du Corsaire, 215
Brasserie Lorraine, 215
Brasserie McAuslan, 42, 43, 196
Brasserie Nationale d'Haiti, 215
Brasseries Beauce Broue Inc., 196
Bratney Equipment Company/Ken Bratney
    Company, 220
Brauhaus Schloss, 154
Brauhaus Systems Caspary, 220
Brauindustrie (video), 362
Brauwelt International, 357
Bray's Brewpub and Eatery, 152
Brazos Brewing Company, 175
Breckinridge Brewery and Pub, 25, 139
Breckinridge Brewery Colorado, 139
Breckinridge Brewery Denver, 22, 139
Breckinridge Brewery in Buffalo, 22, 163
BREW, 358
Brewbakers, 183
Brew Brothers Brewing Company Ltd., 47
Brew Brothers/Eldorado Hotel and Casino, 160
Brew City, 132
Brewers & Bottlers Equipment Corp., 220, 241
Brewers Association New South Wales, 340
Brewers' Association of America, 338
Brewers Association of Canada, 340
Brewers Association of Japan, 340
Brewer's Bier Haus, 160
Brewers Bulletin, 358
*Brewers Digest/Annual Buyers Guide & Brewery
    Directory*, 358
Brewer's Guardian, 358
Brewers' Guild, 340
Brewers Retail, 42, 44
Brewers' Society, 340
Brewery at 34 Depot Street/Arrowhead Brewing
    Company, 155
Brewery at Lake Tahoe, 132
Brewery Atlantis, 202
Brewery Creek Brewing Company, 184
Brewery Operations, Volume 6 (Thomas), 349
Brewery Operations, Volume 7 (Thomas), 349
Brewery Planner (Mendel and Gold), 349
Brew Free or Die! Beer and Brewing, Volume 11
    (Loysen), 348

Index

Brew Hawaii, 20, 358
Brewhouse Inc., 36
Brew House of Danvers, 155
Brewing (Lewis and Young), 349
Brewing and Beverage Industry International (video), 362
Brewing & Distilling International, 358
Brewing Industry Council, 341
Brewing Matters, 338
Brewing Mead (Gayre and Papazian), 350
Brewing operations ratios, 113 (table)
Brewing Products (U.K.) Ltd, 268
Brewing Quality Beers (Burch), 350
Brewing Research Foundation International, 341
Brewing Science, Volumes 1-3 (Pollock), 350
Brewing Society of Japan, 340
Brewing Techniques, 358
Brewing the World's Great Beers (Miller), 350
Brewing under Adversity: Brewery Operations, Volume 8 (Thomas), 350
Brewlab, 344
BrewMakers/Venture Brewing Inc., 22, 132
Brewmaster's Pub, 184
Brewmeisters/Palm Springs Brewery Inc., 132
Brew Moon (No. 2), 155
Brew Moon Enterprises, 34, 155
Brewpub Manual, The (Owens), 349
Brewpubs, 1, 8; Canada, 53 (figure); chain, 9-10; closing of, 53 (figure); defined, 49; estimated total taxable shipments by, 77-78 (table); opening of, 53 (figure) Brewpubs, U.S., 51 (figure); closing of, 51 (figure); estimated total taxable shipments, 62-73 (table); opening of, 51 (figure)
Brewski's Brewing Company, 132
Brewsters Brewing Company and Restaurant (No. 1), 47
Brewsters Brewing Company and Restaurant, 197
Brewsters Brewing Company and Restaurant (No. 2), 47, 190
Brewsters Brewing Company and Restaurant (No. 4), 190
Brewsters Brewing Company and Restaurant (No. 5), 47, 197
Brewsters Brewing Company and Restaurant (No. 6), 47, 190
Brewsters Brewing Company and Restaurant/ Cornerstone Inn (No. 3), 47, 197
Brew Store, 220
Brew Tee's, 262
Brick Brewing Company Ltd., 44, 193
Bricktown Brewing Company, 37, 168
BridgePort Brewing Company, 8, 11, 14, 168
Briess Malting Company, 268
Brimstone Brewing Company, 34, 154, 205
Bristol Brewing Company, 23, 139

British Columbia Liquor Distribution Branch, 316
British School of Brewing, 344
Broad Ripple Brewing Company, 150
Broadway Brewing Company, 23, 139
Brooklyn Brewery, 207
Brouwer Brewery, 139
Brown and Moran Brewing Company. *See* Troy Brewing Company
Brown Forman, 11
Brown Manufacturing Company, 249
Brown-Miller Communications, 262
Brown Porter, guidelines for, 373
Bruce Brewing System—Brewery Builders, 220
Brunswick Corporation, 33
Brürm at Bar, 143
B. T. McClintick Brewing Company, 184, 209
Buccaneer Brewery Ltd., 215
Buchanan Brewing Corp., 180
Buckhead Beer Company, 147
Buckhead Brewery and Grill, 144
Buckingham Mountain Brewing Company/McGallen Brewing Company, 172
Buffalo Bill's Brewery, 132. *See also* Owens Brewing Company
Buffalo Brewing Company, 163
Buhler (Canada) Inc., 220
Bulut, Anetta: on Great Lakes Brewing, 45
Burch Bottle & Packaging, 241
Bureau of Alcohol, Tobacco, and Firearms (BATF), 286-288, 365; Compliance Matters, 322-333 (table) Bureau of Alcoholic Beverages and Lottery Operations (Maine), 298
Burkhardt Brewing Company, 166
Burlingame Station Brewing Company/Golden State Brewing Company, 132
Burns, Shawn: on Yakima Brewing and Malting, 14-15
Bushwakker Brewing Company Ltd., 47, 197
Busse Inc., 241
Butterfield Brewing Company, 22, 132

C

CAE Screen Plates, 220
Cafe on the Square and Brewpub, 175
Cafe Pacifica/Sankt Gallen Brewery, 132
Calhoun's BBQ and Brewery, 175
California Brands Flavors Inc., 280
California Brewin (RedBrick), 350
California Brewing Company, 132
California Cafe company, 10
California Department of Alcoholic Beverage Control, 290
California Glass Company, 249
California Small Brewers Association, 338
California State University Stanislaus, 344

Callahan's Pub and Brewery, 132
Cambridge Brewing Company, 155
Cambridge Inc., 241
Campaign for Real Ale (CAMRA), 11, 340, 341
Canada Malting Company Ltd., 268
Canaday, Dayton, 14
Canadian Custom Stainless, 45
Canadian Liquid Air Ltd., 280
Cape Cod Brew House/Nantucket Brewing Company, 155
Capital Brewing Company, 30, 184
Capitol City Brewing Company, 144, 149
Capitol City Brewing Company (No. 2), 144
Captains City Brewing Inc., 180
Cardinal Brewing, 183
Cargocaire Engineering Company, 222, 241, 249
Caribbean Development Company Ltd., 216
Carling National Brewing Company, 154
Carlsbad Brewery and Public House, 132
Carlsberg, 39
Carlson Filtration Ltd., 222
Carlson's Brewery Research, 262, 365
Carmel Brewing Company, 132
Carnegie Hill Brewing Company, 35, 163
Carolina Brewery, 165
Carolina Brewing Company, 165
Carolina Mill Bakery Brewery, 165
Carson Depot, 160
Carstens, Kyle, 23
Carver Brewing Company, 140
Cascade Lakes Brewing Company, 168
Cascade Microbrewery and Public Firehouse, 169
Casco Bay Brewing Company, 153
Cask Brewing Systems, 43, 222, 269
Cask-conditioned beers, companies brewing, 11
Catamount Brewing Company, 15, 33, 179
Catholic University of Leuven Laboratory of Brewing Science, 344
C. B. & Potts, 17, 139
CBS Insurance, 255
C. C.'s Brew Pub, 193
CDC Inc., 222
Cedar Brewing Company, 150
CEEPS Barney's Ltd., 193
Celebrator Beer News, 363
Celis Brewery Inc., 8, 36, 176
Celite Corp., c/o World Minerals Inc., 222
Cellar Tap, 193
Cemcorp Ltd., Consulting Engineers, 255
Center for Brewing Studies, 278, 344
Centrico Inc., 222
Century Mfg. Inc., 34, 222
Ceramem Separations, 224
Cerevisia, 358
Cerveceria Bohemia, 215

Cerveceria Cuauhtemoc: Baja California (Sur), 212; Ciudad Juarez, 212; Culiacan, 212; Guadalajara, 212; Monterrey, 212; Navojoa, 212; Nogales, 212; Toluca, 212
Cerveceria del Pacifico, 212
Cerveceria India Inc., 186
Cerveceria Moctezuma, 212
Cerveceria Modelo, 212, 215
Cerveceria Modelo de Guadalajara, 212
Cerveceria Modelo del Noroeste, 212
Cerveceria Modelo de Torreon, 212
Cerveceria Nacional Dominicana, 215
Cerveceria Vegana, 215
Cerveceria Yucateca, 212
Chambre Syndicale de la Malterie Francaise, 341
Champion Billiards and Cafe, 179
Champion Brewing Company, 26, 140
Chapter House Brewpub, 163
Charley's Tavern, 193
Chateau St. Michelle Winery, 8, 11, 15
Checkers Brewpub/MacBradee's Brewing Company, 197
Cheers Brew Pub & Restaurant, 197
Cheers Roadhouse Inn, 47-48, 198
Chemdet Inc., 224
Chemgrate Corp., 224
Cherry Creek Brewing Company, 203
Cherryland Brewing Company, 184, 209
Cherry Street Brewery, 168
Chester-Jensen Company Inc., 224
Chicago Brewing Company, 149
Chicago Brew Pub, 173
Chrislan Ceramics Inc., 224, 249, 263
Chubby's Brew Pub & Sports Bar, 197
Chuckanut Bay Brewing Company, 181
Cia Cerveceria del Tropico, 212
Ciao! Travel, 263
Circle V Brewing Company, 150
Cisco Brewers, 155
C. I. Shenanigan's, 17
C. J.'s Brewpub Inc., 180
Clamtown Brewery Inc., 155
Clark's Crossing Brewpub, 198
Classic English-Style Pale Ale, guidelines for, 370
Classic Irish-Style Dry Stout, guidelines for, 373
Clement's Brewing Company. *See* Vernon Valley Brewery
Climax Brewing Company, 161
Clipper City Brewing Company, LP, 154
Clubhaus Brewpub, 157
CM Supply and Consulting, 255
Coastal Brewing Inc., 205
Coasters, 145
Coast Range Brewing Company, 132
Cobblestone Pub and Brewery, 179

Coddington Brewing Company, 173
Coeur d'Alene Brewing Company/T. W. Fisher's Brewpub, 23, 148
Coffee beer, 12
Cold Spring Brewery Company/Beverage International Group Ltd., 29-30, 157
Colorado Brewing Company, 140
Columbia Brewing Company, 174
Columbine Mill Brewery Inc., 140
Columbus Brewing Company, 30, 166, 207
Commonwealth Brewing Company, 11, 36, 155, 205
Compania Cerveceria de las Antillas, 215
Compania Cerveceria International, 215
Conners Brewery, 45, 193
Consolidated Beverages America Ltd., 269, 278
Continental Pilsener (Miller), 350
Contract brewing companies: defined, 49; estimated sales by, 73-75 (table)
CooperSmith's Pub and Brewery, 26, 140
Coophouse Brewery, 140
Coors, Peter: on mega brands, 40
Coors Brewing Company, 13, 40, 140, 175, 179; F.X. Matt and, 9; microbrews by, 10; seasonal beers by, 10
Coors Brewing Company Technical Library, 365
Copper Canyon Brewing Ale House, 130
Copperhead Brewing Company Ltd., 193
Copper Tank Brewing Company, 36-37
Copper Tank Brewing Company (No. 1)/Austin Microbrewers LLC, 176
Copper Tank Brewing Company (No. 2)/Austin Microbrewers LLC, 176
Cornelius Pass Roadhouse and Brewery/McMenamins, 169
Cottonwood Grille & Brewery, 165
Covany Brewing Company, 21, 132
Coyote Springs Brewing Company and Cafe, 26, 130
Craft-brewing index, U.S., 50 (figure), 52 (figure)
Craft-brewing industry, growth of, 1, 8, 41
Craft-brewing industry, Canada, percentage growth of, 54 (figure)
Craft-brewing industry, U.S.: dollar volume for, 54 (figure); percentage growth of, 54 (figure); top fifty companies, 55 (table)
Crane River Brewpub & Cafe, 160
Cream Ale, guidelines for, 381
Creemore Springs Brewery Ltd., 42, 44, 193
Crescent City Brewhouse, 37, 152
Crested Butte Brewing Company, 23, 140
Crisp Malt, 269
Criveller Company, 45, 224, 241, 250
Crooked Creek Brewery, 208
Crooked River Brewing Company, 30, 167
Crosby and Baker, 270, 274, 281
Cross Distributing Company Inc., 224
Cross Plains Brewery Inc., 209
Crown City Brewery, 132
Crystal Ballroom, 15
Crystalite Corp., 263, 281
Cusack's Brewpub and Roaster, 129
Custom Brew Beer Systems, 224
Custom Deco Inc., 250
Cuvee de la Marmite, 43-44
CZ Tech, 270

D

Dairy Engineering Company, 224
Dakota Brewing Company, 207
Dale W. Woys & Associates, 263
D. & F. Engineering Inc., 241
Danse-Skjold Brewing Company, 202
DATOGRAF Apparatebau GmbH & Company, 241
Dave's Brewpub, 151
Dave Miller's Homebrewing Guide (Miller), 352
David & Mark Brewing Company, 204
Davis and Small Oldtime Sign & Photo Company, 263
Dayton Superior Corp., 281
DCI Inc., 224
DCV ULTRAMALT, 270
Dean, Shirley, 22
Delaware Alcoholic Beverage Control, 292
Delmar Stuft Pizza and Microbrewery, 133
Denison's Brewing Company, 45, 193
Denver Chop House and Brewery, 24, 140
De Objective Bierproevers, 341
Department of Alcoholic Beverage Control (Kentucky), 297
Department of Liquor Control (Ohio), 306
Department of Liquor Licenses and Control (Arizona), 289
Department of Public Safety, Liquor Control Division (Minnesota), 300
Department of Revenue (South Dakota), 309
Department of Revenue, Liquor Division (Montana), 302
Department of the Treasury, Bureau of Alcoholic Beverages and Taxes (Puerto Rico), 314
Desai Capital Management, 9
Deschutes Brewery (No. 2), 169
Deschutes Brewery and Public House, 13, 169
Desert Edge Brewery at the Pub/Desert Edge Brewing Company, 178
Desnoes & Geddes Ltd., 215
Detroit & Mackinac Brewery Ltd., 30, 206
Detroit Stool & Chair Mfg. Inc., 250
Deutscher Brauer-Bund E.V., 341
Devil Mountain Brewing Company/Bay Brewing Company, 22
D. G. Yuengling & Son Inc., 33, 173
Diamond Knot Brewery, 181

Dicalite/Grefco Inc., 224
Dictionary of Beer and Brewing, The (Forget), 351
Dilworth Brewing Company, 165
Dilworth Micro Brewery, 165
Dimmer's Brew Pub Inc., 140
Dino & Luigi's Stuft Pizza Sports Bar and Brewery, 133
Distilled spirits, per capita consumption of, 88 (figure)
Diversey Corp., 224
Diversey Inc., 225
Diversified Management Services Ltd., 255, 263
Diversified Packaging Products Inc., 241
Division of Alcoholic Beverage Control (New Jersey), 303
Division of Liquor Control (Missouri), 301
Dixie Brewing Company Inc., 152
D. L. Geary Brewing Company Inc., 34, 153
DME Brewing Services, 225, 255
DMS Group, 255
Dock Street Brewery and Restaurant (No. 2), 144
Dock Street Brewing Company, 33, 208
Dock Street Brewing Company Brewery and Restaurant, 172
Doemens School, 344
Dogfish Head Brewing and Eats, 144
Dogwood Brewing Company, 147
Dolan's Pub, 43
Don Gambrinu's Brewpub Inc., 145
Dorette Company, 250
Dornbusch Brewing Company Inc., 205
Dortmunder/European-Style Export, guidelines for, 378
Downtown Brewing Company, 174
Downtown Joe's Brewery and Restaurant, 133
Doyle, Richard: on Mass. Bay Brewing, 31-32
Draft Service Inc., 250
Dragon's Breath Pale Ale, 46
Draught Horse Pub and Brewery, 176
D.R.B. & Associates, 255
Drinktec U.S.A. Ltd., 225, 242, 250, 281
Drummond Brewing Company, 46
Dry Lager, guidelines for, 380
Drytown Brewing Company, 163
DuBois, 225
Dubuque Brewing & Bottling Company, 23, 26, 34, 150
Duclaw Brewing Company, 154
Dunedin Brewery/Prospector Brewing Services, 145
Durango Brewing Company, 23, 140
Düsseldorf-Style Altbier, guidelines for, 375
Duster's Micro-brewery, 156

E
E. Z. CAP, 242
Eagle Brewing Company Inc., 148, 181
Earnings, 92 (figure)
Eastern Rivers Brewing Company, 208
Ebbets Field, 158
Eddie McStiff's Brewing Company, 23, 178
Edgar A. Weber & Company, 281
Edgefield Brewery/McMenamins, 169
Edme Ltd., 270
Ed Tringali & Associates, 255
Edwards Engineering Corp., 225
Eel River Brewing Company, 133
Egan Brewing Company, 184
El Dorado Brewing Company: Mount Aukum, 133; Stockton, 133
Eldorado Canyon Brewing Company, 140
Electro-Steam Generator Corp., 225, 250
Elephant Butte Brewery and Pizzeria, 162
Elk Grove Brewing Company Inc., 133
Ellensburg Brewing Company, 181
Ellicotville Brewing Company/S&W Company LLC, 163
Elliott Bay Metal Fabricating Inc., 225, 250
Elm City Brewing Company/The Brewery, 34, 143, 203
Elora Brewery Ltd./Taylor & Bate, 193
El Toro Brewing Company, 133
Embudo Station/Preston Brewery, 162
Emerald Isle Brew Works Ltd., 11, 173
Empire Brewing Company, 163
Employment, 92 (figure)
ENCORE!, 242
Enerfab Inc., 225
Engine House #9/The Power Station, 181
England Worthside Ltd., 225
English (Extra Special) Strong Beer, guidelines for, 370
English Old Ale, guidelines for, 372
English Ordinary Bitter, guidelines for, 370
English (Special) Best Bitter, guidelines for, 370
English Strong Ale, guidelines for, 372
English-Style Brown Ale, guidelines for, 372
English-Style Dark Mild Ale, guidelines for, 371
English-Style Light Mild Ale, guidelines for, 371
Epsen Hillmer Graphics Company, 242
Equipment Enterprises Inc., 281
Erie Brewing Company/Hoppers Brewpub, 172
Ertel Engineering Company, 226
Eske's Brew Pub/Sangre de Cristo Brewing Company, 162
Essentials of Beer Style, The (Eckhardt), 351
Estes Park Brewery, 140
Etched Images, 263
Etna Brewing Company, 133
ETS Laboratories, 278
Eugene City Brewing Company/West Brothers Bar-B-Q, 169

Index

Europeanbeer (Eurobeer), 44
European Brewery Convention (EBC), 341
European Low-Alcohol Lager, guidelines for, 378
European-Style All-Malt Pilsener, guidelines for, 377
European-Style Dark, guidelines for, 379
European-Style Pilsener, guidelines for, 378
Europe 1992 Connection, 250, 281
EUROSOURCE Inc., 242
Evaluating Beer (Gold), 351
Evansville Brewing Company, 150
Excise taxes, 40, 334-336 (table)

F

Falco Stainless Steel Equipment Ltd., 226
F. & M. Breweries Ltd., 44-45, 193
Farmington River Brewing Company, 143
Faultline Brewing Company Inc., 133
Feathers, 193
Feinberg, Mark, 22
Ferment, 359
Fertitta Enterprises, 9, 20
F. H. Steinbart Company, 270, 274
Field's Restaurant & Brewpub, 169
50 Great Homebrewing Tips (Weisberg), 351
Figgie, 226
Filter Equipment Company Inc., 226, 242, 338
Filtrine Manufacturing Company, 226, 242
Finest Beers, closing of, 45
Firehouse Brewery and Restaurant, 167
Firehouse Brewing Company, 145, 174
First Fabrics Inc., 226
First Key Industrial Corp., 255
Fischer Brewing Company Inc., 203
Fish Brewing Company/Fishbowl Pub, 15, 181
Fitzpatrick's Brewing Company, 150
Five Star Products and Services LLC, 282
Flagstaff Brewing Company, 130
Flat Branch Brewing Company, 30, 158
Flatlander's Brewing Company, 149
Fleetside Pub & Brewery, 26, 140
Flo-Pac Corp., 226
Florida Beer Brands, 36, 204
Florida Brewery Inc., 145
Florida Division of Alcohol, Beverages, and Tobacco, 293
Flying Dog Brewpub, 23, 140
Foreign-Style Stout, guidelines for, 374
Forsely, Fred: on Shipyard, 32-33
Fort Garry Brewing Company Ltd., 47, 192
Fort Spokane Brewery, 181
Fort Wayne Brewing Company, 204
Foster's, 39
Four Peaks Brewing Company, 130
Fox & Hounds Brewpub, 198
Foxboro Company, 227, 263
Fox River Brewing Company/Fratello's Italian Cafe, 184
Foxx Equipment Company, 227
Franchises, popularity of, 9
Frankenmuth Brewery Inc., 30, 156
Franklin Street Brewing Company, 206
Frederick Brewing Company, 8, 34, 154
Fredimo Bottlers Inc., 208
Fredricksburg Brewing Company Inc., 176
Free State Brewing Company, 151
Fremont Brewing Company, 133
French-Style Biére de Garde, guidelines for, 377
Freshops, 274
Frick/Reco Division, York International Corp., 227
Friends Brewing Company, 204
Friesen of Iowa Inc., 227, 250
Frio Brewing Company, 176
Fromm, Meyer-Bass Inc., 274
Frontier Brewing Company, 205
Front Street Ale House/San Juan Brewing Company, 181
Front Street Brewery, 151, 165
Fruit beers, guidelines for, 382
Fullerton Hofbrau, 22, 133
Full Moon International Inc./Lake Highland Brewing Company, 204
Full Sail Brewing Company, 12
Full Sail Brewing Company/White Cap Brewpub and Tasting Room, 169
Full Sail Brewing Company (No. 2)/Pilsener Room at Riverplace, 169
Fulton Pub and Brewery/McMenamins, 169
F. X. Matt Company, 9, 10, 31, 33, 34, 163

G

Gabelli and Company, 10
Gafco-Worldwide Inc., 227, 243
Galena Main Street Brewpub/Kingston Inn Restaurant, 149
Galveston Brewery, 176
Gamajet Cleaning Systems Inc., 227
Gambrinus Brewing Company, 8, 167
Gambrinus Malting Corp., 270
Gamse Lithographing Company, 243
G. & D. Chillers Inc., 227
G. & H. Products Corp., 227
Gate City Brewing Company, 207
GATT. *See* General Agreement on Tariffs and Trade
GEA Ecoflex, Division of NIRO Inc., 242
Gem State Brewing, 148
General Agreement on Tariffs and Trade (GATT), 40
General Filtration, Division of Lee Chemicals Ltd., 227, 282
General Press Corp., 263

Genesee Brewing Company/Dundee's Brewery, 10, 40, 163
Gentle Ben's Brewing Company, 26, 130
Gentlemen Jims, 163
German Agricultural Marketing Board—CMA, 275
German Glass & Gift Imports Inc., 250
German Leichtbier, guidelines for, 378
German-Style Bock Bier, guidelines for, 379
German-Style Brown Ale, guidelines for, 375
German-Style Helles Bock, guidelines for, 379
German-Style Kölsch, guidelines for, 374
German-Style Märzen, guidelines for, 379
German-Style Pilsener, guidelines for, 377
German-Style Schwarzbier, guidelines for, 379
German-Style Strong Doppelbock, guidelines for, 379
German-Style Strong Eisbock, guidelines for, 380
German Wheat Beer (Warner), 351
G. Heileman Brewing Company Inc., 12, 29, 30, 40, 154, 184
G. Heileman Brewing Company Inc. Corporate Headquarters, 149
G. Heileman Brewing Company Inc./Lone Star Brewing Company, 176
Gilbert Insect Light Traps, 251
Gilbert Robinson Inc., 206
Gimson Engineering Ltd., 227
Glacier Peak Brewing Company, 181
Glasses, Mugs & Steins, 263
Glatt Bros. Brewing Company, 194, 270, 275, 278
Glencastle Brewing Company, 133
Glenwood Canyon Brewing Company, 140
Global Brewing Services Inc., 256
Goggins & Whalen Insurance Agency Inc., 256
Gold Coast Brewing Company, 206
Gold Crown Brewing Company, 45, 194
Golden Ale Canadian-Style Ale, guidelines for, 374
Golden City Brewery, 140
Golden Lion Pub and Brewing Company, 196
Golden Pacific Brewing Company, 22, 133
Golden Valley Brewery & Pub, 169
Goodall Rubber Company, 227
Good Beer Guide 1996 (Evans), 351
Goose Island Beer Company, 30
Goose Island Brewing Company, 11, 30, 149
Goose Island Brewing Company (No. 2), 149
Gordon, Dan: on Gordon Biersch, 20-21
Gordon Biersch Brewery (No. 1), 133
Gordon Biersch Brewery Restaurant (No. 1), 133
Gordon Biersch Brewery Restaurant (No. 2), 133
Gordon Biersch Brewery Restaurant (No. 3), 133
Gordon Biersch Brewery Restaurant (No. 4), 134
Gordon Biersch Brewery Restaurant (No. 5), 147
Gordon Biersch Brewery Restaurants, 9, 20-21, 22
Gorrill, Stephen, 36
Gottberg Brew Pub/Gottberg Auto Company, 160

Grace Davison, 282
Grain Millers Inc., 270, 282
Grain Systems Inc., 228
Grandes Brasseries Antillaises, 215
Grand Rapids Brewing Company, 156
Grandstand Sportswear, 263
Granite Brewery (No. 1), 43, 192
Granite Brewery (No. 2), 194
Grant, Bert and Sherry, 8-9
Grant's Ales, 15
Grant's Brewery Pub, 181
Grant's Yakima Brewing and Malting Company, 14-15
Grant's Yakima Brewing Company, 181
Granville Island Brewing Company, 190
Graphic Nature, 263
Gray Brewing Company, 30, 184
Great American Beer Cookbook (Schermerhorn), 351
Great Baraboo Brewing Company, 157
Great Basin Brewing Company, 160
Great Cooking with Beer (RedBrick), 352
Great Dane Pub & Brewing Company, 30, 184
Great Divide Brewing Company, 23, 141
Great Lakes Brewing Company, 30, 42, 44, 45, 167, 194
Great Northern Brewing Company, 23, 159, 166
Great Western Brewing Company, 47, 198
Great Western Malting Company, 271
Green Bay Brewing Company, 184
Greenshields Pub and Brewery, 37, 165
Grenada Breweries Ltd., 215
Gritty McDuff's, 11, 34, 153, 205
Gritty McDuff's (No. 2), 153
Grizzly Bay Brewing Company, 134
Grizzly Peak Brewing Company, 157
Guardian Labs, 228
Guinness Jamaica Ltd., 215
Gulfstream Brewing Product, 228
G. W. Kent Inc., 227, 243, 270, 275, 278

H
Haffmans B. V., 228
Hair of the Dog Brewing Company, 169
Hale's Ales Ltd. (No. 1), 181
Hale's Ales Ltd. (No. 2), 181
Hale's Ales Ltd. (No. 3), 181
Hammer and Nail Brewers, 144
Handbook of Brewing (Hardwick), 349
Handy Button Machine Company of New York Inc., 263
Hangtown Brewery Inc., 134
Happy Valley Brewing Company, 190
Harbor Lights Brewing Company, 22, 134
Harp & Star Brewing Company, 176
Harrison Hollow Brewhouse, 148

Index

Hart Brewing Company Inc., 12, 17, 22, 45, 46, 181, 194
Hartford Brewery Ltd., 144
Harvest Moon Brewery/The Ales Company/Sullivan Brewing, 161
Haupenthal, Peter, 45
Hazel Dell Brewpub, 181
H. C. Berger Brewing Company, 10, 23, 141
Heartland Brewing Company, 163
Heather Motel and Brewpub, 192
Heavenly Daze Brewery & Grill, 141
Heavy Duty Products Inc., 228, 243
Heckler Brewing Company, 202
Hedwin Corporation, 243
Heidelberg Restaurant and Brewery, 194
Heineken, 39
Heinrich Ceramic Decal Inc., 282
Henry Weinhard's, 19, 40
Herb beers, guidelines for, 382
Hereford and Hops, 157
Heriot-Watt University International Centre for Brewing and Distilling, 345
Heritage Brewing Company, 22, 134
Heuft U.S.A. Inc., 243
Hickenlooper, John: on Wynkoop, 23-24
Hierman's Hofbrau, 176
Highland Brewing Company, 165
Highland Pub and Brewery/McMenamins, 169
Highlands Brewery, 145
High Point Brewing Corp., 203
High Range Graphics, 264
High Street Brewery and Cafe/McMenamins, 169
Hilge/Shanley Pump, 228, 243
Hill Country Brewing and Bottling Company, 36, 176
Hillsdale Brewery and Public House/McMenamins, 169
Hilton Head Brewing Company, 174
Himmelberger Brewing Company, 159
Hoboken Brewing Company, 161, 206
Hoffbrau Steaks Brewery (No. 1), 176
Hoffbrau Steaks Brewery (No. 2), 176
Hogshead Brewpub, 134
Hohensteins Inc., 338
Hollow, David: on RAM International, 17-18
Holy Cow! Casino, Cafe & Brewery, 160
Homark Group Ltd., 251
Home Brewers Companion, The (Papazian), 352
Homebrew Favorites (Lutzen and Stevens), 352
Homebrew Today, 359
Home on the Range PhotoTops, 251
Hometowne Breweries Ltd., 45, 194
Hoover Materials Handling Group Inc./SABCO Industries/Sav-a-Barrel Corp., 228
Hopfen und Malz GmbH, 228, 243, 256
Hop Growers of America Inc., 275

Hoppers Brooker Creek Grille and Taproom, 145
Hoppy Brewing Company, 202
Hops (Neve), 352
Hops and Bistro Brewery (No. 1), 130
Hops and Bistro Brewery (No. 2), 134
Hops and Bistro Brewery (No. 3), 130
Hops and Bistro Brewery (No. 4), 130
Hops Grill and Bar, 10, 37, 39; Boynton Beach, 145; Bradenton, 145; Carrollwood, 145; Clearwater, 145; Jacksonville, 145; Lakeland, 145; North Tampa, 145; Ocala, 145; Orange Park, 145; Orlando, 145; Palm Harbor, 145; Port Richey, 145; St. Petersburg, 145; South Tampa, 145
Hoptech, 275, 282
Hop Town Brewing Company, 134
Hopunion U.S.A. Inc., 275
Hornell Brewing Company, 207
Horseshoe Bay Brewing Company Ltd., 190
Hoster Brewing Company, 167
Hours, 92 (figure)
Houston Brewery, 37, 176
Howe Sound Brewing Company Ltd., 47, 190
How to Build a Small Brewery (Owens), 352
How to Open a Brewpub or Microbrewery (Winner, Smith, Lewis), 352
Hubcap Brewery and Kitchen, 10, 25-26, 141
Hubcap Brewery and Kitchen (No. 2), 176
Hub City Brewery, 176
Huber Verpackungen, 243
Hudepohl-Schoenling Brewing Company, 11, 167
Hugh Baird & Sons Ltd., 271
Humboldt Brewery, 19, 134
Humes Brewing Company Inc., 134
Humpback Brewing Company, 202
Humperdinck's, 17
Humphreys Bar & Grill, 185
Hunter Gatherer, 174
Huntington Beach Beer Company, 134
Hybrid styles, guidelines for, 381-382
Hyde Park Brewing Company, 163

I

IDD Process & Packaging Inc., 228, 243, 256, 275, 283
Illinois Liquor Control Commission, 295
Il Vicino Wood Oven Pizza, 162
Il Vicino Wood Oven Pizza (No. 2), 141
Imperial Stout, guidelines for, 372
Import INSIGHTS, 353
Imports: leading, 82 (table); sales of, 39, 81 (table)
Incorporated Brewers' Guild, 341
Indcon Design Ltd., 228, 244
Independence Brewing Company, 172
Independent Family Brewers of Britain (IFBB), 341
Indiana Alcoholic Beverage Commission, 295
Indianapolis Brewing Company, 15, 150

India Pale Ale, 12, 21, 23, 28, 33; guidelines for, 370
Industrial Dynamics Company Ltd.—Manufacturers of Filtec Inspection Systems, 244
Industrial Filter & Pump Mfg. Company, 229
Initial Public Offerings (IPO), 8
Inland Printing Company/Inland Label, 244, 264
Innozyme Ltd., 229
Institute for Brewing Studies, 1, 19, 36, 339
Institute of Brewing (Australia), 340
Institute of Brewing (U.K.), 341
Insurance Associates of Northern California, 256
Integrated Restaurant Software, 264
Interbrew SA, 42, 48
International Brewing & Manufacturing Inc., 229
Interurban Brewpub, 39, 168
Introduction to Brewing Science and Technology, Parts I, II, and III, An (Rainbow and Float), 353
Ion Exchange Products Inc., 229, 283
IPO. *See* Initial Public Offerings
Ipswich Brewing Company, 34, 155
Irish Times Pub & Brewery, 145
Irons Brewing Company, 23, 141
ISO—Insurance Services of San Francisco, 264
ISP (International Specialty Products), 229, 283
Issaquah Brewhouse/Eagle River Brewing Company, 181
Italian Oasis Restaurant & Brewery, 160

J

Jack Daniel's Brewery, 11, 36, 151
Jack Daniel's Corporate Headquarters, 151
Jacob Leinenkugel Brewing Company, 12, 28-29, 184
Jacob Leinenkugel Brewing Company (No. 2), 184
JACO Equipment Corp., 229
Jaenicke Inc., 275
Jaipur Restaurant and Brewpub, 160
James Bay Restaurant & Brewery, 163
James Gate, 194
James Page Brewing Company, 157
James River Brewing Company, 180
James R. Van Liere Structural Engineer, 256
Jamestown Brewing Company, 203
James Vickers & Company Ltd., 283
Japan Microbrewers Association, 340
Jaxson's Restaurant and Brewing Company, 176
Jenkins/Athens Insurance Services, 256
J. E. Siebel Sons' Company, 229
Jet Carboy & Bottle Washer Company, 229
Jet City Brewing Company, 15, 209
J. M. Swank Company, 271, 275, 279
Joe-Joe's Brewing Company, 134
Joe's Brewing Company, 149
Joe's Millhill Saloon and Restaurant, 161
Joey's Inc., 176
John Barleycorn's/McMenamins, 170

John Harvard's Brewhouse, 11, 155
John Harvard's Brewhouse (No. 2)/The Brewhouse LLC, 36, 147
John H. Bergmann Associates Ltd., 256
John I. Haas Inc., 275
John Labatt Ltd., 42, 48 *See also* Labatt's Breweries of Canada
Johnson Beer Company, 36, 165
Johnson Litho Graphics of Eau Claire Ltd., 264
Johnstown Brewing Company, 208
Jones Brewing Company, 172
Jones Street Brewery, 30, 160
Joseph Huber Brewing Company, 184
Joseph L. Owades & Company, 256
Journal of the American Society of Brewing Chemists, 359
Journal of the Institute of Brewing, 359
Journeyman Metal Services, 16
JTECH Inc., 251
J. T. Whitney's Brewpub and Eatery/Kicks, 184
Judge Baldwin's Brewing Company/B. F. Coleman Brewing Corp., 141
Just Brew It! Beer and Brewing, Volume 12 (Loysen), 353
J. V. Northwest Inc., 14, 20, 30, 229

K

Kalamazoo Brewing Company Inc., 30, 157
Kal Grafx, 244
Karl Strauss Breweries/Associated Microbreweries, 134
Karl Strauss Brewery Gardens, 134
Katie Bloom's Irish Pub and Brewery, 39, 177
Kawartha Lakes Brewing Company, 45, 194
KBC Brewpub and Grill/Kentucky Brewing Company, 151
K. C. Brewing Company, 134
Keg Club, 229
Kegs Brewery and Fine Dining/Alamogordo Brewing Company, 162
Kehoe, Tom, 11
Keith's Brewery, 192
Kelley Creek Brewing Company, 182
Kelly's Caribbean Bar & Grill, 146
Kenerik/Golden Gate, 229, 244
Kennebunkport Brewing Company, 153
Kennebunkport Brewing Company/Federal Jack's Brewpub, 33
Kennedy School, 15
Kershenstine Diamond, 206
Kessler Brewing Company, 23, 159
Key West Overseas Brewery, 146
Kgalagadi Brewers, 339
KHS Machines Inc., 229
King Brewing Company, 157

Index

Kingston Brewing Company Ltd., 45-46, 194
KLR Machines Inc., 229
KMS Consultants, 256
Kobor and White Brewery Inc., 207
Koch, Jim, 11
Köln-Style Kölsch, guidelines for, 374
Kona Brewing Company, 147
Koospol, 341
Kramer Stainless Systems, 230
Krones Inc., 32, 34, 230

L

Labatt's Alberta Brewery, 190
Labatt's Breweries/British Columbia: Creston, 190; New Westminster, 190
Labatt's Breweries of Canada, 39, 194 *See also* John Labatt Ltd.
Labatt's Manitoba Brewery, 192
Labatt's Newfoundland Brewery, 192
Labatt's Ontario Breweries: Etobicoke, 194; London, 194
LaBelle Brewing Company Inc., 185
La Brasserie Labatt's Limitee, 196
Le Brasserie les Maskoutains de Saint-Hyacinthe, 43
La Brasserie Portneuvoise, 196
La Brasseurs de l'Anse, 43
La Cervoise, 43-44, 196
La Conner Brewing Company, 182
Lafayette Brewing Company, 150
La Futel, 44
Lager beers, guidelines for, 377-381
Laguna Beach Brewing Company, 134
Lagunitas Brewing Company, 135
La Jolla Brewing Company, 134
Lake City Brewing Company, 163
Lakefront Brewery Inc., 30, 185
Lakeport Brewing Corp., 194
Lake St. George Brewing Company, 153
Lakeside Brewery and Wine Inc., 209
Lake Superior Brewing Company, 158
Lake Tahoe Brewing Company Inc., 22, 202
Lake Titus Brewery, 163
Lakewood Bar and Grill, 17
Lallemand Inc., 279
Lambic (Guinard), 353
Lancaster Malt Brewing Company, 172
Lang Creek Brewery, 159
Large brewers: defined, 49; market share of, 80 (table); shipments by, 79 (table)
Larson, Geoff: on Alaskan Brewing, 13-14
Last Straw, 198
Latchis Grille and Windham Brewery, 179
La Traverne de Sergeant, 196
Latrobe Brewing Company, 172
La Villa de Torrimar, 186

Lawler Brewing Company, 130
Law Offices of Earle D. Bellamy II P.C., 256
Lawson Mardon Packaging, 244
Lax & Noll, 257
Lazar & Company, 230, 251, 257, 264
Lazlo's Brewery and Grill, 160
Lazy Hound Restaurant and Brewery, 151
L. C. Thomsen Inc., 230
Leavenworth Brewery, 182
Le Cheval Blanc, 197
Left Hand Brewing Company, 23, 141
Legend Brewing Company, 180
Les Brasseurs du Nord, 42-43, 197
Les Brasseurs GMT, 43, 197
Le Vintage Collection (Designer Labels), 283
Lewis Twice Consultancy, 257
Lexington Brewing Company, 205
Lexington City Brewery, 152
Liberty Steakhouse and Brewery at Broadway at the Beach, 174
Liberty Street Brewing Company, 167
Library Restaurant and Brewing Company, 186
Lift Bridge Brewing Company, 167
Lighthouse Brewery and Public House/McMenamins, 170
Lind Brewing Company, 11, 135
L'Inox, 43, 196
Lion Brewery and Museum, 33, 194
Lion Inc./Gibbons-Stegmaier Brewery, 172
Liquid Assets Brewing Systems, 20, 251
Liquidtech Inc., 251
Liquor Commission of the City and County of Honolulu (Hawaii), 294
Liquor Control Administration (Rhode Island), 308
Liquor Control Commission (Connecticut), 292
Liquor Enforcement Division (Colorado), 291
Liquor License Board of Ontario, 318
Little Apple Brewing Company, 151
Loeffler Chemical Corp., 283
Lonetree Brewing Ltd., 141
Lone Wolfe Brewing Company, 141
Long Island Brewing Company, 34, 163
Long-Kesh Funding, 257
Long Trail Brewing Company, 33, 179
Long Valley Pub & Brewery/Long Valley Brewing Company, 161
Los Gatos Brewing Company, 135
Lost Coast Brewery & Cafe, 22, 135
Louie's Custom Tap Handles, 251
Louisiana Alcoholic Beverage Control, 297
Louisiana Brewing Company/Brasserie de la Louisiane, 152
Louisiana Jack's/Silo Brewpub, 152
Lowell Brewing Company, 34, 155
Lucky Labrador Brew Pub, 170

Lupofresh Inc., 276
Lupofresh Limited, 276

M

McAuslan, Peter: on Brasserie McAuslan, 43
McCall Brewing Company/Cerveceria Inc., 148
McCloud Pest Control, 251
McCormick Distribution and Marketing, 264
McDonald, John: on Boulevard Brewing, 26-27
McFarlane Brewing Company, 130
McGuire's Irish Pub and Brewery, 146, 204
McKenzie River Partners, 202
MacLean Brewery Equipment Ltd., 230
McMenamin, Mike: on McMenamins Breweries, 15-16
McMenamins/Columbia, 182
McMenamins/Mill Creek, 182
McMenamins/Murray and Allen, 170
McMenamins/Roy Street, 182
McMenamins/Six Arms Pub, 182
McMenamins/West Linn Pub, 170
McMenamins Breweries, 10, 12, 15-16
McMenamins Edgefield Brewery, 15, 16
McNeill's Brewery, 179
Maas Brewing Systems, 230
Mac & Jack's Brewery Inc., 182
Mackie, Keith, 15; on McMenamins Breweries, 16
Madison Brewing Company/Pub and Restaurant, 179
Mad Monk Brewing Company Ltd., 207
Mad River Brewing Company, 20, 135
Magic City Brewery, 37, 129
Magic Hat Brewing Company, 34, 179
Magnotta Brewery Ltd., 194
Magyar Sorgyart Szovetsege, 341
Maibock, 28; guidelines for, 379
Maine Coast Brewing Company, 153
Mainline Brewing Company, 135
Main Street Brewery/Four Corners Brewing Company, 141
Main Street Brewery/Queen City Brewing Company, 30, 167
Main Street Brewing Company (MA), 155
Main Street Brewing Company (TX), 177
Major's Brew House, 45, 194
Maletis, 13
Malnove Corp., 244
Malt & Hop Distributors of Canada Inc., 271
Malt Advocate, 359
Malt beverages: consumption of, 86 (figure), 110 (figure), 111 (figure); consumption of (per capita), 83 (figure), 86 (figure), 87 (figure), 112 (figure); consumption of (percentage change), 111 (figure), 112 (figure); non-alcoholic, 382; population and, 83 (figure); shipment of, 86 (figure), 93 (figure), 94-109 (figure); sales of (by state), 84 (figure); total tax paid withdrawals of, 85 (figure)

Malteries Franco-Belges, 272
Malting and Brewing Science, Volumes 1 and 2 (Briggs, Hough, Stevens, and Young), 353
Malt Products Corp., 271
Mammoth Brewing Company, 135
Manayunk Malt & Hops Company, 172, 208
Mangel, Scheuermann & Oeters Inc., 230
Manhattan Beach Brewing Company, 135
Manhattan Brewing Company, 36
Manitoba Liquor Control Commission, 316
Marcon Wine & Filters, 230
Marin Brewing Company, 22, 135
Maritime Pacific Brewing Company, 15, 182
Maritimes, openings/closings in, 43 (table)
Mark's Brewing Company, 141
Market Street Mill, 174
Market Street Pub, 146
Maroney Sausage Est./Widmer Brothers Brewing Company, 170
Martha's Exchange, 160
Marthasville Brewing Company, 36, 147
Martin Velas, 257
Maryland Wire Belts Inc., 244
Mass. Bay Brewing Company, 31-32, 155, 205
Master's Brasserie and Brewpub, 194
Matter Company, 257
Maui Beer Company, 204
Maui Kine Brewery Ltd., 148
Maumee Bay Brewing Company, 167
Maytag, Fritz: on Anchor, 18-19
MBAA Technical Quarterly, The, 359
Mechanical Welding Service, 230
Medicine Bow Brewing Company, 186
Meheen Brewing Company, 182
Meheen Manufacturing, 244
Menasha Corp., 264
Mendocino Brewing Company, 19, 135
Mercury Cafe, 141
Merriman, Michael: on Alcatraz, 10
Metz, Douglas: on wine/spirit wholesalers, 11
Meyer Supply Inc., 230
MHD Canada Inc., 45, 272, 276
Miami Brewing Company, 36, 146
Michelob, 10, 19, 40
Michigan Brewing Company, 157
Michigan Liquor Control Commission, 299
Mickey Finn's Brewery/Libertyville Brewing Company, 30, 149
Microbreweries: defined, 49; growth of, 1, 8, 42
Microbreweries, Canada, 42, 53 (figure); closing of, 53 (figure); estimated total taxable shipments by, 76-77 (table); opening of, 53 (figure)
Microbreweries, U.S., 51 (figure); closing of, 51 (figure); estimated total taxable shipments by, 57-62 (table); opening of, 51 (figure)

Index

Microbreweries Across America, 12
Micro Brew Express—Beer-of-the-Month Club, 257, 264
Micro Matic U.S.A. Inc., 244
MicroPure Filtration, 230, 245, 257, 339
Mid-Atlantic Association of Craft Breweries, 339
Mid-Coast Brewing, 209
Middle Ages Brewing Company Ltd., 163
Middlesex Brewing Company Inc., 156
Midnight Sun Brewing Company, 129
Midwest Beer Notes, 363
Mile High Brewing Company, 13, 141
Milestown Brewing Company/The Golden Spur, 159
Mill Brewery, Eatery, & Bakery, 39; Birmingham, 129; Fort Myers, 146; Knoxville, 175; Winter Park, 146, 204
Mill Creek Brewery & Restaurant, 158
Miller Brewing Company, 9, 10, 12, 13, 32, 40; California, 135; Celis Brewery and, 8, 36; Georgia, 147; North Carolina, 165; Ohio, 167; Shipyard Brewery and, 8; Texas, 177; Wisconsin, 185
Millipore Corporation, 230
Millrose Brewing Company, 149
Millstream Brewing Company, 30, 151
Minnesota Brewing Company, 15, 18, 158
Mishawaka Brewing Company, 150
Mission Bridge Brewing Company, 47, 190
Mississippi Delta Microbrewery, 204
Mixed styles, guidelines for, 381-382
M. J. Barleyhoppers Brewery and Sports Pub, 148
Modelo Especial, 39
Modern Brewery Age, 40, 359
Molson Breweries, 19, 39, 194, 366
Molson Breweries/Atlantic Region/St. John's Plant, 192
Molson Breweries/Ontario Division: Barrie Plant, 195; Etobicoke Plant, 195; North York Plant, 195
Molson Breweries/Québec Division/La Brasserie Molson O'Keefe, 197
Molson Breweries/Western Division, 191; Alberta Region/Edmonton Plant, 190; British Columbia Region/Vancouver Plant, 191; Manitoba Region/Winnepeg Plant, 192; Saskatchewan Region/Regina Plant, 198
Momentum Management, 264
Monitek Technologies Inc., 231
Montana Brewing Company, 159
Montgomery Brewing Company/Alabama Brewpubs LLC, 129
Mon Village Brewery, 197
Moonlight Brewing Company, 135
Moosehead Breweries Ltd., 192
Morgan Street Brewery, 158
Morris Hanbury Jackson Le May Ltd., 276

Morris Hanbury U.S.A. Inc., 276
Motor City Brewing Works Inc, 30, 157
Mountain Brewers. *See* Long Trail Brewing Company
Mountain Sun Pub and Brewery, 12, 26, 141
Mountain Valley Brewpub, 34, 164
Mountain West, openings/closings in, 25 (table)
Mount Airy Brewing Company/Firehouse Pub and Restaurant, 154
Mount Angel Brewing Company, 170
Mount Baker Brewing Company, 182
Mount Begbie Brewing Company Ltd., 191
Mount Hood Brewing Company, 170
Moxcey, Tom: on Rock Bottom, 24-25
Moylan, Brendan, 22
Moylan's Brewing Company, 22, 135
MSK Covertech Inc., 245
Mueller, 20, 31
Multiplex Company Inc., 251
Multnomah Brewery, 170
Münchner Dunkel, guidelines for, 379
Münchner-Style Helles, guidelines for, 378
Munton and Fison PLC, 272
Murphy's, 17
Murphys Creek Brewing Company, 135
MVE Inc., 252
Mystic River Brewing Company, 144

N

Nacho Mama's Brewery, 36, 164
Nail City Brewing Company, 24
Naisbitt's Brewery, 178
Namaqua Brewing Company, 141
Napa Valley Ale Works, 135
Napa Valley Brewing Company, 135
National Beer Wholesalers Association, 339
National Brewing Company Ltd, 216
National Chemicals Inc., 231, 252
National Research Institute of Brewing, 344
NDA Engineering Group, 231
Nebraska Brewing Company, 206
Nebraska Liquor Control Commission, 302
Nelson Brewing Company, 191
Neptune Brewery, 164
Neuweiler Brewing Company Inc., 208
Nevada City Brewing Company, 135
Nevada Department of Taxation, 302
New Amsterdam Brewing Company, 207
New Belgium Brewing Company, 22, 141
New Brewer, The, 359
New Brewing Lager Beer (Noonan), 353
New Brunswick Liquor Corp., 317
Newcomer Carmel Brewing Company, 21
New Complete Joy of Home Brewing, Second Edition, The (Papazian), 353

New England Brewing Company/Brewhouse Restaurant, 34, 36, 144
Newfoundland Liquor Corp., 317
New Glarus Brewing Company, 30, 185
New Haven Brewing Company, 36. *See also* Elm City Brewing Company
New Jersey Brewery LLC, 161
Newlands Services Inc., 47, 232
Newport Beach Brewing Company, 136
New World Brewery, 146
New World Brewing Systems Inc., 17, 231
New Zealand Hop Marketing Board, 276
Niagra Falls Brewing Company, 195
Nielsen's Equipment & Design Inc., 252
Nightwing Enterprises Inc., 252
Nigrelli Systems Inc., 232
1996 Brewers' Market Guide, 358
'93 Beer Log Update (Robertson), 348
'94 Beer Log Update (Robertson), 347
Nobra, 339
Noel/Greaves Inc., 257
Non-alcoholic malt beverages, guidelines for, 382
Norman Brewing Company, 168
Norman R. Soine—Consulting Brewing Chemist, 258
Northampton Brewery/Brewster Court Bar & Grill, 34, 156
North Central, openings/closings in, 29 (table)
North Coast Brewing Company, 21, 136
North Country Smokehouse, 264
Northeast, openings/closings in, 35 (table)
Northern Breweries Ltd.: Sault Ste. Marie, 195; Sudbury, 195; Thunder Bay, 195
Northern Lights Brewing Company, 182
Northern Lights Brewing Company/Shannon's Cafe, 129
North Rock Brewing, 215
Northwest, openings/closings in, 17 (table)
Northwest Beer Journal, The, 363
Northwestern Extract Company, 283
Northwest Territories Liquor Commission, 317
Nor'Wester Brewery and Public House, 12-13, 170
  IPO by, 8, 13
Norwich Inn/Jasper Murdocks Ale House, 179
No Tomatoes Restaurant/Great Falls Brewing Company, 153
Nova Scotia Liquor Commission, 318
Nutfield Brewing Company, 161
Nuttings Lake Publishing, 245

O

Oaken Barrel Brewing Company, 150
Oak Creek Brewing Company, 130
Oak Hills Brewpub/McMenamins, 170
Oasis Brewery and Restaurant, 23, 25, 142
Oasis Brewery Annex, 23, 25, 142

Oatmeal Stout, guidelines for, 373
Ocean Avenue Brewing Company, 136
Odell Brewing Company, 23, 142
Oertel Brewing Company, 205
Office of Audit and Examination, Department of Revenue (Tennessee), 309
Office of State Treasurer (North Dakota), 306
O'Herin Enterprises, 264
O'Hooleys Pub and Brewery, 167
Okanagan Spring Brewery Ltd., 44, 46-47, 191
Oktoberfest, 10; guidelines for, 379
Oktoberfest, Vienna, Märzen (Fix and Fix), 354
Oland Breweries Ltd., 192
Old Baldy Brewing Company, 136
Old Broadway, 166
Old Chicago Brewery & Pub, 24, 170
Old City Brewing Company, 36, 208
Old Colorado Brewing Company/Casa de Colorado, 142
Old Columbia Brewery, 19, 136
Old Credit Brewing Company, 195
Old Dominion Brewing Company, 33, 180
Olde Heurich Brewing Company, 203
Olde Hickory Brewing Company, 165
Oldenberg Brewing Company, 152
Olde Salem Brewery, 156
Olde Stone Brewing Company, 45, 195
Old Florida Brewing Corp., 204
Old Hampton Brewers Ltd., 164
Old Harbor Brewing Company/The Pilgrim Brewery, 34, 156
Old Market Pub & Brewery, 170
Old Marlborough Brewing Company, 206
Old North State Brewing Company, 165
Old Peconic Brewing Company Ltd., 207
Old Peninsula Brewpub, 157
Old Raleigh Brewing Company, 165
Old River Brew Company, 136
Old Towne Tavern & Brewery, 34, 154
Old West Brewery, 162
Old West Brewery (No. 2), 177
Old World Brewing Company, 34, 207
Oliver Breweries/Wharf Rat Camden Yards, 11, 154
Oliver, Garret, 33
Omniart, 265
Onalaska Brewing Company, 182
One-Keg Brewhouse, 26, 142
Only the Best Brewing Company Inc., 26, 142
On Premise Magazine, 359
On Tap: A Field Guide to North American Brewpubs and Craft Breweries (Johnson), 354
On Tap: The Guide to Brewpubs—U.S. East of the Mississippi and Canada (Johnson), 354
On Tap: The Guide to Brewpubs—U.S. West of the Mississippi (Johnson), 354

Index

Ontario, openings/closings in, 45 (table)
Orbisphere Laboratories, 232
Orchard Street Brewing Company, 182
Oregon Ale and Beer Company, 12, 207
Oregon Brewers Festival, 27
Oregon Brewers Guild, 12, 339
Oregon Brewing Company/Rogue Ales, 11, 13, 171
Oregon Fields Brewing Company, 170
Oregon Fruit Products, 283
Oregon Liquor Control Commission, 307
Oregon Trader Brewing Company, 170
Oregon Trail Brewery, 170
Original Saratoga Springs Brewpub, 164
O'Ryan's Tavern & Brewery/Oregon Mountain Brewing Company, 162
Osprey Ale Brewing Company, 170
Otter Creek Brewing Company Inc., 34, 179
Otto Brothers' Brewing Company, 186
Oud Bruin Ale, guidelines for, 376
Ould Newbury Brewing Company, 156
Ouray Brewing Company, 142
Outterson Brewing Services Inc., 232, 258, 283
Overland Park Brewing Company, 151
Overland Stage Stop Brewery, 142
Owen O'Learys Restaurant, 156
Owens Brewing Company, 21, 202
Owens-Brockway, 245
Oxford Brewing Company, 11, 34, 180, 205
Ozark Brewing Company, 37, 130

P

Paar Scientific (Export) Ltd., 232
Pabst Brewing Company, 40, 182, 185
Pacific, openings/closings in, 21 (table)
Pacific Brewing Company, 136
Pacific Coast Brewing Company, 136, 170
Pacific Coast Container, 245
Pacific Hop Exchange, 136
Pacific Northwest, openings/closings in, 17 (table)
Pacific Northwest Brewing Company, 182
Pacific Rim Consulting Group, 258
Pacific Western Brewing Company, 191
Packaged sales, 85 (figure)
Paddy's Pub and Brewery, 192
Padre Island Brewing Company, 177
Page, Ron, 34, 36
Paguag GmbH & Company, Hose Division, 232
Pale Ale (Foster), 354
Pall Corp., 232
Pall Ultrafine Filtration Company, 232
Palmer Lake Brewing Company, 142
Palmetto Brewing Company, 174
Panther City Brewery & Cafe, 177
Papazian, Charlie, 36
Paper City Brewing Company, 156

Parker Hannifin Corp., Process Filtration Division, 232
Park Slope Brewing Company, 164
Parlor City Brewing Company, 164
Parrots Ferry Brewing Company, 136
Party Pig/Quoin, 245
Paul Mueller Company, 232
Pauls Malt Ltd., 272
Paul Zaft Copper Works, 232
Pavichevich Brewing Company, 149
Peak to Peak Brewing Company, 142
Pearl Brewing Company/Pabst Brewing Company, 177
Pelican Brewing Company/Sazerac Company, 11, 205
Pend Oreille Brewing Company, 148
Pennsylvania Brewing Company, 33, 208
Pennsylvania Liquor Control Board, 308
Pepe and Joes, 24, 212
Pepperwood Bistro, 195
PepperWorks, 284
Perlick Corp., 232, 252
Pete's Brewing Company, 8, 9, 11, 15, 18, 40, 202
Pete's Place, 168
Peter Austin Projects, 32, 33, 43
Phantom Canyon Brewing Company, 26, 142
Philadelphia Brewing Company/Samuel Adams Brewhouse, 172
Philadelphia's, 171
Philip Morris, 9
Phoenix Brewing Company, 147
Phoenixx Ltd., 265
Photo Marketing Products Company, 265
Picaroons Brewing Company, 43, 192
Pico-Brewing Systems Inc., 233
Pierre Rajotte, 233
Pike Brewing Company/Merchant du Vin, 11, 15, 182, 209
Pikes Peak Brewery Inc., 142
Pin Center, 265
Pinch Penny Pub Inc., 149
Pinehurst Village Brewery, 165
Pine Street Brewing Company, 203
Pint Post, The, 360
Pittsburgh Brewing Company, 172
Pizza Port Solana Beach Brewery, 136
Platte Bottom Brewery, 142
Pleasanton Main Street Brewing Company, 136
Pneumatic Scale, 245
Polar Ware Company, 233
Pony Express Brewing Company, 30, 151
Ponzi, Nancy: on BridgePort, 8
Popular Head Mule Company Brewpub and Grill, 129
Port Arthur Brasserie and Brewpub, 45, 195
Port City Brewery, 37, 129
Porter (Foster), 354
Port Jackson Mfg., 233

Portland Brewing Company, 12, 171
Portland Brewing Company (No. 2), 171
Portsmouth Brewery, 161
Post-Production Bistro/O'Toole's, 195
Potomac River Brewing Company, 34, 180
Potts, Blair, 36
Power Flame Inc., 233
Powerhouse Brewing Company, 136
Power House Restaurant and Brewery, 182
Powers Brewing Company/Powers Colorado Brew, 142
PQ Corp., 283
Practical Brewer, The (Broderick), 355
Prairie Inn, 47
Prairie Rock Brewing Company, 149
Premier Malt Products Inc., 272
Prescott Brewing Company, 130
Preservation Ale, 202
Price-Schonstrom Inc., 233
Prime Time Printing, 284
Prince Edward Island Liquor Control
    Commission, 319
Principles of Brewing Science (Fix), 355
Private Brewer's Guide, The (ZymoScribe), 355
Production: adjusted, 90 (figure); draught sales, 85
    (figure); seasonal index of, 84 (figure)
Profamo Analytical Services Inc., 233
Profit and loss statement, comparative, 91 (figure)
PROGINOX Inc., 233, 258
Prolong Systems Inc., 233, 253
Prosser/Enpo (Sellers), 233
Pub Brewing Company, 39
Pugsley, Alan: on Shipyard, 32-33
Pugsley's Brewing Projects International/Shipyard
    Brewing, 33, 233, 258
Pumphouse Brewery, 142
Pure Colorado Inc. *See* Beverage International
Pyramid Alehouse and Brewery at Berkeley, 136

Q

Quality Assured Brewing, 144
*Quality Brewing, Share the Experience: Brewery
    Operations, Volume 9* (Thomas), 355
Quebec, openings/closings in, 43 (table)
Queen City Bakery and Brewery, 165
Quinn's on the Danforth, 45
Quinte Brewery, 195

R

Raccoon River Brewing Company, 24
Ragtime Taproom, 37, 146
Railhouse Restaurant and Brewery/R. Ales Inc., 185
Railway Brewing Company, 129
Rainbow Bridge Brewing Company, 204
Rainier Brewing Company Inc., 182
R. A. Jones & Company Inc., 246

RAM Border Cafe, 17
RAM International/Big Horn Brewing Company, 10,
    16-17, 17-18
Randy's Restaurant/Fun Hunter's Brewery, 185
Rapids Wholesale Equipment Company, 234, 253
Rascher & Betzold Inc., 284
RASTAL GmbH & Company KG, 265
Rattlesnake Creek Brewery, 166
Raven Ridge Brewing Company, 129
Read Systems, Inc., 234
Red Ass Brewing Company, 203
Red Bank Brewery Company, 161
Red Bell Brewing Company, 173
Redhook Ale Brewery, 8, 12, 17, 182
Redhook Ale Brewery (No. 2), 183
Redondo Beach Brewing Company, 136
Red Rock Brewing Company, 26, 178
Red White and Brew, 136
Redwood Coast Brewing Company/Tied House Cafe
    and Brewery (No. 1), 21, 137
Reedy River Brewing Company, 174
Refrigeration Service 6, 234, 253
Regal Eagle Brewing Company/North Slope Brewing
    Company, 129
Regional breweries: Canada, estimated total taxable
    shipments by, 76 (table); defined, 49; U.S., esti-
    mated total taxable shipments by, 56 (table)
Regional specialty breweries: Canada, 53 (figure);
    defined, 49; U.S., 51 (figure)
Registration Tax Division/Oklahoma Tax
    Commission, 307
Remcor Products Company, 234
Remington Watson Smith Brewing Company Inc., 185
Reno Brewing Company, 23, 206
Republic Brewery, 186
Richbrau Brewing Company, 180
Richen, John, 16
Rikenjaks Brewery, 152
Ringneck Brewing Company/The Brew Kettle
    Inc., 167
Rio Bravo Restaurant & Brewery, 162
Rio Grande Brewing Company Inc., 162
Ripley Stainless, 47
River City Brewing Company, 137, 146, 151
River Market Brewing Company, 158
Riverosa Company, 207
Riverside Brewing Company, 21, 137
Rixie Paper Products, 265
R. J.'s Ginseng, 204
R. J.'s Riptide Brewery, 136
RLS Equipment Company Inc., 234
R. M. Yates Company Inc., 265
Robert J. Ryan Inc., 258
Robinson Brewing Company, 195
Robust Porter, guidelines for, 373

Index

Rock'n M Brewing Company, 159
Rock Bottom Brewery, 11, 15, 24, 142
Rock Bottom Brewery (No. 2), 158
Rock Bottom Brewery (No. 3), 37, 177
Rock Bottom Brewery (No. 4), 171
Rock Bottom Brewery (No. 5), 37, 177
Rock Bottom Brewery (No. 6), 151
Rock Bottom Brewery (No. 7), 149
Rock Bottom Brewery (No. 8), 167
Rock Bottom Restaurants Inc., 8, 10, 18, 24-25
Rock Creek Brewing Company, 208
Rockford Brewing Company, 35, 144
Rockies Brewing Company/Pub at Rockies, 22, 142
Rockslide Brewpub/Snowy Mountain Brewpub, 142
Rocky Mountain Brews, 363
Rogue Ales/Oregon Brewing Company, 11, 13, 171
Rogue River Brewing Company. *See* Siskyou Brewing Company
Rohrbach Brewing Company, 36, 164
Rohrbach Brewing Company (No. 2), 164
Roller Coat Products, 284
Roosters 25th Street Brewing Company, 178
R-P Products, 234
Roskamp Champion, 234
Roslyn Brewing Company, 183
Rotterdam Brewing Company, 195
Rounders Restaurant, 10
Routh Street Brewery, 177
Rowland's Calumet Brewery, 185
Royal Bavaria Brewhaus and Restaurant, 168
Rubicon Brewing Company, 137
Ruby Mountain Brewing Company Inc., 160
Russell Brewing Company, 47, 162, 191

S

SABCO Industries/Sav-a-Barrel Corp., 228, 234
Sacramento Brewing Company, 137
Sagba, 215
Sailor Hagar's Brewpub, 191
St. Andrew's Brewing Company, 177
St. Arnold Brewing Company, 11, 36, 177
St. Croix Beer Company, 206
St. Kitts Breweries Ltd., 216
St. Louis Brewery/The Taproom, 30, 159
St. Maarten Breweries, 216
St. Stan's Brewery Pub and Restaurant, 19, 138
Salado Creek Brewing Company, 208
Salt Lake Brewing Company Corporate Office, 178
Salt Lake Brewing Company/Fuggles, 178
Salt Lake Brewing Company/Squatters Pub, 178
Salvadore Machinery Corp., 234, 246, 258
Samuel Adams, 30-31, 40
San Andreas Brewing Company, 137, 202
San Diego Brewing Company, 137

SandLot Brewery at Coors Field/Coors Brewing Company, 10, 143
S&P Corporation, microbrews by, 10
San Francisco Brewing Company, 137
San Juan Brewing Company, 143, 203
San Marcos Brewery and Grill, 137
Santa Barbara Brewing Company, 137
Santa Clarita Brewing Company, 137
Santa Cruz Brewing Company/Front Street Pub, 137
Santa Fe Brewing Company, 162
Santa Monica Brewing Company, 137
Santa Rosa Bay Brewing Company, 146
Santa Rosa Brewing Company, 137
Santa Rosa Stainless Steel, 234
Saranac beers, 9, 33
Sarasota Brewing Company, 146
Sasib Beverage & Food North America Inc., 234
Saskatchewan Liquor and Gaming Authority, 319
Saskatoon Brewing Company/Cheers Roadhouse Inn, 47-48, 198
Savannah Brewing Company, 24
Saw Mill River Brewing Company, 164
Saxer Brewing, 171
Sazerac spirits company, 11
Schafer Container Systems, 234
Schenk Filter Systems Inc., 236
Schirf Brewing Company/Wasatch Brewery, 23
Schirf Brewing Company/Wasatch Brewing Company (No. 2), 23, 178
Schirf Brewing Company/Wasatch Brewpub, 178
Schlueter Mfg., 236
Schreier Malting Company, 272
Schumacher & Associates, 258
Schwarzen, John: on Hops Grill and Bar, 37, 39
Scotch Ale (Noonan), 355
Scottish Export Ale, guidelines for, 371
Scottish Heavy Ale, guidelines for, 371
Scottish Light Ale, guidelines for, 371
Scottish-Style Ales, guidelines for, 371
Scott Laboratories Inc., 236, 279
Scott Laboratories Ltd., 236, 279
Seabright Brewery Inc., 137
Sea Dog Brewing Company, 153
Sea Dog Brewing Company (No. 2), 153
Seagram Company Ltd., 366
Seagrams Beverage Company, 11, 204
Sea Moss Inc., 284
Seaport Pub & Brewery, 137
Seattle Brewers, 183
Secret Life of Beer (Eames), 355
Service Training Systems, 265
Seven Barrel Brewery, 161
75th Street Brewery, 158
Shaftebury Brewing Company Ltd., 42, 46, 191
Shanley Pump, 236

Shannon Kelly's Brewpub, 158
Shannon Pub, 164
Sharkey's Brew Club, 26, 143
Shark Tooth Brewery and Steakhouse, 148
Shea's Brewery, 164
Shed Restaurant and Brewery, 179
Sheepscot Valley Brewing Company, 36, 153
Sherlock's Home, 11, 158
Shields Brewing Company, 138
Ship Inn Inc., 161
Shipyard Brewing Company, 8, 11, 32-33, 34, 153
Siebel Institute of Technology, 258, 279, 344, 365
Sierra Nevada Brewing Company, 18, 40, 138
Signature Beer Company, 30, 206
Silbrico Corp., 284
Siletz Brewing Company, 171
Silk's Grill and Brewing Company, 177
Silver Plume Brewing Company, 143
Sioux Falls Brewing, 174
Siskyou Brewing Company, 18, 171
Sisson's/South Baltimore Brewing Company, 154
SKA Brewing Company, 143
Skagit River Brewing Company, 183
Sleeman Brewing & Malting Company Ltd., 44, 47, 195
SLO Brewing Company, Inc., 138
Slopeside Brewing Company, 204
Sly Fox Brewhouse & Eatery, 173
Small Independent Brewers Association, 341
SMB Technik, 34, 236, 246
Smiling Moose Inc., 143
Smith & Reilly, 209
Smoke-flavored beers, guidelines for, 382
Smokey Mountain Brewery, 165
Smoky Mountain Brewing Company, 37
Smuttynose Brewing Company, 34, 161
Snake River Brewing Company/Jackson Hole Pub and Brewery, 23, 186
Snapple Beverages, 9
Snow Dog Brewing Corp., 203
Snowshoe Brewing Company, 138
Societe Anonyme des Brasseries de Cote-d'Ivoire, 339
Societe des Alcools du Quebec, 319
Societe Malienne de Boissons, 339
Societe Nationale de Brasseurs, 339
Sommer, Mark, 26
Sonoco Engraph Label Group, 237, 246, 253, 259, 265, 272, 277, 279, 284, 339, 344, 365
Sonoma Brewing Company, 138
Sonora Brewing Company, 130
Sound Brewing Systems Inc., 237, 259
South, openings/closings in, 38 (table)
South Carolina Department of Revenue, 308
Southeastern Brewing Company, 174
Southend Brewery and Smokehouse, 37, 166

Southern California Brewing Company, 138
Southern Draft Brew News, 363
Southern Wine and Spirits, 21
South German-Style Dunkel Weizen/Dunkel Weissbier, guidelines for, 375
South German-Style Weizen/Weissbier, guidelines for, 375
South German-Style Weizenbock/Weissbock, guidelines for, 375
South Pointe Seafood House and Brewing Company, 146
South Shore Brewery, 185
Southwest Brewing News, 364
Spanish Peaks Brewing Company, 22, 159, 206
Spartanburg Steel Products Inc., 237, 246
Spear Inc., 246
Specialist Joinery Fittings, 253
Specialty beers, guidelines for, 382
Specialty Products International Ltd., 272
Specific Mechanical Systems Ltd., 24, 47, 237
Spencer's Restaurant and Brewhouse, 171
Spice beers, guidelines for, 382
Spider Roll Brewing LLC, 259
Spinnakers Brewpub Inc., 191
Spirits companies, beer by, 11
Spoetzl Brewery Inc., 8, 177
Sprecher Brewing Company, 30, 185
Spring Garden Brewing Company, 166
Spring Street Brewing Company, 207
S. S. Steiner Inc., 276
StabiFix Brauerer—Technik GmbH, 237, 279
Stainless Steel Containment Systems Inc., 237, 246
Stainless Steel Specialists Inc., 43, 237
Standard Box Corp., 246
Standard Paper Box Corp., 246
Star Brewing Company, 15, 171
Starbucks coffee, 12
Star Garnet Brewing, 148
Stark Mill Brewery and Restaurant, 34, 161
Star Spangled Beer (RedBrick), 355
Star Union Brewery Company, 150
Starview Brewing Company, 208
State Liquor Authority/Division of Alcoholic Beverage Control (New York), 305
State Liquor Commission (New Hampshire), 303
State of Utah Alcoholic Beverage Control, 311
State Street Brewing, 204
State Tax Commission (Mississippi), 300
Station Casinos Inc., 20
Steamboat Brewery and Tavern, 143
Steamship Brewing Company, 34, 180
Steam Works Brewing Company, 47, 191
Steelhead Brewery & Cafe, 171
Steelhead Brewing Company, 15, 22, 138
Steensen U.S.A. Inc., 237

Steinecker brewhouse, 22
Stevens Point Brewing Company, 29, 185
Stewart's Brewing Company, 144
Stimson Lane Vineyards, 8
Stingray Brewery Ltd., 215
Stoddard's Brewhouse & Eatery, 22, 138
Stone Coast Brewing Company, 153
Stone Mountain Brewers, 204
Stonhard Inc., 237
Stord Inc., 237
Storm Brewing Company Ltd., 47, 191
Stoudt Brewery, 33, 173, 208
Stout (Lewis), 356
Stout Marketing, 265
Strahman Valves Inc., 238
Strand Brewing Company, 177
Straub Brewery, 173
Strauss, Karl, 19
Stroh Brewery Company, 11, 18, 177; Heileman and, 40; microbrews by, 10; North Carolina, 166; Pennsylvania, 173; Pete's and, 9
Stroh Brewery Company Corporate Headquarters, 157
Stroh Brewery Company St. Paul Plant/Northern Plains Brewing Company, 158
Stroh Brewery Company Tampa Plant, 146
Strong Scotch Ale, guidelines for, 372
Stutrud, Mark: on Summit Brewing, 27-28
Style guidelines, 367-382
Suds 'N' Stuff, 360
Sudwerk Privatbraueri Hubsch, 21, 138
Sugarloaf Brewing Company, 153
Summit Brewing Company, 26, 27-28, 158
Summit Commercial, 253
Summit Products Inc., 259
Sunday River Brewing Company, 153, 205
Sun International Trading Ltd., 265
Sunrise Milling, 272
Sun Valley Brewing Company, 23, 148
Superb Gas Products Company, 238
Sussman Electric Boilers, 238
Sutter Brewing Company Inc., 138
Svenska Olframjandet, 341
Swancock Designworks, 265
Swans Brewpub/Buckerfield Brewery, 47, 191
Sweet Stout, guidelines for, 373
Swiss Brewers Association, 341
Syracuse Suds Factory, 164

T

Tabernash Brewing Company, 23, 143
Table Rock Brewing Inc., 23, 148
Table Rock Brewpub and Grill, 148
Tall Ship Ale Company, 191
Tapps Brewing Company, 183
Tapsters Brewhouse and Restaurant, 196
Taste for Beer, A (Beaumont), 356
Taylor Brewing Company, 150
T-Bonz Gill & Grill, 174
Team Industries Inc., 238
Telluride Beer Company, 203
Tel-Tru Manufacturing Company, 238
Ten-Penny, 26, 27
Terrific Pacific Brewery and Grill, 138
Terriss Consolidated Industries, 238
Texas Alcoholic Beverage Commission, 310
Textbook of Brewing, A (DeClerck), 356
Thai Orchid Restaurant, 39, 146
Thai Orchid Restaurant/Thai Orchid U.S.A. Inc., 146
Thames Valley Brewing Company, 196
Thielmann Container Systems, 246
Third Street Ale Works, 138
Thompson, Howard: on Creemore Springs, 44
Thompson Brewpub/McMenamins, 171
Thunder Bay Brewing Company Inc., 161, 253
Thunder Mountain Brewery, 148
Tied House Cafe and Brewery (No. 1), 21, 137
Tied House Cafe and Brewery (No. 2), 22, 138
Tied House Cafe and Brewery (No. 3), 138
Tin Whistle Brewing Company, 47, 191
Titletown Brewing Company, 24
Tivoli Brewery/(america!), 26, 143
Tobler, Stefan: on Okanagan Spring, 46-47
Toby Jug Bop System, 238
Tod, Rob, 36
Tombstone Brewing Company, 130
Tomcat Brewing Company, 166
Tommyknocker Brewery & Pub, 23, 143
Topeka City Brewing Company, 151
Tordon, Shawn: on La Cervoise, 43-44
Tortuga's, 146
Tosca Limited, 238
Total Brewing International Ltd., 238
T. Pauls Beer Company, 207
Tracks Brewpub, 196
Trader & Trapper, 158
Trade Winds Brewing Company, 148
Traditional Bock, guidelines for, 379
Traditional English-Style Bitter, guidelines for, 370
Trafalgar Brewing Company, 196
Traffic Jam and Snug, 157
Trailhead Brewing Company, 159
Traverse Brewing Company Ltd., 157
Treasure Coast Brewing Company, 146
Treaty Grounds Brew Pub, 148
Tree Brewing Company Ltd., 47, 191
Trinity Beer Works Inc., 173
Triple Rock Brewing, 138
Triumph Brewing Company/Disch Brewing Company, 34, 161

Tropical Brewery, 215
Tropical-Style Light Lager, guidelines for, 381
Troy Brewing Company, 34, 164
Truckee Brewing Company, 139
Tsingtao Brewery, 46
Tuchenhagen North America Inc., 238
Tugboat Brewpub & Cafe, 171
Tulsa Brewing Company, 37, 39, 168
Tun Tavern/Tun Tavern Brewing Company Inc., 34, 208
Tuppers Hop Pocket Ale, 205
Turner, Van: on Kingston, 45-46
Tuscan Brewery, 139
Twenty Tank Brewery, 139
Twin Falls Brewing Company/Muggers Brewpub, 148
Twinpak Inc., 246
Twisted Pine Brewing Company, 143
Two Angels Beer Company, 203
TwoRows Restaurant and Brewery, 39, 177
Tye Dye Brewing Company, 208
Tynan, Anastasy, 20

U
U-Brew Inc., 259
UCB, 339
Ugly Dog Brewery Inc., 173
Uhlig Brewing Company, 139
Uinta Brewing Company, 23, 178
Umpqua Brewing Company, 171
Unibroue Inc., 42, 197
Union Brewery Company, 160
Union Camp Corporation, 247
Union Colony Brewery, 143
Union Station Brewing/The Brew House LLC, 173
Unipath Company, Oxiod Division, 238
United Canadian Malt Ltd., 272
U.S. Border Brewery Cantina, 36, 147
U.S. Tobacco, 8
Upper Canada Brewing Company, 44, 196
Upstream Brewing Company, 24
UST Inc., 8, 15

V
VAFAC Inc. (Virginia Food and Craft), 238, 259, 273
Val Blatz Brewery. *See* G. Heileman Brewing Company
Valley Forge Brewing Company Restaurant and Pub, 173
Valley of the Moon Brewery, 139
Valu-Wear, 265
Vancouver Island Brewing Company, 47, 192
Vegetable beers, guidelines for, 382
Velo and Seitz, 20
Vendome Copper & Brass Works Inc., 238
Vera Foods, 259

Verband Schweiz Brauerien, 341
Vermont Department of Liquor Control, 311
Vermont Pub and Brewery, 179
Vernon Valley Brewery, 35
Victory Beer Recipes (American Homebrewers Association), 356
Victory Brewing Company, 173
Videojet Systems International Inc., 247
Vienna-Style Lager, guidelines for, 378
Vieux Copenhagen Brasseurs, 43, 197
Villa, Keith, 203
Village Brewery, 37, 177
Vino's, 130
Vinotheque, 238
Vintage F/X, 265
Virginia Beverage Company, 180
Virginia Department of Alcoholic Beverage Control, 312
Vista Brewing Company, 174
Vitro Packaging Inc., 247
Volckening Inc., 247
Volunteer Beer Inc., 208

W
Wachsmann Brautechnik brewhouses, 20
Wachusett Brewing Company, 34, 156
Walker & Lee Advertising/Design, 265
Wallaby's Grill & Brewpub, 167
Walnut Brewery, 11, 24, 143
Wanker Beer Inc., 202
Washington State Liquor Control Board, 312
Watch City Brewing Company Inc., 156
Waterloo Brewing Company, 178
Water Street Brewery, 185
Waukesha Fluid Handling, 239
Waymatic, 284
Weeping Radish Brewery (No. 2), 36, 166
Weeping Radish Restaurant and Brewery, 166
Weidman's Old Fort Brewery, 130
Weinkeller Brewery, 150
Weinkeller Brewpub (No. 2), 150
Wellington County Brewery Ltd., 196
West: Canada, openings/closings in, 47 (table); U.S., openings/closings in, 25 (table)
Westchester Brewing Company, 164
Western Reserve Brewing Company, 167
Westport Brewing Company, 159
West Seattle Brewing Company, 183
Westside Brewing Company, 164
West Virginia Brewing Company, 34, 183
Westwood Brewing Company, 139
Weyerbacher Brewing Company Inc., 173
Weyermann, Heinz GmbH, 273, 284
Wharf Rat Camden Yards/Oliver Breweries Ltd., 11, 154

Index

Whatcom Brewery, 183
What's Brewing, 360
Whidbey Island Brewing Company, 183
Whistler Brewing Company, 192
Whitefish Brewing Company, 159
Whitetail Brewing Company, 173
Widmer Brothers Brewing Company, 9, 12
Widmer Brothers Brewing Company/Widmer Brothers Gasthaus, 171
Widmer Brothers Brewing Company B. Moloch/Heathman Pub, 171
Wigan Richardson International Ltd., 277
Wild Bill's Brewing Company, 174, 208
Wild Boar Brewing Company/Georgia Brewing, 204
Wild Duck Brewery and Restaurant, 171
Wild Goose Brewery, 11, 33, 154
Wild River Brewing and Pizza Company, 15, 172
Wild River Brewing and Pizza Company (No. 2), 172
Wild Wild West Brewery and Gambling Hall, 26
Willamette Brewpub, 18
Willamette Valley Brewing Company. *See* Nor'Wester Brewery and Public House
William & Scott Brewing Company/Rhino Chasers, 19, 202
Williamsville Brewery, 146, 180
Wilmington Brewing Company Inc., 166
Wilson Brewing Systems Ltd., 239
Wiltse's Brew Pub and Family Restaurant, 157
Windrose Brew Pub, 147
Wine, per capita consumption of, 89 (figure)
Wine Bottle & Packaging Inc., 247
Wineries, beer by, 11
Winners Circle (Loysen, Papazian, Raizman), 356
Winstanley Associates, 266
Winter People, 266
Winthrop Brewing Company, 183
Wisconsin Brewing Company, 185
Withdrawals: adjusted, 90 (figure); malt beverage, 85 (figure); seasonal index of, 84 (figure)
Wittemann Company Inc., 239
WMS Inc., 259
W. M. Sprinkman Corp., 239
Wolf Canyon Brewing Company, 162
Wooden Pony Brewing Company, 168
Woodstock Brewing Company, 161, 164

Wordenglass & Electricity Inc., 266
World Division U.S.A., 266
Worshipful Company of Brewers, 342
Wright Metal Signs Ltd., 266
W. W. Reichert, Bavarian Brewhouse Inc., 239, 253
Wyeast Laboratories, 259, 279
Wynkoop Brewing Company, 10, 11, 23-24, 143
Wyoming Liquor Commission, 314

Y

Yakima Brewing and Malting Company/Grant's Ales, 8, 11
Yale Town Brewing Company, 192
Yamhill Brewing Company LLC, 207
Yankee Brew News, 364
Yards Brewing Company, 11, 173
Ybor City Brewing Company, 36, 147
Yeast Culture Kit Company, 279
Yeast Technology (Reed and Nagodawithana), 356
Yegua Creek Brewing Company, 178
Yellow Rose Brewing Company, 178
Yorkville Brewery & Tavern, 164
Young's Brewing Company/Northwest Sausage and Deli, 183
YSI Inc., 239
Yukon Liquor Corp., 320

Z

Zahm and Nagel Company Inc., 239
Zip City Brewing Company, 165
Zumbiel Packaging, 247
Zymurgy, 360
Zymurgy: All-Grain Special Issue, 360
Zymurgy: Hops and Beer Special Issue, 361
Zymurgy: Special Ingredients and Indigenous Beer, 361
Zymurgy: The Brewing Process: Gadgets and Equipment Special Issue, 361
Zymurgy: The Great Grain Issue, 361
Zymurgy: Traditional Beer Styles Special Issue, 361
Zymurgy: Troubleshooting Special Issue, 360
Zymurgy: Why We Brew, 362
Zymurgy: Yeast Special Issue, 360

Advertising Index

Bohemian Breweries	221
Brauhaus Systems Caspary	Color Insert Page 1
Brewers Publications	Color Insert Page 4
Briess Malting Company	269
California Brands Flavors Inc.	280
California Glass Company	Packaging Tab (Front)
Canada Malting Company Ltd.	270
Cask Brewing Systems	222
Century Manufacturing	223
Century Manufacturing Inc. (Tap Handles)	249
Consolidated Beverage/Beeston Malting Company	268
Consolidated Beverage/Coopers	271
Crosby & Baker	281
DME Brewing Services	Color Insert Page 2
Dock Street Brewing Company	10a
Falco Stainless Steel Equipment Ltd.	226
Five Star Products and Services LLC	282
GEA Ecoflex	242
HopUnion	275
Institute for Brewing Studies	10b
JV Northwest Inc.	Brewing Equipment Tab
MVE Inc.	252
New Brewer, The	Packaging Tab (Back)
New World Brewing Systems Inc.	231
Newlands Services Inc.	Inside Back Cover
Outterson Brewing Services Inc.	257
Palmer Promotional Products	Marketing Tab
Premier Malt Products Inc.	272
Pub Brewing Company	Inside Front Cover
Santa Rossa Stainless Steel	235
Schenk Filter Systems	236
SMB Technik Inc.	245
Specific Mechanical Systems Ltd.	Color Insert Page 3
S. S. Steiner Inc.	276
Vera Foods S.A.	258
World Crisa	261

Statistics No Brewery Should Be Without

Industry Revealed offers breweries a competitive edge by presenting the trends, averages and statistics of the industry as a whole. This comprehensive compilation presents figures on topics such as:

- Annual gross revenues, cost of goods per barrel, total start-up costs and other financials

- Six-pack, 22-ounce bottle, pint and half-barrel prices for different *regions* and *sizes* of microbreweries and brewpubs

- Brewpub and brewery/restaurant per customer check totals

- Total number of employees, hours worked and salaries

- Lists of most commonly brewed beer styles

- And much more!

Never-before released statistics compiled from the Institute for Brewing Studies' annual comprehensive Brewery Survey are available now.

Industry Revealed is a 50-page report priced at $48 for non-members and $36 for IBS members.

The Beer Brand Index — just a click away!

The Beer Brand Index — a comprehensive listing of North American breweries, brands, styles and alcohol content — is coming to you on diskette. Once a section in the *North American Brewers Resource Directory*, the ***Beer Brand Index*** is now formatted in a tab-delineated file to make it easier for you to scan companies, search for beer styles and identify brands using your database or word processor.

The ***Beer Brand Index*** (3 ½-inch diskette) is available for $40 ($20 for IBS members) in either PC or Macintosh format. Contact (303) 447-0816, FAX (303) 447-2825, orders@aob.org or http://www.aob.org/aob for more information.

BRDBBI

Brewers Publications presents ...

NEW Brewing Lager Beer

NEW and COMPLETELY REVISED

NEW Brewing Lager Beer
The Most Comprehensive Book for Home- and Microbrewers

by Gregory Noonan

Greg Noonan and Brewers Publications have revised and expanded one of the most popular and trusted technical books on brewing. *New Brewing Lager Beer* details the intricacies of world-class lagers and ales. With chapters detailing beer ingredients, decoction mashing and the most advanced brewing procedures, this is a book no brewer should be without. *New Brewing Lager Beer* delves into scientific brewing and lifts brewers to the next level of their craft.

Completely Revised and Expanded
GREGORY J. NOONAN

5½ x 8½ • 387 pages • four-color soft cover • illustrations • Brewers Publications • ISBN 0-937381-46-2 • $14.95

To place an order or request a free catalog contact Brewers Publications at PO Box 1510, Boulder, CO 80306-1510, U.S.A.; (303) 546-6514; orders@aob.org; or FAX (303) 447-2825. You can also access us at http://www.aob.org/aob on our World Wide Web site.

NBLB

Passionate about beer?

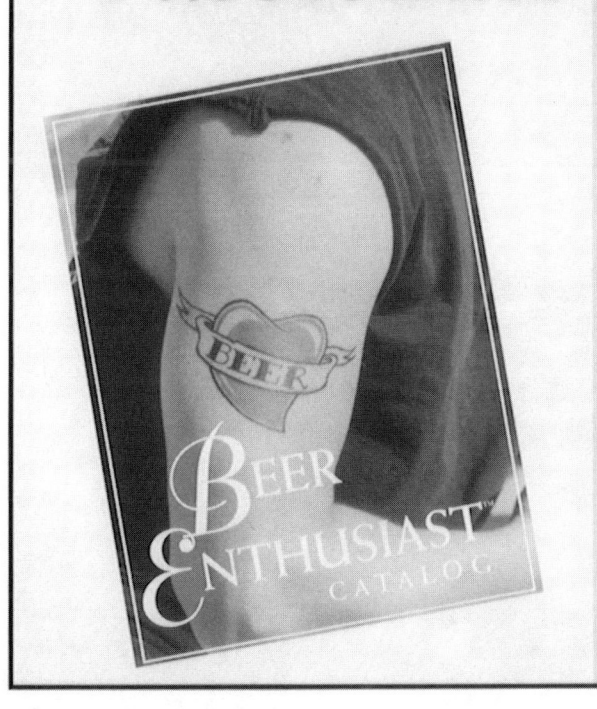

Then you need the #1 resource for every beer lover — the Beer Enthusiast™ catalog. Check out our comprehensive catalog full of books and beerphenalia sure to fuel the obsession of homebrewers, professional brewers and beer enthusiasts alike.

Call us at (303) 546-6514 to order your FREE catalog today!

Association of Brewers
PO Box 1510 • Boulder, CO 80306-1510, U.S.A. •
(303) 546-6514 • FAX (303) 447-2825.
http://www.aob.org/aob • orders@aob.org

BRD

Enjoy the Classics

Brewers Publications presents masterpieces for your brewing library — the *Classic Beer Style Series*. Each volume of the Series details the history, flavor profiles and recipes of the world's most popular beer styles. This timeless collection raises beer to a new level of sophistication.

For more information or a catalog of titles, contact Brewers Publications at (303) 447-0816, orders@aob.org or FAX (303) 447-2825.

"I read it in *The New Brewer.*"

Old Dominion Brewing Co., the Washington, D.C., area's first microbrewery, began brewing in early 1990 and makes a wide variety of ales and lagers and a popular root beer.

**Jerry Bailey, President,
Old Dominion Brewing Co.,
Ashburn, Va.**

> "I rely on *The New Brewer* to keep me up to date on what's happening in the brewing field — from learning about technical issues to tracking industry trends. One article even inspired us to make root beer! I always read each issue from cover to cover."

Industry leaders like Jerry Bailey know that only *The New Brewer* provides the inside information craft brewers from coast to coast depend on. Each issue is packed with vital statistics for business planning, the latest in brewing techniques, alternative technologies, beer recipes, legislative alerts, marketing and distribution ideas — everything you need to succeed in today's competitive market.

Whether you're an established brewery or just in the planning stages, our in-depth coverage will give you information you can put to work immediately. After all, your business is our business.

See for yourself. Subscribe to *The New Brewer* today!

Please complete the following information. We'll rush subscription information your way!

NAME _____
TITLE _____
COMPANY _____
ADDRESS _____
CITY _____
STATE/PROVINCE _____ ZIP/POSTAL CODE _____
COUNTRY _____ TELEPHONE _____

Please return this coupon to: Institute for Brewing Studies, PO Box 1510, Boulder, CO 80306-1510, U.S.A. For faster service contact: (303) 447-0816; FAX (303) 447-2825; orders@aob.org or http://www.aob.org/aob

NB BR

The New Brewer • YOUR INSIDER'S VIEW TO THE CRAFT-BREWING INDUSTRY

BOOKS for Brewers and Beer Lovers

Order Now ... Your Brew Will Thank You!

These books offered by Brewers Publications are some of the most sought after reference tools for homebrewers and professional brewers alike. Filled with tips, techniques, recipes and history, these books will help you expand your brewing horizons. Let the world's foremost brewers help you as you brew. Whatever your brewing level or interest, Brewers Publications has the information necessary for you to brew the best beer in the world — your beer.

Please send me more free information on the following:
(Check all that apply.)

- ☐ Book and Merchandise Catalog
- ☐ American Homebrewers Association®
- ☐ Institute for Brewing Studies
- ☐ Great American Beer Festival®

Ship to:

Name _____

Address _____

City _____ State/Province _____

Zip/Postal Code _____ Country _____

Daytime Phone (___) _____

Please use the following in conjunction with the order form when ordering books from Brewers Publications.

Payment Method

- ☐ Check or Money Order Enclosed *(Payable to Brewers Publications)*
- ☐ Visa
- ☐ MasterCard

Card Number _____ Expiration Date _____

Name on Card _____ Signature _____

Brewers Publications, PO Box 1510, Boulder, CO 80306-1510, USA • (303) 546-6514 • FAX (303) 447-2825 • orders@aob.org • http://www.aob.org/aob

BRD

BREWERS PUBLICATIONS ORDER FORM

PROFESSIONAL BREWING BOOKS

QTY.	TITLE	STOCK #	PRICE	EXT. PRICE
____	Brewery Planner	500	80.00	_____
____	96–97 North American Brewers Resource Directory	505	100.00	_____
____	Principles of Brewing Science	463	29.95	_____
____	Beer Brand Index (Specify PC or Mac)	520	40.00	_____

THE BREWERY OPERATIONS SERIES from Micro- and Pubbrewers Conferences

QTY.	TITLE	STOCK #	PRICE	EXT. PRICE
____	Volume 6, 1989 Conference	536	25.95	_____
____	Volume 7, 1990 Conference	537	25.95	_____
____	Volume 8, 1991 Conference, Brewing Under Adversity	538	25.95	_____
____	Volume 9, 1992 Conference, Quality Brewing — Share the Experience	539	25.95	_____

CLASSIC BEER STYLE SERIES

QTY.	TITLE	STOCK #	PRICE	EXT. PRICE
____	Pale Ale	401	11.95	_____
____	Continental Pilsener	402	11.95	_____
____	Lambic	403	11.95	_____
____	Oktoberfest, Vienna, Märzen	404	11.95	_____
____	Porter	405	11.95	_____
____	Belgian Ale	406	11.95	_____
____	German Wheat Beer	407	11.95	_____
____	Scotch Ale	408	11.95	_____
____	Bock	409	11.95	_____
____	Stout	410	11.95	_____

GENERAL BEER AND BREWING INFORMATION

QTY.	TITLE	STOCK #	PRICE	EXT. PRICE
____	New Brewing Lager Beer	469	14.95	_____
____	The Art of Cidermaking	468	9.95	_____
____	Brewing Mead	461	11.95	_____
____	Dictionary of Beer and Brewing	462	19.95	_____
____	Evaluating Beer	465	19.95	_____
____	Great American Beer Cookbook	466	24.95	_____
____	Victory Beer Recipes	464	11.95	_____
____	Winners Circle	467	11.95	_____

BEER AND BREWING SERIES, for homebrewers and beer enthusiasts, from National Homebrewers Conferences

QTY.	TITLE	STOCK #	PRICE	EXT. PRICE
____	Volume 8, 1988 Conference	448	21.95	_____
____	Volume 10, 1990 Conference	450	21.95	_____
____	Volume 11, 1991 Conference, Brew Free or Die!	451	21.95	_____
____	Volume 12, 1992 Conference, Just Brew It!	452	21.95	_____

Call or write for a free Beer Enthusiast catalog today.

- U.S. funds only
- All Brewers Publications books come with a money-back guarantee.

*Postage and handling: Please include in payment $4 for the first book ordered, plus $1 for each book thereafter. Canadian and international orders please add $5 for the first book and $2 for each book thereafter. Diskette's nonreturnable.
Orders cannot be shipped without appropriate postage and handling.

SUBTOTAL _____
Colo. Residents Add 3% Sales Tax _____
Postage and Handling * _____
TOTAL _____

Brewers Publications, PO Box 1510, Boulder, CO 80306-1510, USA • (303) 546-6514 • FAX (303) 447-2825 • orders@aob.org • http://www.aob.org/aob

BRD

JOIN THE INSTITUTE
The Power of Membership

Three excellent reasons why you should belong to the Institute for Brewing Studies:

1. Information
We research and publish information on all topics affecting brewers: alerts on legislative and tax issues, technical brewing data, new products and statistics, and operating information.

2. Fellowship
Our membership is more than 3,000 strong. These are 3,000 members in a community with common interests.

3. Membership Benefits
Benefits include a year's subscription to **The New Brewer**, substantial discounts for the National Craft-Brewers Conference and Trade Show, representation to associations and the media, Brewmaster for Hire, On-line Brewers Forum, Small Brewers Insurance, *Alcohol Issues Alert* quarterly updates (Brewery Member only), facts and figures on the industry, grass roots initiatives on issues and more.

Complete the membership application below and begin receiving all the benefits of membership in the Institute for Brewing Studies.

Membership to the Institute for Brewing Studies

Join the Institute and start receiving your benefits immediately. Just mark the appropriate membership category below and complete your address information. Thank you for your participation.

Corporate Membership

☐ Operating Brewer (includes all microbreweries, pubbreweries, regional breweries, large breweries and contract brewing companies). Estimate taxable production for current year and check appropriate category. Please remit in U.S. funds.

___ 1 to 15,000 bbl./yr. $195
___ 15,001 to 1 million bbl./yr. $325
___ 1 million plus bbl./yr. $1,400

☐ Allied Trade to the Brewing Industry (includes suppliers, associations, schools, consultants, etc.): $275

☐ Brew-on-Premise: $195

Individual Membership
(Includes breweries in planning.)

☐ $135

Subscription Only to *The New Brewer*

United States:
☐ $55 one-year   ☐ $99 two-year

Canada and International:
☐ $65 one-year   ☐ $119 two-year

Method of Payment:

☐ Check enclosed (must be in U.S. funds)

Charge to:
☐ Visa   ☐ MasterCard

Acct. No. _____

Exp. Date _____

• Make checks payable to: Institute for Brewing Studies. Prices effective through 12/31/97. Contact: (303) 447-0816, orders@aob.org or FAX (303) 447-2825 for credit card orders.

Important: Please indicate your industry affiliation.

☐ Operational brewery
☐ Brewery in planning
☐ Contract brewing company
☐ Distributor or importer
☐ Equipment manufacturer
☐ Industry consultant
☐ Ingredients supplier
☐ Association, government agency, school or library
☐ Publication editor or writer
☐ Other: _____

Please complete the following:

Name _____

Title _____

Company _____

Address _____ City _____

State/Province _____ Zip/Postal Code _____ Country _____

Telephone _____

Return this form to: Institute for Brewing Studies, PO Box 1510, Boulder, CO 80306-1510, U.S.A.; or FAX (303) 447-2825.

OPENING A BREWERY?
THE INSTITUTE FOR BREWING STUDIES WANTS TO HEAR ABOUT IT!

Please fill out this form and send it to the Institute to make sure we know about your new brewery and to help us serve the industry better.

(please print or type)

Company Name _____

(dba) _____

Mailing Address _____

Street Address (if different) _____

City _____ State/Province _____ Zip/Postal Code _____

Country _____

Telephone _____

FAX _____ E-mail _____ WWW _____

Principals _____

_____

_____

_____

Head Brewer _____

Primary Contact _____

Names and styles of the beers you intend to produce _____

_____

_____

Date of first commercial sales (projected if not open yet) _____

_____

Check one only: ❏ Microbrewery   ❏ Brewpub   ❏ Contract Brewing

Annual production capacity (check one) _____ ❏ U.S. Barrels _____ ❏ Hectoliters

Total square footage (including storage, offices) _____ square feet

Number of seats (if applicable) _____

Copy this form and send with any press releases, photographs suitable for printing or newspaper clippings concerning your brewery to: Institute for Brewing Studies, PO Box 1679, Boulder, CO 80306-1679, USA or FAX (303) 447-2825.
Thank you very much.